MIDDLE EAST CONTEMPORARY SURVEY

Volume XXIV: 2000

MIDDLE EAST CONTEMPORARY SURVEY
Published for
The Moshe Dayan Center
for Middle Eastern and African Studies
The Shiloah Institute
Tel Aviv University

Haim Shaked, Founding Editor

Editorial Advisory Board

MIDDLE EAST CONTEMPORARY SURVEY

Volume XXIV
2000

BRUCE MADDY-WEITZMAN
Editor

**The Moshe Dayan Center
for Middle Eastern and African Studies
The Shiloah Institute
Tel Aviv University**

Middle East Contemporary Survey

Published in 2002 in Israel by The Moshe Dayan Center for Middle Eastern and African Studies, Tel Aviv University

Typeset in Israel by The Moshe Dayan Center for Middle Eastern and African Studies, Tel Aviv University

Printed and bound in Israel by A.R.T. – Offset Printing Ltd.

Library of Congress Catalog Card Number: 78-648245
ISBN: 965-224-054-0
ISSN: 0163-5476

About the Series and Editor

Established in 1977, the *Middle East Contemporary Survey (MECS)*, was designed to be an up-to-date reference for scholars, researchers and analysts, policymakers, students and journalists. It therefore examines in detail the rapidly changing Middle Eastern scene in all its complexity.

In each volume, the material is arranged in two parts. The first contains a series of essays on broad regional issues and on the overall relations of the region with other parts of the world. Subjects explored in detail include inter-Arab relations, Islamic affairs, economic developments, and the relations between major world powers and the Middle East. The second part consists of country-by-country surveys of seventeen Arab states and the Palestinian Authority, as well as Iran, Israel and Turkey. The course and various aspects of Arab-Israeli relations are detailed in both the relevant country chapters and in the essays in Part One. Regional aspects of foreign policies and internal developments that have wider implications are discussed in the chapters on inter-Arab relations and Islamic affairs, respectively. The emphasis in Part Two is on elucidating the inner dynamics of each country's politics and society.

Bruce Maddy-Weitzman is Senior Research Fellow at the Moshe Dayan Center at Tel Aviv University.

Preface

The present volume of *Middle East Contemporary Survey* is the twenty-fourth in an annual series which provides a continuing up-to-date analytical account of the political and economic developments in an exceptionally complex part of the world. As always, every effort has been made to use the widest range of source material and maintain the highest possible academic standards.

While *MECS*, like all collective works, has an editor responsible for its merits and shortcomings, it is — perhaps more than most such publications — a team project. Most of the essays in this volume have been researched and written by the members of the Shiloah Institute of the Moshe Dayan Center for Middle Eastern and African Studies at Tel Aviv University. Other contributions have been made by academics and experts from other institutions in Israel and abroad.

The period surveyed in this volume, unless otherwise indicated, is from January to December 2000. In order to avoid excessive repetition while achieving a comprehensive survey of the affairs of each country individually, extensive cross-references have been used.

MECS would never be able to meet its demanding schedule were it not for the efforts of a number of people, whom I wish to acknowledge here. Asher Susser and Martin Kramer, current and former directors of the Dayan Center, have provided valuable support, drive and vision for the entire enterprise. Amira Margalith, assistant to the Head of the Center, fulfilled a variety of executive tasks with skill and continuous care. Judy Krausz continued to be an important stylist and critical reader for *MECS*. Virginia Myers made a highly-valued contribution as a stylist. Juliet Landau-Pope meticulously copyedited and proofread the entire volume, and in the process provided an important additional critical eye to the text. Lydia Gareh furnished vital production assistance, based on her wealth of experience in the Dayan Center. David Levinson's proofreading talents were essential, as always. The exacting work of indexing was carried out by Rahel Yurman. Ruth Beit-Or prepared the maps for publication, in consultation with Ami Ayalon. Others who must be singled out for special thanks are Ilana Greenberg, Roslyn Loon, Rachel Schenker, and the Center's documentation specialists: Haim Gal, Curator of the press archive; Marion Gliksberg, librarian of the Center, assisted by Dorit Paret; and Aryeh Ezra, systems manager. Elena Lesnick, the Dayan Center's Managing Editor was responsible for the entire in-house production of a camera-ready manuscript, maintaining her usual high standard while always remaining calm in the eye of the storm.

I remain indebted to, and appreciative of Daniel Dishon, the Shiloah Institute editor of *MECS* during its formative years.

All good things must come to an end. This volume of *MECS* will be the final one, after nearly a quarter-century of informed analysis of the tumultuous developments in the Middle East: from Sadat's visit to Jerusalem to the Iranian revolution, the Iran-Iraq war and the second Gulf War, the Madrid process and the Oslo accords, and their breakdown. I am proud to have been associated with *MECS* for most of its existence, and for having served as co-editor of Volume XVIII and editor of volumes XIX-XXIV. Whether or not the Middle East is better off now than it was in 1976 is up to the individual reader to judge. What can be said is that the twenty-four volumes of *MECS* provide an indispensable basis for such a judgment, and constitute a lasting contribution to the study of the Middle East.

The Editor

Table of Contents

PART ONE: CURRENT ISSUES

THE MIDDLE EAST IN PERSPECTIVE

INTERNATIONAL AND REGIONAL AFFAIRS

PART TWO: COUNTRY-BY-COUNTRY SURVEY

List of Maps

Transliteration

The **Arabic** language has been transliterated as follows:

b	for	ب	q	for	ق
d	for	ض، د	r	for	ر
dh	for	ذ	s	for	ص، س
f	for	ف	sh	for	ش
gh	for	غ	t	for	ط،ت
h	for	هـلـح	th	for	ث
j	for	ج	w (or u)	for	و
k	for	ك	y (or i)	for	ى
kh	for	خ	z	for	ظ، ز
l	for	ل	'	for	ا،'
m	for	م	'	for	ع
n	for	ن			

In addition, the following should be noted:

Long vowels are not marked for distinction from short ones. Thus ناظر = *nazir*, but also نظير = *nazir*.

The *hamza* is used only in the middle of a word.

The *shadda* is rendered by doubling the consonant containing it.

The *ta marbuta* is not shown, except in construct phrases. Thus *madina, madinat Nasr.*

The definite article is always shown as "al-," regardless of the kind of letter following it.

Exceptions to the above are Lebanese and North African proper names which have adopted a French or common Maghribi spelling.

In transcribing **Persian**, frequent allowance is made for pronunciation; thus Khomeini (not Khumayni). Names appearing in both Arabic and Persian texts are transcribed according to the language of the relevant text. Thus Hizballah (Arabic) or Hizbollah (Persian).

Recommended Method for Citation from *MECS*

In the interest of accuracy, consistency, and simplicity, the following method of citation is recommended. Based on the classification of *MECS* as a periodical, published annually, the method conforms to the *Chicago Manual of Style*.

In a footnote: Asher Susser, "Jordan," *Middle East Contemporary Survey*, Vol. X (1986), p. 445.

In a bibliography: Susser, Asher, "Jordan," *Middle East Contemporary Survey*. Vol. X (1986), pp. 425–64.

The accepted abbreviation of the periodical's title is *MECS*. The year is that covered by the volume as indicated on the volume binding and title page, not the year of publication. No mention need be made of editors or publishers, who have changed several times since the establishment of *MECS*. Some styles may require mention of place of publication, usually in parentheses following the title of the periodical. For Volumes I through VII, the place of publication was New York; for Volumes VIII and IX, Tel Aviv; for volumes X-XXII, Boulder, Colorado; for volumes XXIII-XXIV, Tel Aviv.

List of Initials and Acronyms

AI	Amnesty International
AIS	Armée islamique du salut (Algeria)
AMU	Arab Maghrib Union
APN	Assemblée populaire nationale (Algeria)
ANAP	Anavatan Partisi (Motherland Party; Turkey)
ANFD	Association nationale des familles des disparus
ASEZ	'Aqaba Special Economic Zone
ATACMS	Army Tactical Missile System
AUB	American University of Beirut
BCP	Banque centrale populaire (Morocco)
b/d	Barrels per day
BIAD	Birleşmiş İslam Akvam Devletin (United Islamic Peoples' State, Turkey)
CDR	Council of Development and Reconstruction (Lebanon)
CEDAW	Convention on the Elimination of All Forms of Discrimination Against Women
CEPA	Council of European Parliamentarians Assembly
CHP	Cumhuriyet Halk Partisi (Republican People's Party; Turkey)
CIA	Central Intelligence Agency (US)
CIS	Commonwealth of Independent States
CNLT	Conseil national pour les libertés en Tunisie (Tunisia)
COMESA	Common Market for Eastern and Southern Africa
COMESSA	Community of the Sahel and Sahara States
CR	Council of Representatives (Yemen)
DFLP	Democratic Front for the Liberation of Palestine
DHKP-C	Devrim Halk Kurtulus Partisi-Cepke (Revolutionary People's Liberation Party-Front; Turkey)
DOP	Declaration of Principles
DSP	Demokratik Sol Partisi (Democratic Left Party; Turkey)
DUP	Democratic Unionist Party (Sudan)
DUP	Democratic Unionist Party (Tunisia)
DYP	Doğru Yol Partisi (True Path Party; Turkey)
ECC	Economic Consultative Council (Jordan)
ECHR	European Court of Human Rights
EIA	Energy Information Administration (US)
EIR	Executives of Iranian Reconstruction
EIU	Economist Intelligence Unit
ESDI	European Security and Defense Identity
EU	European Union
FAR	Forces armées royales (Morocco)
FFS	Front des forces socialistes (Algeria)
FIS	Front islamique du salut (Algeria)
FLN	Front de libération nationale (Algeria)
FP	Fazılet Partisi (Virtue Party, Turkey)
FSA	Final status agreement

FRD	Further (Israeli) redeployment
FTA	Free trade agreement
FTZ	Free trade zone
GCC	Gulf Cooperation Council
GDP	Gross domestic product
GIA	Groupe islamique armée (Algeria)
GIS	General Intelligence Service (PA)
GPC	General People's Congress (Libya);
	General People's Congress (Yemen)
GPCom	General People's Committee (Libya)
GSM	Global system for mobile communications
GSPC	Groupe Salfaiste pour le prédictation et le combat (Algeria)
HADEP	Halkin Demokrasi Partisi (People's Democratic Party; Turkey)
Hamas	Harakat al-Muqawama al-Islamiyya (Islamic Resistance Movement; PA)
	Harakat Mujtama' al-Silm (Algeria)
IAF	Islamic Action Front (Jordan)
IAPC	Islamic Arab Popular Congress (Sudan)
IBDA-C	Islam Büyük Dogu Akincilar-Ceple (Islamic Great Eastern Raiders Front; Turkey)
ICJ	International Court of Justice
ICO	Islamic Conference Organization
IDB	Islamic Development Bank
IDF	Israel Defense Forces
IEA	International Energy Agency
IGAD	Inter-Governmental Authority on Drought
IIPF	Islamic Iran Participation Front
IIRO	International Islamic Relief Organization
ILO	International Labor Organization
IMF	International Monetary Fund
IMI	Israel Military Industries
IMU	Islamic Movement of Uzbekistan
INC	Iraqi National Congress
IPF	IGAD Partners Forum
IRMO	Islamic Revolution Mojahedin (Iran)
IUMK	Islamic Unity Movement of Kurdistan
JBA	Jordanian Bar Association
JCG	Justice and Charity Group (Al-'Adl wal-Ihsan; Morocco)
JPA	Jordan Press Association
JPF	Jordan Press Foundation
JRM	Jame'eh-ye Ruhaniyyat-e Mobarez (Militant Clergy Association; Iran)
JRTC	Jordan Radio and Television Corporation
KDP	Kurdistan Democratic Party
KPC	Kuwait Petroleum Corporation
LADDH	Ligue algérienne pour la defence des droits de l'homme (Algeria)
LF	Lebanese Forces
LNG	Liquid natural gas
LRA	Lord's Resistance Army (Uganda)

LTDH	Ligue tunisienne des droits de l'homme (Tunisia)
MAFTA	Mediterranean Arab Free Trade Area
MBT	Main battle tanks
MDS	Mouvement des démocrates socialistes (Tunisia)
	Mouvement démocratique et social (Morocco)
MGK	Milli Güvenlik Kurulu (National Security Council; Turkey)
MHP	Milliyetçi Hareket Partisi (Nationalist Action Party; Turkey)
MIT	Milli Istihbarat Teşkilati (National Intelligence Agency, Turkey)
MK	Member of Knesset (Israel)
MKO	Mojahedin-e Khalq Organization (Iran)
NC	National Congress (Sudan)
NDA	National Democratic Alliance (Israel; Sudan)
NDP	National Democratic Party (Egypt)
NGO	Non-governmental organization
NIF	National Islamic Front (Sudan)
NOP	National Oil Company (Libya)
NPT	Nuclear Non-Proliferation Treaty
NRP	National Religious Party (Israel)
NSC	National Security Council (US, Turkey)
OAU	Organization of African Unity
OECD	Omnium Nord Afrique (Morocco)
OPEC	Organization of Petroleum Exporting Countries
OSU	Office for Strengthening Unity (OSU)
PA	Palestinian Authority
PDF	Popular Defense Forces (Sudan)
PFLP	Popular Front for the Liberation of Palestine
PKK	Parti Kerkeren Kurdistan (Kurdistan Workers' Party; Turkey)
PLC	Palestinian Legislative Council
PLO	Palestine Liberation Organization
PNC	Palestine National Council
	Popular National Council (al-Mu'tammar al-Watani al-Sha'bi; Sudan)
Polisario	Popular Front for the Liberation of al-Saqiyya al-Hamra and Rio de Oro (Western Sahara)
PPS	Parti du progrès et du socialisme (Morocco)
PPP	Palestinian People's Party
	Purchasing power parity
PRA	Parti du renouveau algérien
PSF	Preventive Security Forces (Palestine)
PSP	Progressive Socialist Party (Lebanon)
PUK	Patriotic Union of Kurdistan
PUP	Popular de l'unité populaire (Tunisia)
RCC	Revolutionary Command Council (Iraq)
RCD	Rassemblement constitutionnel démocratique (Tunisia); Rassemblement de la culture et la démocratie (Algeria)
RP	Refah Partisi (Welfare Party; Turkey)
RSP	Rassemblement socialiste progrèssive (Tunisia)
SADR	Saharan Arab Democratic Republic

SANG	Saudi Arabian National Guard
SCF	Special cash facility
SCPM	Supreme Council for Petroleum and Mineral Affairs (Saudi Arabia)
SLA	South Lebanese Army
SLP	Socialist Liberal Party (Egypt)
SPLA	Sudan People's Liberation Army
TKP/ML-TIKKO	Türkiye Kommunist Partisi/Marksist-Leninist-Türkiye İşçi Ve Köylü Kurtuluş Ordusu (Turkish Communist Party/Marxist-Leninist-Turkish Workers' and Peasants Liberation Army)
UAE	United Arab Emirates
UDI	Unilateral declaration of independence
UGTA	Union générale des travailleurs Algeriens
UJ	University of Jordan
UN	United Nations
UNDOF	United Nations Disengagement Observer Force
UNESCWA	United Nations Economic and Social Commission for Western Asia
UNIFIL	United Nations Interim Force in Lebanon
UNMOVIC	United Nations Monitoring, Verification and Inspection Commission
UNSCOM	United Nations Special Commission on Iraq
USFP	Union socialiste des forces populaires (Morocco)
USTR	United States Trade Representative
WB	World Bank
WEOG	Western European and Others Group (UN)
WMD	Weapons of mass destruction
WRM	Wye River Memorandum
WTO	World Trade Organization
YRG	Yemeni Reform Grouping
YSP	Yemeni Socialist Party

List of Sources
Newspapers, Periodicals, Irregular Publications, and Electronic Services

Name (Place, Frequency of Publication)	Abbreviation
ABC (Madrid, daily)	
Abrar (Tehran, daily)	
Afarinesh (Tehran, daily)	
Africa Confidential (London, bi-weekly)	AC
Africa Research Bulletin (Oxford, monthly)	ARB
Aftab-e Yazd (Yazd, daily)	
Al-Ahali (Cairo, weekly)	
Al-Ahram (Cairo, daily)	
Al-Ahram al-'Arabi (Cairo, weekly)	
Al-Ahram al-Iqtisadi (Cairo, weekly)	
Al-Ahram Weekly (Cairo, weekly)	AW
Al-Akhbar (Cairo, daily)	
Akhbar al-Khalij (Manama, daily)	
Akhbar al-Yawm (Khartoum, daily)	
Akhbar-e-Eqtesad (Tehran, daily)	
Akhir Sa'a (Cairo, weekly)	
Alif Ba (Baghdad, weekly)	
Alwan (Khartoum, daily)	
Amnesty International Report (London, annual)	
Al-'Arab (Doha, daily)	
Al-'Arab al-Yawm (Amman, daily)	
Al-'Arabi (Cairo, weekly)	

Name (Place, Frequency of Publication)	Abbreviation
Arab News (Saudi Arabia, daily)	
'Asr-e Azadegan (Tehran, daily)	
'Asr-e Ma (Tehran, bi-weekly)	
L'Authentique (Algiers, daily)	
Al-'Ayn (Nazareth, weekly)	
Al-Ayyam (Manama, daily)	
Al-Ayyam (Ramallah, daily)	
Babil (Baghdad, daily)	
Bahar (Tehran, daily)	
*Bahrain News (Occasional publication of the Bahrain Freedom Movement)	
Al-Ba'th (Damascus, daily)	
Al-Bayan (Dubai, daily)	
Christian Science Monitor (Boston, daily)	CSM
Civil Society (Cairo, monthly)	
Corriere della Sera (Milan, daily)	
Country Analysis Brief (Occasional publication of the Energy Information Administration)	
Country Profile (London, annually)	
Country Report (London, quarterly)	CR
The Daily Star (Beirut, daily)	
The Daily Telegraph (London, daily)	DT
Al-Da'wa	

Name *(Place, Frequency of Publication)*	Abbreviation
(London, monthly)	
Demain (Casablanca, weekly)	
Al-Dustur (Amman, daily)	
The Economist (London, weekly)	
El Pais (Madrid, daily)	
Entekhab (Tehran, daily)	
Europe in Israel (Newsletter of the EC delegation to Israel)	
Fath (Tehran, daily)	
Filastin al-Muslima (London, monthly)	
The Financial Times (London, daily)	FT
Foreign Affairs (New York, five per year)	FA
Frankfurter Rundschau (Frankfurt, daily)	
Future News (Beirut, daily)	
Gazeta Shqiptare (Tirana, daily)	
*Il Giornale (Vicenza, daily)	
The Globe and Mail (Toronto, daily)	
Globes (Tel Aviv, daily)	
The Guardian (Manchester, daily)	
Gulf News (Abu Dhabi, daily)	
Gulf States Newsletter (West Sussex, biweekly)	GSNL
Ha'aretz (Tel Aviv, daily)	
Hadith-e Qazvin (Qazvin, daily)	
Ham-mihan (Tehran, daily)	
Hambastegi (Tehran, daily)	
Hamshahri	

Name *(Place, Frequency of Publication)*	Abbreviation
(Tehran, daily)	
Hatzofeh (Tel Aviv, daily)	
Al-Hawadith (London, weekly)	
Al-Hayat (London, daily)	
Al-Hayat al-Jadida (Gaza, daily)	
Hayat-e No (Tehran, daily)	
The Hindu (Chammai, daily)	
Horizons (Algiers, daily)	
Hürriyet (Istanbul, daily)	
The Independent (London, daily)	
The International Herald Tribune (Paris and Zurich, daily)	IHT
Iran (Tehran, daily)	
Iran News (Tehran, daily)	
Iran Vij (Tehran, daily)	
Iran Weekly Press Digest (Tehran, weekly)	IWPD
Al-'Iraq (Baghdad, daily)	
Al-Istiqlal (Gaza, weekly)	
Al-Ittihad (Baghdad, weekly)	
Al-Ittihad (Haifa, daily)	
Jane's Foreign Report (London, weekly)	
Jane's Intelligence Review (London, monthly)	
Jang (Rawalpindi, daily)	
Javan (Tehran, weekly)	
Al-Jazira (Riyadh, daily)	
The Jerusalem Post	JP

Name	Abbreviation	Name	Abbreviation
(Place, Frequency of Publication)		*(Place, Frequency of Publication)*	

Name (Place, Frequency of Publication)	Abbreviation
(Jerusalem, daily)	
The Jerusalem Report	JR
(Jerusalem, biweekly)	
Jeune Afrique/L'Intelligent	JAI
(Paris, weekly)	
Le Jeune Indépendent	
(Algiers, daily)	
Jerusalem Journal of International Relations	
(Jerusalem, quarterly)	
The Jewish Chronicle	
(London, weekly)	
Jomhuri-ye Islami	
(Tehran, daily)	
Jordan Times	JT
(Amman, daily)	
Journal of Democracy	
(Ann Arbor, Michigan, quarterly)	
Journal of Palestine Studies	JPS
(Berkeley, CA, quarterly)	
Al-Jumhuriyya	
(Baghdad, daily)	
Al-Jumhuriyya	
(Cairo, daily)	
Kar ve Kargar	
(Tehran, daily)	
Kayhan	
(Tehran, daily)	
Kayhan International	KI
(Tehran, daily)	
Al-Khabar	
(Algiers, daily)	
Al-Khalij	
(Sharja, daily)	
Al-Khartoum	
(Cairo, daily)	
Al-Khartoum	
(Khartoum, daily)	
Kiyan	
(Tehran, monthly)	
Kull al-'Arab	
(Paris, weekly)	
Kuwait Times	
(Kuwait City, daily)	
Libération	
(Paris, daily)	
Liberté	
(Algiers, weekly)	
*Libya: News and Views	LNV

Name (Place, Frequency of Publication)	Abbreviation
(daily)	
Al-Liwa	
(Amman, weekly)	
Al-Liwa al-Islami	
(Cairo, weekly)	
The Los Angeles Times	LAT
(Los Angeles, daily)	
Ma'ariv	
(Tel Aviv, daily)	
Al-Majalla	
(London, weekly)	
Al-Majd	
(Amman, weekly)	
Al-Manar	
(Jerusalem, weekly)	
Manilla Phillipine Daily Inquirer	
(Manilla, daily)	
Maroc Hebdo International	MHI
(Casablanca, weekly)	
Le Matin	
(Algiers, daily)	
The Middle East	ME
(London, monthly)	
Middle East Economic Digest	MEED
(London, weekly)	
Middle East Economic Survey	MEES
(Nicosia, weekly)	
*Middle East Forum Wire	
(Washington, DC, biweekly)	
Middle East Insight	
(Washington, DC, bimonthly)	
Middle East International	MEI
(London, biweekly)	
Middle East Journal	MEJ
(Washington, DC, quarterly)	
Middle East Report	
(Baltimore, quarterly)	
*Middle East Review of International Affairs	MERIA
(Ramat Gan, Israel, quarterly)	
Middle East Research and Information Project	MERIP
(Washington, DC, irregular)	
Middle East Quarterly	MEQ
(Philadelphia, PA, quarterly)	
Middle East Times	MET
(Cairo, weekly)	
Mideast Mirror	MM
(London, daily)	

Name	Abbreviation	Name	Abbreviation
(Place, Frequency of Publication)		*(Place, Frequency of Publication)*	

Midstream (New York, monthly)		*Oman Daily Observer* (Muscat, daily)	
Milliyet (Istanbul, daily)		*Orient* (Hamburg, quarterly)	
Le Monde (Paris, daily)		*The Ottawa Citizen* (Ottawa, daily)	
Le Monde Diplomatique (Paris, monthly)		*Pakistan* (Islamabad, daily)	
Mosharaket (Tehran, daily)		*Palestine Times* (Leeds, monthly)	
Al-Mukhtar al-Islami (Cairo, monthly)		*Panorama* (Tayba, weekly)	
Al-Musawwar (Cairo, weekly)		*Peacewatch* (Washington, DC, irregular)	
Al-Mushahid al-Siyasi (London, weekly)		*Philadelphia Inquirer* (Philadelphia, weekly)	
Muslim Students Association News (Columbus, OH, daily)	MSANEWS	*Policy Watch* (WINEP, Washington, DC, irregular)	
Al-Mustaqbal (Beirut, daily)		*Publico* (Lisbon, daily)	
Al-Mustaqbal al-'Arabi (Beirut, monthly)		*Al-Quds* (Jerusalem, daily)	
Al-Mustaqila (London, weekly)		*Al-Quds al-'Arabi* (London, daily)	
Al-Nahar (Beirut, daily)		*Al-Rafidayn* (Baghdad, biweekly)	
The Nation (Islamabad, daily)		*Al-Ra'y* (Amman, daily)	
The Nation (Nairobi, daily)		*Al-Ra'y al-'Amm* (Kuwait, daily)	
Nawa-I-Waqt (Rawalpindi, daily)		*Relations* (Jerusalem, quarterly)	
The News (Islamabad, daily)		*Resalat* (Tehran, daily)	
Newsweek (New York, weekly)		*Rossiyskaya Gazeta* (Moscow, weekly)	
New Vision (Kampala, daily)		*Ruz al-Yusuf* (Cairo, weekly)	
New York Daily News (New York, daily)		*Ruzegar-e Now* (Tehran, weekly)	
New York Review of Books (New York, bi-weekly)		*Sabah* (Istanbul, daily)	
The New York Times (New York, daily)	NYT	*Al-Sabah* (Tunis, daily)	
Nezavisimaya Gazeta (Moscow, daily)		*Al-Safir* (Beirut, daily)	
The North Africa Journal (Boston, MA, monthly)		*Al-Sahafa* (Khartoum, daily)	

Name	Abbreviation	Name	Abbreviation
(Place, Frequency of Publication)		*(Place, Frequency of Publication)*	

Saudi Gazette
(Riyadh, daily)
*Sawt al-Qozaz
(Bulletin of the Chechen opposition to
Russian rule)
Al-Sha'b
(Cairo, weekly)
Al- Sha'b al-'Arabi
(London, weekly)
Al-Sharq al-Awsat
(London, daily)
Sobh-e Emruz
(Iran, daily)
La Stampa
(Turin, daily)
Sudan Democratic Gazette   SDG
(London, monthly)
The Sunday Times
(London, weekly)
Survival. Journal of International
Institute of Strategic Studies
(Oxford, quarterly)
Syria Times
(Damascus, daily)
Al-Tadamun
(Baghdad, weekly)
Tehran Times   TT
(Tehran, daily)
Al-Thawra
(Baghdad, daily)
Al-Thawra
(Damascus, daily)
Time
(New York, weekly)
The Times
(London, daily)
The Times of Oman
(Muscat, daily)
Tishrin
(Damascus, daily)
La Tribune
(Algiers, monthly)

Turkish Daily News   TDN
(Ankara, daily)
'Ukaz
(Jidda, daily)
Uktubar
(Cairo, weekly)
Al-Usbu'
(Cairo, weekly)
Al-Usbu' al-'Arabi
(Beirut, weekly)
Al-Usbu' al-Adabi
(Damascus, weekly)
US News and World Report
(Washington, DC, weekly)
Al-Wafd
(Cairo, daily)
The Wall Street Journal   WSJ
(New York, daily)
Al-Wasat
(London, weekly)
The Washington Post   WP
(Washington, DC, daily)
El Watan
(Algiers, daily)
Al-Watan
(Muscat, daily)
Al-Watan al-'Arabi
(Cairo, weekly)
Al-Watan al-'Arabi
(Paris, weekly)
Ya le-Tharat al-Hosein
(Tehran, weekly)
Yedi'ot Aharonot
(Tel Aviv, daily)
Al-Yawm
(Algiers, daily)
Al-Zaman
(London, daily)
Al-Zawra
(Baghdad, weekly)

* Electronic publications

News Agencies

Full Name   *Abbreviation*

Agence France Press (Paris)   AFP
Anatolia News Agency (Ankara)
Associated National Press Agency (Rome)   ANPA
Associated Press (New York)   AP
Bulgarska Telegrafina Agentsia (Sofia)   BTA
Deutsche Presse-Agentur   DPA
Informatsionnoye Telegrafnoye Agenstvo Rossii—
   Telegrafnoye Agenstvo Suverennykh Stran (Moscow)   ITAR—TASS
Iraqi News Agency (Baghdad)   INA
Iran Press Service (Paris)
Islamic Republic News Agency (Tehran)   IRNA
Islamic Students News Agency   ISNA
Italian News Agency   ANSA
Jamahiriyya Arab News Agency (Tripoli)   JANA
Jordan News Agency (Amman)   Petra-JNA
Kuwaiti News Agency (Kuwait)   KUNA
Maghreb Arabe Presse (Rabat)   MAP
Middle East News Agency (Cairo)   MENA
Panafrican News Agency   PANA
Reuters (London)
Russian Information Agency (Moscow)   RIA
Saudi Press Agency (Riyadh)   SPA
Seoul Yonhap (Republic of Korea)
Syrian Arab News Agency (Damascus)   SANA

Radio and Television Stations, and Monitoring Services

(Radio stations known by the location of their principal transmitters and national television stations which are not referred to with abbreviations are not listed, since their names are self-explanatory.)

Name	Abbreviation	Notes
British Broadcasting Corporation	BBC Monitoring	London
Cable News Network Inc.	CNN	Atlanta, GA
Daily Report: Near East and South Asia	DR	Monitoring reports published in English translation by the US Foreign Broadcasting Information Service
Enterprise Nationale de la Télévision Algérienne	ENTV	Algiers
Lebanese Broadcasting Television	LBCTV	
Radio Free Europe/Radio Liberty		
Al-Jazira Television		Doha, satellite channel
Voice of Israel	VoI	Israeli national radio
Voice of Palestine	VoP	Official station of the PA, Broadcast from Jericho
Wireless File/Washington File	WF	Published by the United

Note: Radio and news agency material not otherwise attributed is available in Hebrew translation at the Moshe Dayan Center archives.

Notes on Contributors

OFRA BENGIO, PhD (Tel Aviv University, 1994). Senior Research Fellow at the Moshe Dayan Center. Senior Lecturer at the Department of Middle Eastern and African History, Tel Aviv University. Fields of specialization: contemporary Middle Eastern history; modern and contemporary politics of Iraq; and the Arabic language. Author of *Saddam's Word: Political Discourse in Iraq* (1998), *Saddam Speaks on the Gulf Crisis, A Collection of Documents* (1991), *The Kurdish Revolt in Iraq* (1989, in Hebrew), and articles. Co-editor of *Minorities and the State in the Arab World* (1999), and co-translator and editor of a collection of poetry by Abu Nuwwas, *Wine and Love Poetry* (1999, in Hebrew).

MITCHELL BENNETT, BA (Rutgers University, 2000). MA student in Middle Eastern History, Tel Aviv University.

KEREN BRAVERMAN, BA (Tel Aviv University, 2002). Junior Research Fellow at the Moshe Dayan Center.

DAN ELDAR, PhD (Tel Aviv University, 1979). Adjunct Research Fellow at the Moshe Dayan Center. Previously, Senior Head of Department in the Analysis Division of the Israeli Prime Minister's Office, in charge of research on political and strategic Middle Eastern affairs (1978–98). First Secretary at the Embassy of Israel in Japan (1989–92). Commentator on international affairs in the Israeli daily *Ha'aretz* (1976–78). Author of articles on the contemporary history of the Middle East.

WILLIAM W. HARRIS, PhD (University of Durham, 1979). Senior Lecturer in Political Studies, University of Otago, New Zealand. Fields of specialization: Middle East politics and political geography. Author of *Faces of Lebanon: Sects, Wars and Global Extensions* (1997), *Taking Root: Israeli Settlement in the West Bank, the Golan, and Gaza-Sinai 1967–1980* (1980), and articles on Lebanese political developments, particularly relating to Syrian interventions.

MEIR HATINA, PhD (Tel Aviv University, 1998). Lecturer at the Department of Middle Eastern and African History, Tel Aviv University. Fields of specialization: modern Islamic thought, and the history and politics of Egypt. Author of *Islam and Salvation in Palestinian Politics: The Islamic Jihad* (2001), *Islam in Modern Egypt: Studies in the Writings of Faraj Fuda* (2000, in Hebrew), and *Palestinian Radicalism: The Islamic Jihad Movement* (1994, in Hebrew).

JOSEPH KOSTINER, PhD. Senior Research Fellow at the Moshe Dayan Center. Associate Professor, Department of Middle Eastern and African History, and Head of the Aranne School of History, Tel Aviv University. Fields of specialization: modern and contemporary history of the Arabian Peninsula states. Author of *From Chieftaincy to Monarchical State: The Making of Saudi Arabia 1916–1936* (1993), *South Yemen's Revolutionary Strategy* (1990), *The Struggle for South Yemen* (1984), and articles. Co-editor of *Tribes and State Formation in the Middle East* (1991). Editor of *The Gulf*

States: Politics, Society, Economy (2000, in Hebrew), and *Middle East Monarchies: The Challenge of Modernity* (2000).

MARTIN KRAMER, PhD (Princeton University, 1982). Senior Research Fellow at the Moshe Dayan Center, and former director of the Center. Fields of specialization: modern Arab history; Islamism, Islam and the West. Author of *Islam Assembled* (1986), *Arab Awakening and Islamic Revival* (1996), *Fadlallah: Compass of Hizballah* (1998, in Hebrew), and *Ivory Towers on Sand* (2001). Editor of *Shi'ism, Resistance and Revolution* (1987), *Middle Eastern Lives* (1991), *The Islamism Debate* (1997), *The Jewish Discovery of Islam* (1999), and the *Middle East Quarterly* (Philadelphia).

MEIR LITVAK, PhD (Harvard University, 1991). Senior Research Fellow at the Moshe Dayan Center. Senior Lecturer at the Department of Middle Eastern and African History, Tel Aviv University. Fields of specialization: modern Shi'i history; Palestinian politics and Islamist movements. Author of *Shi'i Scholars of Nineteenth Century Iraq: The 'Ulama of Najaf and Karbala* (1998) and articles on Palestinian issues and Shi'i history. Editor of *Islam and Democracy in the Arab World* (1998, in Hebrew).

BRUCE MADDY-WEITZMAN, PhD (Tel Aviv University, 1988). Senior Research Fellow at the Moshe Dayan Center. Fields of specialization: modern and contemporary Middle Eastern history; inter-Arab relations; and the modern Maghrib. Author of *The Crystallization of the Arab State System, 1945–1954* (1993), and articles on regional Arab politics and Maghrib affairs. Editor of *Middle East Contemporary Survey,* volumes XIX-XXIV, 1995-2000 and co-editor for Volume XVIII, 1994. Co-editor of *Religious Radicalism in the Greater Middle East* (1997).

UZI RABI, PhD (Tel Aviv University, 1999). Lecturer at the Department of Middle Eastern and African History, Tel Aviv University. Fields of specialization: history and current affairs of the Arab Gulf states. Author of *New Oman* (2000, in Hebrew).

RAMI REGAVIM, BA (Tel Aviv University 2002). Junior Research Fellow at the Moshe Dayan Center.

ELIE REKHESS, PhD (Tel Aviv University, 1986). Senior Research Fellow at the Moshe Dayan Center and Director of the Program on Arab Politics in Israel, established in the Center in 1996, in cooperation with the Konrad Adenauer Foundation. Fields of specialization: political history of the Arabs in Israel; Islamic movements in Israel; and Palestinian affairs. Author of *The Arab Minority in Israel: Between Communism and Arab Nationalism* (1993, in Hebrew). Editor of *Arabs in Israeli Politics: Dilemmas of Identity* (1998, in Hebrew), *Arab Politics in Israel at a Crossroad* (1996, in Hebrew), and *The Arab Minority in Israel: Dilemmas of Political Orientation and Social Change* (1994).

PAUL RIVLIN, PhD (University of London, 1984). Senior Research Fellow at the Moshe Dayan Center, Tel Aviv University. Field of specialization: the Middle East economy and its historical development. Author of *Economic Policy and Performance in the Arab*

World (2001), *The Israel Economy* (1992), *The Dynamics of Economic Policy Making in Egypt* (1985).

YEHUDIT RONEN, PhD (Tel Aviv University, 1997). Research Fellow at the Moshe Dayan Center. Lecturer at the Department of Political Science, Bar Ilan University. Fields of specialization: Sudan, Libya and the Maghrib. Author of *Sudan in a Civil War: Between Africanism, Arabism and Islam* (1995, in Hebrew), and articles on the modern political history of Sudan, Libya and Maghrib affairs. Editor of *The Maghrib: Politics, Society, Economy* (1998, in Hebrew).

BARRY RUBIN, PhD (Georgetown University, 1978). Deputy Director of the BESA Center for Strategic Studies, Bar Ilan University, and editor of *Global Journal* and *The Middle East Review of International Affairs.* Author of, among others: *The Transformation of Palestinian Politics* (1999); *Revolution Until Victory: The Politics and History of the PLO* (1994); *Cauldron of Turmoil: America in the Persian Gulf* (1991); *Modern Dictators* (1987), and *Paved with Good Intentions: The American Experience and Iran* (1982).

ARYEH SHMUELEVITZ, PhD (University of Wisconsin, 1981). Professor for Middle Eastern History and former chair of the Department of Middle Eastern and African History; co-founder of the Shiloah Institute for Middle Eastern and African Studies and its annual publication, *The Middle East Record;* Senior Research Fellow at the Moshe Dayan Center. Fields of specialization: history and society of the Ottoman Empire, Turkey and Iran; the Jews of the Ottoman Empire and Turkey. Author of *The Jews of the Ottoman Empire in the Late 15th and the 16th Centuries* (1984), *Turkey in the 20th Century — Between Tradition and Modernization* (1997, in Hebrew), *Turkey's Experiment in Islamic Government, 1996–97* (1999), *Ottoman History and Society — Jewish Sources* (1999). Editor of *Seder Eliyahu Zuta by Rabbi Eliyahu Capsali* (History of the Ottomans in three volumes, 1983, 1977, 1975, in Hebrew). Co-editor of *The Hashemites in the Modern Arab World* (1995) and *The Middle East Record*, volumes I-V, 1960, 1961, 1967, 1968, 1969-70.

LESLIE SUSSER, PhD (Oxford University, 1989). Senior Writer, *The Jerusalem Report.* Fields of specialization: Israeli politics and the Arab-Israeli peace process. Co-author of *Yitzhak Rabin: Soldier of Peace* (1996). Author of articles on fascist movements in Britain.

JOSHUA TEITELBAUM, PhD (Tel Aviv University, 1996). Senior Research Fellow at the Moshe Dayan Center. Lecturer in the Overseas Students Program, Tel Aviv University. Fields of specialization: the history of the Arabian Peninsula, specifically Saudi Arabia; Palestinian history and politics. Author of *The Rise and Fall of the Hashimite Kingdom of Arabia* (2001) and *Holier Than Thou: Saudi Arabia's Islamic Opposition* (2000).

ESTHER WEBMAN, MA (Tel Aviv University, 1996). Research Fellow at the Moshe Dayan Center and Research Fellow at the Stephen Roth Institute for the Study of Anti-Semitism and Racism, Tel Aviv University. Fields of specialization: contemporary Muslim-Jewish relations; Muslims in Britain; Islamist movements; and antisemitism and the perception of the Holocaust in the Arab world.

DANIEL ZISENWINE, MA (Hebrew University, 1997). Junior Research Fellow at the Moshe Dayan Center. Doctoral candidate in History of the Modern Middle East, Tel Aviv University. Field of specialization: North Africa. Author of articles on modern North African affairs.

EYAL ZISSER, PhD (Tel Aviv University, 1992). Senior Research Fellow at the Moshe Dayan Center. Senior Lecturer at the Department of Middle Eastern and African History, Tel Aviv University. Fields of specialization: history and politics of Syria and Lebanon. Author of *Asad's Legacy — Syria in Transition* (2000), *Lebanon — the Challenge of Independence* (2000), *Syria's Asad — At a Crossroads* (1999, in Hebrew) and several studies on modern Syrian and Lebanese politics.

PART ONE: CURRENT ISSUES

THE MIDDLE EAST
IN PERSPECTIVE

The Middle East in 2000:
Things Come Undone

MARTIN KRAMER

In the first year of the new millennium, the Middle East turned back the clock. An intense diplomatic effort to resolve the very essence of the Israeli-Palestinian conflict failed. By the year's end, the two parties were locked in a violent confrontation. This was no repetition of history, but the casual observer could be excused for thinking that 2000 looked like a rerun of 1987, or 1982, or 1967, or 1948, or 1936, or 1929. At various moments, the renewed confrontation between Israelis and Palestinians evoked each of these past landmarks in their long history of confrontation. And this round, like its predecessors, promised to be bloody and impassioned, superficially decisive but fundamentally inconclusive.

The US also sustained damages in the crash. This was the last year of the presidency of Bill Clinton, a man who had put his heart and mind into the effort to bring peace. His failure was not a matter of too little involvement, but of too much. As his own political clock ran down, his urgency only raised the stakes still higher, culminating in a marathon three-way summit at Camp David. This presidential retreat, long associated with Egyptian-Israeli peace, would ever more be remembered as the place where Palestinian-Israeli relations went into a tailspin. For the US, the debacle posed a new challenge to its prestige as sole hegemon.

Even before the meltdown, the attempt to bring Israel and Syria over the threshold also failed, followed a short time later by the death of Syrian president Hafiz al-Asad. The prospect of a Syrian-Israeli peace receded, but Israel did end its twenty-two-year occupation of South Lebanon, removing at least one point of friction. Israelis would remember this as the one major achievement of Israeli prime minister Ehud Barak — if they could ignore its negative impact on Israel's deterrent posture in Arab eyes.

In the Arab world, there was concern about the dangerous turn in Israeli-Palestinian relations. But nowhere did it have a destabilizing effect. Asad on his death was succeeded by his son, Bashshar, in a process that demonstrated the deep personalization of Arab politics. Saddam Husayn of Iraq survived yet another year of sanctions, and the debate in the West over their efficacy grew heated. Elsewhere, it was politics (or, more precisely, the absence of politics) as usual. But in Iran and Turkey, arenas of genuine political contestation, the struggle over priorities intensified, as both countries wrestled with the need for reforms.

Did anyone prosper in the Middle East in 2000? In September, the price of oil hit a ten-year high of almost $37/b. In desert palaces and Swiss banks, coffers overflowed.

SYRIA–ISRAEL

At the end of 1999, American mediation had finally provided a formula for a renewal of Israeli-Syrian negotiations, the first since 1996 (see *MECS* 1999, pp. 64–68). The talks took place from 3–11 January in Shepherdstown, West Virginia, between Israeli prime minister Barak and Syrian foreign minister Faruq al-Shar'. The two men never shook hands.

The state of the negotiations became clear following the leak of a confidential US bridging document, which the Americans presented to both sides at the close of the talks, and which was promptly leaked to an Israeli newspaper. On many issues — normal relations, security, water — there had been progress. But the document, by its omissions, also made it evident that the core territorial issue had not been resolved.[1]

Syria insisted on a return to the "line of 4 June 1967," comprised of positions Syria held on the eve of the 1967 war. This included the northeastern shore of the Sea of Galilee, which Syria had occupied in 1948. Asad was wont to tell of how, as a young officer, he swam in the lake and cooked fish on its shores. Syria demanded a return to those shores, and the rights of a riparian state.[2]

But the "line of 4 June 1967" was not the international border which Britain and France had established between British-mandated Palestine and French-mandated Syria in 1923. That line had placed the whole of the lake in Palestine. It was Israel's position that Israel had exclusive right to control of the lake — the principal source of Israel's water. The late prime minister Yitzhak Rabin had been willing to accept a face-saving gesture: Israel would accept "4 June" as a basis. But since no such line existed on any map, it would have to be negotiated. In such a negotiation, Israel would insist that "4 June" be demarcated in such a way as to leave the entire lake in Israel.

No progress was made on this issue at Shepherdstown, and the Israeli leak of the American bridging document greatly embarrassed Syria, since it omitted the territorial *quid pro quo* of full Israeli withdrawal to the "line of 4 June." Syria immediately began to backtrack, engineering its own leaks to a Lebanese newspaper in order to rescind many supposed Syrian concessions.[3]

Clinton made a last effort to revive the negotiations on 26 March, when he met Asad for three hours in Geneva. Clinton again conveyed Israel's position on the lake; Asad replied by repeating his fish story to Clinton: "Until 1967, I would swim in the Sea of Galilee, I would have barbecues there, I ate fish."[4] The summit broke up in failure, with both Clinton and Asad believing they had been misled as to its chances for success.

The diplomatic train had reached the end of the Syrian track. Clinton decided to lay blame, announcing that Barak's proposal was "serious, detailed, and comprehensive." "The ball is in Syria's court now," he added, "and I'm looking forward to hearing from [Asad]."[5] But the chance for an Israeli-Syrian agreement had died, and it was buried with Asad himself, when he died some two weeks later (see below).

The precise history of this failure would be written by future historians. Was Israel short-sighted to insist on holding the last few hundred meters on the northeastern shore of the lake? Was Syria foolish in not stroking Israeli public opinion?[6] Whatever the verdict, it seemed unlikely that a similar exercise would be attempted any time soon. "The Syrian story is over," announced Barak. "The window of opportunity will be closed for a long time."[7]

ISRAEL EX-LEBANON

Barak, in his 1999 election campaign, had promised an Israeli withdrawal from South Lebanon by the end of his first year as prime minister. His obvious preference was to end the twenty-two-year occupation in the framework of a peace agreement with Syria. But Barak was prepared to exit unilaterally, if Syria failed to come to terms.

Through the winter and spring, ambiguity surrounded Barak's commitment. Israel made no visible preparations for withdrawal, and there was confusion as to how complete the withdrawal would be. But on 5 March, the Israeli cabinet voted to depart by early July. Israel began practical preparations, and announced its willingness to withdraw to a line determined by a UN technical team. Over three days in late May, Israeli troops abruptly scampered back across the border, without sustaining casualties. Israel's client militia, the South Lebanon Army (SLA), collapsed immediately. On 16 June, the UN Security Council confirmed that Israel's withdrawal was complete.

In the aftermath, an uneasy equilibrium prevailed on the Israeli-Lebanese frontier. However, tensions remained high in the area of the so-called Shab'a farms. Israel had occupied this ground in 1967, and the UN regarded it as occupied Syrian territory. According to UN cartographers, Syria still had sovereignty over the Shab'a farms.[8] Lebanon, however, claimed it as Lebanese territory.

Hizballah seized this opportunity to declare the Israeli withdrawal incomplete. "So long as the Shab'a farms area remains under occupation, we can't describe what happened as a total withdrawal," announced Hasan Nasrallah, Hizballah secretary-general. "This means we have to continue our jihad to liberate this occupied area."[9] The area remained a potential flashpoint which Hizballah and Syria could ignite at will, if they were prepared to run the risk.

The Israeli withdrawal from Lebanon probably had a negative impact on the concept of peace through diplomacy. It gave sustenance to the notion that Israel could be forced to make concessions through "resistance," without the need for laborious negotiations and treaties. "The way to recover our usurped rights is not through secret talks or security coordination with the usurpers," announced a Gaza weekly, "but through determined resistance, strong faith and patience."[10]

"The Lebanese example should not be generalized," a senior American diplomat told an Arab newspaper. "Attempts to draw conclusions that Hizballah's methodology should be emulated" were "extremely dangerous."[11] But before the year was out, the Palestinians seemed to have drawn precisely that conclusion.

PALESTINE REVERSAL

The collapse of negotiations with Syria brought Barak back to the Palestinian track, and to an intimate engagement with Palestinian Authority (PA) chairman Yasir 'Arafat. Barak, a former general, mounted the diplomatic equivalent of a blitzkrieg assault. He imploded faster than anyone imagined was possible, even in Israel's volatile politics. 'Arafat, a former guerrilla, launched the political equivalent of a hit-and-run, hide-and-seek campaign. He weathered the storm once again, despite the volatile politics of Palestine. By year's end, no one could say whether Israel or Palestine enjoyed the advantage. But there was no doubt which leader would pay the price of the confrontation.

PAVED WITH GOOD INTENTIONS

In the winter months, it had been business as usual. On 6–7 January, Israel turned over 5% of the West Bank to the PA, constituting the second phase of the second West Bank redeployment, as agreed upon in September 1999 at Sharm al-Shaykh (see *MECS* 1999, p. 61). But Barak and 'Arafat could not reach an agreement on the third and final Israeli redeployment, as stipulated by the Oslo II agreement (see *MECS* 1995, pp. 139–41). Barak wanted to fold it into a final agreement, whereas 'Arafat insisted on receiving a foothold in the vicinity of Jerusalem. As talks languished, 'Arafat threatened to declare a Palestinian state on 13 September, the deadline for a final status agreement. But Israel made counter-threats, and 'Arafat found no international support for a unilateral move.

On 9 March, Barak and 'Arafat met in Sharm al-Shaykh, under the baton of Egyptian president Husni Mubarak. There they committed themselves to reaching a framework agreement on permanent status (FAPS) by May, with the goal of a final agreement by September. Intensive negotiations began on 3 May in the Israeli resort of Eilat, and Israeli chief negotiator Oded Eran gave some indication of the Israeli offer. The PA would receive Gaza and three cantons constituting some two-thirds of the West Bank, linked by "safe passages." Later, more land might be transferred, putting some 80% of the West Bank in Palestinian hands. Israel would annex three major settlement blocs. The parties did not discuss Jerusalem.[12]

The Palestinians rejected this proposal and broke off the talks. American special envoy Dennis Ross then assured 'Arafat that this was not Israel's final offer, and "secret" talks were resumed in Stockholm. On 15 May, the Israeli government and Knesset voted to turn over three villages on the periphery of Jerusalem to PA control. 'Arafat would be put at the gates of Jerusalem.

But that very same day, an outbreak of violence presaged the future. On Palestinian "Nakba Day," marking the "catastrophe" of 1948, Palestinian crowds marched to Israeli checkpoints across the West Bank and Gaza. They heaved stones and petrol bombs; they were met by rubber bullets and tear gas. Fatah's armed Tanzim used live fire; so did Israeli troops. Four Palestinians died. According to one Palestinian, "there seems to be an element of truth to Israeli charges that 'Arafat and the PA leadership had a hand in encouraging the unrest," with the objective of "strengthen[ing their] negotiating position."[13] The battles subsided, but the Nakba Day violence indicated that the Palestinian leadership did not regard negotiation as its only option.

Yet Barak remained adamant about pushing forward to an "end-of-conflict, end-of-claims" agreement. He had always been critical of the incremental nature of the Oslo process. Rather than negotiate interim measures, he preferred a make-or-break, now-or-never, do-or-die negotiation. Only an American president, Barak reasoned, could bring this about, and no American president had more of a commitment to the process than Bill Clinton. Barak persuaded Clinton that enough progress had been made in Stockholm, and that he would make it worth the president's time. Clinton cornered a reluctant 'Arafat. On 5 July, Clinton called Barak and 'Arafat to a marathon summit at the presidential retreat in Camp David, Maryland. The summit opened on 11 July.

CAMP DAVID II

Camp David II was predicated on one basic assumption: neither of the parties could afford to send Clinton away empty-handed. Camp David symbolized the maximum possible investment of presidential time and prestige.[14]

Barak knew better than to send Clinton away empty-handed. He decided to make an offer at Camp David that exceeded past Israeli proposals, and put aside many old assumptions about Israeli security requirements. Israel now offered to surrender 89.5% of the West Bank. It would retain the three large settlement blocs, home to 140,000 of the estimated 180,000 settlers. In exchange for the remaining 10.5%, Israel agreed to a land swap, which would involve relinquishing uninhabited desert in Israel in exchange for the settlement blocs. (Israel initially proposed a 10:1 ratio of West Bank land for Israeli land.)[15] The Jordan Valley, long regarded by Israeli strategists as an essential security buffer, would be given to the Palestinians, but Israel would lease much of it, and keep six army bases there. According to some reports, the Palestinians replied by insisting on 97% of the West Bank, and a land swap giving them territory of comparable "size, quality, and value" to the annexed settlements. This gap was not closed at Camp David, but in accepting the notion of a land swap, the negotiators laid the foundation for agreement on the territorial issue.

But the gaps on Jerusalem and the refugees could not be bridged. Israel proposed the creation of a Palestinian city, Al-Quds (the Arabic name of Jerusalem), under Palestinian sovereignty. It would include some Palestinian-inhabited neighborhoods presently within the municipal borders of Jerusalem, as well as outlying villages. Israel offered Palestinian municipal autonomy elsewhere in Jerusalem, a "special regime" inside the Old City, and Palestinian "permanent custodianship" over the sacred places. But Israel would retain sovereignty.

'Arafat rejected all of these proposals, insisting on Palestinian sovereignty over the Arab neighborhoods and the Old City, excluding the Jewish quarter and the Western Wall, but including the Temple Mount/Haram al-Sharif. When the depth of disagreement became clear, Clinton suggested deferring Jerusalem and going for an agreement on all other issues. But 'Arafat rejected a partial agreement. Jerusalem proved to be the prime obstacle to a framework agreement at Camp David.

But Camp David also threw another obstacle in sharp relief: Palestinian refugees. The Barak government had no objection to an unlimited influx of Palestinian refugees into the projected Palestinian state. But Israel refused to concede, on principle, any moral, legal, or political responsibility for the refugees' plight. Israel was prepared to consider reunification of families, and to contribute financially to refugee rehabilitation. But there could be no general license for several millions of Palestinians to claim the "right of return" to lands that became Israel in 1948.

Palestinians, in their turn, insisted on just that. They demanded that Israel acknowledge its (sole and full) responsibility and offer all refugees the free choice between return or compensation. Thus, Palestinians sought to reverse not only the consequences of 1967, but at least some of the consequences of 1948.

On 26 July, the summit finally ended, without an agreement. The Clinton administration decided to go public with its dissatisfaction over 'Arafat's positions. "The Israelis were more willing to be creative and flexible," said National Security Adviser Samuel Berger. The Palestinians "were not as prepared to compromise and to let go of some of their traditional positions."[16] In the past, the US had declared itself willing to accept any agreement reached by the parties. At Camp David II, the Clinton administration effectively rejected two of the most cherished "traditional positions" of the Palestinians, on Jerusalem and the refugees. Not only had Barak made his final offer; so, too, had the Clinton administration. "Labor Zionism and Pax Americana offered the Palestinians the best that could be hoped for in a practical world," wrote American-Lebanese analyst Fouad Ajami, "and were rebuffed."[17]

Camp David II failed because only two of the three parties shared a sense of urgency. Barak, elected on a peace platform, needed an agreement for his political survival. Clinton wanted one for his "legacy." But for 'Arafat, who had made no effort to prepare his public for conceding on territory, Jerusalem and refugees, the summit looked like a trap.[18] The situation was captured by the most famous video footage to emerge from Camp David: 'Arafat and Barak dithered over who would go first through an open door, Barak seeking to push 'Arafat over the threshold. At Camp David, 'Arafat refused to be pushed through a door he had no intention of entering.

INTIFADA II

The political impact of the failure, on Barak and 'Arafat, could not have been more different. Barak came home to find his minority government in danger of imminent collapse. His critics, even within his own camp, used his Camp David concessions against him. 'Arafat, in contrast, returned to a hero's welcome. He had given nothing; Palestinian "rights" were intact. The Israelis had made unprecedented concessions, and even if they were taken off the table with the summit's failure, they established a new baseline. In fact, the Palestinians were soon urging another Camp David summit. This time, Barak and Clinton were reluctant, unless it was a "signing summit" for a done deal.[19]

But after Camp David, some Palestinians began to debate the merits of resorting to violent confrontation. In July, a Jerusalem-based reporter sympathetic to the Palestinians reported Fatah's mood in these words: "Certain Fatah leaders air the view that a clash is required for the world to intervene 'on the weaker side' to force the Israelis to address rights the Palestinians have been unable to persuade them to address through negotiations."[20] In a late July poll, 57% of Palestinians thought that a violent confrontation would win them political gains, and 63% thought that Hizballah's resistance methods should be emulated if an agreement were not reached in the coming months.[21] Hearts and minds were being prepared for an uprising, with the goal of reshuffling the political deck.

Most Israelis failed to see it coming. Talks continued, and on 25 September, Barak hosted 'Arafat at his home outside Tel Aviv. "We met with Arafat and the entire Palestinian leadership for a warm, open meeting," said Barak, "that I believe will help us in our efforts to renew the negotiations."[22] Israel's leading Arab affairs journalist wrote: "There isn't a scrap of evidence to support the claims of prophets of doom that he ['Arafat] is planning some kind of super-intifada."[23] A few weeks later, he found himself writing a column entitled "Super-Intifada" — and tracing its origins precisely to a decision by 'Arafat.[24]

On 28 September, Likud leader Ariel Sharon visited the Temple Mount/Haram al-Sharif in Jerusalem. The next day, Palestinians rioted, and Israeli police killed five in an attempt to control them. Over the following days, thousands of young Palestinians, backed up by armed members of Fatah's Tanzim organization and Palestinian police officers, marched to Israeli checkpoints in search of confrontation. There had been violent clashes between PA and Israeli forces before. This time, however, the PA worked to transform sporadic riots into a sustained uprising, which the Palestinian media immediately dubbed the al-Aqsa Intifada.

The resulting images became etched in the collective consciousness of Palestinians and Israelis. There was the image (30 September) of a Palestinian father and his eleven-year old son pinned down by cross fire in Gaza. They were filmed crouching against a wall, with Israeli bullets flying around them. The boy was killed, the father wounded. And there was the image (12 October) of two Israeli reservists who were taken to a Palestinian police station in Ramallah, and there lynched by a crowd. A camera captured their bodies being hurled from an upstairs window. Israeli helicopter gunships retaliated by destroying targets in Ramallah and Gaza. In the first weeks, the violence also spilled over into the Israel Arab community, and thirteen Israeli Arabs were killed in clashes with the police. The battles and the funerals, all conveyed into every home in this most media-saturated of all modern conflicts, systematically dismantled the Israeli-Palestinian track.

The American fire brigade tried to quench the flames. Secretary of State Albright met with 'Arafat in Paris on 4 October; when he walked out of one session, she had to chase after him. Clinton tried his hand: on 17–18 October, he presided over an "emergency" summit in Sharm al-Shaykh. It extracted a commitment from both sides to take "immediate concrete measures to end the violence," and established an international commission, headed by former US senator George Mitchell, to investigate the causes of the violence. The establishment of the commission was to have been a ladder, allowing both sides to climb down from their confrontation. But they did not, and as the weeks wore on, the battles took on a different character. Street clashes were replaced by exchanges of gunfire. Palestinian gunmen based in PA-controlled Bayt Jala opened fire nightly on the Jewish neighborhood of Gilo in Jerusalem; Israeli forces responded with return fire and tank shells. The images evoked the battles for Jerusalem in 1948 and 1967. The uprising, which was never wholly spontaneous, became a low-intensity war between the PA and Israel.

'Arafat's role, at least at the outset, remained a disputed issue. "The hero is the one who can keep his balance on the waves," said Faysal al-Husayni, the PA's point man in Jerusalem. "But the hero is not making the waves alone. The waves are caused by more than one element — wind, temperature, the gravity of the moon. And Yasir 'Arafat maybe is one of those elements."[25] Whatever the case, 'Arafat soon developed a clear objective: extracting some unilateral Israeli concession in exchange for a cease-fire. At a minimum, Palestinians wanted "international protection," as a counter-weight to the US. But Israeli opinion was so inflamed that no Israeli government could consider "rewarding" violence. Israel responded instead with what one observer described as a "soft siege" of the PA.[26] Barak also came under siege, and as his coalition buckled beneath him, he had no choice but to seek a new mandate from the voters. On 9 December, he announced his resignation of the premiership, precipitating new elections in 2001.

(This did not end efforts to reach an agreement. On 23 December, Clinton announced his "parameters" for a settlement. The Palestinians would receive 94 to 96% of the West Bank; the remainder would be annexed by Israel, and in exchange for empty Israeli territory. Refugees would have the right to return only to the Palestinian state, but some would be allowed into Israel on humanitarian grounds. This served as the basis for another last round of negotiations in Taba, Egypt, in 2001.)

By the end of the year, at least three-hundred Palestinians and more than sixty Israelis had died in the clashes, and there was no end in sight. The violence exposed the flaws in the construction of the Oslo "peace process." Almost since its inception, the process had been criticized by extreme voices on both sides. But it was always assumed that the original partners — the Israeli Labor Party and the PLO leadership — had some implicit understanding about where the process would end. In 2000, it turned out that they did not. The PLO leadership believed that it had made its last major concession back at Oslo. The remainder of the "peace process" would consist of a series of Israeli concessions, up to and including total Israeli withdrawal, the refugees' "right of return," and sole Palestinian control of the Haram al-Sharif. The Labor Party assumed that the "peace process" consisted of mutual concessions at every stage, and that Palestinian concessions would be forthcoming in exchange for Israeli concessions, especially on the "right of return" and the Temple Mount. The core deal of land-for-peace and a two-state solution could not be translated from principle into practice.

Israelis and Palestinians seemed destined to battle it out in a test of resolve. The outcome could not be predicted, but one thing seemed certain: conflict management, not conflict resolution, would define the next phase of Israeli-Palestinian relations. The Oslo "peace process," envisioned as an unfolding series of confidence-building measures, culminating in a "grand bargain," was finished.

ARAB PREDICAMENT

The Arab world continued to undergo generational change at the top. In 2000, Syria added a new twist, by producing a case of hereditary succession in an ostensible republic: Hafiz al-Asad was succeeded by his son Bashshar. Few observers thought this first instance would be the last. Fouad Ajami dubbed the hybrid system "ibnism" (after the word *ibn*, son). Egyptian sociologist Sa'd al-Din Ibrahim called it "republarchy" (*jumlukiya*). Whatever it was called, Syria exemplified the procedure.

SYRIAN SUCCESSION

Bashshar had been preparing for the succession for six years, yet the process was not complete on 10 April when his father died, at the age of sixty-nine. The formalities were concluded hastily. Within a few hours, the People's Assembly voted to amend the Syrian constitution, lowering the minimum age of the president from forty to thirty-four — precisely Bashshar's age. The next day, he was promoted from staff colonel to lieutenant-general, and made commander-in-chief. On 25 June, the Ba'th party congress nominated him for the presidency, and a referendum was scheduled for 10 July. A Damascus-based journalist wondered whether "the incoming president's commitment to the trappings of openness [will be] reflected in a more modest 'yes' vote at the referendum than the 99% plus approval ratings his late father routinely scored."[27] As it happened, Bashshar received a "yes" vote of 97.3%, leaving ample room for improvement.

It was remarkable that the Syrian system could continue to coexist in so intimate a proximity to the Lebanese system. Despite the heavy legacies of civil war, Israeli occupation, and Syrian hegemony, Lebanon still managed to practice something that remotely resembled democracy. Its press showed some pluck, and the Lebanese electorate could surprise, as it did in parliamentary elections held in two stages over the summer. Rafiq al-Hariri, who had served as prime minister from 1992 to 1998, staged a spectacular comeback against incumbent Salim al-Huss. He and his loyalists swept the election, and he became prime minister on 26 October, forming a broad-based thirty-member cabinet, supported by 106 delegates in the 128-member parliament. No one had any illusions about Hariri (a cross between a CEO and a Saudi prince), or about the limits of Lebanese "democracy." Still, Lebanon had moved a step toward a plural order.

THE IMMOVABLE STATE

Egypt, by contrast, gravitated toward a Pharaonic one. The Islamists had already been defeated, and there were no terrorist acts in 2000. The regime was free to turn upon its other critics.

In the run-up to parliamentary elections in Egypt, authorities arrested Sa'd al-Din Ibrahim, whose Cairo-based Ibn Khaldun Center planned to monitor the vote for irregularities. The indictment and trial of the Arab world's most internationally prominent social scientist, reflected the determination of the regime to intimidate critics of all stripes, not just Islamists. The elections delivered 87% of the seats in the new People's Assembly to the ruling National Democratic Party.[28]

As for the Islamists, the so-called "second wave" of Islamism had washed over the Arab world without effecting any regime change. Rulers continued to consolidate their grip, and some even felt sufficiently confident to amnesty Islamist opponents. In Morocco, Islamist leader Abdessalame Yassine was released from house arrest. In Algeria, the Islamic Salvation Army (AIS), the armed wing of the Islamic Salvation Front (FIS), disbanded itself, and members took advantage of a government amnesty. In Syria, the regime amnestied 380 imprisoned Muslim Brethren, including twenty who were serving life sentences. Amnesties were the clearest proof that the Islamists no longer frightened the denizens of the palaces.

True, Usama bin Ladin, the Saudi extremist who had taken refuge in Afghanistan, still had cells in some Arab countries. But he did not expend energies trying to overthrow regimes. Instead, he targeted the Americans. On 12 October, suicide bombers in a dinghy blew a gaping hole in an American destroyer, the USS Cole, in the Yemeni port of Aden, killing seventeen sailors. Bin Ladin remained a thorn in the side of the US, but he would only become a top priority after 11 September 2001, when his operatives attacked America itself.

The US worried more about the efforts of Saddam Husayn to break the grip of UN sanctions, as a sequel to his earlier elimination of UN weapons inspections. Most notably, Iraq managed to break up the air embargo, a weak link in the sanctions system. Russia, France and Jordan sent in "humanitarian" flights, later followed by commercial flights. By year's end, flights to and from Saddam International Airport had become routine. A new American administration would have to make difficult choices about the eroding sanctions regime.[29]

IRAN AND TURKEY: MODELS UNDER STRESS

Iran and Turkey continued to provide a striking contrast to the Arab world. Both had open political systems, characterized by contested elections and robust parliamentary life. Yet both came under great stress in 2000, as they struggled to come to terms with needed reforms.

IRANIAN REFORMISTS AT BAY

Whenever Iranian voters went to the polls, they consistently cast their ballots for reform. The parliamentary elections of 18 February were no exception. Some 80% of 38.7m.

eligible voters participated, casting ballots for five thousand candidates who contested 290 Majlis seats. The reformists, comprised of the left-wing Mosharekat (led by Khatami's brother) and the centrist Kargozaran (formed around former president Rafsanjani), swept the poll. After a run-off election on 5 May, the reformists commanded about two hundred seats in the Majlis.

But whenever the reformists swept the polls, the conservatives mobilized the judiciary to silence them. On 23 April, the courts invoked a new law to crack down on the press. Police closed twelve newspapers and periodicals; another two were closed on 27 April. Later closures brought the total to some thirty reformist publications. In the autumn, the courts rounded up seventeen reformists who had participated in a Berlin conference on the political future of Iran, and put them on trial. Attempts by Majlis reformists to reverse the conservative drive failed.[30]

The power struggle in Iran fed a never-ending debate in the West, and especially in Washington, over how best to encourage the cause of reform. The result was a policy of mixed signals. On 17 March, Secretary of State Albright gave an address announcing the lifting of import restrictions on Iranian carpets and foodstuffs. She also described the CIA-backed overthrow of Prime Minister Mohammad Mossadeq in 1953 as "a setback for Iran's political development."[31] Yet the State Department continued to list Iran as the foremost state sponsor of terrorism. Any change in US-Iranian relations would have to await some unforeseeable shift in Iran, or in the Middle East.

TURKEY IN OVERDRAFT

Turkey lurched from crisis to crisis — first, political, and then, financial. These were the result of the country's chronic inability to effect reforms.

On 12 January, the ruling coalition agreed to suspend the execution of Abdullah Öcalan, leader of the outlawed Parti Kerkeren Kurdistan (PKK; Kurdish Workers' Party), pending a ruling from the European Court of Human Rights. It was a measure that endeared Turkey to the European Union (EU), the club Turkey hoped to join. But on 19–20 February, three Kurdish mayors were arrested for alleged affiliations with the PKK. The arrests drew a wave of criticism from Europe and even the US, and the mayors were released and reinstated after nine days of detention. Despite the defeat of the PKK, Turkey had yet to stabilize a new policy on the Kurds.

In the spring, the question of extending the presidency of Süleyman Demirel preoccupied Turkish political life. The seventy-five-year-old Demirel, who had been a domineering president, represented the old guard of Turkish politics; his friends had come and gone, but his enemies had accumulated. His eight-year term stood to end on 16 May. Only a constitutional amendment, requiring a three-fifths majority of parliament, could prolong it. Turkish prime minister Bülent Ecevit favored the extension, and the issue became a test of his ability to marshal his ruling coalition.

In the end, Ecevit failed: the parliament rejected the proposed amendment, and on 5 May, it elected a new president, Ahmet Necdet Sezer, head of the Constitutional Court and a fallback candidate nominated at the last minute by Ecevit. Many thought Sezer, lacking a political base, would adopt a lower profile than Demirel, and that he favored a more ceremonial presidency. They were wrong. The president defied the prime minister over every controversial issue, from civil service dismissals to bank privatization. Ecevit and Sezer eventually became the two opposite poles of Turkish politics. Their spats created the impression that no one was in charge.

In October, the Turkish banking regulatory board took over ten insolvent banks, and assumed their obligations. Thus began a rolling financial crisis that exposed all of the flaws of Turkey's political and economic system. Word soon spread that other banks had bad loans, and in November, a run on the banks drained $6bn. out of Turkey almost overnight. The crisis of confidence spread to the stock market, which fell by 40% in two weeks. Under US prodding, the International Monetary Fund (IMF) stepped in, pledging a $7.5bn. loan on 6 December. Turkey had a young, dynamic, and entrepreneurial population, and a sclerotic, plodding, and corrupt political system. By year's end, the country was closer than ever to experiencing another coup—this one, by the IMF.

NOTES

For the place and frequency of publications cited here, and for the full name of the publication, news agency, radio station or monitoring service where an abbreviation is used, please see "List of Sources."

1. Robert Satloff and Patrick Clawson, "The US Draft Treaty for Syria-Israel Peace: A Textual Analysis," *Peacewatch*, No. 242 (14 January 2000).
2. This issue was summarized by Frederic C. Hof and Patrick Clawson, "Who Will Control the Shore and Waters of the Galilee?," *Peacewatch,* No. 254 (13 April 2000).
3. Robert Satloff, "Syria's Critique of the US Draft Treaty: A Textual Analysis," *Peacewatch*, No. 243 (27 January 2000).
4. Ross Dunn, "Assad's Price is the Return of Galilee Shore," *The Times*, 29 March, and *JR*, 24 April 2000, quoting transcript of the talk as broadcast by MBC.
5. Quoted by Jane Perlez, "Clinton Says Next Move for Peace Is Assad's," *NYT*, 29 March 2000.
6. Journalist Patrick Seale, ever-sympathetic to the Syrian position, admitted that "Syria's negotiating style — its stiffness, its refusal to engage in public relations, its scornful neglect of Israeli domestic opinion — must also bear some part of the blame for failure....Damascus has refused to make the gestures which might have softened the Israeli public's deep distrust." Patrick Seale, "Obituary of the Syrian Track," *MEI*, 19 May 2000.
7. Quoted in *JR*, 8 May 2000.
8. Ranwa Yehia, "Farms Foreshadow Withdrawal," *AW*, 18 May 2000.
9. Nasrallah interview in *al-Wasat* (no date given), via *MM*, 30 May 2000.
10. *Al-Istiqlal*, quoted by Khalid Amayreh, "Hizbullah vs. Arafat," *MEI*, 2 June 2000.
11. Aaron Miller, quoted by Lamis Andoni, "The Washington Spin," *MEI*, 2 June 2000.
12. Leslie Susser, "The Carrot of Statehood," *JR*, 5 June 2000.
13. Khalid Amayreh, "The Territories Erupt," *MEI*, 19 May 2000.
14. This summary relies on the few published accounts available at the time of this writing, including Leslie Susser and Isabel Kershner, "The Tragedy of Errors," *JR*, 16 July 2001; and Hussein Agha and Robert Malley, "Camp David: The Tragedy of Errors," *New York Review of Books*, 9 August 2001.
15. According to Agha and Malley, "Camp David," Israel offered 91% of the West Bank.
16. Donald Neff, "The US Piles on the Pressure," *MEI*, 18 August 2000.
17. Fouad Ajami, "Intifada: The Future as History," *US News & World Report*, 4 June 2001.
18. David Makovsky, "Arafat's Resistance to a Summit," *Peacewatch*, No. 267 (28 June 2000).
19. Leslie Susser, "Heading for a Second Summit?," *JR*, 28 August 2000.
20. Graham Usher, "The 'Make or Break' Summit," *MEI*, 14 July 2000.
21. Jamil Hilal, "Polls Apart: Israeli and Palestinian Public Opinion after Camp David," *MEI*, 1 September 2000.

22. Deborah Sontag, "Arafat's Visit to Barak's Place Broke the Ice, Both Sides Say," *NYT*, 26 September 2000.
23. He also added that "Mubarak of Egypt confirms this adamantly." Ehud Ya'ari, "Less for Less in Jerusalem," *JR*, 25 September. Another journalist ruled out "another intifada, a regression to the black days of closed schools and shops and daily casualties on the firing line. There are too many factors mitigating against it." Hirsh Goodman, "Oslo Osmosis," *JR*, 10 October 2000. (This issue of the weekly was published just before the outbreak of the intifada.)
24. Ehud Ya'ari, "Super-Intifada," *JR*, 23 October 2000.
25. Quoted by Lee Hockstader, "Arafat: Missing in Action," *WP*, 22 October 2000.
26. Ehud Ya'ari, "Soft Siege," *JR*, 6 November 2000.
27. "Consolidating Bashar," *MEI*, 14 July 2000.
28. Amy W. Hawthorne, "Egyptian Elections: Rumblings of Change, But NDP Dominance Maintained," *Policywatch*, No. 506 (27 November 2000).
29. Nicholas Lehmann, "The Iraq Factor," *The New Yorker*, 22 January 2001.
30. Michael Rubin, "The Ebb and Flow of Reform in Iran," *Policywatch*, No. 459 (1 May 2000).
31. Text of Albright speech, *MM*, 20 March 2000.

INTERNATIONAL AND
REGIONAL AFFAIRS

The United States and the Middle East

BARRY RUBIN

During the year 2000, the US made its greatest effort ever to negotiate comprehensive Arab-Israeli peace agreements in the Middle East. At the same time, it continued efforts to maintain sanctions on Iraq and to explore how pressures or détente might change Iran's policies.

With Middle East peace a top foreign policy goal at the start of the year, President Bill Clinton was prepared, said his spokesperson, "to invest as many days" as necessary to achieve a negotiated settlement. "We're at a unique time in this process," the spokesperson suggested, "where [Israelis, Syrians, and Palestinians]...have a high level of trust in the president, built over...seven years of working on this process."[1]

National Security Advisor Samuel Berger proclaimed, "For the first time...Israel, Syria and the Palestinians have a common goal in sight, and the common sense to see that they have a historic opportunity to achieve it now."[2] The approaching end of Clinton's term also became a factor in the negotiations, adding a sense of urgency to his efforts.

Yet these expectations and efforts ended in total disappointment. The Syria-Israel negotiations in January quickly broke down. On the Israel-Palestinian front, US attempts to mediate a major breakthrough suffered delays in the first half of the year, followed by the failed Camp David summit in July, the outbreak of violence in September, the inability to broker a cease-fire in October, and the Palestinian rejection of Clinton's own peace proposal in December.

THE ARAB-ISRAELI ARENA

SYRIA-ISRAEL TALKS

Syria-Israel talks under US sponsorship began on 3 January at Shepherdstown, West Virginia (for the lead-up to the talks, see *MECS* 1999, pp. 23–24). Secretary of State Madeleine K. Albright described these negotiations as "a huge historic opportunity."[3] Clinton was closely involved, coming to participate four times in the first week and saying the talks were "off to a good start."[4] At first, the US played down the likelihood of success, with Albright saying,"We are at the beginning of a process here, not at the end of it."[5]

The meetings' format was modeled on the 1978 Camp David and 1998 Wye Plantation talks (see *MECS* 1977–78, pp. 29–30; 1998, pp. 21, 68–71). The intent was to isolate the negotiating teams to ensure an extended series of meetings, which included US-hosted social interaction, proximity talks with the US team shuttling between the two sides, and direct high-level exchanges. These discussions were supposed to sufficiently define and narrow the gaps to enable US bridging proposals to be presented along with offers of potential financial aid to implement any resulting agreements. State Department spokesperson James Rubin suggested, "A deal this big is going to carry with it a price tag....But we believe the peace is so important, and our vital interests could so be strengthened by a peace agreement, that it is worth our playing an important role."[6]

After the first day of talks, the US claimed success in creating four committees. In Rubin's words, "We are proceeding apace" and working to develop a work plan encompassing all issues.[7] But progress was soon seen as slow, attributed by US officials to the leaders' desire to please their constituents.

In an attempt to move the talks forward, Clinton presented a seven-page working paper to both sides on 8 January. "This is difficult stuff," Clinton said as he canceled other business in Washington to join the talks. "They are trying to imagine the end of the road." The document was a proposed text for an agreement, including each side's position and summarizing disagreements on points where they differed.[8]

Nevertheless, on 9 January, the talks adjourned, and though they were supposed to restart on 19 January, they never reconvened. Rubin remarked, "We believe that we cannot urge the parties to go faster in pursuing this agreement than they are comfortable with, that it's their decision; they are the ones that are going to have to make the decision as to whether to make the essential decisions to get an agreement."[9]

Clinton put a positive spin on the cessation of the talks: "The good news is I'm convinced they both still want to do it. They're not as far apart as they might be; they're not as far apart as they have been." Albright called the situation a "delay," adding:

> all this activity reflects that negotiations are now moving ahead....We are coming closer to settling one of history's longest and most enduring conflicts. Both sides genuinely desire peace, but overcoming a legacy of mistrust is not easy. But despite these tribulations, a key underlying reality is emerging: the logic of peace has become compelling for Arabs, Israelis and the Palestinians alike. Their leaders will have to take hard, fateful, even painful decisions. But they have increasingly come to understand that there is no better alternative.[10]

The administration was careful not to blame either side for the breakdown.[11] "It's certainly not a step forward," remarked a senior official, but attributed the problems as an inevitable part of the ups and downs of negotiations. Clinton and Albright talked to the leaders, and experts were to come to Washington for detailed talks.[12]

The administration tried one more time to find some way out of the impasse, a direct meeting in Geneva between Clinton and President Hafiz al-Asad of Syria. Berger said that differences between Syria and Israel regarding a peace agreement "may not be irreconcilable" and that the US hoped that the two sides "over the next few weeks will reach the conclusion that they can enter into a serious round of negotiation. But that's by no means certain."[13]

A three-hour Clinton-Asad meeting on 26 March, however, yielded no positive result as Asad rejected the proposals Clinton presented to him. The basic idea was a phased Israeli turnover of the Golan Heights to Syria in exchange for security guarantees, a peace agreement, and the step-by-step development of normal relations. Syria rejected the plan because it also demanded a small strip of territory along the Sea of Galilee shoreline which it had taken control of in the 1950s. A US official reported afterward that Asad was "immovable" and appeared to have come with the misconception that Barak and Clinton would meet all his demands (see chapter on Syria).

The administration knew that the meeting was a gamble but believed it had a better chance of success than proved to be the case, another diplomat said. Clinton said that it was now up to Asad to make the next move but it was generally — only privately — acknowledged that the Syria-Israel track was now dead.[14]

ISRAEL-PALESTINIAN NEGOTIATIONS

At the beginning of the year, Clinton administration officials expressed great optimism regarding the Palestinian track. The US had been promoting the peace process since the original agreement was signed on the White House lawn in 1993 (see *MECS* 1993, pp. 35–40). Periodically, the US had stepped in to mediate when progress seemed possible but was not happening. By 2000, though, the often-delayed process seemed to be at the point of final decision-making.

Even while dealing with the Syrian track, the US acknowledged the centrality of Israel-Palestinian negotiations. State Department spokesperson Rubin told reporters during the Syria-Israel talks in West Virginia on 4 January, "We have been in touch with both sides on a daily basis....We've always said...that it is possible to pursue both of these tracks....They each have their own logic, and their own rationale...and I think it shows that you can move forward on both tracks."[15]

On 20 January, Palestinian Authority (PA) leader Yasir 'Arafat visited Washington and lunched with Albright at her home. The US still hoped to complete an Israeli-Palestinian framework agreement by mid-February and US officials urged 'Arafat to show the flexibility needed to achieve this goal. In the Oval Office before he and 'Arafat met, Clinton said, "As in any process like this, there must be inevitable and difficult compromises. No one can get everything that either side wants." He added that he believed that 'Arafat and Barak, would "reach a comprehensive peace in a reasonably short period of time."[16] Clinton and 'Arafat met briefly also at the World Economic Forum in Davos, Switzerland on 29 January.[17]

In late February, after the failure to meet the deadline for a framework agreement, US peace envoy to the Middle East Dennis Ross visited the region. After meeting 'Arafat on 28 February, he predicted, "We will see a permanent status agreement by September of this year." Israeli and Palestinian negotiators met for two rounds of talks at Bolling AFB in Washington DC under US auspices in March and April in an attempt to reach a framework agreement that could lead to a final peace treaty by September. Clinton also consulted with President Husni Mubarak of Egypt during his 28 March visit to Washington.[18]

Barak and 'Arafat came to Washington to meet Clinton, on 11 and 20 April, respectively. Ross was then sent to the area for further exchanges. At this point, the administration was evaluating the state of the talks, points of agreement or differences, and the best steps to take next in trying to mediate the conflict.[19]

A senior administration official stated, "We are beginning a new phase in this process, obviously one in which the US will play a more intensified role."[20] Ross explained, "What is very clear to me is that there is a readiness on each side to get down to business in a serious way. They are continuing an effort that began at Bolling. We are in a new...more intensive phase....I will go back and forth between the leaders and the negotiators."[21]

Clinton met once again with Barak on 1 June. Barak and his own investigations had apparently convinced Clinton that the time was ripe for a summit. An administration official said the exchange showed "a very determined effort on Prime Minister Barak's part to seize the moment and to see if, in fact, from his standpoint it's possible to reach an agreement. [Clinton] feels, based on his conversation on the phone yesterday with Chairman 'Arafat, that he, too, has a commitment also to try to seize the moment and end this conflict."[22]

The next step in preparing for the summit was to send Albright to the region on 5 June, for the first time in six months. The following day she met with 'Arafat who agreed to come to Washington for consultations.[23] "The moment of truth is fast approaching in the pursuit of the Israeli-Palestinian peace," Albright said. "If the Israelis and the Palestinians are willing to accept that neither can get 100% of what they want, and that each side must address the other in a spirit of partnership, then they will succeed."[24]

Clinton and 'Arafat met on 14 June in a long session discussing all the major issues involved in a final peace accord, paying special attention to the proposed borders of a Palestinian state. According to a US official, the White House wanted a summit meeting but not one that would collapse in failure. As a senior official explained on 15 June: "For a summit we have to be in a position to have at least a reasonable chance to reach bridging solutions."[25]

In announcing the summit on 5 July, Clinton explained in detail the basis for holding the meeting and his expectations:

> The objective is to reach an agreement on the core issues that have fueled a half-century of conflict between Israelis and Palestinians.
>
> Why this summit, and why now? While Israeli and Palestinian negotiators have made real progress, crystallizing issues and defining gaps, the truth is they can take the talks no further at their level. Significant differences remain, and they involve the most complex and most sensitive of questions.
>
> The negotiators have reached an impasse. Movement now depends on historic decisions that only the two leaders can make. I will be there with them, and I intend to do all I can to help them in this endeavor.
>
> To delay this gathering, to remain stalled, is simply no longer an option, for the Israeli-Palestinian conflict, as all of us have seen, knows no status quo. It can move forward toward real peace, or it can slide back into turmoil. It will not stand still. If the parties do not seize this moment, if they cannot make progress now, there will be more hostility and more bitterness, perhaps even more violence, and to what end? Eventually, after more bloodshed and tears, they will have to come back to the negotiating table. They will have to return to face the same history, the same geography, the same demographic trends, the same passions, and the same hatreds, and, I am sure, the exact same choices that confront them here and now.
>
> The leaders have to make the decisions that are still there to be made, and the longer we wait, the more difficult the decisions are likely to become.[26]

During the spring of 2000, US officials had been briefed on secret Israel-Palestinian talks held in Europe. The two sides had agreed to go directly to a final status resolution and to produce a framework for such an agreement. On one hand, these discussions seemed to be making progress toward an agreement on most issues. But, on the other hand, without decisions by Barak and 'Arafat no more progress would be made and no deal could actually be closed. Given the approaching end of Clinton's term and 'Arafat's own threats of making a unilateral declaration of independence (see chapter on the PA), it seemed reasonable to bring the two leaders together for a summit that would try to bridge differences and try to reach a comprehensive agreement.

Clinton told a newspaper interviewer, "I would be totally misleading if I said I had an inkling that a deal is at hand." Yet despite his caution, Clinton and other US officials also expressed tremendous optimism over the prospects of success, with the president noting, "I think if we work hard we can get it done in a few days."[27] On leaving for the meeting on 11 July, Clinton stated, "The parties have proven that peace is possible when they are determined to make it. In the process, they have passed the point of no return."[28]

Nevertheless, while the talks continued from 11 to 24 July, they did not succeed but rather ended in total deadlock. Clinton was generally careful to avoid blaming either side, though he was more critical of 'Arafat. In an interview, he told Israeli television, "The Palestinians did make some moves at these talks that have never been made before. And while I made it clear in my statement, I thought that the prime minister was more creative and more courageous...I saw changes emerge on both sides, including within the Palestinian camp."[29] Talking to the London Arabic daily newspaper *al-Hayat*, Clinton asked for Arab help in reaching an agreement.[30]

The talks had failed to produce the hoped-for agreement but diplomatic efforts continued. Ross returned for talks with Israeli and Arab officials in August, conveying Clinton's readiness to hold additional summit meetings with Barak and 'Arafat. But there seemed no prospect for progress in the negotiations.[31] After the outbreak of violence in late September (see chapters on Israel and the PA), US efforts were given added impetus. The US urged both sides to calm the situation.[32]

This goal was said to cover the US decision to abstain on 7 October regarding a controversial UN Security Council resolution criticizing Israel for allegedly using "excessive force" in responding to the violence. US Ambassador to the UN Richard Holbrooke stated, "The focus of our efforts should not be on finger pointing and recrimination. What is critical now is to end the violence and restore calm throughout the region."[33] "Everything that the United States does," Clinton said, "should be designed toward, number one, trying to preserve the calm, and number two, trying to restore the peace process."[34]

After meetings with Barak and 'Arafat, Albright said that both leaders made clear their commitment "to find a way out of the tragic circumstances in which they are now caught up."[35] This effort led to the October Sharm al-Shaykh summit meeting, involving Barak, 'Arafat, Clinton, Mubarak (the host), and Jordan's King 'Abdallah. Clinton said the meeting "made real progress" because both sides "agreed to issue public statements unequivocally calling for an end of violence" as well as "immediate, concrete measures to end the current confrontation, eliminate points of friction, ensure an end to violence and incitement, maintain calm, and prevent recurrence of recent events." The US would facilitate security cooperation between the parties and also help create a fact-finding committee "on the events of the past several weeks and how to prevent their recurrence." Finally, Clinton called for a return to negotiations seeking a permanent status agreement.[36]

Yet this agreement was not implemented, despite Clinton's continued contacts with Barak and 'Arafat, including an offer in early November to invite them to Washington. The administration, however, continued to sound optimistic. For example, on 3 November, State Department spokesperson Richard Boucher declared that, Albright, following talks with Israeli and Palestinian negotiators, had found that the parties "agreed with each other on the steps needed to go forward."[37] Asked about US attitudes toward 'Arafat,

Boucher responded: "As long as the violence continues...the leaders, need to do more....They need to fully implement the understandings thoroughly and quickly. So it's not a question of...'It's out of my hands' or 'I don't have control.'"[38] The US urged Israel to lift economic restrictions on the Palestinians, saying the US government does not believe that "exerting economic pressure can be productive."[39] But it also rejected 'Arafat's call for UN observers in the territories.[40]

At the request of the US, once again, on 19 December, Israeli and Palestinian negotiators returned to Bolling AFB to discuss a final status agreement. Clinton and Albright joined the talks at times. On 23 December, Clinton presented his own comprehensive plan to both sides for the first time.[41] He stated, "I put some ideas on the table. They go beyond where we were at Camp David; they meet the fundamental needs that both sides expressed at Camp David."[42] On 26 December, the State Department announced that the "parties have taken back ideas to consult with their leaders. We expect to hear from them later this week on whether these ideas are the basis for moving forward."[43] Clinton urged the Israelis and Palestinians to reach a peace agreement by the time he left office on 20 January. "I think that if it can be resolved at all, it can be resolved in the next three weeks," Clinton said at a 28 December press conference. "I don't think the circumstances are going to get better. I think, that in all probability, they'll get more difficult."[44]

The efforts by Clinton during the year 2000, and especially at Shepherdstown, Camp David and in presenting his own personal plans, marked a culmination of US peacemaking efforts not only during his term but over the past quarter-century. For the first time, the US had talked directly to the parties about its own vision of a comprehensive peace. The failure of this effort seemed to be a landmark in US Middle East policy. For if the countries directly involved were unwilling or unable to come to an agreement, the priority and hope of the US brokering a peace deal would be dramatically lowered.

LEBANON

The US supported Israel's unilateral withdrawal from South Lebanon (see chapters on Israel and Lebanon) — though it had not pressured Israel toward such a move — and sought to ensure the peacefulness of that border. Asked if he expected violence after the pullout, Clinton responded on 11 April: "If Israel pulls out in accordance with the UN resolution [425], what justification will anyone have for violence? [The Lebanese] have been asking for this for years."[45] The US also nominally supported Syrian withdrawal but did not actively seek this outcome.[46]

The US did, however, seek to ensure the end of fighting in that area. As Defense Secretary William Cohen stated on 25 May, "It is important that the UN confirm the Israeli withdrawal as quickly as possible. Once that has been done, the role of the UN will be to restore international peace and security and to assist the government of Lebanon in ensuring the return of its effective authority in the area." The State Department urged Lebanon's government to "move quickly" to maintain peace in the area with the help of UN observers. Albright urged Syrian foreign minister Faruq al-Shar' to use Syrian influence to restrain the Lebanese Hizballah movement which had spearheaded the fight against Israel in South Lebanon. The State Department reiterated US support for the Ta'if accords of 1989, mandating the disbanding of all Lebanese militias (see *MECS* 1989, p. 29).[47]

Albright noted that the US had told those who "have control over the Hizballah" (i.e., Syria and Iran) "that violence is not the solution here." The US was working with the

UN to press for calm along the border. "We believe that the Lebanese army and their police forces need to get down into south Lebanon; and then the UN, through [its peacekeeping] operation there, should be able to help maintain the calm."[48]

THE US AND IRAQ, IRAN AND THE PERSIAN GULF

IRAQ

Regarding Iraq, US policy had three basic principles. First, it continued efforts to preserve international sanctions while slowly letting them become weaker to avoid more drastic reductions in restrictions. Second, the US supported attempts to restart inspections but was aware that Iraq was unlikely able to permit them. Thus, maintaining sanctions was a more important priority than making concessions to ensure new inspections. Third, the US maintained a sporadic but continuous bombing campaign against Iraqi efforts to interfere with reconnaissance flights. These bombings also served the purpose of letting the US hit suspected weapons' and military sites.

In January, the Clinton administration fought against Iraqi attempts to block creation of a new commission to restart arms monitoring after a year in which inspections had been completely suspended (see *MECS* 1999, pp. 282–85) by Baghdad. "If we allow Iraq to make the decisions as some seem to want, we are putting the whole system on its head, and we're never going to get the disarmament the resolutions require," State Department spokesperson Rubin said.[49]

At the same time, US intelligence reports and officials warned that Iraq was using the inspectors' absence to develop chemical and biological weapons and rebuild military installations destroyed in earlier bombings. US policy was in a quandary. It had no additional means to force Iraqi compliance, given the already existing sanctions and allies' unwillingness to tighten them. The administration was not ready to use all-out force against Iraq nor did it have any faith in Iraqi opposition groups that Congress was touting as a way to replace Saddam Husayn. Consequently, the best option seemed to be to maintain sanctions and maximize the international isolation of Iraq. If Iraq's refusal to cooperate on inspections postponed the end of sanctions, this outcome coincided with US interests and goals.

US officials said there remained three "red lines" that could lead to the use of force: a threat against a neighboring country like Kuwait or Saudi Arabia; an attack on the Kurdish autonomous area in northern Iraq; or a renewal of nuclear, chemical or biological weapons programs.[50] Yet clearly, despite its rhetoric, the Clinton administration wanted to avoid escalating the conflict with Iraq, concerned about the potential consequences of such action and worried about its lack of international support.

At the same time, the US knew that sanctions were eroding in several ways: through cheating; pressure from countries like China, France and Russia to reduce the penalties; and concessions made by the US in the face of this pressure. In terms of cheating, the State Department concluded that illicit oil exports from Iraq averaged 100,000 b/d in the year 2000, double the level for 1998 when oil prices were much lower (see *MECS* 1998, pp. 58–60).[51] But the US could not easily counter this leakage since it went through Turkey and Jordan, allies whom the US did not want to antagonize, and Iran, a state where the US had no leverage.

In addition, US businesses were involved with Iraq through the legal "oil-for-food" program. American companies purchased about 700,000 of the 2 m. b/d exported daily by Iraq, mainly through foreign go-betweens who then sent the oil to US ports.[52]

A case study in the US tactical retreat was a proposal introduced to the UN in March to allow Iraq to spend $600m. (up from $300m.) on importing spare parts and other equipment for its oil industry in order to increase production and thus provide more money to pay for civilian goods and projects.[53]

The US thus recognized that sanctions were gradually being loosened but accepted this in order to maintain an international coalition to keep some sanctions in place and also to counter accusations that the sanctions were hurting the Iraqi people. Secretary of State Albright presented this strategy in a September Senate Foreign Relations Committee hearing. Saddam Husayn, she said:

> is now selling more oil for food and medicine than ever before....We allowed that because we wanted the Iraqi people to have what they needed....[But] we are [not] the ones that are keeping the Iraqi people from having food and medicine. There never has been an embargo on food and medicine. The only thing that has been lacking was the money for Saddam Husayn to allow that, and the pumping of oil has now allowed that.[54]

The US did, however, have two direct ways to affect Iraqi policy or to weaken the regime: carrying out bombing or missile raids and supporting the opposition. There were many such air attacks — averaging once every three days — and Iraq claimed they caused high civilian casualties. The Pentagon said more than 280,000 sorties were flown in the almost ten years since no-flight zones were imposed, without a single loss of aircraft to hostile fire. Still, the Iraqi decision to challenge reconnaissance patrols from mid-1998 onward led to an escalation of US attacks on radar and anti-aircraft installations.[55]

As for covert measures, *Washington Post* columnist Jim Hoagland wrote that the program to topple Saddam, instituted in the previous year (see *MECS* 1999, pp. 273–75) "has ground to a halt" and that CIA briefers told congressional committees the "covert program...has only a 10% to 15% chance of success." The CIA, Defense Department, and White House officials all had a low opinion of the Iraqi exile groups that Congress ordered them to support. "Next to nothing is being spent on military and civilian training for the opposition," wrote Hoagland, "and the money is mostly used for travel, office rentals, and salaries."[56]

The Republicans criticized Clinton's efforts as insufficient. While administration officials kept insisting that they are interested in ousting Saddam, complained Sen. Sam Brownback (R-Ks), "not one official...has been willing to take even the most minimal steps towards that end." Republican presidential candidate George W. Bush said that he would take a tough stand against Iraq if he were elected.[57]

IRAN

The US continued efforts to promote détente with Iran. Despite some hopeful signs, there was still little concrete progress and nothing approaching a real breakthrough or change. Some events were symbolic, like the visit of an Iranian soccer team to the US in January for the first time since the 1979 revolution.[58] In March, the Clinton administration eased import bans on such Iranian consumer goods as pistachios, caviar and carpets.

White House spokesperson Joe Lockhart said Clinton had been looking at a variety of ways to "encourage a constructive dialogue" with Iran.[59]

The administration heartily welcomed the February Iranian parliamentary elections that turned into a landslide victory for the moderates (see chapter on Iran). James Rubin called the election "an event of historic proportions. The Iranian people have demonstrated unmistakably that they want policies of openness and engagement with the rest of the world [and] greater freedom within Iran."[60] He added that the administration would watch closely to see whether the new parliament would lead Iran to change its opposition to the Middle East peace process, cease support of terrorist groups seeking to derail the negotiations, and reexamine Iran's efforts toward developing weapons of mass destruction (WMD). These were the three US conditions for normalizing relations with Iran.[61]

At the same time, US efforts to prevent Iran from obtaining WMD continued. In March, Clinton signed into law the Iran Non-Proliferation Act of 2000 to punish countries or companies helping in Iran's weapons' development programs. Clinton stated that its goal was to combat "Iran's efforts to acquire weapons of mass destruction and missile delivery systems. This issue remains at the top of the agenda with Russia as well as with other countries whose companies may be providing such assistance to Iran."[62] The US continued careful monitoring of Russian institutions suspected of helping Iran obtain WMD.[63]

OTHER GULF ISSUES

The US continued to supply strategic support and arms to the Gulf Cooperation Council states. For example, in March the US finalized the sale of eighty F-16 fighter jets, with more advanced capabilities than those then being deployed by the US air force, to the United Arab Emirates for $6bn. Vice-President Al Gore stated, "The sale is part of US efforts to help Gulf allies defend their interests in the region." He also praised the sale for providing jobs to Americans.[64]

The US was very concerned about petroleum price hikes during the year. Clinton warned that this situation could damage the US economy, particularly at a time when US inventories were at a twenty-four-year low, and urged OPEC countries to increase production (see chapter on Middle East economic developments).[65]

NOTES

For the place and frequency of publications cited here, and for the full name of the publication, news agency, radio station or monitoring service where an abbreviation is used, please see "List of Sources." Only in the case of more than one publication bearing the same name is the place of publication noted here.

1. AP, 3 January 2000; White House daily briefing (Shepherdstown, West Virginia), 3 January 2000 <www.usembassy-israel.org.il/publish/peace/archives/2000/january/me0104g.html>.
2. *NYT*, 7 January 2000.
3. *NYT*, 3 January 2000.
4. *NYT*, 4 January 2000.
5. *IHT*, 4 January 2000.

6. *NYT*, 4 January 2000.
7. US Department of State briefing, 4 January 2000 <www.state.gov/www/regions/nea/000104sb_va_peace.html> or <www.usembassy-israel.org.il/publish/peace/archives/2000/january/me0104i.html>.
8. This paper's text was published in *Ha'aretz*, 13 January 2000. Detailed accounts of US involvement are provided in *NYT*, 9 and 10 January 2000.
9. US Department of State briefing, 11 January 2000 <secretary.state.gov/www/briefings/0001/000111db.html>.
10. "Remarks by Secretary of State Madeleine K. Albright, On 'Sustaining Democracy in the Twenty-First Century,'" The Rostow Lecture Series, School of Advanced International Studies, Johns Hopkins University, 18 January 2000 <secretary.state.gov/www/statements/2000/000118.html>; Clinton is Convinced Israelis, Syrians Still Want Peace Talks, 17 January 2000 <www.usembassy-israel.org.il/publish/peace/archives/2000/january/me0118c.html>; Albright on Delay of Third Round of Israel-Syria Talks, 17 January 2000 <www.usembassy-israel.org.il/publish/peace/archives/2000/january/me0118b.html>.
11. *WP*, 18 January 2000.
12. Reuters, 18 January 2000.
13. AP, 26 March 2000.
14. *NYT*, 28 March 2000.
15. US Department of State briefing, 4 January 2000.
16. *NYT*, 21 January 2000.
17. AP, 30 January, 2000.
18. AP, 28 March 2000.
19. Background briefing on Clinton-Barak meeting, 11 April 2000 <www.usembassy-israel.org.il/publish/peace/archives/2000/april/me0412a.html>.
20. Senior official briefing on Clinton-'Arafat meeting, 20 April 2000 <www.usembassy-israel.org.il/publish/peace/archives/2000/april/me0421b.html>.
21. Press Q&A by Ambassador Dennis Ross, prior to start of negotiations session, Eilat, Israel, 3 May 2000.
22. AP, 1 June 2000; senior official briefing on Clinton-Barak meeting in Lisbon, 1 June 2000 <www.usembassy-israel.org.il/publish/peace/archives/2000/june/me0601c.html>.
23. US Department of State briefing, 1 June <secretary.state.gov/www/briefings/0006/000601db.html>; Reuters, 5 June; Department of State briefing, 6 June 2000 <secretary.state.gov/www/briefings/0006/000606db.html>.
24. *NYT*, 6 June 2000.
25. Reuters, 15 June; *NYT*, 16 June 2000.
26. Announcement by President Bill Clinton on Mideast summit at White House briefing, 5 July 2000 <www.usembassy-israel.org.il/publish/peace/archives/2000/july/me0705c.html>.
27. AP, 5 July 2000.
28. Clinton Remarks Upon Departure For Camp David Peace Summit (The only way for the Israelis and Palestinians now is "forward"), 11 July <www.usembassy-israel.org.il/publish/peace/archives/2000/july/me0711c.html>. See also his column in *Newsweek*, 17 July. See also Dennis Ross in US Department of State, Mideast Coordinator Ross' interview on CNN's "Late Edition," 10 July <www.usembassy-israel.org.il/publish/peace/archives/2000/july/me0710d.html>; *New York Daily News*, 17 July 2000.
29. Clinton Interview by Israeli Television on Peace Talks, 28 July 2000 <www.usembassy-israel.org.il/publish/peace/archives/2000/july/me0728a.html>.
30. Clinton Interview with *al-Hayat* on Middle East Peace, 11 August 2000 <www.usembassy-israel.org.il/publish/peace/archives/2000/august/me0811b.html>.
31. *NYT*, 19 August 2000.
32. US Department of State briefing, 29 September 2000 <secretary.state.gov/www/briefings/0009/000929db.html>.

33. Holbrooke's remarks on UN resolution on Mideast violence, 10 October 2000 <www. usembassy-israel.org.il/publish/peace/archives/2000/october/me1010b.html>.
34. Clinton Q & A with Reporters on the Middle East, 11 October 2000 <www.usembassy-israel.org.il/publish/peace/archives/2000/october/me1011a.html>.
35. Albright Press Conference on Mideast Violence, 5 October 2000 <www.usembassy-israel.org.il/publish/peace/archives/2000/october/me1005b.html>.
36. Clinton-Mubarak Statement at End of Mideast Summit, 17 October 2000 <www. usembassy-israel.org.il/publish/peace/archives/2000/october/me1018a.html>.
37. US Department of State briefing, 3 November 2000 <secretary.state.gov/www/briefings/ 0011/001103db.html>.
38. US Department of State briefing, 3 November 2000.
39. US Department of State spokesman on Mideast Developments, 6 December 2000 <www. usembassy-israel.org.il/publish/peace/archives/2000/december/me1206b.html>.
40. US Backs UN Rejection of Mideast Observer Mission, 19 December 2000 <www. usembassy-israel.org.il/publish/peace/archives/2000/december/me1219a.html>. See also, Ambassador James B. Cunningham, Deputy US representative to the UN statement following the Security Council's Failure to Adopt a Draft Resolution Calling for Establishment of an Observer Mission in the Occupied Palestinian Territories, 18 December 2000 <www.usembassy-israel.org.il/publish/peace/archives/2000/december/ me1219a.html>.
41. "The Clinton Plan," 23 December 2000 in Ha'aretz, 31 December 2000.
42. Clinton on Mideast Peace Prospects, 29 December 2000 <www.usembassy-israel.org.il/ publish/peace/archives/2000/december/me1229a.html>.
43. US Department of State spokesman on Middle East Development, 26 December 2000 <secretary.state.gov/www/briefings/0012/001226db.html>.
44. Clinton on Mideast Peace Prospects, 29 December 2000 <www.usembassy-israel.org.il/ publish/peace/archives/2000/december/me1229a.html>.
45. Clinton and Israel's Barak Remarks before Meeting, 11 April 2000 <www.usembassy-israel.org.il/publish/peace/archives/2000/april/me0412b.html>.
46. Senior Official Briefs on Clinton-'Arafat Meeting, 20 April 2000 <www.usembassy-israel.org.il/publish/peace/archives/2000/april/me0421c.html>.
47. JP, 25 May 2000.
48. Albright Interview Telecast 26 May on CBS-TV's "Early Show", 26 May 2000 <secretary. state.gov/www/statements/2000/000526.html>.
49. NYT, 20, 27 January, 2000.
50. NYT, 1 February, 2000.
51. AP, 7 February, 2000.
52. WP, 21 February, 2000.
53. NYT, 1 April, 2000.
54. Albright Before Senate Foreign Relations Committee, 27 September, 2000 <secretary. state.gov/www/statements/2000/000926.html>.
55. WP, 17 June, 2000.
56. WP, 2 March, 2000.
57. NYT, 3 July, 2000.
58. NYT, 16 January, 2000.
59. NYT, 15 March, 2000.
60. US Department of State Spokesperson James Rubin, US Calls Iranian Elections: Event of Historic Proportions, 22 February, 2000 <secretary.state.gov/www/briefings/0002/ 000222db.html>.
61. NYT, 21 February, 2000.
62. White House, "Statement by the President," 14 March 2000 <clinton6.nara.gov/2000/03/ 2000-03-14-president-signs-iran-nonproliferation-act-of.html>.
63. US Department of State, "Statement by James P. Rubin, Spokesman," 24 April, 2000 <www.usembassy-israel.org.il/publish/peace/archives/2000/april/me0424a.html>.

64. Vice-President Gore Lauds Lockheed Martin Sale of F-16s to the United Arab Emirates, 5 March <www.usembassy-israel.org.il/publish/peace/archives/2000/march/me0306b. html>. See also Reuters, 21 March 2000.
65. Clinton's Remarks on Mideast Peace Meetings and Oil Prices, 7 September 2000 <www. usembassy-israel.org.il/publish/peace/archives/2000/september/me0907a.html>.

Western Europe, Russia and the Middle East

DAN ELDAR

Throughout the first year of the twenty-first century, the European Union (EU) was mainly preoccupied with molding its identity and structure for the coming decade. Significant progress was achieved in the process of EU enlargement eastward. By contrast, European expectations of progress in the Arab-Israeli peace process, heightened in 1999 following the election of Ehud Barak as prime minister in Israel, were partially deflated in March 2000 in light of the failure of a summit meeting in Geneva between US president Bill Clinton and Syrian president Hafiz al-Asad. Disappointment grew in the wake of an unsuccessful tripartite conference between the US, Palestinian and Israeli leadership at Camp David, Maryland in July-August. The outbreak of a new cycle of Arab-Israeli violence at the end of September, culminating in Barak's resignation early in 2001, ended European expectation of an imminent settlement. However, France, which assumed the presidency of the EU in the second half of 2000, attempted to fill a perceived vacuum in the Middle East peace process following the failure of the Camp David summit. In September, President Jacques Chirac, struggling with a sharp loss of prestige domestically, explored the possibility of a French initiative but without success.

The EU, and most of its member states, retained by and large their basic policy toward the Arab-Israeli peace process during the year, namely, avoiding any competition with the US and perceiving their own role as complementary to and supportive of American diplomatic activity. Given President Clinton's intensive involvement in the process until the very last days of his term, there was little room for effective European intervention (see chapter on the US and the Middle East).

In contrast to the EU's minimal impact and frustration with the Arab-Israeli peace process, the process of normalization of relations between the West European states and Iran proceeded apace. Highlights of this included visits by Iranian foreign minister Kamal Kharrazi to London at the beginning of the year and of President Mohammad Khatami to Berlin in July.

In another sphere, namely Iraq, France, along with Russia, continued to press for lifting the sanctions against Baghdad, and permitted French humanitarian flights to Iraq.

West European relations with Libya warmed during the year following the agreement by Libyan leader Mu'ammar al-Qadhdhafi to permit the two Libyan suspects in the 1988 bombing of a Pan Am aircraft to stand trial before a Scottish court at The Hague (see chapter on Libya). Notably, the European dialogue with Libya, as with other North African countries, including Egypt, shifted from the Middle Eastern context adhered to by the EU in the past to an African context, reflected in the first Euro-Africa summit, held in Cairo in April.[1]

Russia's new president, Vladimir Putin, retained the ambition of his predecessor, Boris Yeltsin of restoring his country's influence in the Middle East. Emphasizing Russia's official role as co-sponsor of the Arab-Israeli peace process, Foreign Minister Igor Ivanov engaged in intensive diplomatic activity, shuttling in the region in the manner of one of his predecessors in office, Yevgeny Primakov (see *MECS* 1997, pp. 40, 64). In contrast to its policy in the Arab-Israeli arena, where like EU member states, Russia yielded to US primacy, Putin defied the American policy of banning exportation of military equipment and nuclear technology to Iran and significantly upgraded political and military relations with it.[2] Russia also maintained close relations with Iraq. The protracted conflict between the Russian army and the Muslim rebels in Chechnya did not harm Putin's policy in the Middle East; Middle Eastern states did not publicly contest the new Russian president's portrayal of the Chechnya conflict as a struggle against international terrorism and not a conflict with the Muslim world.

WESTERN EUROPE AND THE ARAB-ISRAELI PEACE PROCESS

AN AVALANCHE OF VISITS
The EU, under the acting presidency of Portugal, launched a round of official visits to the Middle East at the start of 2000, aimed at building up personal contacts on the part of the European office holders and projecting a higher EU profile in the peace process. British prime minister Tony Blair was one of the European leaders to maintain frequent consultations with both Israeli prime minister Barak and Palestinian Authority (PA) chairman Yasir 'Arafat. Blair was optimistic at the beginning of the year regarding peace prospects for Israel and its neighbors.[3] French president Chirac also conveyed goodwill toward Barak; the Israeli leader responded with telephone updates to the French president on developments in the peace process.

Portuguese foreign minister Jaime Gama led a three-day round of talks with Middle Eastern leaders in the region in mid-January, accompanied by EU foreign policy chief Javier Solana and EU special envoy for the peace process, Miguel Angel Moratinos. The delegation visited Israel, the PA, Egypt, Syria and Jordan. The EU, Gama stated, was "extremely worried" that negotiations between Israelis and the PA, "held up by difficulties which must be overcome without delay."[4] Although Israel showed a distinct lack of enthusiasm regarding EU attempts to play a more active role in the peace process, Solana stressed the EU commitment to assist the process on all its tracks.[5]

The president of the European Parliament, Nicole Fontaine, visited the region in February,[6] reiterating the EU intention to support the Israeli-Palestinian peace process in every possible way. Initially, she refused to meet PA officials in East Jerusalem, probably yielding to pressure by her Israeli hosts. Only after heavy pressure by political leaders in Europe, including Chirac, did Fontaine acquiesce, meeting the Palestinian leaders in East Jerusalem in a chilly atmosphere. Fontaine, however, in a statement in Jordan, reiterated a previous 1999 EU statement regarding the problem of Jerusalem in the peace process, namely that the city must be viewed as a "corpus separatum"[7] (see *MECS* 1999, p. 33).

Concurrently, French prime minister Lionel Jospin paid a three-day visit to Israel and the PA. The aims of the visit were: to demonstrate a new chapter in relations between France and Israel; to showcase Jospin's independence in shaping French foreign policy under Chirac's presidency, with an eye to the presidential elections in France in 2002;

and to prepare the ground for the forthcoming presidency of France of the EU. Jospin headed a delegation of cabinet ministers that included Foreign Minister Hubert Vedrine. The visit turned stormy when Jospin, in a press conference in Israel, referred to the Lebanese Hizballah as terrorists and expressed understanding for Israeli retaliatory activity in Lebanon (see below). Palestinians were fearful that Jospin's remarks signaled a change in France's traditionally pro-Arab policy. As a result, he was met by violent protests by Palestinian students at a West Bank university in a visit there and was slightly injured by a stone on the back of his head. Chirac, the French Foreign Ministry and Jospin himself, upon returning to Paris, hastened to assure the Arab world that no substantial change of policy had occurred.[8]

Soon afterward, the president of the European Commission, Romano Prodi, paid his first visit to Israel and the PA, pressing for greater political and economic EU involvement in the peace process.[9]

EU commissioner of external relations, Chris Patten, made a week-long fact-finding tour in the region in early April. During meetings with leaders from Egypt, Israel, the PA, Jordan and Syria, Patten cautioned that Europe would not automatically bankroll the peace agreements.[10] Reiterating the EU stance, he defined the union involvement in the peace process as complementing the leading role played by the US. The EU would assist the parties in the negotiations only where they sought such help.[11]

Overall, the wave of European officials' visits to the Middle East in the early part of the year failed to inject any significant momentum into the sluggish Israeli-Palestinian negotiations. Early in May, Moratinos acknowledged the absence of progress and dispelled any illusions about meeting the 13 May deadline for the signing of the framework agreement for a final settlement between the two sides.[12] Nevertheless, EU officials remained engaged.

Antonio Gutrerres, Portuguese prime minister and current president of the European Council, brought up allegations of accelerated Israeli construction in the West Bank settlements.[13] At the same time concern was voiced in Israel about possible EU recognition of a Palestinian state should it be declared on 13 September, the date announced by the PA as its new deadline for reaching a framework agreement on the final settlement with Israel.[14]

THE PALESTINIAN-ISRAELI TRACK

On the day that France took over the EU presidency, 1 July 2000, President Chirac, in a symbolic gesture, received PA chairman 'Arafat in Paris, at 'Arafat's request. Presumably, the Palestinian leader wanted to sound out the French view regarding the unilateral declaration of independence (UDI) scheduled for 13 September. France had joined other EU member states in 1999 in supporting the postponement of UDI, initially scheduled for May 1999.[15]

However, the secondary status of the EU was quickly highlighted by the fact that the EU was not invited to take part in the US-sponsored Israeli-Palestinian summit at Camp David from 26 July–7 August. Moratinos had to be satisfied with maintaining continuous contact with the participants.[16] Following the summit, Israel launched an intensive diplomatic campaign to convince EU member states to refrain from supporting the mooted UDI. Most of the European countries expressed sympathy for the Israeli positions presented at the Camp David summit.[17] The UN Millennium Assembly in September was an opportunity used by the Israeli prime minister to hold a series of meetings with the EU leaders present. They tended to support the Israeli positions put forward at Camp David, while exerting pressure on 'Arafat to refrain from a UDI and to demonstrate greater flexibility regarding the proposals raised at Camp David.[18]

Just prior to the UN General Assembly meeting, EU foreign ministers meeting in Evian on 1 September had already indicated opposition to a Palestinian UDI on 23 September. The end of October was mentioned as a possible new deadline for reaching a settlement, given the approaching end of Clinton's term of office. Mention of a Palestinian UDI was carefully avoided. Britain, the Scandinavian countries and the Netherlands were of the opinion that any EU intervention in the negotiations should be delayed until an agreement was reached. Italy, France, Belgium and Spain, on the other hand, felt that it was "frustrating for the EU to go to the region with its checkbook only once a peace agreement has been reached, and that it must act now."[19] Although the entire first day of the summit was devoted to the peace process, no joint declaration on the subject was issued.[20]

At the same time, Chirac, anxious to step into a perceived vacuum in the wake of the failed Camp David summit, hosted Egyptian President Husni Mubarak, his closest Middle Eastern ally. Their discussion focused on the various solutions to the Jerusalem question. Chirac concluded the talks with the Egyptian leader on an optimistic note, observing: "There is a feeling that we are close to the goal and only a small effort is needed to reach the anticipated peace."[21]

The shift in the EU stance disappointed the PA, which announced the postponement of the UDI at that time. The EU foreign ministers participating in the assembly praised this decision, at the same time reiterating the Palestinian right to a sovereign state.[22]

THE EU AND THE COLLAPSE OF THE PEACE PROCESS
The sudden violence between the Palestinians and the Israelis that erupted on 28 September evoked a quick response by the EU acting president, Jacques Chirac. On 1 October, he issued a statement "on behalf of the EU" that the clashes in Jerusalem were sparked by an act of "provocation," thereby accepting the PA version that blamed Israeli opposition leader Ariel Sharon's visit to the Temple Mount for triggering the outburst. The EU called on both parties to end the confrontations and "prevent further acts of violence." Referring implicitly to Israel, it warned "against an unjustified use of force."[23]

This step marked the end of the EU's relatively sympathetic stance toward the Barak government. Chirac now adopted a more activist approach toward the Arab-Israeli arena hitherto restrained by several other EU member states. In a second statement, on 2 October, Chirac expressed dismay and concern over the upsurge of violence caused by an "irresponsible act of provocation...which ignited predictable conflagration."[24] France then pushed for the formation of an international commission of inquiry into the outbreak of the violence.[25] Responding affirmatively to a PA appeal for the EU to take part in such a commission, French foreign minister Vedrine emphasized his "unreserved condemnation" of "Mr. Sharon's deliberate provocation for internal political reasons, which is even more serious."[26] Israeli political leaders considered French support for the formation of a commission of inquiry as "total capitulation to the Palestinian demands."[27]

The pointed blame by the French of Israel for the outbreak of violence, and the pressure to hold an international inquiry, dominated the atmosphere of a four-way summit meeting in Paris on 4 October between Barak, 'Arafat, Chirac and US secretary of state Madeleine Albright to discuss a solution to the crisis. Chirac, adhering to the Palestinian version of the outbreak of the intifada, spoke harshly to Barak, particularly in the wake of his objection to an international inquiry. Barak subsequently blamed Chirac for the failure of the summit and for encouraging new terrorism in the Middle East.[28] Several days later, Chirac tried to balance his policy by publicly condemning the Palestinian destruction of the Tomb of Joseph in Nablus, a Jewish holy site, along with a Palestinian terror attack in Jerusalem. The Israelis viewed these declarations as too little and too late to repair the damage caused to French-Israeli relations.[29]

Concerned with the shift toward support for the Palestinian side, the Israeli government made efforts to elicit a more balanced attitude from EU leaders and the public. Shimon Peres, the Israeli minister for regional cooperation, embarked on a diplomatic blitz in Western Europe, including Biarritz, France, where he held talks with leaders participating in the EU Council conference there.[30] A statement issued by the council reflected a measure of neutrality, addressing a "solemn appeal" to the Israeli and Palestinian leaders and peoples to stop the escalation and bring an immediate end to the violence. It also requested Javier Solana to continue his fact-finding mission in the Middle East.[31] The statement omitted mention of a commission of inquiry or any other initiatives, but expressed support for the prospect of holding an Israeli-Palestinian summit at Sharm al-Shaykh in Egypt. Moreover, Chirac acknowledged at a news conference that the EU involvement with the peace talks was "marginal," and that "if the parties request it, then we will be present. In no way do we wish to complicate matters." In an unusually frank admission, he also acknowledged being traumatized by the crisis in the Middle East. "We had the feeling a fortnight ago that we were very close to reaching a peace agreement...maybe in a wave of optimism. It was a cruel disappointment to us."[32]

Referring to this sense of frustration, Belgian foreign minister Louis Michel spoke out at Biarritz in favor of a stronger political role for the EU in the Middle East peace process to counter-balance that of the US.[33] In this context, EU envoy Solana, received an invitation from Mubarak on his Middle East mission to participate in the Sharm al-Shaykh summit agreed upon by the Israelis and the Palestinians.[34] The invitation to the EU, as well as to the secretary-general of the UN, was approved by the US, Israel and the Palestinians. Solana also took part in the negotiations leading to the summit, which was held on 16–17 October.[35] Moreover, he was appointed to the five-member international fact-finding committee agreed upon at Sharm al-Shaykh to examine the crisis, headed by former US senator George Mitchell.[36]

The upgrading of EU participation in the efforts to resolve the Israeli-Palestinian crisis did not mean that there was a consensus of views among EU member states. On 19 October, Germany, Britain, the Netherlands and Denmark abstained in a UN General Assembly vote condemning Israel for "using violence and exaggerated force against Palestinian civilians." This was a setback for France as acting president of the EU.[37] Still, in the battle between Israel and the Palestinians over European public opinion and the support of the EU leaders, the Palestinians won greater sympathy and understanding. Responding to a Palestinian request, the European Commission authorized a payment of 27m. euro to the PA on 8 November to help meet urgent current expenses, including salaries for public sector employees, drawn from a special cash arrangement agreed upon in 1998.[38] The EU also applied pressure on Israel to verify the origin of products exported to Europe in order to bar exports produced in the Israeli-ruled areas of the West Bank and Gaza from benefiting by tax exemption.[39]

The escalating Palestinian-Israeli violence was discussed at the fourth annual Euro-

Mediterranean foreign ministers conference (Marseilles, 15–16 November) devoted to fostering relationships within the region based on the Barcelona process (see *MECS* 1997, p. 65). Syria and Lebanon boycotted the conference. The closing communiqué reaffirmed the Berlin (1999) and Biarritz declarations supporting the establishment of a sovereign democratic Palestinian state, and, moreover, at an early date, preferably through negotiations.[40] While the Arab countries participating in the summit deplored the EU failure to become more involved in the peace process,[41] Israeli officials interpreted the communiqué, and in particular the notion of establishing a Palestinian state "at an early date," as a significant and negative deviation from previous EU declarations.[42] The adoption of the Euro-Mediterranean Charter of Peace and Stability — the main goal of the conference — was postponed owing to the unsettled political situation in the Middle East, further evidence that the Barcelona Euro-Mediterranean process had fallen hostage to the lack of progress in the Arab-Israeli peace process (see *MECS* 1997, p. 65; 1998, pp. 33–34; 1999, p. 31). EU leaders and officials could only issue a mild statement calling the reactivation of the Barcelona process in a long-term context.[43]

The collapse of the Middle East peace process played only a marginal role in the annual gathering of the EU Council, held in Nice on 7–9 December. It was, however, included in a declaration issued by the council after the conference, which cited five "vital" conditions for the resumption of negotiations in the Middle East. The declaration was sharply criticized by the Israelis for an implicit linkage between the Israeli settlements in the territories and the Palestinian violence.[44] Showing empathy with the Palestinians, the EU approved a special cash facility (SCF II) of up to 90m. euro for the PA areas.[45]

Before the year's end, the EU generally, and France as acting president in particular, attempted to step into the vacuum created by the imminent end of Clinton's term in office and make some impact on the peace process. EU special envoy Moratinos shuttled between the sides in the region conveying messages. French foreign minister Vedrine, visiting the region in mid-December, made a last-ditch effort to generate momentum. His initiative called for halting violence, implementing the provisions of the transitional agreement, and starting intensive negotiations for a final status agreement based on Israeli flexibility regarding Jerusalem and Palestinian flexibility on the refugee issue.[46] However, at that stage, with the far less ambitious Sharm al-Shaykh agreements for defusing the crisis still unimplemented, the French foreign minister's tour proved unproductive.

The only tangible result of the EU activist diplomatic approach following the outbreak of violence was the inclusion of Javier Solana in the Mitchell fact-finding committee, dispatched to the region on 11 December.[47]

FRANCE AND THE ISRAELI WITHDRAWAL FROM SOUTH LEBANON

Shortly after the failure of the summit meeting between Clinton and Asad in Geneva in March, Israel, convinced that the window of opportunity for achieving a peace agreement with Syria had been shut, decided on a unilateral withdrawal from South Lebanon in fulfillment of UN Security Council Resolution 425 (see *MECS* 1977–78, p. 190), with or without an overall peace settlement.[48] The decision evoked support from the EU commissioner for external relations, Chris Patten, in a statement made from Damascus.[49] Nevertheless, special EU envoy Moratinos, convinced that priority should be given to the Syrian track, continued to shuttle between Damascus and Jerusalem, urging both sides to resume negotiations.[50]

Upon Israel's official announcement on 16 April of its decision to pull out its forces from South Lebanon, French minister of defense Alain Richard, who was visiting Israel, accused Syria of refusing to arrive at a peace agreement with Israel, as this would undermine the legitimacy of its domination of Lebanon. Richard's statements recalled similar remarks by French prime minister Jospin during his visit to Israel in February (see above), namely that the Hizballah's activities in Lebanon were acts of terror, justifying Israeli retaliatory strikes, and that Syria was blocking progress in negotiations with Israel. At the time, Jospin's statements put France in an awkward position vis-à-vis Syria and Lebanon, impelling Chirac to promptly reassure them about France's unwavering policy in the Middle East.[51]

In the wake of Richard's remarks, Lebanese prime minister Salim al-Huss summoned the French ambassador to protest interference in Lebanese internal affairs,[52] while Syrian foreign minister Faruq al-Shar' visited Paris for talks with Chirac and Vedrine.[53] Attempting to play down his colleague's criticism of the Syrian role in Lebanon, Vedrine reiterated the readiness of France to provide peacekeepers for the UN force in South Lebanon, provided the IDF pullout was part of a wider peace agreement, which Paris favored.[54]

France was particularly interested in promoting an international peacekeeping force in South Lebanon in line with its self-perception as the traditional protector of Lebanon. Diplomatic contacts were initiated on the issue during April, starting with frequent phone consultations between Chirac and Barak. Israel sought French support for maintaining peace in South Lebanon after its pullout. France, however, preferred to expand the existing UNIFIL (UN Interim Force in Lebanon) contingent deployed in South Lebanon rather than establishing a new multinational force following the Israeli pullout.[55] Israel's acting foreign minister, Shlomo Ben-Ami, visiting Paris to discuss the issue, appeared disappointed by Prime Minister Jospin's refusal to send French troops to the region unless Syria agreed and the UN Security Council approved it in a resolution.[56] Predictably, Syrian Foreign Minister Shar', visiting Paris, did not support such a move, cautioning the French against sending forces in the event of a unilateral Israeli withdrawal.[57] French prevarication regarding sending forces to South Lebanon prior to the Israeli withdrawal, which took place on 23 May, continued until the end of the year, highlighting the dissonance between the French claim to a special role in Lebanon and its severely constrained policies.

An unexpected development affecting the Syrian-Israeli track of the peace process occurred in June with the sudden demise of the Syrian president, Hafiz al-Asad (see chapter on Syria). Chirac, accompanied by Vedrine, was the only Western leader to attend the funeral, a move criticized in France both by the political majority and the opposition.[58]

DIALOGUE WITH IRAN

The gradual rapprochement between EU member states and Iran, begun with the election of President Mohammad Khatami (see *MECS* 1998, pp. 43–45; 1999, pp. 41–42), continued in 2000. An important milestone was a visit by Iranian foreign minister Kamal

Kharrazi to London in January, the first by a foreign minister of the Islamic Republic of Iran to Britain. Kharrazi met both with his counterpart, Robin Cook, and with Prime Minister Tony Blair, who underlined Iran's regional importance and the determination by Britain to begin a new chapter in relations with the Islamic Republic. Both parties underscored the progress made in improving the relations between them on bilateral issues. However, differences of opinion on regional and international issues, especially regarding the Arab-Israeli peace process, were acknowledged by British foreign minister Cook. Iranian hostility toward Israel was cited by the British media, which criticized the timing of the visit and depicted Iran as being still a "dangerous place." Both Blair and the media also raised the question of thirteen Iranian Jews detained in Iran for nearly a year on charges of spying (see *MECS* 1999, p. 319; and chapter on Iran). Another controversial subject of media attention was Iranian efforts to develop weapons of mass destruction (WMD). Nevertheless, the visit ended with a joint declaration of intention to expand cooperation in cultural and economic affairs and in combatting drug trafficking, an issue on which Iran was praised by other EU members as well.[59]

Despite this diplomatic overture, and a certain upgrading of British-Iranian economic relations, a reciprocal visit by Cook to Tehran in 2000 was postponed twice in an atmosphere of recriminations in both countries. In Britain, Labor Party MPs criticized Cook's overtures to Iran despite the absence of any apparent change in its human rights record, Khatami's claims of liberalism notwithstanding.[60] Nevertheless, bilateral trade relations were eased significantly in October when the British government's Export Credits Guarantee Department confirmed the restoration of medium-term coverage for British exporters to Iran for the first time since 1993. The confirmation was announced by British minister of trade Richard Cabron on a visit to Tehran.[61]

Germany, too, invested considerable efforts in normalizing relations with Iran. It was at the forefront of the EU policy of restoring the "critical dialogue" with Iran following the "Mykonos trial" in Berlin of Iranian officials convicted of murdering Kurdish exiles there (see *MECS* 1997, pp. 49–50; 1998, pp. 45–47). In March, German foreign minister Joschka Fischer, together with a high-ranking political and economic delegation, paid an official visit to Tehran, the first by a German foreign minister since 1991. A principal aim of the visit was to arrange the upcoming July visit by President Khatami to Germany, the first by an Iranian leader since 1967.[62] The visit took place as scheduled, against a background of demonstrations in Berlin of Iranian opposition groups in exile, and a petition signed by 175 members of parliament urging that the visit be canceled because of Iran's reputed involvement with international terrorism. Khatami held meetings with President Johannes Rau and Chancellor Gerhard Schroeder during his stay.[63] According to Schroeder, both leaders "want to create a really substantial new start" in the relations between the two countries. However, in a private talk with Khatami, held in a "frank atmosphere," the chancellor criticized the human rights situation in Iran.[64] As was the case in other EU member states, the German hosts were anxious to boost Khatami's liberal image internationally and thereby strengthen his position in Iran. In a meeting in September at the UN between German foreign minister Fischer and his Iranian counterpart, Kharrazi, Fischer referred to the Iranian president's visit to Germany as a turning point and a new chapter in bilateral German-Iranian relations.[65]

Italy, Iran's leading trading partner among EU member states, had been in the economic vanguard of the change of climate between the EU and Iran in 1998, when Italian foreign minister Lamberto Dini first visited Tehran. Dini followed this up with another visit in

March 2000, which was devoted mainly to bilateral economic issues. He termed Rome-Tehran ties as "comprehensive and extensive."[66]

France, in contrast, highlighted Iran's human rights abuses. Throughout the year, it led the protest against the conviction of the Iranian Jews held on charges of spying. On the day that France assumed the presidency of the EU, French prime minister Jospin declared that the verdict against ten of the thirteen Iranian Jews accused of spying for Israel, which was issued days before, was unacceptable.[67] In December, France decided to send a low-ranking official to a meeting between Iran's deputy foreign minister and an EU delegation scheduled to take place in Paris. Tehran protested and called off the meeting, accusing France of "hegemonic behavior."[68]

BREACH OF THE AERIAL EMBARGO ON IRAQ

The divergence of views in the EU regarding the policy toward Iraq remained basically unchanged from late 1999, when the British, in alliance with the US, began carrying out joint air strikes against Iraq (see *MECS* 1999, pp. 43–45). France, together with Russia, attempted to reach an international agreement to lift the sanctions and the air blockade against Baghdad. In January, France joined Russia in opposing the nomination of the Swedish disarmament expert Rolf Ekeus as head of a new UN monitoring verification inspection commission (UMOVIC), tasked by the UN with supervising the disarmament of Iraq. France viewed him as incapable of providing the complete overhaul of the agency that it sought. Their objection facilitated Iraq's refusal to allow the new commission to carry out its duty.[69] Eventually, the UN Security Council unanimously approved the appointment of the candidate favored by France, Hans Blix, Swedish diplomat and former director of the International Atomic Energy Agency (IAEA), as head of the commission. France then called on Iraq to cooperate with the Security Council.[70]

The British government, in contrast, retained its view of Saddam Husayn as a regional risk in possession of a "formidable arsenal" intended for offensive purposes.[71] British Foreign Office minister Peter Hain warned in May that Husayn was rebuilding his supply of WMD, thus once more becoming a threat to the world. He called on Iraq to allow the UN arms inspectors to return, and condemned those who demanded the lifting of the sanctions against Iraq as pursuing a policy of appeasement.[72] Blair, refusing to yield to pressure from his own party to suspend the sanctions, declared that "while Saddam continues to try to develop weapons of mass destruction, I think it would be a serious mistake to lift those sanctions."[73]

Politicians, as well as private NGOs in Britain and France, organized civilian aid flights to Baghdad in defiance of the sanctions. In Britain, an aid flight organized by Labor MP George Galloway in March was banned by the Foreign Office and the UN, its aid cargo eventually diverted through Amman to Iraq.[74]

In France, delegations of politicians and academicians organized direct chartered flights to Baghdad in February and in September as part of a campaign to lift the sanctions and the civilian air embargo against Iraq. Some of the flights were canceled, but by September, the French Quai d'Orsay was less determined to ban them, claiming that non-commercial flights did not necessarily contradict the UN resolutions.[75] The first such flight from Paris in a decade landed in Baghdad on 25 September. The flight, which did not have UN approval, included French doctors, artists, sports figures and other celebrities. France also proposed that the UN allow flights in Iraqi aerial space without prior approval from the sanctions committee of the Security Council, a proposal rejected by the US.[76] French foreign minister Vedrine, in Moscow at the time, closed ranks with the Russians, stating that both had similar, although not identical, views on Iraq (see below). Defending the first direct French flight to Baghdad, Vedrine said: "It was a humanitarian act." He did, however, call on Iraq to cooperate with the international community on the basis of relevant UN resolutions.[77]

By then, the French government, which had assumed the presidency of the EU, legitimized and even endorsed direct flight initiatives to Baghdad. The second such flight took place on 1 December, and included delegates of the National Assembly and Senate among its passengers. It, too, lacked UN approval.[78]

UNEASY RELATIONS WITH LIBYA

Contacts between the EU and several of its member states with Libya were fitful. Qadhdhafi's intense interest in ending his international isolation met with a restrained West European response, motivated essentially economically.

Seeking to join the Euro-Med Partnership, Qadhdhafi, in an encounter in Tripoli with diplomats from the EU demanded that Israel and the Palestinians be banned from it, so long as their dispute remained unsolved. The EU rejected this condition unequivocally, thus setting the limits and tone of the rapprochement with Libya. EU Commissioner Chris Patten made it clear that an invitation to Qadhdhafi was conditional on a written commitment by him to accept the Barcelona process (Libya, Albania and the former Yugoslavian republics were the only Mediterranean countries that were not members of the Euro-Med Partnership). "If Libya doesn't change its mind on Israel and Palestine, it will be left outside the [Barcelona] process," an EU spokesperson stated.[79]

The tough position adopted by the EU, and in particular by Patten, was undoubtedly influenced by the revelation in January that parts for Scud missiles bound for Libya had been smuggled through London's Gatwick Airport in November 1999 under a bill of lading describing them as car parts.[80] British foreign minister Cook instructed the newly appointed British ambassador to Libya — the first in fifteen years — to voice Britain's "deep concern" at the attempt to evade the arms embargo against Libya and to warn Qadhdhafi that there must be "no repetition of such an abuse."[81]

Following this setback in EU-Libyan relations, the next opportunity for reconciliation was presented during the first Euro-Africa summit, which took place in April in Cairo. Several heads of EU member states made overtures to Qadhdhafi there, including German chancellor Schroeder, French president Chirac, the prime ministers of Italy, Spain and Austria, and officials from the Netherlands and Ireland. Qadhdhafi, however, discomfited the European partners at the summit by a tirade against Western colonialism. According to an EU Commission spokesperson, the Libyan leader's speech reconfirmed that he remained "a very difficult interlocutor." EU Commission president Romano Prodi of Italy, one of the staunchest supporters of rapprochement with Libya, admitted that "maybe we need more time than we thought, but talks go on."[82]

Although no breakthrough was achieved, several EU member states individually set the wheels of reconciliation in motion, motivated by economic considerations. Italy, Britain and France attended an international exposition held in Tripoli in April. France was represented by its minister of state for industry, Christian Pierret, the first visit to Tripoli by a French governmental minister since the imposition of international sanctions against Libya in 1992.[83] A visit to Tripoli in April by the British permanent under-secretary at the Foreign Office — the highest-ranking British official to visit since relations had been restored in July 1999 — signaled British interest in improving relations with Libya.[84]

In August, with the release of European hostages held by Muslim insurrectionists in the Philippines and their arrival in Tripoli, French foreign minister Vedrine thanked Libya for its mediation. Nonetheless, he emphasized there was no linkage between Libyan involvement in the affair and concurrent prospects of improved relations between the two countries, on the one hand, and the judicial process underway in France against Qadhdhafi, on the other.[85] German foreign minister Fischer also arrived in Tripoli, in September, to thank the Libyan government for its intervention during the hostage-taking episode in the Philippines. Fischer met with Qadhdhafi's son, Sayf al-Islam, which members of the German delegation referred to as a "symbolic courtesy visit."[86]

Italy, Libya's most important EU economic partner, had no inhibitions in promoting rapprochement. Addressing an Italo-Libyan joint partnership held in Rome, Italian foreign minister Dini declared that "a new phase" of collaboration had begun between the two countries. In a reference to the colonial period as well as recent events, he observed that "a page [had] been turned" in bilateral relations.[87]

RUSSIA AND THE MIDDLE EAST

Russian foreign policy in the Middle East was characterized by increased activism following Vladimir Putin's assumption of the presidency at the beginning of the year. Two main aspects were discernible in the Russian effort to rehabilitate its position in the Middle East: intensive diplomatic activity related to the Israeli-Palestinian track of the peace process, legitimized by Russia as a co-sponsor of the 1991 Madrid peace conference (see *MECS* 1991, p. 123); and a reversion to the traditional Soviet policy of arms sales to Iran, Iraq, Syria and Libya. Although the export of arms was primarily a means to improve its balance of payments rather than a political lever, a political dimension was present as well, particularly regarding Iran and Iraq. With the US monopolizing the Arab-Israeli peace process, Russia's long-term strategy was to counterbalance its political and diplomatic inferiority by developing an independent policy toward its nearest Middle East neighbors — Iran and Iraq.

MARGINALIZATION IN THE ARAB-ISRAELI PEACE PROCESS

The peace process was one of the first foreign policy domains in which the new leadership in the Kremlin applied diplomatic activity. Early in January, Russian foreign minister Igor Ivanov announced that Moscow intended to host a forthcoming meeting of the multilateral steering committee for peace in the Middle East, scheduled for February.[88] Addressing the plenary session of the meeting, acting president Putin stressed the desire of the international community to advance the peace process. He praised the roles of the EU, the US, Egypt, Jordan and Norway, while noting that Russia, too, regarded it as a priority foreign policy issue. With this, he assured the delegates that "we are not fighting for a zone of influence in the Middle East."[89] The importance of the conference was in its convening, which allowed for recognition of Russia's role in a Middle East settlement and provided proof that Russia was not isolated internationally. The developments in Chechnya, Russian spokespersons also noted, had not affected the atmosphere of the conference.[90]

In May, Russia undertook an initiative of its own, which was presented to Israel, the Palestinians, Syria and Lebanon by special presidential envoys. The initiative proposed methods of reviving negotiations on the Syrian and Palestinian tracks, with special emphasis on the Syrian, under the assumption that following the Israeli withdrawal from South Lebanon according to the terms of UN Security Council Resolution 425, the way would be paved for a settlement with Syria.[91]

Following his election to the presidency in June, Putin entered into an intensive dialogue with Israeli prime minister Barak, and an empathy developed between the two. Barak regularly updated the Russian president on developments in the peace process by phone. Besides Russia's ambition to play a more important diplomatic role, the two leaders shared common concerns about Islamic terrorism. Nevertheless, Israeli Foreign Ministry officials had reservations about Russia's sporadically intensive diplomatic activity in the peace process.[92]

Late in June, the Russian president's special envoy to the Middle East, Deputy Foreign Minister Vasily Sredin, visited Jerusalem, bringing a personal message from Russian foreign minister Ivanov to his Israeli counterpart, David Levy. Following talks with Israeli officials, Sredin expressed optimism about the possibility of reaching a final settlement between Israel and the Palestinians in the year 2000. The Russian envoy also met with PA chairman 'Arafat, conveying a message of support to him from Putin and Ivanov.[93]

The limits of Russian diplomatic involvement in the Israeli-Palestinian process were made clear, however, by Russia's exclusion from the tripartite meeting between Israel, the Palestinians and the US at Camp David in late July. Ivanov welcomed the US initiative, noted that "there is no room for rivalry here," and expressed Russian hopes for concrete agreements to be reached during the meeting. Russia, he averred, had not distanced itself from the problem but had actually stepped up its participation.[94] Russia thereby implicitly acknowledged American leadership of the peace process, notwithstanding its ambition to play a greater role. In the same vein, Russia, like the EU, refrained from any official comment on the unproductive conclusion of the Camp David summit.

Thereafter, talks between Russian officials and their Israeli and Palestinian counterparts continued both in Moscow and in the Middle East. A visit by 'Arafat to Moscow in August was referred to as very important by Foreign Minister Ivanov. Against the background of the declared Palestinian deadline for proclaiming UDI (13 September), Putin, Ivanov and Russia's envoy to the Middle East, Sredin, reiterated their recognition of the Palestinian right for an independent state. However, the Russians advised "restraint and thoughtfulness" on 'Arafat's part regarding the timing of the declaration, and welcomed the PA decision at the beginning of September to defer it.[95] Sredin expressed regret that the Palestinians and Israelis "still have serious differences over the entire spectrum of a permanent settlement."[96] Putin, meeting with Barak during the UN General Assembly session in New York in September, warned that if the Israeli negotiations were not "crowned with success, a dangerous regression could occur."[97]

The outbreak of violence between the Palestinians and Israelis at the end of September elicited a strong denunciation by telephone from Ivanov, who castigated 'Arafat and acting Israeli foreign minister Shlomo Ben-Ami alike for provocative acts by extremists on both sides.[98] A similar condemnation was voiced by the Russian permanent representative to the UN Security Council.[99] Nevertheless, Russian officials expressed hope that the Israeli-Palestinian negotiations would continue. In the wake of the new violence, Ivanov embarked on a regional tour, meeting with leaders in Syria, Lebanon, Israel and the PA. Although he had no illusions for an immediate solution to the crisis, he was optimistic that an agreement could soon be reached for ending the violence and resuming the negotiations.[100]

Upon his return, Ivanov was instructed by Putin to prepare proposals for solving the new crisis. Claiming that his visit had resulted in a "principled agreement" to hold an urgent summit, Ivanov called for the participation in it of the co-sponsors of the peace process, the UN secretary-general, Chairman 'Arafat and Prime Minister Barak.[101] The similarity of this proposal to the overall framework of the Sharm-al Shaykh summit of 16–17 October (see above) was apparent, although with a significant difference — Russia was not invited, despite a statement it had issued on the eve of the summit declaring its wish to participate.[102] Russia's desire for an active role in the peace process was thus rebuffed again, this time in a particularly conspicuous way, given the participation of the US, the EU, the UN secretary-general, Egypt, Jordan, Israel and the PA. Once again, however, the Russian reaction was mild, at least officially. Putin expressed hopes for a successful meeting, praising President Clinton's courage. Ivanov explained apologetically: "For Russia, it's not the format but the results which are fundamentally important."[103] Despite the inconclusive outcome of the summit, both Putin and Ivanov referred positively to the understandings reached for quelling the violence.[104] By contrast, delegates of the Russian Duma, along with the Russian media, criticized Russia's non-participation in the summit, accusing the US of "monopolizing" settlement of the conflict in the Middle East.[105]

Nevertheless, Russia's exclusion from the inner diplomatic circle of actors in the peace process did not deter its foreign policy decision-makers from pursuing an active stance. Putin maintained telephone contact with Barak and 'Arafat. Russian diplomats, headed by Foreign Minister Ivanov, visited the region frequently, issuing a plethora of statements calling for an end to the violence and a resumption of negotiations. Ivanov, visiting Israel as part of a regional tour in mid-November, proposed that the international observer force posted in Hebron be increased and deployed for a limited two-month period in other areas of friction — an idea gently rejected by Barak. Ivanov promptly clarified that his government would not promote the idea without Israeli consent.[106] Avoiding calls for the resumption of the peace process, Ivanov stressed the importance of creating the necessary conditions to implement the understandings reached at Sharm-al-Shaykh.[107] A visit by 'Arafat to Moscow on short notice, on 24 November, signaled the possibility of an increased Russian role. Putin, however, stated pessimistically that the settlement efforts "are currently on the brink of catastrophe, and all the striving and attempts will be futile unless the level of violence and confrontation is reduced."[108]

IRAN — A STRATEGIC PARTNER

Relations between Russia and Iran during 2000 moved forward at an accelerated pace in what appeared to be a distinct strategy by the Putin administration. In January, the chairperson of the Iranian Supreme National Security Council, Hasan Rouhani, visited Moscow, at which time Russian foreign minister Ivanov described relations between Russia and Iran as strategic, with long-term implications. The two countries were like-minded, they proclaimed, in their rejection of global uni-polarity, the preservation of the 1971 US-Soviet anti-ballistic missile (ABM) treaty, the protection of human rights, and combatting international terrorism. Both agreed to cooperate in molding the world order of the twenty-first century.[109] Indicating the underpinning of the strategic partnership between Iran and Russia, the Russian defense minister, Marshal Igor Sergeyev, at a meeting with Rouhani, expressed satisfaction that "the impetus of ties in the military, military-technical, scientific-technical and energy fields is being maintained."[110] That same day, the Russian commission on military industry, headed by acting president Putin, announced that it would supply Iran with three reactors for its Bushehr nuclear power plant.[111] According to the Russian minister for nuclear energy, Yevgeny Adamov, who pressed for the acceleration of the Bushehr project, Russia could earn up to the "incomparable" amount of $1bn. for each nuclear reactor.[112]

A law passed by the US Congress and signed by Clinton in March imposing sanctions against any country assisting Iran in developing WMD, evoked a series of conflicting Russian reactions. Adamov denied that Russia was supplying Iran with expertise that could be used to develop nuclear weapons, claiming that doing so would pose more danger for Russia than for the US. Other Russian officials gave assurances that their country abided by the Gore-Chernomyrdin agreement of 1995 drawn up in context of the US-Russian Commission for Technological Cooperation.[113] Moreover, Russian spokespersons defended the Iranian nuclear program as "peaceful" and in conformity with the Non-Proliferation Treaty.[114] The imposition of sanctions by the US against several Russian bodies for their alleged support of Iran's missile and nuclear projects was criticized by the Russian Foreign Office as "ignoring realities."[115]

That the Iranian issue was regarded by Putin as major was reflected in his reference to it in his first public speech following his election. Laying out his foreign policy priorities, the Russian president called for reducing nuclear arms stocks and turning Russia's economy into a market economy, explicitly stating that this economic interest necessitated nuclear cooperation with Iran.[116] With the passage of time, it became clear that Putin's reference to Iran was an indication of a turning point in Russian nuclear policy. On 7 May, he published a new regulation allowing the sale by Russia of nuclear materials to countries that did not possess nuclear weapons. The decree abrogated a previous, contrary regulation issued by Boris Yeltsin in 1992. The sudden and unexpected repeal of Russian nuclear export limits clearly held the potential of facilitating and accelerating Iranian nuclear activity, causing concern in the US and Israel.[117]

A new level of Russian-Iranian military rapprochement was reached when the head of the military cooperation department of the Russian Defense Ministry, Col.-Gen. Leonid Ivashov, arrived in Iran for a five-day working visit in June. His meetings with Iranian military officials resulted in a decision by both countries to cooperate in the military field on a basis.[118] They also found "common interests...pinpoint[ed] a common threat" to their security, and "determine[d] ways of neutralizing it." Although Russia continued to pledge to the US that it had no new military contacts with Iran, the foundations for future Russo-Iranian strategic military relations were being laid.[119]

In July, Iranian president Khatami and Russian president Putin extended reciprocal invitations to visit each other in their respective countries,[120] although their first encounter took place in New York during the UN General Assembly millennium summit in September.[121] Following this meeting, officials in both countries began preparing for a future visit by Khatami in Moscow.

The ongoing process of Russo-Iranian strategic rapprochement and military cooperation reached a peak in November with a decision by Russia to retract the Gore-Chernomyrdin agreement and formally resume military-technical cooperation with Iran. According to the terms of the annulled agreement, Russia had committed itself to complete the implementation of all outstanding military-technical cooperation projects with Iran by December 1999, and not conclude any new ones. The retraction of the agreement merely legitimized an existing reality.[122]

The strategic turning point was underscored by a historic visit to Iran by Russian defense minister Igor Sergeyev at the end of 2000, the first of its kind since the Islamic Revolution in 1979. The visit was openly described as aimed at developing military cooperation.[123] Prior to the visit, Russian foreign policy officials made efforts to deflect the negative American reaction to their country's shift in policy.[124] Their argumentation emphasized the importance of the Russian-Iranian military cooperation for the security of both countries and for regional stability. Avoiding sharp responses to US criticism, Sergeyev and other officials attempted to assure the international community that "the two countries abide by the international rules of conduct and that the military cooperation is of a non-offensive character."[125] Besides wide-ranging talks with his military counterparts, Sergeyev met with President Khatami and Foreign Minister Kharrazi. Announcing the opening of a new chapter in bilateral relations with Iran, Sergeyev reiterated publicly that Russia had resumed military-technical cooperation with Iran that had been "virtually put on hold" in 1995.[126] The year thus ended with a synchronized Russian strategic move to build up Iran as its Middle East cornerstone.

SUPPORT FOR IRAQ

Continuing its ongoing efforts to lift the sanctions against Iraq, Russia initiated talks on resuming direct flights to Iraq in March between Aeroflot and the Iraqi airline. The talks were later joined by the Vnukovo airline, which made its first flight to Iraq on 17 September. This charter flight, and others that followed, were encouraged by the Russian government, and were made without obtaining UN approval. Foreign Minister Ivanov, underlining their humanitarian purpose, stated that these flights did not indicate the start of regularly scheduled flights.[127]

Concurrently, high-ranking bilateral political and military meetings resumed. In April, Iraqi defense minister Sultan Hashim Ahmad arrived in Moscow and met with his Russian counterpart, Igor Sergeyev. Reportedly, the sale of Russian arms to Iraq was discussed during the visit, although this was denied by the Russian authorities. Sergeyev insisted that "Russia is strictly observing all international sanctions regarding Baghdad but is ready to fully restore cooperation between the two countries."[128]

Russia, for its part, consistently condemned the ongoing joint US-British bombing of Iraqi military installations as violating international law and UN Security Council resolutions.[129] The issue was discussed in July by Putin during a meeting in Moscow with the Iraqi deputy prime minister, Tariq 'Aziz. The reception given to 'Aziz in the Kremlin was the subject of criticism by the US State Department, which held that UN Security Council members should not host Iraqi officials.[130] Responding, Russian foreign minister Ivanov asserted that Russia "will continue to maintain a very active dialogue with Iraq."[131] Ivanov, significantly, began his tour of the Middle East in November with an official visit to Baghdad, the first by such a high-ranking Russian official in a decade. He was hosted by 'Aziz, and handed over a message from Putin to Saddam Husayn.[132] Shortly thereafter, 'Aziz returned to Moscow for talks with his Russian counterpart on various bilateral issues and on strategies to lift the sanctions against Iraq (see also chapter on Iraq).[133]

NOTES

For the place and frequency of publications cited here, and for the full name of the publication, news agency, radio station or monitoring service where an abbreviation is used, please see "List of Sources." Only in the case of more than one publication bearing the same name is the place of publication noted here.

1. MENA, 2 April 2000 (DR).
2. For an analysis, see E. Rumer and S. Avineri, "Russian Resurgent?" *Policy Watch*, No. 508, 27 December 2000.
3. *JP*, 2 January 2000.
4. ANSA (Internet version), 17 January 2000 (DR).
5. Ibid.
6. *Europe in Israel*, No. 54, May 2000.
7. *JP*, 22 February; *Ha'aretz, al-Hayat*, 23 February; *JT* (Internet version), 24 February — BBC Monitoring, 26 February 2000.
8. *Ha'aretz*, 23, 25, 27 February; *Le Monde*, 26, 28 February; *The Times*, 28 February; *Time*, 13 March 2000.
9. *Europe in Israel*, No. 54, May 2000.
10. VoI, 5 April — BBC Monitoring, 7 April 2000.
11. *Ha'aretz*, 4 April 2000.
12. VoP, 2 May — BBC Monitoring, 4 May 2000.
13. *Ha'aretz*, 2 June 2000.
14. *Ha'aretz*, 19 June 2000.
15. *Le Monde*, 4 July 2000 (DR).
16. ABC (Internet version), 26 July 2000 (DR).
17. *Ha'aretz*, 13 August 2000.
18. *Ha'aretz*, 3, 6, 7 September 2000.
19. AFP, 2 September 2000 (DR).
20. Ibid.
21. *Ha'aretz*, 3 September 2000.
22. *Ha'aretz*, 25 September 2000.
23. AFP, 1 October 2000 (DR).
24. AFP, 2 October 2000 (DR).
25. AFP, 3 October 2000 (DR).
26. AFP, 2 October — BBC Monitoring, 4 October 2000.
27. VoI, 3 October — BBC Monitoring, 5 October 2000.
28. *NYT*, 5 October; *Ha'aretz*, 5, 6 October; *Yedi'ot Aharonot*, 13 October 2000.
29. AFP, 7 October; *Ha'aretz*, 8 October 2000.
30. *Ha'aretz*, 11 October 2000.
31. *Europe in Israel*, No. 57, December 2000.
32. AFP, 13 October (DR); R. France, 13 October 2000 (DR).
33. RTBF Radio 1, Brussels, 13 October — BBC Monitoring, 16 October 2000.
34. Efe, 14 October 2000 (DR).
35. *Ha'aretz*, 18 October; *Europe in Israel*, No. 57, December 2000.
36. *Europe in Israel*, No. 57, December 2000.
37. *Ha'aretz*, 22 October 2000.
38. *Ha'aretz*, 9 November; *Europe in Israel*, No. 57, December 2000.
39. *Ha'aretz*, 5 November 2000.
40. *Europe in Israel*, No. 57, December 2000.
41. R. France, 16 November 2000 (DR).
42. *Ha'aretz*, 17 November 2000.
43. *Le Monde*, 17 November; *Europe in Israel*, No. 57, December 2000.
44. *Ha'aretz*, 12 December 2000; *Europe in Israel*, No. 58, February 2001.

45. *Europe in Israel*, No. 58, February 2001.
46. *Al-Sharq al-Awsat*, 8 December (DR); MENA, 14 December 2000 (DR).
47. *Europe in Israel*, No. 58, February 2001.
48. *Ha'aretz*, 30 March 2000.
49. *JP*, 9 April 2000.
50. *Ha'aretz*, 3 April; *al-Hayat*, 21 April 2000.
51. Syrian TV, 28 February — BBC Monitoring, 1 March 2000.
52. *Le Monde*, 22, 26 April 2000.
53. *Le Monde*, 24 April 2000.
54. *JP*, 21, 24 April 2000.
55. VoI, 3 April — BBC Monitoring, 5 April 2000.
56. *Ha'aretz*, 14 April 2000.
57. *Ha'aretz*, 27 April 2000.
58. AFP, 14 June — BBC Monitoring 16 June; *Le Monde,* 16 June 2000:
59. *FT*, 11 January; *JP*, 11 January; *Ha'aretz*, 12 January; Iranian TV, 10 January — BBC Monitoring, 12 January 2000.
60. *FT*, 29 June 2000.
61. IRNA, 2 October — BBC Monitoring, 7 October 2000.
62. IRNA, 6 March 2000 (DR).
63. *WP*, 11 July 2000.
64. *Ha'aretz*, 11, 13 July; *WP*, 11 July 2000.
65. IRNA, 19 September 2000 (DR).
66. IRNA, 5 March — BBC Monitoring, 7 March 2000.
67. AFP, 1 July — BBC Monitoring, 3 July 2000.
68. *TT* (Internet version), 4 December 2000 (DR).
69. *IHT*, 19 January 2000.
70. AFP, 27 January 2000 (DR).
71. PANUKR, 19 April 2000 (DR).
72. PANUKR, 25 May 2000 (DR).
73. PANUKR, 22 November 2000 (DR).
74. PANUKR, 6, 12 March 2000 (DR).
75. AFP, 16 February (DR); AFP, 4 August — BBC Monitoring, 7 August; *Le Monde*, 13 September 2000.
76. *Ha'aretz*, 24, 29 September 2000.
77. ITAR-TASS, 28 September 2000 (DR).
78. R. France, 1 December (DR); AFP, 2 December 2000 (DR).
79. ANSA, 10 January 2000 (DR).
80. Ibid; AFP, 10 January 2000 (DR).
81. *The Times*, 10 January; *WP*, 10 January 2000.
82. *JP*, 5 April; *Ha'aretz*, 4, 5 April; *Policy Watch*, No. 454, 17 April 2000.
83. *Le Monde*, 18 April 2000.
84. *The Times*, 26 April 2000.
85. *Ha'aretz*, 30 August 2000.
86. *Frankfurter Rundschau* (Internet version), 14 September 2000 (DR).
87. ANSA, 13 December 2000 (DR).
88. *JP*, 7 January; MENA, 9 January 2000 (DR).
89. Interfax, 1 February 2000 (DR).
90. Ibid.
91. *Ha'aretz*, 5 May; ITAR-TASS, 4 May — BBC Monitoring, 6 May 2000.
92. *Ha'aretz*, 5 May 2000.
93. Interfax, 30 June, 3 July (DR); VoP, 30 June (DR).
94. ITAR-TASS, 10 July 2000 (DR).
95. ITAR-TASS, 11 August (DR); Russian TV, 11 August — BBC Monitoring, 14 August; ITAR-TASS, 1 August — BBC Monitoring, 11 August; ITAR-TASS, 20 August 2000 (DR).

96. Interfax, 11 September 2000 (DR).
97. Interfax, 7 September 2000 (DR).
98. ITAR-TASS, 1 October 2000 (DR).
99. RIA, 4 October 2000 (DR).
100. Interfax, 11 October 2000 (DR).
101. Interfax, 13 October 2000 (DR).
102. Interfax, 15 October 2000 (DR).
103. Interfax, 16 October 2000 (DR).
104. Interfax, 17 October 2000 (DR).
105. ITAR-TASS, 8 October 2000 (DR).
106. *Ha'aretz*, 16 November 2000.
107. Interfax, 15 November — BBC Monitoring, 17 November 2000.
108. ITAR-TASS, 24 November (DR); *Ha'aretz*, 29 November 2000.
109. ITAR-TASS, IRNA, 13 January 2000 (DR).
110. ITAR-TASS, 14 January — BBC Monitoring, 17 January 2000.
111. R. Moscow, 14 January — BBC Monitoring, 17 January 2000.
112. Interfax, 10 February 2000 (DR).
113. Interfax, 15 March 2000 (DR).
114. Interfax, 4 April 2000 (DR).
115. ITAR-TASS, 26 April 2000 (DR).
116. *Ha'aretz*, 2 April 2000.
117. *Ha'aretz*, 6 June 2000.
118. ITAR-TASS, 25 June 2000.
119. ITAR-TASS, 30 June — BBC Monitoring, 1 July 2000.
120. IRNA, 15 July — BBC Monitoring, 17 July 2000.
121. ITAR-TASS, 7 September 2000 (DR).
122. Interfax, 23 November 2000 (DR).
123. IRNA, 25 December 2000 (DR).
124. Interfax, 26 December (DR); *WP*, 29 December 2000.
125. ITAR-TASS, 26 December 2000 (DR).
126. RIA, 28 December 2000 (DR).
127. Interfax, 20 March (DR); ITAR-TASS, 14, 18, 21 September 2000 (DR).
128. Interfax, 16, 18, 20 March 2000 (DR).
129. Interfax, 17 May (DR); Interfax, 28 July 2000 (DR).
130. Interfax, 27 July 2000 (DR).
131. Interfax, 28 July 2000 (DR).
132. Interfax, 13 November (DR); *Ha'aretz*, 14 November 2000.
133. ITAR-TASS, 29 November — BBC Monitoring, 30 November 2000.

Inter-Arab Relations

BRUCE MADDY-WEITZMAN

The inter-Arab system entered the new millennium with a bevy of question marks. The implications for the Arab world of accelerating globalization (*'awlama*) was a favorite topic of commentators and scholars; most agreed that Arab governments and societies had failed to develop policies which would benefit the general Arab interest, and that the Arab Middle East was being left further and further behind the globalizing train. Domestically, at least five factors militated against the likelihood of significant change in the near term: (1) the proven staying power of authoritarian regimes; (2) the absence of a robust civil society and genuine pluralism; (3) the durability of Islamist opposition movements and their impact on the tenor of public discourse; (4) the failure to develop productive, competitive economies; and (5) uncertainties surrounding the assumption to power of a younger generation of leaders, which dictated cautious approaches to policy issues. In June 2000, Syrian president Hafiz al-Asad joined the list of leaders who had passed away the previous year, and his son Bashshar was hastily named his successor.

Regional difficulties, which were both symptoms and causes of collective Arab weakness, compounded matters further: (1) the decade-long unfinished business of the Gulf War, which left Iraq an embittered pariah state albeit with considerable mischief-making ability and growing sympathy among Arab populations; (2) the halting, unconcluded Arab-Israeli peace process, and the resulting uncertainty throughout the region; (3) the relative strength of regional, non-Arab powers (Turkey, Israel and Iran); and (4) the failure to develop concrete collective policies toward regional issues and build more formal collective mechanisms to manage inter-Arab disputes. Given the absence of a common regional agenda, the "Arab world" seemed at times a misnomer, in political terms, masking the reality of a series of zones of conflict and concern (the Maghrib, the Nile Valley, the Levant, the Fertile Crescent, the Arabian Peninsula and the Gulf) in which states pursued their particular agendas with scant reference to wider, common goals.

Hasan Naf'a of the al-Ahram Center for Strategic and Political Studies aptly captured the prevailing mood among Arab nationalist analysts: "Unlike other regions in the world, the new Arab millennium appears very ominous indeed. All Arab countries without exception are facing a crisis of some sort or another." These ranged from internecine conflicts (e.g., Algeria, Sudan, Yemen), to the ravages imposed by international sanctions (upon Iraq and Libya), to the "international blackmail" of the Gulf states "designed to bleed them dry and cripple their wills," to the concerns of succession, and social and economic difficulties brought on by the switch to a market economy and entry into the international market system. Inter-Arab affairs, he continued, were no less gloomy. "The Arab world," he wrote, "seems like a paralyzed wreck, badly in need of a complete new nervous system." For Naf'a, the immediate problem was the mostly negative implications of what he believed was an imminent Arab-Israeli peace settlement which, in the absence of strong and creative Arab policies, well-functioning collective Arab institutions and an Arab common market would primarily serve Israeli interests in being a regional hegemon.[1] Al-Ahram managing editor Salah al-Din Hafiz echoed Naf'a's dour view, emphasizing the negative implications of an apparently imminent Israeli-Syrian peace agreement on the Palestinian question, the hegemonic aspirations of Israel and the future regional role of Egypt.[2] One could take issue with Naf'a's description of the causes of Arab difficulties and of his, and Hafiz's analyses of the implications of an Arab-Israeli peace and the contours of the post-peace era. Still, there could be little doubt that the Arab political order was far from what its practitioners and intellectuals hoped that it would be.

Naf'a's focus on the centrality of the Arab-Israeli peace process for regional Arab affairs was prescient, but not in the way he had intended. The dynamics of inter-Arab politics during 2000 were heavily shaped by the course of Arab-Israeli relations. Contrary to expectations, no final peace settlement was concluded by Israel with either Syria or the Palestinians. A direct outcome of the failure of Syrian-Israeli diplomacy in the early months of the year was Israel's unilateral withdrawal in late May from South Lebanon, after twenty-two years. The move resulted in a fair degree of tension between Egypt, which welcomed the withdrawal, and Syria, which feared a worsening of its strategic situation in Lebanon and beyond. The failure of Palestinian-Israeli diplomacy in the summer led to the outbreak of sustained violence, beginning in late September, which almost completely monopolized the collective Arab agenda for the remainder of the year. Arab governments had to face the challenges triggered by the al-Aqsa Intifada and maneuver delicately between their own inflamed domestic publics, the resolute opposition of most regimes to the widening of the conflict with Israel, the requirements of inter-Arab diplomacy, and the views of their Western, mostly American patrons. The immediate outcome of these conflicting pressures was an emergency Arab summit in Cairo in October, the first all-Arab gathering of heads of state in four years. Like most previous Arab summits, it was noteworthy as much for its having been held as for its actual decisions. Host Egypt played its traditional role as leader of the Arab bloc, such as it was, making sure that the summit resolutions were commensurate with its interests. For Yasir 'Arafat and the Palestinian Authority (PA), which he headed, the nature of the support tendered by the summit was, at best, half-hearted; the implementation of the decisions was even more disappointing.

Elsewhere, incremental change was registered in the ongoing saga of Iraqi efforts to lift the decade-long international sanctions against it. Syria, in particular, strengthened its ties with Iraq, while avoiding excessive criticism from either Kuwait and Saudi Arabia, or their American patrons. So did Jordan, which led the way in breaking down the air embargo against Iraq. Iraqi vice president 'Izzat Ibrahim al-Duri represented President Saddam Husayn at the October Cairo summit, the first time Iraq had been admitted to the summit forum since August 1990. Arab sub-regional groupings continued to register little in the way of concrete achievement. The Gulf Cooperation Council (GCC) went about its routine business, while divisions on key regional issues and an overriding concern with protecting sovereign prerogatives prevented its six members from forging more meaningful institutionalized ties. Regarding the two immediate neighbors of the GCC, namely Iraq and Iran: Saudi Arabia and Kuwait were in a minority regarding Iraqi policy, with the others favoring a more proactive, conciliatory approach. Most GCC governments sought to improve ties with Iran, willfully oblivious to their own declared collective position in support of the United Arab Emirates (UAE) against Iran in their dispute of three Gulf islands. In North Africa, the long-delayed Arab Maghrib Union (AMU) summit remained out of reach, despite the expressed desire of the parties. Algerian-Moroccan differences, particularly over the Western Sahara issue, remained the biggest stumbling block to the proposed summit and to the revival of AMU activities.

Efforts to institutionalize the anti-Iraq Gulf War alliance in the Arab world had resulted in the establishment of the eight-nation Damascus declaration framework, consisting of Egypt, Syria and the six GCC states. This, in turn, was underpinned by a loose Egyptian-Saudi-Syrian axis. By the end of 2000, the Damascus declaration framework appeared entirely emasculated, and the Egyptian-Saudi-Syrian core triangle also seemed of diminishing value as well. Thus, while Egypt continued to set the overall direction of what passed for collective Arab action, the actual content of that action was meager, as each individual state pursued its particular interests against the background of regional uncertainty.

(For developments in the bilateral and triangular relationships of Libya, Sudan and Egypt, and bilateral developments involving Algeria and Morocco, and Yemen and Saudi Arabia, respectively, see the appropriate country chapters.)

THE ARAB-ISRAELI PEACE PROCESS AND INTER-ARAB AFFAIRS

The election of Ehud Barak as prime minister of Israel in May 1999 (see *MECS* 1999, pp. 298–305) had rejuvenated the atmosphere and substance of Arab-Israeli diplomacy. The year 2000 opened with Syrian-Israeli negotiations at a decisive stage and apparently close to resolution. On 22–23 January, Egyptian president Husni Mubarak traveled to Damascus and Amman for talks with President Hafiz al-Asad of Syria and King 'Abdallah of Jordan. Speaking at the conclusion of the Mubarak-Asad talks, Egyptian foreign minister 'Amru Musa issued a call for an Arab summit. Delaying such a summit, he said, would be "a big strategic mistake." Mubarak's trip, and the summit call, were clearly an attempt by Egypt to reassert its leadership of the Arab camp, particularly on Arab-Israeli issues. But the Syrians had little interest in a summit while in the midst of its own negotiations with Israel.[3] That, plus a host of other obstacles, made it impossible to convene a summit, until circumstances changed radically later in the year (see below).

One by-product of the revival of the peace process was the tentative resuscitation of the multilateral track of the peace process, via a steering committee meeting in Moscow on 1 February. The gathering came on the heels of a meeting on the sidelines of the World Economic Forum gathering in Davos, Switzerland between the Bahraini heir apparent and commander-in-chief of the Bahraini armed forces, Shaykh Salman bin Hamad Al Khalifa, and veteran Israeli leader Shimon Peres, and created a bit of a stir among Arab observers. The apparent interest among the GCC states and others to revive links with Israel before peace agreements had even been concluded drew caustic comment from Arab observers,[4] echoing longstanding Syrian refusal to participate in the multilateral track prior to the satisfactory conclusion of bilateral negotiations with Israel. Egypt was sensitive to the criticism and took pains to explain why its proactive approach was preferable. Foreign Minister 'Amru Musa, who prior to the Moscow meeting had had an acrimonious public exchange with Peres at Davos, emphasized that the multilateral gathering was designed primarily to spur progress on the various bilateral tracks of the peace process and that substantive Arab-Israeli normalization could only follow a comprehensive peace.[5] At the same time, Musa declared, it was incumbent on "visionaries" not to wait, and to start brainstorming regarding the future shape of the Middle East in ten to twenty years time, "provided we are sure that Israel is ready" to enter into a "better, safer...and more balanced Middle East." Referring to the new era of globalization, he expressed the hope that Egypt would be:

> the center of a new and positive and different way of life, of trade, of investment, of interaction — culturally, economically, politically and security-wise....We want to compete — but in economics, in culture, in the scientific and technological fields....We must adopt a positive attitude toward [the new era] and work to make sure that this new era opens vistas for everybody under conditions of justice and fairness and peaceful relations. But you cannot have peaceful relations and a sense of justice and fairness unless the Palestinians are comfortable and secure.

Egypt, he told his interviewer, was ready and willing to bear its historical responsibility in the region, and to help rebuild the region, "not necessarily as a big driver, but rather as a partner — a big partner, an important partner."[6]

Egypt was to follow up the Moscow meeting by hosting a meeting of the working group dealing with displaced persons (from the June 1967 War), and dates were set for a number of other working groups.[7] However, the renewal of tension over events in Lebanon interceded, and the subsequent Arab League foreign ministers meeting in March (see below) officially conditioned the renewal of the multilateral process on progress in the bilateral sphere.

THE LEBANESE ARENA

Contrary to expectations, the Syrian-Israeli negotiating track stalled, and the Palestinian-Israeli track showed no movement either. This, plus a new round of violence in South Lebanon between 25 January and mid-February, marked by Lebanese Hizballah units killing a number of Israeli soldiers and Israel retaliating by targeting power stations in the Beirut area, occasioned a flurry of inter-Arab diplomatic interactions. The lead was taken by Egypt and Saudi Arabia, which together with Syria constituted the dominant pillars of what passed for a collective Arab grouping in the post-Gulf War era. President Husni Mubarak of Egypt made a brief high-profile visit to Lebanon on 19 February, where he emphasized the Egyptian commitment to Lebanese security against Israeli threats, and readiness to help Lebanon rebuild all the installations that were destroyed by Israel. It was the first visit ever by an Egyptian president to Lebanon, a Syrian preserve since the mid-1970s, and formerly a target for the regional ambitions of radical pan-Arabism led by Jamal 'Abd al-Nasir of Egypt. Despite Mubarak's staunch backing for Lebanon against Israel, his visit could not have entirely pleased Syria, which preferred exclusivity over Lebanese foreign relations. In late February–early March, the Saudi crown prince and de facto ruler, 'Abdallah bin 'Abd al-'Aziz bin Sa'ud, journeyed to Cairo, Damascus and Beirut for meetings with Mubarak, Asad and Lebanese president Emil Lahhud. The trip was preceded by visits to Riyadh by Syrian foreign minister Faruq al-Shar' and an unnamed envoy of Mubarak.[8] Both Cairo and Riyadh were keen on putting up a public united Arab diplomatic front vis-à-vis Israel while also containing the violence; they most likely urged Syria to exercise restraint over Hizballah actions and thus avoid further Israeli retaliations and a widening of the conflict. Some reports had Saudi Arabia quietly encouraging Syria to conclude a peace agreement with Israel, with American encouragement.[9] As for Lebanon, Saudi Arabia pledged to take the lead in paying for the restoration of the Lebanese power grid, which had been seriously damaged by recent Israeli air raids.[10]

The Saudis were also interested in dampening renewed calls for the convening of the long-delayed Arab summit conference, explaining that such a gathering needed to be carefully prepared. Much of the Saudi reluctance (which was publicly denied) was due to its opposition to rehabilitating Iraq: Baghdad had been absent from the last summit, held in 1996, and it was understood by all that it would participate in the next one, whenever it convened. Egypt showed interest in the summit idea, particularly as a means to reconfirm its centrality in the Arab world. However, at this stage, with the peace process in flux, Syria and the PA still not on good terms, and the Iraqi "file" still open, Egypt did not pursue the idea further. Instead, Egypt supported the proposal by Arab League secretary-general 'Ismat 'Abd al-Majid to make the summit an annual event, regardless of the circumstances (a perennial idea; see *MECS* 1996, p. 79; 1999, p. 87). Egypt and Yemen took the lead in seeking approval of the proposal at the upcoming regularly scheduled meeting of Arab League foreign ministers in mid-March. *Al-Ahram* recommended that the eight Damascus declaration states — Egypt, Syria, Saudi Arabia and the five other members of the GCC — first hold an "economic" summit.[11] Egypt also adopted an activist posture in the Maghrib, encouraging Algerian-Moroccan dialogue and reiterating its interest in observer status in the AMU, and on the question of Iraqi status, which Foreign Minister Musa discussed with his Kuwaiti counterpart Sabah al-Ahmad Al Sabah.[12]

Concurrent public anger toward Israel and sympathy toward Lebanon led King 'Abdallah of Jordan to postpone a planned visit to Israel, and visits by the foreign ministers of Kuwait and the PLO to Beirut. In a show of solidarity with Lebanon, the meeting of Arab foreign ministers was held on 12–13 March in Beirut, and not at its regular site, Arab League headquarters in Cairo. But to Syrian displeasure, the meeting was preceded by a Mubarak-hosted summit meeting between Israeli prime minister Barak and PA chairman 'Arafat on 8 March in Sharm al-Shaykh, where they announced the resumption of Israeli-Palestinian negotiations, beginning later in the month in Washington. Three days earlier, the Israeli government had unanimously endorsed the withdrawal of all Israeli forces from South Lebanon to the international boundary, with or without an agreement. With Israel about to be pilloried at the Arab foreign ministers meeting, and with its own negotiations with Israel hanging in the balance, Syria viewed the renewal of the Israeli-PA track weakening the Arab collective stance and the Syrian position. A possible unilateral Israeli withdrawal from South Lebanon left Damascus no less uneasy.

The meeting itself was preceded by a different sort of flap, between Secretary-General 'Abd al-Majid of the Arab League and Iran. At issue was the projected presence of Iranian foreign minister Kamal Kharrazi. He had been invited to be an observer of the opening session in his capacity as representative of the rotating presidency of the Islamic Conference Organization (ICO). However, the Iranians sought his attendance at the closed sessions of the Beirut conference as well, piquing 'Abd al-Majid, and Egypt. The invitation was then redirected to the ICO secretary-general, 'Azzadin al-Laraki, a former Moroccan prime minister.[13]

The eighteen-point final statement of the conference dealt exclusively with Lebanon, although other issues were discussed as well during the meetings. On the declarative level, support for Lebanon was unequivocal, including its "resistance" against the occupation and its legitimate right to self-defense (language which legitimized Hizballah actions, to Syrian satisfaction), and its longstanding demand for Israeli withdrawal from the south according to UN Resolution 425 of 1978. The harsh language of the statement was exemplified by its support of any Lebanese government endeavors to seek reparations or initiate international war crimes proceedings. Israeli actions were sharply condemned, as were recent statements by Israeli officials (particularly by Foreign Minister David Levy), threatening Lebanese civilians, as well as statements made by "some officials from friendly countries" that "equated the aggressor with the victim" (referring to comments critical of Hizballah by Prime Minister Lionel Jospin of France). Practical measures, however, were limited. The perennial Syrian demand for the cessation of all Arab-Israeli ties was watered down to a call on those Arab states that had relations with Israel "to reconsider" them following the latest Israeli aggression against Lebanon (Egypt, Jordan and Mauritania had full diplomatic ties; Morocco, Oman, Tunisia and Qatar had lower-level ones). According to one report, the Saudis had also pressed for a somewhat more binding commitment, while Jordan was utterly opposed, Oman expressed "reservations" and Egypt eventually accepted, and helped fashion the more watered-down language which was actually adopted.[14] Similarly, those countries involved in the multilateral track were asked to "reconsider their participation until substantive and tangible progress is achieved on all tracks." The statement called on the Arab states to support Lebanese "steadfastness and reconstruction" and fulfill previous aid commitments pledged at the Tunis (1979) and Baghdad (1990) Arab summit conferences.

The communiqué also reiterated the commitment of Arab states to the peace process with Israel on all tracks, including their backing for the linkage between the Lebanese and Syrian tracks. This stood in implicit contradiction to the demand for unconditional withdrawal according to Resolution 425, a contradiction which was about to have practical implications.

The linkage between all the tracks was made especially explicit in the statement's endorsement of the right of return of Palestinian refugees. This right had traditionally been a sacred Arab principle. What was noteworthy was that it was referred to specifically with regard to Lebanon, this to the satisfaction of its Christian communities, and in line with Syrian requirements. The issue, if not resolved on the basis of return to Palestine, "was a time bomb threatening security and stability in Lebanon." Lebanese president Lahhud drove the point home by declaring that there would not be peace on the Lebanese-Israeli border even after an Israeli withdrawal so long as the Palestinian refugee camps in Lebanon were bristling with arms, enabling residents to continue launching guerrilla operations against Israel. According to a number of reports, Egyptian foreign minister Musa, tacitly backed by Jordan and Qatar, had argued that Lebanon should welcome the anticipated Israeli withdrawal without linking it to a solution of the issue of Palestinian refugees living on its soil. Lebanese prime minister Salim al-Huss "categorically denied" that there had been any differences over how to handle the Israeli decision to unilaterally withdraw from South Lebanon by July in the absence of an agreement.[15] Lahhud's statement, the cynical Syrian manipulation of the Palestinian refugee question and the sidelining of the Palestine question at the conference, complained Palestinian journalist and publisher 'Abd al-Bari 'Atwan, all demonstrated that Syrian and Lebanese hostility toward the Palestinians was general, and not directed merely at 'Arafat because of the

Oslo accords. Moreover, the hostility weakened Syrian efforts to block the normalization of relations between other Arab states and Israel.[16]

The statement concluded by declaring that their meeting remained in open session, to reconvene in the event of there being a "repeat of Israeli aggression against Lebanon."[17]

No mention of convening an Arab summit was made in the final statement. Nonetheless, according to one report, the issue provoked disagreement between Egypt and Saudi Arabia, in line with their pre-summit positions on the subject. Saudi foreign minister Sa'ud Al Faysal was reportedly active behind the scenes, pressuring other Arab ministers to oppose the idea of a regular annual gathering at this time. The agreed-on compromise was the appointment of a committee charged with holding contacts aimed at convening an Arab summit. The committee was chaired by Omani foreign minister Yusuf bin 'Alawi, with the participation of the foreign ministers of Egypt, Syria, Tunisia and Yemen, and Arab League secretary-general 'Abd al-Majid.

As Syrian-Israeli negotiations entered into a deep freeze following the failure of a Geneva meeting on 26 March between President Bill Clinton of the US and President Asad of Syria, and the reality of an imminent unilateral Israeli withdrawal from South Lebanon hit home, inter-Arab consultations moved into higher gear. The Syrian foreign minister hosted his Egyptian and Saudi counterparts on 3–4 May in Tadmur (Palmyra). Their concluding statement welcomed the impending withdrawal in accordance with UN Resolutions 425 and 426, and supported the deployment of UNIFIL peacekeeping forces on the Israeli-Lebanese border after the withdrawal, "so as to deprive Israel of any pretext to hold Lebanon or Syria responsible for any security incidents that might endanger security, peace and stability in the region." The declared acquiescence of Syria to the UN deployment marked a departure from its previous opposition. In return, Syria received full backing vis-à-vis Israel in two areas: the ministers asserted their determination "to torpedo any attempt aimed at creating a rift" between the Syrian and Lebanese peoples or "undermining internal stability in Lebanon"; and they blamed Israeli intransigence for the stalled Syrian-Israeli negotiations, which should result in Israeli withdrawal to the 4 June 1967 lines, as Syria demanded.[18] Syria also pushed for an early meeting of the leaders of all three countries to further reinforce its stand, but Egypt saw no urgency to do so.[19] (They had last met in December 1994 in Alexandria; see *MECS* 1994, pp. 88–89; the most recent tripartite meeting of their foreign ministers was in March 1998, see *MECS* 1998, pp. 100–101.) An Egyptian pro-government weekly subsequently reported that the Egyptian and Saudi foreign ministers pledged that their countries would provide moral and military backing to Syria if it was attacked by Israel.[20]

The following week, on 8 May, Asad flew to Cairo to meet with Mubarak. The Egyptians were keen to reassure Syria that the Israeli withdrawal, which Faruq al-Shar' had earlier called a "suicidal" act, would not lead to the isolation of Syria or weakening of its negotiating position vis-à-vis Israel.[21] Just as importantly, Egyptian reassurance was designed to encourage Syria to work for stability on the Lebanese-Israeli front, and not allow it to develop into a new flashpoint of tension. In that spirit, Mubarak advised Asad not to express reservations about the form of the Israeli withdrawal. Egypt also served as a courier of sorts between Israel and Egypt. The meeting was preceded by a telephone call from Barak to Mubarak, in which he reportedly expressed Israeli readiness to be responsive to the Syrians if they presented positive proposals. According to official Egyptian sources, Asad tendered two proposals, which Egypt then conveyed to Israel: the first would give Syria full control of the northeastern part of Lake Tiberias if the

Israelis agreed to provide regular annual water quotas from the lake with US and UN-sponsored guarantees of compliance; the second promised speedy normalization of relations.[22]

Egyptian determination to stabilize the area following the withdrawal was further driven home by the high-profile visit of the Egyptian prime minister to Lebanon on 17–19 May, to co-chair meetings of their joint cooperation committee. At their conclusion, the two sides issued a joint statement which welcomed "Lebanon's victory in liberating its land," praised the major improvement of Egyptian-Lebanese ties (Lahhud had reciprocated Mubarak's February visit with one to Cairo during April), and expressed Lebanese appreciation for Egyptian help in repairing the Beirut power stations damaged in the Israeli attack in February. Lebanon also welcomed the decision of the tripartite Palmyra meeting to endorse the UNIFIL role after the Israeli withdrawal in line with UN resolutions. Arab countries were called on to adhere to the resolutions of the March foreign ministers conference, "particularly with regard to the provision of financial, political and medical support necessary for Lebanon's steadfastness and its reconstruction." In line with Syrian requirements, the statement warned Israel of attempting to "drive a wedge" between the Syrian and Lebanese negotiating tracks.[23]

On 4–5 June, Cairo hosted the seventeenth meeting of the Damascus declaration foreign ministers. Issued with great fanfare in March 1991 by the six GCC states, Egypt and Syria, the core of the anti-Iraqi Arab coalition during the Gulf War, the declaration was designed to serve as the framework for a new, more stable and purposeful Arab order (see *MECS* 1991, pp. 141–44). However, it quickly became clear that expectations and realities were two different matters; and the framework receded in importance, serving merely as a periodic forum for consultations, as a companion to the Egyptian-Syrian-Saudi leadership grouping of the Arab world.

On Arab-Israeli issues, the meeting generated little debate; the final statement reiterated support for Syria and Lebanon against Israeli "threats," endorsed UN efforts to implement Resolution 425 and implicitly backed demands by Syria and Lebanon for Israel to withdraw from the disputed Shab'a farms area. The Iraqi question, by contrast, exposed growing divisions among the eight states over the issue, differences which heavily impeded inter-Arab cooperation (for details, see section on Iraq). The Cairo meeting would be the only gathering of the Damascus declaration states during 2000. By year's end, Egyptian officials, were cynical about the framework's utility and openly skeptical regarding its future.[24]

THE DEATH OF HAFIZ AL-ASAD

President Hafiz al-Asad of Syria died on 10 June. Although his ill-health during the preceding months was widely known, his passing seemed sudden. Over the course of nearly three decades of rule, he had transformed Syria from a weak, unstable entity where inter-Arab rivalries were frequently played out, to a stable power capable of weathering both regional and domestic crises and carving out a measure of influence in challenging geopolitical environs. Asad had not achieved many of his major foreign policy goals: developing Syria as an effective regional counterweight to Israel; bringing Jordan and the Palestinian movement under Syrian tutelage, as he had successfully done with Lebanon; achieving an Arab-Israeli political settlement in accordance with Syrian requirements; and blocking Arab diplomatic initiatives which were not in line with Syrian needs. The adventurous foreign policy of Iraq and hostility toward the Syrian Ba'th was a source of constant difficulty; Turkey had forced him to abandon support of the Turkish Kurdish opposition; Asad's Soviet backer had withdrawn much of its support even before the fall of the USSR; he had proved unable to convince the US to remove it from a list of states sponsoring or sheltering terrorists. On the plus side, Asad had weathered all of the Lebanese storms, including outside pressures, to effectively transform Lebanon into a Syrian satellite, of sorts; he also successfully nurtured Syria's strategic relationship with the Islamic regime of Iran. With the succession process uncertain, governments throughout the region watched keenly for signs which would indicate Syria's course in the days ahead.

Like most funerals of heads of state, Asad's provided a window into the nature of Syrian foreign relations. Unlike the funeral of King Husayn a year earlier (see *MECS* 1999, p. 343), Western leaders stayed away, apart from President Jacques Chirac of France, indicating the problematic international standing of Syria. By contrast, many Arab heads of state did attend, as did the presidents of Iran and Turkey. They included President Mubarak of Egypt, Crown Prince 'Abdallah of Saudi Arabia (in lieu of the ailing King Fahd), King 'Abdallah of Jordan, the emirs of Kuwait and Bahrain, 'Ali 'Abdallah Salih of Yemen, President Lahhud of Lebanon, President 'Abd al-'Aziz Bouteflika of Algeria and President Muhammad Hasan 'Umar al-Bashir of Sudan. Yasir 'Arafat of the PA also flew to Damascus to pay his respects: it was his first trip to Syria since 1993, and he clearly hoped that it would be a harbinger for improved relations with the new Syrian regime. The Iraqi representative was the relatively low-level vice president Taha Muhyi al-Din Ma'ruf, indicating Saddam Husayn's unwillingness to overly dignify the memory of his old foe.

The hasty installment of Bashshar al-Asad as president seemed unseemly, and even embarrassing to some in the Arab world.[25] Egyptian officials and commentators, in particular, took pains to distance themselves from the "presidential monarchy" style of government which Syria had adopted, and toward which Iraq was well on the way. Official Egypt was especially sensitive to the matter: Mubarak had never designated a vice-president, who under the constitution would automatically succeed him (as he himself had succeeded Anwar al-Sadat in 1981), and his son Gamal, a businessman by profession, was taking an increasingly active role in public life. Indeed, Mubarak was so sensitive about the subject that merely a hint of the possibility of being succeeded by his son, and not by a proper institutional process, was enough to bring down his full wrath against the prominent Egyptian scholar Sa'd 'Iddin Ibrahim (see chapter on Egypt). However, the swift and pain-free installment of Bashshar by the ruling Syrian elite was reassuring to Syria's neighbors, who always favored stability.

Bashshar's ascension to power occasioned considerable speculation that Syria was likely to enter a new era of domestic reform and liberalization, and a more flexible foreign policy, particularly vis-à-vis the Arab-Israeli arena. As it happened, the remainder of the year was marked more by continuity than by change in Syrian domestic and foreign policies (see chapter on Syria). There was, however, a notable improvement in Syrian relations with both Jordan and Iraq (for the latter, see section on Iraq, below). Syrian-Egyptian relations, on the other hand, were marked by periodic friction.

Syrian-Jordanian Relations
One of King 'Abdallah's foreign policy priorities upon succeeding his father in 1999 was to improve Amman's frosty relations with Damascus. This would allow Jordan to

be in the very center of the inter-Arab system, on good terms with all three sides of the Egyptian-Saudi-Syrian triangle. Syrian-Jordanian relations, historically, had been characterized by long periods of animosity and suspicion, and occasional, usually brief periods of amicability and consultation. The latest cold wind emanating from Damascus had originated in 1994, with the Jordanian decision to sign a separate peace treaty with Israel, regardless of Syrian disapproval (see *MECS* 1994, pp. 85–87, 428–29). Relations subsequently fluctuated, but were generally unsatisfactory, as far as Jordan was concerned.

The year 2000 began with Jordan complaining that Syria had failed to brief Jordanian officials about its negotiations with Israel; one official characterized Syrian behavior as "almost deliberate." Moreover, Syria proved utterly unresponsive to a Jordanian suggestion that it host a round of Syrian-Israeli talks.[26] Failure to keep Arab partners informed about negotiations with Israel, let alone coordinate tracks, had long been a Syrian complaint. Thus, the Jordanians, while perhaps genuinely desirous of more information and certainly preferring to play a more active role, if possible, undoubtedly enjoyed tossing Syria's traditional accusation against it back at Damascus. In any case, the Jordanians remained unsatisfied on bilateral issues as well: e.g., the hundreds of Jordanian prisoners languishing in Syrian jails, and the small amount of water supplied by Syria, following the fanfare which accompanied the Syrian offer in 1999 to compensate Jordan for the reduction in the amount of water supplied by Israel (on both matters, see *MECS* 1999, pp. 362–63, 564). The cold shoulder given to Jordanian officials by Syrian foreign minister Faruq al-Shar' rankled, as did the continuing failure to appoint a Syrian ambassador to Amman.[27] A visit by the Jordanian speaker of the Senate, former prime minister Zayd al-Rifa'i, who historically had good relations with the Syrian leadership, failed to produce tangible improvement.

In April, King 'Abdallah visited Israel. Among other things, the visit signaled to Syria that Jordan had a variety of regional options. But 'Abdallah balanced the visit with one to Damascus on 21 May. The Jordanian press emphasized Jordan's desire to improve relations, but, in the words of one analyst, "it takes two to tango."[28]

The initial response by Jordan to the change in Syria was one of guarded optimism. As time passed, it became clear that a substantial thaw was in progress. Both sides undertook confidence-building measures: Syria released several dozen Jordanian prisoners, spurring Jordanian hopes for a general amnesty,[29] and Jordan banned two senior leaders of the Syrian Muslim Brotherhood from returning to their Amman residences after they had left for London to campaign against the new Syrian regime.[30] 'Abdallah visited Bashshar on 19 July with a delegation which included his prime minister, chief of the royal court, head of the joint chiefs of staff and speaker of parliament. The visit seemed to symbolize a new, more cooperative era in inter-Arab relations, led by a younger generation of leaders who were slowly but surely assuming power.

From that point on, Jordanian-Syrian relations improved significantly. Their joint higher committee, chaired by their respective prime ministers, convened in mid-August. Discussions resumed on linking the electricity networks of the two countries as part of a larger project designed to link their grids with those of Egypt, Iraq, Lebanon and Turkey. Their ministers of trade and transportation signed an agreement on operating a rail line; other agreements dealt with agriculture and the creation of a free trade zone, and discussions were held regarding joint oil and gas exploration, construction projects, and cultural and scientific cooperation.

Water was a subject of much mutual interest. In late July, the water ministers of both countries took steps to resuscitate the long-delayed al-Wahda Dam on the Yarmuk River (see *MECS* 1987, pp. 647–48; 1994, p. 98). During 'Abdallah's July visit, Syria agreed to provide Jordan with 3.5m. cubic meters of water, as a stopgap measure, until September, to be taken from Syria's own irrigation water. The actual supply of the water began in mid-August.[31] The International Monetary Fund (IMF) granted a loan for a joint water project to be initiated in 2002 by the Syrian-Jordanian Drip Irrigation Company.

The thaw in Jordanian-Syrian relations was highlighted by their responses to the Palestinian al-Aqsa Intifada, which broke out in late September. To be sure, Jordan and Syria did not see eye-to-eye on the substance of the issue, with Jordan fearing the collapse of the peace process and the negative spillover effect of the Israeli-Palestinian confrontation on Jordan. Syria, for its part, was delighted with the renewed confrontation, especially since it had feared that an Israeli-Palestinian peace agreement would weaken its strategic position vis-à-vis Israel in the absence of a Syrian-Israeli peace agreement. However, unlike past occasions, Jordan and Syria maintained high level consultations during the initial crisis period. Jordan's foreign minister 'Abd al-Ilah Khatib met with the Syrian leadership in Damascus on 9 October, and on 18 October, Bashshar himself arrived in Amman for talks with 'Abdallah, on the eve of the emergency Arab summit conference in Cairo. It was the first official working visit to Jordan by a Syrian president since 1986.[32] (For the actions of the two leaders at the summit, see below.)

Syrian-Jordanian differences on the Arab-Israeli conflict did not prevent an overall warming of bilateral ties, neither did their subtle competition to pioneer the breakdown of taboos in relations with Iraq (see below) have any overt effect on the atmosphere between them. One further concrete demonstration of the thaw in relations pertained to the issue of the Syrian failure to appoint an ambassador to Jordan after a seven year absence. Following Bashshar's ascent to power, the Syrian chargé d'affaires in Amman said the matter was merely technical, and would be remedied shortly. On the day of Bashshar's arrival in Amman, *The Jordan Times* reported that an ambassador had been appointed, but his identity was only announced officially two months later.[33]

THE PALESTINIANS AND THE INTER-ARAB ENVIRONS

The priority given by Israel to the Syrian negotiating track at the beginning of the year left the Palestinian leadership concerned. This mirrored Syrian discontent whenever the Palestinian-Israeli track moved forward at the apparent expense of Syria. The poor state of their bilateral relationship reflected these mutual suspicions. Syrian unwillingness to normalize relations with 'Arafat and the PA rankled the Palestinians no end, and no amount of Egyptian and Jordanian prodding could get Syria to budge from its hostility. For Damascus, as long as 'Arafat insisted on being treated as an equal, and as an independent actor, unwilling to define Palestinian collective interests and policies in ways which were commensurate with all-Arab requirements (as defined by Syria), he would remain *persona non grata* in the Syrian capital.

As with the Iraqis and Jordanians, the death of Hafiz al-Asad raised hopes among the Palestinian leadership that a new page could be turned. However brief 'Arafat's stay during the funeral, it was noteworthy. A large Palestinian parliamentary delegation, headed by Salim al-Za'nun, chairperson of the Palestine National Council (PNC), paid a condolence visit at the end of the forty-day mourning period, at the invitation of the Syrian National Assembly.[34] Coming after the conclusion of the Camp David summit (see below), Palestinians hoped that the combination of proven Palestinian steadfastness at the summit and the official nature of the invitation meant that the changing of the guard in Syria portended a breakthrough in relations. To that end, 'Arafat turned down the overtures of Rif'at Asad, the exiled brother of the late president and pretender to the Syrian presidency, for a meeting.[35] However, in substance, the Syrian posture remained unchanged, leaving the Palestinians disappointed.

Some signs of progress were registered in the PA relations made with Kuwait. The latter had blamed the Palestine Liberation Organization (PLO) bitterly for allegedly siding with Iraq in 1990 (see *MECS* 1990, p. 517), and had steadfastly refused to include the Palestinian leadership among the Arab parties with which it had gradually normalized relations — the North African states, Jordan and Yemen. A warm embrace between 'Arafat and Kuwaiti foreign minister Shaykh Sabah al-Ahmad Al Sabah, the leading Kuwaiti official to advocate improving relations with the *duwal al-dadd* (the "contrary" states, i.e., those that had tilted toward pro-Iraqi sentiments in 1990–91) occurred during the May celebrations in San'a which marked the tenth anniversary of Yemeni unification (see *MECS* 1990, pp. 709–12). Duly noted was the contrast between Sabah's warmth and the refusal of Crown Prince Shaykh Sa'd al-'Abdallah Al Sabah to shake 'Arafat's outstretched hand during the funeral of King Hasan of Morocco in July 1999 (while at the same time eagerly shaking hands with the Israeli prime minister). Still, their embrace raised many eyebrows in Kuwait, and a group of Kuwaiti parliamentarians drafted a statement demanding that Shaykh Sabah apologize to the Kuwaiti people for committing "a strategic blunder worse than the Iraqi invasion of Kuwait."[36]

Additional signs of a thaw in the Kuwaiti attitude came in the wake of the renewed Palestinian-Israeli violence (see below).

Camp David and the Aqsa Intifada

Egypt, Jordan and Saudi Arabia kept a close watch on the Camp David proceedings. The Jordanians were particularly anxious regarding any possible agreement on the question of Palestinian refugees which would directly impact on Jordan[37] while the leaders of all three countries were exercised over the Jerusalem question. At one point during the talks, the US and Israel sought Egyptian pressure on 'Arafat to demonstrate greater flexibility, but without success; the US was clearly disappointed with both the Egyptians and the Saudis. Indeed, Cairo and Riyadh were concerned primarily with insuring that 'Arafat resist Israeli and American demands for concessions on the issues of Jerusalem and borders. Following telephone consultations between Mubarak and King 'Abdallah, the Jordanian foreign minister 'Abd al-Ilah al-Khatib flew to Alexandria on 22 July to meet with his Egyptian counterpart, 'Amru Musa, to discuss the summit, which was still in progress. The next day, Mubarak flew to Saudi Arabia, where he and the Saudi leadership "reaffirm[ed] the shared and solid Egyptian-Saudi position in support of the Palestinian stance at Camp David, and reiterate[d] the Arabs' adherence to Palestinian sovereignty over East Jerusalem."[38] The conclusion of the summit without an agreement was greeted with a palpable sigh of relief among both officials and commentators throughout the Arab world, where it was widely feared that 'Arafat would bow to American pressure and tender unacceptable concessions on core issues.[39] President Clinton's subsequent complaint that the Palestinians had been too inflexible was refuted by Musa, who said that flexibility would be needed in matters related to details, but not the principles enshrined in UN Resolution 242. 'Arafat, he emphasized, had full "Arab, Islamic and Christian" backing on the Jerusalem issue.[40] Mubarak was irritated with the criticism emanating from the West: "Some accused us of not having helped the Camp David negotiations," he told Egyptian students. "How were we supposed to help when we did not know the details and what was happening in the Camp David kitchen? And if Egypt and Saudi Arabia are required to help, does help mean relinquishing [one's rights] to the other side?"[41] In any case, both Egypt and Jordan interpreted the Camp David meetings not as a failure but as a way-station toward further American-sponsored negotiations.

Inter-Arab consultations intensified after Camp David, reflecting widespread uncertainty over what was to come next, and what the policies of Arab states should be. As in the past, there loomed the possibility of a unilateral Palestinian declaration of independence on 13 September, the seventh anniversary of the Oslo accords. 'Arafat was peripatetic, hopping from one capital to the next in order to confirm Arab, Muslim and international backing and thus strengthen his position vis-à-vis the US and Israel, in advance of his next moves. His Arab itinerary included five visits to Egypt, as well as trips to Algeria, Morocco, Libya, the UAE, Sudan, Tunisia, Yemen, Qatar, Saudi Arabia, and Bahrain. King 'Abdallah of Jordan met him in Morocco on 31 July and again in Ramallah on 22 August (for the degree of tension between the PA and Jordan, see chapter on Jordan). The contrast between Syria and the rest of the Arab "central stream" regarding relations with the PA was highlighted again by the fact that 'Arafat conspicuously avoided Damascus, where he remained unwelcome.[42] By contrast, he did visit Iran, Syria's "strategic ally" for more than twenty years. It was 'Arafat's first "bilateral" visit to Tehran since February 1979, when the new Islamic revolutionary government handed the PLO the keys to the Israeli embassy (he attended the Tehran ICO summit in December 1997). 'Arafat entreated President Muhammad Khatami of Iran, current president of the ICO, to convene a special ICO summit on the Palestinians' behalf, but to no avail.

Overall, the Palestinians were unhappy with the level of Arab and Muslim support, a theme which would recur shortly, and far more acutely.[43] The only multi-nation forum which did convene was the ICO Jerusalem Committee. Meeting on 28 August in Agadir under the patronage of King Muhammad VI of Morocco, the sixteen-member committee, which included eight Arab parties, endorsed all Palestinian and Arab demands, and called for international recognition and UN membership of the soon to be proclaimed Palestinian state.[44] However, regarding a possible declaration of independence on 13 September, 'Arafat found practically no actual support. Egypt and France, in particular, took the lead in advising against such a move, favoring continued diplomatic efforts to bring about a softening of the Israeli position. 'Arafat also sounded out Arab leaders regarding the convening of an Arab summit, which he considered vital in order to "provide local and international cover" to the Palestinians, and lay down "specific [red] lines " to which Palestinian negotiators could then point in rejecting American and Israeli pressures for further concessions.[45]

However, the cause was not sufficiently urgent to allow for existing obstacles to be overcome. Again, it was Cairo which had the deciding say, and Cairo preferred additional quiet diplomacy with American and European involvement to collective Arab spectacles. An alternative suggestion was an Egyptian-Syrian-Saudi summit, but this, too, failed to materialize. On 21 August, Mubarak received in Alexandria, 'Arafat and Syrian foreign minister Shar' separately. The next day, King 'Abdallah of Jordan traveled to Ramallah to meet with 'Arafat, after first visiting with Israeli prime minister Ehud Barak in Tel Aviv. Shar' criticized 'Arafat for keeping the other Arab parties in the dark regarding the

Camp David discussions. As usual, the Egyptians were interested in simultaneously promoting Palestinian-Israeli negotiations, a coordinated Arab stand under its leadership, and no Palestinian unilateral acts (e.g., a declaration of independence) which could backfire against them by inviting Israeli unilateral moves. Syria, for its part, preferred that the negotiations be halted, and that the Arab world stand as a single unit vis-à-vis Israel. Other minority voices, apart from perennial rejectionists Libya and Iraq, included Qatar and Yemen. While on a state visit to Yemen, Emir Shaykh Hamad bin Khalifa Al Thani of Qatar called for an Arab summit to discuss the declaration of an independent Palestinian state. His host, President 'Ali 'Abdallah Salih, characterized the Camp David talks as fruitless and advocated the use of force to win back Arab rights, a method, he said, which Hizballah proved successful in Lebanon.[46]

With Egypt firmly in the inter-Arab driver's seat, at least with regard to formal collective action, there was little that 'Arafat could do. He thus deferred the declaration of statehood yet again, and continued to keep his options open.[47] Egypt, for its part, was hopeful that its post-Camp David diplomacy with the US, the EU countries and Russia, would bear fruit, as Egypt detected what it viewed as new flexibility in the American position.[48]

In early September, Arab foreign ministers (minus the Saudi and Kuwaiti foreign ministers who delegated officials of lower standing) met in their regularly scheduled semi-annual meeting in Cairo. To the surprise of many, the five-member committee, which had been charged with working out a "mechanism" for convening the summit on an annual basis, decided that an Arab summit would convene in early 2001 in Cairo, and that a regular summit would henceforth be held annually during the month of March. Egypt would chair the first summit, Morocco the second, and subsequent ones would be chaired on a rotating basis. An annex confirming the process was to be attached to the Arab League charter.[49] For the Palestinians, a January summit was too far away to be of immediate value. For the Egyptians, however, the January date and the commitment to a regular annual summit confirmed anew their regional leadership and ability to shape the collective Arab agenda. More specifically, it bought Egypt time, time to witness the unfolding of the peace process and to try and advance the cause of Iraqi-Kuwaiti healing.

However, the explosion of Israeli-Palestinian violence in late September, altered all calculations. What quickly became known as the Aqsa Intifada triggered waves of anger throughout the Arab world. Fed by daily, real-time televised images of Palestinian casualties broadcast by Arab satellite networks across the region, popular protests took place in nearly every Arab country, from Morocco to the Gulf, and on a scale not seen since the Gulf War. In Morocco, half a million persons marched peacefully, led by Prime Minister Abderrahmane El Yousouffi. Normally placid Gulf countries also witnessed noisy street protests, including Oman, which hosted an Israeli commercial office, and even Kuwait, despite the country's decade-long animosity toward the Palestinians. In Jordan, protestors clashed with security forces, resulting in a ban on all further demonstrations; in Egypt, repeated student demonstrations were watched carefully by the authorities. Egypt, Jordan, Morocco, Saudi Arabia, and subsequently Kuwait all provided hospital treatment to wounded Palestinians, and funds were raised in many countries for medical treatment. Nonetheless, criticism from columnists and opposition figures of Arab governments and the Arab League was savage, with one columnist describing the league as the "league of the living dead."[50] Fifty-five leaders and intellectuals from Islamist movements across the Arab and Muslim world issued a joint statement which denounced "Arab [governments'] submissiveness and willingness to give in," demanded that Arab and Islamic states "expel Israeli missions [and] halt all overt and covert ties of normalization with the Zionists," and called for Palestine to be liberated by mass action and armed resistance.[51]

In the midst of this increasingly charged atmosphere, Arab governments scrambled to take stock of the developing situation and its potential impact at home. On 2 October, Asad visited Mubarak in Cairo to discuss the situation. Both issued public calls for an Arab summit. However, Mubarak still wanted the summit to take place only in January, preferring not to convene Arab leaders during a time of crisis, but rather to try to help shepherd the protagonists back to the negotiating table and away from armed conflict. Barak's rejection of Mubarak's offer to host a meeting in Sharm al-Shaykh on 5 October between him and 'Arafat led Mubarak to advance the dates of the summit to late October. He was eager not to appear to be behind the curve of Arab public opinion so as to be able to shape it to Egyptian requirements. To be sure, Libya and Iraq adopted a militant, dismissive line regarding the summit. Libyan leader Mu'ammar al-Qadhdhafi, visiting Damascus on 9 October, charged that the purpose of the summit was to call a halt to the current intifada, instead of supporting its continuation.[52] Saddam Husayn, for his part, sent an open letter to Mubarak expressing "regret" that Arab governments had been so tardy in convening a summit on behalf of the Palestinians, which Arab publics would view suspiciously.[53] But Saddam also knew that the summit would benefit Iraq simply because Iraq would be able to attend. In any case, Mubarak chose to ignore their criticism.

In the midst of the Israeli-Palestinian confrontation, three Israeli soldiers were abducted from the disputed Shab'a farms border area by Hizballah units on 7 October. The move raised immediate fears of an Israeli military response against Syria and Lebanon, thus generating intensive inter-Arab and international diplomatic activity. Syria's partners in the "core" Arab triangle — Saudi Arabia and Egypt — were publicly supportive of Syria in the face of Israeli threats, while privately advising it to rein in Hizballah and act with restraint in the event of Israeli actions. Regional war, Mubarak never tired of saying, was no longer an option. After visiting wounded Palestinians in a Riyadh hospital, Crown Prince 'Abdallah of Saudi Arabia warned that "no one should think that the Kingdom of Saudi Arabia and the whole Arab and Islamic world would just watch with their arms folded," if Israel were to carry out its threats.[54] Egyptian foreign minister Musa visited Damascus twice in three days (8,10 October) to confer with Asad. For years, Egypt had unsuccessfully attempted to mediate Syrian-Palestinian differences. Now, to its satisfaction, Asad agreed to take a telephone call from 'Arafat on 10 October, indicating that the now imminent summit would be conducted according to Egyptian wishes.[55]

The degree to which Egypt continued to lead the diplomatic process was again highlighted on 16–17 October, when it hosted an Israeli-Palestinian-US summit in Sharm al-Shaykh. Syria had had significant disagreements with Egypt over both its very convening and the content of the summit. Saudi intervention, including a three-way foreign ministers meeting in Riyadh on 14–15 October, helped to damp down, but not eliminate the differences, as the Syrian media remained sharply critical of the Sharm al-Shaykh gathering.[56] The four-way summit produced a fragile agreement to implement a cease-fire and resume political negotiations. Arab reactions, official and unofficial, more or less followed established lines. Officially, Egypt strongly defended its active diplomatic role as necessary for Palestinian well-being, as well as being politically shrewd. Mubarak claimed to have spoken to several Arab heads of state, all of whom urged him to do something for the Palestinians.[57] The Sharm summit, wrote al-Ahram editor Ibrahim

Nafi', in no way obviated the need for an Arab summit in support of the Palestinians. Rather, they complemented one another.[58] Writing in *al-Sharq al-Awsat*, a Paris-based Syrian columnist warned against "rhetorical one-upmanship" and "outbidding" by various Arab and Muslim parties (implicitly including Hizballah). Such acts, he said, while ostensibly supportive of the Palestinians, were really designed to upstage, and even destabilize Arab regimes, the only ones capable of extending material and political support to the Palestinians. The summit's main task, he declared, should be precisely that.[59]

Columnists, opposition figures and leaders of countries belonging to the militant fringe criticized the agreement as essentially taking the wind out of the collective Arab sails, denuding the upcoming Arab summit of any potential leverage on behalf of the Palestinians. Significantly, President Asad of Syria alluded critically to Mubarak's assertion that the Sharm al-Shaykh agreement had been designed to spare Palestinian blood. If the Palestinian people had wanted their blood spared, he declared, they would have remained in their homes instead of confronting the Israeli army on the streets.[60]

Qadhdhafi acted in his own inimitable fashion. On 17 October, he revealed on al-Jazira satellite television that the upcoming Arab summit conference had already drawn up its resolutions, which fell far short of what was required, in his view. Reading out portions of the draft text, he scoffed at its threat to prosecute Israeli leaders on war crime charges. Thus, in both form and content, he regarded the summit meeting as a sham. Instead, he said, there should be a carefully prepared summit, which would devise a strategy that would satisfy "the revolting Arab street," with regard to Israeli occupation of Arab lands, the requirements of globalization, or the need to put the Arabs on the map of the new world.[61] Foreign Minister Musa, for his part, downplayed the whole matter, saying that Qadhdhafi's purported text was a "preliminary" document designed for discussion. On the eve of the summit, Mubarak attacked those Arab regimes which were calling for a "hardline stand." "What is [it] supposed to mean?...A declaration of war? War is not a joke. Anyone who speaks of a declaration of war should be aware of its meaning, its gravity and its impact on his people — unless those who say so [intend to fight] until the last Egyptian soldier."[62]

The Cairo Arab Summit

The summit opened on 21 October in Cairo, following a preparatory conference of foreign ministers on 19 October. Given the pre-summit dynamics, expectations for dramatic decisions were practically nil. Nonetheless, the atmosphere was charged, thanks to the general atmosphere of anger among wide sectors of the public. Demonstrations took place across the Arab world that day, the largest being in San'a, the Yemeni capital, under official patronage. Numbering at least hundreds of thousands, with "most carrying weapons," the marchers called for "jihad" to liberate Jerusalem.[63]

The list of those present and absent from the summit was of special interest. Most notable was the presence of Iraq, for the first time since August 1990, with 'Izzat Ibrahim al-Duri, vice-chairman of Iraq's ruling Revolutionary Command Council, leading the delegation in Saddam Husayn's stead. Indeed, the Palestinian-Israeli confrontation had been a boon to Saddam Husayn. To be sure, sanctions against Iraq were already eroding, most Arab countries were gradually upgrading their ties (see below), and it had been clear for some time that the Iraqi presence at the next Arab summit conference was a foregone conclusion. But the ongoing violence provided Saddam with an opportunity to cultivate more public support in the Arab world by reminding others of his militancy on behalf of the Palestinians. One concrete manifestation of his support were direct cash payments to families of "martyrs". The Kuwaitis were particularly concerned that the Palestinian-Israeli crisis was accelerating Iraq's reentry into the Arab fold and eroding the standing of the US in the region.

In contrast to Iraqi satisfaction with returning to its place at the summit conference table, Qadhdhafi wanted no part of it, sending as low a level representative as possible: the permanent Libyan delegate to the Arab League, 'Abd al-Mun'im al-Hawni. On the other end of the political spectrum, President Maaouyia Ould Taaya of Mauritania and Sultan Qabus of Oman both sent lower level delegations as well, in order to avoid being personally lambasted for maintaining formal relations with Israel. Mauritania was represented by its prime minister, Shaykh El Avia Ould Muhammad Khuna, and Oman by Fahd bin Mahmud Al Sa'id, deputy prime minister for cabinet affairs.

All together, of the twenty-two Arab League members, fifteen were represented by their heads of state; the ailing monarch of Saudi Arabia, was represented by de facto ruler Crown Prince 'Abdallah; that of Kuwait by acting prime minister Sabah al-Ahmad Al Sabah, and that of the UAE by Shaykh Maktum bin Rashid Al Maktum, vice president and prime minister. For the first time in many years, the president of war-torn Somalia, one of the three peripheral league members in the Horn of Africa (along with Djibouti and the Comoros Islands), attended, a fact which was noted with satisfaction in the summit's final statement. Overall, the level of participation was extremely high, a reflection of the perceived gravity of the Palestinian-Israeli situation.

While the summit's actual discussions and final communiqué were bereft of significant controversy, the contrast in the rhetoric of the participants was especially sharp. Their sensitivity to the anger in the Arab "street" was unprecedented, as least as far as public expressions were concerned. Mubarak's opening speech to the conference, as the host, emphasized the three main themes of Egyptian policy toward the conflict: the exclusive responsibility of Israel for the outbreak of violence and the fate of the peace process, the Arab world's commitment to achieving an "equitable,…just and comprehensive peace in accordance with the international legitimacy resolutions and in implementation of the land-for-peace principle," and Egyptian determination to play a central diplomatic role to help bring about the cessation of the fighting and progress toward a diplomatic solution, which had been embodied by the Sharm al-Shaykh summit. Mubarak also emphasized the relationship between the summit and the deeply felt anger in the Arab world:

> We embody the Arab people's rejection and express the overwhelming and justified anger that has gripped all the Arab and Islamic peoples without exception at the aggression on their sanctities. We are here to express our peoples' wishes and feelings and the nation's conscience and collective sentiment.

At the same time, Mubarak cautioned his counterparts against being led by the "street." "Our mission ultimately as leaders of this nation is to proceed on the road that achieves this nation's interests, insures its stability, and protects it from surrendering to emotional stands," he declared.[64]

Mubarak's insistence on maintaining course, despite widespread Arab doubts over Israeli intentions, was echoed by King 'Abdallah of Jordan and King Muhammad of Morocco. 'Abdallah linked the three main issues facing the Arab world: the pressing need for wider Arab economic cooperation in the face of globalization processes which had left the Arab world "on the sidelines"; the Arab-Israeli conflict, and especially the

Palestinian cause; and the unjust isolation and threat to Iraq. "We can either regain the nation's trust by working together," he concluded, "or consolidate doubts that the Arab system is no longer capable of fulfilling the nation's aspirations."[65] Muhammad's speech, his first summit appearance as head of state, was perhaps the least militant, as he vowed not to go back on his father's choice of making peace with Israel, while being in accord with the overall Arab insistence on compelling Israel to modify its policies.[66]

By contrast, the public rhetoric of Syrian president Asad, Yemeni president Salih and the PA leader 'Arafat was especially harsh. Making his first appearance at an Arab summit, Asad presented a militant posture, in line with longstanding Syrian positions, and against the background of the failed Syrian-Israeli negotiations earlier in the year and the events in Lebanon. Israel's ongoing "criminal, bloody acts" against the Palestinians, proved that:

> the Israeli leaders are unable to hide their racist, aggressive nature. In fact, they have gone beyond that by declaring this nature as a method of dealing with the Arabs... aiming [live bullets] directly at the head and the chest...clear proof of an overwhelming desire by the Israelis to kill. They have planned this in advance and at the highest levels.

In remarks which were guaranteed to disturb the Egyptians, Asad criticized calls to cease the intifada on the pretext of halting the shedding of Palestinian blood. "We have not heard any Palestinian struggler ask for [a] stopping [of] the bloodshed," he declared. "The blood that was shed was not shed so that we may come and stop this shedding, but in order for Israel to pay the price." Asad extolled the Israeli "defeat" in Lebanon, the first such outcome since the October 1973 War. It had been achieved, he said, thanks to the "unwavering resolve, determination, and faith" of the Lebanese resistance, which was determined to change the facts on the ground. "The Palestinian brothers in the West Bank and the 1948 Palestinian territories" (i.e., pre-1967 Israel), he said, appeared to have learned the lesson of Lebanon. "Therefore, as Arabs at this summit, we cannot stay in between. We should either be with the victim or the killer, and we must certainly spell out our stand." As a first step, "all forms of cooperation with Israel must be stopped and the decision to boycott Israel must be activated." While insisting that his was not a call for war, he also insisted that the Arabs must only pursue a "peace of the strong" (in contrast to what he called a "peace of the weak," or a "war of the weak"). One could not also fail to note the deliberate contrast between Asad's "peace of the strong" and 'Arafat's mantra-like "peace of the brave" which he had pursued with the late Israeli prime minister, Yitzhak Rabin.

Salih of Yemen positioned himself firmly on the side of the "Arab masses" who, he said, were waiting for "crucial decisions" in the face of the "genocide" being inflicted on the Palestinian people by Israel. "Normalization," he declared, "did not grant us strength. It is as if we approached them from a point of weakness, begging them for peace." Israel, he stressed, was "a cancer in the Arab body," which needed to be confronted on all levels, not with war but through "resistance...jihad...donations...and sending money to buy weapons." International forces should be introduced to protect Palestinian civilians from Israel aggression.[67] But these were not to be Arabs. At one point during the summit discussions, 'Arafat suggested that Jordanian and Egyptian forces should be introduced to protect the Palestinians. Salih immediately expressed disapproval, saying that it would not be in either country's interest, to which King 'Abdallah of Jordan wholly concurred.[68]

'Izzat Ibrahim of Iraq representing Saddam Husayn, went even further than Salih in claiming to speak for the "Arab masses" against "those who were imposed on them as rulers." It was the latter, he said, who "try to make [the Arab nation] move backward and to undermine its will, morale, and resources." The clear stand of Iraq, he announced, was:

> to call and work for the liberation of Palestine through jihad... which can liberate Palestine and the other Arab territories that the filthy Jews had occupied and incorporated into their deformed Zionist entity....Those who speak about another course...the so-called peaceful solution...should remember the futile attempts that lasted for twenty years to enhance our resolve and regain Arab sovereignty over Palestine and grant the nation a serious opportunity for pride and glory.....Let the one who claims he has another alternative defend this alternative before the Arab masses, and not implicate all the Arabs in what is not feasible.

Once the goal of liberation was agreed on, he declared, the specific roles and actions expected from each Arab state could then be determined.[69]

Befitting the centrality of the Palestinian issue at the summit, 'Arafat's speech was the longest of the opening addresses. Detailing its "barbaric" practices and "bloody massacres," he accused Israel of introducing a dangerous "religious dimension" to the conflict. In this context, he condemned Israel for claiming sovereignty over the Haram al-Sharif (Temple Mount) in Jerusalem on the basis of a fabricated history of the Jewish Temple, and for allowing opposition leader Ariel Sharon to visit the site and thus spark the violence in a premeditated manner. At the same time, he also emphasized the PA commitment to a "just, lasting and comprehensive peace," praising the diplomatic efforts of President Clinton, while also making specific mention of UN Resolutions 181 (partitioning Palestine) and 194 (enshrining the "right of return" of Palestinian refugees). 'Arafat thus adroitly straddled the line between the militancy and anger being expressed among his own population and in many Arab quarters, fundamental Palestinian positions on Jerusalem and refugees, and the diplomatic efforts by his Egyptian patron and the peace process sponsor, the US, to damp down the violence and restore the momentum of negotiations. He concluded by calling on Arab leaders to put their differences aside, "for the sake of the children of Palestine, Iraq, Lebanon, Syria, and the rest of the Arab nation," and achieve "genuine inter-Arab reconciliation." Doing so would inaugurate a "new Arab era that is in line with the status of our nation and the greatness of our pan-Arab goals."[70]

'Arafat also scored a symbolic success of sorts at the summit, winning the public embrace of Kuwaiti acting prime minister Shaykh Sabah. Sabah's defense of the act to irritated critics at home was simple: "When a brother comes to greet you, do you tell him 'no'?" In any case, he said, "there are no differences with the Palestinian people ...We hope that differences with the PA will be eliminated as soon as possible." Underscoring his words, Kuwait flew a number of wounded Palestinians from Amman for treatment in Kuwaiti hospitals, and Sabah himself visited them there."[71] Kuwait also pledged funds to the Palestinians, in line with a Saudi initiative to establish two special funds, one for the preservation of the Arab and Islamic character of Jerusalem, and one for the families of Palestinian "martyrs" (see below). A week after the summit, the Kuwaiti cabinet issued a statement stressing Kuwaiti commitment to "preserving the rights of the Palestinian people and supporting them to establish their independent state on their national soil." The PA sought to capitalize on the new atmosphere, designating senior 'Arafat aide Nabil Sha'th to be in charge of promoting a dialogue with the Kuwaiti leadership. To that end, Sha'th hinted that the Palestinians might try to mediate between Iraq and Kuwait over the fate of Kuwaiti prisoners missing since the 1991 Gulf war. KUNA quoted him as praising Kuwaiti support for the Palestinian intifada and calling on Iraq to release Kuwaiti prisoners.[72]

By contrast, President 'Abd al-'Aziz Bouteflika of Algeria gave the cold shoulder to 'Arafat, only meeting him briefly at the end of the summit, and popular expressions of support for the Palestinians were strongly discouraged in Algiers. Bouteflika even refrained from addressing the summit at all. As one of the Palestinians' leading supporters, historically, the shift in the Algerian position was noticeable. It apparently stemmed from a desire to curry greater favor in the West at the expense of involvement in all-Arab affairs. It also derived from concern that permitting popular expressions of support for the Palestinians might contribute to domestic instability.[73]

With the basic text of the final statement already determined at the outset, there was little rancor expressed during the closed summit sessions. Almost ritually, Qadhdhafi's representative walked out of the gathering before it ended, declaring that it "would take no concrete decision likely to end Israel's aggressive practices."[74] Iraq's Ibrahim expressed "reservations" with the draft final communiqué. Couching his criticism in Islamic terms, he bemoaned the "inadequate...way the Arab nation's capabilities were viewed," and the fact that:

> knowledge of the faithful Arab and Muslim people was not as it should be....If we do not...go back to the nation's past, civilization and symbols, and stand as one man, then [additional] lands and rights will be lost....[Thus] we are called upon as Arab Muslims by God to resort to jihad.[75]

The wording of the final communiqué was especially harsh, in line with the images of bloodshed which had dominated the Arab public sphere for the last month. Israel, the leaders declared, was solely responsible for the violence, for it had "turned the peace process into a war operation against the Palestinian people, using military force to besiege it, isolate it and take it hostage inside the West Bank and Gaza Strip." Seeking to demonstrate their responsiveness to the Arab 'street,' even as they sought to contain it, Arab leaders commended "the response of the Arab masses — from the Atlantic to the Gulf — to the intifada of the heroic Palestinian people" against "Israeli aggression and the brutal actions of the occupation forces." The summit participants called on "the sons and daughters of the Arab nation to donate one day's wages as a popular Arab contribution in support of the intifada and the Palestinian national struggle."

With an eye to the international arena, Arab leaders made a number of demands. The first was the establishment of an "impartial international commission of inquiry" sponsored by the UN Security Council and UN Human Rights Commission to determine the causes and apportion blame for the violence, including the "massacres" perpetrated by Israeli forces. The Security Council, they said, should "continue to monitor developments in the occupied Palestinian and Arab territories which threaten international peace and stability." Moreover, the UN should consider establishing an "international force or presence" to protect the Palestinians living under the Israeli yoke. In addition, they demanded that the Security Council "set up a special international criminal court to try the Israeli war criminals who committed the massacres...along the lines of the two courts formed by the Security Council to try war criminals in Rwanda and the former Yugoslavia. They pledged to follow up the matter of bringing the alleged perpetrators of "these barbaric practices" to justice "according to the statutes of the International Criminal Court."

At the same time, Arab leaders reiterated their commitment to a "just and comprehensive peace" based on the concept of "land-for-peace" enshrined at the 1991 Madrid peace conference and anchored by UN Resolutions 242 and 338, which would entail Israeli withdrawal from the territories it conquered in 1967, and UN Resolution 194, which guaranteed the Palestinian refugees "right of return." All past summit conferences had also endorsed the "right of return," drawing little attention. Its usage reflected the centrality of the refugee question in Palestinian-Israeli negotiations and the unwavering public support of Arab states of the Palestinians.

For years, Arab summits had been lambasted by all and sundry in the Arab world as being long on rhetoric and short on action. The question raised by the Cairo summit was what, if any, concrete steps the participants would take. If there was one immediate demand from radical Arab states and the Arab "street" during the preceding month of violence, it was that Arab governments sever all the various forms of diplomatic and commercial ties established with Israel over the last seven years. Indeed, the summit's final statement faithfully echoed the widespread anti-normalization sentiment in the Arab world, especially in light of the deadlocked peace process. They thus "affirm[ed] their commitment to firmly challenge Israel's attempts to infiltrate the Arab world under any guise." The statement did not spell out explicitly its preference for the severance of ties, emphasizing only that Israel would bear responsibility for any actions taken, including the severance. Regarding the multilateral track, which had tentatively been re-started earlier in the year, the final statement was more explicit. Under current circumstances, it said, "talk of a joint future in the region was irrelevant." Arab states would therefore not participate in further regional negotiations or economic development schemes until a "just and comprehensive" peace was achieved. For Syria, the condemnation of normalization was especially satisfying, for it had been in a distinct minority on the subject for years.

It was clear to all that Egypt and Jordan, the two front-line states which had signed full-scale peace treaties with Israel, would not actually cut diplomatic relations. Those with lower-level ties, however, were expected to do so, being vulnerable to such pressures. Oman had already announced on 12 October that it was shutting the Israeli trade office in Muscat. Almost immediately after the summit, Morocco and Tunisia closed their diplomatic missions in Israel. Morocco had recalled the chief of its liaison office for consultations two weeks before the summit. Having played a supporting role in the Arab-Israeli peace process for years, the Moroccan decision to cut diplomatic relations entirely was especially notable, and probably stemmed from the new ruler's desire to bolster his own legitimacy in the face of widespread pro-Palestinian support.[76] Qatar held out for a time but soon succumbed to Saudi and Iranian pressure in order to save the ICO summit it hosted three weeks later (see below, and chapter on political Islam). Only Mauritania, among the most peripheral of all Arab League members, both geographically and socially, refused to downgrade its full relations, with the US apparently playing a key role in the decision.

Acting on a Saudi initiative, the summit also decided on the establishment of two funds: (1) the $800m. "al-Aqsa Fund" to "provide for projects intended to preserve the

Arab and Islamic character of Jerusalem, preventing its obliteration, and to wean the Palestinian people from the Israeli economy"; and (2) the $200m. "Intifada Fund" to be directed to the "families of Palestinian martyrs in the intifada and for raising and educating their children." The Saudis pledged to contribute a quarter of the sum earmarked for the two funds. One week later, the Kuwaiti cabinet, following the emir's instructions, reportedly agreed to contribute $150m. to the two funds.[77] The emir of Qatar, Shaykh Hamad bin Khalifa Al Thani, agreed to bear the costs of the UN inquiry into human rights violations in the West Bank and Gaza set up by the UN Human Rights Commission on 19 October. A follow-up committee, made up of the foreign ministers of Egypt, Syria, Jordan, Lebanon, Morocco, Bahrain, Tunisia, Saudi Arabia and "Palestine," and Arab League secretary-general 'Abd al-Majid, was established to ensure the implementation of the resolutions.

The final statement reaffirmed the intent of Arab leaders to hold regular annual summits, to "enhance the joint Arab endeavor in all fields, particularly the economic field which has become more pressing than at any time before, particularly [now] that international and regional developments have made Arab economic integration a pressing matter." The next one was scheduled for March 2001, in Amman. The emphasis on economic integration, enhancing the role of the Arab League, and holding regular annual summits conformed precisely to Egyptian inter-Arab policy.[78] Although the Libyan representative had already withdrawn from the summit, Libya quickly assented to the decision to hold regular summits.[79] (For the full text of the final statement, see Appendix I.)

The Egyptian government was thus satisfied that Arab anger and frustration had been channeled in ways that would exert pressure on Israel but prevent a slide towards regional confrontation and instability. But it also needed to defend the summit results before skeptics in the Arab press and in some official quarters. Foreign Minister Musa declared that the summit resolutions complemented "the rebellious, objecting members of the Arab people," even if they were "not completely identical with what the angry Arab public wants," and noted that a number of Arab governments had already cut official relations with Israel.[80] Senior Mubarak adviser Usama al-Baz strong rejected criticism that the summit had taken no practical measures, pointing to the funds pledged, the intent to establish an international criminal tribunal to investigate the violence perpetrated against the Palestinians, and the recognition that building a strong Arab economy was crucial to changing the regional relations and thus compelling Israel to change its policies. Baz also denied charges that the US had intervened to water down the summit resolutions.[81] Criticizing Arab radicals, the Egyptian minister of information, speaking on behalf of the cabinet, stated that "those who resorted to outbiddings" constituted "a fifth column to divert attention from Arab action."[82]

For his part, having achieved the all-important invitation to the conference, Saddam Husayn quickly blasted the prevailing Arab order. Wrapping himself in the mantle of 'the Arab nation,' he called on it to sweep away their illegitimate rulers, mentioning specifically the Saudi royal house, " the primary cause of all evil." Castigating the "frail resolutions issued by that failing and suspicious summit," he declared that "those who are responsible for manipulating the nation's resources and those who disregarded its will have joined the ranks of the enemies of the nation. Those people have turned into official and public agents...acting on behalf of the United States and Zionism...without any shame."[83]

While no doubt irritated, Egypt could afford to ignore the Iraqi outburst. But even small public signs of Palestinian discontent drew stinging rebukes from their Cairo patron. A statement by the Palestinian news agency WAFA criticizing the summit for not adopting tougher measures, 'Arafat's reported characterization of the resolutions as "weak," and demonstrations in the West Bank castigating Mubarak and allied Arab monarchs all incurred the wrath of Egyptian commentators over a number of days. They, in turn, accused the Palestinians of everything from ingratitude, corruption and disloyalty to low morals. The PA quickly organized a pro-Egyptian demonstration, 'Arafat flew to Sharm al-Shaykh to smooth Mubarak's ruffled feathers, and the episode passed like "a summer cloud," according to Egyptian foreign minister Musa. But it provided evidence of considerable tension and mutual mistrust beneath the surface of the Egyptian patron-Palestinian client relationship.[84] Egypt also was extremely perturbed by the unflattering tone and content of al-Jazira television broadcasts, and Information Minister Safwat Sharif urged Egyptians not to listen to its "vituperations," even hinting that its Qatari owners were colluding with Israel to divide Arab ranks by attacking Egypt.[85]

THE AFTERMATH OF THE ARAB SUMMIT

The Doha ICO Summit

As the host of the imminent, regularly scheduled summit of the ICO, Qatar found itself in the hot seat. Consistently iconoclast in its policies during recent years, it was now torn between maintaining its low-level, albeit formal links with Israel and hosting a successful summit of the fifty-six-nation body, with all of its attendant symbolic value for the numerically tiny (pop. 200,000) principality. Ironically, it was the Doha-based al-Jazira satellite television station — "the biggest inciter of the Arab masses to commit suicide and to boycott," in the cynical words of the Saudi editor of *al-Sharq al-Awsat*[86] — which had contributed significantly to the anti-Israel ferment in the Arab world, making it more difficult for Qatar to maintain its distance from the Arab consensus as formulated by the Cairo summit. With the summit only four days away, Saudi Arabia announced that it would boycott the summit as long as Qatar maintained ties with Israel. Qatari foreign minister Shaykh Hamid bin Jasim bin Jabir Al Thani had hurried to Riyadh the day before to try to dissuade Crown Prince 'Abdallah from boycotting, but to no avail.[87] Heads of a number of other states, notably Iran, planned to stay home and send lower-level delegations, and the summit rapidly threatened to be an acute embarrassment for its host. The Egyptian media, for their part, criticized Qatar vociferously, particularly for al-Jazira's portrayal of alleged Egyptian and Arab deficiencies in supporting the Palestinians. Thus, on 9 November, three days before the summit opening, Qatar ceded to the pressure and closed the three-person Israeli trade office in Doha. Qatar linked the decision to the deaths of nearly two hundred Palestinians during the six weeks of the intifada and to the need to "create the necessary atmosphere" for holding the summit.[88]

With Qatar having bitten the bullet, the summit proceeded without controversy. Most of its public aspects were taken up with the Palestinian intifada, which generated little controversy and considerable militancy. A clause in the final statement of the conference expressing trust in the PA leadership under 'Arafat was removed after Syria objected.[89] Behind the scenes, considerable efforts were made to promote conciliation between Iraq and the international community, and Iraq and Kuwait, with Qatar being assigned a significant mediating role, in the latter case (see section on Iraq, below; for more details on the summit, see chapter on political Islam).

Implementing the Cairo Summit Resolutions — or Not?
One week after the Doha summit, following Israeli military strikes in Gaza, Egypt recalled its ambassador from Tel Aviv, for the first time since the 1982 Lebanon War. In conjunction, Jordan affirmed previous suspicions that it would not be naming a new ambassador to Israel to fill the vacant post as long as Israel continued to violently repress the Palestinians. Thus, with the exception of Mauritania, the "normalizing" Arab states had all, in some measure, toed the line laid down at the Cairo summit. But the financial support pledged at Cairo was less unwavering. Arab finance ministers, meeting in Cairo at the end of November, pledged approximately 70% of the $1bn. agreed on in October. In addition to the Saudi contribution, Kuwait and the UAE each committed $150m., Qatar promised $50m., Egypt and Algeria promised $30m. each, Oman and Yemen each promised $20m., Syria promised $7m., Jordan $2m. and Sudan $1m. The money, it was agreed, would be dispensed through the Saudi-based Islamic Development Bank (IDB). But the Palestinians were extremely disappointed. 'Arafat, who personally led the Palestinian delegation, had hoped to receive immediate, emergency funds of over $200m. to help pay overdue wages of Palestinian employees, held up due to the Israeli economic blockade of the PA areas. Even a loan, he told them, would be welcome. But Arab countries, concerned with the level of corruption within the PA, preferred to establish proper supervision and accounting procedures through the IDB. Kuwait, it was reported, had even conditioned its funding on its not being given to the PA. The PA then asked for an urgent $100m. loan, but was turned down, drawing Palestinian anger. The bank's chairman, Ahmad Muhammad 'Ali, retorted that it was not authorized to lend the money, but was studying a number of aid projects which could be funded according to the rules governing the operation of the two funds.[90]

The gap between financial promises and fulfillment was the central topic of discussion at the 10–11 December meetings in Damascus of the foreign ministers committee mandated by the Cairo summit to follow-up the implementation of its resolutions. Aware that it was likely to be discomfited, Saudi Arabia chose not to send its foreign minister to the meeting, substituting its deputy foreign minister as delegation head. League secretary-general 'Abd al-Majid reported that there had been "many shortcomings…which require immediate resolution at the highest political levels." He noted that only $30m. had been disbursed by Saudi Arabia (much of it apparently to cover the salaries of PA employees) while Palestinian losses amounted to more than $1bn. By contrast, the EU and the World Bank had extended emergency loans to the PA of 28m. euros and $12m., respectively. 'Abd al-Majid urged Arab governments to transfer money immediately to the two IDB-managed funds and to authorize emergency loans to the PA to enable it to meet urgent needs.

The Palestinian and Syrian representatives were both sharply critical of Saudi behavior. Faruq al-Qaddumi of the PLO declared that the economic siege that Israel was imposing on the West Bank and Gaza Strip was designed to "kill the intifada," and that "the delay in transferring the financial aid is helping to kill it too." The mechanism for disbursing aid via the IDB, he said, was far too complex to be effective, and that one-third of all Palestinians in the West Bank and Gaza were in urgent need of income from which they had been deprived by Israeli actions. Another Palestinian delegation member, Nabil Sha'th, urged Arab states to help the Palestinians by allowing the tariff-free import of produce from the West Bank and Gaza. He also lambasted the Arab states' "questioning of the transparency of the PA," noting that international donors had testified to its honesty and the fact that it had not "wasted a single penny" of aid. Peeved, the Saudi deputy foreign minister, asked the Palestinians to provide written proposals for aid to the Arab League drafting committee, in order to include them in the recommendations of the ministerial meeting — and for some of those recommendations to be made public and others to be kept unpublicized. Faruq al-Shar' of Syria was openly critical of the Saudis. Pressing the Arab states to do more, given the urgency of the situation, Shar' reported that Syria, despite being a "confrontation state" and thus bearing its own burdens, had at least deducted one day's pay from all private and public sector employees in aid to the Palestinians, on top of its $7m. cash pledge, in line with its summit commitments.[91] Their common cause held out the possibility of an improvement in relations, with speculation that 'Arafat would make a trip to Damascus.

To be sure, leading Saudi officials did make some additional funds available. Prince Nayif bin 'Abd al-'Aziz, the interior minister, transferred $26m. for the families of the dead and wounded, and Prince Talal bin Walid transferred a sum of $22m. to the PA for workers unemployed because they could not enter Israel.[92] But these sums fell far short of the $1bn. pledged at Cairo, and did little to dissipate the image of the rich Arab oil producers dithering on their financial commitments. By contrast, Iraq eagerly jumped into the fray, seeking to further rehabilitate its regional standing, by demonstrating solidarity with the Palestinians through financial aid. Each family of a Palestinian "martyr" was allocated a cash grant of $10,000, distributed through Iraqi supporters in the PA areas, with the cooperation of the PA. In late October, a Palestinian airliner flew into Baghdad from Amman, in defiance of the UN air embargo, with a group of wounded Palestinians who were transferred to Baghdad hospitals. On 11 December, Iraqi television reported that Iraqi foreign minister Muhammad Sa'id al-Sahhaf had informed the UN Security Council and UN secretary-general Kofi Annan of the decision to allocate 1bn. euros "for supporting the Palestinian people's struggle against the Zionist aggression." Iraq also reportedly sought to strengthen its influence among the Palestinians by reviving its Palestinian client body, the Arab Liberation Front, in the PA areas. Five Iraqi divisions had already camped for an extended period of time on the Jordanian and Syrian borders during the month of October in a gesture of support for Syria and the Palestinians. At the beginning of December, a convoy of sixty-eight trucks delivered 4,000 tons of medicine and basic food stuffs — rice, flour, oil, lentils, tea and coffee — to West Bank and Gaza Palestinians, via the Allenby Bridge crossing, where their goods were transferred to Palestinian and Jordanian trucks. Saddam's popularity among Palestinians was obvious, with his picture being hoisted prominently during demonstrations and at funerals. Mubarak, for his part, reportedly warned 'Arafat about expanding Iraqi influence in the West Bank and Gaza.[93]

The year ended in uncertainty, as the violent Palestinian-Israeli confrontation showed no sign of abating. In analyzing the consequences of the uprising thus far, one Arab analyst wrote that it "had created new conditions that are redrawing the picture of the contemporary Palestinian and Arab reality." It had "restored the Palestinian cause to its central position in Arab hearts and minds, even if it has yet to resume such a central place in official Arab policy." Of particular import was that it had "mobilized the youth, who had been brought up in a climate in which the Palestinian cause and pan-Arabism had been sidelined, replaced by a demoralizing discourse about the requirements of realism and the constraints imposed by globalization." Arab governments, he said, could only ignore the Arab 'street' at great risk. No matter the outcome of the Palestinian intifada, it had "opened up wide new horizons in Arab life."[94]

Most Arab governments, for their part, remained cautious, simultaneously keeping an eye on the domestic, regional and international arenas, while seeking to avoid a slide into a broader Arab-Israeli confrontation. In inter-Arab terms, the Palestinian question, while again central to the public agenda, and the tool for "outbidding" by individual states or opposition movements, brought about no alterations in inter-Arab alignments. Nor did it threaten to trigger a destabilization process within any of the Arab countries. For all of the shortcomings of Arab governments, and for all of the emotive appeal of the Palestinian cause, Arab regimes were more immune, and less vulnerable to "pan-Arab" criticism than in decades past.

IRAQ — TEETERING SANCTIONS, PARTIAL REHABILITATION

Iraq registered steady, incremental progress during the year in its efforts to undermine a decade of imposed international isolation and return to an active role in inter-Arab and regional affairs. Its presence at the October Arab summit (see above) was one concrete marker of its success, even though the summit treatment of the Iraqi issue was unsatisfactory to Baghdad. Another achievement was the upgrading of formal diplomatic relations in the spring by Bahrain, which returned its chargé d'affaires to Baghdad after a ten-year hiatus, and the UAE, which reopened its embassy, closed for ten years, leaving only Kuwait and Saudi Arabia as holdouts among the GCC states. Even the Saudis made occasional noises regarding the need to ease the suffering of the Iraqi populace and the need to deepen popular, societal links between their two countries. To that end, Saudi exporters had steadily increased their dealings with Iraq, and the Saudis successfully pushed for UN permission to open a crossing point on the Saudi-Iraqi border for the passage of Saudi goods.[95] However, the Saudis also repeatedly blocked efforts in inter-Arab forums by Qatar and others to begin rethinking collective Arab policies toward Iraq (see below). Kuwait, for its part, was increasingly aware of the need to avoid appearing unduly intransigent with regard to the terms for easing Iraq's reentry into the Arab system. Nonetheless, it was insistent that its basic conditions be met and continued to regard Iraqi policies as the root cause of the region's problems.

Outside the Gulf, Iraq continued to make strides. Vice President Taha Yasin Ramadan was an honored guest at the Yemeni reunification celebrations in late May. Egyptian officials repeatedly spoke of the need to break the diplomatic deadlock and restore a semblance of normalcy to Iraqi-Arab relations. Economic links with Egypt deepened substantially. On 6 November, just days before the Doha ICO summit, Egypt raised the flag over its embassy in Baghdad, which had functioned as an interests section of the Indian embassy since the break in Egyptian-Iraqi relations in 1991.[96] Ties with both Syria and Jordan also improved qualitatively.

Iraq derived considerable political and public relations benefit from the outbreak of the Aqsa Intifada, linking the suffering of the Palestinian and Iraqi peoples at the hands of the "Zionists"/"Westerners," and adopting an uncompromising stand against Israel and in support of the Palestinians. One concrete offshoot was the severe weakening of the air embargo against Iraq. In late September, Jordan and then a host of other Arab countries followed the lead of Russia and France in dispatching special flights bringing humanitarian aid and solidarity missions to Baghdad in defiance of the UN ban. The flights generated considerable anger in Kuwait,[97] but to no avail. All of this was achieved without Iraq making any substantive concessions, or apologizing for its 1990 invasion, as the Kuwaitis demanded.

Even prior to the renewal of the Palestinian-Israeli confrontation, Iraq was becoming more bold in its criticism of its Arab neighbors. "The sole concern of rulers and kings is to sit on their thrones and give the impression that they are governing," declared Saddam on one occasion. "Is it not a disgrace to them that the aggressors' warplanes take off from their territory and territorial waters to attack the citadel of Arabism, destroy the property of the Iraqis and murder Iraqi women, men and children?"[98] Iraq didn't refrain from attacking the UAE either, for suggesting at the UN millennial summit that Iraq had further to go regarding compliance with UN resolutions.[99] On 4 September, an Iraqi airplane violated Saudi airspace. Concurrently, Iraq accused Kuwait of stealing oil for the Rumayla and Zubayri oil fields which straddle their common border. Similar accusations preceded Iraq's 1990 invasion.[100] Neither the Saudis, Kuwaitis, nor the Egyptians, were happy with Saddam's hostile rhetoric. But the Egyptians, and even the Saudis to an extent, favored engaging Iraq on the economic sphere. The year ended with the UN and Iraq still at an impasse, but with Iraq having more "normal" relations with the bulk of the Arab world than at any time since 2 August 1990.

IRAQI-SYRIAN RELATIONS

Iraq acutely desired closer relations with Syria, as it sought to break down the decade-long international sanctions regime against it. Since 1997, Syria had begun taking steps to normalize ties with Iraq, particularly in the economic sphere, but had refrained from bold political steps which would be construed by the US, Saudi Arabia and Kuwait as violating the sanctions regime. As time passed, and support for easing or lifting the sanctions entirely grew in the Arab world, Syrian actions became more overt. As was the case with Syrian-Jordanian relations, the death of Hafiz al-Asad and his replacement by Bashshar led to an improvement in Syrian-Iraqi ties, in this case, an acceleration of the existing warming trend.

During the first part of 2000, Iraq continued its pattern of courting Syria, notwithstanding the latter's sometimes standoffishness. In January, for example, at the time of the Syrian-Israeli talks in Shepherdstown, an Iraqi diplomatic source signaled that his country would not interfere with Syrian diplomatic efforts, and supported them.[101] The failure of the talks was blamed by the Iraqi press on the US and Israel.[102] More directly, Iraq, following Jordan, signaled that it would take measures to restrict the activities of the Syrian Muslim Brotherhood opposition operating in Baghdad.[103]

Iraq's representative at the Asad funeral was a lower-ranking official than that of most other Arab states (see above). However, ten days after Asad's death, Iraqi foreign minister Sahhaf made a condolence call to Bashshar; five days later, Sahhaf came back to Damascus to meet with his counterpart Shar'. From that point on, the warming of economic ties proceeded apace, effectively chipping away at the sanctions regime. In the fall, Syria took more overt steps to challenge them, along with many other Arab states. However, when it came to the overt political gestures which Iraq desired, e.g., restoring full diplomatic relations, the Syrians held back.

In early August, the joint economic committee of the two countries met for the first time since the abortive union efforts of 1978–79 (see *MECS* 1978–79, pp. 236–40), in Damascus. They expressed their wish to double their trade volume to $1bn.[104] They also signed an agreement to export Iraqi goods via Tartus port, and Iraq began building a free trade zone near its border with Syria.[105] Their trade ministers followed up the joint committee sessions with a meeting on 11 September; that same month, an official Iraqi delegation attended the Damascus International Exhibition. At the end of September, Syria industry minister concluded a five-day visit to Baghdad by signing agreements to export Syrian goods to Iraq within the UN's "oil for food" program.[106]

Particularly noteworthy were the steps taken to reactivate the Kirkuk-Banyas oil pipeline, closed by Syria at the height of the Iraq-Iran war in 1982 at the behest of its Iranian ally (see MECS 1981–82, pp. 233). An agreement to reopen the pipeline had been signed in 1998 but not implemented. In mid-November, the pipeline, with a capacity of 300,000 b/d, began to operate on an experimental basis. One report spoke of the two sides' intention to build a second, parallel line.[107] The following month, the two sides reached agreement on another strategic commodity — Euphrates river water — and accused Turkey of trying to avoid implementing an existing agreement governing its exploitation by the three littoral states.[108]

The transportation arena witnessed a number of concrete measures. The Iraqi national airline declared its intention to reopen its office in Damascus, after almost twenty years of closure, in order to enable Iraqi officials and businessmen to bypass the sanctions and travel to various destinations.[109] Throughout the decade, Amman had played this role exclusively. Syria's apparent willingness to serve as a transit point for Iraqi travelers, who could still leave Iraq only via road transport, placed it in competition with Jordan. Earlier, on 20 July, Syria and Iran signed an agreement to link their railway networks via Iraq, following the cancellation of a similar agreement to use Turkey as the transit country. Ten days later, Iraq and Syria signed an agreement to open a rail line between Mosul and Aleppo.[110] During August, the two countries reached a final agreement on the demarcation of their common border.

Tariq 'Aziz, first deputy prime minister of Iraq and long-time diplomat, visited Damascus nine times during the second half of the year, meeting Bashshar twice and paving the way for visits by other high-ranking officials. According to some analysts, he promoted the creation of an economic grouping in the Fertile Crescent which would, by definition, erode the trade embargo imposed on Iraq. Syria was obviously a key in any such scheme. Syria for its part, sought to find the right balance between improving ties with its important, and potentially threatening neighbor to the east, and not antagonizing its backers in the Gulf, and the US and Britain.[111]

IRAQI-JORDANIAN RELATIONS

Throughout the decade, Iraqi-Jordanian relations had been both fraught with tension and rooted in overlapping interests. As a result, they witnessed considerable ups and downs, but apart from the brief period in 1995–96 when King Husayn of Jordan actively encouraged Saddam's overthrow (see MECS 1995, pp. 74–78, 414–19; 1996, pp. 83–84), they were conducted within parameters well-understood by both sides. After periodic fluctuations during 1999 (see MECS 1999, pp. 288–89) and the first part of 2000, relations improved significantly at mid-year, following the ascent of 'Ali Abu al-Raghib as prime minister of Jordan. From then on, political and economic ties improved substantially, and Jordan became an important asset in Iraqi efforts to end the sanctions regime. Nonetheless, Jordan was very careful not to let the improvement jeopardize its relations with other key Arab and international actors, i.e., Saudi Arabia, Egypt and the US. Every move Jordan made towards Iraq was done only after consultations with them.

Several incidents reflected the chill in ties during the first half of 2000. Jordanian authorities made difficulties for Iraqi delegations and officials seeking to enter the country. Jordan also showed no willingness to solve outstanding bilateral problems such as the matter of the Iraqi commercial airplanes grounded at the Amman airport and Iraqi ships anchored in 'Aqaba port since the 1991 Gulf War.[112] Furthermore, Jordan placed on trial foreign pilots who sought to fly their private airplanes from Amman to Baghdad to protest against the flight sanctions.[113]

Iraq acted similarly. In June, it executed a Jordanian civilian charged with "conspiring against Iraq's higher interests." According to Jordanian minister of information Salih Qalab, official Iraqi delegations demonstrated contempt for Jordanian sovereignty by contacting Jordanian opposition activists during their visits.[114]

At the same time, basic diplomatic and economic ties were maintained, for they served both sides: Jordan remained an important lifeline for an isolated Iraq, while Iraq remained Jordan's number one trading partner in the Arab world, sanctions and all. Indeed, Jordan was almost desperate for an easing of the sanctions, which would enable a renewal of the transit trade from 'Aqaba to Baghdad and increased direct Iraqi purchases from Jordan. Politically, Iraq, even in its weakened condition, provided Jordan with an important counterweight to Syria and Saudi Arabia. Moreover, the suffering of the Iraqi people under the sanctions regime was an important issue for wide swaths of the Jordanian populace. Thus, Jordanians of all stripes consistently urged the easing of international sanctions, and sought ways to circumvent them.

In January, Jordanian parliamentary and governmental delegations visited Baghdad and King 'Abdallah sent Saddam Husayn a telegram of congratulations on the occasion of 'Id al-Fitr. Jordan also imposed restrictions on Iraqi opposition activists. The most concrete sign of continuing close ties was the conclusion in late January of their annual oil agreement, which would supply Jordan with 4.8m. tons of crude oil, its entire annual needs, half for free and half at low cost. In conjunction, the two sides also agreed to increase the volume of bilateral trade by 50%.[115]

Abu Raghib's ascent to office marked a qualitative turning point, even though Jordan remained unwilling to take unilateral actions in defiance of the UN. Iraqi vice president Taha Yasin Ramadan led a large delegation to Jordan in mid-July for discussions with King 'Abdallah and other senior Jordanian officials on economic and political issues.[116] In the wake of Ramadan's visit, the Jordanian media spoke out in favor of Iraq and criticized other Arab countries for not helping to end the Iraqi people's suffering, even while acknowledging Jordan's interest in not acting against the US and the UN. Jordanian economic and public figures now called on their government to move closer to Iraq due to the dire economic situation in Jordan, and non-governmental groups organized demonstrations in Amman against the sanctions regime.[117]

The Iraqis drew much satisfaction from the positive shift in Jordan. Nonetheless, it made sure to emphasize its frustration with Jordan's continued "over-obedience" to the UN sanctions. Playing the Arab-Israeli card in response,[118] Iraqi officials even threatened to draw up a blacklist of Jordanian companies doing business with Israel. The contrast between Jordanian and Iraqi positions toward the Arab-Israeli peace process was highlighted anew at the October Cairo summit, following the outbreak of the al-Aqsa Intifada (see above). However, King 'Abdallah did make sure to meet with 'Izzat Ibrahim of Iraq, who was seconding for Saddam Husayn at the summit. It was the highest-ranking meeting between Jordanian and Iraqi officials since August 1990. Moreover, in a measure of renewed concern with its own outraged public opinion and the need to avoid the arrows of its more militant and powerful neighbor, Jordan permitted Iraq to use it as a platform to deliver humanitarian aid to the Palestinians (see above).

For Iraq, the complete ban on civilian airflights into and out of the country had especially rankled, leaving it almost completely dependent for access to the outside world on the highway to Jordan. As the summer wore on, Arab countries increasingly showed interest in testing the UN enforcement of the ban. Shortly after taking office, Abu Raghib's government tendered a formal request to the UN to permit flights from Jordan, claiming that the Amman-Baghdad road was very dangerous.[119] In late September, Russia and France both sent flights to Baghdad, demonstrating their view that UN sanctions did not include an air embargo. With the barrier broken, Jordan did the same, on 27 September, becoming the first Arab country to dispatch a flight to Baghdad since August 1990. One factor prompting the Jordanians to move quickly was fear that other Arab countries, such as Syria, Libya and Yemen, were about to flout the flight ban, and thus deprive Jordan of the potential political benefits of having been first.[120]

With the precedent set, Syria, Egypt, Tunisia, Yemen and the UAE followed with their own flights of solidarity missions and humanitarian aid. During the autumn months, Royal Jordanian Airlines made regular weekly flights to Baghdad, and Jordanian civil groups organized their own special flights. However, heavy pressure from the UN sanctions committee forced the Jordanian national carrier to cease its regular flights and limit itself to irregular ones based on humanitarian considerations.[121]

The breakthrough on flights was paralleled by steadily deepening relations in other areas. Jordanian prime minister Abu Raghib led a delegation to Iraq on 1 November. He was the highest-ranking Arab official to visit since the 1991 Gulf War. The trip was applauded in the Jordanian press as "an overdue assertion of where Jordan's true interests lay."[122] It resulted in the signing of several economic agreements, including the laying of an oil pipeline between Iraq and Zarka.[123] On 21 November, an Iraqi trade fair was opened in Amman. With Jordan more dependent on the Iraqi market than any other Arab country — Iraq took 26% of its exports to Arab markets, and sold Jordan 67% of its imports from Arab countries — Jordan was more keen than ever to maintain its special relationship. The fact that Iraqi-Syrian ties were showing distinct signs of improvement was certainly not lost on Amman, which could only look uneasily on the prospect of enhanced Syrian competition, notwithstanding its genuine desire to end the sanctions regime.

THE IRAQI QUESTION AT OTHER MULTILATERAL MEETINGS

The Damascus Declaration Foreign Ministers Meeting

The widespread desire to break the status quo regarding the sanctions regime and ease Iraq's reentry into regional and international affairs was forcefully articulated by Egyptian foreign minister Musa at the opening session of the Damascus declaration foreign ministers conference in Cairo on 4–5 June:

> We cannot stand idle before the suffering of our brotherly people in Iraq...All Arab governments are required to exert necessary efforts in cooperation with the United Nations to lift economic sanctions on Iraq according to a specific program...It is not possible, either politically or humanely, to maintain the embargo on our brothers in Iraq without any light at the end of the tunnel.[124]

One month earlier, Qatari foreign minister Shaykh Hamad bin Jasim had jolted his Kuwaiti listeners by urging Kuwait not to remain captive of the wound inflicted on it by Iraq, and by advocating a Gulf initiative to end the regional impasse and return to a state of normalcy in relations with Iraq.[125] He raised the proposal at a GCC foreign ministers meeting in Jidda on 3 June, the day before the Cairo conference, but without results. Hamad tried again in Cairo, provoking a heated argument during the closing session over his insistence that the final statement refer to the initiative. The Saudi, Kuwaiti and Bahraini foreign ministers were also strongly opposed, and the Egyptian and Syrian representatives were "not sympathetic" either. Thus, although both official and popular Arab opinion increasingly favored a change in the status quo, the final statement of the conference stuck to established formulas, referring only to the need to alleviate the suffering of the Iraqi people, for which the Iraqi regime was responsible, and for Iraq to comply with UN resolutions, with no reference to the lifting of the sanctions.[126]

The Doha Summit and Iraq

Between the Damascus declaration meeting of early June and the Doha ICO summit four months hence, the climate shifted in Iraq's favor. Moreover, the ICO forum was more congenial for a pro-active approach than the Arab forums. Thus, Qatar, the summit's host, was able to introduce language in the its final communiqué which was far less antagonistic and more accommodating toward Iraq than in the past. In addition to Qatar, Egypt, Saudi Arabia, and Oman all had a hand in brokering the text or preparing the diplomatic ground for its acceptance.

The title of the section in the final communiqué dealing with Iraq was altered from the traditional "Sequels of the Iraqi aggression against the State of Kuwait" to the more neutral "The Situation between Iraq and Kuwait." Iraq was asked to "complete" the implementation of its commitments in line with relevant Security Council resolutions, and Iraq and the Security Council were asked to undertake "a comprehensive dialogue" in order to peacefully implement the resolutions and lift the sanctions. The summit also mandated the emir of Qatar, Shaykh Hamad bin Khalifa Al Thani, in his capacity as ICO chairman for the next three years, to:

> use his good offices, in consultation with Iraq and Kuwait, to establish the appropriate groundwork for the resolution of the existing disputes between them in accordance with the principles and aims of the United Nations, the relevant Security Council resolutions, and the principles and aims of the Islamic Conference Organization.

While reiterating Kuwait's longstanding demand to ascertain the fate of Kuwaitis missing since the war, the statement also called, for the first time, on the International Committee of the Red Cross to do the same with regard to missing Iraqis. The statement also affirmed that there was nothing to prohibit air flights to and from Iraq, ratifying the spate of recent flights to Iraq by Arab, Muslim and other countries. Moreover, it condemned "the illegitimate actions to which Iraq is being subjected outside the framework of Security Council resolutions," i.e., the American-British air strikes on Iraq.

To be sure, the lack of Kuwaiti and Saudi objections to the latter clause did not reflect their true positions. The Kuwaitis were not entirely pleased with the outcome, but preferred to accept the resolution in order to demonstrate its goodwill and flexibility.

Iraq, for its part, was quite satisfied, and Foreign Minister Muhammad al-Sahhaf implied that Iraq had accepted Qatari mediation of its dispute with Kuwait. Shaykh Hamad called the developments a "qualitative breakthrough," and said that it constituted the most significant aspect of the summit.[127] The new atmosphere was somewhat reflected at the GCC summit at the end of December (see below). However, no substantive diplomatic movement was registered during the remainder of the year. The main diplomatic arena for altering the sanctions regime remained the UN, and despite Iraqi-UN contacts, no substantive change was registered.

THE GCC

GCC institutions continued to function routinely. However, the particular interests of its six members and the overriding concern of ruling elites with the jealous preservation of their sovereign prerogatives effectively blocked the path to more meaningful multilateral cooperation. The Iraqi question pitted Kuwait and Saudi Arabia against the other four, who all favored more flexible policies of engagement with Baghdad. The UAE dispute with Iran over the status of the three Gulf islands created tension between the UAE and Saudi Arabia, owing to the qualitative warming of Saudi relations with Iran (see chapters on Saudi Arabia and Iran). The Saudis were followed by the other four GCC members, leaving the UAE diplomatically isolated vis-à-vis Iran, notwithstanding official GCC proclamations of solidarity. The long-running tension between Bahrain and Qatar had abated somewhat in late 1999 and early 2000, but flared up again, despite Saudi and UAE mediation (see chapters on Bahrain and Qatar). The Arab-Israeli arena was less controversial, as Qatar and Oman essentially toed the line laid out by the Arab League summit.

One departure from past patterns was that the GCC held two summit conferences: in addition to its annual end of the year meeting, a "consultative" summit was held in Muscat on 29 April. (For the text of the final statement, see Appendix II.)

The 30–31 December summit in Manama was noteworthy for its proclamation of a joint defense pact, subject to ratification by each state. Under its terms, which were not released, an attack on one would be considered an attack on all. It was believed to include plans to upgrade and link communications and missile warning systems, and link them to the US systems in the region as well. Bahrain was reportedly successful in spearheading a proposal to expand the five-thousand-member "Peninsula Shield" joint rapid deployment force to 22,000. Upgrading and deepening defense cooperation had long been a proclaimed ideal. However, it was not clear whether deeds would live up to intent. Crown Prince 'Abdallah of Saudi Arabia acknowledged the difficulties, noting "it was absurd to talk about a unified military front in the absence of a unified and cohesive political front."[128]

On other issues dealing with the "GCC march," the goal of establishing a unified tariffs schedule by the year 2005, declared at the 1999 summit (see *MECS* 1999, pp. 102–103) was reiterated. The common tariff was essential for signing a free trade agreement with the EU, the GCC major trading partner. The only movement made toward achieving currency unification was an agreement to peg their currencies to the US dollar, compelling a change by Kuwait, which had used a currency basket. GCC states agreed to allow their nationals to own property, work in the civil service and be given similar treatment as the other national employees, and freely own businesses in member countries, but with some unspecified professions being limited to the nationals of each country.[129]

The language of the final statement regarding Iraq was more conciliatory than in the past, reflecting a compromise between Saudi Arabia and Kuwait, on the one hand, and Qatar and the UAE, on the other. Under the heading "The situation in Iraq," rather than the situation resulting from "Iraq's invasion of Kuwait," the summit commniqué called on Iraq to implement all UN resolutions and cease its aggressive attitude. It refrained, however, from speaking of the need to replace the Iraqi regime and emphasized the desire of the GCC states to alleviate the suffering of the Iraqi people.[130]

On the Iran-UAE dispute, GCC leaders essentially acknowledged that the tripartite committee established in 1998 to mediate between the two countries had failed, owing to Iranian unwillingness to cooperate. The disputed islands, it reiterated, rightfully belonged to the UAE, and appropriate measures should be taken to insure that right, including a judgement by the International Court of Justice at the Hague.[131] On the Israeli-Palestinian conflict, GCC states unequivocally condemned Israeli "aggression" and supported all Palestinian demands, including the "right of return" of Palestinian refugees. Falling oil prices (see chapter on economic developments in the Middle East) were of immediate concern: GCC oil ministers were instructed to reduce production levels at the upcoming January meeting of OPEC and "take any other measures to maintain equilibrium in the market and achieve the targeted price" of $25/b.[132] (For the full text of the summit's final communique see Appendix III.)

APPENDIX I: FINAL STATEMENT OF ARAB SUMMIT CONFERENCE, CAIRO, 21–22 OCTOBER 2000

Answering the urgent invitation extended by His Excellency President Muhammad Husni Mubarak, president of the Arab Republic of Egypt, in his capacity as chairman of the 1996 extraordinary Arab summit in Cairo, their majesties, excellencies and highnesses the kings, presidents and princes of the Arab states held an extraordinary summit in Cairo on October 21–22, 2000. The summit was held at a crucial juncture in our nation's history and a new stage in the life of our peoples, when dangerous developments have led to a deadlock in the peace process between the Arabs and Israel and at a time when Israel has turned the peace process into a war operation against the Palestinian people, using military force to besiege it, isolate it and take it hostage inside the West Bank and Gaza Strip.

The summit hails the intifada of the Palestinian people in the occupied Palestinian territories which has clearly expressed bitter frustration resulting from long years of anticipation and waiting for the outcome of a political settlement, which yielded no results because of Israel's intransigence, procrastination and failure to fulfil her commitments. The Arab leaders ask the Almighty to bless the souls of the Palestinian martyrs and consider their virtuous blood a valuable asset for the sake of liberating the land, setting up the State and establishing peace. The Arab leaders commend the response of the Arab masses — from the Atlantic to the Gulf — to the intifada of the heroic Palestinian people and their national, wall-to-wall condemnation of Israeli aggression and the brutal actions of the occupation forces.

The reaction of the Arab masses was an expression of [pan-Arab] national feelings and strong solidarity with the struggle of the Palestinian people for its sovereignty, dignity and sanctities.

The Arab leaders hold Israel responsible for returning the region to an atmosphere of tension and to manifestations of violence resulting from her practices, aggressions and siege of the Palestinian people in violation of her obligations, as an occupation power, under the 1949 Fourth Geneva Convention; [in violation] of international law; and [in violation] of efforts to build peace in the region.

In addition, Israel's rulers have been dealing disdainfully with the issue of holy al-Quds (Jerusalem) only to satisfy their lust for irresponsible showmanship and deliberate provocation built on abhorrent racism. They request her to desist forthwith from all provocative actions and the policy of reprisals against Arab citizens.

The Arab leaders reaffirm that the al-Aqsa intifada erupted as a consequence of the continuation and perpetuation of the occupation and Israel's desecration of Jerusalem's al-Haram al-Shariff and other Moslem and Christian sanctuaries in the occupied Palestinian territories.

The Arab leaders evoke the memory, and remind the world, of the martyrs who sacrificed their lives in defense of their occupied land and holy sites in a fearless challenge to the war machine which Israel lined up to confront the unarmed Palestinian people.

They reaffirm the Palestinian people's right to seek fair compensation from Israel for human and material damage and losses incurred. They decide, in answer to the proposal by the Kingdom of Saudi Arabia, to set up two funds.

One — of $800m. and called "al-Aqsa Fund" — will be to provide for projects intended to preserve the Arab and Islamic character of Jerusalem, preventing its obliteration, and to wean the Palestinian people from the Israeli economy. The second — of $200m. and called "The Intifada Fund" — will be to provide for the families of Palestinian martyrs in the intifada and for raising and educating their children. They greatly appreciate the decision of the Custodian of the Two Holy Places [King Fahd], whereby the Saudi kingdom will contribute a quarter of the sum earmarked for the two funds.

The Arab leaders call on the sons and daughters of the [pan-]Arab nation to donate one day's wages as a popular Arab contribution in support of the intifada and the Palestinian national struggle at this critical phase facing our Arab nation.

The Arab leaders demand that an impartial international commission of inquiry be set up — in the framework of the United Nations and reporting back to the UN Security Council and the UN Human Rights Commission — to determine the causes and apportion blame for the serious deterioration in the occupied Palestinian territories, including the massacres committed by the Israeli occupation forces against the Palestinian and Lebanese peoples and against other Arab citizens in occupied lands.

In this respect, they underscore the provisions of UN Security Council Resolution 1322 of October 7, 2000 and the resolutions passed by the emergency session of the UN Human Rights Commission on October 19, 2000 and by the UN General Assembly on October 20, 2000. They ask that the Security Council continue to monitor developments in the occupied Palestinian and Arab territories which threaten international peace and stability. They want the Security Council and General Assembly to assume the responsibility of providing the necessary protection for the Palestinian people living under the yoke of Israeli occupation — this, by considering the establishment of an international force or presence for this purpose, given that the United Nations remains incessantly responsible for the Palestinian land and people until such time that the Palestinian people can realize its inalienable rights in Palestine in keeping with international legitimacy.

The Arab leaders affirm that the Arab states will prosecute, according to international law, those behind these barbaric practices and demand that the Security Council set up a special international criminal court to try the Israeli war criminals who committed the massacres against the Palestinians and Arabs in the occupied territories along the lines of the two courts formed by the Security Council to try war criminals in Rwanda and the former Yugoslavia. They will follow up the matter of bringing them to justice according to the statutes of the International Criminal Court.

The Arab leaders strongly denounce and condemn Israel for resorting to escalation through her aggressive actions and provocative stands at a time when the region was bracing itself for just and comprehensive peace — particularly after the Arabs decided, in the wake of the [1991] Madrid Conference, that the option of just and comprehensive peace paves the way for the final settlement of a conflict that has lasted more than half a century.

The Arab leaders condemn Israel's negative response to the peace option and her failure to seriously seek just and comprehensive peace. They warn Israel against persisting in acts and practices which threaten peace and undermine stability in the region.

The Arab leaders affirm that the [pan-Arab] nation has constants which are immutable, rights which are non-negotiable and objectives which they will pursue relentlessly to realize the Arabs' higher interests.

The Arab leaders affirm that the two pillars of peace are comprehensiveness and justice — they are the sine qua non for peace's acceptance and durability. They affirm that this Arab perception requires a parallel commitment from Israel. She should reciprocate this perception with an unambiguous stand, committing herself to international legitimacy as expressed in UN Security Council Resolutions 242 and 338; General Assembly Resolution 194 pertaining to the Palestinian refugees' right to repatriation and compensation; other relevant UN resolutions; and the bases and principles of the peace process, foremost among them the concept of land-for-peace.

The Arab leaders affirm that just and comprehensive peace will not be realized except through the return of holy al-Quds (Jerusalem) to full Palestinian sovereignty; the recognition of the Palestinian people's legitimate rights, including its right to an independent state with holy al-Quds as its capital, given that the latter is Palestinian land occupied since 1967 and is of particular spiritual and religious significance; the recovery of all occupied Arab territories, entailing Israel's full withdrawal from the West Bank, the Gaza Strip, Syria's Golan Heights back to the 4 June 1967 line and completion of the pullback from South Lebanon to the internationally recognized border, including the Shab'a Farms; the release of Arab prisoners held in Israeli jails, in keeping with UN resolutions; and the dismantling of Israeli settlements, in implementation of UN Security Council Resolution 465 of 1980. In this context, the Arab leaders reaffirm once more their support for the brethren in Syria, Lebanon and Palestine and they reiterate their commitment to the full recovery of their [brethren's] legitimate rights and occupied territories. In this context, they affirm their rejection of any attempts to impose an unjust or unbalanced peace based on Israeli claims and at the expense of Arab rights and interests.

In light of the setback in the peace process, the Arab leaders affirm their commitment to firmly challenge Israel's attempts to infiltrate the Arab world under any guise, and to stop building any kind of relation with Israel. They hold Israel responsible for any steps or decisions taken by Arab states in respect of relations with Israel, including their severance because of the peace deadlock and the ensuing dangerous developments as well as the repercussions that these have had on the Arab and Islamic arenas. This, until just and comprehensive peace is attained.

Underscoring the fact that the deadlock in the peace process on all its bilateral tracks has effectively derailed the multilateral track, the Arab leaders affirm that tackling issues of regional cooperation cannot be done without a genuine breakthrough toward the achievement of just and comprehensive peace in the region. Moreover, the peace process logjam, resulting from Israel's policies and provocative practises, renders any talk of a joint future in the region irrelevant. They resolve not to resume any official or unofficial activity in the framework of the multilateral track and to stop all steps and activities concerning regional economic cooperation with Israel in the said framework, not to participate in any such endeavors and to link their resumption to tangible progress toward the realization of just and comprehensive peace on all tracks of the peace process.

The Arab leaders commend the resolutions of the [ICO] Jerusalem Committee, chiefly the closing statement of its latest session in the Moroccan city of Agadir, which supported the State of Palestine's position in insisting on full sovereignty over East Jerusalem, including al-Haram al-Sharif and all the other Moslem and Christian sanctuaries which are part and parcel of the occupied Palestinian territories, and on holy al-Quds being the capital of the independent State of Palestine.

The Arab leaders recall UN Security Council Resolution 478 of 1980 which urges the nations of the world not to relocate their embassies to Jerusalem and the resolution of the eleventh Arab summit held in Amman in 1980 which undertook to sever all relations with states which relocate their embassies to Jerusalem or recognized Jerusalem as Israel's capital.

The Arab heads of state affirm that the realization of permanent peace and stability in the region requires Israel to join the Nuclear Non-Proliferation Treaty and to open all her nuclear facilities to international inspection and monitoring. In this context, they underscore the importance of ridding the Middle East of nuclear arms and all weapons of mass destruction. They consider this a precondition for regional security arrangements in future.

The Arab leaders express their conviction that the momentum of change on the international scene requires that joint Arab action be enhanced and that the Arab League be supported and that its institutions be developed and modernized to shore up its national role.

In this context, the Arab leaders, meeting at this critical juncture, decided that Arab summits be held regularly and hosted on a rotational basis alphabetically, as approved by the Arab League Council in its Session 114 and endorsed in final form by the Arab foreign ministers in their meeting preceding the current summit.

The kings, presidents and princes decide to hold the thirteenth Arab League Council regular meeting at summit level in March 2001 in Amman under the chairmanship of the Hashemite Kingdom of Jordan.

The Arab leaders are confident that regular Arab summits will enhance the joint Arab endeavor in all fields, particularly the economic field which has become more pressing than at any time before, particularly that international and regional developments have made Arab economic integration a pressing matter and that the Arab states possess human, natural and strategic resources which contribute to economic stability, growth and prosperity in the region and the world at large.

The Arab leaders commend the spirit of full solidarity which prevailed at the summit and the delegations' constructive deliberations which reflected a deep feeling among the leaders, their governments and their peoples that the juncture is critical and that it was imperative to hammer out a unified Arab position in the face of Israeli threats, liable to return the peace process to the proper course of just and comprehensive peace in the region.

The Arab leaders express their appreciation to His Highness Shaykh Hamad bin Khalifa Al Thani, the emir of Qatar, for his decision to bear the costs of the UN inquiry into human rights violations in the occupied Palestinian territories set up by the UN Human Rights Commission in its fifth Emergency Session [in Geneva] on October 19, 2000. This would enable the inquiry to go ahead and achieve its objective.

The Arab leaders affirmed their determination to continue enlisting Arab potentials in the service of their [pan-Arab] nation's causes and to mobilize all resources to liberate occupied Arab lands and to support the Palestinian people's struggle to recover its land, set up its state on its national soil, with Jerusalem as its capital, and to preserve Moslem and Christian holy sites in Palestine.

The Arab leaders agreed to remain in touch over developments facing the Arab nation. They expressed their deep gratitude and appreciation to His Excellency President Muhammad Husni Mubarak, president of the Arab Republic of Egypt, and to the fraternal people of the Arab Republic of Egypt, for their generous hospitality and for the successful preparation and organization of this conference. They wish His Excellency President Muhammad Husni Mubarak and the fraternal people of Egypt success and prosperity.

SOURCE: *MM*, 23 October 2000.

APPENDIX II: PRESS STATEMENT ISSUED AT CONCLUSION OF GULF COOPERATION COUNCIL'S CONSULTATIVE SUMMIT, MUSCAT, 29 APRIL 2000

Their majesties and highnesses leaders of the Gulf Cooperation Council states, held their second consultative meeting in Muscat, capital of the Sultanate of Oman, on Saturday, 24th Muharram 1421 AH, corresponding to 29th April 1999.

Their majesties and highnesses the GCC leaders taking part in this meeting have expressed appreciation for their brother His Majesty Sultan Qabus bin Sa'id of Oman for hosting this fraternal consultative meeting in a true brotherly atmosphere.

The conferees believe that this meeting is another proof of their joint eagerness to continue meetings and exchange views on all issues that would reinforce the GCC march and respond to its peoples' aspirations.

Their majesties and highnesses the GCC leaders also expressed great satisfaction with latest developments in Bahraini-Qatari relations in terms of fraternal unity and eagerness to promote them further in the wake of the visits exchanged by Qatari emir His Highness Shaykh Hamad bin Khalifa Al Thani and Bahraini emir His Highness Shaykh Hamad bin 'Isa Al Khalifa, as well as their talks that resulted in a determination to bolster cooperation between the two countries in the interest of their people and the peoples of the GCC states.

The leaders said they were pleased with the several successive bilateral visits they exchanged, which, they noted, enriched the work of the GCC through economic, border and diplomatic agreements signed at the end of these visits. They particularly pointed to the agreement facilitating the travel of GCC citizens to most of the GCC states using identity cards. The leaders expressed the desire to see all GCC states implement this procedure.

The leaders looked at a report on the work of the GCC tripartite committee, which is tasked with finding a mechanism for negotiations between the United Arabs Emirates (UAE) and the Islamic Republic of Iran pertaining to their dispute over the islands of Greater Tunb, Lesser Tunb and Abu Musa, which belong to the UAE.

They asked members of the tripartite committee to continue their efforts and hoped the Iranian government would respond favorably to the noble goal for the sake of which the committee was formed. They underlined keenness to establish strong relations between the GCC countries and the Islamic Republic of Iran based on mutual trust, good neighborliness, respect for the two sides' rights, non-interference in others' affairs, and working for the well-being of the region.

The conferees also discussed the state the Middle East peace process has reached and the situation in Iraq. They underlined the political constants the GCC countries expressed towards these two issues in the political statements issued at the end of the periodic meetings of the Higher Council and the Ministerial Council.

They also looked into a proposal presented by Bahrain to enhance military cooperation among the GCC countries through reinforcing the GCC laws pertaining to this issue.

The GCC secretary-general then briefed the leaders on what has been accomplished in the sphere of joint work since the convening of the Riyadh Summit last December, especially with regard to the issues of customs federation, power link-up, and negotiations with the EU to sign a free trade agreement between the EU and the GCC countries.

SOURCE: Omani TV, 29 April — BBC Monitoring, 1 May 2000.

APPENDIX III: FINAL STATEMENT OF GCC SUMMIT CONFERENCE, MANAMA, 30–31 DECEMBER 2000

In the name of God, the Compassionate, the Merciful.

In response to the kind invitation of His Highness Shaykh Hamad bin 'Isa Al Khalifa, the emir of Bahrain, the Supreme Council [of the GCC] held its twenty-first term in Manama, Bahrain, on Saturday and Sunday, 4 and 5 Shawwal 1421, corresponding to 30 and 31 December 2000 under the chairmanship of His Highness Shaykh Hamad bin 'Isa Al Khalifa. His Highness Shaykh Maktum bin Rashid Al Maktum, UAE vice-president, prime minister and Dubai governor; His Royal Highness Crown Prince 'Abdallah bin 'Abd al-'Aziz, Saudi deputy prime minister and commander of the National Guard; His Majesty Sultan Qabus bin Sa'id, sultan of Oman; His Highness Shaykh Hamad bin Khalifa Al Thani, emir of Qatar; His Highness Shaykh Jabir al-Ahmad al-Jabir Al Sabah, emir of Kuwait, attended the meetings. GCC Secretary-General Jamil Ibrahim al-Hujaylan also attended the meeting.

Their majesties and highnesses, leaders of the council's member states, expressed their delight for the return of His Highness Shaykh Zayid bin Sultan Al Nuhayyan, president of UAE, to good health after receiving treatment abroad. They beseeched God to keep his highness in good health and help him to continue to lead UAE and serve the issues of the Arab and Islamic nation.

The Supreme Council reviewed the results of joint work in the economic, social, political, military, security, educational and media fields. The Supreme Council expressed its satisfaction with the achievements and its desire and honest will to push forward the march of the GCC to follow up on regional and international developments to meet the aspirations and noble objectives as represented in the council's basic law. It also stressed the need to resume efforts to bolster security, stability and development among the council's states and peoples.

Economic issues: The Supreme Council discussed the march of economic cooperation among member states based on the reports and recommendations received from the ministerial council, ministerial committees and the general assembly. The Supreme Council instructed the relevant committees to expeditiously reach an agreement on the principles, laws and procedures necessary to set up a customs union among GCC states according to the specified time. The Supreme Council commended the steps taken by Bahrain to lower customs tariffs in accordance with the trends of their majesties and highnesses, the leaders of GCC states, in accordance with all the steps and measures necessary to activate the customs union.

In an endeavor to apply Item 22 of the unified economic agreement on coordinating financial, fiscal and banking policies, and in an attempt to increase cooperation between the ministries of transport and central banks and to unify currencies to complete the desired economic cooperation among these states, the Supreme Council has adopted a common measuring unit for the currencies of the GCC states as a first step towards this goal. The Supreme Council directed the financial and economic cooperation committee, the committee of governors, financial institutions and central banks to put together a work plan according to a set timetable to accomplish that goal and present it to the Supreme Council in its next session. It also directed the committee of governors to reach an agreement on the necessary mechanisms and measures to facilitate interaction of the currencies of the GCC states at the markets of member states.

The Supreme Council has decided to allow the natural and corporate persons of the GCC council to practice all economic activities and professions, except for a few, which will be limited to the nationals of the same country at this stage. It also agreed to expand the scope of retail trade for the citizens of the council in other member states by endorsing the amendment rules of retail trade within GCC states.

The Supreme Council has agreed to extend implementation of the unified customs law within GCC states as a guideline for one more year and to make it compulsory in all GCC states as of January 2002.

The Supreme Council also passed the veterinarian quarantine law and decided to make it compulsory after it was modified to conform with the rules and regulations of the World Trade Organization in this regard.

The Supreme Council approved a long-term strategy in terms of the GCC states' relations and negotiations with other countries that belong to regional blocs and international organizations. It also decided to endorse a declaration of principles for cooperation between GCC states and the European Free Trade Association (EFTA), that was signed between the two sides.

The Supreme Council examined the situation in the oil market and noted with satisfaction the fruit of efforts the GCC states exerted in cooperation with other producers inside and outside OPEC over this past year and confirmed by the OPEC summit in Caracas. These efforts aimed to strike a balance in the market at levels suitable for both producers and consumers.

The Supreme Council affirmed that its states will continue to follow the same approach next year in order to keep the market balanced and prices stable within OPEC's agreed-upon range. In this context, the Supreme Council has instructed the GCC states' oil and energy ministers to work on decreasing levels of production in the next OPEC meeting, and to take any other measures to maintain the balance in the market and reach the target price.

The Supreme Council underlined the importance of cooperation between producers and consumers. It praised the outcome of the seventh International Energy Forum recently held in Riyadh and welcomed the suggestion of His Highness 'Abdallah bin 'Abd al-'Aziz, Saudi crown prince, deputy prime minister, and commander of the National Guard, to establish a secretariat at the forum to enhance dialogue between producers and consumers.

The Supreme Council has agreed to treat GCC nationals who are serving as civil servants in any member state in the same way that the nationals of that country are treated according to the privileges listed in the decisions of the ministers in charge of central civil service bodies in the GCC states.

The Supreme Council underscored the need for the parties concerned in the public and private sectors to continue increasing employment opportunities for GCC nationals and inform the council's next session of the extent of progress made in this regard. The Supreme Council has endorsed the recommendations and mechanisms submitted by the joint committee to examine the demographic composition and effects of foreign labor. It stressed the need for member states to take the necessary measures to put these recommendations and mechanisms into practice.

Moreover, the Supreme Council has endorsed the joint plan to develop education curricula submitted by ministers of education, as well as measures for their implementation.

The Supreme Council has examined the Consultative Council's assessment of economic cooperation between GCC states and its proposals for the activation of the comprehensive and long-term development strategy in building scientific and technical capabilities in the member states. It decided to refer these proposals to the relevant ministerial committees in order to develop and strengthen joint economic action based on them.

The Consultative Council has been charged with examining the following topics and submitting its findings to the Supreme Council:

* The development of a comprehensive educational system.
* Energy and the environment.
* Water strategy.
* Scientific and technical research.

The Supreme Council has endorsed the Riyadh document on a unified law for penal measures in the GCC states as a guiding principle for four years.

The Supreme Council has agreed to extend work by the Muscat document for a unified civil affairs system for the GCC states as a guiding principle for another four years.

The Supreme Council has viewed the measures taken and research conducted in the field. It expressed satisfaction with the flow of military cooperation and the practical measures implemented in enhancing collective defence and military cooperation, which were crowned by the Supreme Council's endorsement of the Joint Defence Pact among GCC states. Their majesties and highnesses, the GCC leaders, have signed the pact, which will be endorsed by each member state according to the measures observed in each state.

The Supreme Council has adopted the resolutions of the nineteenth meeting of their highnesses and excellencies the interior ministers, which was held in Riyadh on 24 and 25 October 2000. Special attention was paid to resolutions strengthening follow-up and communication mechanisms between interior ministries in order to facilitate the movement of citizens and trade between the GCC states and enhance cooperation in combating drugs.

The Supreme Council discussed the developments in Iraq's implementation of the Security Council resolutions on the Kuwait-Iraq situation and the results of its occupation of the state of Kuwait. Out of the Supreme Council's eagerness to provide the suitable conditions for achieving security, peace and stability in the Gulf region, the Supreme Council renews its call on Iraq to complete its fulfillment of the commitments stipulated in the Security Council resolutions on cooperation with the International Committee of the Red Cross and the trilateral committee, which is seeking to find a quick and final solution to the problem of Kuwaiti prisoners and other third-country nationals and returning all Kuwaiti property in its possession.

The Supreme Council also asks Iraq to resume cooperation with the United Nations to end the outstanding issues regarding weapons of mass destruction and means of monitoring. The Supreme Council asks Iraq and the Security Council to engage in a comprehensive dialogue to implement these commitments in a fair and comprehensive manner on a sound foundation so that this will lead to the lifting of sanctions.

The Supreme Council stresses that Iraq should respect the security, independence, sovereignty and territorial integrity of the State of Kuwait. Iraq should also adopt all the necessary steps to show its peaceful intentions towards the GCC states, in a manner that achieves security and stability in the region. The Supreme Council renews its permanent welcome of, and its readiness to participate in, any humanitarian initiative that contributes to alleviating the suffering of the fraternal Iraqi people.

The Supreme Council reiterates its determination to continue the GCC states' efforts, which seek to lift this suffering, within the context of international resolutions. The Supreme Council stresses the need to respect Iraq's independence, unity of its land, territorial integrity and non-interference in its domestic affairs.

The Supreme Council also listened to a report by the trilateral committee, which is assigned the job of finding a mechanism to start direct negotiations to resolve the issue of Iran's occupation of the three islands that belong to the UAE by peaceful means. The report noted that the Islamic Republic of Iran refused to cooperate with the trilateral committee concerning the mission it was assigned by the GCC. This confirmed Iran's rejection of the previous peaceful initiatives by the UAE. After a thorough assessment of the developments in Iran's occupation of the three islands, the Supreme Council decided to ask the Ministerial Council to examine all the available peaceful means, which lead to regaining the legitimate rights of the UAE to its three islands — Tunb al-Kubra (Greater Tunb), Tunb al-Sughra (Lesser Tunb), and Abu Musa — which are still occupied by the Islamic Republic of Iran. This is based on the following principles.

1. Supporting the UAE's right to its three islands — Tunb al-Kubra, Tunb al-Sughra and Abu Musa — which are occupied by the Islamic Republic of Iran, and rejecting Iran's continued occupation of the three islands that belong to the UAE.

2. Asserting the UAE's full sovereignty over these three islands, which are an integral part of the UAE; the UAE reserving all its rights to them; and not recognizing any other sovereignty on the three UAE islands, its territorial waters, airspace, continental shelf and the economic zone that belongs to it.

3. Rejecting the Iranian claims about the island of Abu Musa and the measures carried out by the Islamic Republic of Iran and all the other consequences of these measures. All these measures threaten security and stability in the region and increase tension in it. Consequently, this threatens international peace and security. The GCC states categorically reject the continued Iranian occupation of Tunb al-Kubra and Tunb al-Sughra.

4. Condemning the Iranian violations and military maneuvers on the occupied islands of the UAE and its territorial waters and asking Iran to stop conducting these maneuvers, which are considered provocative acts that threaten security and stability in the Arabian Gulf, constitute a source of grave concern and do not help to build confidence.

5. Supporting all the steps taken by the UAE to restore its sovereignty over its three islands by peaceful means, stemming from the principle of collective security of the GCC states and asking the Islamic Republic of Iran to accept referring the dispute to the International Court of Justice.

The Supreme Council reviewed the bloody incidents in the occupied Palestinian territories as a result of the savage attacks, suppressive measures and policies of closure and siege practised by Israel against the brotherly Palestinian people, who are demanding all their legitimate rights, including their right to repatriation and the establishment of their independent state with al-Quds al-Sharif (Jerusalem) as its capital. While expressing its denunciation and condemnation of these attacks and measures, the council calls for providing protection for the Palestinian people against these attacks. It reiterates its constant and declared stands towards the establishment of a just and comprehensive peace in the region, based on the resolutions of international legitimacy, especially Resolutions 242 and 338 and the land-for-peace principle.

The Supreme Council also affirms that comprehensive peace will only be achieved through the Palestinian people's achievement of their full legitimate rights and the establishment of their independent state with al-Quds al-Sharif as its capital and full Israeli withdrawal from the occupied Syrian Golan Heights to the 4 June 1967 line, as well as the completion of Israeli withdrawal from the Lebanese territories to the internationally recognized borders, including Shab'a Farms, in accordance with UN Security Council Resolutions 425 and 426. It also calls for the release of all Lebanese prisoners and detainees in Israeli prisons.

The Supreme Council expresses its hope that the efforts under way will lead to a peaceful settlement that restores the legitimate rights of the Palestinian people. It asserts its full confidence in the Palestinian negotiator and appeals to the international community to exert more efforts to pressure the Israeli side and ask it to comply with the foundations and principles approved by the Madrid peace conference. This should lead to the restoration of all the legitimate Arab rights.

The Supreme Council renews its request to the international community to work towards making the Middle East region, including the Arabian Gulf, into a zone that is free of all weapons of mass destruction, including nuclear weapons. It emphasizes the necessity for Israel to join the Nuclear Non-Proliferation Treaty and to submit all its nuclear installations to the international inspection system of the International Atomic Energy Agency.

The Supreme Council expresses its support for the resolutions of the Ninth Session of the Islamic Summit Conference that was held in Doha in the period 12–13 November 2000. It also expresses its full confidence that the State of Qatar under its emir, His Highness Shaykh Hamad bin Khalifa Al Thani, will strive during its presidency of the Organization of Islamic Conference [ICO] to assume its responsibility wisely and capably so as to raise the organization's standard of performance and efficiency and achieve the Islamic nation's interests, increase its effectiveness and strengthen its presence in the international arena.

The Supreme Council expresses its great appreciation and gratitude to the true and sincere efforts that have been exerted by the Kingdom of Saudi Arabia under the custodian of the two holy mosques, King Fahd bin 'Abd al-'Aziz Al Sa'ud, and his brother His Highness Prince 'Abdallah bin 'Abd-'Aziz Sa'ud, the crown prince, deputy prime minister, and National Guard commander, during its presidency of the twentieth session of the Supreme Council and the accomplishments that have been made. They gave the blessed march a push forward towards the achievement of more progress and prosperity for the peoples of the region.

The Supreme Council also expresses its great appreciation and gratitude to the emir of Bahrain, His Highness Shaykh Hamad bin 'Isa Al Khalifa, and his government and people for the warm welcome, hospitality and feelings of true brotherhood with which the GCC heads of state were received. The GCC heads of state also note the care and attention, which His Highness Shaykh Hamad bin 'Isa Al Khalifa, president of the current session of the Supreme Council, has given to this meeting. They praise his wise management, which has had the biggest effect in reaching important results and decisions. They express their belief that Bahrain under his highness will contribute to strengthening this blessed march and leading it to new horizons and the fulfillment of the ambitions and aspirations of the GCC states.

The Supreme Council looks forward to the twenty-second session, which, God willing, would be held in the Sultanate of Oman in December 2001 at the kind invitation of His Majesty Sultan Qabus of Oman.

Issued in Manama, 5 Shawwal 1421, corresponding to 31 December 2000.
SOURCE: Bahraini TV, 31 December 2000 — BBC Monitoring, 3 January 2001.

NOTES

For the place and frequency of publications cited here, and for the full name of the publication, news agency, radio station or monitoring service where an abbreviation is used, please see "List of Sources." Only in the case of more than one publication bearing the same name is the place of publication noted here.

The author wishes to thank Nahum Shilo for his help in the writing of the sub-sections on Jordanian-Syrian, Jordanian-Iraqi, and Syrian-Iraqi relations, and Ariel Avraham, for his assistance in data collection.

1. *Al-Ahram*, 14 January 2000 (*MM*).
2. *Al-Ahram*, 5 January 2000 (*MM*).
3. Ben Lynfield, in *JP*, 24 January 2000.
4. *MM*, 2 February 2000.
5. MENA, 3 February 2000 (DR).
6. Interview with Patrick Seale in *al-Hayat*, 4 February 2000 (*MM*).
7. *JP*, 18 January; *Ha'aretz*, 29 May 2000.
8. *Al-Hayat*, 29 February 2000 (*MM*).
9. *Al-Quds al-'Arabi*, 29 February 2000 (*MM*).
10. *Al-Quds al-'Arabi*, 1 March 2000 (*MM*).
11. *Al-Ahram*, 1 March 2000 (*MM*).

12. *MM*, 10 February, quoting *al-Ahram* editor-in-chief Ibrahim Nafi' on the need for an "emergency summit" to discuss the stalemated peace process; Tariq Massarwa, in *al-Ra'y*, 21 February (*MM*); *AW*, 24 February 2000.
13. *Al-Ayyam* (Manama), cited by *MM*, 10 March 2000.
14. *Al-Quds al-'Arabi*, 13 March 2000 (*MM*).
15. Text of statement in *MM*, 13 March; *al-Hayat*, 13 March (*MM*); *al-Safir*, 15 March 2000 (*MM*).
16. *Al-Quds al-'Arabi*, 13 March 2000 (*MM*).
17. *MM*, 14 March 2000.
18. R. Damascus, 4 May 2000.
19. *Al-Ahram al-'Arabi*, 6 May 2000.
20. *Al-Ahram al-'Arabi*, cited by *Ha'aretz*, 17 May 2000.
21. *Al-Mustaqbal*, 3 May 2000 (*MM*).
22. MBC TV, 8 May 2000 (BBC Monitoring).
23. MENA, 19 May 2000 (DR).
24. *MM*, 7 June 2000.
25. See, e.g., Muhammad Hasanayn Haykal's commentary in *al-Usbu'*, cited by *MM*, 10 July 2000.
26. *Al-Ayyam* (Ramallah), 25 January 2000 (DR).
27. Bassam Badarin, *al-Quds al-'Arabi*, 20 March 2000 (*MM*).
28. *Al-Dustur*, 21 May 2000 (DR).
29. *JT*, 18 July 2000 (DR).
30. *Al-Majd*, 24 July 2000 (DR).
31. *JT*, 27 July, 2 August, 14 August; *al-Ra'y*, 1 August 2000.
32. The late Syrian president Hafiz al-Asad had paid a condolence call to King Husayn in April 1994 following the death of the king's mother. Earlier, in 1987, he had attended the Amman Arab summit conference. Apart from these two visits and the 1988 (Algeria) and 1990 (Cairo) Arab summits, all of their many meetings between 1986 and 1994 were held in Damascus.
33. *Al-Dustur*, 7 July; *JT*, 18 October; *al-Hayat*, 24 December 2000.
34. The delegation was made up of members of both the PNC and the PA Legislative Council.
35. *Al-Quds*, 8 August 2000.
36. *Al-Quds al-'Arabi*, 26 May 2000 (*MM*).
37. See remarks by Jordanian prime minister 'Ali Abu Raghib in *al-Hayat*, 10 July 2000 (*MM*).
38. Ibrahim Nafi', in *al-Ahram*, 27 July 2000 (*MM*).
39. For a sample of reaction among Arab commentators, see *MM*, 26 July 2000.
40. MENA, 27 July 2000 (DR).
41. *Al-Ahram*, 24 August 2000 (*MM*).
42. 'Adli Sadiq, in *al-Hayat al-Jadida*, 18 August 2000 (DR).
43. *Al-Hayat*, 14 August 2000 (*MM*).
44. The committee met on the foreign ministerial level. Neither 'Amru Musa of Egypt, and Salim al-Huss of Lebanon (also prime minister) attended. For the text of the final statement, see *MM*, 29 August 2000.
45. *Al-Hayat*, 14 August 2000 (*MM*).
46. *MM*, 7 August 2000.
47. *Al-Hayat*, 14 August 2000 (*MM*).
48. Ibid.
49. *Al-Hayat*, 4 September 2000 (*MM*).
50. Assayid Zahra, *Akhbar al-Khalij*, cited by *MM*, 2 October 2000.
51. *Al-Quds al-'Arabi*, 6 October 2000 (*MM*).
52. *Al-Quds al-'Arabi*, 11 October 2000 (*MM*).
53. Ibid.
54. SPA, 9 October — *MM*, 10 October 2000.

55. *Al-Quds al-'Arabi*, 11 October 2000 *(MM)*.
56. AFP, 15 October; *al-Sharq al-Awsat*, 17 October 2000 *(MM)*.
57. *Al-Ahram*, 19 October 2000 *(MM)*.
58. *Al-Ahram*, 16 October 2000 *(MM)*.
59. *Al-Sharq al-Awsat*, 17 October 2000 *(MM)*.
60. *Al-Quds al-'Arabi*, 8 November 2000 *(MM)*.
61. *Al-'Arab*, 19 October 2000 *(MM)*.
62. *Al-Ahram*, 19 October 2000 *(MM)*.
63. AFP, 21 October 2000.
64. ESC TV, 20 October — BBC Monitoring, 23 October 2000.
65. JTV, 21 October 2000 (BBC Monitoring).
66. AFP, 21 October 2000.
67. Ibid.
68. *Al-Sharq al-Awsat*, 14 December 2000 *(MM)*.
69. JTV, 21 October 2000 (BBC Monitoring).
70. Palestinian satellite TV, 21 October — BBC Monitoring, 23 October 2000.
71. AFP, 24 October 2000.
72. *MM*, 30 October 2000.
73. *Al-Hayat*, 3 November 2000 *(MM)*.
74. AFP, 22 October 2000.
75. R. Baghdad, 22 October — BBC Monitoring, 24 October 2000.
76. Muhammad Sayyid al-Sa'id, *al-Hayat*, 3 November 2000 *(MM)*.
77. *MM*, 30 October 2000.
78. *MM*, 23 October 2000.
79. AFP, 24 October 2000.
80. *Al-Safir*, 24 October 2000 (DR).
81. *Al-Sharq al-Awsat*, 26 October 2000 (DR).
82. MENA, 28 October 2000. (DR).
83. Iraqi TV, 22 October — BBC Monitoring, 24 October 2000.
84. AFP. 24 October; *MM*, 26, 30 October; MENA, 26 October 2000 (DR).
85. *MM*, 27 October 2000.
86. 'Abd al-Rahman al-Rashid, in *al-Sharq al-Awsat*, 9 November 2000 *(MM)*.
87. *Al-Sharq al-Awsat*, 8 November 2000 *(MM)*.
88. QNA, 9 November 2000 *(MM)*.
89. *Al-Quds al-'Arabi*, 14 November 2000.
90. *AW*, 30 November; *al-Sharq al-Awsat*, 8 December 2000 *(MM)*.
91. *Al-Mustaqbal*, quoted by *MM*, 11 December 2000.
92. Roni Shaked, *Yedi'ot Aharonot*, 13 December 2000.
93. *Al-Hayat al-Jadida*, 7 December; Iraqi TV, 11 December; Middle East News Online, 12 December; *Iraq News*, 13 December 2000.
94. Qusayy Salah Darwish, *al-Hadath al-Dawli*, cited by *MM*, 30 November 2000.
95. *Al-Mustaqbal*, 5 October 2000 *(MM)*.
96. *Al-Hayat*, 8 November 2000 *(MM)*.
97. Bassam Badarin, *al-Quds al-'Arabi*, 29 September 2000 *(MM)*.
98. *Al-Quds al-'Arabi*, 13 September 2000 *(MM)*.
99. *Al-Sharq al-Awsat*, 12 September 2000 *(MM)*.
100. *Al-Watan* (Kuwait), 15 September 2000 *(MM)*.
101. *Al-Sharq al-Awsat*, 16 February 2000.
102. *Al-Thawra* (Baghdad), 9 February 2000.
103. *Al-Sharq al-Awsat*, 16 February 2000.
104. *Al-Sharq al-Awsat*, 6 August 2000.
105. IPR Strategic Business Information Data Base, 19 September 2000.
106. SANA, 29 September 2000.
107. *Al-Safir*, 23 November 2000.

108. *Al-Sharq al-Awsat*, 26 December 2000.
109. IPR Strategic Business Information Data Base, 10 October 2000 (DR).
110. R. Baghdad, 1 August 2000 (DR).
111. Analysis by Ibrahim Hamidi, *al-Hayat*, 30 November 2000 (*MM*).
112. *Babil*, 15 May; *al-Dustur*, 29 May; *al-Quds al-'Arabi*, 15 July 2000.
113. *Al-Quds al-'Arabi*, 24 July 2000 (*MM*).
114. *Al-Quds al-'Arabi*, 15 July; *al-Sharq al-Awsat*, 24 July 2000 (*MM*).
115. Iraqi TV, 24 January (DR); *al-Sharq al-Awsat*, 25 January 2000.
116. *JT*, 16 July; *al-Hadath*, 24 July 2000.
117. *Al-Dustur*, 10 July; *JT*, 7 August 2000.
118. *Al-Quds al-'Arabi*, 12 September 2000 (*MM*).
119. *Al-Sharq al-Awsat*, 23 July 2000.
120. Bassam Badarin, *al-Quds al-'Arabi*, 29 September 2000 (*MM*).
121. *JT*, 5, 15 November, 4, 11, 25 December; *al-Majd*, 18 December 2000.
122. *MM*, 1 November 2000.
123. *JT*, 1 November; *al-Dustur*, 4 November 2000.
124. *Al-Ahram*, 7 June 2000 (*MM*).
125. *Al-Quds al-'Arabi*, *al-Watan* (Kuwait), 15 May 2000 (*MM*).
126. *Al-Watan* (Kuwait), Reuters, *al-Hayat*, 7 June 2000 (*MM*).
127. *Al-Hayat*, 14, 16 November 2000 (*MM*).
128. Simon Henderson, "The Gulf Cooperation Council Defense Pact: An Exercise in Ambiguity," *Policy Watch*, No. 511, January 16, 2001; *Gulf News*, 1 January 2001.
129. *Gulf News*, ibid.
130. Ibid.
131. *AW*, 4 January 2001.
132. *NYT*, 1 January 2001.

The Undiminished Threat of Political Islam

ESTHER WEBMAN

The viability of Islamism as a political force seemed to have reached a low point in early 2000. The three Islamist regimes — Sudan, Iran and Afghanistan — were widely perceived to be in deep trouble. Drawing on the lessons of the Sudanese situation, the Muslim Brotherhood in Jordan acknowledged in its annual political report that the Islamist movement was not "a unified force, despite its adopting the rhetoric of unity," and was not immune to "the diseases of dictatorship and tyranny once [the Islamists] arrive to positions of power." The political crisis in Sudan demonstrated the difficulty faced by Islamist movements in translating theory into practice, as well as the problem of more than one center of authority in a single country.[1] The Afghan people under the rule of Taliban were described by Tunisian journalist 'Afif al-Akhdar as being hostage in their own country, while those who govern in the name of Islam in Iran might be ruining Islam, dissident Iranian Ayatollah Mahdi Yazdi warned.[2] Conversely, Islamists in Arab countries continued to suffer from their identification with violence and terrorism, and were pursued by an international effort aimed at striking at the infrastructure of Islamist movements everywhere.

On the threshold of the new century, Islamist intellectuals and commentators continued to be preoccupied with the failure of Islamists to attain their goals and the insurmountable problems they confronted while in power. All agreed that Islamism was in a transitional phase, reassessing its goals and modus operandi while struggling for survival.[3] Iraqi writer Salah al-Nasrawi, who praised the contribution of Islamism to the Islamic revival and to the exposure of the ailments of Muslim societies, urged that self-criticism and reform be accompanied by reconciliation and the reintegration of Islamists in their societies to prevent the recourse to violence.[4] Going a step further, Jordanian Islamist Yasir Za'atra,[5] Jordanian researcher Hisham Ja'far and Egyptian psychologist Ahmad 'Abdallah[6] contested the very use of the term "political Islam" to define Islamic movements, viewing the term as misrepresenting the variety of Islamic movements. All the movements had been pushed into the political context, which became the only criterion of their success, while in reality each of them represented a different experience and many had long since favored cooptation in the extant political systems.

Discussing the Egyptian movement, al-Jama'a al-Islamiyya, Islamist lawyer Muntasir al-Zayyat posited four causes for its deterioration, which could be applicable to other Islamist movements not in power:

(1) Some opinion in the movement favored a truce with the government;
(2) The authorities had defeated the Islamists militarily;
(3) Popular support had been lost;
(4) Many of its leading members were in prison.

With this, Zayyat pointed out, an ongoing process of revision had occurred, leading to the formulation of a "new social covenant" redefining and deepening the relationship between the Islamic movements and society, and between society and government.[7]

Two events in the course of the year instilled new hope in the Islamists: the Israeli withdrawal from South Lebanon in May; and the outbreak of the Palestinian al-Aqsa intifada at the end of September. The Israeli withdrawal was generally interpreted by Arab Islamists as a victory for Hizballah and as proof that the Islamist way was the right solution to the Arab predicament of the past two centuries. The Hizballah experience was portrayed as a model for emulation, not only because of its successful struggle against the Zionist/Jewish enemy, but also because it exemplified the adaptability of the Islamist movement to changing circumstances. The intifada prompted a resurgence of pan-Islamic and pan-Arab feeling throughout the Arab countries and Muslim communities worldwide and legitimized radical anti-Israeli and anti-American slogans of Islamists. Moreover, the Islamists seemed to be regaining popular support throughout the region and dominated the discourse of the intifada.

With this, the threat of religious extremism and terrorism emanating from the Taliban control in Afghanistan and their guest and sponsor Usama Bin Ladin, did not recede and remained a focus of concern for the US.

FIGHTING ELUSIVE VILLAINS

PATTERNS OF INTERNATIONAL TERRORISM

Following the deadly bombings of the American embassies in Tanzania and Kenya in 1998 that killed 224 people (see *MECS* 1998, pp. 131–32), Usama Bin Ladin's attempts to carry out terrorist acts aimed at the US, Jordan, Albania and other countries were foiled as a result of joint efforts by intelligence officials around the world. Dozens of terrorists allegedly trained in Afghanistan and linked to him were arrested in Britain, Germany, Canada, the US, Jordan and Pakistan during 1999 and 2000. The net result of the arrests, the increased surveillance, cooperation among intelligence services and infiltration was to weaken Bin Ladin's terrorist infrastructure and limit his freedom of movement. Consequently, according to a senior US intelligence source, he changed some of his standard operating procedures.

The cumulative evidence from investigations of arrested suspects pointed to a loosely knit global network of terrorists bound by a common ideology. While these terrorists operated independently or were affiliated with various non-governmental organizations, they could, at times, join forces against their perceived common enemy. A series of new phenomena in this context were revealed during the investigations:

(1) Bin Ladin was using proxies who shared his jihad philosophy but were not members of al-Qa'ida (base) to carry out the attacks, such as members of the Algerian Groupe islamique armée (GIA) who were trained in camps in Afghanistan funded by him;

(2) His personal fortune was essential for continued terrorist activity. Similarly, terrorist groups relied on millions of dollars contributed annually by religious donors in the Arab world through a complex system of financing. A significant number of Islamist groups involved in terrorism used charitable organizations as fronts to conceal their activities and sources of funds;

(3) Freelance Muslim terrorists worked concurrently for several organizations and

charged high fees. Operating mainly from Lebanon, they were experts in passport counterfeiting, arms supplies and bomb assembly;

(4) Bin Ladin's organization, which was entirely his own creation, included cells in over fifty countries, many of them self-sufficient. Moreover, he strengthened links between extremist groups devoted to terrorism around the globe. He was believed to determine the worldwide objectives for all Islamic terrorist groups;

(5) While the broad agenda of religious extremism predated Bin Ladin, he tapped into a powerful and growing wave of religiously motivated hatred of the West during the late 1990s. These terrorists were driven not by a cult of personality but by a world view in which they were perceived as vanguard of a divinely ordained battle to liberate Muslim lands;

(6) The terrorists allied with Bin Ladin were not constrained by political concerns;

(7) They sought the acquisition of chemical and even nuclear weapons;

(8) Bin Ladin began focusing on "soft" targets for terrorist acts, such as hotels and tourist sites, rather than embassies or government buildings;

(9) Bin Ladin had been empowering second-tier leaders with more authority, although he continued to make the key decisions; and

(10) Britain was a site of growing Islamist activity, including funding, proselytizing and locating recruits.[8]

This new terrorism was typified by a combination of "religious motivation and a desire to inflict catastrophic damage," wrote Daniel Benjamin and Steven Simon, former directors of counter-terrorism in the US National Security Council.[9] US President Bill Clinton proposed allocating $300m. in new federal spending to combat global terrorism, urging the US to cooperate extensively with other nations to detect and thwart potentially deadly plots by groups with access to increasingly sophisticated weapons. He warned that the miniaturization of weapons would enable small groups or "free agents" to pose serious threats that once were possible only from hostile nations. "The advent of globalization and the revolution in information technology have magnified both the creative and the destructive potential of every individual, tribe and nation," he said.[10]

UNRAVELING THE STRANDS OF THE MILLENNIAL CONSPIRACIES

Harsh Sentences for Plotters in Jordan

A major trial began in the State Security Court in Jordan in March 2000 of twenty-eight men, accused of plotting terrorist attacks in Jordan on the eve of the new millennium. Fifteen of the suspects (thirteen Jordanians, one Iraqi and one Algerian) had been in custody since December 1999 while thirteen others, including Jordanians, Palestinians and a Yemeni, were fugitives in Pakistan, Afghanistan, Britain, Lebanon and Syria, and were tried in absentia. The charges leveled against them included possessing explosives and unlicensed automatic weapons, plotting to carry out terrorist acts, belonging to an illegal organization linked to Usama bin Ladin, and counterfeiting and circulating bank notes. The defendants had allegedly planned to plant explosives in the Radisson SAS Hotel in Amman on 3 January, and to attack American and Israeli tourists at Mount Nebo and at a site on the Jordan River.[11]

On 18 September, the court handed down eight death sentences, six in absentia. Fourteen of the defendants were sentenced to prison terms ranging from seven and a half years to fifteen years at hard labor. Six others were acquitted. The main defendant in the case, Khadhr Abu Hawshar, was condemned to death, as was Usama Husni Kamil Sammar, but the court immediately commuted their sentences to life at hard labor. Abu Hawshar, a veteran of the Afghan war who later joined the Jaysh Muhammad (Muhammad's Army — a radical Islamic group that perpetrated terrorist acts in Jordan in the late 1980s — see *MECS* 1991, p. 498), was identified as the ringleader. Following his release from a Jordanian prison in 1993, he moved to Yemen, where he joined the Egyptian Jihad. Defendants sentenced to death in absentia included: Munir al-Maqdah, a Palestinian Fath commander from the 'Ayn al-Hilwa refugee camp in Lebanon; Ra'id Muhammad Hasan Hijazi, considered to be Hawshar's assistant, who was subsequently arrested in October by the Syrian security authorities and handed over to Jordan; and Muhammad Husayn Zayn al-'Abidin, also known as Abu Zubayda, a Palestinian living in Pakistan who was believed to be a key aide to Bin Ladin and coordinator of his "external operations." A Jordanian Islamist living in Britain, 'Umar Abu 'Umar Abu Qatada, was sentenced in absentia to fifteen years for his alleged role in financing the group.

Abu Hawshar's lawyer, Salah Badr, claiming that the defendants were being "persecuted because they only want to uphold Islam and fight the Jews," denied their links to Bin Ladin or to any militant activity.[12]

The Trial of the Millennial Conspirators in the US
Several arrests were made in connection with the bomb plot discovered in the US on the eve of the millennium (see *MECS* 1999, p. 131). The plot appeared to have been centered in the Canadian cities of Montreal and Vancouver, although its targets were not discovered. The case turned into the biggest counter-terrorism inquiry since the embassy bombings in 1998.

In January, authorities in Senegal arrested Muhammad Walad Salahi, brother-in-law of one of Bin Ladin's key lieutenants, who was believed to be operating the Algerian group in Canada. Salahi had arrived in Canada in the fall of 1999, and, while in Montreal, worked closely with Mukhtar Hawari, an Algerian who was detained in mid-January in Montreal and charged with arranging the logistics of the plot. Another Algerian, 'Abd al-Ghani Maskini, was arrested in New York, for having been allegedly in contact with Ahmad Ressam (a.k.a. Abu Rida), also an Algerian. Ressam had been arrested on 14 December 1999 at the Canadian-US border, driving a carload of explosives.

Another Algerian suspected of involvement in the plot was Hamid 'Aysh, who had lived in Vancouver for three years, until May 1999. 'Aysh subsequently moved to Ireland and was associated with the Mercy International Relief Agency, a Kenya-based Islamic charity that American prosecutors linked to the embassy bombings and Bin Ladin. 'Aysh was briefly detained in Ireland in December 1999, but was released before the authorities learned that the evidence tied him to the American bomb plot.[13]

On 24 June, the French police arrested 'Abd al-Salim Boulanouar, a French citizen of Algerian origin, who had been deported from the Philippines, where he had served a six-month sentence for possession of explosives. Boulanouar was believed to have close ties with Ahmad Ressam. Both men were part of a group led by Fatih Kamil, an Algerian veteran of the Afghan war against the Soviet Union, who maintained homes in both France and Montreal.[14]

In October, 'Abd al-Majid Dahuman, indicted in absentia in Seattle in January on charges of conspiring to bring explosives into the US as part of the millennium bomb plot, was reportedly arrested in Algeria. The American authorities had offered $5m. for information leading to Dahuman's arrest. He and Ressam had shared a hotel room in Vancouver during the month before Ressam's attempt to cross the border into the US, and the two may have prepared the explosives together.

American officials suspected that Bin Ladin's group was involved in assisting Ressam and his alleged co-conspirators. However, evidence regarding Bin Ladin's possible involvement in the American plot remained inconclusive by the end of the year. The American investigators were reportedly frustrated in their efforts to find out what the Algerians intended to target in the US and when they planned to act. Ressam was scheduled to stand trial in Los Angeles in March 2001, while 'Abd al-Ghani Maskini and Mukhtar Hawari (see above) were to be tried in New York on charges of conspiring to support a terrorist group and to conceal their support for Ressam.[15]

PURSUING THE CASE OF THE EMBASSY BOMBINGS IN KENYA AND TANZANIA

The trial of the defendants in the case of the 1998 American embassy bombings in Nairobi and Dar as-Salam (see *MECS* 1998, pp. 133–34) was set for 5 September in the Manhattan District Court but postponed to 3 January 2001 to give the defense attorneys more time to prepare. Bin Ladin, along with sixteen other men, was accused in the indictment. Six defendants were being held in New York, three in other countries, and eight were fugitives. Extradition proceedings were underway for those jailed abroad, and a $5m. reward was offered for the capture and conviction of each fugitive.[16]

Five more fugitives, indicted on 20 December, raised the total number of accused in the case to twenty-two. The indictment portrayed the five new defendants as key members of al-Qa'ida. Two of the five — identified as Sayf al-'Adil, an Egyptian, and Anas al-Libi, of Libya — were allegedly members of a consultation council for al-Qa'ida, which discussed and approved terrorist operations. The three others were Egyptian Islamists. The amended indictment also charged a defendant already in custody, Mamduh Mahmud Salim, with attempted murder and other counts for an attack on a guard at a federal jail in New York on 1 November 2000. The four men awaiting trial in New York included one US citizen, Wadi' al-Hajj, and three foreign nationals who had been arrested abroad: Khalfan Khamis Muhammad, Muhammad Siddiq 'Awda and Muhammad Rashid Da'ud al-'Awhali. They were charged by the federal government in a 319-count indictment with plotting to bomb the embassies and kill Americans in different parts of the world.[17]

Federal prosecutors painted a most detailed picture of Bin Ladin's worldwide terrorism conspiracy. They depicted an organization that used international companies and a relief organization as covers for its operations; obtained blank passports from the government of Sudan; recruited a network of operatives living in the US; and communicated by fax, satellite phone and coded letters, often in language that was only partially veiled.

Evidence emerged that Wadi' al-Hajj, known as Abu 'Abdallah al-Lubnani, aged thirty-nine, a Lebanese Maronite who had procured American citizenship, was one of Bin Ladin's most trusted and dangerous aides, and a personal courier. Hajj allegedly met with Bin Ladin in Afghanistan in 1997, and conveyed orders to his operatives in Kenya, which led to the 1998 embassy attacks. Hajj also served as a front man, creating fictitious companies to hide Bin Ladin's activities. Documentary evidence also showed that Bin Ladin used the Mercy International Relief Agency (see above) as a front for terrorist operations.[18]

The first direct link between Bin Ladin and the bombings was provided by a former sergeant in the US Army, 'Ali A. Muhammad, who on 20 October pleaded guilty to participating in a terrorist conspiracy against Americans. Muhammad, aged forty-eight, a naturalized American citizen born in Egypt, had worked for Bin Ladin for a ten-year period after his stint as a supply sergeant assigned to a Special Forces unit at Fort Bragg, North Carolina, during 1986–89. The prosecution described him as one of Bin Ladin's oldest and most trusted lieutenants. Muhammad revealed that Bin Ladin's organization used tactics inspired by the Shi'i Islamist suicide bombers who blew up the US Marines barracks in Beirut in 1983, killing 241 soldiers and leading to the evacuation of the American troops from Lebanon (see *MECS* 1983–84, p. 553), as well as by the 1985 hijacking to Beirut of a TWA flight by Shi'i Islamists (see *MECS* 1984–85, p. 544). His confession also linked Bin Ladin with 'Imad Mughniyya, a Hizballah security chief who was believed to have masterminded these acts and the bombing of Israeli and Jewish institutions in Argentina in 1992 and 1994. Mughniyya worked closely with Bin Ladin's top aides, including Wadi' al-Hajj (see above). A car business was set up to create income, and a fictitious charity organization was created to provide al-Qa'ida members with forged identity documents. Muhammad also implicated Saudi dissident Khalid al-Fawwaz, head of the Islamist Advice and Reform Committee office in London, who had been arrested in 1998 by British security forces and whose extradition was sought by the US.[19]

THE PURSUIT OF ISLAMISTS IN THE WEST

International cooperation in combating terrorism led to the stepped-up pursuit of Islamists in the West in 2000. The parents of an Israeli-American teenager who was killed in a 1996 Islamist terrorist attack in Jerusalem filed a $600m. lawsuit in Chicago in May against several Islamic charities, non-profit organizations and individuals, contending that they raised money in the US for the Palestinian Hamas. This was the first attempt by individuals to use federal anti-terrorism laws against front organizations in the US that raise money in the name of Islamic causes. Among those named in the suit were Muhammad Salah, a naturalized US citizen accused of being a high-ranking fund-raiser for Hamas; the Qur'anic Institute; and the former head of Hamas' political bureau, Musa Abu Marzuq (see *MECS* 1995, pp. 120–21). The suit also named several other Islamic groups and individuals as members of the covert Hamas network in the US, including the Holy Land Foundation for Relief and Development, a charity with branches in Texas and Illinois; the Islamic Association for Palestine, a non-profit group dedicated to disseminating information about the Israeli-Palestinian conflict; and the United Association for Studies and Research in Virginia.[20]

In July, eighteen people were arrested in the Charlotte, NC area and accused of immigration violations and illegally profiting from cigarette smuggling and money laundering as part of an organized plot to raise and funnel money and equipment to Hizballah. Eight were jailed without bond, eight others were released on bail, and two were put under 24-hour house arrest. The affidavit alleged that the leader of the group, Muhammad Yusuf Hammud, solicited contributions for Hizballah, received military training in Lebanon, and communicated with Hizballah via the Internet. One of those arrested, 'Ali Husayn Darwish, had allegedly transported over $1m. to Lebanon. An additional $360,000 in cashier checks was also traced to Lebanon.[21]

In August, Bulgaria expelled a Jordanian, Ahmad Musa, to Jordan for engaging in unregulated religious activities that constituted a threat to national security. He was allegedly running a Muslim foundation used as an aegis for sending Bulgarian Muslims for religious and military training abroad.[22]

In October, the Italian authorities arrested eleven Muslims suspected of belonging to an Algerian branch of the Islamist organization al-Takfir wal-Hijra. Responsible for forging documents for Islamists in Italy, helping to smuggle arms into Algeria, and providing funds for Jihad, they were charged with criminal association for the purpose of carrying out acts of terrorism abroad. The Italian operation, code-named Crusade, reportedly led to the dismantling of a full-fledged terrorist network centered in Naples, which was part of a broader European network.[23]

A twenty-year-old Egyptian, Sabir Sulayman, suspected of being an associate of Bin Ladin, was declared persona non grata in October and deported to Egypt by the Albanian secret service, only minutes after he landed in Albania. His name had reportedly appeared on blacklists supplied by the CIA and the Egyptian information service.[24]

In November, British authorities accused two Bangladeshis, Munil 'Abidin and Mustafa 'Abidin, of setting up a network to carry out terrorist operations in Birmingham. Allegedly members of an Islamist group associated with Bin Ladin, they were arrested on the basis of their involvement in cases of international terrorism and after police seized quantities of explosives in their homes. The British police also investigated another group of Islamists based in a religious center in Birmingham, who had entered England on false passports in 1998 and recruited and trained supporters for Bin Ladin.[25]

German authorities arrested four suspected terrorists with ties to Bin Ladin and seized weapons and explosives in a search of two Frankfurt apartments in December. The four were charged with membership in a criminal organization, arms and explosives violations, and falsifying documents.[26]

BIN LADIN'S BURGEONING ACTIVITIES

Threatened by the ongoing war in Chechnya (see *MECS* 1999, p. 129), Russia insistently charged that Islamist recruits were being sent to Chechnya and that many more were receiving training in camps in Afghanistan. Quoting an alleged military instructor of Bin Ladin's organization, ITAR-TASS reported that a unit of four hundred fighters was sent to Chechnya in May, and that hundreds of Arabs and Afghans had been dispatched there since the outbreak of fighting in 1998.[27] Russia believed that without massive support from international terrorists, the Chechen rebels would not have been able to carry on their resistance. Bin Ladin, Russia claimed, had sent Chechen warlord Ibn al-Khattab $5.5m. to pay these "mercenaries," and in May, signed a protocol on cooperation with representatives of the Chechen separatist president Aslan Maskhadov, together with a representative of the Taliban government, at a meeting in Mazar-i-Sharif, Afghanistan. The document reportedly dealt with assistance in personnel, arms and munitions.[28]

Taliban spokespersons and Chechen foreign minister Ilyas Akhmadov denied the existence of any official ties between them, or that Bin Ladin was sending fighters to Chechnya.[29] However, Afghan opposition leaders claimed that on 2 November, Bin Ladin met with Chechen emissaries in Qandahar, Afghanistan, gave them $5m. and promised to reinforce them with well-trained recruits.[30] The leader of the London-based al-Muhajiroun Islamist organization, Shaykh Omar Bakri Muhammad, confirmed in December that some 600 to 700 volunteers were trained in Britain, ready to be sent to Chechnya, Afghanistan, Kashmir and other areas to continue the "sacred war."[31]

Russia also accused the Saudi-based international Islamic organization, al-Haramayn al-Sharifayn, originally formed to support the Afghan fighters against Russia, of being a major source of funding for the Chechen rebels through its offices in Georgia and Azerbaijan. The Egyptian al-Jama'a al-Islamiyya, the Turkish Refah Party and the People's Movement nationalist party in Turkey were also said to be raising funds for ammunition and medicines for the rebels in Chechnya. The London-based Islamist Hizb al-Tahrir and Afghanistan's ruling Taliban movement were reportedly the most prominent groups to expand their presence in the North Caucasus and Central Asia.[32]

Bin Ladin was believed to have provided support to the Islamic Movement of Uzbekistan (IMU), which sought to replace President Islam Karimov's regime with an Islamic theocratic state. A high-ranking IMU leader, Tahir Yuldash, tried in absentia and condemned to death by the Uzbek Supreme Court, was reported to be hiding in Afghanistan. The IMU launched armed incursions into Uzbekistan and neighboring Tajikistan and Kyrgyzstan during the summers of 1999 and 2000.[33]

Islamist groups in the Philippines also received support from Bin Ladin. An American intelligence report published in August confirmed that Bin Ladin subsidized the training camps used by both the Moro Front and its rival, the Abu Sayyaf group.[34] It also disclosed that the International Islamic Relief Organization (IIRO), set up in 1992 by Bin Ladin and his brother-in-law, Muhammad Jamal Khalifa, served as a front organization for funding terrorist activities in the Philippines. The IIRO, according to the report, was working under the aegis of the Muslim World League, an organization wholly financed by the Saudi Arabian government, and was used for the purchase of arms and other logistical requirements of the Abu Sayyaf. Only 10%–30% of the foreign funding of the IIRO was used for its stated relief and livelihood projects.[35]

In October, Kuwaiti security authorities arrested eleven people, including two police officers, and seized large quantities of powerful explosives earmarked for use in attacks in Kuwait and abroad. Although the political affiliation of the suspects was not specified, they were believed to be Islamists targeting US installations in and around Kuwait. The detainees included an Egyptian physician and a Yemeni carrying a Bosnian passport, who were immediately deported. The arrests were made less than a week after US forces in the Gulf were put on a high state of alert following the attack on the USS Cole (see below). The group's leader, Muhammad 'Abdallah, who was arrested on 31 October, was a Kuwaiti suspected of belonging to an Islamist group.[36] A London-based Islamist organization, the Islamic Observatory Center, claimed that a Moroccan aide of Bin Ladin's escaped from Kuwait to Iran with a forged Saudi passport hours before the arrests.[37] Kuwait did not comment on reports that the group was linked to Bin Ladin. The Kuwaiti daily al-Ra'y al-'Amm quoted Bin Ladin as denying links with the group that was arrested.[38]

HEIGHTENED ISLAMIST COOPERATION UNDER IRANIAN AUSPICES

According to the US State Department report on terrorism in 1999, released in May 2000, Iran had "stepped up its encouragement of, and support" for such militant Palestinian groups as Hamas and Islamic Jihad, known for their rejection of the peace process.[39] Iran was also presumed to be behind the growing cooperation between these movements and Hizballah, reflected in various developments. An Iranian delegation headed by 'Ali Akbar Velayati, the former Iranian foreign minister and now adviser to

Supreme Leader Ayatollah 'Ali Khamene'i, visited Syria and Lebanon in July and met with rejectionist Palestinian groups, including Hamas leaders. They reportedly discussed the possibility of mounting a new intifada to foil the chances of a peace agreement between Israel and the Palestinians, and apportioned about $2.5m. from Iran among the various groups.[40] Velayati assured the three Hamas leaders deported from Jordan in November 1999 (see *MECS* 1999, p. 114), Khalid Mash'al, Musa Abu Marzuq and Ibrahim Ghawsha, who attended the meetings, along with representatives of Hamas in Damascus and Tehran, of Khamene'i's support in their struggle against the "Zionist regime." They agreed that the concurrent Camp David talks between Palestinian Authority (PA) chairman Yasir 'Arafat and Israeli prime minister Ehud Barak under the auspices of the American president was dangerous for the Palestinian cause, for the status of Jerusalem, and for the Palestinian refugees' right of return.[40]

The London-based *al-Sharq al-Awsat* reported that Iran was also working on reorganizing the ranks of the Palestinian Islamic Jihad movement and settling differences between its leaders. Quoting Palestinian sources, the paper claimed that the Iranian intelligence agency had requested a $200,000 increase in financial aid to the Islamic Jihad movement for this purpose. Khamene'i reportedly urged Hizballah to speed up the implementation of the first stage of a plan to organize the al-Jaysh al-Thawri al-Sirri al-Islami (Secret Islamic Revolutionary Army), which would consist of joint cells from the Islamic Jihad and Hizballah to carry out operations inside the Palestinian territories. The joint organization was to be commanded by Hizballah activist 'Imad Mughniyya, together with Islamic Jihad leaders. An Israeli report claimed that Iran set up an office to coordinate the activities of Hamas, the Palestinian Islamic Jihad and Hizballah, with Mughniyya as its head.[41]

Details of the investigations of the defendants in the millennium plot in Jordan (see above) revealed that the Palestinian Fath commander in Lebanon, Munir Maqdah, who was accused of being a conspirator, and other Fath activists in Lebanon were in close contact with Hizballah and the Islamic Jihad. Moreover, following the expulsion of Hamas leaders from Jordan, relations between Iran and Hamas improved continuously on both the operational and political levels.[42]

Israeli intelligence reports also indicated that both the Islamic Jihad and Hamas, especially the international political arm of Hamas, had infiltrated certain elements of the Islamic movement in Israel. According to one report, Israeli Muslim bodies intensified cooperation with Muslim elements in Egypt, and that young Israeli Muslims were sent to train with Hamas in Iran and to Bin Ladin's camps in Pakistan and Afghanistan.[43]

FUTILE ATTEMPTS TO HUNT DOWN BIN LADIN

NEGOTIATING WITH THE TALIBAN

The Taliban authorities continued to shelter Bin Ladin despite international pressure. Even the US-sponsored sanctions imposed by the UN on the Taliban regime in Afghanistan in November 1999 failed to deter them. A Taliban delegation that met with Karl Inderfurth, US assistant secretary of state for South Asia, in Islamabad in January ruled out handing over Bin Ladin. Instead, the Taliban demanded that the US provide evidence of his alleged involvement in terrorism to the Afghan Supreme Court, or agree to assign the issue to Islamic scholars to decide upon an acceptable solution. Another proposal by the Taliban was to authorize the Islamic Conference Organization (ICO) to monitor Bin Ladin's activities in Afghanistan.[44] Taliban officials reiterated this position throughout the year, insisting that they had restricted Bin Ladin's movements and closed his training camps.[45] He had reportedly complained in private about the Taliban's restrictions on his freedom of movement, which had become harsher as external pressure mounted. Reports suggest that he approached Pakistani leaders, who were considered to be close to the Taliban leaders, to persuade them to relax the ban. In the wake of the intifada (see below), he reportedly sought the Taliban leaders' permission to issue a public statement denouncing the Israeli aggression against the Palestinians on two occasions, only to be refused.[46]

Pakistan remained actively involved in facilitating a dialogue between American officials and the Afghan government on the Bin Ladin issue. In May, an FBI team arrived in Islamabad to meet high-ranking Pakistani officials and share evidence supporting the allegation of Bin Ladin's terrorist activities. The evidence consisted mostly of court statements by Islamists arrested in Canada, Pakistan and Jordan. Ongoing diplomatic contacts culminated at the end of May in a futile meeting in Pakistan between US Undersecretary of State Thomas Pickering and the Afghan deputy foreign minister, Mawlavi 'Abdul Rahman Zahid, who flew in from Qandahar.[47]

Afghanistan's rulers renewed an offer for dialogue with the US over Bin Ladin in July, possibly in response to comments by Inderfurth at a congressional committee hearing on "The Taliban: engagement or confrontation." The assistant secretary of state revealed at that time that Washington and Moscow were in agreement over the threat of terrorism emanating from Afghanistan.[48]

In September, the Taliban sent a delegation to several Western and Muslim capitals and launched a campaign at the opening session of the UN General Assembly to solicit support for their bid to have Afghanistan seated in the UN. Taliban deputy foreign minister Zahid met with senior State Department officials, urging them to help the regime gain international recognition. Failing in this effort, the Taliban blamed the US for penalizing them because of their refusal to expel Bin Ladin and because of their religious policies.[49] The Six-Plus-Two Group (China, Iran, Pakistan, Tajikistan, Turkmenistan, Uzbekistan, plus Russia and the US; see *MECS* 1999, p. 132) met in New York in November to consider a fresh peace proposal by the UN. In a report to the group, the deposed Afghani president, Burhanuddin Rabbani, said Bin Ladin's supporters were fighting alongside the Taliban against the small opposition-controlled region in northern Afghanistan.[50]

Following mounting fears in Afghanistan of a US military strike, a meeting took place on 2 November between US Ambassador to Pakistan William Milam and the Taliban ambassador in Islamabad, 'Abd al-Salam Zayf. Milam informed the Taliban that the US had "concrete evidence" of Bin Ladin's involvement in the embassy bombings in 1998, and that it would be prepared to hold Bin Ladin's trial in a third country.[51]

Although the discussions between the Taliban and the US were not productive, they continued at intervals throughout the year, at the request of both the Taliban and the US. In a report released on 30 November, UN Secretary-General Kofi Annan deplored the failure of the Taliban to deliver Bin Ladin for trial, as called for by several Security Council resolutions.[52]

CONTEMPLATING MILITARY ACTION

Tension grew in the Pakistan-Afghanistan region at the end of March, whether due to reports that Bin Ladin had issued a new call for jihad, or of American preparations to deliver a blow to Bin Ladin. Jihad poster messages were said to be circulating in the North West Frontier Province in Pakistan, evoking a prompt denial by Taliban leader Mullah Muhammad Omar, who questioned their authenticity. He claimed that the Taliban controlled Bin Ladin's activities and access to him and viewed the circulation of such reports as part of a plan by the US or its allies to malign the Taliban and harm Afghanistan.[53]

American diplomats in Pakistan were said to have sent their families back home and reduced staff in the American missions in advance of a US strike.[54] Fazlur Rahman, leader of Pakistan's Islamist party, Jami'at-i 'Ulama-i-Islam (JUI), warned that agents of American agencies were moving about in Pakistani tribal areas without any restriction and were planning to co-opt tribal leaders in an operation against Bin Ladin.[55] Such information on possible American moves prompted rumors that Bin Ladin had relocated to the Philippines but these were denied by his spokespersons.[56]

Reports originating from Pakistan in July again alluded to a possible US attack on Bin Ladin, citing the establishment of CIA camps in Pakistani territory across the Afghanistan border.[57] The Taliban Foreign Ministry reiterated assurances that Afghan soil would never be used as a base for attacks against other nations.[58] An unconfirmed report in September said that Bin Ladin had escaped unharmed from a rocket attack by an unknown source on his convoy near Taliban headquarters in Qandahar. The rockets destroyed several cars belonging to his bodyguards.[59]

The bombing of the USS Cole in Yemen in October (see below) evoked conjecture that the US was preparing an attack on positions in Afghanistan. Reports in mid-November indicated that the US had positioned its naval ships off the Pakistani coast in readiness for a strike, and pointed to mounting pressure on Clinton to act before the presidential elections in November.[60] Afghanistan threatened to retaliate with full force if the US ever tried to attack it. Afghan foreign minister Mawlavi 'Abdul Wakil Mutawakil stated that the presence of American forces in the Gulf was unjustified, and demanded that the US and Russia be expelled from the Six-Plus-Two Group. He also accused the UN of playing a provocative role in relation to Afghanistan.[61] Pakistan declared that it would not allow the US to cross its airspace to attack Afghanistan,[62] while Turkey announced that it would not grant permission to the US to launch an air attack against Afghanistan from its territory.[63] Countries in Central Asia distanced themselves from the US plans as well, stating that they were not willing to provide land facilities for the US forces. By mid-December, the Clinton administration appeared to be backing off. According to Pakistani sources, the reason for the delay in carrying out the strike was lack of evidence against Bin Ladin combined with US fear of violent reactions by Islamist groups.[64]

An Afghan source reported in November that due to the imminent threat of a US missile strike in response to the Cole attack, Bin Ladin had left his main camp in Qandahar and moved to a secret base in the Hindu Kush mountains.[65]

CRACKDOWN ON "ARAB AFGHANS" IN PAKISTAN

Pakistan, concerned about its own stability and/or American retaliation, tightened the noose around Bin Ladin's associates in Pakistan and reportedly decided to hand over individuals wanted by various countries — especially Muslim states — for involvement in terrorist acts. The decision was also aimed at countering allegations that Pakistan sponsored terrorism, and at improving ties with countries such as Saudi Arabia and Egypt which accused both Afghanistan and Pakistan of harboring persons sought by them.[66]

Pakistani security forces reportedly launched a countrywide crackdown on Arab Afghan militants in Peshawar, deporting eighteen people in May and June, including nationals of Libya, Yemen and Turkey.[67] A Palestinian, Samir Mustafa, was arrested at the Karachi airport for attempting to travel to Italy on forged documents,[68] and a Yemeni citizen, Ahmad 'Abdallah, was arrested when attempting to cross the border into Afghanistan, along with two Pakistanis without visas who were carrying a large amount of money. Mustafa was suspected of having ties with Bin Ladin.[69] Four more Arabs — two Kuwaitis, one Egyptian and one Algerian, all suspected of ties with Bin Ladin's organization — were also arrested during this same period. The Egyptian detainee, Muhammad Sha'ban, was extradited in May to Egypt. [70]

An indirect result of this crackdown was the arrest by the Taliban in Kabul of a Syrian soldier, Rahim Janco, and a Kurd, Arkun Ilyas, who were allegedly trained by a joint Israeli-American intelligence network and tasked with collecting information about routes used by Usama bin Ladin and Muslim mujahidin to enter Chechnya. The Syrian reportedly confessed that he had been blackmailed by money and sex while visiting the UAE. Bin Ladin consequently replaced his Arab bodyguards with Bengals and Pakistanis, and moved his headquarters from Qandahar.[71]

Some twenty-five to thirty Arab nationals left Pakistan for Afghanistan during the first half of 2000 to avoid arrest and deportation, according to a report published in July.[72] An Iraqi national, Salih Sulayman (also known as Abu Dajana), believed to be a close associate of Bin Ladin, was arrested in Peshawar in October.[73]

INTERNATIONAL COOPERATION TO THWART THE TALIBAN AND CURTAIL BIN LADIN'S ACTIVITIES

The war in Chechnya and growing unrest in the other Muslim Central Asian republics led Russia to join international efforts to combat terrorism. This was reflected in a summit held in Dushanbe, Kazakhstan in July by the Shanghai Five Forum, comprising Russia, China, Kazakhstan, Tajikistan and Kyrgyzstan. The forum, originally set up in mid-1990s to resolve border disputes between China and the constituent republics of the former Soviet Union, now expanded its agenda to include the growing threat posed by terrorists and separatists trained and armed by the Taliban. They discussed measures to counter this threat. In a declaration issued at its close, the forum singled out Afghanistan as the chief source of instability in the region and called for coordinated efforts to combat international terrorism.[74] India, Iran and Uzbekistan displayed interest in joining the group.[75]

At the same time, a dialogue initiated in May between Russia and the US regarding closer cooperation in combating the threat of terrorism led to an agreement in July to form a bilateral working group on Afghanistan. Russia threatened to carry out preemptive strikes against the Taliban, whom it accused of helping train Islamic militants to fight in Chechnya and Central Asia, while the CIA and FBI established intelligence stations in Dushanbe, Tashkent and Bishkek. Russian soldiers were reportedly stationed along Tajikistan's border with Afghanistan.[76]

Incursions by the Taliban during August and September into areas controlled by the Afghani opposition — the Northern Alliance (see *MECS* 1996, pp. 107–109) — raised concern in Russia, the Central Asian republics bordering on Afghanistan, India and Iran, all of which supported the opposition government under Burhanuddin Rabbani. Both Russia and the West believed that the Taliban success was sending a powerful signal to other militant groups about the use of Islam as a rallying point for political and military forces in the region. The Taliban, they feared, might adopt even more aggressive measures than Iran to export their ideology by helping Islamic movements which were already challenging the successor regimes to the Soviet Union in Central Asia. Additionally, it was feared, the completion of the Taliban triumph in Afghanistan would encourage Islamist groups in Pakistan to intensify their efforts to establish a more rigidly Islamic state. The combination of a Taliban-ruled Afghanistan, a fundamentalist government in Pakistan and Islamic Iran would be a nightmare for both the West and Russia.[77]

In the belief that Islamic extremists were trying to redraw the map of Central Asia, Russian defense minister Igor Sergeyev met with leaders of the anti-Taliban alliance attending a session of the Russian and CIS Defense Ministers Council on 26 October in Dushanbe. The discussions concerned military support for Gen. Ahmad Shah Mas'ud, who was considered the only effective opponent to the Taliban.[78]

The Russian-American working group on Afghanistan, meeting for a second time in October in Moscow, contended that "the situation in and around Afghanistan continues to pose a threat to regional and international security." It resolved to pursue efforts to induce the Taliban to stop supporting terrorism, close terrorist training camps and hand Bin Ladin over to justice.[79] Russian-American cooperation on this issue culminated in their co-sponsorship of a UN Security Council resolution on 19 December imposing additional sanctions on Afghanistan.

IMPOSITION OF NEW SANCTIONS ON AFGHANISTAN

The Security Council resolution demanded that the Taliban surrender Bin Ladin and close terrorist training camps within a month or face new sanctions. (Previously imposed sanctions banned flights to and from Afghanistan; see *MECS* 1999, pp. 132–33). The Security Council called on foreign backers of the Taliban — an apparent reference to Pakistan — to withdraw any "officials, agents, advisers and military personnel" engaged in supporting the Taliban war effort. In addition, the Security Council called for a freeze on Bin Ladin's assets and those of members of his alleged terrorist network; barred international aircraft from landing in Afghanistan without the council's approval; urged countries to reduce diplomatic representation by the Taliban abroad; and placed restrictions on travel by senior Taliban officials. The sanctions also placed an arms embargo on the Taliban and a ban on exports of acetic anhydride, used in the manufacture of heroin — a bid to deprive the militia of opium revenue.

Several council members, including France, the Netherlands and Canada, expressed concern over the implications of the new sanctions for the impoverished Afghanistan people, but none were willing to block the resolution, since opposition would have amounted to support for the Taliban. Responding to the resolution, the Taliban information minister, Qadratullah Jamal, accused the US and Russia of using the issue of Bin Ladin and terrorism as a pretext for destroying the Islamic system of Afghanistan. The Taliban announced that it would protect Bin Ladin, called for a boycott of American and Russian products, and urged other Muslim states to join them in this campaign. It also threatened to absent itself from the UN-sponsored talks for a negotiated solution to the Afghan issue, which were ongoing throughout the year.[80]

In a press release issued following the imposition of the sanctions, al-Muhajiroun, the London-based Islamist group associated with Bin Ladin's World Islamic Front umbrella network (see *MECS* 1998, pp. 129–30 and below), accused the international body and its "pro-Israel leader Kofi Annan" of exposing "its ugly face of Islamophobia." Al-Muhajiroun also organized a demonstration against the sanctions outside the UN Information Center in London.[81]

Despite cumulative evidence in the hands of the US about Bin Ladin's network activities, some critics argued that the US, by portraying him as the mastermind behind Islamist terrorist activities worldwide, was responsible for aggrandizing him and his cause. Harvey Kushner, an expert on terrorism at Long Island University, contended that viewing Islamic fundamentalism as a global monolith was erroneous. Rather, Bin Ladin's operation was a loose network, not an organization that could sustain an orderly succession of leaders. "The danger of Bin Ladin is not the structure but the randomness of this configuration," he said. Fawaz Gerges, a professor of Middle Eastern studies at Sarah Lawrence College who studied Middle East Islamic movements, called the American insistence on describing Bin Ladin as the top terrorist unrealistic. Bin Ladin, he believed, was "a spent force" with little support outside Afghanistan. Not only was he under siege by the American and other intelligence organizations, his organization itself was splintered. Reportedly, some sixty Arab veterans of the war in Afghanistan in the 1980s had defected from Bin Ladin's movement after the 1989 Soviet withdrawal to form a breakaway pro-Taliban faction led by 'Umar 'Abd al-Hakim Abu Mus'ab Suri, one of Bin Ladin's oldest associates. Suri and Bin Ladin were reunited in 1996, when Bin Ladin put him in charge of indoctrination at his training camps in Khost. They soon became estranged, however, over ideological differences, with Suri becoming more of a religious radical than his former boss.[82]

ISLAMIST DISCORD AND DISCONTENT

Differences within some of the Islamist organizations, especially the Egyptian Jihad and the Jama'a al-Islamiyya, the Palestinian Hamas and the Algerian Front islamique du salut (FIS), weakened their popularity. The major issues of contention, common to all the groups, were the use of violence and participation in existing political systems. According to Egyptian security sources, the rivalry between the leaders of the two Egyptian organizations enabled the authorities to contain the armed activity of these groups and cut off their fighting cadres in Egypt from sources of finance and weapons abroad. The military containment of Hamas and of Algerian Islamists also weakened their standing.

COORDINATION BY ARAB STATES TO COMBAT TERRORISM

Twenty Arab ministers of interior, meeting in Algiers in late January to coordinate measures to combat terrorism, adopted a revised version of the "Arab strategy for combating terrorism" that provided for "strengthened cooperation between Arab security agencies in combating cross-border crime," which had been adopted in 1999 (see *MECS* 1999, p. 122). Until then, only twelve Arab countries had approved the agreement. President 'Abd al-'Aziz Bouteflika of Algeria urged the remainder to do likewise in his opening remarks to the conference. The ministers also endorsed what was described as an Egyptian initiative to convene a UN-sponsored international conference on combating terrorism, while adding the usual proviso that a distinction had to be made between terrorism and the right of peoples to struggle against foreign occupation.

While the Saudi-owned daily al-Sharq al-Awsat portrayed the conference results as a step toward building a worldwide "front" to combat international terrorism and organized crime, other Arab commentators considered them a "smokescreen" for a joint endeavor to suppress all forms of political opposition. Inter-Arab cooperation against terrorism "is a byword for Arab regimes scratching each other's backs by helping each other suppress political dissent or criticism, the only field in which they ever really cooperate," argued 'Abd al-Bari Atwan, the Palestinian editor of the London-based al-Quds al-'Arabi.[83]

Cooperation in confronting terrorist groups again topped the agenda of another conference of Arab ministers of interior which took place in Tunis in May. Habib al-'Adili, the Egyptian representative, commended his country's close cooperation with the European countries — a policy which resulted in the handover to Egypt during 1998-2000 of some of the most wanted militants living abroad, who for years had plotted anti-government attacks and collected funds to finance terrorist activities back home.[84]

FRICTION BETWEEN EGYPTIAN ISLAMIST LEADERS

In a startling move in February, the Egyptian Jihad movement announced the dismissal of Ayman al-Zawahiri as its leader. Zawahiri, who was viewed as Bin Ladin's right-hand man, had been sentenced in absentia in Egypt to death for his role in several terrorist acts (see above) and was living in Afghanistan. Commentators linked his departure to personal rivalries in the movement coinciding with the ongoing debate over the issue of a truce with the authorities and the end of violence inside Egypt, announced in 1997 (see MECS 1997, p. 144). Friction reportedly arose between Zawahiri and Sayyid Imam al-Sharif, alias Dr. Fadl, spokesperson of the organization, and between Zawahiri and his deputy, Muhammad Makkawi.[85]

Reports of Zawahiri's dismissal were followed by a statement issued by one of the Egyptian Jihad leaders, living in exile in Germany, Usama Siddiq Ayyub, openly calling for an end to violent acts both inside and outside Egypt and for focusing all efforts on the liberation of the al-Aqsa Mosque by force. Ayyub's lawyer, Sa'd Hasaballah, confirmed that the initiative represented an extraordinary strategic change in the Jihad group's thinking, and that a number of leaders inside and outside Egypt supported it. Islamist writer Kamal Habib noted that the appeal reflected a new stage of maturity reached by the Islamist movement after long and bitter experience. Zawahiri, he pointed out, was unable to accept this initiative because of his ongoing strategic alliance with Bin Ladin.[86] Zawahiri's brother, Muhammad, also a leader in the organization, was turned over to the Egyptian authorities in June by the UAE.[87]

In August, eleven Jihad members jailed in the Wadi al-Natrun prison in Egypt issued an appeal to the movement leaders inside and outside Egypt to accept the initiative proposed by Usama Ayyub and unify all efforts toward the goal of the liberation of Jerusalem.[88]

Similar divisions emerged in the positions of al-Jama'a al-Islamiyya. The Jama'a's spiritual leader, Shaykh 'Umar 'Abd al-Rahman, imprisoned in the US since 1995 for his role in the bombing of the World Trade Center (see MECS 1995, pp. 116–17), announced that he was revoking his support for the cease-fire with the Egyptian authorities declared unilaterally by the movement in 1997. The truce had been opposed all along by the exiled military commander of the Jama'a, Rifa'i Ahmad Taha, who also operated closely with Bin Ladin. Both leaders charged that "the unilateral truce has not achieved anything, that the state has not reciprocated, and that it will never allow Islamist groups to engage meaningfully in peaceful politics." 'Abd al-Rahman's announcement created confusion among the movement's followers. Taha relinquished his role as leader of the Shura Council of the organization abroad, while adamantly denying that he had been the victim of an internal coup to depose him. The Shura Council of al-Jama'a al-Islamiyya consisted of two parts, explained Islamist lawyer Muntasir al-Zayyat in an interview to *al-Sharq al-Awsat*. One part was the original council established by the founding leaders, now jailed in the Tarra prison in Egypt. They included Shaykh Karam Zuhdi, Shaykh Najih Ibrahim, Shaykh 'Isam Dirballah, Shaykh 'Asim 'Abd al-Majid, Shaykh Usama Hafiz, Shaykh Hamdi 'Abd al-Rahman, Shaykh Fu'ad al-Dawalibi, Shaykh 'Ali al-Sharif and 'Abbud al-Zummar. It was they who had unanimously launched the truce initiative. The second part was the Shura Council of the Jama'a abroad, headed by Mustafa Hamza, who announced that the decision made by the movement to cease armed operations was still in force. Rifa'i Taha, however, declared from Afghanistan that he opposed the continuation of the initiative.[89]

'Abd al-Rahman's U-turn exacerbated an existing split within the Jama'a between two camps: a majority camp led by Mustafa Hamza, which supported the decision to cease all military operations inside and outside Egypt, and a hard-line faction led by Rifa'i Ahmad Taha, which opposed the move.[90] In the wake of the war of statements prompted by 'Abd al-Rahman's announcement, he issued an appeal to all parties to refrain from further declarations. 'Abdallah 'Abd al-Rahman, 'Umar's son, explained that his father "did not mean to annul the initiative to halt violence, did not incite violence, but only voiced his opinion of its futility by withdrawing his backing for it."[91] Islamist lawyer Zayyat, thought to have engineered the move in 1997 to renounce violence, viewed 'Abd al-Rahman's declaration as a "reminder" that the Jama'a could still cause trouble for the government if it did not continue releasing the movement's jailed activists, as the Jama'a demanded. The declaration may have also sought to draw attention to the conditions in which 'Abd al-Rahman was being held in the US — in solitary confinement and denied visits.[92] A meeting of Islamists in Afghanistan in September, attended by Bin Ladin, Rifa'i Ahmad Taha and Ayman al-Zawahiri, reaffirmed their determination to work for the release of 'Abd al-Rahman. Video footage of the meeting, produced by a company called the Jihad Media Center in Afghanistan, was broadcast by Qatar's al-Jazira satellite TV on 21 September.[93]

Friction resurfaced with the bombing of the American destroyer USS Cole in October (see below). Taha issued a statement praising the attack as a retaliation for the acts of the Israeli occupation against the Palestinian people. Other Jama'a leaders, however, fearing that such statements could embroil the organization in a new cycle of violence, disassociated the movement from it.[94]

THE DIMINISHING EFFECTIVENESS OF HAMAS

The deportation from Jordan in 1999 of the head of the Hamas political bureau and three prominent bureau members, to Qatar, and the resumption of the Syrian-Israeli talks at the end of that year, had a negative impact on the viability of Hamas. On the one hand,

Hamas was less able to fight the Israelis than in the past, as its military wing had been dealt a number of successive blows. On the other hand, the political situation in the PA had changed dramatically. Aware of the decline in its popularity, Hamas showed signs of flexibility in its stance, observed Prof. Nasir al-Sha'ir of al-Najah University, noting two important developments. Firstly, the movement proposed a temporary truce as an alternative to the process of attaining a permanent peace with Israel. Secondly, Hamas accepted in principle the Palestinian people's stand regarding the proposed political settlement. This meant, Sha'ir said, that the issue was not religious, and that Hamas, although committed to a certain perception of the Palestinian issue, would not impose its view on the people.[95]

The four deported Hamas leaders — Khalid Mash'al, Ibrahim Ghawsha, Sami Khatir and 'Izzat Rishq — made sustained judicial and political efforts throughout the year to return to Jordan. Assisted by members of the Jordanian Muslim Brotherhood and the Islamic Action Front (IAF), they filed an appeal in January to the Jordanian Higher Court of Justice against the prime minister, the cabinet and the interior minister, contesting their expulsion, arguing that it was unconstitutional.[96] A ruling by the court rejected their appeal.

In July, they attempted to make contact with the newly formed government of 'Ali Abu al-Raghib through various mediators in a bid to be allowed to return to Jordan.[97] The new government, however, was not interested in overturning the decision, contending that it was a sovereign decision and that no non-Jordanian political party was allowed to operate in Jordan. Hence the deportees could be allowed to return to Jordan only as Jordanian citizens.[98] A mediation initiative between the Jordanian prime minister and the deportees took place at the Doha ICO summit in November (see below), when Abu al-Raghib met with Khalid Mash'al in the presence of the Qatari foreign minister.[99] None of the deportees, however, were allowed to return during 2000 (see also chapter on Jordan).

AMNESTY FOR ALGERIAN ISLAMISTS

Despite the National Reconciliation Law proposed by President 'Abd al-'Aziz Bouteflika of Algeria in July 1999 (see *MECS* 1999, p. 127), offering Islamists an opportunity to surrender to the authorities without penalty, the situation of Islamists in Algeria did not improve (see chapter on Algeria). The amnesty offer, due to expire on 13 January, was extended informally to allow more militants to surrender. In January, the Armée islamique du salut (AIS), the armed wing of the FIS led by Madani Mizraq, officially dissolved itself, and its members were granted amnesty by the state. Saudi Arabia reportedly granted Algeria $800m. to help it rehabilitate Islamist rebels who returned to civilian life, and also offered asylum to Mizraq. Algerian newspapers reported that by January 2000, 4,200 people had taken advantage of the National Reconciliation Law since it was first announced. Of them, 2,400 belonged to the AIS while the rest belonged to the GIA and other militant groups. A statement issued by the FIS welcomed the amnesty granted to the AIS while stressing that it needed to be followed up by moves to effect political reconciliation in the country, including releasing its jailed members and lifting the ban on its activities.

Still, the government amnesty offer seemed to sow even further dissension within the Islamist groups. Leading FIS figures opposed to the agreement between Mizraq and the authorities were presumed to be behind unconfirmed reports that one of Mizraq's aides tried to assassinate him. An FIS leader in exile, Rabah Kabir, while announcing his support of the truce reached between the AIS and the army, did not deny that there were differences within the group over how much had been gained by it. A member of another Islamist faction, the Salafi Group for Call and Combat, headed by Hasan Hattab, who was reportedly negotiating with government security forces on terms of surrender and amnesty when the deadline passed, was assassinated by dissenters in the faction in January. The GIA, together with two other small groups, announced their rejection of the reconciliation law and vowed to continue their anti-government attacks.[100]

Egyptian pro-Islamist writer Fahmi Huwaydi believed that disbanding the AIS and pardoning its fighters was aimed primarily at weakening the FIS. FIS leaders, 'Abbasi Madani and 'Abd al-Qadir Boukhamkham supported Bouteflika's initiative, while others — 'Ali Belhaj and 'Ali Jeddi — had reservations. FIS leaders in exile, such as Kabir and Anwar Haddam, also adopted conflicting positions. The effects of these differences could be seen in a statement issued by the spokesperson for the FIS coordination council, which disassociated the FIS from the "naive political positions adopted by some of its members inside Algeria and abroad." Referring to reports that the presidential pardon included Kabir, Huwaydi asserted that by excluding mention of other FIS leaders, the reports, if true, showed that the FIS was still being subjected to government pressure, and that the authorities were exploiting the front's weakness in an attempt to dismantle it completely.[101] The controversy over the National Reconciliation Law among FIS members resurfaced in a statement issued in October by Ja'far Houari, a member of the FIS overseas executive committee headed by Kabir, in which he reneged on his former support of Bouteflika's reconciliation policy.[102]

Anwar Haddam, who had been jailed in the US since 1995 (see *MECS* 1995, p. 119) on charges of belonging to a terrorist organization, won a case contesting his deportation before the Board of Immigration Appeals in November. He was granted political asylum and released from prison after an immigration tribunal found that the classified evidence against him did not support the accusation that he was a terrorist.[103]

THE CHANGING FORTUNES OF THE ISLAMIST MOVEMENTS

THE EFFECT OF THE ISRAELI WITHDRAWAL FROM SOUTH LEBANON

The Islamist movements registered a historic achievement in their otherwise gloomy situation during 2000 with the unconditional, non-negotiated Israeli withdrawal from South Lebanon in May. The Israeli withdrawal was interpreted as a victory for Hizballah, its philosophy and its strategy. It was perceived as proof that the Islamist option was the right solution to the 200-year-old Arab predicament. The Muslim nation (*umma*) was encouraged to follow the example of Hizballah in its struggle against the Zionist/Jewish enemy, who was revealed as either meek and cowardly, or as a "spider web" when confronted by death and destruction.[104]

Statements by the Iranian-based Islamic Revolution Guards Corps and the Martyr Foundation viewed the pullout as a victory "of right over evil" and as "a heavy blow to the weak body of...Zionism and...global arrogance" by an unflinching resistance.[105] In a message of congratulations to the Lebanese nation and the Islamic resistance movement,

Ayatollah 'Ali Khamene'i of Iran lauded Hizballah's victory over "the usurper Israeli enemy," emphasizing that it revealed that the solution to the Arab-Israeli conflict lay solely "in the logic of resistance, Jihad and devotion."[106]

In light of Hizballah's experience, Hamas openly called for the "Lebanonization" of the Palestinian territories, praising the Lebanese model of resistance and asserting that "the language of resistance" was the only language understood by the Israelis. Hamas confirmed Israeli press reports that the Hamas external command was working toward establishing a military wing in the territories by recruiting Palestinian students abroad. These students were reportedly sent to an Iranian military college, trained in various fighting techniques, and sent back to the Palestinian territories.[107] Hamas spokesperson Isma'il Abu Shanab said in an interview that Hamas hoped to replicate the Lebanese experience of Hizballah in the Palestinian territories.[108]

With this, the withdrawal posed new challenges to Hizballah. Having achieved its main objective and reaching a zenith of popular adulation, Hizballah faced an unclear future. It needed to define how to maintain its constituency and translate the popularity it had gained from resistance into formal representation and political power.[109] In an apparent shift of focus away from armed resistance to domestic concerns,[110] Hizballah Secretary-General Hasan Nasrallah portrayed the victory of his organization as the victory of all Lebanese.[111] However, Hizballah was unprepared to lay down its arms and turn into a purely political party.[112]

Sudanese Islamist commentator 'Abd al-Wahhab al-Effendi contended that the price Hizballah now had to pay for its victory and for its recognition as a legitimate party "almost without enemies inside Lebanon" was altering its identity as an Islamic party. It had to concede its ultimate objective of creating an Islamic state in Lebanon and acquiesce to coexistence with other political parties in a secular framework. The newly sanitized message of Hizballah, its newly adopted conciliatory approach vis-à-vis other Lebanese political forces, and its emphasis on the non-violence of its Islamist philosophy reflected considerable maturity along with a degree of shrewdness rarely found in Islamist movements. Effendi pointed out, however, that not much remained of its original Islamic message. Could this indicate the future direction of other Islamic movements, especially since many of them were moving toward adaptation to international circumstances and domination by local secular forces, Effendi wondered.[113]

The response of Hizballah to the Palestinian intifada reflected its predicament. Hizballah vociferously supported the intifada and urged the Palestinians to keep up its momentum. It also called on Arab countries on the eve of the Arab emergency summit convened in October (see below) to open their borders with Israel to those wishing to carry out resistance acts and jihad, to supply weapons to the Palestinian people for self-defense, and to sever relations with Israel.[114] Yet, Hizballah ruled out launching cross-border operations against Israel from Lebanese territory. Even the kidnapping of three Israeli soldiers on 7 October along the Lebanese border at the disputed Shab'a Farms area, and the abduction of an Israeli civilian a few days later were tangential to the uprising. They were meant primarily to serve as bargaining chips for the release of Hizballah and Lebanese detainees in Israel (see chapter on Lebanon).[115] While they demonstrated Hizballah's propensity for violent struggle, they also reflected its pressing need to remain in the political limelight, observed the Lebanese daily al-Mustaqbal. According to Hizballah deputy secretary-general, Shaykh Na'im Qasim, the need for cooperation between Hizballah and the Palestinian intifada in order "to confuse the enemy" was only one of three messages that Hizballah wanted to deliver by means of the abductions. The others were the release of Lebanese and other Arab prisoners still in Israeli jails, and the right of the organization to carry out operations in the Shab'a Farms region, which it viewed as occupied Lebanese territory.[116]

IMPROVED POSITION OF THE ISLAMISTS IN LIGHT OF THE AQSA INTIFADA

The Aqsa Intifada, which broke out at the end of September following a visit by Israeli opposition leader Ariel Sharon to the Temple Mount (al-Haram al-Sharif — the area of the holy mosques; see chapter on the Palestinian Authority), evoked an unprecedented demonstration of pan-Arab and pan-Islamic rage. This was accompanied by incitement and antisemitic manifestations throughout the Arab world and in Arab and Muslim communities globally. The intifada highlighted the religious dimension of the Arab-Israeli conflict, which is a basic tenet of Islamic fundamentalist ideology, blurring the lines between nationalist and Islamist discourse. This led to the radicalization of the discourse against Israel, Zionists and Jews, as well as against the US; elevated the status of Hamas and the Islamic Jihad in the Palestinian street; and enhanced cooperation between them and Hizballah. "Although Islamist political movements have taken a battering at the hands of Arab governments," wrote *The Economist*, "the rousing language of Islamic revival" continued to make inroads.[117]

Popular Expression of Support and Solidarity

Tens of thousands of people from all walks of life in the Arab and Muslim worlds took part in demonstrations to vent their fury at Israel and the US. They carried banners equating the swastika and the Star of David, chanted "Death to Israel" and, calling for jihad, burned Israeli and American flags.[118] Demonstrations were also held in Saudi Arabia where they are generally prohibited. Some of the demonstrations were dispersed by police when they threatened public order. In Jordan, the police dispersed protesters who tried to march on the Israeli embassy. Syrian police used tear gas to disperse angry demonstrators who tried to reach the US embassy in Damascus. Clashes between security forces and university students occurred in Cairo and Alexandria.[119] During a demonstration led by the Muslim Brotherhood at Cairo University on 16 October, a mobile phone was used to call Shaykh Ahmad Yasin, leader of Hamas in Gaza. Yasin's response was broadcast to the students over a loudspeaker.[120] Addressing a rally in Tehran, Hamas leader Khalid Mash'al declared that the State of Israel should be destroyed and praised the Iranian supreme leader Khamene'i for calling on the Islamic world to wage jihad against the Jewish state.[121]

This "demonstration of rage," wrote London-based Islamist scholar Azzam Tamimi, was "an expression of hostility and hatred for a project that is seen by Arabs and Muslims alike as an imperialist invasion aimed at sustaining the weakness and even paralysis of the Muslim umma."[122] The strong Arab and Muslim reactions elicited by the intifada were further proof of the capacity of the religious dimension to mobilize Muslims worldwide. Palestinian anthropologist Rema Hamami and sociologist Salim Tamari of Bir Zeit University claimed that "the idea of shared sovereignty over the Haram al-Sharif proposed by Israeli prime minister Ehud Barak in the Israeli-Palestinian negotiations at Camp David in July exposed the sensitive religious dimension of the conflict — control over a sacred site deeply contested by Arabs and Israelis. That "the protests would take on a religious character" was inevitable. Strong media emphasis on the religious dimension of the uprising, Hamami and Tamari asserted, also reinforced popular notions in Israel, in the Arab world and in Muslim communities in the West that the Israeli-Palestinian conflict was "a Jewish-Muslim conflict: eternal and insoluble."[123]

The demonstrations were also directed against the US, not only for its allegedly biased role as peace process mediator but as a reflection of anti-Western sentiment. The US was perceived as leading an anti-Islamic and anti-Arab struggle in collaboration with Israel and Zionism. In Egypt, acts of vandalism were carried out against American targets. An act that seemed to symbolize opposition to American support of Israel was the destruction of a Kentucky Fried Chicken outlet.[124] Egyptian students in Cairo also vented their anger on the British-based supermarket chain, Sainsbury, erroneously thought to be owned by Jews; stores were damaged and some of the firm's three thousand employees were injured.[125] Cars and property were also destroyed by demonstrators in Amman.[126] Hamas sympathizers in Gaza and Nablus attacked several cafes and stores, reportedly owned by PA officials, which sold alcoholic beverages.[127]

Two attempts on the lives of Israeli embassy staff members occurred in Amman on 19 November and 6 December, amidst heightened public pressure on the Jordanian authorities to close down the embassy altogether. Two previously unknown groups claimed responsibility for the first attack: the Jordan Islamic Resistance Movement, and "The Group of the Warrior Ahmad Daqamsa" (Daqamsa was the Jordanian soldier who shot dead seven Israeli schoolgirls and injured several others in the Baqura area in northern Jordan in March 1997; see *MECS* 1997, pp. 477–78).[128] Two other groups claimed responsibility for the second shooting, vowing that more would follow until Jordan severed diplomatic relations with Israel. The Muslim Brotherhood — the largest opposition political movement — warned after the second incident that so long as Israeli diplomats were present in Jordan, they were bound to be vulnerable to attacks by Jordanians retaliating against Israel's brutal attempt to suppress the Palestinian uprising.[129]

Enhanced PLO Cooperation with the Islamists

Religion played a major role in the first weeks of the uprising, as a rallying and symbolic force. Ironically, however, the participation of Hamas and other Islamic forces was minimal at first, confined essentially to raising the Hamas flag at funeral processions, observed Hamami and Tamari. With the PA driving the intifada, Hamas the main opponent of the PA regime, was initially reluctant to assume a central role.[130]

Operating in the context of the National and Islamic Higher Committee for the Follow-up of the Intifada, a united front of national and Islamist forces (composed of all the Palestinian Liberation Organization [PLO] political factions and the Palestinian Islamic movements — Hamas, Islamic Jihad and the Hamas-affiliated political party, Hizb al-Khalas), Hamas and Fath (the main PLO faction) agreed to coordinate activities relating to the continuation of the intifada and to issue all statements and leaflets under the umbrella of the unified intifada leadership.[131] About one hundred Hamas and Islamic Jihad activists were released, or escaped, from PA jails in Gaza and the West Bank after the first week of the uprising, removing a crucial divisive issue with the PA and enabling them to organize for a more active role.[132] Hamas leaders outside the PA became active during the intifada in heightening support for the Palestinian cause by meeting with Arab leaders. Khalid Mash'al, for example, visited Iran and Syria in October,[133] and Yemen in November.[134]

The intifada also highlighted and enhanced the influence of Hizballah in the PA and indirectly that of Iran. Yellow Hizballah flags were ubiquitous in Palestinian demonstrations and funerals at this time, even more numerous than the green flags of Hamas.[135]

Worldwide Islamist Support for the Intifada

Al-Muhajiroun, the Islamist group associated with the World Islamic Front for Jihad Against the Crusaders and the Jews founded in 1998 by Bin Ladin (see *MECS* 1998, pp. 129–30) and headed by Shaykh Omar Bakri Muhammad, together with the Islamic Observation Center, led by Egyptian Islamist Yasir al-Sirri, organized a mass demonstration in London in support of the intifada after Friday prayers on 13 October. Al-Muhajiroun also distributed a leaflet threatening to kill Jews and wage war against Israel and against American targets. Demonstrations were also organized by the Islamist London-based organization Hizb al-Tahrir, and by a hitherto unknown group, the Islamic League in Britain.[136]

In the US, the jailed leader of the Egyptian al-Jama'a al-Islamiyya, Shaykh 'Umar 'Abd al-Rahman, called on Muslim clerics to issue a fatwa sanctifying the indiscriminate killing of Jews. "Jihad is now a duty for the entire [Islamic] nation until Palestine and the Aqsa mosque are liberated and Jews are either pushed into their graves or back where they came from," the shaykh declared.[137] A similar call was issued by the Pakistani Islamist movement, Hizb al-Mujahidin, which also announced that a contingent of mujahidin was ready to leave for Palestine.[138]

In a telephone interview with the Italian daily, *Il Giornale*, al-Muhajiroun leader Bakri stated that the World Islamic Front was recruiting Muslim volunteers from Italy, France and Spain to fight for the liberation of Palestine from Israeli occupation. Thirty-four mujahidin had already been sent to the Middle East to provide support for the uprising, he said, but the real objective was to prepare 300 to 400 combatants ready to die for the cause. Bakri added that his and similar organizations helped Hamas, the Palestinian Jihad and any Islamic force by collecting funds, recruiting fighters and sometimes carrying out propaganda for these groups in Europe.[139]

Emir Shamil Basayev, leader of the Chechen rebels, declared that a group of 153 Chechen fighters was prepared to be sent to the Middle East, and that Jerusalem was the concern of all Muslims.[140] Shortly after the ICO conference in November, the Chechen fighting forces issued a "second Aqsa declaration," in which they renewed the pledge to fight the Jews, who were "defiling the Holy Land." More basically, however, the declaration reflected disappointment at the ICO failure to support their cause. It criticized the "so-called 'Islamic' organization which had conveniently removed the word 'jihad' from its dictionary," and "blessed the brutal disbeliever invasion of Chechnya, by conveniently declaring it a Russian internal affair."[141]

Bin Ladin, too, was dissatisfied by the overall Islamic response to the uprising; during a meeting with his followers in Afghanistan he reportedly expressed consternation over the impotence of the leaders of Islamist movements, who did not take advantage of the agitation by the Arab peoples to support the intifada more vigorously.[142]

Islamist Encouragement of Jihad and Sanctification of Martyrdom

Friday sermons at mosques throughout the Arab world were dominated by angry denunciations of what was termed Israeli brutality, and calls for jihad. Jihad was presented as a religious duty incumbent on all Muslims and the conflict was portrayed as a conflict between truth and falsehood.[143]

Shaykh Muhammad bin 'Abdallah Al Subayl, imam of the Grand Mosque in Mecca, called on Muslims worldwide to take up jihad against "the enemies of God and Islam and humanity" and stop "Zionist oppression and carnage against the Palestinians."[144] Similarly, Egyptian al-Azhar Grand Imam Shaykh Muhammad Sayyid al-Tantawi called for jihad against Israel: "As long as the Jews attack us, violate our rights and shed our blood, it is our duty to fight them." He justified the abduction in October of the three Israeli soldiers by Hizballah in this context.[145] Iraqi clerics, too, issued a fatwa calling for jihad.[146]

Hamas urged the Palestinian people to pursue the intifada and called on Arabs and Muslims worldwide to support it financially and morally out of a conviction that Israel and Jews should be destroyed.[147] Shaykh Ahmad Yasin, the spiritual leader of the movement, reiterated the notion that Israel was "a foreign body, imposed by force and will be eliminated by force."[148] Preaching from his mosque in Gaza, PA appointee Shaykh 'Abd al-Fattah called war inevitable, "part of a final, apocalyptic battle that will drive the Jews off Islamic soil." The intifada, he believed, would spread to the entire Arab world, and would unite all the Muslims behind the Palestinian struggle, driving all the Jews out of Palestine.[149]

Generally, these appeals remained unheeded. Jordanian commentator Ibrahim Alloush, present at a Friday sermon in the Central Mosque in Amman, argued that such sermons were "hypocritical rhetoric" typical of "the Islam of the sultans." He pointed out that "the preacher spoke up at length against Zionists, Arab regimes, and oppression" but in the end urged his listeners to disperse quietly and avoid demonstrations.[150]

Boycott as a Religious Duty

Muslim scholars also urged Arabs and Muslims around the world to boycott American and Israeli products. Grand Imam Tantawi asked the faithful to "boycott Israel and all who support it in aggression and injustice" and urged that a blacklist of goods be drawn up. The mufti of Egypt, Nasir Farid Wasil, issued a religious edict prohibiting Muslims from buying Israeli and American products. Boycotting Israeli and American products was a "religious Muslim duty" and "a form of jihad against oppression," the mufti said, and Muslims who buy or consume American and Israeli products must be considered "sinful" and "criminal."[151] Another Muslim scholar, Shaykh Yusuf al-Qaradawi of Qatar, issued a fatwa during an interview on 8 October with the al-Jazira TV, ruling that the boycott was a duty (farida) for Muslims. "Every dollar paid for these products is translated into a bullet fired at the heads and hearts of Palestinian children," Qaradawi said.[152]

In Beirut, spiritual leader Shaykh Muhammad Husayn Fadlallah also advocated a boycott of American and Israeli products. "This is the simplest expression of support for the Palestinians," he stated. To continue to use American products while the US government was "helping the Zionists murder our brothers and sisters in Palestine" was morally unacceptable. The US, Fadlallah charged, was the "most sinister enemy of Islam and Muslims." Boycotting American goods and products was not only an Islamic duty but "a form of self-defense."[153]

These appeals, however, remained on the declarative level only, wrote journalist Fu'ad Matar. When Arab governments failed to take steps to support the intifada, he argued, it was natural for people to turn to religious figures for guidance as to how to channel that anger into action. To what extent these clerical messages, issued in the form of statements or sermons, were made out of conviction, and to what extent they were merely designed to assuage public anger, was unclear. They might have been well-intentioned appeals, said Matar, but they were not binding fatwas. An effective fatwa would have to be issued by a conference of muftis from Arab and Islamic countries convened specifically to discuss the boycott issue and taking into account official dealings between the Arab countries and the US, he pointed out. "Such a flood of fatwas is liable to cause confusion."[154]

ATTACK ON THE USS COLE IN YEMEN

Suicide bombers attacked the US destroyer Cole on 12 October during a refueling stop in the Yemeni port of Aden. Two men in a small boat edged up to the ship at a fueling dock in the harbor and detonated a package of explosives. The explosion killed seventeen crew members and injured thirty-nine, opening a hole at the midsection of the ship.[155] A day later, another explosion occurred at the British embassy in San'a, causing only minor damage.[156] A man thought to belong to the militant Yemen-based Islamic Jihad was arrested a week later on suspicion of carrying out the second attack.[157]

The perpetrators of the first attack, however, proved to be more elusive. The US deployed over one hundred investigators in the Middle East to track down those responsible for the bombing. Relations between the US and Yemen were strained when the Americans were excluded from the direct interrogation of detainees, and friction arose over a number of related issues. This culminated in the denial by Yemen of landing rights to several small American ships and a helicopter, all ferrying FBI agents. In early December, however, an agreement was reached allowing FBI agents to observe the interrogation of suspects and witnesses.[158]

The investigation revolved around two Yemen-based groups, the Islamic Jihad and the Aden-Abyan Islamic Army. Early in the investigation, the plot against the Cole was revealed as having involved a network of cells, each with one to three operatives. Some seventy persons were immediately detained and questioned in connection with the incident. They included police and government officials at a regional government office in Lahij, north of Aden, where Islamists returning from the Afghan war had settled in the early 1990s. A false driver's license and other documents had been issued at that office to a man named 'Abdallah Ahmad Khalid al-Musawa, identified as the operational leader of the bombing and as one of the two men aboard the explosive-laden boat that rammed the Cole. The two men were natives of Yemen, both veterans of the Afghan war.[159]

Six men believed to be key accomplices were also detained. Yemeni president 'Ali 'Aballah Salih confirmed their detention in an interview on 25 October, identifying the detainees as leaders of the Islamic Jihad organization in Yemen. They were, he said, of Yemeni, Egyptian, Algerian and other nationalities. He refrained from providing any details on their ties with Bin Ladin, emphatically refuting suggestions that high-ranking Yemeni officials with known links to Bin Ladin dating back to the mid-1980s may have played a role in the bombing. According to Yemeni prime minister 'Abd al-Karim al-'Iryani, non-Yemenis organized the attack, namely "international terrorist elements," whom he identified as "Arab Afghans." They view Islam solely as a source of jihad against non-Muslims, with the US as a primary target, 'Iryani said.

Salih sharply criticized the US for failing to take better security measures to protect the Cole, while refuting a State Department report describing Yemen as "a safe haven for terrorists." The main conspirator behind the attack, he disclosed, was Muhammad 'Umar al-Harazi, born in Mecca of Saudi and Yemeni parentage, who had fought in Afghanistan. Harazi, who was still at large, had been sought by the FBI in connection with the 1998 American embassy bombings in East Africa. Allegedly operating from a base in the UAE, he had provided money, equipment and training for the Cole bombers. He was said to be the cousin of a man identified in a US federal indictment as the driver of the suicide truck bomb that had devastated the American embassy in Nairobi. At least two other individuals who allegedly played a major role in the planning and execution of the attack on the Cole were also still at large.[160]

The Cole attack had several parallels with the 1998 bombings of US embassies in Kenya and Tanzania, including the use of TNT, outside explosive specialists, sophisticated electrical detonation devices, and the activation of longstanding local terrorist cells. However, no explicit evidence tying Bin Ladin to the blast emerged. The strongest clue that Bin Ladin might have been the ultimate mastermind of the Cole attack was the relationship between Harazi and the suicide truck bomber in the Nairobi attack.[161]

By the end of November, the Yemeni investigators concluded the interrogation of the six Yemeni suspects and turned them over to the state prosecutor. The suspects, who were not publicly identified at that stage, were to be charged with carrying out the bombing, threatening state security, forming an armed band and possessing explosives.[162] Ignoring American appeals to delay the trial, since many investigation leads remained to be followed up, Yemen scheduled the trial of the six for January 2001. Included among the suspects were "Arab Afghans," who were said to have provided false documents, the skiff used in the attack, equipment and several hundred pounds of explosive.[163]

Although there was no solid indication that Bin Ladin was involved with the Cole attack, he was considered a potential suspect, and several American investigation agents focused exclusively on him.

According to Omar Bakri Muhammad, a group calling itself Muhammad's Army (Jaysh Muhammad, see above) claimed responsibility for the attacks on the American ship and on the explosion in the British embassy. Linking the two terrorist actions to the intifada, Bakri Muhammad vowed to continue the battle until Palestine was free of Jews and until US troops left the holy places in the Arabian Peninsula.[164] Arab commentators generally tended to think that since the attack coincided with the intifada, it was carried out in retaliation for American support of Israel.[165]

In a statement published in al-Sharq al-Awsat, Rifa'i Ahmad Taha, leader of the Egyptian al-Jama'a al-Islamiyya, and Bin Ladin's close associate, lauded the attack on the destroyer as adding a new dimension in the struggle against the West. Although he denied responsibility for the attack, he claimed that it could not be condemned because the target was military, "belonging to a hostile country that supports the Zionist entity."[166]

As the investigation continued, US forces in Bahrain, Qatar and Turkey were placed on the highest state of alert because of specific and credible threats of terrorism.[167] Unsubstantiated reports of a planned American retaliatory military action against Bin Ladin circulated until the end of the year, but none materialized.[168] Reacting to these reports, Bin Ladin and the Taliban promptly denied any involvement in the Cole attack. The Taliban, fearing that the world might blame Afghanistan for the attack and impose additional sanctions on it, insisted that "nobody living in Afghanistan had anything to do with the attack on the US warship." The Taliban information minister, Qudratullah

Jamal, insisted that Bin Ladin was under constant surveillance and could not have conducted such an operation from such a distance.[169] Several Pakistani newspapers published a brief statement by Bin Ladin on 17 October denying his involvement and warning the US against making any attempt on his life. Taliban officials, in simultaneous denials from Kabul, Islamabad and the office of their representative in New York, claimed that Bin Ladin's statement was fabricated by those who "want to malign Afghanistan and Bin Ladin and drag them into crimes they had not committed."[170]

In November, the Kuwaiti daily *al-Ra'y al-'Am* published a telephone conversation with Bin Ladin from his base in Afghanistan in which he denied any links with the perpetrators of the attack or with the suspects apprehended in Kuwait for planning suicide attacks on US military convoys (see above). The paper also quoted Bin Ladin as saying that neither he nor his followers had any intention of attacking US civil or military installations in any Arab country. A few days later, however, an Afghan, identified only as Muhammad, told a newspaper in Pakistan that he was instructed by Bin Ladin to deny these remarks and to reiterate Bin Ladin's adherence to his fatwa issued in 1998, declaring jihad against the US and Israel.[171] A similar denial was published a month later in a Saudi paper.[172] Other newspapers quoted Bin Ladin as expressing satisfaction with the attack.[173]

Former deputy director of the FBI Buck Revell explained in an interview that Bin Ladin was not involved in the specific day-to-day operations of his network, but that he was both the spiritual and the de facto leader of an international organization with infrastructures in many countries, including the US. Although the evidence did not lead to him conclusively, the modus operandi and the motive for the Cole incident fell within the confines of his agenda.[174] Another expert on terrorism, Harvey Kushner, stated that there was reason to believe that Bin Ladin had been investigating methods of launching attacks by sea, as he had tried to acquire small, personal submarines. The Cole attack was seen by American experts on terrorism as a significant technical advance over earlier terrorist attacks, such as the bombing of the US embassies in Kenya and Tanzania.[175]

By the end of the year, it became evident from the investigations in Yemen, as well as the investigations of the millennial conspiracy cases, that the bombing of the Cole had originally been part of Bin Ladin's broad plan to hit American targets worldwide during the first days of the millennium. An earlier plot to attack another American destroyer, USS The Sullivans, also during a refueling stop in Aden on 3 January, had gone awry when the attack boat with the explosives sank on its way to carry out its mission.[176]

The Cole incident spotlighted Yemen as a crossroads of international terrorism, its hinterland serving as a stronghold for Islamic terrorist groups with links to Bin Ladin. Yemen had been in the limelight in this context since the kidnapping of sixteen Westerners in December 1998, resulting in the killing of tourists, and the trial of leaders of the Aden-Abyan Islamic Army in 1999 (see *MECS* 1999, pp 124–26). The timing of the Cole attack two weeks after the outbreak of the intifada, and amidst strong anti-American manifestations in Arab countries, magnified its significance along with confusion and fear regarding the prospect of additional terrorist attacks.

CHANGING OF THE GUARD IN THE ISLAMIC CONFERENCE ORGANIZATION

Iran concluded its three-year presidential term of the ICO in 2000. The presidency won by Iran in 1997 (see *MECS* 1997, pp. 161–63) held significance for it as it symbolized the end of Iran's isolation in the Arab and Muslim worlds. Iran pinned many hopes in the ICO, aiming to turn it into a more vigorous and influential international organization and thereby enhance her own standing. As the end of the term approached, Iranian officials attempted to highlight the organization's achievements. Shortly before the ICO foreign ministers meeting in June (see below), the Iranian deputy foreign minister for international affairs, Mohammad Javad Zarif, cited the accomplishments of the organization with international crises, especially issues concerning Muslims since 1998. The ICO, he said, was active in Chechnya as an international intermediary organization; had put forward a peace initiative for Afghanistan, welcomed by all the belligerent parties; had held two meetings, in Jidda and Tehran, to review plans for implementing the Dialogue of Civilizations, the brainchild of President Khatami; expanded international cooperation with the European Union, the Organization for Security and Cooperation in Europe, and the Organization of African Unity, and had gained recognition as an active international organization.[177] Qatar took over the presidency of the ICO from Iran.

FOREIGN MINISTERS MEETING IN JUNE

The twenty-seventh annual meeting of ICO foreign ministers, held in Kuala Lumpur on 26–29 June, was attended by one thousand delegates from fifty-six member states. Malaysian prime minister Mahathir Muhammad, who delivered the keynote address on the conference theme, "Islam and Globalization," warned that the Muslim world was unprepared to face globalization and the information age because it was technologically "backward and poor." The Muslim world, he said, faced a series of threats: "petty rivalries"; information technology, which threatened Islamic values; e-commerce, which threatened to wipe out importers, distributors, retailers and government revenues, reducing Muslim states to the level of "banana republics"; the liberalization of trade by the Western world's banks, industries and services, which threatened to control the Muslim world economically and politically; and "punishment" for acts of frustration which the Western nations judged as "terrorism."

In a joint communiqué issued at the end of the meeting, the ministers pledged to enhance solidarity and economic ties, and to defend the rights of Muslims worldwide. The ministers condemned "international terrorism," such as air hijackings; expressed "deep concern" over the linkage of Islam and human rights violations in the international media; and reiterated support of the Islamic world for an independent Palestinian homeland with Jerusalem as its capital. They affirmed support for the Middle East peace process and called on the international community to exert pressure on Israel to halt its settlements in the occupied Arab territories. They also called on Muslim states that had taken steps toward establishing relations with Israel within the framework of the peace process to reconsider such moves and close offices until Israel complied with UN resolutions.

Regarding Chechnya, the ICO offered to play a role in facilitating contacts with Russia to bring about a peaceful settlement of the conflict. It also decided to send a fact-finding mission to investigate the plight of Filipino Muslims in the southern Philippines, and agreed to a proposal to include Malaysia and Brunei in its six-member committee monitoring the situation in the southern Philippines.

On economic issues, which were given prominence at the meeting for the first time, the ICO agreed to take prompt steps to upgrade economic cooperation between Muslim nations with the ultimate aim of creating a common Islamic market.

Some one hundred resolutions and documents on various political, economic, social and cultural issues were ratified by the foreign ministers. Turkey was unusually active in the meeting. It proposed the candidacy of one of its veteran diplomats and an adviser at the foreign ministry, Yasar Yakis, for the position of ICO secretary-general. But Moroccan statesman 'Abd al-Wahid Belqaziz was selected as the new secretary-general, replacing 'Azzadin al-Laraki, whose term was due to end in 2000.[178]

THE NOVEMBER ICO SUMMIT IN DOHA: FOCUS ON THE INTIFADA

Three issues of contention nearly caused the Iranian, Saudi and Bahraini leaders to stay away from the summit: Qatar's retention of its low-level ties with Israel; Bahrain's longstanding maritime border dispute with Qatar; and Egypt's anger over the critical reportage of the Qatar-based al-Jazira TV satellite channel. Ultimately, however, the summit was held as scheduled on 12-14 November in Doha, after Qatar submitted to pressure to sever its relations with Israel (see chapter on inter-Arab relations).

The continuing Palestinian intifada gave rise to expectations among Arabs and Muslims alike that the summit would constitute an important milestone in the history of the organization and the Muslim world. "With no public forums through which to make their voices heard, Muslims have nowhere else to pin their hopes other than on their leaders," wrote al-Quds al-'Arabi on the eve of the summit.[179] As expected, the Palestinian issue headed the conference agenda. Although only six of a total of eighty-seven items on the agenda related to the conflict — namely, Jerusalem, the Golan Heights, Lebanese territory still under Israeli occupation, Lebanese citizens held in Israeli jails, the ICO Jerusalem Fund, and the Middle East peace process — they dominated the summit.

Along with the expectations, however, was the sober realization that the three-day summit was unlikely to produce any practical resolutions on Palestine.[180] Talal Salman, publisher of the Beirut-based al-Safir, attributed the weakness of the Muslim states to the fact that Islam, as Arabism before it, had weakened as an ideological force for unity. "In many cases, it, too, has turned into a burden — especially since political Islam has been abused to...a degree that repelled most Muslims, and turned into a weapon in the hands of the enemies of Islam." However, Egyptian Islamist columnist Fahmi Huwaydi asserted in al-Sharq al-Awsat that even if the summit achieved nothing more than forcing Qatar to close down the Israeli mission, it was worth convening. In his view, summits — whether Arab or Islamic — were never devoid of value, even if their achievements were modest and fell far short of the nation's aspirations. Assuming that the liberation of Palestine from Israeli occupation was a goal on which the Muslim nation was agreed, he argued, any measure to support Palestinian rights and condemn Israeli aggression was a step in the right direction. Any form of resistance became a jihad serving the ultimate goal. Stone-throwing, political and diplomatic condemnation, cutting off all relations with Israel — all were legitimate steps, Huwaydi concluded.[181]

Appeals to the conference included one by the secretary-general of the Jordanian-based al-Quds Committee, who called on participants to take practical steps toward the liberation of Jerusalem and Palestine, such as severing political and economic ties with Israel and contributing financial aid to the al-Quds Fund.[182] Another appeal came from Hamas spiritual leader Shaykh Yasin, who urged Muslim states to "wake up from their long dormancy" and demanded action rather than the verbage of denunciation and condemnation; financial support; and Muslim volunteers to carry out jihad in Palestine.[183] Palestinian civic leaders and political activists also sent an appeal in the same vein.[184]

In his address to the summit, Iranian President Khatami, defined Israel as a "terrorist, racist Zionist regime" and proposed deciding upon the following measures:

(1) Unequivocal condemnation of the systematic crimes of the Zionist regime against Palestinians;

(2) Comprehensive sanctions on Israel by Islamic countries;

(3) Creation of a comprehensive mechanism to support the intifada;

(4) Attempt at formation of an international war crimes tribunal for occupied Palestine under the auspices of the UN;

(5) Diplomatic coordination for the establishment of an impartial fact-finding mission for the tragic events in occupied Palestine;

(6) Prevention of the economic blockade against the Palestinian people;

(7) Support for the establishment of the state of Palestine with Jerusalem as its capital.[185]

Crown Prince 'Abdallah of Saudi Arabia urged Muslim countries to freeze or drastically curtail their relations with Israel. In a warning to the US, he also called on Muslim leaders to break off relations with any country that opens an embassy in Jerusalem. UN Secretary-General Kofi Annan counseled restraint, urging participants not to promote violence and hatred.

Despite the show of support for the Palestinian cause, the delegates were split on how to show their displeasure with Israel. Some of the more traditionally hostile states, such as Iran, Syria and Sudan, called for a full boycott of Israel. However, twenty of the ICO members — most of them African and Central Asian nations, and led by Egypt, Turkey and Jordan — openly rejected the more radical calls for a complete severing of relations with Israel.

The final communiqué "invited" the member states to reduce their contacts with Israel and stop all forms of normalization, and urged the US administration to "revise its biased stance" toward Israel. The statement also supported Palestinian and Arab appeals for the formation of a UN peacekeeping force to protect Palestinians in the West Bank and Gaza.[186]

While the Palestine question may have dominated the public declarations, it was in its approach to Iraq that the ICO made a qualitative breakthrough. The Iraqi issue, namely, relations with Kuwait and the need to implement relevant UN resolutions, was among the vast array of items on the original conference agenda.[187] The summit called on Iraq to implement the commitments contained in the resolutions and to enter into a comprehensive dialogue with the Security Council in order to bring about the lifting of the sanctions. It also mandated the emir of Qatar, Shaykh Hamad bin Khalifa Al Thani, in his capacity as the newly elected chair of the ICO, to establish the appropriate groundwork for resolving the existing disputes between Iraq and Kuwait.

An appeal sent to the conference by the Taliban demanding once again the Afghanistan seat in the ICO — another bid to expand international recognition — was apparently not discussed.[188]

Meeting on the sidelines of the conference, Arab foreign ministers held their first follow-up meeting since the Arab summit of 21–22 October (see chapter on inter-Arab relations). A committee comprising Egypt, Syria, Saudi Arabia, Lebanon, Tunisia, Morocco, Jordan and Palestine discussed methods of collecting and distributing the $1bn. al-Aqsa Fund and the Jerusalem Intifada Fund approved by the summit.[189]

Summing up, the pan-Arab al-Quds al-'Arabi saw little cause for satisfaction over the contribution made by the Islamic summit, claiming that the "poetic" statements it issued in support of the intifada were never intended to be put into practice. However, the paper said, the softened attitude toward Iraq, and the decision to establish an Islamic Court of Justice to settle disputes among member states, were two aspects that differentiated it from previous summits.[190]

According to the UAE daily al-Khalij, the Islamic summit emulated the earlier Arab summit in Cairo in failing to take serious steps to counter Israeli aggression and American support for it. The Arab summit, it claimed gave priority to narrow interests over collective Arab interests, thereby squandering an opportunity to take effective action, which it concealed by a carefully worded communiqué. "The Islamic summit followed suit, labeling itself 'the al-Aqsa summit,' upping the rhetoric a little, but committing the member states to nothing."[191]

Palestinian journalist Khalid Amayreh defined the outcome of the two summits as "virtually a big, fat zero," writing that "in both cases, the member states, whether individually or collectively, demonstrated a startling degree of impotence, incompetence and powerlessness."[192] The Palestinian Islamist weekly al-Manar reproached Arab leaders for delays in turning over funding. All the declarations about donations to the Palestinians, it contended, were aimed at assuaging the rage of the Arab public. The paper accused Arab leaders of weakening the PA, suffocating the intifada and increasing the pressure on the Palestinian people by withholding the donations.[193]

Complying with the summit decision to demand the creation of a war crimes tribunal to probe "Israeli crimes," an ICO delegation led by Qatari foreign minister, Shaykh Hamad bin Jasim bin Jabir Al Thani, arrived in New York on 27 November to discuss the issue with Kofi Annan and member states of the Security Council.[194]

RALLYING AROUND JERUSALEM

Prior to the outbreak of the intifada, opposition to the Camp David negotiations and to the proposal reiterated by the US to transfer its embassy in Israel from Tel Aviv to Jerusalem evoked angry reactions from most Islamist movements in 2000. The national popular assembly for the support of Jerusalem and Palestine in Jordan, composed of various political groups, declared its a priori rejection of any concessions that the Palestinian delegation might make during the negotiations. Supporters of the Muslim Brotherhood in Zarqa staged a rally on 12 August to protest the American intention to transfer its embassy to Jerusalem. Following Friday prayers that day, hundreds of protesters shouted anti-Israeli and anti-US slogans calling for jihad to liberate Jerusalem from Israeli occupation. Hamas leader Isma'il Abu Shanab called the American decision a declaration of war against the Palestinians and their "most cherished holy place," in that the Americans would be seizing Palestinian land to build their embassy. 'Abdallah Shallah, secretary-general of Islamic Jihad, also announced that the relocation of the embassy would amount to a declaration of war on the Palestinian people, and, in line with Hizballah's stance, threatened to retaliate.[195]

Iran launched a diplomatic campaign within the Muslim world on the Jerusalem issue immediately after the failure of the Camp David-2 negotiations. Khatami, in his capacity as ICO president, sent several envoys to member states in early August, urging them to adopt a firm stance on the issue.[196] The eighteenth meeting of the ICO Jerusalem Committee, held in Agadir, Morocco on 28 August, confirmed its support for a Palestinian state with sovereignty over Arab Jerusalem and all the holy Islamic and Christian shrines.[197]

Jerusalem Day, observed in the Muslim world since 1979 on the last Friday of the month of Ramadan to express support for the Palestinian cause, was marked on 22 December by demonstrations in Iran, Syria and Lebanon denouncing Israel and the US and encouraging the continuation of the intifada.[198] The Iranian embassy in Damascus organized a two-day meeting named "Resistance, a symbol of freedom." It was attended by a delegation from the Iranian Islamic Consultative Assembly, leaders of Palestinian rejectionist organizations, ambassadors from the Muslim countries, and Palestinians living in Syria, Jordan and Lebanon.[199]

Islam remained "a powerful political symbol and ideology throughout much of the Muslim world," argued Middle East researcher John Esposito.[200] The reaction of the Muslim world to the intifada validated this assertion to a great extent. However, it also showed its limitations. While Islamism as an ideology and Islamist movements generally had lost much of their momentum, they remained forces to be reckoned with. This dichotomy was perhaps best reflected by the experience of Hizballah and the Islamic regime in Iran. The vibrant internal contest within Iran between conservatives and reformers, which culminated in the reformers' victory in the February parliamentary elections led pro-Islamist writer Fahmi Huwaydi to write: "The issue of Islam and democracy started to be seen in a new light....The old hostility was gone, and the issue was being looked at more neutrally, with some observers genuinely asking whether the two can actually coexist."[201]

Even al-Hayat's liberal editor, Hazim Saghiya, hoped that Khatami would show the boldness needed to establish an "Islamic democracy" along the lines of Europe's "Christian democracy" and possibly chart a "third Shi'ite way" that was neither subservient to the US nor blindly hostile to it.[202]

As much as Huwaydi's assertions and Saghiya's hope might be viable over the longer term, their immediate relevance paled in view of the impending threat of radical Islamic forces.

NOTES

For the place and frequency of publications cited here, and for the full name of the publication, news agency, radio station or monitoring service where an abbreviation is used, please see "List of Sources." Only in the case of more than one publication bearing the same name is the place of publication noted here.

1. "A Reading of the State of the Arab World by Jordan's Muslim Brothers," *MM*, 28 July 2000.
2. *Al-Ahali*, 17 May 2000.
3. *AW*, 10 February; *al-Watan al-'Arabi*, 7, 14, 21, 28 April 2000.
4. *Al-Hayat*, 16 April 2000.
5. *Al-Hayat*, 30 April 2000.

6. *Al-Mustaqbal al-'Arabi*, September 2000, pp. 140–50.
7. *Al-Watan al-'Arabi*, 21 April 2000.
8. *WP*, 21 February, 11 March, 24 December; *Ma'ariv*, 23 August; *al-Sharq al-Awsat*, 25 December 2000 (DR).
9. *NYT*, 4 January 2000.
10. *WP*, 18 May 2000.
11. *Al-'Arab al-Yawm*, 31 January; *al-Hayat*, 5 February, 21 April, 8 May, 20 July; *NYT*, 4, 29 February, 29 March; *Ha'aretz*, 21 April; *JT*, 23 May, 18 June, 13 July; R. Amman, 12 July 2000 (BBC Monitoring).
12. UPI, 18 September (BBC Monitoring); *Ha'aretz, The Times, The Independent, al-Hayat*, 19 September; *al-Sharq al-Awsat*, 4 December; *al-Ra'y*, 9 December (DR); *WP*, 24 December 2000.
13. *Ha'aretz*, 2 January; *al-Hayat*, 1, 14, 22 January, 2, 22 February; *NYT*, 27 January; *WP*, 27 January, 21 February 2000.
14. *Al-Hayat*, 28 June; *IHT*, 29 June 2000 (DR).
15. *NYT*, 7 December; *WP*, 8, 24 December 2000.
16. AP, 7 August 2000 (BBC Monitoring).
17. *Al-Hayat*, 7 August; *al-Sharq al-Awsat*, 19 November; AP, 20 December; *WP*, 31 December 2000 (BBC Monitoring).
18. *NYT*, 22 January; *al-Hayat*, 24 January, 22 April, 17 December; *al-Sharq al-Awsat*, 24 January, 24 December 2000.
19. *NYT*, 21 October, 7 November; *JP, The Nation* (Nairobi), 22 October (BBC Monitoring); *al-Sharq al-Awsat*, 26 October(DR); *al-Quds al-'Arabi*, 1 December 2000.
20. *NYT*, 13 May 2000.
21. AP, 21 July; *WP*, 27 July 2000.
22. TRUD, 8 August 2000 (DR).
23. ANSA, 17, 18 October (DR); *Corriere della Sera*, 17 October 2000 (BBC Monitoring).
24. *Gazeta Shqiptare*, 1 November 2000 (BBC Monitoring).
25. *The Times*, 19 November; *al-Sharq al-Awsat*, 23 November 2000 (DR).
26. AP, 28 December 2000 (BBC Monitoring).
27. ITAR-TASS, 4, 14 April; 22 May; 19 July; 29 August (DR); Interfax, 8 August (DR); *The News*, 28 September 2000 (DR).
28. Interfax, 22 May; 31 August 2000 (DR).
29. DPA, 29 August (BBC Monitoring); Letter to the executive director of AP, 6 September 2000 (MSANEWS).
30. ITAR-TASS, 14 November 2000 (DR).
31. ITAR-TASS, 28 December (BBC Monitoring); *Ha'aretz*, 29 December 2000.
32. ITAR-TASS, 19 May, 23 July (DR); Interfax, 25 August 2000 (DR).
33. UPI, 29 November 2000 (BBC Monitoring).
34. *IHT*, 29 June 2000 (DR).
35. *Manila Philippine Daily Inquirer*, 9 August (DR); *DT*, 21 December 2000.
36. *Al-Sharq al-Awsat*, 8, 11, 20 November 2000 (DR).
37. *Al-Sharq al-Awsat*, 11 November 2000 (DR).
38. *Al-Ra'y al-'Amm*, 13 November; *al-Hayat, al-Watan*, 14 November 2000 (*MM*).
39. *WP*, 9 June 2000.
40. *NYT*, 6 August 2000.
41. *Al-Sharq al-Awsat*, 8 July, 13 September; IRNA, 25 July 2000 (DR).
42. *Al-Sharq al-Awsat*, 13 September 2000.
43. *Hatzofeh*, 29 November 2000.
44. AFP, 21 January 2000 (DR).
45. *Al-Sharq al-Awsat*, 27 January; IRNA, 27 May; *The Times*, 18 June; Voice of the Islamic Republic of Iran, 10 July (DR); *The News*, 15 July; 26 October; UPI, 10 November 2000 (BBC Monitoring).
46. *The Nation* (Islamabad), 23 December 2000 (DR).

47. AFP, 19 May (DR); *The News, Jang,* 30 May 2000 (DR).
48. AFP, 23 July 2000 (DR).
49. *NYT,* 21 September; *Pakistan,* 10 October 2000 (BBC Monitoring).
50. UPI, 4 November 2000 (BBC Monitoring).
51. AP, DPA, 2 November; *Pakistan,* 3 November 2000 (BBC Monitoring).
52. AP, 30 November 2000 (BBC Monitoring).
53. *The News,* 18 April; *Jang,* 23 April (DR); *WP,* 9 May 2000.
54. *Nawa-i-Waqt,* 19 April 2000 (DR).
55. *Nawa-i-Waqt,* 18 April 2000 (DR).
56. *Jang,* 1 April 2000 (DR).
57. *The Pioneer,* 16 July 2000 (DR).
58. AFP, 16 August 2000 (DR).
59. *Pakistan,* 18 September 2000 (BBC Monitoring).
60. *Al-Sharq al-Awsat,* 12 November; *The Guardian,* 24 November 2000.
61. *The News,* 27 October (DR); *al-Sharq al-Awsat,* 6 December (DR) 2000.
62. *The News,* 29 October 2000 (DR).
63. *Milliyet,* 16 November 2000 (DR).
64. *Al-Sharq al-Awsat,* 6 December (DR); UPI, 29 November, 16, 21 December (BBC Monitoring); CNN, 13 December 2000.
65. *The Guardian,* 7 November; ITAR-TASS, 14 November 2000 (DR).
66. *Pakistan,* 29 June 2000 (DR).
67. *The Pioneer,* 16 July; *The News,* 17 July 2000 (DR).
68. AFP, 14 April 2000 (DR).
69. *Nawa-i-Waqt,* 4 April; *The Nation* (Islamabad), 1 June 2000 (DR).
70. *Nawa-i-Waqt,* 12 April; *The Nation* (Islamabad), 1 June 2000 (DR).
71. *Nawa-i-Waqt,* 3 May; *Jang,* 30 June (DR); *The Guardian,* 28 July; *The Ottawa Citizen,* 30 July; *al-Quds al-'Arabi,* 1 August (BBC Monitoring); *al-Sharq al-Awsat,* 7 August 2000 (DR).
72. *The News,* 17 July 2000 (DR).
73. UPI, 20 October 2000 (BBC Monitoring).
74. *The Pioneer,* 19 July 2000 (DR).
75. *The Hindu,* 5 April; *The Telegraph,* 24 May; *The Pioneer,* 19 July 2000 (DR).
76. AFP, 24, 25, 27 May, 23 July, 6 August; ITAR-TASS, 26 May, 8 December 2000 (DR).
77. UPI, 5 October 2000 (BBC Monitoring).
78. *Nezavisimaya Gazeta,* 27 October (DR); *The Times,* 28 October 2000.
79. Interfax, 18 October (DR); UPI, 18 October 2000 (BBC Monitoring).
80. IRNA, 20 December (DR); *WP,* AP, 20 December (BBC Monitoring); *DT,* 21 December; *The Nation* (Islamabad), 23 December 2000 (DR).
81. Al-Muhajiroun press release, "Hands off Bin Ladin and Afghanistan, United Nations of America: Continuous Onslaught against Muslims," 20 December 2000 (MSANEWS).
82. *IHT,* 5 July (BBC Monitoring); *The Ottawa Citizen,* 30 July (BBC Monitoring); *The News,* 31 July (DR); *Newsweek,* 7 August 2000.
83. *Al-Sharq al-Awsat, al-Hayat, al-Quds al-'Arabi,* 31 January 2000 (*MM*).
84. *AW,* 4 May 2000.
85. *Al-Sharq al-Awsat,* 6, 7 February 2000 (DR).
86. *Al-Sharq al-Awsat,* 8 February 2000 (DR).
87. *IHT,* 5 July 2000 (BBC Monitoring).
88. *Al-Sharq al-Awsat,* 13 August 2000 (DR).
89. *Al-Sharq al-Awsat,* 19 June (*MM*), 25 June 2000 (DR).
90. *Al-Hayat,* 15, 22 June, 23 August (*MM*); *al-Quds al-'Arabi,* 19 June (*MM*) 2000.
91. *Al-Sharq al-Awsat,* 24 June 2000 (DR).
92. *Al-Sharq al-Awsat,* 19 June (*MM*), 25 June 2000 (DR).
93. Al-Jazira Satellite TV, 21 September (BBC Monitoring); *al-Quds al-'Arabi,* 23 September 2000.

94. *Al-Sharq al-Awsat*, 13, 14 November 2000 (DR).
95. *Al-Ayyam* (Ramallah), 22 January 2000 (DR).
96. *JT*, 19 January; *al-Safir,* 24 January 2000 (DR).
97. *JT*, 4 July 2000.
98. *Al-Quds*, 17 July (DR); *al-Majd*, 4 September 2000 (DR).
99. *Al-Dustur,* 14 November 2000 (DR).
100. *Al-Hayat, al-Sharq al-Awsat*, 14 January (*MM*); *WP*, 17 January; *AW*, 20 January; *al-Quds al-'Arabi,* 20 January (*MM*); *NYT,* 27 January 2000.
101. *Al-Sharq al-Awsat*, 18 January 2000 (*MM*).
102. *Al-Sharq al-Awsat*, 30 October 2000 (DR).
103. American Arab Anti-Discrimination Committee (ADC), Action alert No. 41, 1 December (MSANEWS); *Al-Sharq al-Awsat*, 4 December; ADC press release, 7 December (MSANEWS); CAIR alert No. 278, 8 December (MSANEWS); *al-Hayat*, 9 December; *WP*, 12 December 2000.
104. Statements by Hasan Nasrallah on Jerusalem Day, 31 December 1999 and after the Israeli withdrawal on 26 May 2000 <www.hizbollah.org>.
105. IRNA, 24 May 2000 (DR).
106. *Kayhan*, 24 May (DR); IRNA, 25, 27 May 2000 (DR).
107. Reuven Paz, "Hamas's Lessons From Lebanon," *Peacewatch*, No. 262, 25 May 2000.
108. *Al-Majalla*, 12 November 2000 (DR).
109. *WP,* 26 May; *AW*, 8 June; *al-Majalla*, 18 June 2000 (DR).
110. Steven Hecker, "Hizballah and the Upcoming Lebanese Elections: Shifting Priorities," *Policy Watch* No. 481, 18 August 2000.
111. Nasrallah statement, 26 May 2000 <www.hizbollah.org.>.
112. *Al-Sharq al-Awsat*, 7, 8 July (DR); IRNA, 9 July (DR); *al-Mustaqbal*, 10 July (*MM*) 2000).
113. *Al-Quds al-'Arabi,* 6 September 2000 (*MM*).
114. *Future News*, 5 October 2000 (MSANEWS); Hizballah TV, 20 October 2000 (BBC Monitoring).
115. *MM*, 9 October; *NYT*, 10 October; *WP*, 17 October, 24 November; Michael Young, "Hizballah Outside and In," *MERIP*, press information note 37, 26 October 2000.
116. *Al-Mustaqbal*, 31 October 2000 (*MM*).
117. *The Economist*, 21 October 2000.
118. *Al-Hayat al-Jadida,* 1 October; *al-Liwa*, 4 October; *al-'Iraq*, 5 October; *The Economist*, 7 October; *JP*, 17 October; *Ha'aretz*, 9, 17, 18, 25 October; *Filastin al-Muslima*, November 2000.
119. IAP-Net, "Imam of Mecca's Grand Sacred Mosque Calls for Jihad against Zionist Carnage," 10 October (MSANEWS); *Arabia News* <www.ArabiaNews.com>, 13 October (MSANEWS); *AW*, 19 October; *al-Haramayn*, No. 47, 5 November 2000 (MSANEWS).
120. *AW*, 26 October 2000.
121. AFP, 5 October (BBC Monitoring); *al-Hayat al-Jadida*, 5 October 2000.
122. Azzam Tamimi, "The Days of Rage and the Beginning of the End," 8 November 2000 (MSANEWS).
123. Rema Hamami and Salim Tamari, "Anatomy of Another Rebellion," *MERIP*, Vol. 30, No. 4 (Winter 2000), p. 7.
124. *AW*, 19 October 2000.
125. *DT*, 17 October, 27 December 2000; *Ha'aretz*, 3 January 2001.
126. *JT*, 25 October 2000.
127. *Al-Ayyam*, 15 October; Hamami and Tamari, "Anatomy of Another Rebellion," p. 1; Chris Hedges, "The New Palestinian Revolt," *FA*, January 2001 (MSANEWS).
128. *AW*, 23 November 2000.
129. *Al-Sharq al-Awsat, al-Quds al-'Arabi*, 6 December 2000 (*MM*).
130. Hamami and Tamari, "Anatomy of Another Rebellion," p. 13.
131. IAP-Net, 4 November 2000 (MSANEWS); <www.iap.org>.

132. *Al-Ayyam*, 9 October (DR); al-Jazira TV, 13 October (BBC Monitoring); *The Economist*, 21 October 2000.
133. *AW*, 19 October 2000.
134. Yemen TV, 4 November 2000 (BBC Monitoring).
135. IAP-Net, 16 October 2000 (MSANEWS).
136. *Al-Sharq al-Awsat*, 14 October (DR); JP, 17 October; *DT,* 19 October; *The Jewish Chronicle*, 27 October 2000.
137. CNN, 5 October; *JP*, 6 October 2000.
138. *Pakistan*, 18 October 2000 (DR).
139. *Il Giornale*, 14 October 2000.
140. Statement by Shamil Basayev, *Sawt al-Qoqaz*, 10 October 2000 (MSANEWS).
141. *Sawt al-Qoqaz,* 24 November 2000 (MSANEWS).
142. *NYT, al-Hayat*, 5 November 2000.
143. *Al-Hayat al-Jadida*, 1, 2, 3, 8, 9, 14, 15, 21, 22, 24 October; *AW*, 19 October 2000.
144. IAP-Net, "Imam of Mecca's Grand Sacred Mosque calls for Jihad against Zionist Carnage," 10 October 2000 (MSANEWS).
145. *Al-Hayat al-Jadida*, 10, 11, 12 October 2000.
146. *Al-'Iraq*, 12 October; *al-Hayat al-Jadida*, 15 October 2000.
147. Hamas statements, 3, 15, 26 October, 9 November, <www.palestine-info.org.>; *al-Hayat al-Jadida, La Stampa,* 14 October 2000 (BBC Monitoring).
148. *Al-Hayat al-Jadida*, 11 October 2000.
149. *Yedi'ot Aharonot*, 16 October; Hedges, "The New Palestinian Revolt," *FA*, January 2001 (MSNEWS).
150. Ibrahim Alloush, A report from the street battles of Amman, *Free Arab Voice*, (private website) October 6, 2000.
151. MENA, 16 October 2000 (DR).
152. *Al-Hayat al-Jadida*, 9 October; *al-'Arabi*, 29 October; al-Jazira TV, 28 November (DR).
153. *Al-Hayat al-Jadida*, 9, 14, 19, 23, 27, 31 October; *JP*, 17 October; *AW*, 19 October; *al-Ahram*, 23 October; *Ha'aretz*, 25 October, 3, 8 November; IAP-Net, 29 November; *al-Ayyam*, 5 December; *al-Quds al-'Arabi, al-Sharq al-Awsat*, 6 December; <www.arabicnews.com>, 23 December 2000.
154. *Al-Sharq al-Awsat*, 6 December 2000 *(MM).*
155. AP, 12, 28 October (BBC Monitoring); *Ha'aretz, MM*, 13 October; *The Times*, 15 October; *al-Sharq al-Awsat*, 6 December 2000 (DR).
156. *DT*, 14 October; *Ha'aretz,* 15 October 2000.
157. *The Guardian*, 19 October 2000.
158. CNN, 14 October; *AW*, 19 October; *NYT, al-Hayat*, 29 October; 1 November; *WP*, 25 October, 2 November, 7 December; *al-Mustaqbal, al-Sharq al-Awsat*, 3 November 2000 *(MM).*
159. *NYT*, 26 October, 9, 26 November; *WP*, 26 October, 1, 17, 20 November; *al-Hayat,* 27 October, 2 November 2000.
160. *WP*, 26 October, 7 December; *NYT*, 26 October, 13, 15 December; *Ha'aretz*, 27 October; AP, 28 October (BBC Monitoring); *al-Hayat*, 9, 11 December; *IHT*, 16 December; *al-Sharq al-Awsat*, 24 December 2000 (DR).
161. *WP*, 20 November, 3 December; *IHT*, 27 November 2000.
162. *WP*, 27 November, 3 December 2000.
163. *WP*, 7 December; *NYT*, 13 December; *al-Sharq al-Awsat*, 24 December 2000 (DR).
164. *Il Giornale*, 14 October 2000.
165. *MM*, 13 October; *AW*, 19 October 2000.
166. *Al-Sharq al-Awsat*, 12 November 2000 (DR).
167. *WP*, 26 October; CNN, 24 October 2000.
168. *Jang*, 17 October; *WP*, 3 December 2000.
169. *The News*, 17 October (DR); *The Times*, 28 October 2000.
170. *The Guardian*, *NYT*, UPI, 18 October 2000 (BBC Monitoring).

171. DPA, *al-Ra'y al-'Amm*, 13 November; *The News*, 15 November 2000 (DR).
172. *Al-Watan*, 12 December (BBC Monitoring) 2000.
173. *Al-Hayat*, 4, 5 November; *NYT*, 5 November 2000.
174. CNN, 19 October 2000.
175. *The Guardian*, 19 October 2000.
176. *WP*, 24 December 2000.
177. IRNA, 12 June 2000 (DR).
178. Malaysian News Agency, 27 June (BBC Monitoring); IRNA, 27 June (DR); ITAR-TASS, 28 June; *Saudi Gazette*, 29 June (BBC Monitoring); *The Nation* (Islamabad), 29 June (DR); DPA, 30 June (DR); Islamic Republic of Iran Network 1, 30 June 2000 (BBC Monitoring).
179. *Al-Quds al-'Arabi*, 6 November 2000 (*MM*).
180. *Al-Quds al-'Arabi*, 13 November 2000 (*MM*).
181. *Al-Hayat, al-Sharq al-Awsat, al-Safir*, 13 November 2000 (*MM*).
182. IRNA, 9 November 2000 (MSANEWS).
183. IAP-Net, 12 November 2000 (MSANEWS).
184. IAP-Net, 11 November 2000 (MSANEWS).
185. IRNA, 13 November 2000 (DR).
186. *WP*, 12 November; *NYT*, 13 November 2000.
187. *Al-Sharq al-Awsat, al-Quds al-'Arabi, al-Hayat*, 8, 9 November (*MM*); *AW*, 9 November; *al-Safir*, 10 November 2000 (*MM*).
188. IRNA, 8 November (DR); *Pakistan*, 12 November 2000 (BBC Monitoring).
189. *Al-Quds*, 13 November; *al-Hayat, al-Mustaqbal, al-Ahram, JT*, 14 November (*MM*); IRNA, 14 November (DR); *Ma'ariv*, 15 November 2000.
190. *Al-Quds al-'Arabi*, 15 November 2000 (*MM*).
191. *Al-Khalij*, 15 November 2000 (*MM*).
192. *Palestine Times*, No. 114, December 2000.
193. *Al-Manar*, 11 December — *Middle East Media Research Institute*, Dispatch No. 178, 16 January 2001.
194. IRNA, 27 November (DR); AFP, 27 November (MSANEWS); *Iran News*, 28 November 2000 (BBC Monitoring).
195. *Al-Dustur*, 25 July (DR); *al-Safir*, 2 August; *al-Istiqlal*, 7 August (BBC Monitoring); *JT*, 13 August 2000.
196. *TT*, 26 July; IRNA, 2 August; DPA, 2, 3 August 2000 (BBC Monitoring).
197. IRNA, 19 September 2000 (DR).
198. AP, 22 December 2000.
199. IRNA, 24 December 2000 (DR).
200. John Esposito, "The Next American President," *Middle East Insight*, November 2000.
201. *Al-Sharq al-Awsat*, 22, 28 February 2000 (*MM*).
202. *Al-Hayat*, 23 February 2000 (*MM*).

Economic Developments in the Middle East and North Africa

PAUL RIVLIN

The huge increase in oil revenues that occurred in 2000 had major effects on the economies of the Gulf states, Algeria and Libya, and to a lesser extent on other, more diversified oil-producing economies. Many countries in the region, including the Gulf oil producers, continued to implement economic reform programs and benefited from so doing. In Turkey, and to a lesser extent in Egypt and Lebanon, the banks faced difficulties as a result of structural weaknesses and economic policies. The problems posed by rapid population and labor force growth continued to threaten living standards and political stability. There was also some evidence of a rise in the number of people in the region living in poverty in the late 1990s. Egypt, Tunisia and Jordan benefited from an increase in tourism from the European Union (EU) as the economy there expanded. EU demand rose for agricultural and certain industrial goods produced in the Middle East and North Africa. However, the prospects for tourism, investment and trade in Israel, the Palestinian Authority (PA) and Jordan worsened following the outbreak of the Palestinian intifada in September 2000 (see chapter on the PA). This, together with financial difficulties in Egypt and Lebanon, resulted in higher risk assessment ratios for some countries in the region by foreign credit agencies.

OIL PRICES

In 2000, on an annual average basis, the OPEC basket price for oil was 58% higher than in 1999 when it had already risen by 42% (see Table 1). The sharp increase in oil prices in 2000 was even more dramatic considering that the OPEC basket price had fallen to below $10/barrel (b) in December 1998. Although oil prices increased sharply during 1998 and early 1999, prices had been running at their lowest levels since 1973, prior to the Arab oil embargo late that year. In many respects, the price of oil in 1999 and especially in 2000, was the result of the preceding price collapse. The latter led to a large number of well closures and a reduction in oil exploration and production in non-OPEC countries. Low prices stimulated oil demand, and reduced investment in new oil exploration and production, thus putting pressure on prices. OPEC also restricted production in order to push prices up.[1]

OIL REVENUES

The increase in oil revenues in 2000 was mainly due to higher prices but increased production also played a role. This was in contrast with 1999, when Middle East OPEC production declined slightly.[2] Table 2 shows that in 2000 oil revenues in the Middle East OPEC rose by 71%. In the Gulf Cooperation Council (GCC) countries they rose by 62%.[3]

In constant 2000 prices, Middle East OPEC revenues peaked at $456bn. in 1980 and were at their lowest, almost $81bn., in 1986.[4] In per capita terms, oil revenues in Middle East OPEC countries averaged $5,310 in 1980, $746 in 1986, $705 in 1999 and $1,200 in 2000. The rise in 2000 was dramatic but it should be viewed in context. Given the population increase in the region, oil revenues needed to increase so as to maintain their per capita level.[5] The US Department of Energy's Energy Information Administration (EIA) estimates for Middle East OPEC oil export revenues for 2000 showed that oil export revenues were at their highest level in real terms since 1984, the year before the oil price collapse of 1985/1986 (see *MECS* 1984–85, pp. 259–75; 1986, pp. 227–42). This massive inflow of oil revenues helped the balance of payments, budgets, and overall economic conditions in those countries.

Countries of the GCC generally based their 2000 budgets on a $15/b oil price, more than $12/b less than actual oil prices in 2000. Maintaining fiscal discipline and economic reform efforts, however, remained important for most OPEC countries; the question remained whether the rise in oil export revenues would make it easier for countries to delay various reforms and economic liberalization.[6]

OIL PRODUCTION

Middle East members of OPEC increased their average annual production by 1.4m. b/d or 6.8% in 2000, following a fall of 418,000 or 2% in 1999. Output in Saudi Arabia rose by 8.8% after a 6% decline in 1999. Nearly half of the rise was accounted for by Saudi Arabia, which produced 38% of Middle East OPEC oil in 2000 (see Table 3).

ECONOMIC GROWTH

The increase in oil revenues, based on higher oil production, led to a sharp rise in growth rates in the Gulf states, listed in Table 3. The exception was Bahrain, that produced little oil. Overall growth in the GCC was 5.8% in 2000, compared with 2% in 1999 and 0% in 1998. Outside the Gulf, the pattern was mixed, with the diversified economies in Western Asia, as a group, experiencing a second year of decelerating growth. According to the UN Economic and Social Commission for West Asia (UNESCWA), this growth rate was not fast enough to absorb the increase in the labor force and as a result unemployment rose.[7] This was likely to have had implications for poverty levels in the region (see below). In North Africa, Algeria and Libya benefited from increased oil revenues but the non-oil states did much less well. Growth in Tunisia decelerated as a result of drought and the recovery in Morocco was very modest.

FINANCIAL DEVELOPMENTS

The sharp increase in oil revenues had significant effects on government budgets, as shown in Table 5. All of the GCC states were estimated to have had budget surpluses in 2000, following large deficits in most of them in 1999. In Egypt and Jordan, tough fiscal policies resulted in reductions in the deficits measured as shares of GDP. In Lebanon, Yemen and the PA, budget deficits widened (see Table 5). The increase in oil revenues in 2000, unlike that in 1996, did not cause governments in the GCC to ease fiscal policies and abandon structural reform programs. Although state investment rose, it did so much less than revenues and the role of the private sector increased as a result of an improved investment climate.[8]

According to the 2000 International Monetary Fund (IMF) report on international capital markets, total net private capital inflows into emerging markets in 1999 amounted to $80.5bn., or 7% higher than the previous year. Private capital flows replaced official flows as the largest external source of capital for developing countries and accounted for 80% of net flows to all developing countries. In the Middle East and North Africa, it was estimated that net resource inflows nearly doubled in 1999 to $20bn. This compared with a net resource flow of only $3bn. in 1995 and an average of $8.7bn. for the period 1990–1997. Most of the increase in 1999 consisted of an $8bn. rise in private flows. This did not result in an equivalent increase in foreign investment; the region accounted for only 1.7% of total foreign investment in 2000, compared to 0.6% in 1992 (see Table 6).

Two factors enabled this inflow to take place. The first was the rise in oil prices, which resulted in a huge transfer of income from the rest of the world to the region. The second was the improvement in the region's financial framework as a result of reform and liberalization. In recent years, the GCC countries partially opened up their capital markets to the rest of the world. Many countries in the region had strengthened their financial systems, mainly by reducing government deficits. This did not prevent the development of problems in the banking sectors in several countries.[9]

BANKING CRISES

In November, Turkey was hit by a major banking crisis that reflected weaknesses in the banking system and, more generally, problems of economic management during a period of rapid inflation. The government wanted to privatize banks in the public sector, including those that it had to take over when they collapsed financially. Not all of the Turkish banks were able to adjust to a new reality. This meant that they would have to rely on alternative sources of income rather than on interest earned on government bills or recycling the debt of sister companies (see section on Turkey, below). In Lebanon, a bloated banking system relied on government debt to earn a living. With a very large budget deficit, the government issued a continuous stream of treasury bills with high interest rates. Banks found it easier to recycle this debt than to lend funds to the private sector. In Egypt, banks were affected by a liquidity squeeze, falling foreign exchange reserves and a slowdown in the level of economic activity. These problems highlighted the slow pace of privatization and the lack of transparency in management and control of the financial sector (see section on Egypt below).[10]

POVERTY

There is evidence that during the late 1990s the number of people living in poverty in the Middle East and North Africa region rose. A World Bank (WB) study showed that the number of poor, defined as those living on an income below $1.08 a day at 1993 purchasing power parity (ppp) rose from 5m. in 1996 to 5.5m. in 1998. The share of the population that lived in poverty rose from 1.8% to 1.9%.

This followed a sharp fall in poverty in the late 1980s, when the number fell from 9.3m. (4.3%) to 5.7m. (2.4%) in 1990. Using a wider definition of poverty, those who lived at below $2.15 per day on a 1993 ppp basis, the number rose from 60.6m. in 1996 to 62.4m. in 1998. The share fell slightly from 22.2% to 21.9%. It should be noted that the share of those living in poverty, according to both definitions, was much lower in the

Middle East than in any other part of the developing world, including those areas that have experienced faster growth such as East Asia and Latin America.[11] The main reasons for the rise in poverty were the effects of stabilization and structural change programs.[12]

ECONOMIC PERFORMANCE IN 2000 BY COUNTRY

ALGERIA

Following years of civil war and low oil prices, Algeria experienced significant economic improvements in 1999 and 2000. Gross domestic product (GDP) growth in 2000 was estimated at 5.2% by the EIA and at 3.8% by the Algerian Central Bank.[13]

The combination of higher oil prices and slightly higher oil exports in 2000 compared to 1999 resulted in much higher oil export revenues. According to the EIA, they reached an estimated $10.6bn. in 2000, an increase of 63% on 1999 and more than double their 1998 level. Algeria exported around one million b/d of crude oil. Oil and gas continued to account for more than 90% of Algerian export earnings, and about 30% of GDP.

The rise in oil revenues relieved pressures on government finances (Algeria's budget had been based on an assumed oil price of $15/b, some $13/b lower than actual prices) and helped the country's overall economic growth. Foreign reserves increased sharply, external debt fell, the current account balance improved dramatically and pressures on government finances were reduced. Unemployment remained high at around 30% and low-level political and labor unrest continued. A large black market equal to up to 20% of the GDP, and continued weakness in the non-oil economy (a severe drought hurt the agricultural sector in 2000) prevailed.

In September 2000, the IMF urged the government to proceed with privatization and banking reform, lower tariffs aimed at protecting domestic industry and reduce dependence on hydrocarbons. It praised the Algerian government for its strong fiscal discipline (and careful monetary policy as well), and for permitting a devaluation of the dinar against the dollar. Finally, the IMF noted that high oil prices gave Algeria an opportunity to make progress on implementing reforms and address the country's many problems.

BAHRAIN

The economy grew by an estimated 5.2% in 2000 compared with an average of 4% in the preceding four years. Crude oil and natural gas accounted for 16.6% of GDP in 1999, the lowest share among member states of the GCC. The current account of the balance of payments improved from a deficit of $300m. in 1999 to a surplus of $700m. in 2000. Bahrain benefited from the increase in oil income elsewhere in the Gulf, which has strengthened its position as a trading center.[14]

EGYPT

The economy grew at an estimated rate of 3.9% in 2000, compared with 6% in 1999.[15] The slowdown was the result of a monetary squeeze that reduced investment and consumption growth rates. The origins of the squeeze lay in the balance of payments difficulties experienced in 1998. In that year, government spending on social programs was high and in 1998/99, the budget deficit rose to 4.2% of GDP, compared with 1% in 1997/98. In 1999, the government introduced more restrictive policies, but was determined to maintain the exchange rate of the Egyptian pound against the US dollar, and thus sold dollars and bought pounds. This led to a scarcity of pounds, reflected in the fact that the narrowly defined money supply (M1) rose by only 1% in 1999, following a 20% expansion in 1998. The shortage of liquidity continued in 2000. In January, the overnight interest rate on Egyptian pounds rose to 17%.[16]

Another reason for the shortage of liquidity was large government allocations to a number of high prestige investment projects. One such project was the multi-billion dollar New Valley project, designed to resettle millions of Egyptians from the Nile Valley in the desert. Another was the Al Salaam irrigation project in the Western Sinai desert. According to an international investment bank, the scale of these projects was so large that financing them put strains on the state budget, on interest rates and on the balance of payments.[17]

In April, President Husni Mubarak ordered the repayment of $7.5bn. to local companies. In May, Prime Minister 'Atif 'Ubayd admitted that the liquidity shortage was partly due to delays in making repayments and said that the privatization program would be accelerated in order to bring in funds. The economy was also affected by depressed corporate results, rumors that prominent business leaders had fled abroad and debt problems in the private sector. In June, the Supreme State Security Court found thirty-one business owners, bankers and members of parliament guilty of profiteering, and the illegal acquisition of public funds. This, together with the liquidity problems, caused fears about the stability of the banks.[18]

IRAN

The Iranian economy which was heavily reliant on oil export revenues for about 80% of total export earnings, and 40%–50% of the government budget, was hit hard by low oil prices during 1998 and early 1999. From 2000, with the rebound in oil prices, the economy began to recover. In the financial year (March–March) 1999/2000, GDP grew by 2.5%; in 2000, it was estimated to have grown by 5.1%.[19]

In 2000, Iranian oil export revenues were estimated at $23.2bn., up 67% from 1999 and more than double 1998 revenues. To cope with its economic problems, the government proposed a variety of privatization and other restructuring and diversification measures. It also set up a "stabilization fund" for above-budget oil revenues.

The 2000–2001 budget was based on a forecast price of oil at around $16/b, compared to an average price for Iranian crude oil of around $26/b during 2000. Budget deficits were a chronic problem, in part due to large-scale state subsidies — totaling some $11bn. per year — including foodstuffs and especially gasoline. In June 2000, the Majlis rejected a proposal to raise gasoline prices by 28%, opting instead for a 10% increase. Higher oil export revenues helped to ease this situation as Iran gained around $800m. in revenues for every $1/b increase in the price of its oil. Iran was estimated to have exported about 2.5m. b/d of crude oil in 2000, slightly more than in 1999. In 2000, Iran experienced a severe drought and as a result food imports rose. The drought also resulted in power shortages.

A sweeping critique of the management of the economy made by one of the most distinguished Iranian economists, Jahangir Amuzegar, highlights many of the problems facing the economy during 2000. According to Amuzegar, the Khatami administration had neither a clear economic philosophy nor a credible economic agenda. The only blueprint — the Economic Rehabilitation Plan — announced after a year's preparation and input from many experts, was a list of well-known problems that were to be relieved by superficial remedies. Disjointed reform proposals were either not vigorously pushed by the government or blocked by the conservative-dominated Majlis due to ineffective leadership. Furthermore, the side effects of the economic policies, were not properly forecast at the time, and thus tended to aggravate already difficult economic conditions.

The Central Bank's efforts to service the foreign debt and the already twice-rescheduled arrears in the face of declining oil revenues and falling foreign exchange reserves were made at the expense of imports. Drastic cuts in foreign supplies in turn starved local import-dependent industries of inputs and resulted in increased inflation. Deflationary measures designed to keep consumer prices in check resulted in reduced private liquidity and further deflation. Allowing the currency to depreciate in order to cover budget deficits and encourage non-oil exports undermined market confidence, squeezed private investment and encouraged capital flight. Disputes between economic officials on major policies (e.g., interest rates, exchange rates, money supply) reduced public trust in the government. In the end the president's main supporters — students, unemployed youth, women and intellectuals — had very limited praise for his administration's handling of the economy. They were hurt financially as the benefits of modest economic growth were still consumed largely by the *bazaari*s (private trade monopolists), the *bonyad*s (Islamic "charitable" foundations) and others close to the regime.

There were also successes: the reduction of external debt, financing of budget deficits through public borrowing instead of drawing on Central Bank credits, slowing the rate of inflation, signing a number of oil and gas contracts with foreign energy companies, the resumption by the WB of lending to Iran, infrastructure improvements, and the completion of some long-term projects. These went almost unnoticed because their impact on the daily life of ordinary people had not yet been felt.[20]

IRAQ

Since 1990, the economy shrank dramatically as a result of a decade of UN sanctions. In 2000, however, it was estimated to have grown by 15% due to increased oil export revenues.

Iraq continued to be subject to UN sanctions. These sanctions constrained both the dollar value that Iraq could export and also controlled how oil export revenues could be spent. (In December 1999, the limit on the revenues that Iraq could earn from oil exports — $5.3bn. per six months — was ended by the UN Security Council.) In March 2000, the Security Council voted to double the amount of money Iraq could spend on oil industry spare parts to $600m. every six months.[21]

Oil exports were estimated to have averaged 2.3m. b/d in 2000. Oil export revenues were estimated at $21.6bn. in 2000, up 89% from the $11.4bn. earned in 1999. Since late 1996, Iraqi oil production increased by over 2m. b/d — from 550,000 b/d in November 1996 to around 2.7m. b/d forecast for 2000. In 1997 and 1998, rapidly increasing Iraqi oil exports played a significant role in creating a world oil glut and causing a price collapse.

In late September 2000, the UN Compensation Commission awarded Kuwait $15.9bn. in damages stemming from the Iraqi invasion and occupation of Kuwait in 1990/1991. As part of a compromise, the commission also agreed to reduce the portion of Iraqi oil proceeds set aside for reparations from 30% to 25%. Since 1996, the UN "oil-for-food" program generated around $26bn., most of which was supposed to go to humanitarian efforts in Iraq, with the remainder going toward war compensation payments to Kuwait and others. The economic affairs committee of the Council of Ministers prohibited all state institutions from dealing in the US currency. Iraq also tried to transfer its UN-monitored escrow petroleum account from dollars to euros and to halt all foreign trade transactions in dollars. The aim was to minimize the influence the US had on the country's international economic and financial transactions, which were significantly curbed by the US-backed UN sanctions. The ban included all agreements and trade contracts concluded with foreign parties. The Central Bank of Iraq announced that it planned to buy European currencies including the French franc, the German mark, the Austrian schilling, the Dutch florin and the Italian lira against their equivalent in dollars.[22]

ISRAEL

In 2000, GDP grew by 5.9%, the fastest rate since 1968. This was entirely due to a huge surge in high-tech exports. Economic growth would have exceeded 6% but for the Palestinian intifada which affected tourism, construction and other sectors to a lesser extent. GDP per head rose by 2.5%. Inflation was zero as a result of a prolonged monetary and fiscal squeeze and the high external value of the shekel. The strong exchange rate was due to high real interest rates and inflows of funds due to large foreign investments in the high-tech sector. The budget deficit declined to 0.6% of GDP as a result of a prolonged squeeze on spending and much higher than expected tax revenues. The latter were largely due to the boom in the high-tech sector. The inflation and budget targets were undershot but although nominal interest rates were reduced by the Bank of Israel, high real rates and tight fiscal policy squeezed much of the economy with the exception of high-tech that relied on foreign funds. With the fall in share values on the NASDAQ in the last quarter of 2000, the high-tech sector also experienced a slowdown.

The acceleration of economic activity resulted in very rapid job creation — nearly 100,000 new jobs in the year ending in the third quarter of 2000 — but unemployment remained stable at a very high 9%. Industrial exports, excluding diamonds, rose by 25.4% compared with 7.2% in 1999. The current account deficit fell because exports increased much faster than imports.[23]

JORDAN

The first half of 2000 saw the emergence of some positive trends in the Jordanian economy, with GDP increasing at an estimated annual rate of 4%. Tourism revenues rose, as did public and private sector investment but the economy was affected by the Palestinian intifada in the final quarter of the year. As a result GDP was estimated to have increased by 2.5% in 2000. The budget deficit was on target at 6.5% of GDP. A fall in revenues in the second half of the year was matched by a cut in expenditure. The government was reluctant to reduce wages in a period of regional tension and so most of the reduction fell in the area of capital spending.[24]

Foreign investors were attracted by Jordanian membership in the World Trade Organization (WTO) which began in 1999 and by the so-called Qualified Economic Zones which give duty-free access to US markets for goods produced with minimal Israeli content.

KUWAIT

With oil revenues accounting for about 90%–95% of government income (and around

40%–50% of GDP), sharply increased oil prices since early 1999 obviously had positive implications for financial, budgetary, and economic conditions in Kuwait. In the fiscal year ending in June 2000, for instance, Kuwait's state oil company, the Kuwait Petroleum Corporation (KPC), earned a net profit of $2.6bn., nearly $800m. above previous projections. Kuwaiti crude oil prices were likely to have averaged $25/b in 2000, approximately double the $13/b currently being used to calculate the KPC financial statement (as well as the Kuwaiti budget). Following a serious recession in 1997 and 1998, the Kuwaiti economy grew by 5.5% in 2000. Oil export revenues were estimated at $17.7bn., 79% higher than in 1999 and more than double their 1998 level. Net crude oil exports in 2000 were estimated at about 1.9m. b/d, up slightly from 1.7m. b/d in 1999. Per capita oil export revenues, was estimated at $8,161 in 2000, or 70%–75% below levels reached in the mid- to late-1970s.[25]

LEBANON

The Lebanese economy continued to be plagued by high and rising public debt. Interest payments accounted for a very large share of government spending and were the main cause of the increase in the budget deficit. As a result of the high debt level, interest rates were high, despite the recession which plagued the economy. Unemployment was estimated at 20% in 2000, as a result of two years of virtual stagnation. The economy did not grow in 2000, although this was an improvement following a fall in GDP of 1% in 1999.[26]

LIBYA

Libya earned an estimated $12.5bn. from oil exports in 2000, up 69% from 1999 revenues and more than double 1998 earnings of $5.5bn. Oil export revenues accounted for about 98% of hard currency earnings and around 90% of government expenditures. Over the past several years, Libyan oil export production and export earnings were affected by UN and US sanctions imposed in the years following the 1988 bombing of Pan Am flight 103 over Lockerbie, Scotland. On 5 April 1999, Libya handed over the two suspects, prompting the UN (but not the US) to suspend sanctions. As a result of both sanctions and low oil prices, the Libyan economy barely grew in several years (0.6% growth in 1997, a decline of 1.5% in 1998, and 1.9% growth in 1999). GDP growth was expected by the EIA to reach 3.2%, and by the Economist Intelligence Unit (EIU) at 6.5%. Both sets of estimates also reflect an accelerating growth trend since 1998.[27]

Libya had been forced to adopt a more conservative fiscal policy and limit public infrastructure spending to a few main projects, such as the Great Man-Made River, a $25bn. project to bring water from underground aquifers beneath the Sahara to the Mediterranean coast. Given the rebound in oil prices (and the suspension of UN sanctions), the Libyan economic situation (and outlook) had improved somewhat. On the other hand, higher oil earnings threatened to remove some of the incentives for Libya to restrain spending and to implement needed economic reforms. Also, per capita oil export revenues in constant dollars are only 12% of 1980 levels, even with the 1999–2000 surge in prices. Libya continues its attempts at diversifying the economy away from oil and toward natural gas, and generally has kept government spending under tight control in recent years. Libya was expected to have exported around 1.2m. b/d of crude oil in 2000, up slightly from 1.1m. b/d in 1999.

MOROCCO

Morocco's real GDP grew by an estimated 0.7% in 2000, compared with a fall of 0.7% in 1999, when the country was hurt by a serious drought. In 2000, agricultural production, which accounted for a large share (around 17%–20%) of the economy and workforce (around 40%–50%), contracted by about 18%. Vulnerability to erratic rainfall patterns encouraged the government in its attempts at economic diversification, particularly towards manufacturing and services, including a strong tourism sector. The manufacturing sector accounted for about 17% of the economy. Progress in the privatization of state-owned companies, alleviation of poverty and unemployment, and deficit reduction, was slow although in late December 2000 the national telecommunications company was partially privatized. In 2000, an oil and gas discovery (of unknown magnitude) near the border with Algeria raised hopes that the energy import bill (of about $1bn.–$1.5bn. per year) could be reduced and that more foreign investment could be attracted.

Tight fiscal and monetary policies helped to reduce the fiscal deficit from 10% of GDP in the 1980s to less than 3%. Inflation was 1.9%. The trade deficit was $4.5bn. in 2000. (Morocco traditionally ran a merchandise trade deficit and a surplus on transfers — largely from worker remittances.) Foreign investment, which increased in 1999 to $1.9bn. (partly in response to government policies aimed at creating a positive environment for such investment) appears to have fallen once again in 2000.[28]

OMAN

The GDP was estimated to have increased by 4.6% in 2000 following a fall of 1% in 1999. The current account improved from a deficit of $200m. in 1999 to a surplus of $3.2bn. in 2000. Both of these developments were due to increased oil export revenues, which rose from $3.6bn. in 1999 to $6.7bn. in 2000, a rise of just over 85%. Net oil revenues in the state budget rose by 67% between 1999 and 2000 and the budget deficit declined 64%.[29] In 2000, Oman joined the WTO.[30]

THE PALESTINIAN AUTHORITY

After the economic and social crisis in 1996, caused by prolonged border closures in the early months of that year, the Palestinian economy entered a period of recovery. From early 1997 until September 2000, the recovery was marked by significant employment growth. The unemployment rate declined from an average of 25% in 1996 to about 11% in the first half of 2000. Economic improvement came to a halt at the end of September 2000 when the intifada broke out. Subsequently, the economy went into a massive decline. The closure of borders with Israel disrupted trade and led to large losses of labor income. Large-scale damage was inflicted on Palestinian infrastructure as a result of the violence. According to official Israeli sources, the number of Palestinians from the PA employed in Israel fell from 120,000 to 20,000-30,000 by November. This resulted in a $20m. loss of labor income per week. Commerce between Israel and the PA fell by more than 90% to an estimated $10m. per week. For a few days at the beginning of the unrest, the PA barred the movement of goods from Israel through the crossing points. The main result was a blow to the Palestinian economy and the restrictions were lifted shortly after they were imposed.[31]

A UN source estimated that the crisis had resulted in a 50% reduction in domestic productive activity in the period September–November 2000, valued at about $8m. a day. The UN also estimated that in 1999, Palestinian workers earned about $750m. from jobs in Israel and Israeli settlements and industrial zones. In the first half of 2000, an average of about 125,000 Palestinians were employed in Israeli-controlled areas on a daily basis. As a group, these workers earned about $3.4m. for each normal working day prior to the crisis. On an annualized basis, assuming no border closures and no change in the average number of workers or their average wage, Palestinian workers in Israel could have earned an estimated $822m. in the year 2000. Internal movement restrictions and border closures substantially reduced such income-generating opportunities in the last quarter of the year.

An immediate effect of the crisis was that about 110,000 workers formerly employed in Israel lost their jobs. Within days of its onset, the core unemployment rate rose from less than 11% to nearly 30% of the labor force. To this must be added the effect of the disruption in normal internal economic activity due to mobility restrictions and border closures. The combined effects raised unemployment in the PA to at least 40% of the labor force.

External trade was an important part of the Palestinian economy and had important effects on the size of the GDP, since the production of goods for export generated significant employment and income. The scarcity of resources and other inputs in the PA required the import of raw materials, equipment and machinery. Thus, the disruption of external trade reduced domestic production, income and employment.

The economic impact of the intifada came to about 10% of GDP in 2000. These losses were calculated in relation to the level of economic activity prevailing prior to the crisis, rather than in comparison to the maximum income-generating potential of the Palestinian economy. Total losses of income and production, at an annual rate, were estimated at about $3bn..

Prior to the crisis, there were approximately 70,000 unemployed Palestinians. As a result of the effects described above, it was estimated that another 190,000 persons lost their jobs. At the end of 2000, there were more than 260,000 unemployed persons in the PA. The average employed Palestinian supported himself/herself plus four other people, a high dependency ratio. Therefore, in addition to the negative impact on the livelihoods of 190,000 workers, the crisis reduced the income of 760,500 other Palestinians. In total, more than one million individuals — or about one-third of the population in the PA — were affected by mobility restrictions. If previously unemployed persons and their dependents are included — some 350,000 persons — the number of Palestinians affected came to 1.4m. or 45.5% of the population.

In addition to significant physical destruction of private and public assets — buildings, infrastructure, and vehicles — there have also been significant losses to the public sector in the form of lost revenues. Domestic income and VAT revenues have been reduced due to the lower levels of domestic income caused by disruptions in production and reduced labor flows to Israel. External revenues, mainly customs and VAT revenues associated with imports from Israel and abroad, have been reduced by lower commodity flows caused by movement restrictions and by reduced consumer demand. In 1999, 63% of all PA revenues were in the form of transfers of receipts collected by Israeli authorities under the terms of the 1994 Paris Protocol. Since early October, the clearance revenues transferred by Israel to the PA were well below the anticipated amount owed, seriously straining the liquidity position of the PA.

On the expenditure side, the PA has increased the level of spending to cope with the large number of killed and wounded Palestinians, the destruction of homes, and the rising needs generated by rising unemployment and hardship. The PA Ministry of Finance warned that the crisis would increase the budget deficit sharply in 2000, as a result of reduced revenues and higher spending. In 1999, some 55% of PA expenditures were for public employee salaries. Reduced revenue transfers would make it more difficult for the PA to provide regular salary payments for upwards of 115,000 public sector employees in November.[32]

There were also serious long-term effects, the most important of which was the decreased willingness of foreigners to invest in the PA or in Palestinian-Israeli industrial parks or joint ventures. They are likely to wait for a final settlement before risking investing again.

QATAR

GDP was forecast to increase by 4.6% in 2000, up from 3.3% growth in 1999. Oil remained the dominant sector of the economy, although natural gas became increasingly important and the government pushed diversification efforts. Oil accounted for some 70% of government revenues, and also had an impact on production of condensates and associated natural gas. Increased oil prices since early 1999 helped in several ways: the increase in revenues was used to balance the budget for the first time in twelve years, and to pay for a huge liquid natural gas and petrochemicals development program. Qatar has the third largest gas reserves in the world, after Russia and Iran. Qatar's oil export earnings for 2000 were estimated at $6.8bn., up 68% from 1999 and more than double their 1998 level. Until 2000, Qatar maintained relatively tight fiscal and monetary policies. The increase in oil revenues enabled the government to announce the resumption of several projects, including a new airport, which had been shelved for lack of funds, kept inflation under control, and helped to improve the balance of payments. Oil exports were estimated at 685,000 b/d of crude oil in 2000, up from 649,000 b/d in 1999.[33]

SAUDI ARABIA

In 2000, oil production averaged 8.8m. b/d compared with 7.8m. b/d in 1999. In 2000, Saudi Arabia was estimated to have earned about $67bn. in crude oil export revenues, up 76% from the $38bn. earned in 1999, and double 1998 earnings. The large increase in oil production was the main factor behind the sharp acceleration of economic growth.

The dramatic decline in oil revenues which Saudi Arabia experienced during 1998 and early 1999 represented a major challenge for the government (since oil export revenues account for nearly 90% of total Saudi export earnings, 70% of state revenues and 40% of GDP). The subsequent sharp increase in oil prices significantly improved Saudi Arabia's economic position, with 5.4% real GDP growth forecast for 2000, as well as a record current account surplus. On the other hand, despite the high level of oil prices, Saudi Arabia's per capita oil export revenues (in inflation adjusted dollars) remain far below high levels reached during the 1970s and early 1980s (about $2,352 per person today, versus $17,373 in 1980, for instance). This was due in large part to the fact that the Saudi population had more than doubled since 1980.[34]

Despite attempts to diversify its economy, Saudi Arabia remained heavily dependent on oil revenues. The oil price decline of 1998 and early 1999 came just as the Saudi economy appeared to be recovering from the 1990/91 Gulf War, and seriously hurt short-term economic and financial situations. The dramatic turnaround in Saudi oil revenues in 1999–2000 resulted in faster economic growth as well as greatly improved external trade and budgetary balances.

Saudi Arabia faced major economic challenges despite the recovery in oil revenues. For instance, the need to create jobs for young Saudis remained a challenge, as did reducing the $150bn.–$170bn. public debt, increasing capital investment in the infrastructure, overhauling the tax code, reducing state subsidies, privatizating state-owned firms, and diversifying the economy. Saudi Arabia's per capita oil export revenues (in constant dollars) were only around 14% of the peak reached in 1980. In 2000, GDP growth was estimated at 7.6%.

In the 2000–2005 development plan, the government accepted the need to reduce state involvement and increase private sector and foreign participation in the economy. However, it moved very slowly in this direction, largely due to fears of job losses for Saudi citizens, as well as resistance by the private sector and some members of the Saudi royal family. Large state corporations like Saudi Aramco (which had a monopoly on Saudi upstream oil development) and the Saudi Basic Industries Corporation (SABIC) dominate the Saudi economy. No state assets were sold to the private sector, and privatization was limited to allowing private firms to take on certain service functions.

Desire to join the WTO was behind some of the push toward economic liberalization in the country. Saudi Arabia had hoped to be admitted to the WTO by the end of 2000, although it appeared that this would be delayed by a variety of issues, including the degree to which Saudi Arabia was willing to increase market access to its banking, finance, and upstream oil sectors. Ultimately, WTO membership would likely result in significant changes to the Saudi economy, which was characterized by relatively high tariff rates, subsidies, and a variety of restrictions on the free market. The goal of WTO membership was in part due to Saudi desire to attract foreign investment (up to $200bn. over the next twenty years, according to Foreign Minister Prince Sa'ud al-Faysal), and in part to its push for new markets for the petrochemical industry. In November 1999, King Fahd stated that "the world is heading for...globalization" and that "it is no longer possible for [Saudi Arabia] to make slow progress." In the context of successfully becoming integrated into the global economy, Fahd also emphasized the importance of regional unity among Gulf states — economically, politically, and militarily. A customs union, for instance, among GCC countries, was agreed upon at the December 1999 GCC summit (see *MECS* 1999, pp. 103–107). The union was to take effect in March 2005. As it were, goods from GCC countries were exempt from all Saudi import duties, as long as 40% of their value had been added within the GCC, and the producing company was owned at least 51% by GCC citizens.

Saudi Arabia also had a policy known as "Saudiization," the goal of which was to increase employment of its own citizens by replacing 60% of the estimated 7.2m. foreign workers in the country. In order to do so, Saudi Arabia had stopped issuing work visas for certain jobs, moved to increase training for Saudi nationals, and set minimum requirements for the hiring of Saudi nationals by private companies. State subsidies and losses by unprofitable state-owned enterprises were large contributors to the Saudi budget deficit. The Finance Ministry called for an increased private sector role. The private sector accounts for around 40% of Saudi Arabia GDP (and 89% of employment), but only 5%–10% of those employed in the private sector were Saudi nationals. Saudi Arabia asked private companies to increase their Saudi staff by 25% over the coming year, and then by 5% per year after that.[35]

SUDAN

The economy grew by an estimated 7.2%, the fourth consecutive year of healthy growth. The quality of Sudanese economic data was not good and there was much uncertainty about how the economy had developed. Broadly speaking, in recent years, the economy was managed within guidelines determined by the IMF. In 2000, the economy benefited from a rise in oil income that particularly helped the balance of payments. Oil export revenues rose from $608m. in the first half of 1999 to $861m. in the first half of 2000, an increase of 42%. The total for 2000 may have reached $1.1bn., or about 70% of total exports. The completion of the Al-Jeili oil refinery reduced the need to import refined oil products and was one of the factors resulting in a trade surplus. The current account recorded a deficit because of the rise in profits remitted by international oil companies.[36]

Agriculture, which accounted for almost half of GDP did well in 2000, with sugar production up 32% on 1999 and cotton production 11% higher. Despite this, the UN World Food Program reported in January 2001 that 600,000 people in Sudan needed food aid and the number was growing.

SYRIA

The economy was estimated to have grown by 1.5% in 2000 following a 1.5% decline estimated for 1999. This improvement was due to the increase in oil revenues resulting from higher oil prices. Oil export revenues in the first quarter of 2000 rose by 50% over their level in the first quarter of 1999 and the EIU forecast that they would reach $3bn. in 2000, compared to $1.3bn. in 1998 and about $1.9bn. in 1999. Oil production was slightly lower in 2000 than in 1999, part of a long-term trend.[37] Oil accounted for between 55% and 60% of Syrian export earnings and more than one-third of its GDP.

Oil output and production continued to decline due to technological problems and depletion of oil reserves. Since peaking at 604,000 b/d in 1996, Syrian oil output had fallen steadily, to an estimated average for 2000 of 530,000 b/d, as older fields have reached near exhaustion levels. The decline is expected to continue over the next several years, while consumption rises, leading to a reduction in net oil exports. Syria hope to reverse this trend through intensified oil and gas exploration and production efforts.[38]

Syrian population growth rate was one of the highest in the world, as was that of its labor force. Some 200,000 new job seekers entered the labor market a year. According to official data, the unemployment rate in 2000 was 9.5% which meant that about 430,000 were without work. Among those aged 15 to 24, the problem was acute with unemployment reaching 72% in 1999. Most of the unemployed were illiterate or with a low level of education. These factors coupled with the fact that half of the labor force earned less than $100 a month in 1999, put pressure on the government to increase public sector wages. With the increase in revenues from oil exports, this became possible in 2000.

Higher revenues accruing to the government from oil were used to increase the salaries of 1.4m. state employees by 25% in May 2000.[39]

Agriculture, which accounted for about 30% of GDP and employed 32% of the labor force, suffered from the effects of severe drought and this limited the growth of the economy as a whole.

Plans were announced to legalize private sector banks and permit foreign investment in the financial sector. Privately owned banks were nationalized in 1963 and since then the financial sector was underdeveloped. Under the new regulations, banks in Syria would have a minimum of 25% government ownership and Syrian nationals or institutions would own at least 51% of the shares, with no individual having more than 5%. Foreigners or foreign institutions would be allowed to own up to 49% but would require approval from the prime minister. Syria also planned to establish a stock exchange, to float the Syrian pound and end the system of multiple exchange rates.[40]

According to a report quoting official sources, estimates of private savings abroad stood at $60bn. Other sources said the figure could have been as high as $100bn. The reforms were designed to help Syria repatriate some of these funds, but attracting both deposits and banks back to the domestic financial system was likely to prove challenging given the nature of Syrian bureaucracy and political uncertainty.[41] In 2000, the European Investment Bank extended its first development loan to Syria in ten years. This followed the completion of agreements with Germany to reschedule $572m. of debt. The $66m. loan was to be used for the development of the electricity network.[42]

TUNISIA

The Tunisian economy was estimated by the EIU to have grown by 4.7% in 2000, compared with 6.2% in 1999. The slowdown was due to a fall in agricultural production due to drought. Other sectors grew healthily: manufacturing by 5.8%, commercial services by 7%, tourism by 4.5%, transport by 5.5% and communications by 20%.

The economy, one of the strongest in the Arab world, grew by 5.7% on average in 1996–2000 while the population grew by about 1.1% a year. As a result, average living standards rose. Unemployment remained a serious problem as the labor force increased faster than the population. The government estimated unemployment at 15.5% in 2000.[43]

TURKEY

During the last ten days of November and in early December 2000, Turkish financial markets experienced a period of high volatility. The financial difficulties of one medium-sized bank, that was subsequently taken over by the government-controlled Savings Insurance Fund (managed by the Regulatory and Supervisory Board for Banking), and the sell-off by that bank of large stocks of government paper in the secondary market, led primary dealers to suspend the posting of the rates on government paper. This triggered massive capital outflows, in spite of the rise of interest rates to 100%-200%. At the same time, the Central Bank of Turkey increased the supply of net domestic financial assets well outside the range envisaged in the economic stabilization program, out of concerns for the effect that excessively high interest rates would have on the banking system. Those events, together with weaker international market sentiment for emerging economies, led to a loss of $6bn. of foreign exchange reserves. On 30 November, the Central Bank announced that it would stop providing liquidity to the market, halting in this way the loss of reserves. Interest rates, however, skyrocketed to over 1,000%. The pressure on financial markets eased only with the announcement of a tougher policy and the request for access to the IMF Supplemental Reserve Facility.[44]

During most of 2000, the stabilization program announced in December 1999 had made progress in strengthening public finances, lowering inflation, and reviving economic growth. The public sector primary balance (which excludes interest payments) moved from a deficit of 1.9% of GNP in 1999 to an officially projected surplus of 3% of GNP in 2000. The operational deficit (which includes interest payments) was estimated to have fallen even more, as a result of the drop in domestic interest rates. Consumer price inflation was projected to fall to about 38% in 2000, its lowest level since the mid-1980s, but still thirteen percentage points above target. GNP growth was expected to be somewhat above the program range of 5%–6%, sustained by strong domestic demand, after a year in which the economy had shrunk by 5.1%.[45]

However, the external account deficit was estimated to have widened from almost 1% of GNP in 1999 to about 5% of GNP in 2000. At least 2% of this increase was due to the rise in international oil prices, the appreciation of the dollar, which negatively affected Turkish competitiveness in European markets, and the rise in international interest rates. Thanks to increased confidence in macroeconomic policies, this deficit was readily financed for most of the year. Up to mid-November, international bond issues amounted to $7.5bn. (compared with a plan of $6bn. for 2000) and international reserves had increased by $3.5bn.

These developments reflected a combination of policy factors, the nature of the Turkish economy, and external shocks. The change in the monetary framework, coupled with the strong fiscal and structural reform package, resulted in the rapid fall in domestic interest rates early in 2000. While the introduction of a pre-announced exchange rate path provided an anchor for interest rates, the effect on inflation expectations was not as strong. This combination of a sharp decline in interest rates and inertia in inflation expectations boosted domestic demand to a level well-above program expectations. The surge in domestic demand and external shocks — the increase in international energy prices and interest rates, and the appreciation of the dollar vis-à-vis the euro — lay behind the deterioration of the external current account. In addition, delays in structural reform, and particularly in banking and privatization, emerged.

The reaction of financial markets to these developments was muted until late November. Then a crisis began to develop as a liquidity problem of some medium-sized banks, although its roots were deeper. The deterioration in the external current account and a weakening of confidence hit parts of the banking system as rises in interest rates caused a fall in banks profit margins due to a mismatch in the asset/liability composition. Following a major relaxation of liquidity, a disturbance in the inter-bank market resulted in a substantial loss of foreign reserves.

THE UAE

The UAE was expected to earn $20.7bn. in oil export revenues in 2000, up 73% from 1999 and more than double 1998 revenues. As with other OPEC countries, the sharp increase in oil prices of the past year significantly improved the UAE economic, trade, and budgetary situations. Real GDP was forecast to grow by 4.8% in 2000, compared to a 5% decline in 1998, while the current account has moved sharply into surplus. The UAE economy was more diversified than others in the GCC, and moved increasingly toward tourism, banking, re-exports, and information technology. The UAE was estimated to have exported about 2m. b/d in 2000, slightly higher than its 1999 level.[46]

TABLE 1: THE OPEC BASKET PRICE ANNUAL AVERAGE, 1997–2000 (Dollars per barrel)

1997	1998	1999	2000
18.68	12.28	17.47	27.60

SOURCE: *MEES*, 15 January 2001.

TABLE 2: MIDDLE EAST OPEC STATES: OIL REVENUES 1998–2000 ($ billions)

	1998	1999	2000
Algeria	4.8	6.5	11.0
Iran	19.5	13.9	23.6
Iraq	6.2	11.4	19.3
Kuwait	8.4	10.4	17.7
Qatar	2.9	4.1	6.7
Saudi Arabia	29.7	38.3	66.0
UAE	9.3	11.9	20.7
Total	80.2	96.5	165.0

SOURCE: US Department of Energy, *Energy Information Administration, OPEC Revenue Factsheet, September 1999*, April 2001.

TABLE 3: OPEC MIDDLE EAST OIL PRODUCTION (thousands of barrels a day)

	1998	1999	2000
Algeria	823	758	818
Iran	3,616	3,541	3,709
Iraq	2,115	2,542	2,520
Kuwait	1,990	1,901	2,094
Libya	1,352	1,328	1,421
Qatar	650	625	696
Saudi Arabia	8,110	7,662	8,336
UAE	2,190	2,071	2,217
Total	20,846	20,428	21,811

SOURCES: *MEES*, 15 February 1999, 12 February 2001.

TABLE 4: ANNUAL GROWTH RATE OF GDP IN THE UNESCWA REGION, 1998–2000 (percentages)

	1998	1999	2000
Bahrain	4.8	4.0	4.1
Kuwait	-1.8	0.5	3.6
Oman	2.7	-1.0	3.0
Qatar	8.4	3.5	6.0
Saudi Arabia	1.6	0.4	5.1
UAE	-7.1	8.3	10.2
GCC average	0.0	2.0	5.8
Egypt	5.6	6.0	5.0
Jordan	1.7	1.6	3.5
Lebanon	1.0	0.0	2.5
Syria	-1.8	1.5	2.5
West Bank and Gaza	9.6	7.0	-3.5
Diversified economies	5.4	3.9	3.6

SOURCE: UNESCWA, *Preliminary Overview of Economic Developments in the ESCWA Region in 2000* (New York: UN, 2000), p. 3 (hereinafter: UNESCWA, *Preliminary Overview*).

TABLE 5: BUDGET BALANCE/GDP IN THE UNESCWA REGION, 1998–2000 (percentages)

	1998	1999	2000
Bahrain	-6.5	-2.5	0.7
Kuwait	-5.9	4.3	7.1
Oman	-6.9	-7.7	0.5
Qatar	-4.5	-0.6	5.0
Saudi Arabia	-10.1	-7.0	1.0
UAE	-16.6	-14.8	1.0
Egypt	-1.0	-4.2	-3.6
Jordan	-6.9	-4.2	-2.7
Lebanon	-14.2	-14.5	-16.5
Yemen	-6.4	0.1	-1.7
West Bank and Gaza	-2.4	-1.2	-5.0

SOURCE: UNESCWA, *Preliminary Overview*, p. 9.

TABLE 6: NET PRIVATE CAPITAL FLOWS TO EMERGING MARKETS, 1992–99

	1992	1993	1994	1995	1996	1997	1998	1999
Worldwide Emerging Markets (WEM)								
Total Net Private Capital Inflows	112.6	172.1	136.3	226.9	215.9	147.6	75.1	80.5
Net Foreign Direct Investment	35.4	59.4	84.0	92.6	113.2	138.6	143.3	149.8
Net Portfolio Investment	56.1	84.4	109.6	36.9	77.8	52.9	8.5	23.3
Bank Loans and Other	21.0	28.3	-57.3	97.4	24.9	-44.0	-76.7	-92.5
Middle East								
Total Net Private Capital Inflows	33.7	22.3	18.6	9.1	5.6	14.6	19.9	20.6
(as percentage of WEM)	29.9	13.0	13.7	4.0	2.6	9.9	26.5	25.6
Net Foreign Direct Investment	0.2	3.5	5.4	4.6	1.4	2.3	2.0	2.6
(as percentage of WEM)	0.6	5.9	6.4	5.0	1.2	1.7	1.4	1.7
Net Portfolio Investment	12.7	5.1	7.6	3.8	3.0	3.3	6.7	7.3
(as percentage of WEM)	22.6	6.0	6.9	10.3	3.8	6.2	78.8	31.3
Bank Loans and Other	20.8	13.6	5.6	0.8	1.2	9.0	11.2	10.8
(as percentage of WEM)	99.0	48.1	-9.8	0.8	4.8	-20.5	-14.6	-11.7

SOURCE: IMF, *International Capital Markets, Developments, Prospects and Key Policy Issues* (Washington DC: IMF, September 2000).

NOTES

For the place and frequency of publications cited here, and for the full name of the publication, news agency, radio station or monitoring service where an abbreviation is used, please see "List of Sources." Only in the case of more than one publication bearing the same name is the place of publication noted here

1. Paul Rivlin, *World Oil and Energy Trends: Strategic Implications for the Middle East,* Jaffee Center Memorandum, No. 52 (September 2000), pp. 15–25.
2. UNESCWA, *Preliminary Overview of Economic Developments in the ESCWA Region in 2000* (New York: UN, 2000), p. 4.
3. <www.eia.doe.gov/cabs/opecrev.html>, October 2000.
4. Ibid.
5. Calculated from EIA, WB, *World Development Report 2000/2001* (New York: Oxford University Press for the WB, 2000), pp. 278–79; WB, *World Development Indicators* (Washington DC: WB, 2000), pp. 38–41; IMF, *International Financial Statistics Yearbook 1999* (Washington DC: IMF, 1999); *International Financial Statistics, January 2001* (Washington DC: IMF, 2001).
6. OPEC Revenues Fact Sheet, March 2001, <www.eia.doe.gov/cabs/opecrev.html>.
7. UNESCWA, *Preliminary Overview,* p. 2.
8. Ibid., p. 4.
9. *MEES,* October 2000.
10. *MEED,* 22 December 2000, pp. 21–24; *FT,* "Survey of Egypt," 10 May 2000.
11. Shaohua Chen and Martin Ravallion, "How Did the World's Poorest Fare in the 1990s?", *World Bank Policy Research Working Paper,* No. 2409 (August 2000), pp. 27–28.
12. Paul Rivlin, *Economic Policy Making and Practice in the Arab World* (Boulder CO: Lynne Rienner, 2001), Chapter 2.
13. *Country Analysis Brief,* Algeria, January 2001 <www.eia.doe.gov/emeu/cabs/ algeria.html>; *CR,* Algeria, January 2001.
14. *CR,* Bahrain, February 2001, pp. 6, 11.
15. *CR,* Egypt, November 2000, p. 5.
16. *CR,* Egypt, 1st quarter, 2000, p. 20.
17. *FT,* "Survey on Egypt," 10 May 2000.
18. *CR,* Egypt, November 2000, pp. 15–16.
19. <www.eia.doe.gov/emeu/cabs/iran.html>, September 2000.
20. *MEES,* 6 November 2000.
21. *Country Profile,* Iraq 2000, p.12.
22. *MEES,* 30 October 2000.
23. *Ha'aretz,* 2 January 2001.
24. UNESCWA, *Preliminary Overview,* pp. 6, 10; *CR,* Jordan, February 2001, pp. 5, 19.
25. <www.eia.doe.gov/emeu/cabs/kuwait.html>, August 2000.
26. UNESCWA, *Preliminary Overview,* pp. 6, 10.
27. <www.eia.doe.gov/emeu/cabs/libya.html>; *CR,* Libya, February 2001, p. 5.
28. *Country Analysis Brief,* Morocco, January 2001 <www.eia.doe.gov/emeu/cabs/ cabsme.html>.
29. *CR,* Oman, January 2001, pp. 5, 19, 31.
30. UNESCWA, *Preliminary Overview,* p. 4.
31. Israel Ministry of Finance, *Economic Research and State Revenue Division, Economic Outlook November 2000* <www.mfa.gov.il>.
32. UN, Office of the UN Special Co-ordinator, *The Impact on the Palestinian Economy of Confrontations, Mobility Restrictions and Border Closures,* 28 September–26 November 2000 <www.arts.mcgill.ca/mepp/untso>.
33. *CR,* Qatar, January 2001, pp. 25, 30, 35–39.

34. *Country Analysis Brief,* Saudi Arabia, November 2000 <www.eia.doe.gov/emeu/cabs/saudi.html>.
35. *CR,* Saudi Arabia, February 2001, p 11.
36. *CR,* Sudan, February 2001, pp. 5, 11, 17–22, 29.
37. *CR,* Syria, January 2001, pp. 5, 6, 29.
38. *Country Analysis Brief,* Syria, February 2001 <www.eia.doe.gov/emeu/cabs/syria.html>.
39. UNESCWA, *Preliminary Overview,* p. 6, 10.
40. *CR,* Syria, January 2001, pp. 27–28.
41. *MEES,* 11 December 2000, pp. B1 and B2.
42. *MEED,* 22 December 2000, p. 5.
43. *CR,* Tunisia, January 2001, pp. 5, 19.
44. OECD, *Economic Survey, Turkey 2001* <www.oecd.org>.
45. *CR,* Turkey, January 2001, p. 5.
46. *Country Analysis Brief,* UAE, October 2000 <www.eia.doe.gov/emeu/cabs/uae.html>.

PART TWO:
COUNTRY-BY-COUNTRY SURVEY

Middle East Countries
Social and Economic Indicators

	Population Midyear (m) 2000*	Population Growth (average annual %) 1980–90	1990–2000	GDP 2000 ($m.)	Purchasing Power Parity Estimate of GNI per Capita 2000 ($)**	GDP Annual Average Growth 1980–90	1990–2000	Inflation (GDP Deflator) 2000	Life Expectancy at Birth (years) 2000	Adult Literacy (%) 2000
Algeria	30.0	2.9	1.9	53.8	5,500	2.7	2.1	23.7	71.0	66.2
Bahrain	0.7	5.0a	3.2	8.0	12,130	—	—	—	73.1	87.6
Egypt	64.0	2.5	2.0	98.3	3,690	5.4	4.6	5.8	67.5	55.3
Iran	64.0	3.3	1.6	99.0	5,900	1.7	3.6	22.3	69.1	76.3
Iraq	23.3	3.3a	2.5	—	—	—	—	—	61.1	55.9
Israel	6.0	1.8	2.9	110.3	19,320	3.5	5.1	1.7	78.4	94.6
Jordan	5.0	3.7	4.3	8.3	4,040	2.5	4.8	-0.6	71.5	89.7
Kuwait	2.0	4.4	-0.7	29.7	—	1.3	—	25.6	76.6	86.0
Lebanon	4.0	3.4	1.7	16.6	4,530	—	5.9	-0.4	70.4	80.0
Libya	5.5	—	2.3	—	—	—	—	—	71.0	82.0
Morocco	29.0	2.2	1.8	33.4	3,140	4.2	2.2	1.6	67.5	48.9
Oman	2.4	8.4	3.9	10.6b	8,690c	8.3	—	—	73.6	71.3
Qatar	0.6	7.5	1.9	14.5	17,690c	—	—	—	74.8	81.3
Saudi Arabia	20.7	5.2	2.7	174.3	11,050b	0.0	—	16.1	72.5	76.3
Sudan	29.7	3.3	2.1	11.5	1,298b	1.5	5.6	8.0	56.2	57.8
Syria	16.0	3.3	2.8	16.4	3,230	3.3	4.7	1.1	69.7	71.0
Tunisia	10.0	2.4	1.6	19.5	6,070	5.4	3.7	2.4	72.1	70.0
Turkey	65.0	2.3	1.5	199.9	7,030	-2.0	—	50.6	69.7	85.0
UAE	2.9	10.1	4.5	48.7c	19,720c	—	—	—	75.3	75.0
West Bank & Gaza	3.0	—	4.3	4.4	1,660	—	—	6.8	—	—
Yemen	18.0	3.3	3.9	8.7	780	—	—	15.9	56.5	46.3

a   1986–90
b   1998
c   1999
*   Estimate, includes non-nationals
** GNI — gross national income or gross national product. The use of official exchange rates to convert national currencies to US dollars does not reflect the relative purchasing powers of currencies. Purchasing power parity is used as an alternative conversion factor. This is defined as the number of units of a country's currency to buy the same amount of goods and services in the domestic market as one dollar would buy in the US.

SOURCES: WB, *World Development Report 2002*; *World Development Indicators* <www.worldbank.org>.

Algeria
(Al-Jumhuriyya al-Jaza'iriyya
al-Dimuqratiyya al-Sha'biyya)

MEIR LITVAK

President 'Abd al-'Aziz Bouteflika's civil concord policy for ending the Islamist insurgency in Algeria that had raged since 1991 achieved only partial success. In the six months from the passing of the civil concord law in July 1999 to its deadline in January 2000 about six thousand rebel fighters reportedly surrendered. Most were members of the Armée islamique du salut (AIS), the military arm of the Front islamique du salut (FIS). However, the majority of groups affiliated with the more radical Groupe islamique armée (GIA) kept fighting, mainly in the countryside. Their activities appeared to combine ideological motivation, local power struggles and banditry. Although they suffered mounting casualties, these organizations were able to replenish their ranks by young men in despair over the dire socioeconomic conditions in Algeria, leading to a resurgence of violence toward the year's end.

The civil concord policy remained limited to the military sphere, as the authorities refused either to legalize the FIS or enable it to resume political activity in a different form. Most political parties welcomed the concord, although some opposition politicians contended that it fell short of addressing structural, political and social problems. The FIS, which acknowledged its military defeat and accepted the concord grudgingly, grew increasingly bitter at its own political exclusion, but could do little to change things. Many of the former Islamist insurgents, however, resumed their Islamic propagation (da'wa) in and around mosques, which the government could do little to check.

The implementation of the civil concord revealed once again the friction between Bouteflika and the military, which remained the real power broker in the country. The army reportedly vetoed Bouteflika's plan to extend the amnesty to some of the GIA-affiliated organizations, and may have initiated press criticism of the president. The dispute coincided with the largest reshuffle of the military high command since 1988. This completed the takeover of the army by officers who had served in the French military, at the expense of the generals who had originally fought in the guerilla struggle against France and had received their advanced training in Arab countries.

Bouteflika's much publicized efforts to reform the bureaucracy, which he accused of being "out of touch with real situation," and his calls for greater transparency remained unrealized. His attack on a group of journalists who visited Israel in late June was largely intended to deflect criticism from the government's poor performance, but it also demonstrated the limits to liberal reform that he was willing to tolerate. The resignation of Prime Minister Ahmad Benabitour in August after only eight months in office, and the appointment of a new cabinet headed by Bouteflika's confidant, 'Ali Benflis, strengthened the president's hand in running the government, but did not change his overall relations with the army.

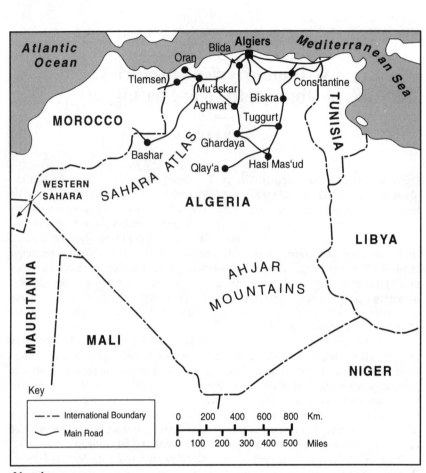

Algeria

The continuing economic crisis was a major cause for the cabinet's resignation. Although enhanced revenues, thanks to rising oil prices, had improved macroeconomic indicators, structural problems — inefficient public sector industries, underdeveloped agriculture, and a bloated bureaucracy — remained unresolved.

Foreign policy continued to be Bouteflika's favored arena. He sought to fashion a leading role for Algeria in Arab and African affairs, to consolidate Arab cooperation in the struggle against Islamic insurgency, and to improve the Algerian image in the West. Relations with Morocco, however, remained problematic due to the dispute over the Western Sahara and the historical antagonisms between the two countries. Bouteflika's trip to Paris in June was largely a symbolic reconciliation with the former colonial power, and produced few tangible economic or strategic results. At the same time, Algerian relations with the US grew ever warmer.

INTERNAL AFFAIRS

THE CIVIL CONCORD

President Bouteflika's civil concord policy for ending the seven-year Islamist insurgency was to be concluded on 13 January, the deadline for Islamist rebels to surrender peacefully. However, AIS commander Madani Mezraq suspended the process on 3 January, charging the government with depriving AIS activists who had surrendered before that date of their "civilian rights," in violation of previous agreements between the AIS and the Algerian army. Following negotiations with army representatives, the AIS, which had ceased fighting since October 1997, agreed to dissolve its organization. In return Bouteflika announced on 11 January a full amnesty and restoration of civil rights for AIS fighters who would lay down their arms, rather than the stricter terms of the 1999 civil concord law (see *MECS* 1999, pp. 170–73). The army rejected an AIS request to incorporate its activists into special units that would fight the more radical organization alongside the military, perceiving this as an Islamist ploy to penetrate its ranks.[1]

Overall, about six thousand fighters are said to have surrendered between the enactment of the civil concord law in July 1999 and the end of January 2000. According to Interior Minister Yazid Zerhouni, these amounted to 80% of those who had taken up arms against the state. While Mezraq reportedly left for exile in Saudi Arabia, some AIS leaders saw the amnesty as an opportunity to resume their campaign for an Islamic state by other means. One indication of the continued support for the Islamist cause was the hero's welcome from villagers in various regions to AIS fighters who came down from the mountains. Saudi Arabia reportedly awarded Algeria financial support to help rehabilitate Islamist rebels, and other unnamed Gulf countries assisted the authorities to launch a trial project in Western Algeria helping "repentant" Islamist fighters to set up small business enterprises. The government also pledged to implement a more comprehensive reconstruction plan to aid the families of the victims of terrorism.[2]

The terms of the amnesty created a paradox whereby the regime, primarily the army, enabled those who took up arms against the state to return to normal life, while keeping FIS political leaders in prison or excluded from political activity. The regime apparently regarded the fighters as a more manageable threat than the Islamist politicians, who continued to pose a long-term ideological and political challenge to the army's grip on power.

Bouteflika refused to legalize the FIS or allow its political leadership to engage in politics under a different guise so long as Algeria "still tends its wounds," from the bloodshed. While he expressed some understanding of the circumstances that had led some young people into violence, he maintained that he had no national mandate to resolve the problem of those who were "at the root of the idea of violence."[3]

Most of the radical Islamist groups rejected the civil concord. The Algerian media reported that government representatives held talks with Hasan al-Hattab, leader of the Salafist Group for Propagation and Combat (Groupe Salfaiste pour le prédication et le combat; GSPC) based in the Kabyle region, on the terms of surrender and amnesty. They failed to reach an agreement, apparently because of internal dissension within the Islamist group. Some surrendered their weapons, while the majority continued to fight. Other groups, most notably the GIA, which operated mostly in Western Algeria, and the Baqun 'ala al-'Ahd group, rejected any truce or agreement with the state and proclaimed their determination to pursue holy war until the Islamic state was set up. They denounced the AIS as "apostates" and "renegades" who deserved to be "exterminated." The hard-liners reportedly killed dozens of their number who sought to take advantage of the amnesty.[4]

The cessation of armed struggle and the dissolution of the AIS deprived the FIS of significant leverage over the government, producing diverse reactions within the movement. Rabah Kebir, head of the FIS Executive Committee Abroad, welcomed the amnesty as a "commendable and bold initiative" that would enable the fighters to be reintegrated into civilian life. He urged Bouteflika to speed up the pace of national reconciliation, by legalizing the FIS and releasing all its prisoners, headed by its two leaders, 'Abassi Madani and 'Ali Belhaj.

Other FIS spokespersons were less conciliatory. Kamal Guemazi argued that the civil concord law would remain "mere legislation" — a "publicity stunt" according to another FIS leader, 'Ali Jeddi — as long as it was not accompanied by a political solution and the release of FIS leaders. Guemazi accused the government of not being interested in a political solution to the Algerian crisis, claiming that Algerians were reverting to despair, as the "language of eradication and violence" replaced previous promises of "security, peace, and concord." Ja'far Houari, a member of the Executive Committee Abroad, maintained that the 1997 truce agreement (see *MECS* 1997, pp. 273–74) also allowed the FIS to form a political party, and demanded that Bouteflika implement the agreement. "No one, not even the president," could deny the FIS its constitutional, "sacred right" to return the political scene, concluded another FIS leader, 'Abd al-Qadir Boukhamkham. The more hard-line FIS Coordination Council dismissed the amnesty as a "non-event" and a continuation of the regime's policy of "treachery adopted since 11 January 1992." It denounced the "naive political stances" adopted by mainstream FIS activists, which "dwarfed and diluted its demands and compromised the sincere strugglers into the service of the junta."[5]

Most other parties welcomed the amnesty as an "important step" in realizing a "comprehensive national reconciliation among Algerians." Some opposition politicians contended that the civil concord policy merely suppressed, rather than repaired, the imbalances in Algerian political and social life that had originally caused the conflict, insisting that greater political liberalization was essential to address the structural crisis. Women's organizations and the association of the families of victims of terrorism held a demonstration in Algiers on 10 December 1999 protesting the pardon to "terrorists."[6]

The supposed end of hostilities again raised the question of the "missing persons." On 17 February, the Sumud [Steadfastness] Association sent an open letter to Bouteflika, in which it claimed that ten thousand people had been kidnapped by Islamists and army personnel since violence began in 1992. It urged the government to check sites, particularly wells, for the bodies of abducted people. Louisa Hanoune, leader of the Algerian Workers Party, claimed she had proof that the security services were involved in the kidnapping of c. 4,600 people. The Association nationale des familles des disparus (ANFD) handled 7,023 cases of missing persons, while lawyers close to the association estimated that c. twenty-two thousand had vanished at the hands of the various security organizations since 1992. The ANFD organized demonstrations and sit-ins of families, and also took their cases to the first Euro-Mediterranean meeting for the families of missing people on 8–11 February in Paris. It joined a delegation of the families of missing people from seven Mediterranean countries that presented their grievances to Mary Robinson, the UN human rights high commissioner, on 20 March during the fifty-sixth session of the UN human rights commission in Geneva. It also campaigned for a tribunal on human rights to be set up at the International Court of Justice [ICJ] at The Hague to investigate the matter. Although mass graves containing several dozen corpses each were found throughout the year, Bouteflika rejected the families' demand for a hearing. According to Arab observers, the government decision to transfer the missing "file" from the Interior Ministry to the Ministry of Justice signaled its determination to remove the issue from its working agenda. ANFD lawyer Mahmud Khelili stated that he had "evidence of abductions carried out by the security services," and complained that there was a "group of criminals" who were "exercising [a] public function in the Algerian state, whom the state is protecting."[7]

Following Bouteflika's declaration that the authorities would "crush" those who spurned the amnesty offer, on 19 January the army launched Operation Sayf al-Hajjaj (Sword of al-Hajjaj) against GIA strongholds in the wooded mountainous region south of Relizane (450 km. southwest of Algiers). The operation was named after the eighth-century Umayyad governor of Baghdad, known for his cruelty. It was the first in a long series of attacks on Islamist strongholds throughout the country in the following months, in which the army repeatedly claimed successes in killing "terrorists" and "bandits." While the cities were relatively quiet, the Islamists continued their attacks in the countryside, and even managed to hit gas pipelines in March, threatening the most important source of government revenue. They also continued to kill civilians, causing occasional mass flights of terrified villagers to nearby towns. Secularist journalists argued that Islamism and large-scale banditry had become intertwined, as personal ambitions for power and wealth lurked behind the uncompromising ideology of some of the Islamist commanders. Chief of Staff Muhammad Lamari claimed in April that "terrorism has been overcome. Only banditry remained," but the reality was far grimmer.[8]

Critics of the regime argued that the army high command was not genuinely interested in ending the fighting, as this would deprive it of the justification for retaining decisive political power in Algeria. While it was difficult to confirm this claim, it is clear that following its victory over the AIS, the military saw no need to negotiate with the smaller more radical organizations and rejected any political solution that would have compromised its own dominant role. Rather, it was bent on a military solution that would preserve its position. In addition, thousands of pro-government militia members, who had asserted their leadership in rural Algeria by force of arms, resented the amnesty.

They saw it as threatening their hard-won victory and were reportedly bent on taking revenge on the Islamists, whom they blamed for the wartime atrocities. Later in the year, however, about four thousand militia members refused to continue fighting the Islamists, in protest against the government decision to stop paying their wages. Representatives of the Ligue algérien pour la défense des droits de l'hommes (LADDH) denounced the "grave violations of human rights committed with full knowledge of the facts, concealed and often committed under orders of the highest authorities."[9]

Bouteflika and the Army

The failure of the civil concord policy to end violence brought to the fore once again the tension between Bouteflika and factions within the military high command. While he owed his election to the military backing, Bouteflika continually sought to expand his sphere of influence. He repeated his insinuations of corruption in the military, while his confidants leaked to the press his desire to amend the constitution in order to further enhance the presidency.[10]

A central point of contention between Bouteflika and army hard-liners revolved around the extension of the scope and duration of the amnesty, which the military hard-liners appeared to oppose. Bouteflika stated on several occasions during March and April that Islamists who had remained active and now chose to surrender could still benefit from an amnesty even after its expiration. The implication that they would enjoy the same terms as the AIS fighters marked a clear concession from previous government positions, which had been partly responsible for the failed negotiations with the GSPC. Alluding to some disagreement with the army, Bouteflika deplored the fact that he did not have "all the prerogatives to grant a general amnesty." He also expressed some "understanding" with regard to previous demands by the GSPC commander, saying that "Hattab had attacked military targets only and he did not kill civilians."[11]

Probably with the backing of some factions in the military, Bouteflika appointed Ret. Gen. Muhammad 'Ata'illah to conduct secret talks with Hattab and other GIA leaders to arrange their surrender in return for full clemency, but to little avail. The secularist press and the former ruling party, the Front de libération nationale (FLN), echoing the hard-line military faction, criticized Bouteflika for appeasing terrorists who had massacred civilians. Members of the families of victims of terror in Algeria marked the first anniversary of Bouteflika's entering office by demonstrating against him with the slogan, "you have crossed the red line, Bouteflika." 'Ata'illah himself came out in favor of a general amnesty that would include the GIA units as well as those imprisoned for their political views, seeing this as the only way to end the ongoing bloodshed in Algeria.[12]

The dispute over the amnesty coincided with the largest reshuffle of the military high command since 1988. Announced on 24 February, it involved the retirement of sixteen senior generals, and included four of six military regions, commanders of the navy, the gendarmerie and the Republican Guards. All but two of the retirees were supporters of former president Liamine Zeroual. Some of them reportedly supported the candidacies of Ahmad Talib al-Ibrahimi and Mouloud Hamrouche in the 1999 presidential campaign. The Algerian and Arab media presented the reshuffle as Bouteflika's initiative to promote younger officers who would be more dependent on him. However, the four most senior positions held by the real power brokers in the military, headed by Chief of Staff Muhammad Lamari, were left untouched. Lamari emerged as the major beneficiary of the change, as the new appointees, primarily Maj. Gen. Ibrahim Fodeil Cherif, new commander of the first military region, were his allies. The reshuffle completed the takeover of the army by those officers, like Lamari himself, who had served in the French army and had joined the struggle for independence at a very late stage. This group had come to prominence after 1988 under the leadership of former defense minister Khalid Nizzar. The losing faction was comprised of generals who had originally fought in the guerilla struggle against France and had received their advanced training in Arab countries. The reshuffle signified the victory of the professionals, who sought to abolish national conscription and to remodel the army along contemporary Western lines into a fully professional force, over the historic "mujahidun." These generals were also determined to retain their grip on the political and economic arenas.[13]

The political implications of the reshuffle became evident on 8 March when former president 'Ali al-Kafi (1992–94) castigated the former French army officers as a "fifth column." He contended that since coming under the control of the "French Army" faction, the military had been incapable of addressing the terrorist challenge. Nizzar, a former French army officer, came out against al-Kafi, but also against Bouteflika. He described the civil concord policy as a failure and called for the extermination of the Islamist insurgents. Retired members of the French faction published articles defending their service for the Algerian revolution and state. The public row reflected deeper rivalries between different wings of the ruling elite. The "French generals" viewed the criticism against them as jealousy, because they had appeared to be more successful in running the country and holding onto power since independence. Their opponents contended that Algerian independence remained deficient so long as they retained the upper hand, as France effectively continued to rule the country through them.

The dispute also revolved around the perception and legitimacy of the various periods of post-independence Algerian history. Thus, 'Ata'illah suggested that the origins of the crisis went back to the advent of former president Chadli Benjedid, which, among other things, had led to Bouteflika's removal from the post of foreign minister and the rise of the "ex-French-army" faction. Former prime minister Sid Ahmad Ghozali, on the other hand, criticized Bouteflika for encouraging attacks on the army and dismissed Bouteflika's term in office as a "lot of talk but very little action." Ret. Gen. Rashid bin Belis went further, calling for Bouteflika's dismissal. A youth activist lamented that "the facade [and] image changes, but it is still the military in power," and Bouteflika was "just another card they can deal with." Recognizing his weakness, Bouteflika praised the army on several occasions for having saved Algeria from destruction and for working to guarantee its unity. To the foreign media, he still asserted — unconvincingly — that he maintained overall control over the military.[14]

The Limits of Administrative Reforms

The continued violence, as well as the government failure to address the ongoing economic and social crises (see below) undermined Bouteflika's popularity and status. Seeking to reverse this trend, he launched a public campaign to improve government performance. He criticized "corruption, preferential treatment and the misuse of the law at the expense of the weakest." He accused the administration of being "out of touch with real situation" in the country and with indifference to the "concerns expressed by the citizens." He called for greater transparency and better communication between all levels of government, stressing the need for greater efficiency and decentralized management. On 1 March he amended the 1997 governorate law by a presidential decree which bypassed the parliament. This amendment abolished the ministerial position responsible for the Greater Algiers Governorate held by Sharif Rahmani, who had twelve commissioners under him, and placed the new governor on an equal footing with all other governors. Apparently, Bouteflika saw Rahmani's dual status as a challenge to the central government authority.[15] In a symbolic action two months later, on 12 May, he dissolved the Higher Education Council, the Higher Youth Council and the National Watchdog for Monitoring and Preventing Corruption as being useless and costly bodies.[16]

The appointment of 311 new judges and prosecutors during July–August marked the peak of a government campaign to reform the judiciary. This followed the publication of government reports on the need to take action against corruption and state interference in the judiciary. Bouteflika himself issued a circular directive for new emergency measures to enforce the rule of law in all government institutions. He also issued a decree allocating more funds to the Justice Ministry, aimed at providing more humane prison conditions. It appeared, however, that these efforts were mainly designed to "portray the government as acceptably proactive to Western governments" and to "serve a sop" to various human rights groups." They failed, therefore, to produce significant results.[17]

While Bouteflika presented himself as a benevolent champion of the people, he was determined to restrict political liberalization to the limits established by the ruling elite, and to prevent the emergence of opposition movements that would be too independent or too popular. The political parties which remained outside the governmental coalition frequently complained about the blackout imposed by the public media on their activities. The authorities also amended the internal regulations of the Assemblée populaire nationale (APN), in order to prevent independents from establishing a pro-Islamic caucus in the parliament.[18]

Equally important, Interior Minister Zerhouni declared on 10 May his opposition to license Harakat al-Wafa wal-'Adl (Fidelity and Justice Movement), led by former presidential candidate Ahmad Talib al-Ibrahimi, for being a facade for the "dissolved party" — a code name for the FIS. The claim had some foundation because Ibrahimi, scion of a distinguished clerical family, was the pro-Islamist candidate in the 1999 elections, and the FIS supported his campaign. In addition, El Watan claimed that 17 out of the 40 official founding members of the Wafa party were former FIS activists and that 23 of its central council were "known for direct links" with the FIS. Ibrahimi denied the charges, saying that the FIS had its own leadership and that, unlike the FIS, his movement sought to fuse together the Islamic and nationalist trends. According to the foreign media, it was conceivably this approach that made the new party popular, and therefore a source of concern to the authorities. Following repeated requests by the Wafa party, Zerhouni announced on 8 November his final refusal to legalize it, claiming that it was a reincarnation of the banned FIS. A week later he ordered the national security services to close down local Wafa offices throughout the country. Bouteflika himself reiterated his adamant refusal to legalize the FIS, pointing to popular opposition to such measures, particularly among families of terror victims. The constitution, he insisted, did not provide for the FIS existence at all, adding that as far as he was concerned the "FIS does not exist." The government also procrastinated in licensing the pro-military Front démocratique of Sid Ahmed Ghozali, possibly for being too vocal. "We have a deceptive political discourse that calls for the rule of law and for respect of public liberties, but the practice is the exact opposite," charged Muhammad Sa'id, a spokesperson for the Wafa party. Elsewhere, Bouteflika justified the restrictions on democracy, saying that in western democracies all parties respected "broad strategic outlines," whereas Algerians "measured democracy on the basis of escapism."[19]

The government was increasingly concerned that "repentant" AIS fighters were resuming their "political proselytism" — their religious propagation — particularly in mosques, after having laid down their arms. The secularist *Liberté* complained that former AIS men had "reconquered the mosques from which they are delivering almost daily sermons with a rare virulence," adding that "religious tapes, veils," and other "subversive material" were being sold in public squares and outside mosques." The media reported that the Islamists demanded that the people not watch government TV, as it contradicted Islamic principles. In August, the government announced its intention to improve its supervision of the mosques around the country, which had served as recruiting grounds for the Islamist movements.[20]

Bouteflika and the Press
Bouteflika's tenuous relationships with the independent press continued to reflect his political status and style as well as the complex nature of Algerian authoritarianism. In January, the government ended the printing press monopoly, allowing the private press to have its own printing and distribution facilities. It also promised to respect the media's right to free expression.[21]

However, when a group of Algerian journalists visited Israel on 26 June — 3 July at the invitation of the Israeli Foreign Ministry, Bouteflika attacked the trip as "an unforgivable misdeed." He denounced the journalists as "traitors to the sacred values of freedom," accusing them of stabbing the Palestinians in the back, as well as the Syrians and Lebanese. Since Bouteflika himself had spoken in favor of peace with Israel (see below), his attack was largely interpreted as a response to Algeria's domestic politics. The privately owned French-speaking press had consistently criticized Bouteflika for granting full amnesty to Islamist fighters and for his high-handed style reminiscent of "the days of the one-party state." Many of these attacks were apparently inspired and sanctioned by factions within the military-political establishment that were at odds with Bouteflika over other issues. It was also widely speculated that Bouteflika was not fully informed of the journalists' trip, and saw it as an attempt by his rivals within the regime to embarrass him, or as an infringement of what he regarded as his own preserve — foreign policy. In addition, Bouteflika probably sought to enhance his popularity among Islamist and nationalist circles that opposed any ties with Israel. He also demoted Communications and Culture Minister 'Abd al-Majid Tebboune to the rank of a junior minister at the Interior Ministry for allowing the trip to take place.

Bouteflika's associates complained that factions within the military were disseminating "damaging" information via the Internet highlighting the president's failures to bring about peace, and that he sought to impose restrictions on the press. The legal Islamist parties, Harakat Mujtama' al-Silm (Hamas Movement of the Society for Peace), the Nahda and the Parti de renouveau algérien (PRA), called for a judicial inquiry into the visit. The majority party, the Rassemblement national démocratique (RND), defended the freedom of the journalists to make the visit. Despite their condemnation, the authorities took no measures against the journalists after they returned.[22]

The independent press denounced Bouteflika's criticism as an incitement to violence, and accused him of trying to divert attention from his domestic failures. The National Union of Journalists declared itself "revolted to the utmost extent," while *Le Matin* likened Bouteflika's "hysterical campaign" and "inquisition-style speech" to a "Goebbels-style campaign" [alluding to Nazi Propaganda Minister Joseph Goebbels]. It argued that the "witch hunt" was "based on settling old scores" with the press.[23]

In a revealing statement after the storm had subsided, Bouteflika declared on 17 August that journalists were "required to serve the interests of the Algerian state" and to distance themselves from "partisan and political affiliations." In October, he boasted that the Algerian press was "the freest of the freest media in the world," adding that it was hurling "insults and abuse and no one harasses it." Still, in November a court fined *Liberté* and *El Watan* for publishing articles exposing corruption in government offices and on 8 December the minister for communications and culture, Muhyi al-Din 'Amimour, threatened to restore censorship on security reporting unless the press mended its ways.[24]

Coalition Troubles

The governing coalition also suffered from internal divisions, mainly between secularists and Islamists. Sa'id Sa'di, leader of the Berber-dominated Rassemblement de la culture et la démocratie (RCD), criticized the Islamist-conservative groups in the coalition for showing "very little enthusiasm and support" for Bouteflika's political program. He maintained that Bouteflika needed "soldiers" who would selflessly defend his policy and would reject any compromise with the Islamists. In response, Hamas leader Mahfuz Nahnah, demanded on 13 July that Bouteflika avoid any concessions to the "westernized secular" groups, especially in regard to security policy. Nahnah later lashed out at Bouteflika for failing to push forward a real national reconciliation. He contended that the status of Algerian "Arab-Islamic identity" was being "devalued," and derided the "flagrant violations" of the "constitution and the laws" committed under the pretext of "breaking taboos." He also complained that changes made in the judiciary (see above) and the universities harmed Arabic-educated cadres, a reference to the longstanding social problem of the preferred status of French-educated elites in Algeria. As a solution, he advocated "reconciliation between the state and the mosque, and the promotion of Islam and the Arabic language," thus ignoring the constitutional provisions forbidding parties to use religion for political purposes.[25]

Bouteflika's relations with Prime Minister Benabitour worsened during the year. Benabitour resigned in June, but retracted his decision following pressure from army Chief of Staff Lamari. Bouteflika's frustration at the slow pace of government reforms, and Benabitour's problematic working relations with the president's own men in the cabinet, led him to resign again, this time for good, on 26 August, after only eight months in office. With unusual public candor, Benabitour attributed his resignation to Bouteflika's efforts to manage "all the major issues by himself" without leaving the prime minister "any room to maneuver." He pointed to the legislation through presidential decree behind the parliament's back, and to the economic reform programs formulated by Bouteflika's staff that contradicted the government program without even informing the cabinet. They also disagreed on managing the privatization of state enterprises. Bouteflika favored immediate and unconditional privatization as the only way to revitalize and rescue public sector corporations, while Benabitour preferred gradual privatization because of the heavy social cost of laying off thousands of workers at a single stroke. Benabitour also protested that he was not allowed to pick his own ministers and propose them for presidential approval, although the constitution allowed him that privilege.[26]

Bouteflika, who had sought the resignation, immediately appointed as prime minister 'Ali Benflis, his close personal ally, and former director of his presidential office, having also previously held the post of justice minister, Benflis was a stalwart of the FLN, and was known to be affiliated with the regime's liberal wing. The new cabinet retained most of Benabitour's ministers, including all the core group of economic reformers whom Bouteflika had brought in to overhaul the economy, most notably the minister responsible for privatization, Habib Temmar, and the finance minister, 'Abd al-Latif Benachenhou. The six coalition parties preserved their representation: The RND, the largest party, received five — albeit minor — portfolios; Hamas received three; the secularist Berber RCD and the Islamist Nahda received two portfolios each, and the smaller PRA and Alliance nationale républicane one each. The new cabinet signified a comeback for the FLN, as two of its members, both close allies to Bouteflika, were given senior ministries. Muhyi al-Din 'Amimour became minister of information and culture and 'Abd al-'Aziz Belkhadem — regarded as one of the "bearded FLN," a reference to his pro-Islamist leanings — was appointed foreign minister. As former speaker of parliament, Belkhadem supported a political settlement of the Algerian crisis including a dialogue with the FIS. Their appointment in the face of the military's displeasure was seen as a gesture to Islamist circles and signified Bouteflika's determination to control Algerian foreign policy himself, as Belkhadem lacked diplomatic experience. Like its predecessor, the new cabinet was beset by internal disputes among ministers representing sharply opposed ideological orientations, prompting the angry Bouteflika to demand that they should forget their party ideologies and abandon their focus on purely sectoral programs.[27]

Some political parties dismissed the change of cabinet as a non-event that would not bring about any significant change in politics and the economy. The RND, the largest coalition party, expressed its disapproval with Belkhadem's appointment as foreign minister, because of his pro-Islamist views. Opposition parties saw the change of cabinet as an indication of government bankruptcy of ideas in tackling Algerian problems. They criticized the senior roles given to FLN men as an unjustified rehabilitation of the party that was held largely responsible for plunging Algeria into its economic crisis in the 1970s and 1980s. "The men in power do not want any change in our society," said 'Abdallah Jabjallah, leader of the small Islamist National Reform Movement, and "[w]hat matters most to them is their own interest." The FIS, in contrast, gave a cautious welcome to the cabinet change, saying that it brought in figures known for their positive stance on national reconciliation. It expressed the hope that the new cabinet would base the future economic direction on an integrated political plan aimed at national reconciliation, which would not exclude anyone and would mark a shift from the practice of change for its own sake which had marked political life in Algeria.[28]

Some foreign observers claimed that the cabinet change and appointment of his own man as prime minister had enhanced Bouteflika's stance vis-à-vis the army. Further, the army was said to be displeased with the appointment of Belkhadem and 'Amimour, in view of their pro-Islamist sympathies. The replacement of eight department heads at the Defense Ministry, coinciding with the cabinet change, was seen as another move by Bouteflika to exert control over the military. Others maintained that it was the army which had chosen Benflis as Bouteflika's 1999 presidential campaign manager and had initiated the reshuffle in the Defense Ministry. More importantly, the person succeeding Benflis as chief of the president's staff was Ret. Gen. Larbi [al-'Arabi] Belkheir, a former interior minister considered to be one of the most powerful individuals in Algeria. It was Belkheir who sponsored Bouteflika's presidential effort and convinced the decision-makers *(les décideurs)* in the army to back his candidacy. In addition to keeping an eye on the president, Belkheir's new function appeared to be to mediate between Bouteflika, who sought to expand his powers, and the military, which was reluctant to give him a wider margin for maneuver. Other points of friction between Bouteflika and the army were his intentions to revise the constitution, differences over the Western Sahara, and the declared goal of wholesale privatization, which threatened the generals' control over lucrative export and import businesses.[29]

The new government announced its intention to institutionalize administrative reforms and liberalize the economy, while Bouteflika himself launched a renewed campaign against corruption and mismanagement. He set up investigative committees and a special police task force reporting directly to him, which focused on municipal and provincial administrations and the "real-estate mafias" that seized urban property. These measures were seen as a special threat by the RND officials who controlled most of these bodies" and who complained that Bouteflika's measures were undermining the stability of state institutions. Foreign reporters, however, pointed to the dominant role of retired generals who had forged partnerships with wealthy contractors and importers in order to amass huge fortunes through trade monopolies. In October, Bouteflika reshuffled the top personnel of six ministerial administrations, and declared once again his intention to reform the judicial system and cultural institutions. In addition to administrative measures, he traveled around the country in order to spread his message that the state was "bankrupt and relying on the state [would] not solve anything." Some of Bouteflika's critics described these tours as an attempt to take his conflict with the army to the streets. In the meantime, foreign observers commented that he had been "strong on rhetoric but weak on delivery," and that "many of the fundamental economic and social problems, which fed the Algerian crisis," had not been addressed.[30]

Bouteflika's invitation to Amnesty International (AI) to send a fact-finding delegation, in an effort to improve the Algerian image in the eyes of the international community, proved another source of tension with the army. The delegation arrived on 5 November, announcing its intention to meet government officials, representatives of civil and human rights organizations and parliamentarians. It demanded interviews with Chief of Staff Lamari, chief of intelligence Maj. Gen. Muhammad Mediene and chief of military security Gen. Isma'il Lamari in order to get their views on violations of human rights. The generals refused, as did most government officials.[31]

The army high command was reportedly angered by Bouteflika's silence over the delegation's request to meet its members, which they interpreted as an attempt to embarrass them, and by the publication of the AI report in the FLN organ *El Mojahed*, apparently authorized by Bouteflika. "Somebody" is "busy making a case against the military institution," concluded former prime minister Ahmad Ghozali, himself an ally of the army.[32]

The indirect elections on a provincial basis of forty-six members of the Conseil de la nation, the upper house of parliament, on 30 December had little impact on the political scene. Some coalition parties were obliged to form alliances with legal opposition parties, mainly the Berber-dominated Front des forces socialistes (FFS), in order to secure some representation. The main struggle took place between the majority party, the RND, which was apparently backed by the military following the resignation of President Zeroual, and the FLN, affiliated with Bouteflika. The RND lost one seat but retained its majority of 79, while the FLN gained 2 seats, taking its total to 12. Hamas gained one seat, giving it three, while the FFS retained its 4 seats.[33]

Surging Violence
By the year's end, it seemed that the civil concord policy had reached a deadlock, with the violence only increasing. As a public relations gesture, Bouteflika pardoned four thousand prisoners, none of whom was affiliated with Islamist organizations. At the same time, he sent out feelers to the FIS. The government reportedly held secret talks with 'Ali Belhaj, the FIS second-in-command who had been imprisoned since 1992 and had wielded a measure of influence on the radical groups. He was allegedly offered release from prison in return for giving up politics and endorsing the truce, but declined. FIS officials contended that they had exerted pressure on GIA and GSPC fighters to lay down their weapons in return for a general amnesty, claiming that success depended on the release of the two imprisoned FIS leaders, 'Abassi Madani and Belhaj. Foreign Minister Belkhadem told FIS activists who operated in Europe that they were welcome in Algeria.

However, nothing came out of these initiatives, indicating that the gap between the Islamists and the government was too wide to be bridged. FIS activists accused the government of reneging on the agreement reached with the AIS, which, they argued, entailed the legalization of their movement. They expressed bitter disappointment in the national concord policy, describing it as "a desperate attempt by the regime to consolidate its former policies of eradication, depict them as something different, and market them inside and outside the country." Nonetheless, they conceded that return to armed struggle was not a viable option. The FIS could claim one minor victory when the US authorities released Anwar Haddam, FIS representative in the US, following his detention.[34]

As in previous years, the holy month of Ramadan (27 November–27 December) witnessed increased violence, with c. three hundred people killed by Islamist attacks. By the end of the year the number of fatalities exceeded 2,500, more than in 1999. In two of the worst incidents, 22 people were killed with knives and axes in a coastal village west of Algiers and 15 schoolchildren were murdered in a school dormitory in Medèa. The mounting casualties aroused widespread criticism of Bouteflika from the usually compliant APN, with deputies demanding a drastic change of policy and some even calling for his removal. The growing violence showed that despite military claims of success against the Islamists, the radical groups were able to replenish their ranks with young men driven mainly by alienation and despair from dire socioeconomic and political conditions, and the absence of hope for the future.[35]

THE ECONOMY
Enhanced revenues thanks to rising oil prices (see chapter on Economic Developments in the Middle East) improved macroeconomic indicators, but its structural problems — inefficient state-owned industries, a bloated bureaucracy and poor agriculture — remained serious. Exports of oil and gas reached $21bn., with the balance of trade recording a large surplus of $12.3bn. By July 2000, foreign exchange reserves had increased to $7.8bn. from $4.5bn. at the end of 1999. That same month, improved political risk perceptions and the higher oil prices persuaded the OECD consensus committee to raise the credit rating of Algeria from category 7 to category 5, with other export credit agencies

following suit. Nevertheless, the economy grew by only 3.6% — a disappointing rate due mainly to a poorer than expected harvest and insufficient investment in non-hydrocarbon industrial sectors. This growth rate was well below the 6%-7% needed to lower unemployment significantly. Private sector companies, whose production increased by 6.4%, were the main engines of this growth, while public sector companies recorded a 2% production fall. The industrial sector achieved a 2% production growth. Inflation was contained to a mere 0.3%, reflecting the weakness of domestic demand. Thanks to rising revenues, the budget was revised in July, raising public expenditure to AD 346.01bn. from AD 290.24bn.[36]

The inefficient public sector remained the greatest economic problem, besides the $20bn. damages caused by the fighting since 1992. The level of non-performing loans by state-owned enterprises amounted to 85% of GDP. Consequently, efforts to reform the banks that were forced to buy uncoverable debts were at a standstill. Unemployment rocketed to c. 2.4m. by mid-2000, or 29.8% of the active population. Worse, about 75% of the jobless were under the age of thirty, as every year another 350, 000 young people joined their ranks. The rural exodus to overcrowded cities continued unabated, propelled by the structural problems of Algerian agriculture and the impact of terrorism. It exacerbated the already serious shortage of urban housing that drove many young men to social alienation and political radicalism. The Union générale des travailleurs Algeriens (UGTA) repeatedly warned the government of widespread social unrest if the large-scale privatization leading to the lay-off of hundreds of thousands of workers continued. Indeed, demonstrations and strikes of employees were not uncommon.[37]

Most state-owned companies, which continued to provide the bulk of industrial production, operated below their 1992 capacity. Algeria made little use of funds offered by the World Bank and EU to restructure its industries. While dozens of French industrial managers met Bouteflika during his Paris visit, actual investment, which appeared to be confined largely to the hydrocarbon sector, registered only a 1.9% real growth. Potential investors insisted that Algeria had to quicken the pace of reforms in order to attract a further inflow. The trend of Arab investors to buy into Algerian assets, strongly promoted by Bouteflika, continued but of itself was too small to change the gloomy overall picture.[38]

The oil industry remained the mainstay of the economy. The Algerian OPEC quota rose to 852,600 b/d. The state energy company Sonatrach attracted more loans from the US Export-Import Bank and the Saudi Islamic Development Bank, among other major export credit agencies, to help finance its development plans.[39]

FOREIGN AFFAIRS

Foreign policy remained Bouteflika's favorite activity, arising from his diplomatic experience and increasing frustration with his inability to bring about major changes in Algerian domestic affairs. By December 2000 he had been on thirty-two trips abroad since his election, including minor international events. As part of this policy, on 29–31 January Algeria hosted the seventeenth session of the Council of Arab Interior Ministers, which stressed the need for consolidating Arab coordination in combating terrorism. However, Bouteflika's efforts to convene an Arab summit in Algiers failed. In his capacity as OAU chairman, he also mediated between Ethiopia and Eritrea, and hosted the signing of the ceasefire and peace agreements between the two countries on 18 June and 12 December respectively. While Bouteflika could claim to have increased his personal prestige and that of Algeria abroad, this had little impact on Algerian internal problems or his position within the country.[40]

ALGERIA AND THE MIDDLE EAST

Bouteflika exerted particular effort to improve Algerian relations with North African states (for Morocco, see below). Algerian foreign minister Youcef Yousfi came to Cairo on 17 January where he met President Mubarak, while Egyptian foreign minister 'Amru Musa visited Algiers on 9 February, conveying Mubarak's thanks for Algerian assistance in convening an African-European summit in Cairo. Bouteflika himself attended the summit on 4 April.[41]

Algerian relations with Tunisia were based on mutual opposition to radical Islamism and remained firm. Tunisian foreign minister Habib Ben Yahya and Defense Minister Muhammad Jegham visited Algiers on 6 March and 1 April, respectively. Bouteflika himself held talks with President Zayn al-'Abidin ben 'Ali of Tunisia on 4 April, during the African-European summit. Following these talks, Algerian chief of staff Lamari came on a five-day visit to Tunis on 10 April to discuss bilateral military cooperation. In May, the two countries signed an accord on combating smuggling and easing cross-border travel. Bouteflika came to Tunis on 28 June to celebrate the completion of the land border markers between the two countries. They agreed to set up a committee for political consultation chaired jointly by their two foreign ministers. They also paid the necessary lip service to the idea of the Arab Maghrib Union (AMU), although no concrete steps were taken toward this.[42]

Relations with Libya, which had thawed in 1999, improved significantly, with Bouteflika calling throughout the year for the lifting of UN sanctions on Libya, in spite of the expressed displeasure of Algeria's Western backers. Libyan foreign minister, 'Abd al-Salam al-Turayki, came to Algeria on 27–28 March, and Bouteflika met Libyan president Mu'ammar al-Qadhdhafi on 4 April during the African-European summit. The two countries exchanged military delegations, the Libyan one coming on 18 April and the Algerians reciprocating on 17 May. As part of this improvement, the Jamahiriyya Libyan Arab Airlines resumed their flights to Algiers in August. Following Bouteflika's visit to Tripoli on 22 October, the two countries established follow-up committees to expand their relations and on 23 November signed a cooperation protocol agreement.[43]

Morocco

While Bouteflika seemed to want a diplomatic thaw with Morocco, Algerian-Moroccan relations remained unstable, a result of the historical antagonism between them and the dispute over the Western Sahara, to which hard-line factions in Algeria remained deeply committed. As before, it was Morocco that first pushed for improving bilateral ties, while Algeria rejected any significant progress so long as the Western Sahara issue remained unresolved. In addition, Algeria seemed more interested than Morocco in reviving the AMU, probably as a means to securing a greater regional leadership role.

On several occasions in February, Moroccan prime minister Abderrahmane Youssoufi expressed his country's dissatisfaction with the state of relations with Algeria, insisting that there was no obstacle to reopening the border between the two countries. He reiterated Moroccan denial of Bouteflika's accusations, made in September 1999, that Morocco was interfering in Algerian internal affairs (see *MECS* 1999, p. 184). Algerian officials, while denying any Arab or European mediation between Algeria and Morocco, stated that relations with Morocco had not reached the "proper level," although they were "moving in that direction" and were "bound to develop gradually for the better once efforts to resolve the outstanding disputed issues begin." Bouteflika, for his part, on the occasion of the eleventh anniversary of the AMU on 17 February, sent a message to King Muhammad VI expressing Algerian "readiness" and "sincere determination" to boost "fraternal relations" and cooperation with Morocco. King Muhammad responded by sending the Moroccan youth and sports minister, Ahmed Moussaoui, to Bouteflika with a verbal response.[44]

As a gesture to Morocco, Algeria supported the candidacy of Omar al-Kabbaj of Morocco to head the African Development Bank for a second term. However, when Morocco sent a second envoy, Abdeslam Znined, minister delegate to the minister of foreign affairs and cooperation, to Algiers on 2 March he was received by Prime Minister Benabitour, with Bouteflika reportedly refusing to see him. Bouteflika did confer with King Muhammad during the African-European summit in Cairo on 4 April and denied the existence of any mediation between the two countries, since "[b]etween brothers and friends, we do not need the mediation of other brothers and friends."[45]

The thaw in bilateral relations continued with the visit of Moroccan interior minister Ahmed Midaoui to Algiers on 29 April, to discuss security and terrorism problems along the Algerian-Moroccan border following the infiltration of Moroccan territory by a GIA group. Algerian interior minister Zerhouni described on 10 May a willingness on both sides to improve relations, but noted a difference in approach. Morocco preferred a summit between the two rulers to solve outstanding issues, where "the decision to reestablish relations and lift border restrictions would be taken." Algeria, for its part, preferred to set up "a balanced" mechanism at the bureaucratic or ministerial level to resolve the core disagreements so as to avoid uneven gains by the two parties, implying that Morocco had more to gain from focusing on the bilateral track alone. Algeria apparently preferred to advance the AMU, which it believed enhanced its position vis-à-vis Morocco.

Yet, Zerhouni welcomed Moroccan readiness to help Algeria in its fight against Islamist insurgents along the borders. Algeria had its way, as the two countries agreed to set up joint committees to deal with the various issues pending between them before making any dramatic change of policy. The visit of the Algerian speaker of the Conseil de la nation, Bachir Boumaza, to Morocco on 9 May in Prime Minister Youssouffi's words helped to "clear the air between the two countries," and capped the process.[46]

Nevertheless, a breakthrough in Algerian-Moroccan relationships was not achieved mainly due to the unresolved Western Sahara issue. Algeria continued to support the Polisario independence movement fighting Morocco over the Western Sahara territory. In particular, it backed Polisario's adamant insistence on implementing the UN-sponsored referendum plan (see chapter on Morocco). It was reluctant to have the European-African summit in Cairo deal with the problem, preferring to keep it under OAU sponsorship, where it enjoyed greater support. An Algerian delegation headed by Minister of Justice Ahmed Ouyahya took part as an observer in the unsuccessful UN-sponsored talks between Morocco and Polisario on 14 May, and on 28 June. The Algerian press held Mauritania and former US secretary of state James Baker, the UN secretary-general's personal representative to the Western Sahara, responsible for the failure. They accused them of supporting the Moroccan position of finding "an uncertain third way" to resolve the conflict, and abandoning the UN peace plan which provided for a referendum.[47]

Bouteflika reacted angrily to King Muhammad's assertion that the Western Sahara issue was in essence an Algerian-Moroccan problem because the SADR was "Algeria's creation," calling this an "insult" and an attempt to "falsify facts." He pledged that Algeria would not change its stance on the Western Sahara issue "whatever the consequences," adding that it rejected the "fait accompli policy," the "law of the jungle" and "hegemony of the strongest over the weakest. Under government sponsorship, twelve civil associations organized a campaign of solidarity with "the Saharan cause." Hopes of a reconciliation between Algiers and Rabat were fading, commented *Le Jeune Indépendent*, accusing Morocco of reverting to its old hawkish position against the holding of a free and fair referendum, knowing that it would lose should the vote take place. Continuing the critical tone, Bouteflika commented that the AMU was "at a standstill" even though he had allegedly complied with Moroccan wishes to regard the Sahara as a separate issue from other bilateral problems. He also reiterated his complaint that Morocco was the source of drugs, from which Algeria suffered "terribly."[48]

Further Morocco-Polisario talks were held in Berlin on 28 September, but produced no results. Algeria reiterated on several occasions its unequivocal support for Saharan self-determination, insisting that it was a "matter of decolonization" which needed to be settled by the UN through a "free and fair referendum" that, would enable the Saharan people to choose its political future.[49]

In a final twist, Algerian Interior Minister Zerhouni arrived in Rabat on 16 November declaring that Algeria and Morocco were both "hoping to establish strong relations based on complete confidence and common and balanced interests." In their joint communiqué, both countries agreed to a "realistic, practical" rapprochement, which would take into account the "balance of interests," and a common will to normalize relations. They also agreed to hold similar meetings periodically. Yet, by 26 December, Zerhouni, talking on the civil concord policy, spoke of "a set-up by Rabat and some countries of the Middle East to destabilize Algeria in the wake of its strong return to the international scene." The deep-seated suspicions prevailed once again (see also chapter on Morocco).[50]

Iran
Algerian contacts with Iran continued in the early part of 2000. Bouteflika met President Mohammad Khatami of Iran at the funeral of Syrian president Hafiz al-Asad on 14 June (see chapter on Syria). They met again on 8 September during the UN millennium summit and announced the resumption of full diplomatic ties between their countries, which had been severed by Algeria in 1993. The two men agreed "not to interfere in each other's internal affairs," since Algeria had previously accused Iran of supporting the Islamist insurgents. Khatami expressed "regrets" following the "suffering endured by the Algerian people and Algeria," which the Algerian press interpreted as a formal "act of penitence" by the Iranian authorities toward the Algerian tragedy.[51]

ALGERIA AND EUROPE
Improving relations with the European Union (EU) was a high priority for Bouteflika, who hoped to alleviate Algerian debts, upgrade its trading status with the EU to that of Morocco and Tunisia, and attract European investment. Speaking at a UN trade conference in Bangkok on 18 February, Bouteflika complained that the desire of the West to tear down barriers to trade and the movement of capital, in addition to the crippling levels of debt and plunging overseas aid from developed countries, meant that Africa would remain

locked in misery. He contended that huge debt levels meant that the "poor" were "financing the rich," and that developing nations were excluded from consultations because powerful countries refused to open their markets. Bouteflika reiterated these themes during the Euro-African summit in Cairo on 2–4 April, charging that what Europe had offered to African states was "a drop of water in a vast and very thirsty desert."[52]

Algerian negotiations with the EU on a free trade agreement, which had started in 1996, resumed in April 2000. The European Commission accepted the Algerian demand to recognize the principal of "specificity and uniqueness" of the Algerian economy, after Algeria had consistently maintained that its agricultural sector was not competitive compared with agriculture in EU or neighboring countries. Algeria also sought to force EU officials to recognize that the dismantling of customs barriers would immediately damage its fragile domestic industries, which were still undergoing painful restructuring. While further talks in May and December reported progress, no agreement was concluded by year's end.[53]

Concurrently, in order to improve Algeria's image internationally, Bouteflika invited representatives of AI, Human Rights Watch, the International Federation of Human Rights Leagues [FIDH] and Reporteurs sans frontières to visit Algeria, lifting the ban imposed on them in 1996. The AI delegation arrived on 2 May and the FIDH mission on 31 May. Radio Algiers stated that the AI delegation concluded that the security situation had "noticeably improved and that the security measures taken by the Algerian authorities reflected their concerns over human rights issues. The reports published by the two organizations, however, were far less congenial.[54]

Following its second visit to Algeria in November, the AI delegation issued two reports on 9 and 21 November which noted the improvement in the security situation. Still, it expressed frustration that the Algerian authorities had "not taken concrete measures with a view to remedying the numerous alarming problems Algeria is grappling with regarding human rights." Rather, it charged that "impunity and the absence of investigation still constitute the norm even when violations of human rights are immediately brought to the attention of the authorities." It complained that the authorities did not respond to "a single one of the requests for information submitted to them" regarding "specific cases" of human rights violations. "Nor have they communicated the statistics and the essential factual information that were requested of them." It expressed concern that state-armed militias, which had been suspected of involvement in killings, were not brought under the effective control of the law.[55]

Interior Minister Zerhouni, the APN, the RND and various civil organizations denounced the reports as "a flagrant aggression against the nation and its institutions," and for being ignorant of the "reality of the political situation in Algeria." They accused AI of employing double standards of "biased standing with blind terrorism and those behind it who wanted to destroy the country," whose activities had been prevented by the "alertness of the National People's Army."[56]

Russia
Algerian relations with Russia improved considerably during 2000. On 28 March, Bouteflika received Russian Duma speaker Gennadiy Seleznev, who handed him a letter from Russian president Vladimir Putin. Russian foreign minister Igor Ivanov visited Algeria on 7–8 October, when he discussed with Bouteflika economic cooperation and particularly the Algerian debt problem. A week later Russia agreed to supply Algeria

with 22 Sukhoi Su-24 bombers. These exchanges culminated in the visit of Algerian chief of staff Lamari to Moscow to sign a military cooperation agreement with Russia.[57]

France

France continued to occupy a pivotal role in Algerian European policy, being its major foreign creditor and commercial partner, as well as having influence on the other Algerian creditors, the Paris Club and the IMP. Algeria also believed that if Paris normalized its relations with Algiers, other EU countries would follow suit. The visit of Algerian foreign minister Youcef Yousfi to France on 25–26 January was the first in six years by an Algerian foreign minister. He met French president Jacques Chirac and prime minister Lionel Jospin, and their talks marked an improvement in the two countries' complex bilateral relations. Among other issues, Yousfi discussed Algerian external debt relief, its presidency of the OAU, governmental guarantees to French investments in Algeria and the resumption of Air France flights to Algeria — delayed due to disagreements over security arrangements. Other outstanding bilateral issues concerned the status of the more than a million Algerian immigrants in France and their links to their native country.[58]

On 5 February, Bouteflika sent a personal message to Chirac stressing the importance of Algerian relations with France, which, he said, would be a top priority for the new Algerian cabinet. Chirac responded by stressing his determination to deal "seriously" with all the issues on which the future of French-Algerian cooperation depended. Consequently, with government prodding, a delegation of 130 French businessmen arrived on 5 February to discuss investment opportunities in Algeria. It concluded five partnership projects, with others under way, although one French businessman summed up the visit as "plenty of fine sentiments, few concrete results." In March, COFACE, the leading French source of credit information and the manager of French government export guarantees, stated that Algeria was no longer a risk to foreign investors, thereby lifting conditions imposed on the country in 1994, such as the compulsory need to provide security.[59]

On 16–17 May, Algerian Conseil de la nation speaker Boumaza visited France where he met Chirac and other officials hailing the revival of the relations of friendship between both countries. Significantly, he also met Henri Hadjenberg, president of the Representative Council of Jewish Institutions in France (CRIF), signalling Algeria's conciliatory approach toward former Algerian Jews who had emigrated to France on the eve of independence, and a gesture toward Israel as well. Interior Minister Yazid Zerhouni followed on 23–24 May to discuss security issues and the movement of people between both countries, as well as paving the way for Bouteflika's visit to France.[60]

One factor behind the French desire to improve relations with Algeria was its concern that the US was using the painful historical legacy of French-Algerian relations in order to supplant French influence in Algeria and the Maghrib region as a whole. Thus, following US Defense Secretary William Cohen's declaration in February that the US intended to expand military cooperation with Algeria, France dispatched a senior official to Algiers to discuss French military cooperation. While the US Sixth Fleet held joint naval exercises with the Algerian navy in early May, Algeria cancelled joint maneuvers with the French navy, ostensibly because of its reservations about EU security policy in the Mediterranean. The cancellation prompted a visit by Vice-Admiral Paul Habert, commander of the French Mediterranean naval region, to Algeria on 27 May in order to discuss bilateral military cooperation with Chief of Staff Lamari.[61]

Bouteflika's own visit to France on 14–16 June, the first full state visit by an Algerian president (President Chadhli Benjadid's visit in 1993 was merely an "official" one), marked a new stage in the reconciliation process as well as its difficulties. His main objective was to elevate Algerian relations with France to a new level. However, the visit started acrimoniously when the French press published dismissive assessments by French officials of Bouteflika's real authority in Algiers vis-à-vis the military, and his performance in office. They also highlighted critical reports on Algeria by FIDH. Human rights activists and relatives of the victims of the violence during the 1990 demonstrated against Bouteflika throughout the visit.[62]

Almost every aspect of this visit was carefully loaded with symbolism, as both parties sought to seize the moral high ground in preparation for later financial bargaining. Bouteflika met Chirac, Jospin, the president of the Senate, Christian Poncelet, Interior Minister Jean Pierre Chevènment and Finance Minister Laurent Fabius, as well as French businessmen. He also traveled to the Verdun battlefield, where he paid homage to the 180,000 Algerian Muslims who served in the French army during the First World War and the 26,000 who were killed. However, Bouteflika's address at the French National Assembly was ostentatiously boycotted by various deputies, on grounds ranging from Bouteflika's own "terrorist" past to the undemocratic nature of Algeria and its alleged failure to address the issues of the Harkis (Algerians who collaborated with France during the war of independence between 1954–1962, thousands of whom were massacred following the French withdrawal).[63]

His speech to the Assembly, the first by an Algerian president, was given in French — the language of the former occupier. Bouteflika called on France to face up to its colonial past and change its attitude toward the Algerian struggle for independence as a crucial step in building new relationships with Algeria. He stressed the burden placed on Algeria by years of terrorism and requested France and the EU to increase their aid. He stressed the pivotal role of Algerian-French cooperation in cementing an agreement with the EU, which was so essential for Algeria.[64]

Algerian officials heralded the visit as the start of a fresh chapter in relations with France. Chirac, for his part, declared French readiness to support Algeria economically, to tirelessly support it before the international financial institutions, and to "promote imaginative solutions concerning debt." The actual results were more modest. France agreed to convert Fr.F. 400m. of Algeria's $26bn. external debt into investments. It also promised that, following its successful swapping of official debt for investment funds with Morocco, it would arrange a similar facility to retire Algerian debt. Such a measure would allow potential French investors to finance their projects from credits, which otherwise would have been repaid in the form of official debt. At the same time, however, France refused to sell advanced weapons to the Algerian army.[65]

Clearly disappointed, Bouteflika stated that he was leaving France "empty handed" and did not believe "any gestures whatsoever were made" during his visit. He explained that the ties between Algeria and France should be either "privileged, exemplary, exceptional ones," or they were "not worth the trouble."[66]

ALGERIA AND THE US

The unequivocal American support for the civil concord and economic reform policy reflected the ongoing improvement in bilateral ties. US assistant secretary of state for Near Eastern affairs Edward Walker, visited Algeria on 2-3 February. He discussed with

Bouteflika and Prime Minister Benabitour how to advance bilateral economic cooperation, and conveyed US president Bill Clinton's support for Bouteflika's policy. Several other US officials visited Algeria during the year, while Bouteflika met US secretary of state Madeleine Albright on 9 September during the UN millennium summit in New York. President Clinton himself praised Bouteflika's efforts in dealing with Algerian "political challenges."[67]

As part of the warming American attitude, Algeria became the sixth Arab state (in addition to Mauritania, Morocco, Tunisia, Egypt and Jordan) to join a dialogue with NATO as part of the NATO Mediterranean initiative. In May and August, Algeria and the US held joint naval exercises along the Algerian coast. Arab observers described the exercises as an important indication" that Algerian-US military cooperation could be improved. According to the US ambassador to Algeria Cameron Hume, the levels of ties remained "limited" compared to the US relations with both Tunisia and Morocco.[68]

The release of Anwar Haddam, head of the FIS parliamentary delegation abroad, who had been in prison since 1996, attracted criticism and protests by Algerian anti-Islamist groups. But Algerian government spokespersons did not allow this episode to mar the broader relations with the US.[69]

NOTES

For the place and frequency of publications cited here, and for the full name of the publication, news agency, radio station or monitoring service where an abbreviation is used, please see "List of Sources." Only in the case of more than one publication bearing the same name is the place of publication noted here.

1. *Le Matin*, 4th January (BBC Monitoring); R. Algiers, 6 January (BBC Monitoring); Algerian TV, 11 January (BBC Monitoring); *MM*, 12 January 2000.
2. R. Algiers, 19 January (BBC Monitoring); *MM*, 20 January; *NYT*, 27 January; <www.ArabicNews.com>, 3 February; *al-Sharq al-Awsat*, *MEI*, 11 February; *El Watan*, 14 March 2000.
3. *MM*, 18 January; LCI TV, 1 February 2000 (BBC Monitoring).
4. *Al-Majalla*, 2 January; R. Algiers, 13, 30 January (BBC Monitoring); *WP*, 17 January; *Le Matin*, 19, 21 January; *al-Khabar*, 22 January; *El Watan*, 26 January; *al-Sharq al-Awsat*, 2 February; *al-Hayat*, 14 April 2000.
5. *MM*, al-Jazira satellite TV, 12 January (BBC Monitoring); *al-Hayat*, 14 January; *al-Sharq al-Awsat*, 14 January, 25 February; FIS Coordination Council website, 15 January 2000 (BBC Monitoring).
6. *Al-Hayat*, 11 December 1999; R. Algiers, 13 January (BBC Monitoring); *MEI*, 11 February 2000.
7. *Le Matin*, 3, 21 February, 20 March; *al-Hayat*, 20 March; *El Watan*, 13 May; *al-Wasat*, 15 May; *FT*, 17 June 2000.
8. *WP*, 17 January; *El Watan*, 19 January, 23 May; *Liberté*, 7 February, 23 March; *Le Matin*, 4, 23 March, 5 April, 7, 12 June; *al-Khabar*, 29 April; *Le Monde*, 16 June; *al-Khabar al-Usbu'i*, 24 July; *AW*, 27 July; *Le Jeune Indépendent*, 4 October; *L'Authentique*, 5 November 2000.
9. *NYT*, 27 January; *MEI*, 11 February; *El Watan*, 13 May; *al-Youm*, 12 July (BBC Monitoring); *al-Hayat*, 19 October 2000.
10. *Al-Hayat*, 3 March, 14 April; *al-Watan al-'Arabi*, 17 March; *MEI*, 24 March 2000.
11. *Le Matin*, 21, 27 March; R. Algiers, 7 April (BBC Monitoring); ENTV, 6 June 2000 (BBC Monitoring).

12. *Le Matin*, 21 March; *al-Hayat*, 25 March, 14 April; *al-Watan al-'Arabi*, 21 April; *al-Quds al-'Arabi*, 25 April; *El Watan*, 13 May 2000

13. *MM*, 25 February; *al-Wasat*, 6 March; *al-Ahram al-'Arabi*, 11 March; *MEI*, 24 March 2000.

14. *WP*, 15 March; *al-Hayat*, 21 March, 3, 8, 21 April, 12, 25 May; *al-Wasat*, 24 March; *MEI*, 19 May; *MM*, 11 April; R. Algiers, 11 May (BBC Monitoring); *Liberté*, 17 June 2000 (BBC Monitoring).

15. ENTV, 1, 3, 20 March (BBC Monitoring); *CR*, Algeria, April 2000, p. 17.

16. *MM*, 14 April; R. Algiers, 12 May (BBC Monitoring); *El Watan*, 23 June 2000.

17. *CR*, Algeria, October 2000, p. 15. See, *al-Hayat*, ENTV, 21 September, 8 October; R. Algiers, 5 November 2000 (BBC Monitoring).

18. *La Tribune*, 30 March; *Le Matin*, 17 May 2000.

19. *El Watan*, 13 April, 1, 19 May; *al-Hayat*, 23 May; *al-Wasat*, 17 July; *FT*, 11 August, 14 November; *Le Matin*, 4 September, 23 October, 14 November; *al-Sharq al-Awsat*, 12 September; ENTV, 28 October (BBC Monitoring); R. Algiers, 8 November 2000 (BBC Monitoring).

20. *Le Quotidien d'Oran*, 1 April (BBC Monitoring); *Liberté*, 4 July; *al-Hayat*, 11 August 2000.

21. R. Algiers, 26 January 2000 (BBC Monitoring).

22. *Ha'aretz*, 26 June; *MM*, 28 June; 3 July; *MEI*, 14 July; *al-Watan al-'Arabi*, 28 July; *CR*, Algeria, October 2000, p. 17.

23. *Le Matin*, 2, 3 July; *Le Monde*, 4 July; *al-Watan al-'Arabi*, 7 July; *MEI*, 14 July; *MWM*, No. 86, 5 July 2000.

24. R. Algiers, 17 August (BBC Monitoring); ENTV, 28 October (BBC Monitoring); *Liberté*, 9 November; *Le Matin*, 19 December 2000.

25. *Le Jeune Indépendent*, 15 July; *El Watan*, 12 August 2000.

26. R. Algiers, 26 August (BBC Monitoring); *El Watan*, *al-Sharq al-Awsat*, 27 August; *MM*, 7 September; *MEI*, 15 September 2000.

27. Algerian TV, 26 August (BBC Monitoring); *al-Wasat*, 4 September; *al-Quds al-'Arabi*, 1 November 2000.

28. *El Watan*, 27 August, 4 September; *al-Zaman*, 12 September 2000.

29. *Al-Hayat*, 28 August, 1 November; *MM*, 7 September; *MEI*, 15 September; *al-Wasat*, 18 September; *Le Matin*, 5 December; <www.ccFIS.org>, 22 December 2000; *CR*, Algeria, January 2001, p. 13

30. *FT*, 11 August; *al-Wasat*, 28 August, 16 October; *al-Sharq al-Awsat*, 16 September; ENTV, 21 September, 8, 28 October (BBC Monitoring); R. Algiers, 5 November (BBC Monitoring); *al-Hayat*, 12 November, 23 December 2000.

31. *Liberté*, 7 November; *al-Hayat*, 9 November; *Le Jeune Indépendent*, 19 November 2000 (BBC Monitoring).

32. *Al-Hayat*, 3 December; *Le Matin*, 5 December 2000.

33. *Al-Hayat*, 31 December; *CR*, Algeria, January 2001, p. 14.

34. *Al-Sharq al-Awsat*, 30 October; ENTV, 31 October (BBC Monitoring); *al-Zaman*, 13, 18 November; *Le Matin*, 14 November 2000.

35. *Al-Youm*, 21 December; *AW*; 21 December; *al-Sharq al-Awsat*, 22 December; *al-Hayat*, 23 December; *CR*, Algeria, January 2001, p. 12.

36. *MEI*, 28 July; *CR*, Algeria, October 2000, p. 21, January 2001, pp. 10, 13, May 2001, p. 21; *CP*, Algeria, 2001, p. 31.

37. *El Watan*, 20 February; *al-Hayat*, 20 May; *al-Wasat*, 17 July; *MEI*, 28 July; *CR*, Algeria, January 2001, p 20.

38. *MEI*, 28 July; *CR*, Algeria, October 2000, p. 27; *CP*, Algeria, 2001, p. 30.

39. *CR*, Algeria, October 2000, p. 23.

40. R. Algiers, 29, 30 January, 18 June (BBC Monitoring); ENTV, 21 February, 12 December (BBC Monitoring); al-Zaman, 7 March; *MM*, 14 April; *al-Hayat*, 23 December 2000.

41. ENTV, 18 January; R. Algiers, 9 February 2000 (BBC Monitoring).

42. ENTV, 6 March, 1, 4 April, 3 May; R. Algiers, 10 April 2000 (BBC Monitoring).
43. R. Algiers, 28 March (BBC Monitoring); ENTV, 4, 18 April, 23 November (BBC Monitoring); JANA, 17 May; Libyan TV, 22 October (BBC Monitoring); *CR*, Algeria, July 2000, p. 19.
44. ENTV, 9 January, 17, 23 February (BBC Monitoring); *al-Sharq al-Awsat*, 4, 17 February; R. Algiers, 15 February (BBC Monitoring); *Le Matin*, 20 February 2000.
45. ENTV, 2 March, 4 April (BBC Monitoring); *al-Hayat*, 3 March; *Horizons*, 5 April 2000.
46. *Liberté*, 23 April; R. Algiers, 29, 30 April, 10 May (BBC Monitoring); RTM TV, 9 May (BBC Monitoring); *al-Hayat*, 11 May 2000.
47. ENTV, 12, 15 January, 27 June (BBC Monitoring); Sahara Press Service (SPS), 10 January; R. Algiers, 28 June (BBC Monitoring); *El Watan*, 29 June 2000.
48. *Time*, 26 June; *Le Matin*, 1 July; *La Tribune*, R. Algiers, 16 August (BBC Monitoring); *Le Jeune Indépendent*, 26 August; ENTV, 3 September 2000 (BBC Monitoring).
49. R. Algiers, 24, 28 September (BBC Monitoring); R. Polisario, 6 November 2000 (BBC Monitoring).
50. ENTV, Moroccan TV, 16 November (BBC Monitoring); *Liberté*, 26 December 2000.
51. *Al-Khabar*, 14 June; R. Algiers, 9 September; *El Watan*, 10 September; *MM*, 13 September 2000.
52. AFP, 17, 18 February; MENA, 4 April 2000.
53. *The North Africa Journal*, 22 April; ENTV, Algiers, 12 May (BBC Monitoring); R. Algiers, 14 December (BBC Monitoring); *CP*, Algeria, 2000, p. 15.
54. *Al-Hayat*, 31 March; R. Algiers, 2, 14 May (BBC Monitoring); *Horizons*, 31 May 2000; <www.fidh.org/magmoyen/algerie.htm>; <www.web.amnesty.org/web/ar2000web.nsf/nafr_mideast>.
55. <www.amnesty.org>, Index: MDE 28/11/00, 8 November, MDE 28/016/2000 21/11/2000.
56. *Al-Sahafa*, 4 November; ENTV, 9, 12 November 2000 (BBC Monitoring).
57. ENTV, 28 March (BBC Monitoring); ITAR-TASS, 7, 13 October, 20, 21 November 2000.
58. *Le Monde*, *al-Hayat*, 26 January; *CR*, Algeria, April 2000, p. 18.
59. R. Algiers, 5, 6 February, 31 March (BBC Monitoring); *Le Matin*, 6 February; *MEI*, 30 June 2000.
60. R. Algiers, 16, 17, 24 May; ENTV, 23 May 2000 (BBC Monitoring).
61. *Al-Hayat*, 28 May; *MM*, 14 June; *MEI*, 30 June 2000.
62. *Le Monde*, 14, 15, 17 June; *Libération*; 14, 15 June; *FT*, 15, 17 May; *MEI*, 30 June 2000.
63. *FT*, France Inter Radio, 15 June (BBC Monitoring); ENTV 17 June (BBC Monitoring); *Le Monde*, 16, 17 June; *MEI*, 30 June 2000.
64. LCI TV, 14 June 2000 (BBC Monitoring).
65. France Info Radio, 15 June (BBC Monitoring); *CR*, Algeria, July 2000, p. 20.
66. France 2 TV, 16 June 2000 (BBC Monitoring).
67. R. Algiers, 12 January, 2 February, 22 March, 29 April, 24 June, 17 August, (BBC Monitoring); ENTV, 3 February, 9 September 2000 (BBC Monitoring).
68. *Al-Sharq al-Awsat*, 22 March; R. Algiers, 23 March (BBC Monitoring); *al-Hayat*, 24 April, 8 May; *al-Khabar*, 7 May; R. Algiers, 5 August 2000 (BBC Monitoring).
69. ENTV, 8 September (BBC Monitoring); *al-Khabar*, *El Watan*, 10 December 2000.

Bahrain

(Al-Bahrayn)

JOSHUA TEITELBAUM

In 2000, Bahrain, led by Emir Hamad bin 'Isa Al Khalifa, made some progress toward the encouragement of greater political participation, although not enough to entirely satisfy the largely Shi'i opposition. A new Consultative Council was appointed, which included a Jew and a Christian. Hamad also announced that the council would be elected within four years, and that it would coexist with a fully elected parliament, amounting to a bicameral system. The emir further declared that the emirate would become a kingdom. Relations were unsettled with Qatar, as the two countries continued to dispute control of the Hawar Islands. Attempts at reconciliation were many, but results were few. Following the Saudi lead, Bahrain continued to improve relations with Iran; following the US lead, it took a hard line on Iraq, and even offered to once again host UN monitors of the Iraqi arms program. Military cooperation with the US continued apace. With respect to economic issues, increased oil revenues during the year contributed to a rise in real GDP of 5%.

INTERNAL AFFAIRS

The year opened with Emir Hamad displaying typical tribal largesse: the palace announced that he would fund the weddings of two thousand nationals to mark the passing of the millennium. As in other Gulf countries, Bahraini bachelors were tempted to marry foreign women because of the high price of the dowry. Hamad's munificence thus demonstrated both his generosity and the royal family's desire to limit the growth of the non-Bahraini population.

The first year of Hamad's rule, which ended on 6 March, had generated some expectation that the young monarch would restore previously suspended political freedoms (such as bringing back the elected National Assembly, which was dissolved in 1975). The release of opposition members from jail added to this assessment on the part of many Bahrainis. Although in December 1999 he had announced that he would establish municipal councils elected by universal suffrage (see *MECS* 1999, p. 195), the predominately Shi'i opposition was not satisfied by this minor, yet still unfulfilled gesture.[1]

And the opposition was waiting for more. It continued to report violations of human rights, including arrests and the prevention of Shi'i celebrations, while the government took measures to bolster security. During the year it appointed governors to three of the four administrative districts. All were members of the Al Khalifa, and all were veteran security officials. The Bahrain Freedom Movement noted that the Human Rights Committee had done nothing since it had been created by the emir in 1999, and was only called upon to defend the emirate from the criticism of foreign human rights groups. An attempt to set up a human rights NGO was thwarted by the government. The opposition

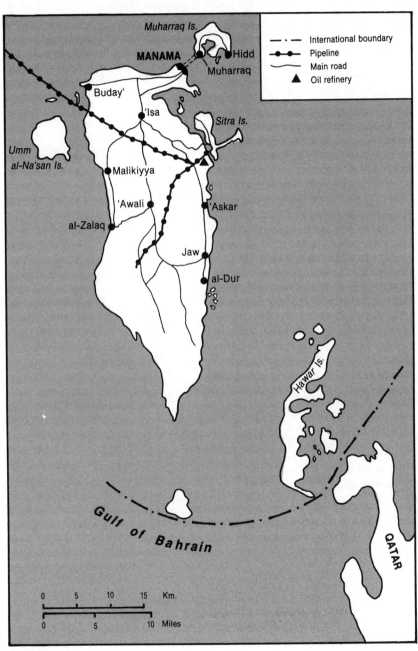

Bahrain

reported on numerous small demonstrations. A journalist who worked for the London-based *Economist* was arrested and then released in November. Amnesty International (AI) continued to express its concern about the human rights situation in the country; the US State Department estimated that "as many as" 750 detainees remained in prison.[2]

Hopes of further political participation in the emirate were raised in May, when the prime minister, Shaykh Khalifa bin Salman Al Khalifa, announced that women would be added to the appointed Consultative Council during the year, and that the next council, four years hence, would be freely elected.[3] But the institution itself, even if freely elected, had virtually no power.[4]

The emir made new appointments to the Consultative Council in late September. The forty-member (plus chairman) council included nineteen new members. There were four women amongst the new appointees, including a Christian. A Jew of Iraqi origin, Da'ud Nunu, was also among the new appointees. In September 1999, the emir had hailed "the efforts of the Nunu family over several decades to consolidate the role of Bahrain in the banking sector." According to the minister of information, Muhammad Ibrahim al-Mutawa'a, the council representatives had been selected "from every category of society which will contribute to the enrichment of the democratic process and in political, administrative, and economic decisions." When all was said and done, the council had nineteen Shi'is (one was Isma'ili), nineteen Sunnis, one Jew, one Christian, and a Shi'i chairman.[5] The appointment of women and minorities, particularly a Jew, to a Majlis al-Shura, which was essentially a Muslim concept, was an interesting step for the emir. The US hailed the move, although the opposition believed that its only aim was to satisfy the US, and pointed out that the council was not in accordance with the Bahraini constitution.[6]

In October, the emir announced that Bahrain would adopt a new national charter after the people had discussed it. The charter would "set the principles...for a new conception for the state and Bahraini democracy, which will adopt the best part of the past." The opposition, however, wondered how the emir could change the constitution without a constitutional process, and expressed its concern that the forty-six-member committee, appointed in November and asked to comment on an initial draft document, would be a rubber stamp for the emir's wishes to bypass the constitution. Emir Hamad's plan was termed "dictatorship consolidated in the name of reform."[7]

The opposition also complained that the committee formed to examine the national charter was dominated by the Al Khalifa. Six members of the committee resigned in early December, objecting to attempts to circumvent the constitution and turn the country into a monarchy. According to Shaykh Khalid bin Ahmad Al Khalifa, minister of state in the emir's court, the Bahraini system was a hereditary monarchy anyway, and therefore it could be called a kingdom, emirate, or sultanate.[8] But becoming king was certain to raise the international profile of the Bahraini leader.

In mid-month, the emir announced that the country would gradually install a fully elected parliament and hold municipal elections. He termed the planned elections "the foundation stones for democratic and political development" in a National Day speech broadcast live to the nation. But the elected parliament was to exist alongside the appointed consultative council, "which comprised experienced and specialized people," according to the emir.[9] The opposition stated that the move did not go far enough, since the emir had yet to release all political prisoners and allow the return of exiles, but it was cautious in its criticism. The opposition acknowledged that Emir Hamad had "started to behave in a more serious manner on political and economic issues," but it still demanded the restoration of parliament. It further called for national reconciliation before Manama went ahead with a proposed referendum on the elections.[10]

In a further conciliatory move, the emir commuted the death sentences of three Shi'is convicted of a 1996 arson attack on a Manama restaurant.[11]

The ruling family experienced a slight scandal beginning in July, when it was discovered that a US Marine had married a member of the Al Khalifa, Maryam, aged eighteen. They eloped to the US, with the marine, Lance Corporal Jason Johnson, spiriting his bride out the country dressed as a marine and carrying fake military documents. The ruling family opposed the marriage. "I did the worst thing possible in my country, to fall in love with a non-Muslim," said Al Khalifa. "To make it even worse, he's an American."[12]

ECONOMIC ISSUES

The rise in oil prices helped the economy of Bahrain, leading to a 5% growth in real GDP during the year, up from the 4% of 1999. This led the government to slash taxes on food and consumer goods. In April, Emir Hamad ordered the creation of a Supreme Council for Economic Development to devise a strategy for the economy, which was too dependent on an oil resource that was running out. The council was to be chaired by the prime minister, Shaykh Khalifa bin Salman Al Khalifa, who was to appoint at least nine ministers and experts to serve on it. The council was charged with determining the future strategy of economic development and follow up on implementation. It was also to propose policies for economic growth and determine the nature of economic development. Seeking foreign investment was to be a priority of the council.[13]

FOREIGN AFFAIRS

Crown Prince Salman bin Hamad's visit to the US in mid January, combined with the emir's strong support for US Gulf policy and hosting the American Navy's Fifth Fleet, all demonstrated Manama's position as a strategic US ally in the Gulf.[14]

Relations with Qatar continued to be bumpy, as the two sides awaited the decision of the International Court of Justice (ICJ) on the dispute concerning the Hawar Islands and other territories claimed by both countries. In January the emir of Bahrain paid a visit to Doha, which followed December 1999 visit of the Emir Hamad bin Khalifa Al Thani of Qatar to Manama (see MECS 1999. p. 196).[15] In February, Qatari crown prince Jasim bin Hamad visited Bahrain to meet with his counterpart, Shaykh Salman, in order to co-chair the first meeting of a joint high commission set up in December 1999. The commission was also set to examine a project to build a 50km. causeway connecting the two Gulf states. Both sides seemed determined to avoid a confrontation. Following the commission meetings, statements were issued by both sides urging patience with respect to their mutual dispute.[16] In March, Shaykh 'Abdallah bin Thamir bin Muhammad Al Thani was announced as Doha's ambassador to Manama. Crown Prince Salman visited Doha in April for another meeting of the joint commission, while at the same time, Qatar Airways resumed its flights to from Doha to Manama.[17]

But this newfound optimism received a blow in May, at the end of which the ICJ was supposed to start hearing arguments in the case. Bahrain had expected that the commission would lead Qatar to withdraw its suit from the ICJ and rely on the commission and the mediating efforts of the UAE and Saudi Arabia. When Doha failed to withdraw the suit,

Manama announced that it "had no choice but to set aside the work" of the commission. Qatar expressed "surprise" at the move, particularly since relations had seemed to be on the mend, but it probably believed that it had a better case than Bahrain to present to the ICJ. Doha emphasized that the suspension of the commission's work had been a Bahraini decision taken without consultation with Qatar. Saudi Arabia and the UAE sought to mediate — they brought about a meeting between the two emirs late in the month — but it yielded no forward movement.[18]

The rhetoric heated up as the ICJ began to hear the case. The Bahraini prime minister, Shaykh Khalifa bin Salman Al Khalifa, warned that Bahrain would not give up a single inch of its territory. "Justice will not be done unless it confirms a right that is anchored in history and backed by law," he stressed. Qatari papers ridiculed Bahrain for noting to the court that its troops on the islands had gone on alert. Bahraini newspapers scoffed at Doha's opening arguments, which stressed the proximity of the Hawar Islands to Qatar. All the same, the countries' leaders called for calm during the ICJ deliberations. The emir of Bahrain stated that Manama "has a sincere wish to set up a rapprochement, cooperation, even a union with our brothers in Qatar," but the Qatari emir was not as sure, replying that the decision would have to be that of the people of the two countries. Desire for union aside, Bahrain was non-committal about whether or not it would accept the ICJ decision. A visit by Emir Hamad of Qatar to Manama in late May did little to calm the situation.[19] Significantly, the Bahraini opposition stood by the emir in his dispute with Qatar, writing that "we hope the ICJ will soon announce an amicable solution that retains Bahrain's sovereignty over the islands of Hawar."[20]

In July, Bahrain announced that it was pushing ahead with tourism development on the Hawar Islands, so that the islands "become an important pillar of the national economy."[21]

As the Doha Islamic Conference Organization (ICO) summit approached in November, Bahrain announced that it would boycott the meeting because of the dispute. Emir Hamad of Bahrain stated that it was not right to go to Doha before the ICJ had issued its verdict, and that "Qatar's pretensions on Bahrain's state territory and waters have affected relations between the two countries and prevented their development." Shaykh Hamad of Qatar did, on the other hand, attend the Gulf Cooperation Council (GCC) summit in Manama in December.[22] During the summit, Bahrain protested a GCC publication that affirmed Qatari sovereignty over the Zubara, an area on the west coast of Qatar, which was claimed by Bahrain.[23]

Israel hinted during the year at contacts with Bahrain. Its foreign minister, David Levy, stated in February that normalization with Bahrain was on course. The crown prince met with Israeli regional cooperation minister Shimon Peres at the Swiss resort of Davos during the World Economic Forum in late January. Following the meeting, Salman said, "We will take two steps for each step they take for the sake of peace. We will never fall behind." He was referring to Israel's consent to open negotiations with Syria. Although the official Bahraini press played down the importance of the meeting, it appears that Bahrain may have been motivated by a desire to compete with Qatar, with a view to firming up commercial contacts with Israel following the signing of a peace agreement.[24]

Following the outbreak of Palestinian violence in late September, Bahrain backed calls for an urgent Arab summit, and flew medical aid to the injured. On Friday 20 October, following prayers, around two thousand Bahrainis shouted anti-Israel and anti-

US slogans during demonstrations in front of the US embassy. No arrests were made. A Bahraini official was quoted as saying that "there can be no arrests of citizens who have expressed, in a peaceful manner, their feeling about what is happening to Palestinians in Jerusalem." The opposition, however, said that "scores" were arrested at the October demonstrations, as well as at further pro-Palestinian demonstrations on the Iranian-influenced 'Jerusalem Day' in December. The government denied that there were arrests in the December demonstrations. Playing host to a meeting of GCC foreign ministers in November, Bahraini foreign minister Shaykh Muhammad bin Mubarak Al Khalifa called the Israeli response to the violence "savage attacks."[25]

Relations with Iran continued their steady improvement, as Manama followed the Saudi lead on rapprochement with Tehran. Bahraini minister of commerce 'Ali Salih 'Ali signed a memorandum of understanding with his Iranian counterpart Muhammad Shariatmadari at the end of the first meeting of a joint economic commission in Tehran in March. Iranian foreign minister Kamal Kharrazi visited Manama at the end of the month for talks of the joint political committee. His visit followed on the heels of a statement by the Bahraini prime minister, Shaykh Khalifa bin Salman Al Khalifa, stressing that normalization with Iran would happen much more rapidly if Tehran ended its "occupation" of three disputed Gulf islands claimed by the UAE (see chapter on the UAE). Both sides stressed the progress made in the talks and Kharrazi announced that the two countries would soon launch a sea link to increase trade.[26]

Bahraini support for US policy in the Gulf continued to cloud relations with Iraq. Manama offered in February to host a planned new UN arms control body for Iraq, UNMOVIC (see chapters on the US and the Middle East, and Iraq). It had also played host to the previous body, UNSCOM. Baghdad slammed Manama for its offer, saying it meant that Bahrain was "ready to commit new crimes against the people of Iraq." In October, Bahrain sent a plane loaded with medicine and food to Baghdad, in a gesture designed to show that it was supportive of the Iraqi people.[27]

Bahrain signed a series of mostly trade-related cooperation accords with Sudan in January, following a visit by Sudanese president 'Umar al-Bashir.[28]

In defense affairs, Bahrain signed a defense cooperation protocol with Jordan in February during a visit by King 'Abdallah II. The protocol stipulated cooperation in training senior officers and the exchange of military expertise. During a visit to Britain later that month, the crown prince and commander in chief of the Bahraini Defense Force, Shaykh Salman signed an agreement to upgrade the 1994 joint defense pact with London. Manama was a stop for US secretary of defense William Cohen during his swing through the Gulf in April. Cohen was trying to sell the Gulf countries on the US idea for a missile defense system known as the Cooperative Defense Initiative. The idea was not well received in Manama, where Defense Minister Shaykh Khalifa bin Ahmad Al Khalifa said that it was too expensive and had not been discussed by the GCC countries. In June, Bahrain took delivery on the first of its new production F-16 aircraft from Lockheed Martin. In August, the US announced that it intended to sell Bahrain the Army Tactical Missile System (ATACMS), a system designed to hit high-value targets, such as missile batteries and tank formations, using short-range ballistic missiles fired from a multiple-rocket launcher carried on a tracked vehicle. Concerned that the technology might fall into foreign hands, the US military intended that Bahraini military personnel would not have access to the launch codes, and that the ATACMS storage compound would be placed under 24-hour video surveillance by CENTCOM (Central

Command), the organization of the US military responsible for operational control of US combat forces in the Middle East and Central Asia.[29]
The length of Cohen's stay in Bahrain during his Gulf tour was indicative of the importance both countries attached to the defense relationship. The presence of the US Navy's Fifth Fleet in Bahrain also contributed to Manama's economy, amounting to around $187m. in 1999, including food and fuel purchased and spending by US personnel on liberty or living in Bahrain. The US was spending an additional $200m. on a building project for the military, using Bahraini contractors.[30]

NOTES

For the place and frequency of publications cited here, and for the full name of the publication, news agency, radio station, or monitoring service where an abbreviation is used, please see "List of Sources." Only in the case of more than one publication bearing the same name is the place of publication noted here.
      The author thanks Itamar Inbari for his excellent work in assembling source material for this chapter.

1. Bahrain Freedom Movement member Sa'id Shihabi, *al-Quds al-'Arabi*, 10 March 2000 (MEM).
2. *CR*, Bahrain, Qatar, May 2000, p. 15; *Bahrain News*, 18, 20 February, 5, 13, 14 March, 29 October, 2 November (MSANEWS); AFP, 7, 14 November; AI News Release, 21 November 2000; US Department of State, *Bahrain, Country Report on Human Rights Practices, 2000*, February 2001.
3. AFP, 30 May 2000.
4. *Al-Quds al-'Arabi*, 23 June 2000 (MEM).
5. AFP, 26, 27 September 2000.
6. *MM*, 28 September; AFP, 29 September, 1 October 2000.
7. AFP, 3 October; *Bahrain News*, 27 November (MSANEWS).
8. *Bahrain News*, 5 December (MSANEWS); AFP, 7 December; *MM*, 10 December 2000
9. AP, AFP, 16 December 2000.
10. AFP, 17, 19, 20 December 2000; *CR*, Bahrain, Qatar, February 2001, p. 12.
11. AFP, 26 December 2000.
12. AFP, 10, 17 July 2000.
13. AFP, 3 January, 1 April; US EIA report on Bahrain, October 2001.
14. AFP, 15 January; *CR*, Bahrain, Qatar, 1st quarter, 2000, p. 15.
15. AFP, 6 January; *al-Sharq al-Awsat*, 28 January 2000.
16. AFP, 20, 22 February 2000.
17. AFP, 22 March, 24 April 2000.
18. AFP, 19, 20, 21, 22, 24 May; *al-Quds al-'Arabi*, 25 May 2000 (*MM*).
19. AFP, 30 May, 3, 9, 29 June, 18 July; *CR*, Bahrain, Qatar, August 2000, p. 15.
20. *Bahrain News*, 30 June 2000 (MSANEWS).
21. AFP, 8 July 2000.
22. AFP, 6 November, 26 December 2000.
23. AFP, 29 December 2000.
24. AFP, 1 February; *CR*, Bahrain, Qatar, 1st quarter, 2000, p.15.
25. AFP, 3, 14, 20 October, 25 November, 24, 25 December; MENA, 14 October (DR); *Bahrain News*, 22 October, 22 December 2000 (MSANEWS).
26. IRNA, 2 March, 29 March, 22 May (DR); AFP, 28, 29, 30 March 2000.
27. AFP, 10, 12 February, 18 September, 15 October 2000.
28. AFP, 15, 16 January 2000.

29. AFP, 8, 27, 28 February, 5 April; Reuters, 2 May; PRNewswire, 23 June; *Defense News*, 11 September 2000.
30. *CR*, Bahrain, Qatar, May 2000, p. 16.

Egypt
(Jumhuriyyat Misr al-'Arabiyya)

MEIR HATINA

Parliamentary elections occupied the center stage of Egyptian political life in 2000. For the first time, they were comprised of three rounds, held during October–November. The judiciary, which supervised the elections, gained in prestige as a central pillar of the rule of law in the country, evoking an acknowledgment by the opposition that this was a positive, albeit insufficient, development on the path to genuine democracy. The limits of political pluralism and civic activity, however, were evident throughout the year.

Islamist violence diminished, but Islamists demand for legal inclusion in national politics remained unaddressed. Moreover, the government suspended the opposition Socialist Liberal Party (SLP) in May, for alleged irregularities. This was followed by the postponement of elections in all professional associations to an unspecified date, and the arrest of the prominent liberal activist-scholar, Sa'd al-Din Ibrahim, on a variety of charges including receiving foreign funding with the intent of tarnishing Egypt's image. The struggle over Egypt's cultural orientation was also palpable during the year. A new law defining personal status, which, inter alia, awarded women the right to sue for divorce in court, was ratified by the parliament in January only after a highly charged debate led to the adoption of amendments designed to appease the mostly Islamist opponents. In a similar vein, a new edition of the novel by Syrian author Haydar Haydar, *Walima li-a'shab al-bahr* ("A Banquet for Seaweed"), evoked a public outcry against its perceived insult to Islam and incited student riots.

The decade-long economic reform program in Egypt also evoked public grievances. It had not fulfilled the expectations of the bulk of the population for social relief, or of local and foreign investors for a substantive liberalization of the Egyptian market. Caught between these two divergent sets of priorities, the government showed more responsiveness to the social agenda, its main source of legitimation, and rejuvenated efforts to reduce poverty and unemployment. Accordingly, although the goals of privatization and integration in the global economy continued to guide economic policy makers, the implementation of these policies was slowed by concerns about their likely social repercussions. Monetary policy, too, seemed to favor ensuring a relatively stable exchange rate of the Egyptian pound vis-à-vis the US dollar, in order to impose a degree of market stability and boost public confidence in the local currency. Minister of Economy and Foreign Trade Yusuf Butrus-Ghali prudently noted that the country's economic policy shifts were subtle. "This is not a system of large shocks."[1] While government officials emphasized that economic caution reflected a sense of national responsibility and concern for the poorer sectors of society, the business community perceived it as lack of commitment to building a market economy.

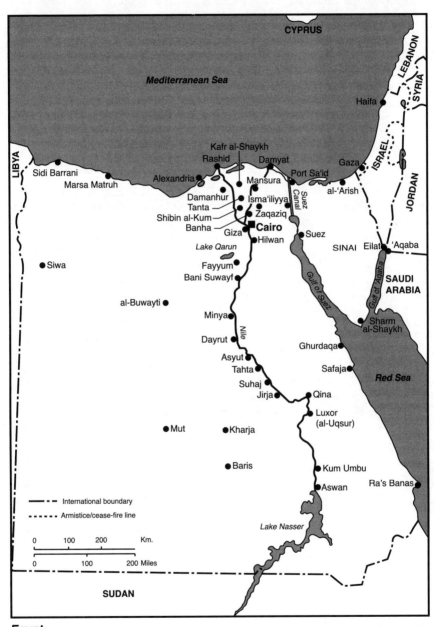

Egypt

Egypt's regional agenda was no less burdened than its domestic one. The promise of a comprehensive regional peace held out by Israeli prime minister Ehud Barak granted Egypt a further opportunity to exhibit its mediation skills. Once again, Cairo became a busy center of Arab diplomacy. Palestinian Authority (PA) Chairman Yasir 'Arafat, as well as Barak, were frequent visitors, while Syrian diplomats, too, made sure to stop in Cairo for consultations. However, Cairo's diplomatic optimism rapidly turned to frustration. Syrian-Israeli negotiations, after gaining momentum early in the year, quickly reached a dead end. The death of President Hafiz al-Asad in June and his son Bashshar's preoccupation with establishing his credentials to retain power, further reinforced the diplomatic impasse. In addition, the Israeli-Palestinian negotiations for a permanent settlement, which reached a climax at talks in Camp David in July, ended inconclusively and set the stage for widespread and sustained Palestinian-Israeli violence, beginning in September.

The violence in the West Bank and Gaza areas had repercussions throughout the region, impelling the Arab governments to consolidate a joint anti-Israeli stand and dealing a heavy blow to the Egyptian peace diplomacy. Cairo, appeasing domestic and regional Arab public opinion, felt compelled to recall its ambassador from Tel Aviv for consultations and express its support for an Arab embargo of Israeli products. However, Mubarak made it clear that a regional war was out of the question and that Egypt would continue to promote the peace process. The moderating influence of Egypt was also reflected in the relatively restrained decisions adopted at the emergency Arab summit conference in Cairo in October and the Islamic Conference Organization (ICO) summit in Doha in November, which left the issue of severing all ties with Israel to the discretion of the countries involved (see chapter on political Islam). Egypt also invested effort among the Palestinians and in the Arab world to promote an American proposal for a final status agreement between Israel and the PA. These attempts, however, were unsuccessful, revealing the limits of Mubarak's influence on 'Arafat, particularly when Palestinian and Egyptian agendas did not converge.

The regression in the peace process placed Egypt in a delicate diplomatic position, caught between its desire to eliminate the risks of regional instability by expanding the perimeters of peace in the region and its aspiration to promote closer inter-Arab cooperation under its own tutelage. This last ambition faced other obstacles as well, such as the continued failure to bring about national reconciliation in Sudan, and the Gulf Arab states' ongoing obstruction of Iraq's return to the Arab fold. Both issues — that of Sudan and of Iraq — were also on the Egyptian-American agenda, as Egypt demanded US support for Sudanese territorial integrity, and an easing of the sanctions on Iraq. These, along with domestic concerns, including the status of the Egyptian Coptic minority and civil rights in general, continued to fuel bilateral tension between Cairo and Washington, albeit without destabilizing their strategic partnership.

INTERNAL AFFAIRS

ISLAM IN THE STATE
Mubarak's initial policy of conciliation toward the Islamist trend in the 1980s, namely, dialogue with the militants and the integration of the Muslim Brotherhood in party politics, gave way in the 1990s to a decisive policy of military and political suppression. As a

result, Islamist violence gradually diminished, becoming more of an ongoing security concern than an existential threat to the regime. The distinctive Egyptian entity, defined by geography (the Nile Valley) and history (an entrenched central government), reinforced Egypt's highly cohesive state structure and functioned as a protective barrier against the risk of disintegration. A term sometimes used to describe the Egyptian polity was a "state of institutions."[2]

The growing distress of the militant groups in light of state repression was reflected both on the ideological and the organizational levels, exacerbated by further internal strife and the withdrawal of members seeking to establish legal political parties. The announcement in 1999 of a unilateral cease-fire by the largest militant organization, al-Jama'a al-Islamiyya (hereinafter, the Jama'a), attested to the decline in power of the militants (see *MECS* 1999, pp. 204–206). Although the cease-fire was maintained into 2000, and was joined by the Jihad group, intense debate continued internally over the justification for this step, especially given the state's ongoing harassment aimed at denying the militants a public platform.

Friction within the ranks of the radical Islamists was evident during the year. In January, the former head of the military arm of the Jama'a, Mustafa Hamza, replaced Rifa'i Ahmad Taha as leader of the movement. Apparently, Taha was ousted for attempting to draw the Jama'a into a pact with the network of the dissident Saudi militant, Usama bin Ladin, a step deemed too dangerous by the other movement leaders.[3] Bin Ladin's attacks in recent years on American targets in Africa and the Gulf (see *MECS* 1998, pp. 131–34) made him a primary target for seizure by the US security forces, thereby exposing all his allies, including Egyptians, to harassment and extradition in various Western countries.

A similar development was evident in the ranks of the Jihad movement, which until 2000 had rejected the notion of ending violence. Reports in February announced that Ayman al-Zawahiri, founder of the Jihad, was ousted as leader of the movement because of his ideological rigidity, centralist tendencies and moves to forge a link between the Jihad's agenda and that of bin Ladin.[4] This development bolstered the pragmatically oriented wing of the movement, which supported a cease-fire and was anxious to show that violent revolution was not the Jihad's only strategy. According to Usama Sadiq, one of the leaders of this group, the armed struggle should be directed at Palestine in a campaign to liberate the al-Aqsa Mosque.[5] The widening consensus over a cease-fire, however, failed to put an end to internal disputes in the radical camp.

In a letter in June to Jama'a leaders in Egyptian jails, 'Umar 'Abd al-Rahman, the movement's ideological leader jailed in the US for his involvement in the 1993 World Trade Center bombing (see *MECS* 1993, pp. 129–30), expressed reservations over the cease-fire. It "had achieved nothing other than disunity," he stated.[6] This message elicited a fierce debate between supporters and opponents of an end to violence. Taha, the Jama'a's former leader and an advocate of a hawkish stance, announced that the movement was currently reconsidering the decision regarding the cease-fire. In contrast, other Jama'a leaders outside Egypt reiterated their commitment to the cease-fire, which they said had produced a number of achievements, including an end to frequent arrests and torture in jails and the release of hundreds of Islamists held in detention. They attributed 'Abd al-Rahman's declaration to the harsh conditions of his solitary confinement, which precluded sufficient awareness of the facts.[7] Still, a previous statement issued by 'Abd al-Rahman in October 1999, which banned Muslims from taking part in the "infidel" Egyptian parliament, gained wide support in the radical camp.[8]

The regime remained indifferent to the confusion in the militants' ranks regarding a unilateral cease-fire. In February, two Jihad leaders who had been extradited from Albania in 1998 were executed. In June, four persons charged with membership in a terrorist organization were sentenced to prison. In October and November, three militants were killed in Aswan by security forces and another fourteen individuals were arrested.[9] Governmental pressure was also kept up on former radicals by denying their demands for legal representation in national politics.

Spokespersons for the Shari'a (Islamic law) Party and the Islah (Reform) Party, whose members had seceded from their respective parent movements, the Jama'a and the Jihad, reiterated their renunciation of violence and their loyalty to the state (see *MECS* 1999, p. 206). However, they criticized the regime's hostile attitude, manifested in the legal sphere in the consistent rejection of the licensing requests submitted by the two parties, and in the security area in the systematic harassment of party members. In light of these repressive measures, leaders of the parties doubted that their appeal to the Political Party Tribunal would have any practical consequences.[10]

The marginalization of the militants weakened their pro-jihad, revolutionary strategy. However, it benefited the other Islamist approach — the legalist one represented by the Muslim Brotherhood, which advocated the gradual Islamization of the Egyptian polity and society by educational and political means (*da'wa*). Like the militant groups, the Brotherhood was also excluded from national politics and from civic power bases in professional associations through a series of legal and military maneuvers, and was forced to maintain a low profile. However, its grass roots popularity and its communal networks of social, health and educational services provided it with more stamina than the militants.[11]

The ongoing offensive by the government against the Brotherhood continued into 2000, focusing on the elections for the Bar Association scheduled for July and for parliament in October–November. Nineteen student members of the movement were arrested in Alexandria in January on the charge of membership in an illegal group. Forty activists in Cairo and Giza were arrested on the same charge in May. Meanwhile, the trial continued of twenty Brotherhood leaders arrested in October 1999, accused of conspiracy to undermine the social order.[12] The Brotherhood maintained that arrests and trials would not deter its members from seeking office in the professional associations and parliamentary elections, as withdrawal from them would be considered an act of suicide.[13] However, in order to temper the government attitude toward the movement, the Brotherhood announced that it would submit a shorter list of candidates than in the past.[14]

In anticipation of the elections to the Bar Association, following four years of state supervision of its activity due to alleged financial irregularities, the Brotherhood presented eight candidates, in contrast to approximately twenty candidates in the 1992 elections. The elections, however, were postponed due to a disagreement between the government and the association's lawyers regarding electoral procedures.[15]

The three-round parliamentary elections, based on individual lists, included a list of seventy-three Brotherhood candidates. It was half the number which had been fielded in the 1995 elections. For the first time in the movement's history, the list of candidates included a woman. The movement instructed activists to maintain a low profile at pre-election assemblies.[16] While welcoming the establishment of judicial supervision over the voting process, the Brotherhood expressed concern over possible government repression of its members in the preliminary stages of the process prior to the submission of the lists of candidates. This concern was not groundless.[17]

In May, the Party Affairs Commission of the Shura Council (the upper house of the Egyptian parliament) suspended the activities of the SLP and the publication of its journal, al-Sha'b (see below). The official justification for this injunction was internal rivalry over the party leadership and apparent misappropriation of funds. Clearly, however, the step was designed to prevent the Brotherhood from making use of the significant propaganda assets derived from its close relationship with the SLP.[18] Additionally, in order to deny a large number of Brotherhood members an opportunity to stand for election, the government announced that any individual with a criminal record was prohibited from participating in political activity.[19] With the approach of the elections in October, arrests became frequent.[20] Still, despite this systematic abuse, the Brotherhood won an impressive electoral achievement: seventeen of its seventy-three candidates were elected, making it the largest party in the opposition bloc, significantly larger than the total number of seats won by all other fifteen opposition parties combined. The cancellation of election results in Alexandria prevented the Brotherhood from gaining an additional two seats.[21]

The Brotherhood's successful electoral performance reflected, on the one hand, the relative freedom in which the elections took place, and on the other, the organizational capabilities of the movement, especially in light of official harassment. The results illuminated its political potential and reaffirmed its status as a permanent feature of Egyptian public life. The electoral achievement buoyed Brotherhood morale after a decade of systematic exclusion from national politics. Brotherhood leaders now demanded official recognition, and hinted their intention to contend in the Shura Council elections in April 2001.[22] However, the regime quickly dampened their enthusiasm. Fifteen Brotherhood members were sentenced to prison terms of 3–5 years in November, and twenty others were arrested in December.[23] The relationship between the state and the Brotherhood continued to be a vicious cycle of governmental offensives followed by a low, defensive profile by the movement in anticipation of future opportunities to demonstrate its strength.

Islamist politics claimed a hold on governmental institutions but also a monopoly over religious truth and the shaping of individual thought and conduct. This was the underlying point of departure for the assertiveness of Islamists with regard to the public sphere, i.e., in the struggle over public morality. Denunciations by Islamists of alleged insults to Islam had become a regular feature of cultural discourse, putting liberal thinkers on the defensive on issues of faith and forcing the government into an ambivalent position.

A typical episode in 2000 was the outcry over a new edition of the novel "A Banquet for Seaweed," first published in 1983 by Syrian author Haydar Haydar. Set in Algeria, the story is an account of society and its suffering under the military regime, climaxed by the suicide drowning of a dim-witted religious skeptic.[24] The book caused a public storm over its alleged insult to Islam, involving three elements that played a prominent role in the early stages of the debate: the Islamist opposition, the Ministry of Culture and al-Azhar University, the center for Islamic learning in Egypt and beyond. The Islamists denounced the author as a second Salman Rushdie and demanded that those responsible for the publication of the book be prosecuted. They also called for the resignation of Minister of Culture Faruq Husni for permitting its publication in Egypt, and blamed Shaykh al-Azhar Muhammad Sayyid Tantawi for authorizing the publication.[25] Minister Husni, refusing to resign, accused the Brotherhood of incitement for the purpose of political gain prior to the upcoming elections to the parliament. Nevertheless, he ordered the book removed from all bookstores.[26] Shaykh Tantawi claimed that the Ministry of Culture had not sought the authorized opinion of the Islamic Research Center of al-Azhar prior to the publication of the book, as required by the law of 1961.[27]

Both the decision by the minister of culture to remove the book from the stores and the explanations provided by Shaykh al-Azhar failed to quell the uproar, which soon turned into protest rallies by Azhar students. This development necessitated the intervention of a fourth player — the government — which had hitherto focused on examining Islamist complaints against the individuals involved in the book's publication. The police arrested seventy-five students (releasing them a few days later), and charged another forty Brotherhood activists with incitement.[28] In addition, the government appointed a committee of experts to investigate the charges against the book and its author. The committee's conclusions cleared the book of any suspicion of insulting religious values, but no copies of the book reappeared in the stores.[29] The government, in deciding to forcibly remove the issue from the public agenda, thereby revealed its inability to mold the national cultural agenda.

In contrast to its dominant position in politics, the government was only one of several elements in the struggle over shaping social values and image in the public sphere. The most conspicuous of these elements was the Islamist trend, which offered a more "authentic" and pristine narrative than the official one. This trend was supported by a large number of state-appointed 'ulama, who were the ideological rivals of Shaykh al-Azhar Tantawi. They criticized what they viewed as excessively liberal fatwas issued by Tantawi on social issues, aimed, they believed, at appeasing his government patrons.[30] The Islamist trend initiated the storm surrounding Haydar's book and dictated the terms of the ensuing controversy. Another element, the liberal trend, played a secondary role in this episode, with liberal Egyptian writers rallying to the defense of freedom of expression and insisting on literary, not political criticism of the book. They also demanded the abolition of al-Azhar's supervisory authority over published material on religious topics, claiming that the institution was a civil agency whose role was to provide guidance in faith-related issues only.[31] However, their voice was politically ineffective, especially in light of the government's ambivalent stance in the cultural realm.

By contrast, the government displayed far greater determination in promoting the status of women, with the new law of personal status presented to parliament in January. The bill granted women the right to sue for divorce in an accelerated court procedure pending the return of their dowries and a relinquishment of their financial rights, including alimony payments. Formerly, a woman seeking divorce was forced to prove that her husband was either infertile, insane or unable to provide economic support, as a condition for a suit. Furthermore, the new bill granted legal recognition to customary (unofficial) marriage (zawaj 'urfi), and permitted wives to travel abroad without their husband's permission.[32] All these clauses evoked heated public debate during the formulation of the bill and its submission to parliament. Most objections were Islam-based, as family matters were legally grounded in the Shari'a.

The government emphasized that the proposed law had received the approval of the religious authorities. Shaykh al-Azhar Tantawi appeared before the parliament and pointed out that Islam recognized equality between man and woman in some cases. "It is not that man is made of gold and woman is made of bronze," he said. While the right of divorce is granted unconditionally to men, he acknowledged, the problem lay in the abuse of this right, which the new law sought to rectify.[33] Tantawi's support of the government policy failed to mollify the parliamentary opposition. Opponents of the law — mainly Islamist-oriented and socially conservative delegates — contested the validity of the report written by the Islamic Research Center of al-Azhar, alleging that only twenty-three 'ulama of fifty had been present during the discussions of the issue.[34] Reportedly, many 'ulama had spoken out against the bill during the discussion, viewing it as a clear violation of the Shari'a, which requires the absolute obedience of wife to husband. Their major concern was the potential destabilization of family life through a flood of divorce applications, currently only a few thousand annually.[35] The debate revealed the segmented nature of the religious establishment and its limitations in mobilizing its members to promote the government's social agenda.

The 'ulama's reservations were supported by spokespersons of the Islamist opposition, members of the Brotherhood and militant groups, all of whom wished to use the debate over the law as a lever to oppose government policy and demonstrate their own stature.[36] In contrast, civil rights and women's organizations applauded the significant contribution to enhancing the status of women, although they feared that the law would benefit only affluent women who could allow themselves to relinquish their financial rights in exchange for a divorce. They voiced resentment against the intensity of the religious opposition to the law despite its support by Shaykh al-Azhar.[37]

Ultimately, the religious-based arguments of the opposition forced the government to amend the law: women were required to participate in a three-month period of discussion and conciliation in court prior to submitting an application for divorce, and the right of women to travel abroad without their husband's consent was dropped.[38]

SETTING BOUNDARIES: THE GOVERNMENT-CIVIL SOCIETY RELATIONSHIP

Egypt witnessed a significant increase in a new type of non-governmental organizations (NGOs) during the two decades of relative political openness under Mubarak. These organizations, similar to the more traditional NGOs, provided social services, but combined this activity with advocacy of civil and political issues. In this respect, they helped enrich public discourse on issues related to democratization, women's status and civil rights, yet their political impact was slight and in some cases their adherents were even exposed to government harassment.[39]

Opposition parties remained weak and professional associations were increasingly subjected to governmental supervision as a barrier against Islamist takeover. This policy of containment was reflected in Act 153 of 1999, which strictly regulated NGO functioning and instituted sanctions against such infractions as receipt of unapproved external funding or intervention in politics (see *MECS* 1999, pp. 209–11). Although the law was repealed in June 2000 under the pressure of local and Western public opinion,[40] the government continued to intervene in the internal affairs of NGOs. A prominent example was the elections to the Bar Association, scheduled by court order for July after a four-year period of government supervision due to alleged misappropriations of funds. Association lawyers opposed the voting procedures proposed by the government, including the placement of the voting stations, which they claimed would invite irregularities. In response, the government postponed the date of the elections, a move aimed at undermining the presumed strength of the Brotherhood showing in the Bar Association elections so close to the elections to parliament.[41]

The regime exhibited a low threshold of tolerance not only for the Brotherhood but for its allies. In May, the Party Affairs Commission suspended all activity by the SLP and closed its journal, al-Sha'b. The official justification was the internal dispute over the party leadership, which reached a peak when the leader, Ibrahim Shukri, was replaced by two different candidates on two consecutive occasions. In reality, however, the suspension was a response to the aggressive campaign conducted by al-Sha'b against the minister of culture in light of the publication of Haydar's book (see above).[42] Al-Sha'b had continuously tested the limits of governmental tolerance with its attacks on senior public figures over a period of years. Most prominent among these targets was the deputy prime minister and minister of agriculture, Yusuf Wali, who in 1999 was accused of ruining Egyptian agriculture by employing Israeli experts. Frequent confrontations with the government generally ended in trials and incarcerations of the paper's staff. In the current confrontation, besides the closure of the paper and the suspension of all party activities, the party leaders were investigated for receiving contributions from foreign bodies and for their ties with the Brotherhood.[43]

This episode evoked a flurry of responses from the opposition parties and civil rights organizations. Most of them held that the SLP and al-Sha'b had indeed exceeded the boundaries of accepted ethical behavior by politicizing religion and using ideological terror to the point of breaching public order. However, they criticized the extreme response of the government, emphasizing that any violation of the law should be treated exclusively through judicial channels.[44] Clearly, their desire to exploit the political distress of an Islamist-oriented rival on the eve of the elections was outweighed by their fear of a further erosion of Egyptian civil society.

Although disappointed with the criticism of civic groups and opposition parties, the SLP was pleased with their objection to the government moves against the party and its organ.[45] The SLP leaders sought to bring about internal reconciliation in order to remove the cause of the suspension, concurrently conducting a campaign in the courts against the Party Affairs Commission's decision to punish the party. In September, an administrative court permitted al-Sha'b to reopen, but the suspension of the SLP remained in force. The government promptly appealed to a higher court regarding the reopening of al-Sha'b, signaling its determination to redefine the limits of acceptable criticism in public discourse.[46]

The government also directed its efforts to curb civil activism in liberal circles and civil rights organizations. In July, the police closed the Ibn Khaldun Center for Development Studies in Cairo and arrested the director of the institute, Sa'd al-Din Ibrahim, together with fifteen other employees. The center was devoted to promoting democracy and civil society in the Arab world. Ibrahim had been a target for attacks by both the governmental and the opposition press because of his open treatment of such sensitive issues as the status of the Coptic minority in Egypt and his ongoing relationships with Israeli colleagues. His involvement in the drafting of an educational curriculum in Egypt in 1999 which expanded the study of the Coptic heritage in the public school system evoked further antagonism toward him.[47]

Ibrahim was arrested on charges of possession of forged identity cards with the intention of using them to vote in the parliamentary elections; preparing a distorted documentary film on the elections; and receiving funds from foreign donors without prior approval. Denying these charges, Ibrahim claimed that his arrest was politically motivated. It was his arrest, and not the activities of the Ibn Khaldun Center, he asserted, that damaged Egypt's reputation abroad. It sent a message to the world that no honest Egyptian could possibly function in the fields of human rights and democracy, i.e., that all were hired agents motivated by foreign bribes.[48] However, Ibrahim's fate was sealed by the Egyptian press, which systematically accused civil rights organizations of constituting a lever for foreign intervention in the country's internal affairs.[49] While a few commentators presented a more balanced view, criticizing the rush to condemn Ibrahim in the press without waiting for the conclusion of the legal procedures, these voices were overshadowed by the hard line taken in the government-owned media.[50]

The added issue of Ibrahim's American citizenship served to cloud the Egypt-US relationship. Despite a demand by the US for Ibrahim's immediate release, backed by international human rights organizations and the academic community, Egypt extended his detention, filing an indictment against him in September.[51] In taking this step, Egypt wished to warn the NGOs against overstepping the limits of civic activism, and at the same time to caution the West to refrain from using the civil rights issue as a justification for intervening in Egypt's sovereign affairs. The pronounced assertiveness of the government, even at the price of an international uproar, remained constant throughout Ibrahim's trial, which ended in May 2001 with a sentence of seven years imprisonment.[52] Viewed in a wider perspective, the heavy-handed approach of the government to civil rights organizations was designed to ensure that economic liberalization did not foster a corresponding liberalization of politics.[53] This strategy of mitigating the impact of economic reform on the civic arena was described by Robert Springborg as "crony capitalism," i.e., the government divests some of its ownership and permits the growth of a private sector linked closely to the state, thereby preserving the political status quo.[54]

THE PARLIAMENTARY ELECTIONS

The elections to parliament constituted the focus of political activity of both the government and the opposition parties during most of the year. A short while after his election to the presidency for his fourth term in November 1999, Mubarak pledged that the parliamentary elections in late 2000 would be honest and reliable. He also reiterated that the opposition was an integral part of the political fabric and functioned as a watchdog to protect the public interest.[55] However, the opposition parties, accustomed to hearing similar declarations in the past, viewed the test of Mubarak's statements in the implementation of genuine electoral reform that would advance Egypt along the road to true democracy.

The government rejected consistent demands by the opposition to revert to the electoral system of 1984 and 1987 based on party lists, fearing that reintroducing this format would allow the Brotherhood to gain parliamentary representation. Similar demands to revoke the constitutional clause allocating half the seats to fellahin (peasants) and laborers as being anachronistic and discriminatory were also rejected.[56] With this, the demand to transfer the supervisory authority over the elections from the Ministry of Interior to the judiciary was accepted by the government, thereby appeasing the opposition and allaying concerns by international bodies regarding the integrity of the elections.[57] Mubarak also approved the establishment of a new political party — a first in twenty-two years — the centrist National Accord Party (Hizb al-Wifaq al-Qawmi), raising the number of official parties to fifteen. Most of the founders of the new party were older former members of other parties, especially the SLP and the Democratic Nasserite Party. The party was headed by Ahmad Shuhib, a former member of the Free Officers group responsible for the 1952 coup which overthrew the monarchy. The new party lacked a clear ideological platform, with the exception of its rigid stance on the Israel-Arab conflict.[58] The party application was approved just two weeks after its submission in March, while longtime requests for approval submitted by two Islamist parties — the Wasat and the Shari'a — as well as the neo-Nasserite Dignity Party, were denied.[59]

The opposition suspected, not without basis, that the approval of the National Accord Party was a government tactic to split the opposition vote on the eve of the elections while giving the appearance of enhancing democracy for the benefit of the international community.

The amending of the election law in April to institute judicial supervision of the electoral procedure presented a complex logistical problem for the government because of the requirement that judges supervise each of the 42,000 voting stations. The solution was a three-stage electoral process — in Upper Egypt, Lower Egypt and metropolitan Cairo — over a three-week period, between 18 October and 8 November, along with a reduction in the number of voting stations to 18,000.[60] Although these technical arrangements were accepted by the opposition parties, they were not happy with the excessive emphasis placed by government spokespersons on the judicial supervision of the elections as a reflection of a free and fair democracy.[61] The opposition argued that the vaunted supervision was limited to election day only and did not replace the need for a genuine liberalization of the political arena.[62]

In preparation for the elections, the National Democratic Party (NDP), the president's ruling party, made efforts to improve its image and performance, initiating changes in the composition of the party leadership, the politburo and the general secretariat for the first time since 1993. More women, Copts, business-owners and younger members were co-opted into these bodies. To be sure, however, purges made within the NDP ranks excluded Mubarak's most trusted colleagues, such as cabinet ministers Yusuf Wali, Safwat al-Sharif and Kamal al-Shadhili. Two prominent figures among the newcomers were Yusuf Butrus-Ghali, minister of economy and foreign trade, who was of Coptic origin and nephew of former UN Secretary-General Butrus Butrus Ghali, and Jamal Mubarak, the president's son.[63] The addition of the younger Mubarak to the general secretariat evoked speculation in the Egyptian press regarding Mubarak's personal plans in light of the trend of grooming sons as heirs in a number of Arab republics, including Iraq and Syria.[64]

In a significant move, the party decided to support twelve Coptic candidates in Cairo and other regions,[65] a step taken in the aftermath of bloody events in the village of Kushh and nearby areas in the province of Suhaj in Upper Egypt in January. There, an economic dispute between Copts and Muslims developed into sectarian violence in which nineteen Copts and one Muslim were killed and thirty-three were wounded.[66] The government, in elevating more Copts within the NDP and putting them forward as parliamentary candidates, was anxious to appease the Coptic community in Egypt and abroad and to defuse international criticism of alleged sectarian persecution in Egypt.

In contrast to NDP efforts to enhance its image and reorganize its ranks in anticipation of the elections, the opposition parties were preoccupied by internal power struggles. The Wafd was embroiled in a rivalry over a successor to its late leader, Fu'ad Siraj al-Din who died in August. The Nasserite Party contended with internal tension exacerbated by the debt incurred by its organ, *al-'Arabi*, and the decision to privatize it. The Liberal Party found itself in a dual crisis: a leadership vacuum following the death of Mustafa

Kamil Murad, and an identity crisis in light of ideological ambiguity. The SLP, which was expected to play a key adversarial role in the opposition camp during the elections, was hard hit by the government's suspension of its activity following its aggressive campaign against Haydar's book (see above).[67] The fragmented state of the legal opposition had an adverse impact on its preparations for the elections and left the arena clear for two major actors — the government and the Muslim Brotherhood.

The three-stage elections, based on individual lists, commenced on October 18 with a record total of 3,965 candidates competing for 444 seats in the assembly. The electoral process was conducted in relative calm. Scattered violent episodes resulted in the death of nine persons and the wounding of dozens of others, as compared to the elections of 1995 when fifty-one were killed and 878 wounded (see *MECS* 1995, pp. 261–62). Nonetheless, opposition candidates protested against police abuse and a strong bias in the media in favor of candidates from the ruling party.[68] According to estimates, only 25% (24.6m.) of the 67.2m. eligible voters exercised their right to vote. The results of the vote, announced by the minister of interior on 15 November, indicated that the NDP retained its parliamentary dominance with 388 of the total of 444 elected seats, or 87.7% (as against 416 seats, or 93.7%, in 1995). The opposition parties won a total of 33 seats, or 7.4% (as against 14 seats, or 3.15%, in 1995): 17 Brotherhood, 7 Wafd, 6 NPUG (National Progressive Unionist Grouping), 2 Nasserites and 1 Liberal. Another 21 seats went to unaffiliated independents. As in the past, President Mubarak used his constitutional prerogative to appoint ten additional assembly members, including 4 women and 4 Copts. This brought the number of women and Coptic delegates to 12 and 6, respectively (as against 6 and 6 in the previous assembly).[69]

Although the NDP continued to enjoy an overwhelming majority in parliament, their victory did not obscure the fact that the elections constituted a pronounced public protest against the ruling party, stemming primarily from disappointment with the government's economic policy (see below). Only 170 of over 400 official party candidates won seats. A number of key party figures, including nine heads of parliamentary committees, two former cabinet ministers and two former governors, lost their seats. The party's majority in the assembly was retained only by virtue of the 218 independent candidates who joined its ranks. Most of these were NDP affiliates not included in the party's official list, who preferred to run independently and thereby avoid pledging full allegiance to the party line.[70] This was clearly evident in the opening session of the new assembly on 13 December. NDP loyalist Fathi Surur was reelected speaker for the tenth successive year. However, one of his two deputies was only narrowly reelected after a fierce contest, while 156 delegates, including over one hundred from the NDP, supported the Wafd candidate for the post.[71]

The relatively poor performance of the NDP in the elections evoked widespread criticism in the government-sponsored press and heightened the urgency of the issue of reorganizing the structure of the party. In this, a major role was assigned to Jamal Mubarak, who stated that the rejuvenation of the party depended on restoring its popularity by active involvement in public affairs.[72] The electoral embarrassment to the ruling elite, however, had no effect on the stability of the regime. The assembly, still submissive to the all-powerful presidency and to wide-ranging emergency laws, continued to play a distinctly subordinate role in national politics, although the presence of a vocal thirty-three-member opposition, headed by the Brotherhood, insured livelier debate over state policy.

ECONOMIC REFORM: PROSPECTS AND RISKS

Economic liberalization and structural reform progressed slowly over the year. Frustrated local and foreign investors felt that the reform program, ratified in 1991 and designed to transform the Egyptian economy into a model of development in the Arab world, had proved to be overly ambitious.[73] Nonetheless, they acknowledged that the macroeconomic foundations of the Egyptian economy had proven to be stable, having weathered a series of crises in recent years. These included a drop in tourism following the 1997 Luxor massacre (see *MECS* 1997, pp. 306–307), the erosion in foreign currency reserves in the wake of falling oil prices, and reduced foreign investment in light of the Asian financial crisis in 1998. Egypt had rebounded from each of these setbacks. The recovery of the tourism industry was impressive, with 4.8m. tourists and receipts of $3.9bn. in 1999, a trend which continued well into 2000. Oil prices rose again in the second half of 1999 (see *MECS* 1999, pp. 142–43), and Cairo resumed its promising position in the eyes of the international business community.[74] In addition, Egypt became an exporter of natural gas on a world scale when large reserves were discovered early in 2000.[75]

These important achievements, however, did not alleviate the need to cope with urgent problems that had developed in the process of redesigning the national economic structure. The major one, which continued to cast a heavy shadow on the pace of economic liberalization, was the danger of widening social gaps between the richer and poorer strata. This fear was clearly reflected in Mubarak's instructions to his cabinet early in the year to give priority to rebuilding the educational, health and welfare systems and to increase social spending in the state budget. The 2000/2001 budget, approved in May, showed a 12.3% increase in social spending — £E 112.6bn. ($32.8bn.), compared to £E 100.3bn. ($29.2bn) in the previous budget.[76] Government officials also announced the establishment of a fund to aid small businesses, grant loans to graduates of institutions of higher education, and invest in development projects to create thousands of new jobs annually.[77]

The need for a social security net to alleviate socioeconomic problems was pressing in light of Egypt's demographic time bomb — with 500,000 individuals joining the labor force and an annual natural population growth of 1.4m. (even though the rate of annual growth steadily declined, reaching 1.7% in 2000). Moreover, the official unemployment rate of c. 12%[78] reinforced the ongoing slowdown in the privatization of public enterprises.[79] Despite attractive incentives offered by the government to the public to leave the densely populated urban centers, the number of individuals who sought a new life in the desert towns was extremely minimal. Furthermore, the socioeconomic conditions of the agrarian population in the countryside continued to be aggravated by the new land reform program implemented in 1997 (see *MECS* 1997, pp. 321–22), allowing landowners to fix rentals according to market values. As a result, many *fellahin* were forced to sell their assets in order to meet higher tenancy rates, and some 420,000 lost their land.[80]

Another pressing problem impeding economic growth was the national monetary crisis, reflected in a growing shortage of US dollars in the local market as a result of more restrictive regulation of foreign currency aimed at reducing imports and lowering the trade deficit ($2.921bn. in the first quarter of the year). The determination of the government to keep the exchange rate below £E 4:$1, and its refusal to inject dollars into private banks in order to prevent a further depletion of foreign currency reserves

($15bn. in early 2000), evoked harsh criticism in business circles. The result was an adverse impact on the scope of imports and a consequent decrease in government income.[81] Under pressure, the central bank initiated a depreciation of the Egyptian pound in the last quarter of the year, which in December reached c. £E 3.85:$1 as compared to £E 3.40:$1 at the beginning of the year.[82] In addition, although inflation was stable at around 3.5%, the GDP fell to 3.9%, down from 6% in 1999. The limited potential domestic growth impelled Egyptian enterprises to search for alternative markets regionally and overseas.[83]

Prime Minister 'Atif 'Ubayd and Minister of Economy and Foreign Trade Yusuf Butrus-Ghali, the navigators of economic policy, stressed that the process of reform was proceeding consistently but cautiously, designed to prevent strong shocks. They also spoke of the need to reinforce the global status of the Egyptian economy, while acknowledging fears of increased dependency on foreign bodies and the risk of exposing the domestic market to imports.[84] These fears were also the source of the delay in signing a partnership agreement with the European Union (EU), although the formulation of the agreement had been completed in June 1999 after five years of discussion. Ultimately, the partnership agreement was signed in January 2001. It provided Egypt access to the Euro-Med free trade zone, scheduled to be established in 2010.[85]

With this, Egypt was interested in diversifying its markets, especially in Africa through its membership in COMESA (Common Market for Eastern and Southern Africa). The motives for joining this organization in 1997 were political no less than economic, as the Nile River flowed through nine of the twenty member countries. Cairo hosted a COMESA convention in February and a follow-up conference in April, to which a number of European countries were invited.[86] Still, COMESA provided Egypt with minimal economic benefit. The African market purchased no more than 2% of Egyptian exports in 1999, compared to 44% by the EU market and a potential 14% in the Mediterranean Arab Free Trade Area (MAFTA), which Cairo sought to promote without much success.[87]

FOREIGN AFFAIRS

EGYPT, ISRAEL AND THE PEACE PROCESS

Mubarak's initial aim, upon taking office as president after Anwar al-Sadat's assassination in 1981 (see *MECS* 1980–81, pp. 437–39), was to break out of the inter-Arab isolation imposed on Egypt in the wake of the 1979 peace treaty it concluded with Israel. By the late 1980s, this aim was almost completely achieved as a result of several factors: the Iran-Iraq War (1979–88), in which material assistance from Egypt to Iraq was recognized as vital; the Lebanon War (1982), which revealed the importance of Egypt as a counterbalancing force to Israel; the inability of the Arab rejectionist front, headed by Syria and Iraq, to foil the peace process, reinforced at the end of the decade by the collapse of the Warsaw Pact and the emergence of the US as the single global superpower; and Mubarak's cautious promotion of Egypt as a moderating, yet indispensable power in Arab politics. Once Egypt returned to the fold of the Arab world, it resumed a key position there, reflected, inter alia, by leading the Arab portion of the international coalition against Saddam Husayn in the Gulf crisis of 1990–91. As such, Egypt was expected to both defend and represent Arab interests vis-à-vis Israel and the US.[88]

Following the Madrid conference in October 1991 (see *MECS* 1991, pp. 104–105),

Egypt's peace strategy became the relevant option for most Arab states. The collective Arab agenda shifted its former focus on military rivalry with Israel to a focus on the terms of Israel's acceptance as a legitimate player in the region, highlighting the "land for peace" formula and nuclear disarmament. However, Arab diplomacy consistently set boundaries to Israel's regional inclusion by rejecting normalization with it, which was viewed in the Arab world as a cover for Israeli expansionist ambitions as well as too blatant an admission of defeat. This restrictive stance was reflected in the bilateral relationship between Egypt and Israel, both culturally and commercially. Cultural contacts with the Israeli intellectual community were discouraged in Egypt, while commercial ties were limited to oil, gas and textiles.[89]

Ideologically, the normalization issue became a major component of Egyptian intellectual discourse. Most writers expressed aversion to any normalization with Israel, arguing that Israeli economic, political and cultural inroads in the Middle East would serve Israel as an additional asset, alongside its military strength and nuclear capability. Moreover, normalization would provide Israel with "regional depth," which was perceived as an underlying Western goal. According to the opponents of normalization, Israel served as the front line in preserving the strategic and economic interests of the West in the Middle East and in obstructing any real Arab unity. As such, normalization with Israel would further promote the Western-sponsored process of globalization in the region, which was aimed at divesting the Arabs of their national assets and self-identity.[90]

With the adversaries of normalization with Israel in the lead, its few supporters found themselves marginalized and exposed to public censure. One of them, the political commentator Amin al-Mahdi, attributed the hostility to normalization with Israel to the lack of democracy in the Arab world and the consequent "single opinion" ideology. This rigid ideology, he wrote, was sustained by the traditional sacred alliance between the military elites and orthodox Islam, which held a monopoly over the Arab-Israeli conflict for over fifty years, yet produced only destructive results. Another commentator, Tariq Hajji, attacked the anachronistic conspiracy theories which, he said, dominated Arab thought, engendering nothing but passivity and backwardness. Instead, he advocated the principle of acceptance of the "other" in a world that was becoming a global village, characterized by close interactions between states and peoples.[91]

The Egyptian government, for its part, claimed that moving ahead with normalization was conditional upon progress in the peace process,[92] which proved to be fragile and subject to reversal. The peace process stagnated for most of the period of the Netanyahu government in Israel (1996–99), thereby also preventing Egypt from demonstrating its mediation skills. Under the Barak government, from June 1999, the diplomatic dialogue became more intense and substantive, dealing with the basic questions of the permanent peace settlement. Even so, it failed to achieve much progress either in the Palestinian track or in negotiations with Syria. Mubarak, nevertheless, continued to credit Barak's peace agenda and also expressed support for Israel's unilateral withdrawal from Lebanon in May 2000 (see chapters on Israel and Lebanon), even at the price of tension with Syria.

Both 'Arafat and Barak visited Cairo frequently. Both also gained Mubarak's blessing on the eve of the crucial Camp David summit sponsored by President Clinton in July.[93] The summit, however, culminated in failure, repositioning the charged issues of Jerusalem, control of the Haram al-Sharif (Temple Mount) and the Palestinian refugee problem squarely on the Arab agenda. Although Cairo perceived itself as the patron of the peace process, it was also the leader of the Arab world. Accordingly, Mubarak stressed that no Arab leader, including 'Arafat himself, was authorized to make any concessions regarding East Jerusalem or the al-Aqsa Mosque located on the Mount.[94]

The violent events of September in the West Bank and Gaza Strip (the al-Aqsa intifada; see chapter on the PA) and the uproar they created in the Arab street placed Egyptian diplomacy in a delicate position. Israel's punitive actions against the PA provoked demonstrations on university campuses in Egypt and triggered belligerent statements by both intellectuals and high-ranking 'ulama. The mufti of Egypt and the Shaykh al-Azhar called on Arabs everywhere to contribute money and guns to the Palestinians and to boycott Israeli products. Should the political and economic jihad fail to effectively contain Israeli aggression, they declared, the solution would be a military jihad.[95] These and many other 'ulama represented a quietist, state-sponsored Islam that was, nevertheless, assertive in its stance on Israel.

Government spokespersons expressed their support for a firm, cohesive Arab stand and a ban on Israeli goods, but continued to display diplomatic restraint. The Egyptian efforts to reestablish stability and revive the peace talks culminated in hosting of the Sharm al-Shaykh summit in October. Despite the failure of the summit, Egypt persevered in projecting its peace treaty with Israel as a fait accompli which no Arab or Muslim party had the right to undermine. For this, Egypt was subjected to heavy pressure not only from marginal Arab countries such as Yemen and Libya, which called for a declaration of war against Israel, but also from key countries such as Syria and Saudi Arabia, which demanded aborting diplomatic relations with Israel.[96]

Egyptian counterpressure for restraint bore fruit, resulting in relatively moderate decisions adopted in Cairo at the Arab summit on 21 October and at the summit of the ICO on 11 November, which left the issue of relations with Israel up to each country (see chapters on inter-Arab relations, and political Islam). Nonetheless, Egypt was expected to make supportive gestures to the Palestinians. The most important of these was the recall of the Egyptian ambassador from Tel Aviv in November for consultations in Cairo as a response to Israel's use of helicopters against PA installations. This was the harshest diplomatic step taken by Egypt since it recalled its ambassador following the Israeli invasion of Lebanon in 1982 (see *MECS* 1981–82, pp. 463–64).[97] At the same time, Egypt also put pressure on 'Arafat to halt the violence in the territories and to reach an agreement with Israel, this time on the basis of an American mediation proposal.[98]

Egyptian officials described the American proposal as positive, although not conclusive. It had the potential to solve two major obstacles: first, the issue of Jerusalem, which evoked angry Arab public opinion directed, inter alia, at the local regimes for their helplessness in dispelling the alleged Jewish threat to al-Aqsa; and second, the issue of the borders of the Palestinian state, which, according to the proposal, would encompass 95% of the West Bank and Gaza territories. This proportion would satisfy the principle consistently promoted by Egypt ever since Sadat's peace initiative, i.e., "the return of all occupied territories" from the 1967 war.[99] Egypt, however, was limited in its ability to persuade 'Arafat to reach a compromise on the third and most sensitive obstacle, namely the refugees right of return. So entrenched was this ethos in the Palestinian collective memory that any Arab attempt to put pressure on the PA would appear as illegitimate or immoral interference.[100] The episode involving the American proposal revealed the limits of Mubarak's influence on 'Arafat: the Palestinian leader conveyed deep respect and esteem for Mubarak as an advisor and mediator vis-à-vis Israel, but not as a patron.

Further Egyptian attempts to restart the peace process failed, first when Barak refused to participate in a tripartite meeting with Mubarak and 'Arafat in Sharm al-Shaykh on 28 December, and again when Israeli-Palestinian talks in Taba broke down on 27 January 2001 without any firm agreement.[101] These failed attempts marked the prelude to a twilight period, as Clinton left the White House and Israel began preparing for new elections, which were to be won in February 2001 by Ariel Sharon, leader of the right-wing camp.

EGYPT, THE ARAB WORLD AND IRAN

Commitments by Israeli Prime Minister Ehud Barak to a comprehensive peace in the Middle East provided Egypt with a valuable opportunity to play its favored role as regional leader. Cairo again became the nerve center of Arab diplomacy, giving precedence to the Palestinian track yet energetically promoting the Syrian-Lebanese track as well, in light of the window of opportunity created by the Barak government.

Mubarak, in separate meetings with Syrian president Hafiz al-Asad and Barak, played a key role in paving the way for the renewal of peace talks between Israel and Syria in Shepherdstown, Maryland, in February. Cairo-Damascus relations briefly improved as a result, only to take a step backward when the talks were suspended.[102] Mubarak came to realize that he had almost no impact on Asad's diplomatic moves, and that the Syrian leader was determined to prove Syria's ability to achieve a more favorable peace agreement than that achieved by Egypt.

Improved Egyptian-Lebanese relations were another cause of friction between Egypt and Syria. Mubarak traveled to Beirut on 19 February to meet with President Emil Lahhud, marking the first trip to Lebanon by an Egyptian president in fifty years. The visit, coming in the wake of Israeli air raids on Beirut power stations, signified Mubarak's wish to send a message of Arab solidarity in the face of Israeli aggression but also to express support for the sovereignty of Lebanon. Mubarak's visit led to a reciprocal visit by Lahhud to Cairo in April and a subsequent reinforcement of bilateral trade and economic ties.[103]

Damascus was not pleased with this Egyptian-Lebanese intimacy, and was even less pleased with Egyptian support of Israel's announced unilateral withdrawal from South Lebanon scheduled for July. Egypt's argument that withdrawal from occupied territory served national Arab interests led to a confrontation between the Egyptian and Syrian delegations to the Arab foreign ministers' meeting in Beirut in April. Eventually, to maintain a united front, Egypt acceded to the meeting's final statement supporting a demand for Israeli withdrawal by mutual agreement, yet it continued to adhere to its original position.[104] When the Israeli forces left Lebanon in May, Mubarak conveyed congratulations to the leadership in Beirut, calling the evacuation a "great victory for the Lebanese people and an important step to realize a just and comprehensive peace."[105]

Syria under Asad had indeed proved to be a difficult ally for Egypt. The death of Asad in June and the succession of his inexperienced son Bashshar (see chapter on Syria) was perceived in Egypt as removing a major obstacle to Mubarak's efforts to consolidate a more unified Arab policy on diplomatic issues and relations with the US. President Bashshar, in selecting Egypt as the destination of his first official visit outside Syria (in October), acknowledged Mubarak's senior diplomatic status and his own desire for a greater degree of Egyptian support than his father had wanted.[106] However, like his father, Bashshar voiced views that were discordant to Egypt, especially on the issue of the peace process, as demonstrated at the October Arab summit and in November at the ICO summit (see chapter on Syria).

King 'Abdallah of Jordan provided a more convenient relationship, displaying full coordination with Mubarak. The Egyptian leader was perceived in Amman as a source of moderation and stability in the inter-Arab arena, especially in light of the violent Israel-PA conflict, which put the Hashemite kingdom under pressure (see chapter on Jordan).[107]

Although Egypt's mediation skills in the peace process were sidelined by the violence in the Palestinian arena, they continued to have an impact on the issue of Sudan. The Egyptian-Libyan initiative of 1999, designed to promote national reconciliation in Sudan (see MECS 1999, pp. 220–21), continued to dominate the agenda of the government in Khartoum and the Sudanese opposition during 2000. Egyptian interests in this conflict were more immediate than in the Palestinian case. The concern over the sources of the Nile river, prompted continued Egyptian assertiveness in promoting its peace initiative based on the principle of preserving Sudan's territorial integrity.[108] This also impelled Egypt to firmly reject the US-supported initiative of the Inter-Governmental Authority on Drought (IGAD), which viewed the right of self-determination for Christian and animist southern Sudan as an option (see chapter on Sudan).[109]

Cairo's advancement of the Egyptian-Libyan initiative took place in an atmosphere of considerably improved bilateral relations with Sudan. Longtime issues of contention were resolved, e.g., the return of Egyptian assets in Khartoum appropriated in 1992–93 because of ideological and political disputes between the two states; or were under negotiation, e.g., control over the disputed Hala'ib triangle zone. Another obstacle that had clouded relations between the two states was removed in late 1999 following steps taken by President 'Umar al-Bashir to neutralize his former mentor and ally, Hasan al-Turabi, speaker of the parliament and leader of the Islamic National Front (see MECS 1999, pp. 529–31).[110] Mutual visits by high-ranking officials of both countries, and joint trade treaties, rare in the immediate past, became common events.[111] These bilateral developments peaked with the return of the Egyptian ambassador to Khartoum in December after a six-year absence. The ambassador, summing up the significance of the Sudanese issue in Egyptian foreign policy, declared that it was no less important than the problem of peace in the Middle East.[112]

Egyptian diplomatic efforts also continued to be directed to the Iraqi issue in light of the ongoing international sanctions against Baghdad. The diplomatic relationship between Iraq and Egypt was upgraded in the course of the year, reflected in mutual visits by senior officials and increased bilateral trade, with Egypt becoming Iraq's leading source of imports.[113] Egypt continued its efforts to persuade the US and the UN to show greater flexibility on the embargo issue.[114] Still, Egypt shied away from the full restoration of diplomatic ties, in deference to the US, Saudi Arabia and Kuwait. Baghdad, for its part, welcomed improvement in its ties with Cairo, yet voiced frustration at the pronounced asymmetry between their economic and political ties.[115]

Iran also expressed frustration, and even anger, at the discrepancy between the levels of bilateral economic and diplomatic relations with Egypt. In this case as well, bilateral relations, including in the cultural and religious realms, continued improving, accompanied by optimistic statements by spokespersons on both sides regarding the forthcoming restoration of diplomatic relations. Significantly, Mubarak telephoned President Muhammad Khatami in June congratulating him on the co-option of Iran to the G-15 group of developing states. The call was described by the Iranian minister of culture as "historic," namely the first personal contact in twenty-two years between the presidents of the two states.[116] These developments, however, remained on the declaratory level for the time being. Furthermore, mutual reproaches in the state media of both countries did not entirely cease. Cairo criticized the continued use by Tehran of the term "Persian Gulf" as a reflection of continued Iranian hostility toward the Gulf Arab countries. Tehran, for its part, attacked Cairo's "language of peace," which had failed in light of Israeli "aggression" toward the Palestinians in the al-Aqsa intifada, while praising "the language of power" as having proven itself in driving Israel out of Lebanon. Accordingly, Iranian officials urged Egypt to sever all ties with Israel and join hands in conducting a real jihad for the liberation of Palestine.[117]

In both cases — Iraq and Iran — Egypt was aware of the limits of its regional maneuverability. It evaded the restoration of diplomatic relations in order to both preserve its intimate relations with its economic benefactors from the Gulf (as well as with the West)[118] and maintain its position at the center of the Arab consensus. Cairo officials and commentators were careful to emphasize that the stability of the Gulf was an important Egyptian interest. So long as territorial and political disputes involving Iraq and Iran with their neighbors continued, they added, the resumption by Egypt of full diplomatic relations with these two states would remain in abeyance.[119]

RELATIONS WITH THE US

The Egyptian-US relationship continued to involve a number of regional and bilateral issues. Cairo and Washington shared many interests in both arenas, but their differences became increasingly public.

Close political and military cooperation and mutual visits by high-ranking officials were in evidence during 2000, illustrating the viability of the Cairo-Washington axis. Mubarak's visit to the US in March was followed by reciprocal visits to Cairo by the American secretaries of defense and state over the course of the year, demonstrating the American acknowledgment of Egypt's moderating role in Arab diplomacy. Secretary of Defense William Cohen declared that Egypt's military needs would always be satisfied, while Secretary of State Madeleine Albright cited Egypt's role as a strategic partner in the pursuit of Arab-Israeli peace.[120] Still, a number of issues overshadowed the relationship between the two states over the year, some of which were related to the peace process and others to Egyptian domestic issues.

Immediately prior to and during the crucial discussions on a permanent settlement between Israel and the PA at Camp David in July, Washington expressed discontent at Mubarak's refusal to try and induce 'Arafat to make concessions on the issue of Jerusalem. With this, statements by Clinton suggesting that the transfer of the American embassy to Jerusalem was under consideration evoked fierce disapproval in Cairo. Egyptian officials explained that such statements could only drive the region toward another round of bloody violence.[121] Similar friction surfaced over the rigid American stance on the international sanctions against Iraq, and over the possibility of US support for a separate status for southern Sudan as part of the IGAD initiative.[122]

Friction and exchanges of allegations were even more explicit over bilateral issues in light of sectarian violence in Upper Egypt, in which nineteen Copts were killed in January,[123] and the arrest of the Egyptian civil rights activist, Sa'd al-Din Ibrahim, in July (see above). The arrest of Ibrahim, who also held American citizenship, was defined by the White House as a "civil rights rather than criminal issue." The US exercised quiet yet intense pressure on Egypt for his release. In response, Egypt claimed that Ibrahim's citizenship did not grant him immunity from legal processes aimed at investigating the charges against him. The Egyptian press went even further, accusing Ibrahim of being a secret US agent and a NATO spy.[124]

The exchange of accusations reached a peak in August with the publication of a column by *New York Times* journalist Thomas Friedman. The piece, which was written as a personal letter from Clinton to Mubarak, raised doubts about the benefits to the US of the $30bn. aid package which Egypt had received from it since 1978. Friedman accused Mubarak of hardening 'Arafat's stance on the issue of Jerusalem, as well as suppressing democracy and violating civil rights in Egypt.[125] The article did not reveal anything new, yet it exposed Egyptian sensitivities regarding relations with the US. The Egyptian response to the article, following the lead of the official press, was to brand it a political indictment inspired by the White House as part of an Israeli-Jewish conspiracy to discredit Egypt.[126]

The Egyptian press attacked the American presumption to disseminate liberal values to the world while social and racial abuse still existed within its own borders. The press also rejected the claim that the US received little benefit from the aid to Egypt. According to Ibrahim Nafi', editor of *al-Ahram*, this charge was no more than an American posture, because a large part of the aid was devoted to military acquisitions and strategic needs which served US interests. In addition, he wrote, Cairo had opened up the local and Arab markets to American goods and ensured it a supply of cheap oil, a factor that had facilitated the US economic upsurge of the 1990s.[127]

The violent regression in the peace process between the PA and Israel in the last quarter of the year, and Egyptian sensitivity to domestic and Arab regional public opinion, heightened tension in the Egyptian-US relationship. Attempting to diffuse it, Foreign Minister 'Amru Musa denied the existence of a crisis in the relationship, commenting only that "the relationship is not at its best."[128] Mubarak's foreign policy advisor, Usama al-Baz, emphasized that bilateral ties were based on mutual respect and joint interests, and warned against attributing responsibility to the US for decisions made by Israel. The Arab interest, he pointed out, was to broaden collaboration with the US in order to promote the Arab perspective on the nature of the desirable peace settlements in the Middle East.[129]

NOTES

For the place and frequency of publications cited here, and for the full name of the publication, news agency, radio station or monitoring service where an abbreviation is used, please see "List of Sources." Only in the case of more than one publication bearing the same name is the place of publication noted here. Unless otherwise stated, all references to *al-Jumhuriyya* are to the Cairo daily.

1. *FT*, 10 May 2000.
2. See, for example, Gabriel Ben Dor, "Stateness and Ideology in Contemporary Middle Eastern Politics," *The Jerusalem Journal of International Relations*, Vol. 9, No. 3 (September 1987), pp. 1–9.
3. *Al-Mukhtar al-Islami*, 23 November 1999; *al-Hayat*, 12, 15 March 2000.

4. *Al-Sharq al-Awsat*, 7 February; *al-Watan al-'Arabi*, 11 February. See also Hani al-Siba'i, quoted in *al-Wasat*, 20 April 2000.

5. *Al-Hayat*, 7 February 2000.

6. *CR*, Egypt, August 2000, pp. 14–15.

7. Ibid.; *al-Sharq al-Awsat*, 24, 25 June, 13 August; *al-Wasat*, 26 June. See also *al-Hayat*, 15 March 2000.

8. *Al-Wasat*, 7 August 2000.

9. *Al-Hayat*, 25 February; MENA, 13 April, 20 June, 26 October. On the government stance toward the unilateral cease-fire declared by the militants, see *FT*, 10 May 2000.

10. *Al-Sharq al-Awsat*, 20 January; *al-Wasat*, 3 July 2000.

11. On the relations between the government and the Muslim Brotherhood, and its vicissitudes during Mubarak's tenure, see Husayn Tawfiq Ibrahim, *al-Nizam al-siyasi wal-Ikhwan al-Muslimun fi Misr min al-tasamuh ila al-muwajjaha 1981–1996* (Beirut: Dar al-Tali'a, 1998).

12. MENA, 18 January, 22 July; *al-Da'wa*, February; *al-Hayat*, 15 March; *The Economist*, 19 May 2000. See also *Le Monde*, 1 June 2000.

13. Ma'mun al-Hudaybi, quoted in MENA, 22 January; Mustafa Mashhur in *al-Da'wa*, April, pp. 4–5, May, pp. 4–5. See also *al-Wasat*, 25 May 2000.

14. *Al-Hayat*, 24 May; *al-Wasat*, 25 May, 12 June 2000.

15. *Al-Hayat*, 19, 21 May; *CR*, Egypt, August, p. 13; *al-Sha'b*, 15 September 1992. The elections to the Bar Association were finally held on 17 February. They resulted in an electoral achievement for the Brotherhood, whose eight candidates all won seats on the board. *CR*, Egypt, May 2001, pp. 12–13.

16. On the Brotherhood's preparations for the elections, see *al-Wasat*, 24 July, 28 August; *al-Hayat*, 20 August; *al-Sharq al-Awsat*, 25 August. The release early in the year of 'Isam al-'Aryan, a prominent leader of the Brotherhood, after five years in prison, had an important effect on the movement's performance in the electoral process. On 'Aryan, see *al-Wasat*, 6 March, 25 May 2000.

17. *Al-Wasat*, 18 September 2000.

18. *Al-Hayat*, 21 May; *al-Majalla*, 4 June; *CR*, Egypt, August 2000, p. 14.

19. *Al-Wasat*, 18 September 2000.

20. See, for example, *al-Hayat*, 17 September; MENA, 31 October; *CR*, Egypt, November 2000, p. 14.

21. An estimated 2,400 Brotherhood members were arrested during the elections. See R. Monte Carlo, 24 October; *AW*, 16 November; *CR*, Egypt, November 2000, p. 14; *al-Hayat*, 19 December 2000.

22. *Al-Musawwar*, 17 November; 'Isam al-'Aryan, quoted in *AW*, 23 November; *al-Sharq al-Awsat*, 5 December 2000; Mustafa Mashhur and Ma'mun al-Hudaybi, quoted in *al-Mukhtar al-Islami*, 9 February 2001; *CR*, Egypt, February 2001, p. 13.

23. *Al-Mukhtar al-Islami*, 10 January; *CR*, Egypt, February 2001, p. 13.

24. Haydar Haydar, *Walima li-a'shab al-bahr* (Beirut: n.p., 1983).

25. *Al-Hayat*, 10, 19 May; *Ha'aretz*, 19 May; *Civil Society*, June 2000, pp. 6–7.

26. *Al-Hayat*, 19 May 2000.

27. MENA, 17 May. On al-Azhar's censorship authority in matters of faith, see, *Hurriyyat al-ra'y wal-'aqida* (Cairo: al-Munazzama al-Misriyya li-Huquq al-Insan, 1994), Vol. 2, pp. 13–24. According to a report in *al-Majalla*, 4 June 2000, al-Azhar censored over 320 books in the preceding few years.

28. MENA, 10, 12 May; *al-Hayat*, 19 May 2000.

29. *Ha'aretz*, 19 May; *Civil Society*, June 2000.

30. See, *al-Nur*, 16 December 1998; *al-Wasat*, 20 February, 10 April, 18 September 2000.

31. *Al-Hayat*, 19, 20 May; *al-Majalla*, 4 June 2000.

32. *Al-Wasat*, 10 January; *MEI*, 11 February, pp. 17, 19; *CR*, Egypt, February, 2000, p. 17.

33. Tantawi, quoted in *al-Hayat*, 17 January 2000. See also his previous statements in *al-Liwa al-Islami*, 18 February 1999.

34. *Al-Hayat*, 26 January 2000.
35. *Al-Hayat*, 17 January; *al-Sha'b*, *Ha'aretz*, 21 January; *Civil Society*, February 2000. See also *Statistical Year Book 1992–1998* (Cairo: Central Agency for Public Mobilization and Statistics, June 1999), p. 25.
36. See, *al-Sha'b*, 21 January; *al-Da'wa*, February 2000.
37. *Al-Wasat*, 10 January; *Ha'aretz*, 21 January 2000.
38. *MEI*, 11 February 2000, pp. 17, 19.
39. See, *Middle East Report*, Spring, pp. 38–41; *FT*, 10 May 2000.
40. *Al-Ahram*, 4, 5 June 2000.
41. *Al-Wasat*, 12 June; *CR*, Egypt, August 2000, p. 13.
42. MENA, 16, 17, 18 May; *al-Hayat*, 21 May; *Uktubar*, 28 May. For the Brotherhood's response to the suspension of SLP activity, see *al-Da'wa*, July 2000.
43. MENA, 21, 23 September 2000.
44. *Al-Hayat*, 19, 21 May; *al-Ahali*, 24 May 2000.
45. See,'Adil Husayn, secretary-general of the SLP, quoted in *al-Hayat*, 19 May 2000.
46. MENA, 9, 14 September. For other examples of the government determination to redefine civic activity, see *Civil Society*, February; *JP*, 2 April; *al-Hayat*, 2 June; MENA, 26 September 2000.
47. On Sa'd al-Din Ibrahim's thought and activities, see, Iliya Harik, "Democratic Thought in the Arab World: An Alternative to the Patron State," in Charles E. Butterworth and I. William Zartman (eds.), *Between The State and Islam* (Washington: Woodrow Wilson Center, 2001), pp. 143–44. See also Ibrahim's writings, *Ta'ammulat fi mas'alat al-aqalliyat* (Cairo: Ibn Khaldun Center, 1991); *The Copts of Egypt* (Cairo: Ibn Khaldun Center, 1996).
48. *AW*, I July; MENA, 2, 4 July; *Akhir Sa'a*, 5 July; *al-Ahali*, 19 July; Sa'd al-Din Ibrahim, "A Reply to My Accusers," *Journal of Democracy*, Vol. 11, No. 4 (October 2000), pp. 58–63.
49. See, *al-Hayat*, 7 July; *al-Wafd*, *al-Musawwar*, *al-Akhbar*, 22 July 2000.
50. See, *al-Ahram*, 11 July; *al-Hayat*, 14 July; *al-Wafd*, 19, 22 July 2000.
51. *Al-Hayat*, 15 July; *al-Quds al-'Arabi*, 28 July 2000.
52. *NYT*, 22 May 2001.
53. See also Lars Berger, "The Case of Saad Eddin Ibrahim and the Current Relationship between State and Civil Society in Egypt," *Orient*, Vol. 41, No. 4 (December 2000), pp. 668–71; Nissim Rejwan, "The Plight of the Arab Intellectual," *Midstream*, Vol. 47, No. 3 (April 2001), pp. 26–30.
54. Robert Springborg, *Political Structural Adjustment in Egypt: A Precondition for Rapid Economic Growth?* (San Domenico: European University Institute, June 1999), pp. 22–29.
55. *CR*, Egypt, February, 2000, p. 16.
56. Ibid.
57. *CR*, Egypt, May, p. 16; MENA, 9, 12 July 2000.
58. *Al-Hayat*, 3 February; *al-Wasat*, 13 March 2000.
59. Regarding the Wasat (Center) Party, whose members had split from the Brotherhood in 1996 (see *MECS* 1999, pp. 208–209), the government did permit it to operate a cultural association aimed at promoting dialogue among different ideological streams, thereby signaling its tolerance of cultural rather than political activities. See MENA, 2 March; *al-Wasat*, 24 April; *Ha'aretz*, 5 May; *CR*, Egypt, May 2000, pp. 15–16.
60. *CR*, Egypt, August 2000, pp. 12–13.
61. See, for example, *Uktubar*, 23 July 2000.
62. *CR*, Egypt, May 2000, p. 16.
63. *Al-Hayat*, 3 February, 8 August; *al-Majalla*, 20 February; *al-Musawwar*, 8 September 2000.
64. See, for example, *al-Wafd*, 14, 15, 17 June; *al-Musawwar*, 16 June; *Ruz al-Yusuf*, 17 June; *al-Usbu'*, 19, 23 June; *al-Ahali*, 28 June; *Ha'aretz*, 30 June 2000.

65. *Al-Wasat*, 28 February; *al-Musawwar*, 8 September 2000.
66. On the sectarian strife in Upper Egypt and its political ramifications, see *JP*, 4 January; *al-Wasat*, 10 January; MENA, 11 January; *MEI*, 28 January; *Civil Society*, February; *al-Hayat*, 4 July 2000.
67. *Al-Hayat*, 15 March, 17 May; *al-Sharq al-Awsat*, 27 August; *al-Wasat*, 4, 11 September 2000.
68. See, *al-Wafd*, 9, 15, 16 November; *AW*, 16, 23 November 2000.
69. On the parliamentary elections, see *al-Ahram*, 16 November; *AW*, 16, 23 November; MENA, 20 September, 18, 24 October; *CR*, Egypt, November 2000, pp. 12–14.
70. *Al-Musawwar*, 3, 17 November; October, 12, 26 November 2000; *CR*, Egypt, February 2001, pp. 12–13.
71. *CR*, Egypt, February 2001, p. 14.
72. *Uktubar*, 12 November 2000.
73. For observations about Egypt's economic policy in the 1990s, see Paul Rivlin, *Economic Policy and Performance in the Arab World* (Boulder: Lynne Rienner Publishers, 2001), pp. 105–12; Ahmad al-Sayyid al-Najjar (ed.), *al-Itijahat al-iqtisadiyya al-istratijiyya 2000* (Cairo: al-Ahram Center for Political and Strategic Studies, January 2001), pp. 225–54.
74. *FT*, 10 May; *CR*, Egypt, August 2000, pp. 24–25, May 2001, p. 31.
75. *Ha'aretz*, 7 January; *FT*, 10 May 2000.
76. MENA, 18 April, 11 May; *CR*, Egypt, November 2000, p. 16.
77. MENA, 18 April 2000.
78. *FT*, 10 May 2000.
79. Only 156 of the 314 state enterprises designated for sale by the year 2001 had been sold. Total revenues from privatization of public enterprises amounted to $4.4bn. *FT*, 10 May 2000; *CR*, Egypt, February 2001, p. 19.
80. *FT*, 10 May 2000.
81. Ibid.; *CR*, Egypt, November 2000, pp. 20–21.
82. *CR*, Egypt, February, pp. 21–23, May 2001, pp. 11–12, 19, 22.
83. *FT*, 10 May 2000; *CR*, Egypt, February 2001, p. 11.
84. *FT*, 10 May. See also *al-Ahram al-Iqtisadi*, 15 May 2000.
85. *FT*, 10 May; MENA, 7 June, 4 July 2000; *CR*, Egypt, February 2001, p. 32.
86. *CR*, Egypt, May 2000, p. 17; February 2001, pp. 32–33.
87. *FT*, 10 May 2000. For statistics on Egyptian foreign trade, see *Statistical Year Book 1992–1998*, pp. 294–96. On the difficulties in promoting the idea of a common Arab trade zone, see Yusif A. Sayigh, "Arab Economic Integration," in Michael C. Hudson (ed.), *Middle East Dilemma* (London: I.B. Tauris, 1999), pp. 233–58.
88. On Egyptian foreign policy after the Gulf War, see, Raymond A. Hinnebusch, "Egypt, Syria and the Arab State System in the New World Order," in Haifaa A. Jawad (ed.), *The Middle East in the New World Order* (London: Macmillan, 1997, 2nd edn.), pp. 169–72.
89. See, e.g., *FT*, 10 May 2000.
90. For Egyptian perception of normalization with Israel and the "new Middle East" vision, see, Salama Ahmad Salama (ed.), *al-Sharq Awsatiyya hal hiya al-khiyar al-wahid* (Cairo: Markaz al-Ahram lil-Tarjama wal-Nashr, 1995); Nadia Mahmud Mustafa (ed.), *Misr wa-mashru'at al-nizam al-iqlimi al-jadid fi al-mintaqa* (Cairo: al-Ahram Center for Political and Strategic Studies, 1997); Salah al-Din Hafiz, *Tahafut al-salam* (Cairo: Dar al-Shuruq, 1998).
91. Amin al-Mahdi, *al-Sira' al-'Arabi al-Isra'ili* (Cairo: al-Dar al-'Arabiyya lil-Nashr, 1999); Tariq Hajji, *Naqd al-'aql al-'Arabi* (Cairo: Dar al-Ma'arif, 1998); idem., *al-Thaqafa awalan wa-akhiran* (Cairo: Dar al-Ma'arif, 2000). See also Lutfi al-Khuli, *'Arab? na'am wa-Sharq Awsatiyyun aydan* (Cairo: Markaz al-Ahram lil-Tarjama wal-Nashr,1994); *Ha'aretz*, 31 March 2000.
92. See, *Ha'aretz*, 23 January, 20 February; *FT*, 10 May 2000.
93. *FT*, 10 May; MENA, 7 July 2000.
94. *Ha'aretz*, 4, 13 August 2000.

95. *Ha'aretz*, 16 October; *al-Musawwar*, 13 October; MENA, 16 October; *al-Istiqlal*, 2, 9 November 2000.
96. *Ha'aretz*, 22 November; *CR*, Egypt, November 2000, pp. 15–16.
97. *Al-Ahram*, 23, 29 November; *al-Jumhuriyya*, 27 November 2000; *CR*, Egypt, February 2001, pp. 15–16.
98. *Ha'aretz*, 28 December 2000.
99. *Al-Ahram*, 17 December; *Ha'aretz*, 28 December 2000.
100. *Ha'aretz*, 28 December 2000.
101. *CR*, Egypt, February 2001, pp. 15–16.
102. MENA, 12, 22 January, 8 April, 8 May 2000.
103. Ibid., 19, 20 February, 21 April, 19 May; *al-Watan al-'Arabi*, 25 February 2000.
104. *Ha'aretz*, 5 April; MENA, 8 April 2000.
105. MENA, 24 May 2000.
106. *Al-Wasat*, 9 October 2000.
107. On Egyptian-Jordanian relations during the year 2000, see *JT*, 23 January, 29 November; *al-Hayat*, 24 January; MENA, 16 April, 2 July 2000.
108. *Al-Hayat*, 4 January; MENA, 28 February, 29, 30 March, 8 April, 9 May 2000.
109. *Al-Hayat*, 4 January; MENA, 8, 29, 30 March.
110. On the power struggle between Bashir and Turabi, see *al-Da'wa*, 22 January; Stefano Bellucci, "Islam and Democracy: The 1999 Palace Coup in Sudan," *MEJ*, Vol. 7, No. 3 (June 2000), pp. 168–75.
111. See, MENA, 6 July, 2, 5 September 2000.
112. MENA, 13 December 2000.
113. See, MENA, 2, 30 March; *al-Sharq al-Awsat*, 2 September; *al-Wasat*, 13 November 2000.
114. *Al-Sharq al-Awsat*, 23 January; MENA, 29, 30 March; *al-Hayat*, 20 October 2000.
115. *Al-Sharq al-Awsat*, 2 September 2000.
116. See, IRNA, 4 January, 14, 21 June; *al-Musawwar*, 3 March; *Ha'aretz*, 3 July; October 30 July 2000.
117. *Al-Sharq al-Awsat*, 21 January; *TT*, 29 January, 3, 11 July; *Jomhuri-ye Islami*, 5 August 2000.
118. On Egypt-Gulf states relations, see, *al-Sharq al-Awsat*, 1 March; MENA, 23 April, 7, 28 June, 23 July, 16 August, 29 November 2000.
119. See, *al-Hayat*, 25 July; *AW*, 3 August 2000.
120. MENA, 25 March, 7 June, 21 November; *The Economist*, 5 April; *MEI*, 7 April 2000; *WF*, 24 November 2000.
121. MENA, 29 July; *NYT*, 1 August; *al-Ahram*, 4 August; *al-Hayat*, 28 August 2000.
122. See, MENA, 8, 30 March; 'Amru Musa, quoted in *al-Hayat*, 20 October 2000.
123. See, *Ha'aretz*, 4 January; MENA, 25 March 2000.
124. *WP*, 13, 17 July; *al-Sharq al-Awsat*, 19 July; *al-Musawwar*, 21 July; *Ha'aretz*, 28 July; *al-Wasat*, 14 August 2000.
125. Thomas Friedman, "The Egypt Game," *NYT*, 1 August 2000.
126. *Ha'aretz*, 6, 9 August; *al-Hayat*, 28 August 2000.
127. Ibrahim Nafi', in *al-Ahram*, 5 August; *Ha'aretz*, 9 August 2000.
128. *Al-Hayat*, 20 October 2000.
129. MENA, 23 November 2000.

Iran

(Jomhuri-ye Islami-ye Iran)

MEIR LITVAK

The struggle over the nature of the Islamic system of government waged between the dominant conservative camp, backed by Supreme Leader Ayatollah 'Ali Khamene'i, and reformists supporting President Hojjat ul-Islam Mohammad Khatami continued unabated during 2000. The reformists, although factionalized, won an absolute majority in the elections for the sixth Majlis held in February. Their victory reflected the deep frustrations of the Iranian electorate — particularly young people and women — with the failure of the Islamic regime to address the socioeconomic problems of Iran, and their craving for greater political and cultural openness.

The conservatives, empowered by Khamene'i's sanctioning of "legitimate violence," launched a multifaceted post-election offensive aimed at preserving their hegemony. The Council of Guardians annulled election results in eleven constituencies and manipulated the Tehran ballots in order to facilitate the election of former president Hashemi Rafsanjani to the Majlis. The judiciary closed more than twenty reformist newspapers and put journalists, along with several liberal politicians and clerics on trial. A leading reformist, Sa'id Hajjariyan, was shot, and the reformist minister of culture 'Ataollah Mohajerani resigned under conservative pressure.

Khatami, torn between his loyalty to the Islamic system and to his supporters, could only urge his supporters to respect the Islamic constitution that secured clerical rule and the leader's supremacy, while appealing for the preservation of the people's rights, which he claimed, were enshrined in the constitution. He conceded, however, that he lacked the "necessary tools" to implement these very parts of the constitution.

Reformist journalists continued to open new newspapers, while the Majlis worked on advancing the reformist agenda through legislation, but the Council of Guardians vetoed most of its initiatives. Khamene'i personally blocked amendment of the harsh press law, further enhancing his stature as the supreme arbiter of Iranian politics. By year's end, little remained of the reformists' hopes.

Growing revenues resulting from the boost in oil prices gave the Islamic system a crucial respite. Yet, it also enabled the triumphant conservative faction to avoid addressing of structural socioeconomic problems in Iran.

Iranian foreign policy, which sought a balance between pragmatic strategic and economic interests and ideological commitments, depending on the arena and the issues, remained unchanged. While reformists aspired to a rapprochement with the US, the conservatives, headed by Khamene'i, rejected any American gesture toward Iran as insufficient and as a ploy to subject Iran to American hegemony. Both factions supported the consolidation of Iran's strategic and economic alliance with Russia and closer ties with Europe and its Middle Eastern neighbors, particularly in the Persian Gulf. Still,

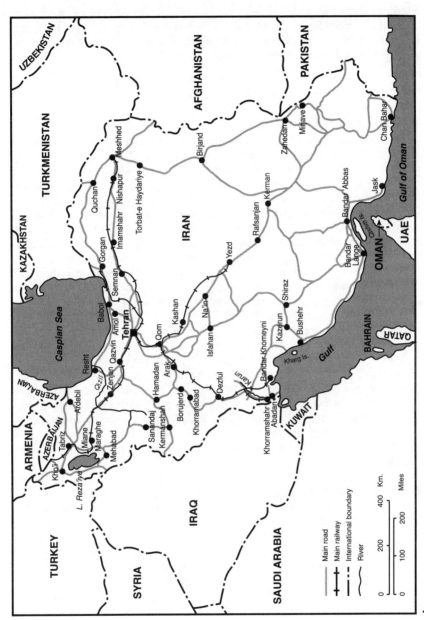

Iran

efforts to improve ties with Turkey, Iraq and Egypt were marred by past recriminations, or mutual distrust due to ideological reasons and conflicting strategic aspirations. Concurrently, Iran remained faithful to its rejection of the Arab-Israeli peace process and persistently called for the destruction of Israel.

INTERNAL AFFAIRS

THE MAJLIS ELECTIONS

The elections for the sixth Majlis, scheduled for 18 February, became the main arena in the struggle between the reformist Second-Khordad (23 May) Front (named for President Khatami's 1997 election date) and the conservative camp. By 14 January, Interior Ministry supervisory boards had disqualified 758 out of 6,860 candidates running for the 290-seat parliament, and transferred the lists to the conservative-dominated Council of Guardians for its final endorsement. The reformers had swamped the nominating process, daring the conservatives to order wholesale disqualifications, as they had done in the 1996 elections and risk mass protest. A more limited disqualification procedure, the reformers hoped, would leave a sufficient number of candidates in the running.[1]

The Council of Guardians published its final tally of 576 rejected candidates on 7 February. The main reasons cited for disqualification were membership of "illegal political groupings" or "lack of practical commitment to Islam, infraction of the law and disloyalty to the absolute rule of *velayat-e faqih*" [guardianship of the supreme Islamic jurisprudent]. Among those who were dropped were prominent reformists such as Hojjat ul-Islam 'Abdollah Nuri, the imprisoned former interior minister (see *MECS* 1999, p. 235), and such critics of the system as former foreign minister Ebrahim Yazdi, head of the banned (but tolerated) Freedom Movement (Nehazat-e Azadi-ye Iran). Some thirty serving Majlis members were also disqualified. The disqualifications, however, were less massive than those of 1996, whether because the council feared a public outcry, or because it hoped that the reformists' votes would be diluted due to the large number of candidates, thereby giving the conservatives an advantage. Overall, it confirmed 6,083 candidates, 513 of whom were women, a 56% and 60% increase, respectively, compared with the 1996 elections.[2]

The Struggle over Voting Lists

While the Council of Guardians deliberated, the various political groupings began to draft lists of recommended candidates, as voters were to elect candidates in each district on a personal basis. The conservative coalition — the Followers of the Imam and the Leadership Path — sensing their waning popularity, put former president and current head of the powerful conservative-dominated Expediency Council, 'Ali Akbar Hashemi Rafsanjani, at the top of their Tehran list. Rafsanjani set his sights on the speakership of the Majlis, confident of the backing of two factions with which he was linked — the dominant conservative clerical faction the Tehran Militant Clergy Association (Jame'eh-ye Ruhaniyyat-e Mobarez; JRM), and of the technocratic Executives of Iranian Reconstruction (Kargozaran-e Sazendegi-ye Iran; KSI). Rafsanjani, projecting the image of a centrist and of the only candidate capable of preventing a political deadlock between the conservatives and reformists, hoped to attract some of those who voted for Khatami in 1997 and thereby split the reformist coalition.[3]

To help Rafsanjani, Khamene'i pardoned the former Tehran mayor and Rafsanjani's protégé, Gholam-Hosein Karbaschi, who had been imprisoned in May 1999 for corruption after helping engineer Khatami's election. Khamene'i apparently hoped that Rafsanjani would earn popularity for securing Karbaschi's release and Karbaschi would head his patron's campaign.[4]

While the KSI rallied behind Rafsanjani, other Second-Khordad groups, mainly the Jebhe-ye Mosharekat-e Iran-e Islami (Islamic Iran Participation Front; IIPF) and the Militant Clerics Association (Majma'-e Ruhaniyyun-e Mobarez; MRM), refused to put his name on their lists. Liberal commentators criticized his presidential policies, holding him responsible for a number of ills in the Iranian polity and economy, and in particular condemning his silence during the serial murders of intellectuals in 1998 (see *MECS* 1998, p, 241).[5] The loose pro-reform coalition was divided over the composition of the recommended candidate's lists, particularly in Tehran, which sent the largest delegation to the Majlis. A major bone of contention was the number and identity of clerics in the lists. By 10 February, the Second-Khordad Front's eighteen member groups agreed to support two hundred joint candidates in the provincial constituencies and to present separate candidates for another forty seats. In Tehran, however, the front's major groups, the IIPF, MRM, KSI and the more radical Office for Strengthening Unity (OSU; Daftar-e Tahkim-e Vahdat), published separate lists only. Overall, 290 reformists ran nationwide, some of whom appeared on several lists, including in Tehran, but in different rankings.[6]

The IIPF list contained ten of its own founding members, headed by Mohammad Reza Khatami, a forty-year-old physician and political neophyte seeking to appeal to young voters in particular by capitalizing on the popularity of his illustrious brother, the president. The list included five clerics, four of whom were MRM leaders headed by Mehdi Karubi, former Majlis speaker and MRM secretary-general in the sixteenth place. The MRM list included its own leaders as well as IIPF and Islamic Revolution Mojahedin Organization (IRMO) figures whose common denominator was support for Khatami. Neither list included Rafsanjani, pointing to discord with the KSI. Greater unity was evident in the candidate lists fielded by the conservative Islamic Coalition Association and the JRM, which also included several KSI candidates headed by Rafsanjani.

The reformists also feared that many candidates, running as independents, were actually conservatives. Consequently, in order to avoid splitting pro-reformist votes, 890 reformists withdrew their candidacy nationwide during the week before the elections.[7]

The Platforms

Although the official campaign started on 9 February, clerics, politicians and the press launched the contest long beforehand. Their campaigns reflected two conflicting political cultures. Khatami, traveling extensively around the country in support of the reformists, called for mass participation, particularly of young people and women, his two most important power bases. He implicitly criticized the Council of Guardians' screening and the excessively stringent standards of social conduct imposed upon the candidates in the name of Islam. Conversely, Khamene'i declared that massive participation would "slap America's face" and refute the "enemy's" claim that the people had distanced themselves from the revolution. He urged voters to elect religiously committed candidates and reject those "scared or fascinated" by the West.[8]

The IIPF ran under the nationalist slogans "Iran for all Iranians" and "Justice, freedom and spiritual values" that were associated with the 1979 revolution, underscoring the message that reform sprang from, rather than clashed with, the revolution. It advocated limiting judicial power, addressing the issue of serial killings of political dissidents, liberalizing the economy, amending the press laws to strengthen freedom of expression, eliminating censorship of books and films, strengthening elected local councils, and reassessing Iranian policy vis-à-vis the US and the Arab-Israeli conflict. Seeking to allay conservative fears, Reza Khatami contrasted Western-style democracy with the democratic system that the IIPF advocated, which, he emphasized, was linked to Iranian "culture, religion and civilization." However, while professing allegiance to the doctrine of *velayat-e faqih*, he argued that the people could exercise supervision over it through the election of their representatives in the Council of Experts, that elected the leader.[9]

Pro-reform candidates emphasized their role in bringing about Khatami's 1997 victory, while downplaying their participation in the 1979 revolution. They stressed their academic qualifications or technical experience, promising to build a better future and focusing on economic reform, pluralism, greater individual freedom, and the equality of all citizens before the law. The conservatives highlighted their religious qualifications, stressing "spiritual integrity," faith in the *velayat-e faqih*, the defense of the revolution, and the "cleansing of society." They also warned of "Zionist and American conspiracies" against the revolution. The conservatives accused the reformists of sacrificing economic growth to political and cultural change, whereas reformists argued that political reform was essential for addressing the economic ills of Iran.[10]

Pro- and anti-reform candidates were also distinguishable by their contrasting political and cultural vocabularies. Reformers used nationalist and modernist discourse replete with such terms such as political renovation (*baz-sazi-ye siyasi*) and expanding freedoms (*gostaresh-e azadiha*), addressing the people as fellow citizens (*ham-mihanan*). Typical conservative phraseology was Islamic nation (*ummat-e Islam*), "protecting the revolution's values," and "Western cultural onslaught."

Reformists employed Western campaigning techniques focusing on young people, holding rallies and question-and-answer sessions in sports stadiums and universities. These events were lively, even joyous affairs, with audiences sometimes chanting "Khatami, we love you" and singing previously banned nationalist songs. Conservative newspapers, by contrast, denounced fraternization between male and female students, singing, dancing, immodest dress and "heavy make-up" at reformist rallies. They concentrated their rallies in mosques, where the atmosphere was more sober with women often kept outside.

Since the government banned the display of electioneering posters in the streets, the reformists resorted to circulating leaflets. The candidates' pictures that appeared in the press and in leaflets provided another distinctive marker. Reformists were often pictured smiling — emulating Khatami — and wearing suits and even ties — the latter a symbol of "Western cultural decadence" in the conservative view. The hard-liners, by contrast, appeared grim-faced, mostly shabbily dressed and sporting bushy beards following the model Khomeini, founder of the Islamic Republic. Reformist women candidates wore robes and scarves in light colors, as opposed to the strict black chador of the conservative female candidates.

The pro-reform candidates, on average, were more educated — often at the university level — as compared to their hard-line rivals. Many of the reformists were modern-style business-owners, journalists, university teachers and writers, while many of the conservatives hailed from the bazaars, the clergy and the civil service. The reformers sought to appeal more to the middle class and to urban industrial workers, while the conservatives were the standard-bearers for peasants, small shopkeepers, the traditional merchant classes and the elements of the *lumpenproletariat* that always acted as the shock troops of the regime.[11]

Conservative vigilante groups occasionally disrupted pro-reform rallies or attacked their rivals' election headquarters. Additionally, the outlawed Iraq-based armed opposition organization, Mojahedin-e Khalq, carried out mortar attacks on Tehran government buildings on 5 February, killing one person with the aim of disrupting the election campaign.[12]

The Vote

The voting process was chaotic, as voters had to select candidates from huge lists (861 candidates in Tehran for thirty seats) and fill in their names by hand, based on listings prepared by factions or newspapers. Voter turnout on 18 February was 70%, well below the 88% turnout in the 1997 presidential elections or the 75% rate in the 1996 Majlis elections. The province of Ohkiluyeh-Boyerahmad had the highest vote rate with 96.1%, while Tehran Province ranked last with 57.1%. The low turnout in Tehran was attributed to insufficient opportunities for face-to-face contact between candidates and voters. The vote counting, which was not computerized, proceeded slowly. The results, announced on 26 February, showed that the reformists had won 148 parliamentary seats, the conservatives 37, independents 35, and religious minorities 5. Sixty-five seats in 52 constituencies where no candidate reached the 25% threshold, were left for a second round.[13]

The reformist victory was particularly pronounced in the big cities. In Tehran, reformist candidates took 29 of the 30 seats, only 4 of them clerics. Mohammad Reza Khatami came in first, followed by Jamileh Kadivar, sister of the imprisoned liberal cleric Mohsen Kadivar and wife of 'Ataollah Mohajerani, minister of culture and Islamic guidance — and 'Ali Reza Nuri, brother of 'Abdollah Nuri. As relative newcomers to politics, they probably owed their high places to their association with illustrious relatives. A third of the top thirty contenders in Tehran had family links in the highest political echelons. Reformists also swept all 5 seats in Isfahan and Mashhad; 3 out of 4 in Shiraz; and 2 in Tabriz, with the other 4 left to the second round. IIPF-backed candidates won 20 of the 41 seats in rural areas, which traditionally supported the conservatives.[14]

The major loser was Rafsanjani, one of the regime's most powerful figures. Following a week of vote counting, the Council of Guardians' supervisory commission ranked him in the twenty-ninth place, barely crossing the 25% threshold. His daughter Fa'eza, until then regarded as a liberal, lost her seat, probably because of her proximity to her father. The former intelligence minister, 'Ali Fallahian, who was implicated by the press in the murder of intellectuals in 1999, failed to get elected in Isfahan. Neither were other leading conservatives, such as deputy speaker Hasan Ruhani and Mohammad Reza Bahonar reelected. Overall, only 52 out of 200 incumbents retained their seats.[15]

Most of the newly elected deputies were political novices, fifteen years younger on average than members of the fifth Majlis — representative of the generation that grew up following the 1979 revolution. Although the number of elected women dropped from 13 to 9, they were all reformists.[16]

The elections cannot be said to have constituted a second revolution, as they were conducted entirely within the existing political structure and according to the 1979 constitution. Consequently, they excluded secularists and other opposition trends. However, reinforcing the trend of the preceding presidential and municipal elections, they may be seen as an attempt to redefine the significance of the 1979 revolution and resolve some of its contradictions. As in all revolutions, the regime's ideology had lost much of its appeal when dealing with reality twenty-one years after assuming power. Since most Iranians had grown up under the Islamic regime — 70% were below the age of thirty — they were unreceptive to its claims of great achievements as compared with the pre-revolutionary period, which they did not experience. The regime's failure to solve the economic problems of Iran together with rampant corruption (see below) rendered its claim that an Islamic political system guaranteed a harmonious and moral society increasingly hollow. Economic prosperity appeared more appealing than the religious asceticism advocated by most clerics. Consequently, even government spokespersons conceded the erosion of religious values, with 75% of the population as a whole and 86% of young students failing to recite the obligatory daily prayers.

Paradoxically, the expansion of education — one of the government's greatest achievements — highlighted the sophistication of the population compared to previous generations. Similarly, the lowering of the voting age to fifteen and the politicization of women and the traditional sector led to rising expectations among the populace. Khatami's insistence on the "rule of law" and the slogan "Iran for all Iranians," with their promise of equal treatment, resonated strongly with those who felt excluded: intellectuals, nationalists, secularists and, above all, women and young people who longed for more freedoms and a less rigid social atmosphere. Many also wanted better relations with the West in order to stimulate economic growth and facilitate travel and contact with relatives living abroad. Furthermore, most Iranians favored greater political liberalization, which would increase public accountability and the prospects for economic reform.[17]

Reactions to the election results among reformists varied. "Khatami, you are no longer alone in your reform battle," exclaimed *Sobh-e Emruz*, while *Iran* commented that the country was experiencing a "national sense of satisfaction." Newly elected Majlis deputies laid out ambitious plans to reform the cultural and judicial domains to enhance personal and political freedoms and reduce the intrusion of the religious authorities into lives of the citizens. A few warned against "intoxication in victory," cautioning that "people should not have unrealistic expectations from the reformists." Seeking to allay conservative fears, Khatami stressed that the Iranian nation would never put aside the principles of the revolution.[18]

The conservatives initially sought to belittle the significance of the elections. The hard-line *Kayhan* contended that in going to the polls the people had responded to their leader's call to express their "hatred toward America" and the "racist Zionists," and renew their "bond with the lofty ideals of the late imam Khomeini." Rafsanjani described the elections as "rivalries among members of a family" and warned against the American- and Israeli-inspired interpretation of them as signifying the demise of the revolution. Adopting a more hostile tone, Mas'ud Dehnamaki, editor of *Jebheh*, attributed the reformist victory to the psychological warfare they conducted against the conservatives, and recommended that the Basij militia and the police should become stricter as of late spring so that people would feel bitter and the reformists incompetent. Violence should be committed in certain periods and in "flash-like moves." A few conservatives conceded the need for "some soul searching" although without changing "principles and positions."[19]

Initially, the reformists' expectations seemed to materialize in the form of increased cultural openness. The Tehran Museum displayed a collection of Western art that had been stored in its basement for years. For the first time since the 1979 revolution, a female singer performed in public during a classical music festival on 8 February. Interestingly, these tokens of cultural liberalization survived the conservative crackdown on political liberalization later in the year (see below). Despite clerical disapproval, the authorities allowed mass celebrations on 14 March of the Chaharshanbeh-ye Suri fire festival dating from Zoroastrian times. In another gesture of broadened social freedom, the Supreme Court ruled that the possession of videos and audio cassettes that "corrupt public ethics" was no longer a crime if kept for personal use only.[20]

THE CONSERVATIVE BACKLASH

Amending the Election Results

Determined to preserve its hegemony, the conservative establishment launched a multifaceted offensive against the reformist tide. In March and April, the Council of Guardians annulled the election of eleven reformist deputies, alleging technical violations of the election law and naming their conservative rivals as victors. Responding, deputy interior minister Mustafa Tajzadeh, a reformist who headed the national election headquarters and the IIPF charged that the council failed to offer any evidence for its action. Demonstrations protesting the annulments erupted in each of the constituencies involved, but to no avail.[21]

The Council of Guardians focused special attention on Tehran, ostensibly in the wake of conflicting mutual accusations by reformists and conservatives of fraud regarding Rafsanjani's ranking, but more likely in order to elevate his standing in the capital's delegation to the Majlis. Initially, it ordered a recount of five hundred ballot boxes, but when the desired outcome failed to materialize, it broadened the recount to a thousand ballot boxes, claiming the discovery of a "plot" against Rafsanjani. In a series of statements on 1, 4 and 7 May, it canceled parts of the elections and ordered a recount of all the ballot boxes in Tehran. Conservative figures followed suit, demanding the annulment of the entire Tehran vote. Presumably, they sought to bar the ratification of the IIPF leaders elected in the capital, who were tipped to become the new leaders of the Majlis due to be inaugurated on 27 May.[22]

In addition, the Council of Guardians in April and subsequently the Expediency Council in late July, vetoed the motions to grant the Majlis the authority to monitor institutions and organizations that were under the direct control of the supreme leader. These bodies included religious foundations (bonyads) that, in effect, were economic conglomerates which functioned as sources of political patronage.[23]

The second round of elections took place on 5 May, with 132 candidates vying for 66 seats in 52 constituencies. The IIPF, deprived of effective means to reach the population following the closure of their newspapers (see below) and facing pressure by the Council of Guardians in Tehran, appealed, nevertheless, for calm and patience, wary of open confrontation with the conservatives. By contrast, Ayatollah Ahmad Jannati, secretary of the Council of Guardians, urged voters to oppose candidates who had "anti-revolutionary" thoughts. In the event, pressures by the government did not affect popular preferences, as Second-Khordad Front candidates won 47 seats, the conservatives 10 and independents 9. Overall, the reformist IIPF and IRMO won approximately a hundred deputies, while the conservative retained about 65 deputies. The remaining seats went to several centrist groups — KSI, MRM, the Islamic Labor Party and the Islamic Solidarity Party — and independents. The 65 seats retained by incumbents in the fifth Majlis stood in marked contrast to the 220 seats won by first-timers. Notably, the number of elected clerics dropped from 51 to 25, continuing a trend of declining clerical share in the Majlis that had begun in the second Majlis. Following the Council of Guardians' overturning of the first-round results, by-elections in twelve constituencies were rescheduled for 2001.[24]

Confronted with the voters' clear message, Khamene'i decided to put an end to the bickering over the Tehran vote and instructed the Council of Guardians to approve the vote while discounting only the suspected ballots. On 20 May, the Council of Guardians published the final results for Tehran awarding the reformists 26 seats, the conservatives 2 — with Rafsanjani as number twenty — and ordering a reelection for two additional seats. Observers described the decision as a compromise that provided Khatami with strong parliamentary support, while saving Rafsanjani's honor. All the reformist factions criticized the decision. The Interior Ministry filed an unprecedented lawsuit against the Council of Guardians for raising unfounded accusations of fraud in the electoral process. Some three thousand students demonstrated at Tehran University on 22 May, accusing the council of tampering with the election results. Seeking to spare himself further humiliation, Rafsanjani announced his resignation from the Tehran delegation on 25 May. While the conservatives lost a powerful figure in the Majlis, the reformists appeared to have earned his hostility.[25]

Political Violence

On 12 March, Sa'id Hajjariyan, a former radical turned liberal who served as managing editor of *Sobh-e Emruz* and advisor to Khatami, was shot and gravely injured. The assassins escaped on a motorcycle of a type that only the security forces were allowed to have, raising widespread suspicions as to their institutional affiliation. The IIPF and the reformist press pointed to conservative leaders who called for violence against reformers, declaring that they could not "bend the will of the people to reach their goals." By contrast, the conservatives, headed by Khamene'i and Rafsanjani, blamed the attack on foreign "enemies," particularly the US and "global Zionism."[26] On 20 March, the authorities announced the arrest of the "main culprit" and five accomplices, claiming they had acted out of "personal motivation." However, the government policy of releasing only partial information, and the pressure exerted on journalists to abandon their investigations of the assassins' connections with the Revolutionary Guards increased the widespread perception of a cover-up. *Sobh-e Emruz* wrote of "a shadow government of assassins" who were active in the "halls of power in the Islamic republic," and of theoreticians of "slaughter-therapy" in extremist conservative circles. Mosharekat suggested that government officials focus on domestic reform, rather than resort to unconvincing propaganda that unfailingly pointed to foreign conspiracies. The main suspect was put on trial on 25 April and sentenced to a fifteen-year prison term on 17 May.[27]

The Berlin Conference

The participation on 7–9 April of seventeen prominent reformists at a conference in Berlin titled "Iran after the Elections" provided the regime with the pretext to launch an offensive. Statements by some of the participants, e.g., an appeal by attorney Mehranguiz Kar for a "complete revision" of the constitution, or criticism by Hojjat ul-Islam Hasan Yusefi Eshkevari of the absence of freedom and democracy in Iran and his argument that various Islamic laws should be changed, were perceived by conservatives as verging on open rebellion. Moreover, Iranian opposition groups in exile disrupted the conference, accusing both the guests and the organizers of promoting merely cosmetic changes on Khatami's behalf.[28]

The conservative press in Tehran charged conference participants with "anti-nationalist and anti-revolutionary" advocacy in the service of hostile Western and Zionist circles.[29] Footage of the exiles at the conference screened by the state television focused on scantily-clothed female demonstrators in order to shock viewers regarding their immorality, linking the "anti-Islamic" disruptions to the reformists. Demonstrations and rallies were held in several cities charging the reformists with betraying the Islamic Republic and demanding "exemplary punishments" against the participants.[30]

A Revolutionary Guard statement on 16 April described the "champions of American-style reforms in Iran" as "atheists fighting God," who had resurfaced "like a malignant tumor." If necessary, it warned, the enemies of the revolution would "feel the reverberating impact of the hammer of the Islamic revolution on their skulls" so that they would never be able to concoct plots or commit crimes. Upon returning to Iran, the conference participants were temporarily detained and subsequently tried for "scandalous propaganda" against the political system in Iran (see below).[31]

In guiding the conservative offensive, Khamene'i took care to avoid excesses. In the Friday sermon in Tehran on 14 April, he rejected "US-style" reforms — a code term for reformist demands — as destructive to the principles of the Muslim faith. Vowing that the Islamic regime would act "with strength and violence" against all those resorting to force, aggression and "violation of the law," he drew a distinction between unacceptable and "legitimate violence." Other conservative figures were less subtle. Ayatollah Mohammad Taqi Mesbah-Yazdi warned that reformists were trying to revive 2,500-year-old apostate traditions, but should bear in mind that the penalty for apostasy was death. Charging the reformists with violating Islamic sanctities, Ayatollah Abu-l-Qasem Khaz'ali urged: "Kill them wherever you find them." Khatami sought a middle course, criticizing some of the themes of the Berlin conference but also expressing displeasure with persons "creating intrigue to push our society to lawlessness and brutality in the name of defending values."[32]

Khamene'i, seeking to set firm boundaries to the factional strife, called for greater tolerance and understanding among the different factions within Iran. In a sermon on 12 May, he commented that there was "nothing wrong" with disagreement within the Iranian community. He expressed support for Khatami, thereby preventing the president's backers, especially young people, from coming out against the system as a whole, while at the same preserving the basic tenets of the Islamic system and restricting Khatami's actual authority. He signaled his reservations regarding the ultra-conservatives by conceding that Iran needed "revolutionary reforms, innovation and progress" and calling on the religious seminaries (*madaris*) to embrace "new thoughts and ideas." Concurrently, he rejected "American reforms" advocated by radical reformists for they would allow their "American masters" to "take control" of the Iranian economy and culture. Both the conservative clerical JRM and the pro-reform clerical MRM announced their support for Khamene'i's statement.[33]

Silencing the Press

Both conservatives and reformists regarded the liberal press as instrumental in mobilizing popular support for the reformists. The participation of several outspoken journalists at the Berlin conference heightened conservative animosity to the liberal press. Before disbanding, the outgoing Majlis on 18 April amended the press law, prohibiting criticism of the constitution, of Islam and of the states' security policy. On 20 April Khamene'i declared his determination to confront the "danger" posed by "press circles" who had become "a center of the enemies of Islam" with the "sole aim" of undermining the revolution's achievements. Given a green light, the judiciary ordered the closure during 23 and 27 April of twelve dailies, three weeklies and one monthly — the most extensive press closure since 1979 — for publishing material that "disparaged" Islam and the Islamic revolution. It also demanded that the Ministry of Culture withhold permission for new publications, hitherto granted by the ministry alone, without the prior approval of the judiciary. By the year's end, the judiciary had closed another sixteen publications.[34]

In addition, the judiciary initiated a series of trials against managing editors — seventeen in May alone — as well as journalists of the banned publications on a variety of charges, including "activities against national security" and "scandalous propaganda" against the Iranian political system. Reporters Without Frontiers charged that following Burma, Iran constituted the "biggest jail for journalists in the world."[35] Not surprisingly, the conservative dailies gave full support to the struggle against their more widely circulated rivals.[36]

In a joint statement, the reformist newspapers criticized the closures pledging to "fight for their rights through legal channels," while also calling on people to adopt a strategy of "active calm" (*aramesh-e fa'al*) as a counter to the efforts of "totalitarians and extremists" to push the reformists to violence and anarchic conduct. Thousands of students held protest rallies against the closures in nine universities, and over 110,000 people, mostly students, petitioned the judiciary to release the jailed journalists. In a joint letter to the chief of the judiciary, Ayatollah Mahmud Hashemi Shahrudi, some 151 Majlis deputies censured the "incorrect action" against the press as "an affront to the nation," and criticized the imprisonment of journalists as "insensible or unnecessary."[37]

Khatami was torn between his loyalty to the system and to his supporters, who urged greater liberalization. He stressed the "rights of the people" to freedom of speech and assembly, "including [the right] of being opposed to the Islamic Republic," as being among the "great achievements of the Islamic revolution." Concurrently, he emphasized the need to enforce the law of the state, rejecting those who sought to "hurt our religion and culture" in the name of freedom and those who harmed the people's rights in the name of religion.[38] In an unpublicized "constitutional warning" to Shahrudi, Khatami protested in June against the wave of newspaper closures, warning that people would lose trust in the Islamic system itself should factional pressures influence the judiciary. Khamene'i, however, declared full support for the judiciary.[39]

The conservatives also targeted Minister of Culture 'Ataollah Mohajerani, who censured the closure decision as contradictory to the constitution. A statement by the judiciary on 30 April argued that if the ministry had "stood against the poisonous atmosphere created by some press circles," the closures would have been unnecessary." Conservative Majlis members and dailies followed suit, demanding Mohajerani's resignation. On 9 May, the secretary of the Expediency Council, Mohsen Reza'i, told the Islamic Republic News Agency (IRNA) that Khamene'i supported Khatami and his entire government except for Mohajerani. Mohajerani expressed his readiness to resign should such a measure relieve Khatami of political pressure, but the Khatami cabinet opposed this step nearly unanimously. Meanwhile, Khatami bid for time, hoping that the conservative campaign would subside.[40]

The Conservative Political Program

Outlining the guidelines of the conservative position, Khamene'i spoke on 9 July of an American-British attempt to replicate in Iran the "plots" that had destroyed the Soviet superpower, namely the use of reformist slogans. This stratagem, he said, would never work for Iran. Concurrently, he sought to "disarm" the reformers by propagating a conservative version of reforms. He described reform as "intrinsic" to Islam and the revolution, but maintained that "real" reform, which is "Islamic and revolutionary," meant looking after the people's welfare.[41]

The conservative press, taking its cue from Khamene'i, warned of an American-Zionist plot to topple the revolution under the guise of reformism.[42] The conservatives also attacked the reformists, including the Khatami administration, for an excessive preoccupation with "marginal" political issues, which were nothing but a blind imitation of Western "liberal democracy" focused on American capitalism. Comparing Khatami and his reforms with Gorbachev's perestroika and the collapse of the USSR, the conservatives accused the reformists of failing to tackle socioeconomic problems, thereby exacerbating the social, cultural and moral crisis in Iran. They called for "real reforms" based on "Islamic principles" which would deal with poverty, unemployment and corruption, while warning that "Yeltsin-prescribed reform" threatened to "shatter Iran" as it did the USSR. However, the conservatives remained vague regarding the reforms they supported. A few praised the Chinese example of implementing reforms without endangering the integrity of the system.[43]

The Sixth Majlis in the Shadow of the Conservative Offensive

The sixth Majlis was convened on 27 May in a milieu of palpable conservative pressure. Its first task, electing the speaker — the fourth-ranking official in Iran, and members of the presiding board of the Majlis — produced splits within the reformist coalition. The MRM and KSI supported the conservatives in the tradition of electing a cleric as speaker — MRM Secretary-General Hojjat ul-Islam Mehdi Karubi, former speaker of the third Majlis (1989–92), who was the reformist closest to the conservatives. The IIPF, which favored a layperson for the post, yielded the speakership to Karubi, who on 11 June gained 193 votes with 63 abstentions. IIPF leaders Behzad Nabavi and Mohammad-Reza Khatami were elected as first and second deputy speakers, respectively. Soheila Jelodar-Zadeh, an engineer and spokesperson of the Islamic Labor Party, was the first woman ever elected to the presiding board.[44]

In light of Khatami's weakness, the Majlis took the lead in advancing the reformist agenda. On 14 June, it tabled a motion barring security personnel from entering universities without the university chancellor's request, a move related to the police raid on a university dormitory that had sparked the July 1999 demonstrations (see *MECS* 1999, pp. 242ff).[45]

One of the first priorities of the Majlis was to lift the restrictions imposed on the press law passed by the preceding legislature. However, when the Majlis convened to debate the new law on 6 August, Khamene'i sent it a letter pointing out that the current law was capable of preventing a "great calamity": the takeover or infiltration of the press by the enemies of Islam and the revolution. Therefore, any amendment of the law by the Majlis was "illegitimate," as it would "threaten the security, unity and the faith of the People."[46] Karubi, a staunch advocate of *velayat-e faqih*, adjourned the session forthwith, explaining that Khamene'i's letter was a governmental order, and that the constitution gave him, as the *vali-ye faqih* (ruling jurist), "absolute powers." Scuffles broke out in the chamber, and some sixty deputies walked out in protest. Several members of the Majlis threatened to resign in protest, arguing that Karubi should have put the matter to a vote.[47]

The conservative press hailed Khamene'i's "historic" decision. Clerics in Qom called for the removal and trial of Majlis deputies who had insulted the *velayat-e faqih*, and conservative protestors outside the Majlis called for their death. Unnamed reformist Majlis deputies claimed that Khamene'i's decision was illegal, but, acknowledging their weakness in the face of overwhelming conservative power, they expressed hope for a compromise that would liberalize the press law. Moderate clerics in Qom, notably Ayatollah Hosein 'Ali Montazeri and Yusuf Sane'i, hinted that Khamene'i's decisions bordered on one-man rule, anathema in the historically pluralistic Shi'i tradition.[48]

Since both the Council of Guardians and the Expediency Council could have vetoed the changes to the law, had it passed, Khamene'i's personal intervention apparently reflected determination to draw clear red lines regarding the reform process and show the reformists that they faced him directly, not just his proxies. Reportedly, he perceived the reformers' attempt to expand freedom of expression as a direct personal challenge, given that the previous parliament had introduced the restrictions after he himself led the campaign against pro-reform journalism.

The entire episode heightened the tension between the elected governmental bodies, dominated by the reformists, and the conservative-controlled appointed ones. Responding to an unprecedented insistence by several reformist parliamentarians that Khamene'i's letter about the press law be read into the legislative record, the Council of Guardians spokesperson Ayatollah Reza Ostadi, and its secretary, Ayatollah Ahmad Jannati, threatened to revoke the credentials of any member who failed to demonstrate overt loyalty to the *velayat-e faqih*.[49] These threats prompted a major debate about the powers of the Majlis vis-à-vis those of the Council of Guardians. Some parliamentarians, including Karubi, insisted that the council was not entitled to oust a deputy after his election and the approval of his credentials. Deputies, they claimed, had the constitutional right to express views on all matters, and could not be penalized for that. Faced with this opposition, Jannati backed down.[50]

Khatami maintained a low profile during the press law affair, although he vented his frustration in a rare television interview on 21 August. Terming the press crackdown as "painful," he was, nevertheless, unable to promise a change in this policy. He implicitly criticized the hard-liners by claiming that the late Ayatollah Khomeini, the founder of the Islamic system, had always "respected the people and attached great importance" to their vote. More importantly, he conceded that although, as president, he was in charge of implementing the constitution, he sometimes lacked the "necessary tools" to do so. Reports on constitutional violations by various state bodies that he had submitted to the leader and to the previous Majlis were ignored. Still, while acknowledging disagreements with other governmental branches and "major problems," he pledged that he would not resign.[51]

The Khoramabad Affair

As if to demonstrate Khatami's impotence, anti-reform vigilantes attacked students at the annual national convention of the radical reformist OSU student wing held in the southwestern city of Khoramabad on 24 August. The vigilantes' aim was to prevent the liberal philosopher, Abdol-Karim Soroush, and the reformist Hojjat ul-Islam Mohsen Kadivar from addressing the students. The next day, the preacher at the Khoramabad Friday prayers called for the rest of the "unwanted guests" to be driven out. Violence escalated as the vigilantes rampaged, burning banks and government offices and clashing with students and townspeople who demanded that the conference continue. One police officer was killed and sixty students were hospitalized. The conference was cut short when the Revolutionary Guards threatened a "punishing response" if rioting continued "in the name of reform." In a rare direct challenge, OSU activists called on Khamene'i to define his relationship with "pro-violence groups using his name." The IIPF, increasingly concerned that the students who had put them in office were turning too radical, urged them to remain calm and avoid falling into the trap of conservatives who sought violent confrontation.[52]

The affair reflected a broad pattern of conservative activity: vigilante groups calling themselves "the people" were dispatched to attack reform rallies and headquarters or to provoke violence. Then, the conservative dailies printed sensational headlines to discredit the movement and Khatami's government, writing that civil society caused instability, and that a free press spread anti-Islamic sentiments and tacitly served enemies like secularists and the US. Lastly, conservative judges banned offending reformist newspapers or jailed activists.[53]

A further indication of the conservative resolve to use force against popular discontent, the Basij militia command announced its intention to recruit fifteen million new members in the Third Development Plan period (2000–2005) in line with establishing a force of twenty million and to arm all full-time Basij members. Basij commander Brig. Gen. Mohammad Hejazi stated that while full-time, salaried Basijis were banned from political activity, "ordinary" members were free to be politically active, giving a green light to Basijis who acted as vigilantes against reformists. The Revolutionary Guards were also slated to grow from 1,000 to 1,500 battalions by the year's end. In another manifestation of the use of the military for political means, the judicial branch of the Iranian armed forces set up a new office to deal with the "rampant social vices" in the country.[54]

POLITICAL TRIALS

The Trial of the "Jewish Spies"

The judicial offensive against reformists culminated in three major political trials in 2000. The first was the closed-door trial of thirteen Jews and eight Muslims accused in June 1999 of espionage for Israel and the US (see *MECS* 1999, p. 319), which opened on 13 April. Most foreign observers regarded the trial as a conservative ploy to foil any Iranian rapprochement with the West by putting Khatami in an impossible situation as he would not be able to challenge the judiciary and would thus lose credibility in the West. Observers cited the defendants' social background, the precarious status of Jews under the Islamic republic, the regime's hostility to Israel, and the fact that the Muslim defendants were tried only following international criticism over the likelihood of fabricated accusations against Jews.[55]

As in the past, some of the defendants confessed on television the charges against them.[56] However, they recanted their confessions on the last day of the trial, stating that they had been extracted under duress. The defense also claimed that the courtroom confessions were full of inconsistencies and that the prosecution had failed to provide adequate evidence for the charges, insisting that "only a show trial could find them guilty." Some of the Muslim defendants also denied the charges. Various foreign observers concluded that the charges were "more of an indictment of the Iranian judicial system than of the accused." American Jewish organizations claimed that the incitement in the Iranian media against the defendants, and their broadcast confessions, evoked anti-Jewish acts in various Iranian cities.[57]

On 1 July, the court convicted ten of the defendants and acquitted the other three. Despite previous pronouncements by leading clerics that the defendants deserved death, the sentences varied from thirteen to two years, reflecting fears by the court and government of excessive damage to Iran's foreign relations in the event of capital punishments. The US and various European Union (EU) governments condemned the trial as a miscarriage of justice that flouted international norms for free and fair trial procedures.[58] Iran rejected this criticism as undue intervention in its domestic affairs, attributing it to "Zionist manipulation" of the world media and insisting that the accused had been "treated kindly according to Islamic principles." The conservative press expressed disappointment with the verdicts and demanded the death sentence. Khatami, who defended the verdicts, suggested that "leniency" be shown in the event of appeals.[59]

Following appeals by the defendants, who maintained that they were innocent, a higher court reduced the sentences on 21 September by two to six years. Apparently, Iran took into account international criticism despite previous declarations to the contrary. The conservative *Jomhuri-ye Islami* charged that the sentences led to widespread suspicions that the judiciary backed down over "international Zionist" political and propaganda pressure.[60]

The Trial of Hojjat ul-Islam Hasan Yusefi Eshkevari

Hojjat ul-Islam Eshkevari, the most senior cleric to participate in the Berlin conference (see above) was put on trial in the Special Court for Clergy (Dadgah-e Vizhe-ye Ruhaniyyat) on 7 October. He had angered the conservatives with statements that the social edicts of Islam were changeable, including parts of edicts mentioned in the Qur'an. Prior to his return to Tehran in August, he observed that the mixing of religion and politics "spoils, corrupts and empties both of their substances" and expressed his opposition to a leader of the revolution (i.e., Khamene'i) whose power exceeds the constitution.[61]

Following a closed-door trial, the court convicted Eshkevari on 17 October on five charges: apostasy (*ertedad*) and waging war against Islam (*moharebeh*) — both capital offenses according to Iranian law; statements and acts constituting threats against national security; negative propaganda against the Islamic system and spreading of lies to distort public opinion; insulting Khomeini the late founder of the Islamic Republic; and slandering the clergy.[62]

While dissident clerics had been imprisoned and defrocked before under the Islamic regime, Eshkevari's trial and the unprecedented harsh verdict aroused a storm of protest in Iran. During the trial 321 intellectuals signed a letter to Khatami expressing anxiety over Eshkevari's fate. Khatami himself expressed "concern" at the verdict stating that "the power-holder must not condemn his critics as apostates" and observing that "a man's ideas will not go away, even if he does." The Second-Khordad Front condemned the Special Court as an unconstitutional tool to eliminate opponents of the regime and described the verdict as "reminiscent of the medieval inquisition" and a threat to the "republican" nature of Iran's political system.[63]

Majlis Speaker Karubi rejected the apostasy charge, arguing that even if Eshkevari's views were controversial, he was still a Muslim. Moreover, Grand Ayatollah Montazeri — Khomeini's deposed heir-designate — under house arrest himself — ruled that nothing Eshkevari had stated or written was illegal, let alone contrary to Islam, and that expressing a critical view against Islam was not sufficient cause for imprisonment. Religious-based accusations brought against people like Eshkevari, Akbar Ganji (see below), and Abdollah Nuri had nothing to do with Islam, but were "political pretexts to silence dissidents," Montazeri stated. Submitting to these pressures, an appeals court commuted the death sentence in May 2001 and scheduled a retrial, while Eshkevari remained in prison.[64]

The Berlin Conference Trial

The trial of the seventeen other participants in the Berlin conference started on 5 November. Most of the defendants rejected the blanket charges that they had gone to Berlin with the intention of harming national security or "spreading propaganda against the regime." Rather, they argued, they had "bravely defended the Islamic Republic." The trial, they said, was notable for lack of prosecutory evidence and for procedural ambiguity.[65] The leading defendant, investigative journalist Akbar Ganji, opted for attack as his line of defense. Known for his articles accusing intelligence operatives and conservative clerics of ordering the serial killings of pro-reform intellectuals in 1998, he had labeled Rafsanjani "the Red Eminence" because of his behind-the-scene responsibility for bloodshed. His books, including "The Dungeon of Ghosts" (*Tariqkhaneh-ye ashbah: asibshenasi gozar be dowlat-e demokratik-e towse'egara*, Tehran, 1999) which detailed his investigations into the killings, dominated Iran's bestseller lists.[66]

In scenes rarely witnessed in Iran's revolutionary courts, Ganji accused former intelligence minister 'Ali Fallahian of being the "master key" in ordering the 1998 serial murders, and pointed to Hojjat ul-Islam Mohseni-Eje'i, head of the Special Court for Clergy and of the Press Court, as ordering the death of dissidents. He emphasized the role of the "Haqani circle" — graduates of the Haqani religious seminary who served in the judiciary and intelligence services — as instigators of the murders of dissidents as apostates. He challenged Khamene'i himself, saying that he had "the right not to agree with the leader," in his attacks on the press, and that he "should not be punished for disagreeing" with him. On 13 January 2001 the court sentenced Ganji to a ten-year-prison term and five years of internal exile. Most of the other defendants were acquitted.[67]

The Trial of Intelligence Officials

The reformists could claim a minor victory when the trial of eighteen Intelligence Ministry officials charged with committing the 1998 serial murders of dissident political and intellectual figures began on 22 December, after prolonged procrastination by the judiciary. Earlier, the judiciary had closed the lawsuit against former intelligence minister Qorban 'Ali Dorri Najafabadi and had dismissed Ganji's accusations against other officials. Bowing to public pressure, it put on trial eighteen lower-rank operators, who were, according to the Intelligence Ministry, "rogue" agents who had carried out orders given by their immediate superiors without the knowledge of the seniors. The reformists, however, maintained that the case exposed only a fraction of an intricate state-sponsored "killing machine" that had murdered as many as eighty political opponents since 1990. On 28 January 2001, the court sentenced three of the defendants to death and twelve to prison terms ranging from two years to life, acquitting three.[68]

Reformists Fighting Back

Confronting the conservative offensive, and in light of Khatami's weakness, the Majlis reformists struggled to take the lead in promoting the reform agenda through legislation. Their major dilemma was how to operate within and yet against the state, abiding by the very rules that were being used to undermine reform. Their efforts largely failed as the conservative Council of Guardians rejected 15 of the 42 bills approved by the Majlis, compared with 2 out of 22 bills approved by the previous Majlis.[69]

Among the bills that passed was an amnesty to Iranians who had fled abroad because of anti-government activities or ties to outlawed political parties. The bill aimed at bringing back some three million exiled Iranians — many of them academics and business owners — whose return could bring in badly needed investment and technological expertise. The Majlis also passed a bill calling for the relaxation of the strict background check that state employees had to undergo before employment. In November, it reversed a decision by the previous Majlis and lowered the voting age from 16 to 15 in order to increase the share of young voters, who tended to support reform.[70]

The cabinet, for its part, submitted a bill on 24 September designed to provide a clear definition of political offenses, instead of the broad guidelines in the constitution that allowed the judiciary to prosecute defendants for almost any political activity. The conservative press attacked these bills as opening the door to "anomalies and corruption." Mas'ud Dehnamaki, editor of the banned conservative *Jebhe* urged against permitting the Second-Khordad Front any peace as the Evin prison and the firing squads should await "their highnesses." The Council of Guardians vetoed the bill, saying it should have been drafted by the judiciary. Undeterred, the Majlis passed "outlines of legislation" giving defendants the automatic right to have a lawyer present at all stages of an inquiry or trial — a first since the 1979 revolution. It also set up a committee to expedite the procedure for acting on complaints filed by political detainees at the pre-trial stage. Majlis members visited political detainees in the notorious Evin and Qasr prisons and described the prison situation as highly "deplorable."[71]

Paying tribute to the importance of women's support for the reformists, the Majlis approved a bill on 27 August allowing single women to study abroad. More importantly, it amended the Personal Status Law expanding women's opportunities to divorce their husbands. It also raised the marriage age for girls from 9 to 13 and mandated court approval for marriage by boys under 18 or girls under 15. Conservatives attacked the changes in prerequisites for marriage as violating Islamic law, but the reformists won the debate in the Majlis by arguing that the measure would help prevent the practice of selling young girls, some of whom ended up as prostitutes. Nevertheless, the Council of Guardians vetoed both laws. The marriage law, however, was passed by the Majlis again and passed on to the Expediency Council for final arbitration.[72]

Seeking greater legislative expediency, the Majlis set up a joint committee with the judiciary to review all the judicial laws which had been passed since the Islamic revolution, sift out "unnecessary regulations," and propose new laws which the judiciary would then present as bills to parliament. However, in December, the Expediency Council acceded to the Council of Guardians' position on legislation by handing over the responsibility of submitting judicial bills directly to the judiciary, practically depriving the reformists — both in the legislative and executive branches — of essential rights of governing.[73]

The struggle over freedom of the press brought to a head the conflict between the Majlis and the Council of Guardians. Undeterred by persecution, reformist journalists launched new newspapers to replace those that had been closed down. The Ministry of Culture reported that it was reviewing license applications for two thousand periodicals, 530 of them submitted since April when the mass closures began. By December, however, the judiciary had processed — and rejected 132. Equally important, the provincial media tried to fill the gap left by the large-scale closure of Tehran newspapers. However, in addition to the threat of closure, these publications contended with lower revenues from sales, advertising and state subsidies, along with a dearth of modern printing facilities, resulting in low circulation and limited exposure. Another indication of the public thirst for information was the publication in Iran of 9,564 separate book titles between March and September, a 23% increase from the previous year, 18% of them translations of foreign titles.[74]

On 31 October, the Majlis passed a bill requiring only the permission of the Press Supervisory Board for the change in status of a publication from a weekly to a daily, or from local to national distribution, instead of approvals by the more conservative Justice Ministry, the law enforcement forces and the Intelligence Ministry, as decreed by the judiciary. The Council of Guardians vetoed the bill as "un-Islamic" and as contradictory to Khamene'i's August guidelines (see above). In response, reformists argued that clarifying laws fell within the responsibility of the Majlis and, moreover, that Khamene'i's August guidelines did not refer to this issue. Defying the Council of Guardians veto, and seeking to assert its prerogative, the Majlis reapproved the bill, but the Council of Guardians vetoed it once again and the bill was sent to the Expediency Council for adjudication. Even the usually pliant Karubi expressed anger at the Council of Guardians decision, criticizing it as the wrong way "to defend the supreme leader, Islam or the regime." Retreating from a confrontation, however, Karubi removed the bill from the agenda.[75]

Other Majlis deputies were more defiant in challenging the Council of Guardians "unprincipled rejection of Majlis ratification." They argued that the council weakened the leader's position and prestige by placing him in confrontation with the people's right to determine their fate through their elected representatives. Continuing this trend would lead to factional distrust, they warned, urging that the Council of Guardians rise above personal interest and avoid factional politics. Some deputies spoke of the need to reduce the council's constitutional powers, while others threatened to investigate complaints against it, knowing full well that they were powerless to do so. The council remained unimpressed, insisting on its superiority vis-à-vis the Majlis, including the right to prosecute its members. In the same vein, Iran rejected a UN General Assembly resolution adopted on 4 December, expressing "deep concerns" about press freedom in Iran, dismissing it as failing to "correspond to the reality of Iranian society."[76]

The reformist setback was capped by Khatami's yielding to pressure by Khamene'i to accept on 14 December the resignation of his ally Mohajerani as minister of culture. Conservatives described the resignation as overdue, but a joint statement by 190 Majlis deputies hailed his "invaluable achievements." Others described the development as Khatami sipping "from the bowl of hemlock," just as Khomeini had been forced to accept a cease-fire to end the Iran-Iraq War. They expressed fear that Mohajerani's removal meant increased restrictions on culture. Not only had Khatami lost an ally, he was unable to dismiss any of his conservative ministers, a legacy from his predecessor, Rafsanjani. "Khatami spends his time in the cabinet defending rather than leading," commented one analyst.[77]

Overall, the Majlis reformists lacked a strategy for maintaining unity in parliament, with some deputies who were elected on a pro-reform ticket shifting to the right in the course of the year. By way of example, the MRM and KSI joined the conservatives in rejecting Khatami's nominee as minister of post and telecommunications in October. Conceding their weakness, Second-Khordad Front leaders resolved to "pursue a policy of rapprochement with the pillars of the system in order to dry up all roots of tension and suspicion in the country."[78]

The Role of the Students

As in the previous four years, students remained the most vociferous advocates of radical change and therefore a major target for repression by the conservatives. In June alone, prior to the first anniversary of the Tehran University dormitory incident on 8 July 1999 (see *MECS* 1999, pp. 242–44), the authorities arrested dozens of undergraduates and university lecturers in Tehran, Isfahan, Shiraz, Tabriz and Mashhad.[79] On 8 July, Basij and Ansar-e Hezbollah (Champions of the Party of God) vigilantes attacked a rally at Tehran University and the students, who were joined by thousands of ordinary Iranians, turned violent, chanting slogans that challenged the very foundations of the regime such as: "The clerics live like kings, while the people are reduced to poverty," "Death to the clerical establishment," "Long live liberty," and "Khatami, Khatami, show your power or resign."[80]

While the campuses remained relatively calm during the months that followed, several protests were staged over the Berlin conference trials. Students also memorialized the late nationalist prime minister, Dr. Mohammad Mossadeq, who was vilified by the Islamist government, and demanded the release of Montazeri from house arrest. Aware of the students' revolutionary potential, the conservatives, headed by Khamene'i, warned of "politically motivated hidden traps set both inside and outside the universities," while continuing to harass leading student activists.[81]

Students Day on 6 December marked a peak of public protest. The Interior Ministry forbade a rally planned by the reformist Islamic Union of Students and Graduates, led by Heshmatollah Tabarzadi. Instead, thousands of students used the occasion of Khatami's speech at Tehran's Tarbiat-e-Modarres University to air their demands with relative impunity. They drowned out Khatami's remarks with chants demanding freedom for jailed activists, the resignation of hard-line officials, a referendum on the constitution, and bolder action by Khatami against the conservatives. Decrying the free atmosphere during students' rallies, the conservative *Kayhan* complained that boys and girls exchanged flowers, "greeted each other by shaking hands," and were not fasting even though it was the holy month of Ramadan.[82]

The Roles of Khatami and Khamene'i

Although by December, Khatami and the reformist faction could claim several foreign policy successes (see below), the great hopes in the domestic sphere generated by the Majlis elections were all but dashed. The president, who was part and parcel of the Islamic system and sought to preserve it, was either unable or unwilling to confront the conservatives. As a result, a rift appeared among his frustrated supporters. The moderates adhered to the strategy of "active calm," which advocated reform from within the system and frowned on open confrontation with the conservatives. The radicals, particularly students, maintained that this policy had outlived its usefulness and had become an excuse for inactivity. Many of them came to consider Khatami's presidency a failure, asserting that the reformist movement was too frail a vehicle for the sweeping changes they envisioned. Instead, they advocated radical steps, including civil disobedience, to bring about change. As before, however, the students were unable to rally mainstream Iranian society behind them.[83]

Khatami persisted in his cautious conduct. Speaking to students — his most enthusiastic constituency — he complained that Iranians always waited for a hero who would "resort to a miracle to create fundamental changes overnight," and when changes did not take place, or failed to "take place the way they wanted them," they despaired. Instead, he urged people to "cooperate with their leaders to pave the way for progress," criticizing those who advocated the concept of "bypassing Khatami" by pursuing more radical reforms. He also criticized conservatives who opposed all reform as undermining the revolution. "Suppose we silence the critics" for a while, he said. "These people will remain dissatisfied, and no one will be able to prevent the resulting damage." Thus, "secularism and fundamentalism will both lead to the collapse of the Islamic revolution," he warned.[84]

Khatami's associates reported his growing frustration and reluctance to run again in the 2001 presidential elections. Such messages were probably aimed at deterring radicals from "bypassing" him but also at persuading the conservatives that only his moderate policies could keep the lid on more radical manifestations of public frustration.[85]

Seeking to justify his failures vis-à-vis his supporters, Khatami conceded to a student audience on 26 November that "the president does not possess sufficient authority in order to perform this duty." In particular, he complained that he was unable to halt violations of the constitution, or enforce its implementation. The president, he emphasized shortly thereafter, "should be provided with necessary tools to uphold the constitution." Chiding the conservatives further, he stated that although Iran had emerged twenty years earlier from the "heavy weight" of dictatorship, it had not yet been "completely delivered from it, and dictatorship continues to haunt us all."[86]

Rejecting Khatami's remarks, the chief of the judiciary, Ayatollah Mahmud Hashemi Shahrudi, warned that Khatami was playing politics with the constitution, while other conservative politicians described Khatami's assertions as an "excuse" and a cover-up of his failures, as well as an expression of lust for more power. They insisted that he was duty bound to respect the terms of the constitution that subordinated him to the leader and warned that his claim would lead the country into an "incurable crisis," as greater power for the president would produce "absolute rule." Conservative legal experts accused the executive branch, i.e., Khatami personally, of systematically breaching the constitution. Some conservatives dismissed his complaints as a ploy to gain votes in the next presidential elections. By contrast, the IIPF announced its readiness to coordinate activity with the executive branch in order to pass the necessary laws concerning the presidential powers. The reformist *Iran News* attributed Khatami's failure to carry out his duties to the activities of numerous influential centers of power, "pressure groups" and foundations that were directly subordinate to the leader and served as instruments of control for the clergy outside the president's purview.[87]

Seeking to lower expectations among his more radical supporters, and possibly as a response to conservative opposition, Khatami denied that he sought constitutional change, noting that revamping the constitution was "an insult to the Iranian nation." Rather, he insisted that he be provided with the necessary tools to enforce the constitution.[88] Thus, regardless of his frustration, Khatami remained committed to the framework of the Islamic system and refrained from challenging its foundations. By the same token, the conservatives, including Khamene'i, did not seek to oust Khatami, their criticism notwithstanding. They preferred that he continue as a crippled president who would keep the lid on widespread public dissatisfaction and preserve the Islamic system, including their own status and authority.

As the conservative-reformist struggles wore on, Khamene'i enhanced his position, expanding his divine mandate to include the daily affairs of governance. Apparently he attempted to isolate Khatami from the more radical reformists, while allowing him to continue courting the public, who revered the president. However, he no longer had the president standing as a buffer absorbing public criticism that was directed at the Islamic system. Consequently, Khamene'i's hands-on mode of action managed to demystify his elevated post as a supreme leader who was above political squabbles. He now appeared more as a factional leader who could be criticized like any other political figure. University students had begun chanting slogans against him at rallies, and, more importantly, several Qom clerics distributed leaflets criticizing him on theological and political grounds.[89]

ECONOMIC AFFAIRS

Enhanced revenues due to rising oil prices gave a short-term boost to the Iranian economy but were insufficient to overcome its structural problems. A sprawling bureaucracy, mismanagement, lack of transparency particularly in the religious foundations [bonyads], which were subordinated to Khamene'i's office and controlled large sectors of the economy, contradictory regulations and laws favoring unprofitable nationalized industries vis-à-vis the private sector, along with huge subsidy programs absorbed much of the state income. These factors, and poor tax collection (accounting for c. 30% of total annual revenues) produced fiscal imbalance, a low investment rate, low growth and an external payments deficit. Official unemployment exceeded 16%, with unofficial figures significantly higher.[90] In addition, the worst drought in thirty-two years, affecting 17 out of Iran's 28 provinces in 2000, caused damages amounting to c. $1.7bn., mostly in crop and livestock losses, and accelerated rural-urban migration. Wheat imports increased to c. 6m. tons making Iran among the world's largest wheat purchasers.[91]

The Islamic Republic's Third Development Plan (2000 to 2005), which went into effect in March at the start of the Iranian fiscal year, called for increased productivity by reducing the involvement of the state in the economy, and the encouragement of competition by eliminating monopolies. It set an exceedingly high investment target of 7% a year, and 6% in annual economic growth (compared with an actual growth rate of 3.2% in the previous five years), in addition to creating 750,000 jobs annually by providing incentives for private investment, adjusting the tax system, and lowering inflation to below 15% by 2005.[92]

As in other fields, the struggle between conservatives and reformists dominated the molding of economic policy. While many conservatives sought to preserve state control over the economy, Khatami supporters were divided between those who favored greater market liberalization and those who stressed social justice. In February, the Council of Guardians rejected as unconstitutional sections of the five-year plan positing large-scale privatization. The outgoing Majlis endorsed the ruling, scuttling the reformers' hopes that a revote would force arbitration by the Expediency Council. The Guardians also rejected a government proposal to borrow up to $47bn. in foreign currency to meet the needs of its development plan, limiting net borrowing to half that amount. The Majlis, while passing the budget's initial vote on 6 March, limited fuel price hikes to 10%, thereby quashing government hopes to reduce excessive consumption and balance income and expenditure. It also rejected government proposals to allow the operation of private insurance firms or foreign investment in Iranian mines. The Majlis did, however, pass legislation permitting the establishment of privately owned banks, a move that served the interests of the powerful bazaar constituency.[93]

Attracting foreign investment of at least $10bn. annually was essential for attaining sustainable economic growth. Yet, Iran had attracted only $3bn. in investment in the previous five years, mostly in the oil sector. The major obstacles to foreign investment were restrictions on foreign ownership of property and on investment in the most attractive sectors, such as mining and energy; vague and even punitive tax laws and multiple foreign exchange rates; high inflation; a lack of legal frameworks providing investment security and an absence of transparency in economic data. As a partial remedy, the government promoted free trade zones (FTZ), and in February allowed foreign companies to invest in the offshore island of Qishm independently of participation by Iranian companies.[94]

The election of the reformist-dominated sixth Majlis resulted in greater economic policy cooperation between the executive and legislative branches. In June, the government launched talks with foreign companies to develop its mining and metals sector. It also invited applications from foreign banks to operate in its FTZs, the first such foreign involvement since the 1979 revolution. In October, Iran published international tenders for foreign participation in 1,250 construction projects. It also launched a comprehensive plan on national tourism in cooperation with the World Tourism Organization and the UN Development Program. Overall, Iran registered thirty-one new foreign companies operating in the country in 2000, a 121.4% increase from the previous year. However, it still ranked 154th out of 160 countries in attracting foreign investment, with the FTZ proving a major disappointment. Significantly, c. three thousand Iranian companies were registered in the economically inviting United Arab Emirates, while in the previous three years alone Iranians invested c. $13bn. in Turkey.[95]

In August, the Majlis passed legislation allowing foreign investors for the first time to have a majority shareholding in Iranian companies, including guarantees against seizure of assets, provisions for repatriating hard currency, and the removal of a requirement that any financial dispute between foreigners and their local partners must be settled in an Iranian court. The Majlis also abolished various duties on exports designed to offset the drop in sales of Iran's five main non-oil exports — carpets, pistachios, chemicals, steel and copper. In December, it approved the merger of the Ministry of Mines and Metals with the Ministry of Industries, complying with the government policy to eliminate parallel administrative bodies that competed for influence and resources.[96]

The hydrocarbons sector remained the dominant industry in Iran, its main — 80% —

foreign exchange earner and its largest employer outside agriculture. Iran maintained its position as OPEC's second-largest oil producer although annual production was slightly lower than its 3.7m. b/d OPEC quota. However, rising domestic demand, which forced it to double gasoline and natural gas imports, threatened its position as a net oil exporter. Iran acknowledged a "lack of access to modern technology and scarcity of funds" as hampering its optimal production capacity to produce oil in recent years. In order to maintain its 14.3% share in the OPEC production ceiling, Iran needed at least $3bn. in investment to increase production capacity and another $2.5bn. to make up for the depletion of old oil wells. While Iran signed over twelve buy-back contracts with European and Japanese firms to develop existing and new oil fields, this could not compensate for the absence of investment by American companies with their superior technology and greater resources.[97]

Higher world prices (see chapter on economic developments in the Middle East) increased Iran's revenues from oil and its derivatives to $18.6bn. in 2000, a 63% gain. For the first time in years, Iran achieved a trade balance and current account surpluses. Likewise, its foreign exchange reserves roughly equaled its debt burden, which fell to $10.3bn., compared with $30bn. in 1997, when Khatami entered office. Short-term debts fell from 65% of currency reserves to 40%. The flow of foreign revenues raised the Iranian rial to a two-year high of IR 8,000:$1. With Majlis approval in October, the government added IR 30bn. (c. $4bn.) to the 2000/01 budget for development projects, but also for salaries and drought compensation.[98]

Still, the overall economic picture remained mixed. The annual growth rate stood at 5.2%, largely due to oil revenues, but falling short of the minimum 6% target rate set by the five-year development plan. More importantly, up to 200,000 new jobs were officially created from March, the beginning of the Iranian fiscal year, until December 2000, far short of the 750,000 target, with the reformist Iran reporting a far lower figure — 40,000. Labor Minister Hosein Kamali blamed the country's labor woes on an influx of nearly two million refugees, mostly Afghans. Labor union officials, however, argued that factories all over Iran were losing money and were no longer able to pay their workers. Strikes by dismissed or unpaid workers abounded during the year.[99]

Living standards continued to decline as the average annual income rose by only 2.2%, while average urban household expenses rose by 22.6%. After twenty-five years of Islamic rule, government officials conceded the failure of Islamic economics to solve Iran's social ills, pointing out that over twelve million people lived below the poverty line and 20% of the population did not have "enough to eat," while the richest 20% of the population owned 80% of the national wealth.[100] Economic difficulties also encouraged emigration, both legal and illegal, particularly of young people, estimated at several thousand a month, which exacerbated the country's longstanding brain drain.[101]

Growing frustration among young people due to economic and social difficulties, coupled with Iran's proximity to the vast opium-growing regions of Afghanistan, produced a disastrous drug-addiction problem with severe societal implications. Notwithstanding government claims of intercepting hundreds of tons of drugs annually, and the death of 2,500 law enforcement officers fighting traffickers since 1979, government statistics reported two million addicts (3.2m. according to health officials) who consumed c. 600 ton of drugs annually. The crime rate was rising steadily and every six days a woman was raped, murdered or mutilated in Tehran, Iran reported. Prostitution among high school students driven by poverty and drug addiction rose by 635% during the preceding decade, lowering the average age of prostitutes from 27 to 20, while suicides grew by 109% during 1998 and 1999 alone. Minister of Health Mohammad Farhadi warned that hepatitis and AIDS resulting from drug abuse by injection were a "time bomb" waiting to rip through Iranian society, prompting other officials to break a cultural taboo and urge that AIDS education be added to school curricula.[102]

FOREIGN AFFAIRS

Iranian foreign policy during 2000 remained unchanged. Both conservatives and reformists shared the same view of establishing Iran as a regional power, diverging only on the right balance between pragmatic needs and ideological commitment, depending on the specific arena and issues.

IRAN AND THE MIDDLE EAST

Turkey

A visit by Iranian foreign minister Kamal Kharrazi to Turkey on 17–18 January reflected the two faces of Iranian-Turkish relations: a shared interest in expanding economic ties, and mutual distrust due to opposite ideological orientations. During a discussion of economic ties, the Turks raised allegations, denied by Iran, that Iran harbored fighters belonging to the radical anti-government Parti Kerkeren Kurdistan (PKK; Kurdistan Worker's Party; see chapter on Turkey). More importantly, Iranian spokespersons and the Iranian press slammed the close Turkish-Israeli military relationship as threatening regional security and stability warning that Iran would not "tolerate" Israel's presence in Turkey and that Turkish ties with the "Zionist aggressors" would jeopardize its relations with Iran and the Arab countries. Iran also accused Israel and the US of obstructing the implementation of its natural gas deal with Turkey signed in 1996. These threats notwithstanding, Kharrazi signed a memorandum of understanding with his hosts regarding mutual cooperation in various political, economic and cultural areas, in addition to fourteen extant joint economic commissions.[103]

No sooner did Kharrazi leave Ankara, then Turkish officials and the Turkish press accused Iran of providing training and financial support to a Turkish Hizballah terrorist organization apprehended by Turkish security forces the week before. Iran rejected the accusations, declaring that it had always respected the principles of "non-interference in others' domestic policies and of good neighborly relations." The Turkish press, however, continued to publish captured documents disclosing the magnitude of Iranian support for Hizballah and the PKK.[104] Iran, in turn, protested a statement by Turkish prime minister Bulent Ecevit following the reformist victory in the Majlis elections expressing the hope that Iran "would stop exporting its brand of hard-line Islam." The Iranian press chastised Turkey for its anti-democratic conduct and poor human rights record toward its own Islamists and minority groups.[105]

Revelations by the Turkish press in May of Iranian involvement in the 1993 murder of the secularist journalist, Ugur Mumcu, exacerbated the tension between the two countries. The friction culminated in an announcement by Turkey that newly elected President Ahmet Necdet Sezer would not attend the ten-member Economic Cooperation Organization (ECO) summit scheduled in Tehran.[106]

Iran, adamantly denying all charges of links to the murder, spoke in two voices. The conservative press accused Turkey of acting under "provocation and orders" from both Washington and Tel Aviv and called on the Iranian authorities to "downgrade" relations with Ankara. It also officially protested the "illegal and unacceptable" attitude of the Turkish authorities following the arrest of hundreds of Iranian citizens during the investigations into the Hizballah and PKK activity. With this, Kharrazi stressed on 8 June that both countries should rely on diplomatic means to solve any bilateral problem. In a signal to Turkey that Iran had other regional options, he highlighted the importance of Iran's cooperation with two of Turkey's erstwhile rivals, Greece and Armenia. Khatami, for his part, twice extended personal invitations to Sezer to attend the ECO summit. Sezer, however, declined until "the expected improvements in Turkish-Iranian relations" occurred, primarily, the "creation of an atmosphere of security."[107]

Nevertheless, the two countries concluded a series of memoranda of understanding aimed at expanding bilateral trade and economic ties, which had witnessed substantial growth during the year.[108] In October, they signed an agreement reinforcing their joint effort against rebel border-crossing and drug trafficking. Tension increased once again when, on 31 October, Turkey forced an Iranian civilian aircraft en route to Damascus to land in Diyarbakir for inspection on suspicion of carrying weapons to the Lebanese Hizballah. Iran protested the "illegal and unfriendly" act, while the Iranian press accused Turkey of obeying "Zionist" orders.[109]

Azerbaijan

Iranian relations with Azerbaijan remained tense due to a series of ongoing problems. Iran suspected Baku of backing Azeri nationalists in Iranian Azerbaijan. It also opposed the construction of a pipeline that would transport Turkmenistan's natural gas to the West via Azerbaijan, bypassing its own territory. Additionally, the two countries disagreed over rights to the Caspian Sea resources. While Iran and Turkmenistan believed that the states bordering the Caspian should have a 20% share each of the seabed, surface and waters, Azerbaijan, Russia, and Kazakhstan advocated dividing the seabed and leaving the surface and waters in common use. Furthermore, Iran resented Azerbaijan's close ties with the US, Turkey Israel. Yet, another problem was the disruption of Iranian electricity supplies to the Nakhichevan enclave.[110]

Azerbaijan accused Iran of backing religiously-motivated disturbances and subversion initiated by Azeri clerics. It also resented Iranian support for Armenia in the dispute between Azerbaijan and Armenia over control of Nagorno-Karabagh and charged Iran with supplying the enclave with arms and ammunition. Azerbaijani border troops complained in July about Iranian violations of their territorial waters and airspace. The conservative media in Tabriz just across the border, whether intending to convey a veiled threat to Azerbaijan to mend its ways, or reflecting deep-seated Iranian aspirations to regain Azerbaijan, claimed that the "thirst" of "the Muslims of the Caucasus" to return to "the main body of the Islamic Republic" and to be "annexed to their motherland" had intensified since the 1989 collapse of communism. Visiting Ardabil province on 27 July, Khamene'i praised the "love" of many Azeris for the Iranian clergy, while accusing Azerbaijan of harboring unjustified territorial claims regarding the Caspian Sea. In October, reflecting Azerbaijan's concerns, President Heidar Aliyev postponed his planned visit to Iran "indefinitely," explaining that bilateral relations had not reached the "desirable level."[111]

Iraq

Political differences and the residue of the Iran-Iraq War, rather than economics, continued to shape Iranian relations with Iraq. An Iraqi trade delegation arriving in Tehran on 11–17 January seemed to signal a mutual will to upgrade economic and political ties. Foreign Minister Kharrazi reiterated Iranian recognition of Iraqi territorial integrity, while Expediency Council chairperson Rafsanjani announced Iranian readiness to establish a political and military alliance with all its Arab neighbors, including Iraq, in order to safeguard regional stability.[112]

However, the continued sponsorship by Iraq of the Mojahedin-e Khalq Organization (MKO) that carried out attacks in Tehran and in the provinces bordering on Iraq foiled whatever chance there was for such an improvement. Iran submitted an official protest to the UN and to Iraq for allowing cross-border raids, accusing Iraq of twenty-seven cease-fire violations during 1999, while the commander of the Revolutionary Guards, Gen. Yahya Rahim Safavi, warned on 7 February of a strong Iranian response should Iraq fail to prevent future raids. The conservative media was less diplomatic, calling for military action to "destroy the centers of dissent deep within Iraqi territory." Iran voiced similar accusations throughout the year. Iraq, however, claimed that it did not interfere in MKO internal affairs or armed activities, just as Iran denied any involvement in attacks by Shi'i opposition organizations in Baghdad.[113]

The fate of prisoners of war (POWs) was another bone of contention between both sides. Iran asserted that Iraq still held 2,800 Iranian prisoners, while Iraq charged that Iran held 29,000 Iraqi POWs (a figure Iran denied) and that an additional sixty thousand were still missing. In a gesture toward Iraq, Iran released c. 3,390 Iraqi POWs between April and June.[114]

In April, Iran seized ten tankers in its territorial waters which were illegally exporting Iraqi oil. Hitherto, it had allowed coastal trade with Iraq — particularly oil smuggling — in violation of UN Security Council sanctions, allegedly exacting hefty fees amounting to c. $500m. annually from the smugglers. The change of policy was apparently designed to pressure Iraq over the MKO issue or to raise smuggling fees. After enforcing the UN sanctions for two months, Iran reopened its sea lanes to enable Iraq to smuggle out c. 100,000 b/d of oil. Foreign analysts linked these fluctuations to Iran's domestic power struggle and to internal financial interests: Khatami had ordered a halt to the oil smuggling, but the conservative-controlled Revolutionary Guards, which exacted c. $20m. a month from the smuggling, restored it.[115]

Apparently in response to Iranian measures at sea, Iraq temporarily barred Iranian pilgrims in late July from visiting the holy Shi'i shrines in its territory, in violation of previous agreements. Seeking to defuse the situation, Iran unilaterally released three thousand Iraqi POWs, rejecting Iraqi claims that thousands of others remained captive.[116]

The acrimonious atmosphere notwithstanding, Kharrazi met his Iraqi counterpart, Muhammad Sa'id al-Sahhaf, during the opening UN General Assembly session in September. That same month, Khatami himself met with Iraqi vice president Taha Yasin Ramadan during the OPEC conference in Caracas. The meeting — the highest-level encounter between the two sides since the 1991 Gulf War — revolved around upgrading diplomatic relations, security issues — mainly Iraqi support for the MKO, the exchange of POWs, and Iranian pilgrimages to holy sites in Iraq. While reporting progress, Iranian sources noted that the "book on disputes with Baghdad" was too large and "contains some bloody chapters" that could not be resolved in a single meeting alone.[117]

The meeting in Caracas initiated a hesitant thaw in relations. The Iraqi minister of transport and communications, Ahmad Murtada Ahmad, arrived in Tehran on 3 October to discuss cooperation in the field of trade and transport. More importantly, Kharrazi came to Baghdad ten days later expressing the hope that a new page would open in Iran-Iraq relations. He conferred with Iraqi president Saddam Husayn in order to convey Iranian determination "to settle all outstanding problems relating to the Iran-Iraq War.[118] The conservative Iranian press was less sanguine. While pointing to agreement with Iraq on the Palestinian question and the need to oppose the US, it stressed Iraq's 1980 aggression against Iran, its support of the MKO, and its overall untrustworthy nature. More visits by high-level Iraqi officials followed in December and the two countries agreed on a new formula to resolve the POW issue, but the basic distrust remained intact.[119]

Saudi Arabia

Iran continued efforts to improve relations with Saudi Arabia as a lever against Iraq and in order to weaken Saudi links with the US, and thereby diminish the American naval presence in the Gulf. The Saudis, who were also interested in such an improvement eased visa regulations to Iranian business owners and those coming to the *'umra* (minor) pilgrimage. In a symbolic gesture, they invited Khamene'i to visit the kingdom, the first such invitation since the 1979 revolution, but Khamene'i did not act on it, apparently for domestic reasons.[120]

During the first ever visit of an Iranian defense minister to Saudi Arabia in April, Admiral 'Ali Shamkhani proposed the formation of a Gulf defense pact that would include the six Gulf Cooperation Council nations and Iran. The Saudis declined, unwilling to jeopardize their relations with the US.[121] Still, during a visit to Iran by Saudi foreign minister Sa'ud Al Faysal on 7–8 October, President Khatami described Iranian relations with Saudi Arabia as "very successful," stressing bilateral cooperation in OPEC and on the Palestinian problem.[122]

Facing terrorist attacks on its soil, some of them apparently linked to Iran (see *MECS* 1996, pp. 582–86), Saudi Arabia was more interested than Iran in signing a security pact dealing with joint combat against drug trafficking and terrorism. Iran sent a delegation to put the final touches on such an agreement only on 21 November in response to Saudi exhortations. The treaty was eventually signed on 17 April 2001.[123]

Egypt

Iranian relations with Egypt constituted another arena where ideology and pragmatism clashed. As part of his regional policy of détente, Khatami pushed for restoring diplomatic ties with Egypt, severed since the 1979 revolution, by first expanding economic and cultural cooperation. On 21 June, Egyptian president Husni Mubarak telephoned Khatami — the first direct contact between the leaders of the two states in twenty-one years — to congratulate him on Iran joining the Conference of Developing Countries. A week later, the two foreign ministers, Kharrazi and 'Amru Musa of Egypt, met in Kuala Lumpur to discuss the normalization of bilateral relations, and held several telephone conversations thereafter. The two countries also organized trade fairs in each other's capital city.[124]

Still, several issues prevented the restoration of diplomatic ties. While sanctioning the improvement of economic ties, the conservatives attacked Egypt for its relations with Israel. Egypt, for its part, demanded that Tehran change the name of Khalid al-Islambuli

Street, which commemorated the assassin of Egyptian president Anwar al-Sadat in 1981. The conservatives, however, vetoed any such change. In January, conservative-backed hooligans ransacked the offices of the newly established Iran-Egypt Friendship Society. Foreign sources contended that the Iranian Revolutionary Guards provided aid to the radical al-Jama'a al-Islamiyya organization that was fighting the Egyptian government.[125]

Syria

While Iran stated its support for Syrian efforts to restore its "legitimate rights" by negotiating with Israel, it was evidently concerned with the impact of a successful outcome of such talks on its relations with its most important Arab ally. Iran, vehemently criticizing Egypt and the Palestinians for negotiating with the "Zionist regime," while explaining that Syrian policy stemmed from heavy American pressure. Still, the Iranian media scolded Syria for ignoring Israeli failures to honor its commitments and "advised" Syria to "proceed with caution."[126] Iran was clearly relieved when the negotiations broke down in April, praising Syria for its steadfastness.[127]

The death of Syrian president Hafiz al-Asad on 10 June did not alter the relationship between the two countries. Iran declared a three-day mourning period and Khatami came to the funeral to embrace Asad's son and successor, Bashshar, and ensure the continued functioning of the alliance. In a message to Bashshar al-Asad, Khamene'i praised his late father as "one of the superior figures in the Arab world" who resisted Zionism. Several other Iranian officials visited Syria in the following months, while Syrian prime minister Mustafa Miru visited Tehran on 21 November. Underscoring Syria's importance, Defense Minister Shamkhani warned that Iran would not "remain silent" should Israel attack either Syria or Lebanon.[128]

Lebanon

Lebanon remained a central sphere of influence for Iran in light of the close Hizballah connections. Iran supplied weapons to Hizballah to continue its fight against the Israeli presence in South Lebanon, while Iranian envoys frequented Beirut throughout the year to express support for the organization and its role in Lebanese politics. A visit to Iran by Lebanese president Emile Lahhud on 18–19 April, and his meetings with Khamene'i, Khatami and other senior leaders pointed to the importance of Lebanon in the Iranian view.[129]

While hailing the unilateral Israeli withdrawal in May from South Lebanon as a major victory for Lebanon and the entire Muslim nation, Iran was anxious to ensure that its influence would not wane once a major motivating element — fighting Israel — was removed. It backed the Hizballah position on the disputed Shab'a region (see chapter on Lebanon), maintaining that Hizballah alone would determine the future shape of resistance. With Iran continuing to supply the organization with arms, it appeared that Hizballah was seen by Iran as offering it the chance to perpetuate the longer-term struggle against the very existence of Israel.[130]

Israel and the Peace Process

Iran's ideological conviction since the inception of the 1979 revolution that Israel was a "cancerous tumor" in the region which should be "destroyed and shattered" remained unchanged.[131] This was a rare instance where ideology and state interests did not clash;

hostility toward Israel served Iranian aspirations for regional leadership, while not entailing any cost in terms of its relations with the West.

Iran vehemently opposed the Arab-Israeli peace process as a betrayal of Palestinian and Arab usurped rights. Instead of pinning their hopes on negotiations, the Iranian media insisted, Palestinian leaders should mobilize their people for an "armed struggle to liberate their homelands." It warned that increased contacts with Arab countries enabled Israel to gain a foothold in the region, with "destructive" political, economic, cultural and social consequences for those countries. The Arab world, it argued, need not "please the Zionists and their mentors in Washington." Instead, Arab leaders could rest assured of the full support of the Muslim world if they decided to erase Israel from the Middle East.[132]

Concurrently, seeking to project a more agreeable image to foreign countries, the secretary of the Supreme Security Council, Hojjat ul-Islam Hasan Ruhani, asserted that while Iran opposed the peace process, it had done nothing to thwart it. Israeli and foreign sources, however, maintained that Iran supported radical Palestinian groups opposed to any compromise with Israel and advocating armed struggle against it. In a rare example of dissent on foreign policy, Majlis candidate 'Ali-Reza Nuri of the IIPF, echoing his brother 'Abdollah Nuri's position (see *MECS* 1999, pp. 253–54), argued that the countries actually involved in the peace process knew better what decisions to make than uninvolved countries, i.e., Iran, implying that Iran should desist from adopting a more radical stance than the Arabs themselves.[133]

Iran hailed the unilateral Israeli withdrawal from South Lebanon (see chapter on Israel) as a great victory for the global Islamic movement and for "all those believing in the violent struggle against the Zionist regime." It showed, Khamene'i stated on 25 May that the only solution to "atrocities of the usurper Zionists" lay "in the logic of resistance, jihad and devotion."[134]

Insisting that the lessons of Lebanon be applied in the Palestinian arena, Iran lashed out at the Camp David summit of American, Israeli and Palestinian leaders (May 2000; see chapter on the Arab-Israeli peace process) as a sellout of the Palestinian cause. The "so-called" peace process, Khatami explained, ignored the roots of the problem, i.e., Israel's existence and Palestinian displacement. In addition to ideological arguments, Iran maintained that Israel refused to comply with the UN resolutions regarding the Palestinian issue. Consequently, Khamene'i predicted, any Palestinian compromise with Israel would fail because of resistance by Islamic Palestinian groups. Israel is a false and fictitious entity, he said, which is why it would "vanish," while followers of all religions would "live in Palestine in peace." Khatami, Rafsanjani, Karubi and other officials met with the leaders of Palestinian Islamic Jihad, Hamas and Hizballah in Tehran, Damascus and Beirut during the latter part of the year in order to coordinate activity against any future Palestinian-Israeli agreement.[135]

Iran welcomed the failure of the Camp David summit as a defeat of US policy. It blamed Israel for rejecting "even the minimum demands of the Palestinians," while its demands were so "harsh" that even the "timid" Yasir 'Arafat could not have accepted them. Jerusalem, Khatami declared, was not "solely a subject of conflict between Palestinians and Israelis," but was "Islam's primary holy site and the very symbol of the Islamic cause." Therefore, no individual or group had the "right to bargain over this sacred Islamic cause."[136]

Although critical of 'Arafat for formerly being "shamefully submissive" toward

"Zionist" pressure, Iran, as current chair of the Islamic Conference Organization (ICO), received 'Arafat on 10 August, with Khatami promising him that Iran would "take every possible action" to resolve the Palestinian issue. In addition, Iranian officials made repeated trips to the region in order to establish a joint Islamic position regarding Jerusalem. Khamene'i's personal representative, 'Ali Akbar Velayati, visited Damascus and Beirut in July, while deputy foreign minister Mohammad Sadr traveled to Amman, Beirut, Tunis, Damascus and Riyadh.[137]

Iran regarded the outbreak of violent confrontations between the Palestinians and Israel on 28 September (see chapters on the PA and Israel) as a further vindication of its position. Setting the general line, Khamene'i accused Israel of conspiring to destroy the al-Aqsa Mosque in Jerusalem and of "massacring" Muslim Palestinians. He reiterated the original Iranian position that the only way to resolve the Middle East crisis was to destroy "the Zionist regime," the "root and cause of the crisis." Pledging Iranian support of the Palestinians in attaining this goal, he expressed confidence in the ultimate victory of the Muslims as both Israel and the US were "disintegrating and rotting from within." Khamene'i packaged his ideas in positive terms, calling for the return of all Palestinian refugees to their homeland, followed by the holding of referendum by the "original people of Palestine," i.e., excluding those Jews who came as part of the Zionist enterprise. The referendum would determine the political regime that the people wanted, in the certainty that the result would be a Muslim Arab state.[138]

The conservative press urged using the opportunity of the outburst of violence to destroy Israel and criticized 'Arafat for discussing the cessation of the violence with the Israelis.[139] Significantly, the reformists, some of whom had previously pointed to the need for a revised attitude toward Israel, joined the mainstream.[140]

Iran used the confrontation to present itself as the champion of the Palestinian cause, condemning the "indifference" of Arab governments. Khatami, on a more cautious note, maintained that "the least" Muslim countries should do was sever ties with Israel.[141] Complementing its words with deeds, Iran flew dozens of injured Palestinians to receive medical treatment in Iranian hospitals. Khamene'i called on Iranians to donate money to help the Palestinians, while Grand Ayatollah Fazel Lankarani authorized the allocation of monies from religious funds to support the Palestinian struggle. Iran also hosted officials of the Lebanese Hizballah, Hamas, the Islamic Jihad of Palestine and the Popular Front for the Liberation of Palestine-General Command to coordinate their operations against Israel. Qods (Jerusalem) Day on 22 December marked the peak of the state-organized vilification of Israel, with rallies held in dozens of cities. Revolutionary Guards commander Gen. Rahim-Safavi declared on the occasion that Iran was "in a state of open non-military war with the Zionist regime."[142]

IRAN AND THE WORLD

The US

Iran's relationship with the US was the major foreign policy arena in which ideology prevailed over pragmatic economic considerations. Reflecting Khatami's position, government spokespersons challenged the US to lift its sanctions against Iran, release Iranian assets in America, withdraw its military forces from the Persian Gulf, and halt hostile propaganda as preconditions for thawing bilateral relations. With this, they welcomed immediate investment by American companies in Iranian development projects. Concurrently, Iran denounced the US for seeking cultural domination and for its policies in the Persian Gulf, the Caspian Sea and the Arab-Israeli conflict. Statements by US president Bill Clinton on 14 February in favor of a "constructive partnership" with Iran, evoked a retort by Kharrazi that Iran wanted "tangible signs of goodwill" rather than words.[143]

The conservatives still regarded the US as the antithesis of the Islamic government, fearing that the restoration of ties with it would adversely influence Iranian domestic politics and culture. In addition, they viewed the Iranian alliance with Russia (see below) as improving its bargaining position and diminishing the appeal of economic ties with the US. They condemned US secretary of state Madeleine Albright's stated hope that the Majlis elections — i.e., a reformist victory — would improve bilateral ties, perceiving this as an unacceptable interference in Iranian domestic affairs. Conversely, a few reformists stressed the need to remove the taboo on discussing the prospect of negotiations with the US, proposing a dialogue based on mutual national interests rather than ideology to settle bilateral differences. IIPF candidate 'Ali-Reza Nuri stated that Iranian citizens rather than the government should decide the fate of Iranian-American relations by a referendum.[144]

US officials welcomed the election results, expressing the hope that Iran would modify its opposition to the Arab-Israeli peace negotiations, cease its support of terrorist groups, and reexamine the utility of developing weapons of mass destruction (WMD). While hinting that the results of such change might lead to reciprocal rewards, the US ruled out as premature the removal of Iran from its list of states which supported terrorism or supporting World Bank (WB) loans to Iran. Moreover, in February, Congress passed the Iran Non-Proliferation Act linking US aid for Russia's space program to the cessation of Russian aid for the Iranian weapons programs, a move which elicited Russian and Iranian condemnation.[145]

In a gesture toward Iran, however, Secretary Albright announced on 17 March the removal of a ban on importing carpets, caviar, dried fruits and pistachios from Iran and the relaxation of restrictions on visits by Iranian academics and athletes. She stated American readiness to settle "outstanding" bilateral legal claims estimated at several billion dollars, through the US-Iran claims tribunal in The Hague. She also admitted, but did not apologize for, past US meddling in Iranian internal affairs, including the CIA-backed coup in August 1953 that overthrew the government led by Mohammad Mossadeq and restored the monarchy.[146]

The Iranian cabinet welcomed the American move "as far as ending the hostilities" were concerned, but cautioned that the change in US policy was insufficient to warrant an immediate restoration of long-broken ties. It rejected American allegations of human rights abuse and the production of WMD.[147] Reformists, who argued that Albright's speech required a "positive response at the same level," emphasized the economic and political benefits from normalizing relations with the US and contended that most Iranians favored this approach. Stressing the Iranian need for American technology and capital, *Iran News* viewed diplomatic relations with the US as "inevitable."[148]

However, Khamene'i, and the entire conservative camp, upholding their ideological position, dismissed Albright's statements as "deceitful and belated confessions" that could not compensate for the harm done, but rather aimed at perpetuating the enmity with Iran. The Iranian nation, Khamene'i stated, considered the US its "enemy" because Iranian history was "fraught with animosities and treacheries by the US." In a subsequent rebuttal of the reformists' reasoning, Khamene'i argued that "none" of Iran's problems would ever be solved by establishing relations with the US because the Americans were more concerned about their own interests than about those of the nations with which they dealt.[149]

Tension between the two countries increased following a series of contentious developments. The US tried but failed to block approval by the WB on 18 May of a $232m. loan to Iran, the first in seven years. The conviction in July of ten Iranian Jews on charges of spying (see above) prompted American condemnation, which Iran rejected. On 11 July, a US federal judge ordered Iran to pay $327m. to the families of two Americans killed in a suicide bombing in Israel, ruling that the evidence showed Iranian involvement in the attack. Iran rejected the decision as "worthless and politically motivated." In a symbolic response, the Iranian Organization of Victims of Weapons of Mass Destruction filed a lawsuit to the Preliminary Commission of the War Crimes Tribunal in the Hague against US officials whom it held responsible for the downing of an Iranian passenger plane in 1988 (see *MECS* 1988, p. 31). The US continued pressuring Russia not to sell Iran laser technology that could be used to produce fuel for nuclear weapons (see below).[150]

A test by Iran on 15 July of a medium-range missile, Shahab-3, capable of reaching Israel as well as US troops based in Saudi Arabia, evoked American criticism as a "serious threat to the region and to US non-proliferation interests." Retorting, *Kayhan International* wrote: "If Washington honestly desired global peace," it would have abandoned its "bigoted and criminal policies."[151]

Responding, nevertheless, to popular desire to initiate a dialogue with the US, Khamene'i explained that Iran's anti-American policy followed thorough "study and calculations" and was based on three major principles:

(1) Iran rejected a unipolar world dominated by the US because "America" lacked the "moral or the political competence to lead the world." All the US had to offer was "its superior industry, its complex technology, its advanced sciences, and its wealth," but Iran could not "accept this."

(2) "[No] matter how many concessions you grant them," the US still demanded more and would be in a position to impose its will.

(3) The US opposed political Islam as a threat to itself. In the current state of affairs, anything said "in favor of rapprochement" with America was "an insult and betrayal of the Iranian people."[152]

Still, Khamene'i and the conservatives supported the reformists' efforts to induce a change in American policy toward Iran. Taking advantage of the Inter-Parliamentary Union summit in New York in late August, Speaker of the Majlis Karubi held a meeting with two US senators — the highest-ranking bilateral exchange since the 1979 takeover of the American embassy in Tehran (see *MECS* 1979–80, pp. 474–79). He called on Congress to "stop its hostile behavior towards Iran" and cease pressuring foreign and American firms that sought relations with it. He also stated that his country welcomed promoting relations between Iranian and American cultural and scientific institutions. Additionally, Karubi conferred with heads of US oil companies, who were forbidden by the US government to invest in Iran, encouraging them to work for the removal of all sanctions against it. Furthermore, he met with American Jewish leaders, who raised issues related to the Jewish community in Iran. Presumably, following conservative pressure, Karubi subsequently claimed that his meetings with the senators and Jewish leaders were "accidental," stressing that he had criticized US congressional policy against Iran.[153]

In a related gesture, three American officials came to Iran to attend for the first time since the 1979 embassy takeover a conference sponsored by the UN Food and Agriculture Organization.[154]

Khatami pursued a similar line at the UN millennium summit in New York. In his address to the plenum on 5 September, he stressed that the US could restore political and economic ties with Iran by apologizing for its misdeeds, particularly its role in the 1953 coup and the damage incurred thereafter, criticizing the US for failing to do so. He later demanded that the US "compensate" for the problems it had "created in the past." Radio Tehran, in similar vein, urged the US to stop supporting the MKO and release frozen Iranian assets as additional preconditions for dialogue. Secretary of State Albright, seeking to convey a message that the US was "willing to listen" to Iranian arguments, attended the session at which Khatami spoke, but the two leaders did not hold any direct talks. In a more important gesture, President Clinton extended his stay at the summit in order to be present at Khatami's address.[155] In what appeared as a precedent, Kharrazi and Albright both attended an eight-nation meeting at the UN to promote peace in Afghanistan (15 September), albeit without holding direct talks. Furthermore, the US allowed Kharrazi to attend several conferences at US colleges during his visit, as part of its policy of "people-to-people dialogue."[156]

In contrast to the administration's approach, the US House of Representatives issued a statement on 10 October urging the State Department to drop its policy of quiet rapprochement with Iran. Pointing to "executions, torture, attacks on dissidents abroad and the trial of thirteen Iranian Jews," as well as Iranian efforts to acquire nuclear capability, the statement concluded that "any talk of political openness or moderation" in Iran was "ill advised." Instead, American recognition and support for the National Council of Resistance of Iran (an MKO-led organization) was recommended. Iran condemned the resolution as a "futile reaction" to its growing international stature.[157]

The US Senate enacted legislation on 11 October allowing American victims of terrorism to collect court-awarded damages from countries that sponsored terrorism. Consequently, the Clinton administration allocated c. $400m. in frozen Iranian assets to secure payment of indemnities awarded by courts to eight families in class action suits against Iran. Iran accused the US of viewing itself as the absolute power in international relations and of securing its interests through bullying and aggression. On 30 October the Majlis passed legislation authorizing "victims of US interference" to sue the US in Iranian courts for "actual, compensatory or moral damages sustained as a result of any such interference."[158]

The difficulties in finalizing the results of the American presidential elections in 2000 provided the conservative media in Iran with an opportunity to heap scorn on Western democracy and on the US in particular.[159] Still, reformists expressed the hope that pressure by American oil companies anxious to invest in Iran would force the next president to change US policy. Ironically, the very ambitions harbored by American oil companies that had alarmed and infuriated Iranian nationalists during the early 1950s had now became a source of hope.[160]

Russia

The "strategic partnership" between Iran and Russia grew stronger during 2000. Both countries were allied against the Taliban government in Afghanistan and shared similar interests in the Caspian region.[161] Russia was Iran's major arms provider in addition to constructing a nuclear power plant in Bushehr. A steady stream of visiting delegations from both sides concluded numerous agreements on bilateral economic and strategic cooperation during the year.[162]

These interests superseded Iran's ideological commitment to Islamic solidarity with the Chechen people. In a quasi-official division of labor, the conservative press accused Russia of committing atrocities in Chechnya and described acting president Vladimir Putin as "the butcher of Chechnya,"[163] while official Iran adopted a more restrained tone. In a congratulatory message to Putin on 4 January, Khatami expressed his hope that the Chechen crisis "would end in a peaceful manner." Both deputy foreign minister Mohammad Javad Zarif, who led an ICO delegation to Russia on 17 January, and Foreign Minister Kharrazi warned Russia that the war would negatively affect its relations with ICO member states. Both urged the use of political means to resolve the crisis. Iran was also the leading Muslim nation providing aid for Chechen Muslim refugees. Still, Iranian officials stressed their country's respect for Russian territorial integrity and for the status of Chechnya as part of Russia, a position influenced by Iran's own fear of irredentism by its ethnic minorities. Iran hailed the Russian initiative in April to hold talks with the Chechen leadership, offering its services as a mediator, but refrained from other action. As the year progressed, Iran seldom addressed the Chechen issue.[164]

Iran's shared interests with Russia regarding the Caspian region was a major factor overshadowing their differences over Chechnya. Both were concerned about growing US economic involvement in Azerbaijan's oil industry, particularly in the construction of the Baku-Ceyhan and Trans-Caspian gas pipelines that competed with the line that Iran and Armenia were trying to complete. Seeking to keep the US out, Iran floated in May the idea of a South Caucasus security system encompassing only the countries of the region, but did not elicit much response. Kharrazi and his Russian counterpart, Igor Ivanov, agreed during a meeting on 26 July on the need to adopt a Caspian Sea legal framework that would exclude external players. However, while Iran agreed with Russia's position of developing disputed oil fields on a 50–50 basis, Russia, which had the largest Caspian coastline, rejected Iran's proposal that each of the five Caspian Sea states receive 20% of its area.[165]

Such disagreements did not interfere with the tightening of bilateral military links. A high-level Russian military delegation — the first since 1991 — arrived in Tehran on 3 July, with both countries announcing their intention to move toward "planned military cooperation." A meeting between Khatami and Putin during the UN General Assembly session in New York on 6 September was another symbol of the alliance. A visit to Tehran of Sergey Ivanov, secretary of the Russian National Security Council, on 18–20 October resulted in agreements to expand cooperation in the nuclear, military, economic and technical domains. This overshadowed a Russian decision in September, made under US pressure, to temporarily suspend the sale of laser technology which could be used in building nuclear weapons.[166]

Disturbed by a series of Taliban victories over the opposition Northern Alliance in October, Iran joined in Russian efforts to reassure the Central Asian states in the face of threats by the Taliban and pressure the Afghan rulers to negotiate with the opposition. However, short of an open confrontation, Iran had little leverage over the Taliban.[167]

Iran applauded the Russian announcement on 23 November to scrap a 1995 pledge to the US not to sell tanks and battlefield weapons to Iran. A visit to Tehran by Russian defense minister Igor Sergeyev on 24–26 December — the first by a Russian defense minister since 1979 — capped the Russo-Iranian military tie. The visit was devoted to determining the "state of the Iranian army and its needs."[168]

Europe

Iranian relations with the EU countries generally improved during 2000 in light of a joint interest in expanding economic relations. Moreover, for Iran, closer links with Europe did not carry the same ideological baggage as did the prospect of ties with the US; rather, it diminished the importance of economic considerations in renewing ties with the US. The EU countries took advantage of US economic sanctions that kept American companies away from Iran, and expanded their own trade with it (see chapter on Europe and the Middle East).

NOTES

For the place and frequency of publications cited here, and for the full name of the publication, news agency, radio station or monitoring service where an abbreviation is used, please see "List of Sources." Only in the case of more than one publication bearing the same name is the place of publication noted here. All references to *Kayhan* are to the Tehran daily.

1. IRNA, 29 December 1999, 3, 14 January 2000.
2. *Iran News*, 10 January, 16 February; IRNA, 29 January 2000.
3. *'Asr-e Ma*, 22 December 1999 (DR); *Hamshahri*, 10 January (DR); *Iran News*, 13 January; AP, 31 January 2000.
4. IWPD, 1 January; IRNA, 24, 25 January; *TT*, 29 January 2000.
5. *KI*, 22 January; *Iran News*, 25 January; *TT, Abrar*, 29 January 2000 (DR).
6. *Iran News*, 16 January; *TT*, 25 January; *Resalat*, 13 February 2000.
7. *Iran News*, 31 January, 9 February (DR); *Akhbar-e-Eqtesad*, 2 February (DR); IRNA, 6, 7, 16 February 2000.
8. IRNA, 19, 31 January, 2, 15 February (DR); *NYT*, 16 February 2000.
9. Reuters, 2 February; *MM*, 11 February; DPA, 13 February; *al-Sharq al-Awsat*, 17 February 2000.
10. *Kayhan*, 29 January (DR); *Mosharekat*, 2 February; *KI*, IRNA, 16 February; *Resalat*, 17 February 2000 (DR).
11. *MM*, 11 February; *The Times*, 14, 17 February 2000; Haleh Esfandiari, "Is Iran Democratizing? Observations on Election Day," *Journal of Democracy*, Vol. 11, No. 4 (October 2000), pp. 109–12.
12. Iranian TV, 6 February (BBC Monitoring); *Sobh-e Emruz*, 12 February; *Iran News*, 13, 14 February; *Kayhan, Iran*, 16 February 2000 (BBC Monitoring).
13. IRNA, 20, 22, 26 February; IWPD 25 February, 3 March 2000.
14. IRNA, 26 February; *Iran*, 29 February 2000.
15. *'Asr-e Azadegan*, 22 February (DR); *Kayhan*, 25 February 2000 (BBC Monitoring).
16. *Akhbar-e Eqtesad*, 20 February 2000 (DR).
17. *LAT*, 14, 26 February; AFP, 5 July; IRNA, 1 August; Mark J. Gasiorowski, "The Power Struggle in Iran," *Middle East Policy*, Vol. 7, No. 4, October 2000.
18. *'Asr-e Azadegan*, 19 February (DR); *WP*, 20, 21 February; *Sobh-e Emruz*, 21 February (DR); *TT, Ham-mihan*, 22 February; *The Independent*, 23 February; Reuters, 26 February; *Iran*, 27 February 2000.
19. *Kayhan*, 20, 21 February (DR), 1 March; *Iran News*, 21 February (DR); *Javan, Iran Vij*,

22 February; R. Tehran, 25 February (DR); *Fath*, 2 March 2000 in <www1.columbia.edu/sec/cu/sipa/GULF2000/>.

20. *WP*, 2 March, 26 November; *The Globe and Mail*, 7 March; AFP, 14 March; AP, 5 March; IWPD 11 March 2000.

21. IRNA, 11, 13 March, 8, 9, 19, 23 April; RFE/RL Iran Report, Vol. 3, Nos. 15, 17, April 2000.

22. *Fath*, 26 February (DR); IRNA, 29 February, 26 April, 1, 7, 20 May; *TT*, 7 March; IWPD March 4; *IPS*, 6 May; *Bayan*, 8 May; *Iran News*, 15 May 2000 (DR).

23. IRNA, 18 April; *Hayat-e Now*, 31 July 2000.

24. IRNA, 5, 6 May; *WP*, 6 May 2000; Yasuyuki Matsunaga, "Iran's Domestic Politics and Foreign Economic Relations After the Sixth Majlis Elections," in Gulf2000 website.

25. *Iran*, 15 May; *al-Sharq al-Awsat*, 17 May; IRNA, 18, 25 May; AFP, 20 May; *Iran News*, 24 May (DR); RFE/RL Iran Report, Vol. 3, No. 21, 29 May 2000.

26. R. Tehran, 12, 15 March (BBC Monitoring); IRNA, 13, 14, 16 March; *Bayan*, 13 March; Iranian TV, 15 March 2000 (BBC Monitoring).

27. IRNA, 20, 21 March, 17 May; *Sobh-e Emruz*, 21, 29 March; *al-Sharq al-Awsat*, 22 March; RFE/RL Iran Report, Vol. 3, No. 13, 27 March 2000.

28. IPS, 9, 10 April; *Resalat*, 10 April 2000 (DR).

29. *Resalat*, 10 April (DR); *Kayhan*, 11, 22, 25 April (DR); *Abrar*, 20 April (DR); *Jomhuri-ye Islami*, 25 April, 1, 7, 11 May 2000 (DR).

30. IPS, 19 April; *Kayhan*, 22 April; IRNA, 24, 30 April; *KI*, 25 April 2000 (DR).

31. *MM*, 12, 17 April; Tehran TV, 16 April (BBC Monitoring); *al-Sharq al-Awsat*, 18, April; IRNA, 20 April; *Jane's Intelligence Review*, 1 June 2000.

32. R. Tehran, 14 April (DR); *Fath*, 19 April; *Sobh-e Emruz*, 19 April; *Kayhan*, 24 April 2000 (DR).

33. R. Tehran, 12 May (DR); IRNA, 14, 15 May 2000.

34. Iranian TV, 18 April (BBC Monitoring); R. Tehran, 20 April (BBC Monitoring); IWPD 15 April; IRNA, 23 April, 23 May, 23 October; RFE/RL Iran Report, Vol. 3, No. 37, 2 October, No. 39, 16 October 2000.

35. IPS, 12 April; IRNA, 30 April, 9, 20 May, 21 August; AFP, 7 August; RFE/RL Iran Report, Vol. 3, No. 31, 14 August, No. 39, 16 October 2000.

36. *Resalat*, 22 April (DR); *Jomhuri-ye Islami*, 3 May; *Kayhan*, 3, 21 May 2000 (DR).

37. *Mosharekat*, 26 April; IRNA, 18 June; AFP, 26 June 2000.

38. IRNA, 25 April; R. Tehran, 22 May 2000 (DR).

39. IRNA, 27, 28 June; R. Tehran, 27 June 2000 (DR).

40. *Jomhuri-ye Islami*, 22 April (DR); *Iran News*, 25 April; IRNA, 27 April, 9, 23 May; *Kayhan*, 30 April; *Bahar*, 14 May (DR); *Resalat*, 16, 20 May 2000 (DR).

41. Iranian TV, 9 July 2000 (BBC Monitoring).

42. *Resalat*, 12, 15 July; *Jomhuri-ye Islami*, 15, 18, 21 July; *Kayhan*, 15, 23 July, 13 August; *Iran*, 19 July 2000 (DR).

43. *Ya Le-Tharat al-Hosein*, 14 June (DR); *Jomhuri-ye Islami*, 11 July (DR); *Resalat*, 13, 20, 26 July; *TT*, 15 July; IRNA, 26 July 2000.

44. *TT*, 21 May; *Bahar*, 24 May (DR); IRNA, 30 May, 11 June, 14 August; *Hamshahri*, 31 May 2000 (DR).

45. IRNA, 14 June, 1 July; *TT*, 14 June; *Iran News*, 26 June 2000.

46. IRNA, 6 August 2000.

47. IRNA, 6 August; *Jomhuri-ye Islami*, 13 August; RFE/RL Iran Report, Vol. 3, No. 30, 7 August 2000.

48. Reuters, *Iran News*, 7 August; IRNA, *TT*, 7, 8 August; AFP, BBC, 8 August; *NYT*, *MM*, 9 August; RFE/RL Iran Report, Vol. 3, No. 31, 14 August; *IHT*, 21 December 2000.

49. *Jomhuri-ye Islami*, 15 August; R. Tehran, 18 August 2000 (DR).

50. IRNA, *Iran News*, 17th August; Iran, 17, 19 August; *Hayat-e Now*, 17, 21 August; *Abrar*, 20 August (DR); R. Tehran, 22 August 2000 (BBC Monitoring).

51. Iranian TV, 21 August 2000 (DR).

52. IRNA, 27 August; *Jomhuri-ye Islami*, 28 August; *FT*, 30, 31 August; *Iran News*, 31 August; Patrick Clawson and Ray Takeyh, "Iran Dialogue Abroad, Violence at Home," *Policy Watch*, No. 483, 1 September 2000.
53. Ali Mudara, "Iran's Reform Dilemma: Within and Against the State," *MERIP Press Information*, Note 30, 12 September 2000.
54. *Kayhan*, 14 September; RFE/RL Iran Report, Vol. 3, No. 35, 11 September, Vol. 3, No. 39, 16 October; *Hayat-e Now*, 7 October; *TT*, 10 October; IRNA, 24 November 2000.
55. RFE/RL Iran Report, Vol. 3, No. 15, 17 April; *The Economist*, 20 May 2000.
56. For an analysis of televised confessions in Iran, see E. Abrahamian, *Tortured Confessions: Prisons ad Public Recantations in Modern Iran* (Berkeley: University of California Press, 1999).
57. IRNA, 3, 8 May; AFP, 24 May, 13 June; AP, 24 May; *FT*, 25 May, 14 June; *The Independent*, 30 May, 4 June; Reuters, 1 June; *WSJ*, 7 June; R. Tehran, 21 June 2000 (BBC Monitoring).
58. IRNA, AFP, 1 July; *NYT*, 2 July; RFE/RL Iran Report, Vol. 3, No. 26, 3 July; *FT*, 3 July; Reuters, 5 July 2000.
59. IRNA, 2, 7, 8 July; Iranian TV, 2 July (BBC Monitoring); *Iran News*, 2 July; Reuters, 3, 12 July; *TT*, 4 July; *Jomhuri-ye Islami*, 5 July 2000.
60. AFP, 20 July; AP, 21 September; *FT*, 22 September; *Jomhuri-ye Islami*, 23 September 2000.
61. *Kayhan*, 19 April; IPS, 10 October 2000.
62. IRNA, 16 October 2000.
63. *Hamshahri*, 15 October; IRNA, 16, 22 October; *Hambastegi*, cited by Reuters, 18 October; *Hayat-e Now*, *Aftab-e Yazd*, 19, 23 October 2000.
64. IPS, 16 October; AFP, 19 October; *Hambastegi*, 23 October; *Resalat*, 24 October 2000; *Hayat-e Now*, 10 October 2001 (DR).
65. *Hamshahri*, 4 November (DR); *The Economist*, 9 November 2000.
66. For Ganji's activities, see David Menashri, *Post Revolutionary Politics in Iran: Religion, Society and Power* (London: Frank Cass, 2001), pp. 31–32, 157–58, 309, 321–23.
67. *Iran News*, 22 November; IRNA, 30 November 2000, 13 January 2001; *FT*, 1 December; AFP, IPS, 2 December 2000.
68. *Hambastegi*, 21 November; *Aftab-e Yazd*, 26 November; *The Economist*, 7 December; IRNA, 9 December 2000, 28 January 2001; RFE/RL Iran Report, Vol. 3, No. 49, 23 December; *Hamshahri*, 24 December 2000.
69. *IHT*, 15 August; *The Guardian*, 21 August; IRNA, 26 November, 2 December 2000.
70. <www.ParDaily.com>, 3 September; *Jomhuri-ye Islami*, 9 September; *Iran News*, 18 September (DR); Reuters, 1 October, 15 November; *Hamshahri*, 1 October; *TT*, 2, 24 October 2000.
71. *Resalat*, 27 September, 15 October (DR), *TT*, 2 October; Iranian TV, 19 October (BBC Monitoring); IRNA, 23, 29 October; *Iran*, 23 October 2000.
72. *TT*, 11 July, 2 October; *NYT*, 9 August; IRNA, 30 October 2000.
73. R. Tehran, 28 October (BBC Monitoring); IRNA, 3 December 2000.
74. IRNA, 14 September; RFE/RL Iran Report Vol. 3, No. 36, 18 September; *TT*, 1 October; IRNA, 24, 28 October; *Hayat-e Now*, 6 December 2000.
75. IRNA, 31 October, 4, 5, 6, 7, 8, 15 November; *Aftab-e Yazd*, 2 November 2000.
76. *Iran News*, IPS, 4 November; IRNA, 4 November, 2, 5, 14 December; *Hamshahri* 8 November (DR); *Aftab-e Yazd*, 7 December 2000.
77. IRNA, 14, 15, 20 December; *Hambastegi* (DR), *Iran News*, 19 December; *Hamshahri*, 24 December 2000.
78. *Entekhab*, 5 October; IRNA, 19 December 2000.
79. *MM*, 19 June; IRNA 28 June 2000.
80. IRNA, 8 July; *IHT*, 2000.
81. IRNA, 16, 17 October; IPS, 7 November 2000.
82. AFP, 6 December; *Kayhan*, cited in RFE/RL Iran Report, Vol. 3, No. 47, 11

December 2000.

83. *Hadith-e Qazvin*, 15 October (DR); *Kayhan*, 18 November; *The Guardian*, 21 November; *MEED*, 24 November; *Resalat*, 26 November; *WP*, 28 November; *IHT*, 1 December; RFE/RL Iran Report, Vol. 3, No. 46, 4 December 2000.

84. Iranian TV, 17 October (BBC Monitoring); *Iran News*, 18 October 2000.

85. AFP, 17 October; *WP*, 28 November 2000.

86. Iranian TV, 26 November (DR); IRNA, 29 November 2000.

87. *Abrar*, 30 November (DR); *Resalat*, 3 December (DR); *Iran*, 3, 6 December; *Aftab-e Yazdi*, *Iran News*, 4 December (DR); IRNA, 6, 7 December 2000.

88. IRNA, 6 December 2000.

89. Reuters, 6 August; *NYT*, 7 August; *MM*, 9 August; *The Guardian*, 21 August; *Jane's Intelligence Review*, 1 September; *IHT*, 20 December 2000.

90. Charles Recknagel, "Iran: Divisions Hinder Economic Recovery" and "Iran: Economy Needs Sweeping Changes" RFE/RL, 6 April 2000.

91. Dow Jones, 15 February, 5 March; IRNA, 11 June; *FT*, 23 August 2000.

92. Recknagel, ibid.; *CP*, Iran, 2000/2001, p. 23.

93. AFP, 29 February; Reuters, 6 March, 6 April; IRNA, 7 March; Charles Recknagel, "Iran: Battle Looms On Reforms," RFE/RL, 23 March 2000; *CR*, Iran, June 2000, p. 21.

94. *FT*, 17 March; Charles Recknagel, "Iran: Battle Looms on Reforms," and "Iran: Foreign Investors Willing But Wary," *RFE/RL*, 23 March 2000. On the FTZ, see *MEED*, 31 January; IRNA, 18 February; *Dow Jones*, 22 May 2000.

95. IRNA, 13 March, 10 October; AFP, 29 June; Reuters, 11 September, 13 December; *TT*, 29 November; *Asia Pulse*, 5 December; *FT*, 6 December; *Iran News*, 21 December 2000.

96. *FT*, 23 August; IRNA, 25 September, 3 December; IWPD, 2 September; *MEED*, 1 November 2000.

97. *Iran News*, 8 February; IRNA, 7 March, 14, 1 June, 28 November; Reuters, Iranian TV, 23 March (BBC Monitoring); *CR*, Iran, December 2000, p. 26.

98. *Dow Jones*, 20 July; *FT*, 22 August; IWPD 30 September, 6 October; *MEED*, 20, 27 October; AFP, 18 November 2000; *CR*, Iran, March 2001, p. 33.

99. AFP, 26 June; IRNA, 15 November; *Iran*, 29 October; Reuters, 28 November 2000.

100. IRNA, 15 July; Iran, 20 July; *CR*, Iran, December 2000, p. 23.

101. *Bayan*, 20 June, cited by <www.payvand.com>; *FT*, 16 November; IRNA, 20 November 2000.

102. *Kar ve Kargar*, 24 June (DR); IRNA, 24, 25 June, 11, 20 September, 27 November; *Hamshahri*, 5 July; <www.ParDaily.com>, 6 July; AFP, 6 September; *Iran*, 16 October 2000.

103. *TT*, 16, 17 January; *Abrar*, R. Tehran, 17 January (DR); IRNA, 18 January 2000.

104. Anatolia, 20 January (DR); *Milliyet*, 21, 29 January (DR); *Hurriyet*, 27 January (DR); RFE/RL Iran Report, Vol. 3, No. 12, 20 March 2000;

105. Anatolia, 24 February (DR); *Abrar*, 22 February (DR); IRNA, 25 February; *KI*, 26 February; *Resalat*, 2 March 2000.

106. *Milliyet*, 9, 17 May (DR); *Hurriyet*, 11, 12 May (DR); IPS, 19 May 2000.

107. IPS, 19 May, 25 August; IRNA, 22, 24 May, 5 June, 18 July, 22, 23 August; *Kayhan*, 22 May; *Jomhuri-ye Islami*, 29 May, 12 June; IWPD, 3 June; Anatolia, 7 June, 23 August; *TT*, 13 July; *Abrar*, 19 July 2000 (DR).

108. IRNA, 7 March, 9 May, 29 July; Anatolia, 14 May, 2 August 2000 (DR).

109. IRNA, 15 October; IWPD, 14 October; *TT*, 1, 2 November; *Resalat*, 2 November 2000.

110. RFE/RL Iran Report, Vol. 3, No. 2, 10 January, No. 4, 24 January, No. 26, 3 July; *Resalat*, 8 June 2000 (DR).

111. IPS, 16 March; RFE/RL Iran Report, Vol. 3, No. 12, 20 March, No. 26, 3 July, No. 28, 24 July; Interfax, 22 July, 13 October; AFP, 27 July; *Trend News Agency*, 25 October 2000.

112. R. Baghdad, 11 January (DR); IRNA, 17, 27 January; al-Jazira satellite TV, 25 January 2000 (DR).

113. Reuters, 4 February; R. Baghdad, 7 February (DR); *Abrar*, 7 February, 14 March, 9 April

(DR); *TT*, 7, 8 February; R. Tehran, 18 August (BBC Monitoring); IRNA, 18 September 2000.

114. IWPD, 6 May; IRNA, 28 June; AFP, 5 July 2000.

115. *NYT*, AFP, 6 April; IRNA, 11 April; *LAT*, 3 July; AP, 15 July; *CSM*, 20 July; RL/RFE Iran Report, Vol. 3, No. 36, 18 September 2000.

116. IRNA, 31 July, 9, 13 August; AFP, 6 August 2000.

117. R. Baghdad, 21 September (BBC Monitoring); *TT*, 30 September; *al-Sharq al-Awsat*, 4 October 2000.

118. R. Baghdad, 3 October (DR); IRNA, 14 October 2000.

119. *Abrar*, 8, 30 October (DR); R. Tehran, 15 October (BBC Monitoring); *KI*, 15 October; *Aftab-e Yazd*, 24 October (BBC Monitoring); IRNA, 5, 14, 15 December 2000.

120. *TT*, 23 January; IRNA, 19 February 2000.

121. *Gulf News*, 26 April; IWPD, 22 April 2000.

122. IWPD, 7 October 2000.

123. <www.ArabicNews.com>, 19 October; AFP, 26 October; IRNA, 21 November 2000, 17 April 2001.

124. AP, 21 June; IRNA, 28 June, 2 July, 23 October, 30 November; Reuters, 2 July; IWPD, 8–14 July; <www.ArabicNews.com>, 20 October 2000.

125. *Jomhuri-ye Islami*, 25 April, 27 June, 2, 3 July; *KI*, 3 July; *Jane's Foreign Report*, 3 August 2000.

126. *TT*, 2, 4, 19 January; IRNA, 3 January; Iranian TV, 6, 11 January (DR); *Resalat*, 10 January, 3 February; *Iran News*, 13 January; *al-Dustur*, 14 February 2000.

127. *TT*, 10 April; IRNA, 15 April 2000.

128. IWPD, 1 June; <www.ParDaily.com>, 13 June; IRNA, 13 June, 24 July, 8 August, 21 November; *TT*, 29 December 2000.

129. IRNA, 28 February, 6, 27 March, 18, 20 April; *Ha'aretz*, 29 March 2000.

130. IRNA, 25, 26, 28 May, 8 October; *LAT*, 23 October 2000.

131. *Jomhuri-ye Islami*, 10 January; *Resalat*, 11 January 2000 (DR).

132. *TT*, 2,12 January; *Resalat, Jomhuri-ye Islami* 11 January (DR); IRNA, 19 January; *KI*, 22 February 2000.

133. DPA, 13 February; *JP*, 14 February; *Ha'aretz*, 29 March; AFP, 4 April 2000.

134. IRNA, 24, 25 May; Iranian TV, 24, 28 May, 3 June (BBC Monitoring); *Iran News*, 24 May; R. Tehran, 25, 26 May (BBC Monitoring); *Jomhuri-ye Islami*, 1 June 2000.

135. IRNA, 24 June, 11, 24, 25 July; *MM*, 26 June; *al-Sharq al-Awsat*, 8 July; *al-Hayat*, 11 July; R. Tehran, 11, 13, 23 July (BBC Monitoring); RFE/RL Iran Report, Vol. 3, No. 29, 31 July 2000.

136. IRNA, 25, 26 July; *Entekhab*, 26 July; *Jomhuri-ye Islami*, 26, 30 July; *Abrar*, 29 July 2000 (DR).

137. IRNA, 10 August; RFE/RL Iran Report Vol. 3, No. 31, 14 August 2000.

138. Iranian TV, 4 October (BBC Monitoring); R. Tehran, 20 October 2000 (BBC Monitoring).

139. *KI*, 3, 5 October; *Abrar*, 5 October; Iranian TV, 5 October (DR); IRNA, 13 October; *Jomhuri-ye Islami*, 14 October; *TT*, 17 October 2000.

140. IRNA, 13, 17 October; *Kar ve Kargar*, 14 October 2000 (DR).

141. *Kayhan*, 7 October (DR); *Jomhuri-ye Islami*, 9, 22 October (DR); *KI*, 17 October; R. Tehran, 20 October (BBC Monitoring); IRNA, 7 November 2000.

142. IRNA, 3 October, 9, 21, 22 December; IPS, 6 October; AFP, 18 October; R. Tehran, 20 October (BBC Monitoring); Reuters, 9 November; Iranian TV, 24 December 2000 (DR).

143. IRNA, 11, 26 January, 6, 15 February; *Resalat*, 18 January; R. Tehran, 19, 29 January (DR); Iranian TV, 24 January (DR); *TT*, 25 January; <www.CNN.com>, 15 February 2000.

144. AFP, 11 February; IPS, 14 February; *Iran*, 1 March (DR); Karbaschi to RFE/RL, 2 March at <www.RFERL.org>; *Sobh-e Emruz*, 7 March 2000.

145. IWPD, 5 February; AFP, 10, 24, 25 February; *NYT*, 21 February; Reuters, 23 February; IRNA, 25 February; *Abrar*, 26 February 2000 (DR).

146. IRNA, 17 March 2000.
147. *NYT*, 15, 18 March; IRNA, 19, 22 March, 5 April; RFE/RL Iran Report, Vol. 3, No. 13, 27 March 2000.
148. *Ham-mihan*, 27 March, 7 April (DR); *Sobh-e Emruz*, 22, 27 March; *Iran News*, 18 April 2000.
149. IRNA, 25 March, 7, 20 April; *Jomhuri-ye Islami*, 6 April; *Resalat*, 6, 8 April; *Kayhan*, 12 April 2000.
150. *NYT*, 19 May, 19 September; Reuters, 1 July; *MM*, 11 July; *WP*, 12 July; R. Tehran, 12 July 2000 (BBC Monitoring).
151. AP, 17 July; *Abrar*, 18 July (DR); *KI*, 19 July 2000.
152. AFP, 27 July; IRNA, 16 August 2000.
153. IRNA, 31 August, 1 September; *NYT*, AFP, AP, 1 September 2000.
154. *LAT*, 31 August 2000.
155. *LAT*, 5 September; IRNA, 7 September; R. Tehran, 8 September (DR); *IHT*, 11 September; RFE/RL Iran Report, Vol. 3, No. 35, 11 September 2000.
156. AP, 15 September; *NYT*, 16 September; AFP, 20 September; *Iran*, 24 September 2000.
157. Reuters, 11 October; IWPD, 7 October; Iranian TV, 14 October (BBC Monitoring); *TT*, 14 October 2000.
158. *NYT*, 12 October; *Abrar*, 28 October; IRNA, 31 October 2000.
159. *Resalat*, 11, 21 November; *KI*, 15 November; *Jomhuri-ye Islami*, 6 December 2000.
160. IRNA, R. Tehran, 24 December 2000 (DR).
161. Robert O. Freedman, "Russian-Iranian Relations in the 1990s," *MERIA Journal*, Vol. 4, No. 2, June 2000.
162. Iranian TV, 14 January (DR); ITAR-TASS, 17, 26 January (DR), 9 July (BBC Monitoring); IRNA, 17, 18 February, 1 March, 1 August; Interfax, 14 March 2000.
163. *Jomhuri-ye Islami*, 6, 17 January; *Resalat*, 17 January (DR); *KI*, 22 January, 20 February; IRNA 10 February; ITAR-TASS, 14 February 2000 (DR).
164. Iranian TV, 4, 19 January (DR); Interfax, 17 January, 17 February; IRNA, 18, 26 January, 19, 25 April 2000.
165. RFE/RL Iran Report, Vol. 3, No. 20, 22 May, No. 22, 5 June; *Resalat*, 8 June; IRNA, 29 June; Interfax, RIA, 1 August 2000 (DR).
166. ITAR-TASS, 30 June, 6 September (BBC Monitoring); IRNA, 18 October; IPS, 20 October 2000.
167. IPS, 27 October; *Afarinesh*, 29 October 2000 (BBC Monitoring).
168. R. Tehran, 24 November, 6 December (BBC Monitoring); IRNA, 24, 28 December; *WP*, 29 December 2000.

Iraq

(Jumhuriyyat al-'Iraq)

After a decade of severe international sanctions, Iraq began to see some light at the end of the tunnel. Three developments, all of them external, contributed to this change: the sharp rise of oil prices, a lowering in the degree of American engagement with the Iraqi issue, and the eruption of the second Palestinian intifada. Iraq capitalized on these developments to further erode the sanctions, improve its regional and international standing, and drive a wedge between the shrinking anti-Iraq camp and those countries anxious to do business with it.

Although Baghdad had refused to accede to UN inspection of its weapons of mass destruction (WMD), its pleas to lift the sanctions fell on ground more fertile than at any time in the past. More and more countries were willing to challenge the US and its ally, Britain, by doing business with Iraq, raising their level of diplomatic representation and breaching the decade-long air embargo against flights to Baghdad. Iraq also managed to lessen its isolation in the Arab world by improving bilateral relations with three key countries — Egypt, Syria and Jordan — and, no less important, by taking part in an Arab summit, also for the first time in a decade. In this context, it was the Palestinian intifada that provided Iraq with the opportunity to attain significant legitimation as a stalwart defender of Arab rights and revived Iraqi aspiration for a leadership role in the Arab world, or at least of its radical camp.

On the home front, President Saddam Husayn typically initiated changes and personnel reshuffling in order to prepare the ground for, or preempt various contingencies. An issue of great concern to him was the kind of regime that would succeed him, and how he would be remembered. This concern was reflected in a best-selling novel published at the end of 2000, transparently based on his life story. In real life, Husayn was faced with the decision as to which of his two sons, 'Udayy or Qusayy, would be his heir apparent. All indications pointed to the younger Qusayy. 'Udayy, undoubtedly aware of this, attempted to fight back by fostering a personality cult reminiscent of that of his father and by promoting his status in the rubber-stamp National Assembly. These moves, however, constituted a rearguard battle as Husayn conferred important actual powers on Qusayy during the course of the year.

Husayn also took steps to inject new blood into the decaying Ba'th system. Additionally, he put nearly all the governorates under the rule of former high-ranking military officers, in order to reinforce the loyalty of the military and forestall any possible upheaval against the regime. Another area of concern was the Shi'ite south, which, despite continuous repressive measures, remained restive. Of even greater concern was the Kurdish region to the north, a major part of which had been beyond the regime's control since the 1991 Gulf War. The passage of time increased the difficulty of bringing this territory back into

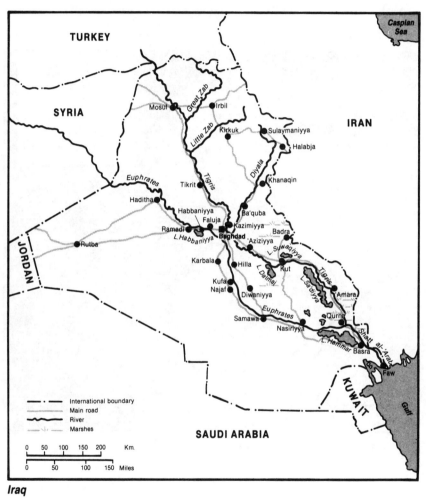

Iraq

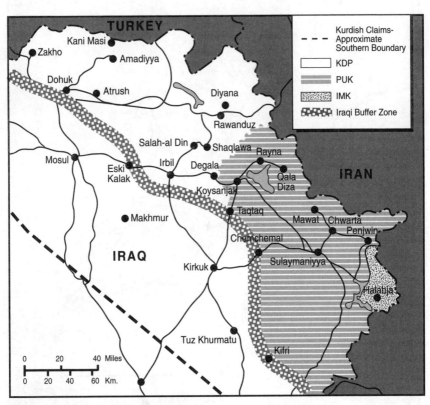

Iraq: Kurdish Autonomous Zone

the fold, as it had developed some of the trappings of an autonomous entity, a distinctive political style and culture, and independent ties with the outside world. Restoring it to Iraq would certainly necessitate the use of considerable force, which only the military possessed.

INTERNAL AFFAIRS

FICTION AND REALITY IN SADDAM'S IRAQ

A significant event in Iraq at the close of 2000 was the publicity given to the appearance of an anonymous novel, titled *Zabiba wal-Malik* (Zabiba and the King), a love story between a king named 'Arab and a simple, young, beautiful and courageous woman, Zabiba.[1] She has mobilized the people around the king in his struggle against his enemies. The king meets the woman in her humble house and invites her to his palace, where they hold long discussions about nationalism, the openness of the government, conspiracies and love. The king falls in love with Zabiba and marries her secretly. When war is declared against the king, she volunteers to fight and is killed in battle. The king proclaims Zabiba a martyr (*shahida*) and is applauded by the people for this and for having married a simple woman. After her death, he calls for a meeting of the people's representatives to discuss the merits of a monarchical regime. The discussion reveals who is loyal and who is treacherous toward the king and the people. The traitors include princes, big merchants and Jews. Notably, the debate leaves the question of hereditary rule unanswered.

The author of the novel was rumored to be none other than Saddam Husayn himself.[2] Conceivably, Husayn encouraged such rumors and, at the very least, inspired the ideas and messages of the story, as the style was identical to his own. He reportedly met with writers and playwrights at the beginning of the year, urging them to produce novels, stories and plays that would convey the feats of "the mother of battles" (the Gulf War) to the Iraqi people, along with other events and ideas which required dramatization. He declared his own intention to write a play that would appeal to the young generation.[3] Later in the year, he informed the cabinet about a novel that had impressed him greatly — "Martyrs Without Shrouds" (*Shuhada bila Akfan*), written by an Iraqi prisoner of war who had returned from Iran, which, Husayn pointed out, had treated the prisoners even worse than the Nazis. Husayn ordered the novel to be broadcast on television and radio, read out during seven meetings of the Ba'th Party, and distributed in the Arab world and beyond.[4] In August, he called upon poets to write a new national anthem based on his ideas about martyrdom, glory and love of the homeland.[5]

The emphasis placed on this type of activity suggests that the Iraqi public was deemed weary of constant war and struggles, impelling Husayn to find new ways to raise morale and reinforce popular support for his regime. Epics and melodrama seemed to him a better tool for firing the popular imagination and transmitting his messages rather than the traditional kinds of rhetoric and propaganda.

Husayn's burst of creative activity, however, did not cause him to lose sight of power politics, which he orchestrated as meticulously as ever. Turning over a number of responsibilities to his son Qusayy at the expense of 'Udayy (see below), he retained a strong grip on power. Reports during the year of his deteriorating health due to cancer, as evidenced by reputed haggardness, could not be corroborated by an objective source.

Not only did he not relinquish his powers, he acquired additional ones, e.g., the decision-making power to use chemical weapons, previously conferred by him on commanders of Iraqi regions.[6] He also "acquired" the much desired post of secretary-general of the Ba'th Party All-Arab (qawmiyya) National Command.[7] Practically speaking, Husayn had assumed the post after the death of the former secretary-general, Michel 'Aflaq, in 1989. However, publicizing it officially in early June 2000, a few days before the death of Syrian president Hafiz al-Asad, was designed to convey the message that from now on, he would be the sole National Command leader. Until Asad's death, there were two rival National Commands, one based in Damascus and headed by Asad, and the other based in Baghdad and headed, after 'Aflaq's death, by Husayn. The move signified Husayn's intention to intensify his pan-Arab activities. An Iraqi artist had previously depicted this theme figuratively, showing Husayn standing behind a large tent, holding the tent peg in one of his hands, as a symbol of his love of and care for all Arabs (in Husayn's terminology, the tent).[8]

These manifestations of Husayn's personality cult were intensified around the annual commemoration of his birth date on 28 April (1938), celebrated sometimes for the entire month. In April 2000, the Baghdad weekly Alif Ba went so far as to quote al-Farabi, the renowned tenth century Arab philosopher, in a description of the outstanding characteristics of Saddam Husayn.[9] A former high-ranking military commander, Tahir Jalil al-Habbush, published a book in the growing genre of tributes to Husayn, titled "The Beginnings (awa'il) of Saddam Husayn."[10] An exhibition opened on this occasion displaying over 15,000 gifts that Husayn had received from Iraqis, other Arabs and individuals worldwide.[11] Earlier, Husayn made a donation to the Qa'id al-Nasr (Leader of Victory) Museum of Gifts of seven gold-plated cigar holders which he no longer used because, as he wrote in an attached note: "We are all for the state, we are all for the country. Our blood is for the people. Every possession is the property of God."[12]

Most Iraqis were probably resigned to the cult, but some actively opposed it. According to a report in October, Husayn ordered the execution of eight Iraqis charged with forming an opposition organization and defacing several murals depicting Saddam Husayn.[13] Similarly, another non-Iraqi source reported the implementation of a new type of punishment in Iraq, tongue amputation for slandering the president.[14] If true, this was an addition to a long list of punishments meted out to Iraqis who dared challenge Saddam's infallibility, or were suspected of doing so. One of the victims during 2000 was the mother of Saddam's late son-in-law Husayn Kamil, who had fled to Jordan in 1995 and was later killed together with his brother and father upon their return in 1996 (see MECS 1996, pp. 326–29). Kamil's mother was found stabbed to death after reportedly calling for the murder of her sons and husband to be avenged.[15] Even if the report were untrue, Saddam Husayn's dynasty undoubtedly ranked high among ruling families that consumed their kin.

Husayn had to tread very cautiously in his relations with his two sons, 'Udayy and Qusayy. He turned over a measure of power to them, but sparingly, anxious to prevent a struggle between them, and at the same time to shield them against revenge from family and other sources, such as had occurred in 1996 with the assassination attempt on 'Udayy. According to one report, Saddam Husayn declared Qusayy as the heir apparent in a family meeting in April, and 'Udayy gave his consent.[16] While the report appeared far-fetched, the indications were that Husayn trusted Qusayy more than his brother, having already granted him in previous years key posts in the state security apparatus, including that of supervisor of the Republican Guard. One such chilling demonstration of Qusayy's power came to light during the year; in March 1998, he had ordered the killing of two thousand prisoners, some of whom were awaiting appeal decisions. On the whole, Qusayy kept a low profile, but his closeness to his father was evident from his participation in meetings with the military command, and from cables of support he sent to his father on various important occasions. One such cable, broadcast on Radio Baghdad, harshly attacked Kuwait on the tenth anniversary of the Iraqi invasion, describing the Iraqi move as the liberation of Kuwait. 'Udayy did not have this privilege but his ambition found other outlets.[17] Husayn gave him a certain amount of leeway but not so much as to threaten his own rule or to compete with Qusayy.

'UDAYY SADDAM HUSAYN: ASPIRING TO BECOME THE HEIR APPARENT

The year 2000 witnessed strenuous efforts by 'Udayy to project himself as a hero and as the heir apparent to his father, President Husayn. The change of guard in a number of Arab countries; his aging (and possibly ailing) father; the rising star of his younger brother Qusayy; and his own intense ambition prompted him to make his move. Yet he remained aware of the almost insurmountable obstacles to overcome before he could reach his goal, as both his physical and moral stature put him at a great disadvantage. He had become disabled after the failed assassination attempt on him in 1996 (see *MECS* 1996, pp. 329–30), and had acquired an infamous reputation as a killer, sadist, warmonger and womanizer, along with being greedy and unstable.[18] Most importantly, Saddam did not seem to have given 'Udayy his blessing and, worse still, appeared to be trying to reign him in.

'Udayy sought to use the media, his own political clout and his father's prestige to surmount these hurdles. His control of part of the media, including the newspaper *Babil*, several other dailies and weeklies, and the radio and television youth stations, proved invaluable for promoting his political agenda.[19] The most urgent task was to refurbish his image and initiate a personality cult reminiscent of that of his father. The need to rid himself of the image of a disabled person was perceived as acute. His photographs, which saturated his media outlets, showed him either seated or standing but never walking. Surgery to remove a bullet lodged in his spine had failed once again, leaving him as disabled as before, although his media claimed he had regained the ability to walk.[20]

Projected as physically fit and energetic, he was shown on Youth TV riding a horse, hunting birds (with his brother) and swimming in the Tigris River.[21] This last activity could not fail to remind his audience that he was following his father's path, as Saddam had similarly swum in the Tigris as proof of his health and youthfulness (see *MECS* 1992, p. 451; 1997, p. 375). In his propaganda, 'Udayy habitually imitated his father in the way he dressed and in his speech. Appealing to various sectors of society (journalists, students, sports groups, etc.), 'Udayy typically peppered his speech with Qur'anic verses, as did Saddam, and sometimes employed the royal "we" in addressing an audience.[22]

He made the most of the ceremony in which his father had decorated him with five medals of valor and three of high merit, printing large pictures of the event in his newspapers.[23] The fact that he had been decorated together with high-ranking officers was highlighted to show both his importance in his father's eyes and his closeness to him. That 'Udayy even surpassed his father in certain areas was alluded to in a nuanced manner. His doctorate (in political science)[24] was mentioned during the election campaign for the National Assembly (see below), which meant that he was more educated than his father. He also grew a beard, which made him appear more pious than Saddam. Much was also made of his ability to appeal to young people, his pursuit of "democratic norms" and his propensity to teach "lessons in democracy."[25]

'Udayy's main opponent, however, remained his younger brother Qusayy, who was closer to his father (significantly, Qusayy had been decorated militarily before his brother). 'Udayy hoped to beat Qusayy in the political field through his activity in the Ba'th Party,[26] various socio-political associations (youth, students and sports), and his election to the National Assembly. Although the assembly, a parliament of sorts, was known to be devoid of any power, 'Udayy was determined to use it to improve his credentials by enhancing its standing.

In January 2000, 'Udayy received a cable from the secretary of the National Assembly wishing him well on the occasion of the 'Id al-Fitr feast, a gesture signalling his entry into the political arena. Early in March, he declared his decision to run in the assembly elections.[27] Two days before the elections, 'Udayy published an article in *Babil* entitled "The Termites," signed with his pen name, Abu Sirhan, sharply attacking the government intelligence apparatus (*mukhabarat*) for corruption.[28] Overnight, he wrote, "the intelligence organ had shifted its great national role of fighting spying...to that of tracking down various types of smuggled animals and putting them up for auction for the benefit of the organ." The article ended with a warning that if the intelligence organ were not healed quickly, it would become, "sooner or later," like the termite that destroys a large tree, or the cancer "that kills the body of a thirty-one-year-old athlete" (a reference to the Ba'th regime).[29]

Timed to prepare the groundwork for his election, the article could be read as a criticism of his father, his brother (who controlled the intelligence apparatus) and the assembly itself (for not checking its authority).[30] By contrast, 'Udayy, in exposing this "inside story," portrayed himself as untamable and willing to fight corruption even inside his own house. 'Udayy may have had another, hidden agenda for attacking the intelligence services. He himself was known to have been deeply involved in smuggling, and this may have been a means to protect his own vested interests. Whether related to the article or not, the assistant to the chief of intelligence, Khalil Ibrahim, together with thirty other officers, were reportedly dismissed.[31]

'Udayy received 99.99% of the votes cast in his assembly district, Baghdad.[32] Perhaps not coincidentally, 'Udayy's results were even higher than those of his father, who received 99.96% of the vote in the 1995 presidential election (see *MECS* 1995, pp. 321–23).

Initially hinting at his desire to become speaker of the assembly, 'Udayy told al-Jazira TV: "Electing a speaker of the National Assembly is a democratic practice that is based on voting. This will be decided when the voting takes place, God willing."[33] Soon, however, he announced his decision not to nominate himself for a senior position in the assembly "in order to give a chance to the more senior members" of the Ba'th Party. In a veiled criticism, however, he added that he hoped the elected speaker would "live up to the honor and responsibility borne by the nominee to this post."[34] Clearly, it was his father who had thwarted the move. While Saddam Husayn wanted to promote his older son, or channel his energies, in a rubber-stamp body such as the assembly, 'Udayy appeared to him too overtly ambitious and too outspoken. Hence the need to reign him in. Possibly, he also wanted to avoid criticism for nepotism, and prevent friction between a younger man who had vowed to bring new blood into the assembly and old colleagues of the Ba'th Party. The need to keep 'Udayy at bay vis-à-vis his brother Qusayy may have also been a consideration for Husayn.

'Udayy, however, was not content to have his wings clipped. The easiest channel for him to pursue was that of the personality cult. Prior to the elections, *Nabd al-Shabab* devoted a full page to "the hero" (*batal*) 'Udayy, and his feats in organizing, military training and leading high school student commandos, thus proving "his love of the homeland, religion and the struggle."[35]

Later, *al-Ittihad* referred to him in superlatives that approached those reserved for his father: he had "a rare personality," "deep general knowledge," "an ardent love of the nation's heritage" and "knowledge of the holy Qur'an by heart." People who had met him, it wrote, were astonished by his personality, testifying that they had never met "a son of a leader like him," for he was the "lion's cub" and "a copy of the spirit and will of his father, the leader."[36]

'Udayy's aspiration to become the heir apparent was also reflected in the prominence given in *Babil* to the ascent to power of Bashshar al-Asad in Syria in June 2000, covered with large photos and numerous articles, unlike the reportage in the government-controlled papers.[37] The clear message was that, like Bashshar, 'Udayy had the right to inherit power. He was close to the Syrian successor in age (36, 37, respectively), education (both had doctorates), openness to modern life (each controlled the Internet set-up in their respective countries), and involvement with youth. As in the past, 'Udayy continued to place great emphasis on his activities on behalf of youth in the belief that they could determine not only the fate of the nation but his own personal career. Inter alia, he criticized various ministries and governmental bodies for failing to employ more young people, as the president had directed. According to one set of statistics, the ratio between job seekers (141,800) and those who found work (14,100), was ten to one.[38]

Enhancing his appeal to young people was also a means by which 'Udayy could counter-balance Qusayy's growing influence among the armed forces, to which 'Udayy seems to have been denied access. 'Udayy was said to wield some power as supervisor of the Fida'iyyu Saddam (Saddam's Fedayeen, a paramilitary body), which numbered between 10,000–15,000;[39] and, he reportedly managed to bring about the rehabilitation of over fifty officers who were supporters of his late uncle Khayrallah Talfah. Yet he could not match his brother in this arena. The two appeared to be pulling in opposite directions: Qusayy entrenching his power base in the military and security services, and 'Udayy paving his way to power by increasing his visibility. 'Udayy's chances of beating his brother with such a weapon, however, appeared slim.

ELECTIONS TO THE NATIONAL ASSEMBLY

The generally predictable and essentially inconsequential elections to the 250-member National Assembly generated a measure of political interest in 2000 when 'Udayy presented his candidacy. His intention to infuse new blood into the assembly was illustrated in an article published in his paper *Babil*, criticizing negative aspects of the 1996 elections, including the influence of tribal loyalty in voting patterns; the non-participation of women, especially in the countryside, or the delegating of others to vote for them; abuses of the propaganda law by candidates; and the laxity of election supervisors.[40] Such criticism, albeit mild by Western standards, was exceptional in Iraq.

The elections to the assembly took place on 27 March, exactly four years after the previous ones, signaling the stability and continuity of the regime. This contrasted sharply with the previous presidential elections, which were held only once, in 1995. Ba'th Party conclaves, too, were held irregularly, showing that when real power was at stake, proper procedures were not meticulously observed. To qualify as a candidate, one had to believe in God and in the Ba'th revolution of July 1968 and have contributed to the war effort during the Iran-Iraq War and/or the Gulf War. Those who had evaded military service; were married to a foreigner; or had engaged in trade during the sanction period (a ban which would extend through two assembly elections subsequent to the lifting of the sanctions) were disqualified.[41]

A total of 512 candidates ran for 220 seats (the remaining thirty places were not contested since the Kurdish region did not take part in the electoral process). The remaining seats were filled with nominees by the president. Non-Iraqi sources reported that the candidates came from various sectors of society and included officials, former army officers, journalists, industrialists, physicians, engineers, religious leaders and tribal chiefs.[42] Notably, 70% of the 165 Ba'th Party candidates stood for election for the first time, evidence of the intention to bring younger people into the assembly.

The results of the election showed that the voter turnout had been high — 88.6% of the 9.2m. eligible voters. All 165 Ba'th Party candidates were elected, along with 85 independents, 30 of the latter appointed by Husayn to represent the Kurdish autonomous zone. Of 25 female candidates, 18 were elected (down from 27 in the 1989 assembly; see *MECS* 1989, p. 380).[43] The elections demonstrated once again that despite declarations promoting democratization and openness, the Ba'th would not relinquish its monopoly even on a rubber-stamp institution such as the National Assembly.

It was precisely this image that 'Udayy set out to change. Initially, he distanced himself from the Assembly, pointedly absenting himself from the opening session, presumably to show his indignation at not being allowed to become speaker and having to relinquish the post to the seventy-year-old incumbent Sa'dun Hammadi. Indeed, friction between the two was rumored. This may have prompted Hammadi to activate the assembly somewhat and enhance its contact with the Iraqi people, e.g., by initiating citizen access to it twice weekly in order to present their complaints.[44] At the end of the year, 'Udayy changed course and began to show some involvement. Attending an assembly meeting for the first time on 24 December, he presented a paper on the "work and performance of the state agencies" and spoke about the organizational, administrative and financial affairs of the assembly, including "the means of improving the performance of the assembly and activating the role of the assembly members in order to serve Iraq."[45] With most of the key political and military venues closed to him, 'Udayy had evidently decided to try to capitalize on the assembly and turn it into a springboard for attaining his other goals. Whether the assembly as an institution could gain anything from his race to the apex of power was a moot question.

THE BA'TH PARTY: ATTEMPTS AT REJUVENATION

After thirty-two years in power, the Ba'th Party was perceived as losing vigor. Husayn spoke of the need "to train new Ba'thists, on the principle that the struggle is not over yet." He also announced an original way to rejuvenate the system: requiring all party members to pass a formal Ba'th Party examination intended "to increase the members' political and organizational consciousness and to strengthen their leadership abilities."[46]

The examinations were given simultaneously (2 February) in all parts of the country. They included such topics as the history of the Ba'th Party struggle, Saddam Husayn's biography (*sira*), his writings on various political, religious and intellectual issues, and "the challenge of the present phase." The examination was uniform, whether for students, teachers, workers, peasants or military personnel, with a view to achieving "unity (*wahda*) of thinking, organizing, planning and leading."[47] Not surprisingly, both the examiners and the examinees, all of whom were Ba'thists, succeeded in fulfilling this mission. *Al-Jumhuriyya*, calling it "a unique, glorious experience," pointed out that even the "best universities in the world" could not have matched the speed and efficiency in administering and evaluating the examinations.[48] Clearly, the regimentation of the Ba'th membership was the order of the day.

Another step was granting a measure of visibility to female members of the party. Virtually all but nonexistent in the public mind heretofore, female activists began to receive publicity. Saddam Husayn issued directives to establish branches (*shu'ba*) for women in every section (*far'*), while special elections were held for women, marking "a real turning point in the Ba'th march."[49] This attention to women may have been attributable to dwindling Ba'th ranks, the need to mobilize women in a sanctions-stricken society, and the benefits of demonstrating a degree of openness and liberalization in the system. The role of Zabiba as a symbol of the people in the novel discussed above was another indication of this new trend.

Children and youth also received their share of attention from the party. To encourage young people to join the party, Husayn directed the granting of credit to graduates of the Ba'th Party secondary vocational schools to help them open workshops in mechanics, electricity, carpentry, etc. Priority would be given to those who received "backing from the party branch."[50] On another level, children — "Saddam's Cubs" (Ashbal Saddam) in all parts of the country underwent military training in summer camps organized by the Ba'th Party. The children also received lectures there on such subjects as history, religion and manly values (*rujula*).[51] At the conclusion of the camp, the children sent a cable to Saddam Husayn written in their own blood, promising to give their all for "God, the homeland, the leader."[52]

Husayn made a point of holding personal meetings with Ba'th Party members to raise morale. One such meeting exposed the existence of problems facing the Ba'th in three Shi'i governorates: Basra, Dhi-Qar and Maysan. "The party in these governorates," Husayn said, "is under daily examination" and had to lead a jihad there against enemies [who believed]...that they could "create a breach in the south." In these circumstances, Ba'th Party members should behave as if they were in the period of "clandestine struggle," a factor that should improve their performance. Praising the men and women in the daily struggle, and awarding them medals of valor, Husayn also alluded to certain older party members who, when they drop down in the Ba'th ranks, "lose their impetus" for the struggle.[53] Meanwhile *al-Hayat* reported that eighty leading Ba'th members were expelled from the party for "corruption" and for "distorting the party image."[54] Although this particular report could not be corroborated, the party was undoubtedly aging and needed a face-lift.

PLACATING THE ARMY

Another pillar of power that demanded Husayn's constant attention was the army. As in the past, non-Iraqi sources continued to report various failed coup attempts against Husayn and the execution of army officers (forty on one occasion) implicated in these attempts, which allegedly took place almost monthly. There were also occasional reports about the flight from Iraq of high-ranking military officers, the most prominent in 2000 being Hamid Sha'ban, a former air force commander.[55] While these reports were unverifiable, the regime was clearly under strong pressure as a result of the ongoing American and British attacks in the no-fly zones in the north and the south. An indication of difficulty was the unprecedented media publicity given to the commander of the air force, Lt. Gen. Shahin Yasin, breaking a tradition of secrecy that did not even allow citing the chief of staff by name. Yasin's picture appeared in the newspapers, he gave interviews to the media, and he met with Husayn regularly and publicly.[56] At mid-year he was referred to as "commander of air defense forces," but whether he relinquished his earlier post was not known. The publicity given to Yasin may have reflected a fear of demoralization in this specific branch of the military and the need to build up goodwill. Simultaneously, concerted attempts were made to attract young people to the air force. Secondary school graduates were called upon to enrol in the air force college and were promised various financial incentives both during their studies (e.g., monthly salary of ID 14,000) and upon joining the force (ID 66,000).[57]

Husayn sought to appoint former high-ranking military officers to key governmental posts, e.g., as governors, both to gain the goodwill of the military and to preempt possible unrest in certain sensitive areas, such as the Shi'ite south. Another likely motive was to build up loyalty for the succession of his son Qusayy. In May, he named Lt. Gen. Najm al-Din 'Abdallah Muhammad, Lt. Gen. Nuri 'Alwan and Maj. Gen. Fawzi Humud 'Ulawi as governors of Wasit, al-Ta'mim and Diyala, respectively.[58] Oddly, the new governors were cited in this announcement by their military rank, making it unclear whether they assumed office while still in service or after retirement. Undoubtedly, however, their ranks were mentioned in order to inspire awe. Other military officers appointed to key governmental posts were the former chief of staff, Iyad Futayyih al-Rawi, named head of the Youth Committee Association (Hay'a), and Iyad Khalil Zaki, former deputy chief of staff for ordinance, named governor of al-Muthanna. In 1999, all but one governors were former military officers (see Table 1). With this, Husayn was careful not to elevate military figures to the top echelon in the Ba'th Party or in the Revolutionary Command Council (RCC) — the highest legislative and executive authority in the state, probably to keep them at arm's length from real political power. Another of Husayn's ongoing tactics was to bedeck high-ranking officers with medals of valor. One such hero, Ahmad Hammad al-Zawba'i, dean of the Military Leadership College, was awarded no less than fifteen such medals.[59]

Late in June, President Husayn took yet another step that seemed to be geared to gain favor with the military. He ordered the suspension of Ba'th Party regional commands set up by the RCC in December 1998.[60] The establishment of these commands was, at the time, a precautionary measure against a possible Kurdish or Shi'i uprising that might have followed the anticipated Anglo-American attack at the end of that year. The appointment of Ba'th Party members to head them, however, may have been interpreted as a lack of faith in the loyalty of the military and its ability or willingness to fight such an uprising, requiring the appointment of party officials to supervise or even take command in case of emergency. By suspending these commands, Husayn sought to signal, first, that the country had resumed its normal state, and second, that the military could be trusted to protect the country from both internal and external enemies. Ibrahim Khalil Ibrahim, president of al-Bakr University, spoke of the importance of providing military training to the Iraqi people and developing ties between them and the armed forces, emphasizing, inter alia, the need for coordination between the Ba'th Party and the army.[61] Husayn himself lost no opportunity to praise the feats of the Iraqi army and boost its morale. Significantly, the novel focused on the strong bonds between the king, the Iraqi people and the army. Typically, Husayn declared on one occasion: "Defeat them [the enemies] using the determination of the people. Let the air defence of the armed forces act as your frontline spear." Similarly, he called on nuclear scientists "to take part in the fight against the nation's enemies."[62] More concretely, he granted the military and the security services priority in housing with the announcement that 320,000 plots of land for housing would be distributed to them in all parts of the country, while families of military personnel killed while serving were given free housing in Basra and Karbala.[63]

Clearly, Husayn's moves to control as well as reward the military, alongside his insistence on the development of the Iraqi military machine, most importantly non-conventional weapons, helped keep the military in line.

THE SOCIOECONOMIC PICTURE: THE CONSEQUENCES OF SANCTIONS AND CORRUPTION

The economic situation improved significantly by the end of the year due to the sharp increase of oil prices in 2000, although this betterment occurred mainly on the macro level. In October 2000, Iraq exported crude oil at the rate of 2.8m. b/d[64] (compared to 3.2m. b/d before the Gulf War), earning $7.2bn. in the second half of the year (compared with total exports of $1.5bn. in 1996, and $5.5bn. in 1997). Iraq was also reported to have $11bn. in monetary reserves in France (apart from frozen accounts there and in other countries).[65] Commerce was also said to be booming unprecedentedly since the imposition of the embargo a decade earlier, with a number of countries (the latest being Germany and South Korea) reactivating their embassies and staffing them with commercial officers.[66]

Saddam Husayn attempted to boost the economy by activating the decaying, almost nonexistent private sector. He announced in March that foreign currency would be made available to private sector and mixed companies at 50% below market price, provided that it was used for purchasing raw materials for production. The encouragement of the private sector did not mean giving up the role of the state, he explained, but rather, the increase of production in any sector would eliminate goods and services paid for by foreign currency and would provide employment to a large number of Iraqis.[67] This explanation may have failed to sufficiently buoy potential private industrialists or allay the fear of those with vested interests in the extant socialist system, for in June, Husayn reiterated his call, adding an additional element: establishing industrialization centers to be run by state employees. These centers would be transferred to the private industrial sector in a phased plan, and would enjoy private sector privileges. This meant, Husayn explained, that the employee would work for the state by day and elsewhere after official hours.[68] The establishment of a special fund of ID 50bn. ($50m.) to help activate all sectors of the economy was announced in July. The fund was to grant loans to entrepreneurs, with priority given to those who had been awarded medals.[69] Additionally, the government announced that it would allow citizens to open foreign currency accounts. The issue of the absence of private sector participation in enterprises was discussed yet again, in September, with no solutions found to this chronic problem.[70] Presumably, potential entrepreneurs lacked trust in the government support and feared fluctuations in the economy, especially under the sanctions. Another disincentive may have been a government campaign to improve income tax collection, launched at the beginning of the year.[71]

The improved financial situation did not necessarily improve the lot of ordinary Iraqis. According to a UN report, the per capita GDP had fallen from $3,100 in 1989 to $250 in 2000. The school dropout rate, which had been almost nil in 1989, was now almost 20%, and literacy had plummeted from 90% to 66% over the "last decade."[72] These statistics, however, hid the growing gap between the thin layer of society comprising the ruling elite, especially in Baghdad, which was becoming increasingly wealthier; and the vast majority of Iraqis, especially in the south, among civil servants, and in the cities, who had become impoverished. By way of example, a box of eggs cost ID 2,250 (slightly over $1), while the monthly salary of a retired official was around ID 2,500, or, as one retiree said, "The price of one box of eggs." This compared with a salary of $720, or ID 240, before the sanctions and the resultant inflation.[73] The situation of retirees became so difficult that at the end of the year the RCC issued a resolution stipulating that "the minimum monthly income of a retiree, including his salary, allowances and ration allowances, should be ID 8,000."[74] This could not have been much of a comfort at a time when ID 1,800–1,950 was worth $1.[75] In sharp contrast, the nouveau riche of Baghdad, including ministers and other high-ranking officials, were reproached by Saddam Husayn for their extravagance and ostentatiousness, in their wedding parties, for example, thereby hurting the poor. He asserted that such excess had not existed to that extent before the sanctions, at a time when the overall economic situation was much better.[76]

As in the past decade, the poor wages, the decline in work opportunities and the rising rate of unemployment continued to cause a variety of negative trends, including increased begging, which the government attempted to stop by imposing prison sentences on anyone caught begging. Students were reported to be dropping out of high school and resorting to begging in order to provide for their families.[77] Another phenomenon was the growing number of gangs and cases of robbery and theft. In one case, three young girls attempted to rob a jewelry shop.[78] Attempting to combat this phenomenon, which was especially rampant in Baghdad, night watchmen were appointed by the authorities. However, it soon became clear that the watchmen themselves took part in the crimes, leading to a promise by Baghdad governor 'Abd al-Wahid Shinan al-Ribat to compensate citizens who were victims of watchmen. Another method of combating theft and corruption was granting financial bonuses to informers.[79] Corruption and cases of fraud, especially in the food industry, continued unabated, prompting the government to close forty-eight factories on such charges.[80]

Corruption became rampant in the education system, too. Teachers resorted to opening private classes at school during school hours, and even threatening to fail students who did not enroll in them, whether because they could not afford them or because they did not need them. Similarly, parents were now forced to pay for such school expenses as electricity and water.[81] In an unprecedented move, the RCC decided at the end of the year to open private kindergartens and schools, to be funded by the parents. Earlier, the cabinet announced increases in tuition fees at universities and technical institutes.[82] All this further widened the gap between the rich and the poor. Significantly, the government also decided to require uniform dress for university students, presumably with a view to reducing socioeconomic tensions.[83] On another level, the government decided to provide work that families could do at home, such as sewing. President Husayn also attempted to convince women to work at home in order to economize on clothing. This and other steps taken by him[84] to limit women's freedom, however, prompted women to begin to demand equal rights to men, such as entitling women civil servants to acquire subsidized land for housing.[85]

Housing was another branch that underwent a severe crisis. Although the need for housing units was estimated at 3.4m. for the year 2000, little work was begun in the construction of new houses.[86]

A contentious issue was that of the Internet. As in other Arab countries, the main concern of the government was losing control of this medium, prompting measures to slow down its spread and impose supervision. According to one official, while there was no possibility of attaining total control over Internet access, the government promised to "do our best to protect the citizen" from it.[87]

In sum, despite improvement on the macro level, the lot of ordinary Iraqis continued to be harsh, partly because of the sanctions and partly because of their cynical exploitation by the regime.

COPING WITH UNREST BY MEANS OF REPRESSION AND ISLAMIZATION

Although the Ba'th did not admit it, unrest among the Shi'is was ongoing, the result of long years of discrimination, the sanctions and repression. The last included the killing of religious leaders, most recently Ayatollah Muhammad Sadiq al-Sadr and his two sons, murdered in February 1999 (see *MECS* 1999, pp. 270–72). While martial law had not been declared in the Shi'i areas, many of the governors there over a long period were former high-ranking military officers, signifying that a strong hand was needed to combat unrest. The population in these areas was regularly called upon to undergo training in arms in "popular training" centers (*tadrib sha'bi*) to combat "traitors" and counteract "plots" fomented against the Arab nation and humanity generally.[88]

Non-Iraqi sources and the Iraqi opposition reported occasional clashes in the south, including armed attacks against Ba'th Party officials. The authorities, in turn, demanded the establishment of night patrols.[89] A previously unknown group — the Islamic Unity Party — claimed that it had carried out eighteen operations in February against Iraqi intelligence and security forces in the south and center of Iraq to mark the first anniversary of the "martyrdom" of al-Sadr. The group reported that twenty-seven persons were killed in these operations.[90] The authorities, for their part, were said to have marked the occasion by executing twenty-five officers imprisoned for showing laxity in confronting the attackers in the unrest that erupted at the time.[91] Rocket attacks in Baghdad in April, May and September were claimed by other Islamist factions, including another previously unknown group, the Islamic Observer Group Inside Iraq (*Majmu'at al-Raqib al-Islami Dakhil al-'Iraq*).[92] The authorities acknowledged these attacks but blamed them on Iran and described them as having been directed against civilian targets. The Islamist groups claimed that the republican palace had been targeted.[93]

The combination of restiveness and abiding Ba'th fear of a Shi'i uprising in Iraq prompted heightened repression of the Shi'i population under the guise of the sanctions. Iraqi journalists who visited Najaf, Karbala and Hilla reported that in Najaf, for example, the population had only two hours a day of electricity — one hour during the daytime and one hour at night. Requests for the use of generators, as was the practice in other governorates, were refused on the pretext that this "would harm the national network."

The supply of water and other municipal services was also cut back severely or was nearly nonexistent. The Najafis were said to be jealous of Karbala for the "rapid development" that it was witnessing,[94] but if Karbala were better off than Najaf (probably as a premeditated move by Saddam; see *MECS* 1982–83, p. 579), it too suffered from severe cutbacks in the supply of water and other facilities. Hilla, once a flourishing city, also endured a long period of negligence, exacerbated during the sanctions.[95] Not a single new street was laid out since 1970, nor was any street paving carried out, although the population had paid for this service. Hilla, too, suffered from a lack of electricity most of the time. One journalist reported observing students studying in the streets around the Ba'th Party building because only there were the streetlights lit. Municipal facilities were almost nonexistent.[96] Such reports (by Salam al-Shamma' and 'Ali Ghani in *Alif Ba*) were quite rare and daring by Iraqi standards. Generally, the media were filled with reports of a contrasting situation, i.e., the allocation of vast sums of money for the development of these very places, popular indignation at the sanctions, and the love of Iraqis for and gratitude to Saddam Husayn.

Tribal issues were also disturbing to the regime. A decree issued in November punished an impostor who falsely claimed a kin relationship to descendants of Imam 'Ali bin Abi Talib with a seven-year prison sentence, and anyone who claimed a false relationship to a particular clan, a three-year sentence.[97]

Maintaining an inclination of several years' duration, Husayn counteracted this restiveness in the Shi'i and other sectors of the Iraqi population by leaning increasingly toward Islam, or, rather, manipulating Islamic symbols and messages for political purposes. He declared on one occasion that "every part of Iraq had become a prayer rug and a *mihrab* (prayer niche) for the believers."[98] Despite the sanctions, renovation of old mosques and the construction of new ones in various parts of the country continued at an increased rate. The most important of these projects, commissioned and supervised by Husayn himself, were the al-Rahman, the Saddam and Umm al-Ma'arik Mosques.[99] He also initiated the opening of a new Qur'an radio station, inaugurated on the occasion of his birthday on 27 April.[100] The opening of the station was part of the national campaign of faith, initiated by Husayn in June 1993 (see *MECS* 1993, pp. 391–92) and carried on vigorously ever since. Other Qur'an teaching centers were opened in prisons, especially for the benefit of child prisoners — boys and girls as young as nine years of age.[101] The climax of this campaign was a Qur'an written in the blood of President Husayn, which evoked exceptionally laudatory speeches from his close associates.[102] Evidently, Husayn needed a supply of ingenious devices which could serve to repress the Islamic tide but at the same time link up with it in order to maintain his control over the country.

CHRONIC WEAKNESS OF THE IRAQI OPPOSITION ABROAD

The Iraqi opposition abroad — excluding the Kurds — continued to suffer from chronic weakness stemming from a lack of unity and direction, the absence of a real power base at home, and insignificant outside support. These weaknesses may have become even more pronounced during 2000, as the improved regional and international standing of the Ba'th neutralized the attraction of the opposition abroad to outside supporters/ manipulators.

Representatives of the opposition (including Kurds) met with American Vice President Al Gore on 26 June and were promised that the US would not "flag in supporting" their efforts, and that the policy of the administration continued to be committed to the objective of removing Saddam Husayn from power.[103] However, beyond these solemn promises, which were mainly related to promoting Gore's presidential campaign, nothing was done. Even the minimal US support of $97m. promised to the opposition in 1998 (see *MECS* 1998, p. 294), remained largely undelivered.

The reasons may have been a lack of confidence in the opposition, or fears that it would misuse the funding or become neutralized by internecine rivalries in the rush for a piece of the American pie. Indeed, two main groups abroad vied for influence: the veteran Iraqi National Congress (INC), whose representative, Ahmad Chalabi, met with Gore, and the more recent Democratic Centrists (Tayyar al-Wasat), formed in 1999. The latter group met in London on 12 February 2000 in order to initiate "independent" political action that would put an end to "the opposition paralysis." Previously cooperating with the INC, the Democratic Centrists now criticized the older group and its leader, Chalabi,[104] designated as the main recipient of American political and financial backing earmarked for the Iraqi opposition. The INC itself, which was split internally, had failed to become an umbrella body for the Iraqi opposition.[105] The policy line adopted by the Democratic Centrists, in complete contradiction to that of the INC, eschewed dependence on any foreign party and opposed the continuation of the sanctions and the no-fly zones.[106] The group elected a fifteen-member executive committee which included 'Adnan Pachachi, a former foreign minister, who was named secretary-general; 'Arif 'Abd al-Razzaq, a former prime minister; and Ghassan 'Atiyya, a former diplomat who became the group's spokesperson.

Meanwhile, the Ba'thi regime increased its pressure on the opposition abroad, targeting Ghassan 'Atiyya in particular. An appeal to "shed the blood" of 'Atiyya was published in *al-'Iraq* on 25 March in the name of the shaykhs of the al-Humaydat tribe (of the Shamiya administrative district in the middle Euphrates) to which he belonged. In September, a special court in Baghdad issued a death sentence in absentia against 'Atiyya and Mustafa al-'Ani, on charges of meeting with Israelis.[107] President Husayn also reportedly approved the allocation of $2m. to his intelligence director, Tahir 'Abd al-Jalil al-Habbush, to implement a plan for "tracking down oppositionists abroad, preventing them from having any influence on the Iraqis in the states providing a safe haven, and monitoring their activities."[108]

A group of Iraqi defectors also claimed that Husayn had dispatched teams of female agents to target dissident Iraqis in Britain. The exiled Iraqi general Najib al-Salihi reported receiving a video cassette showing one of his female relatives being raped by a member of the intelligence service in order to blackmail him to stop working for the opposition.[109] Although these specific reports could not be corroborated, Baghdad clearly attempted to persecute the opposition in any way possible. Another example was the refusal of the regime to sign trade contracts with the Czech Republic so long as the "hostile" Radio Free Europe/Radio Liberty station (financed by the US and managed by the Iraqi opposition) continued to broadcast from Czech territory. The Czech explanation that it had no say regarding broadcasts failed to convince Baghdad.[110]

It appeared that in the war of nerves between Baghdad and the opposition, the former had the greater likelihood for victory.

IRAQI KURDISTAN: BETWEEN NATION-BUILDING AND FRATRICIDE

THE KURDISH REGION AND THE CENTER COMPARED

After a decade in which Iraqi Kurdistan was outside the control of the central government, significant differences between that region and the center were observable. Some of these differences were inherent, while others were more transitory, the result of changing domestic, regional and international circumstances.

One striking difference was that while political activity in the center was all but frozen, the Kurdish region brimmed with it. Moreover, while in the center a single political party — the Ba'th — monopolized power, a host of parties, groups and outside interests vied for influence within Iraqi Kurdistan. Similarly, while the media in the center were monopolized by the Ba'th, in the Kurdish north they were diverse, owned by several main parties. Eight television stations operated in the north along with a large number of radio stations. The Kurds also had unrestricted access to the Internet (where it existed) and satellite television, media which Iraqis in the center and south could only dream of.[111]

The openness in the Kurdish region had its impact on the social level as well. Kurdish women were better integrated in the political system than in the center. The Kurdistan Democratic Party (KDP), although considered more traditional and tribal than its rival, the Patriotic Union of Kurdistan (PUK), had a female minister of development and construction, Nasrin Barwari.[112] The more important role played by women in Kurdish society was symbolically reflected by the statue of a woman at the entrance to Zakho, a city under KDP control.[113] Notably, Jalal Talabani, the head of the PUK, promised that women from various regions of Kurdistan would be brought into the leadership of the party.[114]

The Kurds were better off economically than the population in the center and the south. The UN-supervised oil-for-food program in the Kurdish region, instituted in 1996, made for greater efficiency than in the center. Moreover, fifteen active NGOs were devoted to rehabilitation.[115] Additionally, the region's income grew significantly, as it had become the major outlet for Iraqi trade and other economic transactions with the outside world. According to one observer, Iraqi Kurdistan was flourishing as never in the previous twenty years.[116]

These developments also changed the nature of relations between the north and the center. Ten years of the absence of control by the central government enabled the Kurds to develop the trappings of independence, e.g., self-government, a parliament, an army (Peshmerga), security forces, flags, an anthem, Kurdish-language media and books in Kurdish. Paradoxically, interdependence between the two parts of Iraq grew significantly as well. Since it no longer controlled the area, Baghdad was forced to depend on the Kurds both for the flow of water (the PUK controlled the region in which the two major dams, Darbandikhan and Dokan, were located) and the flow of oil in the strategic pipeline to Turkey (located in the area controlled by the KDP). The Kurds, for their part, depended on Baghdad for such necessities as electricity and commerce. All this gave further impetus to the notion of a federal Iraq, so cherished by the KDP and so feared by Baghdad.

During the year 2000, however, the main preoccupation of the region was less with Baghdad and more with the interrelationship between the groups and organizations within Kurdistan.

THE KURDISTAN KALEIDOSCOPE

To the outside observer, Iraqi Kurdistan seemed a kaleidoscope of groupings and elements constantly shaping and reshaping alliances and rivalries. The main players in the region during the period under review were the two leading parties — the KDP headed by Mas'ud Barzani, and the PUK, led by Jalal Talabani; various Islamist groups; a leftist communist group; Turkoman organizations; and the Turkish Kurdish Workers' Party (Party Kerkeren Kurdistan; PKK).

While relations between the KDP and the PUK were typically tense, at no point did they revert to warfare, as during 1994–96. Confrontation was prevented not by any sudden amity between the two, but more likely by popular pressure against such a move. They also appear to have realized that fighting would not serve their interests, that both were inextricably enmeshed in each other's problems, and that certain outside forces, especially the US, were trying to broker peace between them. Until the middle of the year, regular contact was kept up between the parties (excluding direct contact between Barzani and Talabani) regarding the exchange of prisoners and discussions of various outstanding issues. The fifty-second ordinary meeting of the Higher Peace Committee was held on 20 May 2000, attended by representatives of the two parties.[117]

The meeting with Gore and other American officials in Washington on 26 June marked the first time that such a high-ranking American official met publicly with Kurdish representatives. Addressing the PUK and KDP representatives, Gore reaffirmed the US commitment to "the protection of the people of Iraqi Kurdistan."[118] He also urged the parties to speed up the implementation of the 1998 Washington Agreement which sought to normalize relations between the two. While Talabani himself attended the meeting, Mas'ud Barzani did not, instead sending his nephew and son-in-law, Nechirvan Barzani, who headed the KDP-led regional government. Mas'ud Barzani's absence may have been prompted by distrust of American motives and intentions (i.e., that Gore wished to use the Kurdish card to promote his candidacy for presidency by issuing a challenge to Saddam Husayn); Barzani's self-confidence, which allowed him the luxury not to attend such a meeting (in contrast to the Kurdish yearning for such an open meeting in the 1970s); his desire to leave the door open to Baghdad; or in order to disparage Talabani by signaling that Nechirvan was a good enough counterpart for him.[119] Presumably, this was viewed as a personal slight by Talabani.

In the event, the Washington meeting did not improve relations between the two parties, rather it worsened them. Regular meetings ceased and a war of words ensued, with each party blaming the other for the lack of progress in solving outstanding problems and normalizing relations.

The Washington encounter illuminated an inherent imbalance in the status of the KDP vis-à-vis that of the PUK. For various reasons, the KDP perceived itself as stronger and better off than its rival, the PUK. The end of the Kurdish internecine fighting in 1996 left the KDP with a better territorial position than the PUK. The KDP controlled the governorates of Dohuk and Irbil, which enjoyed the protection of the no-fly zone (set up in 1991) as well as direct access to Turkey, stimulating an economic boom in the KDP territory. The PUK, which controlled the Sulaymaniyya governorate, enjoyed neither advantage, and was in fact under constant threat from Baghdad. Indeed, it repeatedly warned that Baghdad was massing troops and "Arabizing" the adjacent oil-rich Kirkuk region. In August, for example, it reported that from January 2000 onward, 997 Kurds had been deported from Kirkuk to Sulaymaniyya.[120] Talabani asserted in a speech that the Kurds were not prepared "to abandon this sacred city" [Kirkuk], not only because of its economic importance but also because of its strategic, cultural and historical importance to Kurdistan.[121]

Due to its strategic location, and probably because of its more pragmatic political approach as well, the KDP enjoyed better relationships with various regional and international actors than did its rival. Ever since its surprising appeal for help to Baghdad in August 1996 (see *MECS* 1996, pp. 337–38), the KDP assiduously kept the door open for contacts with the government. Furthermore, it did not keep these relations secret. Barzani emphasized continuously that the Kurds sought nothing more than federation with Baghdad.[122] While this formula was not to the liking of the central government, it was less frightening for it and for other regional players than an independent Kurdish state. A symbolic reflection of KDP-Baghdad relations was a visit in November of a delegation of "Iraqi artists" to "Iraqi Kurdistan." A member of the delegation stated that a hundred works by artists "from Iraqi governorates" would be exhibited "as a means to consolidating the bridge of amity between the two sides."[123]

The KDP also had strong relations with other important elements in the region, namely, Turkey. These ties were based on joint economic interests as well as political expediency, i.e., the need to curb the Turkish-based secessionist PKK, their common enemy. So confident of these relations had the KDP become, that its representation in Ankara held a reception marking the Kurdish festival of Nevruz for the first time, with the KDP representative, Safeen Dizayee, and the tourism minister of the "northern Iraqi region," Huseyin Fincare, receiving the guests in Peshmerga uniforms. However, no representatives from the Turkish Foreign Ministry or the government attended the reception.[124] Possibly because of this bold Kurdish step, or because of the more crucial problem of the Turkomans (see below), relations between the KDP and Ankara cooled somewhat during the latter part of the year. Still, regular contacts, meetings and transactions continued as before, with Mas'ud Barzani himself visiting Ankara and meeting with Turkish officials in October 2000.

The KDP also sought to develop relations with Syria, as evidenced by the three-day mourning period it declared following the death of Syrian president Hafiz al-Asad in June, and Barzani's visit to Damascus in November, when he held talks with President Bashshar al-Asad. Notably, the two parties "affirmed" the need to work toward lifting the embargo on Iraq during the visit.[125] Attempts by the KDP to develop relations with the Arab states were also reflected in the establishment of an Arab-Kurdish Friendship Society in Irbil in March 2000.[126]

In addition to Syria, Barzani visited other Arab countries in November, including Libya, Egypt, Saudi Arabia and Jordan, where he reiterated his message that the KDP opposed the sanctions and was committed to the unity and territorial integrity of Iraq. However, he stressed, this unity should be implemented in the form of a federation which left only foreign policy, national defense and financial affairs in the hands of the central government.[127] Barzani's visits to the Arab countries and his statements there clearly aimed to ingratiate the KDP with Arab leaders and perhaps prepare the ground for the time when the sanctions were lifted and the possibility that Baghdad might clamp down on the Kurds. Earlier, in October, Barzani visited Turkey, Britain, France and Austria. Both tours were quite unusual for Barzani, as for most of the host countries, indicating changing times and a degree of recognition for the emerging Kurdish entity. Moreover, as one Kurdish official maintained, the KDP (and possibly the PUK, too) had representations in "the European countries, North America, and neighboring Arab countries."[128] An additional motive for Barzani's visits may have been to balance those of Talabani, who habitually circulated in various capitals. One of Talabani's visits was to Ankara in July (see below), constituting yet another twist in the complex intra-Kurdish as well as Kurdish-Turkish relationship.

DIALOGUE AND CONFRONTATION

Relations between the PUK and Ankara were soured for several years because the Turkish government suspected Talabani's group of sheltering the PKK and supporting them in their fight against Turkey. In May, however, the PKK, in an about-face, accused the PUK of supporting the Turkish army in an operation against them, a charge vehemently denied by the PUK. Earlier, in March, a PUK delegation visited Ankara at the invitation of the Turkish foreign minister, followed by a visit by another high-ranking PUK delegation seeking Turkish economic support. Talabani's visit there in July, and his meeting with Prime Minister Bülent Ecevit to inform him of "the latest developments in Kurdistan," elicited a forthcoming response by Ecevit, who said: "Recently the institution headed by Talabani has begun to take more effective measures against the terrorist organization PKK. He gave detailed information to me concerning this issue. We appreciate this."[129]

Clearly, Talabani had reached the conclusion that in order for him to improve the situation of the PUK and alter the balance of power between it and the KDP, he would have to ally himself with Ankara. The quid pro quo would be to fight the PKK. Indeed, less than two months after Talabani's visit to Ankara, intense clashes broke out between the PUK and the PKK, lasting until the end of the year. Each party blamed the other for the violence. Additionally, the PUK blamed Baghdad for supporting the PKK, while the PKK accused Ankara of supporting the PUK. The extent of these clashes could be inferred from a PUK report claiming that it had killed 120 PKK members in one attack.[130] During the course of 2000, therefore, the PUK replaced the KDP as militant foes of the PKK, presumably hoping to raise their political standing in Ankara.

Conversely, the KDP relationship with Turkey became clouded. This was the result of growing tension between the KDP and the Turkoman minority in the Kurdish Autonomous Zone, who were represented by the Turkoman Front. The Front, claiming that it had bureaus and headquarters stretching from Zakho to Kifri, accused KDP officials of ignoring its "fraternal efforts" and of standing "against the Turkoman people's aims and aspirations."[131] Responding, the KDP denied that it had placed obstacles before Turkoman schools or "persecuted" the Turkomans, in other such ways, and insisted that the Turkomans enjoyed freedom of expression and movement, had their own schools, newspapers, radio and television, and, above all, had a minister to represent them in the (KDP-established) cabinet.[132] The two parties initiated a dialogue in May to try to solve outstanding problems. However, in July the KDP reportedly attacked the Turkoman Front headquarters in Irbil, killing two and injuring six others. This evoked a charge by the Front that the KDP sought "to annihilate the 2.5 million-strong Turkoman population in Iraq," and that Barzani was worse than Saddam Husayn.[133] The Front called on Turkey to support the Turkomans against the KDP repression, which Ankara promised to do.

Clearly, the Turkoman population figure cited by their spokesperson was greatly exaggerated. Nonetheless, the Turkomans were a power that the KDP had to reckon with, all the more so since Turkey backed them with a view to counterbalancing the growing power of the KDP in the region. Moreover, the Turkomans tried to ally themselves with the PUK, in light of the two common "enemies" they both confronted: the KDP and the Iraqi government (Baghdad was accused of increasingly persecuting Kurds and Turkomans in the Kirkuk governorate adjacent to the Sulaymaniyya governorate under PUK control). The PUK and the Turkomans were also concerned with the alleged expulsion of Kurds and Turks from the oil-rich Kirkuk region and the settling of Palestinians in their place. Talabani, calling attention to this policy, advocated reinforcing Kurdish-Turkoman brotherhood in order to face this danger. Palestinian officials in Iraq and journalists, however, denied the existence of such a policy.[134]

Both the KDP and the PUK had to deal with yet another rival, common to both — Kurdish Islamist groups. One of these groups, (Islamic Movement in Kurdistan) controlled the Halabja region, which in 1994 had been the scene of fighting between the Islamists, backed at the time by the KDP, and the PUK (see *MECS* 1994, p. 343), and which ended in a full-fledged war between the KDP and the PUK. Attempting to widen their influence in their respective regions thereafter, both the KDP and the PUK had to contend with the growing power of a variety of Islamist groups.[135] The Islamists were accused of masterminding terrorism and sabotage in various parts of Kurdistan. A member of one of the groups, the Islamic Unity Movement of Kurdistan (IUMK), confessed.[136] In August, the KDP clashed with the militia of another group, the Islamic Unification, killing twenty-one. The PKK, too, was said to have attacked an Islamist group, the Islamic Mujadidin Movement, and to have killed thirty.[137] Bombs and booby-trapped cars thought to be set by Islamists exploded throughout the year in various parts of Kurdistan, but their perpetrators were rarely found.

In summary, the Kurds appeared to have improved their civic and economic situation, and to some extent managed to introduce themselves and their agenda into the international arena. Still, as in the past, they failed to achieve a modicum of unity among themselves, and the struggle for power between different groups, parties and states involved in the Kurdistan region went on unabated. Thus, if the US, Britain or any other party envisioned using Kurdistan as a springboard from which to orchestrate the downfall of the Ba'th, they had their work cut out for them.

FOREIGN AFFAIRS

THE IRAQI BATTLE TO LIFT THE SANCTIONS

The Iraqi battle to annul the sanctions imposed on it since 1990 scored several important successes during the year. Although the sanctions were not lifted entirely, a growing number of countries, commercial concerns and individuals were willing to challenge or defy them openly. The causes of this development ranged from genuine humanitarian concerns to cold political and economic considerations. The Iraqi contention that the sanctions were the cause of suffering to the Iraqi people could no longer be brushed aside, as it provided statistics, and photographic evidence to support its version, particularly visual images connecting the death of children to the lack of medicine.[138] The counter-arguments by the US and its allies that Husayn himself was the real cause of this suffering, since he continued to spend huge sums of money on the construction of palaces and the fueling of his personality cult propaganda machine, were comparatively ineffective. The US and its allies were no more successful in their argument that, left unrestrained, Husayn would be much more dangerous to his people and to other nations alike.

In January, the US-based NGO, Human Rights Watch, demanded a lifting of the sanctions, which it considered a violation of human rights.[139] Even more dramatic was the decision by the head of the UN oil-for-food program, Hans von Sponeck, to resign from his post in protest against the sanctions, stating: "I do not want to be associated with a Band-Aid that is inadequate to end the plight of the civilian population."[140] Sponeck's move was all the more gratifying for Iraq and embarrassing for the US and its ally, Britain, as it came on the heels of the resignation of the previous UN director a year earlier, and was quickly followed by the resignation of the head of the World Food Program in Iraq, Jutta Prughart, on the same grounds. Adding to US-British discomfort was Sponeck's final report, which criticized not only the sanctions but also what he described as the "devastation" caused by the US and British air strikes on Iraqi territory in the no-fly zones (on the air strikes, see *MECS* 1999, pp. 282–83).

No less damaging for the American and British stance was UN Secretary-General Kofi Annan's appeal in March for "smarter sanctions," warning that the UN was in danger of losing the propaganda war with Saddam Husayn. He maintained that the humanitarian situation in Iraq posed a serious moral dilemma for the UN, since "the UN has always been on the side of the vulnerable and weak....Yet here we are accused of causing suffering to an entire population."[141]

Russia, France and China had long been applying pressure to lift the sanctions altogether. They scored a point against the US and Britain when they blocked the appointment in January of Rolf Ekeus, the American choice, to head the new UN Monitoring, Verification and Inspection Commission (UNMOVIC). However, UNMOVIC, successor to UNSCOM (United Nations Special Commission on Iraq; first headed by Ekeus), never set up operation in Iraq during 2000. Although the statements of the agreed-on appointee, Hans Blix, were more conciliatory to Iraq than those of his predecessor, Richard Butler, Iraq refused to allow him and his staff into the country. Iraq announced that it opposed any form of weapons inspections so long as the sanctions were in place. UNMOVIC thus remained a dead letter.

The sanctions were being eroded in various ways. Italian and French businessmen landed in Baghdad in April, marking the first such defiance in ten years of the ban on flights to Iraq. This was followed by other such arrivals in September, a trickle that became a flood in November when more and more countries began to defy the ban. Iraq itself activated internal flights, too. Moreover, from the beginning of 2000, Iraq was granted a significantly more liberal program of oil sales to enable it to pay for civilian goods. In effect, Iraq was no longer limited regarding the quantity of oil it could sell, a move that the US did not oppose.[142] With this, Iraq also smuggled out growing quantities of oil via its neighbors, Turkey, Syria and Iran,[143] so as to have a free hand in using oil revenues for its own purposes. One such purpose was the continued development of its military industry, evidenced by its testing in July of the Sumud short-range ballistic missile. Although the development of a missile of that range was not banned by the sanctions, the test evoked growing fears that Iraq could easily use this expertise to develop long-range missiles. No less damaging to the viability of the sanctions regime and its initial purpose were reports and warnings from various quarters, chief among whom was Richard Butler, that Iraq was moving ahead in its development of nuclear, biological and chemical weapons.[144]

The ineffectiveness of the sanctions was further demonstrated by the fact that not only did they not weaken or isolate Saddam Husayn, but they enabled him to manipulate the suffering of the Iraqi people to regain entry into the Arab fold and the international community at large. That the ostracization of Iraq was disintegrating rapidly was evidenced by the appeals of more and more countries to lift the sanctions alongside their resumption of diplomatic relations with Iraq. No better display of the international courting of Iraq could be found than the Baghdad trade fair of November 2000, in which c. 1,500 firms from a total of forty-five countries participated.[145] The great leap in oil prices in 2000 and the prospects of doing business with Iraq, coupled with the lack of American interest in, or policy on Iraq, turned Baghdad into a pilgrimage site despite the sanctions.

BAGHDAD'S ATTEMPT TO ENGAGE THE US

Iraq tried to engage the US during 2000, both through dialogue and through the more traditional war of words and other symbolic acts. The two-pronged approach was motivated by the rise in oil prices and by growing demands within the US by individuals and humanitarian groups to loosen or lift the sanctions altogether. Moreover, American aloofness vis-à-vis Iraq increased, as domestically the focus was on the November presidential elections, and externally President Clinton put all his efforts into the Israeli-Palestinian peace process. What little attention was devoted to the Iraqi issue was characterized by inconsistency and indecision. Whereas presidential candidate Gore declared in March that the US was trying to oust Saddam Husayn from power, Secretary of State Albright stated later that force was not the answer to getting cooperation from President Husayn on arms inspections.[146] While Gore met with representatives of the opposition and promised US support, in practice the Clinton administration did nothing to fulfill these promises. Evidently, both Clinton and Gore had made a decision to keep the subject of Iraq out of the election campaign so as to preclude any Iraqi reaction that might jeopardize the Israeli-Palestinian peace process or Gore's chances to win the elections.

Iraq, in a mirror reaction, took great care not to provoke an American military attack on it. Rather, it sought to use all its diplomatic and political propaganda resource to isolate the US administration, both internally and externally, on the issue of the sanctions. Occasional Iraqi hints at a willingness to initiate a dialogue with the US alternated with harsh verbal attacks on Clinton, Albright, Gore and the US generally as constituting the main cause of Iraqi suffering.[147] Baghdad also capitalized on pressure developing within the US for a change in the sanctions policy.[148] Additionally, Iraq signed a cooperative agreement with CNN, the first such agreement with an American communications medium since the Gulf War.[149]

Some of the pressure in the US for easing the sanctions was motivated by the desire to do business with Iraq. American firms were already quietly engaged in aiding the reconstruction of the oil industry in Iraq and other commercial ventures.[150] Other voices earnestly calling for the repeal of the sanctions, included, surprisingly, that of Scott Ritter the former UN arms inspector who two years earlier had resigned from the UN in protest over the American failure to support tougher UN inspections. Now Ritter was invited to Iraq to judge whether Iraq had rebuilt its arsenal. A more skeptical figure, Democratic Party Congressman Tony Hall, visited Iraq in April 2000 to examine the effects of the sanctions on the health of Iraqi children and ended up recommending not to lift the sanctions. Immediately thereafter, 126 members of Congress urged Clinton to keep the sanctions in place.

Faced with the adamant official American stance, Baghdad resorted in October to an economic gimmick: it decided to stop using the American dollar for its international transactions and shift instead to the euro. Baghdad explained that the move resulted from American hostility to Arabs and to humanity in general, and Iraqi determination "to thwart the US dream of controlling Arab resources and using them to promote its economic and hostile purposes." Husayn, meanwhile, once again predicted the imminent collapse of the US.[151]

In summary, Iraq failed to bring about a change in the official American stance before Clinton left office. The new administration, it feared, was likely to be worse.

THE RETURN OF RUSSIA TO IRAQ

Iraqi-Russian relations improved significantly during 2000 against a background of tension between Russia and the US, Russian efforts to reestablish itself in the Middle East, and growing economic and military opportunities in Iraq. Anxious to take advantage of these opportunities, Russia stood at the forefront of those countries willing to challenge American policy in Iraq as well as fill a certain vacuum left by the US because of its other preoccupations. Russia hoped to use its clout in order to lift the sanctions altogether, or at least erode them further, thereby enhancing its status in Iraqi eyes.

Its first successful move was to challenge the appointment of Rolf Ekeus as head of UNIMOVIC, a nominee opposed by Iraq (see above). While a US official described the decision as an "unprecedented" gesture of defiance toward UN Secretary-General Kofi Annan,[152] it was in fact a challenge to the US itself, which was powerless against it. Meanwhile, Russian officials, including President Vladimir Putin and Foreign Minister Igor Ivanov, became increasingly vocal in their demands to lift the sanctions and end American and British air attacks in the no-fly zones. Iraq regarded the attacks as illegal, a view which Russia "fully shared."[153] Russia also continued to contribute to the de facto erosion of the sanctions. Two Russian oil tankers were apprehended, in February and April, in attempts to smuggle out Iraqi oil under the guise of purchasing Iranian oil. Clearly, the trade in oil outside the oil-for-food parameters was beneficial both to Iraq and its partners, in this case Russian companies. In another breach of the sanctions, official Russian delegations and commercial representatives began arriving in Iraq on direct flights when Baghdad's international airport was reopened in mid-August.[154]

Concurrently, diplomatic, cultural and military relations continued to expand. Baghdad intensified its contacts with Moscow, sending Deputy Prime Minister Tariq 'Aziz for talks and consultations with high-ranking officials in Russia, including President Putin, on several occasions. Russian foreign minister Ivanov, visiting Baghdad in November, met with President Husayn. Oil continued to be the primary basis for the bilateral relationship. As one Russian official explained: "Russian business considers Iraq as one of the most promising markets, both from the point of view of oil production,...supplies of Russian equipment and machinery, and setting up transport communications."[155] Reportedly, Russian companies purchased 40% of the Iraqi oil exports under the UN oil-for-food program.[156]

At the end of the year, Iraq and Russia signed a memorandum drawn up by the Iraqi and Russian oil ministries aimed at formalizing bilateral links. The two countries also signed an accord in May for scientific and cultural cooperation, which included exchange visits by scientists and experts and the teaching of each country's language, history and civilization at the other's universities.

Military cooperation with Russia was the most important aspect of the relationship for Iraq. In February, *The Sunday Telegraph* reported that Russian military officials breached the UN arms embargo against Iraq by signing a $90m. deal through Belarus for upgrading Iraqi air defense systems and reequipping its military aircraft. Belarus also agreed to overhaul seventeen Soviet-made Iraqi warplanes located in Belarus since the late 1980s.[157] Iraqi defense minister Sultan Hashim Ahmad, arriving in Moscow in April, was believed to be secretly negotiating with Russian companies for the development of long-range missiles. Iraq was known to have set up a large network of front companies to disguise procurement deals for projects forbidden under the UN sanctions.[158]

Overall, Iraq registered considerable success in recreating the Cold War atmosphere that would allow it to exploit the rivalries between the US and Russia for its own benefit.

REENTERING THE ARAB FOLD

Iraqi efforts to return to the Arab fold began to bear fruit during 2000. This was due to a combination of pressure from the Arab 'street' and the realpolitik approach of some of the Arab rulers, along with the skillful use of cards in the Iraqi hand. The suffering of the Iraqi people due to the sanctions, the sharp rise in oil prices, and the second Palestinian intifada which erupted at the end of September 2000 were all mobilized by Baghdad for this goal.

The main Iraqi argument with regard to the sanctions was that they were "Arab," i.e., if the Arab countries were to disobey them, they would no longer be viable. On the other hand, were they to continue to observe them, they too would be responsible for the suffering inflicted on the Iraqi people. To be sure, even if, in principle, some Arab countries were willing to go all the way to meet the Iraqi demands, they had to weigh three considerations: the American reaction, Kuwaiti and Saudi opposition, and their own fears of Saddam Husayn's ambitions and designs. Nevertheless, after ten years of sanctions, these factors had lost some of their potency, while pressure from the Arab 'street' and, more importantly, economic considerations began to gain ground. This gradual shift in the Arab attitude was reflected in various moves. More and more officials in various Arab countries, including Egypt and Syria — partners in the original anti-Iraqi coalition — called for lifting the sanctions. Once the air embargo was broken by Russia and France in September, Arab countries starting with Jordan and followed by Morocco, Yemen, Libya, Tunisia, the UAE, Syria and Egypt flew airlines into Baghdad's newly reopened international airport.[159] Although the flights were not yet scheduled on a regular basis, and were boarded mainly by businessmen, journalists, artists and intellectuals who came on "humanitarian" missions, bringing medicine and food, they had an important psychological and political impact. Their message was that Baghdad was no longer isolated, and that the Iraqi argument that the ban on civilian flights to and from Iraq was dubious and illegal from the start had merit.

Another important move was the elevation of various Arab diplomatic representations in Iraq from interest section to ambassadorial level. The most important Arab country to take this step was Egypt, which in November followed the lead taken by the UAE in April.[160]

Besides improving its bilateral relations with many of the Arab countries, Iraq managed to rehabilitate itself on the pan-Arab level as well, most importantly by participating, for the first time in ten years, in an Arab summit conference — the emergency Arab summit held on 21–22 October 2000 in Cairo (see chapter on inter-Arab relations). Although the summit dealt mainly with the Palestinian intifada and not, as Baghdad would have wished, with the issue of the sanctions against Iraq, the very fact of Iraqi participation (in the person of RCC Vice Chairperson 'Izzat Ibrahim al-Duri, representing Saddam Husayn) signified the diminishing power of the anti-Iraqi Arab camp and, most importantly, of the veto power of Kuwait and Saudi Arabia. It also pointed to Baghdad's newly acquired importance in the wake of the eruption of the intifada, or, as one pro-Iraqi paper described it, "Iraqi victory in an age of Arab defeat."[161] Not that Baghdad entirely shed its vitriolic rhetoric against other Arab governments. Husayn periodically urged the overthrow of various Arab regimes[162] even at a time when relations were improving on the bilateral and pan-Arab levels. Nevertheless, the return of Iraq to the Arab fold continued apace, despite its occasional bellicosity, essentially due to the sharp increase of oil prices, which impelled many of the Arab countries to seek business links with it.

With its three Persian Gulf neighbors — Iran, Kuwait and Saudi Arabia — still harboring various degrees of animosity toward it, Baghdad focused its attention at the end of the year on the Fertile Crescent. Deputy Prime Minister 'Aziz began to propagate the idea of an economic union between the countries of the Fertile Crescent — Iraq, Syria, Lebanon and Jordan — as a first step toward full political integration. The Iraqi media and academic community followed this lead, seeking to play up the benefits of such a project to all countries concerned.[163] The Iraqi charm offensive toward the Fertile Crescent countries was occasioned by three important developments: the succession in Jordan (1999) and in Syria (2000) of two young and inexperienced rulers — King 'Abdallah and President Bashshar al-Asad, respectively; the collapse of the peace process between Israel and Syria, followed by that with the Palestinians; and the eruption of the Palestinian intifada at the end of September. Armed with its newly potent oil weapon, Iraq sought to heighten its influence in Syria and Jordan, inter alia, by playing one neighbor against the other.

The main concern of Baghdad was to engage Syria, its long-time rival in the Fertile Crescent. This process, begun under President Hafiz al-Asad, was accelerated under his son Bashshar (see also *MECS* 1996, pp. 349–50; 1997, pp. 400–401; 1998, pp. 312–13; 1999, p. 287). After twenty years of severed relations, the two countries opened interest sections in February 2000. Reportedly, Tariq 'Aziz visited Damascus no fewer than nine times in the latter part of the year, meeting with Bashshar twice. No less important was a visit by RCC vice chairperson Duri, in November 2000, and his meeting with Asad.[164] Damascus, for its part, took a step forward by calling for the lifting of the sanctions, even at the risk of antagonizing Kuwait and Saudi Arabia. The two countries also exchanged visits by economic delegations, reactivated the Mosul-Aleppo passenger train service, established their long-disputed final border points on the basis of the 1923 British-French demarcation; and, most importantly, reactivated the Iraqi-Syrian oil pipeline which had been closed since 1982 at the end of the year. Overall, Iraq was eager to develop relations on all levels, especially the political one, while Syria was more guarded, laying the emphasis on the economic sphere.

Jordan was the other target for the charm offensive. Baghdad used the Syrian-Jordanian rivalry, the growing economic dependence of Amman on Iraqi oil, and the radicalization in the Jordanian 'street,' reflecting mounting support for Iraq, to revive and extend its influence there. The most impressive result of this effort was a three-day visit by Jordanian prime minister 'Ali Abu al-Raghib to Baghdad in late October-early November. The visit, which was termed 'historic' in the Jordanian media, was the first by a high-ranking Arab official to Baghdad in ten years, signifying a clear Jordanian tilt toward Iraq and yet another challenge to the sanctions region. Underlining this shift, Abu Raghib stated that the visit aimed "at expanding and strengthening the relationship between the two fraternal countries, leading to political, economic and social integration."[165] Indeed, the talks, which were supervised by Husayn, laid the basis for doubling the volume of trade; selling Iraqi oil to Jordan at preferential prices ($21 per barrel); renewing the Iraqi oil grant to Jordan, amounting to half the Iraqi supply; constructing a 750km. oil pipeline from Iraq to Jordan; and retaining the 'Aqaba port (and not Syrian ports) as the major port of entry for Iraqi imports.[166] Jordan, which relied on Iraqi crude and derivatives to meet nearly all its energy needs,[167] had now come almost full circle in resuming the intimate relations of the 1980s with Iraq (see *MECS* 1981–82, p. 604).

In addition to Syria and Jordan, Iraq managed to improve its relations with other Arab countries, including Egypt, Libya, the UAE, Qatar and others (see chapter on inter-Arab relations).

PROBLEMATIC NEIGHBORS: KUWAIT, SAUDI ARABIA, IRAN
In contrast to the rapprochement which Iraq managed to effect with many of the Arab countries, its relations with Kuwait and Saudi Arabia remained hostile. Viewing these countries as the source of many of its troubles, Iraq escalated its war of words against them with the hope of isolating them in the Arab world or at least neutralizing their influence on other Arab countries. Both Saudi Arabia and Kuwait, the Iraqis maintained, were responsible for prolonging the sanctions. Moreover, Baghdad accused them of direct aggression against it by allowing American and British airplanes to use their bases to carry out attacks on Iraq. "The Saudi and Kuwaiti regimes are real partners in the continuing US-British aggression against our people and our country and the resulting crimes of murder and destruction," wrote the government-sponsored *al-Thawra*.[168]

Another "hostile" act by Kuwait, specifically, was its continued demand that Iraq return Kuwaitis missing since the Gulf War period (see *MECS* 1999, p. 289). Iraq insisted that it had no Kuwaiti POWs, charging that the Kuwaiti refusal to close the "so-called missing files" revealed its "malicious practice."[169] Iraq also countered this demand by raising the issue of 1,150 Iraqi POWs and nationals who allegedly went missing in Kuwait during the first half of 1991. Simultaneously, it kept up a campaign of veiled and open threats against Kuwait which reached a peak in August, the anniversary of the Iraqi invasion of Kuwait. Saddam Husayn, his two sons and the media reiterated that "the Day of Call" (the invasion of Kuwait) was fully justified, hence no regret or apology for it (as Kuwait kept demanding) was due; the Iraqis' patience had its limits; Iraq would not hesitate to teach Kuwaiti rulers an "extra lesson"; and, lastly, a warning that Kuwait was pushing Iraq "to the road of confrontation."[170] Despite these threats, Iraq declared that it had no intention of attacking Kuwait, an assertion that hardly reassured the Kuwaitis. By the end of the year, the tense atmosphere seemed to have been somewhat eased by Kuwaiti acquiescence in November to the depiction by the Islamic summit conference organization of the 1990 invasion as "the situation between Iraq and Kuwait" and not "the Iraqi aggression (see chapter on Islam)."[171] At bottom, however, relations between Iraq and Kuwait remained as hostile as ever.

Saudi Arabia, which in Iraqi eyes belonged to the same camp as Kuwait, also toned down its overt hostility toward the end of the year, when it decided to open land borders at the Jadidat 'Ar'ar border crossing for what was described by an Iraqi official as "trade diplomacy." In addition, Saudi Arabia declared its support of Iraqi independence and territorial integrity.[172] However, apart from symbolic gestures, real rapprochement seemed remote.

Relations with Iran remained as ambiguous as ever: cycles of hostility were punctuated by short periods of détente or even rapprochement. "Terrorist" attacks and counterattacks by the "agents" or the opposition of each country against the other were reported throughout the year. The use of each other's opposition for a war by proxy was both a symptom and a cause of tension. The main explanation for the ambiguity in Iraqi-Iranian relations was the carryover from the past combined with the interests of the present. The eight-year Iran-Iraq War (1980–88) remained the basic obstlacle to establishing a peaceful relationship between the two, for although the war had ended, the enmity was unresolved (see *MECS* 1988, pp. 213–18, 511–18). Iran continued to demand that Iraq accept the 1975 Algiers agreement between the Shah and Saddam Husayn as the basis for the solution of the conflict, and that Iraq pay reparations to it, as had been decided by the UN. This, according to Tehran, could be accomplished through "its most valued asset — oil."

In addition, Iran demanded that Iraq stop its support for the "despicable" Mojahedin Khalq Organization, which "continued" the war against Iran "through various acts of sabotage."[173] Another thorny problem for both countries was that of POWs and missing soldiers. Iraq claimed that seven thousand Iraqi POWs still remained in Iran, while Iran claimed that 2,806 Iranians were still being held in Iraq.[174] Though these figures may have been inflated, the fact that prisoners of war remained twelve years after the end of the war indicated the depth and the intensity of the conflict. In April, Iran released another 450 Iraqi POWs (who, upon returning to Iraq, received $150 as a gift from President Husayn). Many others, Iran claimed, had sought asylum in Iran. Iraq maintained that it held no Iranian POWs but that Iranians had sought asylum there.[175]

Another contentious issue was the Iraqi demand that Iran return the 125 Iraqi civilian and military aircraft which had taken refuge there on the eve of the 1991 Gulf War. Iran, however, refused to do so, linking the return of the aircraft to acceptance by Iraq of Iranian reparations terms based on Iraqi responsibility for starting the war in 1980.[176] Iraq, for its part, continued to claim that it was Iran which had begun the war on 4 September. Only on 22 September had "the wise Iraqi leadership made its historic, firm and bold decision to deliver a decisive and comprehensive response to the Iranian aggression" (see *MECS* 1979–80, pp. 516–22).[177] Mirroring Iranian demands, Baghdad insisted that Tehran end its support of the Iraqi Shi'i opposition.

Despite this continuous contention, the two parties were said to be cooperating in smuggling oil. Reportedly, Iran charged $5 for each ton of Iraqi oil it allowed to pass through its territorial waters.[178] Furthermore, by the end of September, signs of a thaw and even rapprochement between the two parties were apparent, and were confirmed by a meeting at the October OPEC conference in Caracas between Iranian president Mohammad Khatami and Iraqi vice president Taha Yasin Ramadan. The meeting, which was "requested" by Ramadan, was described by Khatami as "a very important and crucial event."[179] In addition to oil politics, the Palestinian intifada also contributed to a closing of ranks. The rapprochement momentum continued with the visit of Iranian foreign minister Kamal Kharrazi to Baghdad later in October, when he met with President Husayn.

The two sides continued to host reciprocal visits by delegations and individuals until the end of the year, but despite the improved atmosphere, none of the basic bilateral problems were solved.

THE INTRICATE IRAQI-TURKISH RELATIONSHIP

Ever since the Gulf War, relations between Iraq and Turkey were determined more by external factors than by direct bilateral ones, in contrast to the situation prior to the war. Iraq had two major grievances against Turkey, namely, that it continued to be part of the anti-Iraqi camp, and that it had forged a strategic alliance with Israel. It accused Turkey, along with Saudi Arabia and Kuwait, of responsibility for the daily "acts of aggression" against Baghdad by allowing American and British planes to fly from its bases in order to carry out attacks against Iraq. It claimed that a total of 4,306 flights had been made by American and British planes from the Incirlik base in Turkey between December 1998 and June 2000.[180] Iraq submitted a complaint to the Arab League on the matter, requesting Arab support against Turkey, although without any tangible result. The Iraqi media, too, attacked Turkey, ridiculing its tilt to the West as hopeless and arguing that its interests lay in befriending the Arabs rather than turning into a "mere geostrategic basis for the West."[181]

No less worrisome for Baghdad was the Turkish-Israeli strategic alliance (see *MECS* 1996, p. 349). Two issues in this context came in for special criticism during the year: the construction by Turkey of a spy satellite, and the mooted sale of water to Israel. Reports of the Turkish decision to cooperate with Israel in building the first Turkish spy satellite came under harsh attack by Iraq, which questioned what need Turkey could have for such a satellite if not to spy against Arab countries and harm them further.[182] As an Iraqi Foreign Ministry spokesperson stated: "Choosing the Zionist entity as an ally to supply Turkey with a spy satellite can only be viewed as a negative step, a miscalculation and a wrong view of the present and future of the region."[183] Similarly, Iraq expressed strong opposition to the intention of Turkey to sell water to Israel, even though the supply in question would not be drawn from the Euphrates or Tigris Rivers, which run through Iraq, but from the Manavgat River.

The issue of water remained a thorny problem between the two countries on the bilateral level, and the impasse regarding how Tigris and Euphrates water should be shared between the littoral countries, alongside anger at the Turkish-Israeli alliance, were probably the main causes of the rapprochement between Iraq and Syria. So grave was the issue of water for Iraqis that even the opposition outside Iraq formed a committee "to defend Iraq's water rights" against Turkish encroachment at a time when Iraq was "weak" and incapable of reacting. The Turkish military incursions into Iraqi Kurdistan for the purpose of rooting out the Turkish Kurdish PKK forces were another cause for Iraqi concern, even though they were, by now, familiar occurrences. Iraq could do nothing to prevent them except issue protests and denunciations. Linked to this were Iraqi[184] fears regarding the deepening Turkish involvement with and support for the Iraqi Turkomans,[185] Turkish allies in Iraqi Kurdistan (see above).

With this, certain strong common interests helped balance out the negative aspects of their relationship to some extent. These concerns were maintaining the flow of oil through the Iraqi-Turkish pipeline or by smuggling routes, and the containment of the Iraqi-Kurdish autonomous region. Significantly, both countries highlighted the large losses incurred by Turkey because of the sanctions.[186] However, it was only in October that

Turkey took the symbolic step of violating the sanctions by sending a plane to Baghdad. Following the lead of various other countries, Turkey, too, initiated a new approach to Baghdad, focusing on Iraqi plans for three new projects: the opening of a new border crossing for increased trade between the two countries; the establishment of a joint Turkish and Iraqi consortium to extract and ship natural gas through Turkey; and the laying of a new pipeline parallel to the Kirkuk-Yurmurtalik pipeline. Presumably, these lucrative projects were dangled before Turkey to encourage it to quit the American-British camp and ignore the sanctions altogether. Turkey, however, still viewed its interests as lying essentially with the West. For all their importance, the implementation of these ambitious projects would have to wait for better times.

RIDING THE WAVE OF THE PALESTINIAN INTIFADA

The second Palestinian intifada, which erupted in September 2000 (see chapter on the PA), provided Iraq with an opportunity to reassert its militant posture with greater vigor. Baghdad sought to use the intifada as a lever to promote a series of cherished aims:

(1) Avenge the decade of sanctions and the suffering of the Iraqi people by targeting Israel, the regional "alter ego" of the US;

(2) Undermine the two pillars of American policy in the region: dual containment and the Arab-Israeli peace process;

(3) Bring about the complete erosion of the sanctions against Iraq;[187]

(4) End Iraq's regional and international isolation and accelerate its return to the Arab fold;

(5) Lead the radical Arab line regarding Palestine, in opposition to Egypt's moderate stance;

(6) Goad the Palestinians in Jordan to press their government to adopt a pro-Iraqi and anti-Israel line; and

(7) Reinforce Iraqi-Palestinian ties.

Iraq pursued its objectives declaratively and in practice. Saddam Husayn escalated his anti-Israeli rhetoric by calling on all Israeli Jews — Ashkenazi and Sephardi alike — to leave the country forever, and by vowing to liberate Palestine "from the [Jordan] river to the Mediterranean." His pronouncements and others in the Iraqi media, were increasingly peppered with antisemitic themes, including quotations from the Qur'an referring to the "ugly" Jew.[188] At the same time, Saddam moved five Iraqi divisions to the Syrian border, declaring that if the Iraqi army were given access, it would be able to defeat Israel by itself.[189] This act was designed, in part, to impress upon the young and inexperienced rulers of Syria and Jordan that the regional balance of power favored Iraq.

Saddam also used the intifada to mobilize popular support. The Iraqi case in this respect was unique, as the perceptions of the Palestinian issue in the Arab "street" were in harmony with the view of the Iraqi regime. Consequently, the regime could itself promulgate a radical line, rather than being forced to respond to popular pressure, as was the case in Egypt, Jordan or even Syria. Saddam reportedly enlisted more than six million "volunteers," including two million women, to fight for the Palestinian cause. He also provided material support to the Palestinians, the most dramatic example being grants of $10,000 to the families of "martyrs" (Palestinians killed in clashes with Israel).[190] This drove home the message that the Palestinians and the Iraqis were one people, and that despite its own severe financial problems, Iraq was willing to sacrifice for this cause as no other Arab country had done. Moreover, Saddam transferred this money through his own agents, allowing him to circumvent the Palestinian Authority (PA), infiltrate the Palestinian 'street' and increase his popularity.

However, the magnanimous behavior of Iraq toward the Palestinians was for export only. Its treatment of resident Palestinians was among the worst in the Arab world. The percentage of Palestinians in the total population was lower than in any other Arab country,[191] the result of a policy of systematic exclusion. In 1975, when Baghdad opened its gates to all Arabs and provided them with full citizenship, it excluded the Palestinians from this offer.[192] During the Iran-Iraq War, when it welcomed more than a million Egyptian workers into the country, it continued to exclude Palestinians. The same was true following the Gulf War, although the Palestinians had supported Iraq in its conflict with Kuwait. Until recently, Palestinians in Iraq were forbidden to purchase a house or a car or even install a telephone line. By 2000 they were permitted to buy these things, although not to inherit them.[193]

If the Palestinians were aware of this duality in the Iraqi attitude toward them, they did not allow it to influence their perception of Saddam. For them, he was an authentic Arab hero who in 1990–91 had dared challenge the only superpower in the world and had survived its massive assault against him, and who boosted their morale by launching missiles against Israel and sending its residents scurrying to their shelters. The intifada and the developments in Iraq strengthened these bonds further.

LIST OF GOVERNORS IN THE YEAR 2000*

Name	Name of Governorate	Previous Military Position
1) 'Abd al-Wahid Shinnan al-Ribat	Baghdad	Army Chief of Staff
2) Ahmad Ibrahim Hammash	Basra	Assistant Chief of Staff for Administration
3) Najm al-Din 'Abdallah Husayn al-Dur Muhammad	Wasit	Assistant Chief of Staff for Administration
4) Sabah Nuri 'Alwan	Al-Ta'mim	Commander of the 3rd Corps
5) Fawzi Humud 'Ulawi	Diyala	Staff Maj. Gen.
6) Muhammad 'Abd al-Rahman 'Abd al-Qadir	Ninwa	Assistant Army Chief of Staff
7) Latif Mahal Humud	Anbar	Staff Brig. Gen.
8) Mahmud Fayzi al-Hazza' Muhammad	Maysan	Commander of the 1st Corps
9) Iyad Khalil al-Rawi Zaki	Muthanna	Assistant Chief of Staff for Supplies
10) Qa'id Husayn Humaydi al-'Awwadi	Al-Najaf	
11) Al-Hakan Hasam 'Ali	Babil	Air Force Commander
12) 'Abd Tariq Sadiq al-Husayn	Al-Qadisiyya	Staff Lt. Gen.
13) Tariq Fayzi al-Hazza'	Salah al-Din	Staff Maj. Gen.
14) Sabir 'Abd al-'Aziz al-Duri	Karbala	Head of Military Intelligence

15) Ahmad 'Abdallah Salih Hammadi al-Jaburi	Dhi-Qar	Staff Maj. Gen.

* The table was prepared with the help of Ayelet Baruch.

SOURCES

1. *Al-'Iraq*, 22 September 1997; 1 February 2000.
2. *Babil*, 12 July 1994; *al-'Iraq*, 29 September 2000.
3. *Alif Ba*, 26 February 1997; Iraqi TV, 20 May 2000 (BBC Monitoring).
4. *Babil*, 23 April 1994; Iraqi TV, 20 May 2000 (BBC Monitoring).
5. Iraqi TV, 20 May 2000 (BBC Monitoring).
6. R. Baghdad, 26 April 1993 (DR); *al-'Iraq*, 23 June 2000.
7. R. Baghdad, 26 January 1992 (BBC Monitoring); Iraqi TV, 12 January 2000 (BBC Monitoring).
8. *Al-Wasat*, 26 June 1994; Iraqi TV, 8 May 2000 (BBC Monitoring).
9. Michael Eisenstadt, "Like a Phoenix from the Ashes," *The Washington Institute Policy Papers*, 36 (1993), pp. 1-99; *al-'Iraq*, 23 June 2000.
10. *Al-'Iraq*, 19 May 2000.
11. *Babil*, 23 April 1994; *al-'Iraq*, 19 May 2000.
12. *Al-Thawra*, 28 September 1997 (DR).
13. VoIP, 16 September 1997 (BBC Monitoring); *al-'Iraq*, 4 August 2000.
14. *Al-Thawra*, 28 August 1988; *al-'Iraq*, 23 June 2000.
15. VoIP, 16 September 1997 (BBC Monitoring); *al-'Iraq*, 23 June 2000.

NOTES
For the place and frequency of publications cited here, and for the full name of the publication, news agency, radio station or monitoring service where an abbreviation is used, please see "List of Sources." Only in the case of more than one publication bearing the same name is the place of publication noted here. All references to *al-Thawra* and *al-Jumhuriyya* are to the Baghdad dailies.

1. Anonymous, *Zabiba wal-Malik* (n.p.: Matba'at al-Bilad); *al-Thawra*, 17, 18 December 2000.
2. *Al-'Iraq*, 31 May 2001 (BBC Monitoring).
3. *Al-Hayat*, 15 February 2000.
4. Iraqi TV, 3 April 2000 (BBC Monitoring).
5. *Al-Jumhuriyya*, 27 August 2000.
6. *Ha'aretz*, 11 August 2000.
7. *Babil*, 8 June 2000.
8. *Al-'Iraq*, 29 February 2000.
9. *Alif Ba*, 26 April 2000.
10. *Alif Ba*, 3 May 2000.
11. *Alif Ba*, 6 May 2000.
12. *Al-Jumhuriyya*, 25 January 2000.
13. *Al-Sharq al-Awsat* (Internet version), 6 October 2000.
14. *Al-Hayat*, 17 September 2000 (BBC Monitoring).
15. *Al-Hayat* (Internet version), 22 February 2000.
16. *Al-Watan al-'Arabi*, 14 April 2000.

17. *Babil*, 7 January; *al-'Iraq*, 8 February, 5 December; *al-Thawra*, 17 July; *al-Sharq al-Awsat*, 4 August; *al-Jumhuriyya*, 15 October 2000.

18. R. Free Europe, 20 November 2000. Another account about him circulated following the defection of a member of his inner circle, Majid Kamil 'Aziz. *The Times* (Internet version), 13 February 2000.

19. 'Udayy's "media empire" included the newspapers and periodicals *Sawt al-Talaba*, *al-Ittihad*, *al-Shabab*, *al-Rafidayn*, *Nabd al-Shabab*, *al-I'lam*, *al-Zaman*, *al-Ra'y*, *al-Ba'th* and *al-Riyadi*. Some of these were available on the Internet, to which he controlled access.

20. *Babil*, 9 March 2000.

21. *Al-Tadamun*, 14 August; *al-Quds al-'Arabi*, 14 December 2000.

22. E.g., *Babil*, 28 January, 29 March 2000. One photograph showed him seated on a throne-like chair. *Zawra*, 9 April 2000.

23. E.g., *al-Shabab*, 2000 (no date); *Babil*, 28 February; *al-Rafidayn*, February 2000.

24. *Babil*, 9 March 2000.

25. *Al-Ittihad* (Baghdad), 2 May 2000.

26. 'Udayy claimed to have become a Ba'th Party member in 1975, namely, at the age of 11 (he was born in 1964). Al-Jazira TV, 27 March 2000 (BBC Monitoring).

27. *Babil*, 22, 23 January, 9 March 2000.

28. *Babil*, 25 March 2000.

29. Ibid.

30. *FT*, 1 April 2000.

31. *Al-Hayat*, 16 May 2000.

32. The list of candidates was published in *al-Jumhuriyya*, 15 March 2000.

33. Al-Jazira TV, 27 March 2000 (BBC Monitoring).

34. *Babil*, 30 March 2000.

35. *Nabd al-Shabab*, 28 February 2000. An essay in *al-Rafidayn* reviewing a century of Iraqi history included an account of the attempt on his life in 1996, transformed into a story of heroism and sacrifice for the homeland. *Al-Rafidayn*, February 2000.

36. *Al-Ittihad*, 2 May 2000.

37. E.g., *Babil*, 11, 15, 22 June 1999.

38. *Babil*, 24 June 2000.

39. *The Military Balance, 2000–2001*. London: The International Institute for Strategic Studies, 2000, p. 149.

40. *Babil*, 22 January 2000.

41. *Al-'Iraq*, 1 February 2000.

42. *Al-Hayat*, 22 March; *al-Sharq al-Awsat*, 28 March 2000.

43. R. Baghdad, 26 March (BBC Monitoring); Iraqi TV, 28 March 2000 (BBC Monitoring).

44. *Al-I'lam*, 21 June 2000.

45. Iraqi TV, 24 December (BBC Monitoring); al-Jazira TV, 24 December 2000 (BBC Monitoring).

46. *Al-'Iraq*, 2 February; Iraqi TV, 2 April 2000 (BBC Monitoring).

47. *Al-'Iraq*, 4 February 2000.

48. *Al-Jumhuriyya*, 22 February 2000.

49. *Al-'Iraq*, 5, 7, 9 September 2000.

50. *Al-Jumhuriyya*, 1 March 2000.

51. *Al-'Iraq*, 23, 27 June, 8, 22 July, 3 August; *al-Jumhuriyya*, 2, 6 August 2000.

52. *Al-Thawra*, 9 July 2000.

53. *Al-Jumhuriyya*, 24 May 2000.

54. *Al-Hayat*, 6 July 2000.

55. Iraqi Communist Party website, 6 January (BBC Monitoring); *'Ukaz*, 26 January (BBC Monitoring); *al-Zaman*, 28 February, 6 April (BBC Monitoring); *al-Sharq al-Awsat*, 12 April (BBC Monitoring); *al-Hayat*, 25 April 2000 (BBC Monitoring).

56. Iraqi TV, 6 April (BBC Monitoring); *Babil*, 8 April; Iraqi satellite TV, 13 August (BBC Monitoring); *al-Jumhuriyya*, 20 August 2000.

57. *Al-'Iraq*, 8 July 2000.
58. Iraqi TV, 20 May 2000 (BBC Monitoring).
59. *Al Jumhuriyya*, 12 February 2000.
60. Iraqi Satellite TV, 25 June 2000 (BBC Monitoring).
61. *Al Jumhuriyya*, 27 February 2000.
62. Iraqi TV, 10 September 2000 (BBC Monitoring).
63. R. Baghdad, 11 July (BBC Monitoring); *al-Thawra*, 14 December 2000. The land was tax free and could also be sold.
64. *CR*, Iraq, November 2000, p. 23.
65. *Al-Sharq al-Awsat*, 28 November 2000.
66. *JP*, 2 May 2000.
67. Iraqi TV, 21 March 2000 (BBC Monitoring).
68. Iraqi TV, 11 June 2000 (BBC Monitoring).
69. *Al-'Iraq*, 4 July 2000.
70. *Al-'Iraq*, 5 September 2000.
71. *Al-Hayat*, 26 February (BBC Monitoring); *Alif Ba*, 24 May 2000.
72. *The Middle East*, July 2000.
73. *Babil*, 22 January; *al-Zawra*, 4 May 2000.
74. Iraqi TV, 17 December 2000 (BBC Monitoring).
75. *CR*, Iraq, November 2000, p. 22.
76. *Al-'Iraq*, 1 September 2000.
77. *Al-Sharq al-Awsat*, 26 March (BBC Monitoring); *al-'Iraq*, 12 May 2000.
78. *Nabd al-Shabab*, 5 June; *al-Thawra*, 11 December 2000.
79. *Al-Ra'y*, 12 March; *Alif Ba*, 5 April 2000.
80. *Alif Ba*, 3 May 2000.
81. *Al-Rafidayn*, February 2000.
82. Iraqi TV, 7 May (BBC Monitoring); *al-'Iraq*, 5 December 2000.
83. *Al-Jumhuriyya*, 8 August; *Alif Ba*, 30 September 2000.
84. *Al-Hayat*, 25 June; *al-Thawra*, 2 July 2000.
85. *Alif Ba*, 26 April 2000.
86. *Alif Ba*, 31 May 2000.
87. *Alif Ba*, 9 February 2000.
88. *Al-'Iraq*, 11, 22 February 2000.
89. *Al-Zaman*, 2 February 2000 (BBC Monitoring).
90. IRNA, 17 February (DR); *al-Ayyam* (Manama), 15 March 2000 (BBC Monitoring).
91. *Al-Hayat*, 29 February 2000 (BBC Monitoring).
92. *Al-Quds al-'Arabi*, 4 April 2000 (BBC Monitoring).
93. *Al-Sharq al-Awsat*, 13 May; *al-Hayat*, 18 September 2000 (BBC Monitoring).
94. *Alif Ba*, 8 March 2000.
95. *Al-'Iraq*, 12 February; *al-Zawra*, 6 April 2000 (BBC Monitoring).
96. *Alif Ba*, 14, 28 June 2000.
97. Iraqi TV, 27 November 2000 (BBC Monitoring).
98. *Alif Ba*, 28 June 2000.
99. *Al-Thawra*, 2 July; *al-Jumhuriyya*, 10 July 2000.
100. R. Baghdad, 29 April 2000 (BBC Monitoring).
101. *Alif Ba*, 12 January 2000.
102. *Alif Ba*, 27 September 2000.
103. *MM*, 27 June 2000.
104. An anti-hero by the name of Chalabi appeared in the novel.
105. *Al-Wasat*, 17 July 2000.
106. *MM*, 14 February; *al-Hayat*, 15 February, 13 December 2000 (BBC Monitoring).
107. *Al-'Iraq*, 25 March; *al-Hayat*, 27 September 2000 (BBC Monitoring).
108. *Al-Hayat*, 12 March 2000 (BBC Monitoring).
109. *The Times* (Internet version), 9, 31 July 2000.

110. Prague CTK, 17, 18 January 2000 (DR).
111. *WSJ* (Internet version), 6 January; Kurdistan TV International (Salah al-Din), 19 February (BBC Monitoring); *al-Sharq al-Awsat*, 5 May 2000.
112. *Khabat* (Internet version), 14 January 2000 (BBC Monitoring).
113. *Al-Hayat*, 5 November 2000.
114. *Kurdistani Nuwe* (Sulaymaniyya, Internet version), 15 November 2000 (BBC Monitoring).
115. *Al-Mushahid al-Siyasi*, 10 December 2000.
116. *Al-Sharq al-Awsat*, 5 May 2000.
117. *Brayati* (Irbil, Internet version), 21 May 2000 (BBC Monitoring).
118. Kurdistan satellite TV (Salah al-Din), 27 June 2000 (BBC Monitoring). According to the PUK, Gore promised protection to the "liberated" area of Kurdistan; KurdSat (Sulaymaniyya), 27 June 2000 (BBC Monitoring).
119. The PUK quoted a KDP source as saying that Barzani did not want to meet with Talabani to discuss problems. *Kurdistani Nuwe* (Internet version), 9 July 2000 (BBC Monitoring).
120. *Kurdistani Nuwe* (Internet version), 14 August 2000 (BBC Monitoring).
121. *Kurdistani Nuwe* (Internet version), 25 March 2000 (BBC Monitoring).
122. *Al-Sharq al-Awsat*, 9 May 2000 (BBC Monitoring).
123. Kurdistan satellite TV, 23 November 2000 (BBC Monitoring).
124. Anatolia News Agency, 20 March 2000 (BBC Monitoring).
125. Kurdistan satellite TV, 11 June (BBC Monitoring); R. Damascus, 21, 22 November 2000 (BBC Monitoring).
126. *Al-Hayat*, 13 March 2000.
127. *Al-Sharq al-Awsat*, 6 December 2000 (*MM*).
128. Kurdistan TV International, 13 January 2000 (BBC Monitoring).
129. Anatolia News Agency, 25 July 2000 (BBC Monitoring).
130. KurdSat TV, 7 December 2000 (BBC Monitoring).
131. *Turkoman Eli* (Irbil), 22 March 2000 (BBC Monitoring).
132. KDP satellite TV, 28 March 2000 (BBC Monitoring).
133. Anatolia News Agency, 14 July 2000 (BBC Monitoring).
134. *Kurdistani Nuwe* (Internet version), 25 March (BBC Monitoring); *MM*, 29 June 2000.
135. *Al-'Iraq*, 2 February 2000.
136. Kurdistan satellite TV, 10 March 2000 (BBC Monitoring). The group denied the authenticity of the confession. Kurdistan satellite TV, 31 August 2000 (BBC Monitoring).
137. Anatolia News Agency, 21 September 2000 (BBC Monitoring).
138. See, for example, a film by John Pilger, "Paying the Price: Killing the Children of Iraq," 57 min., 2000.
139. *Le Monde*, 7 January 2000.
140. *WP* (Internet version), 20 February 2000.
141. *FT*, 15 March; *NYT* (Internet version), 25 March 2000.
142. *NYT* (Internet version), 27 January 2000.
143. *The Times*, 9 March 2000.
144. *NYT* (Internet version), 8 February; *El Mundo* (Internet version), 2 April; *JP*, 25 May 2000.
145. UPI, 13 November 2000.
146. *JP*, 10 March; *NYT* (Internet version), 13 September 2000.
147. *Al-Malaf al-Iraqi*, March 2000 — *MM*, 1 March 2000.
148. See, e.g., "Americans Against Sanctions," *MERIP*, No. 215, Summer 2000, pp. 36–37.
149. *WP* (Internet version), 20 February 2000.
150. *Le Monde*, 28 April 2000.
151. R. Baghdad, 28 October (BBC Monitoring); *al-Quds al-'Arabi*, 14 November 2000.
152. *WP* (Internet version), 18 January 2000.
153. Interfax, 31 May (BBC Monitoring), 2 June; ITAR-TASS, 13 September (DR), 22 September (BBC Monitoring); RIA, 9 November (DR), 2000.
154. ITAR-TASS, 23 September (DR); R. Baghdad, 27 October 2000 (BBC Monitoring).

155. Interfax, 25 September 2000 (DR).
156. Interfax, 16 May 2000 (BBC Monitoring).
157. Quoted by *JP*, 17 April 2000.
158. *The Times* (Internet version), 14 August 2000.
159. *Al-Hayat*, 27 September, 5 October; *MM*, 5 October; *JT* (Internet version), 10 October; *AW* (Internet version), 19–25 October; *NYT* (Internet version), 31 October 2000.
160. *Al-Wasat*, 13 November 2000.
161. *Al-Quds al-'Arabi*, 27 November 2000 (*MM*).
162. INA, 13 October; Iraqi TV, 23 October (BBC Monitoring); *NYT*, 31 October 2000.
163. *Al-Safir* (Internet version), 20 November (DR); *al-Quds al-'Arabi*, 20 December 2000 (*MM*).
164. Ibid.
165. *Al-Dustur*, 2 November 2000 (DR).
166. *Al-Dustur*, 4 November (DR); *al-Quds al-'Arabi*, 8 November 2000 (*MM*).
167. *JT* (Internet version), 1 November 2000 (DR).
168. *Al-Thawra*, 10 April 2000 (BBC Monitoring).
169. *Al-Jumhuriyya*, 30 April 2000.
170. *Al-Jumhuriyya*, 2 August; *Babil*, 7 August (DR); *al-'Iraq*, 29 September 2000.
171. *Al-Sharq al-Awsat*, 4 November 2000.
172. Ibid.; *al-Quds al-'Arabi*, 14 November 2000.
173. IRNA, 15 October 2000 (DR).
174. *JP* (quoting Reuters), 10 April; *AW* (Internet version), 13 April 2000.
175. Ibid.; *al-Hayat*, 7 October 2000 (BBC Monitoring).
176. *Al-Hayat*, 3 January 2000 (BBC Monitoring).
177. *Al-Thawra*, 22 September 2000 (DR).
178. *Al-Hayat*, 7 October 2000 (DR).
179. *Iran* (Internet version), 2 October 2000 (BBC Monitoring).
180. *Al-Thawra*, 10 July 2000.
181. *Babil*, 8 June; *al-Thawra*, 10 July; *al-'Iraq*, 22 July 2000.
182. *Al-'Iraq*, 22, 29 July; *al-Thawra*, 17 July 2000.
183. R. Baghdad, 17 July 2000 (BBC Monitoring).
184. *Al-Sharq al-Awsat*, 23 September 2000 (DR).
185. R. Baghdad, 29 July (BBC Monitoring); *al-'Iraq*, 29 September 2000.
186. According to one inflated estimate, Turkish losses since the Gulf War were $40bn. *Milliyet*, 31 October 2000 (DR).
187. Sa'dun Hammadi, speaker of the parliament, declared that Baghdad rejected offers to recognize Israel in return for lifting the sanctions. *Al-'Arab al-Yawm*, 21 February 2000 (BBC Monitoring).
188. *Al-'Iraq*, 29 September, 20 October; Iraqi TV, 8, 21, 22 October, 2 December (BBC Monitoring); *al-Thawra*, 7 December; *al-'Iraq*, 26 December 2000.
189. Iraqi TV, 3 October 2000 (BBC Monitoring). Even the supposedly moderate Tariq 'Aziz declared that there was no way to liberate Palestine other than jihad and armed struggle. R. Baghdad, 6 October 2000 (BBC Monitoring).
190. This figure was quoted to the author by a journalist who works in the PA. According to an Iraqi announcement, the martyrs of Palestine would be given the same rights and privileges as the Iraqi martyrs of the Iran-Iraq War. Iraqi TV, 5 October 2000 (BBC Monitoring). The privileges given to the families of Iraqi martyrs were two monthly salaries; a car, or ID 5,000 = $16,722; and a house or apartment (see *MECS* 1980–81, p. 583). A few days later, Iraq declared that it would contribute c.$5m. (Iraqi TV, 8 October 2000 (BBC Monitoring).
191. The figure, according to a Palestinian source, was 65,000: 35,000 refugees and 30,000 residents. *Al-Ayyam* (Ramallah), 12 March 2000 (BBC Monitoring).
192. Ibid.
193. *Al-Hayat*, 27 June 2000.

Israel

(Medinat Yisrael)

LESLIE SUSSER AND ELIE REKHESS*

The year 2000 was dominated by the disintegration of Prime Minister Ehud Barak's government and the breakdown of the peace process with the Palestinians. The two developments were not unconnected. The more concessions Barak seemed willing to make to the Palestinians, the more coalition partners he lost; and when peacemaking degenerated into violent confrontation in late September, his implicit working assumption — that a final peace deal with the Palestinians was attainable — was seriously discredited. By the end of the year he had resigned, was awaiting elections and trailing Likud leader Ariel Sharon in the opinion polls.[1]

Barak's failures created optimal conditions for former prime minister Benjamin Netanyahu to make a dramatic political comeback. After Attorney General Elyakim Rubinstein decided not to indict Netanyahu on charges of bribery and corruption, the way was clear for the former prime minister's return to public life. Barak's failure on the peace front seemed to vindicate Netanyahu's hard line toward the Palestinians, and he seemed almost certain to displace the seventy-two-year-old Sharon as Likud leader and then unseat Barak as prime minister. But he withdrew his candidacy when the Knesset voted for elections for prime minister only, and not for a new parliament.[2]

Whereas Netanyahu made a comeback, three other leading politicians fell from grace. President Ezer Weizmann resigned over gifts he had received from two businessmen friends;[3] former defense minister Yitzhak Mordechai, who just a year earlier had been a candidate for prime minister, withdrew from public life following allegations of sexual harassment;[4] and former Shas party leader Arye Der'i was jailed for three years on charges of fraud.[5] Moshe Katzav of the Likud became Israel's eighth president after a surprise election victory over Shimon Peres of Labor in the Knesset, a result that reflected Barak's political weakness.[6]

Indeed, Barak's overreaching and consequent loss of credibility was not confined to the peace process. He had also promised and failed to bring about sweeping reforms in the area of religion and state. The Tal Committee he established was widely expected to set tighter criteria for deferments for *yeshiva* (Jewish religious seminary) students from army service, and his "civil agenda" was designed to enhance secular freedom and curtail the power of the religious establishment. But both initiatives had little effect on the status quo.[7]

The new Palestinian intifada, by contrast, had an enormous impact on Israeli domestic affairs. For one, it put paid to Barak's hopes of turning the sluggish economy around. In each of the first three quarters, there were encouraging signs of economic recovery, but

* Author of the section on the Arabs in Israel.

Israel, the West Bank, and the Gaza Strip

the intifada broke the pattern of accelerated growth, and precipitated a new bout of stagnation and rising unemployment.[8]

Worse was its impact on relations between the Arab minority in Israel and the Israeli establishment. Intifada-related rioting by Israeli Arabs in October led to thirteen Arab deaths at the hands of the security forces and unprecedented tension and distrust between the Jewish majority and the Arab minority in Israel, as well as between the Arab minority and the Labor-led government and its leader.[9]

Most significantly, though, the intifada disrupted what seemed to be a promising peace process. Although the parties failed to reach agreement at a summit at Camp David in July, they continued negotiating and were significantly closer to a deal when the fighting erupted.[10]

The continuing cycle of violence and retaliation led to tension between Israel and the Arab world, including the countries with which Israel was formally at peace. But concerns that these strains would spark a regional war proved unfounded.[11]

Barak's failure to conclude an agreement with the Palestinians was compounded by an earlier breakdown on the Syrian track. Negotiations that began in January in Shepherdstown, West Virginia, amid predictions of a quick breakthrough and an early peace deal, fizzled out inconclusively and were not renewed.[12]

Barak had hoped to include an Israeli withdrawal from the security zone in South Lebanon as part of an agreement with Syria. But when the talks broke down, he decided to withdraw from Lebanon unilaterally. In late May, Israeli forces pulled back to the international border, ending eighteen years of relentless confrontation with the Shi'i Hizballah militia in South Lebanon.[13] Predictions that the Hizballah would follow the retreating forces and attack Israeli towns and villages across the border after the pullback failed to materialize. The withdrawal was far and away Barak's most significant achievement, although critics charged that it encouraged the Palestinian intifada.[14]

INTERNAL AFFAIRS

BARAK'S FALL

A Credibility Gap Widens

Prime Minister Ehud Barak's political persona, inherent coalition difficulties and colossal policy failures dominated domestic politics and culminated in one of the most dramatic falls from public favor in Israeli political history. Elected in May 1999 with an unprecedented personal majority, he ended the year 2000 facing new prime ministerial elections and trailing his opponent, Likud leader Ariel Sharon, by 13%–21% in public opinion polls.[15]

The year began with the prime minister deep in negotiations with Syria, promising a pullout of troops from Lebanon and speedy completion of a peace deal with the Palestinians. He projected a grand vision of peace on all three remaining fronts: Syrian, Lebanese and Palestinian, but failed comprehensively to deliver. He lost right-wing support for going as far as he did in his peacemaking efforts, and he lost much of the center and the left when, despite his unprecedented peace offer to the Palestinians, the Palestinian intifada erupted in late September.

By then the internal contradictions in his coalition, between ultra-Orthodox Shas and secular Meretz, and between Labor and the right-wing National Religious Party (NRP),

Yisrael ba-Aliya and Shas had already eroded his hold on power. Moreover, his instrumental treatment of people made him many enemies and lost him close friends. Sharp policy swings when the peace process ran into difficulty cost him much of what remained of his tarnished credibility. By the end of the year, the Israeli electorate seemed set to punish Barak for promising so much and delivering so little.[16]

Barak's NPOs
The first crack in the prime minister's credibility came in late January when Attorney General Elyakim Rubinstein ordered a criminal investigation into the 1999 campaign financing of five political parties, including Barak's One Israel electoral slate. The investigation was called after State Comptroller Eliezer Goldberg issued a strongly worded report singling out One Israel for circumventing laws restricting foreign donations. In Barak's case, funds had reportedly been funneled to his campaign through a number of non-profit organizations (NPOs). Commenting on Goldberg's report, Barak said: "I didn't know most of the NPOs, I wasn't involved in fund-raising and I wasn't involved specifically in any one of the activities described in the report." Goldberg ordered the party to pay a fine of 13.5m. shekels (about $3.4m.). At year's end, the criminal investigation was still ongoing.[17]

Coalition Infighting
The NPO affair exacerbated Barak's already acute political problems. But well before it emerged, Barak's sixty-eight-member coalition was showing serious signs of instability. As negotiations with Syria progressed in January, the NRP and the Russian immigrant party, Yisrael ba-Aliyah, threatened to leave the government if Israel agreed to withdraw from the Golan Heights. In mid-March, they were joined by Shas in defying coalition discipline and voting against Education Minister Yossi Sarid's decision to include works by Palestinian poet Mahmud Darwish in the literature curriculum. Shortly afterwards, Shas spiritual mentor Rabbi Ovadiah Yosef launched a vitriolic attack against Sarid, branding the Meretz leader a "devil," and urging that "his name be obliterated."[18]

The reason for the rabbi's ire was Meretz leader Sarid's refusal to allocate funds for the ailing educational network of Shas, Ma'ayan Hahinuch Hatorani. In an attempt to defuse the crisis, Barak met Yosef on 30 April, but despite the prime minister's pledges of financial support for the Shas educational network, the rabbi declined to promise automatic support for Barak's peace moves.[19] Shas's move to the right was highlighted just two weeks later, when, on 15 May, the cabinet approved the transfer of three Arab villages around Jerusalem, Abu Dis, al-'Azariyya and Sawahra to Palestinian Authority (PA) control by fifteen votes to six. The four Shas ministers, NRP Housing Minister Yitzhak Levy and Interior Minister Natan Sharansky of Yisrael ba-Aliya cast the dissenting votes.[20]

In late June, the crisis with Shas over education funding flared up again. In order to put pressure on Barak, Shas had voted with the Likud for early elections, and its four cabinet ministers threatened to resign.[21] In order to stop Shas from bolting the coalition, Barak agreed to provide extra funding and greater autonomy for the school system and to legalize Shas's unauthorized radio network. Meretz also helped Shas remain inside the government by pulling its three cabinet ministers out of it on 21 June, although the party remained in the coalition and continued to support Barak in the Knesset.[22] The next day, the four Shas ministers withdrew their letters of resignation,[23] and then voted with the government to overturn the early election legislation.[24]

The Coalition Collapses

But Barak's reprieve was short-lived and on 9 July his coalition effectively collapsed when six ministers resigned and all three dissident parties, Shas, the NRP and Yisrael ba-Aliyah, pulled out of the coalition in protest at Barak's refusal to consult them on the Israeli-Palestinian summit planned later that month at the American president's Camp David retreat. Shas leader Eli Yishai accused Barak of deciding unilaterally on "dangerous" concessions to the Palestinians and of refusing to indicate what his "red lines" were.[25]

Barak delayed his departure to the summit to attend a Knesset vote of no-confidence in the government on 10 July. Two opposition motions alluded to "dangerous concessions" that Barak was supposedly about to offer the Palestinians. After several hours of heated debate, the final count was just seven short of the absolute majority of sixty-one needed to topple the government. And there was more trouble in store. Foreign Minister David Levy refused to accompany Barak to Camp David, castigating the prime minister for offering too much to the Palestinians. "Israel has offered the maximum without getting even the minimum," Levy declared.[26] And on 2 August, just days after Barak's return from Camp David, Levy resigned. Barak appointed Public Security Minister Shlomo Ben Ami, who had in fact been leading the negotiations with the Palestinians, as acting foreign minister.[27]

Barak was now more vulnerable than ever. Levy's resignation left him with only forty votes he could count on in the 120-member Knesset. Moreover, the right-wing-religious alliance that had disintegrated under Netanyahu had been reconstituted. Sensing an opening, Sharon hired Arthur Finkelstein, the American campaign expert who had worked with Netanyahu during the previous two elections. Netanyahu himself began making public appearances, hinting broadly that he would soon be ready to make a political comeback.[28]

Loyal Troops Desert

In late August, Barak received another blow when Haim Mendel-Shaked, his bureau chief, resigned after publicly accusing Barak of being unable to work in a team. In a front-page article in Yedi'ot Aharonot on 21 August, Mendel-Shaked complained that Barak consistently ignored his advice and failed to delegate authority.[29] His resignation followed that of his deputy, Shimon Batat, and, taken together, the resignations seemed to confirm reports of Barak's instrumental treatment of the people around him, even those who, like Mendel-Shaked and Batat, came from the only peer group Barak seemed to trust — army friends, especially those who had served in the elite Sayeret Matkal commando unit that Barak commanded en route to becoming chief of staff.[30]

Barak's Abortive "Civil Agenda"

With the peace process seemingly on hold and his administration tottering, Barak announced a major new policy initiative in late August. No longer dependent on Shas support, he said he intended to focus on a new civil agenda, which would curb the power of the ultra-Orthodox establishment. But rather than turn things around for the prime minister, the new plan further eroded his diminishing credibility and was dismissed by most pundits as a transparent gambit by a struggling incumbent to retain power.[31] Mid-August polls had shown Labor losing eight of its twenty-three Knesset seats and Barak's support among mainly secular Russian immigrants plummeting to just 17%. And although the immigrants and other secular Israelis welcomed the new plan, they were, in the main, skeptical about the degree of the prime minister's commitment. And when, in the months ahead, there was little movement on the civil agenda, Barak's credibility suffered.[32]

The Intifada and the Prime Minister

The biggest blow by far to Barak's credibility was the outbreak, in late September, of the Palestinian intifada (see chapter on the PA). The eruption of violence after what most Israelis viewed as Barak's generous peace offer to the Palestinians at Camp David suggested that the prime minister had misread Palestinian intentions. No longer dictating timetables for peace deals, Barak seemed to have lost control of events, and, instead of his promise of peace and security, Israelis found themselves facing unprecedented violence and terror. The continuing intifada seemed to confirm the right-wing thesis that the Oslo process would not lead to peace with the Palestinians, and, seeking tougher action against the violence, the Israeli electorate moved to the right.[33]

Moreover, the intifada-related riots in Israel proper in late September and early October, in which twelve Israeli Arab citizens and a visiting West Banker were killed by police, had major political ramifications for Barak and the Labor party. Angry Arab citizens blamed Barak and Public Security Minister Shlomo Ben Ami for the killings. That ruled out the possibility of a narrow coalition which would have rested on the support of Arab MKs. It also seemed certain to hurt Barak's chances of re-election.[34]

National Unity Talks

As the violence continued, Barak formally suspended the peace process with the Palestinians on 20 October, and immediately opened negotiations with Sharon aimed at forming a broad-based emergency government.[35] But the talks foundered over Sharon's insistence that he have a veto on key political and security decisions.[36] Still, on 30 October, the day the Knesset reconvened, Binyamin Ben Eliezer of Labor and Meir Shitreet of the Likud managed to reach agreement on national unity. But Barak, still hoping to bring off an eleventh hour peace deal with the Palestinians, preferred to accept an offer from Shas for a thirty-day "safety net." His compliance with the condition for Shas support, freezing all movement on the civil agenda, was perceived as yet another policy zig-zag by the embattled prime minister.[37]

The Slide to Elections

On 28 November, Barak pre-empted opposition efforts to bring down his government by calling for a general election in 2001. In a speech televised live from the Knesset, and which took even his closest colleagues by surprise, he said he was not "afraid of elections" and that his government had a "proven record." The announcement came as Netanyahu, who was well ahead of Barak in opinion polls, was gearing up to replace Sharon, who still trailed the prime minister in the polls, as Likud leader.[38]

Barak moved quickly. The next day, in a bid to preempt a challenge to his leadership from within the Labor party, he convened the central committee and had himself confirmed as the party candidate for prime minister.[39] The specter of defeat by Netanyahu, however, proved too much for him, and, in yet another turnabout, he changed his mind about full-scale elections for the Knesset and the premiership. On 9 December, he announced his resignation as prime minister, but called for a special election to elect a new prime minister only, and not a new Knesset. The election law restricted special prime ministerial contests to MKs; Netanyahu had resigned his seat in the immediate aftermath of his defeat in the May 1999 election, thus rendering him ineligible.[40]

Initially, however, it seemed that Barak's move against Netanyahu would backfire. Netanyahu's supporters in the Knesset tabled legislation to allow any Israeli citizen, not only MKs, to run for prime minister in a special election, and Labor, unwilling to show that it had anything to fear from Netanyahu's candidacy, decided it would help push it through.[41]

On 14 December, however, Netanyahu declared that he wanted a general election for the Knesset as well, and would not run in a special election for prime minister only, arguing that the Knesset as presently constituted was unmanageable. Netanyahu hoped to persuade Shas to support a move to dissolve the legislature and thereby force a general election. But on 18 December the Shas Council of Sages decided to oppose new Knesset elections, possibly because opinion polls predicted that the Likud would make significant gains at the expense of Shas.[42]

The next day special legislation to allow Netanyahu to run in a special election for prime minister was passed by the Knesset, but the house voted against elections for a new parliament. Netanyahu refused to run under the amended rules and withdrew his candidacy for leadership of the Likud. As a result, elections for the party leadership, scheduled for the next day, were called off and Sharon emerged as the party's unanimously endorsed candidate. With his candidacy no longer under threat, Sharon quickly opened up a huge lead against Barak in the polls.[43]

Indeed, the December polls indicated that Barak had lost about 800,000 of the 1.8m. votes he had won to become prime minister in 1999. Barak had been hurt across the board by the intifada, but also by his alienation of two key voter groups, new immigrants from countries in the former Soviet Union and Israeli Arabs. Russian immigrants, who had backed him following his promises of security and secularism, felt he had let them down on both counts. As for the Arab vote, Barak had won over 90% in the 1999 election; the December polls gave him barely 11%. The erosion started almost immediately after the election when Barak refused to consider three mainly Arab parties as prospective coalition partners. Relations worsened when the peace process soured and broke down completely after the thirteen intifada-related Arab deaths in northern Israel.[44]

To win back disaffected voters, Barak based his re-election hopes on plans for a dramatic last minute deal with the Palestinians.[45] In late December, Barak and Clinton agreed on a package they hoped they could sell to the Israeli people and to the Palestinians. On 23 December, Clinton announced "the parameters of a deal," (see below and chapter on the Arab-Israeli peace process) and Israeli acceptance set the stage for a last gasp negotiation, which Barak hoped would win him the election.[46]

NETANYAHU MAKES A COMEBACK

On 28 March, after six months of investigation, the police recommended that former prime minister Binyamin Netanyahu and his wife Sara be tried on charges of bribery and corruption. The police claimed that the Netanyahus had taken some seven hundred gifts to the state, valued at about $100,000, when the former prime minister left office, and that, while in office, he had accepted free services from a building contractor who hoped to get more extensive work from the government in return. Netanyahu denied the charges and accused the police of trumping up the allegations in collusion with his political opponents.[47]

Six months later, on 27 September, Attorney General Elyakim Rubinstein announced that there would be no indictment for lack of sufficient evidence.[48] The decision paved the way for Netanyahu's return to politics. Netanyahu had actually begun his comeback a few months earlier. He made his first public move in July, when he attended the twenty-fifth anniversary celebration of the settlement at Ofrah in the West Bank. From then on, public opinion polls included Netanyahu in their lists of prospective prime ministerial candidates, and his lead over Barak grew as the months went by. In the Likud, most of the party's nineteen MKs lined up with Netanyahu against Sharon, and, in secret talks, the religious parties promised to back his candidacy as soon he made his comeback official.[49]

To focus all this energy, Yisrael Katz, one of Netanyahu's staunchest supporters in the Knesset, set up a political movement called "Zion for a Jewish and Democratic Israel." The basic idea was to form an electoral pact between the right-leaning and religious parties to be headed by Netanyahu.[50] Although Katz's work came to naught when Netanyahu decided not to run in the special election for prime minister, Sharon picked up support from the groups Katz had been trying to align formally.[51]

WEIZMANN RESIGNS

After a protracted scandal involving gifts worth about $450,000 that President Ezer Weizmann had allegedly accepted from two businessman friends, the president announced in late May that he intended to step down on July 10. The scandal broke when investigative journalist Yoav Yitzhak announced at a press conference on 30 December 1999 that Weizmann had been the recipient of regular, undeclared cash payments between 1988 and 1993 from Edouard Saroussi, a French Jewish businessman of Sudanese origin. During the years in question, Weizmann had served as a cabinet minister and MK.[52]

In a statement issued after Yitzhak's press conference, Weizmann insisted the payments were a legitimate gift from a personal friend who had no business interests in Israel, and were therefore not subject to tax. Subsequent press reports, however, hinted that Weizmann and Saroussi had been involved jointly in lucrative arms deals in Latin America in the 1980s.[53] On 20 January, Attorney General Elyakim Rubinstein ordered a full criminal inquiry after his office had found "alleged evidence of a relationship of a business nature between Mr Weizmann and a firm linked to Mr Saroussi between 1983 and 1984." In an address to the nation, Weizmann said that he would not resign the presidency and would "fight for the truth to the end." He also refused to take a leave of absence, arguing that "a man whose conscience is clear does not run away."[54]

A police report released on 6 April found insufficient evidence of bribery and tax evasion, but concluded that Weizmann had committed fraud and breach of trust by accepting unreported funds and favors from Saroussi and another private businessman, Rami Unger. Although the police did not recommend prosecution because of a statute of limitations, Weizmann was left with little choice but to step down.[55]

A Knesset election for a successor was scheduled for late July, and, in a surprise result, Moshe Katzav of the Likud defeated Labor elder statesman and Nobel Prize laureate Shimon Peres by sixty-three votes to fifty-seven in a secret ballot. The outcome was another blow to Barak's embattled administration, and once again it was apparently delivered by Shas, several of whose MKs had promised to vote for Peres, but in fact, cast ballots for Katzav.[56]

The fifty-five-year-old Katzav, who was born in Iran, was the first *Mizrahi* (Eastern) immigrant to be elected to the high office. He promised to introduce a more informal presidential style and said he hoped to be "the people's president."[57]

MORDECHAI INDICTED

President Weizmann was not the only holder of high office to fall from grace. On 9 July, Transport Minister Yitzhak Mordechai, who just over a year before had been the Center Party candidate for prime minister, was formally indicted on charges of sexual assault against three women. A few days earlier, Mordechai had consented to the Knesset lifting his parliamentary immunity, saying that he would prove his innocence in court. Court hearings began in November with Mordechai pleading not guilty to all the charges against him.[58]

The police investigation against Mordechai was launched on 6 March, after a member of his staff complained that he had sexually assaulted her. Protesting his innocence, Mordechai took a leave of absence while police examined the allegations. He told a press conference on 7 March that "everything I have been accused of is not true."[59]

The police findings, however, were very different. In mid-April, they recommended that Mordechai stand trial on charges of having sexually assaulted three women over the last eight years. Their recommendation that Mordechai be charged with "debased acts carried out with force" constituted a far more serious indictment than the original allegations of sexual harassment by the young transport ministry employee, and seemed almost certain to put paid to his political career. The affair also accelerated the disintegration of the ailing Center Party, which never recovered from its poor showing in the 1999 election. Tourism Minister Amnon Lipkin-Shahak took over as leader of the party but failed to reinvigorate it.[60]

RELIGION

Shas and the Kulturkampf

The fissures in Israeli society between Ashkenazim and Sephardim and between secular and observant Jews came to the fore through the outspoken militancy of the Orthodox, Sephardi Shas and its spiritual leader, Rabbi Ovadiah Yosef. Even the Holocaust became an issue. In early August, Yosef was widely criticized for asserting that the six million Jews who perished had died because of sins committed in previous lives. Yosef said: "The victims of the Holocaust were reincarnations of earlier souls who had sinned time and time again." His remarks deeply offended secular and religious Jews alike, who understood him to be casting a slur on the victims and insinuating that they had met their fate because they had not been observant enough. He also seemed, in a perverse twist of logic, to be implying that the Nazis were not evil, but somehow the agents of God.[61]

His remarks, which were recorded and later broadcast on Israel Radio, were strongly criticized by Barak, prominent rabbis and politicians from secular parties. In reply, Yosef, a former chief rabbi and an outstanding religious scholar, claimed that he had been misinterpreted and insisted that Holocaust victims "were holy and pure and absolute saints."[62]

The deep-seated feelings of antipathy between ultra-Orthodox and secular Israelis resurfaced in September when former Shas leader Arieh Der'i began serving a three-year prison sentence, following his conviction on charges of bribery and fraud. About 25,000 mainly Orthodox demonstrators gathered outside the Nitzan prison in Ramle to express support for Der'i, who addressed the crowd and begged forgiveness from anyone he might have wronged. Senior Shas politicians charged that Der'i had been unjustly convicted because of bias against religious and Sephardi Jews. Rabbi Ovadia Yosef compared his incarceration to that of the biblical Joseph, who emerged from prison "to reign over Israel."[63]

The Tal Committee Report

The blanket deferment of yeshiva students from military service, compulsory for all other Israeli Jews, remained a sore point with many secular and religious Israelis after a committee set up to deal with the issue published a report in mid-April which failed to address their concerns. The committee, headed by retired Supreme Court justice Zvi Tal, recommended that yeshiva students should be allowed to leave their religious seminaries at twenty-three, opt for vocational studies or work without being subject to the draft, and that, on reaching the age of twenty-four, they could choose shortened service or go back to their religious studies. This did not please the army, which complained that the exemption age was too low, and that the recommendations put no cap on the number of annual deferments. The report also caused an outcry among reserve soldiers who complained of unequal distribution of the nation's defense burden.[64]

In early July, a bill establishing procedures for yeshiva student draft deferments passed a first Knesset reading by 52 votes to 43, with 7 abstentions. Ultra-Orthodox parties vowed revenge against Sharon for not supporting the proposal and allowing Likud MKs to vote against it. As reservists on hunger strike demonstrated outside the Knesset building, Sharon declared that his conscience wouldn't allow him to support the legislation.[65] However, when a bill to extend the yeshiva draft deferments was tabled in December, Sharon voted for it.[66]

Both Sharon and Barak oscillated between trying to woo the majority secular electorate and their need for political support from the Orthodox parties. Both took strong secularist positions on key issues, but invariably reversed themselves under orthodox pressure.[67]

Barak's Civil Agenda

After Shas quit the coalition in July, Barak made his move for support from the Israeli secular majority, announcing plans in August for what he called a "new civil agenda," or in bolder moments, a "secular revolution." The proposed moves included legislation to allow civil marriages, abolition of the Religious Affairs Ministry and introduction of a system requiring yeshiva students and other Orthodox Jews to carry out community service as a substitute for military conscription.[68]

Throughout September, Barak continued to focus the domestic political agenda on his campaign for civil reform. On 13 September, the cabinet voted to abolish the Religious Affairs Ministry, and, five days later, Barak convened a special ministerial committee charged with reorganizing the working week in Israel in order to make Sunday an additional day of rest and to force government offices to open until noon on Friday. In addition, El Al, the national airline, would be permitted to fly on the Sabbath, once privatization of the company was completed.[69]

However, the upshot of Barak and Sharon's inconsistency was that very little of the new civil agenda was actually implemented, and all thought of change was held up after Shas's late October offer to support Barak for a month from outside the coalition.[70]

Religious Conversion

The Institute for the Study of Judaism, set up in 1999 to deal with the problem of non-recognition of Conservative and Reform conversions in Israel, produced its first graduates in the fall. Several dozen of sixty potential candidates were converted and registered as Jews by the Chief Rabbinate. The institute's conversion school was jointly sponsored by the Orthodox, Conservative and Reform movements, and rabbis from all three taught the converts. Final conversion, however, was by an all-Orthodox rabbinic court.[71]

THE ECONOMY

Effects of the Intifada

The Palestinian intifada, which erupted in late September, had a devastating effect on the economy which was beginning to show signs of buoyancy. The local stock market and Israeli shares abroad tumbled. Investors turned to the US dollar, causing the shekel to lose value. Tourist reservations were canceled, international conventions postponed, public offerings planned by Israeli companies put on hold and several major foreign venture capital investments deferred.[72]

Moreover, in the violence ridden 4th quarter, economic growth declined by 8% (per annum), the sharpest single three-month fall in the country's history. This upset what had been an extremely promising trend: Record growth of 9.1% (per annum) in the third quarter, following 7.8% in the second quarter and 5.1% in the first. Despite the 4th quarter reversal, GDP grew by 5.9% in 2000. GDP per capita, at $17,700, set a record, up 3.4% from 1999, and business GDP was up 7.7%, compared to a 2% rise in 1999.[73]

Soaring Hi-Tech and Structural Problems

The strong performance of the economy in the first three quarters of the year was largely a result of outstanding successes in hi-tech. In 1995 hi-tech accounted for less than 40% of the $14bn. Israel earned from industrial and agricultural exports. By the turn of the century, the figure had skyrocketed to nearly 60% of $21bn. Two-thirds of the $4.9bn. foreign investment in 2000 went into hi-tech companies. And while the "old economy" of factories and farms stagnated, the income from hi-tech pushed economic growth to a bullish 5.9%, and was largely responsible for an impressive leap in exports and a corresponding drop in the trade deficit.[74] Overall, exports rose by 24% to $28.2bn., the biggest growth of the decade, while hi-tech grew at an annual rate of 58% and generated over half the record $5.5bn. export growth. These figures helped bring the trade deficit down by $900m. to $6.5bn., a drop of 11.5%.[75]

But the intifada and the beginnings of a worldwide downturn in hi-tech based earnings in the fourth quarter highlighted the serious structural problems the economy was facing long before the intifada erupted.[76] Indeed, despite its stunning hi-tech performance, Israel was plagued by high unemployment and signs of recession throughout the year. Economic indicators published by the Central Bureau of Statistics (CBS) in the first quarter showed unemployment peaking at a six-year record of close to 9.5%, a sharp slowdown in the growth of industrial production and capital imports, and a real estate market sinking into deeper and deeper recession. High unemployment was partly a result of the fact that only about 20% of the workforce was employed in knowledge-intensive industries, while the other 80% were in the "old economy," where labor-intensive companies, especially in textiles and food manufacture, were closing at an alarming rate.[77]

Nor was unemployment the only reason for a growing gap between rich and poor. World Bank figures, published early in the year, showed that ex-socialist Israel's pay gap was the fourth largest in the Western world. In 1998, according to the CBS, the average monthly per capita income of the top 10% of wage earners was $4,500, 11.8 times higher than the bottom tenth.[78]

Tax Reform Freeze

Plans by Finance Minister Avraham (Beiga) Shochat to introduce a new tax regime to boost the economy and help narrow wage differentials were indefinitely deferred in mid-June, after the Histadrut Trade Union Federation threatened a national strike. The reforms were intended to modernize the tax structure and bring Israel into line with international conventions, but the Histadrut was fiercely opposed because the proposed new system abolished a number of tax breaks for public sector workers.[79]

Just weeks after the Barak government lost its majority in July and early elections became a realistic possibility, Shochat announced tax cuts of NIS1.3bn. ($380m.) on electrical appliances. The government claimed this had been made possible through a tax collection surplus, and that it would help boost the sluggish economy. But most observers saw it as a transparent electoral ploy.[80]

Tight Monetary Policy and Zero Inflation

David Klein was appointed governor of the Bank of Israel on 9 January, replacing Ya'acov Frenkel, who had announced his resignation the previous November. Klein, who had worked at the Bank of Israel since 1987, had served as head of the monetary department, as controller of foreign exchange and as the bank representative on the board of directors at the Tel Aviv stock exchange. Barak said he had chosen Klein because he wanted someone in the Frenkel mold who would continue the previous governor's unabashed monetarism.[81] Klein obliged, and partly as a result of his tight monetary regime, inflation fell in 2000 to exactly zero, Israel's lowest inflation rate ever. The previous record, 0.2%, was set in 1967.[82]

THE ARABS IN ISRAEL

GOVERNMENT POLICIES

The special ministerial committee to oversee the affairs of the Arab citizens of Israel, headed by Minister Matan Vilna'i, continued to operate according to the guidelines laid down following its establishment in 1999 (see *MECS* 1999, pp. 328–29). In January 2000, the committee received a detailed plan presented by the Civil Service Commission aimed at integrating candidates from the non-Jewish sector into the civil service. The goal was that 10% of the total civil service workforce by the end of 2004 be composed of non-Jews. The government approved the plan, announcing its commitment to it both ideologically and in practice.[83] In May, Vilna'i reported that 145 new Arab employees had been accepted in the civil service by the start of the year.[84]

During the course of the year, a prolonged land dispute in the al-Roha area near Umm al-Fahm, known as "Area 107," was resolved. A decision by the Israel Defense Forces (IDF) in 1998 to expand its training grounds northeast toward Wadi 'Ara had evoked demonstrations by the Arab residents of the area, ending in violent clashes with the security forces (see *MECS* 1998, pp. 352–53). In November 2000, Vilna'i announced that an agreement had been reached with the local leaders of the area whereby the firing zone would be distanced from the surrounding Arab villages, bordering areas were designated as an agricultural buffer zone, and a limit of one hundred training days annually was fixed for the zone.[85] The agreement was signed on 31 December.

According to *The Jerusalem Post*, the agreement marked "the first time that the state has backed off from land appropriations for military use due to pressure from the Israeli Arab community, whose vote is crucial in the upcoming elections."[86] *Ha'aretz*, similarly, viewed the agreement as representing "a positive — even historic precedent," proving that sincere and nonrestrictive negotiations could be fruitful.[87]

The ministerial committee also made a series of precedent-setting decisions regarding the Bedouin population in the Negev. A long-range master building plan was announced in August to solve the problems of the dispersed Bedouin settlements in the south, including the granting of recognized status to sixteen such communities over a seven-year period. Vilna'i stated that an integrated approach would be followed in developing these communities, focusing on environment, sewage, the development of neighborhood facilities and the building of public institutions, so that "the settlements will become attractive venues for Bedouin residence."[88] The committee also directed the Infrastructure Ministry to prepare a plan that would provide an immediate as well as a long-term solution to the problem of water supply for the Bedouins in the south. Additionally, a decision was made for a review of Bedouin land settlement, by the Israel Lands Authority. Reacting to these steps, MK Talib al-Sana', a resident of the Bedouin village of Lakia, stated that while positive in themselves, they were insufficient. "We are not impressed by promises," he pointed out, "because we have been burnt many times in the past."[89] In the event, no concrete progress had been made by the end of the year in advancing the plan.

The major focus of the ministerial committee was the completion of a long-term development plan for the Arab sector. In June, the committee approved a governmental allocation of NIS 4bn. for infrastructure and educational development in Arab towns and villages in an effort to close socioeconomic discrepancies between the Jewish and Arab populations. The plan was prepared as part of the agreement which ended a sit-down strike by the Arab mayors in late December 1999 (see *MECS* 1999, pp. 329–30). According to Vilna'i, the aid plan was based on direct investment in development projects for economic recovery as well as funding for education, infrastructure and job creation. The four-year aid package also included increased spending on housing and industrial start-ups.[90] Presenting the plan in July to the Arab MKs and heads of Arab local councils, Vilna'i explained that NIS 2bn. had already been budgeted, while the rest of the sum, NIS 2bn., would be allocated by the various ministries from their current budgets. The plan would be implemented as of January 2001, he said, although in certain areas, such as vocational training and the completion of zoning plans, implementation would begin sooner.[91]

While Arab leaders welcomed the plan, they expressed reservations regarding what they viewed as the limited scope of the investment, as well as skepticism over the prospects for its actual implementation. They hoped that the development projects would be carried out in full and not remain a "paper exercise."[92] In the view of Muhammad Zaydan, chair of the Supreme Follow-up Committee, composed of Arab MKs, heads of local councils and other leaders, the proposals marked the beginning of a serious attempt to tackle problems in the Arab sector resulting from years of neglect, but the plan did not go far enough and there was "room for improvement and expansion."[93] Similarly, MK al-Sana' believed that the plan reflected good intentions but needed additional budgets. Dr. Faysal 'Aza'iza, spokesperson of the Follow-up Committee, asserted that the actual sum that was required to close the gaps was NIS 10bn.[94]

These doubts proved to be well founded, as the government continuously postponed the formal approval of the plan, a step which would lead to including the project in the forthcoming state budget. Only after violent riots erupted in the Galilee and the Triangle areas in early October (see below) did Prime Minister Barak announce his personal commitment to present the plan for cabinet approval. On 22 October, three weeks after the disturbances began, the cabinet ratified it.

The development plan, designed for some seventy-four Arab localities countrywide, excluded mixed Jewish-Arab towns, the Bedouin population in the Negev, and villages that were not officially recognized as such. It was based on three components:

1) Developing the physical infrastructure, with an emphasis on building new neighborhoods, public buildings, police stations, roads and drainage systems;
2) Economic development through the construction of industrial parks, agricultural modernization and building up of the tourist industry;
3) Developing human resources through investment in classrooms, hi-tech education, vocational training and enhancing the status of women.[95]

Presumably, Barak expedited the approval of the plan in an effort to appease the Arab public, in light of the grave outbreak of violence in October, although government officials denied any connection between the events.

RISING POLITICAL UNREST

Signs of rising tension in the Arab sector were evident during the first half of the year under review, manifested by clear indications of political and ideological radicalization in both attitude and behavior.

A survey of the attitudes of the Arabs of Israel on the issue of their national identity, published in March by the Givat Haviva Institute for Advanced Studies, pointed to radicalization in terms of attitude toward the state and a significant reinforcement of the Palestinian component of their national identity. The survey, conducted in late 1999 using a representative sample of five hundred individuals interviewed in person, found that 46% of the respondents described themselves as "Palestinians" or "Arab-Palestinians," and 21% described themselves as "Palestinian Arabs." Only 11% chose the "Arab-Israeli" option, and 4% indicated "Israeli."[96] A similar survey conducted in 1995 had found 38% defining themselves as "Arab-Israelis" and 8% as "Israelis". One of the compilers of the survey, Dr. As'ad Ghanim of the University of Haifa, emphasized that the findings pointed to the weakening of the Israeli element of their identity and the strengthening of the Palestinian element. This trend toward "Palestinization," he said, was a reflection of bitterness and frustration, revealing "an absence of hope on the part of the Arab sector under the Barak administration in contrast to the period of Rabin's government."[97]

Other findings in the survey indicated that some 25% of the respondents supported the establishment of a Palestinian state in place of the State of Israel, and in "all the Palestinian territories." Regarding the integration of the Arabs in the State of Israel, 22% thought that the Arabs in Israel could have equal rights in Israel as a Jewish state; 26% were doubtful of this; and 21% thought that this was not possible.[98]

Land Day was marked on 30 March with rallies and commemorative processions held in several communities in the Galilee and the Triangle area in central Israel. While most of these events passed relatively calmly, a sharp confrontation developed in Sakhnin between local residents and the police. A procession of local people proceeded to the outskirts of the town to protest the intention of the Ministry of Defense to set up an army camp nearby while refusing to expand the area of jurisdiction of the Arab town of 25,000. The protest was led by young people carrying a flag of Palestine, with others carrying a photograph of Gamal 'Abd al-Nasir. Riots broke out when the demonstrators discovered the presence of police monitoring them covertly. The demonstrators threw stones at the police, and the police responded by shooting tear-gas grenades into the crowd. The rally turned into a "battlefield," in the words of an eye-witness. Twenty residents and eight police officers were lightly wounded. Later, a resident of Sakhnin died, reportedly of tear-gas inhalation.[99]

The violent clashes in Sakhnin, and the protests elsewhere on Land Day reflected growing disappointment with the policies of the Barak government, according to observers. Spokespersons of the Arab population pointed out that most of the local councils contended with paralyzing budgetary deficits; the Arab villages had become foci of unemployment; and the problem of the non-recognized villages, especially in the Negev, had worsened.[100]

A further sign of rising tension in the Arab public was to be seen several days later at the Haifa University, where violent clashes broke out between Jewish and Arab students when the latter held a protest demonstration prompted by the death of the Sakhnin resident. Incidents on the campus continued for two days, during which representatives of the Arab students attacked police who arrived on the scene to arrest one of them. Student demonstrations spread to The Hebrew University of Jerusalem, where some students wrapped their heads in keffiyas, military style, and held up a poster that read: "We have the right to demonstrate in our land of Palestine."[101]

Observers once again attributed the cause of the outburst to the Arab sector's "heightened distress since 1996 both because of their difficult economic condition...and the fitful political process."[102] According to Ha'aretz, the wave of student demonstrations reflected the opposition of the population to government policy and to land expropriation. It expressed a transition "from the stage of disappointment and frustration with the Barak government to the stage of rage and opposition."[103]

The force of the rising bitterness could be gauged by events on Israel Independence Day in May. In contrast to previous years, Minister of Interior Natan Sharansky decided to hold the traditional reception for dignitaries from the Arab community in the town of Shfaram (Shafr 'Amr) rather than in Nazareth, presumably because Shfaram Mayor 'Ursan Yasin was known for his good relations with the administration, his moderate views, and his opposition to the militant line of the National Committee of Heads of Arab Local Councils. That body, along with the Supreme Follow-up Committee and the Arab MKs, announced that they would boycott the reception in protest against what they called "disregard of the Arab sector's claims."[104]

As put by Nazareth Mayor Ramiz Jara'isi, who supported the boycott decision, "Barak shoveled in the Arab vote, and the day after elections forgot about the existence of the Arab sector."[105] On 3 May, a manifesto signed by the nationalist Sons of the Village movement was circulated in Shfaram calling on Arab leaders to boycott the official reception scheduled to be held there. "The State of Israel Independence festivities," the manifesto read, "will remain, from our standpoint, a day of mourning in memory of the holocaust of our people, a memorial day commemorating the Kafr Qasim massacre, the Dir Yasin massacre and the Sabra and Shatila massacre."[106]

'Ursan, however, did not back down. "Independence Day is the holiday of the state, and every citizen is obliged to honor it and celebrate it," he said.[107] The event took place as scheduled on 7 May in the presence of Minister Sharansky. However, the boycott was effective, and only three heads of Arab local councils attended. Some four hundred demonstrators protested outside the reception hall, most of them supporters of the Democratic Front for Peace and Equality (known by its Hebrew acronym, "Hadash" or "Jabha," "front" in Arabic) and the National Democratic Alliance (known by its Hebrew acronym "Balad" or "Tajamu'," "Arkamil"). When the invitees emerged from the hall, violence erupted, and was quelled only several hours later by police using tear gas and rubber bullets. Five local persons were wounded by rubber bullets, four police officers were wounded by stone-throwing, and four local persons were arrested.[108]

THE AQSA INTIFADA

Violent demonstrations swept the Arab communities of the Galilee and the Triangle area early in October as a spin-off of the Aqsa Intifada in the territories, resulting in the death of thirteen Arabs and one Jew. These events evoked profound shock in the Israeli public, marking a turning point in Jewish-Arab relations in the country.

The outburst was the most violent act by the Arab population since the establishment of Israel, involving a level of force never before employed, including the destruction of public buildings, the protracted blocking of major highways, the employment of molotov cocktails and even sporadic use of live ammunition against security forces. The harsh response by the police, who fired at the Arab demonstrators, also marked a significant precedent.

The violence erupted on 1 October in the Umm al-Fahm area of the northern Triangle. Later that day it spread to the western and lower Galilee and to the mixed Jewish-Arab cities of Acre and Tel Aviv-Jaffa. By 2 and 3 October, the situation had deteriorated significantly. Thousands of Arab demonstrators took to the streets, blocking main highways, including the Wadi 'Ara road connecting the coastal plain with the lower Galilee, and the Acre-Safed road. Rioters also threw stones, empty bottles and other objects at cars traveling along these routes. Masked young people hurled firebombs at the police.

Banks, post offices and shops were vandalized and set on fire in Nazareth, Baka al-Gharbiyya and other towns and villages in the Galilee and the Triangle. Rioters tore down street lamps and traffic lights, uprooted road signs and severely damaged bus stops in the main junctions of the Wadi 'Ara road. The road blockages caused the cutoff of Jewish communities, with the result that thousands were confined to their homes. Dozens of fires broke out throughout the country, most of them arson attacks related to the riots.

Jewish-Arab disturbances occurred in Tiberias when anti-Arab protesters attacked Arab passersby and tried to burn down mosque. In Upper Nazareth, hundreds of Jewish and Arab youths hurled rocks and bottles at each other. Jewish demonstrators also tried to break into the home of MK Azmi Bishara, a resident of Upper Nazareth. The police, responding aggressively, used tear gas, rubber bullets and live ammunition. As a result, thirteen Arabs were killed, and hundreds of protesters and dozens of police officers were injured.

Arab leaders accused the police of employing excessive force in dispersing the demonstrators, using live ammunition, and shooting indiscriminately at close range. They singled out the commander of the Police Northern District, Alik Ron, in particular, describing him as having a "racist attitude toward the Arabs."[109] Senior police sources dismissed the allegations, pointing to the intensity of the Arab violence and stressing that in several cases police officers perceived their lives to be in danger and resorted to fire after tear gas and rubber bullets had failed. Internal Security Minister Ben Ami announced that all cases of fatalities would be the subject of a governmental inquiry.[110]

In an attempt to restore calm, Prime Minister Barak met with Arab leaders on 3 October, expressing regret over the wave of violence and the loss of life. An agreement was reached at the meeting that police would refrain from entering Arab towns unnecessarily and would act with restraint. Barak also called on Jewish Israelis to cease attacks against Arabs and Arab-owned property, while urging the Arabs not to allow themselves to be provoked to commit violent acts.[111]

A combination of factors contributed to the eruption of the unprecedented riots. MK Sharon's visit to the Temple Mount on the eve of the Jewish New Year, 28 September (see below), provided the spark that ignited an outburst of religious sentiment and Islamic solidarity. Perceiving a threat in Sharon's move, the Arabs of Israel adopted the Islamic movements' cause of protecting the Aqsa Mosque, claiming that Israel was trying to exert its authority over the third holiest site in Islam. Earlier, in mid-September, the Islamic movement in Israel had held a rally in Umm al-Fahm — its fifth in as many years — under the slogan: "Al-Aqsa is in danger." Some 30,000 Arabs gathered in the city stadium and, according to the organizers, approximately NIS 1m. had been collected for "safeguarding al-Aqsa." Shaykh Ra'id Salah, Umm al-Fahm mayor and head of the movement's more dogmatic faction, declared: We tell the Jews in the clearest way: You have no right to even one stone of the Aqsa stones."[112]

Moreover, the swift response of the Arabs in Israel reflected their sense of solidarity with the Palestinian cause. Undoubtedly, the violent clashes between the Israeli security forces and the Palestinians in Jerusalem, the West Bank and the Gaza Strip, including the televised killing of the Palestinian child Muhammad al-Dura, stirred the emotions of the Arabs in Israel, prompting them to show their identification with their Palestinian brethren. Israeli security sources argued that Fath-affiliated activists of the militant Tanzim had visited Arab towns and villages in Israel after the disturbances began in the PA areas and distributed leaflets calling on the population to take part in "the struggle against the Zionist enemy."[113] However, there was no clear proof of direct PA involvement in the wave of violence. Clearly, however, the mood in the territories had undoubtedly radiated to the Arab sector in Israel.

Yet, the Islamic-Palestinian sense of identification notwithstanding, the major cause for the outburst of violence was largely attributable to domestic factors. Arab MKs had contributed significantly to an evolving atmosphere of incitement and violence during the course of the year. In mid-September, Attorney General Elyakim Rubinstein approved a police request to investigate MK Muhammad Baraka of Hadash on suspicion of inciting

Arab protesters to attack the police during demonstrations against the demolition of illegally built houses.[114] MK 'Abd al-Malik Dahamisha, head of the United Arab List, similarly called upon the Arab public at that time to resist the police, declaring that "any policeman who harms an Arab is a criminal." Referring to the demolition of illegally built houses, he stated: "It is our right to protect ourselves and break his [the police officer's] arms and legs."[115] The police recommended indicting Dahamisha, too, for incitement.

Arab MKs also played an active part in the protest against Sharon's visit to the Temple Mount on 28 September, calling him, and the Likud party members who had accompanied him, "racists" and "killers of Palestinians."[116] In the view of a *Ha'aretz* columnist, "the parliamentary leadership of the Israeli Arabs spearheaded the protest against Sharon's visit and by [doing so] became a [responsible] partner in the bloody riots which took place following the visit."[117]

Essentially, the October riots reflected the disappointment of the Arabs in Israel with Prime Minister Barak personally and with his government policies toward the Arab sector generally. An overwhelming majority of 95% of the Arab electorate had voted for him in the 1999 elections (see *MECS* 1999, pp. 323–24), but many felt betrayed when he declined to invite Arab parties to join his coalition, and did little to address the longstanding socioeconomic needs of the Arab sector. Barak was seen as responsible for keeping the Arabs marginalized in Israeli society. Indisputably, the Arabs of Israel harbored pent-up anger over neglect and discriminatory policies by successive governments. The uprising undoubtedly represented the culmination of a process of growing alienation and discontent over unfulfilled expectations to attain equality, especially by the younger generation. Young people spontaneously took to the streets and played a major role in the Israeli Arab intifada, similar to their counterparts in the territories.

Following sustained harsh criticism over the killing of the thirteen Arab citizens by the police, Barak announced, on 22 October, the establishment of an independent committee of inquiry into the incidents, to be headed by a retired judge, Shalom Brenner. Arab leaders, however, rejected this decision and insisted on a state commission of inquiry to investigate alleged police brutality and excessive use of force. They maintained that a state commission of inquiry would have more investigative power and its findings and recommendations would carry more weight.[118] On 2 November, the Supreme Arab Follow-up Committee, announced that it would not cooperate with the public committee of inquiry. Attempting to press the government further to accede to its demands, the Follow-up Committee mooted setting up a protest tent, launching a hunger strike and announcing general strikes.

This pressure appeared to have been productive. On 8 November, Prime Minister Barak revoked his previous decision and announced the establishment of a state commission of inquiry into the October riots, to be appointed by the head of the High Court of Justice. Judge Theodor Or of the High Court was named chair of the commission, with District Court Judge Suhayl Jarah and Prof. Shimon Shamir of Tel Aviv University appointed as members. The decision was welcomed by the Arab leadership, although the Arab Association for Civil Rights ('Adala) questioned the legality of the commission's mandate, namely, to investigate the factors that led to the events, including the behavior of inciters. 'Adala claimed that the government thus "pre-determined that incitement

[was] an established fact," whereas, 'Adala pointed out, this was something that had yet to be established.[119]

Relations between Jews and Arabs in Israel deteriorated significantly in the wake of the bloody events of October, with implications on various levels. A deep crisis of confidence developed between the two populations. Once the situation was stabilized, attempts at dialogue between Jews and Arabs were made in various places, with "peace tents" set up for this purpose near Arab towns in the Galilee and the Triangle. It soon became apparent, however, that the spirit of coexistence had suffered a hard blow. The Jewish public was stunned and frightened by the force of the Arab disturbances. Anti-Arab racist and hate talk escalated significantly. The high level of Arab violence, and especially the blocking of major roads, evoked a siege atmosphere and prompted the perception by Jews of the Arabs of Israel as a threat and a potential fifth column.[120] Little by little, doubts grew about the Arab citizens' loyalty to the state. A survey carried out in the Jewish population upon the outbreak of the intifada revealed that 74% agreed with a definition of the behavior of the Arabs of Israel as treason.

On the other side, the unprecedented killing of thirteen Arab citizens by the police caused shock and pain in the Arab community and opened a deep fissure. Signs of hostility by the Arab public toward the state mounted. A reflection of this trend was evident in remarks by MK Baraka at Bir Zeit University in the West Bank in early November, praising the Palestinian intifada and calling on the Arabs of Israel to take part in the uprising. "We, the sons of the Palestinian people in the State of Israel, have a mission that goes beyond solidarity.... We are obliged, by virtue of our special status, to take part in the struggle of our Palestinian people for liberation and independence."[121] Baraka later claimed that his remarks were quoted out of context. The deep crisis in Jewish-Arab relations was also reflected in the economic sphere. A near-break occurred between both economies immediately following the violent events. Arabs employed in Jewish workplaces feared coming to work, while the Jewish population avoided Arab locales. This development had far-reaching implications. The scope of commerce in the Arab population centers declined by 40%–50%. Jews stopped frequenting Arab restaurants and markets. Jewish suppliers of foodstuffs, clothing, hardware and building materials refused to enter Arab villages, while public service providers such as electric company and banks conditioned the repair of damages caused during the rioting on the provision of police escorts.

THE FORTHCOMING ELECTIONS

Following the rioting of October 2000 and the growing likelihood of early elections for the office of prime minister and for the Knesset, two central issues occupied the Arab public: its position regarding the re-election of Ehud Barak, and the possibility of forming a unified Arab list for the elections.

Prime Minister Barak's standing in the Arab community was damaged severely as a result of the events of October. A survey of a sample of five hundred Arab residents conducted approximately three weeks after the rioting showed that only 16% supported Barak. The reason for this sharp decline in his popularity was reflected in the survey's finding that fully 77% of the respondents held the government of Israel directly responsible for the events.[122]

Barak's resignation on 12 December, and the decision to hold elections for the office of prime minister only, were openly welcomed by the Arab public in Israel. Many considered him the worst prime minister of Israel ever, a reflection of anger and a sense of betrayal over the non-fulfillment of his election promise to bring about peace and equality. Threats by Barak supporters that if the Arabs did not vote for him they would have to contend with Netanyahu or Sharon as prime minister were dismissed by the Arab public as demagoguery and blackmail.[123]

If the Arab public in Israel was nearly unanimous in opposing Barak's candidacy, it was divided on the issue of forming a unified Arab list should elections for the Knesset be held. Late in September, the Supreme Follow-up Committee chairperson Zaydan, urged the Arab parties to unify in the event of elections. Preliminary discussions regarding a merger were reportedly held by Balad and Hadash, while separate contacts were made between the United Arab List and MK Ahmad Tibi, who had split from Balad following the elections in 1999. Prospects for a unified list, however, seemed remote due to internal splits, ideological disputes and the personal rivalries that typified Arab politics in Israel.[124] According to an evaluation in *Ha'aretz*, the rioting in October did not heighten unity within the Arab leadership, which remained at least as divided, if not more so, as previously. This disunity was reflected not only in the failure of the secular, communist, Jewish-Arab Hadash and the United Arab List to coalesce, but also in signs of a loss of confidence in the Arab sector umbrella organizations (e.g., a decision by the heads of the southern Triangle towns to set up an executive committee separate from the Supreme Follow-up Committee) and dissatisfaction with the performance of the Arab MKs.[125]

The Arab population was also divided over whether to present an Arab candidate for the office of prime minister. The Arab MKs all supported such a move, although they disagreed over the choice of candidate.[126] Ultimately, three positions emerged on the issue. MK Azmi Bashara, who had been the only Arab candidate for the position (in the 1999 elections), proposed holding a referendum in the Arab sector on the issue. Others proposed discussing the topic in the Supreme Follow-up Committee so as to attain its approval for the candidate who would emerge with a majority of its members' votes. A third option, promoted by Hadash, was to form a leftist bloc, or "third axis," in Israeli politics, to be headed by an Arab or Jewish delegate of the peace camp (Shimon Peres and Shulamit Aloni were mentioned in this context). According to a *Ha'aretz* columnist, most of the supporters of the third option insisted that such a candidate be backed unanimously by the Supreme Follow-up Committee, in view of the serious decline in the credibility of the Arab MKs as perceived by the Arab public.[127]

FOREIGN AFFAIRS

WAR AND PEACE WITH THE PALESTINIANS

The year 2000 saw ambitious peace efforts degenerate into the worst violence since the Oslo peace process with the Palestinians began in 1993. In a sequence of intensive negotiations, including a fifteen-day summit at the American president's Camp David retreat, Israel and the Palestinians came close to a framework agreement on "permanent status," outlining the principles for a final peace deal between them. But, although significant progress was made in the months immediately after the collapse of the Camp David summit in July, widespread violence erupted in September, putting paid to hopes for an early peace deal. By year's end, the parties were still trying to negotiate peace, but confidence in each other's intentions had been seriously eroded (for further details, see chapter on the Arab-Israeli peace process).[128]

From Stockholm to Camp David

Persuaded to go ahead by Barak in early July, President Clinton announced that he would host a "make or break" summit meeting on 11–19 July at Camp David in an attempt to secure a final peace accord. Weeks of secret talks at various locations in Israel between April and June, and two intensive sessions in Stockholm in May, had left Israeli negotiators Shlomo Ben Ami and Gilead Sher, a lawyer close to Barak, who would later become the prime minister's bureau chief, convinced that a summit had every chance of success. At the Stockholm meetings with a Palestinian team led by Abu 'Ala and Hasan 'Asfur, the parties made progress on two of the three core issues: territory and refugees. The Palestinians agreed for the first time to Israel retaining three large settlement blocs in the West Bank and Israel agreed to hand over most of the territory to the Palestinians. On refugees, there was agreement on international funding for resettlement and restitution and Palestinian acknowledgement that not all resettlement would be in Israel proper.[129]

Still, despite the Israeli optimism, many vital issues remained unresolved: there was no agreement on the precise percentage of land to be handed over; Israel was demanding a military presence in the Jordan Valley; the Palestinians insisted on affirming the right of all refugees to return to Israel proper even if in practice only few would actually go back; and, at Barak's insistence, the third core issue, Jerusalem, had not been broached in any detail.[130]

Obviously going to a high-profile Camp David style conference with so little sown up was going to be a very risky business. But Ben Ami argued that it was the only way to see whether Palestinian rigidity on what he called the "mythic" issues of Jerusalem and refugees could be broken down; it was also the only way to prepare Israeli public opinion for the quantum leap it would have to make on the core issues, especially Jerusalem. And it was only by holding a summit with the principals present and all the issues being dealt with in parallel, that the big picture, what Barak called the "Gestalt," could emerge, with trade-offs possible not only within the major tracks - Jerusalem, refugees and territory — but between them as well.[131]

Three weeks before Camp David, Sher, Ben Ami and Yossi Ginnossar held a long meeting with PA Chairman Yasir 'Arafat in Nablus. According to Ben Ami, he told 'Arafat that, "we [officials] could not make any more progress, and that this was the moment for leaders to take decisions."[132]

Camp David

The Camp David conference was supposed to last eight days, until President Clinton's departure for the G-8 summit in Okinawa. The idea was that he would take an agreement with him to the G-8 for international approval. But, for the first few days, it seemed that the conference was going nowhere. The Israelis were astounded by what they saw as a solid wall of Palestinian passivity. Sher claimed the Palestinian interlocutors were acting in strict accord with a negotiating stratagem devised by 'Arafat. The Palestinians, he said, were ordered not to make any proposals whatsoever for the first four days of Camp David, and to put forward nothing but the orthodox, dogmatic Palestinian line. Then in the last four days, 'Arafat planned to utilize discrepancies between the positions of the various Israeli negotiators to press for concessions, hoping for support from the American facilitators, anxious to close a deal.

'Arafat, according to Sher, was banking on the Americans serving as concession gatherers, and, since there were none to be had from the Palestinians, they would naturally try to extract more from the Israelis.[133]

The Americans had wanted to present bridging proposals at the very beginning of the conference, but Barak dissuaded them. He also talked them out of having an official note-taker. He didn't want written proposals the Palestinians could appropriate as opening positions later if they failed to reach agreement at Camp David. The result was a deep and destructive Palestinian suspicion that the Israelis and Americans were working in cahoots against them.[134]

By the fifth day of the summit, Jerusalem had become the main issue. The Israelis hoped it would be the "locomotive" that would drive the rest. If they got a deal on Jerusalem, the thinking went, everything else would fall into place. And although there was no final agreement on Jerusalem at Camp David, there was a significant conceptual breakthrough. The parties agreed that the Palestinians would get the Arab suburbs and Israel the Jewish suburbs, including those built on what had been Jordanian territory before 1967. The residual argument was over the Old City and Temple Mount, after 'Arafat rejected various American bridging proposals. Sher recalled that Clinton then proposed deferring Jerusalem and cutting a deal on the rest: "On the last evening but one at Camp David, Clinton proposed delaying either part of the Jerusalem issue — Temple Mount and the Old City — or the entire Jerusalem issue. And even to that 'Arafat said no. 'Do you have a counter proposal?' he was asked, and through Sa'ib 'Urayqat he said, 'no.'"[135]

From his point of view, 'Arafat's rejection was not unreasonable. He felt he was being bullied by the Israeli-American partnership, and that not enough progress had been made on the other two core issues to warrant agreement on them with or without Jerusalem. For example, on the territorial issue, the Palestinians agreed to three Jewish settlement blocs in the West bank — Gush Ariel, Gush Etzion and a block around Jerusalem — but were offered only 91% of the land. In addition, Israel wanted to lease part of the Jordan valley, and to have six army camps there with freedom of movement along roads leading to them. The Palestinians felt they would have difficulty establishing territorial contiguity; moreover, for the 9% Israel intended to annex, they would get compensation at a ratio of only one to nine. According to Robert Malley, a member of the American team, 'Arafat initially accepted the 92% (91% plus 1% compensation) offer, but later relented.[136]

In retrospect, Ben Ami explained the divide between the two sides' thinking:

> The Palestinian perspective was that Oslo was a compromise and that it was the last compromise. We were not aware of this. We all thought that somewhere down the road there would be another compromise, which would then be final. But this is not the way the Palestinian leader saw it. Oslo was the 'Peace of the Brave', he didn't feel he had to be brave again. Rather, the other side now needed to be brave by giving in on all vital issues.[137]

US officials claimed the sides had made considerable progress during the fifteen-day session and had promised to refrain from violence and continue to work toward a negotiated settlement. Barak blamed 'Arafat for the failure of the talks, arguing that he had refused to make crucial decisions over the future of Jerusalem; Clinton publicly endorsed this view, aggravating 'Arafat's sense of having been forced into a corner.[138]

The Negotiations Continue

Following the collapse of the summit, 'Arafat embarked on a round of intensive diplomacy to secure international support for his position. In August he visited France, South Africa, Egypt, China, Japan, Malaysia and Vietnam, but was warned against issuing a unilateral declaration of statehood on 13 September.[139] Days before the deadline, the Palestinian Legislative Council met in Gaza and agreed to delay the declaration indefinitely.[140]

Meanwhile, away from the spotlight, Israeli-Palestinian negotiations were continuing apace, despite the Camp David setback. For nearly two months, the parties held almost daily meetings and by mid-September were ready to discuss new American bridging proposals. Both sides sent delegations to Washington, and, when acting foreign minister Ben Ami came back, he told cabinet colleagues and foreign diplomats that Israel and the Palestinians were just weeks away from an historic peace deal. No one questioned his assessment.[141]

This phase culminated in a tête-à-tête between Barak and 'Arafat at the prime minister's private residence in Kochav Yair on 25 September. According to Sher: "They spent a very pleasant evening and committed themselves to reaching an agreement within a few weeks. They agreed to spare no effort and to give their representatives the mandate they needed." That same night Israeli and Palestinian negotiators flew to Washington to put the finishing touches on the American bridging package. Three days later, the intifada broke out.[142]

Violence Erupts

On 28 September, the peace process was totally disrupted when serious rioting broke out in Jerusalem following a visit to the Temple Mount by opposition Likud leader Ariel Sharon. Ironically, the visit coincided with a breakthrough statement by Barak on Jerusalem, in which he suggested an agreed framework and timetable for further negotiations regarding compromise on Temple Mount.[143]

The next day further rioting occurred on the holy site as over 20,000 Muslims left after Friday prayers. Israeli security forces were stoned and responded with live ammunition and rubber bullets. Four Palestinians were killed and about two hundred injured. The rioting, which Palestinian radio described as the start of the "battle for Jerusalem," quickly spread across the West Bank and Gaza.[144]

Seething Palestinian Anger

Despite the apparent progress in the peace process during the early part of the year, Palestinian anger had been seething under the surface for months. Although Israel had transferred another 2% of West Bank territory to full Palestinian control and 3% to partial Palestinian control in early January, the handover came after months of deadlock and was followed by more postponements, which hurt Israel's already sagging credibility on the Palestinian street.[145]

When, after a delay of two months, Israel transferred a further 6.1% on 21 March, the 341.6sq.km. included villages near Hebron, Ramallah, Bitunya, Jericho, Salfit and Jenin, but none touching Jerusalem, despite earlier Israeli promises on the handover of the village of 'Anabta. Although the transfer meant that 42.9% of the West Bank was now under total or partial Palestinian control, Palestinians continued to question Israel's good faith.[146]

In mid-May, in an attempt to prevent "stalemate and deterioration" in the peace process, Barak won cabinet approval, by a vote of 15 to 6, to hand over three West Bank villages situated on the outskirts of East Jerusalem, Abu Dis, Al-'Azariyya and Sawahra, to Palestinian control. After Barak argued that it would help Israel's claim to sovereignty over the city, the Knesset voted 56–48 for the transfer. But when, on the same day, violence spread across the West Bank and Gaza, Barak, under pressure from the right-wing parties in his coalition, postponed the handover.[147]

On 1 May, 650 of 1,650 Palestinian prisoners in Israel launched a hunger strike to draw attention to their plight. The unrest escalated dramatically on 15 May, when large numbers of Palestinians took to the streets to observe the fifty-second anniversary of *al Naqba*, ("the catastrophe," in Palestinian discourse, marking the establishment of the State of Israel.)

One of four Palestinians killed on 15 May was a police officer and Israel accused Palestinian security personnel of taking an active part in the clashes. For their part, the Palestinian media and leaders intensified their portrayal of Israel as hard-line and untrustworthy. This was partly a tactic to exert pressure on Israel to be more flexible. But it exacerbated the tremendous resentment and mistrust of Israel on the Palestinian street. In parallel, the young Fatah forces, the Tanzim, were growing politically and militarily stronger by the day. In the event of an agreement with Israel, they would help counteract opposition from the rejectionist Hamas and Islamic Jihad; but if there were no agreement, they would lead the armed struggle against Israel. In early July, Muhammed Dahlan, head of the Palestinian Preventive Security Forces in Gaza, warned Israeli cabinet ministers that if they failed to produce a deal at Camp David, there would be an explosion. The Israelis dismissed his warning as a transparent attempt to pressure them into a deal on Palestinian terms.[148]

Violence and the Peace Process

The violent clashes that erupted in September effectively destroyed the peace process. In the first month of fighting almost 150 people, mostly Palestinians, were killed. Some of the worst fighting in the first month was around the Israeli settlement of Netzarim in the Gaza strip. In one of the earliest exchanges, filmed by a French television crew, a twelve-year-old Palestinian boy, Muhammad Dura, was shot dead in his father's arms. The images of the boy's anguish and death became an icon for the new intifada and Israeli brutality, winning the Palestinians worldwide sympathy.[149]

In an attempt to broker a cease-fire, American secretary of state Madeleine Albright held talks with Barak and 'Arafat in the US embassy in Paris. 'Arafat insisted that Israel agree to an international inquiry into the outbreak of violence with officials from Egypt, France, Israel and the Palestinians. Barak argued that a review by Israeli and Palestinian officials mediated by the US had already been agreed on. At one point, 'Arafat stormed out of the talks but was persuaded to return after Albright ran after him and ordered the embassy guards to close the gates. 'Arafat and Barak were due to reconvene for talks with President Husni Mubarak of Egypt the next day, but Barak withdrew, saying he saw no point in further discussion. After meeting 'Arafat and Albright at the Egyptian Sinai resort of Sharm al-Shaykh, Mubarak called an emergency summit of Arab heads of state to convene in Cairo on 21 October (see chapter on inter-Arab relations).[150]

On 8 October, Barak warned 'Arafat that peace negotiations would be totally suspended on the evening of the next day if violent clashes continued. UN secretary-general Kofi Annan hurried to the region and, on 10 October, Barak seemed to bow to US and UN pressure when he announced he was willing to give the Palestinians more time to end the violence. 'Arafat mocked the deadline and its extension, and accused Israel of instigating violence with tanks, artillery and helicopters against civilian demonstrators. Annan, however, welcomed the extension and said that, "I think we can rein in the situation."[151]

The Crisis Deepens

But the crisis deepened when, on 12 October, a Palestinian mob lynched two Israeli soldiers in Ramallah. A picture of a Palestinian raising his bloodstained hands after throwing one of the bodies from the police station in Ramallah became an Israeli icon for the intractable nature of Palestinian hatred. The soldiers on their way to reserve duty had strayed into the Palestinian areas and were taken into custody by Palestinian police, who then failed to ward off the angry mob. Israel retaliated by dispatching helicopter gun-ships to attack military targets in Gaza and Ramallah, after warning the Palestinians to evacuate them. The police station where the reservists had been beaten to death was one of the first to be destroyed. 'Arafat described the attacks as a declaration of war.[152]

At a press conference that evening, Barak announced that he no longer regarded 'Arafat as a peace partner and said that, since the peace process was dead, he intended to form an emergency coalition with the right-wing opposition Likud.[153] Again world leaders stepped in, summoning the parties to another summit at Sharm al-Shaykh on 16 October. The summit, chaired by President Clinton, ended with an agreement to end violence and work toward resolving differences through negotiations. Significantly, the commitment to end violence was made by both sides to the US rather than to each other and was described by both as extremely fragile. Moreover, no substantive agreement was reached on the key issue of an inquiry into the outbreak of the violence, although both sides agreed to the establishment of a fact-finding committee with members chosen by Clinton in consultation with Annan. Both sides also agreed to reestablish security coordination through a trilateral security committee with US officials.[154] But shortly after the summit, violence flared in the West Bank towns of Nablus and Bethlehem. The Israeli neighborhood of Gilo on the southern outskirts of Jerusalem also came under fire.[155]

By this time Barak had had enough and drew up new plans to separate Israel unilaterally from the Palestinian areas. Under the scheme, freedom of movement between Israel and the Palestinian territories would be severely restricted. Sa'ib 'Urayqat dismissed it as a "plan of suffocation and occupation."[156]

As the fighting raged on, Israel's chief peace negotiator, Gilead Sher and Shimon Peres, the Israeli minister of regional cooperation and a former prime minister, met 'Arafat in Gaza on 1 November in a bid to reinstate the short-lived cease-fire brokered by President Clinton at Sharm al-Shaykh. After a two-hour meeting, Peres said he had received assurances from 'Arafat that efforts would be made to restore calm, end the violence and renew security cooperation between the two sides.[157]

Barak and 'Arafat undertook to confirm the cease-fire in simultaneous TV broadcasts. 'Arafat vacillated and the broadcasts were finally canceled when a car bomb went off in Jerusalem's Mahane Yehuda neighborhood. Two Israelis were killed in the bombing, one of them the daughter of former housing minister and NRP leader Yitzhak Levy.

Instead of televised addresses, Barak and 'Arafat both issued statements calling for an end to violence and adherence to the fragile cease-fire.[158]

The First "Targeted Killing"

But the cease-fire failed to take root, and on 9 November, Israeli forces killed Husayn 'Abayat, a senior Fatah commander, in a helicopter attack on his car in the West Bank village of Bayt Sahur. This was the first assassination in a new Israeli policy of deliberately targeting Palestinian military activists. Israel claimed that 'Abayat had been responsible for the deaths of three Israeli soldiers in a gun battle in early November.[159]

On 13 November, the cease-fire collapsed completely as heavy fighting erupted throughout Gaza and the West Bank. The upsurge in violence coincided with a visit by Barak to the US for talks with Clinton. Two Israeli soldiers and two civilians were killed in a string of drive-by shootings near the West Bank settlement of Ofrah and in Gaza.[160]

On 20 November, Palestinians detonated a bomb alongside a school bus in Gush Katif in the Gaza Strip, killing two people and wounding five. Israel retaliated with a series of artillery and helicopter raids against Fatah targets in Gaza and the West Bank and bisected the Gaza strip by blocking the main north-south roads.[161]

The school bus bombing caused outrage in Israel and prompted public demonstrations against what right-wingers saw as Barak's policy of restraint. The conflict escalated further on 22 November, when a powerful car bomb exploded near a bus in the town of Hadera, killing two people and injuring over fifty during the evening rush hour.[162]

Barak oscillated between tough military responses and efforts to get the peace process back on track. He unveiled a new peace plan on 30 November, in which he offered to transfer additional land to the Palestinians in return for an agreement to postpone the thorny issues of Jerusalem, refugees and the future of Jewish settlements in the West Bank and Gaza. But Palestinian leaders continued to insist that the only solution was a final settlement of all the issues.[163]

Regional Implications

Concern over the wider regional implications of the fighting grew in November as the violence escalated. Several Arab states closed offices and special interest sections in Israel. Tunisia, Oman and Morocco had closed their offices in October; Qatar announced the closure of the Israeli trade mission in Doha on 9 November.[164]

The next day, in the run-up to a mid-November meeting of the fifty-six member countries of the Islamic Conference Organization (ICO), President Saddam Hussein of Iraq declared that over six million Iraqis had volunteered to fight Israel. At the conclusion of the conference on 14 November, the Muslim states issued a statement supporting the intifada and condemning Israeli aggression. It also called on member countries to sever any ties with Israel that had resulted from earlier peace efforts. But the statement stopped well short of recommending any military decisions against Israel (see chapter on Islamic affairs). Indeed, throughout the crisis, President Mubarak of Egypt had taken the lead in declaring that he had no intention of allowing the conflict to slide into regional war.[165]

Instead, Egypt took strong diplomatic action, and, on 21 November, recalled its ambassador to Israel following helicopter raids in the Gaza strip. The Egyptian move was followed by a Jordanian decision not to send a new ambassador to Tel Aviv (see below).[166]

Mitchell and the Clinton Parameters

On 7 November, as part of the agreement reached at the Sharm al-Shaykh summit, Clinton named the panel that would review events and determine the causes of the violence. It was to be headed by George Mitchell (the former US senator and the chairperson of the Northern Ireland peace talks which had produced the 1998 "Good Friday" agreement) and included among its members US Senator Warren Rudman, the European Union (EU) high representative for foreign and security affairs, Javier Solana, former Turkish president Suleyman Demirel and Norwegian foreign minister Thorbjorn Jagland.[167]

On 11 December, the members of the Mitchell Commission arrived in the region and held separate meetings with 'Arafat and Barak. Senator Mitchell said he hoped the commission's work would help to reduce violence and facilitate a return to peace negotiations. The commission planned to submit a report to the incoming US president, George W. Bush, in March 2001.[168]

Three days later, 'Arafat opened a new round of talks with acting foreign minister Ben Ami aimed at ending the violence and renewing stalled peace negotiations. It was the first high-level Palestinian-Israeli session since Barak's meeting with 'Arafat in October. After the meeting, Israeli officials intimated that Ben Ami had presented a new package of proposals to 'Arafat as a starting point for further negotiations.[169]

On 19 December, Israeli and Palestinian officials met in the US to discuss the new package, and on 23 December, Clinton announced his "parameters" for a deal. In broad outline, he proposed the following compromise solutions on the three core issues: On territory, 94%–96% of the West Bank to the Palestinians with compensation for the 4%–6% annexed by Israel. The 4%–6% annexation would enable Israel to retain control of Jewish settlements in three blocs close to the 1967 border, in which most of the settlers would be concentrated. On refugees, the right of return would be to the state of Palestine, but some refugees would be allowed to return to Israel on humanitarian grounds. International funds would be set up for refugee resettlement and compensation. On Jerusalem, Israel would get the Jewish neighborhoods, Palestine the Arab, with various options for the parties to choose from on sovereignty over the Old City and the Temple Mount.[170]

On 27 December, Clinton said Barak had accepted the plan and that the two sides were "closer than they have ever been before." On 28 December, Barak clarified his position, saying he would willingly use the US plan as a basis for further negotiation if the Palestinians would do the same. The Palestinians, however, submitted a written request for further clarification of the plan and appeared to be prevaricating over accepting it as a basis for talks. Still, Clinton called on Barak and 'Arafat to attend a new summit in Egypt in January, and intense diplomatic efforts to bring both sides to the negotiating table were continuing at year's end.[171]

ISRAEL WITHDRAWS FROM LEBANON

Barak Keeps a Promise

Israel ended its occupation of South Lebanon on 24 May, when the last of its troops left the security zone in South Lebanon, six weeks before Barak's self-imposed 7 July deadline. Over a thousand Israeli soldiers had died in South Lebanon since Israel first established the security zone in 1978, 728 of them in combat in the 1982 Lebanon War and the eighteen years of confrontation with the Lebanese Shi'i Hizballah militia that followed. Hizballah lost a reported 1,276 militia members in the fighting.[172]

Barak made the commitment to pull out of Lebanon during the 1999 election campaign. However, he had envisaged doing so as part of a comprehensive peace agreement with both Lebanon and Syria. But when peace negotiations with Syria bogged down in March, Barak decided to withdraw unilaterally and formally notified the UN in mid-April.[173]

Demoralization in the SLA

Barak had made plain his intention to withdraw months before. But this did nothing to forestall Hizballah attacks on the Israeli army. Nor did it inspire confidence among Israel's Lebanese allies, the South Lebanese Army (SLA) militia. On the contrary, Hizballah stepped up its offensive, and its increased military pressure coupled with uncertainty over what would happen once the Israelis left demoralized the SLA and helped accelerate its disintegration as a fighting force. The SLA suffered a first major blow to morale in late January when Hizballah forces assassinated its deputy commander, 'Aqil Hashim.[174]

The Fighting Intensifies

Fighting between Hizballah and the Israeli army also intensified. After 5 Israeli soldiers were killed in Hizballah attacks in late January and early February, Israeli fighter planes hit power stations in Ba'albak, near the border with Syria, and on the outskirts of Beirut. The attack on Lebanese infrastructure targets was intended to counteract the deterioration in Israel's deterrent capacity in the run-up to the withdrawal.

Hizballah, however, retaliated the next day with a Katyusha rocket attack on the security zone, in which another Israeli soldier was killed. The government declared a state of emergency in northern Israel and ordered inhabitants into the bomb shelters. On 9 February, Foreign Minister David Levy warned that if "Katyusha rockets fall on our settlements, the soil of Lebanon will burn," and two weeks later, Levy stunned members of the Knesset when, during a debate on Lebanon, he threatened to make Lebanon pay "blood for blood, soul for soul, child for child," if Hizballah attacked northern Israel.[175] On 16 February the security cabinet empowered a subcommittee of Barak, Mordechai and Levy to order immediate retaliation for any Hizballah attacks. The decision followed an appeal by IDF Chief of Staff Shaul Mofaz to allow the army to retaliate when Hizballah fired from within populated areas.[176]

Violence flared up again in the weeks preceding the Israeli withdrawal. This time the clashes centered on installations Israel was handing over to the SLA in preparation for the withdrawal. Hizballah also targeted SLA officials, killing two senior officers in early May and triggering another wave of desertions. After a Hizballah rocket attack on the northern Israeli town of Kiryat Shmoneh in early May, Israeli fighters attacked two Lebanese power stations, and, in a warning to Syria, also rocketed the Beirut-Damascus highway, just 10 km. from the Syrian border and close to a Syrian intelligence post. In another message to Syria, Israel carried out air attacks in mid-May on tanks belonging to the Popular Front for the Liberation of Palestine (PFLP), based inside the Syrian-controlled Biqa' Valley.[177]

The Pullout

Israel began withdrawing troops on 14 May, handing over fortified positions in the "security zone" to the SLA. However, on 21 May, the SLA was forced to abandon the main outpost of Tayba, when hundreds of exiled Lebanese civilians moved into the largely Shi'i sector of the security zone. Other outposts in the central sector, including Markaba and Huleh, were also overrun by civilians as SLA units deserted.[178]

The collapse of the central sector allowed Hizballah forces to cut the security zone in two. The eastern sector fell on 23 May, with civilians and Hizballah fighters taking over the SLA headquarters at Marj 'Ayun and freeing 144 prisoners from the al-Khiyam prison.

Meanwhile, families of SLA officers began gathering at the Tornous and Biranit border crossing points, hoping to find refuge in Israel. With the SLA in total disarray, a slow, orderly Israeli withdrawal became impossible. Troops were rushed out in a secret operation on the night between 23 and 24 May. There were no casualties, but equipment, including some high-powered computers, was left behind.[179]

As soon as the Israeli soldiers left, 250,000 Lebanese civilians flooded into the security zone to celebrate. The Lebanese government declared 25 May "National Liberation Day." In the south, thousands of civilians drove or walked along the newly visible border with Israel, taunting Israeli forces on the other side.

The departing Israeli forces were accompanied by around 6,500 SLA members and their families who fled to escape arrest on charges of collaboration. Prime Minister Salim al-Huss had announced on 9 May that SLA members would not be granted amnesty after the Israeli withdrawal. Still, some of those who fled across the border returned within days to join 1,500 SLA members who handed themselves over to the authorities.[180]

Speaking after the withdrawal on 24 May, Barak warned that he would consider any firing on Israeli territory from Lebanon "an act of war." Chief of Staff Mofaz told reporters that, "if there is any attempt to hit the northern residents of Israel, we will hit all those who exercise power in Lebanon, including Syrian targets."[181]

In pulling out of Lebanon, Barak had taken a huge strategic gamble: For nearly two decades Israel had defended its northern border by holding onto a strip of South Lebanon. The price was being bled by Hizballah, which sought to end the occupation, but also functioned as a Syrian tool prodding Israel to give up the Golan Heights. By withdrawing — against the advice of his generals — Barak robbed the Hizballah of its main justification for fighting, and Syria of its main lever for pressure on Israel. He also created a new strategic balance, in which Israel, having recaptured the moral high ground by withdrawing from Lebanon, would feel free to strike back at Syria, as the major powerbroker in Lebanon, for any violence on the northern border. The very volatility of this new situation, Barak hoped, would create a new deterrent balance.

Even if Barak's gamble on the Lebanese front were to pay off, there was still one glaring weakness in his overall strategy, of which he and the Israeli defense establishment were all too well aware: The Palestinians might interpret the withdrawal as capitulation by Israel in the face of determined military pressure, and adopt similar tactics themselves.[182] And, when the intifada erupted in September, many analysts and politicians were quick to make the connection.[183]

The UN Verifies the Israeli Withdrawal

In mid-June, the UN Security Council confirmed that Israel had withdrawn in strict compliance with Resolution 425, and on 28 July, UN peacekeeping troops deployed in the border area of South Lebanon. The move was limited and involved only fifty soldiers from Ireland and Ghana, but was widely regarded as an important step toward reducing border tensions.[184] On 9 August, a combined Lebanese army and Internal Security Forces unit of one thousand troops deployed in the area vacated by Israel. Some six hundred UN peacekeeping forces maintained their positions on the Lebanese-Israeli border. Lebanese forces deployed in barracks in Marj 'Ayun and Bint Jubayl, but did not advance to the border itself, leaving it to Hizballah and UN troops.[185]

Trouble in the Shab'a Farms Area

Still, tension continued over the ongoing Israeli occupation of the Shab'a farms area. The Lebanese claimed that the territory was theirs; Israel said it was Syrian, and that it was holding it ahead of negotiations with Damascus. The dispute over the Shab'a farms area came to a head when three Israeli soldiers were abducted by Hizballah in the Shab'a sector on 7 October, after having approached the border fence. Hizballah presented the abduction as part of its battle to free the Shab'a area and to get back Lebanese clerics and fighters held by Israel.[186]

On 15 October, Hizballah leader Shaykh Hasan Nasrallah announced the capture of a fifty-four-year old Israeli businessman. Hizballah claimed he was a Mossad agent spying for Israel, a charge Israel strongly denied.[187]

The border area remained relatively quiet until the end of the year. The only serious incident apart from the abductions came in late November, when a roadside bomb planted by Hizballah killed an Israeli soldier in the Shab'a farms area. Israel retaliated with air strikes against three targets in Lebanon and a heavy artillery bombardment of Hizballah positions in the south. The message was clear: now that Israel had withdrawn its forces to the internationally-sanctioned boundary line, any attack on it would be met with considerable force (for further details, see chapters on Lebanon and the Arab-Israeli peace process).[188]

Release of Lebanese Prisoners

After a Supreme Court ruling on 12 April, Israel released thirteen of fifteen Lebanese it had been holding prisoner for between eleven and thirteen years as "bargaining chips" for missing Israelis. The court ruled that Israeli law on administrative detention did not give the Defense Ministry the right to detain individuals who did not pose a security threat. Two prisoners, Shaykh 'Abd al-Karim 'Obayd and Mustafa Dirani, remained in custody on the grounds that they did. The release of the other thirteen came after the court rejected a last minute petition from the relatives of missing Israeli navigator Ron Arad, whose aircraft had been shot down over South Lebanon in 1986.[189]

PEACE EFFORTS WITH SYRIA BOG DOWN

Shepherdstown

On 3 January, amid great hopes for a historic breakthrough, Israeli and Syrian delegations began peace talks under American auspices in Shepherdstown, West Virginia. Optimism was high when public negotiations between the two sides resumed at Blair House in Washington in December 1999, after a break of nearly four years, with both parties seemingly ready to go the extra mile. At Blair House, Barak had intimated that he was ready to pull back from the Golan Heights to the 4 June 1967 lines, and Syrian foreign minister Faruq al-Shar' seemed ready for concessions on normalization, security and water arrangements, leading the Americans to conclude that chances for a deal were good (see *MECS* 1999, pp. 66–68, 568).[190]

The talks got off to a shaky start with procedural wrangling over which aspects of the peace deal would be discussed first. The Syrians wanted to settle the territorial issue, while Israel wanted to discuss normalization and security arrangements. The deadlock was eventually broken by setting up four committees, one on each of the four core issues — territory, normalization, security and water — and convening them simultaneously.[191]

President Clinton visited Shepherdstown on five separate occasions and on 4 January, he hinted that he would work closely with Congress to help pay the cost of the Israeli security package that would be a part of any future agreement. To compensate for giving up the strategic Golan Heights, Israel was reportedly seeking about $1bn. for new fortifications, fighter planes, Apache helicopters, Tomahawk missiles and a ground station to gather US satellite information.[192]

The American Paper
On 7 January, both sides reportedly accepted as a basis for further negotiation a seven-page American working paper, defining the points of convergence and differences between them. According to the American paper, which was leaked to the Israeli newspaper Ha'aretz, Syria was demanding a return to the 4 June 1967 borders, while Israel was non-committal; Syria insisted on the removal of all Israeli settlements on the Golan, while Israel wanted them to be allowed to stay under Syrian sovereignty if they so chose; Syria proposed that the agreed-on early-warning station on the Golan be staffed by American and French nationals, with a symbolic Israeli presence only, while Israel insisted on a permanent, effective presence. Syria demanded equal demilitarization on both sides of the new border, while Israel wanted the entire Golan demilitarized but only a small strip on its side of border. On water rights, Syria proposed a joint council, while Israel sought prior assurance that it could continue to use water from Golan sources.[193]

The talks were suspended on 10 January to give each side time to assess its position, and they agreed to meet for a second round on 19 January. However, two days before the scheduled restart, it was announced that the talks had been postponed.[194]

The American Paper Leaked
The Syrians were incensed at the leak of the American document, which showed them ready to make concessions on which they were not yet prepared to go public. They reconsidered their position and presented Israel with an ultimatum: There would have to be a clear Israeli commitment to full withdrawal from the Golan before the Syrian delegation returned. Barak refused and the talks were not renewed.[195]

The Syrians were also concerned at mounting popular opposition in Israel to returning the Golan, which reached new heights on 10 January, when some 150,000 people demonstrated in Tel Aviv against Israeli withdrawal. The Syrians were afraid Barak might strike a deal, but fail to push it through in a referendum.[196]

Clinton Tries Again
In late February, Clinton tried again. He sent a message to Barak saying he needed more leeway on territory, and that, if he got it, he believed he could wrap up the Syrian package. Barak gave Clinton the go-ahead. There was still a problem over the Syrian demand for a presence on the northeastern shore of the Sea of Galilee, although the Syrians assured the Americans that they were not demanding any consequent water rights.[197]

The new American initiative received a setback when, on 1 March, the Israeli government lost a vote on a preliminary reading of a bill on the proposed Golan referendum. The bill, submitted by Silvan Shalom of the Likud, required that the return of the Golan Heights to Syria be approved by at least 50% of all eligible voters, rather than a majority of the votes cast. That meant that, statistically, Barak would have to get a majority of about two thirds of the votes cast, or, conversely, that a third of those who turned out to vote would be able to sink a peace deal with Syria.[198]

Clinton, however, was undeterred and in an effort to break the deadlock, met the ailing Syrian president Hafiz al-Asad in Geneva on 26 March. Asad's willingness to make a rare trip abroad was itself seen as a cause for optimism. However, Clinton was reportedly taken aback when Asad implied that he wanted water and fishing rights in the Sea of Galilee and he quickly realized that the summit would not produce a breakthrough.[199]

White House spokesperson Joe Lockhart said after the meeting that the differences between Syria and Israel had not narrowed and that consequently the US did not believe that it would be productive to reopen talks. Syrian officials blamed Israel for the failure to achieve any progress, claiming that Clinton had not been authorized to offer a full Israeli withdrawal from the Golan Heights.[200]

The Americans, however, blamed Asad for the breakdown. US ambassador to Israel Martin Indyk said afterwards that "Asad didn't come to negotiate, he came to say no." In Indyk's view, a deal was there to be had and what had gone wrong was the timing. When the Syrians were ready for a deal in January, Barak had taken a backward step on the territorial issue, and by the time Barak was ready in March, the ailing Asad was totally absorbed in the question of succession after his death, and no longer interested in a deal with Israel. According to Indyk, Asad was concerned that his son, Bashshar, whom he was grooming to take over the leadership, might not be able to withstand hard-line criticism for being associated with a deal with Israel.[201]

On 5 April, Syrian foreign minister Shar' sent the formal Syrian reply to Clinton, rejecting most of what the Americans and the Israelis were proposing. There was, he said, no need to set up a joint committee to demarcate the 4 June borders, because the UN had all the relevant maps; Syria opposed any form of early warning for Israel on the Golan; water sharing, Shar' said, should be decided "by international law," without spelling out what this meant for the Sea of Galilee; normalization would come not before or during but only after full Israeli withdrawal from the Golan was complete; and the full withdrawal, Shar' said, should be completed in a year, not eighteen months.[202]

Shar''s reply clearly constituted a hardening of the Syrian line, and both the Americans and the Israelis decided there was no point in trying to continue the negotiations.[203] The possibility of progress appeared to diminish further when, on 13 April, Barak announced an end to the freeze on settlement building activity on the Golan, which had been imposed as a confidence building measure when Israeli-Syrian talks resumed in December.[204] Within days of Barak's announcement, press reports surfaced indicating that Syria was about to close a $500m. arms deal with Russia which would include advanced fighter planes, an air defense system and anti-tank armaments.[205]

Asad's Death

Less than three months after the Geneva summit, President Asad was dead. He died of a heart attack on 10 June aged sixty-nine, thirty-three years to the day after Israel captured the Golan Heights. Within hours, moves were underway to ensure a smooth transition to Asad's son Bashshar. The Syrian constitution was amended, lowering the minimum age for a president from forty to thirty-four, to enable the thirty-five year-old Bashshar to assume power.[206]

In Israel there were hopes that Bashshar, an ophthalmologist who had spent some time in the West, might be more open to peace moves than his conservative father had been. Barak called on the new leader to reengage in peace talks, but Bashshar, intent on consolidating his position in Syria, did not respond (for further details, see chapters on Syria, and the Arab-Israeli peace process).[207]

EGYPT AND JORDAN

Intifada Fall-Out

Egypt and Jordan, the two Arab countries with full peace treaties with Israel, made intense efforts to defuse the intifada, and to get Israelis and Palestinians back to the peace table. Both President Mubarak and King 'Abdallah of Jordan were concerned that pro-Palestinian demonstrations could destabilize their regimes, and that pro-Palestinian sentiment across the Arab world could spark a wider confrontation with Israel, which neither of them wanted. Both tried to exert influence on 'Arafat to reduce the level of violence, and both played a role in setting up an international summit in Sharm al-Shaykh in mid-October, at which the parties agreed on conditions for a cease-fire (see above). Mubarak leaned heavily on 'Arafat to attend the summit, reportedly calling him more than a dozen times in the forty-eight hours before it started.[208]

Mubarak also convened an Arab summit in Cairo on 21 October, at which he took the steam out of bellicose resolutions and rhetoric by militant Arab states which could have escalated the fighting.[209] Indeed, Mubarak's determined anti-war stand was the most important single factor preventing the low intensity Israeli-Palestinian conflict spiraling into regional confrontation. War by the Arab countries against Israel without Egypt was almost inconceivable, and Mubarak took the lead in ensuring that there would be no such war by making it clear that Egypt had no intention of fighting. In a mid-October TV interview, he made his abhorrence of the war option crystal clear: The Arab states, he said, had adopted peace as a strategy, and those who were calling for war had no idea what it was really like. "War," he declared, "is not a game," and, in a reference to more militant Arab leaders (the reference was to Salih of Yemen, Qadhdhafi and Saddam), he mocked those who were bent on fighting "till the last Egyptian soldier."[210]

While Egypt played a key role in ensuring there would be no regional war, it maintained its Arab nationalist credentials by leading the chorus of Arab criticism of the Israeli handling of the intifada. When Israeli helicopter gun-ships attacked PA targets in Gaza in late November, in retaliation for the bombing of an Israeli school bus (see above), Egypt recalled its ambassador from Tel Aviv. Jordan followed suit by not sending its newly appointed ambassador to take up his posting in Israel. The moves were seen as the most significant protests by Arab states since the intifada began and took Israeli officials by surprise. Israel, however, made it clear that it had no intention of recalling its ambassadors to Cairo or Amman. Nor did Egypt or Jordan go all the way and sever ties with Israel. At years' end, their embassies in Tel Aviv were still functioning, albeit without full diplomatic representation, and their peace treaties with Israel did not appear to be under threat.[211]

Still, Egypt continued to see Israel as a threat to its regional hegemony, regardless of the Israeli-Palestinian situation. The Egyptians were particularly concerned by the purported nuclear capacity of Israel, and, in May, even before the failure of the Camp David summit, led another assault on the Israeli nuclear policy. At the UN five-yearly review of the Nuclear Non-Proliferation Treaty (NPT) in New York, the Egyptians drew attention to a resolution passed at the previous review in 1995, calling for a nuclear-free Middle East, and urging Israel to sign the NPT. Then, Egypt had tried to make indefinite extension of the treaty contingent on Israel signing. Israel refused and Egyptian-US compromise was the 1995 resolution the Egyptians were now trying to get enforced. But Israel stood firm in its refusal to sign (see *MECS* 1995, pp. 49–50).[212]

After the eruption of the intifada, the press in both Egypt and Jordan took an increasingly critical stand toward Israel and exacerbated already widespread public hostility (for details, see chapters on Egypt and Jordan).

Twice it spilled over into acts of violence against Israeli embassy personnel in Amman. In separate incidents in late November and early December, an Israeli diplomat and an embassy employee were shot and lightly wounded in attacks on their vehicles in the Jordanian capital.[213]

Earlier in the year, King 'Abdallah paid his first visit to Israel, emphasizing the importance of the economic links between the two countries, despite the misgivings in Amman. On 23 April, he met Barak at the Red Sea port of Eilat to discuss economic relations, especially water management. 'Abdallah also urged Israel and Syria to resume peace talks and called for Jerusalem to serve as capital of both Israel and a future Palestinian state.[214]

THE REST OF THE REGION

Temporary Resumption of Multilateral Peace Talks

With the renewed Israeli-Syrian peace talks ostensibly moving forward in Shepherdstown, Russian foreign minister Igor Ivanov announced on 6 January, during a visit to Israel, that multilateral Middle East peace talks would resume in Moscow in February, after a three-year break.[215]

At a meeting in Moscow on 1 February, chaired by Russia and the US, and attended by representatives from the EU, Japan and Canada, Israeli and Arab officials agreed to resume multilateral contacts. They decided to set up four working groups — on economic cooperation, water, refugees and the environment — to meet in April and May in various locations. It was also agreed that a fifth working group on arms control might meet within a few months. But with the early breakdown of the Israeli-Syrian track, the multilateral process ground to a halt, and, with the outbreak of the intifada, was again suspended.[216]

Promising Beginnings Come to Naught

The fate of the multilateral process mirrored the fluctuations in Israeli relations with several other Middle Eastern countries, where promising beginnings gave way to sharp ruptures. An Omani government delegation visited Israel in early January to discuss the reopening of a trade office in Tel Aviv; in mid-January, Foreign Minister Levy paid a four-day visit to his native Morocco, during which the two countries agreed in principle to upgrade diplomatic relations to ambassadorial level and to allow the Israeli national carrier, El AL, to fly directly to Morocco; in late January, the Bahraini heir apparent, Shaykh Salman bin Hamad Al Khalifa, held talks with the Israeli minister of regional cooperation Peres at the world economic forum in Davos, the first ever meeting between the two countries at such a senior level;[217] in early March, Yemen allowed a first-ever group of Israelis to tour the country on Israeli passports,[218] and in mid-March, Israeli officials announced that Israel would provide technical and military expertise to help Algeria build a counter-terrorism unit.[219] But these promising early signs dissipated with the outbreak of the intifada. The old tensions and rhetoric returned, and, within weeks of the fighting, Tunisia, Oman, Morocco and Qatar severed their formal links with Israel. Only Mauritania, which had established full diplomatic relations with Israel in October 1999, balked the tide and maintained the status quo.[220]

Ties with Turkey Stand the Test

Israeli relations with Turkey suffered slight strains when Education Minister Yossi Sarid announced in May that he intended to include material relating to the purported 1915 Turkish genocide of 1.5m. Armenians in the high school history syllabus. But Turkish protests were mollified by Israeli reassurances about the primacy of the relationship.[221]

The military component of the relationship continued to flourish. It was reported in mid-June that Israel Military Industries (IMI) had been awarded a $1bn. contract to upgrade 170 M-60 tanks for the Turkish army, and in July that Israel would be selling Turkey an Ofek satellite for photographic purposes. An Israeli-Russian consortium also tendered to build 145 attack helicopters for Turkey, a contract estimated to be worth approximately $4.6bn.[222]

Most importantly, the Palestinian intifada did little to affect Turkish ties with Israel. Despite its largely Muslim population, anti-Israel protests in Turkey were relatively minor, and diplomatic, military, economic, cultural and business ties were unimpaired. The volume of bilateral non-military trade neared the projected $1bn. mark and Israel's ready acceptance of former Turkish president Suleyman Demirel as a member of the Mitchell panel was testimony to the abiding strength of the relationship.[223]

THE PHALCON, THE US AND CHINA

Israeli relations with the US went through an uneasy period due to the adamant opposition of Washington to a projected Israeli sale of a highly sophisticated airborne early warning radar system to China. Although the system, known as the Phalcon, was Israeli-developed and contained no American parts, and a contract between Israel and the Chinese had already been signed, the US argued that the sale could harm its global interests and called on the special Israel-US relationship in urging its cancelation. US officials argued that the Phalcon's radar and aircraft tracing technology could endanger US forces in a military conflict with China, for example, over Taiwan.[224]

According to the terms of the contract, Israel had agreed to outfit a Chinese-owned Ilyushin-76 aircraft with the Phalcon system at a reported cost of $250m. China had agreed to buy one Phalcon-equipped plane, with an option for at least three more.[225]

In an early April visit to Israel, US secretary of defense William Cohen voiced Washington's displeasure over the projected deal. The issue came up again when Barak met Clinton at the White House on 11 April,[226] and in the ensuing weeks American officials insisted that Israel would "just have to cancel the whole deal."[227]

As Barak temporized, the administration got tougher, and, in June, the House

Appropriations Committee threatened to cut aid to Israel unless it canceled the deal. The Israeli dilemma was acute. The Israeli National Security Council drew up a secret document arguing that the impasse was compromising Israel's dealings with the administration on a wide range of issues and that ties with the US were far more important than honoring the deal with China. China, however, was an important IMI client and canceling the deal threatened to hamper its ability to compete internationally.[228]

Barak had hoped to win the US round, but when the crunch came, he had little choice, and in mid-July, he canceled the deal. Chinese officials reacted strongly, condemning the US for interfering in China's sovereign ties with another country, and Israel for failing to honor a written commitment.[229]

The Phalcon deal was part of an unprecedented warming of ties between Jerusalem and Beijing, which reached a highpoint in mid-April, when President Jiang Zemin became the first Chinese head of state to visit Israel. The cancelation of the Phalcon deal, however, was a serious setback.[230]

EUROPE GAINS MORE INFLUENCE
With the outbreak of fighting after the failure of American-sponsored peace efforts, Europe became more involved in the Israeli-Palestinian track than before. While the peace process was going forward, the Europeans, despite donating funds to help build the Palestinian economy, had little political relevance. But when the process ran aground, their special ties with the Palestinians became more important. European diplomats, Javier Solana, the top EU foreign and defense policy official and Miguel Moratinos, the EU special Middle East ambassador, played an active role in the mid-October effort at Sharm al-Shaykh to bring about a cease-fire.[231] And whereas in the past, Americans and Europeans, vying for influence in the Middle East, had tended to work at cross-purposes, now they tried to coordinate moves, with each side exerting influence where and when it could (see also chapters on Western Europe, Russia and the Middle East, and the Arab-Israeli peace process).[232]

The EU also took steps to improve its political and economic ties with Israel, upgrading the trade agreement in April, and establishing the "EU-Israel Forum" in May to foster greater understanding for EU policies in Israel. Moreover, after years of vainly knocking on the door, Israel was finally accepted as an official member of the Group of West European and Other Nations (WEOG) in the UN, making it eligible for membership of key UN bodies including the Security Council.[233]

UPGRADING TIES ON THE INDIAN SUB-CONTINENT
Strategic Cooperation with India
During a visit to Israel by Indian foreign minister Jaswanath Singh in July, the two countries announced that they would cooperate closely against terror. There were also reports of nuclear cooperation and the two countries set up a biannual foreign ministers' forum to further "strategic dialogue."[234]

Sri Lanka Renews Ties
In early May, Sri Lanka resumed diplomatic ties with Israel, which had been severed in 1970, after pressure by the Arab states. The decision to renew ties followed an invitation to Israeli defense officials to visit Sri Lanka, where the government was reportedly seeking

to upgrade its military hardware, after suffering heavy losses in an offensive by the separatist Tamil Tigers.[235]

POPE JOHN PAUL II VISITS THE HOLY LAND

A visibly ailing Pope John Paul II paid a historic visit to Israel and the PA in late March. On the only previous papal visit to the Holy Land in 1964, Pope Paul VI had pointedly excluded Jewish Jerusalem from his itinerary, traveled directly from Jordan to Megiddo in northern Israel, and spent just twelve hours on Israeli soil. In contrast, Pope John Paul II's visit was a pilgrimage of reconciliation between Christians and Jews, part of a personal crusade for peace among all faiths.[236]

On 23 March, when the pope visited Yad Vashem, the Nazi Holocaust memorial in Jerusalem, he spoke of his profound sorrow for acts of persecution and antisemitism "against the Jews by Christians at any time and in any place." The event was attended by Prime Minister Barak and broadcast live on Israel television and radio. Barak described the pope's visit to Yad Vashem as "a climax of this historic journey of healing" and said that Israelis appreciated his "noble act most profoundly."[237]

The reconciliation with the Jews, however, did not deflect papal sympathy for the Palestinians. The pope met 'Arafat in the West Bank town of Bethlehem on 22 March, and, in a speech delivered in Manger Square, he told Palestinians that they had "a natural right to a homeland." "No one," he said, "can ignore how much the Palestinian people have had to suffer in recent decades. Your torment is the eyes of the world. And it has gone on too long."[238]

A month before the pope's historic visit, the Vatican and the Palestine Liberation Organization (PLO) had signed a basic agreement, which strengthened and clarified their relations. In the agreement, the Vatican recognized the PLO as the representative of the Palestinian National Authority and reaffirmed its position that Jerusalem be granted a special international status, guaranteeing free access for Christians, Jews and Muslims to the city's holy sites. Israeli Foreign Ministry officials rejected the Vatican position, arguing that free access was guaranteed under Israeli sovereignty.

NOTES

For the place and frequency of publications cited here, and for the full name of the publication, news agency, radio station or monitoring service where an abbreviation is used, please see "List of Sources." Only in the case of more than one publication bearing the same name is the place of publication noted here.

1. *Ha'aretz*, 10 July 2000, *JR*, 18 December 2000; 1 January 2001.
2. *Ha'aretz*, 19 December; *Yedi'ot Aharonot*, 22 December 2000; *JR*, 1 January 2001.
3. *Ha'aretz*, 11, 28 May, 10, 11 July 2000.
4. *Ha'aretz*, 10 July 2000.
5. *Ha'aretz*, 12 July, 3, 4 September 2000; *Keesing's*, Vol. 46, No. 7, p. 43688; Vol. 46, No. 9, p. 43769.
6. *Ha'aretz*, 1 August 2000.
7. *Ha'aretz*, 14 April, 20 August, 1 November; *JR*, 8 May 2000.
8. *JR*, 6 November 2000, 29 January 2001.
9. *Ha'aretz*, 10, 12 October; *JR*, 23 October 2000.
10. *JR*, 16 July 2001.

11. *JR*, 20 November 2000.
12. *Ha'aretz*, 4, 17, 18, 25 January, 27 March 2000; Yossi Beilin, *Manual for a Wounded Dove* (Miskal-Yediot Aharonoth and Chemed Books: Tel Aviv, 2001), pp. 91–92.
13. *Ha'aretz*, 24 May; *JR*, 19 June 2000.
14. *Ma'ariv*, 24 May; *Yedi'ot Aharonot*, 26 May 2000.
15. *Yedi'ot Aharonot*, 29 December; *Ma'ariv*, 29 December 2000.
16. *JR*, 18 December; *Ha'aretz*, 22 December 2000.
17. *Ha'aretz*, 27, 28 January; *Keesing's* Vol. 46, No. 1, p. 43383; *JR*, 31 January, 28 February 2000.
18. *Ha'aretz*, 11 January, 14, 15, 17, 19, 20 March; *Keesing's* Vol. 46, No. 3, p. 43490; *JR*, 10 April 2000.
19. *Ha'aretz*, 1 May 2000.
20. *Ha'aretz*, 16 May; *JR*, 22 May, 5 June 2000.
21. *Ha'aretz*, 8, 20, 21 June 2000.
22. *Ha'aretz*, 22 June 2000; *Keesing's* Vol. 46, No. 6, pp. 43647–8.
23. *Ha'aretz*, 22, 23 June; *JR*, 17 July 2000.
24. *Ha'aretz*, 28 June 2000.
25. *Ha'aretz*, 10 July 2000.
26. *Ha'aretz*, 11 July; *JR*, 31 July 2000.
27. *Ha'aretz*, 3 August 2000; *Keesing's*, Vol. 46, No. 8, p. 43722.
28. *JR*, 31 July 2000.
29. *Yedi'ot Aharonot*, 21 August 2000; *Keesing's* Vol. 46, No. 8, p. 43722.
30. *Yedi'ot Aharonot*, 21 August 2000.
31. *Ha'aretz*, 20 August; *JR*, 25 September 2000.
32. *Yedi'ot Aharonot*, 25 August; *JR*, 25 September 2000.
33. *Yedi'ot Aharonot*, 20 October, 10 November, 15, 22, 29 December; *Ma'ariv*, 20 October, 10 November, 15, 22, 29 December 2000; *JR*, 1 January 2001.
34. *Ha'aretz*, 10, 12 October, 12 December; *JR*, 23 October 2000.
35. *Ha'aretz*, 22, 23 October 2000.
36. *Ha'aretz*, 24 October 2000.
37. *Ha'aretz*, 31 October; *Keesing's*, Vol. 46, No. 10, p. 43824, *JR*, 20 November 2000.
38. *Yedi'ot Aharonot*; *Ma'ariv*, 24 November; *Ha'aretz*, 29 November 2000; *Keesing's*, Vol. 46, No. 11, p. 43881.
39. *Ha'aretz*, 1 December 2000.
40. *Ha'aretz*, 10 December 2000; *Keesing's*, Vol. 46, No. 12, p. 43926.
41. *Ha'aretz*, 11, 12, 13 December 2000; *JR*, 1 January 2001.
42. *Ha'aretz* 15, 19 December; *Yedi'ot Aharonot*, 22 December 2000.
43. *Ha'aretz*, 19 December; *Keesing's* Vol. 46, No. 12, p. 43926, *Yedi'ot Aharonot*, *Ma'ariv*, 22, 29 December 2000.
44. *JR*, 1 January 2001.
45. *JR*, 18 December; *Ma'ariv*, 29 December 2000.
46. *Ha'aretz*, 24, 25, 26 December 2000; *JR*, 15 January 2001.
47. *Ha'aretz*, 29 March 2000; *Keesing's*, Vol. 46, No. 3, p. 43490.
48. *Ha'aretz*, 28 September 2000; *Keesing's* Vol. 46, No. 9, p. 43769.
49. *Ha'aretz*, 6, 10 July; *JR*, 31 July, 11 September 2000.
50. *JR*, 11 September 2000.
51. *Ha'aretz*, 20 December; *Yedi'ot Aharonot*, 22 December 2000.
52. *Ha'aretz*, 31 December 1999, 28 May, 11 July; *Keesing's*, Vol. 46, No. 1, p. 43383; *JR*, 14 February 2000.
53. *Ha'aretz*, 5, 7, 14 January; *Yedi'ot Aharonot*, 5, 7 January, 2000.
54. *Ha'aretz*, 21, 24 January 2000; *Keesing's*, Vol. 46, No. 1, p. 43383.
55. *Ha'aretz*, 7 April, 25, 28 May 2000; *Keesing's*, Vol. 46, No. 4, p. 43544 and No. 5, p. 43596.
56. *Ha'aretz*, 1 August 2000; Beilin, *Manual for a Wounded Dove*, p. 144.

57. *Keesing's*, Vol. 46, No. 7, p. 43688; *JR*, 28 August 2000.
58. *Ha'aretz*, 10 July, 24 November; *JR*, 5 December 2000.
59. *Ha'aretz*, 8 March; *JR*, 27 March 2000.
60. *JR*, 27 March; *Ha'aretz*, 17 April, 10 July 2000.
61. *Ha'aretz*, 6 August 2000; *Keesing's*, Vol. 46, No. 8, p. 43722.
62. *Ha'aretz*, 8 August 2000.
63. *Ha'aretz*, 4 September; *Keesing's*, Vol. 46, No. 9, p. 43769; *JR*, 25 September 2000.
64. *Ha'aretz*, 13, 14, 19 April; *JR*, 8 May 2000.
65. *Ha'aretz*, 4, 5 July; *JR*, 31 July 2000.
66. *Ma'ariv*, 31 December 2000; *Ha'aretz*, 2 January 2001.
67. *Ma'ariv*, 31 December 2000.
68. *Ha'aretz*, 20 August 2000.
69. *Ha'aretz* 14, 20 September 2000.
70. *Ha'aretz*, 31 October, 1 November; *Yedi'ot Aharonot*, 25 August; *JR*, 25 September 2000.
71. *Ha'aretz*, 24 December 2000; *JR*, 29 January 2001.
72. *JR*, 6 November 2000.
73. *Ha'aretz*, 2 January 2000; *JR*, 29 January 2001.
74. *JR*, 23 April 2001.
75. *JR*, 22 May 2000; *Ha'aretz*, 19 January; *JR*, 12 February 2001.
76. *Ha'aretz*, 4 January; *JR*, 29 January 2001.
77. *JR*, 24 April 2000, 1 January; *Ha'aretz*, 10 January 2001.
78. *JR*, 24 April; *Ha'aretz*, 5 May 2000.
79. *Ha'aretz*, 4, 5, 7, 12 June 2000.
80. *Ha'aretz*, 15 August; *JR*, 11 September 2000.
81. *Ha'aretz*, 9, 10 January 2000.
82. *Ha'aretz*, 16 January; *JR*, 12 February 2001.
83. *Al-'Ayn*, 6 March 2000.
84. *Kull al-Arab*, 15 August 2000.
85. *Ha'aretz*, 31 December 2000.
86. *JP*, 1 January 2001.
87. *Ha'aretz*, 24 December 2000.
88. *Kol Hanegev* (Beersheva), 25 August; *Panorama*, 25 August 2000.
89. *Kol Hanegev*, ibid.
90. *JP*, 28 June 2000.
91. *Ma'ariv*, 20 July 2000.
92. *JP*, 20 July 2000.
93. Ibid.
94. *Ma'ariv*, 20 July 2000.
95. *JP*, 23 October 2000.
96. *Yedi'ot Aharonot*, 31 March 2000.
97. Ibid.
98. *JP*, 31 March 2000.
99. *Ha'aretz*, 31 March; *al-Ittihad* (Haifa), 2 April 2000.
100. Ibid.
101. *Yedi'ot Aharonot*, 6 April 2000.
102. Ibid.
103. *Ha'aretz*, 13 April 2000.
104. *Al-Ittihad* (Haifa), 5 May; *Kull al-Arab*, 5 May; *Panorama*, 12 May 2000.
105. *Yedi'ot Aharonot*, 4 May 2000.
106. *Ma'ariv*, 4 May 2000.
107. *Ha'aretz*, 4 May 2000.
108. *Ha'aretz, JP*, 5, 8 May 2000.
109. *JP*, 3 October 2000.
110. *Ha'aretz, JP*, 4, 5 October 2000.

111. *JP, Ma'ariv*, 5 October 2000.
112. *Ha'aretz*, 17 September 2000.
113. *Ha'aretz*, 11 October 2000.
114. *JP, Ha'aretz*, 14 September 2000.
115. *JP*, 17 September 2000.
116. *Hatzofeh*, 29 September 2000.
117. *Ha'aretz*, 20 October 2000.
118. *Ha'aretz, JP*, 24 October 2000.
119. *JP*, 7 November 2000. <www.adalah.org./press-releases/00-11-13.htm>.
120. *Yedi'ot Aharonot*, 6 October 2000.
121. *Ha'aretz*, 7 November 2000.
122. *Ma'ariv*, 22 October 2000.
123. *Ha'aretz*, 12 December 2000.
124. *JP*, 28 September; *Globes*, 13 December; *Ha'aretz*, 31 December 2000.
125. *Ha'aretz*, 10 December 2000.
126. *Ha'aretz*, 10, 11 December 2000.
127. *Ha'aretz*, 11, 12 December 2000.
128. Gilead Sher, *Just Beyond Reach: The Israeli Palestinian Peace Negotiations 1999–2001* (Miskal Yedi'ot Aharonot and Chemed Books: Tel Aviv 2001), passim; *JR*, 16 July 2001.
129. Sher, *Just Beyond Reach*, pp. 80–143.
130. *Ha'aretz Magazine*, 14 September; *JR*, 16 July 2001; Menachem Klein, *Shattering a Taboo: The Contacts Toward a Permanent Status Agreement in Jerusalem 1994–2001*, The Jerusalem Institute for Israel Studies, The JIIS Studies Series, No. 89, Jerusalem 2001, pp. 29–30.
131. Gilead Sher, interview with the author, 18 June 2001.
132. Sher, *Just Beyond Reach*, pp. 139–42; *JR*, 16 July 2001.
133. *JR*, 16 July 2001.
134. Ibid., p. 12, Robert Malley and Hussein Agha, "Camp David: The Tragedy of Errors," *The New York Review of Books*, 9 August 2001, p. 63; Beilin, *Manual for a Wounded Dove*, pp. 126, 131–32.
135. *JR*, 16 July 2001, pp. 12,14; Klein, *Shattering a Taboo*, pp. 43–56.
136. Malley and Agha, "Camp David: The Tragedy of Errors", pp. 60, 62; Klein, *Shattering a Taboo*, p. 46.
137. *JR*, 16 July 2001.
138. *Ha'aretz*, 26 July 2000; Beilin, *Manual for a Wounded Dove*, p. 140.
139. *Ha'aretz*, 28 July 2000; *Keesing's*, Vol. 46, No. 8, pp. 43721–2.
140. *Keesing's*, Vol. 46, No. 9, p. 43770.
141. *JR*, 6 November 2000.
142. Sher, *Just Beyond Reach*, pp. 281–82; *JR*, 16 July 2001.
143. *Ha'aretz*, 29 September 2000.
144. *Ha'aretz*, 1 October 2000.
145. *Ha'aretz*, 5, 16, 17, 18 January; *JR*, 31 January 2000, *Keesing's*, Vol. 46, No. 1, p. 43384.
146. *Ha'aretz*, 20 March 2000.
147. *Ha'aretz*, 15, 16 May 2000. See also Beilin, *Manual for a Wounded Dove*, pp. 111–16.
148. Gershon Baskin, "What Went Wrong - Oslo - The PLO (PA) - Israel - Some Additional Facts," <www.ipcri.org>, p. 5; *Ha'aretz*, 19, 23 May, 2 July 2000; Beilin, *Manual for a Wounded Dove*, p. 124.
149. *Ha'aretz*, 1, 2 October; *IHT*, 2 October 2000.
150. *Ha'aretz*, 5, 6 October 2000; *Keesing's*, Vol. 46, No. 10, p. 43823.
151. *Ha'aretz*, 9, 11 October 2000; *Keesing's*, Vol. 46, No. 10, p. 43823.
152. *Ha'aretz*, 13 October 2000; *Keesing's*, Vol. 46, No. 10, p. 43823.
153. *Ha'aretz* 13 October 2000.
154. *Ha'aretz* 17, 18 October; *JR*, 6 November 2000.
155. *Ha'aretz*, 18 October 2000.

156. Ibid.; *Keesing's*, Vol. 46, No. 10, p. 43824.
157. *Ha'aretz*, 3 November 2000.
158. Ibid.
159. *Ha'aretz*, 10 November 2000.
160. *Ha'aretz*, 14 November 2000.
161. *Ha'aretz*, 21 November 2000.
162. *Ha'aretz*, 23 November; *JR*, 18 December 2000.
163. *Ha'aretz*, 1 December 2000.
164. *Ha'aretz*, 10 Novemebr 2000; *Keesing's*, Vol. 46, No 11, p. 43883.
165. *Ha'aretz*, 14, 15 November; *JR*, 20 November 2000; *Keesing's*, Vol. 46, No. 11, p. 43883.
166. *Ha'aretz*, 22 November 2000.
167. *Ha'aretz*, 8 November 2000.
168. *Ha'aretz*, 12 December 2000.
169. *Ha'aretz*, 15, 17 December 2000.
170. *Ha'aretz*, 19, 20, 24, 25 December 2000.
171. *Ha'aretz*, 28, 29, 31 December 2000; *Keesing's*, Vol. 46, No. 12, p. 43926.
172. *Ha'aretz*, 24, 25 May; *Ma'ariv*, 25 May; *Yedi'ot Aharonot*, 26 May 2000; *Keesing's*, Vol. 46, No. 5, p. 43595.
173. *Ha'aretz*, 18 April 2000; *Keesing's*, Vol. 46, No. 5, p. 43595.
174. *Ha'aretz*, 31 January, 7 March, 24 March, 25, 30 April 2000.
175. *Keesing's*, Vol. 46, No. 2, p. 43436; *Ha'aretz*, 10 February 2000.
176. *Ha'aretz*, 17 February 2000.
177. *Ha'aretz*, 5, 14, 17, 21 May 2000; *Keesing's*, Vol. 46, No. 3, p. 43595–96.
178. *Ha'aretz*, 14, 15, 22, 23 May 2000; *Keesing's* Vol. 46, No. 5, p. 43595.
179. *Ha'aretz*, 24, 25 May 2000; *Keesing's* Vol. 46, No. 5, p. 43595.
180. *Keesing's* Vol. 46, No. 5, pp. 43595–6; *Ha'aretz*, 11, 25, 26 May 2000.
181. *Keesing's* Vol. 46, No. 5, p. 43596; *Ha'aretz*, 24, 25 May; *Ma'ariv*, 24, 25 May 2000.
182. *Ha'aretz*, 25, 26 May; *JR*, 19 June 2000.
183. See, for example, *Ha'aretz*, 11 October, 13 October 2000.
184. *Ha'aretz*, 18, 19 June, 29 July 2000; *Keesing's*, Vol. 46, No. 7, p. 43689.
185. *Ha'aretz*, 6,7, 10 August 2000; *Keesing's*, Vol. 46, No. 8, p. 43723.
186. *Ha'aretz*, 8 October 2000; *Keesing's*, Vol. 46, No. 10, p. 43882–3.
187. *Ha'aretz* 16 October 2000; *JR*, 6 November, 20 November 2000.
188. *Ha'aretz*, 27 November 2000; *Keesing's* Vol. 46, No. 11, pp. 43882–3.
189. *Ha'aretz*, 13, 21 April 2000; *Keesing's* Vol. 46, No. 4, pp. 43543–44.
190. *Ha'aretz*, 4 January 2000; Beilin *Manual for a Wounded Dove*, p. 91.
191. *Ha'aretz*, *Yedi'ot Aharonot*, 5 January 2000.
192. *Ha'aretz*, 4 January 2000; *Keesing's*, Vol. 46, No. 1, p. 43384.
193. *Ha'aretz*, 9, 13 January 2000.
194. *Ha'aretz* 17, 18 January 2000; *Keesing's*, Vol. 46, No. 1, p. 43384.
195. *Ha'aretz*, 16, 20, 23, 30 January 2000; Beilin, *Manual for a Wounded Dove*, pp. 91–92.
196. *Ha'aretz*, 11, 12 January 2000; *Keesing's*, Vol. 46, No. 1, p. 43384.
197. Beilin, *Manual for a Wounded Dove*, p. 103.
198. *Ha'aretz*, 2 March; *Keesing's*, Vol. 46, No. 3, p. 43489; *JR*, 27 March 2000.
199. *Ha'aretz*, 27 March; *JR*, 8 May 2000.
200. *Ha'aretz*, 28 March 2000; *Keesing's*, Vol. 46, No. 3, p. 43489.
201. Indyk to author, 16 July 2001.
202. Beilin, *Manual for a Wounded Dove*, p. 103, *Ha'aretz*, 10 April 2000.
203. Ibid.
204. *Ha'aretz*, 14 April 2000.
205. *JR*, 8 May 2000.
206. *Ha'aretz*, 11 June 2000.
207. Ibid., *Keesing's*, Vol. 46, No. 6, p. 43647; *JR*, 3 July 2000.
208. *JR*, 20 November 2000.

209. *Ha'aretz*, 22 October 2000.
210. *JR*, 20 November 2000.
211. *Ha'aretz*, 22 November 2000; *Keesing's*, Vol. 46, No. 11, p. 43883.
212. *Ha'aretz*, 5, 24 April, 11, 22 May, 5 April; *JR*, 22 May 2000.
213. *Ha'aretz*, 20 November, 6 December 2000.
214. *Ha'aretz*, 23, 24 April 2000; *Keesing's*, Vol. 46, No. 4, p. 43544.
215. *Ha'aretz*, 2 February, 16 April; *Keesing's*, Vol. 46, No. 2, p. 43437, *JR*, 28 February 2000.
216. *Keesing's*, Vol. 46, No. 1, pp. 43383–4.
217. *Ha'aretz*, 12 April; *JR*, 24 April 2000.
218. *Keesing's*, Vol. 46, No. 3, p. 43490.
219. *Keesing's*, Vol. 46, No. 11, p. 43883.
220. *Ha'aretz*, 25 April; *JR*, 22 May 2000.
221. *Keesing's*, Vol. 46, No. 6, p. 43648; *Ha'aretz*, 5 July 2000.
222. *Ha'aretz*, 8, 28 November 2000.
223. *Ha'aretz*, 11 April 2000; *Keesing's*, Vol. 46, No. 4, p. 43544.
224. *Keesing's*, Vol. 46, No. 4, p. 43544; *Ha'aretz*, 25, 30 April 2000.
225. *Ha'aretz*, 12, 13 April 2000; *JR*, 24 April 2000.
226. *JR*, 5 June 2000.
227. *Ha'aretz*, 25, 27, 28, 29 June, 2 July 2000; *Keesing's*, Vol. 46, No. 6, p. 43648; *JR*, 10 October 2000.
228. *Ha'aretz*, 12 July; *Keesing's*, Vol. 46, No. 7, p. 43689; *JR*, 14 August 2000.
229. *Ha'aretz*, 12, 13, 14 April 2000; *Keesing's*, Vol. 46, No. 4, p. 43544; *JR*, 8 May 2000.
230. *Ha'aretz*, 17 October 2000.
231. *Ha'aretz*, 8 November 2000; *JR*, 21 May 2001.
232. *Ha'aretz*, 4 April, 4, 8 May 2000.
233. *Ha'aretz*, 16 June, 3 July 2000.
234. *Ha'aretz*, 5 May 2000; *Keesing's*, Vol. 46, No. 5, p. 43597.
235. *JR*, 27 March 2000.
236. *Ha'aretz*, 24 March 2000; *Keesing's*, Vol. 46, No. 3, p. 43489.
237. *Ha'aretz*, 23 March 2000; *Keesing's*, Vol. 46, No. 3, p. 43489.
238. *Ha'aretz*, 16 February; *Keesing's*, Vol. 46, No. 2, p. 43436; *JR*, 13 March 2000; Klein, *Shattering a Taboo*, pp. 53–54.

Jordan
(Al-Mamlaka al-Urdunniyya al-Hashimiyya)

KEREN BRAVERMAN

Changes which Jordan began to undergo following the ascension to the throne of King 'Abdallah II in February 1999 came into focus more sharply during the year 2000. In many ways, the government of 'Abd al-Ra'uf al-Rawabda, which was formed in March 1999 and dissolved in June 2000, was transitional, reflecting 'Abdallah's inheritance of his father's political associates. Rawabda, like most cabinet members, was a politician of the old guard, wary and prudent about reform and political liberalization. In the opinion of many political analysts, the Abu Raghib government appointed in June was actually the first to reflect 'Abdallah's independent intentions and aspirations for Jordan. While it would be wrong to present one as opposed to the other, it is safe to say that the Abu Raghib government was much closer to 'Abdallah's vision.

The new king's approach was apparent in his dealing with the Islamist groups in Jordan. Specifically, it was his refusal to allow the leaders of the Palestinian Hamas to return to Jordan, after having been deported in the end of 1999 (see *MECS* 1999, pp. 352–54), that distinguished 'Abdallah from the late king Husayn. In 'Abdallah's eyes, the deportation was a positive step toward rapprochement with the US, Israel and the Palestinian Authority (PA), and prevented the Palestinian issue from standing in the way of improving relations with all three and the accompanying benefits. Accordingly, both the Rawabda and Abu Raghib governments upheld the deportation, refusing to compromise.

In the foreign affairs sphere, King 'Abdallah successfully recruited financial assistance and improved Jordan's image as a reliable and responsible state with which agreements would be worthwhile. His persistence brought about the signing of the Free Trade Agreement (FTA) between Jordan and the US. The Jordanian economy, however, remained in a state of distress. Unemployment stayed high, and the budget deficit grew. The positive assessments made at the beginning of the year were not fulfilled. The outbreak of the Aqsa Intifada in the Palestinian areas of the West Bank and Gaza in the last quarter of the year brought about a serious economic slowdown and seriously undermined economic prospects for 2001.

'Abdallah's preference for keeping ties with Arab countries as a high priority and relations with Israel at a lower level continued to dominate Jordan's regional policy. The Abu Raghib government approached Iraq, which led to improved relations between the two countries. In addition to economic benefits, this improvement was a response to constant internal pressure from the parliamentary opposition and from professional organizations, which persistently called on the government to break the UN sanctions.

The outbreak of the intifada in late September only increased the Jordanian tendency to prioritize relations with Arab countries, and Jordan decided to join the Arab world in its declaration of support for the Palestinians. Nevertheless, the mass demonstrations

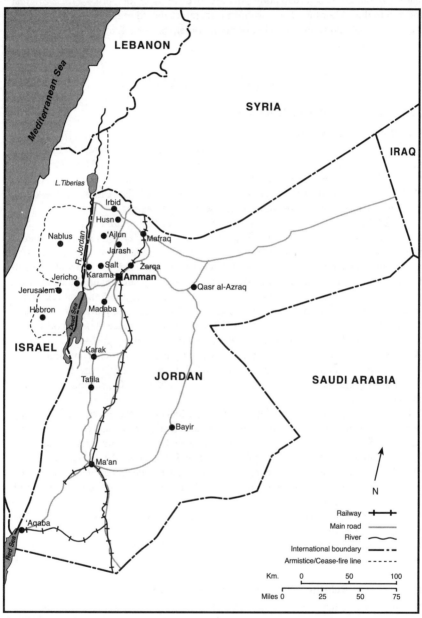

Jordan

that broke out all over Jordan during the first two weeks of the uprising were of great concern to the authorities. The government therefore turned to repressive measures in order to put an end to the violation of public order, and thus forestall any erosion of domestic stability.

INTERNAL AFFAIRS

THE CHANGE OF GOVERNMENTS

The Rawabda Government

The year began with the replacement of the chief of the royal court, 'Abd al-Karim Kabariti — who was already on bad terms with Rawabda by the end of 1999 (see *MECS* 1999, p. 345) — by Fayiz al-Tarawina. The change was interpreted by Salama Ni'mat, *al-Hayat*'s correspondent in Jordan, as a victory for the Rawabda camp over the king's more liberal stream in the government represented by Kabariti.[1]

In mid-January, a cabinet reshuffle took place, the second in the Rawabda administration. Seven ministers were appointed who had never before held ministerial office. They were 'Abdallah Tuqan, minister of post and telecommunications; 'Issa Ayyub, minister of transport; Muhammad Halayqa, minister of industry and trade; Muslih Tarawina, minister of health; Khalaf Musa'ada, minister of justice; Salih Qalab, minister of culture and information; and Wa'il Sabri, minister of energy and mineral resources. Qalab, who originated from the Bani Hasan tribe, was a leading journalist. He was a strong supporter of the PLO during the 1970s and 1980s, and voiced his support for the government crackdown on Hamas in 1999 (see *MECS* 1999, pp. 352–54). Ayman al-Majali was sworn in for the second time as deputy prime minister. Three out of the seven new ministers were of Palestinian origin: Sabri, Tuqan and Halayqa. Halayqa was credited with achieving the Jordanian entry to the World Trade Organization (WTO) at the end of 1999.[2]

The reshuffle followed some criticism from parliament of the government handling of certain economic issues. However, most deputies reacted with indifference, claiming that government policies did not contribute to social and economic reform and that changing ministers would not solve this problem.[3] In February another change was made, when Rima Khalaf, deputy prime minister and minister of planning, resigned, leaving the government with no other women members.[4] Talib Rifa'i was appointed minister of planning to replace Khalaf.[5]

From its inception, the Rawabda government did not exhibit liberal tendencies. The only appointment that introduced a spirit of reform was that of 'Adnan Abu 'Awda as political advisor to the king in March 1999 (see *MECS* 1999, p. 346). He was, however, removed by the king in April.[6]

The Strained Relations between Parliament and Government

In mid-April, tension reached its peak between parliament and government. Deputies expected an extraordinary session to be convened, mainly for economic legislation. Forty-five deputies signed a petition asking the king to grant them authority, in the expected extraordinary session, to discuss issues other than draft laws. Had this been granted, they would have been able to summon the government for a second vote of confidence.[7] A week later, more than fifty deputies, including the speaker of the Chamber of Deputies,

'Abd al-Hadi al-Majali, wrote to the king, criticizing the government and calling for its dismissal.[8] Their main grievance was the government failure to proceed with economic reforms and to move toward political liberalization. One of the claims made in the deputies' petition to the king was that Rawabda's attitude created a rift between East Bank Jordanians and Jordanians of Palestinian origin. According to the petition, Rawabda had asked tribal leaders to come to Amman to show support for the decision to deport the Hamas leaders, and had accepted them dressed in traditional East Bank costume. The events at the universities over the issue of student elections (see below) reflected a negative aspect of government policies as well.[9]

The initial crisis was offset in several ways. A counter-petition, defying the previous one and signed by thirty deputies, was handed to the king.[10] The prime minister and Majali denied the existence of any sort of crisis between parliament and the government, and the king reiterated his confidence in the Rawabda government. However, deputies who signed the criticizing letter speculated that the king would seriously look into it.[11]

At the beginning of May the crisis deepened. Forty-four deputies signed a new petition, calling for an extraordinary session of parliament to debate a vote of confidence in the government.[12] 'Abdallah issued a royal decree summoning parliament to an extraordinary session starting 20 May. The decree detailed a list of fifteen draft bills to be discussed at the session, mostly to do with encouraging foreign investment and privatization.[13] However, it did not grant parliament the authority to summon the government for a second vote of confidence.[14] The decree was accompanied by rumors that the king was expected to dismiss the current government after the extraordinary session and appoint a new prime minister.[15]

There were various explanations of the rift between 'Abdallah and Rawabda. Some claimed that it resulted from the king's tendency to modernize and open up to the West, in contrast to Rawabda's desire to maintain the status quo. According to this view, while it was true that Rawabda had facilitated the signing of the WTO agreement, he had nevertheless prevented its implementation.[16] The senior commentator Fahd al-Fanik, on the other hand, rejected the dichotomous distinction between Rawabda as a conservative, heading a coalition of the old guard who rejected reforms, and the king as leader of the reformers. As proof, he cited the rapid pace of privatization under the Rawabda administration. In addition, he claimed that the source of Rawabda's image as a conservative was the Israeli press.[17] According to another view, the reason for the dislike of Rawabda's government was its failure to implement any of the political or economic reforms advocated by the king.[18] Al-Hayat correspondent Salama Ni'mat pointed to the hostile government attitude toward the Economic Consultative Council (ECC) and its recommendations. The government viewed the ECC, formed by the king in 1999 (see MECS 1999, p. 357) in order to speed up economic reforms, and its liberal-minded recommendations as attempts to bypass government authority. He claimed that the increased focus by the king and the government on economic issues led it to neglect urgent political issues such as the control of the media and the resentment among students and Islamists over students elections at the universities, thus creating an increasing rift between the government and parliament.[19]

The Abu Raghib Government

In mid-June it became clear that the king would replace the prime minister with 'Ali Abu Raghib.[20] Expectations were high that Abu Raghib would improve working relations between parliament and the government. It was believed that the king's choice of Abu Raghib was based on the latter's liberal economic background and private sector experience, since these fitted the king's emphasis on economic issues and therefore his need for a prime minister with a strong economic orientation.[21] Abu Raghib was also an enthusiastic proponent of the 'Aqaba Special Economic Zone project (ASEZ, see below), which the king wanted very much to turn into reality. Abu Raghib headed the project planning committee. In fact, a few weeks before his appointment as prime minister, he had had a fierce argument over the project with Rawabda, who was strongly opposed to it. Rawabda claimed that the ASEZ regulations planned by Abu Raghib deprived the government of any control or influence over Jordan's only port, leaving it in the hands of foreign investors.[22] As well as heading the ASEZ planning group, Abu Raghib chaired the Chamber of Deputies committee on financial and economic affairs.[23]

On 18 June, the king accepted Rawabda's resignation and issued a royal decree appointing Abu Raghib to form a new government.[24] Abu Raghib was quick to do this, probably because he had already started discussions before the Rawabda government resigned.[25] The next day, the new ministers were listed in another royal decree. Nine were of Palestinian origin. This was in line with the spirit of the letter of designation instructing the government to "safeguard national unity."[26] It was a clear sign of Abu Raghib's intention to encourage the political participation of Jordanians of Palestinian origin.

In the letter of designation, the king set out the main government objectives as promoting reforms toward equality in law and speeding up economic reform, including privatization. He instructed the government to "promulgate a modern electoral law that guarantees the representation of all segments of society."[27]

The new government created considerable expectations, based on the reputation and qualifications of the ministers. These were markedly higher than those of the members of the Rawabda government. Besides public sector officials, ministers included private sector figures who were experienced and well-informed in their specific fields. Two of them, Khalid Tuqan and Fawaz Zu'bi, who were appointed to the Ministries of Education, and Post and Telecommunications respectively, had until then served as members of the ECC.[28] Talib Rifa'i, an enthusiastic proponent of privatization in the media, was appointed as minister of information, in line with the king's desire to promote privatization.[29] The appointment of the Islamic Action Front (IAF) official, 'Abd al-Rahim al-'Ukur, as minister of municipal, rural and environmental affairs was seen as a signal to the Islamist parties that the government was sincere in its intention to encourage the political participation of different political groups.[30] However, when Abu Raghib approached individual representatives of Islamic parties, some deputies were critical of his failure to approach the parties themselves. This led to 'Ukur's expulsion from the Muslim Brotherhood[31] (see below).

In the parliament, however, displeasure was evident over Abu Raghib's choice of ministers. Deputies were disappointed with his reluctance to appoint a cabinet drawn from elected representatives.[32] Another concern was that many of the new ministers, who were from the private sector, would find it difficult to adjust to working in the public sector. However, their background was considered essential in bringing much-needed qualities to the government system, such as efficiency, good management and proper planning.[33]

The new government policy statement was presented by Abu Raghib on 9 July. It stressed, among other issues, its intention to change the Election Law. Abu Raghib repeated that objective again in August, but explained that at this stage only certain voting procedures would be altered and not the one-person, one-vote system (see below).[34]

After Abu Raghib presented the policy statement he received the most resounding vote of confidence ever achieved in Jordan — 74 out of 80 deputies[35] — outdoing Rawabda's attainment of 66 votes in 1999 (see *MECS* 1999, p. 346).

Reactions in the Jordanian press to the new government and its policy statement were varied. Many commentators were impressed with the promises made and felt that the government composition meant it might actually achieve the goals it had set. Another widely held view was that this was the first government representing the new era — King 'Abdallah's era, and his plans for Jordan.[36] However, a well-known Jordanian observer, Rami al-Khuri, was skeptical, saying that all governments in the past had presented impressive policy statements, but failed to implement them.[37] In fact, the king himself emphasized in his letter of designation that the new government should be given time before its actions were judged, thus trying to pre-empt the attacks commonly leveled against former governments, namely that they did not produce results fast enough. In his meeting with the parliament, Abu Raghib also stressed that the reforms he was planning would take years to achieve.[38]

Toward the end of the year Abu Raghib ordered the retirement of Samih al-Batikhi, the director of General Intelligence. Batikhi had been one of the "king's men" and the key man in 'Abdallah's court since his appointment as the king's personal advisor in November 1999 (see *MECS* 1999, pp. 345–46). In general, Abu Raghib opposed the involvement of the *mukhabarat* (domestic intelligence) in the political arena. In his opinion, their activities should be confined to security matters. After becoming prime minister he deprived Batikhi of any influence on the formation of government — influential decisions in which Batikhi had been involved under the two previous governments. Moreover, Abu Raghib was dissatisfied with the performance of the *mukhabarat* at the time of the demonstrations in support of the Palestinians in October, when both he and the king were in Washington. In particular, he believed that the use of tear gas by riot police was too violent. Batikhi had also tried to meddle with appointment decisions at the Center for Strategic Studies at Jordan University. He had opposed the polls carried out by the center in regard to sensitive issues in Jordan, such as relations between citizens of Palestinian and Jordanian origin. After Abu Raghib had confided in the king about Batikhi's objections to these polls, he received the king's approval to announce Batikhi's retirement.[39] 'Abdallah then appointed Batikhi to the Senate.[40]

PARLIAMENT, PARTIES AND ASSOCIATIONS
Parliamentary Activity
In the letter of designation to Abu Raghib, the king stressed the need to fight corruption and to modernize public administration. Abu Raghib made many public statements calling on parliament and the government to work together against corruption.[41] The government launched a series of meetings between its own officials and heads of public sector departments, to discuss an administrative reform plan it had prepared.[42]

In parliament, head of the legal committee of the Chambers of Deputies, Mahmud Kharabsha, accused Rawabda's son of taking bribes from two businessmen from the Gulf interested in developing a tourist village next to Queen Alia Airport in Amman and claimed that the prime minister had been involved as well. The Chamber of Deputies appointed an investigation committee of nine deputies to look into these accusations. By mid-February, the committee found the accusations false, and the Chamber of Deputies cleared the prime minister of the corruption charges.[43]

Continuing the trend from 1999 and in accordance with the emphasis in the designation letter, much parliamentary activity was dedicated to economic issues. There was strong opposition to the amendment to the sales tax, as it would increase the list of products subject to a 13% tax. This new amendment was in addition to the sales tax increase agreed in parliament in 1999 (see *MECS* 1999, p. 347). Deputies claimed that it would impose more hardship on the already suffering lower classes.[44] However, in August, Abu Raghib urged the parliament to conclude the amendments to the Sales Tax Law, which were required for the second stage of the International Monetary Fund (IMF) Economic Reform Program and, in his opinion, were long overdue.[45] The Chamber of Deputies endorsed the draft with some minor changes, and the Senate approved the amended draft.[46]

At the end of May, the Chamber of Deputies passed a draft privatization law, which included a problematic article allowing the government to maintain its right of veto over any decision of a privatized company board.[47] The most impressive economic legislation, however, was the endorsement of the 'Aqaba Special Economic Zone Law (see below).

As to political parties in Jordan, Francesca Sawalha of *The Jordan Times* characterized their activity throughout 2000 as "The Politics of Apathy."[48] An interesting development was the formation of the Arab Democratic Union (al-Tajamu' al-'Arabi al-Dimuqrati) by Tahir al-Masri and Ahmad 'Ubaydat, members of the Senate, in mid-October.[49] They presented it as a movement and not a party. Although such a group had been planned for years, 'Ubaydat and Masri explained that it would not participate in the 2001 elections because of its lack of consensus over the election law. They were criticized for not wanting to enter the political fray.[50]

At the end of the year a new party was established. It was named Protectors — The Jordanian Citizens' Rights Movement (Huma — Harakat Huquq al-Muwatin al-Urdunniyya), and Ya'qub Sulayman al-Kiswani was appointed secretary-general. Its main objective was to "protect citizen's rights and to achieve national economic security in the face of Zionist ambitions to establish a Greater Israel (*Isra'il al-Kubra*)."[51]

Civil Liberties
The Struggle to Amend the Election Law
The debate on changing the election law, which had continued in recent years (see *MECS* 1993, pp. 463–65; 1997 pp. 464–67; 1998, pp. 370–71), became very heated in 2000. During the period of the Rawabda government there was wide debate of the issue in the press. One *Jordan Times* editorial called for an open public discussion, and warned against amendment of the law while parliament was in recess, as had happened in 1993, lest it be considered unconstitutional by the Islamic parties.[52]

With the formation of Abu Raghib's cabinet, it was felt that the government would endorse some changes to the controversial election law, but that it would not change the one-person, one-vote system before the 2001 elections.[53] In August, Abu Raghib announced that the government intended to continue a national dialogue with civil society institutions in the kingdom, in order to achieve an egalitarian and modern election law. The recent national dialogue had been initiated by the late king Husayn in 1998 and was resumed by King 'Abdallah in 1999 (see *MECS* 1998, pp. 376–77; 1999, pp. 347–48).

Abu Raghib stressed time and again that initial amendments would not include changing the one-person, one-vote system, and would deal only with voting procedures such as polling stations and voter identification.[54]

In the framework of the dialogue Abu Raghib met with the heads of the professional associations. Their demands included the amendment of the election law and the enhancement of democratization and human rights, in addition to professional issues. Abu Raghib urged them to focus on those and not on politics.[55] Interior Minister 'Awad Khulayfat met with the secretaries-general of the political parties. They asked for government financial support and for backing by the government-controlled media. Khulayfat expressed the government commitment to political development and its intention to bring about a change in the media's approach to political parties.[56]

In late September, the legal committee of the Chamber of Deputies, together with Speaker Majali, started inviting deputies, as well as civil society representatives, including leaders of political parties and professional organizations, and media figures, to participate in meetings about the issue of the election law. They announced their intention to ensure the participation of all sectors of civil society in the dialogue over this issue.[57] However, most of the journalists who were invited to a special discussion with the committee about the election law failed to arrive. Only four out of nearly fifty showed up. *Al-Dustur* chief editor, who said he couldn't attend the meeting due to a tight schedule, explained that journalists didn't arrive because they felt that deputies had never considered their opinions seriously in the past. Therefore, they had developed a measure of apathy with regard to making their opinions heard in parliament.[58]

In September, the government and the Chamber of Deputies discussed the redistribution of electoral districts as a means of achieving a more equitable representation in the next elections.[59] On 25 November, the last session of parliament before the scheduled elections convened. The main issue on the agenda was the amendment of the election law. A proposal for a two-votes-per-person electoral system was prepared by representatives of most parties and handed to the parliament. According to them, the proposed system would create more equitable representation of constituencies that were underrepresented under the one-person, one-vote system. More importantly, the Islamists supported this proposal, thus signaling their possible withdrawal from boycotting the next elections.[60] However, by the end of the year, the election law remained unchanged.

The Media and Press Freedom

After the impressive achievement of amending the Press and Publications Law in September 1999 (see *MECS* 1999, p. 348), a strong desire for more press freedom prevailed. No major changes were made, however, and most of the remaining limitations were left intact. Throughout the year, the argument between those supporting more media freedom and those opposing it continued. The initiative of the Rawabda government, at the end of 1999, to establish a free media zone in Jordan and allow foreign media investment into the country, tailed off unsuccessfully during 2000. Parliament rejected the project, claiming that the Jordanian government was not ready to handle free media. Deputies pointed out the contradiction between allowing unrestricted foreign media in the planned free media zone and continued state-controlled local media in the rest of the kingdom. The government realized there were many obstacles to the realization of the project. In addition to the conservative circles in parliament, many restrictive laws required amendment before any progress could be achieved.[61] The government decided to withdraw the draft legislation, claiming that other recently enacted laws, e.g., the Jordan Radio and Television Corporation (JRTVC) Law and the Investments Law, compensated for it.[62]

Membership of the Jordan Press Association (JPA) remained a precondition for practising journalism in the kingdom, and was a source of discontent to some journalists. The JPA membership subordinated a journalist to strict bylaws, the diversion from which could result in the cancellation or a suspension of one's license. Since journalists from state-controlled or state-owned media dominated the association, it was a means for government control. When Sayf al-Sharif, president of the JPA, was asked about the issue, he explained that until the Jordanian press developed greater maturity, membership would continue to be compulsory.[63]

There were a few cases of JPA involvement in restricting journalistic activity. In September, the JPA expelled its secretary, *al-Hadath* chief editor Nidal Mansur, for one year. The JPA claimed that he was receiving foreign funds and practicing a profession other than journalism, both violations of JPA bylaws. The claim was based on his role as head of the Center for Defending the Freedom of Journalists in Amman, although Mansur repeatedly explained that work at the center was not another profession, but work at an institution dedicated to journalists. Mansur appealed to the High Court, which decided to suspend the JPA decision while investigating it. The verdict was scheduled for January 2001.[64] In July, the *al-Ra'y* cartoonist 'Imad Hajaj was severely criticized for drawing cartoons which allegedly mocked the mobile phone company Fastlink, which was about to advertise in the paper. He was suspended and finally fired. Hajaj claimed that these measures were taken against him because he had been a staunch supporter of press privatization, and that the Fastlink incident was just an excuse.[65] The publisher of *al-'Arab al-Yawm*, Riyad Hurub, was charged with corruption, and subsequently sold his shares in the newspaper.[66] The paper had been the only independent one in the country and, following Hurub's departure, it softened its critical line.

In March, a special court was opened to deal specifically with cases related to press issues. The government presented it as part of the effort to enhance press freedom, claiming that the existence of the court would help to speed up journalists' cases and protect their public dignity.[67]

Prime Minister Abu Raghib had listed reform of the media as a main objective in his policy statement. The minister of information, Talib Rifa'i, expressed Jordan's determination to promote freedom of expression in the kingdom.[68] Indeed, the Abu Raghib government seemed slightly more willing to proceed in this direction than the previous government.

At the beginning of July, the cabinet changed a clause of the Jordan Radio and Television Law which asserted that all broadcasts were the sole domain of the JRTVC. According to the new amendment, the government would have the power to approve both private and foreign broadcasting.[69] The law was passed by parliament in August. However, it did not facilitate the setting up of new stations, since it did not specify regulations for them. Also, the JRTVC board of directors had previously numbered fifteen public sector employees. Under the new law, there were nine members of the board, four from the public sector and four from the private sector. Information Minister Talib Rifa'i was appointed chairperson. While he claimed that the law would enable the JRTVC to become an independent body, critics pointed to the absurdity of appointing the minister as chairperson, thus negating the idea of a media independent of government control.[70]

In December, Rifa'i was about to appoint a new chief editor to the newspaper, *al-Ra'y*. The appointment was opposed by Prime Minister Abu Raghib, Culture Minister Mahmud Kayid, and by the editorial and administrative leadership of *al-Ra'y*. The attempt to force it through went against the general trend of media liberalization. The incident developed into a minor government crisis, with Rifa'i threatening to resign.[71]

Following the suspension of *al-Ra'y* cartoonist Hajaj by the Jordan Press Foundation (JPF) board of directors in July, Khalid al-Karaki, chairperson of the board of the JPF and publisher of *The Jordan Times* and *al-Ra'y*, resigned. He disagreed with the decision to dismiss Hajaj and believed it to be contrary to principles of press freedom. However, at the end of the year, he was reappointed as chairperson, indicating that promoting press freedom might be on the public agenda again.[72]

Freedom of Expression

A draft law on public meetings was discussed by the government, but because of extreme opposition within parliament, was then withdrawn on Abu Raghib's decision. Deputies opposing the draft law claimed that it reduced the public's opportunities to hold rallies and demonstrations even more than the original 1953 legislation.[73]

The Continued Debate on Article 340

The debate regarding the cancelation of this controversial article to the penal code had been going on for years. In cases of real or suspected sexual misconduct by a woman, Article 340 enabled a court to exempt from punishment or give lenient sentences to men guilty of "honor killings" — the murder of female members of one's family to protect the family honor.

In mid-February, a rally was held, calling for cancelation of the article, launched with the participation of members of the royal family, Prince 'Ali and Prince Ghazi. The organizers met with the speaker of the Chamber of Deputies, 'Abd al-Hadi al-Majali, who stressed that the parliament was firmly against canceling the article. The marchers, on the other hand, claimed to be representing King 'Abdallah's position and that of the late king Husayn as well.[74]

The march provoked rage in parliament. At the end of February, fifty-three deputies signed a petition calling for the implementation of *Shari'a* law in Jordan,[75] although approximately thirty of them quickly withdrew their signatures. One of the deputies explained that the purpose of the petition was to protest the canceling of Article 340. The same day, the IAF issued a *fatwa* (religious ruling), stating that canceling the article would be illegal.[76]

Despite the wide support that canceling the article gained from members of the royal family, and although human rights organizations backed the campaign, there was no legal change by the end of 2000. At the beginning of the year, the Chamber of Deputies had rejected the draft law calling for the cancelation, making it the second rejection by the Chamber of Deputies[77] (The first rejection took place in 1999, see *MECS* 1999, p. 351). The Senate, on the other hand, voted on 22 February to cancel Article 340.[78] While there was a lively debate in the press between campaign supporters and opponents,[79] there was also an emphasis on the need for cultural change, requiring government involvement. Legal means alone, it was felt, would not solve the problem.[80] Asma Khadir, a lawyer and human rights activist, criticized the Rawabda government for presenting the draft to cancel the article in a manner that encouraged the objections of the Lower

House, such as saying that it was a result of pressure by international human rights organizations on the Jordanian government. However, even though the article was not canceled, Khadir believed that discussion of the topic had raised public awareness of the issue.[81]

Elections at the Professional Associations

For a decade, the Islamists had gained considerable support in the thirteen professional associations and managed to get their nominees elected to most of the executive council seats and presidencies. In 2000, however, some Islamist nominees faced disappointment in the elections. In the Jordan Pharmacists Association the Islamist candidates lost to a coalition of independent candidates,[82] and in the Jordan Dentists Association the nationalist candidates won all the seats and the presidency.[83] On the other hand, in the Jordan Engineers Association the Islamists won all eleven seats on the executive council as well as the presidency.[84] They were similarly successful in the Jordan Agricultural Engineers Association.[85]

PROLONGED STRUGGLE WITH THE ISLAMISTS

Continued Break with Hamas

On 21 November 1999, four leaders of the Palestinian Hamas organization — politburo chief Khalid Mash'al, spokesperson Ibrahim Ghawsha, editor of the Hamas monthly *Filastin al-Muslima*, 'Izzat al-Rishq, and another member of the politburo, Sami Khatir — were deported to Qatar. The official Jordanian position was that they left of their own free will, but Hamas officials, as well as Muslim Brotherhood members, claimed that they were put on a plane and forced to leave the country. The expulsion followed a crackdown on Hamas, including the closing down of the movement's offices and the arrest of other members (see *MECS* 1999, pp. 352–54).

At the beginning of January, Hamas launched negotiations with the authorities, sending a petition to the king asking him to permit the return of the deportees. At the same time, Hamas made it clear that if these attempts brought no change, they would go to court.[86] Indeed, Salih al-'Armuti, head of the Jordanian Bar Association (JBA), filed a court appeal on behalf of the four. As proof of their coerced departure, they claimed that they were led blindfolded to the plane. In an interview with *al-Safir*, Mash'al said that Hamas was pursuing both legal and political routes to overturn the action, in the hope that at least one of them would work.[87] The deportees turned down the Jordanian offer to visit the country for ten days,[88] and on 12 March 'Armuti presented his arguments to the High Court. These claimed that the Jordanian constitution forbade deportation of Jordanian citizens.[89]

The official Jordanian position throughout the year was that the men would be allowed to return to Jordan if they renounced their official status as members of the Hamas movement.[90] On 14 May, the state presented its final argument in court, rejecting 'Armuti's claim that the four had been deported.[91] At the end of June, the court decided to dismiss the Hamas appeal. Interestingly, the rejection was on procedural grounds. It concluded that the claimants' power-of-attorney was legally invalid.[92] 'Armuti claimed in return that a JBA rule entitled a lawyer to endorse his client's signature, thus enabling the client to reside anywhere so long as the signing had first been carried out in front of the lawyer. In this case, 'Armuti asserted, the claimants had met with a lawyer of his team, and therefore their power-of-attorney was valid.[93]

The appeal was finally rejected just a week before Abu Raghib presented his new government. When that took place, 'Armuti openly expressed his hopes that the new government would reconsider the deportation decision and the Hamas members' request to return to Jordan according to the terms they had proposed.[94] Then, at the beginning of July, the four established the first direct contact with the Jordanian authorities since their deportation.[95] During July, the Hamas movement expressed its optimism that Abu Raghib's attention to the matter was very promising.[96] At the end of the month, Abu Raghib met with Islamist leaders. 'Abd al-Latif 'Arabiyyat, secretary-general of the IAF, who was present, claimed that there was an impression that a compromise could be reached.[97] However, by the end of August, Abu Raghib reiterated the official government stand. Hamas members, he explained, could return to Jordan as ordinary citizens, but not when they were affiliated with a non-Jordanian organization such as Hamas.[98]

In mid-November, Abu Raghib met with Mash'al in Doha. The meeting was arranged by the emir of Qatar, Shaykh Hamad bin Khalifa Al Thani, and was held on the sidelines of the Islamic Conference Organization (ICO) summit conference (see chapter on Islamic affairs). Abu Raghib reiterated the Jordanian condition for the return of Mash'al and the other three, that is, their complete renunciation of their affiliation with Hamas.[99] Both Mash'al and Muslim Brotherhood spokesperson, Jamil Abu Bakr, refused to refer to this information.[100] However, three weeks later 'Armuti announced that he would launch a second appeal to the High Court.[101]

On 6 December, Abu Raghib, during a meeting with members of the national forum for unions and opposition parties, stressed that Jordan would not allow any unauthorized demonstrations in the cities. He emphasized the government's firm refusal to allow any non-Jordanian organization to operate in Jordan, relating this specifically to Hamas.[102] On 30 December, 'Armuti claimed that he had received some positive signs from Abu Raghib about the possibility of solving the problem by mediation. He stressed his strong intention to resolve the issue through political channels, but explained that if this didn't work, he would then appeal to the High Court for a second time.[103]

Hamas did not refrain from taking part in the protests in support of the Palestinians at the time of the outbreak of the Aqsa Intifada. Following Israeli opposition leader Ariel Sharon's visit to the Temple Mount in late September, about six thousand people attended a ceremony in support of the protection of Muslim holy sites in Jerusalem (see chapters on Israel and the PA), held by the Hamas movement in the al-Wihdat refugee camp. The ceremony took place at the entrance to the UN Relief and Works Agency school in the camp. During the ceremony, participants stamped on American and Israeli flags. Shaykh Hamza Mansur, deputy secretary-general of the IAF, addressed the gathering as followers of Hamas, and Hamas leader Shaykh Ahmad Yasin addressed them by telephone, calling for a jihad for the liberation of all Palestinian territories.[104] In late October, Hamas condemned the government for its handling of the "Return [to Palestine] March" (see below).[105]

The State and the Muslim Brotherhood Following the Hamas Crisis

In January the Muslim Brotherhood handed the king a petition asking him to bring back the Hamas leaders who had left the country in November 1999.[106] Although Interior Minister Nayif al-Qadi denied that the events with Hamas were in any way a warning to the Muslim Brotherhood in Jordan, tension did not abate.[107]

A meeting between the king and the Muslim Brotherhood took place in early March, the first since the deportation of the four Hamas men.[108] Another meeting took place later in the month, but did not ease the tension. The Muslim Brotherhood representatives made it clear that their participation in the upcoming elections was contingent on the election law being changed. They also brought up the issue of changes in the laws governing municipal elections and student elections at the universities.[109] In April, a rally in support of the University of Jordan (UJ) Islamist students' struggle took place at the IAF headquarters. Riot police surrounded the place, and only after Interior Minister al-Qadi and Information Minister Salih Qalab arrived and met with IAF secretary-general 'Arabiyyat did the situation calm down.[110]

The government did assist the Muslim Brotherhood in a very embarrassing incident. Ishaq Farhan, head of the Shura Council of the IAF, was denied entry to the US on his arrival there. After the intervention of the Jordanian foreign minister, 'Abd al-Ilah Khatib, a meeting was held between Khatib, Farhan and the US ambassador to Jordan. After the meeting, the US State Department reversed its decision and allowed Farhan to enter the country.[111]

Following the presentation of the new government, the Muslim Brotherhood suspended the membership of IAF member 'Abd al-Rahim al-'Ukur, who had accepted Abu Raghib's offer of a ministry.[112] In September, Muslim Brotherhood spokesperson Abu Bakr announced that the Muslim Brotherhood Shura Council had decided to expel 'Ukur.[113] The IAF repeated its threat to boycott the 2001 election should the election law remain unchanged.[114]

Internal Conflict in the Muslim Brotherhood and its Rift with Hamas

The deportation of the four Hamas leaders caused serious strain between the movement and the Muslim Brotherhood in Jordan, as well as an internal feud inside the Muslim Brotherhood itself. At the beginning of January hardline voices within the Muslim Brotherhood were calling for the creation of a new Islamic party. These were members discontented with the reaction of the Muslim Brotherhood's centrist-dominated, "Golden Center"-controlled executive bureau to the Hamas deportation. They believed it to be both inadequate and too moderate, and demanded a firmer stand.[115] According to al-Sharq al-Awsat sources, the Shura Council called for mass resignations of members against the background of the Hamas crisis, since there was a general feeling that the weakness and bad management of senior members had eased the government's deportation decision. The executive bureau, however, opposed the idea of resignations. In fact, it issued a statement critical of Hamas, blaming it for the crisis with the authorities. It presented this statement to Muslim Brotherhood members at meetings following the deportation.[116] Toward the end of January, Hamas spokesperson Ghawsha said that the Muslim Brotherhood no longer constituted a source of authority for the Hamas movement, because it had "abandoned the Islamic project of the liberation of Palestine."[117] Muslim Brotherhood spokesperson Jamil Abu Bakr responded by stressing that the Muslim Brotherhood had maintained a firm stance of support for the Palestinian resistance movement, and that the Muslim Brotherhood had ideological and moral authority over Hamas.[118] Within two days, Mash'al announced that Ghawsha's statement had expressed only his personal opinion and not the official Hamas position, and Shaykh Yasin, the spiritual leader of the movement, lauded the Muslim Brotherhood role in the Palestinian struggle.[119]

Although the Muslim Brotherhood Shura Council issued a statement after its January half-year meeting, saying that the organization's leadership had succeeded in resolving all differences, internal rifts were soon apparent. The deputy controller-general of the Muslim Brotherhood, 'Imad Abu Dayya, was met by angry reactions when he expressed his opinion that "Hamas was in Palestine and not in Jordan."[120] Members of Palestinian origin expressed their discontent over the fact that the movement had been going through a process of "Jordanization," granting only secondary priority to the Palestinian issue.[121]

Following the Muslim Brotherhood Shura Council mid-year session in July, signs of an internal rift surfaced again. During the session, members proposed some regulatory changes intended to reduce the executive bureau's authority. As an act of protest or manipulation, the six "Golden Center" wing members of the executive bureau resigned by the end of the month.[122] After the Muslim Brotherhood Shura Council withdrew its suggested changes, the six executive bureau members withdrew their resignations. Thus, the centrist executive bureau prevailed over the two other trends in the movement, the hawks, represented by Hammam Sa'id and Muhammad Abu Faris, and the doves, led by 'Arabiyyat and Farhan, who sought their removal from the organization's leadership.[123]

Detentions of Muslim Extremists

During 2000, the issue of Muslim extremists in Jordan attracted serious attention. At the end of 1999 thirteen people, comprising a group linked to Usama bin Ladin, were arrested, suspected of planning terrorist attacks on tourist sites and US government targets in the kingdom (see *MECS* 1999, p. 354). Their arrest and trial drew widespread attention.

Khalil al-Dik, another Jordanian associated with the group, was extradited from Pakistan at the end of 1999 (see *MECS* 1999, p. 354), but denied being involved or having any link to Bin Ladin.[124] Jordan and the US cooperated in the investigation of the group and its alleged plans for terrorist acts[125] and it was decided that Dik's trial would be conducted separately from the main trial.[126] Later, in June, another Jordanian suspect was extradited to Jordan from Pakistan. There were eleven charges against the detainees, including plotting to carry out terrorist acts, possession and manufacture of explosives, possession of automatic weapons, affiliation with an illegal organization and forging official stamps and documents. Officials claimed that the defendants admitted that they had plotted to "undermine the kingdom's stability and target foreign tourists."[127] On 27 March, it was decided to indict twenty-eight of those suspected of supporting Bin Ladin.[128] Out of twenty-eight suspects, only fifteen were held in Jordan. The rest were in hiding, presumably in Pakistan, Afghanistan, Britain, Lebanon and Syria.[129]

When the trial finally opened on 20 April, the fifteen detainees in Jordan pleaded not guilty to plotting terrorist attacks on US targets or on Israeli tourists in Jordan.

In late May, the police succeeded in arresting another suspect from the list of twenty-eight, bringing the number of detainees held in Jordan to sixteen.[130] In mid-July, Prosecutor-General Mahmud 'Ubaydat demanded the death penalty for twelve out of the twenty-eight defendants. They were charged with belonging to an illegal organization linked to Bin Ladin, possession of weapons and planning to attack Western and tourist targets at the millennium celebrations in December 1999. Seven out of the twelve were tried *in absentia*. The other sixteen were accused of planning terrorist attacks, belonging to an illegal organization, selling automatic weapons, planning a robbery and forging documents.[131] 'Ubaydat claimed that the defendants had been collecting weapons since

1996, and had received training in Syria, Lebanon and Afghanistan. The defense brought witnesses who contradicted 'Ubaydat's claims, testifying that the gunpowder and other material found in the defendants' possession was not fit to make explosives. All the defendants pleaded not guilty.[132]

On 18 September the State Security Court convicted twenty-two defendants and acquitted six. It handed down death sentences to six: two who were present, Khadir Abu Hushar and Usama Husni Kamil Samar, and four who had been tried and sentenced in absentia, Ra'id Hasan Khalil Hijazi, Ibrahim Salim Abu Haliwa, Munir Maqdah and Muhammad Sadiq 'Abd al-Nur Ibrahim. Two were sentenced to death, but their sentence was immediately commuted to life imprisonment with hard labor, and fourteen received prison sentences of between seven-and-a-half and fifteen years. Although evidence was found for the existence of contacts, including seeking finance, between the defendants and Bin Ladin, all the defendants were acquitted of the charge of links with Bin Ladin and his organization, al-Qa'ida.[133] During November one of the men sentenced to death in absentia, Hijazi, was extradited to Jordan from Syria. Hijazi confessed during his interrogation that he had visited Afghanistan, received military training in one of al-Qa'ida's bases, and was supposed to carry out attacks on tourist and US targets in Jordan. He was to be brought before court at the beginning of January 2001.[134]

The Islamists' Struggle at the Universities

Another source of friction between the Islamist parties and the authorities was the student elections at the universities. In early March, Islamist students had claimed that the universities' move to change the election system to a one-person, one-vote system was intended to weaken their representation.[135] Later in the month that claim was brought up again, when the Islamists lost the elections at the Jordan University of Science and Technology in Irbid. Since it was an unexpected loss, the Islamists immediately connected it to the changed election system.[136] Another loss followed at the University of Mu'ta student council. The Islamists boycotted these elections.[137]

However, the strongest protests were at the UJ in Amman. After changing the election system to one-person, one-vote, in 1999, the administration of the UJ decided to make further changes. It decided that the nine-member student administrative council would henceforth be appointed by the university president, instead of being elected by the eighty-member student council as in the past. Another change was the appointment of forty out of the eighty members of the student council by the university president. An article allowing students to conduct political rallies was canceled, and the dean was granted authority to send a representative to the meetings of the administrative council. The Islamist parties claimed that all these changes, like those in 1999, were designed to weaken their influence.[138] It is noteworthy that the press was very supportive of the students' struggle and critical of the university authorities.[139]

On 4 April, the students at the UJ started a sit-in on campus to protest the administration's amendments to the student elections law. The sit-in continued for a few days,[140] during which the students threatened to boycott the elections. A day before the elections took place, the Islamist students held a rally on campus.[141] On election day, Islamists clashed on campus with riot police, who used tear gas and colored water to disperse them.[142] Some were arrested, but most were released the same day and only four remained in detention.[143]

The elections, in which 48.3% of eligible voters participated, were won by pro-government and tribal candidates.[144] The protests of the Islamist students did not affect the UJ authorities, and university president Walid Ma'ni appointed a medical student as chairperson of the student council. This was the first time a student council chairperson was appointed by the university president, and not elected by the student council, since 1990.[145] Later on in April, the university authorities decided to refer ten students to a disciplinary council for participating in the rallies.[146] Throughout May and June the UJ continued to delay the graduation of these students, claiming that until the committee investigating their matter had finished its inquiry, they could not graduate.[147] At the time that Abu Raghib announced the new government policy statement, Islamist students staged a sit-in near the parliament, but their hope that he would stop and talk to them was not fulfilled.[148] However, Abu Raghib is assumed to have intervened in their issue by asking the UJ president to ease the punishment of the protesters. The result was a change in the investigating committee decision to expel thirty-nine students who attended the protests, into a warning.[149]

Islamists against the Poet Musa Hawamda

A public attack was launched by Islamic circles against the poet Musa Hawamda and his new book, *My Tree is Higher*. One poem in particular, telling a romantic story about Joseph and the wife of the Egyptian Pharaoh, attracted much criticism from religious clerics and Islamist activists. They claimed that Hawamda should be charged with apostasy. His life was threatened, to the point that an editorial in *The Jordan Times* called on the government to take strong action against those behind the threats. The government response was to ban any further publication and sales of the book.[150]

In June, Hawamda was summoned to the Shari'a court for an investigation of a charge of apostasy.[151] Hawamda claimed that he had been required by the judge to apologize to the Islamists and religious figures. He refused, explaining that his poems did not contradict the Shari'a and that he was a devout Muslim.[152] In July, the accusations against him were dropped by the Shari'a court, and were immediately transferred to a criminal court, charging him of defaming holy Qur'anic figures. Although Hawamda maintained his refusal to apologize, the Shari'a court judge canceled the referral the next day, explaining that he was convinced of Hawamda's innocence and repentance.[153] Nevertheless, in December the Islamic Appeals Court ordered a retrial, claiming that the court should take into consideration expert opinion on the issue, something that did not take place during the first trial.[154]

ECONOMIC DISTRESS

No dramatic change took place in the difficult economic situation. Jordan suffered from an increased budget deficit, and World Bank (WB) officials estimated that the country would have to achieve a 6% annual growth rate in order to accommodate population growth of 3.5%.[155] Unemployment continued to be a major problem. Official figures pointed to 14% unemployed, while non-official data suggested 22%-27%.[156] A major part were university and college graduates. During April–May, c. 150 unemployed Ph.D. graduates staged a forty-five-day sit-in in front of the government offices, and renewed their protests in September.[157]

After joining the WTO at the end of 1999 (see *MECS* 1999, p. 356), Jordan was ready for its next economic milestone. As a result of negotiations held throughout 2000, Jordan and the US finally signed a Free Trade Agreement (FTA) on 26 October (see below).[158]

Work within the framework of the IMF three-year program continued. Accordingly, the IMF granted Jordan a $25m. loan.[159] The WB granted a $34.7m. loan for a higher education project.[160] This was in addition to US and EU financial aid packages (see below).

Foreign debt increased to $9bn., compared to $7.5bn. in 1999 (see *MECS* 1999. p. 355). GDP was $8.3bn.[161] Debt was expected to increase in 2001, since internal and foreign debt combined for 2000 exceeded 100% of GDP.[162]

The IMF pressured Jordan to implement the second stage of the sales tax law, and it was finally endorsed in August (see above).[163] Experts, however, estimated that consumers would not be able to bear the heavier sales taxes.[164]

A key economic development was the endorsement of a draft law to turn 'Aqaba into a special economic zone (ASEZ), a project in which the king was very interested. The ASEZ was planned as a low tax area, where customs barriers would be abolished and taxes lowered to 5% on services and retail sales.[165] It was expected to attract $6bn. from tourism, information technology companies and industry.[166] The Chamber of Deputies approved the draft law in July and it was passed by the Senate in August.[167] The establishment of the ASEZ was set for 1 January 2001. Transport Minister Muhammad Kalalida resigned to assume leadership of the project. In addition, a governing body of five commissioners was appointed. The Transport Ministry was given to deputy prime minister and minister of prime ministry affairs, Salih Irshidat.[168]

Critics of the ASEZ claimed that it would enable foreign countries to purchase land in 'Aqaba. The main fear was of increased Israeli control of land and influence in the area.[169] Commentator Fahd al-Fanik was one of the most persistent critics of the ASEZ, and repeatedly voiced his opposition in the press. In his opinion, 'Aqaba was already packed with industry, while there were other regions in Jordan that required development. In addition, he said the project would encourage Israeli and Saudi investments at the expense of Jordanian investors.[170] In light of the strong opposition, before approving the law the government passed another law that limited the sale of lands in 'Aqaba. It required reciprocity from the investor's country of origin. This automatically excluded Israeli investors as land purchasers, since Israel banned land sales to foreigners.[171]

As Fanik pointed out, the ASEZ project required at least sixteen regulations and decisions to be issued in order for implementation of the plan to begin.[172] In December, the government endorsed three out of twelve bylaws planned for the ASEZ.[173] By the end of the year, however, there was still much legal work to be done.

Another economic project personally promoted by the king was development of the information technology industry. Thanks to his efforts, an agreement was signed with Microsoft CEO, Bill Gates, in September. Under the agreement, all software requirements of the Jordanian government were to be supplied by Microsoft.[174]

More economic legislation took place in the field of privatization. During the months of the Rawabda government, a few companies were privatized: Jordan Cement Factories, Jordan Telecommunications and 'Aqaba Railways Corporation.[175] At the extraordinary session of parliament in May–June, the parliament endorsed the draft privatization law, which allowed the government to maintain a "golden share" in any privatized firm and therefore to veto any decision taken by a board of directors.[176]

FOREIGN AFFAIRS

JORDAN, ISRAEL, AND THE PALESTINIAN AUTHORITY

Keeping a Distance from Israel

Relations with Israel continued along the lines set by 'Abdallah since the beginning of his reign, which were to present a public posture of low priority. In the first half of the year, Prime Minister Rawabda managed a delicate balance between developing ties with other Arab countries while maintaining a certain level of cooperation with Israel.

On 23 April, after a number of cancelations, 'Abdallah finally paid his first visit to Israel since ascending the throne. The meeting took place in Eilat, where he and Israeli Prime Minister Ehud Barak discussed the Palestinian and Syrian tracks in the peace process. Regarding Jerusalem, the king emphasized Jordanian support of the idea of Jerusalem becoming two capitals, for Israel and for the future Palestinian state, while remaining a holy place for the three monotheistic religions. In contrast to the special status promised to Jordan in the Israeli-Jordanian peace treaty (see *MECS* 1994, pp. 412–15, 423–26), the king reiterated Jordanian renunciation of its claim over the Muslim holy sites in Jerusalem. In an interview with Israeli TV during the visit, he said that the future of these sites would be determined by Israeli and Palestinian leaders.[177]

The king expressed his support of the Israeli plan to pull out of Lebanon (see also chapter on Israel), while stressing that the withdrawal must be complete, leaving no outposts.[178] At the king's request the talks concentrated on economic issues, a reflection of 'Abdallah's mission of developing the Jordanian economy as a top priority.[179] Prime Minister Rawabda complained that almost all joint economic projects with Israel had been delayed, and Israeli ministers he spoke to promised that there would be improvement.[180] The Jordanian delegation stressed the importance of securing additional water sources for Jordan.[181]

The Israeli pullout from Lebanon in mid-May, six weeks earlier than Israel's self-declared deadline of 7 July, caught Jordan by surprise. It brought a strong reaction in the Jordanian press, including excited calls for an equivalent pullout from Palestinian territory.[182] When meeting Israeli public security minister Shlomo Ben Ami, King 'Abdallah expressed his satisfaction with the Israeli withdrawal from Lebanon and his hope that there would be a similar withdrawal from Syrian and Palestinian lands.[183]

On 24 June, Israeli soldiers mistakenly opened fire at members of a Jordanian delegation of about 140 professional association and union representatives who were touring South Lebanon. Harsh reactions were expressed by Jordanian political parties and professional unions.[184] An *al-Dustur* editorial attacked Israel, claiming the incident was a direct assault on the Jordanian people, and that it was proof of the Israeli inability to develop good relations with its neighbors.[185] The government also condemned the shooting, stressing that the use of force against unarmed civilians was unacceptable.[186]

On 22 August, King 'Abdallah paid a visit to Ramallah, where he met with PA President Yasir 'Arafat, and then proceeded to Tel Aviv to meet Barak. In diplomatic terms, the visit signaled an improvement in the king's relations with Israel, in comparison to his previous visit to Eilat.

When the tension between Israel and the PA at the end of September erupted into violence (see also chapters Israel, and the PA), Prime Minister Abu Raghib condemned the Israeli actions,[187] and King 'Abdallah put the blame for the events on Israeli provocation.[188] After little more than a week's turmoil, Jordan decided not to send its newly designated ambassador to Israel.[189]

Increasing anti-Israeli sentiment in Jordan came to a head when a diplomat from the Israeli embassy was shot and wounded in Amman in November.[190] On 5 December another Israeli embassy employee in Amman was shot and wounded. The next day, Israel evacuated all families of embassy employees from Amman. The Jordanian government condemned the attack, regarding it as an assault on Jordanian sovereignty.[191]

Israeli Prime Minister Barak's resignation in December, and the prospect of new elections in Israel within a few months, evoked feelings of disappointment and fear in Jordan. The outcome, according to some Jordanian observers, would be the replacement of Barak with a much worse option, namely, the immediately preceding prime minister, Binyamin Netanyahu.[192]

The Anti-Normalization Movement

The movement against normalization of relations with Israel continued to gain support during the year. At the end of April, Amman hosted a conference of the Inter-Parliamentary Union. Over 130 countries were to send their representatives, including Israel. There was wide protest against Israeli participation. Six opposition deputies boycotted the conference,[193] and twenty deputies signed a petition demanding the banning of the Israeli Members of Knesset from the Jordanian parliament.[194] Protesters gathered around the hotel where the conference was being held, carrying banners denouncing Israeli participation, and demanding the lifting of sanctions on Iraq.[195] At the end of August, an anti-normalization conference was held in Amman, with delegates from Jordan and Egypt.[196]

The anti-normalization movement reached an unprecedented level of popularity and activity when the Palestinian Aqsa Intifada broke out at the end of September. After a delay of more than eighteen months (see *MECS* 1999, p. 358), the professional associations' blacklist of figures engaged in normalization with Israel was finally published in November.[197]

Government dealings with the movement during the year were harsher than before. Two weeks after taking office, Abu Raghib set up a meeting with the heads of the thirteen professional associations and warned them against pursuing their political agenda, lest it cause conflict between them and the government. He also used the argument most reflective of his approach, that the associations' rejection of normalization with Israel was hindering economic development.[198]

However, immediately after the outbreak of the intifada, representatives of political parties, professional associations and students staged massive demonstrations in Amman. This was in addition to mass demonstrations of tens of thousands of citizens all over the kingdom. During the first week, from 29 September to 6 October, demonstrations became increasingly larger and more hostile, and called for the expulsion of the Israeli ambassador.[199] On Friday 6 October, 203 marches and 73 rallies were reported. At the end of Friday prayers, around 30,000 people who had prayed at the Husayni Mosque in downtown Amman marched through the city, chanting pro-PA slogans. Another 30,000 attended a rally in the Mahata district of Amman, organized by the Muslim Brotherhood, and called for the expulsion of the Israeli ambassador and the return of the expelled Hamas leaders to Jordan.[200] On 5 October, after six days of demonstration, the authorities resorted to force in al-Baq'a refugee camp, where one person was killed and a number were injured.[201] After a week of clashes, in which Jordanian police had used tear gas and armored vehicles to disperse demonstrators, the government banned all anti-Israel protests.[202]

The government claimed that the death in al-Baq'a occurred when the demonstrators started shooting, and justified the decision to ban all demonstrations by the need to prevent further such incidents.[203] However, it could not stop demonstrations when public excitement was so high, and the professional associations' committee urged the public to continue protesting in violation of the government ban.[204] According to one Jordanian journalist, the government came to a fragile understanding with the opposition parties and the associations, by which demonstrations would be allowed as long as public order was kept.[205]

On 24 October the "Return [of Refugees] March," planned by the professional associations, took place after some negotiation with the government. This procession of thousands started at the professional associations' complex in Amman. From there, buses took participants to the Karama Battle Memorial in the Jordan Valley. The march was supposed to end at the King Husayn Bridge, symbolizing support of Palestinian refugees' right of return to Israel. Riot police dispersed the gathering next to the Karama Battle Memorial, using tear gas and water cannons. The information minister explained that allowing the marchers to reach the bridge would have made the situation uncontrollable[206] — presumably because the immediate proximity of Israeli border personnel might have been incendiary. The organizers of the march claimed that they instructed participants to leave the rally and head back to the buses, since it was raining, and that the riot police started their actions then, for no real reason. The riot police claimed that some of the participants were calling to continue "onto the bridge" when walking to the buses, giving reason to fear they might move toward the bridge.[207]

In early October, anti-Israeli sentiment was running high in parliament as well. Thirty deputies signed a petition demanding the expulsion of the Israeli ambassador.[208] In late October, deputies urged the annulment of the peace treaty with Israel.[209] Anti-normalization groups initiated other acts of protest, such as the boycotting of Israeli currency by the Association of Money Changers, and the professional associations' painting of the Israeli flag on the floor at the entrance to their offices, to be used as a doormat.[210]

Jordan and the Palestinian Authority

Throughout most of the year, Jordan played a supporting role in the Palestinian-Israeli track. There was clear support from King 'Abdallah and the Jordanian press for the idea of the Camp David summit (see also chapter on the PA). The king sent a message of support to 'Arafat through Foreign Minister Khatib, who was in Gaza a few days before the beginning of the summit.[211] Just before the summit, the new prime minister, Abu Raghib, announced his government guidelines. He stressed Jordan's insistence on the implementation of UN Resolution 194, according to which Palestinian refugees were entitled to either repatriation or financial compensation as a basis for a settlement of the Israeli-Palestinian conflict.[212]

At the time of the Camp David summit, Jordan took part in a meeting in Cairo with representatives of Arab states hosting Palestinian refugees, e.g., Egypt, Lebanon and Syria. Its purpose was to discuss a just solution for the refugee problem, in light of the apparent failure of the Camp David summit to do so.[213] The king also participated in the Camp David effort. President Clinton consulted him in order to prevent the summit from failing, after it had lasted little more than a week. The king helped to persuade Barak and 'Arafat to stay on and continue negotiations, when they both seemed to be about to leave, and when Clinton himself had to leave to attend the G-8 summit in Japan.[214]

There was a sense of disappointment in Jordan at the low level of consultation with the PA over negotiations. King 'Abdallah met with 'Arafat in Ramallah in August. However, 'Arafat, who traveled to eleven Arab countries after Camp David (see also chapter on inter-Arab relations), did not visit Amman, and PA officials did not update Jordan. The PA placed more importance on Egyptian advice. Moreover, the Jordanians did not approve of the Palestinian preference for the repatriation of Palestinian refugees from Lebanon.[215] 'Abdallah was most emphatic, noting that the right of repatriation was equal for all Palestinians, wherever they might reside temporarily.[216] It is clear that the king's emphasis expressed Jordanian fears of having to solve the refugee problem inside Jordan.

When the intifada began, Jordanian-PA relations improved and frequent updates replaced the strain that had previously characterized these relations.[217] King 'Abdallah expressed support for the PA and offered condolences for losses as well as every means of assistance to 'Arafat.[218] 'Arafat arrived in Amman on 2 October and was received warmly by the king. The two leaders condemned Israeli actions and encouraged the convening of an Arab summit as soon as possible. On the king's instructions, on 2 October, Jordanian helicopters flew fifteen wounded Palestinians to the Husayn Medical Center in Amman, where they received emergency medical treatment. A Jordanian medical team left for the PA to assist with the wounded, and the king himself donated blood in a nation-wide blood donation campaign.[219] In late November, Jordan pledged $2m. to an Arab League fund which had been established to support the intifada (see also chapter on inter-Arab relations).[220]

The king made several attempts to bring Israel and the PA back to the negotiating table. He urged President Clinton of the US to pursue that course.[221] He also reiterated the PA position on the need for international intervention for the protection of Palestinians.[222]

A positive development had taken place in May, when Israel approved the free entry of Jordanian trucks to the PA, which Jordan and the PA had long requested.[223] However, security measures taken by Israel after the outbreak of the intifada impeded Jordanian-PA economic activity once again as many trucks were held up in queues at the crossing points.[224]

Jordanians and Palestinians — The Domestic Dimension

Events during 2000 fueled some of the deep-rooted tensions in Jordanian-Palestinian relations inside Jordan. The outbreak of the Aqsa Intifada put Jordan in a sensitive position, similar to situations in the past. The spontaneous demonstrations that broke out around the country in reaction to events in the West Bank and Gaza were a powerful reminder of the need for the government to respond, lest Jordan find itself in a situation of public disorder and instability. Indeed, after sustained mass public protests in support of the Palestinian struggle, the government banned all demonstrations and rallies.

Public protest erupted over the continued detention of eighty-three out of the three hundred people arrested by the security forces during the October demonstrations. They were accused of instigating unrest during the rallies. At the end of the year, the trial of seventeen of them began.[225]

Public discussion of the relations between Jordanians of Palestinian origin and Jordanians originally from the East Bank continued. However, each attempt to raise the subject aroused strong emotions. This was especially the case when 'Adnan Abu 'Awda's book, *Jordanians, Palestinians and the Hashemite Kingdom in the Middle East Peace Process*, was published at the beginning of the year. Abu 'Awda had been a political advisor to King Husayn, and held the same post under King 'Abdallah at the time his book was published. The book supported the creation of a confederation between Jordan and the future state of Palestine. Abu 'Awda advocated that Jordanians of both kinds, East Bankers and Palestinians, should live in the Hashemite state, and that the political participation of Palestinians be increased.[226]

In regard to the proposal of a Jordanian-Palestinian confederation, PM Rawabda announced that the idea was inconceivable, since it ignored the Palestinian refugees' right of return and the Palestinian right to an independent state, which were the ideological bases for the peace process.[227] Former prime minister Ahmad 'Ubaydat criticized Abu 'Awda for being sectarian, in wanting to enhance the Palestinian hold on the state. apparatus.[228] The king tried to create a positive atmosphere by stressing the need for national unity and the enhancement of equality.[229]

Immediately after the Abu Raghib government was formed, expectations grew that the election law would be amended in a way which would enhance the representation of Jordanians of Palestinian origin. The press called on the government to delete from official forms the request for a person's place of birth, in order to further equality and combat discrimination against Palestinian citizens.[230] Indeed, in the government policy statement presented by Abu Raghib on 9 July, the new prime minister said that the government would create an election law that would ensure just representation for all Jordanian citizens.[231] However, by the end of the year no real progress had been made.

During the parliamentary debate on Abu Raghib's policy statement, a heated discussion developed on the issue of Jordanian-Palestinian relations in Jordan. A deputy of Palestinian origin, Hamada Fara'ina, spoke of the urgent need for larger representation of Palestinians in the political system. He suggested reforming the Senate, which was appointed by the king, as a first stage toward more equal representation. In response, some deputies declared that Jordanian citizens of Palestinian origin should be deprived of their citizenship.[232] This position evoked bitter responses in parliament and in the press.[233]

Tension over the future of the Palestinian refugees in Jordan continued to simmer. The king and government officials made public announcements reiterating the Jordanian position, which rejected the idea of compensating the refugees in lieu of granting them the right of return to Palestine. Strong opposition to the future arrival of more refugees was repeatedly expressed.[234] On the eve of the Camp David summit in July, Abu Raghib stressed Jordan's inability and unwillingness to receive any more refugees.[235] It seems that the reason behind clarifying the Jordanian position on this issue two days before the tripartite summit at Camp David was concern that pressure would be applied on Jordan to accept additional refugees. Abu Raghib also stressed that Jordan would make sure that Jordanians of Palestinian origin enjoyed their full right of return, and in any case would be able to choose between returning to Palestine or staying in Jordan and receiving compensation.[236]

The kingdom's efforts to achieve financial aid for maintaining the refugee camps continued, with the intention of improving the refugees' living standards as well as easing the burden on Jordan.

JORDAN AND THE INTER-ARAB ARENA

'Abdallah's emphasis on enhancing ties with Arab countries as one of the Jordanian foreign policy priorities was evident throughout the year. Accompanied by a number of officials, the king visited, in addition to other Arab countries, five of the six Gulf Cooperation Council (GCC) countries — UAE, Qatar, Bahrain, Oman and Saudi Arabia. A free trade agreement was signed between Jordan and the UAE.[237] The regime found no contradiction between Jordanian relations with the US and Israel, and its need for close relations with Arab countries.

An interesting rapprochement occurred between Jordan and Libya. Libyan leader Mu'ammar al-Qadhdhafi pledged to help finance the Disi water project[238] at the beginning of the year,[239] and in March agreed to provide c. 70% of the estimated $730m. project. He repeated his pledge in August.[240] 'Abdallah visited Libya and, more important, Qadhdhafi visited Jordan for the first time since 1983.[241]

In addition to Libya, Jordan inquired into the possibility of buying water from Turkey. Even Iran announced it would help finance the Disi project.[242]

The Shift toward Iraq

The most significant improvement in inter-Arab relations occurred with Iraq, during the second half of the year. To be sure, the beginning of the year also witnessed an achievement. After failing to reach agreement in December 1999, on 22 January 2000, Jordan and Iraq finally signed an oil agreement, which was very satisfactory for Jordan. It stated that Jordan would receive a total of 4.8m. tons of crude oil at $19/b, regardless of any price rise in the international market. Half of the oil was free, through an Iraqi grant of $300m.— compared to $250m. in 1999.[243] Iraq and Jordan also decided to increase the volume of the Trade Protocol for 2000 from $200m. to $300m.[244]

However, the relationship continued to be marked by ambivalence and contradictory pressures. Although the Rawabda government declared its support for Iraq and for the general notion of lifting UN sanctions, it was not willing to go too far with these ideas in practice. Tension increased between April and June. On 5 April, an Italian plane carrying human rights activists who defied UN sanctions by entering Iraq entered Jordanian air space on its way back to Europe. It was flying on a course other than the one the pilot had reported, which had not included passing through Jordanian air space. Jordanian authorities forced the plane to land at al-Azraq Airport, northeast of Amman, impounded the plane and detained the pilot. Minister of Information Qalab emphasized that Jordan supported the idea of lifting sanctions, and that in impounding the plane Jordan had not opposed this notion, but had defended international law and Jordanian sovereignty over its airspace.[245] Iraq criticized the Jordanian action, claiming that it contradicted declared intentions by Jordan to help lift sanctions.[246]

At the beginning of June, Iraq started using Damascus airport as its point of departure for flights by officials to other countries, after previously using Amman for that purpose. It seems that this came as a result of new Jordanian restrictions on personal weapons carried by the bodyguards of Iraqi officials. Jordanian officials for their part complained that Iraq had reduced its dependence on the port of 'Aqaba, and had been giving priority to other countries in contracts signed under the oil-for-food deal with the UN.[247]

At the beginning of June, Iraq executed a Jordanian citizen, held in an Iraqi jail since 1993, without notifying Jordan beforehand. Jordan expressed anger and demanded an explanation.[248] The execution was apparently intended to convey Iraqi displeasure with the Jordanian policy regarding the sanctions.

When Abu Raghib's government came to power, things changed dramatically. The new prime minister, known for his pro-Iraqi and anti-sanctions positions, was keen on strengthening ties with Jordan's eastern neighbor, which was also the largest market for Jordan. Iraq received the change in Jordan with satisfaction. Mutual visits by officials and discussions of joint economic cooperation began almost immediately. Although officially denied, Iraq apparently made a request to Jordanian officials to reactivate civilian flights to Baghdad,[249] and Jordan did so for "humanitarian reasons."[250] As an act of good will from the Iraqi side, Iraq announced it would resume passage of trade through 'Aqaba port.[251]

On 27 September, a Jordanian aircraft carrying a number of officials flew to Baghdad, thus making Jordan the first Arab country to violate the decade-long air embargo on Iraq.[252] At the end of October, Jordan stopped using US dollars in trade dealings with Iraq and started using European currencies instead, as a gesture to Iraq, which had announced its refusal to use US dollars in its dealings.[253] On 1 November Abu Raghib flew to Baghdad for a three-day visit. The visit brought enthusiastic responses at home. 'Abdallah was praised in the Jordanian press for his courage and as the first Arab leader to send his premier to Iraq since the 1991 Gulf War.[254] This seemed to be proof that Jordan could improve relations with Iraq while remaining on good terms with the US and Israel. During Abu Raghib's visit, Iraq and Jordan signed an oil agreement for 2001, according to which Jordan would pay $20/b. They also agreed to raise the volume of trade from $300m. in 2000 to $450m. in 2001.[255]

The reasons for King 'Abdallah's determination to enhance relations with Iraq at that particular time were several. The effect of the intifada on Israeli-Jordanian relations, and its damaging impact on Israeli-Jordanian economic cooperation, made it clear that Jordan needed to turn elsewhere. 'Abdallah, positioned uneasily between Israel and Iraq, turned to the old Jordanian ally in the east.

Domestic pressure was another factor. The National Mobilization Committee for the Defense of Iraq was very active throughout the year, and public opinion continued to support Iraq and the canceling of UN sanctions. At the beginning of the year, the committee arranged a special campaign to send 3.5m. pencils to Iraqi students.[256] It also handed the government petitions signed by Jordanian citizens, calling for the embargo on Iraq to be lifted.[257] The movement opposing normalization with Israel coincided with the pro-Iraqi one. From October onwards, the regime tried to compensate for not taking further action against Israel — as the public wanted — by improving relations with Iraq.

At the end of November the first commercial flight left Amman for Baghdad. It was coordinated with the UN, and therefore defined as a humanitarian-commercial flight.[258] However, in the second half of December, Royal Jordanian airlines announced the cancelation of regular flights to Baghdad, as a result of the UN Sanctions Committee objection. The airline decided to run humanitarian and irregular flights instead.[259]

Vacillating Relations with Syria

Relations with Syria, which had improved at the end of 1999 (see *MECS* 1999, pp. 362–63), experienced a certain slowdown after the first few months of 2000. At the beginning of the year there were a few signs of continued improvement, when Syria released seventeen Jordanian prisoners[260] and Jordan closed the offices of the Syrian Muslim Brotherhood in Jordan, forcing the group to hold its Shura Council in Baghdad.[261]

But after the unsuccessful meeting between President Hafiz al-Asad of Syria and President Bill Clinton of the US in Geneva in March (see also chapters on the US and the Middle East, and Syria), in which no progress was achieved on the Israeli-Syrian negotiating track, there was a certain chilling of Syrian-Jordanian relations. In Jordan, there was a general feeling that Syria was not doing enough to improve relations, in contrast to Jordanian gestures of goodwill toward Syria.

Jordanian disappointment was prevalent regarding more than one level. Jordan was unsatisfied with Syrian reluctance to confide in Jordan with regard to its progress on the Arab-Israeli peace process. While there had been some warming of ties during 1999, Jordanian officials claimed that since talks had been resumed on the Israeli-Syrian negotiating track in December of that year, the Syrians were avoiding the Jordanians and keeping them in the dark about developments in the talks. There were also expectations in Amman that Syria would appoint an ambassador when the former chargé d'affaires finished his term, but Syria appointed only a new chargé.[262] Very few Syrian officials visited Jordan. Analysts said the Syrian behavior was an indicator of Asad's desire to subordinate King 'Abdallah to Syrian regional leadership. When 'Abdallah proved in his first few months to be independent, Syrian enthusiasm waned.[263] Jordanians complained of being ignored by Syrian officials, and that Syrian foreign minister Faruq al-Shar' did not contact the Jordanian foreign minister regarding the Syrian-Israeli track. It was suggested that the king's visit to Israel in April was an expression of Jordanian impatience in waiting to receive updates from Syria about Asad's talks with President Clinton.[264]

However, after the death of Hafiz al-Asad in June, relations between Jordan and Syria became warmer. The king telephoned Bashshar al-Asad to offer his condolences to the young president-to-be, and sang Bashshar's praises to all and sundry, including foreign media and world leaders.[265] 'Abdallah was doing young Asad a service, and Asad did not underestimate it. The king visited Damascus and met the new leader immediately after he had been sworn in as president.[266] Soon the two countries embarked on a series of bilateral visits. Meetings took place between Jordanian ministers and their Syrian counterparts in preparation for the convening of the Jordanian-Syrian joint higher committee in Damascus in the second half of August. Jordanians had high expectations of this meeting.[267] During the meeting, Prime Minister Abu Raghib met with Asad.[268] Discussions were held about aviation cooperation, and Syria agreed to allow Jordanian air transport companies to operate flights to Syrian airports without restrictions.[269] Additional agreements were signed on trade, tourism and agriculture.

Signs of good relations and cooperation continued to the end of the year. In August, Syria began supplying Jordan with drinking water, as it had done in the previous summer.[270] In December, Syria extradited to Jordan Ra'id Hasan Khalil Hijazi, who had been sentenced to death *in absentia* two months earlier in Jordan for involvement in the bin Ladin terror group (see above).[271] Syria finally satisfied Jordan by appointing a new ambassador to Amman at the end of the month.[272]

Ties with Egypt

By contrast, there was no dramatic change in relations with Egypt. Differing approaches toward the Arab-Israeli peace process created a degree of competition between the two states. While Jordan was trying to push forward both Palestinian and Syrian tracks, Egypt seemed a little wearied by the Syrian stand and concentrated almost exclusively on the Palestinian track. Egypt and Jordan maintained regular contact throughout the year. A few meetings took place between officials, producing joint statements in support of the peace process and greater Arab cooperation. When the intifada began, meetings and talks became much more frequent, taking place both in Egypt and in Jordan. In October, 'Abdallah attended the Israeli-Palestinian Sharm al-Shaykh summit and the emergency Arab summit in Cairo in October (see also chapter on inter-Arab relations).[273]

JORDAN IN THE INTERNATIONAL ARENA

Because of the economic crisis and King 'Abdallah's emphasis on improving the Jordanian economy, international relations focused on economic affairs. The year started with a long-awaited achievement. In November 1999, Jordan was accepted into the WTO (see *MECS* 1999, p. 356). 'Abdallah, eager to extricate the economy from its longstanding crisis, embarked on another round of international visits (see *MECS* 1999, pp. 355–56), intended to obtain funds, grants and investments, mainly in the sphere of information technology. Already in February, at the World Economic Forum in Davos, he arranged meetings with President Clinton and the owners and chief executive officers of the world's leading IT companies, such as Bill Gates of Microsoft and Stephen Case of America Online. The king convinced Gates to send his representative to check out opportunities in Jordan,[274] which led to a deal, signed in September, to supply Jordanian IT needs (see above).[275] Also in Davos, 'Abdallah met with US Treasury Secretary Lawrence Summers and the representative of the US Trade Representative (USTR) office to the World Economic Forum, Charlene Barshefsky, who were both very supportive of the idea of the US signing an FTA with Jordan.[276]

American aid to Jordan reached a total of $225m., plus a special grant of $100m., which was given also to Israel and the PA.[277] In March, the US granted an additional 180,000 tons of wheat on top of the already promised 200,000 tons.[278] In April, the US approved a special grant of $83m. for water projects, together with $46.1m. to encourage investment.[279] In May, Jordan was removed from the USTR "special 301 watchlist," an annual report examining the adequacy of intellectual property protection in different countries. Jordan's removal was a positive step toward improved economic relations with the US.[280]

There was a measure of tension in June, when the US embassy in Amman went on high alert because of a warning of the US government about a possible terror attack on the embassy. As a consequence, it canceled its scheduled Independence Day celebrations. The Jordanian foreign minister refrained from criticizing US policy, but expressed his doubts about the existence of such a danger.[281]

At the end of the summer, there was some anxiety within the Jordanian government about the possible signing of the FTA with the US. It was feared that if the Republicans won the elections in November, it might be difficult to successfully conclude the agreement. However, Jordan and the US finally signed the agreement on 26 October. President Clinton reiterated US support for Jordan and its importance to the US as a stable country.[282]

The US continued to show its appreciation of the Jordanian role in the Middle East and to express its commitment to Jordanian stability. The US initiated consultations with Jordan regarding the peace process. This was the case after the failure of the Camp David summit in July.[283] After the intifada broke out, 'Abdallah urged the US to help restore quiet in the PA and pushed for the establishment of a US-led international commission to examine the events.[284] The US expressed its gratitude to Jordan for the successful arrest, in December 1999, of terrorists linked to Usama bin Ladin's organization (see above).[285]

The EU likewise expressed its respect for the Jordanian role in the peace process. In November, a delegation from the European Parliament arrived in Jordan as part of the EU effort to bring an end to the intifada.[286] The economy featured in EU-Jordan relations as well. The EU provided an assistance package of 129m. euro,[287] and the European Investment Bank gave Jordan a grant of 60m. euro for industrial projects.[288]

TABLE 1: THE ABU RAGHIB GOVERNMENT, FORMED ON 19 JUNE 2000

Post	Incumbent
Prime Minister and Minister of Defense	'Ali Abu Raghib
Deputy Prime Minister and Minister of Interior	'Awad Khulayfat
Deputy Prime Minister and Minister of Prime Minister's Affairs	Salih Irshidat
Deputy Prime Minister and Minister of Justice	Faris al-Nabulsi
Deputy Prime Minister and Minister of Economic Affairs	Muhammad Halayqa*(P)
Minister of Foreign Affairs	'Abd al-Ilah Khatib*
Minister of Finance	Michel Marto*(P)
Minister of Information	Talib al-Rifa'i*
Minister of Trade and Industry	Wasif 'Azar
Minister of Planning	Jawad Hadid (P)
Minister of Tourism and Antiquities	'Aql Biltaji*(P)
Minister of Transport	Muhammad Kalalida
Minister of Telecommunications and Post	Fawaz Zu'bi
Minister of Energy	Wa'il Sabri*(P)
Minister of Culture	Mahmud al-Kayid
Minister of Health	Tariq Suhaymat
Minister of Public Works and Housing	Husni Abu Ghayda*(P)
Minister of Water	Hatim al-Halawani (P)
Minister of Municipal, Rural and Environmental Affairs	'Abd al-Rahim al-'Ukur
Minister of Education	Khalid Tuqan (P)
Minister of Labor	'Id al-Fayiz*
Minister of Agriculture	Zuhayr Zanuna
Minister of Parliamentary Affairs	Yusuf al-Dalabih
Minister of Social Development	Tamam Ghul (P)

Minister of Youth   Sa'id Shuqum*
Minister of State for Administrative Development   Muhammad Dhunaybat
Minister of Religious Affairs   'Abd al-Salam 'Abbadi*
Minister of State for Judicial Affairs   Dayfallah Masa'ada
Minister of State   'Adil al-Shurayda

* Served in outgoing cabinet
(P) Of Palestinian origin

NOTES

For the place and frequency of publications cited here, and for the full name of the publication, news agency, radio station, or monitoring service where an abbreviation is used, please see "List of Sources." Only in the case of more than one publication bearing the same name is the place of publication noted here.

1. *MM*, 14 January 2000.
2. *JT*, 16 January 2000.
3. *JT*, 17 January 2000.
4. Al-Jazira satellite TV, 24 February 2000 (BBC Monitoring).
5. *JT*, 2 May 2000.
6. *Al-Quds al-'Arabi*, 8 April 2000 (BBC Monitoring).
7. *JT*, 13 April 2000.
8. *JT*, 19 April 2000.
9. *MM*, 18 June 2000.
10. *JT*, 17 April 2000.
11. *JT*, 19, 21 April 2000.
12. *Al-Hayat*, 28 April 2000 (BBC Monitoring).
13. *JT*, 12 May 2000.
14. *JT*, 17 May 2000.
15. Editorial in *JT*, 10 May; and Salama Ni'mat in *al-Hayat*, 1 June 2000 (*MM*).
16. S. al-Khalidi in *JT*, 18 June 2000.
17. Fahd al-Fanik in *JT*, 10 April 2000.
18. Lola Kaylani in *al-Ahram*, 22 June 2000.
19. *MM*, 1 June 2000.
20. *JT*, 15 June 2000.
21. *JT*, 15 June 2000.
22. *JT*, 18 June; *MM*, 16, 18 June 2000.
23. *JT*, 15 June 2000.
24. JTV, 18 June 2000 (BBC Monitoring).
25. *MM*, 19 June 2000.
26. *MM*, 22 June 2000.
27. *MM*, 23 June 2000.
28. *MM*, 20, 21 June 2000.
29. *JT*, 23 June 2000.
30. Musa Kaylani in *JT*, 25 June 2000.
31. *JT*, 22 June 2000.
32. Ibid.
33. *JT*, 6 July 2000.
34. *JT*, 9, 28 August 2000.
35. *JT*, 14 July 2000.

36. *JT*, 20 June 2000.
37. Rami al-Khuri in *JT*, 21 June 2000.
38. Salama Ni'mat in *al-Hayat* as quoted in *MM*, 23 June 2000.
39. *Al-Ahram*, 16 November 2000.
40. R. Amman, 23 November 2000 (BBC Monitoring).
41. *JT*, 21 September, 24 December 2000.
42. *JT*, 22 September 2000.
43. *JT*, 20 January, 17 February 2000.
44. *JT*, 5 June 2000.
45. *JT*, 14 August 2000.
46. *JT*, 16, 21 August 2000.
47. *JT*, 29 May 2000.
48. Francesca Sawalha in *JT*, 6 December 2000.
49. *Al-'Arab al-Yawm*, 12 October 2000.
50. *JT*, 6 December 2000.
51. *Al-'Arab al-Yawm*, 28 November; *JT*, 28 November 2000.
52. *JT*, 6 April 2000.
53. *JT*, 5 July 2000.
54. *JT*, 9, 28 August 2000.
55. *JT*, 29 August 2000.
56. JTV, 10 September 2000 (BBC Monitoring).
57. *JT*, 25 September 2000.
58. *JT*,15 November 2000.
59. *JT*, 18 September 2000.
60. *JT*, 6 December 2000.
61. *JT*, 24 January, 6 November; *MM*, 13 July 2000.
62. *JT*, 30 November 2000.
63. *JT*, 6 February 2000.
64. *JT*, 6 September, 21 December 2000.
65. *JT*, 19, 27 July 2000.
66. *JT*, 3 February 2000.
67. *JT*, 14 March 2000.
68. *JT*, 14 November 2000.
69. *JT*, 9 July 2000.
70. *JT*, 5 September 2000.
71. *JT*, 13 December 2000.
72. *JT*, 24 July, 18 December 2000.
73. *JT*, 30 November 2000.
74. *JT*, 15 February 2000.
75. *JT*, 24 February 2000.
76. *JT*, 25 February 2000.
77. *JT*, 13 February 2000.
78. *JT*, 22 February 2000.
79. *JT*, 10 March 2000.
80. Walid Sa'di in *JT*, 13 March 2000.
81. *JT*, 2 November 2000.
82. *JT*, 30 April 2000.
83. *JT*, 7,8 May 2000.
84. *JT*, 28 February 2000.
85. *JT*, 26 March 2000.
86. *JT*, 17 January 2000.
87. *Al-Safir*, 24 January 2000 (DR).
88. *Al-Hayat* (Internet version), 25 January 2000 (BBC Monitoring).
89. *JT*, 13 March 2000.

90. *JT*, 4 May 2000.
91. *JT*, 15 May 2000.
92. *JT*, 27 June 2000.
93. *Al-Dustur*, 27 June 2000 (DR).
94. *Al-Dustur*, 27 June 2000 (BBC Monitoring).
95. *JT*, 4 July 2000.
96. *Al-Majd*, 10 July 2000 (BBC Monitoring).
97. *JT*, 1 August 2000.
98. *JT*, 25 August 2000.
99. *JT*, 5 November 2000.
100. *Al-Quds al-'Arabi*, 15 November 2000 (DR).
101. *JT*, 5 December 2000.
102. R. Amman, 6 December 2000 (BBC Monitoring).
103. *JT*, 30 December 2000.
104. *Al-Dustur*, 30 September 2000 (DR).
105. *Al-Hayat*, 25 October 2000 (BBC Monitoring).
106. *JT*, 17 January 2000.
107. Petra-JNA, 28 January 2000 (BBC Monitoring).
108. *JT*, 6 March 2000.
109. *JT*, 28 March 2000.
110. *JT*, 11 April 2000.
111. *JT*, 7, 10 May; *al-Dustur*, 8 May 2000 (DR).
112. *JT*, 25 June 2000.
113. *JT*, 27 September 2000.
114. *JT*, 26 June 2000.
115. *JT*, 3 January 2000.
116. *Al-Sharq al-Awsat*, 4 January 2000 (DR).
117. R. Amman, 23 January (BBC Monitoring); *JT*, 25 January 2000.
118. *Al-Ra'y*, 24 January 2000 (DR).
119. *Al-Sharq al-Awsat*, 25 January 2000 (DR).
120. Ibid.
121. Ibid.
122. *JT*, 2 August 2000.
123. *Al-Ra'y*, 1 August 2000 (BBC Monitoring).
124. *JT*, 20 January 2000.
125. *JT*, 31 January 2000.
126. *Al-Sharq al-Awsat*, 18 February 2000 (DR).
127. *JT*, 13 March 2000.
128. *JT*, 29 March 2000.
129. *NYT*, 29 March 2000.
130. *JT*, 24 May 2000.
131. *JT*, 13 July 2000.
132. *JT*, 14 September 2000.
133. *JT*, 19 September 2000.
134. *Al-Sharq al-Awsat*, 18 December 2000 (BBC Monitoring).
135. *JT*, 6 March 2000.
136. *JT*, 14 March 2000.
137. *JT*, 15 March 2000.
138. *JT*, 22 March 2000.
139. *JT*, 23 March, 5 April 2000.
140. *JT*, 7 April 2000.
141. *JT*, 25 April 2000.
142. *JT*, 26 April 2000.
143. *JT*, 27 April 2000.

144. *JT*, 27 April, 4 May 2000.
145. *JT*, 19 May 2000.
146. *JT*, 23 May 2000.
147. *JT*, 23 June 2000.
148. *JT*, 10 July 2000.
149. *JT*, 24 July 2000.
150. *JT*, 23 March 2000.
151. *JT*, 18 June 2000.
152. *JT*, 29 June 2000.
153. *JT*, 13, 14 July 2000.
154. *JT*, 5 December 2000.
155. *JT*, 7 June 2000.
156. *JT*, 19 December 2000.
157. *JT*, 24 April,12 June, 12 September 2000.
158. *JT*, 26 October 2000..
159. JTV, 26 July 2000 (BBC Monitoring).
160. *JT*, 2 March 2000.
161. *CR*, Jordan, December 2001, p. 5.
162. Fahd al-Fanik in *JT*, 25 December 2000.
163. *JT*, 21 August 2000.
164. *Al-'Arab al-Yawm*, 31 May 2000 (BBC Monitoring).
165. *JT*, 5 July 2000.
166. *JT*, 15 September 2000.
167. *JT*, 25 July, 8 August 2000.
168. *JT*, 27 September 2000.
169. Fahd al-Fanik in *JT*, 26 June 2000.
170. Fahd al-Fanik in *JT*, 8 May, 26 June, 24 July, 21 August 2000.
171. *JT*, 27 September 2000.
172. Fahd al-Fanik in *JT*, 4 September 2000.
173. *JT*, 8 December 2000.
174. *JT*, 8 September 2000.
175. *JT*, 6 March 2000.
176. *JT*, 29 May 2000.
177. Israel TV Channel 1, 23 April 2000 (BBC Monitoring); *NYT*, 24 April 2000.
178. Israel TV Channel 1, 23 April 2000 (BBC Monitoring).
179. *NYT*, 24 April 2000.
180. VoI, 23 April 2000 (BBC Monitoring).
181. *Al-Ahram*, 27 April 2000.
182. Editorial in *JT*, 25 May; editorial in *al-Dustur*, 23 May (DR); Hilmi al-Asmar in *al-Dustur*, 25 May 2000 (DR).
183. R. Amman, 24 May 2000 (BBC Monitoring).
184. *JT*, 25 June 2000.
185. *Al-Dustur*, 25 June 2000 (DR).
186. JTV, 24 June 2000 (BBC Monitoring).
187. *JT*, 1 October 2000.
188. *JT*, 2 October 2000.
189. *JT*, 8 October 2000.
190. *JT*, 20 November 2000.
191. Petra-JNA, 5 December (BBC Monitoring); VoI, 6 December 2000 (BBC Monitoring).
192. Editorial in *JT*, 11 December; Michael Jansen in *JT*, 21 December 2000.
193. *JT*, 28 April 2000.
194. *JT*, 25 April 2000.
195. *JT*, 2 May 2000.
196. *JT*, 25 August 2000.

197. *JT*, 20 November 2000.
198. *JT*, 29 August 2000.
199. Petra-JNA, 2 October 2000 (BBC Monitoring).
200. *JT*, 8 October 2000.
201. Petra-JNA, 6 October 2000 (BBC Monitoring).
202. *JT*, 8 October 2000.
203. Petra-JNA, 6, 10 October 2000 (BBC Monitoring).
204. *Al-Majd*, 9 October 2000 (DR).
205. Rami al-Khuri in *JT*, 25 October 2000.
206. *JT*, 25 October 2000.
207. Ibid.; R. Amman, 24 October 2000 (BBC Monitoring).
208. *Al-Dustur*, 8 October 2000 (BBC Monitoring).
209. *JT*, 29 October 2000.
210. *JT*, 7 November 2000.
211. *JT*, 9 July 2000.
212. JTV, 9 July 2000 (BBC Monitoring).
213. *JT*, 20 July 2000.
214. *JT*, 21 July 2000.
215. *Al-Majd*, 18 September 2000 (DR).
216. *Al-Hayat* (Internet version), 9 September 2000 (BBC Monitoring).
217. VoP, 22 November (BBC Monitoring); *JT*, 8, 24 December 2000.
218. *JT*, 2 October 2000.
219. *JT*, 3, 5, 6 October 2000.
220. *JT*, 26 November 2000.
221. Petra-JNA, 21 November 2000 (BBC Monitoring).
222. *JT*, 22 November 2000.
223. *JT*, 7 May 2000.
224. *JT*, 23 October 2000.
225. *JT*, 24 November 2000.
226. Amy Henderson in *JT*, 6 March 2000.
227. *JT*, 7 February 2000.
228. *JT*, 17 February 2000.
229. *JT*, 7 February 2000.
230. *Al-Dustur*, 20 June 2000 (DR).
231. JTV, 9 July 2000 (BBC Monitoring).
232. *Al-Quds al-'Arabi*, 12 July; *JT*, 13 July 2000.
233. *JT*, 13 July; editorial in *JT*, 14 July 2000.
234. *JT*, 6, 10 February 2000.
235. JTV, 9 July 2000 (BBC Monitoring).
236. *MM*, 11 July 2000.
237. JTV, 21 May 2000 (BBC Monitoring).
238. According to the plan, a 325km. water pipeline would be laid leading from the Disi aquifer in south Jordan up to Amman. The project would be able to provide Amman with 100m. cu.m. of water for approximately thirty years and revive the arid areas of south Jordan.
239. *JT*, 25 January 2000.
240. *JT*, 24 March, 24 August 2000.
241. *JT*, 5 October 2000.
242. *JT*, 8 November 2000.
243. *JT*, 23 January 2000.
244. JTV, 22 January 2000.
245. *JT*, 6 April 2000.
246. INA (Internet version), 16 April 2000 (BBC Monitoring).
247. Tariq Ayub in *JT*, 15 June 2000.

248. *JT*, 9 June 2000.
249. *MM*, 18 July 2000.
250. *Al-Sharq al-Awsat*, 23 July 2000.
251. *JT*, 2 August 2000.
252. *JT*, 29 September 2000.
253. *JT*, 26 October 2000.
254. *Al-Dustur*, 2 November (DR); editorial in *JT*, 2 November 2000.
255. *JT*, 5 November 2000.
256. *JT*, 31 January 2000.
257. *JT*, 17 May 2000.
258. *JT*, 1 December 2000.
259. *Al-Majd*, 18 December 2000 (BBC Monitoring).
260. *JT*, 16 March 2000.
261. *MM*, 20 March 2000.
262. *JT*, 13 April 2000.
263. Tzvi Bar'el in *Ha'aretz*, 18 April; *JT*, 13 April 2000.
264. Bassam Badarin in *al-Quds al-'Arabi*, as quoted in *MM*, 25 April 2000.
265. *JT*, 13 June 2000.
266. *JT*, 18 July 2000.
267. *JT*, 14 August 2000.
268. SANA, 17 August 2000 (BBC Monitoring).
269. Petra-JNA, 15 August 2000 (BBC Monitoring).
270. *JT*, 14 August 2000.
271. *JT*, 4 December 2000.
272. *JT*, 24 December 2000.
273. MENA, 16 October 2000 (BBC Monitoring).
274. *JT*, 1 February 2000.
275. *JT*, 8 September 2000.
276. *JT*, 1 February 2000.
277. Ibid.
278. *JT*, 3 March 2000.
279. *JT*, 28 April 2000.
280. *JT*, 5 May 2000.
281. *JT*, 30 June 2000.
282. *JT*, 26 October 2000.
283. *JT*, 4 August 2000.
284. *JT*, 13 December 2000.
285. *JT*, 5 April 2000.
286. *JT*, 21 November 2000.
287. *JT*, 5 April 2000.
288. *Al-'Arab al-Yawm*, 23 February 2000 (BBC Monitoring).

Kuwait
(Al-Kuwayt)

JOSEPH KOSTINER

Public life in Kuwait in 2000 was marred by the convoluted relationship between the Kuwaiti National Assembly (NA) and the government, which had disrupted Kuwaiti political life over the previous decade. The NA sought to provide checks on the power of the government, that was dominated by the Al Sabah royal family. During the year, members of the NA continued to interrogate cabinet ministers, to initiate no-confidence votes and to generally criticize almost every government policy. In short, the NA came to regard itself both as the only legitimate law-making body in the country and as the main political counterweight to the government, which consisted of the prime minister and a cabinet of ministers who were unelected royal family members and other officials. With mounting defiance, NA members demanded the right to challenge government policies and actions, as well as to vote into law those it approved.

The government was dominated by the ruling Al Sabah family, whose members had a majority among cabinet ministers and top-ranking officials, and it sought to resist the NA ambitions. During 2000, however, the government was too weak to defeat the NA in a head-on confrontation. The physical illness of the crown prince and prime minister, Sa'd 'Abdallah Al Sabah, led the emir, Jabir al-Ahmad Al Sabah, to reshuffle the cabinet rather than risk another major clash with the NA, as had happened in February. This delayed but did not stop the political conflict, which was unremitting throughout the year.

In this atmosphere of tension, the government had scarcely enough time or political will to tackle major policy issues. It benefited from an unexpected windfall of oil income in 1999–2000, which produced a small budget surplus. However, deeper structural changes — notably privatization of leading government-owned companies — remained on the drawing board. Moreover, both the government and the NA were unable to resolve widespread anxieties about Kuwaiti security in the face of the Iraqi threat, which was the focus of much public debate. Fears of an Iraqi invasion were not dispelled, and the Kuwaiti reliance on the US defense shield caused much disquiet. Most of all, many Kuwaitis felt threatened by the growing strength of militant Islamists, who tried to impose their behavioral norms on the rest of the population. At the same time, liberal and traditionalist leaders failed to counteract the Islamist initiatives to dominate public life, thus raising serious questions about the cultural and ideological future of Kuwait.

Kuwaiti security interests, namely, concerns vis-à-vis Iraq, dominated foreign relations. As in previous years, Kuwaiti leaders reiterated their distrust of Saddam Husayn's intentions and remained in a state of readiness for a possible clash with Iraqi forces. They therefore resisted any attempts at rapprochement with Iraq and, in the case of border incidents and a rise in tension, such as was initiated by Iraq in September 2000,

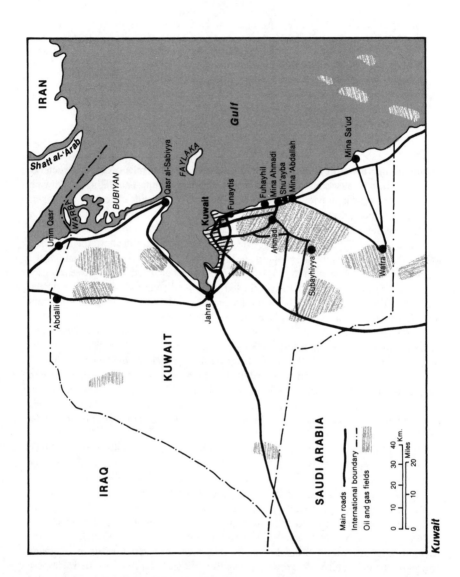

Kuwait

Kuwait put the US forces stationed in Kuwait on alert and its own forces on preparation. The incident was contained, but Kuwait's overriding fear of Iraq remained pervasive.

Kuwaiti leaders, however, had to tread carefully in their commitment to regional policies that were somewhat contradictory. Various Arab states, including fellow members in the Gulf Cooperation Council (GCC), the UAE and Qatar, increasingly supported the lifting of UN sanctions on Iraq. Kuwait, while maintaining its closeness to the US, was nevertheless on friendly terms with the GCC and continued to cultivate relations with member states. Kuwaiti leaders also viewed Iran as an appropriate counterbalance to Iraq in the Gulf, and stepped up their contacts with Tehran.

Finally, disappointed by Saddam Husayn's unrelenting grip on power, Kuwaitis harbored doubts about the interests and effectiveness of the US in the region. Nevertheless, they were aware of their reliance on American forces to counteract any military challenge to their security.

INTERNAL AFFAIRS

THE POLITICAL SCENE: THE GOVERNMENT AND THE NA

The departure on 7 December 1999 of the elderly Kuwaiti crown prince and prime minister, Sa'd 'Abdallah Al Sabah, to the US for medical treatment led directly to a cabinet reshuffle. Sa'd 'Abdallah's deteriorating health had forced him to commit himself to repeated courses of treatment abroad. This raised questions about the shape of the new cabinet and its relations with the NA, given the rivalry and antagonism that characterized relations between the two bodies. There were rumors about Sa'd 'Abdallah's resignation, accompanied by other rumors that an NA member would join the cabinet and become a minister. The rumors were preceded by a cabinet decree closing down two important daily newspapers, *al-Watan* and *al-Siyasa*. This decree encountered fierce opposition from the NA, whose members declared it illegal. Tension between the government and the NA increased, centering around the possibility of a reshuffle.[1] On 17 February 2000, after a heated debate in the NA, the cabinet resigned.[2] The ensuing reshuffle, however, resulted in only a few changes, which were virtually meaningless. 'Adil Khalid Al Sabah remained minister for electricity and water and became minister of state for housing as well. However, the Ministry of Religious Endowment (*Awqaf*) and Islamic Affairs was removed from his control and handed to the minister of justice of the day, Sa'd Jasim Yusuf al-Hashil. The limited nature of the changes appeared to be an attempt by the royal family to maintain the status quo in its power struggle with the NA.[3]

The next few weeks witnessed continued political strife. In April, the assault by Islamists on a female student (see below) stirred up a broad public debate about the conduct of Islamists and gave the government an opportunity to launch a verbal campaign against Islamist NA members. The friction was exacerbated in June by two accidents at state-owned refineries: two technicians died and four were injured in a gas leak at the Shu'ayba refinery, and six workers were killed in an explosion at Mina al-Ahmadi. Because these explosions came in the wake of earlier incidents, NA members called for the resignation of the oil minister, Sa'ud Nasir Al Sabah. After some discussion, both the government and the NA commissioned inquiries into the incidents. The commissions passed on their findings to the prosecutor-general and to the NA investigation committee, in order to consider whether further charges would be laid, possibly against the Chevron Corporation.[4]

Tension between the NA and cabinet members, already heightened over this and other incidents, was further fuelled during 2000. In October, the minister of information, Sa'd al-'Ajami, resigned. As a liberal in Kuwaiti politics, he felt powerless to withstand the Islamist influence in the NA (see below). In November, 'Adil Khalid Al Sabah, the electricity and water minister was summoned to a vote of no confidence in the NA, facing allegations of corruption which he barely survived. The repeated efforts by NA members to weaken the government, compounded by the NA splitting into liberal and Islamist factions, further contributed to the ineffective performance of a government led by an elderly and ailing prime minister. At the same time, there was much uncertainty about the ability of the younger princes in the government.[5] With these deep-seated issues unresolved, the Kuwaiti political system simmered throughout the year, radiating instability upon society at large.

SOCIAL ISSUES: CONFUSION AND SURGING RADICAL ISLAMISM

Kuwaiti society was still affected by the implications of the 1990–91 Iraqi invasion and subsequent war. A sense of insecurity prevailed, emanating from the Kuwaiti assumption that Saddam Husayn had not changed his policies and that a military attack or even an invasion was imminent. Kuwaiti spokespersons, as well as foreign journalists, regularly reported that such beliefs were widely held in Kuwait.[6] These fears were compounded by a growing lack of trust in US security policies. Many Kuwaitis reportedly suspected that the real motive behind the American defense of Kuwait was Washington's intention to establish a lasting military presence in the Gulf, rather than to rid Kuwait of Saddam's expansionist threat[7] (see below).

Uncertainty also surrounded the stateless residents of Kuwait, the *bidun*, an issue which had been high on the public agenda for several years. These were long-time Kuwaiti residents of Bedouin origin, numbering about 130,000, who lacked proper credentials for citizenship. Many were essential manual workers or served in the Kuwaiti armed forces. Public opinion was positive, and favored providing the *bidun* with the rights to medical treatment and livelihood that would follow from granting them citizenship. The NA, on the other hand, feared committing itself to an overly liberal policy of citizenship that could allow a large number of foreigners to become Kuwaiti citizens, and delayed its decision on the issue.[8] However, a change in the citizenship law instituted by the government made it possible for the minister of the interior, Muhammad al-Khalid Al Sabah, to inform the NA that the government intended to grant citizenship to some 36,000 *bidun*, without opening up to an overly liberal policy of citizenship.

The *bidun* issue involved wider questions of foreign workers' conditions in Kuwait. In October 1999, Egyptian foreign workers initiated several days of rioting and looting in protest against their employment and living conditions (see *MECS* 1999, pp. 377). The minister of social affairs and labor, 'Abd al-Wahhab al-Wazzan, was therefore careful to mention that Kuwaiti regulations did not discriminate against foreign workers, and that the national laws and legal policies provided them with adequate protection. Al-Wazzan nevertheless reiterated the policy of "Kuwaitization" of the local workforce. Accordingly, in January 2000, the government endorsed the registration to the Kuwaiti labor force of a second group of five thousand Kuwaiti citizens, who had hitherto not been employed, both men and women.[9] On its own, this reform could hardly change the basic anomaly whereby foreign workers constituted about 70% of the Kuwaiti workforce.

The NA decision in 1999 to block the legislation permitting women to vote (see *MECS* 1999,pp. 372–74) and the resultant public debates, led to a degree of unrest over womens' rights. In early April, six religious extremists were arrested for assaulting an unveiled female student.[10] Women demonstrated in several marches, and commentators emphasized that their protests, supported by liberal politicians, were a challenge to the Islamists' bid to dominate the public agenda.[11]

The Islamists were indeed campaigning to introduce new norms of conduct into Kuwaiti public life. They were trying to overturn the traditional tendency to religious moderation, which to their eyes denoted indifference and laxity. Thus the celebration of Valentine's Day on 14 February, characterized by decorations and exchanging gifts, was denounced as dangerous and its participants as "heretics."[12] Many socially acceptable public customs, such as playing concerts or screening films, were declared *haram* (forbidden) by the Islamists.[13] Arab commentators stressed that groups drawing on the Egyptian al-Takfir wal-Hijra party, on Wahhabis influenced by the Saudi creed and on Shi'i radicals, were active in Kuwait.[14]

In political terms, Kuwaiti Islamists were more impressive and influential during 2000 than their liberal rivals. In June, their influence became evident in two ways: the seven men accused of beating the female student in April were acquitted by a court, on "legal proofs" that the girl had provoked the beating by committing sins. In another development, Islamist members of the NA succeeded in amending a law allowing Kuwaiti and foreign investors to set up private universities in the country, by forcing the building of segregated male and female facilities. Attempts by liberal members of the Assembly to prevent this failed, although a final vote on the new universities' bill as a whole had not yet been taken.[15]

These events demonstrated that the years of fear of Iraqi aggression, and the ongoing parliamentary struggle between the government and opposition groups, as well as internal strife within the latter, had led to an atmosphere of confusion in Kuwaiti society. This was manifested in the difficulties of setting policy on major issues, in feelings of insecurity, and in the growing initiatives by Islamists to take advantage of the unrest and uncertainty to force fundamentalist rules and codes of behavior on society.

ECONOMIC CONDITIONS

The windfall of oil income enjoyed by the Gulf states in 1999–2000 (see chapter on economic developments in the Middle East) brought stability to Kuwait national finances and staunched the immediate budget deficits. Oil prices during this period swung mostly between $20 and $25 per barrel, twice as high as had originally been assumed. An increase in the volume of oil production also worked in favor of Kuwait. Hence, for the first time since 1996, there was a budget surplus of $2.6bn. for the first half of the 1999–2000 fiscal year.[16]

This development did not in itself stimulate other sectors and led to a gain of only about 1% in GDP. Major structural changes were still needed; over 90% of Kuwaiti citizens were still employed by the state, and government expenditure on salaries constituted 37% of general public expenditure, a rise of 3% compared to 1998. The unswerving commitment of the government to full employment and to political stability continued to be a major drain on the national budget.[17]

A series of reforms that the government had introduced into the NA in 1999 were expected to be implemented during the following two years. Under these reforms some of the major Kuwaiti businesses, such as Kuwait Airways and the Kuwait oil tanker company, would be put up for sale (see *MECS* 1999, p. 374). However, fears over potential job losses and the elimination of consumer subsidies deterred the NA from endorsing the privatization of all the companies in question.[18] The government was also reported to be drafting an income tax law and setting up various inducements to indigenous Kuwaitis to join the private sector, policies that had not yet won NA support. In November, the first deputy prime minister and minister of foreign affairs, Sabah Al Ahmad, was appointed to head a special committee to oversee national economic reform. His committee was required to formulate structural reforms and then persuade the NA to endorse them and to cut budget expenditure, which, according to the 2000/01 budget forecast, was supposed to increase by 11.5%.[19] Thus, the windfall of oil income helped keep the Kuwait economy in good condition, but the need for major structural change was clearly evident.

FOREIGN AFFAIRS

POLICY TOWARD IRAQ

Kuwaiti leaders continued to view Saddam's Iraq as their greatest enemy, believing that Iraq harbored ambitions for an invasion or military incursion into Kuwait. In April, Kuwait intercepted Iraqi boats that the Iraqis had called "fishing boats", but which Kuwait regarded as a threat.[20] Kuwait also rejected any Iraqi attempt to "turn over a new leaf" in relations between the two states; with rare unanimity, both government and NA members refused to enter into a direct dialogue with Iraq.[21] In a seminar organized by Kuwaiti businessmen about future relations with Iraq, ambitious plans were discussed for better ties, particularly in economic terms, but it was agreed that this could "only happen once the Iraqi president left power."[22]

In September 2000, there was growing alarm in Kuwait about Iraqi troop movements, a development that often occurred in recent years. In return, Iraq accused Kuwait of stealing Iraqi oil (a claim Iraq had raised against Kuwait before the invasion of 1990) and massed groups of people — many of whom were *bidun*, living in Iraq — along the Kuwaiti border.[23] The tension gradually dissipated in following days.

The six hundred or so Kuwaitis who had been missing since the occupation was another issue on which Kuwaiti leaders were reluctant to give way in any negotiations with Iraq. On the contrary, they demanded the return of these prisoners as another precondition for rapprochement.[24]

Attitudes Toward GCC States

One of the Kuwaiti defense strategies was its alliance with the other members of the GCC. It was clear that the GCC did not count as a military buffer against Iraq, since the armies of its member states were small and relatively inexperienced. The GCC states constituted instead a political alliance that was supposed to back Kuwait in its demands and policies in regard to Iraq. At the seventy-fourth meeting of the GCC foreign ministers that was held in Jidda on 8 April, Kuwait received the kind of supportive statement vis-à-vis Iraq that its leaders had sought.[25]

However, two GCC states, Qatar and the UAE, had developed a relatively pro-Iraq policy (see chapters on Qatar and the UAE), focusing mainly on lifting the UN sanctions. Kuwaiti leaders had to accept that this position was widely supported in the Arab world, mainly by leading states such as Egypt and Syria (see chapter on inter-Arab relations).[26] Kuwaiti spokespersons were critical: they described such a step as "negative" and called for more coordination within the GCC.[27] They did not, however, initiate any move against these policies.

Kuwait's activities within the GCC brought one major success: in early July the Saudi crown prince, 'Abdallah bin 'Abd al-'Aziz, and the Kuwaiti amir, Jabir Al Ahmad, oversaw a final border agreement concerning the shared continental shelf of the two states. The agreement established a basis for further cooperation between the two countries and contributed to greater stability within the GCC.[28]

Following this accord, the Kuwaiti minister of foreign affairs, Sabah Al Ahmad, expressed interest in signing a similar agreement with Iran.[29] This reflected the ongoing Kuwaiti policy of cultivating relations with Tehran (see earlier volumes of *MECS*). Kuwait regarded Iran as a friendly neighbor that might play a counterbalancing role against Iraq, as well as help to reinforce overall Gulf security and stability. Kuwaiti leaders could not afford to sign an official security agreement with Tehran, as the US would oppose this, but they approved of the Iranian naval presence in the Gulf. A continuing dialogue to that effect was carried on [?between naval personnel?].[30]

Kuwait and the US

The main Kuwaiti defense still rested with the US. Ostensibly, Kuwaiti public opinion was often critical of US policies — its support for Israel and its abstention from acting outright to topple Saddam, a stance which, according to certain prominent commentators, attested to Washington's intrinsic interest being the stationary US forces in the Gulf for the long term. In the words of a Kuwaiti academic, 'Abdallah al-Shayeji:

"[We] see Arabs constantly weakened by the US bias towards Israel; and Kuwait [is] no less vulnerable than ten years ago, because here we are at the end of yet another US administration, and Saddam is still in power. And in return what do Kuwaitis see? Cohen [William Cohen, the US Secretary of Defense] coming here every six months to tell us to hold the line."[31]

However, every escalation along the border with Iraq reminded Kuwait of its dependence on American forces. Relying on the ten-year defense agreement from 1991, Kuwaiti leaders were happy to hear reassurances from the US about security during Secretary Cohen's visit in April. In the meantime, the military exercises conducted jointly with the US [in ?date] were an eloquent retaliation to Iraq. Moreover, US forces were there to deter the Iraqi threat in September–October 2000.

NOTES

For the place and frequency of publications cited here, and for the full name of the publication, news agency, radio station or monitoring service where an abbreviation is used, please see "List of Sources." Only in the case of more than one publication bearing the same name is the place of publication noted here.

1. *Al-Sharq al-Awsat*, 17 February 2000.
2. DPA, 17 February 2000.
3. *CR*, Kuwait, 1st quarter, 2000, pp. 10–11.
4. *CR*, Kuwait, 3rd quarter, pp. 13–15; *al-Hayat*, 22 April 2000.
5. *CR*, Kuwait, 4th quarter, pp. 12–14; *FT*, 1 April 2000.
6. Shafiq Ghabra, "The View from Kuwait," *Middle East Forum Wire*, 2 May 2000; *al-Wasat*, 7 August 2000.
7. cf. *FT*, 21 November 2000.
8. *Al-Sharq al-Awsat*, 10 January; *al-Watan*, 25 April; KUNA, 16 May — BBC Monitoring, 1 May 2000.
9. *Kuwait Times*, 10 January 2000.
10. AP, 10 April 2000.
11. *The Independent*, 16 April 2000.
12. DPA, 14 February 2000.
13. *CSM*, 24 April 2000.
14. DPA, 8 April; *al-Majalla*, 22 April; *al-Wasat*, 18 September 2000.
15. *GSNL*, 26 June 2000.
16. *CR*, Kuwait, 2nd quarter, 2000, p. 21.
17. Ibid., pp. 22–23.
18. *ME*, October 2000.
19. *CR,* Kuwait, 4th quarter, 2000, pp. 16–19.
20. BBC Monitoring, 4 May 2000.
21. *Al-Sharq al-Awsat*, 3 January 2000.
22. *Al-Hayat*, 11 May; KUNA, 13 May — BBC Monitoring, 16 May 2000.
23. *FT*, 15 September; 4 October 2000.
24. *Al-Wasat*, 10 April; *The Philadelphia Inquirer*, 27 April 2000.
25. *GSNL*, 11 May 2000.
26. *GSNL*, 10 July 2000.
27. *CR*, Kuwait, 2nd quarter, 2000, p. 14.
28. *Al-Sharq al-Awsat*, 3 July 2000.
29. KUNA, 4 July — BBC Monitoring, 5 July 2000.
30. IRNA, 17 April 2000 (DR).
31. *FT*, 21 November 2000.

Lebanon
(Al-Jumhuriyya al-Lubnaniyya)

WILLIAM W. HARRIS

In 2000, Lebanon witnessed the most significant political developments since the Syrian assault on "rebel" Gen. Michel 'Awn's East Beirut redoubt in October 1990 that ended fifteen years of internal warfare and inaugurated the Syrian-dominated post-war regime (see *MECS* 1990, pp. 533–34).

In May 2000, Israeli forces withdrew from its self-declared "security zone" in South Lebanon, ending eighteen years of Israeli presence in Lebanese territory. This withdrawal, followed within a few weeks by the death of President Hafiz al-Asad of Syria, gave the Lebanese a feeling of transformation in their local and regional environment. Israel receded as a factor in Lebanese politics, and popular attention focused on the poor performance of the regime of President Emil Lahhud and Prime Minister Salim al-Huss, and on the Syrian role in Lebanon.

On 27 August and 3 September, in two rounds of polling in the third post-1990 parliamentary elections, Lebanese voters expressed their dissatisfaction with the Lahhud-Huss regime by giving its opponents a significant victory. On the one hand, this was certainly not a rebellion against Syria. As the new Syrian president, Bashshar al-Asad, observed, "no enemies of Syria" won seats.[1] On the other hand, it was the first time since 1990 that parliamentary elections had involved a genuine contest, albeit within parameters acceptable to Damascus. Former prime minister Rafiq al-Hariri and Druze leader Walid Junblat, targeted by the regime since Lahhud's installation as president in October 1998 (see *MECS* 1998 and 1999, chapters on Lebanon), overrode a fierce blocking campaign to sweep all the Beirut and Mount Lebanon constituencies where they presented lists of candidates. Prime Minister Huss lost his seat in a stunning humiliation, and condemned the elections as "emaciated democracy" (*demoqratiyya hazila*).[2]

The election results encouraged critics of Lahhud's deference to Damascus, and indicated uncertain Syrian management of Lebanese affairs under the new Syrian president. Syrian acceptance of Hariri's resurgence raised questions about the influence of "old guard" elements in Damascus, particularly Hariri's friend, Vice President 'Abd al-Halim Khaddam. On 20 September, the council of Maronite archbishops called for redeployment of Syrian forces in Lebanon "in preparation for their withdrawal."[3] Druze leader Walid Junblat, encouraged by electoral endorsement of his leadership in Mount Lebanon, championed the Maronite position, which made it difficult to dismiss discontent with the Syrian role as a purely Christian phenomenon.

On 23 October, Lahhud named Hariri as the new Lebanese prime minister, after Hariri had received the support of most parliamentary deputies and Syrian backing as well. This was a clear setback for the president. The Hariri cabinet, named on 26 October, marked a return to dividing up government functions among the major Lebanese

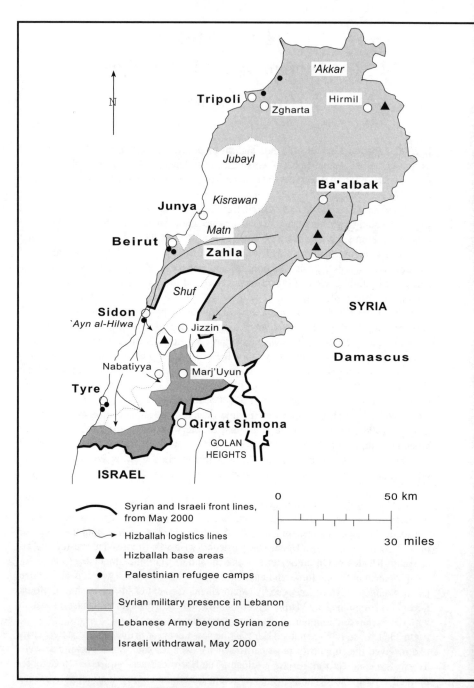

Lebanon 2000: Geopolitical Conditions

politicians and their protégés, after the abortive experiment of technocrat administration under Huss. Accommodating Hariri, Lahhud, Junblat, Parliamentary Speaker Nabih Birri, and Syria's special group of "close allies," while also preserving sectarian balances, required an expansion of the cabinet to thirty ministers.

Hariri resumed his overlordship of economic affairs in late 2000 after a two-year interval during which the Huss government had failed to make any positive impact on the increasingly parlous economic circumstances in Lebanon. Huss had loudly criticized Hariri's financing of Lebanese "reconstruction" via mounting public debt and budget deficits between 1993 and 1998, but in 1999–2000 Huss himself presided over a 60% increase in the budget deficit and a 19% rise in public debt.[4] In 2000, the budget deficit amounted to 24% of GDP, the second highest such ratio in the world after Zimbabwe, and public debt reached 145% of GDP.[5] The economy continued to be in recession, with GDP contracting by 1% in 1999 and 0.5% in 2000.[6] Unemployment stood at over 20%, many small and medium-sized businesses collapsed during the year, and a UN report rated Lebanon as the worst out of twenty-six surveyed countries for corruption in public administration.[7] The 60% of Lebanese who reportedly could not afford basic living costs at the start of the Huss government's term in December 1998 (see MECS 1999, pp. 389–90) had not seen any amelioration of their plight by its end in October 2000. The Huss government also did virtually nothing to rehabilitate the collapsed infrastructure in southern Lebanon after the Israeli evacuation of the security zone.

In the foreign relations sphere, Lebanon had an elevated Middle Eastern profile in early and mid-2000, because of events in South Lebanon. The Israeli bombardment of Lebanese electricity installations on 7 February brought a strong display of verbal Arab solidarity with Lebanon (see chapter on inter-Arab relations). Husni Mubarak made the first ever visit to Lebanon by an Egyptian president, and Arab League foreign ministers held a special meeting in Beirut. In mid-April, President Lahhud visited Saudi Arabia, Kuwait, the United Arab Emirates, and Iran in his first major Middle Eastern tour since taking office. This coincided with the formal notification by Israel to the UN of its intention to implement Security Council Resolution 425 mandating Israeli withdrawal from the south (see MECS 1977–78, p. 190). Iranian leaders showed particular interest in exchanging views with the Lebanese president. In mid-June, after UN Secretary-General Kofi Annan confirmed the Israeli withdrawal from Lebanon, US Secretary of State Madeleine Albright pressed Lahhud to accept Annan's declaration and to deploy the Lebanese army in the vacated area. This was followed by a visit by the UN secretary-general to Beirut, during which Annan had a groundbreaking meeting with Hizballah chief Hasan Nasrallah.

After September 2000, however, Lebanon found its affairs overshadowed by the Palestinian intifada in the West Bank and Gaza (see chapter on the PA). This was ironic because the Israeli withdrawal from South Lebanon, under Hizballah pressure, emboldened the Palestinians to employ violence in their dispute with Israel. Hizballah, uncomfortable about reduction of its activities to the Lebanese domestic arena, projected itself as a regional player after the Israeli withdrawal. It issued statements urging Palestinian activists to follow the Hizballah example, and reportedly advised and trained Palestinian Islamists.[8] Hizballah also used the Lebanese claim to a corner of the Golan Heights known as the Shab'a farms to argue that the Israeli withdrawal from Lebanon was incomplete and that "resistance" could therefore continue in that area. In early October, Hizballah abducted three Israeli soldiers in the Shab'a farms, thereby asserting its identification with the intifada, championing Lebanese dissatisfaction with the UN border demarcation, and reminding Israel of unsettled business with Syria on the Golan.

TRANSFORMATION IN SOUTH LEBANON

ISRAELI ABANDONMENT OF THE SECURITY ZONE

January 2000 marked the beginning of the final six months of Israeli prime minister Ehud Barak's countdown to Israeli evacuation of its self-declared South Lebanon security zone, an area that had been under Israeli influence or occupation since the first Israeli invasion of Lebanon in March 1978. Despite the absence of results from two rounds of talks between Barak and Syrian foreign minister Faruq al-Shar' in December 1999 and early January 2000, optimism persisted that the Israeli withdrawal from Lebanon could be part of a broader peace settlement between Israel, Lebanon, and Syria. This made it easier for Israel to reassure its Lebanese clients, the South Lebanese Army (SLA), that viable arrangements would eventuate for their physical safety.[9] In consequence, the SLA held-up reasonably well into January 2000 in defending security zone installations against Hizballah attacks, important because the SLA manned the majority of the outposts and was expected to cover the thinning-out of Israeli forces. Israeli casualties had been low since Barak's announcement in July 1999 that Israel would leave Lebanon within one year. The reduced death toll related to reduced troop movement, more intensive use of air power against Hizballah, and the SLA performance (see *MECS* 1999, p. 400).

In such circumstances, Israel was not in any hurry to depart early. Barak anticipated using the prospect of unilateral Israeli withdrawal for several months of pressure on Lebanon and Syria to become more amenable to general peace and security arrangements.[10] In January 2000, Israel had still not made serious logistic preparations for abandoning the security zone, and had no plan for a unilateral departure in the absence of an understanding with Lebanon and Syria.

The atmosphere changed dramatically in early February. On 30 January, Hizballah planted a bomb that killed the deputy commander of the SLA, 'Aql Hashim, in his home village of Dibl, deep inside the "security zone." Hashim was the key senior officer in the Israeli-backed militia, and his death was a painful blow to the Israelis.[11] The next day, Hizballah hit an Israeli convoy, killing three soldiers — the most severe Israeli loss in a single incident in nearly a year. The Israelis held back from retaliation for a few days and then, on 4 February, tried unsuccessfully to assassinate a leading Hizballah official by firing a missile at his car from a helicopter. Hizballah Secretary-General Nasrallah termed the attack a violation of the April 1996 "understandings," under which Israel and Hizballah had promised to avoid targeting civilians and civilian areas (see *MECS* 1996, pp. 481–82). On 6 February, Hizballah responded by ambushing an Israeli patrol only a few hundred meters from the international boundary, killing another two soldiers. The ambush caught the Israelis off-guard; evacuation of the wounded took almost two hours because of well-directed fire. In the midst of these exchanges, the Israelis and the SLA abandoned the Sujud outpost, the most exposed position on the security zone perimeter.[12]

Israel resorted to escalation to force Lebanon and Syria to accept a tightened interpretation of the 1996 "understandings," in order to constrain Hizballah use of Shi'i villages as staging-points.[13] On 8 February, Israeli aircraft bombed three electricity sub-stations in Beirut, north Lebanon, and the Biqa', injuring twenty-one civilians and causing damage estimated at $80m. US President Bill Clinton angered the Lebanese and Syrians by indicating that the Israeli assault was a legitimate response to Israeli losses.[14] On 11 February, Israel refused to attend a meeting of the international military committee monitoring the 1996 "understandings." This followed another Hizballah attack killing an Israeli, and the committee thereafter ceased to function.

The surge in Israeli casualties and the shock to the SLA dealt by Hashim's assassination turned Israeli thinking toward early departure from the security zone, regardless of negotiations with Syria. The Israeli daily Ma'ariv reported on 13 February that half of the Israeli government now wanted a unilateral withdrawal within three months.[15] Nonetheless, senior Syrian officials still did not believe that Israel was serious about withdrawal. They interpreted Barak's increasing inclination to "withdrawal without an agreement" as a "tactic to put pressure on Lebanon and Syria," asserting that Israel "will not withdraw...in a unilateral manner because it will create a vacuum."[16] In other words, the Syrians and Lebanese continued to ignore the approaching strategic transformation. Damascus gave no lead to Beirut, where policy rethinking on South Lebanon was paralyzed in the absence of Syrian direction. The underlying reason for this situation was doubtless what the international Arabic daily al-Hayat described as the Syrian president's "incapacity in health terms."[17]

In late February, Lebanon received unusual attention from Arab regimes beyond the Levant. On 19 February, President Husni Mubarak of Egypt made a surprise visit to Beirut without also going to Damascus. Egyptian political sources described the visit as "a sign of Egypt's return in force to the Lebanese arena, and that she won't leave as happened in the [Lebanese] civil war"[18] — a message to Syria as well as to Israel. On 22 February, the Arab League announced that Arab foreign ministers would meet in Beirut in mid-March to demonstrate their solidarity with Lebanon. In Beirut, protesters besieged the US embassy, Hizballah declared the US ambassador persona non grata, and President Lahhud threatened Israel with "painful blows" by the Islamic resistance if it abandoned the 1996 "understandings."[19]

Although Israeli foreign minister David Levy spoke of "burning" the soil of Lebanon if Hizballah continued its operations,[20] Israel reacted to the Arab diplomatic activity in a conciliatory manner. On 28 February, Prime Minister Barak confirmed Israeli readiness to withdraw from the Golan Heights, and on 5 March the Israeli government unanimously endorsed Israeli evacuation of Lebanon, with military redeployment "on the international boundary." On 9 March, Barak had a positive meeting with Mubarak and Palestinian leader Yasir 'Arafat in Egypt, one of the objectives being to take the wind out of the sails of the Arab League's imminent "summit of solidarity" with Lebanon.

Arab foreign ministers assembled in Beirut on 11–12 March, adopted a Lebanese document calling on Arab states with diplomatic relations with Israel to reconsider them in the light of the February "Israeli aggression" against Lebanon. However, Egypt made sure that the condemnations of Israel had no practical content.[21] Syria indicated its irritation with the Egyptian-Palestinian-Israeli meeting preceding the Beirut summit, which "didn't serve the political atmosphere that needed to be preserved."[22] For his part, Egyptian foreign minister 'Amru Musa made caustic remarks about the Lebanese and Syrian attitude toward the prospective Israeli withdrawal from Lebanon, saying that he didn't understand "how we reject the withdrawal that we demand."[23]

Through March, Hizballah and the Lebanese regime expressed divergent assessments of the outlook in South Lebanon. Hizballah chief Nasrallah looked forward with anticipation to his party's "victory," especially if Israel had to withdraw without agreements. He claimed that he was not disturbed by the Israeli boycott of the committee overseeing the 1996 "understandings:" "If Israel wants to be rid of the understandings, the resistance won't weep because it knows how to look after its people."[24] Hizballah's confidence increased following new blows against the SLA. On 2 March, the "resistance" decimated an SLA patrol near the Druze town of Hasbayya, killing five militia members. By targeting the SLA battalion in Hasbayya, Hizballah brought its successful campaign against Jizzin and Sujud closer to the Israeli and SLA headquarters in Marj 'Uyun. The Shi'i Islamists also received a political boost in early March when Crown Prince 'Abdallah of Saudi Arabia put aside his country's coolness toward Hizballah and held a warm meeting with a party delegation during an official visit to Lebanon.

In contrast to the upbeat mood of Hizballah, Lebanese regime leaders viewed the future with foreboding as the reality of having to cope with critical events finally dawned. President Lahhud warned that a unilateral Israeli withdrawal would not give Israel security, because failure to address the situation of the 350,000 Palestinian refugees in Lebanon would lead to new hostilities on the international boundary. He refused to give guarantees to Israel outside the framework of a "just and comprehensive" settlement of the Arab-Israeli conflict, commenting that the Lebanese army was not prepared to constrain Palestinians in the refugee camps and engage in a "new camps war for the sake of Israeli security."[25] Prime Minister Huss hoped that an Israeli-Syrian agreement would relieve Lebanon of the embarrassment of "liberating" its own land while Syria was left in the cold.[26] Parliamentary Speaker Birri referred to unilateral Israeli withdrawal as a "minefield."[27]

President Clinton's announcement on 20 March that he would meet the Syrian president in Geneva on 26 March produced a brief renewal of Lebanese optimism that Lebanon might be rescued by a US-sponsored package deal for the Syrian and Lebanese fronts. The failure of the Clinton-Asad summit (see chapter on the US and the Middle East) canceled all options apart from unilateral Israeli withdrawal.[28] On the Israeli side, Barak had already made it clear to his military command that he wanted withdrawal to a line that the UN would certify as fulfilling the demand in Security Council Resolution 425 for evacuation to the international boundary.[29] He rejected plans for retention of outposts on hills a few hundred meters inside Lebanon — the whole purpose of his withdrawal scheme was to remove any credible justification for Hizballah actions and to give Israel a favorable international context for military responses to provocations.[30]

On 31 March, Barak ordered preparation for withdrawal in May[31] — the collapse of efforts on the Israeli-Syrian "track" made further delay pointless. On 4 April, Israeli foreign minister Levy informed UN Secretary-General Annan that the withdrawal would be complete, unconditional, and "in one step."[32] On 16 April, Israel provided the UN with written notification of its intention to implement Resolution 425. In this situation, the 5,000-strong United Nations Interim Force in Lebanon (UNIFIL) had the important functions of confirming the withdrawal and assisting the Lebanese government to extend its control to the international boundary, according to Security Council Resolution 426. In late March, the Israeli press reported that Israel expected that up to two thousand SLA members and their families would require asylum.[33] There was no longer any hope that an amnesty arrangement might be worked out with the Lebanese. Hizballah chief Nasrallah gave the Israeli allies three options: "Leaving Lebanon, turning themselves over to Lebanese justice, or death by the bullets of the *mujahidin*....It is not permissible that a single collaborator should remain on land liberated by the blood of martyrs."[34]

In the aftermath of the Clinton-Asad debacle, Damascus took the initiative in consulting the Lebanese. Syrian foreign minister Shar' came to Beirut on 1 April and found it necessary to restrain Syria's more enthusiastic friends. Defense Minister Ghazi Zu'aytar, supported by deputy parliamentary speaker Elie al-Firzli, threatened that Lebanon might invite the Syrian army into areas evacuated by Israel, which would put "Tel Aviv within range of Syrian missiles."[35] Plainly concerned that Lebanon was exposing itself to ridicule, Shar' publicly rebuked Zu'aytar.[36] Otherwise, the Syrians dismissed the prospective Israeli withdrawal as a "maneuver" aimed at "sparking discord inside Lebanon and sabotaging the unity of the Lebanese and Syrian [negotiating] tracks."[37] The Lebanese president hinted that Lebanon might refuse UNIFIL deployment on the border if it didn't first confiscate weapons in the Palestinian refugee camps in southern Lebanon.[38] In New York, as its price for endorsing the 20 April UN Security Council declaration that approved the Israeli withdrawal plan and authorized the secretary-general to discuss UN participation in monitoring its implementation with the parties, Syria succeeded in inserting a reference to the importance of achieving a comprehensive peace.[39] Syria even asserted that the 1991 Lebanese-Syrian "Brotherhood Treaty" (see *MECS* 1991, pp. 570–72) required the UN and others to coordinate with Damascus on the Lebanese issue.[40]

The Lebanese and Syrian stances irritated major international actors. The US gave its blessing to unilateral Israeli withdrawal after Clinton's abortive intervention with Asad.[41] Washington sources indicated impatience with the Lebanese attempt to link border security with a solution for the Palestinian presence in Lebanon, and interpreted it as a Syrian-sponsored ploy to disrupt the withdrawal.[42] For his part, UN Secretary-General Annan rejected any UN role in the Palestinian camps as being outside the parameters of Resolution 425.[43]

The French voiced contradictory views — Defense Minister Alain Richard attacked "Syrian hegemony" in Lebanon, while President Jacques Chirac urged Israel to talk with Syria.[44] France initially hoped to use the Israeli withdrawal to recover influence in Lebanon, by leading a new international force in the south, but only if Paris could obtain the assent of Israel, Syria, and Iran. The Syrians scented leverage possibilities, and in late April, after visiting the Lebanese president and prime minister, the Syrian foreign minister headed for Paris to argue the "dangers" of international cover for Israel's withdrawal.[45] However, Shar' found French foreign minister Hubert Vedrine unreceptive. The French advised Syria to encourage the Lebanese to deploy their army after the Israeli evacuation and to tell them to stop complicating matters with the Palestinian issue "because this is not in Lebanon's interest."[46] Vedrine disagreed with his Syrian counterpart's assertion that Israel would not make a complete evacuation.[47] Overall the French position was identical to that of the US on the main issues.

In the meantime, Israel reduced its profile in Lebanon, in some respects grudgingly. On 12 April, the Israeli High Court ordered the government to release Lebanese being held in Israel without trial, principally for prisoner exchange purposes.[48] The government deployed special legislation to retain the two most important detainees, Mustafa Dirani and Shaykh 'Abd al-Karim 'Ubayd [held since 1994 and 1989, respectively], but freed thirteen others on 19 April. The Israelis also thinned out their forces in South Lebanon, and worked on a new electronic fence along the international boundary.[49] On 10 May,

Barak publicly accepted the UN stipulation that the SLA be disbanded and disarmed when Israel departed.[50]

By mid-May, Lebanese security sources estimated that only two hundred Israelis remained in the security zone, that some SLA leaders had already fled, and that several major outposts had been dismantled.[51] Israel continued aerial attacks against Hizballah, and on 3–4 May, two civilians died and twelve were injured in Israeli strikes near Nabatiyya and Jizzin. Hizballah replied by firing forty Katyusha rockets into Israel, leading to Israeli bombing of electricity substations in Beirut and north Lebanon for the second time in 2000. Hizballah fired more Katyushas, but the Israelis decided against further escalation and apologized for the initial civilian deaths.

The flurry of violence paralleled a meeting of the Syrian, Egyptian, and Saudi foreign ministers at Tadmur, in the Syrian desert. Egypt and Saudi Arabia pressed Syria to permit a peaceful Israeli withdrawal, in line with the desire of the international community, and in the 4 May joint communiqué Syria joined its two partners in supporting the UN exercise of "security tasks mandated to it" in South Lebanon.[52] Syria was now looking beyond the withdrawal, and discovered a means by which Hizballah could continue to disturb the Israelis. In late April, Lebanese parliamentary speaker Nabih Birri demanded that the Israeli withdrawal include the Shab'a farms,[53] land on the Lebanese-Syrian border captured by Israel in its June 1967 conquest of the Golan Heights. Most evidence indicated that the area was Syrian territory, despite Lebanese land ownership, and the UN was unsympathetic. The matter had never been raised before, but it suddenly became a Lebanese requirement on the eve of the withdrawal. A clue to the origin of the demand surfaced on 6 May, when "knowledgeable sources" reported Syrian determination that the Israeli withdrawal should encompass the Shab'a farms, sovereignty over which would be settled by Lebanon and Syria "between themselves."[54]

In mid-May, the Israelis accelerated the evacuation of outposts and began dismantling their headquarters in Marj 'Uyun.[55] Hizballah launched a new round of attacks, SLA members deserted in larger numbers, and the Israelis again escalated their aerial activity, notably against Palestinians aligned with Syria in the Biqa'. The Israelis gave no indication of a withdrawal date — possibly they had not yet set one — but events took their own course.[56] On 21 May, the Israelis and the SLA left six villages in the central sector of the security zone, which caused an SLA collapse all the way to the international boundary in this area. Crowds of Shi'i civilians rushed in, four being killed in desultory Israeli shelling. Hizballah and Amal fighters entered behind the civilians. The security zone was now split into two segments, toward the coast and around Marj 'Uyun, and was untenable.[57]

On 23 May, the Israelis pulled out all their remaining soldiers under cover of darkness. Out of about 2,500 SLA personnel, a thousand fled into Israel with their families — a total of 5,670 people — and 1,500 surrendered, all being turned over to the Lebanese authorities.[58] Hizballah spread its forces throughout the security zone in an orderly manner, with virtually no actions against local civilians and no attacks on the retreating Israelis.[59] Even the US State Department commended them; there was presumably a tacit arrangement involving Syria and Iran to avoid superfluous chaos and bloodshed.[60] The Lebanese government declared 25 May a "national holiday," and President Lahhud visited the liberated territory.

LEBANON AND THE INTERNATIONAL COMMUNITY AFTER THE ISRAELI WITHDRAWAL

The Middle Eastern and international situation of Lebanon after May 2000 was almost exclusively related to developments on the Lebanese-Israeli boundary and to the responses of the Lebanese government and Hizballah to the Israeli retreat. The death of President Hafiz al-Asad of Syria on 11 June did not meaningfully affect this reality, despite perturbations in the Lebanese-Syrian relationship in late 2000 (see below), because of the smooth transfer of power in Damascus to Bashshar al-Asad and the fundamental continuity in Syrian policy in Lebanon.

In late May and early June, UN envoy Terje Roed-Larsen shuttled between Lebanon and Israel to discuss delimitation of the international boundary to give the UN a basis for certifying that Israel had implemented Resolution 425. Because of the coarse scale of available maps and uncertainty over the accuracy of boundary peg positions, UN experts had to make their own interpretation of the 1923 boundary between Lebanon and British mandatory Palestine. From the UN perspective, this was simply the best possible international definition of the boundary for the purposes of Resolution 425 — it did not prejudice later redefinition as part of a Lebanese-Israeli peace settlement. Larsen presented the UN "blue line" to the Lebanese and Israelis in the first week of June.[61] This line incorporated both the Lebanese-Israeli boundary and the UN understanding of the Lebanese-Syrian boundary on the Israeli-occupied Golan Heights.

The Lebanese government expressed two objections to the "blue line." First, it maintained that the boundary was demarcated in the 1949 Lebanese-Israeli armistice agreement, and that according to the 1949 version Lebanese territory extended across the "blue line" in three locations.[62] The Lebanese even submitted the aborted 17 May 1983 "agreement" between Lebanon and Israel, long condemned in Beirut and Damascus, as evidence for their claim.[63] The UN objected that there were no Lebanese and Israeli signatures on the 1949 demarcation, the Israelis retorted that the Lebanese were trying to take "Israeli land," and Lebanon hinted that it might declare the withdrawal incomplete.[64]

Second, Lebanon, supported by Syria, continued to demand Israeli withdrawal from the Shab'a farms. UN Secretary-General Annan replied that the existing Lebanese-Syrian border had not been questioned by Lebanon and Syria as the basis for the UNIFIL and UN Disengagement Observer Force (UNDOF) mandates in southern Lebanon and the Golan.[65] UN experts gathered eighty maps, including the map on the Lebanese 1,000 lira banknote, and found only one that placed the Shab'a farms within Lebanon.[66] As a result, the UN required that Syria and Lebanon submit a signed declaration that the farms were part of Lebanon — otherwise there would be no change in the "blue line." The Syrians carefully avoided clarification.

Finding no endorsement for its objections, the Lebanese government reluctantly accepted the "blue line" for verifying implementation of Resolution 425. On 8 June, Prime Minister Huss stated that Lebanon would cooperate with the UN, which enabled UN observers, together with Lebanese military officers, to begin checking that Israeli forces were no longer on Lebanese territory. Lebanon, however, still pressed its claims. President Lahhud wrote to Annan protesting the "blue line," and Huss promised that Lebanon would pursue all diplomatic options for "liberation" of the Shab'a farms.

In the meantime, the Lebanese government refused to deploy its army along the international boundary until there was a peace settlement involving itself, Syria, and

Israel, repeating that it would not be Israel's "border-guard."[67] Lebanon also refused to allow UNIFIL deployment on the boundary before removal of all Israeli infractions. Even formal entry of the Lebanese army to the former security zone was delayed until after UN verification of the withdrawal. This stance left Hizballah as the de facto authority throughout the "liberated" territory, apart from a limited presence of Lebanese security personnel. Despite the good behavior of Hizballah, Lebanese reluctance to assert "government authority" irritated the US and the Europeans.

France, still interested in a security role but wanting guarantees for its soldiers, expressed impatience with Lebanese policy. French sources asked: "Does Lebanon want to be sovereign on its lands or not?"[68] For his part, the UN secretary-general wanted decisions before he toured the Middle East in late June. On 16 June, he announced that Israel had fulfilled his 22 May requirements for withdrawal to a line set by the UN and closing down the SLA. The Lebanese angrily accused Annan of "scandalous errors," because thirteen Israeli infractions of the line had not yet been resolved.[69] At this point, US Secretary of State Albright entered the fray, trying to persuade the Lebanese president to confirm Annan's announcement. Although the UN Security Council gave Lebanon relief by expressing "severe concern" about the infractions, the US was unhappy with Lahhud's rigidity, and its support for financial aid to Lebanon "diminished."[70]

Coordination between Lebanon and the UN improved after Annan's 19–20 June visit to Beirut. In early July, UNIFIL and the Lebanese agreed that nine Israeli transgressions of the "blue line" remained, mainly patrol roads and military installations. The Israelis promised their removal before the end of the month, but on 25 July the Lebanese identified more infractions. On 28 July, the first UNIFIL soldiers entered the former security zone, but only as "patrols."[71] The full deployment of a small force of four hundred observers along the international boundary took place in early August, with Lebanese acceptance that all Israeli violations had ended. Hizballah kept its own observation points on the boundary, and made it plain that UNIFIL should stay away from them. At this stage, the UN secretary-general called for security backup from Lebanese "government forces" rather than the "Lebanese army," a softening of the UN stance.[72] On 9 August, the Lebanese government deployed a joint force of five hundred troops and five hundred internal security personnel in the former security zone. They were stationed in the Marj 'Uyun barracks and the Bint Jubayl technical school and made no move toward the border. Ironically, these UN and Lebanese moves coincided with the first serious incident on the boundary, when the Israelis opened fire at demonstrators throwing Molotov cocktails at the former Fatima Gate crossing point. The Lebanese government refused to do more than contact "local forces" to quieten the situation.[73]

Within South Lebanon, celebration of the Israeli departure could not long conceal the desperate economic circumstances of the inhabitants of the "liberated" area. Out-migration from the security zone had halved the population through the 1990s — from over 200,000 to around 100,000[74] — and many villages were ghost towns in early 2000. With the collapse of the Israeli occupation, about 45% of the remaining working population proceeded either to prison or to Israel, and the area stood to lose more than $100m. of annual income from Israeli wages and smuggling.[75] The Lebanese government made no credible plans for rehabilitation, allowed Amal and Hizballah to occupy facilities like the Marj 'Uyun and Bint Jubayl Hospitals, and sat back to wait for aid from an international conference of potential donor states and institutions.

The fate of the donors' conference illustrated the costs of the Lebanese hard line over security arrangements in the south. Western states were unenthusiastic about pledging funds to a territory where the Lebanese government refused to extend proper security control and where militias held sway. Prime Minister Huss persuaded forty countries and several aid agencies to send representatives to a preliminary meeting in Beirut on 27 July. This meeting established a committee to prepare for a ministerial level conference in Europe in October. Western diplomats, however, told Lebanon to "lower its expectations" and observed that reconstruction in the south was not logical "while there was still a state of war."[76] Huss himself postponed the conference until after the November 2000 US elections. It never took place, and all government promises to the population of southern Lebanon remained unfulfilled into 2001.[77]

Hizballah faced a dilemma about its role after the Israeli withdrawal. On the one hand, its constituency was tired of warfare and the international community told Syria and Lebanon that the Islamists had best not cause trouble on the international boundary. On the other hand, Hizballah did not relish the prospect of giving up its self-assumed regional role as a vanguard of "resistance" to Israel. Through mid-2000 the Syrian leadership transition meant that Damascus had its own reasons for preferring quiet in southern Lebanon, and in mid-June Iranian president Mohammad Khatami reportedly told the UN secretary-general that Hizballah's "resistance role" had ended.[78] Nonetheless, Hizballah leader Nasrallah informed al-Wasat in late May that the Shab'a farms issue meant that "resistance continues" and that the party would keep its weapons because "Lebanon needs all elements of force."[79] At his meeting with the UN secretary-general on 20 June, Nasrallah demanded that Israel release eighteen Lebanese prisoners it still held.[80] On 26 June, Nasrallah and Lahhud agreed that Lebanon would not drop the Shab'a farms issue.

Nasrallah used his early July visit to Iran to shore up the position of Hizballah. He received backing for activism in Arab-Israeli affairs from the Iranian supreme religious guide, 'Ali Khamene'i. Khamene'i called on Hizballah to be "wide awake...for coming phases" and "to continue the road until complete victory, also hoping that Hizballah's example would "push the new Palestinian generation to confrontation and jihad against the Zionist regime."[81] Nasrallah responded enthusiastically in a speech in Farsi at Tehran University. He stressed "the danger that the Zionist entity represents to the region" and predicted "a renewal of the Palestinian intifada."[82] Khamene'i's support was a welcome counterweight to attempts by Khatami and the Syrians to force Hizballah to accept Parliamentary Speaker Birri's supremacy in the Shi'i community.[83] After meeting the Iranian president, Nasrallah brushed aside Khatami's call for Hizballah to turn to "intellectual and cultural concerns," saying that "the time has not yet come to put down weapons."[84]

Hizballah regional ambitions were reenergized in late September with the Palestinian uprising in the West Bank and Gaza. The party ceased all criticism of the Palestinian Authority (PA) and reopened communications with Yasir 'Arafat's Fatah movement.[85] Hizballah now stressed the importance of unity between the PA and Palestinian Islamists, and encouraged escalation of the uprising. On 7 October, Hizballah took advantage of Israeli distraction and the anger with Israel in the Arab world, and seized three Israeli soldiers on the Israeli side of the border fence in the Shab'a farms area. A few days later Nasrallah announced that Hizballah also held an Israeli intelligence officer who had been lured to Beirut; the Israelis referred to a businessman kidnapped in Europe.[86]

Hizballah proposed to exchange the four Israelis for hundreds of Palestinians held by Israel in addition to the eighteen imprisoned Lebanese.

At a single stroke, Hizballah again became a focus for international mediators and the media, inaugurated a new resistance campaign championing the Lebanese claim to the Shab'a farms, and showed that it rather than the Lebanese regime had the initiative in Lebanese foreign affairs. Nasrallah boasted that "the party has outgrown the country and the [Shi'i] community,"[87] while Barak's government in Israel swallowed the humiliation — military retaliation would not free the captives. On 26 November, a Hizballah booby-trap in the Shab'a farms killed an Israeli soldier, but Israel limited its response to local shelling. Contacts via the German government for a prisoner exchange produced no result. Hizballah was inaugurating a new game dangerous for itself as well as for others — further incidents risked Israeli retaliation unwanted by both the Shi'i community and Rafiq al-Hariri's new Lebanese government.

INTERNAL AFFAIRS

TOWARD PARLIAMENTARY ELECTIONS, JANUARY-AUGUST 2000

The government of Prime Minister Huss was at an increasing disadvantage to its principal opponent, former prime minister Hariri, in the early months of 2000. Huss and his largely technocrat cabinet proved unable to alleviate the Lebanese economic recession or to implement bureaucratic reforms, and were overshadowed by security agencies dominated by President Lahhud. The regime's partisan media and judicial campaign against Hariri and his associates through 1999 backfired, enabling the former prime minister to recover public sympathy, especially as the regime was unable to conclude a single court case before the August 2000 parliamentary elections. In December 1999, Huss also presided over the passage of an obviously defective election law. The law divided the six governorates of Lebanon into fifteen constituencies, splitting Beirut into three electorates to weaken Hariri's ability to mobilize votes. Syria backed the law because it was designed to prevent any one political force from gaining preponderance and to protect close allies of Damascus.

Lebanese domestic politics were unusually subdued between December 1999 and late June 2000, in the lead-up to the Israeli withdrawal from South Lebanon. Hariri took care to maintain his November 1999 reconciliation with Lahhud, arranged by the Syrians (see *MECS* 1999, p. 388). He supported the security crackdown against Sunni religious militants in the north in early January 2000, and refused to join protests against the electoral law, stating that "we prefer to go to the judgment of the people."[88] The Syrians indicated their satisfaction with his "flexibility,"[89] and on 5 March, he had a second "excellent" meeting with Lahhud.

In early February, the regime challenged Hariri by proposing a law to restrict election spending and advertising, at the same time that the judiciary charged his close friend, Fu'ad Siniora, the former minister of state for financial affairs, with wasting public funds on the purchase of a large Italian garbage incinerator for the north Matn municipalities. In the event, government opponents in parliament blocked regulation of election spending and advertising. Huss observed that "this leaves the arena open to money and the noise of money...Political money is corruption by definition."[90] Hariri himself said little until early July. He left his ally, Druze leader Walid Junblat, to criticize

Interior Minister Michel al-Murr "who runs the country and distributes the election card to whomever he wishes,"[91] and to attack security agencies associated with the presidency.[92] Such matters involved Syrian sensitivities, and Hariri avoided them.

The election campaign only assumed center stage in Lebanese affairs through July, as the immediate reverberations of the Israeli withdrawal and Hafiz al-Asad's death passed. There were three main battlegrounds. First, in Beirut, Hariri was determined to humble Huss, by showing that constituency gerrymandering by Interior Minister Murr could not corral his public support, and recover his leadership of the Sunni community, thereby asserting primacy in the prime ministerial stakes.[93] Second, in Mount Lebanon, the regime sought to cut down Junblat in the Ba'abda-'Aley constituency and dispose of Nasib Lahhud, a popular opponent of Murr, in the north Matn area.[94] Third, in northern Lebanon, the combination of largely Sunni Tripoli with Maronite Zugharta in one electorate produced a political rift between the Sunni *za'im* 'Umar Karami and his Maronite counterpart Sulayman Tony Faranjiyya. Syrian attempts to mediate reconciliation between their two northern allies proved unavailing.

Otherwise, the continuing electoral alliance of Hizballah and Amal, a cornerstone of Syrian strategy for stabilizing Lebanese politics, made election results in southern Lebanon a foregone conclusion. The same applied in the three Biqa' constituencies, where coalition arrangements between Syrian allies made voting almost irrelevant. President Lahhud sensed Hariri's growing strength and improved position in Damascus, and mediators approached Hariri about a possible return as prime minister early in the election campaign.[95] Lahhud, however, also hoped that Huss, Karami, and Tamam Salam would perform well enough to give the presidency alternatives among Sunni politicians for head of the new council of ministers after the elections.[96]

Hariri had lists of candidates organized for all three Beirut electorates by late July. He sought to cooperate with Salam, head of the Maqasid Foundation and son of the veteran Sunni *za'im* Sa'ib Salam. The cooperation, however, failed because of Salam's promotion of the maverick politician Najah Wakim for an Orthodox Christian parliamentary seat.[97] Hariri wanted former interior minister Bassam Mirhij for this seat, and rejected Wakim, a longstanding opponent. Ironically, Wakim pulled out in early August, citing "canned alliances" and hinting that Lebanon was merely an administrative region of Syria.[98] Salam refused Mirhij and went ahead with his own list of candidates, attacking "financial capabilities that buy the asphalt, the sidewalk, the door, the window, and the balconies" — a reference to Hariri.[99]

Hariri's media, including his Mustaqbal television channel, took the offensive against Huss, Hariri's main opponent in Beirut, through July. Hariri assailed the government proposal to combine the Council for Reconstruction and Development (CDR) and other institutions in a Higher Council for Planning and Development, indicating that it was unconstitutional and had no clear decision-making mechanism.[100] He also impugned Huss's competence in economic policy. Huss responded defensively: "Difficult circumstances have meant that we couldn't achieve what was set out in the [December 1998] government statement, but talk that the government hasn't done anything is untrue."[101] Hariri forced changes in the legislation to integrate state institutions, and accepted the project in order not to appear troublesome in Damascus. Huss announced candidates for one of the Beirut electorates on 7 August, aligning with the Armenian Tashnak party.[102]

Mount Lebanon provided two tests for factions close to President Lahhud vis-à-vis opponents of the regime. In the Ba'abda-'Aley constituency, the presidency favored a coalition including Junblat's Druze opponent, Talal Arslan, the Syrian Social Nationalist Party (SSNP), former Lebanese Forces (LF) chief Elie Hubayqa, and Hizballah.[103] This coalition faced Junblat's Progressive Socialist Party (PSP), backed by Hariri. Hizballah made a controversial decision to stand with Hubayqa, despite the latter's history of ties with Israel, because Junblat had turned against the Islamists in Ba'abda in the 1996 elections, when Syria had wanted Hizballah constrained (see *MECS* 1996, p. 491).[104]

In the north Matn constituency, where all leading personalities were Maronite or Orthodox Christians, Interior Minister Murr joined President Lahhud's son Emil against Nasib Lahhud, a cousin of the president. Murr also managed to link with the veteran opposition deputy Albert Mukhaybar, who had fallen out with Nasib Lahhud. Pierre Jumayyil, son of former president Amin Jumayyil, stood as an independent, aligning with Nasib Lahhud after the government made a clumsy move to prevent his father from returning to Lebanon from exile in France in late July. Murr made strenuous efforts to derail Nasib Lahhud's campaign, having his election posters stripped from billboards and mobilizing internal security personnel to intimidate voters and opposition candidates.[105]

In northern Lebanon, 'Umar Karami of Tripoli feared subordination in a wider coalition of Syrian allies. He made common cause with Nayla Mu'awwad of Zughartá, wife of former president René Mu'awwad, against the alignment headed by Sulayman Tony Faranjiyya, which included 'Umar's cousin Ahmad Karami, prime ministerial hopeful Najib Mikati, and the respected Maronite deputy Butrus Harb. Hariri deferred to Syrian sensitivity about preserving regional political balances and did not present his own candidates.[106] He instructed his representative in Tripoli, Samir al-Jisr, to back the Faranjiyya coalition, despite misgivings about its inclusion of Harb. Karami offended Damascus by his obstinacy and irritated the security agencies by his defense of *shabab* (youth) who had joined the January 2000 "Afghan Arab" insurrection in the Dinniya hills "because of poverty and repression"[107] (see below). Nonetheless, he received backing from Huss, who visited Tripoli on 24 August and observed that "I am visiting my dear friend *ra'is* 'Umar Karami...Naturally I support my friends."[108]

In the last days before the first round of voting on 27 August, the financial power represented by Hariri competed vigorously with the state media and security institutions working for Prime Minister Huss and President Lahhud. State television accused Hariri of "bribing" the American University of Beirut (AUB) when he dedicated a new college that he had funded, while Junblat attacked state security for intervening against him — "we won't let a handful of officers abolish political life."[109] Junblat made comparisons with "the days of [Romanian dictator] Ceaucescu."[110] As regards money power, Hariri was only the most prominent figure among an increasing number of multi-millionaires who were assuming leading positions on candidate lists in 2000.[111] Hariri's wealthy allies Isam Faris (Orthodox) and Yasin Jabir (Shi'i) had major coordinating roles in northern and southern Lebanon respectively, and Najib Mikati and Muhammad al-Safadi (Sunnis) buttressed Faranjiyya's campaign.

Hariri's relations with President Lahhud deteriorated during the final pre-election maneuvers.[112] Lahhud hinted that Hariri was again unacceptable as prime minister.[113] The Syrians, whose domestic preoccupations led them to give the Lebanese regime and other allies more freedom in the Lebanese elections, now intervened to calm the atmosphere. Syria's military intelligence chief in Lebanon, Gen. Ghazi Kan'an, visited

Lahhud twice in late August,[114] and the new Syrian president, Bashshar al-Asad, summoned senior Lebanese politicians to Damascus between 25 and 27 August, "to help Lebanese brothers to overcome personal sensitivities and attain the level of responsibility required to cement national unity."[115]

THE RETURN OF HARIRI

The absence of clear signals from Damascus through the electoral campaign, Hariri's cultivation of the new Syrian leadership, and the sour public mood toward the government meant Interior Minister Murr and the security agencies did not dare to interfere with the actual voting for the new Chamber of Deputies on 27 August and 3 September. The two rounds were therefore relatively free and fair compared with the 1992 and 1996 elections. They produced shattering defeats for the regime and a strong reemphasis of the Lebanese sectarian makeup.[116]

Mount Lebanon and the north voted on 27 August. The main features of the results were the rallying of Druze and Christians to Walid Junblat in the southern parts of Mount Lebanon and setbacks for lists favored by the regime in Tripoli and the 'Akkar hills. Junblat profited from longstanding Druze suspicion of the Lebanese army and security services, exacerbated by Lahhud's espousal of a Syrian-style national security state. Junblat also adopted Christian calls for restructuring Lebanon's relations with Syria after the Israel's withdrawal and Hafiz al-Asad's death, and reached out to old Maronite foes like the Kata'ib party, the LF, and ex-president Jumayyil, who returned to Lebanon on 29 July.[117] Christian votes helped him to break the regime-backed front in the Ba'abda-'Aley constituency, where Hizballah and Talal Arslan only got seats because he left spaces for them. Elsewhere in Mount Lebanon, Nasib Lahhud and Pierre Jumayyil won seats in defiance of Murr in the north Matn, and opponents of the regime wrested three seats from loyalist lists in Kisrawan-Jubayl.

In northern Lebanon, the Faranjiyya list backed by Hariri took thirteen out of seventeen seats in Tripoli-Zugharta, and two of Hariri's allies gained seats at the expense of the Isam Faris list in the constituency centered on the 'Akkar hills. Another Hariri nominee won Sunni votes in the Kharrub hills south of Beirut, displacing the regime's candidate for the Sunni seat in the Shuf electorate. Overall, the regime could count on only 22 of the 63 parliamentary deputies elected in the first round.[118] Against this, Junblat alone commanded thirteen seats. The turnout in Mount Lebanon was a relatively high 57% of registered voters.[119] Here the appeal for participation by the Maronite church outweighed calls for a boycott by exiled Gen. Michel 'Awn and Dory Chamoun's National Liberal Party (NLP). In mainly Sunni Tripoli, however, only 41% of voters went to the polls.[120]

Beirut, southern Lebanon, and the Biqa' voted on 3 September. Hariri triumphed in Beirut, winning 18 out of 19 seats with one Shi'i mandate left vacant for Hizballah. Huss and Salam were removed from parliament. Beirut Sunnis, angry about the demotion of the Sunni prime minister in the Lahhud-Huss partnership, massively supported Hariri.[121] In contrast to Mount Lebanon, a majority of Beirut Christians stayed away from the polls,[122] presumably disillusioned with the candidates. Despite bitter remarks by Huss, Hariri's financial capability was probably a secondary factor in the result. The turnout in Beirut was about 35%, a slight improvement on 1996, but Sunni voters registered an unprecedented 65% participation rate.[123]

In southern Lebanon, the joint Amal-Hizballah list of candidates, formally announced only a few days before polling, took all twenty-three seats. In mainly Sunni Sidon, this list included Hariri's sister Bahiyat al-Hariri and the veteran Nasirite politician Mustafa Sa'd, who had to be reconciled with each other by Parliamentary Speaker Nabih Birri.[124] Birri, who headed the secularist Shi'i Amal movement, dismissed the conservative and leftist opponents of Amal and Hizballah in the Shi'i dominated remainder of South Lebanon as *bakawat* (feudalists) and "frogs" around "the Hizb-Amal lake."[125] In the three Biqa' constituencies, the prearranged coalitions achieved the expected victories. Here, government loyalists and Hariri supporters were mixed with local leaders, Amal, and Hizballah. The only surprise was one loss for the Elie Skaf list in mainly Christian Zahla. The alignment of Amal, Hizballah, and former parliamentary speaker Husayn al-Husayni took all the seats in the predominantly Shi'i Ba'albak-Hirmil constituency. Damascus sponsored Nadir Sukar, once a senior official in the LF in the days of the Christian militia's alignment with Israel, into the Ba'albak Maronite seat. Turnout in the south and the Biqa' was generally mediocre, at 40–45% of registered voters.[126]

Overall, the parliamentary elections emphasized the particularities of the Sunni, Druze, Shi'i, and Christian political arenas. The Sunni electorate made Hariri its unrivalled political representative.[127] Najib Mikati did well in northern Lebanon, but partly on the basis of Hariri's support for the Faranjiyya coalition. As regards the traditional Sunni leading families, 'Umar Karami was reduced and isolated in Tripoli, the Salams were defeated in Beirut, and the al-Sulhs were out of politics. It was an unprecedented state of affairs, and the elections left President Lahhud and Syria no serious option except to appoint Hariri to the reserved Sunni post of prime minister.[128] To do anything else would be to defy the overwhelmingly preference of the Sunni community.

In the Druze arena, Junblat extended his dominance into the 'Aley and Matn districts and resurrected the old Druze-Maronite relationship that had been the foundation of the "principality" of Mount Lebanon between the seventeenth and nineteenth centuries. This was a masterful move that gave Junblat a new salience in Lebanon, and potentially opened the way for a Christian-Druze coalescence vis-à-vis Sunnis, Shi'is, and Syria.

As for the Shi'is, the Amal-Hizballah alignment indicated the political distinctiveness of the largest sect in Lebanon vis-à-vis the other two-thirds of the population. Amal depended on its position within the Lebanese regime to compete with Hizballah's advantages as a successful resistance movement against Israel, and the two parties were only brought together by Syria. Nonetheless, Amal and Hizballah shared the characteristic of being entirely Shi'i phenomena.

In contrast to the more coordinated leadership of Sunni, Druze, and even Shi'i politics, the Christian half of the new parliament was fragmented. This reflected the sectarian heterogeneity of the Christian 35% of the Lebanese population, and the sharp divisions between supporters and critics of the regime. President Lahhud and Interior Minister Murr faced opponents who accepted the 1989 Ta'if agreement, the basis for the "second republic" of Lebanon (see *MECS* 1989, pp. 519–22), including the Kata'ib party, the LF, former president Jumayyil, and various independents, as well as those who rejected the regime, most prominently Gen. 'Awn and NLP leader Dory Chamoun. Because of his close association with Damascus, Lahhud was no more able to represent his Maronite community than his weaker predecessor as president, Ilyas al-Hirawi. Maronite patriarch Nasrallah Butros Sufayr performed this role for Christians, including Maronites, as spiritual leader of the largest Christian sect. The high voter turnout in the Maronite heartland of Mount Lebanon reflected intense local contests between leading families. Added to the varied affiliations of Christian politicians in other regions, such contests produced a fractured collection of deputies co-opted by the regime, Syria, Hariri, and others.

In terms of parliamentary blocs, Hariri and Junblat together secured 35 seats, almost 30% of the new parliament. Hariri's personal following numbered 22, up from 13 in 1996.[129] The major difference from 1996 was Hariri's monopolization of Beirut and Junblat's Christian support. Birri, who could be expected to back Hariri for prime minister if Damascus stood aside, headed a bloc of 17 deputies, six from Amal, as a result of the elections. This was down from 19 in 1996. Hizballah gained a modest increase from 9 deputies to 12, three of whom were Christian clients. The gains, however, merely returned the party to its 1992 position and represented a pre-programmed share of ten in the south and Ba'albak-Hirmil, with the recovery of individual seats in Beirut and Ba'abda, courtesy of Hariri and Junblat. Hizballah lost its status as the largest organized party in parliament to Junblat's PSP. Otherwise there was minor reshuffling among the smaller parties.[130] The Ba'th rose from two to three seats, the SSNP slipped from five to four, the Kata'ib reappeared in parliament with three deputies, and the Armenian Tashnak paid for its split with Hariri by losing four of the six Armenian mandates. Lahhud's sympathizers in the new parliament comprised a scattering of deputies in Mount Lebanon, the north, and the Biqa', while Murr's personal bloc shrank from five to three seats.

Hariri's careful behavior toward Bashshar al-Asad received its reward. On 5 September the Damascus newspaper *al-Ba'th* indicated Syrian support for Hariri's return to office,[131] and on 7 September a "senior Syrian source" told *al-Hayat* that Damascus anticipated "long years" of "cohabitation" between Lahhud and Hariri.[132] Thereafter, the balance of forces within the new government became the main topic of backstage contacts between leading politicians. Junblat even complained that cabinet membership was decided in advance of Hariri's actual appointment as prime minister.[133]

The Lebanese constitution required the president to consult members of the new parliament before naming the new prime minister, which could not occur until the new parliamentary term commenced on 15 October. Lahhud delayed the consultation until after the emergency Arab summit on the Palestinian intifada, held in Cairo on 21 October (see chapter on inter-Arab relations). In the meantime, the deputies voted Nabih Birri into his third term as parliamentary speaker. With Syrian assent for Hariri already secured, there was no doubt about the outcome of Lahhud's contacts with deputies — Hariri received the endorsement of 106 out of 128 parliamentarians. Hizballah declined to name a preferred prime minister, indicating to Lahhud that it would support anyone who followed a program compatible with the party's policies.[134] On 23 October, Lahhud commissioned Hariri to form a government. The extent of the groundwork in the weeks since the election was revealed when Hariri named his thirty-member cabinet within three days, on 26 October.

Hariri's government (see table 1) incorporated the principal political forces, apart from Hizballah.[135] First, Hariri had his own bloc of eight ministers, all Sunnis and non-Maronite Christians. Samir al-Jisr became minister of justice, which meant the instant collapse of the Huss government's judicial pursuit of Hariri's friends. Fu'ad Siniora took the finance portfolio, and the legal case against him vanished. Second, seven positions went to the closest confidants of Syria, and six to Lahhud loyalists. Isam Faris succeeded Michel al-Murr as deputy prime minister, confirming this post as an Orthodox Christian preserve in the hands of a Syrian nominee — a restraint on the Sunni prime minister. Murr's son Elias replaced his father as interior minister, while Khalil al-Hirawi from

Zahla supplanted the Shi'i Ghazi Zu'aytar as defense minister. The latter appointment meant that Christians trusted by the Syrian leadership held all four of Lebanon's top military and security jobs (president, army commander, and the interior and defense portfolios). Third, Birri and Junblat had small blocs of four and three ministers respectively. Birri's friends took development and social welfare ministries, which were relevant to southern Lebanon. Junblat, who remained outside the government, got his friend Marwan Hamada appointed as refugee affairs minister, a post vital for influencing Druze-Christian relations in the Shuf hills.

Overall, the government maintained the sectarian equilibrium of its predecessors as mandated by the Ta'if accord. Maronites, Shi'is, and Sunnis — the three "great" sects — had six ministers each, with the three primary posts of defense, foreign affairs, and finance also being split between them. Shi'is received compensation for the loss of the defense portfolio in the appointment of the professional diplomat Mahmud Hammud as foreign minister. As for the political balance, the Hariri-Junblat alignment roughly equalled the combination of Syrian clients and Lahhud loyalists.

CONTROVERSY OVER THE SYRIAN ROLE IN LEBANON

Fears in early 2000 about an Israeli-Syrian deal at the expense of Lebanon, the Israeli withdrawal from Lebanon in May 2000, and the advent of a new leader in Damascus in June 2000 together precipitated unprecedented public discussion of Syria's domination of Lebanon. Senior Christian personalities, most notably patriarch Sufayr and Gen. Michel 'Awn, had criticized Syrian overlordship since its imposition in 1990, but the new features in 2000 were the boldness of the comments within Lebanon and the public questioning of the Syrian role by non-Christians, particularly Druze leader Walid Junblat. The Sunni, Shi'i, and Druze "streets" resented Syrian hegemony as much as Lebanon's Christians, particularly opposing the uncontrolled influx of hundreds of thousands of Syrian laborers.[136] However, bitterness regarding past Maronite political supremacy and commonality with Syria regarding Arab identity and hostility to Israel had hitherto kept non-Christian leaders quiet or supportive of Damascus, enabling Syria to represent criticism as simply sectarian rancor from some Christians. Junblat's forthright remarks changed this situation, and the Israeli departure removed the most obvious justification for the now twenty-four-year-old presence of 35,000 Syrian soldiers in Lebanon.

The issue surged into public prominence on 24 March when Jubran Tuwayni, chief editor of the renowned Christian centrist newspaper *al-Nahar*, wrote an open letter to Bashshar al-Asad attacking Syrian infringement of Lebanese "dignity, liberty, independence, and sovereignty."[137] Tuwayni, whose father Ghassan had founded *al-Nahar* and who had sympathies with General 'Awn, made his appeal for a new Lebanese-Syrian relationship in the name of all Lebanese. It prompted a fierce response from Fadl al-Shalaq in Hariri's *al-Mustaqbal* newspaper, defending Syria's contribution to Lebanon's "peace and stability" and suggesting that Tuwayni and others wanted "to weaken the Lebanese-Syrian negotiating position vis-à-vis Israel."[138] Al-Shalaq also asserted that he spoke for the "majority of Lebanese." This high-profile media exchange embarrassed Damascus just before the Geneva summit between Clinton and Hafiz al-Asad. It forced the personal intervention of President Lahhud, who claimed that Syria was "not tenacious" about staying in Lebanon.[139]

Junblat began to indicate concern with Syrian-Lebanese affairs in mid-April, as a by-product of his opposition to Lahhud's "intelligence apparatus" and his interest in Christian electoral backing. He made public observations about the contrast between the outflow of Lebanese and the inflow of Syrian workers "as if what is wanted is the replacement of one people by another, and the pauperization and humiliation of what remains of the Lebanese."[140] This coincided with arrests of student supporters of Gen. 'Awn, and an angry demonstration by more than five hundred 'Awnists outside the ministry of justice, demanding Syrian as well as Israeli withdrawal from Lebanon. On 19 April, 'Awn's supporters burned a Syrian flag at St. Joseph's University, and hundreds participated in anti-Syrian protests on five campuses, including the AUB in West Beirut.[141] These manifestations alarmed the Lebanese leadership. Lahhud asked "why do some wake up to the Syrian presence when the [Israeli] occupation is departing defeated;"[142] Huss asserted that "the Syrian presence is legal and its services are welcome";[143] and Birri demanded the release of detained 'Awnists.[144] Amnesty International expressed concern about the use of military courts to try students, and from Paris, 'Awn called on Arab states "to put an end to Syrian exclusiveness [regarding Lebanon]."[145] On 4 May, Junblat openly entered the fray, proposing a dialogue with the Christian opponents of the regime and a debate on relations with Syria.[146]

Junblat provoked Syrian officials when he criticized the anti-corruption campaign in Damascus against "old guard" rivals of President Asad's son Bashshar. In early June, "Syrian sources" responded by postulating that "the corrupt stand together" and that Junblat "feared" the extension of the campaign to Lebanon.[147] After his father's death, Bashshar al-Asad made a minor concession to Lebanese discontent when he spoke of the Lebanese-Syrian relationship as a "model" that needed "completion."[148] This did not get a good reception — a lead editorial in al-Hayat reflected widespread opinion in Lebanon when it defined the "model" as an ambition, not a reality.[149]

In the run-up to the Lebanese elections, other politicians joined Junblat. Nasib Lahhud wanted all aspects of Lebanese-Syrian relations revised, including commercial exchanges and the worker influx. Even Najib Miqati, a Sunni and a friend of the new Syrian president, talked of "reviewing" the relationship "on a healthy…basis," and warned against "bullying from one side against the other."[150] On 25 August, Junblat accused the Syrians of interfering in the elections: "I want to know why some Syrian authorities [marakiz] ask [the village headmen] for the election of the opposing candidate list."[151]

The blows to the Lebanese regime in the parliamentary elections, coming so soon after the Israeli withdrawal and Hafiz al-Asad's death, encouraged Syria's critics. On 14 and 17 September, thousands of LF supporters turned out for commemorations of the 1982 assassination of former LF leader Bashir al-Jumayyil (see MECS 1981–82, p. 723) and LF deaths during the 1975–90 warfare. These were the biggest public manifestations of the LF since the Christian ex-militia was banned in 1994. The demonstrators called for the release of LF leader Samir Ja'ja', repeatedly convicted for murder in what many Christians regarded as show trials, and for the Syrian army to leave Lebanon.[152] On 20 September, the Council of Maronite Archbishops, chaired by patriarch Sufayr, issued a landmark communiqué condemning Syria's "total hegemony" in Lebanese politics, blaming Syria for flooding the Lebanese market with cheap products and cheap labor, and inviting the Syrian army to redeploy as promised a decade previously in the 1989 Ta'if agreement.[153] This represented a dramatic political assertion by the Maronite patriarchate, one of the primary spiritual institutions in Lebanon. It brought immediate reactions from President Lahhud and Sunni and Shi'i religious leaders, who all defended the Syrian presence.

Junblat moderated his own position after the elections. He visited Bashshar in Damascus, and put off a planned meeting with 'Awn in Paris. The Syrians misinterpreted his flexibility as confirming their view that his pre-election comments were merely vote buying.[154] They were therefore caught off-guard when Junblat questioned the Hariri government's policy statement in parliament on 6 November. Junblat noted that the policy statement, which defined the Syrian military presence as "necessary, legitimate, and temporary," did not mention the Ta'if Agreement's requirement for Syrian redeployment.[155] He emphasized that he accepted Syria's strategic arguments and was not endorsing Christian calls for full Syrian withdrawal, but this did not save him from Syria's wrath. From the Syrian perspective, Junblat was exploiting his privileged situation as a Syrian ally to embolden Christian renegades and subvert Muslim solidarity. Syrian officials indicated that Junblat was persona non grata in Damascus, while in the Lebanese parliament the Ba'thist deputy 'Asim Qansu made a death threat against the Druze leader.[156] This had repercussions inside Syria, with pictures of Junblat appearing in the mainly Druze town of Suwayda in defiance of the authorities[157] — a warning that miscalculation in Lebanon could disturb Syrian internal affairs.

Prime Minister Hariri, Parliamentary Speaker Birri, and Syrian officials moved to calm the controversy in the last weeks of 2000. For the new prime minister, the rift between his principal Lebanese partner and his Syrian backers was embarrassing. In a 15 November meeting between Hariri and Hizballah chief Nasrallah, the two men agreed to be conciliatory toward Junblat and to "leave the settlement of his relations with Syria to the time factor."[158] On 17 November, possibly prompted by Syrian vice president 'Abd al-Halim Khaddam,[159] Birri visited patriarch Sufayr to suggest that the reshuffling of Syrian troop dispositions begun in April 2000 would soon develop into a redeployment agreed between the Lebanese and Syrian governments.

Birri's intervention, however, became a fiasco. Syrian foreign minister Shar' disowned the initiative, indicating that Birri had no right to speak for the two governments.[160] Here Shar' buttressed the Lebanese president, who refused to debate the Syrian military presence because doing so would be a "free gift" to Israel."[161] The muddle may have reflected different influences in Damascus as Bashshar worked to consolidate his presidency. Ghazi Kan'an, Syria's security chief in Lebanon, as well as Khaddam and Bashshar, had obvious interests in the "Lebanese file."[162] In any case, the Maronite patriarch was unimpressed by Birri's mission. Sufayr lost no time in declaring that he did not expect Syrian withdrawal in the near future and was more concerned by the "subservience" of the Lebanese regime[163] — a swipe at Lahhud. On 13 December, the Syrians gained some credit when they released forty-six Lebanese from Syrian prisons. For the moment, the continuing Palestinian intifada restricted the impact of the controversy over Lebanese-Syrian relations, particularly on Muslims, and gave Syria a measure of breathing space.

ECONOMY AND SOCIETY

ECONOMIC AFFAIRS

In 2000 the Lebanese economy repeated its poor 1999 performance, with a further 0.5% fall in GDP, compared with average GDP increases of around 4% for countries in the Middle East and North Africa. Almost every indicator pointed to continued recession:

Compared with 1999, the number of new construction permits fell by 20%, investment in new businesses fell by 18%, the volume of imports through Beirut port declined by 14%, and government revenue from property transactions slid by 40%.[164] Solidère, the company responsible for reconstructing central Beirut, experienced a second year of slow land sales and in April 2000 the value of its shares was down to $6.50 from around $15 in the mid-1990s.[165] The slow-down in the previously dynamic construction sector was particularly serious because of the fundamental weakness of Lebanese agriculture and industry. Agriculture, for example, supported 25% of the population,[166] but high costs, poor infrastructure, government neglect, and dumping of Syrian produce meant that most farmers had incomes below the poverty line. In 2000, agricultural output was only 20% of its pre-1975 level, a decade after the war.[167] More than ever, Lebanon depended on its financial and other service functions. In this context, the 25% contraction in the profits of the private banking sector in the first nine months of 2000 was a worrying sign.[168]

The Huss government talked about financial discipline, imposed austerity in salary levels, and raised taxes and fees to improve revenues, but in fact presided over unprecedented deterioration in the public debt and the budget deficit in 2000. Public debt rose from 119% of GDP at the end of 1999 to 145% a year later, and the 2000 budget deficit of $3.9bn. was the largest in Lebanese history.[169] Spending was highly inelastic, with 40% going to interest payments and 40% to funding inadequate wages in the bloated bureaucracy.[170] Apart from debt servicing, the largest single element of government expenditure (15%) was the $1bn. absorbed by the army and the security agencies, jealously guarded by President Lahhud.[171]

Huss and his technocrat ministers lacked the political weight to reform the bureaucracy in the face of determination by senior politicians, particularly Nabih Birri, to defend their patronage networks. They also lacked the international contacts and financial prestige to effectively launch the privatization of such burdensome public enterprises as the Electricité du Liban and Middle East Airlines. The cold relationship between France and the Lahhud-Huss regime because of the latter's campaign against Hariri, who was a personal friend of President Chirac, placed Huss at a disadvantage in the international financial arena.[172] In the months preceding the Lebanese parliamentary elections, it was increasingly evident that the Huss government could not control the Lebanese economy.

In such circumstances, Hariri's return as prime minister was almost inevitable. After two years of stagnation, the electorate remembered the infrastructure improvements and economic growth under Hariri through the mid-1990s — not the debts and deficits he bequeathed to Huss. Hariri proposed to use his political and financial contacts as one of the world's richest men to contract more foreign currency loans and to find buyers for state-owned businesses, using the proceeds to assist debt retirement. His recipe was that Lebanon would spend its way out of recession, regardless of existing debt, and that a 3%–5% growth rate in 2001 would provide the income to escape the debt-deficit trap.[173]

In November, Hariri slashed customs duties — source of half of Lebanon's public revenues — to stimulate demand and lower costs. He also postponed introduction of value added taxes until late 2001. In December, he used his personal prestige to float a $400m. Eurobond issue. This combination of boosted borrowing, lowered public revenues, and higher spending made the commercial banks nervous and unwilling to buy treasury bills.[174] By February 2001, the Central Bank itself held 10% of internal public debt,[175] a situation that increased speculation about the stability of the Lebanese currency and intensified pressure on foreign exchange reserves.[176]

The 1999–2000 recession highlighted negative economic aspects of Lebanon's relations with Syria. In economic terms, Syria needed Lebanon far more than Lebanon needed Syria. Beirut provided Damascus with its window on the West and connections with the global financial system. The Lebanese labor market gave employment to hundreds of thousands of Syrian workers that the Syrian economy could not absorb. In November 2000, *al-Diplomasi News Report* estimated that Syrians took 769,000 jobs "that could be filled by unemployed Lebanese," and transferred $4.3bn. to Syria[177] — equivalent to 25% of Lebanese GDP. The impact on Lebanese workers was made particularly severe by the construction downturn, which meant increased pressure from cheap Syrian labor in seasonal agriculture, industry, municipal services, vending, and taxi driving. A succession of Syrian nominees controlled the Lebanese Labor Ministry after 1992, including Michel Musa in the 1998–2000 Huss cabinet and SSNP leader 'Ali Qansu in Hariri's October 2000 council of ministers, and they removed all impediments to Syrian penetration of the Lebanese labor market. Syrian workers paid no taxes in Lebanon, while the Syrian army "extorted" money "from Lebanese airports, ports and businesses."[178]

SECTARIAN AFFAIRS

The events of 2000 emphasized Lebanese sectarian identities and alignments as the foremost features of Lebanese society and politics. The Israeli withdrawal from South Lebanon and Hizballah elation over its achievement and dilemma regarding its future primarily concerned the Shi'i community, despite celebration of the "resistance" by Lebanese in general. The Maronite patriarchate was chiefly interested in its own people in the former security zone, and the Sunnis of Beirut and northern Lebanon displayed little interest in the new circumstances of the mainly Shi'i southern borderlands of Lebanon. Similarly, sectarianism was the most prominent element in Lebanon's parliamentary elections. Sunnis rallied to Hariri in defense of the prerogatives represented by the Sunni prime minister, and Druze rallied to Junblat as he battled President Lahhud's security apparatus and criticized Damascus.[179] Both Sunnis and Druze felt neglected by the Lahhud-Huss regime.

Druze and Sunni communal preoccupations saw new twists and turns in 2000. The long-running controversy over the spiritual headship (*mashyakhat al-'aql*) of the Druze community (see *MECS* 1997, p. 525; *MECS* 1999, pp. 391–92) resurfaced in early June when Lebanon's Constitutional Council canceled parliamentary authorization for Druze deputies to select the new permanent *shaykh al-'aql* (chief of wisdom).[180] This overturned a deal between Junblat and Talal Arslan, backed by Syria. Junblat angrily accused Lahhud and Birri of backstage involvement, noting: "We don't interfere in Shi'i or Sunni affairs."[181] The issue helped propel Junblat into his new relations with Christian opponents of the Lebanese regime.

As for Sunnis, the bloody "Afghan Arab" rebellion in the Dinniya hills inland from Tripoli in early January (see *MECS* 1999, p. 392), led by a local Sunni activist who had ties with Usama bin Laden and the 'Isbat al-Ansar group in the 'Ayn al-Hilwa Palestinian refugee camp,[182] helped to marginalize religious radicals in the Sunni community. In the 2000 parliamentary elections, the Sunni Islamists lost the last of the five mandates they won in 1992, four of which had already gone in the 1996 elections. With the Islamists reduced to a sideshow, Sunni sensitivities centered on challenges to prime ministerial prestige. In March, Huss refused to sign several death warrants, whereupon deputy prime minister Michel al-Murr promptly signed in his place. Senior Sunni politicians protested, particularly Hariri and 'Umar Karami, and President Lahhud suspended implementation of the warrants. The regime cooled the dispute when it took on a Sunni-Christian "sectarian dimension,"[183] but another episode occurred in April when the Shi'i head of the Public Security Directorate, Jamil al-Sayyid, took it upon himself to define government policy.[184] Huss publicly rebuked al-Sayyid for straying out of "his area."[185] Huss, however, could not erase the negative impressions among Sunnis aroused by such incidents.

Despite their political recession, lack of coherent leadership, and "frustration" with Syrian domination, the Maronites remained Lebanon's center of gravity. They commanded Mount Lebanon — the country's strategic core — and continued to be the majority of Lebanon's global diaspora. Further, the Syrian presence in Lebanon could never be properly stabilized while one of the three great sects in Lebanon seethed openly against Damascus. In 2000, both Shi'i and Druze leaders looked to create an axis with the Maronites, an implicit challenge to the Sunni-Maronite partnership that had been the central feature of Lebanese politics since independence in 1943. Hizballah, which stood aside from the Huss and Hariri governments, cultivated the Maronite presidency. Lahhud responded positively, with his visit to Iran in April, his personal contacts with Hasan Nasrallah, and his outspoken endorsement of the "resistance."[186] Nabih Birri, in contrast, cultivated Maronite patriarch Sufayr, seeking to supply a Shi'i bridge between the patriarchate and Syria. Druze leader Walid Junblat, who knew the Maronites better, sought a more intimate and potent connection — resurrection of the historical Maronite-Druze partnership at the level of popular coalescence rather than strategic calculation. Junblat aimed to make himself the fulcrum of the Christian-Muslim balance in Lebanon, even if a Druze could never occupy one of the primary offices of state.

TABLE 1: MEMBERSHIP OF FOURTH HARIRI GOVERNMENT, 26 October 2000

Portfolio	Incumbent	Sect	Political Affiliation
Prime Minister	Rafiq al-Hariri*	Sunni	—
Deputy Prime Minister	'Isam Faris*	Orthodox	Close to Syria
Minister of Foreign Affairs	Mahmud Hammud	Shi'i	—
Minister of Defense	Khalil al-Hirawi*	Maronite	Close to Syria
Minister of Finance	Fu'ad Siniora	Sunni	Hariri
Minister of Interior and Municipal Affairs	Elias al-Murr	Orthodox	Lahhud/Syria
Minister of Justice	Samir al-Jisr	Sunni	Hariri
Minister of Public Works and Transport	Najib Miqati*	Sunni	Close to Syria
Minister of Health	Sulayman Tony Faranjiyya*	Maronite	Close to Syria

Portfolio	Incumbent	Sect	Political Affiliation
Minister of Labor	'Ali Qansu	Shi'i	SSNP/Syria
Minister of Economy and Trade	Basil Flayhan*	Protestant	Hariri
Minister of Education and Higher Education	'Abd al-Rahim Murad*	Sunni	Hariri
Minister of Displaced People	Marwan Hamada*	Druze	PSP
Minister of Industry	George Afram*	Maronite	Lahhud
Minister of Energy and Water	Muhammad 'Abd al-Hamid Baydun*	Shi'i	Birri
Minister of Social Affairs	As'ad Diyab	Shi'i	Birri
Minister of Environment	Michel Musa*	Greek Catholic	Birri/Syria
Minister of Tourism	Karam Karam	Orthodox	Close to Syria
Minister of Youth and Sport	Sebuh Hovnanian*	Armenian	Lahhud
Minister of Information	Ghazi al-'Aridi*	Druze	PSP
Minister of Culture	Ghassan Salama	Greek Catholic	—
Minister of Agriculture	'Ali 'Ajjaj 'Abdallah	Shi'i	Birri
Minister of Communications	Jean-Louis Qurdahi	Maronite	Lahhud
Minister of State for Administrative Reform	Fu'ad Sa'd*	Maronite	PSP
Minister of State	Bahij Tabbara	Sunni	Hariri
Minister of State	Pierre Hilu*	Maronite	Lahhud
Minister of State	Talal Arslan*	Druze	Lahhud
Minister of State	Bishara Mirhij*	Orthodox	Hariri
Minister of State	Nazih Baydan	Shi'i	Close to Syria
Minister of State	Michel Fir'un*	Greek Catholic	Hariri

* Member of Parliament

NOTES

For the place and frequency of publications cited here, and for the full name of the publication, news agency, radio station or monitoring service where an abbreviation is used, please see "List of Sources." Only in the case of more than one publication bearing the same name is the place of publication noted here.

1. *Al-Hayat*, 1 September 2000.
2. *Al-Safir*, 5 September 2000.
3. *MM*, 21 September 2000.
4. *CR*, Lebanon, April 2001, pp. 9, 21.
5. Ibid., pp. 18, 21.

6. Ibid., p. 11.
7. Ibid., p. 26.
8. Ze'ev Schiff, *Ha'aretz*, 14 February.
9. *JP*, 18 January; Sharon Gal, *Ha'aretz*, 24 January 2000.
10. In a 12 February interview with Israel's Channel Two television, Barak noted that "if there is not an agreement [with Lebanon and Syria] by April or May, and we don't see an agreement on the horizon — we know what to do. Everyone can understand what will happen if there is not an agreement." *Ha'aretz*, 13 February 2000.
11. Tzvi Barel, *Ha'aretz*, 2 February 2000.
12. *Al-Hayat*, 5 February 2000.
13. Amos Harel, *Ha'aretz*, 9 February 2000.
14. *Al-Hayat*, 10 and 13 February 2000.
15. *Ma'ariv*, 13 February 2000.
16. *Al-Hayat*, 10 February 2000.
17. *Al-Hayat*, 11 February 2000.
18. *Al-Hayat*, 20 February 2000.
19. *Al-Hayat*, 19 February 2000.
20. *MM*, 9 February 2000.
21. Mustafa Sarur, *al-Wasat*, 20 March 2000.
22. *Al-Hayat*, 12 March 2000.
23. *Al-Hayat*, 18 March 2000.
24. *Al-Hayat*, 16 March 2000.
25. *Al-Hayat*, 9 March 2000.
26. *Al-Hayat*, 7 March 2000.
27. *Al-Hayat*, 9 March 2000.
28. *Ha'aretz*, 28 March 2000 ("The assessment in the IDF is that the failure of the Geneva summit greatly increases the prospect of a unilateral withdrawal from southern Lebanon"). Also see Dan Margalit, *Ha'aretz*, 30 March 2000.
29. *Ha'aretz*, 23 March 2000.
30. Ibid.
31. Amos Harel, *Ha'aretz*, 3 April 2000 ("Toward the middle of May, when it is finally clear that the chances for a renewal of Israeli-Syrian talks are zero, it seems that Prime Minister Ehud Barak will call Chief of Staff Shaul Mofaz. Barak will order Mofaz to activate the 'Dawn Plan' for unilateral withdrawal from southern Lebanon. The IDF estimates that the plan can be implemented within two weeks of the order. The withdrawal will take only ninety-six hours.")
32. *Al-Hayat*, 5 April 2000.
33. *Yedi'ot Aharonot*, 30 March 2000.
34. *Al-Hayat*, 16 April 2000.
35. *Al-Hayat*, 2 April 2000.
36. *Al-Hayat*, 3 April 2000.
37. *Al-Hayat*, 4 April 2000.
38. *Al-Hayat*, 6 April 2000.
39. *Al-Hayat*, 21 April 2000.
40. *Al-Hayat*, 19 April 2000.
41. *Ha'aretz*, 16 April 2000.
42. *Al-Hayat*, 8 April 2000.
43. *Al-Hayat*, 7 April 2000.
44. *Le Monde*, 22 April; *al-Hayat*, 26 April 2000.
45. *MM*, 27 April 2000.
46. *Al-Hayat*, 27 April 2000.
47. Ibid.
48. *Ha'aretz*, 13 April 2000. The thirteen released men had all been held in Israel since 1986–87.

49. Amos Harel, *Ha'aretz*, 5, 8 May, 2000.
50. *Al-Hayat*, 11 May 2000.
51. *Al-Hayat*, 14 May 2000.
52. *MM*, 4 May 2000.
53. *Al-Hayat*, 30 April 2000.
54. *Al-Hayat*, 7 May 2000.
55. Amos Harel, *Ha'aretz*, 16 May; *al-Hayat*, 18 May 2000.
56. As late as 22 May, the Israeli media reported that 1 June was the most likely date for a withdrawal order (*JP*, 22 May). *Ha'aretz*, 23 May 2000, indicated that even after the 21–22 May collapse of the SLA, Prime Minister Barak still briefly believed that he had "a few days."
57. *Ha'aretz*, 23 May 2000.
58. Mazil Mu'allam, *Ha'aretz*, 1 June; *al-Hayat*, 25 May 2000.
59. *Al-Safir*, 24 May 2000.
60. *Al-Safir*, 8 June 2000, reported US Secretary of State Albright as commenting in Cairo that Syria played "a constructive and cooperative role" during the Israeli withdrawal. Also see Walid Shuqayr, *al-Hayat*, 11 June 2000.
61. *Al-Safir*, 6 June 2000.
62. These locations were adjacent to the Lebanese village of Rumaysh and the Israeli townships of Metulla and Misgav Am (*al-Hayat*, 5 June 2000). The "blue line" also bisected the Syrian 'Alawi village of Ghajjar on the Israeli occupied Golan Heights, placing the homes of many of the villagers inside Lebanon against the wishes of these villagers (*Ha'aretz*, 8, 11 June 2000). The Ghajjar issue was temporarily shelved with a tacit Lebanese agreement not to try to exert Lebanese sovereignty in the village.
63. *Al-Hayat*, 9 June 2000.
64. *Al-Hayat*, 2 and 6 June; *al-Safir*, 6, 8 June 2000.
65. *The Daily Star*, 2 June 2001.
66. *Al-Hayat*, 12, 25 June 2000.
67. *Al-Hayat*, 11 June 2000.
68. *Al-Hayat*, 1 June 2000.
69. *Al-Hayat*, 18 June 2000.
70. *Al-Hayat*, 24 June 2000.
71. *Al-Hayat*, 29 July; Sharon Gal, *Ha'aretz*, 31 July 2000.
72. *Al-Hayat*, 25 July 2000.
73. *Al-Hayat*, 10 August 2000.
74. Gideon Levy, *Ha'aretz*, 9 January 2000.
75. *Al-Hayat*, 13 July 2000.
76. *Al-Hayat*, 16 July 2000. Also see diplomatic editor, *al-Safir*, 15 September 2000 ("Many questions and inquiries, and interested states prefer delay").
77. Lara Sukhtian, *The Daily Star*, 28 May 2001.
78. *Al-Hayat*, 19 July 2000.
79. Nasrallah to *al-Wasat*, 29 May 2000.
80. *Al-Hayat*, 21 June 2000.
81. *Al-Hayat*, 6 July 2000.
82. *Al-Hayat*, 8 July 2000.
83. Ibrahim Bayram, *al-Wasat*, 23 October 2000.
84. *Al-Hayat*, 9 July 2000.
85. Qasim Kasir, *al-Mustaqbal*, 11 October 2000 (*MM*).
86. Ibrahim Bayram, *al-Wasat*, 23 October 2000.
87. Ibid.
88. *Al-Hayat*, 29 January 2000.
89. Muhammad Shuqayr, *al-Hayat*, 31 January 2000.
90. *Al-Hayat*, 31 July 2000.
91. *Al-Hayat*, 26 February 2000.

92. See, for example, *al-Safir*, 2 August 2000.
93. Sarkis Na'um, *al-Wasat*, 17 January 2000 ("Beirut — Electoral 'Mother of Battles' between Huss and Hariri."
94. Nasib Lahhud to *al-Wasat*, 14 August 2000.
95. Walid Shuqayr, *al-Hayat*, 22 July 2000.
96. Ibid.
97. *Al-Hayat*, 20 and 21 July 2000.
98. *Al-Safir*, 7 August 2000.
99. *Al-Hayat*, 9 August 2000.
100. *Al-Hayat*, 7 July 2000.
101. *Al-Hayat*, 6 August 2000.
102. Hariri expressed disappointment that he was unable to bring all the Armenian factions to his side "for reasons that I still don't know, but they don't serve the interests of Armenians and their unity" (*al-Hayat*, 7 August 2000).
103. Hubayqa, a Syrian ally whose past embarrassed his partners, technically ran for parliament by himself for a Maronite seat left empty on the coalition list of candidates. (Niqula Nasif, *al-Wasat*, 21 August 2000).
104. Junblat noted that the PSP opposed the Hizballah candidate in 1996 because of "regional considerations that the Hizballah leadership knows well." (*al-Hayat*, 4 August 2000).
105. *Al-Safir*, 2 August; *al-Hayat*, 2 August 2000.
106. Muhammad Shuqayr, *al-Hayat*, 26 June and 5 August 2000.
107. *Al-Hayat*, 15 July. Also see Muhammad Shuqayr, *al-Hayat*, 7 August 2000.
108. *Al-Safir*, 25 August 2000.
109. *Al-Safir*, 26 August 2000.
110. Ibid.
111. *Al-Hayat*, 21 August 2000.
112. Muhammad Shuqayr, *al-Hayat*, 21 August. Also see Mustafa Sarur, *al-Wasat*, 28 August 2000 ("Arranging 'co-existence' between Lahhud and Hariri needs a detailed understanding, guarantees and reassurances, all of which require more time."
113. *Al-Hayat*, 27 August 2000.
114. Ibid.
115. Ibid.
116. Ibrahim al-Amin, *al-Safir*, 5 September 2000.
117. Ibrahim al-Amin, *al-Safir*, 4 August 2000.
118. *Al-Safir*, 29 August 2000.
119. *Al-Safir*, 27 August 2000.
120. Ibid.
121. Joseph Samaha, *al-Hayat*, 7 September 2000.
122. Turnout in Ashrafiyya (predominantly Christian) was 30%, compared with 84% in Mina al-Husn (predominantly Sunni Muslim). *Al-Hayat*, 4 September 2000.
123. Walid Shuqayr, *al-Hayat*, 5 September 2000.
124. Muhammad Salih, *al-Safir*, 29 August 2000.
125. *Al-Hayat*, 4 September 2000.
126. Ibid.
127. Mustafa Sarur, *al-Wasat*, 11 September 2000.
128. Ibrahim al-Amin, *al-Safir*, 7 September 2000.
129. Niqula Nasif, *al-Wasat*, 11 September 2000.
130. Ibid. Also see Nabil Haytham, *al-Safir*, 5 September 2000.
131. *Al-Ba'th* (Damascus), 5 September 2000 (*MM*).
132. Ibrahim Hamidi, *al-Hayat*, 7 September 2000.
133. *Al-Hayat*, 24 October 2000.
134. Ibid.
135. *Al-Hayat*, 27 October 2000.
136. "The regulation of the presence of Syrian workers is a Muslim demand before being a

Christian one" — Bishara Sharbil, *al-Mustaqbal*, 22 September 2000 (*MM*).
137. *Al-Nahar*, 23 March — *MM*, 24 March 2000.
138. *Al-Mustaqbal*, 24 March 2000 (*MM*).
139. *Al-Hayat*, 26 March 2000.
140. *Al-Hayat*, 17 April 2000.
141. *Al-Hayat*, 20 April 2000.
142. *Al-Hayat*, 22 April 2000.
143. *Al-Hayat*, 23 April 2000.
144. *Al-Hayat*, 21 April 2000.
145. *Al-Hayat*, 28 April 2000.
146. *Al-Hayat*, 5 May 2000.
147. *Al-Hayat*, 8 June 2000.
148. *MM*, 19 July 2000.
149. 'Abd al-Wahhab Badarkhan, *al-Hayat*, 19 July 2000.
150. MENA, 15 July 2000; *al-Hayat*, 16 July 2000.
151. *Al-Hayat*, 26 August 2000. Walid Shuqayr noted "Syrian anger" with Junblat's courting of the Syrian Christian opponents, and an appeal from the Lebanese Ba'th party to Hizballah to support Arslan against Junblat.
152. *MM*, 19 September 2000.
153. *MM*, 21 September 2000.
154. George Bakasini, *al-Mustaqbal*, 7 November 2000 (*MM*).
155. *MM*, 7 November 2000.
156. Ibid.
157. Subhi Hadidi, *MM*, 29 November 2000.
158. Muhammad Shuqayr, *al-Hayat*, 17 November 2000.
159. Subhi Hadidi, *MM*, 29 November 2000.
160. *Al-Safir*, 27 November 2000 (*MM*).
161. Niqula Nasif, *al-Wasat*, 4 December 2000.
162. Walid Shuqayr, *al-Hayat*, 26 November 2000, reported that Birri had meetings with both Bashshar al-Asad and Ghazi Kan'an in the days immediately before his visit to Sufayr. Shuqayr claimed to have information that Birri's contacts with Sufayr were discussed at both meetings.
163. *Al-Hayat*, 26 November 2000.
164. *CR*, Lebanon, April 2001, p. 27.
165. *FT*, 27 April 2000.
166. *The Daily Star*, 8 December 2000.
167. *FT*, 25 April 2000.
168. *The Daily Star*, 13 December 2000.
169. *CR*, Lebanon, April 2001, p. 18.
170. Ibid., p. 19; *FT*, 15 December 2000.
171. Ibid., p. 23.
172. France was particularly discouraging about the proposed October 2000 "donors' conference" for southern Lebanon. *Al-Hayat*, 3 July 2000.
173. *MEED*, 8 December 2000.
174. *CR*, Lebanon, April 2001, p. 21.
175. Ibid.
176. Gross foreign currency reserves declined steadily from 1998 on, mainly because of central bank sales to maintain the exchange rate of the Lebanese lira. Reserves slipped from $7.61bn. in December 1998 to $5.93bn. in December 2000. Reuters, 3 January 2001.
177. *Al-Diplomasi News Report*, November 2000. *MM*, 14 December 2000.
178. Ibid.
179. Thousands of Druze flocked to Mukhtara to show solidarity with Junblat after his 6 November comments in parliament about Syria's role in Lebanon. *The Daily Star*, 13 November 2000.

180. The interim shaykh al-'aql, Bahjat Ghayth, appealed to the Constitutional Council, claiming that parliament had no right to usurp the role of the Druze majlis al-madhhabi (communal council), even on a "one time" basis — *al-Hayat*, 9 June 2000.

181. *Al-Hayat*, 13 August 2000.

182. See series of articles on the "Afghan Lebanese" affair in *al-Hayat*, 18–21 September 2001.

183. *Al-Hayat*, 26 March 2000.

184. *Al-Hayat*, 15 April 2000.

185. *Al-Hayat*, 16 April 2000.

186. Sulayman al-Firzli, *MM*, 1 June 2000.

Libya
(Al-Jamahiriyya al-'Arabiyya al-Sha'biyya al-Ishtirakiyya al-'Uzma)

YEHUDIT RONEN

Following the suspension of seven years of UN-imposed sanctions in 1999, Mu'ammar al-Qadhdhafi could finally invest a substantial amount of energy into domestic affairs to tackle chronic problems in the governmental and economic spheres, and strengthen his grip on power. To achieve these goals, the Libyan leader devolved the responsibilities of cabinet portfolios and state-run institutions to the local level and ordered the revision of the 2000 budget. He also launched an anti-corruption campaign, which targeted some high-level officials. Qadhdhafi needed to resuscitate the national economy, particularly the hydrocarbon-related industries — the backbone of the Libyan economy. The almost exclusive reliance on oil for economic survival, exacerbated by the ongoing decline in oil prices on the world market and the UN embargo, had caused severe cumulative damage during the 1990s. Qadhdhafi, in his thirty-second year of rule, was well aware that improved economic performance could reinforce his political position.

The relatively stagnant economic situation in Libya did not deter approximately a million African migrant workers and their families. Their presence created social and cultural tensions with the local population which eventually sparked unprecedented bloody incidents. While somewhat damaging to Libya's prestige, this violence did not eclipse the regime's satisfaction and heightened political confidence which was due to paralysis of both the Islamist and non-Islamist opposition.

Libya's international standing had improved considerably since the suspension of the UN sanctions. Nonetheless, the success of its newly energized diplomatic efforts was not guaranteed as the failure to restore diplomatic relations with the US plainly indicated. However, diplomatic and economic momentum in relations with Europe were maintained, helped by Tripoli's successful intervention in the release of European hostages from the hands of a Muslim rebel group in the Philippines.

A noticeable rapprochement in foreign affairs occurred with Russia, after a decade-long stalemate following the collapse of the Soviet Union. The greatest proportion of diplomatic efforts, however, were directed southward. Qadhdhafi spared no efforts in promoting his vision of a "United States of Africa," knowing very well that this might serve as a springboard to advance his political interests at home and abroad. He even endeavored to harness Arab countries to join this union plan.

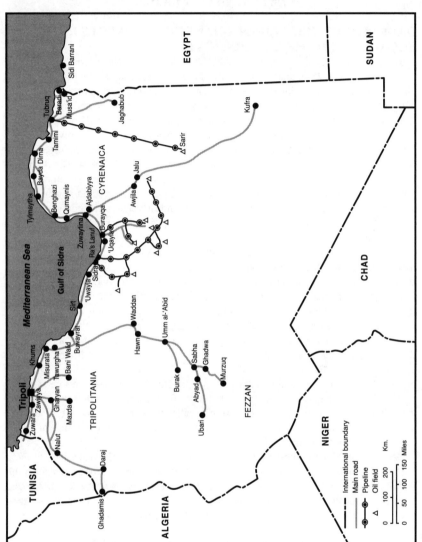

Libya

INTERNAL AFFAIRS

QADHDHAFI'S GUIDELINES: CHANGING PRIORITIES IN THE ECONOMY AND THE GOVERNMENT

Libya's General People's Congress (GPC, the country's highest legislative body), convened in Sirt on 28 January (for the role of the GPC, see chapters on Libya in earlier volumes of *MECS*). A major issue on the agenda of the GPC discussions was the draft budget for 2000, the first since the suspension of the UN sanctions. Although no figures were available, it seemed that the proposed budget generally reflected official and popular expectations for swift economic prosperity, and perhaps even for a revival of the suppressed private sector. Qadhdhafi, however, thought otherwise, and personally took control of discussions of the ostensibly independent GPC. "Oil receipts should not be used for administrative expenses or the import of non-productive goods," he remonstrated. Rather, they should be invested in building essential facilities, including new highways and airports, and in developing vital sectors such as industry, agriculture, defence, health and education.[1] Consequently, he "tore up the budget," ordering it to be revised and the GPC meeting postponed.

Qadhdhafi's strongly-worded message should be viewed within the context of his reinforced bid, which first began in the wake of the sanctions' suspension in 1999, to attract foreign investment to Libya and update the country with modern equipment and technological expertise. This was particularly significant for the hydrocarbon sector whose revenues accounted for close to 95% of the foreign exchange income.

The Libyan leader needed to mobilize public support for investing the major bulk of national resources in medium- and long-term development projects. This involved shelving the expected large-scale financing of short-term projects, including moves to upgrade the standard of living. Although his policy risked an increase in popular discontent, Qadhdhafi appeared determined to stick to his priorities. Thus he attended the GPC forum, seizing the occasion to help fashion the sympathetic atmosphere required to implement the changes. From the rostrum he called for an increase in the efficiency of the executive system, a reduction in bureaucratic expenses and a devolution of power from the center toward the local level.[2]

Qadhdhafi hurried to excuse his flagrant interference in the GPC proceedings, terming it a "revolutionary intervention" (*madhal thawri*) and not a political one.[3] Whatever the semantic parlance, his actions again mirrored the prevailing gap between theory and practice in Libya's "people's power" system, as set out in Part One of Qadhdhafi's *Green Book*, containing the political pillar of his "Third Universal Theory."

IMPLEMENTATION: THE BUDGET REVISION: CABINET RESHUFFLE

The GPC reconvened on 1 March in Sirt to complete the work that had been interrupted in January. It approved the redrafted budget and announced radical changes in the General People's Committee (GPCom., the cabinet). In the revised budget, oil revenues were to provide only 20%, rather than the usual 40% of government income. Expenditure was set at 3.1bn. dinars ($6.65bn.), 12.3% below the 1999 level. The portion spent on development, however, was doubled to 1.8bn. dinars ($3.8bn.), and GDP growth was projected to reach 4.7%, above the 1999 projected 4.2% but below the actual level of

5.4%. In a move that was unlikely to improve Qadhdhafi's popularity, income tax was raised to compensate for the decline in oil revenues.[4]

Qadhdhafi was forced to take drastic measures in order to resuscitate the economy. The 1990s had been a decade of lost opportunities for Libya's economy, caused by declining oil revenues due to developments in the world oil market and the UN-imposed sanctions. The real GDP growth averaged a negligible 0.8% p.a. between 1992 and 1999. Capital stocks had also become depleted due to inadequate fixed investments, limited access to foreign technology and shortages of spare parts and machinery. Libya claimed that the UN embargo cost it about $33bn. in lost growth, non-oil exports and foreign direct investment in the energy sector. Inflation averaged over 12% p.a. between 1990–99.[5] Unemployment stood at around 30%. Corruption spread and the black market, which had mushroomed since the suspension of the sanctions, accounted for around 20% of Libyan exports[6] (for more details on the economic situation in Libya, see *MECS* 1999, pp. 408–409).

Approving the draft, the GPC convention moved further to undertake sweeping changes in the cabinet, eliminating most of its ministries. Of almost twenty portfolios, only five remained intact: foreign affairs, finance, information, justice and public security. Most significant among the abolished ministries was that of energy. Responsibility for hydrocarbon policy was transferred to the state-owned National Oil Company (NOC) headed by 'Abdallah Salim al-Badri, who had hitherto held the oil portfolio in the GPCom., indicating Qadhdhafi's confidence in Badri. The Libyan leader needed the experienced Badri to attract foreign capital in order to modernize the oil sector. This would entail among other things, revising the forty-five-year-old Petroleum Law and providing more promising oil and gas exploration opportunities to foreign oil investors.[7] Libya's propulsion from a modest twentieth position in 1998 to the leading candidate in 2000 for potential oil exploration, development and production ventures, reinforced Qadhdhafi's determination to realize this potential forthwith.[8]

Changes in the GPCom. structure coincided with changes in personnel. Mubarak 'Abdallah al-Samikh became the new prime minister, replacing Muhammad Ahmad al-Manqush, who had held the premiership since late 1997, when the last government reshuffle had taken place. To the two new positions of deputy prime minister were appointed Bashir Bu Janna, to oversee the production sector, and Baghdadi Mahmudi, to oversee services. Both were senior figures in the executive system. Another new appointment was of 'Abd al-Rahman Muhammad Shalqam to head the Foreign Ministry, replacing 'Umar al-Muntasir, who had served since 1992, navigating Libyan foreign policy during the entire UN-imposed sanctions era.[9] Fawziyya Bashir Shalabi, the sole female minister, was appointed to head the newly merged Ministry of Information, Culture and Tourism, having formerly headed the Ministry of Information and Popular Mobilization. The influential 'Ali 'Abd al-Salam al-Turayki, who had served in a series of top political and diplomatic posts since the 1970s, was appointed to the newly-created Ministry for African Unity.[10] These changes should be understood in the context of Qadhdhafi's traditional rotation of influential politicians and technocrats in order to prevent the emergence of threatening power centers.

Concurrently, the GPC announced on 1 March that the functions of "more than eighty companies, offices, hospitals, specialized centers, universities, institutes of higher education and secondary schools" would be transferred from the GPCom. to local bodies.[11] By devolving the power of the dissolved ministries to the local level, Qadhdhafi weakened the political strength of the executive and empowered the "revolutionary" echelon, thus strengthening his control. The move also benefited Qadhdhafi politically as it ostensibly absolved him from accountability for poor executive performance, omissions and corruption, enabling him to remain aloof from public criticism and thus maintain his popularity. "Now," he made it clear, "nobody can complain outside the local communes."[12]

Qadhdhafi presented the government overhaul as a "serious step" amounting to a "real test for the exercise of the 'people's power' authority."[13] It aimed to promote the atmosphere of a mighty, continuous revolution in order to counter the ongoing erosion in revolutionary zeal. In March 2000, a "recent opinion poll" reported that 50% of Libyans questioned claimed to ignore politics and only 10% believed that they could influence political decision-making.[14] Though it was not clear who carried out the poll or exactly where and when it was conducted, it plainly indicated the widespread apathy prevailing among Libyans toward Qadhdhafi's "political revolution." Particularly essential for the perpetuation of Qadhdhafi's political and ideological policies was the need to bring the young generation under the wings of his "revolution." In 2000, 65% of the Libyan population were under the age of twenty-five; many had already been exposed to at least the trappings of a Western lifestyle and referred to it as both positive and tempting.[15] Though born into the "revolution" they did not wholeheartedly subscribe to its political, economic, social and cultural principles, and they presumably expected their head of state to act for the benefit and welfare of the public as a whole.

UNPRECEDENTED VIOLENCE: CABINET CHANGES

On 1 October, the GPC ended its two-day emergency meeting in Sirt. The immediate reason for the convention was the bloody clashes which had erupted between African immigrant workers and Libyans in the town of Zawiyya, west of Tripoli, and in the capital itself, in late September. The number of victims of the violence was unclear, with one source speaking of at least 150, and another of more than five hundred from the Nigerian migrant community alone.[16] A massive exodus of African citizens from Libya back to their home countries soon followed (see below).

According to a somewhat delayed official account, the clashes broke out as a result of a drug war between Libyan dealers and their African competitors ("brothers from beyond the Sahara," in official parlance).[17] Qadhdhafi blamed "hidden hostile hands" for instigating the riots. Though not clarifying their identity, he claimed that they wished to undermine his plan for African unity.[18]

The fact that more than one million out of the total 2.5m. migrant workers in Libya were Africans,[19] most of whom had entered the country illegally since the early 1990s, clearly affected Libyan life. They sought either a refuge from unemployment and civil war or a temporary transit on the way to Europe, providing in the meantime cheap labor for private Libyan enterprises. Not only was there competition for employment (although the migrants were inclined towards unskilled jobs which Libyans sought to avoid), but there was also an upsurge in crimes including drugs, robbery, rape, prostitution and alcohol brewing and drinking. Many Libyans held the African migrants responsible. According to a detailed foreign report, the riots were sparked by a violent incident perpetrated by Africans against Libyans. In response, the report elaborated, Africans were then cornered by the Libyans' relatives who beat them to death and then went on the rampage, attacking any African they met. Organized attempts by groups of Africans to retaliate worsened the riots, until the security forces eventually intervened.[20] Another foreign report claimed that the catalyst for the riots was local resentment of the relationship between a Nigerian and a Libyan schoolgirl.[21]

Whatever the trigger, it was clear that the fatal clashes reflected deep social and cultural tensions. Furthermore, they heavily tarnished Qadhdhafi's vision of an African union and injected a substantial dose of embarrassment into his relations with African states (see below). The riots, the consequent large-scale crackdown and the expulsion of Africans, also damaged Libya's image among the international community, at the height of Qadhdhafi's effort to rehabilitate his country's stature in the West.

Acting to appease primarily the African countries, the GPC not only adopted a series of "organizational measures" in order to prevent the recurrence of the September riots,[22] but also sacked Abu al-Qasim al-Zawi, the minister of public security and justice. He was appointed late in 2001 as the Libyan ambassador in Britain. Zawi was replaced by 'Abd al-Rahman al-'Abbar, a hard-liner with close links to the "revolutionary committees" — a powerful instrument for guarding the regime's grip on power. Zawi's ousting came within a broader reshuffle of the GPCom., which included the dismissal of Muhammad Bayt al-Mal, the finance minister, who had reclaimed his post in early August after being subjected to an undisclosed trial for several weeks. He had been arrested with other Libyan officials in financial and banking institutions on charges of involvement in dissipating Libyan state funds and providing loans to a number of army officers and associates of high-ranking officials without sufficient guarantees.[23] Bayt al-Mal's post was delegated to al-'Ujayli 'Abd al-Salam Burayni, hitherto the acting governor of the Libyan Central Bank. The dismissal of the governor of the Central Bank, Tahir al-Juhaymi, in July, should also be viewed within the context of the anti-corruption campaign, though he was not officially accused of any transgression.[24]

Another change was the naming of former foreign minister, 'Umar Mustafa al-Muntasir as minister of general planning, a portfolio which had been abolished in March (see above). This appointment indicated Qadhdhafi's desire to utilize Muntasir's wide network of foreign contacts in modernizing and reconstructing the Libyan state-run economy. The appointment of 'Abd al-Salam al-Badri as deputy minister for "services affairs" was also announced during the October reshuffle. This was his second shift in 2000 and it was not clear at that time if the new post was an addition, or instead of his position as head of the NOC. Another change was the abolition of the Ministry of Information, Culture and Tourism, headed by Fawziyya Bashir Shalabi. She continued, however, to oversee Libyan radio broadcasting.[25]

THE PARALYSIS OF OPPOSITION ACTIVISM

The opposition threat, particularly that of militant Islam, had largely declined during the previous year and was further shunted to the margins of Libyan politics throughout 2000. The factors which brought about this decline in 1999 remained valid (see *MECS* 1999, pp. 409–11). The Libyan security authorities, however, persisted in their relentless crackdown on Islamists at home as well as extending their activities into Arab and European countries where Libyan Islamists sought refuge. Consequently, more than a dozen Libyan Islamists from Jordan, Egypt, Tunisia, Pakistan and Germany were handed over.[26] Of three militants extradited to Libya, one was reportedly executed.[27]

The debilitating effects of the unceasing pursuit of expatriate non-Islamist opponents continued to pay off for the regime. The opposition remained largely dormant apart from a single, unproductive gathering on 5 August of six opposition organizations. This apparently took place in a London suburb to discuss a joint action strategy against the Libyan regime.[28] A "high-ranking Libyan official" correctly dismissed the significance of the event, describing it as a "desperate attempt by a stray group to prove that it is still able to breathe."[29] The formation of a new expatriate opposition group, the National Reform Congress, was announced on 15 August. It aimed at "establishing a just and civilized multi-party system" in Libya, also lacked political importance.[30] Moreover, the Libyan expatriate opposition was shocked by the "sudden" reconciliation in early September between the Qadhdhafi regime and 'Abd al-Mun'im al-Huni.[31] The latter, a former Revolutionary Command Council member and foreign minister, had gone into self-imposed exile in Cairo in 1976 and had since been considered the most veteran opponent to the regime. This reconciliation resulted in Huni's appointment as Libyan ambassador to the Arab League on 4 September 2000.

FOREIGN AFFAIRS

LIBYA AND THE US

When Libya handed over its two most wanted citizens, both intelligence officers, to the Netherlands to stand trial for the 1988 bombing of a Pan Am flight over Lockerbie, Scotland, and UN-imposed sanctions were suspended in spring 1999, expectations were fanned in Tripoli for an imminent thaw in its chronically strained relations with the US. To Qadhdhafi's dismay, however, the Clinton administration remained firm in its reluctance to mitigate bilateral tension, even after Libya consented to hand over the suspects (see *MECS* 1999, pp. 412–13). Furthermore, in early 2000, the US reiterated its designation of Libya as a sponsor of terrorism, and alleged that Libya sought to acquire long-range missiles capable of hitting American and European territories. Libya immediately denied any such intention, claiming that the allegations were merely aimed at "justifying the American hegemony over Europe and the Mediterranean and consolidating NATO eastward and southward expansion."[32]

A surprise softening in the US attitude toward Libya came in mid-February when the Libyan ambassador to the UN, Abu Zayd 'Umar Durda, was granted a visa to travel from New York to Washington D.C. to attend a conference hosted by the UN International Fund for Agricultural Development. This was the first time in a long period that a top Libyan official was allowed to travel beyond New York. The US explained that the move was due to Libya's cessation of terrorist threats against the US, its expulsion of the Abu Nidal terrorist organization from Libya in 1999 and in its cooperation with the Lockerbie trial proceedings (see *MECS* 1999, pp. 411–13). Libya, stated a senior State Department official, "is not the same Libya it was six years ago."[33] A month later, however, State Department spokesperson James Rubin stated that notwithstanding positive steps to end its involvement in terrorism, Libya still "has a very, very long way to go before it meets the standards required to be removed from the terrorism list."[34] One may assume he was referring to the unresolved Lockerbie controversy, including Qadhdhafi's unequivocal refusal to compensate the families of the Lockerbie victims. Qadhdhafi presumably vetoed the compensation demand, even though such a move could have furthered a resolution of the dispute, since it might have been interpreted as an acknowledgment of personal responsibility for the bombing. Libya, in turn, pressed the US to pay compensation for the "human and material losses" it had caused Libya during the seven-year international embargo, initiated by the US (and Britain) and imposed by the UN.[35]

The oscillation of US policy toward Libya was further attested to by the visit of a State Department team in Tripoli on 25–26 March. This coincided, in fact, with Rubin's statement which reduced the likelihood of an imminent thaw between Washington and Tripoli. This inconsistency in US policy can be partly explained by the lead-up to the US presidential election of November 2000, when the lobbying power of the US families of the victims was most effective. The visit of the US delegation to Tripoli, and the earlier visit of the Libyan UN envoy to Washington D.C., did, however, mark a departure from the longstanding hostility between the two countries. The visit of the US delegation, the first since the break of diplomatic ties two decades earlier, formally aimed at assessing general security arrangements in Libyan airports, hotels and other facilities, in order to consider whether or not travel restrictions imposed upon US citizens should be lifted.[36] Washington banned the use of US passports for travel to Libya in 1981 on grounds that conditions there were unsafe for Americans. Seizing what appeared as American signals towards an easing of hostilities, Libya hurried to declare its wish to resume ties with Washington without preconditions, "except respect for our full independence."[37]

To Libya's disappointment, the US soon ended hopes that relations would improve. Furthermore, in late April, on the eve of the opening of the Lockerbie trial, the US Senate requested that the Clinton administration defer lifting the ban on travel to Libya until the close of the trial, "at the earliest."[38] The administration accordingly decided to maintain the travel ban, and to keep Libya on the State Department list of states sponsoring terrorism. Libya angrily retorted that "the Americans are the losers by their absence from Libya, because oil and non-oil companies from all over the world are flocking into Libya for cooperation, work and gain."[39] The ban did not, however, prevent Louis Farrakhan, leader of the African-American Nation of Islam movement, from visiting Libya in mid-June, to Qadhdhafi's satisfaction (for previous violations by Farrakhan of the ban on travel to Libya, see *MECS* 1996, p. 520; 1997, p. 550).

While certain circles in the US advocated a continued freeze in relations, US firms, led by oil companies, exerted pressure upon the administration to participate in the development of Libya's economic potential, particularly in the oil sector. This followed many years of their exclusion, and after companies from countries within the EU had entered the Libyan economic field the previous year (see *MECS* 1999, p. 413). The eagerness of US oil companies to resurrect their operations in Libya might have been enhanced by a visit of their representatives in late 1999 to inspect assets abandoned in 1986 by order of the Reagan administration (see *MECS* 1986, p. 511).[40] On 4 May, Ronald E. Neumann, deputy assistant secretary of state for Near Eastern affairs, told the Senate that Clinton was not leaning toward warmer relations with Libya.[41] In June of that year, the US State Department changed Libya's status from a "rogue state" to a "state of concern," along with that of Iran and Iraq.[42]

The Lockerbie Trial

On 3 May, following almost a decade of international wrangling, the trial of the two Libyans charged with bombing the Pan Am airliner over Lockerbie opened at Camp Zeist in the Netherlands under the auspices of Scottish law. The suspects, 'Abd al-Basit 'Ali Muhammad al-Maqrahi and al-Amin Khalifa al-Fahima, pleaded not guilty. Qadhdhafi, who had persistently denied any Libyan role in the affair, emphasized that the court was only trying the two suspects and not the Libyan government. While explicitly distancing himself from the trial, he pledged nevertheless to accept its verdict.[43]

The fact that Qadhdhafi himself had not been put on trial strengthened suspicions prevailing since early spring, mainly among the US families of the victims, that he had reached a secret deal with the US and Britain under UN auspices in early 1999, which enabled the extradition of the two Libyans to the Netherlands. The deal, they suspected, assured Qadhdhafi that the trial would not target him as the mastermind of the explosion.[44] In August, in the wake of mounting pressure, the UN released the text of a letter sent to Libya by the UN, wherein the involved parties pledged not to "undermine the Libyan regime."[45] This phrase was interpreted differently by various parties, injecting further doses of complexity into the Lockerbie affair.

Meanwhile, the judicial procedures of the trial were routine, intertwined by a series of adjournments, designed mainly to investigate new evidence. The suspects were accused of three different charges: murder, conspiracy to commit murder, and contravention of the 1982 Aviation Security Act. The defense claimed that responsibility for the bombing lay with members of Palestinian organizations, namely the Popular Front for the Liberation of Palestine-General Command, and the Palestine Popular Struggle Front, and that the forensic evidence was either mishandled or deliberately planted. The two Palestinian organizations promptly denied any involvement in the explosion.[46]

During fall-winter, as the legal proceedings continued, the trial ceased to attract as much attention in the international media. Other issues emerged, including the successful Libyan mediation with a Philippine Islamic rebel group holding Western hostages and their consequent release (see below). The US somewhat spoiled Libya's public relations achievement, however, by criticizing its alleged ransom payment to the kidnappers and by ignoring the Libyan offer to help in releasing the American citizen, Jeffrey Craig Edwards, who was kidnapped by the same Philippine group in late August.[47]

Libya, nonetheless, reiterated in August and September its willingness to resume diplomatic relations with the US immediately, if the relationship was "based on the respect for each other's sovereignty," but to no avail.[48] Frustrated, Libya turned its fury towards the UN Security Council, which had suspended sanctions in 1999 but failed to lift them because of "US stubbornness." Qadhdhafi, therefore, sharply rejected the status of the UN as a world body, telling CNN in a live interview that he would not attend the worldwide UN millennium summit in New York unless the UN underwent reforms. "The UN is a place just to make speeches. It is a decoration," he stated.[49] On 26 October, the UN General Assembly approved a Libyan-sponsored resolution calling for the repeal of all unilaterally imposed extraterritorial coercive economic measures on companies and persons of other countries, given that they were a political means of pressure.[50] Nonetheless, the US extraterritorial sanctions — the Iran-Libya Sanctions Act — which the US passed in 1996 in order to punish non-US firms investing more than $40m. in the Libyan hydrocarbon sector (see *MECS* 1996, p. 521), formally remained in effect, to the strong resentment of Libya (and European companies).

On 25 November, the US extended the ban on American passport holders travelling to Libya by one year.[51] Libya criticized the decision, stating that "Libya's streets are ten times safer than those of the US capital Washington."[52] The US also remained adamant in its reluctance to allow a permanent lifting of the UN sanctions. The Lockerbie trial only concluded in January 2001, returning one guilty and one not-guilty verdict.

INCREASED DIPLOMATIC AND ECONOMIC LINKS WITH EUROPE

Libya's diplomatic and economic relations with EU countries continued to improve throughout 2000, owing to the convergence of interests (for Libya's swift diplomatic reinstatement in Europe in 1999, see *MECS* 1999, pp. 413–15). The EU countries, most prominently Italy, Germany and France, were keen to further penetrate Libya's potentially vast market, particularly that of the hydrocarbon sector.

An embarrassing event occurred in early 2000 following the well-publicized cancellation of an invitation to Qadhdhafi to visit the European Commission headquarters in Brussels, which had originally been extended in December 1999 by Romano Prodi, the European Commission president. Prodi's initiative, however, had infuriated circles within the EU, mostly Britain, and raised questions regarding the proper procedures for determining the EU diplomatic agenda. On 22 January, the EU formally shelved the visit.[53]

Qadhdhafi's meeting with Prodi eventually took place on the sidelines of the Europe-Africa summit in Cairo on 2–3 April. The diplomatic reward Libya reaped from this meeting was certainly much less than the planned "victory trip" into the EU stronghold in Brussels. Nevertheless, Qadhdhafi seized the occasion to hold a series of talks with European heads of state, including the Italian prime minister, Massimo D'Alema, the Spanish prime minister, Jose Maria Aznar, and the German chancellor, Gerhard Schroeder. One may assume that the upgrading of Libya's status in the EU-sponsored Euro-Mediterranean Barcelona process from "special guest" to full member was discussed during these meetings. One of the EU conditions for Libya's full inclusion in this framework was Tripoli's recognition of the State of Israel, which Qadhdhafi had unequivocally rejected. Qadhdhafi, however, allegedly promised Prodi that Libya would not impede the Arab-Israeli peace process.[54] It was plausible that against this backdrop, Qadhdhafi allegedly invited, or gave the impression of inviting an Israeli official to visit Tripoli during his Cairo visit in April. In any case, Libya flatly denied any such gesture.

Aware of the seemingly unbridgeable problems inherent in Libya's joining the Barcelona process, Qadhdhafi subsequently rebuked it. The EU, he stated, "want to take Egypt, Libya, Tunisia, Algeria and Morocco and annex them to the EU, via the Mediterranean. This is tantamount to an aggression on Africa's territorial integrity."[55] Qadhdhafi's reprimand of the EU testified to his growing political confidence at home and abroad, notwithstanding his need for EU support in rehabilitating his diplomatic stature in the international community. This was boosted, inter alia, by his success in attaining the release of Western hostages held for months by a Philippine rebel group (see below).

In gratitude, Germany sent its foreign minister, Joschka Fischer, on a brief visit to Tripoli on 12 September, and a further warming of ties with Berlin ensued. By the end of the year, Germany was the second largest European trading partner of Libya, buying 20% of Libyan exports, and selling 12% of Libyan imports.[56]

In mid-November, Libya reversed an earlier decision to boycott the Euro-Med summit meeting in Marseilles (see chapter on Western Europe, Russia and the Middle East), and sent a high-level delegation headed by Foreign Minister 'Abd al-Rahman Shalqam to attend the forum, thus keeping open the channel to the Barcelona framework.[57]

Libyan relations with Britain, although problematic, improved. The first obstacle was the British announcement concerning the discovery of thirty-two crates of Scud missile parts, disguised as automotive parts, at Gatwick airport. The consignment, allegedly intercepted in late 1999, arrived from Taiwan and was scheduled to be flown by a British Airways cargo flight to Libya.[58] Britain protested at the "unacceptable" use of a British airport for smuggling missile parts into Libya in defiance of the EU arms embargo. Tripoli, however, flatly denied any attempt to smuggle weapons, portraying the whole affair as "simply an air bubble."[59] The British government did not explain the month-and-a-half delay between the alleged interception of the illegal payload and its public exposure. Furthermore, according to some sources, Britain had already impounded the Scud components in May 1999, at the height of Anglo-Libyan negotiations over the renewal of diplomatic relations following a fifteen-year hiatus (see *MECS* 1999, pp. 413–14).[60]

Whatever shaped the timing of the report, it was released on the eve of the scheduled arrival of Sa'd Mujabar, Libya's ambassador to London and only a short while after the British ambassador to Tripoli, Richard Dalton, had taken up his post. The resumption of Libyan Airways flights to Britain on 24 January, proved that the trend of improving bilateral ties had not been hampered.[61] British rejection of Qadhdhafi's invitation to the EU headquarters at the beginning of 2000 (see above), did not disrupt matters. The warming process even survived an incriminating British report on an alleged British plan to overthrow Qadhdhafi in 1996. The supposed plot narrowly failed, but killed six bystanders. British foreign secretary Robin Cook dismissed the alleged plot as "pure fantasy" and said he had seen nothing "which would suggest that the British secret intelligence service has any interest, any role, or any experience in such an escapade."[62] Whatever the truth, the two countries smoothed out their difficulties, as attested to by the visit of the British permanent undersecretary at the Foreign and Commonwealth Office, Sir John Kerr, to Tripoli on 25–26 April, the highest level mission by a British official since the restoration of diplomatic ties in summer 1999.

Libyan contacts with Joerg Haider, former leader of the Austrian far-right Freedom Party, was an interesting development, particularly given Libyan endeavors to strengthen ties with mainstream European powers. Haider visited Tripoli in May and June. Soon afterwards, Libya deposited $25m. into the Austrian Carinthian Bank to ease the strain of the EU blockade on the Carinthian province governed by Haider.[63] This, one may presume, was mainly the outcome of the close friendship established between Haider and Qadhdhafi's politically influential son, Sayf al-Islam, who had studied in Vienna.

Libya's Successful Brokery in the Philippines Hostage Drama
On 23 April 2000, the Abu Sayyaf Filipino Islamic rebel group, a loose collection of several hundred heavily armed rebels fighting for independence in the southern Philippines[64] kidnapped twenty-one people, including ten Westerners, from the Malaysian diving resort of Sipadan and held them on Jolo island in the southern Philippines.

Throughout the summer, the Manila government negotiated for a release of the hostages. Libya played a crucial mediating role, with 'Abd al-Rajab al-Zaruq, a senior Libyan official and former ambassador to the Philippines, spearheading the efforts. Libyan ties in the Philippines dated back to the 1970s when Qadhdhafi — then a self-declared champion of oppressed causes worldwide, particularly those of Islamic character — allegedly financed and militarily backed the Islamic Moro National Liberation Front Filipino rebel group.

The variegated nationalities of the hostages, among them three French nationals, two South Africans, two Germans and two Finns, heightened the prospects of international coverage of the affair and of Qadhdhafi as its hero. Indeed, Qadhdhafi's involvement in the Philippines preoccupied the international media, helping him to further extricate Libya from its prolonged isolation. Furthermore, the portrayal of Qadhdhafi as a responsible, peacemaking leader, enjoying global links with various rebel groups, highlighted his potential to serve Western interests. This was particularly significant for Tripoli as the Lockerbie trial was progressing and Qadhdhafi's bid to ease tension with the US was gathering momentum (see above). Qadhdhafi also hoped that his portrayal as an effective mediator of international crises would ensure, or at least increase, EU backing for Libya's attendance at the forthcoming Marseilles Mediterranean summit as a fully-fledged participant.

Meanwhile, the Abu Sayyaf group insisted upon a ransom of about $1m. in exchange for freeing the hostages.[65] Libya allegedly paid the money, though repeatedly clarifying that it was not paid (as the US claimed) as a ransom to the Abu Sayyaf group but rather to develop economic projects for the impoverished Muslim community in the southern Philippine region of Mindanao. "What Libya did was a sheer human act," stated Hasuna Shayush, a top-level official in Libya's Foreign Ministry. "Libya did not and would not pay a dirham or a dollar for hostages," he added.[66] To lend more credence to this argument, Libya announced that the money came from the Qadhdhafi International Association for Charitable Organizations, headed by Qadhdhafi's son, Sayf al-Islam, and not from the Libyan government. Sayf al-Islam found it politically important to further corroborate this claim.[67]

The apex of the affair came on 27 August, with the release of six hostages. They were air-lifted directly by a Libyan jet to Tripoli, where their welcome was widely covered by the local and international media.[68] At the same time, the Abu Sayyaf group kidnapped more hostages, including an American citizen. Although Libya immediately announced its readiness to act for his release on the basis of a US request, Washington rejected the offer.[69]

This did not, however, affect further Libyan mediation efforts in the Philippines, which led to the release of four additional hostages — two Finns, a German and a Frenchman on 11 September.[70] They too were flown to Tripoli, where they received a red carpet welcome. Qadhdhafi personally gained a public relations boost both at home and abroad, attested to, amongst others, by a remark made by a Libyan citizen. The Libyan release of the hostages, he said, "proves that Qadhdhafi is fighting terrorism and not causing it."[71]

TENSION WITH BULGARIA: MEDICS CHARGED WITH INFECTING LIBYANS WITH HIV VIRUS

In early 2000, six Bulgarian citizens, a doctor and five nurses, who had been jailed about a year earlier, as well as eight Libyans and one Palestinian, were charged with knowingly infecting 393 Libyan children with the HIV virus through contaminated blood. An additional thirteen Bulgarian medics, who had also been jailed in 1999 for the same charges, were freed in early 2000. The affair allegedly took place in 1998 at a pediatric hospital in Benghazi, but was only publicized widely at the beginning of 2000. The tragedy gathered further momentum after the death of twenty-three children and as the Libyan authorities officially accused the Bulgarian medics of "weaken[ing] the security of the state." They also faced charges of violating the rules of Islamic lifestyle. If found guilty, they faced the possibility of capital punishment.[72]

Top-level Bulgarian officials promptly denied that the medics committed "these serious crimes," and expressed concern that they would not receive a fair trial.[73] Toward spring, Sofia undertook diplomatic endeavors in Libya and in other countries, particularly in Russia, South Africa and Egypt, at least to ensure a fair trial for the suspects and to convince Tripoli to return the passports to those medics who had been released from jail. Whether as a result of this diplomatic activity or not, Tripoli returned the passports and delayed the trial of the jailed medics until fall 2000 "at the request of defense lawyers."[74]

Bulgaria remained, however, acutely concerned, fearing its citizens would be used by Tripoli as scapegoats for local negligence. On 30 May, tension mounted further when Tripoli inexplicably banned Bulgaria's Balkan Airlines from flying to Libya and using Libyan airspace.[75] The move clearly signalled dissatisfaction at Bulgaria's high-profile public campaign, casting serious doubts on the Libyan judicial system. The massive protest of Bulgarian citizens in front of the Libyan embassy in Sofia on 4 June further strained mutual relations, urging Libya's embassy in Sofia to express resentment of the "hostile Bulgarian attitude," particularly in the media. Some Bulgarian papers, the embassy argued, "gave grounds for concern with their call for racism in respect to Arabs in general and Libyans in particular."[76]

Observers of the controversy over the Bulgarian medics could not ignore the looming presence of the Lockerbie connection. The Lockerbie trial, which opened in early May (see above) and continued throughout the year, highlighted Tripoli's essential powerlessness. By contrast, the imminent trial of the Bulgarian medics, though entirely different in nature, was used to demonstrate Qadhdhafi's decisiveness and control. Leveling blame for the scandalous affair on the Bulgarians as well as on several Libyans could also be seen within the context of the anti-corruption and efficiency campaign (see above).

Rapprochement with Russia

In late May 2000, Russia reportedly resumed arms deliveries to Libya, in accordance with contracts signed some months earlier.[77] The renewal of military and technical cooperation between Moscow and Tripoli following the collapse of the Soviet Union contrasted with the continuing arms embargo by the EU against Libya despite the suspension of the UN-imposed sanctions. The renewal of cooperation between Libya and Russia had two significant purposes for Qadhdhafi: (1) to update military arsenals and technological equipment after an almost a decade-long paralysis, due to (a) the reduction of income following the drop in oil prices; and (b) the demise of the USSR which had been Libya's military prop, and the UN-imposed embargo; and (2) to exert pressure upon the US to adopt a more accommodating attitude toward Libya unless Washington wished to witness further Russian inroads into Middle East affairs. Ostensibly, this aim seemed irrelevant in the post-Cold War era, but one should remember that Qadhdhafi's formative years as a head of state during the 1970s and 1980s — at the height of the Cold War — deeply influenced his international outlook. The fact that Russia was one of the five permanent members of the UN Security Council presumably motivated Libya further to strengthen relations.

On 30–31 July, Libyan foreign minister Shalqam visited Moscow. He was the first top-level Libyan official to visit Russia since the break-up of the Soviet Union. The Libyan minister exchanged views with the Russian president, Vladimir Putin, and other high-level officials. Among other matters, the two expressed their "mutual commitment" to "enhance bilateral relations in various areas."[78] The visit proved to be a success for Libyan foreign policy, as Putin pledged a call for a "definitive lifting" of the UN sanctions from Libya, and accepted Qadhdhafi's invitation to reciprocate the foreign minister's visit.[79]

During the last months of 2000, political and economic ties increased further. A series of consultations resulted in a $650m. agreement in November for Russia to upgrade a Libyan nuclear power plant and nuclear research center.[80]

QADHDHAFI'S VISION OF A "UNITED STATES OF AFRICA"

Encouraged by his diplomatic success in Africa, which contributed to Libya's escape from the UN sanctions, Qadhdhafi invested considerable energy to advance his position in the continent. Many African countries, motivated by their own interests, warmly cooperated with Qadhdhafi's African policy, hand in glove with his grand design for a "United States of Africa." Since the Sirt declaration, released at the end of the OAU summit meeting in Libya in September 1999, the notion of African unity had become the centerpiece of Libyan African policy. With unity the goal, the Sirt declaration stipulated consent of OAU leaders to the establishment of a central African bank, a supreme court and an African monetary fund (see *MECS* 1999, p. 418).

Foreign, i.e., Western, presence in Africa had long been depicted by Qadhdhafi as one of Africa's worst evils. Libya now positioned itself in the forefront of the struggle to eradicate the foreign presence from the continent. Predictably, therefore, Libya objected to the 20 January "Gabon 2000" military exercise in the Central African region, involving more than 1,200 participants from eight countries including the US, Britain and France. The exercise, aimed at "testing the ability of African countries to intervene in conflicts on the continent,"[81] was perceived by Libya as merely another Western attempt to perpetuate its presence in the region, thus undermining Tripoli's ideological and political impact in Africa.

Libya also consistently sought a role in inter-African politics. The grouping of the Community of the Sahel and Saharan States (COMESSA), established by Qadhdhafi in 1998 and headed by him ever since, continued to serve as an effective platform to nurse Libyan interests in Africa. The COMESSA became increasingly prominent, not due to any political substance but rather because of its tangible activity, repeatedly convening its heads of state under the media's glare (for Libyan African policy and previous COMESSA activities, see *MECS* 1998, pp. 443–46; 1999, pp. 415–18). Interest in COMESSA was further attested to by the inclusion of three new states, Gambia, Senegal and Djibouti, during the summit meeting held in Chad on 2–5 February. The number of COMESSA members was now eleven — including Libya, Niger, Burkina Faso, Mali, Chad, the Central African Republic, Eritrea and Sudan. Assuming his place of honor on the summit stage, Qadhdhafi urged more African countries to join the COMESSA and thus "form the cornerstone of an African union."[82] About a month later, Tripoli reported that Morocco had officially requested to join the COMESSA.[83]

Meanwhile, Qadhdhafi did not miss any opportunity to promote his vision of a "United States of Africa." Within this context, he hosted and visited many African heads of state during the year reviewed. The highlight of this activity was his attendance of the thirty-sixth OAU summit conference, held in Lome, Togo, on 10–13 July. Qadhdhafi arrived in Togo on 8 July, after making a symbolic overland journey across West Africa from Libya via Niger, Burkina Faso and Ghana to reciprocate previous gestures of friendship and further strengthen his country's ties in the region. The OAU summit, financed to a large extent by Libya,[84] dealt with various issues, primarily the promotion of Qadhdhafi's notion of African union. Twenty-seven member countries, just over half of all OAU member states (fifty-three), and two-thirds of those present, signed the union document, stipulating its formation within one year. Nonetheless, the exact shape of the union remained to be determined and in any case, had to be ratified by two-thirds of all OAU member states. Notwithstanding this decision, Qadhdhafi was aware that his vision of African unity had still not advanced as much as he had desired though the OAU summit did agree to devote an extraordinary summit to implementation of the African union document at Sirt, Libya, in March 2001.[85] The fact that the continent's most important powers, namely South Africa and Nigeria, as well as other important countries such as Kenya, Egypt and Algeria, did not line up with the union, displeased Qadhdhafi.[86] So did the absence of a comprehensive discussion during the summit of inter- and intra-conflicts in the continent, which could have further highlighted Qadhdhafi's image as a leading peacemaker. This failing was due to the boycott of the summit by Angola, the Democratic Republic of Congo, Namibia and Zimbabwe, following claims in a UN report, reiterated by Luanda, that Togo — the venue of the summit — "has been supporting the Angolan rebel movement UNITA in return for a share in its so-called 'blood diamonds'."[87] In protest, Qadhdhafi boycotted the reception held in honor of the OAU heads of state in the Togolese capital.[88]

Following the summit, Qadhdhafi continued his tour by road of West Africa, visiting Benin on 12–14 July. During his visits in West Africa, the Libyan leader reiterated his vision. The continent, he stated, should be transformed into a single entity, thus cancelling the borders demarcated by imperialism. Africa, he further accentuated, should rid itself of Christianity, the colonizer religion, and Islam should take its place.[89]

While spearheading the vision of a "United States of Africa" for the sake of the African people, as Qadhdhafi repeatedly stated, Libya itself was the venue of violent "racial attacks" by Libyans against African migrant workers at the end of September.[90] The riots engulfed African nationals indiscriminately, injuring and killing people from Sudan, Niger, Nigeria, Chad, Gambia, Burkina Faso and Ghana.[91] The racial aspect of the riots was reflected by the harassing of some of Libya's one million black indigenous citizens who were mistaken for migrants by their attackers.[92] A short while later, thousands of African migrant workers were deported, or repatriated by their governments.[93] Moreover, later in November and December an additional wave of deportations of illegal Guinean and Cameroonian migrants from Libya was initiated.[94]

Aware of the serious blow these riots could deal to his African unity scheme, Qadhdhafi voiced his regret over the violence, stating that the "enemies" must not be given "the opportunity to impede our unity" and that "we must complete our historical [union] mission." "Africa is one," he reiterated, "one people and one family."[95]

All in all, Libya downplayed the riots. The OAU summit conference held in Tripoli on 7–9 November, was aimed at signalling an atmosphere of "business as usual." The wide attendance of high-level African leaders, among them the heads of Mali, Zimbabwe, Liberia, Uganda and Rwanda, helped Qadhdhafi to enhance Libya's image on the continent. The summit discussed the war in the Great Lakes region, agreeing to send a force of "neutral" African nations to the Democratic Republic of Congo in a bid to end the civil war there.[96] The salience of Africa in Libyan foreign policy, and increasing Libyan importance in African politics, was also mirrored through the increased exchange of visits of high-echelon officials between Tripoli and African capitals. No less than thirteen African presidents visited Tripoli during the year, many of them two or three times. Other noteworthy Libyan diplomatic successes in Africa included the reciprocal opening of embassies with the Seychelles on 19 January, and Tripoli's successful mediation between Djibouti and Eritrea, which led to the resumption of their diplomatic ties on 11 March.[97]

LIBYA AND THE ARAB WORLD

Egypt and Sudan
Qadhdhafi's anger and disillusion with the Arab world for failing to help Libya break the UN sanctions did not abate during 2000 (see chapters on Libya in *MECS* 1992–99).

Egypt, of vital importance for Libya due to its political access to the US and as a buffer against the expansion of militant Islam, remained, however, the first priority on Libya's Arab agenda (see *MECS* 1999, pp. 419–20). The two heads of state, Qadhdhafi and Mubarak, continued to meet periodically using their jointly-conducted diplomatic initiative to end the war in Sudan as a convenient measure for injecting a measure of dynamism into bilateral ties. This initiative which had begun in 1999, also provided Libyan access to Sudanese politics. Libya had a strong interest in curbing the impact of Sudan-based militant Islam and in maintaining Sudanese territorial integrity, fearing that the establishment of an independent state in south Sudan might become a launching pad for US interventionist policies in Africa. It was not surprising, therefore, that Libya supported President 'Umar Hasan Ahmad al-Bashir in his bid to politically eradicate Islamist leader Hasan 'Abdallah al-Turabi (see chapter on Sudan).

It is against this background that one should view the series of meetings held during 2000 within the Libyan-Sudanese-Egyptian "triangle." In early January, the three heads of state met in Khartoum. On 9 March, Qadhdhafi hosted Bashir in Tripoli, meeting him again, together with Mubarak, in Cairo at the Euro-Africa summit on 2–3 April. Bashir arrived in Tripoli for further talks with Qadhdhafi in early June. Mubarak met Qadhdhafi in Tripoli in late July. In early October, Qadhdhafi paid a short visit to Egypt, the first leg of a broader two-week tour he undertook in Jordan, Syria and Saudi Arabia (11–13 October), with whom Libya had already significantly improved relations the previous year (see *MECS* 1999, p. 420). The aim of the visit was to urge the "Arab brothers" to join Libya's Arab-African union plan.[98] On 14 October, Qadhdhafi left Egypt en route to Sudan.

Jordan
On 1–2 September, King 'Abdallah of Jordan visited Libya as the guest of honor for the 1 September celebrations of Qadhdhafi's advent to power in 1969. On 4–7 October, Qadhdhafi reciprocated with a visit to Amman, meeting the king who had returned a short while earlier from a trip to Washington. Talking with the king before and after his visit to the US suggests that Qadhdhafi requested Jordan's mediation services in easing tension with Washington. Libya had already begun to foster ties with Jordan in 1999, pledging to fund the Disi drinking water project in southern Jordan, designed to alleviate the chronic shortages of drinking water in the capital in summer.[99]

Arab Summit

Libya took its customarily militant stance toward inter-Arab summit conferences, this time at the emergency gathering in Cairo on 21–22 October (see chapter on inter-Arab relations). While portraying this summit as "a futile undertaking" and deriding the proposed Egyptian draft of the final declaration in advance,[100] Libya nonetheless attended the forum, represented by its Arab League ambassador, Muhammad 'Abd al-Mun'im al-Huni. Libya wanted the conference to take a radical line toward Israel and sever Arab diplomatic ties with the "Zionist entity."[101] Since Qadhdhafi did not believe such an extreme line would be adopted by the summit, he ordered his representative to walk out in protest on the summit's first day. Libya also staged a nationwide demonstration on 23 October, with a banner denouncing the Arab leaders' actions as "unrepresentative of Arab public opinion."[102]

Arab Maghrib Union

Libya also revealed during 2000 a growing interest in reviving the dysfunctional Arab Maghrib Union and in boosting bilateral ties in this region. The first harbinger of tangible rapprochement in this arena took place with Tunisia. On 3–4 June, the Tunisian president, Zayn al-'Abidin Ben 'Ali, paid a visit to Libya. Qadhdhafi reciprocated with a visit to Tunis on 2–4 August. These two visits served to emphasize their countries' increasing economic cooperation. While in Tunis, the Libyan leader called for the formation of an African-Arab union to work in harmony with the requirements of globalization.[103] Qadhdhafi's bid to rebuild links in the Maghrib was further discernible through the visit of Algeria's president, 'Abd al-'Aziz Bouteflika, to Tripoli on 22 October 2000 (for more details on the Maghrib, see chapters on inter-Arab relations, Morocco, Tunisia and Algeria).

NOTES

For the place and frequency of publications cited here, and for the full name of the publication, news agency, radio station or monitoring service where an abbreviation is used, please see "List of Sources." Only in the case of more than one publication bearing the same name is the place of publication noted here.

1. *Al-Sharq al-Awsat*, 29 January 2000.
2. Ibid.
3. *Al-Hayat*, 29 February 2000.
4. *MEI*, 10 March 2000.
5. *ME*, July 2000.
6. *CR*, Libya, April 2000, p. 14.
7. For details on the Petroleum Law and the required changes, see *MET*, 15 June 2000.
8. *ME*, November 2000.
9. Muntasir died on 23 January 2001 after a long illness.
10. For more details, see *al-Sharq al-Awsat*, 3 March 2000.
11. Libyan TV, 1 March — BBC Monitoring, 3 March 2000.
12. Libyan TV, 2 March — BBC Monitoring, 6 March 2000.
13. *Al-Hayat*, 3 March 2000.
14. *MEI*, 10 March 2000.
15. *Al-Quds al-'Arabi*, 30 October 2000.

16. *Al-Quds al-'Arabi*, 7 October; *The Economist*, 14 October; *al-Hayat*, 19 October; *LNV*, 1 December 2000.
17. The Libyan minister for African unity, 'Abd al-Salam al-Turayki, in an interview with *al-Sharq al-Awsat*, 14 November 2000.
18. R. Tripoli, 9 October — BBC Monitoring, 10 October 2000.
19. PANA (Internet version), 5 October 2000 (DR).
20. *MEI*, 13 October 2000.
21. PANA (Internet version), 5 October 2000 (DR).
22. Libyan TV, 30 September — BBC Monitoring, 4 October 2000.
23. *Al-Sharq al-Awsat*, 17 July, 1 August, 2 October 2000.
24. *Al-Sharq al-Awsat*, 21 July, 1 August 2000.
25. For more details on the reshuffle, see Libyan TV, 30 September — BBC Monitoring, 4 October 2000.
26. *Al-Hayat*, 7 March; R. Islamabad, 30 June (DR); *al-Quds al-'Arabi*, 15 June; *al-Sharq al-Awsat*, 6 August, 4 October 2000.
27. Al-Jazira TV, 6 April — BBC Monitoring, 8 April 2000.
28. *Al-Sharq al-Awsat*, 5 August 2000.
29. *Al-Sharq al-Awsat*, 6 August 2000.
30. *Al-Sharq al-Awsat*, 16 August 2000.
31. *Al-Sharq al-Awsat*, 5, 7 September 2000.
32. JANA, 7 February — BBC Monitoring, 8 February 2000.
33. *WP*, 27 February 2000.
34. <www.CNN.com>, 25 March 2000.
35. Libyan TV, 4 May — BBC Monitoring, 6 May; *al-Hawadith*, 7 July 2000.
36. <www.CNN.com>, 25 March 2000.
37. *Al-Sharq al-Awsat*, 28 March 2000.
38. *LNV*, 29 April 2000.
39. *Al-Quds al-'Arabi*, 2 May 2000, quoting a statement by Libya's Foreign Affairs Ministry.
40. *LNV*, 17 February 2000.
41. For the full text of Neumann's testimony to the Senate, see Federal News Service, 4 May 2000.
42. *NYT*, 19 June 2000.
43. *Al-Sharq al-Awsat*, 13 May 2000.
44. E.g., *The Times*, 6 March; *LNV*, 5 May; *al-Hayat*, 29 August 2000.
45. <www.CNN.com>, 25 August 2000.
46. Al-Jazira TV, 3, 4 May — BBC Monitoring, 5 May 2000. The concise length of the chapter prevented a detailed report on the trial's proceedings.
47. *Al-Quds al-'Arabi*, 24 August 2000.
48. Libyan foreign minister 'Abd al-Rahman Muhammad Shalqam in an interview with *al-Sharq al-Awsat*, 15 September. For other similar clear signals, see also remarks by Shalqam in *al-Quds al-'Arabi*, 25 August and *al-Sharq al-Awsat*, 10 September 2000.
49. <www.CNN.com>, 7 September 2000.
50. Libyan TV, 28 October — BBC Monitoring, 30 October 2000.
51. *LNV*, 25 November 2000.
52. *Al-Sharq al-Awsat*, 26 November 2000, quoting "a prominent Libyan official" in a phone call.
53. *Al-Sharq al-Awsat*, 6 January; AFP, 22 January 2000 (DR).
54. MENA, 3 April 2000 (DR).
55. Libyan TV, 30 August — BBC Monitoring, 2 September 2000.
56. *ME*, November 2000.
57. *Al-Quds al-'Arabi*, 13 November; *LNV*, 16 November 2000.
58. *The Sunday Times*, 9 January 2000.
59. JANA, 10 January — BBC Monitoring, 12 January 2000.
60. *ARB*, January; *al-Sharq al-Awsat*, 12 January 2000.

61. JANA, 25 January — BBC Monitoring, 29 January 2000. Eventually Sa'd Mujabar was appointed a top position at Libya's Foreign Affairs Ministry in early March 2000.
62. Press Association (London), 14, 27 February (DR); *The Times*, 13 February; *ARB*, February 2000.
63. *LNV*, 31 May; *ARB*, June 2000.
64. <www.CNN.com>, 12 August 2000.
65. <www.CNN.com>, 28 August 2000.
66. Libyan TV, 18 August — BBC Monitoring, 21 August 2000.
67. *Al-Quds al-'Arabi*, 31 August, 22 September 2000.
68. For more details, see Libyan TV, 29 August — BBC Monitoring, 31 August 2000.
69. *Al-Quds al-'Arabi*, 13 September 2000.
70. *AW*, 21 September 2000.
71. *LNV*, 10 September 2000.
72. *LNV*, 29 February, 8 June; *MET*, 2 March; BTA, 1, 2, 8 March 2000 (DR).
73. *LNV*, 23, 28 February; BTA, 24 February 2000 (DR).
74. *Al-Quds al-'Arabi*, 5 June; MENA, 10 June (DR); BTA, 22 June 2000 (DR).
75. R. Sofia, 31 May — BBC Monitoring, 2 June 2000.
76. BTA, 28 June (DR); *MET*, 15 June 2000.
77. *ARB*, June 2000, quoting a Russian source.
78. ITAR-TASS, 31 July 2000 (DR).
79. Ibid; Interfax, 31 July 2000 (DR).
80. *JP*, 17 November 2000.
81. *ARB*, January 2000.
82. AFP, 5 February 2000 (DR).
83. Libyan TV, 11 March — BBC Monitoring, 13 March 2000.
84. *ARB*, July 2000.
85. Ibid.
86. For more details, see ibid.; R. Paris, 10 July 2000 (DR).
87. AFP, 10 July 2000 (DR).
88. *Al-Sharq al-Awsat*, 12 July 2000.
89. E.g., *al-Khartum*, 6 July; AFP, 6, 13 July; R. Accra, 7 July 2000 (DR).
90. A wide range of foreign media sources resorted to the term of "racist attacks," quoting the African victims themselves, e.g., *al-Quds al-'Arabi*, 6, 10 October; *MET*, 10, 22 October; *al-Hayat*, 19 October 2000.
91. *LNV*, 27, 30 September; *MM*, 12 October 2000.
92. *The Economist*, 14 October 2000.
93. PANA (Internet version), 8 October (DR); *AC*, 13 October; *The Economist*, 14 October 2000.
94. AFP, 24 November (DR); *LNV*, 20 December 2000.
95. R. Tripoli, 9 October — BBC Monitoring, 10 October 2000, in a message to Ghana's president, Jerry Rawlings.
96. *LNV*, 9 November 2000.
97. JANA, 20 January — BBC Monitoring, 22 January; *al-Khartum*, 14 March 2000, respectively (Djibouti had broken off its ties in November 1998 after the Eritrean president, Issaya Afeworki, accused it of being involved in Ethiopia's war effort against Eritrea. Djibouti, for its part, accused Eritrea of supporting the Afar rebellion).
98. Libyan TV, 4 October — BBC Monitoring, 4 October 2000.
99. *MM*, 19 September 2000.
100. Al-Jazira TV, 17 October — BBC Monitoring, 18 October, an interview with Qadhdhafi, and JANA, 7 October — BBC Monitoring, 8 October 2000.
101. *LNV*, 22 October 2000.
102. *LNV*, 24 October 2000.
103. *Al-Sharq al-Awsat*, 4 August 2000.

Morocco
(Al-Mamlaka al-Maghribiyya)

BRUCE MADDY-WEITZMAN

The first full year of King Muhammad VI's reign was one of considerable uncertainty. His ascencion in mid-1999, following the death of his father, King Hasan II (see *MECS*, 1999, pp. 426–29) generated hopes for a more dynamic, prosperous and liberal era. While still feeling his way, Muhammad's image as a kinder, gentler monarch, aware of Morocco's problems and of the urgent need for their amelioration, remained intact. What was less clear was how far he intended to go in attempting to remake the Moroccan polity, and how exactly he could translate his desires into action. By the end of the year, some of the glow surrounding Muhammad's reign had worn off; the once-promising *alternance* government of Prime Minister Abderrahmane El You y in the government were sympathetic to the reformist agenda. In the meantime, civic groups, from Islamists to liberal human rights activists and women's organizations, were increasingly vocal. The Islamist current appeared increasingly confident that its message was being heard. Indeed, its ability to mobilize support for public activities had never seemed so strong. With traditional opposition parties constituting the basis of the *alternance* government, one was increasingly hard pressed to find any credible political and social opposition in society other than the Islamists. Still, leading Moroccan scholars on its Islamist movements called them a "convenient distraction," enabling the government to keep a tight lid on public life and to avoid meaningful political liberalization.[1] From another direction, demands by various civic groups for the recognition of Berber cultural rights gained momentum with the issuing of the "Berber Manifesto" by 229 intellectuals.[2] All hints of Sahrawi activism in the Western Sahara and in Morocco proper were treated harshly by the authorities.

Efforts to "turn the page" regarding past human rights abuses had been gingerly initiated during the early 1990s by King Hasan, and gradually gathered momentum throughout the decade (see *MECS*, 1993, chapter on Maghrib affairs, and *MECS* volumes 1994-1999, chapters on Morocco). Under Muhammad, the pace continued to accelerate. Emboldened by modest successes, human rights groups continued to press for fuller restitution for abuses perpetrated by the authorities during the political struggles of the 1960s and 1970s. Moreover, they redoubled calls to bring perpetrators of state-sponsored abuses to justice. Other aspects of struggles of the 1960s and the 1970s also intruded on the public agenda. The Ben Barka affair continued to generate new revelations; the accusation that Youssoufi and others on the left had supported the failed military coup against King Hasan in 1972 generated a storm of controversy.

The failure of late winter rains and resulting severe drought for the second consecutive year led to near-zero growth in the GDP. International financial institutions continued to applaud Morocco's record in the macroeconomic sphere. However, they also noted with concern the slow-down in growth rates during the preceding decade and accompanying

413

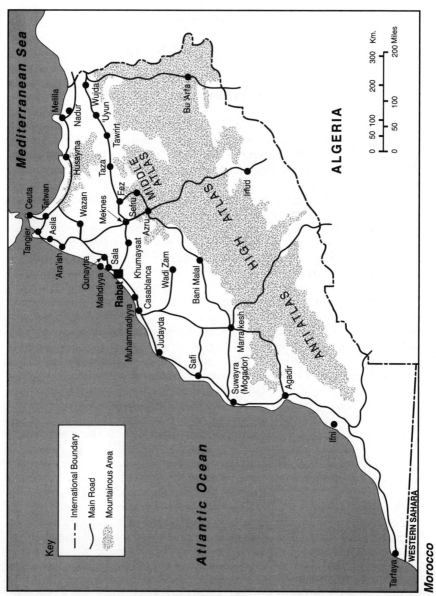

Key

--- International Boundary

— Main Road

Mountainous Area

Mediterranean Sea

ALGERIA

Atlantic Ocean

Morocco

WESTERN SAHARA

0 50 100 200 300 Km.

0 50 100 200 Miles

Melilla
Nadur
Wujda
'Uyun
Bu Arfa
Tawirt
Husayna
Taza
Fez
MIDDLE ATLAS
Ifrud
HIGH ATLAS
Ceuta
Tatwan
Tangier
Asila
Wazan
Meknes
Sefro
Azru
'Ara'ish
Qunaytra
Sala
Khumaysat
ANTI ATLAS
Mahdiyya
Rabat
Casablanca
Wadi Zam
Bani Malal
Muhammadiyya
Judayda
Safi
Marrakesh
Suwayra
(Mogador)
Agadir
Ifni
Tarfaya

rise in poverty and unemployment. According to official figures, the number of Moroccans living in poverty had risen two-thirds between 1991–99, from 3.2m. (13%) to 5.3m. (19%), with children below the age of fifteen the worst affected (44.2%), and rural areas accounting for 65.8% of the total.[3] The pace of privatization slowed substantially, although an important sale was made in December. King Muhammad devoted considerable energy to development and welfare projects designed to cope with the crushing poverty. A government reshuffle in September was designed to inject new dynamism into economic policy-making.

Diplomatic efforts to resolve the Western Sahara issue registered no progress, despite the renewal of efforts by UN special representative James Baker. Baker's attempts to forge acceptable parameters for a referendum in the territory or, alternatively, an agreement between Morocco and the Algerian-backed Polisario movement included a number of meetings between the two sides, but no tangible results. Consequently, Moroccan hopes for a thaw with Algeria remained unfulfilled, and the five-nation Arab Maghrib Union (AMU) remained dormant. King Muhammad made a number of high-profile visits abroad. In particular, his trips to France, Spain and the US were designed to project an image of dynamism and renewal toward Morocco's most important Western allies, attract political and economic support and ameliorate outstanding problems, particularly with Spain. In the Arab-Israeli arena, Muhammad sought to follow his father's traditional policy of engagement with Israel while wrapping himself in the mantle of Islamic piety and support for Arab-Israeli dialogue. But as Arab-Israeli tension increased, reverberating in the Moroccan domestic arena as well, Muhammad was compelled to fall in line with the Arab consensus and break off the low-level diplomatic relations with Israel that had been established in 1994.

INTERNAL AFFAIRS

THE KING, THE GOVERNMENT AND THE *MAKHZEN*
Muhammad had moved swiftly during his first months on the throne to carve out the image of a kinder king bent on improving the lot of the poor, healing past wounds, and liberalizing political life. Nothing seemed to symbolize his intent better than his sacking of long-time Minister of Interior Driss Basri, the man who held many of the keys to the authority of the *makhzen* (establishment), in November 1999, and his replacement of forty-four ministry-appointed *wali*s and governors the following month (see *MECS* 1999, pp. 432-34). In January, the king called for a "new concept of authority," based on fairness, transparency and the rule of law, and this became a regular theme of subsequent speeches. In his Throne Day speech on 30 July, for example, he spoke of making authority "look after public interests, manage local issues, protect security and stability, protect individual and public liberties and open it up through direct contact with them...." What this meant exactly for relations between the monarchy and the state remained to be seen. In the meantime, Muhammad's disdain for some of the more ostentatious aspects of the monarchy (for example, closing down the royal harem and avoiding his father's palaces) helped to project an image of an accessible and concerned ruler. Moreover, in "reminding" the government to "carry out social investments through the formulation of...effective public policy," the king confirmed his commitment to political reform.[4]

Throughout the year, the king continued to be visible, participating in numerous ceremonies to launch various development projects such as water supply facilities, dams and roads, visiting the poor, and allocating funds for social welfare and job creation. The impoverished northern and eastern provinces, long-neglected by the central authorities, received special attention. Muhammad had made a high-profile, historic visit there in October 1999 (see *MECS*, 1999, p. 431), and returned there again in February, as well as visiting the area in disguise. The king's preferred vehicle for promoting development and social welfare was the Hasan II Fund for Economic and Social Development, which he created shortly after ascending the throne. The fund, he said, was a way to ensure a "social economy," one which mixed economic activity with social solidarity.[5] By the end of the summer, it had designated thirty-nine projects for investment, for a total of Dh16bn. ($1.5 bn.), to be financed largely by the proceeds from the funds raised by the awarding of the second Moroccan mobile phone license in 1999. Future earnings from the anticipated privatization of large state-owned firms like Maroc Télécom and Royal Air Maroc were also designated for use by the fund.[6]

The king's Throne Day speech, marking the first anniversary of his ascension, listed the projects and measures he intended to advance. He thereby emphasized continuity with the long reign of his father and the need to innovate in light of "the real and concrete problems of its future generations." A "comprehensive modernization" of state institutions, he said, would enable the construction of a "future democratic, modern and strong Morocco." To that end, Muhammad promised an imminent outline of a "big democratic leap," based on the decentralization of local, provincial and regional councils. Hasan had long mooted the idea, and initial steps had been made in that direction. The councils, said Muhammad, would combine "democratic training and rational [administrative] divisions, and effective, transparent and sound management," and would work in partnership with the state, the private sector and civil society. He also announced the intention to set up an economic and social council, as provided for by the Moroccan constitution, which would be led by "an elite of experts" who would complement elected institutions. Other priorities included "healing the wounds" of past human rights abuses while concentrating on the future, and insuring that the coming decade would be the "decade of education and training," the "second national priority" (after confirming "territorial integrity," i.e,. incorporating the Western Sahara). By the year 2010, the "effect of illiteracy and useless education" would have decreased tangibly.

Interior Minister Ahmed Midaoui complemented the king's efforts by launching a concerted campaign to audit the finances of local authorities in order to tackle corruption and lack of accountability. Corrupt local judges and irregular banking practices were also targeted.[7]

At the same time, a number of tough measures were taken during the year, indicating that the particular brand of authoritarian rule in Morocco was not going to undergo radical revisions in the near future. This was particularly relevant to press freedom. The lively liberal weeklies *Le Journal, Demain* and *al-Sahifa* repeatedly tested the limits of the permissible and ran afoul of the authorities. *Le Journal*'s publication in mid-April of an interview with Polisario Front leader Muhammad 'Abd al-Aziz prompted its temporary banning, together with its sister publication *al-Sahifa,* by order of Prime Minister Youssoufi. The regime's sensitivity to anything which might call into question the Moroccan claim to the Western Sahara was further demonstrated by the firing of the three top officials of the state-run 2M television station for allowing the *Le Journal* interview to be mentioned on its evening newscast. Interior Minister Midaoui reportedly used harsh language in threatening *Le Journal* editor Aboubakr Jamai with further measures if he conducted further interviews with Polisario officials, drawing a protest to the prime minister from the international NGO, Reporteurs Sans Frontières (RSF).[8]

In a separate episode, the publisher of a popular weekly and a journalist were both fined, sentenced to prison and banned from journalism for defaming Moroccan foreign minister Muhammad Benaissa by accusing him of corruption and mismanagement while serving as ambassador to the US in the 1990s. The court action, a response to Benaissa's lawsuit against the two, prompted protests from the journalists' union. King Muhammad intervened, granting them both a royal pardon.

The authorities were also sensitive to media exposure of past human rights abuses. On 8–10 October, three French television journalists were held under house arrest for reporting on the demonstration by the human rights group Forum for Truth and Justice at the notorious former secret detention center, Tazmamart. On 5 November, the AFP bureau chief in Rabat was expelled for an accumulation of reports over several years that the authorities claimed cast Moroccan policies in an unfavorable light.[9]

In December, the authorities' heavy hand was repeatedly felt, apparently to serve notice on all and sundry — journalists, activists, and reformers and critics of any other stripe — that there were clear limits to liberalization. On 26 November, *Le Journal,* and *al-Sahifa* published a letter alleging that Prime Minister Youssoufi and fellow left-wing leaders had been party in 1972 to the failed coup of Gen. Muhammad Oufkir against King Hasan.[10] It quickly became known that the letter had been written in 1974 by Muhammad Faqih Basri. Basri was one of the leading figures of the Moroccan Left who had returned from exile in 1995 (see *MECS*, 1995, pp. 498–99, 502). The letter had been written to Abderahim Bouabid, then the leader of the Union Socialistes des forces populaires (USFP) and also a supposed party to the plot. The accusation created a mini-sensation, of sorts, in the country. On 2 December, the two weeklies, together with *Demain,* which had reported on the letter, were banned indefinitely, with Youssoufi invoking the highly controversial Article 77 of the Press Code. The code allowed both the prime minister and the interior minister to ban any publication that "threatens the kingdom's political and religious foundations." The following day, the three editors-in-chief of the banned publications vigorously criticized the ban as "a manifestation of intellectual terrorism." Domestic and international NGOs also protested the ban, while two of three journals filed suit against the government. *Le Journal*, in the meantime, sought approval for a new publication[11] (for more on the political fallout of the episode, see below). *Le Journal*'s Jamai subsequently wrote that the affair highlighted the existence of a "holy alliance" between the royal administration and the political leaderships who were out of touch with their grass roots. They formed "a real anti-democratic, law-and-order party that cuts across institutions and political parties." The influence of this "undercover party," he said, could only be reduced by transparent elections. Parties needed to be organized along "truly democratic lines," and "a new balance struck between the powers of the monarchy and parliament."[12]

One week after the crackdown on the press, the authorities moved forcefully against striking unemployed graduates, Islamist demonstrators (see below) and human rights activists protesting peacefully on the anniversary of the Universal Declaration of Human Rights. Forty activists from the independent Association marocaine des droits de l'homme (AMDH) and the Forum for Truth and Justice, including AMDH president Abderrahmane Benameur, were arrested after being attacked by security forces. Thirty-three of the demonstrators were to be tried in February 2001.[13] The background to the latest events was a decade-long effort by King Hasan to improve the international image of Morocco on human rights matters, owing to its previously abysmal record. Muhammad had displayed an interest in accelerating those efforts, in order to definitively "turn the page." In July 2000, the Royal Arbitration Commission, which had been established by Muhammad the previous August, announced final compensation settlements for sixty-eight cases, benefiting a total of 354 persons, with payments ranging between $25,000 and $350,000. Preliminary compensation was also paid to a number of Sahrawis and family members who had also been detained or had "disappeared." But critics continued to try to hold the authorities' feet to the fire, citing the arbitrary compensation process and the settling of only a small number of the 5,900 claims filed with the commission. Moreover, even as the authorities permitted the publication of books and articles detailing some of the darker sides of Morocco's past, human rights groups continued to press for full disclosure, compensation and, most disturbingly to some portions of the *makhzen,* bringing the perpetrators of past abuses, mostly from the turbulent 1970s and early 1980s, to justice. In particular, the Forum for Truth and Justice, created in 1999 by victims of forced disappearance and their relatives (see *MECS* 1999, p. 437), demanded public investigations and trials, when warranted.[14]

In February, a retired secret police officer, Muhammad Kholti, became the first member of the security forces to openly admit to torturing political dissidents during the 1970s and 1980s, asking for forgiveness in a letter to two national newspapers. The issue gained further momentum when the AMDH distributed on 23 October an 'open letter to the minister of justice' listing the names of fourteen alleged former torturers and officials involved in disappearances and arbitrary detention. Among those mentioned were the current head of the Royal Gendarmerie and secret services, Gen. Housni Benslimane, as well as former interior minister Driss Basri. In keeping with its independent, critical stance, *Le Journal* was the first Moroccan publication to publish the list.[15] The move clearly upset the security establishment, leading to the violent crackdown in December (against Islamist groups as well; see below). Concurrently, the harsh punishment (five years imprisonment, subsequently reduced to 2 1/2 years) imposed by the army on Capt. Mustafa Adib for exposing corruption among senior officers (leading Amnesty International to identify him as a "prisoner of conscience") indicated the military's sensitivity to challenges to its domain.[16] Where the young king stood with regard to this reassertion of *makhzen* authority could not be determined. His response to those who criticized as inadequate official bodies dealing with human rights issues did indicate, however, that maintaining social and political control was no less important than promoting liberalization.

Political Affairs

Prime Minister Youssoufi pointed to a number of achievements of his government as it entered its third year: bringing order to the management of the national finances, improving the system of taxation, and breathing life into several "very sick" institutions, such as the social security fund. To be sure, the country was "still frail," and the process of change was hard and long, requiring "patience and perseverance." Signs of success were already being witnessed in the main urban areas. However, he said, "the countryside and the mountains are so neglected that we are embarrassed." Nonetheless, Morocco was proceeding on the right path and was now in a "state of convalescence."[17]

As the year progressed, criticism of alleged government immobilism heightened. Youssoufi again refuted the charges in an interview, pointing to the creation of "a new atmosphere conducive to the rule of law and the defense of individual and public freedoms," as well as numerous steps in the field of civil service reform and social affairs. He could sense the people's impatience, he said, and acknowledged that his party had "adopted middle-class values," opening the way for the Islamists to cultivate the "natural electorate," of the left wing, namely the urban poor.[18]

Tension between the USFP and the Istiqlal, the two leading partners of the Kutla Dimuqratiyya (Democratic Bloc) which formed the basis of the Youssoufi *alternance* government, continued to be part of the Moroccan political landscape. Although Istiqlal candidates had received nearly as many votes in the 1997 election as those of the USFP, the USFP had garnered 52 parliamentary seats, and the Istiqlal only 32, making Youssoufi the undisputed candidate of the Kutla for the prime ministership, and the Istiqlal a decidedly junior partner. The Istiqlal had immediately lodged protests against widespread electoral fraud but to no avail. After considerable debate, it decided to participate in the *alternance*, Youssoufi-led government. However, over time, the Istiqlal increasingly voiced criticism of the government performance, and even threatened at times to leave the government. The size of the government — forty-one cabinet members — was a favorite target,[19] and the king himself spoke disapprovingly of its bloated nature. The Kutla itself, formed eight years earlier with much fanfare (see *MECS*, 1993, pp. 88–92), was dormant as a political force. It met rarely as a group, and was not considered by Youssoufi as a "core source" for his policy making. Nor did it act as a watchdog for government action, as the Istiqlal secretary-general Abbas al-Fassi had initially envisaged.[20]

The government streamlining in September resulted in the loss of two ministries previously under Istiqlal control, to the party's chagrin (see below). Some in the party were even more disturbed by the fact that secretary-general Fassi personally benefited from the reshuffle, being appointed minister of employment and social development. On 20 September, Khalid Jamai, Istiqlal Executive Bureau member, was removed from his long-held position as editor-in-chief of the party daily *L'Opinion,* following criticism of al-Fassi for joining the government instead of preparing the party for new elections, and earlier criticism of communications minister Messari's measures against *Le Journal.* The following month, Jamai announced the creation of a "reformist current" within the party which, acting together with like-minded groups in other Kutla parties, would provide the only hope for averting an electoral debacle vis-à-vis the Islamists in the forthcoming 2002 legislative elections.[21] In October, further differences between the Istiqlal and the USFP surfaced during the election to the presidency of the Chamber of Councillors; the USFP were unwilling to support a potential Istiqlal candidate, leading to the election of Mustapha Oukacha of the centrist Rassemblement national des indépendents (RNI).[22] Nonetheless, despite the grumblings and accompanying internal divisions, the Istiqlal continued in 2000 to prefer to try to influence public affairs from the inside, along with the accompanying privileges, to returning to the political opposition. Hopefully, said secretary-general Abbas al-Fassi, the 2002 elections would be fair, and would lead to more suitable results.[23]

As the year wore on, immobilism increasingly appeared to be the defining characteristic of the government. One commentator challenged this perception, arguing, for example, that it had instituted a number of reforms in the areas of health, education, and finance.[24]

But clearly, the effects of the reforms were yet to be felt by the populace, or have an impact on the economy. The mood was reflected in the results of six by-elections for parliamentary seats: only one seat was won by a member of the Kutla. The negative image of the government actions was reinforced by the image of the Chamber of Councillors. Established with much fanfare as part of the ongoing democratization process in Morocco, it was widely perceived as serving no positive function, and perhaps even as a tool to block the government from carrying out far-reaching change. Some commentators suggested that it should be eliminated.[25] Elections for one-third (ninety) of the deputies were held on 15 September, and even Interior Minister Midaoui acknowledged the problem of widespread vote-buying in the elections.[26]

After months of intense negotiations, the long-mooted government streamlining and reorganization was announced on 6 September, with a 33-member cabinet, consisting of twenty-three ministers (including the prime minister), three minister-delegates, six ministers of state, and the government secretary-general. (The outgoing cabinet had had forty-one posts.) Some of its functions were now consolidated and others eliminated, with some ministers assuming different or additional responsibilities, and others not returning to the cabinet. Twenty ministers from the previous cabinet remained in existing or enlarged posts, while nine others assumed other positions. The cabinet included only one woman, down from two in the previous one — Nezha Chekrouni of the USFP, whose enhanced duties as a junior minister included responsibility for the affairs of women, family and children, as well as the disabled.[27] Seven posts were held by independents, including those of the minister of interior and his deputy. The number of cabinet seats held by the USFP was now ten, down from fourteen. USFP ministers who lost their positions were: Khalid Alioua, the influential minister of social development, solidarity, employment and vocational training, who had struggled earlier in the year with the labor unions in order to avoid a general strike; Habib Malki, the minister of agriculture, rural development and fisheries; Hasan Sebbar, minister of tourism; and Ahmad Laraki, a junior-level cabinet member. But the USFP still dominated among the parties. In fact, two of the three economic "super-ministries" were placed in USFP hands, those of Fathallah Oualalou and Ahmed Lahlimi, with the third going to Mustapha Mansouri of the RNI. As minister of employment, vocational training and social development, Fassi of the Istiqlal was also placed in a central and difficult post. The Istiqlal lost two ministries, leaving it with four, and four of its ministers were not returned to the reshuffled cabinet: Minister of Communications Muhammad Larbi Messari, who had sought to liberalize the state audio-visual news media, Minister of Energy and Mines Youssef Tahiri, who was heavily criticized for exaggerating the size of the oil find during the summer (see below), Minister of the Public Sector and Privatization Rashid al-Filali and Minister of Health Abdelouahed al-Fassi. The RNI lost one of its six positions, the Mouvement national populaire (MNP) stayed at three, the Front des forces démocratiques (FFD) one of two, and the Parti du progrès et du Socialisme (PPS) one of three: the secretary of state to the minister of social development in charge of social family and child protection, Muhammad Said Essaadi, who had spearheaded the plan to promote the integration of women in national development which had sparked a strong backlash from Islamist and traditional forces (see below). Thami Khyari of the FFD, who had been the point man in the sensitive fisheries negotiations with Spain, moved to the public health ministry.[28] 'Abdallah Saaf of the Parti socialiste démocratique (PSD) was upgraded from minister-delegate to minister of national education. (For the complete list of the new cabinet, see appendix one.)

Opposition parties belonging to the center-right *wifaq* bloc were dismissive of the government reshuffle. Demanding a change of direction in order to solve the pressing social and economic problems of Morocco, they complained that they had not been considered for cabinet posts, or even consulted.[29]

The Basri letter and the closure of the publications that printed it created considerable controversy. For some time, Basri had been sharply critical of the performance of the *alternance* government, led by his former comrade-in-arms. A copy of the text itself was provided to *Le Journal* by Omar al-Sirghoushni, a veteran leftist opposition figure residing in Paris.[30] But it seemed clear that Basri had approved his action. He had thereby thrown down the gauntlet, reminding the public, and particularly those preparing for the long-delayed USFP party congress in February 2001, that Youssoufi and the Left had once stood for a different, more principled vision than the one being pursued. The facts of history, he said, "need to be resurrected, warts and all, in order to build the future on firm and uncorrupted principles." The closure of the three weeklies, as well as the publication of the USFP youth movement, indicated that hopes for fundamental change were "wishful thinking."[31]

Unable to persuade Basri to disavow the letter, Youssoufi took the offensive; the USFP newspapers, the palace daily and state television all sharply attacked Basri and the offending weeklies, for spreading diabolic falsehoods designed to destabilize the country.[32] The USFP political bureau also rallied to his side.[33] King Muhammad, for his part, expressed "absolute support" for his prime minister.[34] Youssoufi brushed off the charge itself, explaining that he was representing the party in exile at that time, after having been sentenced to death in 1964 for allegedly plotting to kill the king (the sentence was later commuted). He had no problem with the king in those days, he said, only with the undemocratic *pouvoir*.[35] As for the relationship between the past and the present, Youssoufi had already made it clear that he favored repairing damages to citizens caused by past injustices. However, he told an interviewer, it was important to concentrate primarily on the future, and not allow the debate over the past "to be an opportunity for a settling of scores or demands for revenge or a sort of civil war that would take on a legal or intellectual form."[36]

THE ISLAMIST CURRENT

The Islamist current in Morocco displayed increasing confidence and registered a number of important successes in 2000. Shaykh 'Abd al-Salam Yasin, seventy-two year old spiritual leader of the most important Islamist organization, Jama't al-'Adl wal-Ihsan (Justice and Charity Group; JCG) was released from house arrest in mid-May, after more than ten years of confinement. The JCG, together with the Islamist Parti du justice et developpement (PJD; Hizb al-'Adala wal-Tanmiya), which held ten seats in parliament, portions of the Istiqlal and conservative, tradition-minded bodies made an impressive show of force in March, mobilizing 150,000–200,000 marchers in Casablanca against proposed changes in the *mudawanna* (personal status code), changes which were part of a government plan to improve the status of women (see below). As in previous years, the JCG challenged the authorities by running popular summer "camps" at selected Moroccan beaches. Its activities on university campuses also led to clashes with security forces.

The harsh treatment of Yasin by the authorities had begun in 1974, following his missive to King Hasan, "Islam or the Deluge," in which he called for the abolition of the Moroccan monarchy because it was un-Islamic. He was incarcerated, often in psychiatric wards, for almost a decade. In 1989, he was placed under house arrest, which continued uninterrupted apart from a few days in 1995, when he was allowed to preach in a neighboring mosque, only to have the authorities retract their decision following his public comments attacking the regime (see *MECS* 1995, pp. 502–3). The new atmosphere engendered during Muhmmad VI's first months on the throne included speculation regarding Yasin's possible release, in line with the desire of the new ruler and government to remove controversial subjects from the public agenda so as to better pursue reformist goals (see *MECS*, 1999, pp. 439–40). By the end of 1999, Yasin's release seemed to be merely a matter of time.

The late king Hasan had governed adroitly with various combinations of carrot-and-stick policies, co-opting large segments of the political elite, and employing tough measures against those who resisted his blandishments. Yasin was dealt with harshly during his first decade of incarceration, although not nearly as harshly as those from the army who had plotted the king's overthrow in the early 1970s and from the radical left opposition. Throughout the 1990s, during Hasan's more benevolent, reformist phase, the authorities tried any number of times to strike a deal with Yasin in return for his release, but without success. Emboldened by the new atmosphere brought on by Hasan's death, and his standing as a *cause célèbre* among the human rights community in Morocco, he chose to challenge Muhammad with a 35-page memorandum analyzing the current plight of Morocco and providing recommendations to ameliorate it. The memorandum was sent to the king on 14 November 1999; its existence was made public on 28 January 2000; extracts were published in *Le Monde* and *Le Figaro* and the full text was posted on the Internet. It was a unique document, which shed much light on the thinking of the leading Moroccan Islamist at a time of great flux.

The memorandum was written in French, for two reasons: to communicate immediately with diplomatic and "politico-media authorities," and to appeal to the "French-speaking elite," in Morocco which scorns the Arabic language as a "vernacular...used only to communicate with the illiterate people." It was elliptically addressed "to he who is concerned," to avoid violation of Article 23 of the Moroccan constitution which declares the person of the king to be "inviolable and sacred." Cynical, sarcastic and hard-hitting, it blamed the *makhzen*, headed by the late king Hasan, for the underlying social, economic and political problems in Morocco, in a manner which often resembled the longstanding critiques of secular left-wing oppositionists. Destitution, corruption and hopelessness were the characteristics of Moroccan society, he said, and were the direct outgrowth of decades of systematic "looting" of the public patrimony by the royal family and those in its service. This ongoing plundering was epitomized by the activities of Omnium Nord Afrique (ONA), the giant conglomerate, valued at $40m.-50m., which dominated the Moroccan economy and whose privileges "turned it into a monstrous leech that sucks astronomical profits into the accounts of the deceased majesty."

Being "innocent of past crimes," he said, it was up to the "novice" "king of the poor" to make "a decisive break with the past," to demonstrate that he was not a "spineless character and a puppet in the hands of the shrewd and scheming figures of the palace." To be sure, the king's "new style" was a step forward. But "media incantation," which the new king's advisers seemed to think would "easily erase from people's minds the evil memory of the period in which Tazmamart torturers ruled supreme" was not sufficient. "Doing justice to an oppressed person here and delivering a well-structured speech there do not suffice to remedy a difficult situation." What was needed was "effective action that would change the method of government and establish real justice, sensible education and social justice that would abolish privileges and bridge the wide gap between the haves and the have-nots." This gap, he said, was starkly made clear by UN social and economic indicators, which he quoted in detail. Failure to do so would subject Morocco to the "blade" of the open market with Europe due to come into force in 2010. Given the enormous Moroccan debt, on the one hand, and fabulous wealth of the royal family, on the other, he said, there was an "obvious and radical solution" to Moroccan poverty: settle external debt, an estimated $22bn., with the family fortune, and allocate the money used to pay off the debt for public investment in education and infrastructure. Along the way, Morocco would be "liberated...from the yoke of the World Bank," whose "ruthless" strictures regarding structural adjustment had "socially struck Morocco down."

Of course, what distinguished Yasin's critique from the radical left was that its ultimate frame of reference was Islam, an Islam which, in his view, was imbued with the principles of justice and righteousness and utterly opposed to the opulence associated with absolute monarchies. "Poor Hasan II! Instead of behaving like a mortal concerned with his destiny after death...he thought he was eternal. He granted himself sacred status and his poets and flatterers carte blanche to adore him," and annually compelled the kingdom's dignitaries to participate in the "sacrilegious," "pagan" ritual of the *makhzen bay'a* (reaffirming their loyalty to the king).

Yasin recommended that Muhammad follow the lead of a "matchless figure" in early Islamic history, the Umayyad ruler 'Umar (II) bin 'Abd al-'Aziz (ruled 99/717–101/720), who returned expropriated wealth to the population and ordered the royal family to do the same.[37] He also recommended that the king read the Qur'anic verses and teachings of the Prophet detailing the punishment reserved for despots. Restore the "legitimate belongings" of the people, he advised Muhammad, and thus "save your poor father from torment," i.e., sons could redeem the sins of their fathers and actually rescue them from eternal damnation.

To be sure, Yasin said, his movement would remain skeptical regarding "a possible global redemption" by the new king. "However, aware of the gradual nature of any restoration, we are not in any hurry. We will remain, in line with the Islamic logic, the 'tranquille de proposition'[peaceful option]." Nor was he opposed to the monarchy per se. Once the royal family acted in the proper fashion, it would win popular recognition and, most importantly, divine consent. By setting a personal example, he said, Morocco could begin the march towards "genuine democracy...the only way out of dark absolutism. Such a formula would combine modern democratic procedure with the spiritual and moral values of Islam.

Yasin's memorandum was directed nearly entirely inward, toward the woes which the late king Hasan, together with his cronies and sycophants, had brought to Morocco. The West was mentioned only in passing, mostly in the context of the negative consequences of globalization and its pernicious influence on the "Westernized elite" of Morocco. Saudi Arabia, a crucial financial supporter of Hasan's military campaign to incorporate the Western Sahara, drew nary a comment. But Yasin did expound at length on one particular foreign friend of Hasan: "cosmopolitan Zionist Jewry." Hasan, he said, "spared no effort to please the "chosen people," leading some people to characterize his form of rule as a "Judaeocracy." This link, which "betrays our Palestinian brothers and fellow Muslims...seriously offends Islam and morals" and should be disavowed by Muhammad. However, the task would not be easy, since his father's "accomplices" (a reference, among others, to the king's financial adviser Andre Azoulay, a Moroccan Jew) would surely resist. "Jewish connivance" with Hasan, he said, was also evidenced by fact that a published ranking of Hasan as one of the world's richest men was quickly "conjured away," thanks to Jewish control of the Western media ("We know very well who are the media tycoons in America and elsewhere.")[38]

The authorities, while desiring to downplay the importance of the memorandum, were initially unsure how to act. On 5 February, several newspapers that contained the memorandum were temporarily confiscated from newsstands in major cities, but returned that same day. A few days later, Communications Minister Larbi Messari declared that the memorandum had not been banned; in any event it was available on the Internet, the confiscation was "incidental," and censorship was "absurd", and no longer practiced in the country. Concurrently, four members of the JCG were briefly detained in Tangiers and Ben Slimane for distributing the memorandum, but the charges against them — "violating the sacred institution of the monarchy" — were dropped.[39]

While the media generally ignored or downplayed the memorandum, it was widely discussed in private. One journalist reported that it had sent a "shudder of fear" through Moroccan high society.[40] An official of the formerly communist PPS, one of the smaller members of the ruling coalition, declared that the memorandum was "devoid of political sense," while veteran MNP leader Mahjoubi Ahardane declared that Yasin had crossed the line of the permissible.[41] Robert Assaraf, president of the International Center for Research of Moroccan Jewry and long-time confidant of the royal family, attacked Yasin for promoting "religious fanaticism and racism." He contrasted Yasin with Hasan who always advocated peace between Jews and Muslims, and between Israelis, Palestinians and Arabs, and who, as a good Muslim, respected the Peoples of the Book (Jews and Christians).[42] Ahmad Raissouni, one of the leading figures in Islah wal-Tawhid, the Islamist group which underpinned the PJD, agreed with the balance sheet drawn up by Yasin regarding Morocco's difficulties. However, he criticized the memorandum's form and style as damaging, particularly its focus on the royal family's fortune and its failure to recognize the positive changes introduced under the new king's rule. A commentator in *Maroc Hebdo* characterized the missive as an "insidious attack" on the king, who represented a "great hope" for the state, as intolerable, provocative and a violation of the national consensus.[43]

Yasin's letter was denounced by the 'Ulama Councils, an official state body. The missive, they said, was an unacceptable challenge to the legitimacy of the Moroccan ruler, the *amir al-mu'minin* (commander of the faithful; a title of both religious and temporal significance, inscribed in the Moroccan constitution), in violation of the Qur'anic injunction to "obey God, and obey the Messenger and those in authority among you..." Verse 4:59). However, the authorities generally refrained from comment, and took no practical measures against Yasin. On 2 February, Justice Minister Omar Azziman announced that a "negotiated solution" was being discussed which would permit Yasin to carry out his activities while respecting the "rules of democratic law." On 21 February, Yasin's family and a JCG official were prevented from boarding a plane to Saudi Arabia to perform the pilgrimage. They immediately staged a protest at the Interior Ministry, and within a few days, the matter was settled to their satisfaction. The episode indicated the obvious uncertainty of the authorities as how to treat Yasin and his movement.[44]

On Monday 15 May, Yasin notified the authorities that he intended to leave his home on Friday of that week to attend prayers at a nearby mosque in Sale. Interior Minister Midaoui responded the next day, saying that Yasin was "free to go were he liked." Whether this was an attempt by Yasin to force the issue of his continued incarceration or whether it was a pre-arranged script could not be determined. In any case, a large crowd of followers joyfully accompanied Yasin to the mosque. Unlike his aborted release in 1996, he did not preach at the mosque, only prayed. Reactions among the Moroccan political class to the lifting of the ban were favorable: the Kutla parties had long advocated his release, both on human rights and political grounds, favoring a dialogue with non-violent Islamist groups. The USFP deputy head, Housing Minister Muhmmad Yazghi, did warn, however, against any attempt "to turn mosques into political forums."[45]

Yasin's first public comments were delivered the following day, at a well-attended press conference. While naturally happy to be out of confinement (*hisar*), he emphasized that some JCG members were still unjustly imprisoned, and that the authorities continued to harass his organization, despite its legal status. "Who controls this country?" he asked rhetorically. "One does not know."[46] Yasin's daughter and movement spokesperson Nadia warned against excessive euphoria, calling the release part of the authorities' "strategy of diversion, to allow some freedoms as a way of preventing future freedoms." As evidence of the continued squeeze on the movement, she cited the concurrent confiscation of the movement newspaper and the disbanding of its summer camps.[47] Pressed by journalists, Yasin merely emphasized that his movement's rejected violence, and sought dialogue with "honorable democrats" regarding the desired path for Morocco and its understanding of Islam. As for entry into parliamentary politics, he reiterated that his priorities were rather "education first, education second, education third." His movement had time, he said, and would consider electoral competition only when it could be certain that the elections would not be "fixed."[48] In a subsequent interview, Yasin provided additional reasons for not entering the electoral fray. In 1991, he said, the authorities had offered to recognize the JCG as a political party and promised it a place in parliament in return for recognition of the king as *amir al-mu'minin*. He had rejected the offer then, he said, and still maintained the position. Moreover, there was a strong possibility that his organization, being the "leading political force" in Morocco, would win an outright majority in parliamentary elections. This scenario, he emphasized, was one which "our adversaries" spoke of as likely. The risk, he said, was that Morocco would then repeat the terrible experience of Algeria (in which the army intervened following the Islamists electoral victory in 1991, plunging the country into a bloody civil war). For the time being, then, his movement intended to continue concentrating on social and religious activities, while insuring that its voice was heard in the public sphere. Regarding King Muhammad, for example, Yasin spoke favorably of his compassion for the disabled and the poor, and the extension of financial credits to drought victims. In fact, the king's actions had placed the government in an embarrassing situation, highlighting its own failure to ameliorate the country's difficulties. But Yasin also dismissed Muhammad's efforts to promote social and economic development through the reactivation of the Muhammad V Foundation: putting on a bandage was hardly the way to deal with a serious malady, he said.[49]

The authorities' determination to keep a tight rein on the Islamists, and the Islamists equally firm intent to expand their sphere of activities was quickly demonstrated in the renewed confrontation over Islamist "beach camps," which had become a fixture of movement activities in recent years. Just prior to Yasin's release, Interior Minister Midaoui had declared a ban on the camps, effective on 7 June, prompting immediate protests, with beaches in Mahdia, in the Gharb region, and elsewhere being immediately inundated with Islamist supporters. On 7 July, Midaoui reiterated the ban, stating that "the State will not tolerate practices that promote divisions in Moroccan society." Efforts to defy the ban in Mahdia led to clashes between police and Islamists, which resulted in multiple arrests, and scores of injured. A similar confrontation at a Casablanca beach was avoided only at the last minute. Shaykh Yasin urged his followers to avoid violence, and many of those who participated in the confrontations claimed that the police had initiated the violence. JCG spokesperson Fathallah Arsalane called for a dialogue with the state leading to a reconciliation, as opposed to continued repression or ignoring the movement which, he emphasized, was "impossible."[50]

However, the authorities kept up the pressure. In August, two JCG members were sentenced to three months in prison for proselytizing on a public beach in El-Jadida. Publication and sale of the JCG newspapers, al-'Adl wal-Ihsan (a bimonthly) and Risalat al-Futuwwa (a biweekly), was repeatedly hindered. JCG demonstrators, who often combined specific local grievances with anti-Israeli and anti-American slogans, were usually refused permits to stage public protests, and were repeatedly handled roughly by the security forces. Concerned with the JCG influence on university campuses, the authorities used force against JCG student groups on a number of occasions during student election campaigns. The most serious crackdown against JCG demonstrators protesting against the confiscation of their publications and demanding legal recognition of their organization came on the weekend of 9–11 December. Protestors in Rabat and Casablanca were violently dispersed, hundreds were arrested and twenty-two scheduled to be tried.[51] Thus, the year ended with the authorities and the JCG locked in confrontation, with the former trying to restrict the parameters of public activity, and the latter determined to widen them. In this respect, Islamists had much in common with liberal human rights groups and organizations seeking employment for university graduates. All sought to accelerate the expansion of Moroccan "civic space," while the makhzen sought to apply the brakes. But the balance of power remained heavily weighted on the side of the authorities. Prof. Muhammad Tozy remained consistent in his belief that the Islamists did not pose a serious threat. Yasin's memorandum, he said, had ultimately had very little effect, and the Islamists main concern was over what would happen to the movement after Yasin's death.[52]

While the JCG took the lead in setting the agenda of the Islamist current, the PJD also displayed an increased assertiveness. In October, it announced that it was moving away from a position of "critical support" for the Youssoufi government to one of "constructive" opposition. The party national council was sharply critical of the government performance after two years in office, its merely cosmetic cabinet reshuffle, which continued to place personal loyalties above competence, its failure to ensure clean elections unmarred by corruption, and its implementation of the financial "orders of international establishments," despite their negative social impact.[53]

Seeking to counter the Islamists, the king announced in early September a massive mosque-based literacy campaign, to be supplemented by religious, health and civic education, and to be taught by unemployed university graduates.[54] Ideally, in addition to the direct benefits of enhanced literacy, the initiative would deny the Islamists a monopoly on social welfare activities. In December, he sponsored a Dh70m. program organized through the Muhammad V Foundation to provide Ramadan breakfast meals to the poor in collaboration with community groups and associations (the Islamists engaged in similar activities).[55] He also began restructuring the religious establishment with an eye to modernizing Moroccan Islam. A number of new appointments were made to the Higher Council of 'Ulama. In particular, two "modernists" were appointed to key positions in the 'ulama hierarchy: Ahmed Khamlishi, designated head of the influential school Dar al-Hadith al-Hasania, which was responsible for issuing important interpretations of the Qur'an and Hadith; Abbes Jirari, an academic, religious preacher and president of the 'Ulama Council of Rabat-Sale, was appointed as special advisor on theology to the king. In order to placate conservative 'ulama, Muhammad Yussef, who had opposed the plan to integrate women in national development, was named a secretary-general of the Higher Council of 'Ulama. The monarchy also asserted more direct control on religious affairs, transferring power on religious issues from the minister of *habous* (religious endowments) to the king's appointees within the 'ulama system. The 'ulama were now charged with overseeing mosques and reporting directly to the palace. To that end, following the king's "Tetuan speech," the National and Provincial 'Ulama Councils were established on 15 December. The councils, he said, would "provide guidance to citizens to reaffirm their faith and sacred values while sheltering them from movements of deviation," a reference to the growing Islamist current and the increasing influence of Shafi'i and Wahhabi schools of Islamic law and ideology, challenging Morocco's official Maliki rites and practices. With a more active management of religious affairs by the 'Ulama Council, including the issuance of religious rulings (*fatwas*) which would challenge independent rulings being issued by shaykhs affiliated with the Islamist current such as Abdelbari Zamzami, the king and his advisers had clearly identified a crucial field of contention which required greater involvement of the monarchy.[56]

Women, National Development and Islam

Like no other subject, the question of women's status in Morocco was a bellwether subject for a society experiencing rapid social and economic change and political uncertainty. Throughout the 1990s, it had gradually risen in importance. In 1999, it came directly to the fore of the public agenda, as liberal government ministers, in collaboration with the WB, tendered a draft Plan of National Action for the Integration of Women in Development. At the center of the 25-page proposal were radical alterations in the *mudawanna*, which enshrined the inferior legal status of women. The proposals drew strongly negative reactions from both the religious establishment and Islamist groups, and in November, an umbrella body, the National Organization for the Defense of the Moroccan Family, was established to spearhead opposition to the plan. Somewhere in the middle stood King Muhammad, who repeatedly stressed the need to promote women's rights, particularly in light of the high illiteracy and low education rates among women. At the same time, aware of the highly charged nature of the issue, culturally, politically and socially, Muhammad refrained from entering into the specifics of the dispute (see *MECS*, 1999, pp. 437–39). The government itself was divided over the plan, with many of the Istiqlal ministers siding with Abdelbkir Alaoui M'daghri, the minister of *habous* and Islamic affairs, against Essaadi of the PPS and the USFP.[57]

The debate over the subject moved peacefully into the street on 12 March, in unprecedented expressions of civic activism. To mark International Women's Day (8 March), a coalition of women's organizations, the leading liberal political parties and labor unions sponsored a march and rally in Rabat against "poverty, domestic violence and illiteracy" drawing 40,000–50,000 participants. Given the rarity of large-scale demonstrations (owing to the traditional reluctance of the Moroccan authorities to sanction them) the Rabat march constituted an impressive display of the subject's resonance among liberal elements, and the ability to mobilize them. Even more impressive, however, was the counter-demonstration rejecting the proposed changes spearheaded by the Islamists. Initiated by the PJD and joined in the last days before the march by the JCG, hundreds of thousands, many of them women wearing traditional Islamic garb, marched through the streets of Casablanca, under the slogan, "Women are the Sisters of Men."[58]

Aware of the linkage between women's inferior legal status and the country's social and economic misery made by the liberals, JCG spokesperson Yasin sought to answer in the same vein. Moroccan women were indeed in an unfortunate situation, but the source was not Islam. The *mudawanna*, she said, was not a sacred text, and could be altered within accepted bounds, since the Shari'a recognized the rights of Muslim women. It was the heritage of a system of political despotism which needed to be replaced with a just Islamic system, within which women's concerns would be promoted. More generally, the Islamists framed their opposition to the liberal program in cultural terms. Spokesperson Yasin declared that the march constituted rejection of all plans imposed by international organizations, "American imperialism," and local Westernizing elites. The entire debate, declared Ahmad Raisounni, leader of Islah wal-Tawhid, was a false one: whereas secularists claimed to be defending women's liberty, they were actually directing them back toward slavery, treating them as a "miserable object."[59] Islamists also frequently linked the plan to the alleged enemies of Morocco, the "West" and the "Zionists." The plan's author, secretary of state in charge of social protection, the family and children, Muhammad Said Essaadi of the PPS, was branded an "enemy of God," and an "agent of international Zionism."[60]

Interestingly enough, both Islamists and secularists used traditional religious terminology to bolster their cases, referring to the need to employ *ijtihad* (the interpretation of holy law based on individual reason). For the secularists, referring to *ijtihad* was transparently manipulative: unable to provide a widely accepted reading of Islamic texts which would ground their challenge to the prevailing order, they simply declared that the national development plan didn't contradict the spirit of Islam but was a perfect reflection of it. For cultural conservatives and advocates of the political status quo, employment of the *ijtihad* discourse also had a manipulative side, in order to regulate the process of change or redirect the debate entirely. The late king Hasan II, for example, spoke frequently of the need to pursue *ijtihad*-based reform, i.e., to control the pace of change so as to maintain political and social stability.

Stunned, perhaps, by the strength of the Casablanca demonstration, the government quickly shelved the development plan. King Muhammad, while sympathetic with the tenor of the liberal trend, clearly preferred to proceed slowly on the matter. To that end, he established a 20-member panel that included conservative Islamic scholars, representatives from women's groups and other NGOs and the government, to make a thorough study and recommendations regarding the amendment of the *mudawanna*. In this regard, Muhammad's careful actions, designed to defuse political conflict and proceeded slowly and incrementally, were similar to those of his late father. To demonstrate his continued commitment to advancing the status of women, he appointed the first female royal adviser, Zoulikha Nasri, a former secretary of state for the disabled, as well as a small number of female ambassadors.

THE ECONOMY

The government had adopted a draft five-year plan in December 1999 aimed at upgrading national infrastructure, boosting business and alleviating unemployment. The annual growth rate in the plan was targeted at 5%.[61] However, the failure of late winter rains at the beginning of the year resulted in only 0.8% economic growth, following hard on the heels of negative growth in 1999 (see *MECS*, 1999, pp. 446-47). WB and International Monetary Fund (IMF) reports presented a difficult picture. According to the WB, the unemployment rate could reach 27% in 2005 in the absence of sustained annual growth rates of 6%-8%. The IMF commended Morocco for maintaining macroeconomic stability in the face of severe droughts and international financial upheavals, while calling for further structural reforms in the direction of economic liberalization, better fiscal management and the reduction of the public debt.[62] The promised creation of an additional 17,000 jobs to an already bloated public sector, in order to avert a nation-wide strike by unions in June, was noted with chagrin by the WB.[63] In the meantime, unemployment stood at approximately 14% overall, and 22% in urban areas. Another sobering figure was the 40% widening of the trade deficit due to a 65% rise in the cost of oil imports.[64]

On 21 August, King Muhammad announced an important discovery of oil, sparking much speculation and widespread hopes. The estimates of the potential reserves in the new field turned out to be vastly over-optimistic or at least premature.

Beginning in July 1996, the government had calculated the fiscal year from July to June, in order to coincide with the agricultural year. However, this decision was reversed in 2000. Beginning in 2001, the fiscal year would again begin on 1 January, with a six-month transitional budget passed to cover 1 July-31 December 2000. Given the drought, and the government pledge in April to raise the minimum wage by 10% in order to avert a general strike, further injections of cash were sure to be required, and the budget deficit was likely to rise in light of the lower projected growth rates.[65] To that end, in December, 35% of Maroc Télécom, the state telecommunications company, was sold to a French group for $2.2bn., with the funds to be channeled toward the 2001 budget.[66] Early winter rains held out hope for improved economic performance in 2001.

FOREIGN AFFAIRS

THE WESTERN SAHARA AND ALGERIAN-MOROCCAN RELATIONS

The decade-long efforts by the UN to organize a referendum to determine the fate of the Western Sahara (independence or incorporation into Morocco) ground to a halt at the end of 1999 and the beginning of 2000. The inability of Morocco to attain a widening of the eligible voters' roll to include significant numbers of Moroccan residents of Sahrawi origin left it with two choices: either to risk losing an internationally-sanctioned referendum, with all that implied both domestically and internationally, or refusing to cooperate any further with the referendum process (see *MECS*, 1999, p. 441–43). Given the consensus in the country regarding Moroccan rights to the territory, the refusal to cooperate and encouragement of alternative options which would confirm Moroccan

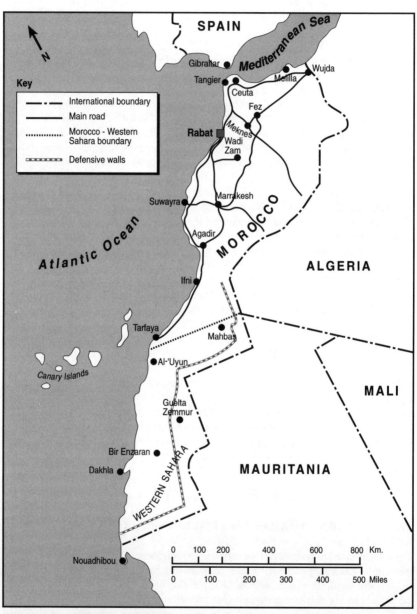

Morocco and Western Sahara

sovereignty over the area was a foregone conclusion. With the Security Council, and particularly the US and France unwilling to force Morocco to accept a UN *diktat*, the UN secretary-general's personal envoy, James Baker, actively sought to nudge the parties toward an agreed-on solution, but without success. The stalemate over the Western Sahara was the single greatest factor in preventing the thaw in Moroccan-Algerian relations which Rabat so eagerly desired (partly in order to weaken long-time Algerian support for the Polisario movement; the Algerians, for their part, refused to hand Morocco this card). In addition, Algeria accused Morocco of harboring, or at least turning a blind eye to Algerian Islamist terrorists on the Moroccan side of their common border. Hence the border, closed since 1994, remained so, and the five-nation AMU remained moribund, notwithstanding the expressed interest of both countries, and Tunisia as well, to revitalize its activities.

On 17 January 2000, the UN transmitted the second part of the provisional voter list, containing the names of individual applicants of three contested tribal groupings, to Morocco and the Polisario. As expected, the vast majority of the 65,000 applicants were rejected, sparking Moroccan anger (for background, see *MECS* 1999, pp. 442–43). As provided for in the UN Implementation Plan, more than 53,000 appeals against exclusion from the provisional voters list were immediately filed. Taken together with previous appeals, the total number of appeal files amounted to more than 130,000. Processing them all, the UN understood, would render impossible the likelihood of holding a referendum any time soon. Consequently, Baker and Annan sought to prod the parties toward an agreement which would obviate the need for a referendum. To that end, Baker visited the region on 8–11 April, and convened the parties in London on 14 May for their first face-to-face meeting since 1997 (see *MECS* 1997, pp. 571–76). Baker stressed to both sides that their fundamental differences over the interpretation of the plan's main provisions meant that "the prospects for holding the referendum were as distant as ever." He then expressed hope that the two sides would come to future meetings with specific proposals to either resolve all outstanding settlement plan issues, "or be prepared to consider and discuss other ways to achieve an early, durable and agreed resolution" to their dispute. On 31 May, UN Security Council Resolution 1301 alluded to the possibility that alternatives to the stalemated referendum process might have to be considered. Now it was the turn of Polisario to be angry.[67]

Two more high-level meetings between Polisario and Moroccan officials were held under Baker's auspices during the year: one in London on 28 June and one in Berlin on 28 September, which, sandwiched by UN-sponsored expert-level technical meetings of the parties in Geneva on 20–21 July, left UN secretary-general Kofi Annan and Baker keenly disappointed. In the midst of the difficulties, the Security Council, in Resolution 1309 on 25 July, had requested that the two parties try to agree on a mutually acceptable political solution, while not ruling out the implementation of the settlement plan. Baker then sought to move the process forward simultaneously in a number of areas: confidence-building measures, such as: the release of 1,686 Moroccan prisoners of war by Polisario and Moroccan accounting for the status of 207 presumed Sahrawi political detainees; expediting the appeals process to determine the eligible voters list for the referendum; and serious discussions on a political agreement which would obviate the need for a referendum, and be based on a combination of Moroccan sovereignty and regional autonomy for the area. But each side stuck to their positions. Morocco insisted that the voter identification process had been fundamentally distorted, and that the appeals process could not satisfy the thousands of rejected applicants. Thus, the implementation plan could go no further. It proposed direct talks with the Polisario to work out a "lasting and definitive solution" that would be based on Moroccan sovereignty and territorial integrity and the "democratic and decentralization principles" which Morocco wished to apply throughout the kingdom, beginning in the south. Polisario refused to discuss anything apart from the settlement plan. Baker and Annan concluded that further meetings of the parties would be useless, and even counterproductive unless Morocco was prepared "to offer or support some devolution of governmental authority, for all inhabitants and former inhabitants of the Territory, that is genuine, substantial and in keeping with international norms." To further nudge Morocco in that direction, they stated that if Morocco failed to act in this manner, the UN mission should begin expediting the pending appeals process for voter identification regardless of the length of time it would take. There matters stood at year's end.[68]

Moroccan-Algerian relations seemed to be heading toward a qualitative breakthrough in the first half of 1999, following the election of 'Abd al-Aziz Bouteflika as Algerian president and the ascension of King Muhammad. Speculation was rife about an imminent meeting between the two leaders and an AMU summit, the first since 1992. However, a major setback occurred in late August, following the massacre of at least twenty-nine Algerian civilians by armed Islamists, allegedly operating from Moroccan soil (see *MECS*, pp. 449–450), and Saudi mediation produced no results.

In a long interview with an Algerian daily on 20 February, Prime Minister Youssoufi expressed regret for the "chill" in bilateral relations, and denied allegations of Moroccan interference in internal Algerian affairs. There was no reason for the border to remain closed, he said. What was needed was simply a decision by Algeria to open it. As for Bouteflika's remarks regarding drug smuggling from Morocco to Algeria, Youssoufi stated that the equation of the "action of Mafia characters" with that of a "neighborly and friendly state" was a "provocation."[69]

Considerable efforts were made to improve relations between the two long-time geopolitical adversaries during 2000. Interior Minister Midaoui met his Algerian counterpart, Noureddine Yazid Zerhouni, in Algiers in January during the annual Arab interior ministers conference. Muhammad sent an envoy to see Bouteflika in February, while Bouteflika sent Muhammad greetings that same month on the eleventh anniversary of the founding of the AMU. Muhammad, Bouteflika, Libyan leader Mu'ammar al-Qadhdhafi and Egyptian president Husni Mubarak met briefly as a group at the Euro-Africa summit in Cairo in April.[70] In May, Muhammad received Bachir Boumaasa, the president of the Algerian senate, and the two countries pledged to expand cooperation between their legislatures.[71] The Moroccans steadfastly denied any interference in Algerian internal affairs, and agreed to the Algerian request to tighten security along its borders to hinder the activities of armed Islamists and drug smugglers, particularly in light of a number of border incidents during April affecting Moroccan villages.[72] In November, the Moroccan authorities sentenced a Moroccan-Algerian network operating in the border region to prison terms.[73] Concurrently, Algerian interior minister Zerhouni made an unusually long 10-day visit to Morocco, holding talks with his Moroccan counterpart Midaoui. At their joint press conference, it was announced that they had decided to set up "mechanisms" to normalize their relations and to re-open their frontiers, and that their joint higher commission would be reactivated in 2001. Now it appeared that it was Algeria which sought to put their differences over the Western Sahara "in parentheses", while Midaoui reiterated that it could never deal with any problem "while forgetting the fulfillment of its territorial integrity in its southern provinces." The Algerians, while certainly not abandoning their Polisario allies, may have been trying to encourage Morocco to be more cooperative with the UN efforts to organize the referendum. In a further sign of an improving atmosphere, Bouteflika and Muhammad exchanged warm greetings at the end of the month to mark the onset of Ramadan.[74] But the year ended without a breakthrough.

As for the AMU and related multilateral projects, efforts to revive its activities continued to come from various quarters, but without achieving a breakthrough. In line with its Eizenstat initiative to promote increased development in North Africa, the US had sought to hold a joint meeting in Washington in December 1999 between the Moroccan, Algerian, Tunisian and American foreign ministers, but without success. The idea was revived in August 2000, with the US hosting a preparatory meeting of lower-level delegations from the three countries, but again without results.[75] A meeting of AMU members at the level of experts dealing with construction, habitat and the environment was held in Rabat in mid-2000. To further advance the discussions, housing minister and deputy head of the USFP Yazghi visited both Tunis and Algiers in June to promote a five-way ministerial-level meeting, to be followed by a similar gathering of all western Mediterranean states. While in Algiers, Yazghi met with Bouteflika.[76] Tunisia continued to initiate efforts to revive the AMU, with Moroccan encouragement. In the meantime, bilateral relations between Morocco and both Tunisia and Libya continued to improve. Muhammad made an official state visit to Tunis on 25–27 May, and two meetings of their joint higher committee were held during the year. The February meeting, held in Tunis, was chaired by the foreign ministers of the two countries; the September meeting, in Rabat, was chaired by their prime ministers, and concluded by the signing of a number of agreements on issues such as trade, infrastructure, and internal security. Bilateral talks with Libya developed slowly and without incident. Relations with the fifth AMU country, Morocco's southern neighbor Mauritania, improved substantially, highlighted by the first ever official visit by a Mauritanian president (up until then, Morocco had always refrained from extending him an official invitation; it had refused to even recognizeMauritania's independence, achieved in 1960, until 1970, claiming the territory as part of Morocco's historical patrimony). Mouaouya Ould Sidi Ahmed Taya of Mauritania met with King Muhammad, Prime Minister Youssoufi and other senior officials in Tangiers on 26 April, and the two countries agreed to set up a joint higher commission to promote bilateral ties.[77]

RELATIONS WITH OTHER ARAB COUNTRIES

Egypt

Relations with Egypt continued develop. Muhammad paid an official state visit to Egypt on 22–24 May. The accompanying fourth session of their joint higher commission resulted in the signing of a number of cooperation agreements, with the aim of boosting trade between them to $100m. In general, the two countries were like-minded on issues pertaining to the region, and to Euro-Med relations.

Qatar

Morocco was added to the growing list of Arab countries angered by Qatar. Dissatisfaction with broadcasts by al-Jazira satellite television, and Doha's failure to support either

Morocco's candidate for the post of secretary-general of the Islamic Conference Organization (ICO) or the unsuccessful Moroccan bid to host the 2006 World Cup were irritating enough. But the Qatari sale of military trucks and equipment to Algeria, which Morocco feared was destined for Polisario hands crossed all of Morocco's "red lines." In mid-July, Morocco recalled its ambassador from Doha. In September, Moroccan officials boycotted the Qatari National Day celebration held by the Qatari embassy in Rabat.[78] But Muhammad and Emir Hamad of Qatar met on the sidelines of the Cairo Arab summit conference on 21 October, following which Morocco returned its ambassador.

THE ARAB-ISRAELI ARENA

Morocco sought to pursue a business-as-usual approach to Arab-Israeli affairs, maintaining links with Israel while encouraging diplomatic efforts on behalf of the Palestinians. But with the failure of the US-sponsored July Camp David summit and the outbreak of Palestinian-Israeli violence in late September (see chapters on Israel and the Palestinian Authority), Morocco was gradually forced to toe the collective Arab line, and break off official diplomatic relations with Israel.

Rabat-born Israeli foreign minister David Levy visited Morocco in January, holding talks with King Muhammad and other Moroccan officials and making a nostalgic visit to his former home. But Israeli hopes that the visit would lead to an upgrading of formal ties and the establishment of a direct air link between the two countries were not realized, as Morocco preferred to maintain the status quo.

Following the unsuccessful Israeli-Palestinian summit in Camp David in mid-July, Israel offered to send acting foreign minister Shlomo Ben Ami (Levy had concurrently resigned) and Tourism Minister Amnon Lipkin-Shahak to brief the Moroccans on the summit discussions, but Morocco declined. Instead, Muhammad concentrated on shoring up his Arab and Islamic flank, hosting a meeting of the ICO Jerusalem Committee on 28 August. Having done so, Morocco then re-opened the Israeli channel. A week later, Muhammad received Ben Ami in Agadir to convey the content of the discussions to him. Pictures of the meeting were broadcast on Moroccan television.[79] In a further sign of continued Moroccan interest in maintaining the relationship, it received in mid-September a large-scale Israeli delegation of commercial representatives specializing in agricultural technology and production for a week of meetings with members of the Moroccan business community. The visit was denounced by the PJD, with al-Tajdid, the party mouthpiece, calling it a "prelude to a flood of agricultural normalization." Accusations were also leveled against Israel as being the origin of the "white fly" disease affecting the Moroccan tomato crop.[80]

The outbreak of Israeli-Palestinian confrontations at the end of September resonated throughout the Arab world, including Morocco. The head of its liaison office in Tel Aviv was called home for consultations. On 8 October, perhaps the largest march in Moroccan history, between 500,000 and one million participants, took place in Rabat in support of the Palestinians. The march was led by the prime minister, and involved all Moroccan political forces, including senior JCG officials (but not Shaykh Yasin himself). The "surprise" of the JCG was a poorly-heard audio link-up with Palestinian Hamas leader Shaykh Ahmad Yasin. The Rabat march was completely peaceful, but in Casablanca, an unauthorized march of 25,000 persons organized by the PJD, degenerated into confrontations with the police.[81]

Muhammad's speech at the emergency Arab summit conference in Cairo on 21–22 October was among the most moderate in tone. As expected, Morocco aligned itself firmly alongside Egypt and Jordan in opposition to any thought of military escalation and in favor of a diplomatic resolution to the Palestinian-Israeli conflict (see chapter on inter-Arab relations). But Morocco also chose to align itself with the Arab consensus and broke off its low-level diplomatic relations with Israel on 23 October. Interestingly, among the reasons given for the move were Moroccan "responsibilities and commitments within the Al-Quds [Jerusalem] Committee, chaired by King Mohammed VI," but no reference was made to the call by the Arab summit conference on Arab states to sever ties.[82] Clearly, the Moroccan authorities wanted to avoid any hint of infringement on Moroccan sovereignty. The real reason for the move was domestic: for some time already, Islamists in particular had been vocal in their criticism of the Israeli diplomatic presence in Morocco. The combination of a new young king more attuned to public sentiment; the increasing space for political activity by parties and "civil society;" and, most of all, the graphic, televised images from the West Bank and Gaza, forced the king's hand and reversed the action taken by his father in 1994.

RELATIONS WITH EUROPE AND THE US

Moroccan-Spanish relations were steadily becoming more intimate and more fraught with tension. A host of subjects crowded their common agenda: the absence of a new fisheries agreement governing EU (mostly Spanish) fishing rights in Moroccan waters, affecting more than five hundred Spanish trawlers; protectionist sentiment, which resulted in attacks by Spanish farmers on vehicles carrying Moroccan tomatoes and other agricultural produce, and accompanying confusion over the terms of the Moroccan association agreement with the EU, which came into effect on 1 March;[83] the status and treatment of some 250,000 Moroccan immigrants and laborers, legal and illegal, in Spain; the problem of illegal immigration and drug trafficking from Morocco to Spain; Spanish unwillingness to discuss Moroccan claims to Ceuta and Melilla; and the considerable non-governmental support in Spain for the Polisario, against the Moroccan claim to the Western Sahara.

Dialogue on the official level was regular, and at a high level. Prime Minister Jose Maria Aznar of Spain made an official visit in May to address some of their differences. To help matters along, he announced that Spain would legalize the status of 90,000 illegal Moroccan immigrants, as well as convert some of the Moroccan debt to investment. King Muhammad made an official, 3-day visit on 18–20 September, during which two bilateral agreements worth $90m. were signed, designed to finance economic projects in northern Morocco and reconvert part of the Moroccan debt into investment.[84]

Muhammad's first official state visit to a non-Arab country as king was to France, Morocco's leading trading partner, on 19–23 March; it followed his "private" visit in mid-January, during which time he nevertheless met with French president Jacques Chirac. Apart from the ceremonial aspects, the visit was marked by French agreement to convert another FF700m. of Moroccan debt to investment.[85] Chirac's support for Muhammad was subsequently exemplified by his granting of FF100m. ($16.9m.), as emergency aid to cope with the drought, as well as by French unwillingness to see the Security Council pressure Morocco on the Western Sahara issue. Neither was the US. US. Moroccan-American relations had deepened considerably in recent years, and were further cemented by Muhammad's high-profile visit to the US on 19–23 June.

TABLE ONE: THE YOUSSOUFI CABINET, ANNOUNCED
ON 6 SEPTEMBER 2000

Post	Name	Party Affiliation
Prime Minister	Abderrahmane El Youssoufi	USFP
Minister of Religious Endowments and Islamic Affairs	Abdelkabir M'Daghri Alaoui	—
*Minister of Foreign Affairs and Cooperation	Mohamed Benaissa	RNI
*Minister of the Interior	Ahmed El Midaoui	—
Minister of Justice	Omar Azziman	—
Minister of Employment, Vocational Training, Social Development and Solidarity	Abbas El Fassi	Istiqlal
Minister in charge of County Planning, Environment, Town Planning and Housing	Mohamed El Yazghi	USFP
Minister of Economy and Finance, and Tourism	Fathallah Oualalou	USFP
Secretary-General of the Government	Abdessadek Rabiaa	—
Minister of Social Economy, Small and Medium Enterprises and Handicrafts, in Charge of General Affairs of the Government	Ahmed Lahlimi Alami	USFP
Minister of Agriculture and Rural Development	Isma'il Alaoui	PPS
Minister of Industry, Commerce and Energy and Mining	Mustapha Mansouri	RNI
Minister of Maritime Fishing	Said Chbaatou	MNP
Minister of Equipment	Bouamor Taghouan	Istiqlal
Minister of Transport and Merchant Navy	Abdeslam Zenined	RNI
Minister of Higher Education and Scientific Research	Najib Zerouali	RNI
Minister of National Education	Abdallah Saaf	PSD
Minister of Health	Thami Khyari	FFD
Minister of Culture and Communication	Mohamed Achaari	USFP
Minister in charge of Relations with Parliament	Mohammed Bouzoubaa	USFP
Minister in charge of Human Rights	Mohamed Aujjar	RNI
Minister of Youth and Sports	Ahmed Moussaoui	MNP
Minister in Charge of Economic Estimates and Plan	Abdelhamid Aouad	Istiqlal
**Minister of Public Service and Administrative Development	M'Hamed El Khalifa	Istiqlal
Minister Delegate to the Prime Minister in charge of the Administration of National Defense	Abderrahmane Sbai	—
Minister Delegate to the Minister of Agriculture and Rural Development, in charge of Rural Development	Hassan Maaouni	MNP
Minister Delegate to the Minister of Employment, Vocational Training, Social Development and		

Solidarity, in charge of the Conditions of Women,Social Protection, Children and the Integration of the Handicapped	Nezha Chekrouni	USFP
*Secretary of State for Foreign Affairs and Cooperation	Taieb Fassi	—
*Secretary of State for the Interior	Fouad Ali-El-Himma	—
Secretary of State delegate to the Minister in charge of County Planning, the Environment, Town Planning and Housing, in charge of Town Planning	Mohamed M'Barki	USFP
Secretary of State delegate to the Minister of Higher Education and Scientific Research, in charge of Scientific Research	Omar El Fassi	PPS
**Secretary of State delegate to the Prime Minister in charge of Post and Information and Communication Technology	Nacer Hajji	USFP
**Secretary of State delegate to the Minister of Social Economy, Small and Medium Enterprises and Handicrafts	Abdelkrim Ben Atiq	USFP

* Joined cabinet in 1999
** New member of cabinet
All others were members of Youssoufi's original 1998 cabinet.

NOTES

For the place and frequency of publications cited here, and for the full name of the publication, news agency, radio station or monitoring service where an abbreviation is used, please see "List of Sources." Only in the case of more than one publication bearing the same name is the place of publication noted here. All references to *Le Monde Diplomatique* are to the English-language version.

1. Muhammad Tozy, quoted in Ignacio Ramonet, "Morocco: The Point of Change," *Le Monde Diplomatique*, July 2000.
2. For the text of the manifesto, see <www.mondeberbere.com>.
3. *CR*, Morocco, April 2000, p. 21.
4. Abdeslam M. Maghraoui, *Journal of Democracy*, Vol. 12, No. 1 (January 2001), p. 85; RTM TV, 30 July — BBC Monitoring, 1 August 2000.
5. RTM TV, 30 July — BBC Monitoring, 1 August 2000.
6. *CR*, Morocco, October 2000, p. 18; *MHI*, 28 July 2000.
7. *The North Africa Journal*, June 2000; *The Economist*, 10 June 2000.
8. *WSWN*, Week 40, 1 October 2000.
9. "Morocco:Country Reports on Human Rights Practices —, 2000," US Department of State, February 2001. (Hereafter: "Morocco: CRHRP," 2000.)
10. C. R. Pennell, *Morocco since 1830* (New York: New York University Press, 2000), pp. 331-32.
12. Aboubakr Jamai, "Morocco, Drifting Towards Authoritarianism," *Le Monde Diplomatique*, January 2001.
13. "Morocco: CRHRP", 2001.

14. Ibid.
15. Ibid.
16. Ibid.; Ignace Dallé, "Morocco: Waiting for Serious Change," *Le Monde Diplomatique*, June 2001.
17. *Al-Sharq al-Awsat*, 4 February 2000 (DR).
18. Ignacio Ramonet, "Morocco: The Point of Change," *Le Monde Diplomatique*, July 2000.
19. *JAI*, 16 May 2000.
20. "A Frozen Coalition," *The North Africa Journal*, May 2000.
21. *Al-Hayat*, 18 September; *Demain*, 4 November 2000.
22. *MHI*, 20 October 2000.
23. *Al-Sharq al-Awsat*, 23 September 2000 (DR).
24. *Le Monde*, 29 July 2000.
25. *Demain*, 22 July; Mustapha Sehimi, *MHI*, 22 September 2000.
26. *Al-Wasat*, 25 September 2000.
27. *CR*, Morocco, October 2000, p. 13.
28. *MWM*, No. 91, 12 September 2000.
29. *Al-Sharq al-Awsat*, 8 September 2000 (DR).
30. *Al-Sharq al-Awsat*, 9 December 2000.
31. *Al-Sharq al-Awsat*, 6 December 2000 (DR).
32. *JAI*, 12 December 2000.
33. *MHI*, 15 December 2000.
34. *Al-Hayat*, 23 December 2000.
35. *El Pais*, quoted by *MHI*, 22 December 2000.
36. *Le Matin* (Internet version), 20 February 2000 (DR).
37. To later generations, 'Umar II was an "exemplar of the Muslim virtues of piety, equality and humility." (P.M. Cobb, "'Umar (II) b. 'Abd al-'Aziz," (EI), new edition, Vol. 10, pp. 221–22).
38. <www.yassineonline.net/letters/index1.html> [English and French versions].
39. "Morocco: CRHRP", 2000.
40. *JAI*, 8 February 2000.
41. *Al-Hayat*, 23 February 2000.
42. *MHI*, 18 February 2000.
43. *MHI*, 4 February 2000.
44. Ibid.
45. *Al-Hayat*, 18 May 2000.
46. <www.yassineonline.net/conferencedepresse/conf.htm>.
47. *Le Monde*, 21 May; *FT*, 20 May 2000.
48. <www.yassineonline.net/conferencedepresse/conf.htm>.
49. *Demain*, 22 July 2000.
50. *MWM*, No. 87, 23 July 2000.
51. "Morocco: CRHRP", 2000.
52. Quoted in Ignacio Ramonet, "Morocco: The Point of Change," *Le Monde Diplomatique*, July 2000.
53. *Al-Sharq al-Awsat*, 3 October 2000 (DR).
54. *MWM*, No. 90, 3 September 2000.
55. *MWM*, No. 96, 16 December 2000.
56. Arzeki Daoud, *MWM*, No. 98, 7 January 2001.
57. *MIH*, 17 March 2000.
58. *Al-Sharq al-Awsat*, 13 March; *al-Wasat*, 20 March 2000.
59. *MHI*, 21 January, 17 March 2000; *Arabies*, February 2001.
60. *JAI*, 21 March 2000.
61. *CR*, Morocco, October 2000, p. 19.
62. Ibid., pp. 19, 24.
63. *The Economist*, 10 June 2000.

64. *CR*, Morocco, May 2001, p. 3.
65. *CR*, Morocco, July 2000, p. 19.
66. *CR*, Morocco, February 2001, p. 3.
67. "Report of the Secretary-General on the Situation Concerning Western Sahara," S/2000/461, 22 May; UN Security Council, S/RES/1301(2000); *WSWN*, Week 22, 28 May 2000.
68. "Report of the Secretary-General on the Situation Concerning Western Sahara," S/2000/1029, 25 October 2000.
69. *Le Matin* (Internet version), 20 February 2000 (DR).
70. Interview with Moroccan foreign minister Muhammad Benaissa, MENA, 5 April 2000 (DR).
71. *Al-Hayat,* 10 May 2000.
72. *Al-Sharq al-Awsat*, 23 April 2000.
73. *Al-Hayat,* 13 November 2000.
74. *WSWN,* Week 46, 30 October; *JAI,* 5 December; *Demain*, 25 November 2000.
75. *Al-Wasat*, 28 August 2000.
76. *Al-Wasat*, 12 June, 18 September 2000.
77. *Al-Wasat*, 8 May 2000.
78. *Al-Hayat*, 20 July; *al-Sharq al-Awsat*, 13 September 2000 (DR).
79. *Al-Wasat*, 11 September 2000.
80. *Al-Sharq al-Awsat*, 19 September 2000 (DR).
81. *Demain*, 10 October 2000.
82. MAP, 23 October — BBC Monitoring, 25 October 2000.
83. *FT*, 4 February 2000.
84. *CR*, Morocco, July 2000, p. 18; PANA (Internet version), 20 September 2000 (DR).
85. *Le Monde*, 19 March 2000.

Oman

('Uman)

UZI RABI

Oman held official celebrations in November 2000 to mark the thirtieth anniversary of Sultan Qabus bin Sa'id's accession to power and the start of the period Omanis referred to as "the renaissance" (al-Nahda).[1] On consolidating his rule, Qabus had inaugurated a major development program to dramatically upgrade the educational and health facilities of Oman. To that end, the early years of his reign saw a massive investment of the national oil income, accumulated since commercial production began in 1967. By 1975, a sizable infrastructure had been established. Schools, hospitals, clinics and roads were built and a welfare system introduced. With its infrastructure in place, Oman began to focus on future economic development. But by the late 1990s, despite the considerable economic and social achievements, Oman confronted a less certain future in light of its diminishing oil reserves. At current production rates, Oman was projected to exhaust its oil reserves within approximately two decades, in contrast to Saudi Arabia and Kuwait, where the reserves would last a century at existing production rates. The problem was exacerbated by the growing number of job seekers entering the market annually, forecast to increase by 212% during the coming two decades, with a concurrent sustained growth in the 0-14-year-old population projected beyond 2020.[2] Little wonder, therefore, that the Omani government was eager to increase the "Omanization" of the labor force, thereby enhancing job opportunities for its expanding young population.[3]

Yet, the real challenge ahead appeared to lie in the political area. In contrast to the enormous development of its social and physical infrastructure, change in the Omani political system came much more slowly. A hesitant move toward greater political participation was marked by the most free ever elections for the Majlis al-Shura (Consultative Council) held in September 2000.[4] Political rallies were banned during the run-up to the election and canvassing in public was discouraged. Most electioneering activity was restricted to door-to-door canvassing for the 540 candidates (519 men and 21 women) who contested eighty-three seats in the fourth Majlis (2001–2003).[5] While the election did not produce any surprises, it helped project a more modern and liberal image for the sultanate.

Caution regarding political change continued to be evident in the sultan's management of his government as well. A cabinet reshuffle carried out during the year appeared to focus on improving public services and supporting privatization, but real change was as unlikely as the results of preceding reshuffles, with loyal ministers continuing to be rewarded by lengthy tenures in office.

If the political order appeared assured, uncertainty continued to surround the succession to the throne. An heir-apparent to the sixty-year-old sultan did not emerge in 2000. The most frequently mentioned candidates for the position, three brothers, were first cousins

440

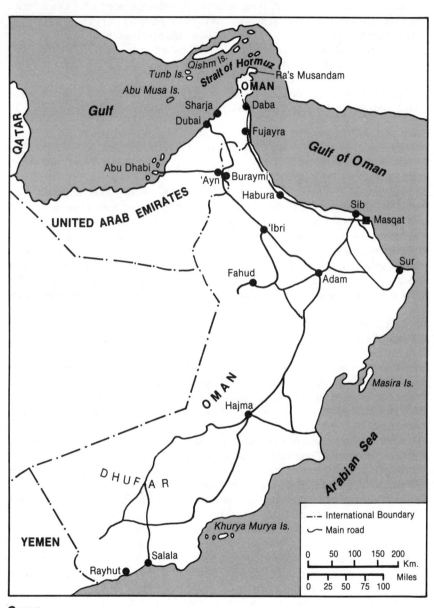

Oman

of the sultan: Sayyid Asad bin Tariq, head of the Higher Committee for Conferences; Sayyid Haytham bin Tariq, secretary-general of the Ministry of Foreign Affairs; and Sayyid Shihab, head of the navy. Qabus, however, did not give any public affirmation to any of these candidates; in the event of his death, the sultanate would rely on provisions made in the Basic Law of the State. Accordingly, on the death of the sultan the royal family would meet to select his successor within three days. If they were unable to agree, the head of the Defense Council would open an envelope left by the sultan containing his choice as successor, and that person would become the new leader.

INTERNAL AFFAIRS

ELECTIONS TO THE MAJLIS

Oman held its first direct election to the Majlis in September 2000, the result of an electoral process that had evolved since 1981. In 1997, the electorate voting for the third Majlis was restricted to some 51,000 Omanis who voted for over seven hundred male and female candidates. The sultan then made the final selection from a list of the candidates elected, picking two of the top four candidates in large constituencies and one of the top two in smaller jurisdictions (see *MECS* 1997, pp. 591–95).[6] In 2000, the delegates were elected by an enlarged electorate of some 175,000, more than three times that of 1997. The top one or two winning candidates in each constituency were chosen by the sultan for seats in the Majlis.[7]

Oman also distinguished itself from most of the other Gulf Arab states by granting women the right to participate in the political process. Beginning in 1994, women were allowed to run for seats in the Majlis.[8] Women throughout the country also participated in the local nomination process, a privilege that had previously been granted only to women in Muscat.[9] Two women, both of whom came from prominent merchant families, won seats in the Majlis. Women were also represented, albeit sparsely, in the cabinet, at the ambassadorial level, on commercial boards of directors and in the chamber of commerce.[10]

While women's participation and increased suffrage were indeed signs of greater political liberalization, the Majlis elections in 2000 were marked by a lack of enthusiasm on the part of both voters and candidates. Only about two-thirds (114,570) of the eligible electorate registered to vote. This voter passivity was coupled with a decrease in the total number of candidates running for office, from 736 in 1997 to 540 in 2000. Conceivably, widespread frustration with the limited powers of the Majlis was the prime reason for this indifference. The cautious approach of the government to political reform evoked impatience among younger, Western-educated Omanis eager for more rapid change. The Majlis had not evolved into a legislative body, it had highly restricted powers, and was prohibited from addressing major policy concerns such as defense and foreign affairs. As such, it held little attraction for would-be members.

Although the government election campaign called on Omanis to "say no to the tribe, yes to Oman" (*na'am li-'uman...la lil-qabila*), tribal patronage remained an important element of Omani society.[11] Since political parties remained prohibited in the sultanate, interest groups played an important role in society, with tribes providing the dominant social structure.[12] Their role was aptly described by the Omani minister of information, 'Abd al-'Aziz Muhammad al-Rawwas:

The tribal nature of our society is a civil society establishment, something which Western thinkers often overlook. This tribal establishment is no less influential than political parties. I do not think we are ready yet for political parties. I do not believe personally we could benefit from them. If we had been run by political parties, I do not think we would have developed so much in the last thirty years. Political infighting would not have allowed this. Our tribal system reinforces national unity.[13]

For all the advances made in terms of suffrage, a large proportion of younger Omanis seemed unhappy with the election results, as the average age of the elected delegates was around forty-five. In the final analysis, the Majlis functioned entirely at the discretion of the sultan. Potential candidates were vetted by the government, thereby constricting the choices available to the voters. The eligibility criteria for candidates — e.g., having a "good reputation" or being "reasonably well-educated" — were arbitrary.[14] The reappointment by the sultan of Shaykh 'Abdallah bin 'Ali al-Qatabi as president of the Majlis al-Shura and Shaykh Hammud bin 'Abdallah al-Harthi as president of Majlis al-Dawla (the State Council; see below) were a vivid example of control from above. With the Shura council president hailing from the Dhahira region and the Dawla council president from the Sharqiyya region — two major Dakhiliyya tribal population centers — the sultan clearly had in mind that the two would balance out the interests of each of these key areas.[15]

Countering press criticism that the Majlis had lost a number of educated delegates because of tribal favoritism in the election procedure, Minister of Interior Sayyid 'Ali bin Hammud Al Bu Sa'idi pointed out that "the Majlis represents varied experiences, abilities and qualifications. Among them are peasants, professionals, fishermen, doctors and engineers. Women also have the right to vote and stand for elections."[16] The charge of tribalism was an insult, he said. "The government does not tell the people to elect anyone because he is of a certain tribe."[17]

The growing frustration on the part of younger and Western-educated Omanis notwithstanding, the authority of the Majlis was enhanced to a degree by the exercise of its right to monitor government activity and summon ministers to report on the performance of their departments. As a result, some ministers attempted to establish a dialogue with Majlis delegates and deal seriously with their concerns. The government focus on development policy and several technocratic changes in 2000 (see below) also reflected the gradual enhancement of the status of the Majlis, particularly in monitoring social policy.

The sultan appeared anxious to balance demands by the younger, urbanized Omanis for greater democracy with the desire of the tribal leaders to maintain the status quo. Political change in the sultanate, therefore, had to be analyzed in light of the paternalistic tradition of tribal and sultanic rule and its confrontation with contemporary pressures for greater participation in decision-making. This consideration was explicitly reflected in the appointment and reappointment by the sultan of delegates to the Majlis al-Dawla, as an appointed upper chamber to counterbalance the elected Majlis al-Shura. The two together constituted the Majlis Oman (Council of Oman). Both houses functioned as conduits of information between the people and the government ministries.

The second Majlis al-Dawla, scheduled to sit for three years starting in January 2001, was appointed in October. It consisted of forty-eight members, including five women, two of them newly appointed. The sultan appeared to have made an effort to keep the membership of the body broadly representative of the various ethnic and religious groups in Oman. Still, over half the delegates had served during the previous term. Among those who were reappointed was Khalfan bin Nasir al-Wahibi, who had served in several ministerial positions before being named to the upper house.[18] Many high-ranking former military officers were also reappointed for second terms, as were technocrats and members of the tribes close to the royal family. A new appointee to the Majlis al-Dawla was Murtada bin Hasan bin 'Ali al-Lawati of a Shi'i mercantile family, who had headed the economic committee of the Majlis al-Shura. Lawati had been defeated at the polls in the September election.[19]

ECONOMIC AND SOCIAL ISSUES

The steady integration of Oman into the global economy took another step forward when the sultanate became a full-fledged member of the World Trade Organization (WTO) in October.[20] For the Omani economy, aiming to move away from its hydrocarbon dependency, this step held the key to a strategy of promoting future growth. However, the coveted membership came with a price, namely a commitment by the sultanate to a 15% dumping tax for all agricultural and industrial products and the liberalization of its service sector, including banking, insurance and telecommunications.[21]

With oil continuing to be the main source of its revenue, Oman remained highly vulnerable to fluctuations in world oil prices. Commerce and Industry Minister Maqbul bin 'Ali Sultan said the first challenge was to utilize the geo-strategic location of the country, optimizing the use of its natural resources, and promoting economic diversification. With Omani oil reserves limited, intensive efforts had to be made in exploration for additional reserves so that depletion would be deferred, he emphasized.[22]

Meanwhile, the government continued its efforts to diversify its sources of revenue, with gas revenue the main element of this strategy. The known reserves of natural gas in the sultanate, though not very large, provided a basis for economic diversification by added value through the establishment of industries utilizing natural gas. The authorities drew up plans to develop gas-based industrial projects, particularly in Sohar, and to accelerate the export of natural gas, which began in April 2000.[23] "We have to add to the proven reserves as quickly as possible," explained Ibn Sultan, "so that commitments could be made for the prospective industries which would require assured and continuous supplies of gas for the entire duration of their life."[24]

Opportunities to generate revenue from sources other than oil and gas remained limited. The issue of taxation remained highly sensitive and the government pledged not to introduce personal income taxes. Corporate taxation was also a controversial issue. Omanization, diversification and privatization remained the three central pillars of economic policy.

The looming domestic issue, however, was unemployment. Minister Ibn Sultan pointed out that:

> despite ongoing efforts to expand the employment of Omanis in various sectors, it has been estimated that the expatriate workers account for about two-thirds of the total employment. While Omanis may account for some 80% of employment in the public sector, their presence in the private sector remains small. Every year, young Omanis are entering the labor market and opportunities have to be found for their gainful employment."[25]

In an attempt to alleviate unemployment, the government increased pressure on the local and foreign private sectors to replace expatriates with Omanis and provide employment opportunities for the rapidly growing and overwhelmingly young Omani workforce.[26]

Rapid population expansion in the sultanate reduced the capacity of the government to provide all the services that it had offered in the past. Budgetary limits prompted increased sales of public assets. Oman was the first of the Gulf states to embrace privatization as a means of dealing with the challenges of a volatile oil market. In March, the government approved the privatization of Sib International Airport.[27] It also considered privatizing the telecommunications and postal services. To this end, the government decided to increase the level of permitted foreign investment, which had been restricted to 49% in any Omani business. In October, Commerce and Industry Minister bin 'Ali Sultan announced that barring a few sectors, such as trading, the government would allow foreign ownership of up to 70%, effective as of 1 January 2001.[28]

FOREIGN AFFAIRS

GULF ISSUES
Regional issues connected to the Persian Gulf continued to be the primary focus of Omani foreign policy in 2000. Meeting in Manama, Bahrain, in December at their annual summit, the Gulf Cooperation Council (GCC) heads of state agreed on a joint defense pact restating a previous commitment from 1987 that an attack on one member state would be considered as an attack on all. In addition, the pact called for a significant expansion of the "Peninsula Shield," a joint GCC force based in Saudi Arabia (see chapter on inter-Arab relations).[29] Oman welcomed the signing of the pact but remained skeptical that it would ever be implemented. It was Sultan Qabus who, in the aftermath of the 1991 Gulf War, had first recommended substantial expansion of the force to 100,000, with troops from all the Gulf states but to no avail (see *MECS* 1991, pp. 596–97). In November 1993, a meeting of GCC defense ministers approved the strengthening of the Peninsula Shield from 8,000 to 17,000 troops, but the decision was never carried out.

Meanwhile, Oman continued to enhance cooperation with other member states. In March, the UAE and Oman fixed their common border after years of acrimony (see *MECS* 1992, p. 650).[30] Oman thereby became the only GCC state to have resolved all its border disputes. It also held discussions with Bahrain concerning the right of their respective citizens to travel to each others' countries using only their identity cards, and on legal and environmental affairs.[31]

RELATIONS WITH IRAQ AND IRAN
Oman appeared to be moving with the Arab mainstream in improving ties with Iraq (see chapter on inter-Arab relations). A decade after the Iraqi invasion of Kuwait, there were increasing signs that Gulf Arab states, apart from Kuwait and Saudi Arabia, wanted to see an end to the international isolation of Iraq, and its reintegration into the regional economy. The sultanate had never actually severed ties with Iraq, although it kept Baghdad at arm's length, consistently urging Saddam Husayn to fully comply with UN resolutions so that sanctions could be lifted. However, the deadlock on the issue in the UN Security Council and the revival of Iraqi relations with other Arab countries prompted a softening

of Omani policy toward Iraq. Sensitive to growing popular outrage over the humanitarian effect of the sanctions and to improving relations between Iraq and other Arab countries, Oman became more vocal in calling for an end to the UN sanctions. Omani Minister for Foreign Affairs Yusuf bin 'Alawi bin 'Abdallah, speaking at the UN General Assembly in September 2000, stressed that "the UN has a historical responsibility to cooperate with Iraq in order to minimize the widespread suffering that may befall the people of Iraq in the future."[32] Meanwhile, he also suggested that sanctions be lifted on the basis that known Iraqi weapons of mass destruction had been destroyed.

Ties with the reformist government in Iran remained stable, although Oman was sensitive to any possible damage they might cause to its relations with the neighboring UAE, which was involved in a dispute with Iran over sovereignty of three Persian Gulf islands — the Greater and Lesser Tunbs (Tanab al-Kubra and Tanab al-Sughra) and Abu Musa. When, following the April meeting of GCC foreign ministers in Jidda, Iranian officials announced the signing of an Iranian-Omani "defense agreement," the Omanis quickly rebutted the statement in order to allay fears in Abu Dhabi. Foreign Minister 'Alawi was swiftly dispatched to Abu Dhabi to reassure President Shaykh Zayid bin Sultan Al Nuhayyan of the UAE about the nature of the "security cooperation deal."[33] Even this wording, however, was subsequently diluted, so that any notion of an agreement with Iran was subsumed within a "routine" and "technical" framework. Ultimately, 'Alawi announced that there had been no agreement, as "there is no need to draw up [an] agreement with Iran, and if there were it would have to include all the countries [of the Gulf]."[34]

RELATIONS WITH ISRAEL AND THE PA

Even more than some of the other Arab countries, Oman wished to see a successful conclusion to the Arab-Israeli peace process, as renewed conflict could potentially destabilize the Persian Gulf, particularly via the mischief-making of radical leaders such as Saddam Husayn. Accordingly, while the Omani government had paid lip service to the Palestinian cause for years, it generally supported a negotiated settlement with Israel. Reiterating the sultanate's stance on the peace process, Foreign Minister 'Alawi stated in September that "Oman had embraced peace and dialogue as a basic principle since the dawn of the blessed Omani renaissance on 23 July 1970."[35] Significantly, Oman participated in the multilateral working group on water. Moreover, it was the site of the Middle East Desalination Research Center, which was supported in part by the Israeli government. Omani and Israeli officials met in April to discuss regional water resources.[36] As 'Alawi stated in an interview in August:

> We [Oman] have said from the beginning that we are ready to turn a new page. That is why we have welcomed Israeli officials here in the early stages of post-Oslo peace talks. We are now ready to forget the hostility of yesterday, but Israel must be willing to take some daring steps, too. Israel must be prepared to show Arabs the peace dividends as well. So far, they have not, and this has bred mistrust.[37]

During the course of the year, however, Oman drew closer to the Arab consensus. Although disappointed with PA chairman Yasir 'Arafat's performance, Omani leaders could not afford to show anything but total solidarity with the Palestinians, calling for the establishment of a Palestinian state, with Arab Jerusalem as its capital, and greater international involvement in the dispute. 'Alawi explained that the aim of a September meeting with Israeli prime minister Ehud Barak, in the aftermath of the failed Camp David negotiations, was to inform him that the Palestinians were not alone in their stance on Jerusalem and that "the Palestinian sovereignty over Eastern Jerusalem was undisputable."[38] 'Alawi's remarks followed official commentary in the local press categorically condemning the Israeli suppression of the Palestinians and demanding that Israel relinquish control of Arab sites.

The renewed outbreak of Israeli-Palestinian clashes at the beginning of October proved too much for the Omani government. Furthermore, the subsequent upsurge of public sympathy in Oman for the Palestinians made the government wary of maintaining ties with Israel in the absence of a final settlement agreement and placed Oman in a uniquely embarrassing spotlight. In mid-October, Oman announced that it was closing both its trade office in Tel Aviv and the Israeli trade office in Muscat. The official statement from the Oman News Agency (ONA) which accompanied the closure announcement stated that "the sultanate will continue to be interested in a just and comprehensive peace...but with terms that will champion the unjustly treated, safeguard the holy sites and restore rights to their owners."[39] Both trade offices were opened in 1996 in the aftermath of a first-ever visit by an Israeli prime minister, Yitzhak Rabin. The closures of the offices reflected Omani government frustration at Israeli reluctance to implement vital elements of the Oslo peace agreements signed in 1993, as well as its more immediate aversion to Israel's suppression of the Palestinian intifada. It also protected Oman from embarrassment at the Cairo Arab summit conference in late October (see chapter on inter-Arab relations).

A further indication of a change in the official position was a statement in mid-October by the senior establishment Ibadhi cleric, the grand mufti Shaykh Ahmad bin Hamad al-Khalili, who stressed that Islamic holy sites in Jerusalem which were "under the control of others" must be "liberated by any means." No peace agreement could be made without the granting of Palestinian sovereignty over the al-Aqsa Mosque, he added. This was followed by an announcement by the sultan calling for the establishment of bank accounts to accept donations in support of the Palestinians. As of early December, *The Times of Oman* reported, donations to the fund totaled OR1.2m. ($1.3m).[40]

These gestures were accompanied by a number of policy statements reinforcing the Omani commitment to the Palestinian cause. The Omani representative to the UN, Fu'ad al-Hina'i, speaking before the Security Council in early October, condemned Israeli actions against the Palestinians as a violation of international agreements providing for the protection of civilians during wartime. In a statement issued to the official press in November, Foreign Minister 'Alawi subsequently stressed that Oman was working directly with the Palestinians and urged other countries to offer their support for the Palestinians. Later in the month, he suggested that the instability in the West Bank and Gaza resulted from the excessive use of force by Israel.[41]

These statements were designed, inter alia, as a response to the dramatic upsurge in pro-Palestinian sentiment in Oman. The clearest manifestation of this sympathy came in early October with a series of peaceful demonstrations in Muscat and other areas around the country over several consecutive days. The first demonstration was organized by students at Sultan Qabus University, with subsequent marches including students from other local institutions and local citizens. Marches were also held after Friday prayers.[42]

There was genuine anger at Israeli actions, but equally, the pro-Western sultanate of

Oman, allied with the US, could not afford to let Islamists or other radicals take the lead in condemning Israel. Protests, albeit carefully contained, were allowed. By the normally quiescent standards of Omani political culture they were sizable, with hundreds of participants in most cases.[43]

While low-key by most standards, the protests represented a sea change in political expression in Omani terms, as politically motivated demonstrations were rare in Oman. Moreover, they were given a warm reception by the government-monitored local press. The laissez-faire attitude of the government to the protests was underlined by assistance given by the police to the marchers. Large numbers of officers were reportedly on hand to stop traffic and assist the demonstrators.[44] Despite initial reluctance, the Omani authorities eventually decided to tolerate the protests rather than curb the demonstrations and lay themselves open to charges of being overly pro-Western or indulgent toward Israel.

RELATIONS WITH BRITAIN AND THE US

Beyond the region, deepening relations with Britain and the US remained a priority. Oman had become a favorite strategic partner of the allied forces in the region due to its pro-Western position on geopolitical issues and its excellent location outside the Strait of Hormuz. As in the past, Oman turned to Britain for expertise in military and technological fields, while a cadre of British expatriates, albeit gradually diminishing in size, acted as advisers. In November, both states announced that their largest joint military exercise since the 1991 Gulf War would take place in September and October 2001. The announcement was made following a meeting in Muscat between British defense secretary Geoff Hoon and Sultan Qabus.[45] During Hoon's visit, a British defense firm signed an agreement with the Royal Army of Oman to improve its response capacity. This agreement with the traditional military ally of Oman followed agreements earlier in the year with two French-led companies to provide the Omani army with a surface-to-air missile system.[46]

Like other Gulf countries, Oman continued to rely on the US as the ultimate guarantor of its security, the GCC defense cooperation agreements notwithstanding. In November, Oman renewed its core military access agreement with the US, first signed in 1980 and renewed for ten years in 1990. The current renewal was also for ten years, and, while details were not released, it was known to contain terms similar to past agreements. Previous agreements provided the US with access to various facilities at the Sib, Thumrayt, al-Khasab and Masira airbases. As part of the agreement, the US paid for upgrading some of the facilities at these bases. While the US had military cooperation agreements of various types with other Gulf states, the Oman agreement was the only formal propositioning agreement that predated the Gulf War.[47]

NOTES

For the place and frequency of publications cited here, and for the full name of the publication, news agency, radio station or monitoring service where an abbreviation is used, please see "List of Sources." Only in the case of more than one publication bearing the same name is the place of publication noted here. However, all references to *al-Watan* are to the Muscat daily.

1. *Al Watan al-'Arabi*, 30 June 2000.
2. The population of Oman has been growing at an estimated 3.5% annually, one of the highest rates in the world. See Oman, *Statistical Yearbook — 1995*; see also *GSNL*, 9 June 1999.
3. *ME*, November 1998, pp. 23–24.
4. *Al-Usbu' al-'Arabi*, 26 September 2000.
5. *Al-Watan*, 15 September; *ODO*, 28 September 2000.
6. *Al-Usbu' al-'Arabi*, 26 September 2000.
7. According to Interior Ministry Undersecretary Sayyid Muhammad bin Sultan Al Bu Sa'idi, 750,000–800,000 Omani citizens aged twenty-one and over would have the right to vote in the 2003 election. See *GSNL*, 6 November 2000.
8. *GSNL*, 25 September 2000.
9. *Middle East Insight*, June 2001, p. 28. See also *GSNL*, 25 September 2000. Not surprisingly, there were more female candidates in the capital and in the prosperous Batina farming region located along the coast than in the more isolated and tradition-bound regions such as the Musandam Peninsula.
10. *Al-Wasat*, 25 September 2000.
11. *Al-Watan*, 14 September 2000.
12. *Al-Watan al-'Arabi*, 22 September 2000.
13. Interview given by 'Abd al-'Aziz al-Rawwas to *Arabies*, July 2000, No. 33, pp. 16–17.
14. *GSNL*, 25 September 2000.
15. *CR*, Oman, January 2001, p. 14.
16. *ODO*, 28 September 2000.
17. Ibid.
18. *CR*, Oman, January 2001, p. 14.
19. *GSNL*, 6 November 2000.
20. The WTO membership protocol was signed on 10 October by Commerce and Industry Minister Maqbul bin 'Ali Sultan. Oman became the 139th member state of the WTO and the fifth GCC country (alongside Bahrain, Kuwait, Qatar and the UAE) to join the organization. *ODO*, 22 November 2000.
21. *Al-Watan*, 17 September 2000.
22. *ODO*, 25 September 2000.
23. *Al-Watan*, 4 September 2000. See also *IHT*, 27 April 2001.
24. *ODO*, 25 September 2000.
25. Ibid.
26. *Al-Watan*, 17, 20 September 2000.
27. *GSNL*, 17 April 2000.
28. *ODO*, 25 September 2000. See also *IHT*, 27 April 2001.
29. *CR*, Oman, January 2001, p. 17.
30. *ME*, May 2001, No. 312, p. 8.
31. *GSNL*, 1 May 2000.
32. *ODO*, 17 September 2000.
33. *GSNL*, 1 May 2000.
34. Ibid.
35. *ODO*, 17 September 2000.
36. *GSNL*, 1 May 2000.

37. Interview given by 'Abd al-'Aziz Rawwas to *Arabies*, July 2000, No. 33, p. 17.
38. *ODO*, 22 September 2000. See also 'Alawi's comment following the GCC foreign ministers' meeting in Jidda. *Al-Watan*, 2 September 2000.
39. *CR*, Oman, January 2001.
40. *Al-Watan*, 19 October 2000.
41. *ODO*, 22 November 2000.
42. *Al-Watan*, 23 October 2000.
43. *GSNL*, 23 October 2000.
44. *ODO*, 19 October 2000.
45. *GSNL*, 20 November 2000.
46. Ibid.
47. *CR*, Oman, January 2001, p. 17.

The Palestinian Authority
(al-Sulta al-Filastiniyya)

ELIE REKHESS AND RAMI REGAVIM

The Palestinian Authority (PA) was confronted in Autumn 2000 by the most profound challenge since its inception in 1994–95: the collapse of the peace process and the descent into violence. The two-week negotiations between the Palestinian, Israeli and US leaderships at Camp David in July failed to culminate with a signing on a final status agreement (FSA). Subsequent attempts to reignite the peace negotiations were abruptly ended with the controversial visit of Israeli Likud opposition leader Ariel Sharon to the disputed Temple Mount (al-Haram al-Sharif) in Jerusalem on 28 September. The visit sparked a series of violent clashes between Israeli security forces and armed PA police officers who joined mass demonstrations throughout the West Bank and Gaza Strip. Early attempts to calm the situation failed and the violent clashes continued in what became known as the Aqsa Intifada. In the first three months of the intifada hundreds of Palestinians and dozens of Israelis were killed and thousands wounded. The Sharm al-Shaykh summit that took place in October in an attempt to stop the violence failed to produce results on the ground, and the intifada continued. While it was unclear who, if anyone, gave the order to start the intifada and who controlled it, younger and local leaders, such as Marwan Barghuthi, used the opportunity to advance their political standing, taking as much credit for the intifada as possible.

During the first half of 2000, the negotiations on a FSA approached the decisive stage. Two Israeli military withdrawals took place during the first months of the year in the framework of the Sharm al-Shaykh agreement of October 1999 (see *MECS* 1999, pp. 473–75), while Palestinian and Israeli negotiating teams conducted several preparatory meetings. The Camp David talks of July were designed to culminate with a signed agreement, but after their failure no such agreement was concluded during the remainder of the year.

While the prospects of the final status talks still seemed favorable, the PA made fervent preparations for the declaration of statehood. In February, 'Arafat managed to convene several of the Palestinian opposition groups in the framework of the PLO Central Council and pass a resolution to declare a state unilaterally on 13 September 2000. After the failure of the Camp David talks, a postponement of two months was declared which stretched out during the remainder of 2000.

On the domestic front, the left-wing opposition parties seemed to increase their cooperation with the PA. The Popular Front for the Liberation of Palestine (PFLP) resumed its activity within the PLO framework after a prolonged period of boycott, and following the retirement of its secretary-general George Habash, the PFLP headquarters relocated from Damascus to PA territory. The Democratic Front for the Liberation of Palestine (DFLP) even joined the PA negotiating team for the Camp David talks. The

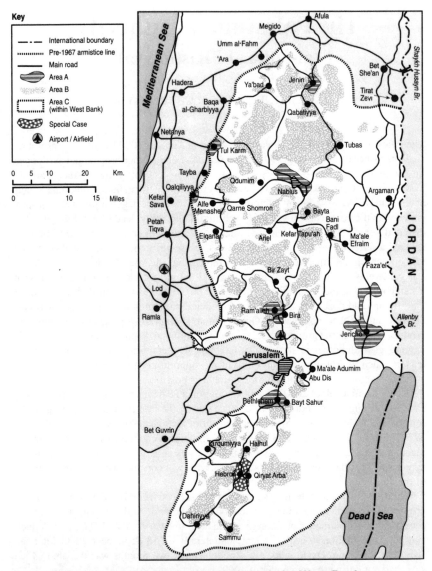

Israeli-Palestinian 1995 Interim Agreement on the West Bank

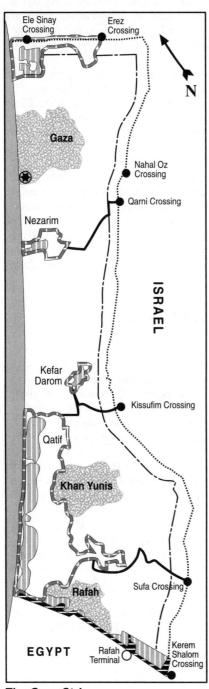

The Gaza Strip

Israeli-Palestinian 1994 Interim Agreement on the Gaza Strip

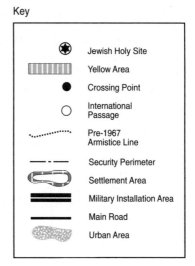

Key

✡	Jewish Holy Site
	Yellow Area
●	Crossing Point
○	International Passage
⋯⋯	Pre-1967 Armistice Line
— · —	Security Perimeter
	Settlement Area
▬	Military Installation Area
—	Main Road
	Urban Area

Islamic opposition, however, maintained its hard-line opposition to the peace process and rejected any compromise with Israel. While Hamas, the main Palestinian Islamic faction, continued to reject any cooperation with the PA, the Islamic Jihad surprisingly agreed to participate in the PLO Central Council deliberations in September over the declaration of statehood.

The cautious optimism in the early months of the year and the continuing improvement in the economic situation in the PA brought a gradual decrease in the public support for the opposition, especially the Islamic opposition. However, the failure of the Camp David talks and the outbreak of the intifada did not bring an automatic increase in the support for these organizations, especially since the PA security and paramilitary forces seemed to be leading the popular struggle.

During the first months of 2000 the PA indeed seemed to be walking along the path of economic development, following the successes of 1999. A continuing decline in the unemployment rate, the issuing of a balanced budget, an improvement in trade and the signing of natural gas production agreement with British Gas, marked the optimistic profile of the Palestinian economy. However, the outbreak of the intifada was an economic disaster for the PA. The unemployment rate soared, trade was cut off almost completely, production slowed to an almost complete halt and huge damages were inflicted upon private and public property due to the heavy fighting in many areas. The year ended with a negative growth of -5.9%.

PALESTINIAN-ISRAELI RELATIONS

DEBATE OVER STATEHOOD

The issue of a unilateral declaration of independence (UDI) gained new urgency in Palestinian quarters early in 2000. Palestinian officials reiterated past assertions of the Palestinian right to declare independence as part of the FSA. PA president Yasir 'Arafat promised that a Palestinian state would be announced during the year 2000, and initiated a campaign to gain international acceptance for such a move.[1] A special two-day meeting of the PLO Central Council, convening in Gaza on 2–3 February, decided on September 2000 to declare statehood.[2]

Once the date for the unilateral proclamation had been set — 13 September — 'Arafat intensified his efforts to gain international support for it. Unlike his campaign in 1999 (see *MECS* 1999, pp. 470–72), this time he appeared to meet with greater success. Notably, both Egypt and Jordan implicitly supported the move, in contrast to their previous response of merely refraining from objecting to it. President Husni Mubarak of Egypt declared straightforwardly in June that Egypt would recognize the Palestinian state, if announced, "under any circumstances."[3] King 'Abdallah of Jordan stressed several times throughout the year that it was the Palestinian right to set up an independent state.[4] He also referred to the long time proposal to form a confederation between Jordan, Israel and the future Palestinian state, and said that "the expression of confederation at this stage of time doesn't exist in our lexicon because it disturbs the peace process and confuses the Palestinian-Israeli track....When peace is reached...Jordanians, Palestinians and Israelis can choose what they see fit in the future."[5]

Reportedly, the European Union (EU) in June began discussing the future status of EU consulates in Jerusalem once the EU countries recognized the Palestinian state.[6] But in August, with the failure of the Camp David talks (see below), the EU reaffirmed its traditional opposition to a Palestinian UDI.[7]

While Palestinian spokespersons speculated that even the US might support the PA in a UDI, the American administration was clear throughout the year about its opposition to such an act. With the failure of the Camp David talks, its objection to a UDI became even more pronounced. In September, the House of Representatives passed a bill imposing sanctions on the PA in the event of a UDI, a step that was harshly criticized by PA representatives.[8]

Public opinion in the West Bank and Gaza was somewhat divided. Most of the Palestinian national factions, including the PA official leadership and the secular opposition groups, expressed enthusiastic support for a UDI. The speaker of the Palestinian National Council (PNC), Salim al-Za'nun, stated in May: "It is our right to declare the Palestinian state and we are ready to bear all the declaration's consequences." The PLO envoy in Washington, Hasan 'Abd al-Rahman, explained in July that "the declaration of a state is a natural right, which nobody can question."[9]

An article published in the East Jerusalem daily *al-Quds* urged the PA to follow the example of the Israeli declaration of statehood in 1948, and not wait for international approval. The article did, however, warn against declaring a state that would extend beyond the pre-June 1967 borders, which were cited in UN Security Council Resolutions 242 and 338, as "no country or international organization would approve it....It would question the reasoning of the Palestinian decision-makers and harm the Palestinian question....This would make the hard-line Israeli stand appear logical and justified."[10]

In March, Na'if Hawatima, secretary-general of the oppositionist DFLP, came out in support of the idea, pointing out that the negotiations between the two parties would henceforth be conducted between two equal sides, each representing a state.[11] George Habash, secretary-general of the oppositionist PFLP, was also favorable, stating in July that "we support the establishment of a fully sovereign Palestinian state, not the state proposed by the Americans as a trade-off for abandoning Palestine, the right of return, the border, and water issues."[12]

The Islamic opposition groups, however, rejected the idea of a UDI altogether. Hamas spiritual leader, Shaykh Ahmad Yasin, said during an interview in July that declaring a state was pointless, since a Palestinian state had already been declared in Algiers in 1988 and nothing had come of it. 'Abd al-'Aziz Rantisi, the Hamas spokesperson in the Gaza Strip, explained that Hamas "is not opposed to the date of declaring the state but to the price that the Palestinian people will pay for it," i.e., that the Palestinians would be gaining only a small portion of historical Palestine.[13]

Opposition was also voiced by secular political figures. The veteran Fath leader, Hani al-Hasan, reiterated in the Ramallah-based daily *al-Ayyam* that there was no need to re-declare statehood, since this had already been done in Algiers in 1988. A future Palestinian state, he said, would require Israeli recognition; otherwise, the significance was declaring a state by means of war. This path could be disastrous for the Palestinians, since "war would be won by the more powerful."[14] Minister of Culture and Information Yasir 'Abd Rabbuh stated similarly, in June, that "we should not declare a Palestinian state unless we will truly be able to impose our sovereignty over all the Palestinian territories, including Jerusalem, under Resolution 242 as a minimum."[15]

On 10 September, three days before the designated date of the declaration of independence, the PLO Central Council decided to postpone the declaration for two months[16] (see below), and the issue subsided for the rest of the year. In the view of some political commentators, Israeli warnings helped preempt the idea of the UDI, which 'Arafat may not in any case have been fully determined to carry out from the start. Conceivably, he used the threat of a declaration of statehood as a means to restart the peace process.[17]

The eruption of the intifada in late September changed the nature of the public discourse on the UDI. Declaration of a state ceased to be a goal to be achieved within the peace process framework and became a central objective of the popular uprising.

THE CAMP DAVID SUMMIT TALKS

The negotiations with Israel over the FSA, which continued during the year, preoccupied public opinion in the PA. In contrast to the Israeli viewpoint, which encompassed various options ranging from partial to nearly total Israeli withdrawal from the territories, Palestinian spokespersons emphasized that only full implementation of UN Resolutions 242 and 338 calling for a full withdrawal from territories occupied in 1967 was a viable option for the Palestinians.[18] US president Bill Clinton's remarks to 'Arafat during the latter's visit to Washington on 20 January, later paraphrased by US secretary of state Madeleine Albright, that the Palestinians should be more flexible and not expect to get everything they demanded, elicited an angry response in the Palestinian press. The Palestinians had already compromised a great deal, and the demand for Resolutions 242 and 338 was the minimum that the Palestinians could ask for, one commentator wrote.[19] Another explained:

> The problem is that, from the start we...did not demand the return of all Palestine so we can offer concessions that would enable us get back the West Bank, the Gaza Strip, and Jerusalem on top....The requests of the "impartial broker" [i.e., the US] have led us to offer concessions to Israel in the 1967 occupied areas. Israel has already guaranteed that the area it seized before the 1967 war was in its pocket and would no longer be the subject of disagreement or even the subject of negotiations with us.[20]

The optimism expressed by Israeli, American and European spokespersons throughout the first part of the year was in stark contrast to Palestinian pessimism regarding the prospects of the peace process.

The atmosphere in the PA did not favor participation in the Camp David talks, held 11–25 July. Members of the Palestinian delegation expressed pessimism about the chances for success prior to the summit, viewing the gap between the sides as too wide to be bridged in just two weeks of talks. Minister of Culture and Information Rabbuh commented in June that "the Washington summit will be held under the worst ever circumstances,"[21] while the speaker of the Palestinian Legislative Council (PLC), Ahmad al-Quray' (Abu 'Ala), stated that there was no point continuing the negotiations so long as the Israelis were not prepared to comply with Resolution 242, and defined the Israeli stand on Jerusalem as "extremely bad."[22]

Several spokespersons, however, thought that the renewed negotiations were worth a try. One was the long-time human rights activist and a critic of the PA administration Dr. Iyad al-Sarraj. Sarraj maintained that the Palestinians must attend Camp David, describing those who rejected the very participation in the talks as cynical and self-righteous, and claiming that 'Arafat would emerge from the summit a winner, whether an agreement was signed or not.[23]

'Arafat, in an attempt to cobble together a unified Palestinian stance representing a wide spectrum of Palestinian viewpoints at Camp David, called on all factions in the PLO Executive Committee to join the Palestinian delegation for the summit, a step described by al-Sharq al-Awsat as "unprecedented." Representatives of the Syrian-based DFLP and the Popular Struggle Front (PSF), along with moderate Palestinian People's Party (PPP), responded positively and were included in the delegation, while the PFLP declined to do so.[24] Explaining his participation in the talks, DFLP secretary-general Hawatima said that although he was not optimistic about the chances for success, there was a need for "responsible coalition leadership" that would guarantee Palestinian rights in the tough circumstances of the summit.[25] Another DFLP representative at the talks, Taysir Khalid, pointed to the need "to face the Israeli and American pressure as a united front."[26]

Not surprisingly, Shaykh Yasin of Hamas, came out vehemently against the summit, calling upon the Palestinian delegation to withdraw from the talks, which he termed "futile."[27] The DFLP, rejecting a critical attack by Musa Abu Marzuq of Hamas for its participation in the talks, issued a statement emphasizing its "clear...policy...since 1973...to arrive at real negotiations based on the international terms of reference in word and deed," and citing DFLP operations against Israel in the 1970s as a reminder of its patriotism.[28]

Essentially, the Camp David talks illuminated the significant, perhaps unbridgeable differences that still existed between the two sides. On some issues disagreement appeared to be as thin as a thread and on others as wide as an ocean. The Israeli ambition to achieve an agreed proclamation of an end to the conflict opened up the debate on all the issues that had either never been officially discussed between the parties, or had not been discussed intensively. Disagreement focused on three major issues: (1) The problem of the refugees; (2) the question of Jerusalem; and (3) the final borders of the Palestinian state.

The Refugees

The longstanding Palestinian position regarding the solution to the refugee problem was an adherence to the right of return (haqq al-'awda), embodied in the full implementation of UN Resolution 194 passed in December 1948. The Palestinian demand was for full repatriation of all the refugees and any of their descendants who desired it, and compensation for the rest. Israel had historically rejected this demand. Official Palestinian spokespersons had shown barely any readiness to compromise. During the latter part of 2000, however, reports in the Israeli press indicated that the Palestinians might consider some flexibility regarding the refugee issue,[29] although these reports remained vague and could not be attributed to specific Palestinian personalities.

In contrast, Palestinian spokespersons reiterated their commitment to the full implementation of Resolution 194 in the Palestinian and Arab press. An editorial in al-Quds, entitled "No Peace Without Solving the Refugee Issue," appealed to the Israeli government to "break out of the hard-line circle in which it placed itself and show responsiveness to fair Palestinian demands...if it actually wants the peace process to be...acceptable [to] the Palestinian people."[30] In a telling statement, the head of the PLO Refugee Department in the PA, As'ad 'Abd al-Rahman, declared: "We in the PLO adhere to Resolution 194, which is the compromise [emphasis added] solution that we accept." Referring to the possibility of reaching an agreement without solving the refugee problem, he called such a solution "a farce that is imposed on us," adding: "an imposed settlement is a rejected settlement."[31]

Leaks to the press during the talks at Camp David revealed that Israel offered to solve the problem by settling refugees — especially those from Lebanon, whose situation was described as extremely difficult — in evacuated settlements.[32] These reports, which were not confirmed by Palestinian officials, evoked anger in refugee circles, mostly in Lebanon and Syria, who rejected such an offer and insisted on their right to return to their original pre-1948 dwellings. According to an *Ha'aretz* commentator, these Palestinian refugees viewed the problem as a personal one involving private property lost in 1948, rather than as a political or national issue. They did not, therefore, regard the PA as an authorized or legitimate negotiator on their behalf with Israel, and refused to waive their right to demand the return of their land.[33]

The failure of the Camp David talks, and the subsequent outbreak of what was widely known as the Aqsa Intifada (see below), evoked an even greater adherence to Resolution 194 in public discourse. A PLC session convened on 22 December adopted the commitment to the right of return stipulated by Resolution 194 as the official policy of the PA, announcing that there could be no solution to the Palestinian problem unless the refugee issue was resolved.[34] Another illustration of this trend was the re-naming the intifada by some as Intifadat al-'Awda (the Intifada of the Return). The return of the refugees was repeatedly cited by Palestinians as one of the goals of the intifada, which, if not fulfilled, would perpetuate the uprising.

Jerusalem

Another point on the agenda hampering the negotiations, and representing an almost unbridgeable divide, was the issue of Jerusalem. Countless statements by Israeli leaders about their commitment to the eternal unity of Jerusalem countered the insistence of demands by Palestinian leaders that Jerusalem — al-Quds — must be the capital of the future Palestinian state. Moreover, the presence of the Jewish neighborhoods in East Jerusalem (perceived by the Palestinians as no different from any of the other West Bank settlements) constituted an even greater obstacle. Broadly, the issue involved two major points of dispute: (1) The status of Greater Jerusalem, namely the Jewish and Palestinian neighborhoods of East Jerusalem; and (2) The status of the Old City and the Temple Mount, with the latter lying at the core of the problem.

Discussions during February and March over the third phase of the second Further Redeployment (FRD), which was agreed upon in the Israel-PA framework agreement signed in September 1999 (see *MECS* 1999, pp. 472–73), involved a demand by the PA that the 6.1% of territory slated for Israeli evacuation redeployment include land and villages bordering Jerusalem, namely the villages of Abu Dis, 'Anata and Bayt Hanina. The Israeli government rejected this demand, reportedly in response to pressures by right-wing activists, and the third phase of the second FRD thus did not include areas bordering on Jerusalem.[35] However, in May, during discussions on the third and final FRD, the Israeli cabinet (and later the Knesset) approved the transfer of three Palestinian villages in the vicinity of Jerusalem, including Abu Dis, 'Azariyya and Sawaharra al-Sharqiyya, as a goodwill gesture prior to the FRD itself. The inclusion of Abu Dis in the proposed transfer was in line with a longstanding Israeli offer to solve the issue of Jerusalem by making Abu Dis the Palestinian capital. Palestinian spokespersons, however, totally rejected the idea. "East Jerusalem alone will be our capital," 'Arafat reiterated in

February.[36] In the event, the third FRD was postponed again by Israeli prime minister Ehud Barak following violent protests in the Palestinian areas on 15 May commemorating the Palestinian *Naqba* ("disaster") of 1948.[37] It did not take place at all during 2000, and was not even discussed after the failure of the Camp David talks and the outbreak of the intifada.

The non-implementation of the third FRD added to the Palestinian dissatisfaction with the Israeli offer. The PA minister in charge of Jerusalem affairs, Faysal al-Husayni, emphasized that a solution could not be reached without negotiating about Jerusalem. Pointing out that the negotiations were not only about East Jerusalem, he argued: "70% of West Jerusalem is owned by Palestinians...why should we only talk about East Jerusalem?"[38] In a similar vein, PA minister of state Hasan 'Asfur insisted that the Palestinian delegation had made significant concessions in the Camp David talks by agreeing to confine the negotiations to East Jerusalem, rather than discussing both East and West Jerusalem.[39]

In June, just prior to the Camp David summit, Prime Minister Barak reiterated his commitment to be faithful to Jerusalem. This statement, in addition to his past declarations where he committed himself to "a united Jerusalem under our sovereignty as the capital of Israel forever,"[40] did not leave much to hope for the Palestinian side regarding the Jerusalem issue.[41] Nevertheless, several conciliatory proposals were reportedly raised by the Palestinian side in Camp David, including the idea that the Jewish quarter of the Old City would remain under Israeli control and that a corridor would connect the quarter to the Western Wall, while the Haram al-Sharif (Temple Mount) area would be placed under Palestinian sovereignty. At one point, the Palestinian delegation suggested that the Temple Mount be placed under "Islamic" sovereignty to be shared by several Muslim countries, headed by Morocco, with the Palestinians holding custody. At another point, the former UN proposal to internationalize the city was also raised. All these proposals were rejected by the Israeli side.[42] The Palestinians, for their part, vehemently rejected a series of Israeli and American proposals, which included: (1) An inter-religious "divine" sovereignty over the Temple Mount, as opposed to sole "Islamic" sovereignty, as the Palestinians proposed; (2) "limited" sovereignty, meaning that the Temple Mount would be declared an area similar in status to that of Area B according to the Oslo accords, under Palestinian civil management and Israeli responsibility for security; and (3) an American proposal to differentiate between "above ground" sovereignty — meaning sovereignty over the mosques — and "below ground" sovereignty — meaning sovereignty over the buried archeological remains of the ancient Jewish Temple (Beit Hamikdash).[43]

As the Camp David negotiations progressed, the issue of Jerusalem, according to Israeli press reports, emerged as the most intractable.[44] Reportedly, the Palestinian stand on Jerusalem grew increasingly resolute, ultimately bringing about the failure of the talks. 'Arafat's adamant stand on Jerusalem, according to commentary in *Ha'aretz*, stemmed from his assumption that he would obtain sovereignty over all of East Jerusalem. While he anticipated that he would be forced to make concessions on such issues as the right of return and the Palestinian demand to remove all the Jewish settlements, he felt he could not compromise on Jerusalem. He had long dreamt of entering Jerusalem as the savior of the city, a modern-day reincarnation of Salah al-Din, who had expelled the Crusaders from Jerusalem in the twelfth century. Reportedly, 'Arafat had delayed the completion of renovation work being carried out on the Aqsa Mosque on the Temple Mount so that he could time his entry into Jerusalem with it.[45]

Although the focus of the talks about Jerusalem was on the status of the Old City, there was no agreement about the future of the rest of East Jerusalem either. Map diagrams of the proposals made at Camp David regarding Jerusalem, prepared after the summit by a Palestinian team operating out of Orient House in East Jerusalem, showed that the entire area of East Jerusalem and its suburbs would consist of a patchwork of Palestinian and Israeli enclaves. In PA minister Husayni's views the maps proved that the Israeli offer at Camp David was neither a compromise nor evidence of generosity, but a plan for territorial fragmentation that would preclude the formation of a sovereign Palestinian state.[46]

The Borders

The disputes over the issue of Jerusalem were directly related to the question of the final borders: the Palestinians insisted on a complete Israeli withdrawal from East Jerusalem, in line with their demand for full Israeli compliance with Resolutions 242 and 338, as they interpreted them (for the Israeli positions, see chapter on Israel).

Reviewing statements by Palestinian spokespersons throughout the year, one would be hard-pressed to find one that did not stress the insistence on a full Israeli withdrawal from all the territories occupied in 1967. Ideas raised in the Israeli media regarding the composition and territorial size of a future Palestinian state did not generate any serious responses on the Palestinian side,[47] e.g., an idea included in the Beilin-Abu Mazin plan, an outline program for the FSA drafted by Labor Minister Yossi Beilin and PLO secretary-general Mahmud 'Abbas (Abu Mazin) during 1994–95, that Jewish settlements would remain in place under Palestinian sovereignty. This idea was also referred to publicly by some settlers, but it was rejected out of hand by Palestinian speakers. Abu Mazin himself promptly declared after the agreement was publicized: "We do not want a single Israeli settler on Palestinian territories, whether or not they would be under Palestinian sovereignty." He proposed that Israel follow the model of complete withdrawal adopted in Sinai following the peace treaty with Egypt.[48]

The Palestinians demanded that Israel comply with "international legitimacy," a Palestinian code word for UN resolutions, especially Resolutions 242 and 338, which stipulated, in the Palestinian interpretation, full withdrawal from the West Bank and the Gaza Strip. As the PA minister for local government, Dr. Sa'ib 'Urayqat, explained, the Palestinians had viewed the peace process from the start as based on the full withdrawal by Israel from the territories it had occupied in June 1967. "When we engaged in negotiations, the goal was to implement rather than negotiate Resolutions 242 and 338," he stressed.[49] In the Palestinian view, the intermediate-stage partial redeployments were, in essence, a prelude to the final status stage, in which Israel would leave the West Bank altogether. "We refuse to relinquish [even] a grain of land in this homeland,"[50] 'Urayqat asserted.

The idea of a limited land exchange between Israel and the Palestinians, implicit in the Beilin-Abu Mazin plan, was discussed by the negotiating teams in the context of the final status negotiations during the year. Reportedly, the Israeli negotiators at the Camp David talks proposed that in return for the annexation to Israel of several blocs of settlements in the West Bank, Israel would transfer an equal-sized territory in the Halutza area, located in western Israel adjacent to the Gaza Strip and the Israeli-Egyptian border, to the Palestinian state.[51] This idea was rejected by the Palestinians shortly before the Camp David talks resumed in July. Veteran Fath leader Hani al-Hasan explained that:

"The maximum which Israel would offer...is to exchange 200 sq. km. of land adjacent to the Gaza Strip with the Palestinians. Brother Abu Mazin did a good thing when he promptly turned down this humiliating offer....the Palestinians are not begging favors from Israel, but are demanding the full Israeli withdrawal from the occupied territories and the recognition of the right of the Palestinian refugees to return home."[52] Similarly, the proposal was rejected by the Palestinian delegation at Camp David, though not in principle. As reported by Minister of Culture and Information 'Abd Rabbuh: "We said that we can exchange, in a very narrow sense, parts of territories, but this should be very limited. The Israelis want...8 or 10 [% of the territories to be exchanged], less or more. Through this action they want to partition the West Bank into three or four cantons."[53]

Summarizing the Camp David talks and the reasons for its failure, 'Abd Rabbuh painted a pessimistic picture: "Some Americans say that the rest of the issues, with the exception of Jerusalem, have been resolved, but this is absolutely untrue....We have disagreements on Jerusalem, the refugees, the territories, and other issues."[54]

THE INTIFADA

THE OUTBREAK OF VIOLENCE
A few days before Rosh Hashana, the Jewish new year, on 28 September, Israeli opposition leader Ariel Sharon visited the Temple Mount site, heavily guarded by police. The visit sparked violent protests on the Temple Mount the following day, during which six Palestinian demonstrators were killed by Israeli security forces. Unrest quickly spread throughout the West Bank and Gaza Strip, with Palestinian police and security forces joining the demonstrators and shooting at Israeli soldiers. American and European attempts to quickly calm the situation failed. On 30 September (only two days after the Sharon visit), a twelve-year-old Palestinian, Muhammad Dura, was shot and killed when he and his father were caught in cross-fire between IDF and PA security forces. The incident, recorded by a French TV photographer, stirred the Arab and Muslim world and further intensified the violent clashes in the territories. The unrest also spread into the Arab cities, villages and neighborhoods in Israel, with thirteen Arab demonstrators killed by the Israeli police (see chapter on Israel).

The following week, the Tomb of Joseph in Nablus, a Jewish holy site guarded by Israeli forces, came under intense attack by PA security forces and demonstrators. On 7 October, after the fatal shooting of an Israeli border police officer, the IDF agreed to evacuate the tomb following an agreement with PA officers that the structure would not be harmed. Shortly after the withdrawal of the IDF forces, however, Palestinian demonstrators stormed the building and nearly demolished it.

On 12 October, two IDF reserve soldiers on their way to their base mistakenly drove their car into an area near Ramallah under PA control. Arrested by PA police, they were taken to the PA police station in Ramallah. Word of the arrest spread around the town and an angry mob besieged the station, broke in and lynched the two soldiers, beating them to death. In response, the IDF bombed the police station and other PA and Fath posts using helicopters and jet fighters. Palestinian casualties at the end of October stood at over one hundred dead and hundreds of injured.

Violence peaked in November, with over 120 Palestinians slain and over a thousand injured in riots and clashes with the IDF, and over twenty Israeli civilians and soldiers dead.[55] Palestinian attacks focused on Israeli civilian and military vehicles traveling in the West Bank and Gaza Strip. Additionally, for the first time since the election of Prime Minister Barak, Hamas resumed suicide attacks inside Israel. A bomb near the center of Jerusalem wounded two Israelis on 1 November, and a remote-controlled car bomb in Hadera killed two Israelis and wounded sixty on 22 November. The IDF began assassinating known Palestinian terrorists in what evolved as a "liquidation policy." Heavy exchanges of fire took place almost nightly when Palestinian guns from Bayt Jalla began shooting systematically at the adjacent Jewish neighborhood of Gilo in southern Jerusalem.

By December, the public demonstrations staged by Palestinian civilians appeared to abate while the number of paramilitary attacks grew, and the intifada assumed the format of a small-scale military confrontation.[56] In an attempt to restrain Palestinian violence, the IDF imposed heavy security measures on the Palestinian population in the form of road closures and increased checkpoints inside and bordering the West Bank and Gaza Strip.

CAUSES, GOALS AND MEASURES ADOPTED

A view widely held by Palestinian commentators was that the outbreak of the intifada was a genuine expression of popular rage against the futility of the peace negotiations and the arrogant manner in which Israel conducted them. This rage had been building for a long time, according to this view. Sharon's visit to al-Haram al-Sharif was merely the spark that ignited the powder keg. Israel was to be blamed for the intifada because of its provocative behavior toward the Palestinians during the years since the signing of the Oslo accords. In an article published in *al-Quds* on 16 October, 'Arafat's advisor, Bassam Abu Sharif, reiterated this oft-repeated viewpoint:

> The real factors of tension essentially revolve around the deep Palestinian feeling...that the Israeli government has thus far shirked...implementing the partial agreements it signed with the Palestinian National Authority.... [This has led to] a realization that this government is continuing with its schemes to gradually swallow up the remaining Palestinian lands and is building more settlements and thousands of new housing units to create a new *de facto* situation on the rest of the land.[57]

This stand was presented as a response to the Israeli claim that the intifada was proof that the Palestinians were not ready for peace with Israel and were not willing to abandon the armed struggle despite generous Israeli offers during the Camp David talks. Developing this theme, Palestinian speakers claimed that the Israeli offer in Camp David was not, in fact, as generous as Israel portrayed it, and was therefore unacceptable to the Palestinians.[58]

Repeated insistence by Palestinian spokespersons that the intifada was a purely popular act, initiated by the Palestinian masses and not guided from above, aimed to counter Israeli arguments that the intifada was planned in advance by the Palestinian leadership and could be halted if 'Arafat wanted to do so. Some Israeli commentators speculated, however, that although 'Arafat may have foreseen the coming of the uprising, he did not initiate it himself and could not have stopped the outbreak of the riots. He therefore, according to this view, behaved as if he were at the helm of the intifada in order to avoid being depicted as dragged along by events.[59]

A noted Israeli military analyst pointed out that Palestinian spokespersons had threatened violent riots as early as the beginning of 2000.[60] Indeed, senior members of the Palestinian negotiating team warned throughout the year that if the negotiations did not result in a satisfactory solution, the Palestinians would be forced to turn to another round of violence. 'Arafat himself threatened in June to "rekindle the intifada inside the Palestinian territories" in response to Israeli threats to use tanks and planes should confrontations result from a Palestinian UDI.[61] Notably, the chief of the West Bank Preventive Security Service, Col. Jibril Rajub, predicted one day before Sharon's visit to the Temple Mount that "riots would not be limited to Jerusalem, but erupt everywhere in the territories," and that the PA "would not try to calm the riots, since they would be the result of a blatant provocation."[62] Moreover, according to an analysis in Ha'aretz, the PA took preparatory steps in September 2000, including stockpiling food and fuel supplies beyond the usual amounts, and rushing sea borne supply shipments that were due to reach Gaza only later in the year.[63]

Analyzing the dynamics of the intifada in regard to both initiation and control, Khalil Shiqaqi of Bir Zeit University claimed that the uprising was neither orchestrated nor led by Yasir 'Arafat, nor was it merely a spontaneous response by an enraged but disorganized Palestinian public to Sharon's visit to the Temple Mount. "The intifada," Shiqaqi held, was "a response by a 'young guard' in the Palestinian nationalist movement not only to Sharon's visit and the stalled peace process, but also to the failure of the 'old guard' in the PLO to deliver Palestinian independence and good governance." The old guard, according to Shiqaqi, was composed of the founders of the PLO, who had spent most of their lives abroad, as had 'Arafat himself and his lieutenants, including Abu Mazin, Abu 'Ala and Nabil Sha'th. The young guard consisted of newly emerging local leaders alongside the leaders of the first intifada, including the head of the Fath Tanzim in the West Bank, Marwan Barghuthi; member of the PLC and leader of the Fath Tanzim in the Nablus area, Husam Khadr; and the Fath Tanzim leader in Beit Sahur, Husayn 'Abayyat, who was killed by the IDF on 9 November.[64]

The question of who controlled the intifada was closely linked to the question of who controlled the PA itself. The rise of younger local leaders apparently prompted 'Arafat and some of his advisors to alter their rhetoric regarding this issue. In an effort to demonstrate that 'Arafat was decisively in control, Minister of Communications 'Imad al-Faluji, together with 'Arafat's advisor, Sakhr Habash, asserted in December that 'Arafat himself had planned the intifada and that it was he who controlled it. (For a detailed discussion of 'Arafat's leadership and Barghuthi's threat, see below).

The goals of the intifada, according to Palestinian spokespersons, were identical to the Palestinian demands at Camp David, which had not been attained. These goals were, namely, the establishment of a state within the borders defined in UN Resolution 242, with Jerusalem as its capital, and the conformation of the Palestinian refugees "right of return" in line with UN Resolution 194. According to Barghuthi, speaking on the radio in October: "Absolutely nobody can stop [the intifada]. Only one thing can end it and...that is the right of return for the refugees, Jerusalem as a capital, and an independent Palestinian state."[65] The intifada, said a press commentator, proved that "there will be no peace or stability in the region unless this people obtains their full rights to an independent, sovereign state, with Jerusalem as its capital, and unless the refugee issue is resolved in line with Resolution 194."[66] An al-Quds editorial described "the issue of Palestinian sovereignty over the Aqsa Mosque [as] the first objective for which the current intifada was unleashed."[67] This was indeed demonstrated in the popular name of the uprising, "Intifadat al-Aqsa" (the intifada of the Aqsa Mosque), used more frequently than "Intifadat al-'Awda."

Some Israeli commentators suggested that the Palestinians wanted the future Palestinian state to emerge from a war of liberation and independence, and not as a result of a political agreement, i.e., to be a product of a decisive military victory and not the outcome of a historical compromise.[68] Typically, 'Arafat's media advisor, Nabil Abu Rudayna, stated that "the future Palestinian state is at the eleventh hour and it will be born imbued with blood."[69] Asked in an interview to describe the "political horizon" of the intifada, Faysal al-Husayni, the minister in charge of Jerusalem affairs, replied straightforwardly: "It is the war of independence."[70]

'Arafat's critics, however, questioned the existence of any comprehensive strategic thinking behind the intifada. Sharply criticizing 'Arafat's leadership style, analyst Yezid Sayigh rejected the attribution of any "strategy" or "pre-planning" to 'Arafat. "Contrary to the Israeli account," he wrote, "his behavior since the start of the intifada reflected [the] absence of any strategy....['Arafat's] political management has been marked by a high degree of improvisation and short-termism, confirming the absence of an original strategy and of clear purpose, whether preconceived or otherwise."[71]

In an effort to maintain the grass roots image of the intifada, many Palestinian speakers called on the public to continue the uprising by "peaceful measures," i.e., public demonstrations and throwing stones and Molotov cocktails,[72] and not to resort to firearm clashes with the IDF. 'Arafat's advisor, Bassam Abu Sharif, warned early in October that "cases of missing discipline or erroneous behavior by radical groups...could lead to a rift in the active defense front."[73] A manifesto published by the Palestinian Democratic Union (FIDA) movement on 24 October called for "broadening the scope of participation by all social sectors," such as "students, women and workers," and warned against "being dragged into armed clashes as much as possible, except within the limits of legitimate self-defense."[74] A statement issued by Fath shortly thereafter called on the public to "refrain from opening fire from among angry crowds and from inhabited houses in order to reduce the number of wounded and martyrs and prevent the shelling of these houses."[75] This appeal was not obeyed. In December, the mayors of Ramallah and al-Bira called on 'Arafat to act against those "who take advantage of the intifada, causing damage and [taking] over by force private and public property."[76] Asked about a popular demand to escalate the intifada, Sakhr Habash (Abu Nizar), a member of the Fath Central Committee answered:

> I am well aware that the balances of power with regard to the concept of war are not in favor of our people. Our people cannot fight a war with the Zionist entity. Thus, a military confrontation is considered a kind of "stupidity." We must identify the nature of the enemy's strength and the sources of our strength. We should not fight this enemy with weapons, in which it is stronger than us. If this happens, we will be the losers.[77]

Another school of thought, representing the advocates of a more aggressive line against the Israelis, mostly representing the security apparatus, claimed that the Israeli "massacre" of the Palestinians, as the Palestinians regularly characterized the killing of Palestinians by Israeli forces, justified and legitimized every sort of Palestinian retaliation. The chief of Palestinian military intelligence, Maj. Gen. Musa 'Arafat al-Qudwa, was quoted as asking rhetorically early in October: "Does Israel expect the PA to take a relaxed view of [its] crimes and the massacres of Palestinians?"[78] Responding to a question about Palestinian violence during an interview in November, Marwan Barghuthi countered: 'What violence? The violence is the tool of the party that uses tanks, helicopter gunships, armored vehicles and live bullets. The Palestinians are unarmed and they resist the enemy with their bare chests."[79] Notably, even the PA militants referred only to the West Bank as the area of confrontation with the IDF, tacitly excluding attacks on civilians and soldiers inside Israel.

While naming the Israeli-Palestinian clashes an "intifada" was intended to establish a cognitive connection between the first intifada (see *MECS* 1987, pp. 263–68; 1988, pp. 283–92, 297–301; 1989, pp. 231–56) and the current uprising, certain obvious differences existed between the situation in 1987 and that in 2000. Asked in an interview of the intifada was sustainable, Barghuthi answered: "The Palestinians went through an intifada for seven years while there was no airport, no ports, no crossings, and not even an authority, and were able to maintain the intifada."[80] In another interview he assessed media coverage in the current intifada as more intensive than in the first intifada. Moreover, he stressed that "the Israeli aggression is much more brutal this time around."[81] According to Fath member Abu Nizar:

> The 1987 intifada happened in a historical condition in which the Palestinian leadership was abroad....The current intifada broke out under different circumstances. Israel has recognized the PLO....[The PA] set up various institutions. We now have a legislative council, flag, anthem, radio, television, and airport. All the elements of a state exist on a part of the 1967-occupied Palestinian territories. We have a government with incomplete sovereignty.[82]

The major difference in goals between the two intifadas was articulated by 'Arafat himself in a speech delivered on 29 November in Tunisia: "Just as our people's intifada in 1987 was crowned with the Declaration of Independence, the Aqsa Intifada will be crowned with the embodiment of this important and historic declaration on our national soil on the blessed land of Palestine." [83]

Appeals for the formation of a national unity government were made after the outbreak of the intifada. Speakers from most factions urged the PA to form a government that would represent all the Palestinian people, this time in order to enhance cooperation in the struggle against Israel. In late October, the prominent local leader Dr. Haydar 'Abd al-Shafi called for the formation of a "national unity authority" and an official popular body to supervise the affairs of the intifada and optimize all resources to confront the Israeli challenges.[84]

A symposium convened in Gaza on 4 December by the Palestinian Press Association (PPA) on the topic "The Intifada — Its Horizons and Developments" discussed, inter alia, the formation of a national unity government. Minister of Communications Faluji confirmed that "the PA has, since the outset, been making persistent endeavors to guarantee the participation of the Hamas movement in the forthcoming parliamentary elections." A Hamas leader, Isma'il Abu Shanab, termed this approach "significant."[85] Still, by the end of the year a national unity government had not yet been established.

THE SHARM AL-SHAYKH SUMMIT

An emergency international summit convened on 16 October in Sharm al-Shaykh to discuss how to stop the violence between the Israelis and the Palestinians. Besides the Israeli and Palestinian teams, headed by Prime Minister Barak and Chairman 'Arafat, respectively, the participants were President Bill Clinton, UN secretary-general Kofi Anan, President Husni Mubarak of Egypt and King 'Abdallah of Jordan. After two days of negotiations, an agreement was reached by the two sides to declare a cease-fire and establish a fact-finding committee under American sponsorship to examine the events that led to the outbreak of the intifada.[86]

In an effort to implement the Sharm al-Shaykh agreement, Israel eased the closures imposed on the Palestinian territories and withdrew some of its military forces, armored vehicles and tanks. The PA, for its part, re-arrested all Hamas activists released since the outbreak of the intifada.[87] A certain decline in the number of violent clashes was indeed registered during the first two days after the summit, but the relative quiet was short-lived. On 18 October, two roadside bombs exploded next to an IDF-escorted convoy of Jewish settlers. IDF special forces operating inside Palestinian-controlled Area A, according to Palestinian sources, arrested eight Palestinians suspected of participating in the 12 October lynching of the two Israeli reserve soldiers (see above). The next day, a group of forty settlers who were hiking in the vicinity of Nablus were pinned down by Palestinian shooting. In the subsequent army rescue operation, one Palestinian and one Israeli settler were killed.[88]

During the Sharm al-Shaykh summit meetings, demonstrations organized in the PA territories called on 'Arafat not to submit to Israeli-American pressure and to reject the demand to halt the intifada. Just before the start of the summit, Barghuthi had announced that Palestinian participation in the Sharm al-Shaykh meetings would not affect intifada activities,[89] and once it ended, he promptly declared that the intifada would continue, since only Israeli compliance with Resolutions 242 and 338, and Resolution 194, could halt it (see below).[90] Spokespersons of various Palestinian opposition factions supported his position, dismissing the summit agreement as useless. 'Abd-al-Latif Ghayth, a member of the PFLP political bureau, stated that the agreement intended to "circumvent and halt the escalating intifada." Taysir Khalid, of the DFLP political bureau, argued that "the results of the Sharm al-Shaykh summit are insignificant and they maintain the explosive situation in the Palestinian territories unresolved." Both stressed that their respective movements would continue the intifada.[91]

Both opposition leaders and high-ranking officials in the PA pressured 'Arafat to reject President Clinton's proposed parameters for a FSA presented to the Israelis and the Palestinians in Washington in late December (see chapter on the US and the Middle East). The Democratic Alliance Bloc, a lobby in the PLC which included Rawiya al-Shawwa, Hasan Khuraysha, Mu'awiya al-Masri, Fakhri al-Turkman and Ra'fat al-Najjar, warned 'Arafat that the ideas raised in the proposal "conflict with the Palestinian firm principles."[92] Barghuthi, while acknowledging that "Israel's positions [represented] an improvement compared to those offered to the Palestinians in Camp David," still claimed that they did not "reach the level of making Israel comply with the resolutions of international legitimacy."[93]

This pressure ultimately led 'Arafat to announce on 27 December that he could neither accept the bridging offer nor refuse it without further clarifications. The main complaint of the PA was that the offer was very clear when it discussed the security arrangements for Israel and the commitments that the Palestinians would have to accept, but it was deliberately blurred about the commitments Israel would have to accept, especially regarding the three controversial issues of the refugees, Jerusalem and borders.[94]

AUTHORITY AND CONTROL: 'ARAFAT'S STATUS AND THE INTIFADA

The complex structure of the Palestinian political entity, made up of numerous elected as well as appointed bodies representing varied ideologies and conflicting interests, mitigated against identifying a potential heir to 'Arafat who would gain wide legitimacy and emerge from a consensus (see *MECS* 1999, pp. 480–82; 1998, pp. 492–94). Historically, the PLO was the national political framework that represented the entire Palestinian people, both in the territories and the diaspora. Its institutions — the PLO Executive Committee, the PLO Central Council and the PNC theoretically represented all Palestinians worldwide. The largest and strongest party in the PLO, Fath, headed by 'Arafat, led the establishment of the PA following the Oslo accords. Its elected parliament, the PLC, represented PA residents only. Tanzim al-Fath was formed in 1994 as the armed wing of the Fath movement to act as a militia loyal to 'Arafat personally, bypassing the regular PA institutions. It was also designed to act as a counterweight to the Islamic opposition by leading demonstrations and engaging in clashes with the IDF.[95]

The problem of determining an orderly succession to 'Arafat was exacerbated by his one-man style of governing which superseded the Fath institutional apparatus. Tanzim leader Barghuthi, a possible contender for the succession, was quoted as describing the situation thus: "There are institutions but the institutions are weak compared to 'Arafat's role. He's bigger than the institutions." In Barghuthi's view, the only way to strengthen the bodies of the Fath movement and help them prepare for a post-'Arafat era was through elections. "If there [are] no elections, the situation in [the] Fath [movement] will be very difficult."[96] Elections had not been held in the PA since the first elections in 1996 (see *MECS* 1996, pp. 138–47). Barghuthi's stand was a bold one, since most Palestinians were not keen to discuss the issue.[97] According to one analysis, Palestinian politicians were afraid to discuss the subject even behind closed doors, and it had never been discussed in any public Palestinian forum.[98]

Although the Palestinian press did not deal with the issue openly, the Israeli media reported that the subject was in fact being discussed in Palestinian circles. Early in the year, the most probable candidates, reportedly, were PLO secretary-general Abu Mazin and PLC speaker Abu 'Ala, in view of their seniority and their close relations with 'Arafat. According to commentary in *al-Sharq al-Awsat* following the Camp David talks, Muhammad Dahlan, head of the PA preventive security police in Gaza, was the figure preparing to succeed 'Arafat, based on Dahlan's impressive political skills demonstrated during the talks in Camp David. Dahlan's functioning, in this analysis, ought to give Israel "the courage to offer a proposal that will achieve a peace agreement, since it eliminated Israel's excuse to avoid offering such a proposition, fearing the uncertain future of the PA after 'Arafat's demise.[99]

The failure of the Camp David talks turned 'Arafat almost overnight into a hero in the PA. Thousands of Palestinians were on hand to welcome him upon his arrival in Gaza airport. His unbending stand and unwillingness to compromise despite Israeli and American pressure gained him support even from the leaders of Hamas. Shaykh Yasin praised 'Arafat "for his firm and principled stance at the Camp David negotiations toward the issue of Jerusalem and the need to restore the city to full Palestinian sovereignty as capital of the Palestinian state."[100]

However, 'Arafat could not rest on his laurels for long. The outbreak of the intifada placed him in a difficult position. Outwardly, particularly vis-à-vis the US and the EU countries, he was anxious to dissociate himself from the violence and to put the blame on Israel for having caused the uprising as an attempt to obstruct him from leading the Palestinians to independence. Yet, domestically, his evasion of responsibility for the intifada soon turned into a double-edged sword in contending with the challenge of potential political heirs such as Barghuthi. Following the conclusion of the Sharm al-Shaykh summit in October, Barghuthi promptly pointed to its failure. In an interview with *Ha'aretz* he emphasized that "the current intifada would not stop with an order, as it did not start with an order,"[101] a hint that it was he who controlled the intifada *de facto*. Barghuthi insinuated that the "street" might not obey 'Arafat should he announce a cease-fire with Israel and a halt to the intifada.[102]

Barghuthi generally avoided direct replies to questions about the measure of his obedience to 'Arafat. In an interview in November with the Egyptian *al-Musawwar*, which described him as "the leader of the intifada," Barghuthi systematically portrayed himself as an authentic representative of the masses, and 'Arafat as the respected yet distant political leader. As in practically all his interviews, Barghuthi made extensive use of the word "we," implying a wide range of meanings: the Fath leadership, Fath al-Tanzim, or simply authentic grass roots. Asked to describe the difference between the PA and the Fath movement, he replied tellingly: "'Arafat...is the chairman of the Fath movement and he enjoys the confidence of its members. We stand by him and respect his decisions, but the intifada expresses the will of the Palestinian people."[103]

The more pointedly Barghuthi emphasized 'Arafat's importance as the symbol of the Palestinian struggle, the more palpable was the implication that he was trying to belittle 'Arafat's role in the actual running of the intifada. This nuance did not escape the notice of 'Arafat's close advisers, and may have prompted the change in the spirit of the statements made by 'Arafat and his retinue in December. Descending from his plane upon his return from a meeting in Tunisia on 5 December, 'Arafat carried a machine gun, a symbolic gesture he had not used in years.[104] The following day, Communication Minister Faluji stated in Gaza that "the PA had begun to prepare for the outbreak of the current intifada since its return from the Camp David negotiations. The preparations were made at the instructions of President Yasir 'Arafat, who expected the outbreak of the intifada as a complementary phase of Palestinian steadfastness in the negotiations, not as a protest restricted to Sharon's visit to the holy Aqsa Mosque."[105] A day after that, 'Arafat's advisor, Abu Nizar, sent a clear message about Barghuthi's type of behavior:

> I can confirm that brother Abu 'Ammar ['Arafat] is, in the end, the authority for all the activities that are taking place. Anyone who thinks differently is not informed of what is happening....But let me say that some faces have been appearing a lot on satellite channels, and some of them thought that they could become leaders by doing this. They started to compete over who would appear more on satellite channels. This phenomenon is not healthy.[106]

THE OPPOSITION AND THE INTIFADA

The beginning of the year marked a period of relative decline in the power and popularity of both the secular and the Islamic opposition movements in the PA due to growing pressure by the PA security forces to curb them, as well as the relative economic prosperity at the time (see below). The failure of Camp David further boosted the popular support of 'Arafat and the Fath movement, reinforcing his image as the hero of resistance to Israeli intransigence. This boost came at the direct expense of the opposition movements' political power. Palestinian public opinion changed dramatically in favor of violent attacks against Israel, actively encouraged by mainstream Fath. However, the growing support for armed struggle was not reflected in a corresponding rise in the popularity of the Islamic opposition organizations during the three months of the intifada (October-December).

Contrary to what might have been expected, the outbreak of the intifada helped reinforce the ruling Fath. The PA security forces, the Fath movement, and its affiliated organizations were depicted as the leaders of the popular struggle against Israel who were now leaving the negotiating table and taking to the streets in order to lead the masses in demonstrations and confront the Israeli soldiers. At the same time, public opinion was still generally opposed to the high-profile sabotage acts and suicide attacks of Hamas and the Islamic Jihad, since they were viewed as damaging to the Palestinian cause and helpful to Israel in gaining international support. Even so, early in the intifada, the PA systematically released many of the key Hamas political and military activists it had detained, in a move that could be interpreted as a tacit approval of the Hamas activities. These included Muhammad Dayf, Mahmud Abu Hunud and Hamas spokesperson 'Abd al-'Aziz Rantisi.[107]

Ever since the adoption of the Oslo accords, the rejectionist front, consisting of the secular Palestinian opposition movements who rejected 'Arafat's leadership and the peace process, together with the Islamic opposition, had urged the return to armed struggle. Upon the outbreak of the intifada, a Hamas speaker, welcoming the renewal of the armed struggle, emphasized that Hamas had never "laid down the banner of resistance" and that "the intifada proves the victory of the resistance option." Hamas urged the PA leadership to abandon the peace process completely and adopt a policy of "Lebanonization" of the territories (see below).[108]

The secular opposition movements, too, welcomed the intifada, insisting that it be maintained until the attainment of the Palestinian goals of an independent state with Jerusalem as its capital and the return of the refugees. Advocating "popular struggle," in contrast to clashes using firearms, the DFLP and PFLP submitted a joint memorandum to 'Arafat urging the convening of a special session of the PLO Central Council to hold elections for the PNC and the PLC, stressing the political aspect of the intifada.[109] This did not mean a rejection in principle of armed clashes, however. In an interview with Radio Monte Carlo, DFLP secretary-general Hawatima denied "distorted" reports that he allegedly recommended disarming the demonstrators. On the contrary, he called "for the distribution of weapons among all the people...who are prepared to defend the homeland and the people and safeguard the intifada until independence."[110]

Still, the adoption by the Fath movement of armed struggle did not benefit the opposition groups. Fath cadres led the popular demonstrations and took all the credit for their actions, pushing the other groups aside. Moreover, while Fath organized members and led violent clashes, Hamas suicide attacks against Israeli civilians were targeted for a certain amount of criticism for not serving the Palestinian cause.[111] Furthermore, Hamas leader Yasin complained that the Fath movement claimed martyred Hamas fatalities as its own, when they were actually Hamas activists.[112]

During a symposium convened in Gaza by the PPA on 4 December, Hamas leader Isma'il Abu Shanab was provocatively asked to explain the reason for the poor participation of the Hamas movement in the current intifada. Explaining the small number of bomb attacks in Israeli cities and the fact that those were not suicide attacks, he replied that "these operations need accurate preparations, selection of the targets, and choice of the right time for carrying out these operations, if they [are] to succeed." He added: "The Hamas movement has gone beyond the phase of martyrdom operations and entered the phase of remote control explosions."[113]

INTERNAL AFFAIRS

THE PALESTINIAN LEGISLATIVE COUNCIL

As in the past, the PLC continued to try to gain greater power and influence at the expense of the presidency, but, as before, with little success. PLC decisions and resolutions had little effect on the conduct of governmental affairs in the PA. During the course of the year, members of the PLC (along with spokespersons of the opposition) complained that the presidential and PLC terms had ended on 9 March 1999, and that parliamentary and presidential elections should have been conducted since then.[114] The head of the PLC political committee, Dr. Ziyad Abu 'Amr, asserted in April: "We cannot continue to talk about 'democracy in Palestine' and 'Palestinian democracy' for long in light of the end of the term of the elected legislative authority and not holding new elections for the PLC and the PNC."[115]

Such declarations, however, made little impression on 'Arafat or his cabinet ministers, who were not considering holding elections at that time. According to the chairperson of the PLC monitoring and human rights committee, Dr. Hasan al-Khuraysha, when he proposed holding elections, the "voting inside the PLC yielded a different result,...and the situation has remained as it is."[116]

The question of a future constitution to be ratified following the anticipated declaration of independence did, however, preoccupy PLC deliberations significantly. A meaningful step was taken on 4 July with the publication of a draft constitution, a week before the start of the Camp David negotiations. This was in preparation to the Palestinian state that was slated to be declared either as a result of the talks, or as a unilateral step on 13 September.

The draft constitution consisted of six major sections and approximately 165 articles. The first and most interesting section, "General and Basic Rules," included basic definitions of the structure of the future Palestinian state and society. The first article stipulated that "Palestine is part of the Arab homeland and the Arab nation." Article 5 stated that "Islam is the official religion" and that "divine religions have their own sanctity and respect." Article 12 described the Palestinian political system as a "parliamentary democracy based on political pluralism," which promised to respect the rights of minorities in a manner that would "protect and respect the decisions of the majority." Section 2, entitled "Rights and Freedoms," stipulated in the first article (No. 23) that "Palestinians are equal before the law and the judiciary. They enjoy equal rights and freedoms without discrimination on the basis of race, color, sex, creed, opinion, or ethnic or social origins, wealth, or official status."[117]

The draft constitution was vague on a large number of issues, and some issues were not covered at all. Examples included the legal mechanism that would allow the Palestinians of the diaspora to "share all forms of power at home and abroad," the exact structure of the parliament (unicameral or bicameral), the dissolution of parliament, and the structure of the proposed position of prime minister. Legal experts were called upon by the PLC to submit proposals as to how these issues should be addressed.[118] A second draft of the constitution, published in September, was clearer about the parliamentary structure, defining it as a bicameral body: a legislative council would represent the domestic Palestinian population and concern itself with internal politics, and a national council would represent the Palestinians outside and would focus on the "fundamental national rights of Palestinians." According to one American researcher, the drafting of the constitution reflected a power struggle between the domestic and the diaspora Palestinian leaders. In drafting the constitution, the PLO sought to entrench its position in the future Palestinian state, protecting its status by the active involvement of PNC speaker Salim al-Za'nun in the wording of the constitution.[119]

The extensive effort to draft a constitution, however, bore no immediate or concrete results. In the event, the state was not declared and, therefore, no constitution was legislated. Whether a constitution would have been legislated if the state had been declared is doubtful. The omission by 'Arafat of any reference to the issue of the constitution during the year suggests that he was not particularly enthusiastic about a development which may have imposed legal restrictions on his authority and control.

CORRUPTION AND HUMAN RIGHTS VIOLATIONS
Following the publication in November 1999 of the "Anti-Corruption Communiqué of the Twenty" denouncing the corrupt conduct of the PA (see *MECS* 1999, pp. 479–80), many of the signatories, including PLC delegates, were arrested by PA security bodies and held for several weeks. One of the detainees, PLC member 'Abd al-Jawad Salah, filed a complaint in January to the Palestinian prosecutor-general claiming that he was attacked by his wardens during his arrest.[120] Released during January and February, none of the signatories showed remorse or any change of opinion. One signatory, political scientist 'Abd al-Satar Qasim of al-Najah University, stated that the tough response of the PA helped draw attention to the manifesto. "We needed the stupidity of the Authority and they were up to our expectations," he commented.[121] Another signatory, Dr. Hasan al-Khuraysha, chairperson of the PLC monitoring and human rights committee, declared: "I am not afraid of anything. I have been doing my job in the legislative council for years without pursuing private interests and without calculations."[122]

Referring in January to the widespread accusations of corruption, Barghuthi blamed the PA for the decline in popular support for the Fath movement by ordinary Palestinians due to the misconduct of its leadership and its security bodies. The public attitude was reasonable, he said. "Since it was Fath which launched the PA project, it is only normal that Fath should pay for the PA's and security organs' mistakes." Linking this accusation to his criticism of the performance of the Palestinian negotiating teams, he cited the ongoing negotiations while the settlements continued growing as a "real tragedy."[123] Significantly, the linkage between PA corruption and criticism of the negotiations had been made in the "Communiqué of the Twenty" as well.

On 17 February, a large-scale teachers' strike broke out, spreading to almost all the cities and villages of the West Bank and Gaza. Protesting low salaries and the absence of provisions for a raise in the PA budget for 2000 despite promises, the teachers halted studies in the Palestinian schools intermittently over several months. In an attempt to break the strike, PA security forces summoned leaders of the striking teachers for interrogation, putting pressure on them to halt the strike and holding some teachers under administrative arrest for long periods of time. The strike eventually faded without any significant results for the teachers, and was finally called off following the Naqba Day disturbances in mid-May.[124]

The Palestinian authorities also had to deal with student unrest in the course of the year. Angered by remarks by French prime minister Lionel Jospin, who during a visit to Israel denounced Hizballah attacks against Israel as terrorist acts, dozens of Bir Zeit University students attacked him and threw stones at him during his visit to the university on 26 February.[125] Suppressing the riots, the Palestinian police arrested large numbers of students (between 30 and 100, according to varying reports) and held them under administrative detention without trial.[126] The detention of the students aroused a large-scale public outcry from human rights organizations, the Bir Zeit faculty and many students. After several weeks of public pressure and a continuous strike at the university, all the detained students were released on 5 March.[127] According to a *Ha'aretz* reporter, the public focused on criticism of the PA reaction to the stone-throwing incident, while ignoring the incident itself, turning "the whole affair of stoning Jospin...into a symbol of resistance to the occupation and the Oslo accords.[128]

THE SECULAR OPPOSITION

'Arafat, exerting strenuous efforts in early 2000 to mobilize the widest possible political support for the negotiations over the final status settlement, made extensive use of the 124-member PLO Central Council, which represented a large spectrum of Palestinian parties both within the PA and abroad. The effort to reach a political consensus was conceived as a continuation of the national dialogue initiated by him in 1999 (see *MECS* 1999, pp. 483–84, 486). Invitations were sent to all political parties to attend a meeting of the central committee convened in Gaza on 2–3 February.[129] In addition to mainstream Fath, the meeting was attended by the DFLP, the Iraqi-based Arab Liberation Front and FIDA, the Islamic Salvation Party.[130] It was boycotted by Hamas, al-Jihad al-Islami, the PFLP, the PFLP-General Command (PFLP-GC) and the pro-Syrian al-Sa'iqa. 'Arafat's advisor, Mamduh Nawfal, sharply criticized the opposition groups who boycotted the meeting, calling the boycott "an evasion of responsibility and abandonment of a required national role at crucial times."[131]

The most significant outcome of the February meeting of the PLO Central Council was a decision by the PFLP to resume its activity within the PLO framework, thereby ending a prolonged period of boycott. The return of the PFLP was facilitated by resolutions passed at the meeting which met its demands. According to Abu 'Ali Mustafa, deputy secretary-general of the PFLP, the council accepted eight of nine points submitted by the PFLP as a condition to resuming its participation in the PLO. The first demand, concerning pursuing the declaration of a Palestinian state regardless of the progress made in the peace process, was accepted by the council. The demand that negotiations with Israel be halted, however, was rejected.[132]

Stressing the existence of an American-Israeli scheme to "liquidate the Palestinian question," the PFLP maintained that "confronting these attempts requires a unified Palestinian stand." The PFLP had decided, therefore, "to assume its role and bear its responsibilities in full by working seriously for the implementation of the decisions and results of the latest session of the PLO Central Council."[133]

An announcement by PFLP secretary-general George Habash of his intention to retire from his post at the end of April evoked a vague explanation by a member of the PFLP political bureau, 'Abd al-Rahim Malluh, that Habash wanted to devote his time to issues that required examination and to form a research center that would deal with the Arab-Israeli and the Palestinian-Israeli conflict. He denied reports that Habash retired due to ill health or to political disagreements within the organization.[134] Press reports, however, claimed that the resignation was indeed related to political differences, namely the more accommodating approach to the Oslo agreements and the PA endorsed by such senior PFLP figures as 'Abu Ali Mustafa. According to the London-based *Mideast Mirror*, if Mustafa were to become secretary-general of the PFLP, "it would likely have an important bearing on the PFLP attitude to the peace process."[135]

Mustafa was indeed elected as the new secretary-general of the PFLP in July.[136] His election was followed by an announcement of the relocation of the PFLP headquarters from Damascus to the PA territory, where Mustafa himself resided. Mustafa explained that moving the headquarters to the territories did not imply a major change in PFLP positions. The PFLP, he declared, remained "opposed to the course that has been followed by influential political forces since the Madrid conference. We will not join this course — neither the negotiations nor the [Palestinian] Authority — before...a new Palestinian approach and a new strategy will be derived."[137]

Concerted attempts to forge a basis of cooperation between the various Palestinian movements were made by PA officials in preparation for the next PLO Central Council meeting in September, which planned to discuss the anticipated unilateral declaration of independence scheduled for 13 September. The Fath movement, the PPP and FIDA jointly issued an appeal for the formation of a national unity government comprising "all the Palestinian political forces and the qualified ones inside and outside the PA in order to confront the political challenges of the coming phase."[138]

Special efforts were made by the PA leadership to come to terms with Hamas and ensure that the organization participated in the September meeting. Shaykh Yasin confirmed in August that Hamas was negotiating with PNC speaker Za'nun over the possibility of its participation in the meeting,[139] but the efforts proved unsuccessful. Both Hamas and the PFLP-GC announced that they would boycott the meeting. Hamas spokespersons charged that the conclave would still be held under the umbrella of the Oslo accords, while the PFLP-GC called the meeting an endorsement of extending self-rule rather than establishing an independent state. However, both the DFLP and PFLP announced that they would participate. PFLP political bureau member Jamil al-Majdalawi attributed his movement's decision to its view of the September deadline as "a decisive juncture between declaring a state and actually beginning to build its institutions and do away with the Oslo accords." Salih Zaydan, a member of the DFLP Central Council, explained the DFLP participation as aiming "to restore unanimity on the Palestinian national principles, based on red lines that cannot be overstepped."[140]

Most surprisingly, the Islamic Jihad movement, too, decided to take part in the meeting. According to the movement spokesperson, Bahjat al-Hilu, the move was meant to "show Palestinian national unity in line with the Islamic Jihad movement's stand that rejects any foreign domination."[141]

THE ISLAMIC OPPOSITION

The popularity of the Islamic opposition movements in the PA appeared to have declined during the first part of the year. Support for Hamas ranged between 10%-15% during January-July, according to a series of public opinion polls conducted by Bir Zeit's Shiqaqi,[142] and reached an even lower ebb of 9% according to a report published in January in *al-Ayyam*.[143] This relatively low rate of support for the major Islamic organization was particularly significant at a time when the popularity of Fath and the PA generally was also declining, indicating that Hamas failed to fill the void. *Al-Ayyam* attributed this loss of popularity in part to the blows inflicted on the military wing of Hamas by both Israel and the PA during 1998–99, i.e., the systematic liquidation by Israel of members of the Hamas military wing, and mass arrests of Hamas activists by the PA. The deportation of four prominent Hamas leaders from Jordan in November 1999 (see *MECS* 1999, pp. 487–89, and below) was another contributing factor. In addition, the declining popularity of Hamas may have been due to: (1) The Israeli-Syrian talks taking place during the first months of the year, which portended the possible loss of an important ally of Hamas; (2) an improvement in the economic situation in the PA; and (3) the approach of the expected FSA.

According to *al-Ayyam*, Hamas leaders, aware of the reduction in public support, had begun to discuss ways to regain their political stature in the Palestinian milieu. Shaykh Yasin's participation in the PLO Central Council convention in April 1999, and his meeting with 'Arafat in September 1999 to discuss the national dialogue were viewed by the newspaper as evidence of an Islamic tilt toward a more pragmatic stance. *Al-Ayyam* quoted Shaykh Jamil Hamami, a former Hamas leader, as pointing to Hamas's "pragmatism and dynamism that allow it to act and move in any new environment while maintaining its firm principles and concepts." Hamami cited a "truce" (*hudna*) offered by Shaykh Yasin as far back as 1994 that could be re-endorsed by the movement as an official stand. The newspapers also cited Dr. Nasir al-Sha'ir, a professor of comparative religion at al-Najah University, who pointed to the truce offer as an important development in the political discourse of Hamas. The latent "acceptance of the Palestinian people's choice and [the] majority's view regarding the proposed political settlement...means that the issue is not 'religious' but is left to the choice of the...people and the view of the majority," Sha'ir wrote.[144]

Still, in their public statements Hamas leaders consistently reiterated unyielding positions regarding the desired solution to the Israeli-Palestinian conflict and the immutability of Hamas's political legitimacy. Referring to the Camp David talks, the head of the Hamas political bureau, Khalid Mash'al, said: "We in Hamas had cautioned against this summit. Our position was to reject it irrespective of its outcome because it is an extension of the Oslo course of concessions that relinquished 78% of our land and rights from the first moment." Asked what gave him the right to speak in the name of the Palestinian people, he stated: "In principle, the representatives of the Palestinian people are those who cling to the rights of the people. Those who give up the Palestinian people's lands, rights, Jerusalem, and their holy sites do not have the right to claim that they represent the Palestinian people."[145]

Hamas spokespersons remained loyal to the ultimate goal of the organization, namely establishing an Islamic state in all of Mandatory Palestine, presenting their goal as acceptable even for non-Muslims. Referring to the status of Christians under an Islamic Palestine, Mash'al declared: "Hamas would put them at its head because they are the sons of this homeland who have worked for it and have sacrificed for it, just like the Muslims."[146] As for Jews, Shaykh Yasin said: "We are calling for a state with an Islamic identity that has room for Israelis who exist now in Palestine." In a reference to the Israeli perception that the Arabs would annihilate its Jewish population if they triumphed over land, he asked rhetorically: "What would we do with the Israelis, throw them in the sea?" His reply was: "No, let them live among us. But their state would not remain over our heads."[147]

The Islamic Jihad movement held a similar position. Interviewed in the press, Dr. Ramadan Shallah, secretary-general of the movement, eschewed any compromises regarding the liberation of the entire land of Palestine. Moreover, he attacked the very concept of liberating the land in stages, as the PLO had advocated as far back as 1974. This, he said, had led to the current compromise stance of the Fath-led PLO. The retrieval of the land in stages should have taken place through struggle and not through negotiations and recognition of Israel. The PLO, he explained, should not have played with such theoretical ideas from the first place.[148]

The Israeli withdrawal from South Lebanon in May (see chapters on Israel and Lebanon), which stirred up the political arena in the PA, was used by opposition spokespersons, especially from Hamas, as proof that Israel could be overpowered through sustained, long-term guerilla activity. According to this argument, the PA was acting against, if not betraying, Palestinian interests by abandoning the path of struggle and opting for negotiations. The "victory" of Hizballah's uncompromising orientation, in this view, illuminated the unsuccessful route of negotiations chosen by the PA leadership, which had brought practically no benefit to the Palestinian masses.[149]

Attempting to rebuff this criticism, the chief of general intelligence in the PA, Amin al-Hindi, rejected the validity of a comparison between the Lebanese and the Palestinian resistance, insisting that the "objective circumstances and the internal conditions are different."[150] Other PA spokespersons pointed out that there were no Israeli settlers in South Lebanon, as even the Israeli right wing did not consider Lebanon part of Israel, in contrast to the situation in the West Bank and Gaza.[151] PA speakers used every possible argument to highlight the complete difference between the Israeli-Lebanese and the Israeli-Palestinian disputes.

Hamas speakers, however, promptly advocated the Lebanese model and claimed that they were the carriers of the Hizballah solution in the Palestinian conflict. Shaykh Yasin called on the PA in November to back his movement, just as the Lebanese government had backed Hizballah, which, he said, forced the Israeli army to withdraw from southern Lebanon under the pressure of armed operations. "Hamas is the corresponding organization to Hizballah," he argued, "but it does not enjoy the support that Hizballah gets from the official Lebanese authorities."[152]

The aftermath of the deportation of the four Hamas leaders from Jordan in November 1999 (see *MECS* 1999, pp. 488–89) heightened friction between the Hamas leadership inside and outside the PA. Attempts to bring about the return of the four to Jordan, both by an appeal to the Jordanian Court of Justice and by appeals on their behalf by various political personalities, failed to result in pardons (see chapter on Jordan). Frustrated by minimal popular protest over the expulsion both in Jordan and in the PA, one of the deportees, Hamas leader Ibrahim Ghawsha, accused the Jordanian Muslim Brotherhood of abandoning the Palestinians.[153] Differences of opinion between the Hamas leadership inside and outside Palestine, which had surfaced in 1999, were exacerbated after the failure of the Camp David talks. While Hamas leaders in the PA, especially Shaykh Yasin, congratulated Chairman 'Arafat for his steadfastness in the talks, Khalid Mash'al scorned 'Arafat and the PA, claiming that the media focus on Jerusalem as the subject that caused the failure of the talks was intended to cover up the Palestinians' concessions on the other subjects.

THE ECONOMY

The first three-quarters of the year saw a significant improvement in the PA economy, largely because the peace process seemed to be moving toward a successful conclusion, or, at the very least, hope for a significant breakthrough was not yet lost. This continuation of the tendency of 1999, when growth in the GDP reached 6%, led World Bank (WB) economists to estimate that the PA economy would grow by over 5% in 2000.[154]

Growth in the GDP was accompanied by a decline in the unemployment rate, which dropped from 13.1% at the beginning of 1999 to 10% at the end of the year. It rose slightly, to 10.9% in the first quarter of 2000, but declined again in the second quarter to 8.8% remaining at that level until the outbreak of the intifada. This also reflected growth in the employment of Palestinians in Israel, amounting to about 125,000 persons on the eve of the intifada.[155]

Israel remained the most important trading partner for the PA, steadily accountable for 85%-86% of Palestinian exports. The monthly average of registered exports until the outbreak of the intifada amounted to c. $42m.[156] Trade activity between Israel and the PA was expected to expand further as a result of an agreement between the two sides signed in August, alleviating various restrictions on the transportation of goods between Israel and the PA.[157]

A national budget was approved by the PLC for the first time in January 2000. The budget, for the fiscal year 2000, was initially presented as balanced, with expenditure amounting to $1.4bn. and revenue optimistically projected at $937m., with an additional $400m. in grants for development expenditures. The major expenditures allocated were 35.1% for police and public security, 18.4% for education, 9.8% for health, and 5.5% for social affairs.[158] The PLC budget committee, however, pointed to $50m. in previous arrears that should have been cited in the budget, creating a deficit. It also recommended including the implementation of the Civil Service Law, stipulating an immediate large salary raise for all public workers, especially teachers, at an estimated cost of $40m. This proposal, however, was not approved, a decision which later evoked the teachers strike (see above).[159]

Minister of Finance Zuhdi al-Nashashibi, warning the PLC during its discussion of the budget not to overload it with demands, called on the private sector to shoulder the burden of economic development in the PA. A member of the budget committee, Da'ud al-Zir, pointed out that while Israel had still not paid some $300m. in tax rebates it owed the PA, the PA had increased salaries in the public sector. He also criticized the budget for its lack of transparency, namely, its failure to reveal the revenues of several public corporations.[160] Other committee members criticized the growing nepotistic practice of awarding public company monopolies to relatives of high-ranking officials in the PA, as well as mismanagement of the donor countries' funds.[161] Partly to ward off these allegations, the director-general of the PA Investment Department, Jamil Harara, attacked the donor countries' practice of selecting projects without considering Palestinian priorities but only their own, criticizing the donors' insistence in channeling their funds to the development of services and professional training. This led to a situation in which "70% of the donations return to the donor states in the form of the contracts their companies sign and the high salaries their experts get," Harara argued, while "the Palestinians receive only 30% of these donations."[162]

The issue of transparency was addressed to some extent in July when, in an unprecedented move, the Planning and International Cooperation Ministry published details of PA investment in local companies and economic ventures through the Palestinian Commercial Services Company. The minister of planning, Nabil Sha'th, called this exposure "steps toward full transparency and accountability in all areas and toward a sound financial system," describing it as the most important achievement of his ministry. The WB vice president for the Middle East and North Africa region, Jean-Louis Sarbib, depicted it as "a step in the right direction."[163]

Jordan and the PA signed an economic agreement in July, which was included in the minutes of the joint Jordanian-Palestinian economic committee. The agreement aimed to strengthen economic cooperation between the two by exempting a range of products from taxes, adopting a joint product-quality standard, encouraging mutual investment, and pursuing efforts to establish a bilateral free trade zone. The minutes also mooted the formation of a joint industrial zone on both sides of their projected common border after the establishment of the Palestinian state.[164]

Implementing an agreement drawn up between the PA and British Gas in November 1999 which allowed the British company to explore and produce natural gas from the seabed off the Gaza Strip, British Gas began experimental drilling in April. The agreement was opposed by Israeli gas-production companies who were involved in gas exploration at a marine site in nearby Ashkelon. The Israeli companies claimed that the PA had no authority to grant gas concessions, since it did not represent an internationally recognized state and therefore had no territorial waters of its own. Rejecting this claim, Minister of Planning Sha'th argued that Israel had no right to intervene in the Palestinian decision, which was a purely internal matter.[165] The discovery of a gas field in early May off the coast of Ashkelon, two-thirds of which lay within the Palestinian marine area, and the discovery of two more, even larger gas fields off the shore of Gaza in July, evoked an enthusiastic reaction in the PA.[166] "This gas find," wrote a commentator in *al-Quds*, "is a good omen and a blessing for the Palestinian people, who have suffered for long from the shortage of revenues and the scarcity of natural resources." The writer expressed the hope that the discovery would give a significant push to the Palestinian economy, which had become a satellite market to Israel after its traditional agricultural character was ruined by the land seizures for the building of settlements and circuitous roads and the competition by Israeli products, which flooded the Palestinian markets.[167] However, the outbreak of the intifada caused an indefinite postponement of production.

Indeed, the outbreak of the intifada engendered a sharp and painful decline in all aspects of the Palestinian economy. Strict road closures were imposed on the Palestinian population, roadblocks increased, and severe restrictions on entry into Israel and transport between the West Bank and Gaza were declared. This situation brought most economic activities to an almost complete halt. The immediate effect was a sharp rise in the unemployment rate. In November, it reached a record peak of 24%, excluding the 10% of the population who had jobs in Israel and could not reach their work places due to the closures.[168]

The economic siege also cut off PA trade routes with the outside world almost completely. Minister of Industry and Trade Sa'di al-Karnaz observed in November that with the halt in Palestinian exports, the agricultural sector was practically "dead," and the same situation faced non-agricultural exports, primarily stone and marble products, textiles and garments.[169] Karnaz, describing the abyss into which the Palestinian economy had sunk, stated: "The Palestinian industry sector has now fallen to below 20% of its normal capacity, which means that about 60,000 workers have lost their jobs....The tourism sector...is ruined. The daily loss is estimated at $1m...the Palestinian economy is down by 80%. The volume of daily losses, not counting damage from the fighting, is estimated at $13m. a day."[170] A special report by the UN special coordinator in the occupied territories, summarizing the economic impact of the first three weeks of the intifada, stated that the events resulted in a 50% reduction of normal economic productivity. It assessed domestic losses at c. $8m. for every normal working day.[171]

A detailed economic report published in November by the Palestinian delegation to the Islamic Conference Organization (ICO) summit in Doha, Qatar, provided the figures concerning losses to the Palestinian economy since the beginning of the intifada: a 100% drop in textile production, 80% drop in the food industries, $3.7m. daily loss in the agricultural and fishing sector, and $500,000 damages to plantations, buildings and industrial plants.[172] The most acute problem was disruption in food supplies to the PA territories. Palestinian spokespersons claimed that Israel was withholding thousands of containers at the Ashdod port, although they did not specify whether these were food containers. The Palestinian report presented at Doha stated that Israel was blocking the transport of any goods into the PA except "what has been billed as humanitarian support."[173] The report also charged that Israel "complicated inspection procedures, which lead to [the] spoiling of Palestinian products."[174] The summit decided to establish a donation fund of $1bn. to support the PA. Palestinian spokespersons, however, complained later that little of the promised funds were transferred to the PA.[175]

The grave economic state was reflected in the final figures for PA economic development in 2000. Per capita GDP dropped approximately 10% during the last three months of 2000, and the overall GDP growth rate for 2000 was -5.9%.[176]

ISRAEL'S UNILATERAL SEPARATION PLAN

Angered by the Palestinian refusal to stop the violence in the early days of the intifada, Israeli prime minister Barak announced a plan at the beginning of October for unilateral separation between Israel and the PA.[177] Designed to eliminate all daily contact between Israelis and Palestinians, although not necessarily to relinquish more land to the Palestinians, the plan was viewed by a Western source as implicitly disastrous for the Palestinians, as it might precipitate more violent unrest even if only partially implemented.[178]

Palestinian reactions to the separation plan were mixed. In a sharp attack on Israel, Minister of Local Government 'Urayqat charged that Israel, under the pretext of the "so-called separation," was trying to "threaten [the Palestinians] with racist designs in order to entrench [the] occupation and annex territories."[179] By contrast, Minister of Supply Abu 'Ali Shahin welcomed the idea of unilateral separation stating that the Palestinians would benefit since the new reality would encourage them to run their own affairs. "We will lose nothing but this dirty occupation," he observed.[180]

Public opinion, however, was opposed to the notion of separation. A poll conducted in the PA in early December showed that about 70% of the Palestinians were against full economic separation from Israel. Concurrently, however, 70% said that they would continue to support the Aqsa Intifada even if it harmed their economic situation.[181]

NOTES

For the place and frequency of publications cited here, and for the full name of the publication, news agency, radio station or monitoring service where an abbreviation is used, please see "List of Sources." Only in the case of more than one publication bearing the same name is the place of publication noted here. Unless otherwise stated, all references to *al-Ayyam* refer to the Ramallah daily.

1. *JP*, 20, 27 January, 8 March 2000.
2. *Al-Quds*, 5 February (DR); *JP*, 2 February 2000.
3. *JP*, 26 June 2000.
4. See for example, *Petra-JNA*, 27 May — BBC Monitoring, 28 May; R. Amman, 6 July — BBC Monitoring, 8 July; R. Amman, 2 August — BBC Monitoring, 4 August 2000.
5. *Petra-JNA*, 27 May — BBC Monitoring, 28 May 2000.
6. *Ha'aretz*, 19 June 2000.
7. *Ha'aretz*, 13 August 2000. According to Palestinian National Council Speaker Salim Za'nun, EU disapproval of a Palestinian UDI led 'Arafat to call a PLO Central Council meeting to delay the declaration of the state. See *al-Ayyam*, 13 August 2000 (DR).
8. *JP*, 29 September; *al-Sharq al-Awsat*, 28 September 2000 (DR).
9. *Al-Quds*, 2 July (DR); MENA, 26 May (DR); *al-Ayyam*, 19 August 2000 (DR).
10. *Al-Quds*, 22 May 2000 (DR).
11. *Al-Quds*, 1 March 2000 (DR).
12. *Al-Safir*, 4 July 2000 (DR).
13. *Ha'aretz*, 4 July; *al-Sharq al-Awsat*, 5 July 2000 (DR).
14. *Al-Ayyam*, 4 April 2000 (DR).
15. *Al-Quds*, 10 June 2000 (DR).
16. *Ha'aretz*, 11 September; *JP*, 11 September 2000.
17. *Ha'aretz*, 30 October 2000.
18. See, e.g., MENA, 19 January 2000 (DR).
19. *Al-Ayyam*, 23 January (DR); *al-Quds*, 22 January (DR); Abu Mazin's interview in *al-Musawwar*, 11 February (DR); 'Arafat's interview in MENA, 9 April 2000 (DR).
20. *Al-Ayyam*, 22 January 2000 (DR).
21. *Al-Quds*, 10 June 2000 (DR).
22. *Al-Ayyam*, 28 June 2000 (DR).
23. *Al-Quds*, 16 July 2000 (DR).
24. *Al-Sharq al-Awsat*, 8 July 2000 (DR).
25. *Al-Quds*, 9 July 2000 (DR).
26. *JP*, 9 July 2000.
27. *Al-Ayyam*, 18 July 2000 (DR).
28. *Al-Dustur*, 12 July 2000 (DR).
29. See, e.g., *Ha'aretz*, 19 May, 26 December; *JP*, 16 July 2000.
30. *Al-Quds*, 12 January 2000 (DR).
31. *Al-Quds*, 23 April (DR). Rahman repeated this view of Resolution 194 as a compromise solution in *al-Dustur*, 26 June 2000 (DR).
32. *JP*, 16 July 2000.
33. *Ha'aretz*, 13 July 2000.
34. *Al-Quds*, 22 December (DR); *Ha'aretz*, 25 December 2000.
35. *NYT*, 22 March 2000.
36. *Al-Nahar*, 1 February 2000 (DR).

37. *JP*, 16 May 2000.
38. *Al-Mushahid al-Siyasi*, 11 June 2000.
39. *Al-Sharq al-Awsat*, 1 September 2000 (DR).
40. Israel TV Channel 2, 18 May — BBC Monitoring, 19 May 1999.
41. *JP*, 2 June 2000.
42. *JP*, 21 July; *al-Quds*, 30 August (DR); *Ha'aretz*, 6 September 2000.
43. *JP*, 19 July; *Ha'aretz*, 10 September; *FT*, 18 September; *Le Monde*, 26 September 2000 (DR).
44. *JP*, 25 July 2000.
45. See *Ha'aretz*, 21, 25 July, 28 August, 18 September, 22 December 2000.
46. *Ha'aretz*, 14 November 2000.
47. See, e.g., *JP*, 25 April; *Ha'aretz*, 19 June. For negative Palestinian references to the Israeli proposals, see *al-Ayyam*, 11, 27 January, 1 March, 15 April, 13 May (DR); *al-Quds*, 10 June 2000 (DR).
48. *Al-Musawwar*, 11 February 2000 (DR).
49. *Al-Ayyam*, 27 January 2000 (DR).
50. *Al-Quds*, 10 June 2000 (DR).
51. *Ha'aretz*, 28 January. In the months preceding the Camp David talks, Prime Minister Barak reportedly opposed the idea of land exchange, though it was later discussed in the Camp David talks. See *MM*, 29 June 2000.
52. *Al-Ayyam*, 1 July (DR). See also *al-Ayyam*, 13 May, 19 September (DR); *al-Quds*, 25 June 2000 (DR).
53. *Ha'aretz*, 31 December 2000.
54. R. Monte Carlo, 20 September 2000 (DR).
55. *Peacewatch*, 1 June 2001.
56. *Ha'aretz*, 13 November, 4 December 2000.
57. *Al-Quds*, 16 October 2000 (DR).
58. *Ha'aretz*, 14 November 2000.
59. *Ha'aretz*, 3, 10, 11 October 2000.
60. *Ha'aretz*, 27 October 2000.
61. *Al-Quds*, 26 June (DR). See also Faysal al-Husayni's declaration that peace is not the only option for the Palestinian people and that they have other options, *al-Ayyam*, 15 June (DR). Also see *al-Ayyam*, 22 April 2000 (DR).
62. *JP*, 28 September 2000.
63. *Ha'aretz*, 27 October 2000.
64. Khalil Shiqaqi, "Palestinians Divided," *Foreign Affairs*, January 2002 (Internet version).
65. R. Monte Carlo, 31 October 2000 (DR).
66. *Al-Ayyam*, 6 October 2000 (DR).
67. *Al-Quds*, 15 October 2000 (DR).
68. *Ha'aretz*, 15 November 2000.
69. *Al-Sharq al-Awsat*, 7 October 2000 (DR).
70. *Al-Hayyat*, 15 November 2000.
71. Yezid Sayigh, "'Arafat and the Anatomy of a Revolt," *Survival*, Vol. 43, No. 3, Autumn 2001, pp. 47–60.
72. *Ha'aretz*, 3 November 2000.
73. *Al-Quds*, 16 October 2000 (DR).
74. *Al-Hayat al-Jadida*, 24 October 2000 (DR).
75. *Al-Quds*, 26 October 2000 (DR).
76. *Ha'aretz*, 4 December 2000.
77. *Al-Hayat al-Jadida*, 7 December 2000 (DR).
78. *Al-Sharq al-Awsat*, 13 October 2000 (DR).
79. *Al-Musawwar*, 10 November 2000 (DR).
80. R. Monte Carlo, 31 October 2000 (DR).
81. *Al-Musawwar*, 10 November 2000 (DR).

82. *Al-Hayat al-Jadida*, 7 December 2000 (DR).
83. *Al-Hayat al-Jadida*, 30 November 2000 (DR).
84. *Al-Quds*, 28 October 2000 (DR).
85. *Al-Ayyam*, 6 December 2000 (DR).
86. *NYT*, 18 October 2000.
87. *NYT*, 19 October 2000.
88. *NYT*, 19 October; *JP*, 19 October 2000.
89. *Al-Quds*, 15 October 2000 (DR).
90. *JP*, 17 October 2000.
91. *Al-Quds*, 18 October 2000 (DR).
92. *Al-Ayyam*, 27 December 2000 (DR).
93. *Al-Sharq al-Awsat*, 24 December 2000 (DR).
94. *Ha'aretz*, 31 December 2000.
95. David Schenker, "Inside the Fatah Tanzim: A Primer," *Peacewatch*, 6 October 2000.
96. *JP*, commentary by Ben Lynfield, 11 February 2000.
97. Ibid.
98. *Ha'aretz*, 15 March 2000.
99. *Al-Sharq al-Awsat*, commentary by Huda al-Husayni, 8 September 2000 (DR).
100. VoP, 26 July — SWB, 27 July 2000.
101. *Ha'aretz*, 19 October 2000.
102. Ibid.
103. *Al-Musawwar*, 10 November 2000 (DR).
104. *Al-Ayyam*, 5 December 2000 (DR).
105. *Al-Ayyam*, 6 December 2000 (DR).
106. *Al-Hayat al-Jadida*, 7 December 2000 (DR).
107. *Al-Ayyam*, 9 October 2000 (DR).
108. *Al-Hayat al-Jadida*, 20 November 2000 (DR).
109. *Al-Quds*, 13 November 2000 (DR).
110. R. Monte Carlo, 1 November 2000 (DR).
111. *Ha'aretz*, 2 November 2000.
112. *Al-Dustur*, 28 November 2000 (DR).
113. *Al-Ayyam*, 6 December 2000 (DR).
114. *Al-Majalla*, 5 March (DR); *Al-Ayyam*, 26 April 2000 (DR).
115. *Al-Quds*, 7 April 2000 (DR).
116. *Al-Majalla*, 5 March 2000 (DR).
117. *Al-Ayyam*, 4 July 2000 (DR).
118. Ibid.
119. *Al-Ayyam*, 16 September (DR); David Schenker, "Statehood, Final Status, and the Future Role of the PLO: Will the Conflict End with Independence?" *Peacewatch*, 12 September 2000.
120. *Ha'aretz*, 20 January 2000.
121. *JP*, 16 January 2000.
122. *Al-Majalla*, 5 March 2000 (DR).
123. *Al-Sharq al-Awsat*, 14 January 2000 (DR).
124. *Ha'aretz*, 26 May 2000.
125. *JP*, 27 December 2000.
126. *Ha'aretz*, 2 March 2000.
127. *NYT*, 6 March; *Ha'aretz*, 8 March 2000.
128. *Ha'aretz*, 8 March 2000.
129. *Al-Ayyam*, 1 February 2000 (DR).
130. *Al-Ayyam*, 2 February 2000 (DR).
131. *Al-Ayyam*, 3 February 2000 (DR).
132. *Al-Quds*, 5 February 2000 (DR).
133. *Al-Quds*, 17 February 2000 (DR).

134. *Al-Quds*, 7 May 2000 (DR).
135. *MM*, 8 May 2000.
136. *Ha'aretz*, 9 July 2000.
137. *Al-Dustur*, 11 July 2000 (DR).
138. *Al-Quds*, 4 September 2000 (DR).
139. *Al-Ayyam*, 13 August 2000 (DR).
140. *Al-Quds*, 8 September 2000 (DR).
141. Ibid.
142. See, e.g., Khalil Shiqaqi, "Palestinians Divided"; *al-Ayyam*, 10 April 2000 (DR); *al-Quds*, 6 March 2000 (DR).
143. *Al-Ayyam*, 22 January 2000 (DR).
144. Ibid.
145. *Al-Majd*, 7 August 2000 (DR).
146. *Al-Quds*, 2 May 2000 (DR).
147. *Al-Dustur*, 28 November 2000 (DR).
148. *Al-Ayyam*, 25 June 2000 (DR).
149. *Ha'aretz*, 29 May 2000.
150. *Al-Quds*, 17 June 2000 (DR).
151. *JP*, 25 May 2000.
152. *Al-Dustur*, 28 November 2000 (DR).
153. *Al-Sharq al-Awsat*, 9 February 2000 (DR). Ghawsha, along with his colleague, Khalid Mash'al, later apologized for the attack.
154. *Country Profile, Israel and the Occupied Territories, 2000*, p. 73; *2001*, p. 86; *CR*, Israel and the Occupied Territories, August, p. 38; November 2000, p. 38.
155. *Country Profile, Israel and the Occupied Territories, 2000*, pp. 77–78; *CR*, Israel and the Occupied Territories, August 2000, p. 46.
156. *Country Profile, Israel and the Occupied Territories, 2001*, p. 96.
157. *Al-Ayyam*, 2 August 2000 (DR).
158. *CR*, Israel and the Occupied Territories, 1st quarter, 2000, pp. 31–32; May 2000, p. 39.
159. Ibid.
160. *Al-Quds*, 27 January 2000 (DR).
161. *Al-Sharq al-Awsat*, 3 January 2000 (DR).
162. *Al-Sharq al-Awsat*, 28 January 2000 (DR).
163. *Al-Ayyam*, 6 July 2000 (DR); *CR*, Israel and the Occupied Territories, August 2000, p. 38.
164. *Al-Dustur*, 7 July 2000 (DR).
165. *Al-Ayyam*, 5 June 2000 (DR).
166. *CR*, Israel and the Occupied Territories, November 2000, p. 51.
167. *Al-Quds*, 28 September 2000 (DR).
168. *CR*, Israel and the Occupied Territories, November 2000, pp. 46–47; *al-Quds*, 16 November 2000 (DR).
169. *Arab News*, 9 November 2000 (DR).
170. Ibid.
171. *CR*, Israel and the Occupied Territories, November 2000, p. 46.
172. *Al-Quds*, 16 November 2000 (DR).
173. Ibid.
174. Ibid.
175. *Arab News*, 9 November (DR); *al-Quds*, 12 December 2000 (DR).
176. *Country Profile, Israel and the Occupied Territories, 2001*, pp. 81, 85–86.
177. *Ha'aretz*, 10 October 2000.
178. *CR*, Israel and the Occupied Territories, November 2000, p. 44.
179. *Al-Ayyam*, 27 October 2000 (DR).
180. *Al-Quds*, 15 November 2000 (DR).
181. *Al-Ayyam*, 8 December 2000 (DR).

Qatar

JOSHUA TEITELBAUM

During the year 2000 several Qataris accused of involvement in a 1996 coup attempt against the emir, Shaykh Hamad bin Khalifa bin Hamad Al Thani, received sentences of life imprisonment. They appealed the ruling. The Al Thani also formed a family council during the year, mostly made up of younger members who supported Hamad's reformist policies. In foreign affairs, the government-funded al-Jazira satellite channel continued to make waves, angering several Arab countries. The station only brought Qatar notoriety, and it gained the appreciation of millions of Arab viewers. Relations with Bahrain remained uneasy (Manama boycotted the Islamic Conference Organization [ICO] summit in Doha in November), as the two sides awaited the verdict of their territorial dispute before the International Court of Justice (ICJ). Doha continued to improve its relationship with Tehran; there were mutual visits by high officials and cooperation agreements were signed. Qatar also tried to improve Gulf relations with Iraq, but to no avail. Relations with Israel suffered a blow in November, when Qatar announced it was closing the Israeli trade office in Doha following the outbreak of Palestinian-Israeli violence. Morocco recalled its ambassador to Doha in July to protest the purchase of arms on behalf of Algeria, which Rabat thought would make their way to the Polisario movement struggling against Morocco for control of the Western Sahara. In defense affairs, Qatar continued to negotiate with the US over granting an airbase on Qatari soil. With respect to economic issues, GDP rose 1.2% due to increased revenue from oil. A $1bn. contract was signed with Exxon-Mobil for the development of an oil field.

INTERNAL AFFAIRS

In the beginning of the year, Qataris were preoccupied with the trial of more than a hundred men accused of plotting a 1996 counter-coup against the emir, Shaykh Hamad bin Khalifa Al Thani (see *MECS 1996*, pp, 570–72). Supporters of the former emir, Shaykh Khalifa bin Hamad Al Thani, formed a support committee overseas for "political prisoners in Qatar," and called for a fair verdict in the trial. It charged the emir with failing to honor a promise to pardon all the accused who turned themselves in. The verdict was announced on 29 February. Eighty-five defendants were acquitted, including twenty who were tried in absentia. A cousin of the emir, former economy minister and police chief Shaykh Hamad bin Jasim bin Hamad, received life imprisonment, along with thirty-two others. Charges that would have carried the death penalty were dropped. The support committee termed the verdicts "unjust and political." During an appeals hearing in September, the public prosecutor called for the beheading of Shaykh Hamad.[1] Certainly, there were members of the royal family who expected a pardon; it was also demeaning to the family to have members imprisoned and undergo a public trial. On the other hand, it seemed that Hamad was balancing two concerns: he wanted serious penalties to deter future plotters, but he also wanted to appear merciful, in the tradition of tribal

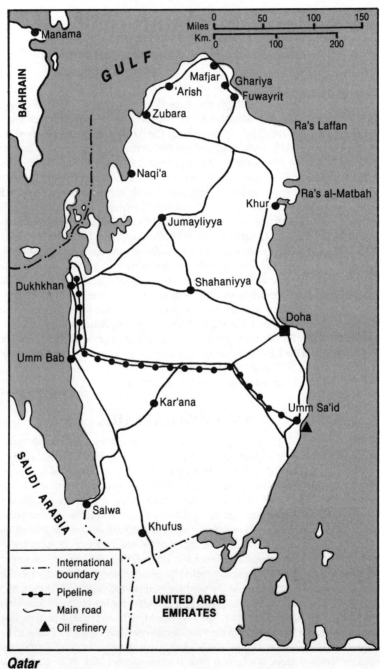

Qatar

leaders. And along with his efforts to increase accountability, he wished to demonstrate that even members of the Al Thani were not beyond the law. The failure to issue pardons showed that the emir was not yet prepared to welcome his father and his entourage back from their exile.

Hamad moved to strengthen his rule in July, when he formed a council of representatives, to be known as the "Council of the Reigning Family." Saudi Arabia set up a similar council in June (see chapter on Saudi Arabia). The emir was chosen to chair the council, and Crown Prince Jasim bin Hamad was chosen as vice chair. Rounding out membership were thirteen other family members, including the foreign minister, Shaykh Hamad bin Jasim bin Jabr and Interior Minister 'Abdallah bin Khalid bin Hamad. "The prerogatives of the council consist of attending to the affairs of the reigning family and to discuss related matters submitted to it by the president," the Qatari News Agency said. The term of membership was designated at five years, renewable indefinitely for equal periods. Hamad probably wanted to use the council to form a consensus among important family members to support his reformist policies; the council was composed primarily of the younger members, who shared his liberalizing agenda. The older members of the family were believed to oppose this agenda, which had led to the erosion of royal family privileges. They had been critical of Hamad's ending of preference given to family members in the granting of high government jobs and free vacation privileges. The local press had also been critical of the annual stipends granted to the Al Thani.[2]

In February, Hamad gave a speech to the Kuwaiti press, in which he called for a "new, open Arab mind" for the new millennium. He attributed many problems in the Gulf to the lack of democracy, and advocated public participation in politics and freedom of the press. There would come a time, he said, when parliaments would have to exist, with ministers being held accountable.[3]

In other internal developments, a poll found that three out of four women in Qatar opposed polygamy, while around the same number of men favored the practice. Most of the women said that they feared losing their husband or that he would not be able to treat his wives fairly, as required by Islam. The men who opposed polygamy said that it cost too much and that they feared the reaction of their first wife. In February, a woman for the first time won the right to practice as a lawyer.[4]

ECONOMIC ISSUES

Real GDP growth in 2000 was an estimated 5.2%, up from 4% in 1999, thanks to the rise in oil prices. Oil-exports earning rose by 32.5% during the year.[5] The rosy fiscal outlook brought about by increased oil revenues led to increased spending in infrastructure. In September and October, the government released QR150m. for the beautification of Doha and for roadworks.[6] The Qatar General Petroleum Corporation signed a $1bn. contact with Exxon-Mobil in May to develop the giant offshore North Field of Qatar.[7] In line with Emir Hamad's reforms, the emirate's newly formed Qatar General Electricity and Water Corporation announced that it would slash 5,300 jobs — two-thirds of its work force — since many workers were entirely unproductive.. According to Energy Minister 'Abdallah al-'Atiyya, this included meter readers who were Qatari nationals but never showed up for work and had their work done by nationals from other countries.[8]

FOREIGN AFFAIRS

The al-Jazira satellite channel of Qatar continued to make waves, while putting the small Gulf state on the map. Emir Hamad told a visiting delegation of Kuwaiti journalists, who criticized the station, that it was not set up "to spite Kuwait." In June 1999, Kuwaiti authorities had banned the station for a month after an Iraqi insulted the Kuwaiti emir during a live broadcast.[9] In April, Libya recalled the head of its diplomatic mission to Doha following criticism of Tripoli on an al-Jazira program. Participants had said that the Libyan system of people's committees was a mere façade for the country's leader, Mu'ammar al-Qadhdhafi, to make all the decisions. Baghdad protested in May that the coverage of Saddam Husayn's birthday was "too pro-American." The Iraqi Ministry of Information wrote the station, noting that "it seems al-Jazira does not want to see Iraqis celebrating, but wants to see the people of Iraq living with disaster and suffering and even dying of hunger." In September, Kuwaiti lawyer Salah al-Hashim filed suit against al-Jazira and popular presenter Sami Haddad for saying that Kuwaitis killed Palestinians, Iraqis, and others by throwing acid on them after the ruling family returned to Kuwait in 1991. Saudi Arabia banned an issue of a Qatari sports magazine because it contained an interview with al-Jazira presenter Faysal al-Qasim, who presented the controversial show "The Opposite Direction," which was rarely kind to Saudi positions. The success of al-Jazira in putting Qatar on the map led officials during the year to consider an Islamic satellite channel. The proposal was made to the ICO when it convened in Qatar in November (see below), and was accepted.[10]

The foreign minister responded to the criticism of al-Jazira by pointing approvingly to precisely what many others feared: its promotion of free expression. "Freedom of choice remains a basic option. We hope to see similar freedom in the rest of the Arab world to enable its citizens to know the truth and to participate in shaping policies and freely expressing their views."[11]

Relations with Bahrain improved for a time, but then slipped backwards again, as the two sides awaited the decision of the ICJ on the long-running dispute concerning the Hawar islands and other territories claimed by both countries. In January, the emir of Bahrain, Shaykh Hamad 'Isa Al Khalifa paid a visit to Doha, which followed the December 1999 visit of Emir Hamad of Qatar to Manama (see *MECS* 1999, p. 502).[12] In February, Qatari crown prince Jasim bin Hamad visited Bahrain to meet with his counterpart, Shaykh Salman bin Hamad Al Khalifa, in order to co-chair the first meeting of a joint high commission set up in December 1999. Both sides seemed determined to avoid a confrontation, and issued statements urging patience regarding their territorial dispute.[13] In March, Doha announced that it was naming an ambassador to Manama, Shaykh 'Abdallah bin Thamir bin Muhammad Al Thani. The Bahraini crown prince visited Doha in April for another meeting of the joint commission, and Qatar Airways resumed its flights from Doha to Manama.[14]

But the budding thaw in relations received a blow in May, at the end of which the ICJ was supposed to begin hearing the case. Bahrain had expected that the joint commission would lead Doha to pull its suit from the ICJ and rely on the commission and the mediation efforts of Saudi Arabia and the UAE. When Doha failed to act, Bahrain announced that it "had no choice but to set aside the work" of the commission. Qatar expressed its "surprise" at the move, particularly in light of the previous improvement in relations, but it probably believed that it had a better case before the ICJ than did Bahrain. It stressed that the suspension of the commission's work had been a unilateral Bahraini decision made without previous consultation with Qatar. The UAE and Saudi Arabia sought to mediate — they brought about a meeting between the two emirs late in the month — but to no avail.[15]

A war of words heated up as the ICJ began to hear the case. The Bahraini prime minister, Shaykh Khalifa bin Salman Al Khalifa, warned that Bahrain would not give up a single inch of its territory. "Justice will not be done unless it confirms a right that is anchored in history and backed by law," he stressed. Bahraini newspapers scoffed at Doha's opening arguments, which stressed the proximity of the Hawar islands to Qatar. Qatari papers ridiculed Bahrain for telling the ICJ that Manama had put its troops on a state of alert on the islands. All the same, the leaders of both countries called for calm during the deliberations of the ICJ. The Bahraini emir stated that "Bahrain has a sincere wish to set up a rapprochement, cooperation, even a union with our brothers in Qatar," but Emir Hamad of Qatar was non-committal, responding that the decision would have to be taken by the people of the two countries. Bahrain was non-committal about whether or not it would accept the ICJ decision.[16]

As the Doha ICO summit approached in November, Bahrain announced that it would boycott the meeting because of the dispute. Emir Hamad of Bahrain stated that it was not right to go to Doha before the ICJ had issued its verdict, and that "Qatar's pretensions on Bahrain's state territory and waters have affected relations between the two countries and prevented their development." Shaykh Hamad of Qatar did, on the other hand, attend the GCC summit in Manama in December (see chapter on inter-Arab relations).[17]

Relations with Iran and Iraq were generally good. Iranian foreign minister Kamal Kharrazi visited Doha in early May and invited Shaykh Hamad to make his first visit to Tehran since the 1979 Islamic revolution. Meanwhile, the Qatari minister of finance, economy, and trade, Yusuf Husayn, paid a visit to Tehran to sign aviation and energy accords.[18]

Emir Hamad arrived in Tehran in mid-July. The Iranians touted Qatari-Iranian relations as "an optimum model for other Persian Gulf states." Qatar was keen to expand commercial ties, while Iran wished to use Qatar as a way to improve relations with other Gulf states, particularly Saudi Arabia. Iranian president Muhammad Khatami held a joint news conference with Emir Hamad, six cooperation agreements were signed in the commercial and educational arenas, and a joint communiqué was issued. The statement expressed approval of the development of bilateral relations and agreement on a wide variety of regional issues.[19] But Iranian dissatisfaction with Doha's maintenance of low-level relations with Israel kept relations from being entirely smooth. The Iranian press and the Majlis were highly critical of Qatar in this regard, and Iran threatened to boycott the ICO summit, scheduled for November in Doha, if Qatar did not break relations with the Jewish state. It eventually did attend (see below).[20]

Iraqi foreign minister Muhammad Sa'id al-Sahhaf visted Doha in January to win support for Iraqi opposition to a new UN resolution on disarmament. In keeping with its determination to assume an outsized regional role, Qatar pushed a policy of removing the sanctions on Iraq. During an academic conference on future relations between Iraq and Kuwait held in Kuwait in May, the Qatari foreign minister surprised many by announcing that the Gulf countries should take the initiative in returning Iraq to the regional fold. This drew fire from the Kuwait press. The Qatari initiative was also discussed by GCC foreign ministers during their June meeting in Saudi Arabia.[21]

In September, an Iraqi armed with a knife hijacked a Qatar Airways jet on its way from Doha to Amman. He forced it to land in Ha'il, Saudi Arabia. The incident was reminiscent of a similar hijacking of a Saudi aircraft to Baghdad during the year (see chapter on Saudi Arabia). The hijacker was reportedly a resident of Basra and a member of the Shammar tribe, which was centered in Ha'il. He was turned over to Qatar by Saudi authorities. The man asked for political asylum in Qatar, saying that he feared he would be put to death if he were returned to Iraq.[22] In November, the US imposed commercial sanctions against a member of the Qatari ruling family, Shaykh Hamad bin 'Ali bin Jabr Al Thani for presenting his personal US-made Boeing 747 to Saddam Husayn as a gift. According to the US, the move was a violation of American policy which prohibited the transfer of goods of US origin to Iraq.[23]

Qatar's relationship with Israel remained on a low flame, and was the cause of a major dispute with Saudi Arabia and other states as the November ICO meeting approached. According to the Qatari daily al-Ray'a, Israeli prime minister Ehud Barak requested in January to visit Doha, but was turned down. An Israeli TV team, however, made it to Doha to cover the Asian Nations soccer qualifying competition and interviewed a Qatari sports official. Barak did meet Hamad at the UN millennium summit in September. The Qatari foreign minister stated that Qatar wanted to show that "there are Arabs ready to extend their hand to Israel if there is a just and fair peace with the Arabs." He also offered a defense of Qatari policy in an interview to al-Jazira: "We do not ask permission to meet with anybody. We also do not mean to harm anybody or compete with anybody... Therefore, I do not think that anybody should be able to dictate to us who we should meet and who we should not."[24]

But the outbreak of violence in the territories in late September was a turning point for Qatar and its relations with Israel. Doha opened its hospitals to wounded Palestinians. In early October, it permitted a large demonstration of Qataris in protest against Israeli policies. The rioting in the West Bank and Gaza led to both local and Arab pressure on Qatar to close the Israeli trade office in Doha. Al-Ray'a called for Doha to sever commercial ties with Tel Aviv. In mid-October, foreign minister Hamad announced that the closure of the office was "possible," but in early November stated that Qatar had no plans to do so. But quite cognizant of its role as chair of the ICO, and with the summit coming up in November, Doha was feeling the pressure. Both Saudi Arabia and Iran threatened to boycott the summit if Qatar let the Israeli office continue to function. Doha was caught between its desire for an independent foreign policy and good relations with the US, and its wish to have a successful summit which would confirm it as a player of some significance in the Islamic world. Qatar finally announced on 9 November that it closing the Israeli office. A government spokesperson stated that the closure "reinforces Arab solidarity and creates the appropriate conditions for holding" the summit. And indeed, the move smoothed the path to a successful meeting. The US lamented the Qatari decision. However, that decision did not interfere with a reported secret meeting between Israeli foreign minister Shlomo Ben-Ami and a senior Qatari official in Geneva in December.[25]

There was a crisis in relations with Morocco, partially caused by al-Jazira as well. On 18 July, Morocco announced that it was recalling its ambassador to Doha to protest what Rabat termed "anti-Moroccan political and media attitudes." Morocco was upset that the Qatari representative voted for Germany to host the 2006 World Cup soccer tournament when Morocco had expected to receive the Qatari vote. A "diplomatic source" in Rabat said that the Qatari deal at the end of May to buy British weapons for Algeria was disturbing, since it was likely that they would find their way to the Polisario. Concurrently, Moroccan newspapers criticized al-Jazira for broadcasting programs they dubbed "anti-Moroccan," including one on "the Israeli penetration of North Africa." A meeting between the crown princes of the two countries later in the month in Riyadh did little to ameliorate the situation. In September, Morocco boycotted Qatar National Day celebrations in Rabat. However, in October, it was reported that the two countries had agreed to normalize relations, following a meeting between Emir Hamad and the king of Morocco, Muhammad VI, on the sidelines of the Arab summit in Cairo.[26]

Determined to be part of the world stage, Qatar continued its mediation efforts in Sudan between President 'Umar al-Bashir and the speaker of the dissolved parliament, Hasan al-Turabi. Foreign Minister Hamad bin Jasim flew to Khartoum in January following a previous visit to Doha by Turabi. Hamad became quite involved in efforts to effect a reconciliation, even offering a proposal himself (see chapter on Sudan). In August, Qatar continued its efforts to mediate between Sudan and Eritrea, following a peace deal it brokered in May 1999 (see *MECS 1999*, pp. 501–502). The emir of Qatar flew to Cuba in September to meet with President Fidel Castro, apparently to reassure oil-dependent Havana, which was worried about high oil prices. Doha was the only Gulf state to maintain diplomatic relations with Cuba at the ambassadorial level.[27]

Relations with Saudi Arabia continued on an even keel, with some progress reported on the implementation of a border agreement between Doha and Riyadh. At the end of April, Saudi minister of interior Nayif bin 'Abd al-'Aziz stated that the "question of the border was "technically resolved...and should soon be signed." Saudi crown prince 'Abdallah bin 'Abd al-'Aziz visited Doha in early May.[28]

Regarding defense issues, Qatar remained fully in the western camp. Crown Prince Jasim visited the US in February–March for a "private working visit," and met with senior US officials. He was accompanied by the foreign minister and other Qatari officials.[29] US secretary of defense William Cohen visited Qatar during a swing through the Gulf in April. Negotiations continued with the US for an agreement that would allow US warplanes the use of a Qatari airbase when US carriers were absent from the Gulf or in times of crisis. Around forty US fighters were to be deployed at a base 35km. south of Doha. The base would be upgraded by constructing prefabricated maintenance buildings, additional hangars, and aprons and sunshades for the planes. Qatar also discussed the sharing of strategic data from US intelligence satellites under the Co-operative Defense Initiative (CDI) proposed by the US to the Gulf states. A dissenting voice was heard, however, from the daily *al-Watan*, which stated that the US presence should be decreased, not increased.[30]

NOTES

For the place and frequency of publications cited here, and for the full name of the publication, news agency, radio station, or monitoring service where an abbreviation is used, please see "List of Sources." Only in the case of more than one publication bearing the same name is the place of publication noted here.

The author thanks Itamar Inbari for his excellent work in assembling source material for this chapter.

1. AFP, 2, 28, 29 February, 17 September 2000.
2. AFP, 12 July; CR, Bahrain, Qatar, August 2000, p. 32.
3. CR, Bahrain, Qatar, 1st quarter, 2000, p. 35.
4. AFP, 31 January (quoting al-Sharq), 16 February 2000.
5. CR, Bahrain, Qatar, February 2001, pp. 20, 35.
6. CR, Bahrain, Qatar, November 2000, p. 38.
7. AFP, 2 May 2000.
8. AFP, 23 April 2000.
9. MM, 13 February 2000.
10. AFP, 24 April, 1 May, 10 September; 11, 16 December 2000.
11. Middle East Insight, September 2000.
12. AFP, 6 January; al-Sharq al-Awsat, 28 January 2000.
13. AFP, 20, 22 February 2000.
14. AFP, 22 March, 24 April 2000.
15. AFP, 19, 20, 21, 22, 24 May; al-Quds al-'Arabi, 25 May 2000 (MM).
16. AFP, 30 May, 3, 9, 29 June, 18 July 2000.
17. AFP, 6 November, 26 December 2000.
18. AFP, 1 May, 19 June; IRNA, 19 June 2000 (DR).
19. AFP, 17, 18 July; IRNA, 18 July 2000 (DR).
20. Jomhuri-ye Eslami, 11 September (DR); IRNA, 5, 8, 9, 11 November (DR); TT, 6 November (DR); Iran News, 6 November (DR); KI, 7 November 2000 (DR).
21. AFP, 6 January, 4 June; al-Quds al-'Arabi, 15 May (MM); al-Watan, 17 May 2000 (MM).
22. AFP, 14, 15, 17 September 2000.
23. AFP, 25 November, 8 December 2000.
24. AFP, AP, 22 January; AFP, 1 April; AP, AFP, 8 September; GSNL, 25 September 2000.
25. AFP, 3, 7, 14, 22 October, 6, 8, 9 November, 17 December 2000;
26. Al-Sharq al-Awsat, 20 July, 13 September; AFP, 23 July, 21 October; WSWN, 30 July <www.arso.org>; CR, Bahrain, Qatar, November 2000, p. 37.
27. AFP, 1, 2, 4 January, 6, 8 August, 13, 14 September; al-Sharq al-Awsat, 6 January 2000 (MM).
28. AFP, 30 April, 1 May, 2000.
29. AFP, 10 March 2000.
30. AFP, 5, 6 April; CR, Bahrain, Qatar, May 2000, p. 38.

Saudi Arabia
(Al-Mamlaka al-'Arabiyya al-Sa'udiyya)

JOSHUA TEITELBAUM

Questions continued to be asked in 2000 about the prospective succession to the ailing Saudi monarch, King Fahd bin 'Abd al-'Aziz. Crown Prince 'Abdallah bin 'Abd al-'Aziz established a family council during the year with himself at its helm. While some suggested that this meant that the succession was imminent, it actually indicated a firming up of power by 'Abdallah, who left Fahd off the council along with Fahd's full brother, Nayif. 'Abdallah pushed slowly forward with his reforms in the area of non-Muslim tourism, more rights for women, and a loosening of media controls. There were several demonstrations during the year in favor of the Palestinians; a rare occurrence in the kingdom. They indicated the growing role of satellite television in spreading the news, demonstrating the inability of the regime to control the flow of information. There were also indeterminate acts of violence, such as a protest by Isma'ilis in Najran, the killing of one foreign national and the wounding of several others, and a hijacking of a Saudi aircraft to Baghdad. The kingdom tried to defend itself against a targeted human rights "attack" by Amnesty International (AI); Saudi Arabia saw the move as an attack on Islam itself. In foreign affairs, relations continued to be close with Iran, and discussions continued apace on the signing of a joint security pact. Riyadh and Baghdad had a vitriolic exchange after Saddam accused the kingdom of being a forward base for US aggression. Border agreements were signed with Yemen and Kuwait. A rise in oil revenues brought some relief, but that was not enough to create jobs for the myriad unemployed. There was some loosening of controls on foreign investment and a few other economic reforms, but the pace remained very slow.

INTERNAL AFFAIRS

THE SUCCESSION

King Fahd continued to hang on to the throne in 2000 despite being hampered by a stroke and other maladies. Crown Prince 'Abdallah continued to pull many of the levers of authority and was active in promoting various reforms, but he was not entirely independent and had to consult with other Saudi princes when making policy.

'Abdallah felt secure enough in power that he allowed himself a ten-day vacation in Morocco in June, followed by another three-day vacation at the Egyptian Sinai resort of Sharm al-Shaykh. But the greatest demonstration of how comfortable he felt as Fahd's successor was the announcement on 4 June that a 'family council' (*majlis al-'a'ila*) had held its first meeting on that day. 'Abdallah chaired the council, and his half-brother Sultan bin 'Abd al-'Aziz, second deputy prime minister and minister of defense and

491

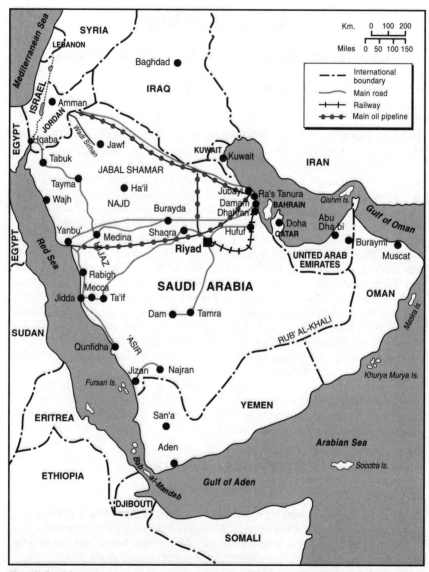

Saudi Arabia

aviation, was deputy chair. It was widely believed that 'Abdallah intended to appoint Sultan as crown prince when the former assumed royal dignity.

The council was composed of eighteen important members of the family from various generations and branches (for membership, see Appendix I). Most noticeably absent from the council was King Fahd himself. A family council, without the head of the family, was a direct signal that 'Abdallah was taking over. Also notably absent was the minister of the interior, Nayif bin 'Abd al-'Aziz, who had reportedly continued to ignore 'Abdallah and report only to Fahd. These two absences seemed to indicate that the council was established with 'Abdallah's prodding and was designed to firm up his hold on power. Noticeably present was Talal bin 'Abd al-'Aziz, the family's *enfant terrible* of the 1960s who had once called for a representative government and had continued to espouse liberalization and more transparency. His inclusion marked his final rehabilitation and signaled that 'Abdallah was going to continue with his reforms.

Although the council contained several persons who held political posts, Nayif denied that the body would have any political role, and declared that it would deal only with internal family matters.[1] It was difficult to say whether the minister of interior was describing the true nature of the new council or was trying to belittle its importance since he had not been included. Talal denied that the council had been set up for succession purposes, or that it had anything to do with politics or affairs of state. "It will look into the affairs of the family, its problems, maybe some mistakes committed domestically or abroad, that reflect badly on the family," Talal told al-Jazira satellite television. Its establishment, however, noted Talal, was "a sign of a wish for reform in the family and a step towards transparency."[2]

In previous successions, a royal council had been convened after the death of the king. But this was the first time the members of the council had been announced, either before or after the king's death.[3] According to the cryptically laconic announcement of the Saudi Press Agency (SPA), the council looked at "its mission and the measures necessary to function in accordance with recommendations of King Fahd, and to make decisions to that effect."[4] The announcement gave the impression that the council had existed for a while, and had just held its first meeting, but this seemed unlikely. It appears that the announcement in this form was designed to demonstrate some sort of continuity with the past, although the council was an entirely new development.

Speculation was rife about the timing of the council's formation. Was Fahd about to abdicate? This thought was strengthened by an evident deterioration in Fahd's mental health. While millions of viewers were watching a soccer game on television in May, Fahd, who was in the stands, was seen to be arguing vehemently with 'Abdallah and other princes. The camera quickly turned to the field, and when it panned back to the royal box, Fahd was no longer to be seen. 'Abdallah presented the winner's cup and medals to the players. The king had also been admitted to hospital earlier in June, although he was released within a day.[5]

The council held a second meeting in early August. Few details were released. Those that were only noted that the meeting had discussed the "internal regulations draft," a document believed by observers to be a kind of a handbook for the behavior of family members;[6] the idea was to combat the image that many family members were corrupt and profligate spenders of the public purse.

BATTLING THE HUMAN RIGHTS ISSUE

AI chose to spotlight human rights abuses in the kingdom in 2000, initiating a worldwide campaign entitled "Saudi Arabia: End Secrecy, End Suffering."[7] The Saudis were accused of arbitrary arrest, torture, executions for acts such as sorcery, and the barring of prisoner access to lawyers and family members. AI issued several reports on Saudi Arabia during the year, and AI members protested at several Saudi embassies. In Washington, the local AI chapter drove around a truck-mounted billboard featuring an amputated hand over the slogan: "This suffering is the secret of Saudi justice."[8]

The Saudis were troubled by the attention, and the day after the beginning of the AI campaign they announced that they had invited a special UN rapporteur to investigate the independence of their judiciary. The kingdom's under-secretary for political affairs, Turki bin Muhammad bin Sa'ud al-Kabir, told the UN Human Rights Commission in Geneva that there was no persecution of non-Muslims and that regulations forbade any form of torture. He added that an independent non-governmental body was being established to help publicize and protect human rights. (By the end of the year, there had been no indication that the organization had been set up.) Prince Turki also echoed the Saudi position that such human rights reports were an attack on Islam, since all Saudi actions were governed by Islamic law. Moreover, he added, the Western concept of human rights ignored other cultures and the Saudis had the right to their own beliefs and to resist the imposition of beliefs from the outside. In May, the Saudi-dominated Gulf Cooperation Council (GCC) announced that it would not brook any discussion of human rights in its discussions with the European Union (EU).[9]

On 6 September, Crown Prince 'Abdallah raised the issue during his speech at the UN Third Millennium Summit: "It is absurd to impose on an individual or a society rights that are alien to its belief and principles," he declared. He stressed that "unbridled globalization" threatened the internal affairs of states "under a variety of pretexts, especially from the angle of human rights." But Saudi Arabia was feeling the pressure, and the next day the kingdom became a party to the Convention on the Elimination of All Forms of Discrimination Against Women (CEDAW — see below). Nayif told the press that "we welcome anyone to see for himself the facts in the kingdom, as it has nothing to conceal," but Foreign Minister Sa'ud Al Faysal seemed to exclude AI when he told the Spanish daily *El Pais*: "If Amnesty International was seeking the truth and it informed itself honestly of the truth, we would consider a visit." This was the essence of 'Abdallah's policy of balancing: he was paying heed to the concerns of the international community, but he was doing so on his own terms. To its satisfaction, Saudi Arabia was elected to the fifty-three-member UN Commission on Human Rights.[10]

'ABDALLAH CONTINUES HIS REFORMS

The introduction of non-Muslim tourism into the kingdom continued to be a Saudi priority. Saudi Arabia needed to diversify its economy and create more jobs for its chronically unemployed — and it had much to show the world in the way of natural beauty. 'Abdallah had already inaugurated a debate on non-Muslim tourism in 1999 (see *MECS* 1999, p. 512); in 2000 the kingdom continued to make very slow — but steady — progress toward international tourism. In April, it was announced that tourist visas were to be granted for the first time. The cabinet approved "certain rules" for issuing visas and visiting "historic and touristic places." It seemed that the rules would eliminate the need for a foreigner to have a local sponsor to visit Saudi Arabia. Later that month, the kingdom set up the Higher Tourism Body, and charged it with "promoting tourist activities and encouraging the kingdom's tourist sector," given, stated the SPA, that tourism represented one "of the country's sources of revenue." In May, Sultan bin Salman bin 'Abd al-'Aziz was appointed to head the organization. Sultan, the son of the governor of Riyadh and the first Arab astronaut, was given the rank of minister — a demonstration of the importance the kingdom attached to tourism. It was reported that about 6,500 tourist visas were issued between the announcement in April and the end of July.[11]

As with the Internet which offered both opportunities and challenges to Saudi society (see *MECS* 1999, p. 551), tourism also potentially threatened Saudi cultural values. But the Saudis were prepared. They aimed at the high end of the tourism market — wealthy people and retirees, who presumably would be more restrained in their public behavior. Tourist sites offered would be for those with an intellectual and historical bent. "Saudi tourism will not be for the masses," said Faruq Ilyas, tourism manager for Saudi Arabian Airlines. "It will be well targeted...pure tourism for archaeology and culture. And it won't be a cheap destination."[12]

There were also some developments with respect to the role of women in Saudi Arabia, following on the heels of the 1999 decision to issue women their own identification cards and to let them observe the meetings of the Consultative Council (*MECS* 1999, pp. 510–12). In July, Princess Jawhara bint Fahd bin Muhammad bin 'Abd al-Rahman Al Sa'ud was named an assistant undersecretary at the Education Ministry, in charge of girls' education. In August, the government acceded to the CEDAW, albeit with reservations. In announcing its acceptance, the government stipulated that it would not comply with "any clause in the agreement that contradicts Islamic *shari'a*." According to a member of the Consultative Council, the reservations were directed at provisions that allowed a woman to give her nationality to her children and the right to choose her husband freely. The first contradicted Saudi law, according to which naturalization was the discrepancy of the authorities, and the second, he said, could technically allow a lesbian marriage. 'Abd al-Rahman al-Rashid of *al-Sharq al-Awsat* was pleased by the signing of the CEDAW, although he expressed his doubt whether this would satisfy Western critics, who viewed Saudi society through the eyes of their own society. But even though Saudi Arabia was improving the status of women, he acknowledged that it had a long way to go. He cited a recent ruling by the government-owned Saudi Telecommunications Company that forbade the selling of mobile or other telephones to women without the permission of a *mahram* (unmarriageable male relative) or a letter from her employer. One small step forward came in August, when it was announced that a new horse-racing track opening east of Riyadh would have stands reserved for women, a move which would finally allow them to attend one of the kingdom's favorite sports. Women at an international Arab conference on security services in Riyadh "nearly caused a riot" when one of the kingdom's most conservative clerics, 'Abd al-Rahman al-Jibrin, objected to their presence.[13]

The media also witnessed some change during the year. There could be no doubt that the ubiquitous presence of satellite television and the censored Internet made official efforts to control the flow of information much more difficult. According to the US State Department, the Ministry of Information relaxed its blackout policy with respect to sensitive news about the kingdom published abroad, although domestic reporting was still strictly controlled. A review of the Saudi press does seem to reveal a certain opening to the discussion of society's ills, although criticism of the royal family was still strictly forbidden. But the openness also owed something to the tone set by 'Abdallah, which was decidedly pro-reform. A new newspaper, *al-Watan*, began publishing from the provincial capital of 'Asir Province, Abha. While it was difficult to say who was behind the paper, its new premises did merit a visit from the crown prince. In June, the SPA reported that the Consultative Council — after studying a report by the Ministry of Information — had proposed that state-run media organs become publicly owned companies that would be allowed to "progress and develop" outside of the ministry's control.[14]

The new openness of the media was not lost on observers. *Al-Quds al-'Arabi*, a daily published in London, which was usually hostile to the kingdom, found some of the candid writing to be commendable. It noted that many papers now regularly tackled formerly taboo issues, criticized government services, discussed Saudi social problems such as unemployment and the economy, and served as a forum for "letting off steam." It ascribed the development to the desire of the government to balance the conservative Islamist tendencies of much of the population with some liberalism. That liberalism was evident in the local television comedy "Tash Ma Tash," which aired each Ramadan before and after the daily fast and satirized Saudi bureaucracy and social problems.[15] It was often the target of the conservatives, but the government did not cancel it.

Additional reforms included a May decision barring cabinet members from taking up positions in companies, except for Saudi Aramco. Those already in such positions would be allowed to serve out their contracts. In June, the Consultative Council endorsed a bill on real estate ownership by non-Saudis. Under the new regulations, non-Saudis would be able to own real estate in all cities of the kingdom with the exception of Mecca and Medina.[16]

In October, Civil Service Minister 'Ali al-Fayiz announced that the government would form a higher administrative committee headed by Sultan to examine ways to reduce public expenditure and improve the efficiency of public employees,[17] who worked in a notoriously bloated bureaucracy. According to a report in the daily *al-Jazira*, Saudi civil servants worked only a maximum of 180 days per year. Apart from the Muslim weekend of Thursday and Friday, religious holidays and annual leave, said the paper, government workers were often absent or took sick leave.[18]

MANAGING THE PALESTINIAN UPRISING — AT HOME

The Palestinian uprising, which began in late September (see chapter on the PA), had a powerful impact on Saudi public opinion. Film of the shooting death of twelve-year old Muhammad al-Dura was broadcast hundreds of times over satellite television, bringing the uprising into the homes of millions across the region. Demonstrations, an extremely rare occurrence in Saudi Arabia, were held in the northern town of Sakaka on 4 October. About two thousand people marched with a police escort. On 6 October, a small group of youths in Riyadh waved Saudi flags and denounced "Israeli massacres." In the northern city of al-Jawf, demonstrators burned the Israeli flag and raised banners in support of the Palestinians. According to residents of al-Jawf who contacted al-Jazira TV, the police confronted the demonstrators and arrested a number of them. Later that week, about forty women marched through Jidda after midday prayers.[19] All things considered, the reaction of the government was mild; the demonstrations were not directed against the regime, and they served the function of letting off steam. But to head off the possibility that pro-Palestinian demonstrations would become anti-government, the government launched fund-raising activities for the Palestinians, including a telethon on state television, and treated Palestinian wounded in Saudi hospitals.[20]

VIOLENT INCIDENTS

There were several violent incidents during the year but no definite trend could be ascertained. Anger at the Russian suppression of the Chechnyan Muslims seemed to have been behind an incident in mid-March. Unidentified men fired what appeared to be blanks at a Russian who worked at his country's consulate in Jidda. Sultan termed the incident a "private" attack, emphasizing that "there was no attack against the Russian consulate."[21]

In April, there was a more serious development: riots in the Yemen border region of Najran by Isma'ili Shi'is of the Banu Yam tribe. The circumstances were not entirely clear. According to the London-based Committee to Protect Legitimate Rights in the Arabian Peninsula, between 14 and 16 April, the authorities arrested three Isma'ili Shi'i scholars for involvement in the outlawed Islamic Action Movement. On 23 April, an Isma'ili cleric, whom the Saudis said was a Yemeni illegal resident, was arrested for "sorcery," a practice outlawed in Saudi Arabia. An associate of the cleric shot and injured a police officer who was searching the cleric's home. When Saudi police then raided an Isma'ili mosque, closing it down and removing books, protesters gathered at the home of the Najran governor, Prince Mash'al bin Sa'ud. The Interior Ministry sent in troops overnight and threatened arrests. During this demonstration, protesters apparently fired weapons and burned cars, killing one member of the security forces and injuring several others.

Wahhabi Islam is severely anti-Shi'i. Shi'is practice what Wahhabis view as shirk, or polytheism. Mash'al, however, stated that the arrests were not linked to religious rights, since, "our Isma'ili brothers have the full freedom to pray in their own way." According to a Yemeni tribal chief, forty people were killed in the clashes. Sa'd al-Faqih, head of the London-based Movement for Islamic Reform in Arabia, said that the Isma'ilis had sparked the protests by commemorating the Shi'i' remembrance of 'Ashura publicly for the first time in many years.[22] An Isma'ili journalist on the scene declared, "we were only defending our religion, or creed, and our honor."[23]

Al-Quds al-'Arabi reported that the Isma'ilis had been emboldened by several AI reports on Saudi human rights violations. It further noted that for years members of the Isma'ili tribe had been co-opted by the government by paying annual stipends to their shaykhs. One of their shaykhs, 'Ali bin Musallim, was related to Defense Minister Sultan by marriage and had been elevated to the position of adviser to the royal court, with the rank of minister.[24]

The Saudis were interested in downplaying the incident, since it drew attention to a dissatisfied sector of the population that had not shown such signs before, and one that was traditionally armed at that. Summing up the clashes, Sultan said that they were caused by "abnormal people who were strange to society and that abnormal people were present all over the world." He asserted that they "did not represent the people of Najran and did not represent the noble tribe of Yam."[25]

In August, a Saudi student opened fire at a housing complex for foreigners in the city of Khamis Mushayt, the location of a major Saudi air force facility, King Faysal Air Base, in 'Asir Province. An air force security officer was killed and two were wounded in the incident. One of the injured was an employee of the British company, British

Aerospace Systems, and the other was an American. The compound housed American, British, and Pakistani personnel and their families. According to the US State Department, the assailant acted alone. Armed with a machine gun, he was injured in the gun battle, which lasted for thirty minutes. Nayif termed the attack a "strange thing with respect to Saudi society."[26]

Also in August, a two-day prison riot broke out in the northern town of al-Jawf. A guard and several prisoners were wounded. Detainees took over the prison to protest against the director, the food, and the lack of newspapers. They held a guard hostage and set fire to mattresses and blankets. After the fire was extinguished, the prisoners asked to meet with the governor of Jawf, Prince 'Abd al-Illah bin 'Abd al-'Aziz, who sent a representative to see them.[27]

The year also witnessed a series of bombing attacks against foreign residents. In September, a British couple was killed in the Bahra desert in the Hijaz. According to the police, they had entered a restricted area used for military training and encountered an explosive device.[28] In November, there were two further bombing incidents in Riyadh. The first, on 17 November, killed a British man and injured the woman traveling with him while they were driving in Riyadh. A few days later, three other Britons were injured in a similar attack. No clear motives for the attacks were initially determined. The latter two attacks led to speculation that they were linked to anger at the West over its support for Israel, or they were carried out by Iraq in retaliation for British participation in "Operation Southern Watch," the enforcement of the no-flight zone in southern Iraq. Saudi officials linked the two bombings, stating that the explosive devices had been similar. In mid-December, there was another bombing with a similar modus operandi: British male victim, car bomb. The driver was badly injured. Saudi officials arrested an American, a Belgian, and a Lebanese in connection with the bombings. They pointed to criminal motives involving money and trafficking in forbidden alcoholic beverages.[29]

In October, a Saudi passenger jet en route from Jidda to London was hijacked to Iraq. The affair appeared to have been either stage-managed by Iraq or carried out with Iraqi cooperation. According to the pilot, a hijacker first demanded that the plane fly to Damascus, and when permission to land had already been granted, ordered the plane to fly to Baghdad. Upon landing, the hijackers demanded negotiations with Saudi authorities, claiming that the Saudi people were oppressed. However, they soon gave themselves up. When the hijackers were presented to journalists, they demanded "justice and equality" in Saudi Arabia and voiced solidarity with the sanctions-hit Iraqi people — sanctions that the Saudis supported and helped enforce. They also denounced the presence of US and British troops in the kingdom, and according to an Iraqi Interior Ministry official, had chosen to fly to Iraq because it "did not bow to American hegemony." But even during discussions with journalists while in the custody of the Iraqis, they claimed that there was still a bomb on the plane and that they wanted to negotiate. The entire event seemed staged. The Saudis later announced that one of the hijackers worked at the Jidda airport as a security officer, while the other was a border guard in Najran. The Saudis demanded their extradition, but the Iraqis refused, eventually granting them political asylum.[30]

The Saudis were at pains to explain these incidents. While they portrayed them as aberrations, their increasing frequency was troubling, and suggested that they were more than simply freak occurrences. What lay behind them remained unclear.

DEVELOPMENTS IN THE OPPOSITION

There were no significant developments in the opposition during the year. Khalid al-Fawwaz, the leader of Usama bin Ladin's London-based Advice and Reform Committee, continued in 2000 to fight his extradition to the US. He had been arrested in 1998 in connection with the August bombings of the American embassies in Tanzania and Kenya (see *MECS* 1998, pp. 27–28). In November, the High Court refused to block his extradition, but the case was still in the courts at the end of the year. A Saudi official was quoted as saying that should he be extradited to the US, the kingdom might request his extradition back to Saudi Arabia.[31]

ECONOMIC AND OIL ISSUES

Major increases in the price of oil during the year contributed to significant growth in GDP. In 2000 it grew an estimated 4%, way up from the 0.4% growth of 1999.[32] But while increasing income, the high price of oil worried the Saudis, who feared that it would lead to a backlash by consuming countries who would cut back on consumption and encourage producers to cheat on their quotas. The Saudis sought to further institutionalize and reinvigorate oil policy in January by creating the Supreme Council for Petroleum and Mineral Affairs (SCPM), headed by King Fahd.[33] The SCPM replaced the Supreme Petroleum Council, formed in 1998.

THE SUPREME COUNCIL FOR PETROLEUM AND MINERAL AFFAIRS (SCPM)

While Fahd was the official chair of the new council, it was widely assumed that ill health would prevent his full participation. Since the deputy chair was 'Abdallah, the establishment of the SCPM, which included tested professionals as well as royals, was a further move by the crown prince to rationalize economic policy-making. It seems that giving Fahd the chair was merely symbolic, and meant to counterbalance the fact that 'Abdallah chaired the Higher Economic Council, which he established in August 1999 (see *MECS* 1999, p. 522).[34]

One important goal of the council was to oversee the attraction and regulation of foreign investment in the oil sector (see below). In February, the council set up a subcommittee, headed by Foreign Minister Sa'ud Al Faysal, to rule on contracts with foreign oil and gas companies; the council immediately began to hold meetings with the heads of the companies. In this regard, October saw the Saudi cabinet authorize the SCPM to take over the management of the national oil company, Saudi Aramco, in order to further coordinate oil policy.[35]

ATTEMPTING TO MANAGE THE PRICE OF OIL

In 1999, oil had dropped below $10/barrel (b). A production cut in March 1999, brought about by cooperation between Riyadh and Tehran, resulted in a recovery (see *MECS* 1999, p. 517). When 2000 opened, benchmark brent crude was trading at more than $24/b; light sweet crude hit over $30/b in mid-February.[36] While pleased by higher prices, which helped the economy recover from the precipitous price falls of 1998–99, the Saudis, the world's largest producers, realized that high prices could backfire. Riyadh stood to gain the most from high prices, but also to lose the most from them in the longer term. Prior to the 27 March OPEC meeting in Vienna, Saudi officials issued conflicting signals about their position on a production increase to bring prices back down. However, as the meeting approached, and following the visit of US energy secretary Richardson to Riyadh in late February, Saudi oil minister Nu'aymi stated that there was a need for a raise in production. Crown Prince 'Abdallah weighed in with a similar view a few days later. Two weeks before the OPEC meeting, oil was trading at $34/b.[37]

The March OPEC meeting was rancorous. The Saudis pushed for increased production, but Iran, which had less reserves, balked. After a two-day dispute, the producers agreed on a small production increase of 1.45m. b/d, but without the participation of Iran, which opposed any production increase. The increase was misleading, however, as it was assumed that at least 1m. b/d were already being produced above quota. A day after the decision, not willing to forfeit market share, Iran announced that they would raise their production along with the other OPEC producers. Oil Minister Nu'aymi said that Saudi Arabia favored a barrel price of around $25 — low enough, he said, to avoid motivating people to look for alternative sources of energy and to avoid a slowdown of the world economy. As a result of the Vienna decision, prices fell back to just under $25.[38]

But that was only temporary relief, as oil prices continued to climb. Meeting in June, OPEC officials could only agree on a small increase of 708,000 b/d. But Saudi Arabia was determined to lower prices. In early July it declared that it would unilaterally boost production by 500,000 b/d if prices did not drop substantially. It had the excess production capacity that the other producers didn't. Psychology was always an important part of the oil market, and prices dropped back below $30/b following the Saudi declaration. In mid-month, OPEC officials said that the extra Saudi oil was indeed being produced and was reaching markets. The kingdom had for many years tried to avoid the role of swing producer, and its move angered Iran.[39]

But again, the effect was not lasting. By mid-August, prices had climbed back up, with Brent futures trading at over $32/b. The SCPM announced at the end of the month that it would work with OPEC to increase output.[40] In early September, even Iran began to be concerned by high prices, and on 10 September, OPEC agreed to increase production by 800,000 b/d. The Saudis pledged an additional 500,000 b/d if prices did not respond to the OPEC production hike.[41]

Bellicose rumblings from Saddam Husayn of Iraq in mid-September sent oil prices over $35/b. Amidst continuing concern, 'Abdallah flew to Caracas in late September for the OPEC summit. At the meeting, he said that Saudi Arabia would play its role in maintaining the stability of the market, and would release more oil should it be necessary. At the same time, he criticized consumer countries for "unjust" taxes on petroleum products. The summit did not announce production cuts, and prices did not drop below $30/b.[42] On 30 October, OPEC brought a price-stabilization mechanism into play, apparently agreed upon secretly. But the mechanism did not work, as many of the countries that were supposed to produce more oil did not have the capacity to do so.

The end of the year only demonstrated the continuing volatility of the market. With a perception that there was enough oil to go around, by December, Brent futures for February 2001 had fallen to around $23/b, lower than the $25/b favored by Riyadh. On the last day of the year, Saudi Arabia called for an oil production cut of up to 2m. b/d to bring prices back up.[43]

In 1998, Saudi Arabia had announced that parts of the Saudi oil sector would be open to foreign investment. With the formation of the SCPM, Sa'ud Al Faysal moved negotiations with the foreign oil companies into high gear. The Saudis jealously guarded the lucrative upstream sector, but were encouraging investment in the gas sector. "The kingdom aims to attract large foreign investments to all stages of its gas sector to respond in the short term to the increasing needs of Saudi industry," said Prince Sa'ud. The projects should be "profitable for foreign companies while also fulfilling the kingdom's objectives of increasing growth, creating jobs for Saudi nationals, and introducing and transferring modern technology," he stressed. At the end of April, Sa'ud completed initial negotiations with twelve foreign firms who had committed to investing $100bn. in the Saudi petroleum sector. The companies submitted more specific proposals in August, and in December, they submitted letters of intent.[44]

In another oil-related development, Japan failed to extend its forty-year concession in the neutral zone Saudi Arabia shared with Kuwait. As a condition for the concession, the kingdom had demanded that Japan finance a $2bn. railway and the development of gas reserves in the zone, as well as increase the import of crude from Saudi Arabia. Japan offered to back Saudi Arabia for World Trade Organization (WTO) membership, but balked at the expense entailed by the Saudi demands. Visits to Riyadh by Japanese representatives were of no avail, and al-Riyad charged that the Japanese were "stingy traders." A visit to Japan by Nu'aymi proved fruitless. Nu'aymi said that the Japanese lost the concession because they refused to increase production for export to Japan, and would not invest in Saudi Arabia. The concession was taken over by Saudi Aramco.[45]

TALKING ABOUT ECONOMIC REFORM

The rise in oil revenues seemed to dampen somewhat the Saudi enthusiasm for reform, although the kingdom remained acutely aware of the need for reform to diversify its economy and provide jobs for its burgeoning population. Population growth had long outpaced oil revenues, leading to a constant drop in per capita GDP. Saudi American Bank warned in September that "oil revenues, even at current high levels, are no longer adequate to sustain growth and job creation." It added that the economy was creating only one new job for every three Saudis who entered the workforce. While Saudi Arabia accepted the need to reduce state involvement and increase private sector participation in the economy, fear of losing control of resources vital to the patronage system of the royal family caused it to move extremely slowly. Despite much talk about privatization, no state assets were sold during the year.[46]

In February, the 'Abdallah-led Supreme Economic Council finalized two bills aimed at easing foreign and domestic private investment. While no details were forthcoming, it was understood by the financial community that the new rules would grant the same basic right to foreign investors as to Saudi nationals. In September, Transportation Minister Nasr al-Sallum revealed that a highway tax was under consideration.[47] These were hopeful signs of reform, but they seemed too little in the face of such a serious situation.

Large-scale spending by princes flew in the face of government claims for the need for economic reform. Fahd's son, 'Abd al-'Aziz, was in the process of building himself a new palace modeled after the Spanish Alhambra. Other senior princes continued to tour the countryside and dole out cars, cash, and scholarships to various and sundry supplicants.[48] 'Abdallah seemed devoted to reform, but in his capacity as crown prince, there was only so much he could do to achieve it.

FOREIGN AFFAIRS

RELATIONS WITH IRAN

Relations between Riyadh and Tehran continued to improve in 2000. Much of the past rancor seemed to have been forgotten, as both countries sought to build on the thaw which first began in 1996. In 'Abdallah's calculations, as long as Iran refrained from meddling with the kingdom's Shi'i population, it served as an appropriate counterbalance to an unstable Iraq.

In January, a large Saudi delegation went to Tehran and agreed to expand trade via joint business ventures to be facilitated by direct shipping and air links.[49] Saudi envoy 'Abd al-'Aziz al-Khuwaytir visited Tehran in mid-February to invite Supreme Leader Ayatollah 'Ali Khamene'i of Iran to visit the kingdom for the pilgrimage. Khamene'i used the opportunity of the visit to thank Saudi Arabia for raising the quota of Iranian pilgrims allowed to make the hajj.[50] Although the pilgrimage had been a site of confrontation in the past, leaders went out of their way to issue conciliatory statements as the occasion approached. For instance, the Iranian official in charge of the Iranian pilgrims, Hojjat ul-Islam Mohammad Reyshari, stated that the Iranians would refrain from any act that might hurt mutual relations. The Saudi authorities permitted the Iranians to hold their "disavowal of the infidel" ceremony in their camp; in previous years, the ceremony had been cause for confrontation (see, for example, *MECS* 1987, pp. 172–74).[51] In March, it was announced that the kingdom had also lifted restrictions on Iranians wishing to come to Saudi Arabia to perform the minor pilgrimage (*'umra*).[52]

Iran was keen to see the removal of US troops from the Persian Gulf. To this end, it sought security pacts with the Gulf Arab countries, and particularly Saudi Arabia. The Iranian minister of defense, Rear Admiral 'Ali Shamkhani, declared in April that Iran-Saudi defense cooperation was on the right track, although there would be no rush.[53] Tehran desired a full-fledged defensive alliance; Riyadh, on the other hand, was more cautious, wanting to limit security cooperation to fighting terrorism and crime. It still believed that Iran was behind the 1996 bombing in Dhahran (see *MECS* 1996, pp. 582–85), but was willing to test the waters of Iranian cooperation.

Later in April, the Saudi cabinet authorized Interior Minister Nayif to hold talks with Iran on a security operation accord that was pointedly limited to combating drug trafficking, terrorism, and organized crime.[54] The fact that the interior minister rather than Defense Minister Sultan was put in charge of these contacts was a strong signal that the Saudis wished to limit the scope of the cooperation.

A further demonstration of the burgeoning relations between the two countries was the landmark visit of Shamkhani to Saudi Arabia in late April; he was reciprocating a similar visit by Sultan in 1999. Shamkhani, who met with top Saudi officials, again expressed the Iranian wish for a "comprehensive security system" in the Gulf. Sultan noted that the visit was "proof of the will of the two countries to get closer and eliminate anything that could impair relations," but emphasized that "any direct cooperation with Iran to guarantee the protection of the Gulf is quite inadmissible."[55] Shamkhani returned aboard the first regularly scheduled Saudi Airlines flight to Tehran in twenty-one years, another sign of growing cooperation.[56]

Numerous news reports suggested that as soon as the Iranians were ready, Nayif would travel to Tehran to sign an accord. Nayif himself said as much in a July interview. He also stressed once again that the accord was only "an agreement of joint security cooperation between the interior ministries of two countries and [had] nothing to do with the rumors about a regional security pact." Regional security, Nayif emphasized, "is a military affair which does not come under the jurisdiction of the interior ministries."[57] In his deprecation of "rumors" about a regional security pact, Nayif was referring to the hopeful commentary in Iranian papers such as *The Tehran Times*, which wrote expectantly about "paving the way for an ultimate military pact" with the Arab countries of the Persian Gulf.[58]

In July, an Iranian diplomat stated that the details of the security pact had been finalized and that it would be signed "within the next few weeks."[59] Saudi foreign minister Sa'ud Al Faysal visited Iran in October, in a further expression of improving ties, and in what was termed by the Iranians as "the third round of the Iran-Saudi political committee."[60] Tehran sent an Interior Ministry delegation to the kingdom in November to discuss the accord,[61] but by year's end, Nayif had not visited Tehran and no security pact had been signed.

The rapprochement with Iran continued to worry Riyadh's GCC ally, the UAE, which had an ongoing dispute with Tehran over the control of three strategic Gulf islands. The islands were an irritant in the Saudi-Iranian relationship and may have been partly responsible for the delay in signing the security accord. In April, in a move apparently meant to coincide with the Shamkhani visit to Saudi Arabia, the UAE expressed its pique by reopening its embassy in Baghdad. Crown Prince Shaykh Khalifa bin Zayd Al Nuhayyan of Abu Dhabi, stated that "the question of our islands is an obstacle to any security arrangement in the region."[62] At a consultative GCC summit in Muscat in late April, the member countries called upon Tehran to allow a mediating committee to resolve the dispute.[63] And at the annual December GCC summit in Manama, 'Abdallah called upon Iran to respond favorably and finally agree to receive a GCC committee formed to mediate the dispute. The summit's final communiqué declared "support for [Abu Dhabi's] right to the three islands and its refusal to go along with their occupation by Iran," and noted with disapproval the Iranian "refusal" to meet with the GCC mediating committee.[64]

A decision by the members at the summit to sign a joint defense pact seemed designed to assuage some UAE worries concerning Iran. The pact committed the member states "to defend any member state victim of an external threat or danger." The pact was to go into force after it was ratified by all the states. The GCC members also discussed enlarging their common Saudi based "Peninsula Shield" rapid deployment force from 5,000 to 22,000 (see chapter on inter-Arab relations).[65]

RELATIONS WITH IRAQ

Saudi Arabia continued to fear the Iraqi potential for acquiring weapons of mass destruction without the supervision of UN monitors. Relations were quite tense during the year and frequently degenerated into mutual name-calling.

In January, Iraq announced that the remains of a Saudi pilot shot down over Iraq in 1991 had been approximately located, apparently in a minefield, and Iraq offered, via the Red Cross, to work with Saudi Arabia to retrieve the remains. In March, it appeared that a way had been found to work together; in May, Iraq reported that the Saudis had backed out. Matters appeared to have been settled in June, and the Red Cross announced that the search would begin in October. Even as the two sides were meeting in mid-October, the Saudis announced that the pilot, Muhammad Nadara, was alive and in an

Iraqi prison. While a body was recovered in the joint search efforts, Saudi officials expressed skepticism that the body was indeed Nadara's.[66]

Saudi skepticism was indicative of its attitude toward Baghdad. For its part, Baghdad was determined to chip away at the decade-old sanctions regime without making any exceptions. In April, the foreign ministers of the GCC deplored Baghdad's refusal to implement UN Resolution 1284, which offered a renewable suspension of sanctions in exchange for full cooperation with a new UN arms control body. The visit of Iranian defense minister Shamkhani to Riyadh that same month led Iraq to fear a new US-Saudi-Iran alliance. Iraq also expressed displeasure at what it saw was Riyadh's efforts to scupper a Qatari initiative to ease the suffering of Iraqis. And in July, Iraq contested a Saudi-Kuwaiti accord mapping out their maritime border (see below); Baghdad said that it did not take into account its "legitimate interests."[67]

It was this constellation of events that apparently led Saddam in August to lash out furiously at Saudi Arabia and Kuwait, calling their leaders "traitors" for lending financial and logistical support to American and British attacks on Iraq. "The people of Saudi Arabia have the right to question their leaders to know how these crimes committed by the leaders against the Iraqi Muslim people serve their interests," said an Iraqi cabinet communiqué. These statements were followed by demonstrations in Baghdad, where King Fahd was burnt in effigy, and slogans were chanted calling the Al Sa'ud "sidekicks of the Jews."[68]

While Defense Minister Sultan tried to quiet matters by stating, "we tell the brotherly Iraqi people that Saudi Arabia has never fired a bullet against an Arab, no matter what the circumstances," the Saudi press blasted Saddam as a "Nazi" and a "rabid camel." Baghdad retorted that the US was acting on behalf of Saudi Arabia and Kuwait in its attacks on Iraq, called Saudi foreign minister Sa'ud Al Faysal a "rotting carcass."[69]

In September, President Saddam Husayn of Iraq branded Saudi leaders as unbelievers for allowing US forces to use bases in the kingdom. "Those who accept that foreigner's boots tread on the land that is home to the holy sites of Islam do not believe in God," he said.[70] The Iraqi oil minister, Amir Rashid, accused Kuwait of stealing Iraqi oil. A similar accusation had preceded the August 1990 Iraqi invasion of Kuwait. On 25 September, Saddam issued a statement in which he accused Saudi Arabia (and Kuwait) of being behind the US air attacks, and he issued a threat: "The ruler of Saudi Arabia and the rulers of Kuwait are the ones murdering Iraqis....They should stop and come to their senses...They had better come to their senses."[71] As usual, Saudi leaders counseled caution, and Fahd said in an interview that relations between Iraq and Saudi Arabia were "based on a common destiny and good neighborliness." But a spokesperson for the Iraqi Ministry of Information and Culture responded by calling for the king to be added to a "list of charlatans and hypocrites."[72]

Saudi Arabia, along with Kuwait, remained the most stalwart among the GCC and Arab countries in their support of UN sanctions against Iraq. Other countries, however, sent humanitarian aid, sometimes without waiting for UN approval. On 29 September, Saudi Arabia halted a Yemeni flight carrying aid to Iraq, even though it had UN clearance; on board were two Yemeni ministers. It was eventually allowed to proceed on condition that it arrive in Iraq via Jordan, not Saudi Arabia.[73]

The Saudis were not eager to have an Arab summit, because Iraq would be present. Even after the outbreak of Palestinian violence, they and the Egyptians favored a summit delayed until January 2001. But the concern for the effects of Palestinian violence on their populations forced the hands of Egypt and Saudi Arabia, and they agreed to a summit, held in October, with the Iraqis present (see chapter on inter-Arab relations).

In November, Saudi Arabia opened its border with Iraq to allow the export of food under the UN-sponsored "oil for food" exception to UN sanctions.[74] Despite ending the year on an upbeat, mistrust and suspicion remained the hallmarks of Saudi-Iraqi relations.

BORDER AGREEMENT WITH KUWAIT

In early June, Saudi Arabia and Kuwait began talks to demarcate their maritime border, an area rich in oil and natural gas. The talks gained greater urgency when Iran began to drill in the Dorra field, which was claimed by both Saudi Arabia and Kuwait. Iran suspended its drilling to avoid tensions after Kuwait protested. On 2 July, the leaders of the two countries issued a joint statement stating that the border had been set. Saudi Arabia ceded to Kuwait the islands of Quruh and Maradim, along with an area of a mile around each of them. Oil and gas revenues from the area were to be shared.[75]

RELATIONS WITH THE US

Two primary issues dominated Saudi-US relations in 2000: high oil prices (see chapter on economic developments in the Middle East), and the deterioration in Israeli-Palestinians relations, which began in late September. Both were responsible for a good deal of tension between Riyadh and Washington. Ahead of the March OPEC session, President Bill Clinton of the US remarked that the tripling of crude prices threatened economic growth in the US and worldwide, and he dispatched Energy Secretary Bill Richardson to Riyadh to plead with the Saudis to work for lower prices. Although Richardson expressed satisfaction with the outcome of the talks, the US attitude was only one of many factors that the Saudis took into account, for they had to balance the needs of consumers with their own desire for higher revenues. Richardson and Oil Minister 'Ali al-Nu'aymi issued a joint statement on 28 February. They both supported price "stability," although that term was open to interpretation. All the same, the statement demonstrated a certain commonality of interest between the world's largest oil exporter and the world's largest oil importer: both countries believed that high prices were generally bad for world economic growth.[76]

In any case, US pressure was increased as the OPEC session approached. The Saudi press criticized the US, saying that it was hypocritical for the US, a free market champion, to try to determine the nature of the oil market. "It is…acting in a way that would put Marxists to shame," wrote the *Saudi Gazette*. The press was particularly incensed by the House of Representative's approval of the Oil Price Reduction Act of 2000. The bill urged Clinton to cut military and economic aid to oil exporters found to be fixing prices to the detriment of the US economy.[77] Nu'aymi denied that the US was pressuring Riyadh, although he admitted that Saudi Arabia had to take the interests of consuming countries into account.[78] 'Abdallah traveled to the US in early September to attend the UN millennium summit. He discussed the oil situation with President Clinton, and asked consuming countries to consider lowering their taxes on fuel.[79]

Under 'Abdallah, the Saudis took a more active role in lobbying the US to pressure Israel to make concessions to its Arab interlocutors. They put considerable effort into restarting peace talks between Israel and Syria, and held intensive talks in this regard with the US in January and February. It was widely reported that 'Abdallah played a role in organizing the Clinton-Asad summit in Geneva in late March.[80] With the failure of Israeli-Palestinian negotiations and the descent into violence beginning in late September, anti-US Saudi rhetoric became increasingly strident. At the 21–22 October Arab summit (see chapter on inter-Arab relations), 'Abdallah publicly upbraided the US for abandoning its self-assumed role as "honest broker" and accused it of being responsible for the outbreak of hostilities since it refused to make Israel recognize Arab rights. In a rare display of pique at the US, he lashed out at American policy, and his umbrage was great. "The United States, sponsors of the peace process, assumes particular responsibility for the collapse of the peace process." Referring first to the US and then to Israel he said: "The sponsor is supposed to hold to account those responsible for such a collapse." Sultan criticized a 25 October resolution in Congress expressing support for Israel and warned US companies, which, he said, were "represented in Congress," of unspecified action if the US continued to act on behalf of Israel.[81]

US Secretary of Defense William Cohen visited Saudi Arabia and the Gulf in April and November to promote the "Cooperative Defense Initiative," an expensive early warning and anti-missile defense program. Cohen's selling point was the danger posed by Iran and Iraq; yet Riyadh was heavily engaged in a rapprochement with Tehran, and Iraq did not seem an immediate threat either. In fact, Saudi Arabia was interested in keeping the US presence "over the horizon," and was not interested in the type of cooperation Cohen had in mind. At a joint press conference on 19 November with Cohen, Defense Minister Sultan noted that there had been discussion of new defense technologies, while downplaying any differences with the US.[82]

In further developments with the US, the Saudis signed several arms contracts. Press reports pegged the value of the deals at over $2bn. Involved were the purchases of maintenance contracts for F-15 aircraft, and an arms package aimed at the modernization of the Saudi Arabian National Guard (SANG), commanded by 'Abdallah. The SANG, which was trained by the US, contracted to buy TW 2A anti-tank missiles, advanced tactical communications systems, and over a hundred light armored vehicles.[83]

SAUDI ARABIA AND THE ARAB-ISRAELI CONFLICT

'Abdallah's frequent travels overseas were part of a strategy to establish himself as the main Saudi voice in the world, in contrast to the nearly incapacitated Fahd. They also signaled a reinvigoration of Saudi foreign policy, whereby the kingdom sought to take initiative, rather than simply follow an existing Arab consensus. For example, as the crown prince headed for South America, Ahmad al-Rab'i of al-Sharq al-Awsat stated that the trip was:

> part of a political move that encompasses the whole planet from top to bottom....Sitting and waiting does not build relations, nor does it solve problems. Initiatives and moves in a politically apprehensive world and changing oil markets is the right way to lay foundations for relations based on mutual trust and understanding.[84]

It was within this framework of increased initiative that the kingdom took a front line position in favor of the Palestinians, seeking to use its relationship with the US to leverage a more favorable position. Bringing the Haram al-Sharif (Temple Mount) in Jerusalem under Palestinian rule was of particular concern.

At the beginning of the year, however, negotiations between Israel and Syria topped the agenda. Syrian foreign minister Faruq al-Shar' visited Riyadh in late February, which was followed by a visit by 'Abdallah to Cairo to coordinate policy with Egypt, all within the framework of a US effort to achieve a successful conclusion of the stalled talks. 'Abdallah followed up his Cairo visit with one to Damascus and Beirut. According to *al-Quds al-'Arabi*, 'Abdallah's Damascus visit was preceded by a secret visit by Riyadh's ambassador to the US, Bandar bin Sultan, who was said to have conveyed American guarantees and Saudi financial "sweeteners" to the Syrians in return for greater Syrian flexibility. The possible convening of an Arab summit was also on the agenda, and Saudi Arabia was also interested in preventing a flare-up of violence following a threatened unilateral withdrawal of Israeli troops from Lebanon.[85]

Prior to the convening of the Camp David summit between Israel and the Palestinian Authority (PA) in July, 'Abdallah again traveled to Egypt to coordinate policy. He also called PA chairman 'Arafat to express his support for the Palestinian position.[86] But the failure of Camp David brought some intense criticism of 'Arafat from the editor of the Al Sa'ud-owned *al-Sharq al-Awsat*, 'Abd al-Rahman al-Rashid, for his refusal to strike a deal. 'Arafat was taken to task for agreeing to participate, if he was not prepared to make difficult decisions: "He wants to be the guest of the American president and have dinner every evening with the prime minister of Israel, but he did not want to offer anything."[87] It seems that Rashid may have been influenced momentarily by sentiments expressed by US officials who were present at Camp David, since the Saudi discourse in general remained resolutely pro-Palestinian, particularly on the issue of East Jerusalem. The *Arab News* wrote: "Palestinians should never acquiesce to Israeli desire to incorporate Jewish settlements in East Jerusalem into Israeli West Jerusalem, including the Jewish Quarter in the Old City."[88]

The outbreak of violence in late September brought a flurry of pro-Palestinian statements, particularly since it involved the al-Aqsa complex. An official Saudi spokesperson described the visit to the Temple Mount by Israeli opposition leader Ariel Sharon as "an affront to the feelings of the Palestinian people and the Islamic nation, and a violation of the sacred nature of the Islamic places" in Jerusalem. The kingdom opened its doors to Palestinian wounded, and Sultan bin Salman bin 'Abd al-'Aziz, head of the tourist authority, offered to pay for the school and university expenses of the siblings of Muhammad al-Dura (see above). During a visit to Palestinian wounded in Riyadh, 'Abdallah stated: "It is time the Israeli side and all those involved in the peace process realized what al-Aqsa means for us, Arabs and Muslims, in terms of history, affiliation, and faith; there can be no bargaining on this."[89]

Following the Sharm al-Shaykh summit between Israeli prime minister Barak and 'Arafat in mid-October, US secretary of state Madeleine Albright flew to Riyadh to brief Saudi officials. At the end of the series of meetings, a US official stated that 'Abdallah had expressed his support for the cease-fire agreement which had been concluded, although much of the Saudi press condemned the agreement as irrelevant: "The continued destruction of Palestinian homes...shows that what is happening on the ground is one thing and what happens in air-conditioned rooms is another," wrote *al-Bilad*.[90]

At the Arab summit held in Cairo on 21–22 October, 'Abdallah called upon Arab countries who had begun to normalize relations with Israel to reconsider (the reference did not include Egypt and Jordan), and proposed the creation of two funds totaling $1bn. to support the Palestinians. The Saudis remained firmly in the Egyptian camp that counseled moderation, but its creation of the two funds was another example of their initiative.[91]

THE ISLAMIC SUMMIT: A DUST-UP WITH QATAR

Riyadh's disdain for the Qatari experiments in liberalization and independent foreign policy (see chapter on Qatar) and the awakening to the Palestinian cause following the outbreak of violence, caused it to threaten a boycott of the November summit meeting of the Islamic Conference Organization (ICO), which was to be chaired by Qatar. 'Abdallah had called at the October Arab summit for Arab states like Qatar, which had begun to normalize relations with the Jewish state, to cut ties to Israel, and now Qatar was to be put to the test.

On 8 November, the SPA published an official statement: "In light of the worsening situation in the occupied territories and Jerusalem,...Saudi Arabia is sorry to announce that it will not participate in the upcoming conference until better conditions are created." While Qatari ties with Israel were not mentioned, Riyadh added that it hoped "that there will be better conditions so that Saudi Arabia can take part." The Saudi move threatened to torpedo the summit, as other countries were tempted to follow the Saudi lead. Following the announcement, a Saudi team that was in Doha to prepare for the summit returned home.[92]

Qatari foreign minister Hamad bin Jasim Al Thani flew immediately to Riyadh in an attempt to rescue the summit. A long meeting with 'Abdallah did not result in a change in the Saudi stance, and on 9 November, Qatar announced that it was closing the Israeli trade office in Doha. 'Abdallah then changed his mind and attended the summit.[93]

'Abdallah's ICO summit speech was as strident as his speech at the Arab summit. He demanded "deeds, not words" from the Muslim leaders worldwide, and again stressed that, as Israel's ally, the US shouldered a special responsibility for the collapse of the Middle East peace process. Muslim countries should cut diplomatic relations with any country that moved its embassy to Jerusalem, he stressed.[94]

'Abdallah's tough speeches were a significant change in the Saudi tone. His attacks on the US, and successful forcing of a Qatari announcement that the Israeli office had been closed demonstrated Saudi resolve, and were sure to increase the price of Saudi stock both at home and in the Islamic world. Following the speech in Doha, al-Sharq al-Awsat's Rashid wrote admiringly of the principled stand of the Crown Prince. While many Arab leaders complained about the "Zionist influence" on US administrations, only the crown prince, he reported proudly, based on personal observation, had taken the issue up directly with President Clinton during his visit to Washington. In the presence of four pro-Israel Jews, including National Security Adviser Sandy Berger, he had asked Clinton how he allowed these Jews to influence him. After the meeting, when one of 'Abdallah's advisers said that he had embarrassed the president, 'Abdallah retorted that if those Jews were not ashamed to attend, why should he be ashamed of expressing his opinion?[95]

RELATIONS WITH YEMEN: BORDER AGREEMENT FINALLY SIGNED

The year opened with continuing suspicion between Riyadh and San'a. The kingdom was still suspicious of experiments in democracy by poor and populous Yemen and its wishes for a greater share in the Saudi labor market. It also harbored resentment over San'a's support for Iraq in the 1990–91 Gulf War. The continued sheltering of Yemeni oppositionists by Saudi Arabia angered Yemen, and the undemarcated border between the two countries was still a sore point. Nevertheless, 'Abdallah, consistent with his policy of ending regional conflicts with Arab and Muslim neighbors, was determined to put matters on an even keel. In June, the two countries signed a border agreement.

A signal that matters might be headed for a change occurred in February, when a Yemeni court imposed a "life ban" on a journalist for damaging ties with Saudi Arabia. The journalist had written an article analyzing a power struggle in the kingdom and its influence on the border negotiations. Concurrently, Riyadh made fresh proposals on two of the hotly disputed border areas, and Yemen reacted favorably. The next month, Yemen invited Fahd and 'Abdallah to the upcoming May celebrations marking the tenth anniversary of Yemeni unification, a development which had never pleased Saudi Arabia and had led it to support the southern secessionists in 1994 (see *MECS* 1994, pp. 561–63). In April, Nayif said that the two countries were close to an agreement.[96] In May, in a major gesture, 'Abdallah attended the unification celebrations at the head of a three hundred-strong Saudi delegation.[97]

On 12 June, a border agreement was signed in Jidda by the foreign ministers of both countries and in the presence of 'Abdallah and Yemeni president 'Ali 'Abdallah Salih. The press in both countries labeled it "historic." According to Salih, it was agreed that the two countries would withdraw their forces about 20 km. from the border to avoid friction, while a commercial company was engaged in demarcating the border.[98] *Al-Quds al-'Arabi* reported that an implicit part of the agreement was that Riyadh would halt its support for Yemeni secessionists, and that the kingdom had even provided San'a with a full list of the Yemenis who had been on its payroll.[99] This development indicated that the border agreement was facilitated more by a change in Riyadh's attitude to Yemen than the actual details of the negotiations.

The text of the agreement was not made public immediately, probably to prevent either side from proclaiming "victory." But Yemeni officials, who also reported that Saudi Arabia had ceded an estimated 40,000 sq. kms., leaked it.[100] Although the agreement was described as "final and permanent," there were still matters to be negotiated. For instance, the border from Jabal al-Thar to the border with Oman had beginning and end points, but no line, although the agreement stated that the two parties would demarcate the border "in an amicable way." The provisional border in this region seemed well to the north of previous Saudi claims, which indicated that a concession had been made by Saudi Arabia. The agreement also included issues that were not directly related to borders by incorporating the 1995 memorandum of understanding signed between the two countries (see *MECS* 1995, pp. 548–50). This included the promotion of commercial ties, and the prohibition of use of one party's territory for "political, military or propaganda purposes against the other party." [101]

The agreement promised to bear fruit for Yemen. In July, during a ceremony in San'a to exchange ratification documents, Saudi foreign minister Sa'ud Al Faysal stated that Riyadh had no objection to Yemen joining the GCC, although it would have to meet the conditions set down by that body. He also welcomed the return of Yemeni laborers to the kingdom; hundreds of thousands had been expelled in retaliation for Yemen's support of Iraq in the Gulf War.[102]

The actual demarcation of the border dragged on throughout the year. In late July, both sides issued a statement saying that they would establish two joint commissions: a military one to discuss redeployment, and one to choose a commercial company to determine the border. Nayif traveled to San'a in August for further discussions, and in

October, the two countries chose the German company Hanzaloft Build to set up markers along the common border. In December, the Saudi-Yemeni Coordinating Council met in Medina, the first such meeting since 1989. Yemen was interested in restoring Saudi aid and lowering its financial debt to Riyadh to about $230m.. A joint statement issued at the end of the meeting determined that a delegation of the Saudi Development Fund would travel to Yemen to settle San'a's debt, and announced that the kingdom would grant a loan of $300m. to finance development in Yemen. As the year drew to a close, however, there was some tension over whose troops would guard a planned oil pipeline running from Saudi Arabia to the Gulf of Aden. Saudi troops were still inside Yemen, pending the demarcation of the border, and Riyadh wanted its troops to guard the pipeline as it passed through Yemeni territory. But Sultan mollified the Yemenis, stressing that "the presence of the Saudi troops cannot prevent investment in Yemen."[103]

APPENDIX I: THE SAUDI FAMILY COUNCIL, 4 June 2000[104]

Crown Prince 'Abdallah bin 'Abd al-'Aziz (chair)
Sultan bin'Abd al-'Aziz, second deputy prime minister and minister of defense (deputy chair)
Muhammad bin 'Abdallah bin Jilawi
Fahd bin Muhammad bin 'Abd al-Aziz
Talal bin 'Abd al-'Aziz
Bandar bin Muhammad bin 'Abd al-Rahman
'Abdallah bin Muhammad bin 'Abd al-Aziz
Badr bin 'Abd al-Aziz, deputy commander of the National Guard
'Abd al-Rahman bin 'Abdallah bin 'Abd al-Rahman
Salman bin 'Abd al-'Aziz, governor of Riyadh
Faysal bin Turki bin 'Abd al-'Aziz bin Turki
Bandar bin Khalid bin 'Abd al-'Aziz
Khalid Al Faysal, governor of 'Asir
Mish'al bin Sa'ud bin 'Abd al-'Aziz, governor of Najran, sitting in for Baha Governor
Muhammad bin Sa'ud bin 'Abd al-'Aziz
Muhammad bin Fahd bin 'Abd al-'Aziz, governor of the Eastern Province
'Abdallah bin Muhammad bin Miqrin bin Mash'ari
'Abdallah bin Fahd bin Faysal bin Farhan
Sa'ud bin 'Abdallah bin Thanayan, undersecretary of the Ministry of Municipal and Rural Affairs, acting chair of the Jubayl and Yanbu' Royal Commission

NOTES

For the place and frequency of publications cited here, and for the full name of the publication, news agency, radio station, or monitoring service where an abbreviation is used, please see "List of Sources." Only in the case of more than one publication bearing the same name is the place of publication noted here.

The author thanks Itamar Inbari for his excellent work in assembling source material for this chapter, and the Gulf2000 project run by Gary Sick of Columbia University for the use of its resources.

1. AFP, 6 June 2000.
2. *FT*, 12 June 2000.
3. "Saudi Family Council Means Transition Is Imminent," *Saudi Strategies*, June 2000, <www.saudistrategies.com>.
4. AFP, 4 June; *al-Wasat*, 12 June 2000.
5. *Al-Quds al-'Arabi*, cited in *MM*, 7 June; Simon Henderson, "Saudi Family Council Suggests Transition is Imminent," *Policy Watch*, No. 469, 9 June 2000.
6. *Saudi Strategies*, August 2000.
7. For this campaign, see <www.amnesty.org/ailib/intcam/saudi/>.
8. *NYT*, AP, 28 March; AFP, 28 March, 1 April; *WP*, 29 March 2000.
9. AFP, 30 March, 22 April, 29 May; *al-Majalla*, 9 April 2000.
10. "Saudi Arabia: Human Rights Developments 2000," Human Rights Watch <www.hrw.org/wr2k1/mideast/saudi.html>.
11. AFP, 4, 17 April, 8, 9 May; *CR*, Saudi Arabia, May 2000, pp. 19–20; *CR*, Saudi Arabia, August 2000, p. 14.
12. AFP, 8 May 2000.
13. AFP, 10 July, 23, 31 August; *al-Sharq al-Awsat*, 26 August; *Arab News*, 6 October 2000; "Saudi Arabia: Human Rights Developments 2000," Human Rights Watch.
14. <www.alwatan.com.sa/info/about_us.htm>; *CR*, Saudi Arabia, August 2000, pp. 14–15.
15. *Al-Quds al-'Arabi*, *al-Sharq al-Awsat*, 6 December 2000 (*MM*).
16. SPA, 13 June; *CR*, Saudi Arabia, August 2000, p. 15. "Saudi Arabia: Human Rights Developments 2000," Human Rights Watch; US Department of State, Saudi Arabia: Country Report on Human Rights Practices for 2000, February 2001.
17. *Arab News*, 15 October 2000.
18. *Al-Jazira*, cited in AFP, 2 February 2000.
19. AFP, 5, 6 October; al-Jazira satellite channel, 6 October (BBC Monitoring); AP, 7 October 2000.
20. *CR*, Saudi Arabia, November 2000, p. 13.
21. AFP, 16, 20 March 2000.
22. 'Ashura commemorates the martyrdom of Imam 'Ali at the hands of the army of the Ummayad Caliph Yazid in 680.
23. "Saudi Arabia: Human Rights Developments 2000," Human Rights Watch; AFP, 24, 25 April 2000.
24. *Al-Quds al-'Arabi*, 25 April 2000 (*MM*).
25. SPA, 26 April 2000 (BBC Monitoring).
26. *Al-Sharq al-Awsat*, *Arab News*, 10 August; AFP, 9, 10 August 2000.
27. AFP, 11 August 2000.
28. AFP, 10 September; *al-Sharq al-Awsat*, 11 September 2000.
29. AP, 17 November; *NYT WP*, 18 November; Reuters, 22, 24 November, 16 December; *Arab News*, 25 November; AFP, 13, 14, 15, 21 December 2000.
30. AFP, 14, 15, 16 October; AFP, 5, 6 November, 7 December; Reuters, 16 October 2000.
31. *Al-Quds al-'Arabi*, *NYT*, *DT*, *The Independent*, *The Guardian*, 1 December; AFP, 1, 2 December; AP, 30 November 2000.

32. *CR*, Saudi Arabia, February 2001, p. 5; EIA, Saudi Arabia, June 2001, <www.eia.doe.giv/emeu/cabs/saudi.html>.
33. AFP, 5 January 2000.
34. Simon Henderson, "Crucial Tests Await New Saudi Oil Council," *PolicyWatch*, No. 435, 24 January 2000; see also Nawaf Obaid, *The Oil Kingdom at 100: Petroleum Policy Making in Saudi Arabia* (Washington, DC: Washington Institute for Near East Policy, 2000), pp. 21–29.
35. AFP, 23 February, 16 October; *CR*, Saudi Arabia, May 2000, p. 25.
36. *FT*, 4 January; AFP, 16 February 2000.
37. AFP, 2, 9 March; *WP*, *NYT*, 28 March 2000.
38. *NYT*, 29, 30 March; AFP, 30 March 2000.
39. *FT*, 5 July; *WP*, 4, 5 July; AFP, 7, 21 June, 3, 15 July 2000.
40. AP, 16, 30 August; *FT*, 16, 18 August; AFP, 30, 31 August 2000.
41. *FT*, 7, 8 September; *NYT*, 10 September; AFP, 8, 11 September 2000.
42. *NYT*, 19 September; AFP, 19, 26, 27 September; *CR*, Saudi Arabia, November 2000, pp. 21–22.
43. AFP, 31 December 2000.
44. AFP, 30 April, 3 May, 12, 17 July 2000.
45. AFP, 8, 10, 16 January, 6, 7, 15, 21, 25, 28 February, 7 March 2000; *CR*, Saudi Arabia, February 2001, pp. 24–25.
46. EIA, Saudi Arabia, June 2001; AFP, 4 September; *WSJ*, 27 June 2000.
47. AFP, 20 February, 17 September 2000; EIA, Saudi Arabia, June 2001.
48. *The Economist*, 20 April; *The Independent*, 8 May 2000.
49. *CR*, Saudi Arabia, May 2000, p. 15.
50. IRNA, 19 February (DR); AFP, 19 February 2000.
51. IRNA, 24 February 2000 (DR).
52. IRNA, 21 March 2000 (DR).
53. IRNA, 9 April 2000 (DR).
54. AFP, 18 April 2000.
55. AFP, 23, 25, 26 April 2000.
56. AFP, 3 May 2000.
57. *Arab News*, 11 July 2000.
58. *TT*, 7 November 2000.
59. Reuters, 4 July 2000.
60. IRNA, 7 October (DR); *Iran News*, 8 October 2000 (DR).
61. IRNA, 21 November 2000.
62. AFP, 23 April 2000.
63. AFP, 29 April 2000.
64. AFP, 30, 31 December 2000.
65. AFP, 31 December 2000; AP, 1 January 2001.
66. AFP, 9 January, 10, 21 February, 13 March, 16 May, 2, 17, 19 October; *al-Sharq al-Awsat*, 3, 24 October 2000.
67. AFP, 8, 9, 23 April; 6 June; 18 July 2000.
68. AFP, 9, 11, 12, 13, 14 August 2000.
69. AFP, 14, 15, 16, 21 August 2000.
70. AFP, 11 September 2000.
71. AFP, 17, 18 September; Iraqi TV, 25 September 2000 (DR).
72. AFP, 3 October 2000.
73. *CR*, Saudi Arabia, November 2000, pp. 14–15.
74. AFP, 7 November 2000.
75. AP, 2 July; *al-Sharq al-Awsat*, 3 July; *CR*, Saudi Arabia, August 2000, p. 17.
76. AFP, 17, 27 February, 7 March; AP, 26 February; *NYT*, 27 February; *WP*, 8 March 2000.
77. AFP, 26 March 2000.
78. AFP, 28 March 2000.

79. AFP, 2, 5, 6 September 2000.
80. AFP, 2 February; Simon Henderson, "Saudi Family Council Suggests Transition is Imminent," *PolicyWatch*, No. 469, 9 June 2000.
81. *Al-Jumhuriyya* (Cairo), 22 October; AFP, 21 October; *WP*, 22 October; *Akhbar al-Khalij*, 7 November 2000 (*MM*).
82. *WP*, 10 April; WF, 20 November 2000.
83. AFP, 8 September, 30 December 2000.
84. *Al-Sharq al-Awsat*, 20 September 2000 (DR).
85. MENA, 29 February (DR); AFP, 28, 29 February; *MM*, 29 February, 1 March; *JP*, 1 March 2000.
86. MENA, 28 June; AFP, 6 July 2000.
87. Quoted in *JP*, 28 July 2000.
88. *Arab News*, 11 September 2000.
89. AFP, 30 September, 4 October; *MM*, 10 October 2000.
90. AFP, 17, 18 October 2000.
91. *Al-Jumhuriyya* (Cairo), 22 October; AFP, 21 October; *WP*, 22 October 2000.
92. AFP, 8 November; "Royal Court Issue Statement on Doha OIC Summit," 8 November 2000, <www.saudiembassy.net/press_release/press_release00.htm>.
93. *Al-Sharq al-Awsat*, 8 November; AFP, 9 November 2000.
94. Reuters, 12 November; *al-Sharq al-Awsat*, 15, 16 November 2000.
95. *Al-Sharq al-Awsat*, 16 November 2000.
96. AFP, 22 February, 26 March 2000.
97. *Al-Quds al-'Arabi*, 13 June 2000 (*MM*).
98. Ibid.; *MM*, 14 June 2000.
99. *Al-Quds al-'Arabi*, 23 June 2000 (*MM*).
100. *Al-Sharq al-Awsat*, 25 June 2000.
101. *Yemen Times*, 3 July 2000.
102. *Al-Quds al-'Arabi*, 5 July 2000 (*MM*).
103. AFP, 14, 15 August, 30 November; 8, 10, 12, 13, 14, 31 December; *al-Sharq al-Awsat*, 12 October; 2000.
104. *MM*, 5 June; *CR*, Saudi Arabia, August 2000, p. 14.

Sudan
(Jumhuriyyat al-Sudan)

YEHUDIT RONEN

Sudan continued to grapple with major unresolved political, social and economic issues in 2000. Most significant was the relentless power struggle between the country's two veteran leaders, President 'Umar Hasan Ahmad al-Bashir and the influential politician and preeminent religious leader Hasan 'Abdallah al-Turabi, and their respective camps. This rivalry dominated the domestic scene, causing further deterioration of the weakened socioeconomic structure.

In line with Sudan's recent political history, anti-government instigation by Turabi supporters fanned widespread discontent, leading to violent protests in major towns. In response, the government exploited the violence to clamp down on Turabi's supporters, especially in view of the presidential elections planned for the end of the year. The elections, held as scheduled, resulted in a victory for Bashir. This not only consolidated his hold on power, but also ensured his victory in this latest round in the ongoing power struggle with Turabi.

Meanwhile, the seventeen-year-old civil war flared up once again, with heavy fighting across the country but especially in the oil-rich east and south. Alarmed, the government intensified efforts at reconciliation with the opposition umbrella body, the National Democratic Alliance (NDA). Surprisingly, Bashir achieved success with Al-Sadiq al-Mahdi's Umma Party (UP), the most influential of the northern opposition parties, to the extent that it returned its base of operations to Sudan after years of self-imposed exile. However, the government failed to improve its relations with other NDA components, especially the northern Democratic Unionist Party (DUP) and the powerful southern-based military group, the Sudan People's Liberation Army (SPLA). With this, Bashir made political gains from the splits in the ranks of the NDA.

Bashir's partial success in the reconciliation effort allowed him to project a moderate and peace-seeking image both at home and abroad. This helped the regime sustain mediation efforts under the auspices of the multinational Inter-Governmental Authority on Development (IGAD; previously, Inter-Governmental Authority on Drought and Development — IGADD) as well as through an Egyptian-Libyan peace initiative. None of these peace endeavors, however, resulted in any tangible progress. The civil war continued unabated, with both the government and the opposition forces unable to claim a definitive victory.

Bashir also devoted considerable effort to improving Sudanese foreign relations both internationally and regionally. The Khartoum government mounted a new diplomatic campaign to end the long-running tension with the US. Although the US welcomed the removal of Turabi from Sudanese power centers and showed signs of a possible reconciliation with Bashir's government, it essentially remained aloof. At the end of the

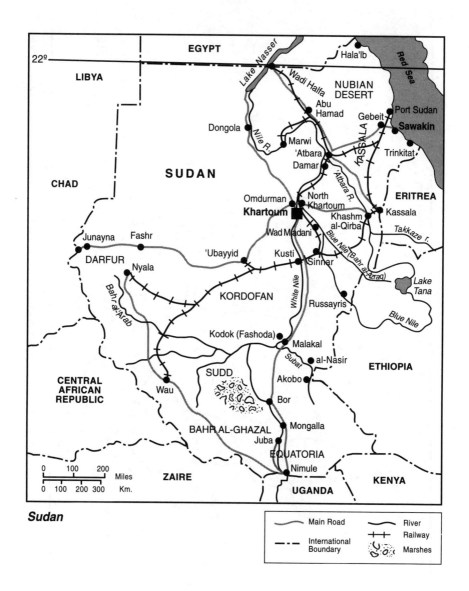

Sudan

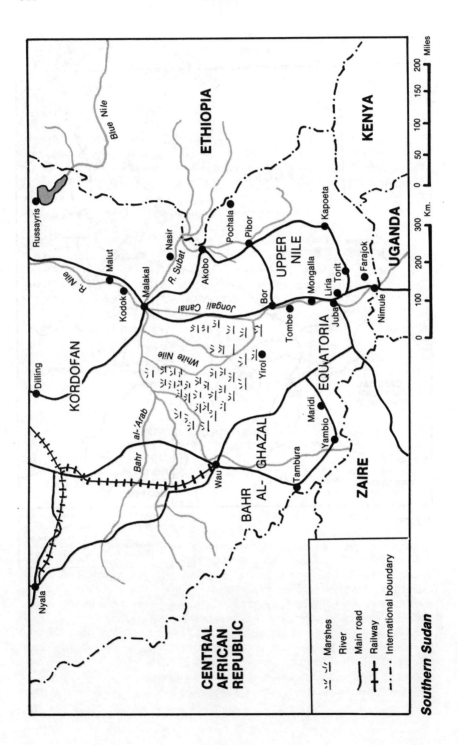

Southern Sudan

year, Washington even toughened its stance, blocking the Sudanese bid for a seat in the UN Security Council. The US held that Sudan continued to sponsor international terrorism and commit human rights abuses. In the same vein, the Americans also flatly rejected Sudan's strenuous diplomatic lobbying to lift the UN-imposed sanctions. Acutely frustrated, the Bashir government pinned its hopes on the installation of the incoming administration in Washington.

The only source of encouragement for Bashir in the realm of foreign relations during the year was the rapprochement with Egypt, boosted by the removal of Turabi from influential governmental positions. Significantly, the initiator of the rapprochement was Egypt, which hoped that Bashir, after sidelining Turabi, would be more responsive to Cairo's interests. Khartoum and Cairo exchanged ambassadors in 2000 after a five-year break. President Husni Mubarak's government continued to treat Bashir with cordiality throughout the year, thereby reinforcing his legitimacy in the face of the ongoing threat posed by Turabi. Relations between Cairo and Khartoum were further enhanced through the joint Egyptian-Libyan mediation apparatus.

Sudan applied itself, with mixed success, to preventing confrontations with its neighbors — Eritrea, Ethiopia and Uganda, which had traditionally provided aid to the NDA opposition. Relations with Eritrea developed favorably at the beginning of the year, culminating in the resumption of diplomatic ties. However, bilateral tension resurfaced in May as a result of suspicions that Asmara was again supporting the NDA in its offensives against the Sudanese army. Relations with Ethiopia, by contrast, reflected a measure of diplomatic and economic cooperation, with the shared border area remaining free of hostilities. A rapprochement with Uganda early in 2000 as a result of mediation led by the US-based Carter Center was short-lived. Both countries traded accusations of supporting each other's opposition movements. Contacts between Kampala and Khartoum in the fall under the auspices of Egypt, Libya and the Carter Center failed to achieve any breakthrough.

INTERNAL AFFAIRS

UNRESOLVED POWER STRUGGLE BETWEEN BASHIR AND TURABI

The power struggle that erupted in late 1999 between the regime's two central leaders, 'Umar Hasan Ahmad al-Bashir and Hasan 'Abdallah al-Turabi, and their respective political camps (see *MECS* 1999, pp. 529–31), gathered momentum throughout 2000.

On 31 December 1999, Bashir began implementing a plan to eject Turabi from the locus of power by "accepting" the resignation of the cabinet and the provincial governors. Justifying this step as necessary to "make way for a climate of freedom," Bashir clearly aimed to purge the government establishment of Turabi's supporters and replace them with his own loyalists.[1] Turabi denounced the move as a "deviation from the constitution."[2] Moreover, mediation undertaken by Qatar early in January to reconcile him with Bashir was depicted by Turabi as a pro-Bashir mission. Qatar conveyed a request that Turabi voluntarily resign from his post as secretary-general of the ruling National Congress party (NC). Turabi promptly rejected the request, which he referred to as an attempted "ouster," and the Qatari mediation effort was soon shelved.[3]

In what was described by observers as a "show of force," Turabi addressed thousands of supporters at the Khartoum headquarters of the NC on the occasion of the 'Id al-Fitr fast on 9 January, declaring war against Bashir: "Those who resist us, we will fight them, and those who join us, we will reconcile with them." He also used the occasion to emphasize his dedication to setting up an Islamic state in Sudan, insinuating that Bashir had betrayed the joint commitment to this cause which they had made when seizing power in 1989.[4] Moreover, Turabi explicitly accused Bashir of ruling the country in a dictatorial fashion.[5]

Late in January, the powerful NC Consultative Council (*Majlis al-Shura*) initiated a series of moves aimed at calming the political maelstrom. It authorized Bashir, as president, to supervise the implementation of NC policies, coordinate between the NC and the other state bodies, and chair the NC nominations and accountability committees. With this, an additional twenty members were elected to the NC Leadership Council, including several Turabi supporters.[6] Moreover, the new cabinet, announced on 24 January, contained several Turabi loyalists. This was aimed at projecting for Bashir a broader base of legitimacy. One of Turabi's most important protégés, former finance minister 'Abdallah Hasan Ahmad, was appointed minister for cabinet affairs, a post viewed as strategic in protecting Bashir's status. Another Turabi supporter, Col. Tayyib Ibrahim Muhammad al-Khayr, the former minister for social planning, filled the role of presidential adviser on security.[7] The new cabinet appeared more security-oriented than its predecessor. The ministers loyal to Bashir, holding the key portfolios of defense, foreign affairs, interior, culture and information, retained their positions, as did the ministers of justice, energy and mining, and federal relations. Concurrently, Bashir named new provincial governors.[8]

In a move to curtail Turabi's influence, Bashir dismissed Turabi's supporters from the National Press Council in early February.[9] A short while later, Bashir closed the Khartoum-based office of the Islamic Arab Popular Congress (IAPC), an influential body in clerical circles headed by Turabi since its inception nearly a decade earlier (see *MECS* 1991, pp. 182–83). Turabi supporters strongly denounced the move, portraying it as the "adoption of a position against Islam...and the implementation of Zionist-US policies."[10] On 22 February, Bashir struck again, annulling the 1998 Association Act (*Qanun al-Tawali al-Siyasi*) (see *MECS* 1998, p. 547). It was replaced by a new Parties and Political Organizations Act, ostensibly allowing for more "flexibility" and "greater political freedom."[11] Fending off Turabi's accusation of betraying the Islamization process, Bashir declared that his government would never retreat from the Islamic Shari'a Law, implying that the political vicissitudes in Khartoum reflected a power struggle rather than any change of policy or conflict of principles.[12]

In mid-March, Bashir extended the state of emergency imposed in December 1999 until the end of 2000.[13] Soon afterward, he announced a decision to hold presidential elections in October 2000 (the elections were originally scheduled for the spring of 2001). Turabi opposed the election decision, which he perceived as a further attempt to curtail his political power, and vowed to fight back. "Our religious values enjoin us not to be the party that initiates aggression," he stated, "but if we are the target of aggression, we can respond in kind."[14]

Minimizing the risk that the NC might not nominate him as its candidate for the presidential elections, Bashir announced on 6 May that Turabi, along with his supporters on the national executive of the NC, had been suspended from the party.[15] Turabi called the move a "political catastrophe."[16] Addressing a large crowd of supporters that had gathered outside his home in Khartoum on 7 May, he said that he awaited "a sign from the Sudanese people before taking the next step." Bashir, he declared, had "used his authority to control the funds and branches of the party all over Sudan by armed force."[17] In a veiled threat, Turabi stated in an interview that "we have grown accustomed to the Sudanese people confronting any military regime in Sudan when the latter seeks to wipe out the political forces, as was the case with [former military rulers] 'Abbud and Numayri."[18]

Police and army forces around Khartoum's key institutions were enlarged. Allegedly, Bashir ordered Turabi's arrest upon his return to the capital from a visit in Port Sudan. Turabi himself predicted that his arrest was imminent.[19] However, Bashir stopped short of taking this step.

Tension culminated in a series of violent clashes in June between the security forces and pro-Turabi students. Early in the month, the police used bullets to disperse students demonstrating at the National Union of Sudanese Youth building in Khartoum. On 20 June, a similar confrontation took place at Sinnar University in central Sudan, resulting in the death of one student and the injury of six police officers. Classes at the university were subsequently "suspended indefinitely."[20]

These events prompted Bashir to convene the 560-member NC Consultative Council on 26 June. It approved a motion by him to dismiss Turabi as secretary-general and expel him, along with a number of his influential supporters, from the party. The council then elected Ibrahim Ahmad 'Umar, former minister of higher education and a close confidant of Bashir, as acting secretary-general.[21] Bashir also appointed another close ally, Naf'i 'Ali Naf'i, a powerful security figure, as cabinet secretary for organizational contacts with the PNC, with the clear task of ensuring that the party fell into line with the wishes of the president.

A day later, Turabi announced the formation of a new political party — the Popular National Congress (PNC; al-Mu'tamar al-Watani al-Sha'bi). This was followed by the resignation of Cabinet Affairs Minister 'Abdallah Hasan Ahmad and Agriculture Minister Hajj Adam Yusuf, who immediately joined the new party in a show of solidarity for Turabi.[22] The PNC promptly launched vituperative attacks against Bashir, accusing him of repressive military rule, using state funds for his own political ends, and leading Sudan toward the separation of religion and state. Threatening a coup, Turabi warned that the "Sudanese people have a way of dealing with military rule that suppresses freedom."[23] This anti-Bashir bellicosity demonstrated Turabi's determination to retain his influential position. Not only had Bashir easily removed him from the foci of power, but he had managed to mobilize only relatively lukewarm popular support in response. Significantly, demonstrative support from the Popular Defense Forces (PDF), the powerful paramilitary body established by Turabi in the early 1990s to combat the southern opposition, was singularly absent. The PDF had hitherto been considered an important pro-Turabi force, counterbalancing the army's pro-Bashir stance.

Still, Bashir appeared to be concerned. He reshuffled his cabinet on 10 July, strengthening his grasp of the executive establishment by staffing it with proven supporters. The two portfolios left vacant by the resignation of the pro-Turabi ministers were filled by 'Abd al-Rahman Sir al-Khatim as cabinet affairs minister, and 'Abd al-Hamid Musa Kasha as minister of agriculture. The position of defense minister, hitherto held by Khatim, was filled by Maj.-Gen. Bakri Hasan Salih. Another important portfolio switch was the appointment of Maj.-Gen. al-Hadi 'Abdallah, formerly chief of security, as minister of the interior, while his predecessor, Maj.-Gen. 'Abd al-Rahim Muhammad Husayn, was appointed advisor to the president and minister of presidency affairs.[24]

Fighting for political survival, Turabi enlisted the help of his staunch student supporters. In mid-August, turbulence erupted at al-Nilayn and al-Quran Universities when the police entered them to suppress unrest.[25]

In a sign of Bashir's confidence that his power was well-entrenched, Turabi's new party, the PNC, was formally approved by the Political Association Registrar on 28 August.[26] Apparently, Bashir favored maintaining a facade of political pluralism, while keeping a close watch on Turabi's activities. However, when in the latter part of September Turabi escalated dissension sharply, Bashir was taken by surprise. This time, the turmoil spread to various parts of the country. Rioting broke out in Nyala in western Sudan, which the police forces promptly suppressed, arresting some forty PNC activists, including former minister of agriculture Hajj Adam Yusuf, who had joined the party a short while earlier.[27] The disturbances then spread to al-Fashr and al-'Ubayyid; to Kusti in central Sudan, about 300 km. south of Khartoum; and to Port Sudan and Qadarif in the east.

Bashir's government acted to crush the riots, while at the same time playing down their effect. The riots were portrayed as a "plot instigated by a small group targeting the country's unity, its social fabric and the security of its citizens by instigating disturbances and causing chaos in various states, exploiting some shortages in services in those states."[28] The socioeconomic aspects of the anti-government protest, however, were significant. As in many violent episodes in Sudan's recent history, political and socioeconomic grievances went hand in hand, manifested by popular unrest. The popular reaction in March 1985 against IMF-inspired measures that resulted in the rise of the price of basic foodstuffs had helped topple the Numayri regime (see *MECS* 1984–85, pp. 621–24). Violent turmoil stemming from socioeconomic distress disrupted the functioning of the administration and the economy during the first half of 1989, causing the downfall of Al-Sadiq al-Mahdi's government. At that time, political subversion led by Turabi converged with popular economic dissatisfaction, engendering the rise to power of both Turabi and Bashir (see *MECS* 1989, pp. 605–609).

Socioeconomic conditions remained a serious burden in the daily life of the population in 2000. The country's external debt was $17bn. and the current account deficit was approximately $700m. Although inflation was contained at below 10%, the value of the dinar against the dollar was maintained, and oil production rose to 185,000 b/d,[29] this was not translated into improved conditions for the population.

Tension between Bashir and Turabi escalated even further at year's end. Discrediting Bashir's presidential election campaign, Turabi called for a "popular revolution in order to restore freedoms."[30] The elections, held on 13–22 December, were widely believed to be a facade for a one-party campaign. The results bore this out: Bashir won by a majority of 86.5% of the vote, while his closest rival, former Sudanese president Ja'far al-Numayri, came in a poor second with 9.6%.[31]

THE CIVIL WAR

Throughout 2000, the NDA opposition reiterated the threat to Bashir's government that the national oil infrastructure would not be secure without a political settlement. This was made clear by the bombing in mid-January of the oil pipeline carrying crude oil for export, at a point approximately 160 km. southeast of Port Sudan. The assault was launched by the Beja Congress, an armed, NDA-affiliated group of the ethnic Beja population living in northeast Sudan. The Beja Congress had long accused Khartoum's government of marginalizing it politically and economically (for background on the NDA's political and military role in the struggle over the control of oil, see *MECS* 1999, pp. 536–37).[32]

In the early spring of 2000, shortly after the withdrawal of the UP from the umbrella NDA (see below), intense fighting erupted between the army and the NDA on Sudan's eastern front, particularly around Kassala, resulting in a series of important military gains for the opposition movement. It captured the towns of Hamash Koreb and Zahana, attacked the Kassala airport, bombed an oil pipeline 30 km. north of Sinkat, and destroyed an Antonov bomber on the ground.[33] The NDA thereby proved that the departure of the UP did not affect its immediate military competence.

Though impressive, the NDA victories failed to signify a turning point in the prolonged, devastating civil war. Nonetheless, the capture of areas in the strategic eastern region and the attack on the oil pipeline constituted a serious threat to Khartoum, politically and economically. Bashir's government, preoccupied with the power struggle within its leadership, needed domestic calm. Bashir, therefore, announced a process of "national reconciliation," declaring a general amnesty on 27 May for the NDA "rebels" fighting in east Sudan along the Eritrean border. Their "tragic living conditions," he stated, were a result of the war between Eritrea and Ethiopia (see below).[34]

The NDA, however, ignored this conciliatory move. Early in the summer, it shifted the focus of its fighting southward, into the central region. The southern-based SPLA launched assaults against government forces in the Gogrial, Aweil and Kuwajina areas of Bahr al-Ghazal. It claimed the destruction of a government convoy and the killing of over four hundred soldiers in the western Upper Nile oil fields during unremitting battles throughout June,[35] necessitating the closure of several oil fields in the region.[36] This fighting, in a region crucial to Sudan's nascent oil industry, endangered the government's sole prospects of ameliorating chronic economic hardships and thereby assuring the political survival of the regime.

Bashir took his reconciliation initiative a step further, announcing an "unconditional amnesty" to opponents of the regime who had committed any act of rebellion since its advent to power in 1989.[37] The opposition, however, flatly rejected the amnesty, strengthening its attacks on the army. In early July, the SPLA claimed the capture of Maban in the southern part of the Blue Nile region near the Khor Adar oil fields.[38] This gain was particularly distressing for the government, as it marked renewed SPLA encroachment into the area of critically important infrastructures: the Russayris Dam, Sudan's only source of hydroelectricity, supplying Khartoum and the entire Nile Valley, and the oil-related projects extending from the oil fields in south and central Sudan to the export terminal at the Bashayir port on the Red Sea. The SPLA had long indicated that one of its main military strategies was the disruption of the flow of oil.

The SPLA offensive continued during July, resulting in the capture of the strategic railway bridge at the Col River near Aweil, thereby endangering the railway link between the garrison town of Wau and the military reinforcements at Aweil to the north.[39]

In a bid to halt the steep military escalation, the army began an aerial bombardment of both military and civilian targets across northern Bahr al-Ghazal and the northeastern Upper Nile.[40] Nevertheless, the SPLA offensive maintained its momentum, capturing the two important railway towns of Maker and Mabior in Bahr al-Ghazal in late July-early August.[41]

In November, a new bout of fighting broke out in the eastern front around Kassala and in the south and central regions in November–December. Army forces reacted with particular vigor to prevent further domestic repercussions, which could have thwarted the election campaign, but fighting continued until the end of the year.[42]

IGAD-Sponsored Mediation: A Cumulative Failure

The US-backed bloc of African states acting as brokers for peace in the Sudanese civil war — the IGAD, consisting of Ethiopia, Eritrea, Kenya, Uganda, Djibouti and Somalia — held a five-day round of talks between Khartoum's government and the SPLA in Nairobi in mid-January 2000. The starting point of the talks was the IGAD Declaration of Principles (DoP) signed by both sides six years earlier, which posited a separation of religion and state, the principle of self-determination for the south, and recognition of the country as multiethnic and multicultural (see *MECS* 1994, pp. 593–95; 1997, p. 634).

With the passage of time, however, it had become apparent that the political and ideological gaps between the two warring sides were as wide as ever and that the DoP had lost much of its relevance. This was reflected in the failure of the January talks. The major bone of contention was the demand by the non-Muslim SPLA for the separation of religion and state. This was a demand that Bashir's government could not afford to meet, at a time when Turabi was accusing Bashir of betraying their joint commitment to the further Islamization of Sudan. Additionally, the disputing sides differed over the delineation of the border between the south and the rest of Sudan, which would be significant in the event of the formation of a southern autonomous region.[43]

The January talks also failed because of Bashir's distrust of the IGAD framework as a whole. He perceived it as biased toward the US, and viewed the African countries who composed it as favoring the non-Muslim SPLA. Another factor that minimized IGAD attractiveness for Bashir was its limited effect on Sudan's conflict politics, as it lacked any effective access to the NDA's northern components. Moreover, Egypt disliked the IGAD initiative, fearing that it might lead to the creation of an independent southern Sudanese state and loss of control over the Nile head waters. Bashir, sorely in need of Cairo's backing in the face of the threat posed by Turabi, could not afford to antagonize Husni Mubarak's government. Additionally, the joint Egyptian-Libyan peace initiative, launched late in 1999 to solve the Sudanese conflict (see *MECS* 1999, pp. 541–42), provided Khartoum with a hospitable alternative to IGAD mediation.

A further round of IGAD-sponsored peace talks, held in Nairobi on 20–26 February, also proved unproductive. Conceivably, Bashir's participation was attributable to his wish to please the US, which Khartoum was courting (see below). Yet another round of talks in Nairobi between the Sudanese government and the SPLA, held in April, broke down once again on the religious issue. According to a southern source, IGAD had become a convenient forum for maintaining the pretense of pursuing a peaceful settlement, with both sides fully aware that nothing of significance would emerge from it.[44]

The cumulative erosion of IGAD appeal as a peace-seeking mechanism was attested by the withdrawal of the SPLA from further talks scheduled for May. The formal justification for this move was the bombing by government forces of civilian targets in southern Sudan.[45] A more convincing reason, however, may have been a new SPLA policy of rapprochement with Cairo initiated late in the spring, along with Egyptian pressure on the SPLA to accept Egyptian-Libyan mediation in place of the IGAD framework. Significantly, the leader of the SPLA, John Garang, called for the amalgamation of the IGAD and the Egyptian-Libyan mediation efforts, as the SPLA "cannot negotiate on two tracks."[46] This position signified a shift, if only tactical, away from the SPLA's insistence on using the IGAD framework alone, and reflected the new position in which the SPLA found itself. The UP had left the NDA and joined the government reconciliation process, (see below) while the other important northern component of the NDA — the DUP, was highly sympathetic to the Egyptian peace proposals and in any case had long resented its exclusion from IGAD. Furthermore, the NDA itself agreed, at a meeting held in Cairo in early July, to hold a dialogue with the Khartoum government, delegating NDA chairperson (and DUP leader) Muhammad 'Uthman al-Mirghani to meet with Bashir.[47]

Thus, although the SPLA was not eager to have its position as the sole negotiating party at the IGAD weakened, it was forced to play the Egyptian card in order not to be marginalized in the politics of the conflict, and risk the disintegration of the NDA. Not only did Garang express his willingness to go along with the Egyptian peace efforts, he vigorously denied promoting the secession of the south, affirming that he stood for a united Sudan based on equality for all Sudanese regardless of religion and race. Only if this option should fail, he asserted, would the SPLA "resort to the self-determination option. Self-determination will be the result of the failure to provide the factors of unification."[48]

The failure of the IGAD forum to achieve productive negotiations led the IGAD Partners Forum (IPF), a consortium of over twenty Western European and North American countries that were supporting the peace-seeking process financially, to rethink the initiative. It delivered a long-overdue ultimatum to IGAD to produce concrete results by September, or face the prospect of the international community discontinuing its backing and seeking more viable alternatives.[49] As if to underline the urgency of the situation, the NDA, at a summit meeting in mid-September at Massawa, Eritrea, formally authorized its reorganized leadership to proceed with reconciliation talks with Khartoum.[50]

However, none of the warring sides, least of all the SPLA, which had a preferred status in IGAD, were prepared to see this forum vanish. Although little was expected from yet another round of IGAD talks, the SPLA and government representatives met again on 21–30 September in Kenya. Two months later Khartoum hosted further IGAD talks. Although no progress was made, the November meeting granted Bashir's isolated government a sense of regional rehabilitation, as the heads of state of Ethiopia, Eritrea, Djibouti and Somalia attended. Notably, however, the Kenyan and Ugandan presidents were absent.[51]

RECONCILIATION BETWEEN THE GOVERNMENT AND THE UP, ALONGSIDE RIVALRY WITHIN THE PARTY LEADERSHIP

The distancing of Turabi from governmental power facilitated Bashir's reconciliation overtures toward the two powerful northern opposition factions, the UP, led by Al-Sadiq al-Mahdi, and the DUP, led by Muhammad 'Uthman al-Mirghani. These two nationalist groups were consistently at odds with Turabi's Islamist camp. Early in January, Bashir returned part of Mirghani's property, which had been confiscated by the government,[52] a gesture that coincided with a round of talks between the government and the UP as part of a dialogue begun in 1999.[53]

The results of these moves were visible at the conclusion of an NDA summit in Asmara in March, when Mahdi announced that the UP was leaving the NDA. Moreover, he hailed the dialogue track with the government as essential, while criticizing the leadership of the SPLA — the most powerful armed component of the NDA — and accusing it of fanning the flames of conflict.[54] Bashir had cause for further satisfaction with the return to Sudan on 6 April of some forty UP members from a long exile in Eritrea. "We have come to bring peace and achieve democracy," stated 'Umar Nur al-Da'im, a senior returnee and secretary-general of the UP. Da'im stipulated that maintaining Sudanese unity was a major goal on the UP agenda,[55] thereby highlighting the gap that had developed between the thinking of his party and that of the SPLA, which advocated secession as an option.

Although the UP withdrawal from the NDA did not immediately lead to the return of its leader, Mahdi, from exile, or the integration of the party into Khartoum's politics, it benefited Bashir's political position substantially. The withdrawal of the UP from the NDA threw the rebel umbrella body into new disarray.

The deep political rivalries endemic to the UP leadership escalated further in the aftermath of Mahdi's announcement of the party's departure from the NDA. Mahdi's move, while supported by his cousin Fadil al-Mahdi, an influential UP figure in his own right, provoked strong denunciation by other senior UP leaders. Nasr al-Din al-Mahdi, another cousin of Al-Sadiq al-Mahdi, and deputy chairperson of the party's five-member secretariat, claimed that the departure of the UP from the NDA undermined the efforts invested by the opposition in trying to topple the Bashir regime. He also questioned the motives behind Mahdi's move, implicitly attributing them to his own personal interest rather than the benefit of the party or the state. Other veteran UP leaders, including 'Abd al-Rahman Nuqdallah and Adam Madibo, demanded that the UP remain under the NDA umbrella.[56]

Conceivably, Mahdi's decision was aimed both at regaining power for the party in governmental politics and at reinforcing his personal status in the party. Since the death two decades previously of Imam al-Hadi, the leadership of the UP had been in contention. On 18 March, the son of the late imam, Wali al-Din al-Hadi, demanded that Al-Sadiq al-Mahdi accept his uncle, Ahmad al-Mahdi, known to be pro-government, as imam.[57] His request was rejected. Instead, Al-Sadiq set up a nepotistic party executive committee portrayed by one commentator as a "breakfast cabinet." Only two of its members were not from Al-Sadiq's immediate family: his faithful lieutenant, 'Umar Nur al-Da'im, who remained party secretary-general, and 'Ali Hasan Taj al-Din, in charge of western affairs. The two represented the main geographic areas of Umma support — the White Nile and the Darfur-Kordofan regions. The other members of the committee were Mubarak al-Mahdi, foreign affairs; Sara al-Fadil (Al-Sadiq's first wife), treasurer; Maryam al-Sadiq (his daughter), women's affairs; and his two sons, 'Abd al-Rahman al-Sadiq, military affairs, and Sadiq al-Sadiq, youth affairs. This move provoked an uproar in the UP. One veteran leader, Bakri 'Adil, charged that the executive body was designed to sideline those who held strong views against the Bashir government.[58]

In late June, over two hundred UP former rebels returned from exile in Ethiopia,[59] further evidence of the progress of the reconciliation process between the government and the UP. The process culminated on 23 November with Mahdi's well publicized return to Khartoum after several years of exile. Addressing UP supporters on arrival at al-Khalifa Mosque in Omdurman, Mahdi once again hailed dialogue with the government, calling on the NDA opposition "to return to the homeland" and declaring his rejection of the war, which "does not serve but foreign interests."[60]

As the year ended, the role of Mahdi and the rest of the UP leadership in government politics was indeterminate, due in part to Bashir's preoccupation with the presidential election campaign. Moreover, Mahdi was forced to devote himself to the consolidation of his own leadership position in his party. Rivalries within the UP and their link to the government were illustrated by a conflict that erupted over the status of the Mahdi home in Omdurman toward the end of the year. Al-Sadiq al-Mahdi's political opponents within his family claimed ownership of the property, whereupon the Bashir government, through its officials in the province of Khartoum, seized the house and placed it under armed guard pending a court decision.[61]

FOREIGN AFFAIRS

RELATIONS WITH THE US

Viewing the Bashir regime as a sponsor of international terrorism, a cause of regional destabilization and a violator of human rights, the US maintained its hostile policy toward Sudan into 2000.

Signs of a possible thaw in bilateral tension did appear at the end of January 2000 when the US administration decided not to allow food supplies to the SPLA opposition in south Sudan.[62] Sudan had made known its unequivocal objection to any American attempt to provide food to the SPLA directly, threatening in late 1999–early 2000 to shoot down any unauthorized aircraft that entered its airspace. The scarcity of food in south Sudan as a result of drought and war had turned foodstuffs into weapons no less valuable than guns.

However, in mid-February, suspicions that Khartoum was using oil revenues to fuel the civil war led the US to impose economic sanctions on Sudan's state-owned oil enterprise, Sudapet, and on a joint venture in Sudan involving Sudapet, the government and three foreign oil companies.[63] Trade and financial sanctions on Sudan had already been imposed three years earlier (see *MECS* 1997, p. 637). Khartoum's officials, anxious not to foil efforts to normalize ties with the US, reacted with restraint. Bashir, in fact, intensified these efforts.[64]

A visit to Khartoum by US special envoy Harry Johnston on 4 March heralded a possible decrease in mutual hostility. The trip was aimed at pressing for an improvement in Sudanese human rights compliance and at monitoring American relief activities in the south. Khartoum initially objected to the mission and referred to it as a plot against Sudanese unity, but later described the talks as a "good start of contacts."[65] Indeed, an improvement in relations between Khartoum and Washington followed. On 20 April, the US reestablished its diplomatic presence in Sudan after a two-year break, although it kept the ambassadorial post in Khartoum vacant, and returned only a skeleton staff to the embassy.[66]

Sudan promptly credited Egypt for this development.[67] Whatever role Cairo may have played, however, it was clear that Washington had its own reasons to defuse the tensions with Bashir's regime. The removal of Turabi from power, and the subsequent projection of Bashir's image as pragmatic and moderate, were viewed positively by the US. Moreover, Bashir's policy of attempted reconciliation with his neighbors (see below) strengthened advocates of diplomatic rapprochement with Sudan within the US administration. Even so, progress in Sudanese-American relations remained "limited and partial," in Foreign Minister Mustafa 'Uthman Isma'il's depiction.[68]

Johnston returned to Khartoum on 12 June for a three-day visit devoted to talks on bilateral ties and on the IGAD peace initiative.[69] Presumably, the encroachment of Egyptian-Libyan mediation efforts on those of the American-backed IGAD, was discussed. The visit was also presumably the occasion for a request by the Sudanese authorities for American help to lift the UN Security Council sanctions imposed on Sudan in 1996. The sanctions were the product of American and Egyptian pressure to force Sudan to extradite Egyptian nationals suspected of carrying out the attempted assassination of Egyptian president Mubarak in Addis Ababa in 1995. The would-be assassins allegedly fled to Sudan thereafter (see *MECS* 1996, pp. 614–15).

Bashir kept up intensive diplomatic efforts in Washington not only to lift the UN sanctions but to obtain a seat in the UN Security Council — one of ten rotating non-permanent seats — as the African representative. The US, however, objected.[70] Tension between the two countries resurfaced in August when the US condemned the bombing of civilians in south Sudan by government forces, while Sudan accused the US of "supporting southern rebels."[71]

Representing Sudan at the UN millennium session in New York in September, Bashir led a delegation that vigorously promoted Sudan's candidacy for acceptance in the Security Council. Sudan, however, failed to be elected in the Council vote on 10 October. Blaming the US for the defeat, Sudan accused it of waging an anti-Sudanese campaign of "intimidation."[72] Sudan's anger at the US deepened in November as a result of a visit by a senior US State Department official, Susan Rice, without Khartoum's clearance, to SPLA-held areas in southern Sudan. Rice, addressing diplomats, legislators and business leaders in Nairobi on 21 March, stated that "the government of Sudan must put an end to the heinous practice of slavery and brutal raids on innocent civilian population."[73] Bashir castigated the visit as an "irresponsible act which violated...international laws and customs."[74]

By then, Bashir's expectations of the Clinton administration had vanished, and Khartoum awaited its successor. On 7 December, Sudan declared Glenn Warren, an American diplomat on the staff of the US embassy in Khartoum persona non grata and expelled him from the country. He was accused by Khartoum of plotting an uprising with NDA opposition figures.[75] Khartoum also charged the US with providing the SPLA with money and weapons, thereby fueling the war in Sudan.[76]

RELATIONS WITH EGYPT

The rapprochement between Sudan and Egypt that began in 1999, following the lengthy deadlock between the two, continued in 2000. Both countries made use of the Egyptian-Libyan mediation initiative to further mutual political interests. A meeting in Khartoum of the foreign ministers of Sudan, Egypt and Libya in January, devoted to peace efforts in the Sudanese conflict, was a case in point. The timing of the meeting — at the height of Bashir's efforts to marginalize Turabi (see above) — was viewed as a gesture of support for Bashir's leadership position against Turabi's. Significantly, the final statement issued by the three foreign ministers focused on the "strategic nature" of their trilateral ties.[77] Egypt and Libya, each for its own motives, rejected Turabi's militant religio-political thrust, perceiving it as undermining their own interests.

Turabi, responding, accused the Egyptian government of conspiring against him.[78] Whether or not Egypt had played a role in helping Bashir weaken Turabi, both Mubarak and Bashir clearly had a shared interest in curtailing Turabi's influence in Sudan's highest political echelon. This paved the way for growing cooperation between Cairo and Khartoum. In February, Egypt and Sudan agreed to reschedule a $70m. Sudanese debt repayment. Shortly thereafter, the new Egyptian ambassador to Sudan, Muhammad 'Asim Ibrahim, arrived in Khartoum.[79] This signified the end of a five-year break in diplomatic relations following the attempted assassination of Mubarak, which Cairo had blamed on Khartoum.

A further indication of growing ties was a tripartite Mubarak-Qadhdhafi-Bashir summit in Cairo on 4 April during the African-Europe summit. The talks, reportedly aimed at providing a further impetus for the Egyptian-Libyan peace initiative in Sudan, constituted a reinforcement of Bashir's leadership.[80]

Concurrently, Egypt initiated intensive mediation aimed at reconciling Bashir and the NDA opposition. Cairo became the venue for a series of meetings during the spring and the summer between Egyptian officials and NDA leaders and between Sudanese officials and the NDA. Egypt's primary motive in reconciling the Sudanese sides was its interest in maintaining Sudanese territorial integrity so as to preclude any potential threat to the supply of Nile water.

At meetings of both countries' higher joint ministerial committee in September, memos of understanding were signed regarding cooperation in the spheres of agriculture, tourism and culture, alongside a trade agreement. Additionally, Egypt committed itself to support Sudan's bid to gain a seat at the UN Security Council (see above).[81] In November, the foreign ministers of Sudan, Egypt and Libya met again in Khartoum to discuss enhancing the peace prospects in Sudan. More specifically, they examined possible coordination between the American-based IGAD peace initiative and the Egyptian-Libyan one,[82] with an eye toward creating a new mediation framework that would encompass all components of the Sudanese opposition and be acceptable as well to the Sudanese government.

RELATIONS WITH NEIGHBORING AFRICAN STATES

Eritrea

Both Sudan and Eritrea carefully fulfilled their commitments to the reconciliation agreement signed in 1999 (see *MECS* 1999, p. 543) following a five-year rupture in mutual relations. The break had occurred in 1995 when Eritrea accused Khartoum's government of supporting anti-government Eritrean Islamic groups. The Eritrean government under President Isaias Afeworki had subsequently joined the US-backed African camp, which included Ethiopia and Uganda and which actively supported the anti-Sudanese NDA opposition.

Sudan and Eritrea restored diplomatic ties on 5 January 2000. Eritrea marked the occasion by handing over the Sudanese embassy building in Asmara — hitherto used demonstratively by the Sudanese NDA opposition as its headquarters — to Khartoum's authority.[83] This gesture was followed by the visit to Khartoum of a high-level Eritrean delegation led by Foreign Minister Haile Woldensae. Bashir, for his part, highlighted the importance attributed by Sudan to the restoration of ties with Eritrea by paying a visit to Asmara on 18 January. Subsequently, the two countries announced the reopening of their joint border.[84] Eritrean president Afeworki soon reciprocated with a visit to Khartoum on 3 February. Shortly thereafter, Sudan Airways resumed flights to Asmara.[85]

In March, however, potential tension surfaced when heavy fighting broke out between Sudanese government forces and the NDA opposition in the east of the country, adjacent to the Eritrean border. Fearing threats by the NDA to involve Eritrea in the conflict, Sudanese foreign minister Isma'il arrived in Asmara to preclude any such development. The visit resulted in a meeting between Sudanese and Eritrean officials to monitor security along the common border.[86]

With the renewal of war between Eritrea and Ethiopia in May, Afeworki found it more difficult to control the border area with Sudan and curb NDA attacks on the Sudanese army launched from Eritrean territory. Furthermore, the rapidly growing influx of Eritrean refugees into Sudan — estimated in early June at seventy thousand[87] — as a result of Eritrea's concurrent war with Ethiopia exacerbated insecurity along the border area. Bilateral tension escalated further in July when Sudan conducted a general mobilization in the Kassala area in eastern Sudan in anticipation of a suspected Eritrean offensive against it. Although Eritrea denied any intention of waging war against Sudan,[88] it accused Sudan of supporting the Ethiopian side, reflecting a basic distrust between the two countries.[89] Sudan, for its part, charged that NDA activity in Eritrea had increased and that Eritrea was allowing the rebels to activate a radio transmitter in Eritrean territory. Sudan preconditioned the normalization of ties on Eritrean expulsion of the NDA from its territory and the closure of the transmitter.[90] Conceivably, the intensive attacks launched by the SPLA against various targets in Sudan's oil infrastructure during the summer reinforced Khartoum's suspicions of an Eritrean-backed NDA raid on the pipeline situated near the Eritrean border.

The government therefore redoubled its efforts to reduce tension with Asmara. On 4–6 October, Bashir and Afeworki and their respective delegations met for talks in Khartoum and agreed on a fresh start in their relations.[91] High-level contacts continued toward the end of the year, with Eritrea reiterating its wish to contribute to Sudanese national reconciliation.[92]

Ethiopia

The resumption of war between Ethiopia and Eritrea in 1999 had opened a window of opportunity to the Sudanese government for political rapprochement with Ethiopia, which was strengthened further in 2000. Sudan and Ethiopia reactivated their joint border commission and agreed on the export of Sudanese oil to Ethiopia.[93] This cooperation was highlighted by an exchange of visits by high-ranking officials between both capitals. Both countries were anxious to keep their border area free of hostility, particularly Ethiopia, which from May onward needed to focus all its energies on renewed fighting with Eritrea.

Uganda

Sudanese relations with Uganda, following a peace agreement signed in November 1999 (see *MECS* 1999, p. 543), oscillated between improvement and crisis during 2000. Honoring the agreement, Uganda released the "last batch" of seventy-two Sudanese POWs taken during the war with Uganda, in January. Sudan responded by releasing fifty-eight Ugandan nationals, mostly children, who had been abducted by the Ugandan rebel Lord's Resistance Army (LRA) headed by Joseph Kony.[94] Uganda had long accused Khartoum of backing the LRA, while Sudan countercharged that Kampala's government supported the Sudanese SPLA opposition.

The rapprochement, however, was short-lived. Uganda complained in March that Sudan had failed to live up to its commitment to the peace agreement: it had not returned all the abducted Ugandan nationals, it had not disarmed "all [LRA] bandits" operating against Uganda from Sudan, and it had failed to extradite the fighters to Kampala. The last, allegedly, remained in south Sudan. Uganda "was not satisfied with the implementation" of the peace agreement, announced President Yoweri Museveni, dampening the rapprochement process.[95] A statement by Ugandan foreign minister Eriya Kategaya that his country would not abandon its moral support of the Sudanese SPLA further fueled tension.[96] Sudan, responding, accused Uganda of violating the peace agreement, which had stipulated an end to support for each other's opposition movements.[97]

Later in March, Uganda reported an air attack over its territory by a Sudanese aircraft, apparently launched against the SPLA rather than Uganda (see above).[98] Both countries' weak control of their remote border areas, and the easy passage of their respective rebel forces across them, blurred the Sudanese-Ugandan boundary and extended each country's war into the other, serving to fuel mutual suspicions.

In July, the US-based Carter Center, which had brokered the peace accord between Sudan and Uganda in 1999, hosted talks aimed at smoothing out difficulties. This mediation was followed by a further series of bilateral talks held in Kampala in September.

Later in the fall, Egypt and Libya initiated efforts to defuse the Ugandan-Sudanese tension. On 6–7 October, representatives from Uganda, Sudan, Egypt, Libya and the Carter Center met in Khartoum to discuss the deployment of border monitors to prevent violations by the respective opposition forces. These efforts were eclipsed, however, by further strain between Sudan and Uganda when Uganda voted against Sudanese membership in the UN Security Council.[99]

NOTES

For the place and frequency of publications cited here, and for the full name of the publication, news agency, radio station or monitoring service where an abbreviation is used, please see "List of Sources." Only in the case of more than one publication bearing the same name is the place of publication noted here.

1. Omdurman TV, 31 December 1999 — BBC Monitoring, 15 January 2000.
2. *Al-Quds al-'Arabi*, 4 January 2000.
3. *Al-Sharq al-Awsat*, 6 January 2000.
4. *MM*, 10 January 2000.
5. *Al-Khartum*, 18 January 2000.
6. *ARB*, 1 January 2000.
7. *Al-Sharq al-Awsat*, 25 January; *MEI*, 28 January 2000.
8. For further details on the composition of the new cabinet and on the newly appointed governors, see Omdurman TV, 24 January — BBC Monitoring, 26 January 2000.
9. *Al-Quds al-'Arabi*, 2 February 2000.
10. *Al-Sharq al-Awsat*, 18 February 2000.
11. SUNA, 23 February — BBC Monitoring, 26 February 2000.
12. SUNA, 28 February — BBC Monitoring, 1 March 2000.
13. Omdurman TV, 12 March — BBC Monitoring, 14 March 2000.
14. *Al-Khartum*, 29 April; R. Monte Carlo, 5 May — BBC Monitoring, 8 May 2000.
15. Omdurman TV, 6 May — BBC Monitoring, 8 May; *MM*, 11 May 2000.
16. *Al-Mustaqbal*, 13 May 2000.

17. *Al-Khartum*, 8 May 2000.
18. Al-Jazira TV, 7 May — BBC Monitoring, 9 May 2000, telephone interview.
19. *Al-Sharq al-Awsat*, 7 May; *al-Khartum*, 10 May 2000.
20. *Al-Ra'y al-'Amm*, 9 June; *Alwan*, 22 June 2000.
21. *Al-Khartum*, 28 June 2000.
22. *Al-Sharq al-Awsat*, 28 June 2000.
23. *MET*, 29 June; *al-Hayat*, 6, 9 July 2000.
24. *Al-Khartum*, 11 July 2000.
25. *Al-Khartum*, 15 August 2000.
26. SUNA, 28 August — BBC Monitoring, 30 August 2000.
27. *AW*, 21 September 2000.
28. Omdurman TV, 15, 20 September — BBC Monitoring, 18, 22 September 2000.
29. *The Economist*, 30 October; *CR*, Sudan, November 2000, p. 3.
30. *Al-Khartum*, 28 November 2000.
31. *AW*, 4 January 2001.
32. *Al-Khartum*, 18 January 2000.
33. *MET*, 6 April; *MEI*, 7 April; Omdurman TV, 1 May — BBC Monitoring, 3 May 2000.
34. *Al-Ray al-'Amm*, 27 May 2000.
35. SUNA, Voice of Sudan, 22 June — BBC Monitoring, 24 June 2000.
36. *MM*, 23 June 2000.
37. SUNA, 21 June — BBC Monitoring, 22 June 2000.
38. AFP, 4 August 2000 (DR).
39. *Al-Khartum*, 15 July 2000.
40. *SDG*, August 2000.
41. *Al-Khartum*, 6 August 2000.
42. *Al-Hayat*, 8 November; *AW*, 16 November; UN Integrated Regional Information Network, Nairobi, 27 November — BBC Monitoring, 29 November; Omdurman TV, 24 December — BBC Monitoring, 29 December 2000.
43. *AW*, 27 January 2000.
44. *SDG*, May 2000.
45. AFP, 3 May — BBC Monitoring, 5 May 2000.
46. *SDG*, June 2000.
47. *MEI*, 18 August 2000.
48. E.g., *al-Ahram*, 13 May, *Akhir Sa'a*, 17 May 2000.
49. *MEI*, 1 September 2000.
50. *SDG*, October 2000.
51. *Al-Hayat*, 24 November 2000.
52. *Al-Sharq al-Awsat*, 3 January 2000.
53. *Al-Ra'y al-'Amm*, 2 February 2000.
54. UP web site, 16, 23 March — BBC Monitoring, 22, 25 March 2000.
55. *MET*, 13 April 2000.
56. *Al-Quds al-'Arabi*, 20 March; *MET*, 7 April 2000.
57. *Al-Quds al-'Arabi*, 24 March 2000.
58. *MEI*, 18 August 2000.
59. *Al-Sahafa*, 28 June. According to a report in *MEI* on 8 December 2000, a total of 700 UP troops had returned home by the end of the year.
60. SUNA, 24 November — BBC Monitoring, 27 November 2000.
61. *SDG*, November 2000.
62. *IHT*, 2 February 2000.
63. *Al-Khartum*, 19 February 2000.
64. R. *Khartum*, 12 February — BBC Monitoring, 14 February; *al-Majalla*, 5 March 2000.
65. State Minister Bishop Gabriel Rorie in an interview to *MET*, 9 March 2000.
66. *Al-Quds al-'Arabi*, 21 April 2000.
67. *Al-Sharq al-Awsat*, 3 March 2000.

68. *Al-Khartum*, 2 May 2000.
69. *Al-Khartum*, 15 June 2000.
70. *Al-Watan al-'Arabi*, 7 July 2000.
71. *Al-Khartum*, 13 August, quoting State Department Spokesperson Richard Boucher; SUNA, 28 August — BBC Monitoring, 30 August 2000.
72. AFP, 12 October 2000 (DR).
73. CNN (Internet version), 21 November 2000.
74. SUNA, 24 November — BBC Monitoring, 27 November 2000.
75. *Al-Hayat*, 8, 9 December 2000.
76. *Al-Musawwar*, 22 December 2000.
77. MENA, 4 January — BBC Monitoring, 7 January 2000.
78. *Al-Quds al-'Arabi*, 5 January 2000.
79. *Al-Ray al-'Amm*, 29 February; SUNA, 12 March — BBC Monitoring, 14 March 2000.
80. For details, see *al-Quds al-'Arabi*, 5 April 2000.
81. MENA, 5 September 2000 (DR).
82. MENA, 22 November — BBC Monitoring, 24 November 2000.
83. *Al-Khartum*, 6 January 2000.
84. SUNA, 20 January — BBC Monitoring, 22 January 2000.
85. Omdurman TV, 7 February — BBC Monitoring, 10 February 2000.
86. *Al-Sharq al-Awsat*, 26 March 2000.
87. *Al-Khartum*, 1 June 2000.
88. *Al-Zaman*, 3 August 2000.
89. *Al-Sharq al-Awsat*, 13 September 2000, quoting Sudanese foreign minister Isma'il.
90. Ibid.
91. Omdurman TV, 4 October — BBC Monitoring, 6 October 2000.
92. *Al-Hayat*, 3 November 2000.
93. *Al-Khartum*, 4 March; SUNA, 5 March — BBC Monitoring, 7 March 2000.
94. *MET*, 13 January; *al-Khartum*, 16 January 2000.
95. *Al-Ahram*, 7 February; *ARB*, 1 February; *AC*, 31 March 2000.
96. *New Vision*, 3 March 2000.
97. *Al-Khartum*, 9 March 2000.
98. *New Vision*, 27 March 2000.
99. *New Vision* (Internet version), 6, 24 October (DR); *AC*, 13 October 2000.

Syria

(Al-Jumhuriyya al-'Arabiyya al-Suriyya)

EYAL ZISSER

Syrian president Hafiz al-Asad's death on 10 June 2000 marked the end of a thirty-year period of rule during which Syria evolved from a weak and unstable state to a regional power. Asad's death came as no surprise, for his deteriorating state of health had been an open secret in the Syrian capital. Apparently, Asad himself had been aware that his demise was imminent, and in the final months of his life he focused on laying the groundwork for his son Bashshar's succession as president. These efforts proved to be successful and facilitated the smooth passage of rule from father to son.

Bashshar's assumption of power had, in effect, begun before his father's death, side by side with broad changes in Syria's highest political echelons. The government was replaced in March, and following the convening of the Ba'th Party congress in June, most members of the party leadership bodies were replaced as well. Broad personnel changes were made in the government information and media apparatuses and the diplomatic corps, and provincial governors were also replaced. Staff changes were also made in the senior military echelon, designed to ensure support for Bashshar in the military-security establishment.

Bashshar's rise to power came at a time when Syria found itself at a crossroads, experiencing growing difficulty in adhering to its past policies, especially in the domestic political, social and economic spheres. Projecting himself as loyal to his father's heritage, Bashshar also conveyed a message that he was the harbinger of change. He advocated openness and transparency in his first speeches after his election in July as president, expressing a desire to allow greater political freedom in the country. These statements encouraged public appeals, especially by intellectuals and the business community, for the introduction of major political and economic changes. Evidence toward the end of the year pointed to the formation of semi-political organizations functioning as periodic cultural or political forums. Bashshar may have hoped that these elements would assist him in promoting change in the domestic, mainly socioeconomic, sphere. However, many Western and Arab analysts believed that his ability to introduce such change was limited. He was viewed as dependent on the security establishment, the Ba'th Party bureaucracy, and a nucleus of veteran leaders who had surrounded his father and assisted him in maintaining his rule. These power bases were generally considered to be opposed to the introduction of any substantial change in Syria, for fear that they might impinge on their own status.[1]

The need for change was obvious, given the difficult economic situation. The Syrian economy remained at a standstill during 2000 in the wake of the sharp recession during the late 1990s, rising unemployment and the collapse of the welfare system. Following the appointment of a new government in March, and the assumption of power by Bashshar

532

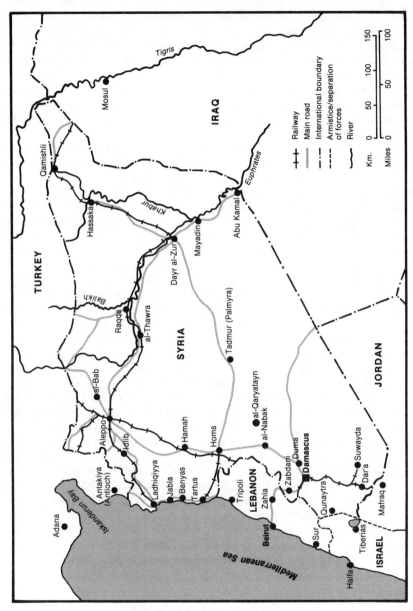

Syria

in June, a discernible effort was made to extricate Syria from its economic crisis and to facilitate its increased integration into the world economy. Plans were drawn up to combat unemployment and encourage investment. A public-sector wage increase was announced, and a series of laws and regulations in the economic sphere were revised. In December, the regional command of the Ba'th Party decided to permit the opening of private banks, a step which was viewed as the beginning of the regime's separation from its socialist legacy.[2] Nevertheless, the government was clearly having difficulty in bringing about significant change, as it feared losing control and harming certain sectors of the population — the party and government bureaucracy, the lower classes and others who formed the regime's base of support.

Syria's regional status declined somewhat with the demise of Hafiz al-Asad. This was especially palpable in Lebanon where, even beforehand, following the withdrawal of Israeli forces from South Lebanon in May (see chapters on Israel and Lebanon), voices were heard, mainly from the Maronite and the Druze communities, calling for the withdrawal of Syrian forces as well, or at least for an easing of Syrian control over Lebanon. Bashshar's ascent to power did not bring about substantial change in the fabric of relations between Syria and Egypt, Saudi Arabia, the Gulf states or Jordan, which continued to be devoid of intimacy and were mainly declarative. Relations between Syria and the Palestinian Authority (PA) continued to be antagonistic.

In the wake of the outbreak of the Palestinian "al-Aqsa intifada" in October (see chapter on the PA), Bashshar attempted at the Arab summit in Cairo and at the Islamic summit in Doha to gain a position of leadership in the radical anti-Israel camp in the Arab world, but with limited success. He was more successful, however, in preserving his alliance with Iran and in promoting a limited thaw with Iraq. Relations with Turkey improved markedly, a reflection of Bashshar's desire to turn over a new leaf with Syria's northern neighbor. However, no improvement was made in relations with the US or Western Europe, mainly because of the lack of progress in the Arab-Israeli peace process.

The early part of the year witnessed efforts to reach a Syrian-Israeli peace agreement, climaxing in a meeting in Geneva between Asad and US president Bill Clinton in March. However, these efforts failed because the differences between the two sides on the question of the borderline between Syria and Israel (the Sea of Galilee shore, as demanded by the Syrians, or a line several dozen meters east of the lake, as demanded by Israel) remained unresolved. Although the transfer of the presidency to Bashshar elicited hopes for the renewal of Syrian-Israeli negotiations, Bashshar preferred to devote himself to bolstering his position in the domestic arena before turning his attention to the peace process. Moreover, Syria toughened its position even further following the outbreak of renewed Palestinian-Israeli violence. Additionally, Lebanon's Hizballah renewed attacks against Israeli targets in the Shab'a Farms region on the border between Lebanon and the Israeli-held Golan Heights, which Israel claimed were encouraged by Syria. These developments evoked fears of the eruption of a new Israeli-Syrian military conflict.

INTERNAL AFFAIRS

ON THE EVE OF HAFIZ AL-ASAD'S DEATH

President Asad's death on the morning of 10 June 2000 was reported to the Syrian public at 18:00 in special radio and television broadcasts.[3] His death did not come as a surprise, as numerous reports had appeared in the Western and Israeli press on the deterioration of his health during the first six months of the year.[4] A leaked CIA report, published in Israel in March, stated unequivocally that Asad was suffering from dementia and that his death was imminent.[5] Apparently, Asad himself was aware that he was nearing the end of his life, as confirmed by his close associate, Defense Minister Mustafa Talas. Clearly, this impelled him to increase his efforts in the first half of the year, to ensure his son's smooth succession.

For several years, Asad and his son had been making systematic changes designed to infuse new blood into the Syrian army. Veteran officers who belonged to Asad's generation were pensioned off and replaced by younger men, most of whom were described as being close to Bashshar. This process continued into the early part of the year, against a background of media reports emanating from Damascus that some veteran army officers still opposed Bashshar's candidacy for the presidency.[7] The most prominent change occurred in February when the chief of the army security department, 'Ali Duba, was pensioned off upon reaching the age of sixty-six. Duba, who had headed the department from 1974, was described as one of the strongmen in the Syrian leadership and as the person responsible for protecting the regime. He was replaced by his deputy, Hasan Khalil, although according to press reports, it was Asaf Shawkat, chief of the security forces branch of the department, who had become the security establishment strongman.[8]

The Establishment of the New Government in March

Another move designed to strengthen Bashshar's position was the dismissal of Prime Minister Mahmud al-Zu'bi, in office since 1987. Zu'bi was replaced by Mustafa Miru, who had served as governor of three provinces successively: Dar'a (1980-86), Hasaka (1986-93) and Aleppo (1993-2000). A graduate in Arab culture from Damascus University, and holder of a doctorate from the Institute for Oriental Studies in Moscow, Miru had joined the Ba'th Party in 1966.[9] The government he formed included 35 ministers, 22 of them new (see Appendix 1). Prominent among the new faces were the minister of information, 'Adnan 'Umran; Naji al-'Atari, deputy prime minister for welfare services affairs; Khalid Ra'd, deputy prime minister for economic affairs; and 'Isam al-Za'im, minister of state for planning. Ministers who retained their portfolios included Muhammad al-'Imadi (economy and foreign trade), Muhammad Khalid al-Mahayani (finance), Mustafa Talas (deputy prime minister and defense minister), Muhammad Hirba (interior) and Faruq al-Shar' (foreign minister).[10]

The main task facing the new government was defined by a Syrian spokesperson as "the effort to improve the economic situation in the country and to lead toward modernization and economic reforms."[11] Indeed the regime's long-term socioeconomic policies had bankrupted the country. Signs of increased activity followed the establishment of the government. New state budgets were approved, with notable alacrity in Syrian terms, for the current and the following year. Economic programs were also approved, namely a long-range program to combat unemployment, plans to computerize the education system, and the updating of a series of economic laws, especially the Investments Law. This trend, led by several of the new ministers, particularly the minister of state for planning, 'Isam al-Za'im, was accelerated when Bashshar al-Asad took office as president (see below).

Nevertheless, these moves did not produce any substantial change in Syria's economic realities. Moreover, the government itself was split between a conservative faction, which feared dramatic change and the loss of its power, and a faction led by Bashshar, who was anxious to spearhead reform.[12]

The Anti-Corruption Campaign

In a move designed to reinforce his status and ward off any challenge to his candidacy as successor, Bashshar mounted an anti-corruption campaign at the beginning of the year. Hundreds of bureaucrats in various government bodies were dismissed, some were charged with crimes, and orders were issued to confiscate property in several cases. The campaign reached a peak with a charge of corruption leveled against former prime minister Zu'bi. Reportedly, charges of "activity contrary to the values of the party and of ethics" had been filed against him, and an order was issued to confiscate his and his family's property. At the same time, an announcement was made that Zu'bi had been removed from the regional command of the Ba'th Party and had been expelled from the party.[13] A report on 22 May stated that Zu'bi had committed suicide when security persons came to arrest him. His funeral was held in his native village of Hirbat Ghazzala in the province of Suwayda, attended by four thousand members of his family.[14] According to reports from Damascus, one of the principal charges against him was his acceptance of a commission for a $250m. purchase by Syria of Airbus planes from France several years previously. Alongside Zu'bi, two other political figures were also accused of involvement in the deal — the former minister of transportation, Mufid 'Abd al-Karim, and the former deputy prime minister for economic affairs, Salim Yasin. Both were arrested and their property confiscated.[15]

The focus of the anti-corruption campaign on Zu'bi, a weak and colorless political figure, bypassing other members of the elite in the regime, evoked some doubt by the Syrian public as to how straightforward the campaign really was. The London daily al-Quds al-'Arabi quoted opinion on the streets of Damascus that Zu'bi had been a small cog in the system, and that the regime had refrained from leveling charges against other senior officials or army officers for fear of undermining its own stabilility.[16]

Reports from Damascus in June stated that the anti-corruption campaign had reached the doorstep of the retired chief of general staff, Hikmat Shihabi, that the regime intended taking steps against him, as well. Reportedly, Shihabi, who had undergone surgery in Beirut, had proceeded from there to Los Angeles, where his son served as Syrian honorary consul, and had no intention of returning to Syria.[17] Apparently, however, Shihabi's high-level connections and his military past stood him in good stead. Defense Minister Talas explained in an interview: "The anti-corruption campaign is not being waged against army commanders who serve their country loyally, and in any case Shihabi is not guilty of anything."[18] Shihabi returned to Damascus in July, met with President Bashshar al-Asad, and declared his support for him.[19]

ASAD'S DEATH AND BASHSHAR'S RISE TO POWER

An April decision to convene the Ba'th Party regional congress in June marked the first time that the congress would be held in fifteen years, although constitutionally it was to convene every four years to determine party policy and elect its institutional leadership. According to assessments in Damascus, the purpose of the announced congress was to elect Bashshar to its central bodies, ensuring his status as successor.[20] A week before the scheduled opening of the congress, however, President Asad passed away.

The Syrian higher echelons moved quickly to fill the vacuum left by the late leader.

With the official publication of Asad's death, the Syrian parliament was convened in an extraordinary session and voted immediately to change Paragraph 83 of the Syrian constitution, which set the minimum age for the president at forty. The revision fixed the minimum age at thirty-four, Bashshar al-Asad's age.[21]

The following day, on 11 June, the acting president, Vice President 'Abd al-Halim Khaddam, promulgated two decrees, one appointing Bashshar al-Asad to the post of commander of the army (Decree No. 9), and the other promoting him to the rank of *fariq* (field marshal), the highest rank in the Syrian army and the one held by his late father (Decree No. 10).[22] That evening, the senior officers of the Syrian army, led by Defense Minister Talas and Chief of General Staff 'Ali Aslan, convened to pledge their loyalty to Bashshar.[23] A week later, the Ba'th Party congress elected Bashshar secretary-general of the party and thereby a member of its highest bodies — the regional command and the central committee.

Toward the end of the congress, the regional command chose Bashshar as its candidate for the presidency. In a sequence stipulated by constitution, his candidacy was then approved by the People's Assembly, following which the Syrian people elected the president in a referendum. Explaining the choice of Bashshar, the regional command stated:

> Bashshar, in his personality and activities, personifies the continuity of the generations — between the generation that ushered in the turning point and the greatest change in the history of Syria, and which gained experience during the years of struggle that it waged, and the younger generation, which grew up under the wing of the Corrective Movement [the term used to describe the rise of Hafiz al-Asad to power] and which today works with all its might for the development and promotion of modernization in the country.[24]

The approval of Bashshar's candidacy was delivered by the People's Assembly on 26 June. The referendum vote was held on 10 July. The entire process was accompanied by demonstrations of support organized by the authorities throughout Syria, beginning on the day of Asad's death.[25]

According to official data, 8.9m. persons cast ballots in the referendum out of a total of 9.4m. eligible voters (94.6%). Voting was held in 1,134 polling stations, 600 of which were stationed in army units, 57 in Internal Security units, 247 at Syrian embassies throughout the world, and 58 in Lebanon. Bashshar received 8.7m. votes, or 97.3% of the votes cast. Votes against him amounted to 22,439 (0.25%), with 219,319 votes declared invalid.[26] Syrian sources pointed to the fact that Bashshar won 97.3% of the vote and not 99.9%, as his father had attained in the referendums during his rule, as evidence of the authenticity of the referendum. Foreign observers, however, doubted the reliability of the results.[27]

Bashshar took his oath of office before the People's Assembly on 17 July. The main thrust of his policy, which he presented in his inaugural address, was "change in the shadow of continuity and stability," i.e., a continued commitment to Hafiz al-Asad's legacy, while introducing changes required by Syrian contemporary needs. He placed special emphasis on the need to "present new ideas in all spheres alongside...reworking and expanding ideas that no longer suit existing realities, or even relinquishing those ideas which are no longer of value." Additionally, the "supervisory apparatus must be strengthened, [as must] the sense of responsibility, respect for the law,...[the] fight [against] waste and corruption, and...transparency values as a permanent phenomenon in the political life in the country." With this, he cautioned:

Democracy is essential, but we must not apply the democracy of others. The Western democracies are the result of a long history, out of which leaders and traditions grew to create the present culture of democratic societies. We, on the other hand, must adopt a democracy unique to us, based on our history, culture and civilization, having its roots in the needs of the society and the reality in which we live.[28]

Bashshar's election to the presidency evoked disparagement in both the Arabic and the Western press for its trappings of monarchy. Foreign observers also cast some doubt on Bashshar's ability to survive.[29] This opinion was aptly expressed by Israel's coordinator of activities in Lebanon, Uri Lubrani, who said: "They have taken a young fellow, thirty-four years old, and crowned him king of Syria, made him commander of the army. I don't give him more than two years, since the generals won't accept it."[30]

Apparently, however, the establishment supported the choice of Bashshar as president. Both the army commanders and the political old guard upheld the succession. Significantly, Vice Presidents 'Abd al-Halim Khaddam and Zuhayr Masharqa were retained in their posts following Bashshar's election.[31] This support had its roots in an awareness of the necessity to fill the vacuum created by Asad's demise promptly. Bashshar, in the absence of any other obvious successor, was viewed as the most fitting and legitimate candidate, as he was his father's choice. Defense Minister Talas explained: "There was the option of Khaddam's candidacy, or even that I also should be one of the candidates. However, it is unthinkable that I, nearing the age of seventy, as is the case with my colleagues, should be considered for candidacy...Bashshar's election is an expression of our thanks to Asad, who gave so much to Syria." Talas added that "Bashshar is a young man of promise who is worthy of trust, and in any event we will assist him."[32]

The only challenge to Bashshar's election came from his uncle, Asad's brother Rif'at, who had been living in exile in Spain for several years. An announcement made in his name over the satellite television station he owned, ANN, cast doubt on the legitimacy of the process of his nephew's election to the presidency. The election process was described as a "knife in the back of the constitution, which could result in the cancellation of the constitutional legitimacy of the institution of the presidency and even to abuse of the will of the people."[33] In a similar vein, Rif'at's son, Sumar, stated that the referendum which approved Bashshar's election was not legitimate. Rather, he claimed, it was his father Rif'at who had the support and legitimation of the Syrian public.[34]

Once it became clear that the transfer of rule to Bashshar had been smooth, and that Rif'at's efforts had not elicited any response in the Syrian public, he ended his criticism. Praising certain parts of Bashshar's inaugural address, Rif'at said that Bashshar's statements reflected the beginning of a "new corrective movement."[35] Syrian sources, however, reported that a warrant has been issued for Rif'at's arrest should he attempt to enter Syria, an indication that the regime feared him.[36] Reportedly, the Saudi leadership, with whom Rif'at had been friendly for years, tried to effect a reconciliation between Bashshar and his uncle at the end of the year. Rif'at himself visited Saudi Arabia in December, meeting with King Fahd and Crown Prince 'Abdallah.[37]

Bashshar's election accelerated the process of rejuvenating the Syrian leadership. Following Bashshar's election, new governors were named and personnel changes were announced in the information and media sphere and in the Ba'th Party bodies. The signal for these changes was given at the party congress convened in June.

The Party Congress

Primary elections in preparation for the congress were held in May in all Ba'th Party branches, sub-branches and cells, with 24,703 candidates vying for 650 elected seats. Three hundred additional members of the congress were appointees in the party leadership bodies and two hundred others were appointed with the status of observers. The elections were held in a more liberal atmosphere than in the past. Instead of prepared lists of candidates recommended by the party leadership, candidates were allowed to campaign against each other. For the first time, several prominent party activists failed in the primaries, including the ministers of electricity, tourism and minister of state for foreign affairs.[38]

According to a party report submitted to the congress, the party membership in early 2000 was 1.4m. By comparison, it was one million in 1992, 374,332 in 1981, and only 65,398 in 1971. According to the report, 67.8% of the members were under the age of thirty, with the 30-40 age bracket comprising 18.7% of the membership. By occupation, 35.7% of the party members were students, 20.6% civil servants and 16.5% peasants. Women comprised 29.1% of the membership.[39]

Despite the impressive increase in the party size, some concern was expressed at the congress over the possibility of a loss of vitality and relevancy and, thereby, a decrease in influence over day-to-day life in Syria.[40] Alluding to this issue in his address to the congress, Bashshar emphasized the need to refurbish the party image. He said:

> Ba'th socialist ideology has never been obsolete: the socialist concept is flexible and cannot be confined to a strict mold, and therefore it can be developed and moved forward....The continuity of the party is ensured to the extent that it can adapt itself to existing realities and is able to progress alongside developments in the various spheres of life.[41]

Appointments to the party leadership bodies were held during the congress, including the regional command and the central committee — the two highest party bodies (see Appendix 2) — a number of veteran politicians and senior officers who had lost their positions in the government or the military in recent years were excluded, e.g., Muhammad al-Khuli, 'Ali Duba, Hikmat Shihabi and Mahmud al-Zu'bi. Eleven new members were appointed to the regional command, headed by Bashshar and Prime Minister Miru. Of the ninety members of the central committee, sixty-two were new, including Mahir al-Asad, the president's brother, and Munaf Talas, a close associate of Bashshar's and the son of the Defense Minister. Military appointees to the regional command dropped from four to two: Mustafa Talas and Chief of General Staff Aslan. The central committee included twenty military appointees.[42]

Following the congress, a number of changes were also made in the local party leadership throughout Syria. New branch secretaries-general and other posts were filled mainly from the ranks of party activists. Extensive changes were also carried out in the governmental system. Of the fourteen provincial governors, ten were removed from office and replaced by party activists, mainly secretaries-general of local party branches, and two others were transferred to new provinces.[43]

Broad changes were made among newspaper editors and media managers as well, in the wake of the replacement of Minister of Information Muhammad Salman by 'Adnan 'Umran. The director-general of the Syrian Arab News Agency, Fa'iz al-Sa'igh, was appointed to the post of director-general of radio and television. His former post was given to 'Ali 'Abd al-Karim, who had been the agency's correspondent in Cairo. A new editor, Khalaf Muhammad al-Jarrad, was appointed for the government-sponsored daily, *Tishrin*, replacing Muhammad Khayr al-Wadi, who was given an ambassadorship. The editor of another government daily, *al-Thawra*, 'Amid al-Khuli,was replaced by Mahmud Salah.[44] These changes were made as part of an effort to improve the level of the media in Syria, which had been severely criticized for years for their poor technical quality. The new information minister himself was quoted as complaining that "we have no real [media] — all we have are three newspapers [*Tishrin, al-Thawra* and *al-Ba'th*] distributed in 60,000 copies each, half of which are returned because they are defective."[45]

More broadly, the attempt to improve the image of journalism in Syria was apparently part of Bashshar's effort to encourage greater openness and transparency in Syrian society. Besides citing this goal in his inaugural address, he highlighted it in a series of newspaper interviews. In the same vein, he ordered the removal of his pictures from the walls of houses, and a toning down of the rhetoric of flattery routinely used by the Syrian press in referring to his father, e.g., the term "the eternal leader." In the event, Bashshar's pictures were not removed from walls, and no noticeable change occurred in the Syrian press regarding references to Bashshar as compared to references to Asad senior.[46]

The Release of Political Prisoners

Bashshar continued the release of political prisoners from Syrian jails, which had begun in April prior to his father's death. Then, several hundred political prisoners, including members of the Communist Labor Party and Palestinians had been released.[47] In November, Bashshar presented a general amnesty law for a series of criminal and political offenses (Law No. 17) for approval by the People's Assembly. This move marked the first acknowledgment by Syria of the presence of political prisoners in its jails, after steadfast denials by the regime.[48] The approval of the law led to the release of some six hundred political prisoners, including members of the Communist Labor Party; members of the Islamic Liberation Party who had been arrested in late 1999 for their opposition to the peace process; activists in the Democratic Ba'th Party; supporters of Salah Jadid; members of the Iraqi Ba'th Party; and activists in the Committee for the Protection of Civil Rights.[49] A particularly important step was the release of fifty Lebanese prisoners, a sensitive issue in Syrian-Lebanese relations (see below).

Bashshar's stated commitment to increased political liberalism, after thirty years of his father's rule, was compared by many to lifting the lid from a boiling pot. Indeed, it did not take long before criticism of the Syrian regime and demands for even more drastic changes in its policy began to be heard from within the country, at first hesitantly and then with growing force. The perception that the iron hand which had ruled Syria in recent decades had eased its grip prompted intellectuals and members of the business community to articulate appeals for greater freedom and democracy, including the right to organize politically. Damascus businessman Riyadh Sayf, who was also a delegate in the People's Assembly, inaugurated a weekly salon in his home on 31 August, which he called the National Dialogue Club (Muntada al-Hiwar al-Watani), with the open intention of establishing, as a next step, an ideological-political framework to be called Friends of Civilian Society (Ansar al-Mujtam'a al-Madani).[50] Similar forums sprang up in Damascus and all over Syria. Khalil Ma'tuk, an attorney associated with the Communist Party, renewed a forum called the cultural body for human rights (Muntada al-Thaqafa Li Huquq al-Insan) devoted to the discussion of human rights.[51] Toward the end of the year, Ihsan Sanqar, a business-owner, announced his intention to seek permission to establish a liberal-conservative party.[52]

In December, Sayf organized twenty-one independent deputies into a faction in the People's Assembly. They included Basil Dahduh of Damascus, associated with the Syrian Socialist Nationalist Party (see below); Mahdi Mahdi Bayk of Ladhiqiyya; and Ma'mun Humsi. This request for recognition as a faction was rejected by the People's Assembly presidency, on the grounds that political activity outside the framework of the National Progressive Front was prohibited.[53] Nevertheless, the members of the group continued to pursue their activities, conspicuously criticizing the regime. Sayf, during a session of the People's Assembly in November, attacked the national budget, with the result that the speaker of the assembly erased his speech from the protocol. In an unprecedented move, Sayf then distributed a copy of his remarks to foreign journalists in Damascus.[54] Going a step further, Humsi dared criticize the security complex, accusing some elements in it of using unacceptable methods that engendered fear and dread among Syrian citizens. Limitations should be placed on the operation of the security organs and they should be monitored, he said.[55]

In another development, ninety-nine Syrian intellectuals signed a petition, published in Beirut in September, demanding "the release of all political prisoners and prisoners of conscience, the return of exiles, the establishment of rule by law, the granting of freedoms and the recognition of political and ideological pluralism, the right to organize, freedom of the press and self expression, and an end to the monitoring of public life." Signatories included several prominent Syrian thinkers, such as a professor of political thought, Sadiq Jalal al-'Azm, the novelist Haydar Haydar, the poet Adunis, civil rights advocate Riyadh Sayf and the economist 'Arif Dalila.[56] No mention was made of the petition in the Syrian media. Lebanese newspapers that reported it were confiscated at the border crossings and distribution was banned in Syria.[57] Moreover, the Syrian media mounted an organized attack on the intellectuals involved. The editor of al-Ba'th, Turki Saqr, wrote: "There are those who are interested in interpreting talk of the stimulation of political life as [meaning] the elimination of existing realities, replacing them with slogans, shiny on the outside and poisonous on the inside." Saqr asserted that "security and stability in Syria are the foundation stones of renewal and development."[58] The editor of Tishrin, Khalaf Muhammad al-Jarrad, sharply attacked the supporters of civil society for:

> having recently taken up the subject...as if it were a lifeline....These ideas have to do with a mere minority of symposium stars and seekers of publicity, honors and power, while the vast majority of the public in the Arab homeland are struggling to find bread, shelter and income. Our main objection to this imported concept is...its detachment from its historic and social roots, and its attachment to individual freedom.... The idea of the separation of the state from civil society is nothing more than an ideological delusion proven false by the history of Western cultures.[59]

Significantly, however, the regional command of the Ba'th Party decided in November to allow the parties in the National Progressive Front to publish their own newspapers, with the aim of encouraging their activities and permitting greater pluralism in the political life of the country.[60] Following this decision, the Communist Party announced its intention to renew the publication of its organ, *Sawt al-Sha'b*.[61] In another step, Bashshar announced the closure of the al-Maza prison in Damascus and the decision to convert it into an institute for the study of history. The move was described in the press as a reflection of the trend toward greater openness, and as "part of turning over a new leaf in the annals of Syria in establishing a dialogue with the Syrian public in general."[62]

The Regime and the Islamic Movement

Asad's death was used by the Muslim Brotherhood as an opportunity to make a new beginning in its relations with the regime in Damascus. The movement's inspector-general, Sadr al-Din al-Bayanuni, declared that despite his objection to the manner in which Bashshar had risen to power, he was prepared to extend his hand to him in the name of the joint struggle to advance Syrian society. His only condition was that Bashshar indeed make a new beginning, release political prisoners, and allow political freedom and pluralism. "Bashshar has come into the weighty inheritance of decades of totalitarian rule...[but] he does not bear responsibility for what happened in the past in al-Hama (see *MECS* 1981-82, pp. 850-51) or any other place, only for what happens after he is sworn in [to office]," Bayanuni stated. He demanded of Bashshar to "allow us to express ourselves," pointing out that "5,000 of our people have been released in the past decade, but 4,500 of our people are in prison and almost 5,000 more are in exile, and they, together with their families, number in the tens of thousands."[63]

The Muslim Brotherhood's need to make peace with Bashshar was acute, as its leader, exiled for years, had become irrelevant in the contemporary Syrian reality. Moreover, the authorities in Jordan, which had become the movement's base, took a number of steps during the year to limit its activities severely, a reflection of Jordan's desire to improve relations with Syria. The Brotherhood's political bureau and information office were closed down in February, and the convening of its Shura Council in Amman was banned. The council convened instead in Baghdad, a development that brought about the start of a dialogue between the Bayanuni faction, considered to be moderate, and the Baghdad-based 'Adnan Sa'd al-Din faction, considered to be radical.[64] Following Bashshar's election, the Jordanians requested that Bayanuni himself leave Amman, where he had resided in recent years. Complying, Bayanuni transferred the focus of his activity to London.[65]

The Muslim Brotherhood's hope to begin a new page under Bashshar were dashed after the new Syrian president essentially ignored the appeal by its leaders. The movement appeared to have lost its foothold in Syria even among Islamic circles in the country. Notably, it was a cleric, Marwan Shaykhu, an independent deputy in the People's Assembly, who read out the announcement of Asad's death over Syrian television, praising the deceased president's religious commitment. Moreover, allegiance to Bashshar was sworn in mosques all over the country. Bashshar himself was careful about fostering his image as a man of religious faith, making sure to attend holiday prayers in the mosques.[66] At the end of the year, he rescinded a standing order forbidding schoolgirls from wearing the veil.[67] Further evidence of the regime's self-confidence was the release of hundreds of imprisoned supporters of the Islamic Liberation Movement, arrested at the end of 1999, because of their opposition to the peace talks with Israel. Reports from Damascus at that time cited the outbreak of riots between the Syrian security forces and Islamic activists during the course of the arrests, with several deaths of security officers.[68]

Additionally, according to reports from Damascus, Bashshar had become engaged to a British-born Syrian, Asma al-Akhras, from a notable Sunni family in Homs.[69]

The bind in which the Muslim Brotherhood found itself brought about the emergence of a more radical offshoot, the Muslim Brotherhood — Jihad Fighters, led by the Baghdad-based Usama al-Maluhi. Announcing his resignation from the Muslim Brotherhood, Maluhi declared that he intended to hoist the flag of democracy in Syria based on the principle of Shura consultation, in classical Islamic thought. He also warned that if the Syrian regime failed to ensure the security and the rights of the Syrian populace, he would lead a jihad against it.[70]

In contrast to its attitude toward the Muslim Brotherhood, the Syrian regime during the previous decade had established close relations with a number of Islamic movements outside Syria, which viewed it as a protective wall against the West and Israel. Following Bashshar's election, these movements called on him to improve the relationship with the Syrian Islamic movement:

> The countries of Greater Syria (Bilad al-Sham) comprise one of the arenas of Islamic activity, and have also played a historic role as a barrier in defending the nation against foreign invasion....Misunderstandings increased in the 1980s at the time of great distress, but we hope that your era will be a new era, and therefore a new leaf must be turned over and Law No. 49 [which stipulates the death penalty for membership in the Muslim Brotherhood] must be repealed.

The signatories to the appeal included leaders of Islamic movements in Tunisia, Iraq, Algeria and Lebanon.[71]

Druze-Bedouin Ethnic Conflict in the Suwayda Province

Clashes in the Suwayda province in southeastern Syria between Bedouins and Druze, who constituted the majority of the population there, were reported in November. A severe drought prompted the Bedouins to encroach on fields belonging to the Druze in the village of Raha near Suwayda. A number of Druze farmers who resisted them were killed. The incident led to a general conflagration throughout the Jabal Druze region. Angry Druze blocked the Suwayda-Damascus road, rioting broke out in the town of Suwayda, and government offices were set on fire by a Druze mob. Demonstrating Druze students on the Damascus university campus demanded that the authorities provide protection for their community. The government quickly sent army units to the district to restore order. Sixty-seven Bedouins, including leaders such as the head of the Shanbila tribe, Sa'ud al-Sa'id, were arrested. The riots subsided after several days, leaving 22 people dead, 18 of them Druze, and 123 people injured.[72] A *sulha* held in Suwayda in December was attended by local dignitaries and prominent figures in the regime. The *sulha* was arranged after the Syrian government announced the payment of compensation amounting to £SY 350,000 (c. $7,000) for each person killed, and c. £SY 3,000 (c. $60) to each person injured, as well as compensation to those whose houses had been destroyed.[73]

The Economy

Reports published during the year revealed that ongoing economic difficulties had not abated. GDP growth for the year 2000 was 1.5%, following a decline of 1.5% in 1999. Considering the high rate of population increase, this meant negative growth in practical terms. The severe recession in the economy also continued, as did high unemployment. Signs of infrastructure collapse were evident in the erratic supply of water and electricity, the communications network, and health, education and welfare services.[74] Although exports in 2000, rose by 45% amounting to $4.8bn.,[75] the increase was entirely the result of the rise in the price of oil, the main source of revenue. Indeed, high oil prices throughout the year improved the economic situation, but shortly at year's end, prices dropped once again. Additionally, the country's oil production declined to c. 510,000 b/d as compared to 604,000 b/d in previous years. Syrian minister of state for planning 'Isam al-Za'im announced that the country must prepare itself for a loss of revenue from oil and needed to develop its human resources.[76]

The grave Syrian economic situation impelled Bashshar to focus on socioeconomic problems with the intention of promoting change and reform — albeit limited in scope — designed to improve the country's economy. This line of thinking, which had its beginnings with the establishment in March of the Miru government, gained impetus with Bashshar's election to office. Policy took the form of a plethora of regulations, e.g., to update the Investment Law, grant permission for the import of private cars by the individual, and ease the law governing the leasing of apartments.[77] Additionally, a decree was issued permitting Syrians residing abroad to be released from military service in return for a monetary payment.[78] Lauding these developments al-Ba'th commented:

> Bashshar's instructions were translated with record speed into dozens of decrees whose aim is to lay the groundwork in the sphere of education, science and information technology and to initiate the revolution in legislation that will amend the legislative and legal infrastructure and bring it up to date....After all, Syria is in desperate need of reform and development, a fact that cannot be ignored.[79]

The Budget

The budget for the year 1999, approved only in January 2000, totalled to £SY 255.3bn. ($5.5bn.), with £SY 121.8bn. designated for investment and £SY 133.5bn. for current expenditures. The explanation given for the delay in preparing the budget was sharp variations in oil prices, which impeded an accurate assessment of anticipated revenue from this central item in the budget.[80] By contrast, the budget for the year 2000 was presented to the People's Assembly for approval within a month after the establishment of the Miru government. The budget, amounting to £SY 275.4bn. ($5.9bn.) broke down as follows: £SY 132bn. for investment and £SY 108.4bn. for current expenditures including debt repayment, price subsidies and incentives for exports. The budget was designed to create 92,300 jobs.[81] In December, the People's Assembly approved a resolution to increase the budget by £SY 66bn. in order to finance debt repayment by publicly owned companies.[82] In contrast to previous practice, the government presented the proposed budget for the year 2001 toward the end of 2000. It amounted to £SY 322.2bn. ($6.9bn.) allotting £SY 161bn. for investment and £SY 161bn. for current expenditures. It was designed to create 65,000 jobs.[83]

Investment

The Miru government highlighted the encouragement of investment as a primary goal, a move made in response to severe criticism in the media and the People's Assembly for several years of the antiquated Investment Law (Law No. 10) of 1991. This law, which had been a linchpin of the Syrian economy, no longer met the country's needs and had lost its relevance to Syrian and global economic realities. In one of his last acts, Hafiz al-Asad published Decree No. 7 on 13 May, introducing amendments to Law No. 10. The main objectives of the amendments was to ease the leasing of land to investors, the retention of, and trade in foreign currency; and taxation.[84] According to official data published by the Central Bureau of Statistics in Damascus, as of August 2000, some 1,520 investment projects had been approved by the government, amounting to a total investment of £SY 311bn. (c. $7.5bn.-$8bn.). These projects contributed to the creation of 100,000 jobs, although Syrian sources admitted that most of the projects had never actually been carried out.[85]

Wage Increases
Another subject addressed by the government was public sector wages, which had not been increased since 1994 and had become seriously eroded. The establishment of a new government elicited hopes for a substantial wage increase. Instead, however, the government mounted an information campaign designed to lower these expectations, explaining that social needs — mainly food subsidies — prevented the allocation of monies for substantial wage increases.[86] On 25 August, Bashshar announced Decree No. 37, granting a 25% wage increase for 1.3m. civil servants and a 20% increase for 461,000 pensioners.[87] According to official data, before these increases, approximately 40% of the country's civil servants earned less than the average monthly wage of £SY 2,000; 7% earned c. £SY 2000; approximately 22% earned £SY 2,200–£SY 3,000; 26.4% earned £SY 4,200–£SY 5,000 (engineers and physicians); 6.7% earned £SY 5,200–£SY 5,700; and 8% (mainly directors-general and senior army officers) earned £SY 5,700–£SY 7,800.[88] At the end of the year, a decree issued by the minister of labor announced a 25% wage increase in the private sector as well. According to press reports, however, many private employers refrained from granting this increase, claiming that the difficult economic situation in the private sector did not permit it.[89] The wage increases were accompanied by the unprecedented cancellation of subsidies for rice and a cut in the subsidy for sugar. However, government spokespersons said that the rest of the prices were still controlled and had remained unchanged.[90]

Unemployment
According to official data, unemployment in the year 2000 was 9.5%, as compared to 9% in 1999. A government spokeperson, however, admitted that the real unemployment rate was about 20%. The 'Alawite region in the northwest and other rural areas had the highest unemployment rates, e.g., Tartus 20.5% and Suwayda 15.7%, as compared to Damascus with a rate of only 7.5%. The data also revealed that 71% of the unemployed were aged 15-24 in a work force of 4.5m., and that 55% of the unemployed were from rural areas.[91] In view of the growing severity of unemployment, the government approved a five-year program designed to create 423,000 jobs.[92]

The Development of the Banking System
In December, the regional command of the Ba'th Party announced preparations for the start of private banking in Syria. This step, according to the Syrian press, was designed "to [carry Syria] forward toward new horizons of development and innovation and to encourage investment in the private and public sectors."[93] Observers viewed the move as a start in relinquishing the commitment to socialist policies that had been in force in

Syria for some four decades. The regional command also announced the establishment of a stock exchange and the adoption of a single rate of exchange for the Syrian pound based on the unification of the three separate existing rates: the rate for trade with neighboring countries, at £SY46 = $1, the rate of exchange for tourists, at £SY11.2 = $1, and the customs rate of £SY23 = $1.[94] Even prior to this decision, a number of Lebanese banks had been granted permission to open branches in Syria and one had been opened in the Damascus free trade zone.[95]

Demography
Updated data on the Syrian population for the years 1994-99 published by the Bureau of Statistics in October indicated that the rate of population growth stood at 2.7%, compared to 3.3% for the years 1981-94, and that by mid-2000 the rate had declined to 2.5%. Female fertility, according to the data, had dropped from 6.1 children per woman in 1980 to 3.7 children in 1998, while the marriage age had risen during this period from 21.4 to 25.1 for women and from 25.7 to 28.9 for men.[96]

FOREIGN AFFAIRS

SYRIA IN THE INTERNATIONAL ARENA
Relations with the US
Relations between Syria and the US remained stagnant throughout the year, largely because of the impasse in Syrian-Israeli peace negotiations. Efforts by the Americans to promote the negotiations at the beginning of the year proved unsuccessful and were discontinued in the wake of the failed summit meeting in Geneva in March between Presidents Asad and Clinton (see chapter on the US and the Middle East). Clinton laid the blame for the failure of the negotiations on Asad for not showing sufficient flexibility. As far as the Israeli-Syrian dialogue was concerned, Clinton declared, the ball was in the Syrian court.[97] Rejecting this accusation, the Syrians claimed that the US was to blame for the failure of the peace effort because of its pro-Israel bias.[98] The chilly relationship between the two countries thereafter was reflected in Clinton's non-attendance at Asad's funeral.[99]

As in previous years, the US State Department report on terrorism, published in April, cited Syria as a state that supported terrorism because of its backing for Hizballah and the Palestinian Islamic Jihad, although it pointed to a decrease in direct Syrian involvement in acts of terrorism.[100] The Syrians dismissed the accusations of their involvement in terrorism as nothing new, asserting that the object of publishing the report was to pressure Syria to adopt a more flexible stand in its negotiations with Israel.[101]

Syria's hardened stance in the wake of the al-Aqsa intifada in October, the renewal of Hizballah attacks against Israel with undisguised Syrian encouragement, and improved relations between Syria and Iraq exacerbated the existing tension between Damascus and Washington. Secretary of State Madeleine Albright, meeting with Bashshar in October in Saudi Arabia, requested him to rein in Hizballah activities. Reportedly, Clinton, in a telephone conversation with Bashshar from Washington, reiterated this message in no uncertain terms.[102] However, this did not deter Syria from supporting Hizballah attacks against Israel. Moreover, the intifada evoked emotional anti-American outbursts throughout Syria. Demonstrators in Damascus attempted to break into the American embassy, but police barred their entry into the building.[103] Syrian intellectuals called for a boycott of American goods and staged a ceremony in Damascus at which American products were burned.[104]

George W. Bush's victory in the American presidential race was welcomed in Damascus, giving rise to expectations that "Bush, the son, will walk in his father's footsteps and end America's pro-Israel bias in favor of a more balanced position demonstrating an understanding of the Arabs' needs."[105] The regime had refrained from publicly expressing support for either of the candidates throughout the election campaign, with Syrian sources quoted as saying that in essence there was no difference between Bush and Gore on anything related to the Middle East question.[106] Nevertheless, a sense of apprehension regarding the possible victory of Al Gore and his Jewish vice-presidential running mate, Joseph Lieberman, was perceptible. Al-Thawra noted on the eve of election: "There are clear Jewish fingerprints in the American election campaign, and the victory of the Jewish lobby could result in a Nazi night falling on the US."[107]

Relations with the EU

Syria continued its efforts to deepen relations with the European Union (EU) countries. Improved relations with Germany was particularly marked once the question of the Syrian debt to it was resolved. Damascus had a $2bn. debt to East Germany, and an additional $1bn. was owed to various West German companies. During a visit to Syria by German chancellor Gerhard Schroeder in October, a debt repayment agreement was signed which canceled c. $500m. of the debt, with Syria pledging to repay the balance of c. $2bn. over a period of twenty years. The agreement allowed Syria to receive aid from the EU in the amount of 570m. euros, as well as smaller loans and grants from Germany.[108]

As in the past, Syria continued to devote its primary diplomatic efforts to France. Relations with France dipped early in the year when French prime minister Lionel Jospin, visiting the region, attacked Hizballah and called it a terrorist organization. French president Jaques Chirac, mollifying the Syrians, insisted that French policies had not undergone any change.[109] The French president was the only Western leader to participate in Asad's funeral.[110]

No substantial progress was made in talks between Syria and the EU regarding finalizing an association agreement, a topic high on the Syrian agenda. Talks at the end of the year during a visit by Syrian minister of state for planning 'Isam al-Za'im, to Brussels were unproductive. Za'im explained that Syria was unable to meet the union's conditions for signing the agreement, for example, the cancellation of customs duties on mutual trade.[111]

Foreign Minister Shar' participated in a conference of foreign ministers of the Barcelona declaration states in May.[112] To French displeasure, however, the Syrians boycotted the conference of Mediterranean states held in Marseilles in November, because of Israeli participation there (see chapter on Western Europe, Russia and the Middle East). Shar' explained: "We will never be able to enter a banquet hall with the Israeli foreign minister, while in Palestine the intifada rages and innocent people are being killed."[113]

SYRIA IN THE INTER-ARAB ARENA

Asad's death diminished Syrian status in the Arab arena significantly. His absence was especially noticeable in the wake of the outbreak of the intifada in October. Bashshar tried but failed to lead the Arab summit in Cairo that month to adopt a radical line regarding Israel. Indeed, the summit, as well as the Islamic conference in Doha that followed adopted moderate resolutions that were far from satisfactory to the Syrians.[114] Syria, Shar' declared, had expected more forceful summit resolutions regarding Israel, and although they were a step in the right direction, they could be expected to remain solely on paper, causing frustration and despair.[115]

Relations with Egypt

Relations between Syria and Egypt continued to be marked by tension and mutual mistrust. The Syrians contended at the beginning of the year that Egypt was making efforts to promote Israeli-Palestinian negotiations at the expense of Damascus. By the end of the year, Egypt's relatively moderate stand regarding the position that the Arab world should adopt in light of the renewed Palestinian-Israeli violence was clearly vastly different from that of Syria.[116] The two countries, however, did take steps to maintain a measure of mutual coordination. Presidents Mubarak and Hafiz al-Asad met in January and in May to discuss the state of the peace process. Attending Asad's funeral in June, Mubarak met with Bashshar. [117] Bashshar, for his part, visited Egypt in September to discuss the peace process, and again in October to attend the Arab summit.[118]

Relations with Gulf States

Syria continued its efforts to maintain close ties with the Gulf states, focused mainly on the economic sphere. These ties were reinforced when, following Asad's death, the rulers of Saudi Arabia and the Gulf states made a concerted effort to assist Bashshar in bolstering his status. Qatar's emir Hamad bin Khalifa visited Damascus in March, thereby ending a long period of tension between the two countries over Qatar's friendly relations with Israel,[119] which Qatar refused to break off. In October, the Syrians threatened to boycott the Islamic conference in Doha if Qatar did not announce the closure of the Israeli representation in the emirate. Qatar responded that it would comply with the Syrian demand (see chapters on Political Islam, and Qatar). However, the Israeli representation there remained intact.[120]

In June, the 1991 Damascus declaration signatory states (Egypt, Syria and the six members of the Gulf Cooperation Council) met for talks on issues that included the situation in Lebanon following the Israeli withdrawal from South Lebanon, the peace process, and the Iraqi question. They also discussed issues related to economic cooperation. The announcement issued at the end of the meeting expressed support for Syrian positions and demanded that the Syrian-Israeli negotiations be renewed on the basis of the acceptance of the principle of international legitimacy (i.e., that Israel withdraw from all territory taken in the 1967 war).[121]

Toward the end of the year, relations between Syria and the Gulf states were clouded by a growing rapprochement between Syria and Iraq (see below). Shar' was quoted as stating that the need to defend Kuwait should not be linked to punishing the Iraqi people. Responding to a complaint issued by Kuwait regarding this statement, Shar' explained that he did not mean that the UN resolution boycotting Iraq should be violated.[122] Syria nonetheless continued to promote better relations with Iraq, to the obvious displeasure of Kuwait and Saudi Arabia. The visit to Saudi Arabia by Bashshar's uncle, Rif'at Asad, in December was interpreted as a Saudi signal to Bashshar that he would do well to discontinue his efforts to draw closer to Iraq.[123]

Relations with Jordan

The year 2000 was marked by efforts by both countries to improve mutual relations, a trend that had begun following the death of King Husayn in 1999 and accelerated after the death of President Asad. King 'Abdallah visited Damascus in April and again in July, following the establishment of the new regime, joining in the efforts to bolster Bashshar's status both domestically and in the inter-Arab and international arenas.[124]

The Jordanian authorities ordered the Syrian Muslim Brotherhood to close down its offices in Amman, and the movement's leader, Sadr al-Din al-Bayanuni, to leave the Jordanian capital[125] (see above). Bashshar, for his part, offered to supply 3.5m. cu.m. of water to Jordan during the summer months to assist in drought relief.[126] Additionally, progress was made in plans by both countries to build the long-delayed Unity Dam on the Yarmuk River, a mainly demonstrative act designed to contrast with concurrent Israeli-Jordanian disagreements over Israeli supply of water to Jordan (see chapter on Jordan). According to reports from Damascus, financing amounting to $200m. had been obtained by Syria and Jordan to begin work on the project.[127] At the end of the year, Syria appointed an ambassador to Amman, 'Abd al-Fatah Amura, filling this post in the Syrian embassy in Amman which had been left vacant for several years.[128]

Relations with Iraq

Mutual efforts by both countries to form closer ties continued. Following Asad's death, Bashshar appeared anxious to turn over a new leaf in Syrian relations with Iraq, inter alia because of fears of a possible flare-up between Israel and Syria. At the same time, Syrian sources reiterated that Syria was not seeking a close alliance with Iraq. In April the Iraqis opened an office of interests in the Algerian embassy in Damascus. However, the Syrians refrained from opening a similar office in Baghdad throughout the year.[129]

A clear reflection of the warming trend between the two countries was the habit of Iraqi politicians of stopping over in Damascus on their way to various world capitals, thereby meeting frequently with senior figures in the Syrian regime. Iraqi vice president Taha Muhyi al-Din Ma'ruf took part in Asad's funeral in June [130] and Iraq's other vice president, 'Izzat Ibrahim al-Duri, arrived in Damascus for an official visit in November.[131]

The two countries also maintained economic ties. Iraqi finance minister Mahdi Salah reported during the year that the scope of bilateral trade had reached $500m. and predicted that in a year or two it would reach $1bn.[132] A railway line between Mosul and Aleppo was inaugurated in August. Senior Iraqi and Syrian officials who participated in the opening ceremony called the event "an expression of the fulfillment of Arab unity."[133] That month, both countries reached a final agreement on the demarcation of their joint border, culminating an eight-year process. In 1995, an agreement had been signed over the demarcation in principle, and the issue was finally settled in 2000.[134] In October, Syria began permitting passenger planes to fly to Iraq, violating the international sanctions against that country. The first plane carried an official Syrian delegation bringing with it medical aid to the people of Iraq. This was followed by other relief aid flights.[135] Additionally, the Kirkuk-Baniyas oil pipeline was reportedly reactivated at the end of the year, which Iraq intended to use for the export of oil to the West. Syrian sources promptly denied these reports. The US State Department refrained from confirming whether the pipeline had been reopened.[136]

Alongside the improving relations with Iraq, Syria continued to maintain contacts with elements opposing Saddam Husayn and with the Kurdish factions in northern Iraq.

The chairperson of the Supreme Council of the Iraqi Islamic Revolution, Muhammad Bakr al-Hakim, visited Syria in February and met with Bashshar.[137] Kurdish leader Mas'ud Barazani arrived in Damascus in October, meeting with Bashshar and other senior Syrian officials.[138]

Relations with the PA

Relations between Syria and the PA remained tense throughout the year. Although PA chairman Yasir 'Arafat was present at Asad's funeral, the Syrians promptly made it clear that the visit did not signify a new chapter in relations with the PA.[139] Indeed, they took steps to block inter-Arab support for 'Arafat regarding possible concessions on Jerusalem, borders and the refugee issue.[140]

While Syria frequently signified support for the intifada, calling for its continuation and intensification, the Syrians pointedly refrained from expressing direct support for the PA. Syria even demanded that any mention of 'Arafat or the authority be stricken from the final communiqué of the Doha Islamic summit, which expressed support for the intifada alone.[141] Similarly, the Syrians refused to receive 'Arafat in Damascus, apparently because of their fear that he might renew negotiations with Israel. Indeed, with the renewal of the Israeli-Palestinian negotiations at the end of the year, the Syrians immediately accused 'Arafat of abandoning the Palestinian intifada and making dangerous concessions to Israel and the US.[142]

Large demonstrations throughout Syria in support of the intifada attested to the strong sentiment in the Syrian public concerning the Palestinian question. Foreign observers believed that it would therefore be difficult for Syria to renew negotiations with Israel so long as the intifada continued and Israel and the Palestinians did not reach a settlement.[143]

Relations with Lebanon

The year 2000 witnessed the diminution of Syria's status in Lebanon, the result of a series of developments. First, the withdrawal of Israeli forces from South Lebanon on 24 May engendered a serious dilemma in Damascus, both because of the loss of a bargaining chip against Israel and because the Syrian military presence in Lebanon lost much of its legitimacy in Arab eyes. Indeed, Lebanese proponents of Syrian withdrawal from the country became more vocal. Secondly, the death of Hafiz al-Asad[144] led to a perception in Lebanon that Syria was weakened, and that challenging Syrian status in Lebanon was no longer dangerous. Third, parliamentary elections held in Lebanon during the summer resulted in a resounding defeat for the government and the return of Rafiq al-Hariri as prime minister (see chapter on Lebanon). Hariri's victory, a purely domestic development, was nevertheless viewed as a blow to Damascus in that the defeated Lebanese government was closely identified with the Syrian regime. To be sure, however, Hariri quickly expressed loyalty to Syria after the elections.

The campaign against the Syrian presence in the country was kicked off by the editor of *al-Nahar*, Ghassan Tuwayni. A frequent critic of Syria for several years, Tuwayni sharpened his attacks in 2000. "Lebanon will not be a free and sovereign state so long as the foreign forces remain in the country," he wrote in May.[145] Another staunch opponent of the Syrian presence in Lebanon, Maronite patriarch Butrus Sufayr, also called for the withdrawal of Syrian forces from the country.[146] Sufayr was joined by the Synod of the Maronite Bishops, which stated in an unprecedented announcement that with the withdrawal of Israel, the time had come to reexamine the question of the Syrian presence in Lebanon.[147] Maronite protest against Syria was accompanied by widespread anti-Syrian demonstrations by students and activists in political parties such as the Free Liberals, sponsored by the Maronite Chamoun family, during which Syrian flags were burned and pictures of Asad and Bashshar were torn off walls.[148]

One of Syria's traditional allies in Lebanon, the leader of the Druze community, Walid Junblat, joined this criticism. Junblat declared that while he understood the need for Syrian forces to remain in strategic places in Lebanon because of the ongoing Arab-Israeli conflict, the 1989 Ta'if agreement should be implemented, i.e., the redeployment of Syrian forces to the Lebanese Biqa' and an end to Syrian intervention in Lebanese internal affairs (see *MECS* 1989, pp. 519-25).[149] Curiously, the Syrian reaction to this public criticism was relatively moderate. The Syrians opted for a dialogue with the Maronite patriarch with the aim of dampening his criticism. Although they took a stiffer line with regard to Junblat, declaring him persona non grata in Damascus, they did not divest him of the villa there which Asad had presented to him, and announced that if he arrived in Damascus as a private person, he would be welcomed.[150]

The source of the outburst of public criticism against the Syrians was apparently the cumulative anger at Damascus for its heavy-handed intervention in day-to-day life in Lebanon. A typical example was a decree announced by the Lebanese minister of education in November allowing any Syrian student to be accepted in Lebanese universities. This time, however, turbulent student demonstrations erupted as a result.[151] In December, the Lebanese government, under pressure from Syria, announced a lowering of customs duties on Syrian agricultural products, a step severely harmful to Lebanese agriculture. The Syrians, however, claimed that the Lebanese decision to substantially decrease customs duties on raw materials imported to Lebanon had been made without coordination with Syria, and was actually harmful to Syrian industry.[152] Another contentious issue was the unresolved question of Lebanese prisoners in Syrian prisons. Although fifty of these prisoners were released in November, and the Syrians claimed that no other Lebanese were being held, reports in Lebanon insisted that the Syrians were holding more Lebanese prisoners, and concern over their fate was expressed.[153] The presence of hundreds of thousands of Syrian workers in Lebanon, who were perceived as taking jobs away from the Lebanese, was also a sore point. Reports from Beirut cited incidents of attacks on Syrian workers that resulted in injuries and deaths. According to Lebanese sources, approximately 1.5m. Syrian workers were registered in Lebanon, with an additional 300,000 unregistered persons, of whom 10% lived there with their families. However, Prime Minister Hariri claimed after his election that there were only about 300,000 Syrian workers in Lebanon.[154]

The Syrians, for their part, took steps to decrease friction with the Lebanese population. In May, following the withdrawal of the Israeli forces from South Lebanon, they began redeploying their forces throughout the country. The process was accelerated at the end of the year in response to mounting demands in Lebanon for Syria to withdraw. Reportedly, the Syrian army decreased the number of roadblocks it had set up on Lebanese roads, and eventually withdrew most of its forces from Beirut. According to reports from Damascus, in contrast to the presence of c. 40,000 Syrian troops stationed in Lebanon at the beginning of the year, only 10,000-15,000 had remained by the end of 2000.[155] Nevertheless, the Syrians stressed, the reference was to redeployment and not an overall withdrawal, which would be effected only after a comprehensive peace was attained in the region.[156] Bashshar was quoted as saying: "If the Syrian army had been deployed in the streets of Damascus over a long period of time, the Syrian public would also have developed disgust toward them, as happened in the Lebanese case."[157]

The renewal of Hizballah operations along Israel's northern border in October, in the wake of the intifada, exacerbated the tension along the Israel-Syria-Lebanon axis. Israel claimed that the Hizballah attacks were carried out with Syrian encouragement and warned that continued offensives could lead to a regional conflagration. The Syrians justified the Hizballah activity as legitimate because it was carried out in the Shab'a Farms area, which Syria claimed was occupied Arab territory. If Israel chose to attack Syria, they declared, it would find the Syrian army prepared for battle.[158] Nevertheless, the Syrians refrained from stating unequivocally that the Shab'a Farms area was Lebanese territory. Foreign Minister Shar' explicitly declared that Israel must withdraw from the area on the basis of UN Security Council Resolution 242 (relating to the Golan Heights captured by Israel in June 1967), and not according to Resolution 425 (relating to areas in Lebanon over which Israel took control in 1978), thus hinting that when the time came, Syria would claim the area for itself.[159]

RELATIONS WITH TURKEY

Syria and Turkey made efforts to improve bilateral ties during the year, after having nearly gone to war in late 1998 (see *MECS* 1998, pp. 585-87). This was reflected in the attendance by Turkish president Ahmad Necdet Cezar at President Asad's funeral. Cezar stated at that time that Turkey was prepared to assist the new Syrian leadership in turning over a new leaf in relations between the two countries.[160] Bashshar was no less eager to improve ties. In September, Syrian minister of interior Muhammad Hirba visited Ankara to discuss the implementation of the security protocol of the Adana agreement signed by both countries in 1998 (see *MECS* 1998, pp. 586-87). Hirba and his Turkish counterpart publicly expressed satisfaction at the manner in which the agreement was being upheld.[161] In November, Syrian vice-president 'Abd al-Halim Khaddam, who in the past had displayed a hostile stance toward Turkey, also visited Ankara. Calling his visit fruitful, Khaddam pointed out that Syria and Turkey shared a long history of hundreds of years, which established the basis for serious cooperation for the benefit of both peoples.[162] Bashshar was reportedly scheduled to visit Ankara at a future date, at which time the settlement of all outstanding problems would be announced.[163]

In practice, however, Syria and Turkey found it difficult to reach agreement on all extant bilateral issues. The question of the Euphrates River waters remained especially contentious. Syria continued to try to foil Turkish plans to build dams along the Euphrates, and even threatened to boycott Western companies if they participated in constructing these dams.[164] The issue grew more serious during the year because of a drop in the level of the river resulting from drought. According to reports from Damascus, the quantity of water that flowed through the Euphrates had fallen to 300 cu.m. per second while Turkey had committed itself to supplying Syria with 500 cu.m. per second in a 1987 protocol.[165]

The question of sovereignty over the Alexandretta region, which the French mandatory authorities had transferred to Turkey in 1939, was another longstanding unresolved point of friction. Reportedly, the Syrians requested deferring treatment of the issue to a later date, but Turkey insisted on an immediate and unequivocal recognition by Syria of the existing border between the two countries.[166]

Turkish-Israeli relations continued to cause apprehension in Damascus, even though

Turkey lowered the profile of its relations with Israel following the outbreak of the intifada.

RELATIONS WITH IRAN

Syria and Iran continued to take steps to preserve and even to further develop their strategic alliance. This did not deter Iran from criticizing Syria early in the year when it appeared that Damascus was about to reach a peace settlement with Israel. Iranian leader 'Ali Khamene'i vigorously attacked "states that were in the past revolutionary and are now in dialogue with Israel, which is actually treason."[167] The failure of the negotiations, however, effectively removed the contentious subject from their bilateral agenda.

The death of President Asad stirred apprehension in Tehran of a possible change in Syrian policy. Radio Tehran stated that with Asad's death the Arab world had lost one of its last fighting politicians and Iran had lost one of its most prominent friends in the region.[168] Iranian president Mohammad Khatami, arriving in Damascus to attend Asad's funeral, stressed his desire to preserve the ties between the two countries.[169]

Syrian reliance on Iran increased toward the end of the year with the deterioration in relations between Syria and Israel as a result of Hizballah activity in South Lebanon. Spokespersons in Tehran promised to stand by Syria should it be attacked by Israel.[170] Their common hostility toward Israel also made it easier for Iran to accept the improvement in Syrian relations with Iraq. Despite Iranian reservations, Tehran agreed to send Iranian planes carrying aid to Hizballah through Iraqi air space, after Turkey required Iranian planes suspected of carrying aid to Hizballah to land in its territory and undergo inspection.[171]

SYRIA AND THE PEACE PROCESS WITH ISRAEL

Syrian-Israeli peace talks resumed on 8 December 1999, with the participation, for the first time, of Israeli prime minister Ehud Barak and Syrian foreign minister Faruq al-Shar'. The resumption of the negotiations at so senior a level, and in effect for the first time at the political level, aroused a wave of optimism in the region and beyond over the prospects of a breakthrough in the negotiations, even the possibility of reaching an Israeli-Syrian peace accord within a few months.[172]

Barak made substantial strides, at least in Israeli terms, toward the Syrians, while taking a number of steps designed to prepare Israeli public opinion for far-reaching concessions on the Golan Heights — in fact, total withdrawal. Members of Barak's inner circle played down the importance of the concessions that Israel would make as part of a peace agreement, while underscoring its advantages. A Syrian-Israeli peace agreement, Barak reportedly said, could completely change Middle East realities and substantially improve Israel's strategic position, and "Israel must not miss this historic opportunity to improve its standing because of intransigence over a few hundred meters of land." In effect, Barak was hinting at his readiness to accept the Syrian demand for an Israeli withdrawal to the 4 June 1967 border.[173]

In Syria, for the first time since the start of the Israeli-Syrian peace negotiations in 1991, and apparently because of a perception that a peace agreement was imminent, the regime was criticized for what appeared to be its readiness to reach a peace settlement with Israel. The chairperson of the Arab Writers' Association in Damascus, 'Uqla 'Ursan, a member of the Ba'th Party, criticized what he called the flexibility that Syria had shown in its negotiations with Israel. "We reject and will continue to reject in the future any possibility of recognizing the Zionist enemy," he wrote. "We will also continue to fight against any evidence of normalization with it, since we view this as a 'struggle for survival' and not 'a struggle for borders'" [a not-so-veiled critique of the phrasing used by Foreign Minister Faruq al-Shar' at the White House lawn in Washington in December 1999] (see *MECS* 1999, pp. 560-61).[174] The embarrassment of the Syrian regime in the wake of such criticism was reflected in Shar''s willingness to appear before the association in February in order to justify government readiness to negotiate and perhaps even reach a peace agreement with Israel. In remarks that were both apologetic and contradictory, Shar' reminded his audience that the Arab world had suffered a defeat at Israel's hands, which had left no choice but to take the road to peace. The conflict with Israel, he reiterated, had turned from a battle for existence into a battle over borders. Still, he stated, he was committed, as a veteran member of the Ba'th Party, to the party's vision and long-range goals, and thus to the destruction of the State of Israel.[175] Shar' stated:

> At the end of the nineteenth century the Zionist vision mounted its path, and at the same time so did the Arab national vision. Each of these visions had its own path, but the difference between them was great: one was an aggressive vision with expansionist ambitions and basically racist. The other, the vision of Arab nationalism wanted to ensure its existence and the unity of its legacy, viewing with humanism the justice of its cause. The Zionist vision has succeeded in realizing most, if not all, of its ambitions, whereas the Arab national vision, unfortunately, experienced upheavals and shock...and over the past several years its light has dimmed and realizing [the vision] became a difficult task. The visit of Sadat to Jerusalem...the Iran-Iraq War and the invasion of Kuwait, all of this was a defeat and even a knife driven into the Arab body.

> Israel is stronger than all the Arab states together, and in addition to that, the United States is its strategic ally, and supplies it with every form of weaponry from the rifle via the missile and up to planes and supercomputers which are not even to be found in Europe...I should like to stress the extent of this aid — both direct and indirect, the official and unofficial — that arrives in Israel from the United States. The Israeli budget is twenty times larger than the Syrian budget, and the military budget of Syria does not reach 7% of the Israeli military budget. It should be borne in mind that world weapons prices are the same for everyone, and there is no inexpensive weaponry, which Syria received or expensive weaponry which Israel procures for itself. All weapons are expensive and all the spare parts are sold at the same price everywhere in the world — in Moscow, Washington and London.

> The real question facing all of us with regard to peace, and I mean genuine peace as Asad's Syria understands it, is: will a peace of this kind allow Israel to expand and establish a 'Greater Israel'? I believe that a war could better assist it to achieve this goal, since there is no military balance between the Arabs and Israel. However, if we turn military confrontation into political, economic, trade and cultural competition, we will neutralize the power of the military weapons that Israel has at its disposal, and thus the result of competition of this sort could be better for us....A situation of peace transforms this conflict into political, ideological, trade and economic conflict, in which we could be in the preferred position....If the Israelis are not prepared to return the occupied lands to their legitimate owners,

they are sending a message to the Arabs that the conflict between us and them is a conflict of existence and not a conflict of borders. In any case, the Israelis hold the concept of a conflict of existence and they treat the Arabs like Indians who have to be annihilated.[176]

After his address, Shar' was asked: "In your address, does not the use of terms such as 'a confrontation between cultures and civilizations that is in the future to replace the military confrontation (between Israel and the Arabs)' create a kind of recognition of the rights of the Zionist movement over Palestine, and does it not clash with the principles of the Ba'th Party?" Shar''s answer was edifying:

> The Ba'th Party contends that the return of all of Palestine is a long-term strategic aim that will not be able to be realized in one stage...Even in the thinking of the Ba'th Party, there is a differentiation between the various stages of the struggle for the liberation of Palestine...According to this differentiation, the first stage is the return of the occupied Arab lands and the ensuring of the permanent national rights of the Palestinian Arab people.[177]

Despite expectations, the two sides failed to achieve a breakthrough, either in Washington on 15–16 December 1999, or in Shepherdstown, Virginia, on 3–10 January 2000. The Syrians apparently arrived at the talks in the hope, probably abetted by the American mediators, that the Israeli side would say the magic words: "withdrawal to the 4 June 1967 line." However, the Israeli side was in no hurry to grant this wish. Even when Israel expressed readiness to withdraw to the 4 June line, what remained unclear to the Syrians was the motive underlying Israel's newfound flexibility, and where the line actually was in Israel's view. During the Washington talks, the Syrians agreed to Israel's demand that the talks focus on setting an agenda for future negotiations. But in Shepherdstown, they rejected the Israeli demand that discussion of the demarcation of the 4 June line be preceded by a discussion about the other components of the peace talks. Following the first round of talks in Shepherdstown, the Syrians announced that they would not continue the negotiations so long as Israel refused to discuss the demarcation of the 4 June line first.[178]

A final effort to get the talks moving was made by the Americans in a meeting between Clinton and Asad in Geneva on 26 March. The mood in both Jerusalem and Damascus on the eve of the meeting was optimistic, apparently deriving from the assumption that the American and Syrian leaders would not have agreed to meet without first ensuring the chances for success of their encounter.[179] During the meeting, Clinton presented Asad with a proposal on behalf of Israeli prime minister Barak designed to extricate the negotiations from the impasse they had reached. The proposal was based on Barak's readiness in principle to accept the 4 June line as the future border between Israel and Syria, but in return, a demand for changes in the line, so that Israel would retain sovereignty over the entire northeastern shore of the Sea of Galilee. Thus Barak demanded an area covering several hundred meters east of the shore, beyond the ten meters that had given the British mandatory government in Palestine control over the sea. He was, however, prepared to leave Hamat Gader (al-Hima) in the hands of the Syrians.[180]

In a later interview, Barak said he had reason to assume that the Syrians would accept the compromise proposal regarding the demarcation of the 4 June line. Israeli sources hinted that Foreign Minister Shar' had led the Americans to believe that Syria would demonstrate some flexibility on this issue. According to Barak:

We had gained [this] impression...not because we had conducted any seances in the evenings there [in Shepherdstown], but rather because that was what the Americans believed, according to what they had been told. We had reason to think that the Syrians understood that Israeli sovereignty over the waters included a strip of ten or thirty or seventy meters from the water, while we believed that we needed several hundred meters. However, at the meeting in Geneva, it became clear that Asad was not prepared to accept even that. Clinton told me that at the very beginning of the meeting he had told Asad that Israel expected to control the shore, and Asad immediately reacted sharply. In other words, that the Syrians were not prepared [for this]. Clinton then said to Shar', "Listen, we understood differently," and Shar' squirmed and stammered.[181]

Indeed, within the first five minutes of the Clinton-Asad summit, it was clear that difficulties had arisen. Asad refused to listen to the compromise proposal presented on behalf of Barak, declaring that Syria demanded the northeastern shore of the Sea of Galilee, and thereby water rights in the sea. Asad also told Clinton that the northeastern shore had been in Syrian hands prior to the Six Day War, and that he himself had swum in the waters of the sea, had fished there and eaten its fish. He informed Clinton that as far back as the time of Salah al-Din, the Sea of Galilee had been Arab and Muslim.[182] This signaled the summit's failure. Thereafter, the Syrian media began voicing explicit demands for the northeastern shore of the Sea of Galilee and partnership in its waters, escalating the rhetoric of the demands to a point from which Syria would find it difficult to retreat in the future.

With the conclusion of the summit, the American president declared that the ball was in the Syrian court and that he awaited responses from Damascus to the proposals presented to them on behalf of Barak. When the answers arrived, Clinton termed them inadequate.[183]

Israeli sources attributed the failed effort to make peace at that time to Asad's state of health. According to this explanation, he was unable to function, to make decisions, or to show the necessary flexibility, mainly because of the feeling that his days were numbered. His primary impetus was ensuring his son Bashshar's succession.[184]

Following the failure of the Geneva summit, officials in Israel and the US promptly laid the Syrian track to rest. The Israeli government made an official and binding decision to withdraw its forces from South Lebanon, a move that Barak had postponed so long as negotiations with Syria were in progress. He had planned to use the issue as a bargaining lever in the anticipated public debate in Israel over the question of a peace agreement with Syria. Until then, he had avoided arousing suspicions in Syria about his intention to withdraw Israeli forces from Lebanon so as not to foil the Israeli-Syrian negotiations.

With the withdrawal of the Israeli forces from South Lebanon on 24 May, Syrian and Lebanese leaders announced that they had no intention of policing Israel's norther border. Israel, they warned, had to take into account that resistance to it would continue even after the withdrawal. Israel could ensure quiet on its northern border only if it reached an agreement with Syria.[185] Israeli sources thought that Syria or Hizballah might incite Palestinians living in Lebanon to perpetrate acts against Israel.[186] Several Israeli leaders, including Chief of Staff Shaul Mofaz and Prime Minister Barak himself, warned that if this occurred, a stiff response would be directed at Syrian targets in Lebanon. Thus, the optimistic forecasts of an imminent Israeli-Syria peace agreement were replaced by fears of a rapid deterioration in the situation, possibly leading to an all-out confrontation between Israel and Syria.[187]

With the passing of Hafiz al-Asad on 10 June 2000, exactly thirty-three years after he had lost the Golan Heights to Israel on 10 June 1967, all eyes turned to Bashshar. The conventional wisdom was that Bashshar would need some time to stabilize his rule at home before he turned his attention to renewing the peace process. Yet, promoting the peace process might prove to be a necessary and even vital step if Bashshar was to extricate Syria from its political isolation, and especially from its economic difficulties. Support for this assessment was to be found in reports from Damascus in July indicating that Bashshar was prepared to renew negotiations with Israel, although he demanded an Israeli withdrawal to the 4 June 1967 border.[188]

However, the intifada, which broke out in early October, pushed aside the possibility of the renewal of the Israeli-Syrian negotiations, at least temporarily. Bashshar chose to adopt a strong anti-Israel policy and to pursue a line calling for the continuation of the struggle, albeit not a comprehensive military struggle, against Israel. In his address at the summit of Arab leaders in Cairo in October (see chapter on inter-Arab relations), he stated that "Syria's aim is to establish a peace of the strong."[189] Demonstrations of support for the intifada in Damascus and elsewhere reflected a deep commitment in the Syrian population to the Palestinian issue. According to foreign observers Syria could be hampered from renewing negotiations with Israel so long as the intifada continued. Moreover, Hizballah, under the aegis of the intifada, renewed its activities against the Israeli northern border region. According to Israeli sources, Syria was encouraging Hizballah activity, a policy that showed Bashshar's lack of experience and maturity, as it could lead to a confrontation between Syria and Israel.[190]

APPENDIX I: THE SYRIAN GOVERNMENT
(March 2000)

Post	*Incumbent*
Prime Minister	Muhammad Mustafa Miru
Deputy Prime Minister and	
Defense Minister	Mustafa Talas
Deputy Prime Minister for Welfare Affairs	Muhammad Naji 'Atari
Deputy Prime Minister for Economic Affairs	Khalid Ra'd
Minister of Foreign Affairs	Faruq al-Shar'
Minister of Interior	Muhammad Hirba
Minister of Economy and Foreign Trade	Muhammad al-'Imadi
Minister of State for Foreign Affairs	Nasir Qaddur
Minister of Finance	Muhammad Khalid al-Mahayani
Minister of Health	Muhammad Iyyad al-Shatti
Minister of Agriculture and	
Agricultural Improvement	As'ad Mustafa
Minister of Communication	Radwan Maratini
Minister of Housing and Utilities	Hisham al-Safadi
Minister of Electricity	Munib bin As'ad Sa'im

Minister of Religious Trusts	Muhammad bin 'Abd al-Ra'uf
Minister of Oil and Natural Resources	Muhammad Mahir bin Husni Jamal
Minister of Local Government	Salam al-Yasin
Minister of Information	'Adnan 'Umran
Minister of Presidential Affairs	Haytham Duwayhi
Minister of Construction and Building	Nihad Mushantat
Minister of Culture	Maha Qanut
Minister of State	Hasan al-Nuri
Minister of Tourism	Qasim Miqdad
Minister of Education	Mahmud al-Sayyid
Minister of State for Environment	Faruq al-'Adli
Minister of Justice	Nabil al-Khatib
Minister of State for Planning Affairs	'Isam al-Za'im
Minister of Higher Education	Hasan Risha
Minister of Transportation	Mukrim 'Ubayd
Minister of State for Governmental Affairs	Mufdi Sayfu
Minister of Social Affairs and Labor	Bari'a al-Qudsi
Minister of Supply and Domestic Trade	Usama Ma al-Barid
Minister of State	Ihsan Sharita
Minister of Industry	Ahmad Hamu
Minister of Irrigation	Taha al-Atrash
Minister of State	Makhul Abu Hamida

APPENDIX II: THE BA'TH PARTY REGIONAL COMMAND AND CENTRAL COMMITTEE (June 2000)

Regional Command
Bashshar al-Asad, 'Abdallah al-Ahmar, 'Abd al-Halim Khaddam, Sulayman Qaddah, Muhammad Zuhayr Masharqa, 'Abd al-Qadir Qaddura, Fa'iz al-Nasir, Ahmad Dighram, Mustafa Talas, Walid Hamdun, Muhammad Mustafa Miru, Muhammad Naji al-'Atari, Faruq al-Shar', Salam al-Yasin, Ibrahim Hunaydi, Faruq Abu al-Shamat, Ghiyyath Barakat, Walid al-Buz, Majid Shudud, Muhammad Sa'id Bakhtayan, Muhammad al-Husayn

Central Committee
Bashshar al-Asad, 'Abdallah al-Ahmar, Sulayman Qaddah, 'Abd al-Halim Khaddam, Muhammad Zuhayr Masharqa, 'Abd al-Qadir Qaddura, Fa'iz al-Nasir; Ahmad Dighram, Walid Hamdun, 'Izz al-Din Bashir, Sa'id Hamadi, Muhammad Mustafa Miru, Muhammad Naji al-'Atari, Faruq al-Shar', Walid al-Buz, Mustafa Talas, 'Abd al-Muhsin bin 'Abd al-Razziq, Ghiyyath Barakat, Faruq Abu al-Shamat, Ibrahim Hunaydi, Salam al-Yasin, Muhammad Sa'id Bakhtayan, Majid Shuddud, Sulayman al-Qadi, 'Ali Aslan, Hasan Turkamani, 'Abd al-Rahman al-Sayyad, Faruq Ibrahim 'Isa, Ibrahim Safi, Ahmad 'Abd al-Nabi, Tawfiq Jalul, 'Ali Habib, 'Adnan Badr Hasan, Hasan Khalil, Mahmud

'Ammar, Kamal Mahfuz, Ibrahim Huwayji, Mahir al-Asad, Manaf Talas, 'Abdallah Ghalyun, 'Ali al-Khuri, Muhammad Hirba, Hasan Risha, Mahmud al-Sayyid, 'Adnan 'Umran, Nabil al-Khatib, Ahmad al-Hamu, Mustafa al-'Ayid, Sa'ad Bakkur, Bathina Shu'ban, Hind Hitti Tani, Ilham al-'Ali, Yusra al-Tawil, Najah Musa al-Sitt, Nahida Qassas, Jamila Jazza, Sana 'Abara, Julya Mikha'il, Hifa Safr, Qamr Ibrahim Muhammad, Maha Shabiru, Shahnaz Fakush, Siham al-Sa'igh, Harbiyya al-Bida, 'Ala al-Din 'Abidin, Faysal Qasim, Subhi Hamida, Nabil 'Umran, Sa'id al-Ahili, Yunis Baghut, Safi Abudan, Ahmad Dashu, Ibrahim Husayn, Rafiq Haddad, As'ad al-'Isa, Salah Kanj, Sulayman al-Nasir, Muhammad Za'al al-Musa, 'Imad al-Asad, Najib Ghazawi, Khayr al-'Ayn al-Sayyid, Muhammad Ayyub, 'Abd al-Qadir al-Husayn, Khalid Salama, Muhammad Ibrahim al-'Ali, 'Abd al-Karim Mustafa Haydar, Sami al-Salih, Ghazi Khadra.

NOTES

For the place and frequency of publications cited here, and for the full name of the publication, news agency, radio station or monitoring service where an abbreviation is used, please see "List of Sources." Only in the case of more than one publication bearing the same name is the place of publication noted here. However, all references to *al-Thawra* and *al-Ba'th* are to the Damascus dailies.

1. See Eyal Zisser, "Will Bashshar al-Asad Last?," *MEQ*, Vol. 7, No. 3, pp. 3-12; *al-Hayat*, 5, 25 December; *al-Nahar*, 13 December 2000.
2. R. Damascus, 2 December; *Tishrin*, 3 December 2000.
3. Syrian TV, 3, 10 June 2000.
4. *Ha'aretz*, 1 May; *al-Quds al-'Arabi*, 29 May 2000.
5. *Ha'aretz*, 6 March 2000.
6. *Al-Safir*, 13 June 2000.
7. *Tishrin*, 16 May 2000.
8. Reuters, 6 February; *al-Quds al-'Arabi*, 14 February 2000.
9. AP, 7 March; *al-Hayat*, 8 March 2000.
10. SANA, 11 March; see also *al-Hayat*, 21 March 2000.
11. R. Damascus, 11 March 2000.
12. *Al-Usbu' al-'Arabi*, 22 May 2000.
13. SANA, 10 May; *al-Ba'th*, 15 May 2000.
14. *Al-Hayat*, 22 May 2000.
15. Reuters, 24 June; SANA, 25 June 2000.
16. *Al-Quds al-'Arabi*, 22 May 2000.
17. *Al-Hayat*, 6, 7 June 2000.
18. *Al-Watan*, 26 July 2000.
19. AFP, 24 June 2000.
20. *Al-Hayat*, 25 April 2000.
21. Syrian TV, 10 June 2000.
22. R. Damascus, 11 June; *al-Hayat*, 12 June 2000.
23. Syrian TV, 11 June 2000.
24. R. Damascus, 25 June 2000.
25. *Tishrin*, 10 July 2000.
26. Syrian TV, 12 July; *Tishrin*, 13 July 2000.
27. *NYT*, 10 July; *al-Hayat*, 13 July 2000.
28. *Tishrin*, 19 July 2000.
29. See *IHT*, 13 June; *al-Wafd*, 12 June; al-Jazira TV, 12 June 2000.
30. *Yedi'ot Aharonot*, 23 June 2000.

31. *Al-Sharq al-Awsat*, 30 July 2000.
32. *Al-Ahram*, 15 July 2000.
33. BBC Monitoring, 13 June 2000.
34. *Al-Hayat*, 13 July 2000.
35. ANN TV, 30 July 2000.
36. BBC Monitoring, 13 June 2000.
37. *Al-Ra'y al-'Amm*, 22 December 2000.
38. *Al-Ba'th*, 14, 22 May; *al-Hayat*, 22 May 2000.
39. *Al-Safir*, 17 June; see also Hanna Batatu, *Syria's Peasantry, the Descendants of its Lesser Rural Notables, and Their Politics* (Princeton, New Jersey: Princeton University Press, 1999), p. 178.
40. *Al-Safir*, 17 June 2000.
41. R. Damascus, 18 June 2000.
42. SANA, 20 June; *Tishrin*, 21 June 2000.
43. SANA, *Tishrin*, 6 October 2000.
44. *Al-Safir*, 26 July; *al-Watan*, 19 August 2000.
45. *Al-Hayat*, 19 June 2000.
46. *Al-Hayat*, 16 July 2000.
47. AFP, 6 May; *al-Hayat*, 9 May 2000.
48. SANA, 22 November 2000.
49. *Al-Hayat*, 18 November; *al-Watan*, 24 November 2000.
50. *Al-Ittihad* (Abu Dhabi), 15 September 2000.
51. *Al-Ra'y al-'Amm*, 15 November 2000.
52. *Al-Hayat*, 2 September 2000.
53. *Al-Wasat*, 19 December; R. Monte Carlo, 23 December 2000.
54. *Al-Nahar*, 9 November 2000.
55. *Al-Ba'th*, 22 November 2000.
56. *Al-Hayat*, 27 September; *al-Safir*, 27 September 2000.
57. *Al-Hayat*, 29 September 2000.
58. *Al-Ba'th*, 14 September 2000.
59. *Tishrin*, 12 September 2000.
60. *Tishrin*, 6 November 2000.
61. *Al-Safir*, 7 December 2000.
62. *Al-Watan*, 20 November 2000.
63. BBC Monitoring, 23 June;AFP, 26 June; *al-Thawra*, 17 July 2000.
64. Al-Jazira TV, 8 February; *al-Majd*, 26 June 2000.
65. *Al-Majd*, 26 June, 24 July 2000.
66. Syrian TV, 10 June, 10 July, 28 December 2000.
67. *Al-Hayat*, 25 December 2000.
68. AP, 4 January 2001.
69. *Al-Sharq al-Awsat*, 2 January 2001.
70. *Al-Quds al-'Arabi*, 23 August 2000.
71. *Al-Quds al-'Arabi*, 22 July 2000.
72. *Al-Nahar*, 9, 12 November; AFP, 11, 12 November 2000.
73. *Al-Hayat*, 19 December; *al-Safir*, 20 December 2000.
74. *CR*, Syria, 3rd quarter, p. 19
75. Ibid.
76. *Al-Safir*, 21 June; *al-Hayat*, 16 December 2000.
77. SANA, 28 November; *al-Thawra*, 3 December 2000.
78. SANA, 30 July 2000.
79. *Al-Ba'th*, 3 December 2000.
80. Reuters, 18 January 2000.
81. Reuters, 9 April; *Tishrin*, 16 May 2000.
82. AP, 31 December 2000.

83. R. Damascus, 5 December 2000.
84. *Syria Times*, 26 April; *al-Ba'th*, 14 May 2000.
85. *Al-Safir*, 9 December 2000.
86. *Tishrin*, 13 August 2000.
87. SANA, 25 August 2000.
88. *Tishrin*, 20 April 2000.
89. SANA, 8 October 2000.
90. *Tishrin*, 31 October; *al-Thawra*, 5 November 2000.
91. *Al-Ba'th*, 7 July; *Tishrin*, 10 September 2000.
92. *Tishrin*, 10 September; *al-Mustaqbal*, 18 September 2000.
93. *Tishrin*, 3 December 2000.
94. *Al-Safir*, 1 December 2000.
95. *Al-Hayat*, 5 June; *The Daily Star*, 9 October 2000.
96. *Tishrin*, 18 October 2000.
97. *Yedi'ot Aharonot*, 31 March 2000.
98. *Al-Hayat*, 27 April 2000.
99. *Ha'aretz*, 14 June; AFP, 17 June 2000.
100. *NYT*, 30 April; *Ha'aretz*, 1 May 2000.
101. Abu Dhabi TV, 2 May 2000.
102. *LAT*, 10 October 2000.
103. AFP, 7 October 2000.
104. *Al-Hayat*, 8 December 2000.
105. *Al-Thawra*, 17 December; see also *Tishrin*, 17 December 2000.
106. *Syria Times*, 25 November 2000.
107. *Al-Thawra*, 28 November 2000.
108. *Al-Hayat*, 14 October; SANA, 31 October 2000.
109. *Al-Ba'th*, 23 April 2000.
110. Syrian TV, 13 June 2000.
111. *Al-Hayat*, 16 December 2000.
112. Syrian TV, 26 May 2000.
113. Syrian TV, 15 November; *al-Hayat*, 31 November 2000.
114. *Al-Hayat*, 22, 23 October 2000.
115. Syrian TV, 15 November 2000.
116. *Al-Quds al-'Arabi*, 6 April 2000.
117. Reuters, 22 January; *al-Quds al-'Arabi*, 6 April; Syrian TV, 13 June 2000.
118. *Al-Thawra*, 2 October; *Tishrin*, 22 October 2000.
119. *Al-Khalij*, 19 March 2000.
120. *Ha'aretz*, 22 October 2000, 22 March 2001.
121. *Al-Thawra*, 4 June; *al-Nahar*, 6 June 2000.
122. *Al-Usbu' al-'Arabi*, 4 September 2000.
123. *Al-Hayat*, 22 December 2000.
124. Syrian TV, 21 May; R. Amman, 19 July 2000.
125. *Al-Majd*, 22, 26 June 2000.
126. *Al-Watan*, 29 July 2000.
127. *Al-Ra'y* (Amman), 27 April 2000.
128. SANA, 19 October 2000.
129. *Al-Hayat*, 1 April 2000.
130. R. Damascus, 25 October 2000.
131. SANA, 13 June 2000.
132. *Al-Thawra*, 18 May; R. Monte Carlo, 6 August 2000.
133. *Al-Ba'th*, 13 August 2000.
134. *Al-Hayat*, 30 August 2000.
135. AP, 10 October; Syrian TV, 1 November 2000.
136. *Al-Hayat*, 1 November; *al-Sharq al-Awsat*, 6 November 2000.

137. *Al-Hayat,* 20 February; *al-Zaman,* 26 July 2000.
138. *Al-Hayat,* 20 February 2000.
139. R. Monte Carlo, 13 June 2000.
140. Reuters, 29 August; KUNA, 4 September 2000.
141. Reuters, 12 November 2000.
142. R. Damascus, 24 December 2000.
143. Reuters, 13 December 2000; Israeli TV Channel 1, 6, 12 March 2001; see also *Tishrin,* 19 December 2000.
144. R. Damascus, 11 June; *al-Hayat,* 12 June 2000.
145. *Al-Nahar,* 22 March, 24 May 2000.
146. *Al-Nahar,* 22 August 2000.
147. Lebanese Broadcasting TV, 20 September; *MM,* 21 September 2000.
148. *Al-Hayat,* 22 April, 4 November; *al-Nahar,* 28 August 2000.
149. AFP, 5, 7 November; *al-Hayat,* 10 November 2000.
150. AFP, 7 November; *al-Safir,* 11 December 2000.
151. *The Daily Star,* 14 November 2000.
152. *Tishrin,* 12 December; *al-Sharq al-Awsat,* 16, 29 December 2000.
153. *Al-Nahar,* 18 November; *The Daily Star,* 23 November; *al-Safir,* 24 November; R. Monte Carlo, 7 December 2000.
154. *Al-Mustaqbal,* 18 November; *al-Nahar,* 26 November 2000.
155. AFP, 22 April; *Ha'aretz,* 25 April; *al-Nahar,* 29 November; BBC Monitoring, 1 December 2000.
156. R. Monte Carlo, *al-Nahar,* 25 November 2000.
157. *Al-Nahar,* 25 November 2000.
158. AFP, 7 October; *Tishrin,* 22 October 2000.
159. Lebanese TV, 24 April; *al-Safir,* 13 May 2000.
160. MENA, 13 June 2000.
161. R. Damascus, 13 June, 27 September 2000.
162. R. Damascus, 3 November 2000.
163. *Al-Hayat,* 7 December; *TDN,* 17 December 2000.
164. *The Independent,* 17 July 2000.
165. AFP, 10 October 2000.
166. TDN, 17 December 2000.
167. *Al-Hayat,* 9 January; *Jomhuri-ye Islami,* 10 January 2000.
168. Iranian TV, 13 June 2000.
169. Syrian TV, 13 June 2000.
170. R. Tehran, 13 November 2000.
171. *Ha'aretz,* 25 December 2000.
172. CNN, 8 December 1999; for the public reaction to Clinton's announcement, see interview with Itamar Rabinovich, Israeli TV, Channel 1, 9 December 1999.
173. See *Ha'aretz,* 10, 17 December; *Yedi'ot Aharonot,* 10, 31 December 1999.
174. *Al-Usbu' al-Adabi,* 12 December; see also 'Uqla 'Ursan, "Bidun Musafaha" (without shaking hands), *al-Usbu' al-'Adabi,* 18 December 1999.
175. *Al-Safir,* 13 February 2000.
176. Ibid.
177. Ibid.
178. *Ma'ariv,* 24, 31 December 1999.
179. *Ha'aretz,* 24, 31 March; see also Israeli TV, Channel 2, 22 March 2000.
180. See *WP,* 29 March; see also *Ma'ariv,* 31 March 2000.
181. See Barak's interview to *Ha'aretz,* 19 May 2000.
182. *Al-Nahar,* 28 March; see also Mustafa Talas' interview to R. al-Sharq, 10 July 2000.
183. CNN, 28 March; MENA, 31 March 2000.
184. Zisser, *MEQ,* Vol. 7, No. 3, pp. 3-12.
185. See *al-Ba'th,* 20 April; *al-Hayat,* 27 April 2000.

186. See interview with Gen. Amos Malka, head of the Israeli military intelligence published in *Ha'aretz*, 31 May 2000.

187. See *Ha'aretz*, 24, 25 May 2000.

188. See *al-Hayat*, 14 July, Reuters, 19 July 2000.

189. See Bashshar's speech at the Arab summit in Cairo, *Tishrin*, 22 October 2000.

190. See *Ha'aretz*, 29 December; *Yedi'ot Aharonot*, 15 December 2000.

Tunisia

(Al-Jumhuriyya al-Tunisiyya)

DANIEL ZISENWINE

The most significant event in Tunisia in the year 2000 was the death in April of Habib Bourguiba, Tunisia's first president and leader of the national struggle for independence. Regarded as the country's founding father, Bourguiba had been involved in virtually every political and constitutional development since Tunisia attained independence in 1956. He was credited with responsibility for many Tunisian achievements, primarily in the social arena. Since the 1987 bloodless coup that removed Bourguiba from office, he had receded from public life and was less familiar to younger Tunisians. Nevertheless, his death at the age of ninety-six caused many Tunisians to reflect on the current situation and future direction of their country.

This introspection occurred amidst palpable signs of public discontent and increased criticism of the regime. Tunisians seemed to have lost confidence in government policies, and various circles exhibited growing impatience over the lack of civil liberties. These sentiments did not lead, however, to widespread action against the government, which continued to rule with impunity, but it seemed clear that the general popularity of the government had eroded, and that it would have to make an effort to regain support among the increasingly impatient populace.

Meanwhile the government gave little indication that it was unduly concerned about its public standing, though it did seem somewhat surprised by the extent of disenchantment. Despite its professed intentions, the government granted little scope for debate and dissent against official policies. The media remained tightly controlled although no official censorship existed, and the country leaders expressed support of a livelier media. Security forces frequently harassed and impeded the free functioning of independent local human rights organizations and activists. Several measures taken by the government in the later part of 2000 suggested that it might be loosening its tight grip over society. Signs that the government genuinely intended to inaugurate a new era of tolerance and greater pluralism, however, were few and far between.

Tunisian opposition parties had no chance during the year to serve as an alternative ideological and organizational framework to the government. They remained locked in internal struggles, and were largely unknown to most Tunisians. Local elections, held in May, reflected this reality, as candidates of the ruling Rassemblement constitutionnel démocratique (RCD; Hizb al-Tajammu' al-Dimuqrati) maintained complete control over municipal councils despite a revised election law aimed at strengthening the opposition.

The economy recorded positive growth rates, larger foreign investments and low inflation. It was unclear, however, whether these figures would be able to sustain an increasingly authoritarian regime and a restless population.

Tunisian foreign relations reflected a mixed record in 2000. Ties with other North

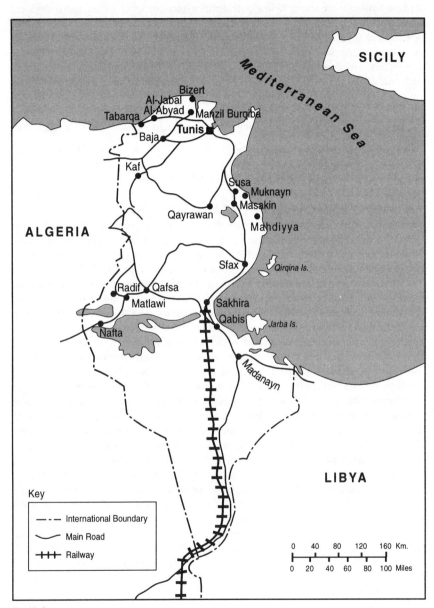

Tunisia

African nations were strengthened considerably, although efforts to revitalize regional frameworks such as the Arab Maghrib Union (AMU) failed to yield substantial results. A similarly high level of coordination was maintained with other Arab countries, especially within the context of the Arab-Israeli peace process. Relations with Europe were affected by international criticism of the Tunisian human rights situation. Relations with traditional allies such as France became noticeably chillier; accordingly, Tunis refocused its diplomacy on contacts with other European countries. Ties with the US remained good and were less troubled by the human rights situation. In addition, several initiatives were undertaken to bolster ties with regions outside Tunisia's traditional diplomatic arena.

INTERNAL AFFAIRS

ANTI-GOVERNMENT FERMENT AND PROTESTS

President Zayn al-'Abidin Ben 'Ali, in his thirteenth year in power and his last five-year term according to the Tunisian constitution, started the year in a strengthened position. He had emerged from the November 1999 presidential elections with a renewed mandate to carry out his political programs and economic initiatives (see *MECS* 1999, pp. 575–78). With the legalized opposition parties limited in their ability to present a serious ideological alternative to the ruling regime (see below), government powers seemed almost unrestrained. But 2000 was less than tranquil for Ben 'Ali and his government. For the first time in more than a decade, instances of overt public discontent and protest against the government were reported. Although these incidents were limited in scope, they highlighted the need for the country's leaders to reconsider some of their policies.

The first public outcry against the government occurred in early February. It involved a protest by taxi drivers in Tunis against new traffic regulations. The striking drivers were reportedly wary of what they described as the zeal by which law enforcement officials implemented these regulations, a situation they described as "unacceptable." The government, to the drivers' satisfaction, accepted their demands; Transport Minister Hassine Chouk announced that the implementation of the new laws would be postponed.[1] Thus ended what was, for Tunisia, a highly unusual three-day strike. But no sooner had the dispute been settled than another series of protests, more substantial in scope, erupted. These protests occurred in the southern part of the country, and reportedly involved high school students in the cities of Zarzis and Jerba. Protests later spread to Gabes, Sfax and Gafsa; frustrated unemployed citizens also joined the students. According to various reports, the demonstrations broke out following rumors about a possible change in the format of high school matriculation exams. As the southern region was experiencing economic difficulties, additional rumors about an increase in the prices of gasoline and bread also fueled these protests.[2] The government, for its part, denied all rumors of an increase in food prices.

This was the first time since 1984 that Tunisians had taken to the streets to protest against economic and social measures. Eyewitnesses reported that protestors blocked roads and closed public buildings. Tunisian security authorities reacted swiftly, and government sources minimized the events, which Ben 'Ali considered "unacceptable to rational people."[3] According to reports circulated abroad, hundreds of demonstrators were arrested as the authorities quelled the disturbances. The city of Zarzis was transformed, according to one report, into a "city under siege."⁴ Several dozen high school students were brought to trial and accused of damaging public buildings and "spreading false rumors." It was later reported that some of the arrested students had been released after their parents signed written pledges to the police guaranteeing that the students would refrain from future protest activities. Many students declared that they had been poorly treated and subjected to violence while in police custody. The Tunis-based Conseil national pour les libertés en Tunisie (CNLT), a dissident human rights group, denounced the arrests and called for the students' immediate release. Dozens of arrested youths were later sentenced to prison terms, which automatically implied their dismissal from universities and obviated the possibility of any future work in the public sector.⁵

Another incident reflecting dissatisfaction with the government occurred less than two months later during funeral services for the late president Bourguiba. According to eyewitness accounts, during the funeral procession bystanders chanted slogans against Ben 'Ali's government (see below).

Another indication of the growing impatience with the regime was a commentary by Tunisian journalist Ryad Ben Fadhel, which was published in May in the French daily *Le Monde*. Ben Fadhel, whose family was part of the ruling élite and considered close to the regime, stressed that Tunisia needed a "new deal" and a change in government policies. He warned Ben 'Ali against clinging to power by not adhering to the constitution, which limited the president to two terms. In what was arguably the most serious incident in 2000 related to anti-government activism, Ben Fadhel was shot three days later near his suburban Tunis home (see below). After the attack on Ben Fadhel, the government appeared to review some of the policies it pursued against its critics.⁶

The government-controlled electronic media and the Tunisian press rarely commented on these incidents. Their significance lay in the fact that they did not involve traditional opposition groups such as the banned Islamists, but often included ordinary middle-class citizens, traditionally considered strong supporters of the regime, despite its shortcomings in areas such as civil liberties and human rights. Although no significant anti-government incidents were reported later in the year, many concluded that the government had lost the confidence of social and political circles that had previously supported its policies. These groups appeared interested in expanding political pluralism, which contrasted with the regime's authoritarian and uncompromising positions toward even minor forms of dissent.

THE DEATH OF HABIB BOURGUIBA

Habib Bourguiba, who led Tunisia's struggle against French colonial rule and served as the country's first president following its independence in 1956 through 1987, died on 6 April at the age of ninety-six.⁷ The ailing Bourguiba, whom Ben 'Ali removed from office in a bloodless coup in 1987 after he was declared medically unfit to govern, had spent his last years secluded in his native town of Monastir. Placed under medical and security supervision, he had receded from public life, and been hospitalized several times over the years. In early March, Bourguiba was diagnosed with a pulmonary infection and admitted to a military hospital in Tunis but was released nine days later. His condition remained poor, and in late March, the government had to dispel numerous rumors that he had died.⁸

Most Tunisians, therefore, were not surprised by the official announcement of

Bourguiba's passing. Ben 'Ali issued a personal eulogy of Bourguiba, and the government announced a seven-day national period of mourning. Ben 'Ali later spoke of Bourguiba as the "leader whom we loved so much" and highlighted the former president as a "reformer and statesman who profoundly influenced the course of our contemporary national history." He noted Bourguiba's pragmatic approach to politics and international affairs, as well as the wisdom and prudence that underpinned his policymaking.[9]

Reactions to Bourguiba's death among Tunisians varied mostly according to age. Many of the younger generation, born after his removal from office, seemed indifferent to the news. Some did indicate in newspaper interviews their appreciation of Bourguiba's social and political achievements, such as the progressive legislation enacted during his tenure that among other things secured legal equality for women. Tunisians who came of age during Bourguiba's thirty-year reign however, expressed more visceral reactions. Some were still angry at the former president's conduct during his final years in office, which were overshadowed by personal scandals among his ministers and senior aides. The memory of Bourguiba's authoritarian and capricious rule remained fresh in their minds. But many, particularly stalwarts and veteran supporters of the "Supreme Combatant" (as Bourguiba was known throughout the country), expressed profound grief upon hearing the news. They spoke of Bourguiba's role in leading Tunisia to independence and establishing a modern state, his uncompromising tenacity and his complete devotion to the country. Some also compared the current administration to that of Bourguiba's, arguing that Ben 'Ali's government had squandered many of Bourguiba's achievements. Bourguiba's ideological and political opponents, however, had little sympathy for the late president. Shaykh Rashid al-Ghannushi, exiled leader of Nahda, the banned Islamist party, criticized Bourguiba in an interview with the Qatari al-Jazira satellite television network, and accused him of being hostile to Islam.[10] In general, however, Bourguiba's popularity endured among many Tunisians. In light of their growing dissatisfaction with the government, increasing numbers questioned the fairness of the former president's removal from office and forced retirement. His death naturally increased some of the government's uncertainties regarding the regime's position toward the former president. In a theme amplified by the government-controlled media, Ben 'Ali spoke at Bourguiba's funeral about the link between the "change" (as the 1987 coup is known in Tunisia) and Bourguiba's political legacy. He attempted to emphasize the similarities between the two administrations at a time when many Tunisians nostalgically recalled the Bourguiba years. Ben 'Ali described the policies of his administration as being part of Bourguiba's legacy and as a new step in reforming the country.[11]

Nonetheless, many Tunisians were angry at the government's handling of Bourguiba's funeral. Many Tunisians were barred from participating in Bourguiba's last rites; the government sought to restrict an outpouring of mass grief for fear that it might lead to anti-government protests. The funeral also fell short in comparison to those of other Arab and North African leaders in recent years. Bourguiba's coffin was transported from Monastir to Tunis on 7 April, where it lay in state at the RCD headquarters. But access to the building was restricted, and crowds were also barred from entering Bourguiba's mausoleum in Monastir. The portrait of the former president that the authorities chose for the funeral was that of an aging Bourguiba, not the image of the younger and vibrant man who championed the struggle for independence — a choice that also angered many. To the surprise and displeasure of many, Bourguiba's internment in Monastir on 8 April was not broadcast live on Tunisian television.[12] According to reports published abroad, some bystanders viewing the funeral procession in Monastir waved signs denouncing the government and shouted slogans against Ben 'Ali, but security forces promptly silenced them. Nevertheless, a number of security officers were reportedly held responsible for the disturbances that accompanied the burial and were therefore dismissed.[13] National observance of the seven-day mourning period was also described as spotty. Dance halls and discos reportedly remained open, for example, and most soccer matches took place as if nothing had happened.

Several prominent foreign dignitaries attended Bourguiba's funeral, including French president Jacques Chirac, Algerian president 'Abd al-'Aziz Bouteflika, Yemeni president 'Ali 'Abdallah Salih, Palestinian Authority (PA) chairman Yasir 'Arafat and the crown prince of Morocco, Moulay Rachid. The limited presence of Arab leaders at the funeral was understandable, some observers commented, particularly from the radical nationalist camp, given Bourguiba's historically testy relations with several of his Arab counterparts. The absence of other Western leaders at the funeral, however, was more puzzling to some Tunisians. They noted Bourguiba's strong pro-Western policies, and were surprised, for example, that no senior American official attended.

Bourguiba was, however, eulogized throughout the world. US president Bill Clinton praised him as a "historic leader, [a] pioneer in the struggle for Tunisia's independence and its economic and social progress." Chirac spoke of him as a "true friend" who complemented Tunisia's image as a humanistic and tolerant country. 'Arafat praised Bourguiba's interest and concern for the Palestinian cause. 'Arafat characterized Bourguiba as the "pioneer of [a] realistic political school [who] achieved great accomplishments and palpable successes," noting the Palestine Liberation Organization (PLO) appreciation of the late president who received the organization after its expulsion from Lebanon following the 1982 Israeli invasion.[14]

The foment surrounding Bourguiba's death quickly subsided and left few, if any lasting marks on Tunisia's political and social landscape. In light of Bourguiba's historical centrality for modern Tunisia, and the controversies that still surrounded him, some argued that the regime could have used his death as an opportunity to foster national unity and public support of the government. Greater participation in Bourguiba's last rites, they said, could have allowed many Tunisians to rid themselves of emotions (whether negative or positive) harbored toward a leader largely responsible for Tunisia's contemporary profile. Such participation would also have allowed the populace to look to the future. Instead, the government ironically turned Bourguiba into a symbol embraced by some opposition circles. In an editorial eulogizing Bourguiba, the French newspaper *Le Monde* argued that the regime's suspicious attitude endangered the late president's heritage, which the government claimed as its ideological foundation. Hele Beji, niece of Bourguiba's ex-wife Wassila Ben 'Ammar, said that Bourguiba did not receive in his death the attention he deserved; her words accurately summarized the feelings of many Tunisians.[15]

THE STATUS OF THE OPPOSITION

Increased displays of public dissatisfaction with the government ironically did little to enhance the position of the legal opposition parties. Locked in internal squabbles, they remained weak, marginal, and ineffective. Many of the parties lacked either credible leaders or strong ideological positions. The continuing lethargy of the opposition, and the fact that the Tunisian élite largely ignored it, baffled some commentators. In recent years, a number of legislative measures had been enacted to increase the opposition's presence in parliament and municipal councils. Some analysts therefore sought to understand why, despite the government's professed interest in enhancing democracy, Tunisian politics remained so obviously anemic.

Part of the explanation for the status of the opposition lay in the parties' internal affairs. The Mouvement des démocrates socialistes (MDS; Harakat al-Dimuqratiyyin al-Ishtiraqiyyin), for example, had the largest number of opposition members in the Chamber of Deputies, but was still reeling from internal disputes that had weakened the party in previous years. As party activists sought to reconcile rival factions and restore unity, they seemed to have had little energy for other affairs. Moreover, the party chairperson, Ismail Boulehya, had adopted a moderate approach to the government, which left little room for criticism (see MECS 1997, 700–701; 1998, 600–601). MDS activists were preoccupied during the year with issues such as when to organize a general convention (that would, among other things, elect new leaders). This was eventually scheduled for March 2001.[16] Another controversy concerned Boulehya's continuing leadership. His position had been disputed since his election in 1997 (see MECS 1997, pp. 700–701), and had led many MDS veterans to quit the party in protest. As many former members and activists began to explore the option of returning, Boulehya's future as chairperson was again called into question. The returning activists were expected to steer the party toward a less conciliatory position vis-à-vis the government. Boulehya, for his part, contended that it was he who had navigated the party through a difficult period after many of its former activists had left, and he said he saw no reason to leave his post. His position for the time being seemed guaranteed, since the government was unlikely to recognize any alternative leadership chosen by only part of the MDS membership.

Other parties, such as the former communist-oriented Mouvement de la rénovation (Harakat al-Tajdid), were in a state of stagnation. The movement had not held a party convention since 1993, and its head, Muhammad Harmel, gave no indication that he was ready to step down. The Parti libéral, which had entered the Chamber of Deputies in the 1999 elections, remained the least visible on the political scene, and its new parliamentary representation did little to enhance its public standing. The Parti de l'unité populaire (PUP; Harakat al-Wahda al-Sha'biyya), whose former secretary-general, Muhammad Belhaj Amor, ran against Ben 'Ali in the 1999 presidential race (see MECS 1999, pp. 576–78), chose a new leader after Amor announced his retirement. Muhammad Bouchiha, a lawyer who had been Amor's top aide, was unanimously elected to replace him. Some PUP activists expressed regret over the unanimous vote, arguing that it did not reflect a proper democratic process. Bouchiha's main rival, Nasser Ben 'Amar, quit the race just hours before the vote, after realizing that his defeat was inevitable. Others were pleased with the vote, noting that they sought to preserve party unity and did not wish to emulate the inner disputes that had plagued the MDS.[17]

Overall, the positions of the opposition parties did not reflect significant ideological disputes with the government, a fact that weakened their public appeal. Over the past few years, the differences between the opposition and the government — if they existed at all — appeared negligible, consisting of form rather than substance. The most vociferous criticism of government policies emanated from small, illegal groups and human rights organizations, which were institutionally weaker than the mainstream opposition parties.[18]

The government legislative initiatives, which secured a larger portion of seats for the opposition in parliament and in the municipal councils, did little to elevate the status of the opposition. The mere presence of a larger number of opposition representatives in these bodies did not alter the basic reality of Tunisian politics, in which the ruling regime and its RCD party dominated political life. Opposition representatives in parliament were unable to compete with the RCD and the powerful executive; nor could they function as serious critics of government policies. The Tunisian media, which trumpeted the government agenda, paid them scant attention. Government spokespersons rarely acknowledged any opposition party or politician. This situation would not have been so perplexing to various observers had the Tunisian government not repeatedly made a point of emphasizing its commitment to democracy and political pluralism.[19] Ben 'Ali, for example, announced additional measures aimed to enhance pluralism, such as increased state funding to political parties and their publications.[20] He expressed satisfaction at the implementation of the democratic-oriented reforms, noting that there was "no ready-made model for democracy" and reiterating that democracy was an "irreversible choice" for Tunisia.[21] As in other realms, however, there was a far cry between the regime's professed intentions and the actual reality. The regime's failure to nurture a propitious climate for a truly pluralistic political system was considered the main reason for the opposition's poor standing in public life.[22] For the time being, hopes that the parties would have a greater opportunity to emerge as a viable political force after the 1999 elections, remained unrealized.

Municipal Elections

Elections for municipal councils, which took place on 28 May, were the most significant political event in Tunisia in 2000. They underscored the inherent weakness of the opposition vis-á-vis the RCD. Ben 'Ali chracterized the elections as an advancement in the country's democratic process.[23] They were conducted under a revised law that allocated at least 20% of municipal council seats to opposition parties, in an attempt to guarantee a greater share of opposition representatives in local municipal bodies (see *MECS* 1997, p. 698). As in the 1999 presidential and parliamentary elections (see *MECS* 1999, pp. 576–78), Ben 'Ali agreed to international supervision of the vote, in an attempt to highlight the elections' transparency.[24] But the vast number of municipal council seats across the country — more than 4,800 in 257 communities — made it virtually impossible for the small opposition lists to field candidates in all locales. Early initiatives to organize united lists of multiple parties did not materialize; opposition groups were able to field candidates in only sixty-two communities. Independent candidates raised the number of communities showing non-RCD lists on the ballot to eighty-two.[25]

The campaign atmosphere was described as lackluster and skeptical, with scant public interest and little suspense. Some opposition figures criticized their limited access to government-controlled radio and television networks. Similar criticisms had been voiced during the 1999 presidential and parliamentary elections; clearly little had changed as far as granting RCD competitors an equal opportunity to propagate their positions. In a bold statement, one opposition party, the liberal Rassemblement socialiste progrèssive (RSP; al-Tajjamu' al-Ishtiraqi) announced shortly before the elections that it was boycotting the vote. It was the only recognized opposition movement not represented in the Chamber of Deputies. RSP chairperson Nejib Chebbi argued that his party refused to take part in a skewed voting process that gave preference to the ruling party, and offered competitors little chance of victory.[26]

Election results were duly predictable. The RCD won the overwhelming majority (94%) of municipal council seats and maintained control of every council. Opposition and independent candidates obtained only 243 seats in local councils nationwide. The elections did little to increase the power of the opposition or alter the nature and image of Tunisian politics, which remained a far cry from the pluralistic system for which the government claimed to be striving.[27]

ISLAMIST OPPOSITION

There were no significant developments concerning the outlawed Islamist Nahda Party in 2000. The ban on the party remained intact, and little change was detected in the official position toward either its leaders or activities. Hopes for a possible dialogue between the government and Nahda, which had accompanied the release of a large number of party activists and supporters in late 1999 did not materialize (see *MECS* 1999, pp. 580–81). There were no reports of any contact between the government and the party throughout the year. Nahda leaders, including Ghannushi, continued to criticize the regime's policies from abroad.[28] A statement issued by the party following the February disturbances, for example, warned the authorities "against the danger of resorting to blind violence in their oppression of their citizens" and called upon the government to review its policies which were "driving the country toward explosion." At the same time, the party reiterated its readiness to engage in a dialogue with the authorities, and called for a general amnesty of prisoners and for the "liberation of political life" in Tunisia.[29] Government officials made no reference to Nahda's statements; given its position toward less vehement critics of the administration, there was little reason to believe that the authorities were ready to alter their uncompromising positions toward the Islamists. Throughout the year, Ghannushi remained an outspoken commentator on general Islamic affairs and politics.[30]

CIVIL LIBERTIES AND HUMAN RIGHTS

As reports of human rights violations made international headlines, foreign governments and the European Union (EU) became more involved in this issue than in previous years, much to the dismay of the Tunisian government. There was evidence that the regime had modified its troubling behavior in this area. The poor maintenance of minimal civil liberties was yet another source of public discontent, adding to the soured political atmosphere within Tunisia.

The human rights situation, coupled with reports of increased harassment of activists and dissidents, resulted in mounting international criticism. Officials denied allegations that the regime had a poor human rights record, and sought to discredit damaging reports. As in previous years, Ben 'Ali admitted that Tunisia had "never claimed perfection" in the sphere of human rights and that there was still much to be done in this area. During a visit to Portugal, Ben 'Ali responded to reporters: "Human rights are respected [in Tunisia]. We have problems, like everyone else, but that is normal." In later statements, while claiming that human rights were "at the forefront of our objectives," he also argued that "no one in the world has the right to tell others what to do, nor claim perfection in this area." Ben 'Ali denied that there were any political prisoners in Tunisia, and as in the past, he likened foreign criticism of the human rights situation to a "pretext to interfere in other people's affairs." In an even tougher stance, he contended that Tunisians participating in "anti-Tunisian campaigns abroad" were taking part in "a form of treason," which would be confronted by law.³¹ But the continuous stream of troubling reports of the regime's human rights record throughout the year suggested that very little had changed.

The Cases of Taoufik Ben Brick and Riad Ben Fadhe

The case of Tunisian journalist Taoufik Ben Brick attracted unprecedented international attention. Ben Brick, who worked as a correspondent for the French newspaper *La Croix* and other European news agencies, had previously written articles critical of the regime and been questioned by the authorities (see *MECS* 1998, p. 604). In 2000, he was again questioned for publishing articles abroad that criticized the human rights situation in Tunisia.³² The authorities also confiscated Ben Brick's passport, harassed his family and disconnected his telephone line. Ben Brick reacted on 3 April by starting a hunger strike that attracted international attention, perhaps owing to the fact that European media groups had employed him. In addition to demanding the return of his passport and the cessation of harassment against his family, he also demanded the right to continue his journalistic work freely. As Ben Brick's hunger strike continued, he received many letters of support from abroad.³³ According to his lawyer, Tunisian security authorities surrounded his residential neighborhood in an attempt to isolate him from visitors. Occasional confrontations between security forces and visitors frequently erupted. The arrest of Ben Brick's brother Jallel on 26 April, after a clash with police stationed outside Ben Brick's house, raised the level of tension even further. Jallel received a three-month prison sentence in early May, and Ben Brick continued his hunger strike while demanding his brother's immediate release. Tunisian authorities also reportedly questioned Ben Brick's close associates and relatives when, as his health deteriorated, the journalist was taken to a private medical clinic in Tunis.³⁴

Many observers viewed the government reaction to Ben Brick's articles and protest as highly disproportionate. Ben Brick's case quickly became an international cause célèbre, embraced by organizations such as the Paris-based media watch group Reporteurs sans frontières. His plight was highlighted worldwide on 3 May, the international day celebrating freedom of the press. Convinced that only the French government could cause the Tunisian regime to yield, Ben Brick's family called on Paris to intervene. In a statement read by his sister at a Paris news conference, Ben Brick criticized Jacques Chirac's support of the Ben 'Ali regime, and called on the French president to join the struggle promoting "the same liberal values embraced by France."³⁵

As Ben Brick's condition grew worse, the French government offered to fly Ben Brick to France to receive medical attention. While French authorities argued that this initiative was purely humanitarian, French officials were forced to admit that the Tunisian government actions to promote human rights were insufficient. As Tunisia's number one foreign trade partner and close European ally, France had previously been reluctant to openly criticize the Tunisian government. But Foreign Minister Hubert Vedrine called on Tunisia to make more progress in the area of human rights, while Philippe Seguin, speaker of the French National Assembly and a Tunisian native, stressed that certain Tunisian practices were no longer acceptable. As a weakened Ben Brick arrived in Paris on 4 May, all parties seemed keen on settling the affair. Ben Brick, who was heckled by security officers as he boarded the Paris-bound plane in Tunis, was warmly received by many public figures in France.

Colleagues in the Arab world and in neighboring North African countries also supported

Ben Brick. In a region with limited, if any, freedom of the press, Ben Brick's plight attracted attention, often to the dismay of governments in the region. His cause was embraced by Algerians who had enjoyed some degree of journalistic freedom in past years and were concerned that they too would ultimately suffer from similar persecutions. The Algerian daily *al-Khabar* awarded Ben Brick the newspaper's annual prize. But Algerian authorities later refused Ben Brick entry to the country. In Morocco, security forces harshly dispersed a small demonstration in support of Ben Brick.[36]

Meanwhile, the Tunisian media ignored his case. His plight did attract domestic interest, though, and provided yet another reason for anti-government ferment, this time among circles previously considered loyal to the regime. Members of the Tunisian Bar Association held a four-hour general strike on 28 May, protesting against "police aggression" encountered by several members who had attempted earlier to visit Ben Brick at his home. Although the association argued that this was not a "hostile act toward the regime," its mere existence reflected increasing dissatisfaction with government policies.

Faced with mounting criticism, especially from abroad, the security forces deployed near Ben Brick's house were removed and his telephone service restored. Government sources reported that the entire affair had been the source of consternation and tension within the security apparatus, and that several officials had been removed from their positions after criticizing the president's actions in the matter. Ben Brick continued his hunger strike, and demanded the release of his brother, who received a three-month prison sentence in early May for attacking a police officer.[37] Ben Brick ended his hunger strike on 16 May after learning that his brother's case was pending a decision before a court of appeals.[38] His brother was eventually released from prison on 18 May.

The events surrounding the shooting a few weeks later of Riad Ben Fadhel, a journalist and media executive, suggested, however, that the government had not changed its policies. Ben Fadhel was shot outside his house in a Tunis suburb just three days after publishing a critique of Ben 'Ali in the French newspaper *Le Monde*. His assailants called him a "traitor dog" before fleeing the scene. Ben Fadhel's injuries were not severe. Although he himself doubted whether high-ranking authorities had orchestrated the assassination attempt, there was little evidence of any motive other than a response to his article. The government-controlled news agency Tunis-Afrique Presse argued that his injuries were the result of a suicide attempt, allegations refuted by Ben Fadhel. He also denied that the attack was related to his business affairs.[39] Regardless of the regime's role in the incident, it appeared to alarm authorities. Ben 'Ali personally received Ben Fadhel at the presidential palace shortly after he was discharged from the hospital, and promised a full investigation of the incident.[40] While the details surrounding the attack remained unclear, the government subsequently appeared to ease its grip somewhat on some dissidents (see below).

Additional Reports of Human Rights Abuses and the Curtailment of Civil Liberties

While the Ben Brick and Ben Fadhel affairs attracted widespread international attention in 2000, other testimonies of human rights abuses abounded. These reports led the US Department of State to conclude in its annual human rights report that there was still room for "significant improvement" in this area.[41]

Two domestic human rights organizations vied for prominence in 2000. The Tunis-based Conseil national pour les libertés en Tunisie (CNLT), which still was denied official recognition (see *MECS* 1999, pp. 581–82), emerged as an important source of information. In a report, the CNLT emphasized that Tunisia was experiencing "one of the darkest periods of oppression" in its history. The report stated that any achievements of the 1970s and 1980s that advanced the cause of civil liberties had vanished, and that the concept of a free press had almost disappeared.[42] The government-recognized Ligue Tunisienne des droits de l'homme (LTDH) debated its future orientation during its conference in October. Its newly elected president, Mokhtar Trifi, considered somewhat of a radical, suggested that the LTDH could employ more aggressive tactics in the future.[43]

Throughout 2000, the distribution of several French newspapers and magazines critical of the Tunisian government (primarily *Le Monde*, *Libération*, *La Croix* and *L'Express*) was disrupted.[44] In a meeting with Tunisian journalists, Ben 'Ali explained that the government had taken these measures because *Le Monde*, in particular, had "ceased to be an objective newspaper." He argued that it did not grant the Tunisian government the chance to respond properly to allegations raised against it and therefore was "not wanted in our country." Broadcasts of the France 2 television network were also blocked.[45]

Other reports included accounts of attacks on offices of attorneys who opposed administrative obstacles that hindered their work. They were frequently denied information by court officials and given little time to defend their clients during court sessions. Telephone and postal service to their offices were often suspended without explanation, and their working conditions were described as increasingly difficult.[46] International human rights organizations accused the government of regularly abusing the judicial system by holding detainees beyond the limit of authorized detention and then falsifying arrest records. Arrested human rights activists claimed that they had been tortured into signing "confessions."[47] Families of political dissidents and human rights activists were denied passports and consequently barred from leaving the country.[48]

The Tunisian human rights situation was discussed by the EU-Tunisia Association Council, which met in Brussels in January, underscoring the fact that the EU considered it an integral part of its developing relations with Tunisia. At the meeting, the Portuguese minister of foreign affairs and acting president of the EU council stressed the importance of respecting human rights and fundamental freedoms. He noted that these issues were essential elements of the 1995 EU association agreement with Tunisia (see *MECS* 1995, pp. 636–37) and that the union would continue to take a "keen interest" in government actions involving human rights.[49]

As the year went on, the government loosened its grip somewhat and expanded the acceptable threshold of internal dissent. Several newspapers, including *Le Monde*, were allowed to resume distribution. Passports were issued to a number of critics and dissidents to whom they had previously been denied. Ben 'Ali himself emphasized that every citizen had the "inalienable right" to travel abroad. He also reiterated his desire to change the nature of the national media. In a meeting with newspaper publishers, he urged them to be more daring in their writing and to avoid any form of self-censorship: "Write as you wish. Be critical as long as what you are saying is true....We never said that everything is perfect," he said. Ben 'Ali made a similar plea to the state-owned television network, and later presented several legislative measures aimed at liberalizing the press code.[50] Very little change was evident, however, as the media continued to adhere to the government agenda.

Several opposition figures reported later in the year that police harassment against them had subsided, but others were arrested and questioned by the police. It was difficult to assess whether these often-inconsistent measures indicated a significant change in government policies, or whether they were only slight modifications aimed at curtailing international criticism and calming internal ferment.[51] Despite various statements, the regime clearly had every intention of maintaining its control over society, and its human rights and civil liberties policies were expected to remain the focus of discussion both within and outside the country.

THE ECONOMY

The Tunisian economy, which recorded robust growth, increased foreign investments and strong macroeconomic performance, was the source of both governmental pride and concern. Ben 'Ali proudly noted the increase in Tunisians' individual income, the drop in inflation, and the shrinking poverty rate inside the country.[52] At the same time, concern grew over potential economic and social unrest. This was in the wake of growing public disenchantment with government policies, a mood that was also fueled by economic factors. "Providing a stable economic environment" was, accordingly, at the top of Ben 'Ali's economic plan.[53] Other government priorities included increasing employment, encouraging foreign investments, continuing fiscal reform, and developing infrastructure.[54]

The Tunisian 1995 Economic Association Agreement with the EU, whose gradual implementation continued during the year, was deemed an important springboard for achieving these goals. The agreement involved a gradual removal of tariff barriers in preparation for the opening of European markets to Tunisian exports, and vice versa (see *MECS* 1996, pp. 685–87; 1997, pp. 712–13; 1998, pp. 611–12) and was expected to propel the Tunisian economy into a new stage of development. Although the government implemented the agreement only in order to cushion expected difficulties, some members of the Tunisian business community argued that the pace in removing tariff barriers was still too fast and that more time was needed to prepare for direct competition with European imports. At the same time, however, international financial organizations were urging the government to move even faster at exposing Tunisia to foreign imports. These bodies did not, however, overlook the important challenges involved in this process. The directors of the World Bank, for example, contended that to meet those challenges, Tunisia would have to create new jobs by facilitating foreign investments and developing the private sector.[55]

The privatization policy, which had accelerated in recent years, gained additional momentum. The sell-off of state-owned companies now included some "strategic" industries (such as electricity production) that the government had previously been reluctant to privatize. Nonetheless, this increased pace still fell short of promises made by official rhetoric. In an attempt to link privatization to the creation of new jobs, potential buyers of firms were also chosen on the basis of their plans for developing the business. This was part of Ben 'Ali's attempt to reduce unemployment and guarantee new jobs. The official unemployment rate was 15.4 %, but was considered to be significantly higher, varying by region and reaching 25% in the southwest.[56] Among the firms put up for sale in 2000 were cement factories and a sugar refinery. Official figures disclosed that forty-one state-owned enterprises had been sold since October 1998, with more sales expected.[57] Reluctance to liberalize the economy at an intensified pace, and government desire to avoid social and economic distress spurred an increase in the minimum wages in early May.[58]

Another priority was developing the national infrastructure. Construction plans for several new highways were presented; work on a new highway connecting Tunis with Bizerete had already begun. Other infrastructure projects included continued work on the Tunisian telecommunication network. Telephone density was still considered low. The number of Internet users had reached 250,000 (roughly less than 4% of the population), according to official statements. In an attempt to promote Internet access, the government announced a reduction of the value added tax imposed on Internet services.[59]

Overall, Tunisia's economic performance won good marks from international financial and banking institutions. The US credit agency Standard and Poor's praised Tunisia's economic growth and low inflation rates, and the economic outlook at year's end seemed positive.[60]

ECONOMIC PERFORMANCE
Tunisia boasted a high growth rate in 2000 — estimated to be about 5% — which Ben 'Ali cited as a major achievement considering international currency fluctuations and an increase in oil prices.[61] Other positive indicators enhanced the microeconomic figures. These included a strong performance by exports, which during the first six months of 2000 reached a 17% year-on-year increase. The tourism sector was set to produce record results in 2000, and served as an important source of income, contributing 6.2% to GDP.[62] Tourism receipts were expected to grow by more than 13% in local currency terms by the end of the year. Foreign investments also grew, totaling more than $459.5m. during the first half of the year. Annual inflation, estimated at less than 3%, was kept at bay.[63]

The Tunisian population exceeded 9.4m., according to a national census conducted in 1999. The annual growth rate was estimated at around 1.15%, far less than that of other developing countries. The census data reflected a population increase in the Tunis area, where 43% of the population resided.[64]

FOREIGN AFFAIRS

THE MAGHRIB, THE ARAB WORLD AND AFRICA
Attempts to revitalize the dormant Arab Maghrib Union (AMU) were Tunisia's departure point for contacts with its North African neighbors. Established in 1989, the AMU became almost completely moribund by 1995, due mainly to tensions between Morocco and Algeria (see *MECS* 1989, pp. 144–47; 1995, pp. 634–35). Tunisia acknowledged that previous efforts to bolster the AMU had not borne fruit; nevertheless it did not desert what Foreign Minister Habib Ben Yahya described as a "strategic choice."[65] Ben 'Ali noted that it was "unacceptable" that the AMU advancement be prevented by "transitory difficulties" and called on its members to overcome their malaise with "renewed enthusiasm, self-confidence, and optimism."[66] To that end, the president dispatched special emissaries to North African capitals in 2000. The situation of the AMU was also raised at bilateral meetings between Ben 'Ali and his Maghribi counterparts, with efforts centering on convening a summit of the leaders of the five member states.[67] But despite

Ben 'Ali's efforts, no major breakthroughs occurred, and the prospects for the AMU remained unclear. Most member countries expressed general support for the AMU, but were reluctant to take any related concrete steps. In an age when member countries had already embarked on diplomatic initiatives that often contradicted those of fellow members (e.g., the differences of opinion between Morocco and Algeria over the Western Sahara region), the role and character of a revitalized AMU were also uncertain.

Tunisian activity with its neighbors was more successful. Relations with Libya, its number one Arab trading partner, had been steadily progressing since the mid-1990s and reached new peaks in 2000. The removal in 1999 of international sanctions on Libya lifted any remaining discomfort in Tunisian circles concerning involvement with a country largely viewed in the international community as a pariah state (see *MECS* 1999, pp. 586–87). Accordingly, the Tunisian-Libyan joint commission met in Tripoli in February and again in October. A number of cooperation agreements were subsequently signed.[68] Ben 'Ali visited Libya in June. His discussions with Libyan leader Mu'ammar al-Qadhdhafi, which focused on means to upgrade bilateral ties, led to an agreement to establish a free trade zone. Following Ben 'Ali's visit, flights between the two countries, which had been suspended as a result of the sanctions were resumed.[69] Qadhdhafi arrived in Tunis on 2 August for a four-day visit, which underscored the positive atmosphere of Tunisian-Libyan relations. In addition to meetings with numerous public figures, Qadhdhafi also visited the late president Bourguiba's grave. This was viewed as a considerable gesture on his part given his historically testy relations with Bourguiba.[70]

Tunisian ties with Morocco were strengthened in 2000 by a flurry of visits by high-ranking state officials, joint committee meetings and new cooperation agreements. Foreign Minister Ben Yahya visited Morocco in February, where he chaired a meeting of the Tunisian-Moroccan joint commission with his Moroccan counterpart, Muhammad Benaissa. Ben Yahya also met with Moroccan king Muhammad, who stressed that both countries had a common resolve to consolidate bilateral relations at all levels.[71] During a similar visit to Tunisia a month earlier, in January, the Moroccan foreign minister met with Ben 'Ali and relayed an invitation from King Muhammad to visit Morocco.[72] Efforts to bolster bilateral ties focused on improving trade relations within the framework of the 1999 free trade agreement between the two countries (see *MECS*, 1999, pp. 585–86), as well as cooperation in the fields of housing and urban planing, transportation, and women and family affairs. To that end, there were a number of ministerial visits such as that of Neziha Zarrouk, Tunisian minister of women and family affairs. Special committees on these subjects met in 2000, and a number of agreements were signed.[73] The warming of relations were crowned by King Muhammad's official visit to Tunis on 24 May.[74] The Tunisian-Moroccan joint commission met again in September.[75]

Relations with Algeria also improved qualitatively. Algerian president 'Abd al-'Aziz Bouteflika paid an official visit to Tunisia in June, in an effort to strengthen bilateral economic relations and revitalize the AMU. This was the first visit of an Algerian head of state to Tunisia since 1994. Bouteflika received a "tumultuous welcome" from Tunisians who lined the capital's streets. He addressed the Chamber of Deputies and met with Ben 'Ali. High on their agenda was the issue of security coordination between the two countries,[76] as Tunisian concerns regarding the effect of internal strife within Algeria continued to be paramount. The Algerian military chief of staff, Muhammad Lamari, visited Tunisia in April and discussed the strengthening of bilateral military cooperation with Ben 'Ali and Defense Minister Muhammad Jegham.[77] Cooperation reportedly increased in the wake of a May attack of Algerian Islamists on a Tunisian border outpost. Two Tunisian border guards were wounded in the attack.[78] Relations with other Arab countries remained sound. Heading Tunisian Arab diplomacy were its bilateral ties with Egypt, as Tunis considered Cairo traditionally close in political and economic orientation. Contacts in 2000 included efforts to increase bilateral trade, promote mutual tourism, and develop cultural exchanges in areas such as visual and performing arts.[79] These issues were discussed in March at the Tunisian-Egyptian joint committee meeting in Cairo, co-chaired by Foreign Minister Ben Yahya and his Egyptian counterpart, 'Amru Musa.[80]

Efforts to bolster cooperation with Gulf states were part of an ongoing improvement in relations that began in the late 1990s (see MECS 1997, p. 708). The emir of Qatar, Shaykh Hamad bin Khalifa, visited Tunis in January. He and Ben 'Ali emphasized the need to increase bilateral cooperation, trade exchanges, joint investments and projects.[81] The Saudi interior minister, Nayif bin 'Abd al-'Aziz met with Ben 'Ali during his May visit to Tunis. The Saudi minister described relations between the two countries as being at their best.[82] Yemen's deputy prime minister and foreign minister, 'Abd al-Qadir Bajamal, visited Tunisia in February and participated in the Tunisian-Yemeni joint committee meetings. He also met with Ben 'Ali and conveyed a message from Yemeni president 'Ali 'Abdallah Salih. Salih visited Tunis in October and met with Ben 'Ali.[83]

Following other Arab countries, Tunisia took further steps away from the UN sanctions regime and appeared ready to engage in more intensive bilateral activity with Iraq. Trade Minister Mondher Zenaidi led an economic and industrial delegation to Iraq, and said that Tunisia was eager to promote cooperation with Iraq in all fields.[84] Iraq's vice president, Taha Yasin Ramadan visited Tunisia in April for high-level meetings. The Tunisian-Iraqi joint commission meetings, held during Ramadan's visit, focused on the need to bolster cooperation in areas such as trade and science.[85] Foreign Minister Ben Yahya met with his Iraqi counterpart in Baghdad on 30 October.[86] Iraqi foreign minister Muhammad Sa'id al-Sahhaf returned the visit in November, meeting also with Prime Minister Muhammad Ghannushi.[87] Tunisia reportedly agreed in principle to return four civilian Iraqi airliners that had been held in Tunis since the eve of the Gulf War.[88] On various occasions, Ben 'Ali stressed the need to lift the UN sanctions.[89]

Tunisia also sought to strengthen relations with Iran. Prime Minister Ghannushi welcomed an "all out expansion" of ties, after meeting with the Iranian minister of culture and Islamic guidance, Mohajerani, who visited Tunis in January. Ghannushi expressed pleasure with the growing trend of political, economic and cultural ties between the two countries. As part of their efforts to intensify relations, Tehran and Tunis agreed on a range of cultural and scientific exchange programs.[90] Iranian foreign minister Kamal Kharrazi visited Tunisia in June and met with Ben 'Ali for what were described as "positive and fruitful discussions."[91]

Tunisia continued to play a modest role and monitor developments in the Arab-Israeli peace process, primarily the Palestinian-Israeli track, and it formulated its positions accordingly. Tunisia remained part of the multilateral peace talks, and participated in the January meeting in Moscow aimed at reviving that track.[92] Tunisian relations with Israel had warmed somewhat following the election of Ehud Barak as prime minister in 1999 (see MECS 1999, pp. 588–89). A further indication of this was the February visit to Israel of Taher al-Sayoud, minister of state for foreign affairs. Sayoud was the highest-ranking Tunisian official ever to visit Israel. Sayoud noted cautiously that Tunisian-

Israeli ties were proceeding gradually, and reiterated Tunisia's policy of linking them to developments in the peace process.[93] However, relations with Israel remained limited, and were opposed by various sections of Tunisian society. Foreign Minister Ben Yahya contended that Tunisia was "not one of those rushing toward normalization" with Israel, and noted Tunisia's "historic obligations" to the Palestinian cause.[94] Throughout the year, Ben 'Ali emphasized the need to recognize the Palestinian right to independent statehood, and said that the Palestinian question was the "main gateway to peace."[95] He was in regular contact with PA chairman 'Arafat, and continued to foster Tunisian assistance to the PA, e.g., by establishing financial and monetary institutions.[96] Over the summer, leading Tunisian intellectuals and public figures established the National Committee against Normalization with Israel which called on the Tunisian government to sever ties with Israel and to refrain from any form of cooperation.[97] The outbreak of the Palestinian uprising in September seriously affected relations, leading to a severing of the formal low-level diplomatic ties, which had been established in 1996 (see chapters on Israel, and the PA). Ben 'Ali participated in the special Arab summit in Cairo in October, convened to discuss the Palestinian uprising. There, he called for an "immediate and unconditional withdrawal of Israeli forces from the Palestinian territories," and proposed the establishment of an international buffer force between Israeli and Palestinian areas.[98] It was during the Cairo gathering that Tunisia announced the severing of diplomatic relations with Israel "in the face of the bloody Israeli aggression" against the Palestinians and in accordance with its stance that linked normalization of relations with Israel with the peace process.[99] Toward the end of the year, Tunisia repeatedly criticized Israeli policies toward the Palestinians.

Tunisia remained committed to promoting ties with other African countries, and expressed the need to bring peace and security to the continent. These general policy outlines, however, generated relatively little diplomatic activity in 2000, compared to other regions with which Tunisia was politically involved.

RELATIONS WITH EUROPE AND BROADER WESTERN ARENAS

Tunisian foreign policy and diplomacy continued to be oriented toward Europe and the West. Its links with Europe, however, became increasingly difficult to sustain in 2000 owing to growing European criticism of the Tunisian human rights situation. Tunisian officials sought to refute these accusations, as they affected relations with some of its traditionally close European allies. At the same time, they sought increased cooperation with other countries, e.g., the US, with whom its ties seemed less prone to such criticism. Tunisia also maintained modest initiatives to widen the reach of its diplomatic activity; contacts with Asia and the Far East, for example, expanded.

The greatest turbulence occurred with France, its number one trade partner and traditional ally. The roots of this tension could be traced back to Tunisia's 1999 presidential and parliamentary elections, which the French media severely criticized. These reports also highlighted the lack of civil liberties inside the country and the abuses of human rights (see *MECS* 1999, pp. 581–82). Tunisian officials argued that the French government had inspired the negative articles; they subsequently adopted measures that Paris viewed as retaliatory, such as limiting the distribution of French newspapers and reviving a campaign to increase the use of Arabic rather than French in government offices nationwide. An immediate outcome of this tension was the French decision to postpone the planned January visit of Prime Minister Lionel Jospin to Tunisia. Officially, France xattributed the postponement to technical reasons. However, French diplomatic sources noted that the visit was rescheduled "for better days."[100] Tunisian sources later asserted that there were no outstanding political issues clouding relations with France, apart from the attitude of elements of the French media toward Tunisia.[101]

A two-day visit of French foreign minister Hubert Vedrine to Tunis in February did little to dispel the chilled atmosphere. Vedrine emphasized at the conclusion of his meetings with Foreign Minister Ben Yahya and with Ben 'Ali that bilateral relations were "good, very constructive and very positive." But a prevailing sense of unease continued to overshadow Tunisian-French relations in 2000, as French officials spoke out against Tunisia's human rights situation, while Ben 'Ali criticized the "smear campaign" conducted by the French media.[102] On a positive note, French president Jacques Chirac attended Bourguiba's funeral, and spoke with Ben 'Ali on several occasions during the year,[103] and Tunisian economic ties to France remained strong.[104]

Cooled relations with France inspired Tunisia to redirect its diplomatic energies toward other European countries, particularly Italy and Spain. Ben Yahya visited Italy in January, where he met with his Italian counterpart, Lamberto Dini. Much of the meeting was devoted to issues that had affected bilateral ties, such as regulating mutual fishing rights. One aspect of their expressed commitment to bolster bilateral relations was a meeting in June of the joint Tunisian-Italian military commission, chaired by the defense ministers of both countries.[105] Contacts with Spain included the January visit of the Spanish foreign minister, Abel Matutes.[106] Other high-level contacts with European countries included a two-day visit by Ben 'Ali to Portugal in May, where he met with President Jorge Sampio. As in other encounters with European leaders, the human rights situation in Tunisia was reportedly raised during the visit, and it remained at the forefront of European concerns in pursuing ties with Tunisia.[107] Overall, Europe's longstanding appreciation of Tunisian economic and social achievements remained intact, but as Tunisia sought to consolidate its ties with Europe even further, issues such as human rights could be expected to receive increased attention from EU members.

Relations with the US, by contrast, continued to focus primarily on political and diplomatic matters, especially regarding the Arab-Israeli peace process. US President Bill Clinton spoke with Ben 'Ali over the summer and emphasized his reliance on the Tunisian president to continue efforts to help boost the peace process.[108] Ben 'Ali's scheduled July visit to the US was postponed at Clinton's request, as it conflicted with the Camp David Israel-Palestinian summit. Tunisian-American contacts continued after the summit, as Edward Walker, US assistant secretary of state for Near Eastern affairs, arrived in Tunis to brief national leaders on the current status of the peace process.[109] Contacts in the military-strategic sphere remained ongoing Defense Minister Muhammad Jegham visited the US in January for the Tunisian-American military committee meetings. Tunisia received special financing from the US government for the purchase of American military equipment.[110] Two American offices affiliated with the US Agency for International Development (USAID) were established in Tunis, as part of efforts to develop bilateral commercial ties.[111]

Tunisia continued modest attempts to enlarge the scope of its diplomatic activity, an effort that had taken shape in the second half of the 1990s. These initiatives were assisted by the fact that Tunisia began in January 1999 a two-year term on the UN Security Council, which raised the interest of other countries in pursuing relations. Especially attentive was China, whose foreign minister, Tang Jiaxuan, visited Tunisia in February and met with Ben 'Ali and Foreign Minister Ben Yahya. The Chinese minister noted that his country had great interest in Tunisia's positive and constructive role in regional and international issues, and extolled the friendship and cooperation between the two countries. He also announced a Chinese loan of approximately $4m. to Tunisia.[112] China's defense minister visited in November and also met with Ben 'Ali, following an October visit to China by Foreign Minister Ben Yahya.[113]

Another emerging market involved contacts with Poland, which Ben 'Ali visited in March. Ben 'Ali had served as Tunisian ambassador to Poland in the 1980s, and his visit was a chance to pursue bilateral ties. Several cultural, scientific and tourism-related cooperation agreements were signed during his visit.[114]

In another development, Tunisia signed a military cooperation agreement with the Czech Republic.[115]

NOTES

For the place and frequency of publications cited here, and for the full name of the publication, news agency, radio station or monitoring service where an abbreviation is used, please see "List of Sources." Only in the case of more than one publication bearing the same name is the place of publication noted here.

1. *Le Monde*, 5 March; *al-Hayat*, 10 February (MSANEWS); statement by Campaign for Human Rights in Tunisia, 8 February (MSANEWS); *al-Quds al-'Arabi*, 18 February (MSANEWS); *Le Monde*, 1 March 2000.
2. *Le Monde*, 5 March; *Libération,* 17 February (MSANEWS); *CR*, Tunisia, 2nd quarter, 2000, p. 14.
3. *CR*, Tunisia, 2nd quarter, 2000, p. 14; R. Tunis, 26 February 2000 (BBC Monitoring).
4. Statement by Nahda, 10 February 2000 (MSANEWS)
5. Statement by the Paris-based Committee for the Respect of Freedoms and Human Rights in Tunisia, 17 February (MSANEWS); statement by the Conseil national pour les libertés en Tunisie, 5, 12 March 2000 (MSANEWS).
6. *Le Monde*, 26, 27 May; *JA/L'Intelligent*, 6 June 2000.
7. Bourguiba's age was a source of controversy among historians and commentators, who pointed to evidence that he was born in 1903, and not in 1906 as he himself claimed. See Derek Hopwood, *Habib Bourguiba of Tunisia: The Tragedy of Longevity* (New York: St. Martin's Press, 1992).
8. *JA/L'Intelligent*, 14 March; <www.arabicnews.com>, 10 March 2000.
9. *JA/L'Intelligent*, 18 April; *al-Sabah*, 7 April 2000.
10. *FT, al-Sharq al-Awsat, al-Sabah*, 7 April; *JA/L'Intelligent*, 18 April 2000.
11. *JA/L'Intelligent*, 18 April; *Le Monde*, 28 April 2000.
12. *Le Monde*, 9 April; *JA/L'Intelligent*, 18 April 2000.
13. *Le Monde*, 11, 30 April 2000.
14. *Al-Sabah*, 7 April; *JA/L'Intelligent*, 18 April 2000.
15. *Le Monde*, 9, 22 April; *JA/L'Intelligent*, 18 April 2000.
16. R. Tunis, 30 October 2000 (BBC Monitoring).
17. *Al-Wasat*, 24 January 2000.
18. *JA/L'Intelligent*, 29 August 2000.
19. See, for example, R. Tunis, 11 May 2000 (BBC Monitoring).
20. See, for example, interview with Ben 'Ali, *Middle East Insight*, July/August; speech by Ben 'Ali, 7 November 2000, Tunisian Information Office, Washington, D.C. <www.tunisiaonline.com; hereinafter: TIO>.
21. TIO, 4 April; speech by Ben 'Ali, 28 July 2000 (BBC Monitoring).

22. *JA/L'Intelligent*, 15 February 2000.
23. TIO, 29 April 2000.
24. <www.arabicnews.com>, 27 April *al-Wasat*, 1 May 2000.
25. *JA/L'Intelligent*, 15 February; *CR*, Tunisia, 2nd quarter, 2000, p. 17.
26. *JA/L'Intelligent*, 11 April; *al-Wasat*, 1 May; *Le Monde, al-Hayat*, 28 May 2000.
27. *Le Monde, al-Hayat*, 30 May; *al-Wasat*, 5 June 2000.
28. *JA/L'Intelligent*, 29 August 2000.
29. Statement by Nahda, 10 February 2000 (MSANEWS).
30. See, for example, *al-Ra'y al-Akhir*, 31 August 2000.
31. R. Tunis, 11 May (BBC Monitoring); R. Tunis, 28 July (BBC Monitoring); interview with Ben 'Ali, *Middle East Insight*, July; *Publico* (Internet version), 10 May (BBC Monitoring); TIO, 9 December 2000.
32. AFP, 18 February; *Libération*, 17 February 2000.
33. *Le Monde*, 12, 23 April 2000.
34. *Le Monde*, 27, 28 April 2000.
35. *Le Monde*, 28 April; 3 May 2000.
36. *Le Matin* (Algiers, Internet version), 17 April, 13 May 2000 (BBC Monitoring).
37. *Le Monde*, 30 April 2000.
38. *Le Monde*, 17 May; <www.arabicnews.com>, 16 May; MSANEWS, 16 May 2000.
39. *Le Monde*, 26, 27 May 2000.
40. *Le Monde*, 31 May; *JA/L'Intelligent*, 6 June 2000.
41. US Department of State, *Tunisia: Country Report on Human Rights Practices for 2000* <www.state.gov>.
42. *Libération*, 18 March 2000 <www.cnlt98.org.>.
43. *JA/L'Intelligent*, 1 August, 7 November 2000.
44. *Le Monde*, 18 January 2000.
45. *Le Monde*, 27 May; *JA/L'Intelligent*, 19 September 2000.
46. Statement by the Committee for the Respect of Liberties and Human Rights in Tunisia, 27 February 2000 (MSANEWS).
47. Summary of Human Rights Watch Report on Tunisia, March 2000 (MSANEWS).
48. Such was the case of Nadia Hammi, the seventeen-year old daughter of Radhia Nasraoui, who was tried in 1999 (see *MECS* 1999, pp. 581–82); statement by the Campaign for Human Rights in Tunisia, 20 March 2000 (MSANEWS).
49. Statement by the Campaign for Human Rights in Tunisia, 28 January 2000 (MSANEWS).
50. TIO, 15 May, 21 June; speech by Ben 'Ali, TIO, 7 November 2000.
51. TIO, 15 May; *al-Hayat*, 16 August (BBC Monitoring); *JA/L'Intelligent*, 19 September; *CR*, Tunisia, 4th quarter, 2000, p. 13.
52. R. Tunis, 11 May 2000 (BBC Monitoring).
53. R. Tunis, 13 February 2000 (BBC Monitoring).
54. *CR*, Tunisia, 1st quarter, 2000, pp. 19–20.
55. *CR*, Tunisia, 3rd quarter, p. 19; 4th quarter, 2000, p. 16.
56. *Country Profile*, Tunisia, 2000, p. 24.
57. *CR*, Tunisia, 2nd quarter, p. 21; 3rd quarter, p. 20; 4th quarter, 2000, p. 17.
58. *CR*, Tunisia, 3rd quarter, p. 21; speech by Ben 'Ali, 7 November 2000 (TIO).
59. Speech by Ben 'Ali, 7 November (TIO); *CR*, Tunisia, 1st quarter, p. 28; 2nd quarter, 2000, p. 27.
60. *CR*, Tunisia, 3rd quarter, 2000, p. 27.
61. Ibid., pp. 9–10.
62. *Country Profile*, Tunisia, 2000, pp. 33–34.
63. *CR*, Tunisia, 2nd quarter, p. 22; 3rd quarter, p. 21; 4th quarter, 2000, pp. 20–21.
64. R. Tunis, 18 January 2000 (BBC Monitoring).
65. <www.arabicnews.com>, 28 February 2000.
66. Speech by Ben 'Ali, 7 November 2000 (TIO).
67. <www.arabicnews.com>, 29 June, 18, 21, July 2000.

68. *Al-Hayat*, 12, 19 February; Libyan TV, 8 October 2000 (BBC Monitoring).
69. <www.arabicnews.com>, 5, 8, 10 June; *CR*, Tunisia, 3rd quarter, 2000, p. 18.
70. Tunisian TV, 2 August; R. Tunis, 3 August (BBC Monitoring); *JA/L'Intelligent*, 5 September 2000.
71. <www.arabicnews.com>, 28, 29 February 2000.
72. <www.arabicnews.com>, 22, 24 January 2000.
73. <www.arabicnews.com>, 25, 27 January, 20 May, 14 June 2000.
74. R. Tunis, 24 May 2000 (BBC Monitoring).
75. Tunisian TV, 21 September; R. Tunis, 23 September 2000 (BBC Monitoring).
76. <www.arabicnews.com>, 28, 29 June, 1 July; *Le Monde*, 30 June, 1 July; R. Algiers, 28 June (BBC Monitoring); *JA/L'Intelligent*, 4 July 2000.
77. Algerian TV, 11 April 2000 (BBC Monitoring).
78. *Al-Hayat*, 20, 22 May; *JA/L'Intelligent*, 23 May 2000.
79. <www.arabicnews.com>, 3, 15, 18 March, 2 November 2000.
80. <www.arabicnews.com>, 13, 14 March; MENA, 13 March 2000 (BBC Monitoring).
81. *Al-Watan al-'Arabi*, 11 February; R. Tunis, 19 January 2000 (BBC Monitoring).
82. R. Tunis, 4 May 2000 (BBC Monitoring).
83. TIO, 11 October; R. Tunis, 10 February 2000 (BBC Monitoring).
84. R. Baghdad, 5 February; Iraqi TV, 6 February 2000 (BBC Monitoring).
85. R. Tunis, 10, 13 April 2000.
86. R. Baghdad, 30 October 2000 (BBC Monitoring).
87. R. Tunis, 3 November 2000 (BBC Monitoring).
88. *Al-Hayat*, 1 November, 19 December 2000.
89. See, for example, R. Tunis, 19 January (BBC Monitoring); R. Tunis, 10 April (BBC Monitoring); speech by Ben 'Ali, 7 November 2000 (TIO).
90. R. Tunis, 12 January 2000 (BBC Monitoring).
91. IRNA, 15 January (BBC Monitoring); R. Tunis, 13 June 2000 (BBC Monitoring).
92. ITAR-TASS, 28 January 2000 (DR).
93. <www.arabicnews.com>, 8 February 2000.
94. MENA, 13 March 2000 (DR).
95. Interview with Ben 'Ali, *Middle East Insight*, July 2000.
96. See, for example, R. Tunis, 10 May (BBC Monitoring); R. Tunis, 23 January; VoP, 24 January 2000 (BBC Monitoring).
97. *Al-Wasat*, 7, 21 August 2000.
98. Speech by Ben 'Ali, Egyptian Satellite TV, 21 October 2000 (BBC Monitoring).
99. R. Tunis, 22 October 2000 (BBC Monitoring).
100. *Le Monde*, 7 January; *JA/L'Intelligent*, 18 January; *al-Wasat*, 31 January 2000.
101. *Le Monde*, 8 February 2000.
102. R. Tunis, 7 February; *Le Monde*, 9 February (BBC Monitoring); *JA/L'Intelligent*, 15 February; TIO, 22 April 2000.
103. *CR*, Tunisia, 3rd quarter, 2000, p. 15.
104. *CR*, Tunisia, 2nd quarter, 2000, p. 19.
105. *Al-Hayat*, 4 February; ANSA, 18 January (DR); Tunisian TV, 19 June; ANSA, 21 June 2000 (BBC Monitoring).
106. R. Tunis, 20 January (BBC Monitoring); *al-Hayat*, 4 February 2000.
107. *Publico* (Internet version), 10 May 2000 (BBC Monitoring).
108. R. Tunis, 6 July 2000 (BBC Monitoring).
109. R. Tunis, 8 July, 5 August 2000 (BBC Monitoring).
110. *CR*, Tunisia, 2nd quarter, 2000, pp. 19–20.
111. *CR*, Tunisia, 3rd quarter, 2000, p. 21.
112. R. Tunis, 17 February; Tunisian TV, 17 February 2000 (BBC Monitoring).
113. XINHUA, 10 October (DR); R. Tunis, 21 November 2000 (BBC Monitoring).
114. R. Tunis, 28 March 2000 (BBC Monitoring).
115. *CR*, Tunisia, 3rd quarter, 2000, pp. 18–19.

Turkey
(Türkiye Cumhuriyeti)

ARYEH SHMUELEVITZ AND MITCHELL BENNETT

The year 2000 started with much optimism in Turkey. The country was recovering from the initial trauma of the earthquakes that had shaken it in 1999. Its European Union (EU) candidacy had been approved and confidence in peace in the predominantly Kurdish southeast was growing. The economy seemed to be improving and the fifty-seventh government of the Turkish republic, a three-way coalition between the Nationalist Action Party (Milliyetçi Hareket Partisi; MHP), Democratic Left Party (Demokratik Sol Partisi; DSP) and Motherland Party (Anavatan Partisi; ANAP), appeared to be stable.

For Turkey to qualify for full EU membership, however, would mean abolition of the death penalty and bringing to an end the fourteen-year-long moratorium on its implementation. But much of the population, as well as one party in the coalition government, the MHP, pressed for one more execution — that of incarcerated Kurdish leader Abdullah Öcalan — before the death sentence was banned. In a tense meeting, the leaders of the three coalition parties decided that it would be in the country's best long-term interests to delay carrying out Öcalan's sentence, at least until the European Court of Human Rights in Strasbourg had reached its conclusions. The Öcalan execution was thus suspended for two to three years.

The changes to comply with EU standards began with the presentation of a plan for comprehensive constitutional reform by the chief justice of the Supreme Court, Sami Selçuk. The envisaged legislation would lead to democratization, judicial reform and genuine separation of the powers of the state, in accordance with European requirements. The aim was to complete all legislation and preparation by 2004 and then to start negotiations for full membership status. In July, the government outlined a timetable for these reforms called the "Road Map to Europe".

Relations with the EU, however, faced many difficulties. A new cause of friction arose in February with EU plans to set up a separate defense organization under the European Security and Defense Identity (ESDI). It was made clear from the start that this would include only full EU members. Nevertheless, Turkey wanted to participate and insisted not only on sending troops to take part in the organization's activities, but also on being a partner in its decision-making authority. The wrangling continued until the end of the year, with the EU and Turkey each holding ground.

Another source of tension was the use of the terms "minority" and "Kurdish" in the EU documents demanding the recognition of cultural autonomy for minorities, which would permit the Kurds to use their mother tongue in education and the media. Prime Minister Bülent Ecevit softened his stance on Kurdish language rights, while trying to stay safely in the middle. Supporting the Kurds were Mesut Yılmaz and his ANAP, the business community, nearly all the leftist parties and the National Intelligence Agency

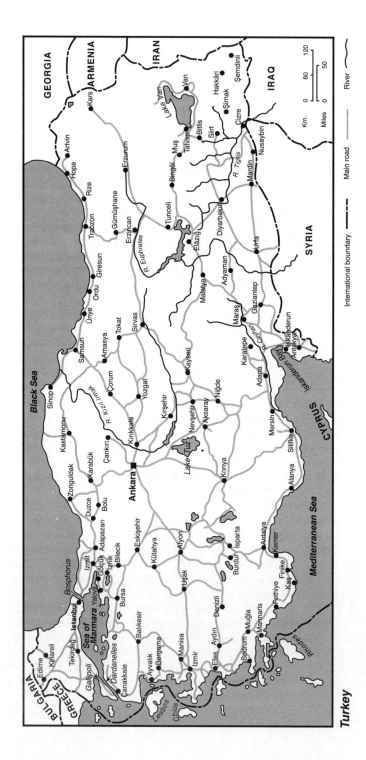

Turkey

(Milli Istihbarat Teşkilatı; MIT). Newly elected President Ahmet Sezer remained silent, but his views on the absurdity of forbidding the language were well known. On the opposing side were the MHP and the military, who were in close agreement on the subject of maintaining national unity. What caused even more tension was the inclusion of the Cyprus question and the treatment of northern Cyprus in the EU Accession Partnership document. The Turkish government stance was that it was ready to sacrifice its relationship with the EU rather than give up control of northern Cyprus. The two sides held firmly to their positions. Negotiations continued, although it seemed that discussions for full membership would now not be before 2010.

In domestic politics, a major issue during 2000 was the presidential election. February, March and April were occupied with efforts to ensure that President Süleyman Demirel could remain in office for a second term. This gave rise to some of the most destabilizing events of the year. Bargaining became the order of the day in Ankara, with special deals offered to the Islamist Fazilet Partisi (FP; Virtue Party) — constitutional and other amendments that would rescue it from threat of closure by the Constitutional Court — in return for its support for the "five plus five" formula (two terms of five years each, instead of one term of seven years) that would save Demirel's presidency. While the coalition went forward with its schemes to protect Demirel, public support for him was steadily declining. By April, the government finally came up with a package of constitutional amendments, including one to grant Demirel a second term. The three coalition party leaders were hopeful that it would be passed in Parliament. To ensure success, Prime Minister and DSP leader Ecevit issued repeated warnings of the chaos in store for Turkey should Demirel not be given a second term.

Much to the humiliation of the coalition government and its weeks of strenuous effort, the vote failed. Neither saving the FP nor the promise of lucrative retirement salaries for deputies had been able to sway the vote. ANAP leader Mesut Yılmaz had refused to order his party how to vote, and deputies in other parties defied the instructions of their party leaders on their secret ballots.

The coalition government had been so confident that it had not even considered an alternative candidate to run for the presidency, in what were potentially four rounds of voting between 27 April and 9 May. An army general was not looked on with much favor and an extra-parliamentary candidate seemed to be an admission of defeat. Nevertheless, such a candidate was found — the chief justice of the Constitutional Court, Ahmet Necdet Sezer. So attractive did he prove that the leaders of all five parliamentary parties marked a historic occasion by announcing, in a joint press conference, their complete consensus on who should be president for the next seven years. Sezer's election in May was met with great enthusiasm. There was considerable expectation that he was the right person at the right time, a legal expert who could represent a Turkey moving decisively to become a nation under the rule of law, as well as in its EU aspirations; someone who would earn respect both at home and abroad. Within a short time President Sezer's star was rising with the public, and his position was firmly established.

Among political parties, the FP was riven by internal conflict and the possibility of disintegration into a reformist faction (with leaders such as Abdullah Gül and Recep Tayyip Erdoğan) and a traditionalist faction (under the leadership of the party leader Recai Kutan), or even into separate parties. However, it remained united because it was waiting for the Constitutional Court to rule on the application to close it down, filed by Chief Prosecutor Vural Savaş. The only hope of the FP was that Turkey, as a candidate for full EU membership, would be loath to blot its democratic record further by closing down yet another political party. The turmoil in the party reemerged at its national convention, when Abdullah Gül from the reformist wing challenged the traditionalist Recai Kutan for party leadership. The antipathy between the two factions deepened during the convention, especially after the undemocratic maneuvers used by the traditionalists to prevent the election of Gül. These resentments could have split the party, but the threat of closure helped to keep it together.

The Republican People's Party (Cumhuriyet Halk Partisi; CHP) held a national convention in September, and former leader Deniz Baykal was restored to power. In November, the MHP reelected Devlet Bahçeli as leader at its own national convention and claimed to represent the "political center." In mid-2000, ANAP leader Yılmaz, was finally cleared of seven charges of corruption by parliament and could take his place in the government as deputy prime minister in charge of relations with the EU.

During the year the coalition government tried to undermine the Kurdish-oriented People's Democracy Party (Halkın Democrat Partisi; HADEP) and to limit its activities, accusing it of cooperation with the Kurdish Workers' Party (Parti Kerkeren Kurdistan; PKK) and of supporting the PKK policy of separation from the Turkish state. Three mayors, all HADEP members, were arrested but released after a few weeks and allowed to return to office. HADEP was supported by the CHP and by interested groups in Europe — the government attitude toward and treatment of HADEP were closely followed by various EU delegations visiting Turkey. HADEP held its national convention in November and restored to power its former leader, Murat Bozlak. The party claimed to be "Turkey's party." In some circles, the tens of thousands who had showed up for the HADEP convention set off loud alarm bells about the rising prospects of Kurdish separatism.

In January, a raid against Hizbullah, a militant Islamist organization, in Beykoz, Istanbul, resulted in the death of the group's leader and an unraveling of its activities. The security operation was followed by weeks of disturbing scenes of dead bodies being pulled from underground torture cells and the graves of the organization's victims. Hundreds of members were arrested and weapons, documents, cassettes and other material confiscated.

The three major issues of the year were the subversive organizations and their activities, especially Hizbullah; the Kurdish question; and relations with the EU and their impact on domestic politics.

INTERNAL AFFAIRS

SUBVERSIVE ACTIVITIES

The raid on Hizbullah was a dramatic beginning to a year in which the security authorities intensified operations against Islamist organizations as well as extreme leftist movements. There were numerous warnings about the growing strength of the Islamist movements and sects and their increasing danger to the regime. Ret. Gen. Nevzat Bolugiray, the general staff martial law coordination chief, claimed that the fight against these organizations became ineffectual when Islamic idealists began to fill positions at the Interior Ministry and the security services during Turgut Özal's administration (1980s), and when the Islamists began to increase in number during the True Path-Welfare Party administration (1996–97). Only when the latter government had gone, he added, did the security services gradually begin to rid themselves of Islamist elements and undertake an effective campaign against these organizations.[1]

Nevertheless, the report of the National Security Council (NSC) following its meeting on 28 March emphasized that many people with militant Islamist views were employed by the ministries, particularly the Ministry of Education, the Ministry of Justice and the Ministry of the Interior. The report claimed that most social science teachers evidently held such views. It concluded that the state was confronted by a serious threat aimed at converting the nation into a religious community and forcing its citizens to submit to fundamentalist control.[2]

The NSC conclusions had been mentioned earlier in a speech delivered by Dr. Abdülkadır Sezgin, chief inspector of the Religious Affairs Directorate, who claimed that the fast-growing religious sects were reaching dangerous proportions, as they were becoming linked to both left-wing and right-wing political parties. It was wrong, he added, for state leaders to perceive the sects as a natural outcome of democracy, and such religious organizations should not be allowed in the political arena. He demanded permission to introduce elective Qur'an courses and courses on religion into the state educational curriculum of the fourth and fifth grades, enabling the government to close down the courses held by the religious sects. He also insisted that Islam should not be the only religion taught in theology faculties in Turkey, but that other religions as well should be included in a school within the faculty.[3]

The subject was discussed again in a report by the intelligence units, in which it was claimed that despite repeated blows dealt to them, the religious sects and congregations continued to present a threat to the secular and democratic regime. It conceded that these organizations had lost a significant amount of power and that their leaders had been apprehended, but stated that their followers remained loyal to them. It warned that they might become active again as soon as they could find an opportunity. The report also discussed the factors contributing to the strength of the various organizations:

(1) They had succeeded in developing strategies to evade regulations introduced during the crackdown initiated by the NSC on 28 February 1997 (see *MECS* 1997, p. 723).

(2) Although they no longer maintained their former religious lifestyles, they had not abandoned the idea of establishing a theocratic state.

(3) They had successfully organized themselves in the provinces to counter economic difficulties.

(4) In the major cities, they evaded certain regulations by carrying out their activities in great secrecy.

(5) Those located in small settlements received support from officials in provinces and municipalities.

(6) They were attracting young people by promising help through their congregations and foundations.

(7) Despite prevailing regulations, they were still using mosques as bases for propaganda activities.[4]

The operations against the militant Islamist movements carried out by the police and the military (mainly the gendarmes) were mentioned by Gen. Atilla Ateş, land forces commander, in a speech in Kayseri in which he discussed the role of the military in defending the secular and democratic character of the republic.[5] Toward mid-February there were reports that the Islamist organizations were planning to kidnap the wives and children of high-ranking police and military officials and would try to infiltrate military installations, using forged documents. The police and the military went to extraordinary measures to prevent both kidnappings and infiltration, and were successful.[6]

The militant Islamist organizations active during 2000 were:

(1) **Hizbullah**. The Hizbullah organization turned out to be the primary target of the security forces during the year and a was major topic in the Turkish media. The process started with the raid by the security forces on 17 January in the Beykoz quarter in Üsküdar-Istanbul, in which the leader of Hizbullah, Hüseyin Velioğlu (according to some sources the leader of the *ilim* group — the most militant in Hizbullah) was killed and other leaders were captured, among them Edip Gümüş, the second in command. The operation resulted in the capture of many floppy disks, tapes, cassettes, documents, maps and photos in the house in Beykoz. The accumulated information from interrogations and seized documents was a breakthrough. It led to an intensification of the struggle against Hizbullah and the uncovering of many cells with much more information, and the arrest of hundreds of members and commanders.

In more than five hundred operations in forty-eight provinces (mainly Adana, Ağrı, Amasya, Ankara, Antalya, Batman, Bayburt, Bingöl, Bitlis, Bursa, Diyarbakır, Elaziğ, Erzurum, Gaziantep, İçel, İstanbul, İzmir, Konya, Malatya, Mardin, Mersin, Osmaniye, Siirt and Van) about five thousand people were detained from the beginning of the year. Approximately 3,500 were arrested, among them teachers, lawyers, physicians, engineers, students, civil servants and religious functionaries (mostly imams ready to cooperate with the Hizbullah). According to the director general of security, Turan Güneş, all leading Hizbullah members except one were captured in the nationwide operations.[7]

About 160,000 pages of documents were found and systematically studied by the Security Intelligence Office. They shed important light on the activities, plans and connections of Hizbullah. They helped lead investigators to the graves of those who had been abducted, interrogated and tortured, and finally assassinated. The corpses were found naked, their hands and feet tied; they had ropes around their necks and bore signs of torture. The tortures and executions were recorded on videotapes that were captured. Those who viewed them were appalled by the cruelty and violence that they portrayed. The minister of justice, Hikmet Sami Türk, said that these cassettes would not be made public, adding that Hizbullah was the most ruthless and brutal organization he had ever known.[8] In addition, the documents and cassettes solved many cases of disappearance and assassination in which members of Hizbullah had been involved since 1992. Among them were the murders of imams in east and southeast Anatolia, who had refused to allow Hizbullah to use their mosques for training and indoctrinating younger generations, as well as evidence of Hizbullah involvement in the assassination of famous advocates of secularism: the journalist Uğur Mumcu, Professors Ahmet Tanır Kışlalı (20 October 1999) and Muammer Aksoy, Dr. Bahriye Uçok, and the famous Islamist feminist writer Konca Kuris (who was identified by her brother, Mehmet Genç).[9]

The detailed evidence of Hizbullah savagery, much of it directed against people from its own camp, was a revelation. The great majority of those killed were bearded, religious and devout people who had had a religious education and were active in religious sects. The slaughter of Islamists by Islamists, even before the establishment of a Shari'a regime in Turkey, forced the religious community into much soul-searching. The general conclusion was that Hizbullah barbarism confirmed the importance of the secular state, because secularism not only guaranteed the non-interference of religious people in the affairs of the non-religious, but proved to be indispensable for protecting religious people as well. As the commentator, Yalçin Doğan wrote: "While Islam rejects savagery, secularism, in contrast to theocracy, protects the individual. This protection is necessary for the Islamic sector above all."[10]

The documents revealed that Hizbullah operated an excellent intelligence network for collecting important information about future targets. For example, in 1994 Hizbullah distributed an internal communiqué instructing its members and sympathizers to do their compulsory military service and send to the organization the plans of military units and any other documents obtained in the course of their training. Documents seized in the raids on Hizbullah safe houses contained data ranging from layouts of the headquarters of military units to the guard patterns of these units, from lists with the names and addresses of military intelligence operatives to General Staff studies. Hizbullah had even started buying houses and land around several military bases, with the intention of attacking the bases and their personnel if faced with armed resistance to its operations. In fact, Hizbullah had mounted meticulous intelligence operations to collect information about every incident, personality, base, society and institution — everything the member knew, saw or heard — which was sent to the upper echelons of the organization. This groundwork served well the operations against individuals or areas. People engaged in illegal business were followed, and money extorted from them by threats or kidnapping. Also found were death lists with the names and addresses of a large number of politicians, as well as a sketch of Prime Minister Ecevit's house and those of some ministers and high-ranking bureaucrats.[11]

According to the documents, the plans were to start a Holy War in October 2001. The war was to begin with street demonstrations and spread in waves to İstanbul, Adana, Mersin, Ankara and İzmir, its primary aim being the elimination of secularist citizens and the military. Velioğlu, in his writings, stated that the Holy War should start without fail before Ramadan 2001 and that the regime to be established would be according to the Iranian model — the only country in the world where true Islam existed.[12]

From time to time, claims had been made by the media and the Turkish government that Iran was cooperating with Hizbullah and providing arms and training. The raids on the organization's safe houses and the interrogation of its leaders proved this to be true. Edip Gümüş, the second in command, admitted under interrogation that the organization had never been short of funds and arms, and that large quantities of arms had been transferred from Russia to Hizbullah camps in Iran. He himself had crossed six times into Iran, trained in a camp near Qom and met many officials of the Iranian Secret Service. Photographs were found of Hizbullah leader, Velioğlu, meeting mullahs in Iran, as well as his Iranian identity card with the description 'foreign staff officer' written in Persian. According to the documents, Velioğlu received military, political and suicide bomber training in Iran in 1988, together with a group of Hizbullah members and leaders.[13]

In addition, records dated 17 February 1994 revealed that Iran had asked Hizbullah to provide information on the deployment and nature of military units along the Turkey-Iran border and on the monitoring and radar equipment in the base in Pirinçilik (not far from the border town Doğu Bayezit), and if these were directed toward Iran. The records also revealed that Iran had asked Hizbullah whether or not an operation could be carried out against the Pirinçilik base. Velioğlu was even asked by Iran on 4 March 1998 to set up a team to attack US and Israeli businessmen. The two sides exchanged information about Turkish policy toward Hizbullah. For example, on 3 November 1999, the Iranians informed Hizbullah that their intelligence agents in Turkey had managed to acquire the report drawn up by the Police Directorate General on Hizbullah.[14] In spite of the records found by the Turkish authorities Iran denied any connection with Hizbullah, and Iranian television described Hizbullah as a gang which had been established by the Turkish security authorities to fight the PKK. However, on 26 January Tehran's *Kayhan Intenational* accused the Turkish authorities of prosecuting Hizbullah on charges of murdering Kurds, although the murders had, in effect, been carried out by the Turkish security forces. In fact, the newspaper accused the authorities of trying to eliminate Hizbullah because they no longer needed them, following the PKK decision in January to cease their militant activities.

There were also rumors that the Lebanese Hizbullah, which had been established and supported by Iran, maintained links with Hizbullah in Turkey. However, the Lebanese Hizbullah denied this and its spiritual leader, Muhammad Husayn Fadlallah, said in an interview with a *Hürriyet* correspondent:[15] "We do not maintain any systematic or other type of relations with Turkey's Hizbullah." On the other hand, there were documented reports that cooperation had been established between Hizbullah and the Kaplancılar in Germany, and that members of the Kaplancılar came from Europe to Anatolia to be trained by Hizbullah.[16] *Al-Sharq al-Awsat* even claimed, based on information from the Turkish Ministry of the Interior, that links had been established between Hizbullah, the Islamic Unity Movement in Iraqi Kurdistan and Bin Ladin's al-Qa'ida, to discuss the idea of establishing a Kurdish Islamic Republic in southeastern Turkey and perhaps northern Iraq.[17]

Because Hizbullah had tried to obtain control by force over the mosques in east and southeast Anatolia, the authorities recruited the head of the Religious Affairs Directorate, Mehmet Nuri Yılmaz, to take action against Hizbullah. Yılmaz, in his attacks on the organization, called it "Hizb-Atrocity" and not Hizbullah.[18] He managed to recover the mosques that had been occupied by Hizbullah and restore them to the control of the Directorate, which took measures to prevent Hizbullah from reestablishing its influence.[19] On the other hand, the religious affairs director admitted that Hizbullah militants had managed to infiltrate the ranks of the Directorate, which acted to remove them as it had done in the mosques.[20]

Hizbullah was, in fact, deeply divided by tensions and clashes. *Milliyet* described no fewer than five factions:[21]

- *Hizbullah Unity and Salutation* included former left-wing supporters among its members and leaders. Its newspaper was *Selam*, a legal publication which published articles from Iran.
- *Hizbullah Vasat* (Moderate) was formed around the periodical *Sahabe* in Gaziantep, and became known when its members bombed a stand selling Old Testaments and Qur'ans at the Gaziantep Fair on 14 September 1997. Its founder-leader, Şahmerdan Sarı, and his nineteen associates were subsequently captured and tried. This group was concentrated in Istanbul, with training camps in Kocaeli and Yalova.
- *Hizbullah İlim* (Knowledge) became famous through its armed struggle against the PKK. It was known to have a large number of militants and sympathizers, who were among those most active against the government.
- *Hizbullah Menzil* (Range) had tried to legalize its activities and had attracted many militants and sympathizers.
- *Hizbullah Vahdet* (Unity) was active in recruiting members with the help of two foundations, one in Istanbul and the other in Diyarbakır.[22]

Despite these divisions, the authorities and the media did not usually identify a group or groups, but used the generic term "Hizbullah." One example was when a huge amount of weapons was seized in Gaziantep in February, and both the official announcement and media reports mentioned only Hizbullah.[23] It might have been the Vasat group, which was active in Gaziantep and also in neighboring Kahramanmaraş, where eighteen of its members — among them six imams — had been arrested while collecting money in the mosques for the group.[24]

The operations against Hizbullah also led to an operation against organizations maintaining certain links with Hizbullah. Among these was the illegal Jerusalem Warriors organization, and the Tevhid and the Selam groups connected with it. The Jerusalem Warriors was formed in 1979 in Iran and modeled on the Revolutionary Guards. Its aim was to set up an Islamic regime similar to that of Iran, through the use of violence. Over the years, most Turkish members of the Jerusalem Warriors had gone to Iran, where they received political and military training. Using information from documents found in the raids against Hizbullah, the Turkish security authorities opened a special operation against the Jerusalem Warriors and the Tevhid and Selam organizations. It was known as the Umut (Hope) operation, and solved the murders of Uğur Mumcu, Bahriye Uçok, Muammer Aksoy, Ahmet Tanır Kışlalı and several foreign diplomats. These murders had been carried out by members of the three organizations in accordance with their policy of exterminating those who advocated secular and Kemalist views. Seventeen people were arrested and brought to trial.[25]

(2) **Islam Büyük Doğu Akıncılar-Cephe (IBDA-C**; Islamic Great Eastern Raiders-Front). This illegal organization, founded in 1985 by Salih İzzet Erdiş, was active in Istanbul, Ankara, Amasya, Bayburt, Bursa, Elaziğ, Erzurum, Kahramanmaraş, Konya, Sakarya, Trabzun, Van, Şanlıurfa, Bingöl and Samsun. It was a Sunni anti-Shi'i organization, pursuing an aggressive, subversive policy against the constitutional government with the aim of establishing a religious regime based on Shari'a law. The IBDA-C became close to İsmailağa, an arm of the Nakşibendi sect, and adopted this group's *Furkan* magazine as its own.[26] One of the main activities of the IBDA-C was planting bombs in major cities with the intention

of sabotaging the tourism industry.[27] The security authorities arrested members of the IBDA-C in various provinces and seized arms and ammunition. Among those arrested were a school headmaster, his wife and another teacher (in Sakarya) who were caught making bombs.[28] The founder-leader had been arrested in 1999 with three other leaders, and his trial continued into 2000.[29] He was replaced by Salih Mirzabeyoğlu, who continued the same policy of violence.[30]

(3) **The Islamic Movement**, established in Batman in 1986/7, was an armed organization whose militants were trained by the SAVAMA in Iran.[31] They were known to be involved in forcible takeovers, bank robberies, abduction and car theft, and were said to be involved in the killing of the journalist Çetin Emeç, the writer Turan Dursun and the Iranian opposition figure Ali Akbar Gorbani.[32] The trial of forty-one members continued during 2000, on charges of murder, bombing and extortion. The prosecution sought heavy penalties for the seven executive board members.[33]

(4) **Aczmendiler** (Seekers of Justice and Truth). These were militants connected with the Nurist sect commemorating Said-i Nursi, the sect's founder. The leader of Aczmendiler, Müslim Gündüz, was sentenced to a prison term of four years and two months for founding and administering an illegal organization active against the secular democratic republic.[34]

(5) **Tufancılar** (*Tufan* = flood deluge). This sect was uncovered in Kahraman province and eighteen members, including its shaykh, Emin Özdemir, were taken into custody. They were accused of slandering secularism.[35]

(6) **Enderun** ("inner part of the palace"). The intelligence agencies identified this sect, which was largely comprised of teachers. It had approximately 1,200 members in about 200 townships in 40 provinces across Turkey. The headquarters was in Nevşehir and the group's publication was *İlk Adım* (first Step). The leader was a retired teacher, Zeki Soyak. When meetings were held in Nevşehir, students from İmam-Hatib schools were invited and a dormitory opened for them. The sect advocated the abolition of all laws starting with the constitution and preached new laws and a new constitution consistent with this nation's aims to form a new order. Secularism, liberalism and Kemalism, it claimed, had gone further than any heresy in history.[36]

(7) **BIAD** (Birleşmiş İslam Akvam Devletin; the United Islamic People's State). This was another new organization uncovered in Nevşehir province by gendarme units, who arrested thirteen of its members. Among them were two imams and the mayor of Karaşehir (a member of the FP), as well as the organization ringleader, Haci Ahmet Didin, who was captured in Ankara. BIAD aimed to unite all Islamic countries under one umbrella and establish an Islamic state under the jurisdiction of a caliphate. Searches did not reveal any weapons or explosives.[37]

(8) **Hizb al-Tahrir al-Islami** (Islamic Liberation Party). An organization active in a number of Middle Eastern countries, particularly Lebanon and Jordan, where the leader was living. Like BIAD, it aimed to establish a caliphate based on Shari'a law that would encompass all Islamic countries. The organization was active in Turkey for many years, but had a low profile and had not staged any armed attacks. However, in March 2000 they did, and the authorities began operations against their leaders and members in the provinces of Kayseri, Erzurum

and Ankara. The main leader, Bülent Çakıcı, was captured.[38] More leaders were arrested a week later, among them Ahmet Kılıçkaya and Mehmet Hanefi.[39]

(9) **Islamic Jihad.** This illegal organization was established through the influence of the Egyptian Islamist group behind the 1981 assassination of President Anwar al-Sadat of Egypt. It sought to establish an Islamic state through armed struggle. The organization was centered mainly in Ankara, with some supporters in southeastern Şanlıurfa province. A traffic accident led to the arrest of seventeen members on a charge of planting ten pipe-bombs in various locations in Ankara.[40]

Parallel to the activities of the Islamic militant organizations were those of the militant leftist organizations. The most active was still the Turkish Maoist movement, the Türkiye Komunist Partisi/Marksist-Leninist-Türkiye İşçi ve Köylü Kurtuluş Ordusu (TKP/ML-TIKKO; the Turkish Communist Party/Marxist-Leninist-Workers and Peasants Liberation Army of Turkey). Its leader, Süleyman Şahin, who had escaped from prison in Malatya in 1993, and three other members were detained in the Czech Republic. Turkey asked for Şahin's extradition to face charges of subversion, murder and armed attack.[41] In March, the bomb expert and secretary-general of the organization, Ali Gülmez, was captured as well as its courier, Ganimet Bozlu. Gülmez was involved in the attack on Çevik on 5 March 1999.[42] The organization was responsible for violence in Tokat and for the attack on a police vehicle in Istanbul in December, in which two police officers were killed and twelve wounded.[43]

Other small illegal leftist organizations were active only spasmodically. The Devrim Halk Kurtuluş Partisi-Cephe (DHKP-C; Revolutionary People's Liberation Party-Front), was involved in explosions that took place in front of four different business premises on the Antalya-Iskenderun highway. Twelve of its members were later arrested in Antalya.[44]

The illegal Communist Revolutionary Union (Devrim Kommunist Birliği) was active in İzmir province and was involved in nineteen attacks there, which led to the arrest of eight of its members in a hide-out in the western part of the province and the confiscation of many documents.[45]

Another group, the MLKP (Marksist-Leninist Komunist Partisi), clashed violently with the security forces in Istanbul while trying to set up a placard of the organization. One of its members was killed in the clash and two were wounded.[46]

THE KURDISH QUESTION

The year brought three major developments in the Kurdish question:

(1) The decision to postpone the submission of Öcalan's file to parliament, as was normal procedure in the case of the death penalty, and to hold it for a period of time in the Prime Minister's Office.

(2) The PKK decision to end their uprising and the party's internal strife about its future.

(3) The discussions in the coalition government about the development of the southeast, and the major debate on Kurdish identity and permission to use the Kurdish language in the education system and the media in the southeast, especially television.

The Turkish decision to become an EU candidate obliged the government to "Europeanize" its penal code, in particular to abolish the death penalty. The procedure was planned to start in mid-January. The main obstacle was the standing death penalty against Abdullah Öcalan, and whether this should be carried out before the code was amended. The MHP was against any postponement of the execution, while the other two members of the coalition, the DSP and ANAP, supported the proposal to wait for the decision of the European Court of Human Rights (ECHR). The two opposition parties were also against postponement, despite the fact that when in power in 1996-97, the government had signed Protocol No. 11. The appendix to this protocol accepted the judicial authority of the ECHR. These parties were therefore asked to be more sensitive on this issue and not to oppose the postponement.[47]

On 12 January, a summit meeting of the three leaders of the coalition parties was called. It lasted about eight hours. Prime Minister Ecevit handed out a report showing how the MIT assessed the postponement. It drew attention to the problems that Öcalan's execution might create for communal peace in the country. The General Staff and other intelligence and security organizations had also prepared reports on the possible consequences of Öcalan's execution. Finally, Bahçeli agreed to the postponement, mainly as a result of ANAP leader Yılmaz's efforts to find the right formula, and the three were able to issue their decision. The Öcalan file was entrusted to the Prime Ministry for a reasonable time, pending a ruling from the ECHR, and if the court decision was delayed inordinately long the deferment could be cut short. The words "for a reasonable time," and the opportunity given to Bahçeli to resubmit the file to parliament should he deem it necessary, convinced Bahçeli and the MHP to accept the formula. The file was to be on permanent stand-by for transfer to parliament at any time, as Turkey would not be obliged to wait for the ECHR ruling if it suspected the court of acting contrary to Ankara's accommodating position.

The decision clearly demonstrated Turkish goodwill and willingness to comply with international obligations. The most important element in the announcement, however, was the government intention to use Öcalan as a bargaining chip in the next phase. This could be taken as a serious warning to the PKK in particular, and Europe, in general. The message to Europe was that Ankara's cooperativeness was not a blank check. From now on, Europe would be obliged to think twice before taking any extreme step concerning Turkey. The message to the PKK was that Öcalan was now a strategic card in the hands of the Turkish government, to force the organization to abandon subversion and violence and to desist from exerting any future pressure to set Öcalan free.[48] Further, the decision made it difficult for the PKK and Öcalan to block Turkish accession to the EU as a full member.[49]

The following day, Prime Minister Ecevit reiterated the conditions for deferral of the Öcalan file: that the postponement was not indefinite, and would come to an end if some countries should be inclined to lay down conditions to Turkey on the matter, if Öcalan were to make threatening statements from his cell via his lawyers, or if efforts were made to use HADEP against the government. It would also end if the length of time requested by the ECHR was arbitrarily extended, conveying the impression that the issue was being exploited.[50]

The opposition parties criticized the government, accusing it of violating the constitution, as no law empowered the prime minister to withhold Öcalan's file from the parliament. How, they asked, did the three leaders establish a procedure that did not exist in the Turkish legal system and was apparently beyond the jurisdiction of the Supreme Court of Appeal and parliament?[51] However, the decision was approved by the parliament. The related problem that continued to preoccupy the coalition government was the protests and demonstrations over the postponement of Öcalan's execution by the families of those killed in the war against the PKK. Political leaders, among them President Demirel, Prime Minister Ecevit and Bahçeli, as well as opposition leaders, met with the families and promised them that the judicial process would be continued following the ruling of the ECHR.[52]

Nevertheless, in the discussions about the death penalty, the justice minister supported its removal from the whole Penal Code, while the MHP opposed its removal from Article 125 of the code, under which Öcalan was sentenced to death.[53] In November, while discussions continued, the minister of state for human rights, Rüştü Kazım Yücelen, recalled that Turkey had not carried out the twenty-five sentences of capital punishment given since 1984, and said that even if it was Öcalan in question, the government would not approve this twenty-sixth capital punishment.[54]

On the eve of the hearing in the ECHR in Strasbourg in November, families who had lost their sons in the war against the PKK gathered in the French town. They demanded the right to attend the hearing and emphasized that there was no discrimination against Kurds in Turkey.[55] On the first day the ECHR heard Öcalan's appeal, which took about three hours, and then the statements of the Turkish legal delegation's attorneys. They refuted the twelve articles in the Öcalan appeal one by one. These included his claims that:

(1) His right to life had not been recognized; their answer was that Turkey had not carried out a death sentence for sixteen years, even on baby killers;

(2) He was mistreated; the answer was that during his trial he stated that he had not been tortured or mistreated;

(3) The trial was not fair; the answer was that he had been tried fairly in front of the world's media.

(4) He was taken from Kenya by force; the answer was that he had entered Kenya illegally, using a false identity;

(5) He could not defend himself; the answer was that he was provided with all the conditions to defend himself;

(6) He could not talk with his lawyers; the answer was that he was not prevented from doing so at any point, but that security forces were present entirely for security reasons;

(7) He did not have freedom of expression; the answer was that he freely communicated within the limits of the law, like any other prisoner.[56]

However, in December 2000 the first chamber of the ECHR decided to consider most of Öcalan's applications and granted him leave to appeal against the sentence.[57]

This deferral of Öcalan's judicial process caused a partial dissolution of the PKK, and many groups of militants either fled surreptitiously from the organization or simply left it. The security forces in the east of the country claimed that the PKK had been almost eradicated within Turkey.[58] Already at the beginning of the year the PKK had convened its Seventh Congress in Iran, attended by 900 to 1,000 people. Conflicts and factionalism were reported to have come to light during the congress. Öcalan had conveyed a "political report" to the congress urging it to disclose that the organization had wholly laid down its arms and requesting that it draw up a peace plan — but at the same time to set up defense units in case Turkey should fail to respond to this peaceful overture.[59] However, the group led by Osman Öcalan (the brother of Abdullah), reportedly enacted momentous decisions to lay down arms altogether and to change the name of the PKK armed wing from People's Liberation Army of Kurdistan to the People's Legitimate Defence Force. The name of the PKK propaganda and political activities wing was also changed from the National Liberation Front of Kurdistan to the Democratic People's Union.

The changes indicated the fundamental shift from an armed struggle to a political campaign, with the slogan "Freedom to Abdullah Öcalan and Peace to Kurdistan." Its main demands were that the PKK be recognized as a legal political party, that minority status be granted to citizens of eastern and southeastern Anatolian origin, and that the Kurdish language be allowed in education and the media. In many of these decisions the congress used the word "Kurdistan."[60]

Giving up the ambition of an independent state in east and southeastern Anatolia caused disappointment among various groups living in camps in northern Iraq and Iran. In particular, the groups of Duran Kalkan and Nizamettin Taş, two senior members of the PKK, opposed the congress decisions.[61] Further, some PKK activists refused to withdraw from Turkey and decided to continue militant action, among them Hamili Yıldırım and his unit which remained active in the provinces of Tunceli and Erzincan.[62] However, without support and supplies from the PKK Chairmanship Council these militants could not sustain their activities, and started to surrender or leave the area. Government operations against these remaining PKK fighters continued, and clashes occurred in various provinces in the east and southeast, resulting in casualties on both sides.[63]

The fact that not all decisions of the Seventh Congress were implemented caused much tension in the Chairmanship Council. Osman Öcalan asserted that as long as the PKK was armed, it was impossible for Turkey and Europe to open negotiations with it and impossible for it to enter legitimate political life. He said that the organization was losing support among the people and asked: "What are we struggling for, and for whom?"[64]

The result was a weakening of PKK activities in the east and southeast, and a subsequent decision by the authorities to abolish the village guard system (established in 1986 to assist the security forces in the struggle against the PKK) and to lift martial law in five provinces in the southeast region. Almost 66,000 village guards were paid salaries, given food aid and granted fifteen days annual leave. By the beginning of 2000, 1,142 village guards had been killed in clashes and 1,186 wounded since these units were set up.[65]

The Turkish government did not accept the resolutions of the Seventh Congress regarding the future of Kurdish citizens in east and southeast Anatolia. Prime Minister Ecevit said that there were only Jewish, Armenian and Greek minorities in Turkey and the Kurds were not a minority.[66] This was the government answer not only to the PKK, but to EU pressure over the rights of minorities to use their language in education and the media. The issue had been raised after the arrest of three mayors of towns in the southeast for trying to introduce the use of Kurdish into their municipalities. It was brought up in February by the deputy prime minister, foreign minister and foreign trade minister of Luxembourg who was paying an official visit to Turkey, and also by the Swedish foreign minister during her concurrent visit to Ankara.[67] This led to an intense public debate about Kurdish identity, especially in the last three months of the year, and whether or not the Kurds were an ethnic group deserving the status of a minority, with the right to use their language in education and the media and to promote their traditions. Within this debate, HADEP was always referred to as the "Kurdish Party."

The question of identity was raised by Gen. Yaşar Büyükanıt, the deputy chief of

General Staff, in a speech about full Turkish membership in the EU. He said that this would be achieved by preserving the unitary and secular structure of the state and taking the necessary measures to ensure this. This led him to the question of the Kurds and HADEP, the party of Turkish citizens of Kurdish origin. The party had received around 1.5m. votes throughout Turkey in the 1999 elections, a little over 4% of the total vote and therefore below the minimum 10% required for entering parliament. By contrast, he pointed out, HADEP had won 39 municipalities in the southeast, including the Diyarbakır metropolitan municipality. It obtained over 40% of votes in the southeast and close to 60% in Diyarbakır. Gen. Büyükanıt claimed that if there had been no pressure by the state in the rural areas of the southeast, HADEP could have increased its ratio of votes even more, which would have reduced the other parties to insignificance.

When Turkish citizens of Kurdish origin were asked why they had voted for HADEP, the response was usually the same: because HADEP was their party. There was no mention of any socioeconomic or cultural reasons. Therefore, Büyükanıt said, if HADEP was closed down the Kurds would establish a new party of their own. His conclusion was that whether the Turks liked it or not, the Kurds existed and they had their own identity — their language and culture — and if both of these were denied then there was a Kurdish problem. This could not be solved only by providing the southeast with food and work. Büyükanıt's suggestions were: (1) to allow HADEP to engage in political activities within the political system on a legal basis, provided, of course, that it would renounce violence, and (2) to pave the way for citizens of Kurdish origin to use, learn and teach their own language, and not to prevent them from preserving and developing their cultural traditions. Such a policy would help other parties to broaden their vote bases in the southeast and would weaken separatist aspirations. It would be right, he added, to moderate the harsh official attitude toward such subjects as Kurdish radio, television and education, because in his opinion the unitary structure of Turkey would not be negatively affected by doing so.[68]

The General Staff did not support this approach, and claimed that broadcasting in Kurdish was a means of persuasion used by the PKK for politicization, which was another dimension of terrorism, and Turkey could not allow itself to be exploited by ethnic differences. Thus there could not even be a debate on the PKK demand to recognize ethnic Kurdish citizens as a separate entity.[69] But Büyükanıt found support for his views in the MIT. Both Senkal Atasagun, the MIT undersecretary, and Mikdat Alpay, its second-in-command, said that media and TV which followed a PKK line was already being watched in the southeast, because satellite dishes were widespread and could pick up Kurdish-language broadcasts from northern Iraq and other bordering states. They added that if the regime wanted to win over its citizens of Kurdish origin it would have to reach them, and the only way was by broadcasting in their own language.[70]

However, there was much political opposition, especially from the MHP, to allowing certain ethnic rights to citizens of Kurdish origin. Minister of State Şuayip Üşenmez (MHP) said that it was wrong to try to establish a different identity. State Minister Abdülhaluk Mehmet Çay (MHP) observed that language was an important part of national culture and a nation should have a single language. Minister of Defence Sabahattin Çakmakoğlu (MHP), stated: "When I take the needs of our national structure into consideration, I believe that Kurdish broadcasts are not necessary." He continued, "Satellite broadcasts in another language is one thing, and to say 'as a start, I will place this issue on legal and legitimate foundations' is another."[71] He stressed that TV broadcasts and education in Kurdish could never be accepted within the framework of Turkish national integrity.[72]

Prime Minister Ecevit supported the right to use the Kurdish language on grounds that modern communications technology could not be confined within borders, and that broadcasts in Kurdish were already being received from northern Iraq and Europe. This, he said, should be taken into account before making a decision.[73] He was supported by Rüştü Kazim Yücelen, minister of state for human rights, who emphasized that Kurdish broadcasts could be made to tell citizens the truth, but that the issue could only be decided by national consensus.[74]

Various civil institutions in Diyarbakır province favored the introduction of Kurdish language broadcasts, in the belief that they would present no problem to national unity.[75] But all efforts to find a way of allowing the use of Kurdish were to no avail. The issue caused confusion in government offices because it was agreed that there was a danger of politicization, as well as a need to respond to EU demands. But the government could not reach a decision — indeed, no decision could be expected from this coalition government.[76]

Despite government objections, HADEP continued to advocate publicly the use of Kurdish in education and the media and even in the administration. In fact, it was forbidden to speak Turkish in the Diyarbakır municipality, as the municipality had decided that Kurdish should be the only spoken language. However, the mayors of Diyarbakır (Feridun Çelik), Siirt (Selik Özalp) and Bingöl (Feyzullah Karaaslan), who were HADAP members, were arrested in February on charges of maintaining secret relations with PKK leaders and members, securing their help in the elections of 1999, and helping them give a political face to the PKK in Turkey and Europe. They were also — especially Diyarbakır's mayor — accused of promoting the use of the Kurdish language and of taking to the EU some of the problems encountered by the municipalities. The mayors admitted having contacts with the PKK, but claimed that they were forced to do so, especially when PKK help in municipal elections was taken into consideration. The mayors were defended by Mustafa Özer, the chairman of the Diyarbakır Bar, and seven lawyers, who alleged that the arrest was contrary to the law and to international agreements. Nevertheless, the Interior Ministry dismissed the three mayors from office, following incriminating statements made by the Diyarbakır representative of the PKK political wing, Abdülkadır Güzel, who was in custody, and by Diyarbakır deputy mayor Ramazan Tekin, accusing the mayors of cooperating with PKK. However, at the end of February, the mayors were released on bail and reinstated by the Interior Ministry.

HADEP continued to be active and its leaders, Ahmet Turan Demir and his successor, Murat Bozlak, insisted that it was not a separatist party. "We want to speak our language, enjoy our culture, and live in peace and brotherhood ... as one state within the borders of the National Pact of 1920," Demir said.[77]

RELATIONS WITH THE EUROPEAN UNION: REFORMS, LEGISLATION AND PARTICIPATION

The decision by the EU in December 1999 at Helsinki to nominate Turkey as a candidate for EU membership caused the Turkish government and parliament to begin the process of reforms and legislation that would bring its constitution, judiciary, administration and economy in line with EU standards. Several ministers were involved in the negotiations and discussions with EU authorities: Prime Minister Ecevit; Yılmaz deputy prime minister in charge of relations with the EU (officially from July 2000); Foreign Minister İsmail Cem; Justice Minister Hikmet Sami Türk and Minister of State for Human Rights Mehmet Ali İrtemçelik.

The number of Turkish people living in EU countries was 3.4m. 70% of them were in Germany, 9% in the Netherlands, 8.7% in France and 4.4% in Austria. Within the EU, 1.8m. Turkish people were working in member countries and the number of Turkish entrepreneurs was 73,200 — an average of 6.2 % — whose annual sales amounted to DM 61.2bn. A total of 366,000 people were employed by Turkish entrepreneurs and their overall investment was DM 15.4bn.[78]

In a public opinion poll held 10–21 August, the results showed that a majority of Turkish people (68.7%) was very much in favor of accession to the EU, with 9.9% opposed and 21.4% didn't know. The supporters of accession gave six reasons:

(1)   It would have positive effects on Turkish economic development.
(2)   It would strengthen Turkey in the world and increase its influence and esteem in the region.
(3)   Turkey would become a law-abiding country which respected human rights.
(4)   Freedom of thought, freedom of expression and freedom of religion would be fully upheld.
(5)   An opportunity would be created to realize Atatürk's dream of a contemporary civilization.
(6)   Accession would contribute toward the establishment of internal peace in the country and a solution of the problem of southeast Anatolia.

The opponents of accession also cited six reasons:

(1)   It would have negative effects on the Islamic identity of Turkey.
(2)   Turkish national identity would be harmed.
(3)   The economy orientation would be limited to Europe, and Turkey might become a colony.
(4)   The conditions laid down for accession might divide the country.
(5)   Turkey could never catch up to Europe in economic development.
(6)   Turkey would lose its sovereign rights.

More than two-thirds — 69.3% — of those who wanted Turkey to join the EU agreed with the conditions that Turkey had to remove the deficiencies in its democracy and improve its human rights in order to comply with international standards, and make sure that all its state organizations respected and upheld the supremacy of law. Much the same number, 70.4 %, agreed that Turkey had to respect freedom of thought and freedom of expression in order to be able to join the EU. 62% agreed that laws should guarantee equality for the cultural rights and identity of all the different groups in the community, to facilitate accession to the EU.[79]

The armed forces also supported accession to the EU. Their views were represented by the deputy chief of General Staff, Yaşar Büyükanıt, who said that entering the EU was a geostrategic and geopolitical "must" for the realization of Atatürk's modernization goal. Nobody doubted this.[80]

Prime Minister Ecevit, who became an ardent supporter of EU membership, often claimed that "Europe needs Turkey and Turkey needs Europe," and that the geopolitical position of Turkey would play an important role in unifying the two continents, Europe and Asia. He based this claim on the fact that Turkey was part of Europe in its geographical, historical and cultural realities, and at the same time part of Asia, Caucasia, the Black Sea region, the Middle East and the Mediterranean. In addition, Turkey imported scientific, technological, administrative and judicial structures and institutions from Europe, and adapted itself to these political and social institutions. On the other hand, Turkey had proved that the Islamic religion was appropriate for secularism, democracy, modernization and gender equality. In this way, he concluded, East and West mixed in harmony in Turkey and this would contribute to the integration of Europe and Asia.[81]

Guenter Verheugen, EU commissioner for enlargement, also stressed that the EU needed Turkey as an equal partner, adding that without Turkey it was impossible to maintain peace and stability in Europe.[82] In a meeting with Foreign Minister Cem (DSP) and the Portuguese foreign minister, Jaime Gama, the issues of Kurdish minority rights, the improvement of Turkish-Greek relations and the need to solve the Cyprus question were discussed; all were considered important elements in the full membership process.[83] However, the inclusion of the Cyprus question in the short-term priorities chapter of the Accession Partnership Document of the EU, and the later addition of the Greek-Turkish problem to this chapter, caused objections on the Turkish side and even a warning from Yılmaz that Turkey did not seek EU membership at any cost. Yılmaz also warned EU countries not to cause any delay to Turkish accession, and that Turkey would not accept any status other than full membership. Nor would it wait longer than the requisite time for preparation.

Despite the obstacles, Turkey did not give up its struggle to join the EU, but initiated a campaign to change those conditions.[84] Minister of Defence Çakmakoğlu (MHP) stated that Turkey did not consider the inclusion of Cyprus or the Aegean issues in the EU Accession Partnership Document to be either right or acceptable. This contradicted the decisions adopted at the Helsinki summit — decisions acknowledged to a considerable extent by Turkey.[85] Volkan Vural, Turkish secretary-general for EU affairs, declared that the EU should stop imposing unnecessary and meaningless political conditions and deal instead with the real agenda.[86] As for the Kurdish people, it was claimed that they were not granted minority status in the 1923 Treaty of Lausanne and therefore had no grounds for any privileges. In fact, within the framework of common law and individual rights the treaty did grant the Kurds and other Turkish citizens the right to use their mother tongue in printing and broadcast media, and to express their identity in this context.[87]

Deputy Prime Minister Bahçeli (MHP) accused the EU of creating obstacles for Turkey by including in the Accession Partnership Document the Cyprus problem, as well as Armenian genocide allegations and issues of democratization and ethnic identity, and said that these were like a wall in front of Turkey. It was not ethical, he said, first to invite Turkey to join the EU and then to plant mines on the road there.[88]

These expressions of anxiety over the delays turned out to be justified when, during the EU summit at Nice, it was revealed in a document related to the required institutional reforms prior to the EU enlargement that the EU did not think Turkey would be ready for full membership until 2010. The French foreign minister, Hubert Védrine, the term president of the EU, in attempting to explain why the schedule of institutional reforms excluded Turkey until 2010, claimed that Turkey was in a special position "because of reasons that were known." He added that Turkey's name was not mentioned in the reform program because full membership negotiations had not started.[89] This was interpreted as an important sign that out of the thirteen candidate nations waiting to enter the EU, only Turkey would have to wait beyond 2010. Prime Minister Ecevit, recalling decisions taken against Turkey a few years earlier, said that Turkey would continue to prepare for full membership as required and on time. When those preparations were completed, the gates of full membership might be opened much earlier than ten years.[90] However, Foreign Minister Cem said that Turkey-EU relations were settled on a particular course, warning the EU that full membership negotiations should start by the end of 2001 or early 2002.[91]

The Reforms on the Way to the EU

The Prime Ministry's Supreme Council for Human Rights Coordination prepared a "road map" for Turkey to follow on its way to full EU membership. It came within the scope of the Copenhagen criteria (Protection of Minorities) and was called "A Timetable for Democracy, Supremacy of Law, and Human Rights." Published in July, the map had fifty-two separate subject headings and envisaged a total rewrite of the Turkish legal system. Turkey aimed to fulfill it by the end of 2002, with the exception of a regulation about "compensation for terrorism."

Road Map to Europe

To be completed in 2000:
(1) Transnational television broadcasting agreement.
(2) Human rights office to be set up under the patronage of the Prime Ministry.
(3) A public inspections board (ombudsman) to be set up to ensure that any administration acted in accordance with its rules and for the purpose intended, and to provide the public with better service.
(4) Witness protection: A draft bill to be legislated concerning witness protection and compensation payments to be made to witnesses.
(5) Status of women: The status of women [and] the General Directorate Organization Law to be discussed by parliament.
(6) Domestic violence: A law to be passed to make domestic violence a criminal offence.

To be completed in 2001:
(1) The Press Law to be amended so as to reduce the scope of what constitutes a press crime and to soften the penalties.
(2) Freedom of organization: A law to be passed to allow public sector workers trade union rights.
(3) Democracy within trade unions: The laws on collective bargaining, strikes, and labor to be amended to ensure democracy within the trade unions and a more democratic working environment.
(4) Health and safety: A vocational health and safety law to be passed, which would include modern forms of organizing.
(5) Modern trades and careers: A law on work permits for foreigners to be passed as a supplement to the law on trades and careers assigned to Turkish citizens in Turkey, which had been in effect since 1932.
(6) Strikes and lockouts: Laws on the Steelworkers' Union, the Press Union, trade unions, and strikes and lockouts to be reformed. Agricultural workers to be covered by the Labor Law.
(7) Labor and employment organization: A labor and employment board to be set up in accordance with EU standards.
(8) Local government reform: Reforms of local government to be enacted so as to increase their authority and efficiency in serving the public.

(9) EU police: A draft to be produced that envisages changes in government decrees in regard to the Law on General Staffing and Procedures, the Higher Education Board and the Security Organization Law, in order to create an up-to-date police force.

(10) Prison overhaul: A prisons law to be passed that would define the duties and powers of prison staff, inmates and those on remand.

(11) EU prison guards: Prison staff to be given contemporary training, and a correctional facility personnel school to be established.

(12) New execution of penalties order: A draft law to be drafted that collates all individual regulations on the execution of a sentence under one separate law that is modern and easy to apply.

(13) Penalty law: A new penalty law to be passed, together with a law of criminal procedure.

(14) ECHR trust: Until the new execution of penalties law is passed, a draft law to be legislated that permits judges and prosecutors to rule on requests by the ECHR to have public prosecutors extend detention time, provided that prosecutors see the individual.

(15) Short trials: A law reducing the burden and processes of the judiciary to be passed.

(16) Civil servants rights: Laws regarding civil servants and pensions to be rewritten to comply with EU norms.

(17) Children's rights: A draft law to strengthen the institutional make-up of the social services and the Council for the Protection of Children to be discussed.

(18) Recourse to ECHR: Abolition of regulations that prevent corrective rulings from being made, or retrials from being carried out should new evidence come to light and in the light of ECHR infringement verdicts against Turkey.

(19) UN agreements: The signing and ratification of the UN Civil and Political Rights Agreement, which had been signed by the EU countries and candidate countries, together with the signing and ratification of the UN Economic, Social and Cultural Rights Agreement and the UN Prevention of Racial Discrimination Agreement.

(20) Death penalty: Protocol No. 6 regarding abolition of the death penalty, and a supplement to the Agreement on Protecting Human Rights and Basic Freedoms, to be signed.

To be completed in 2002:

(1) Freedom of thought: Provisions restricting freedom of thought and expression to be examined. The Penalties Law to be amended in 2001, the Anti-Terrorism Law and the Political Parties Law to be amended in 2002.

(2) Freedom of knowledge: In order to develop the freedoms of knowledge, craft and association, the laws on Police Responsibilities and powers, together with those on cinema, video and music productions, to be amended.

(3) Right to freedom: New regulations to be drawn up on issues that restrict personal freedoms, such as arrest, detention, and torture; the Police Responsibilities and Duties law to be amended.

(4) Freedom of communication: The make-up and powers of the Supreme Radio and Television Board to be rewritten.

(5) General amnesty for the press: Amendments to be passed to prevent writers and journalists from being imprisoned for publishing material that does not imply

the break-up of the unitary state; writers and journalists already in prison to be pardoned.

(6) Freedom for trade unions: The freedom to found an association and to stage meetings and protest marches to conform to the standards of any democratic society.

(7) Solution to unemployment: Article 48 of the constitution to be amended and a new law passed in order to enable to cope with unemployment.

(8) Labor and employment organization: A new law to be passed to bring this organization up to date.

(9) ILO conditions: The provisions of the International Labor Organization (ILO) Agreement on employers terminating contracts to be enacted.

(10) Job security: Legislation to be drawn up to prevent employers from abusing their right to dissolve a service contract.

(11) Agricultural security: Agriculture and forestry workers to come within the scope of the Labor Law.

(12) Aviation law: An aviation employment law to be passed to improve conditions for people employed in the aviation sector.

(13) Shipping law: the working conditions for people employed on boats to be brought up to date.

(14) Justice police force: A Ministry of Justice police force to be set up.

(15) Powers of evidence for lawyers: Lawyers to be given the power to collect evidence.

(16) OHAL: Amendments to be made to the Emergency Rule (OHAL) laws to bring them into line with what is expected of a law-biding state.

(17) Military courts: Amendments to be made to the Military Penal Code and the Trial Procedures Law to stop civilians from being tried in military courts.

(18) Civilian NSC: The ratio of five civilian to five military personnel in the National Security Council (NSC) to be altered in favor of civilians, so that there would be ten civilian and five military personnel on the council.

(19) Political morals: A Political morals law to be passed to help combat corruption.

(20) Wealth disclosure law: Amendment of the existing law so as to prevent the unjust acquisition of wealth.

(21) Women's rights: The position of, and issues surrounding women to be reevaluated and the Turkish Civil Code amended accordingly.

(22) Family courts: The draft law on the founding of family courts to be enacted.

(23) Disabled rights: All the issues surrounding the disabled to be studied in depth and measures taken to help resolve them.

(24) Citizenship: Article 5 of the Citizenship Law, which does away with the principle of equality for Turks married to foreigners, to be amended.

(25) Compensation for torture: Compensation the state is obliged to pay to victims of torture or maltreatment following ECHR rulings to be paid by those who committed the crime.

To be completed in 2004:

Compensation for terrorism: A law concerning compensation for damage resulting from the fight against terrorism to be passed.[92]

In the meantime, the minister of justice convened a special commission to change the Penal Code, including the death penalty, taking into consideration international standards, the realities of the country and, as the minister said, "the needs of the twenty-first century." A new Penal Code was in fact needed because the existing articles were outmoded. Sentences as well as pecuniary punishments were to be reexamined and redefined to take account of human rights and the broader right to freedom of expression. In regard to capital punishment, Turkey was the only country which did not sign the annexed Protocol No. 6, which thereby abolished the death sentence, even though it was a member of the Council of Europe. As mentioned above, capital punishment was to be evaluated within the scope of the new Turkish penal code, but, as the minister of justice said, the commission should take into consideration special conditions in Turkey.[93] Abolition of the death penalty faced certain opposition, especially in regard to Öcalan, but in order to become a full member of the EU Turkey had no choice but to carry out the legal reforms required.

In general, the EU short-term (one year) and medium-term (three years) expectations from Turkey comprised: instituting freedom of expression; adapting the justice system to international norms; abolishing the death penalty; transforming the NSC into a consultative organ; rescinding all laws that prevented Turkish citizens of various ethnicity from using their mother tongue in television and radio broadcasts; recognizing cultural differences and the right of education in mother tongues; and lifting the state of emergency in the southeast. The EU deemed these basic rights and freedoms that Turkey should grant to its citizens, both as a democracy and a state governed by the rule of law.[94] Ecevit declared that Turkey would complete all the preparations required within a period of four years and would be ready for full membership in 2004.[95]

The same optimism was stressed by Treasury Under-Secretary Selcuk Demiralp, who said that the Turkish economy would be prepared for EU conditions within three years, following implementation of the three-year economic program. He added that Turkey had covered significant ground in eliminating its public deficits, and after the government had reduced inflation the EU would raise no further questions in regard to the Turkish economy.[96] Already in February, the Justice Ministry started to examine EU regulations, including Article 6 about capital punishment.[97]

In March, the government approved the Social Security Law to be presented to parliament at the beginning of April. It included a restructuring of the Social Security Authority, the Directorate General of Social Security for Self-Employed Workers and the Employment Authority, and would combine all social security institutions under one roof. The government also started programs at all ministries to raise Turkish norms and standards to those of the EU, and to pass new regulations to remove the concerns of foreign entrepreneurs.[98]

The NSC took a historic step to facilitate accession to the EU by confirming a series of reforms to be implemented in two stages, in 2001 and between 2001 and 2004, with the aim of integrating Turkey with the EU:

(1) Priority should be given to the constitutional changes.
(2) The NSC structure would be changed by increasing its number of civilian members.
(3) Protocol No. 6, which called for the removal of the death sentence, would be signed.
(4) The penal articles against intellectual crimes would be removed.

(5) The Anti-Terror Law and the Political Parties Law would be amended.

(6) A bill on political ethics would be enacted against bribery and corruption.

(7) Human rights would be taken up as a whole, and institutions would be established and fully authorized to protect human rights.

Bills would be enacted to subject past decisions made by military administrations to court rulings.[99]

However, Mesut Yılmaz, deputy prime minister in charge of relations with the EU, said that the Turkish process of adjustment to the EU unfortunately operated very slowly. He suggested work on three areas: (1) combating the racist, discriminative and crusader mentality within Europe that never wanted to accept Turkey in Europe; (2) opposing those in the EU who were not able to defeat Turkey on national causes; and (3) resisting those in Turkey who did not want full EU membership and who felt extremely uneasy about the Copenhagen criteria (on minority rights and human rights) and the Maastricht criteria (on currency unification).[100]

Finally, the minister of justice outlined his suggestions on the constitutional amendments. These, he said, should eliminate all limitations on individual rights and freedoms and translate into reality the ideals of a state of law and the supremacy of the law. Article No. 6 should read: sovereignty is vested in the nation without reservation or condition. Articles Nos. 26 and 28, dealing with linguistic prohibition, should be omitted altogether. The article on the equality of individuals should be changed to state clearly the equality of gender. Political parties which violated the constitution and the Political Parties Law could be disqualified from general elections or by-elections. The age limit for taking up a seat in parliament should be lowered to twenty-five. All authority pertaining to amnesties should be granted to parliament. There should also be an inspection mechanism for administration processes separate from the judiciary. This public inspectorate should be included in the constitution. The authority of the Constitutional Court should be extended and decrees having the force of law, issued in time of war or a state of emergency, should be added to the jurisdiction of the Constitutional Court.[101]

Another field in which legislation was already implemented was that of torture. In an attempt to stop torture, the Human Rights Coordination Supreme Council decided to bring together victims of torture and their torturers in a bid to promote deterrence. Between 25 September and 1 December, assemblies were convened in eighty-one provinces under a program called "The Human Rights Drive." The committees, made up of the secretary-general of the NSC, relevant ministers and high-ranking officials, as well as the minister of state for human rights, Rüştü Kazım Yücelen, toured the provinces one by one. They listened to complaints and allegations of human rights violations, starting with torture, and brought the concerned parties together to discuss or refute the allegations. The highest ranking security officials in each province also attended the meetings, coming face to face with those who made the allegations.[102]

The Kurdish Obstacle

As discussed above, a major obstacle in the dialogue between Turkey and the EU was the regime's attitude to its Kurdish minority and its refusal to allow use of the Kurdish language in Kurdish education and media in southeast Anatolia. The president for economic development, Meral Gezgin Eriş, admitted that Turkey had serious deficiencies in regard to the rights of minorities, and said it should introduce these rights for its own sake and not just for the sake of the EU.[103]

The EU closely followed the Turkish government treatment of Kurdish politicians. Daniel Cohn-Bendit, co-chairman of the European Parliament-Turkish Parliament Joint Committee, requested a meeting with former deputy Leyla Zana in prison, but was refused and decided to cancel a Parliamentary Joint Committee meeting in Ankara.[104] The European Parliament also intervened in the arrest of three HADEP mayors, warning Turkey that such an arrest of elected officials could not be tolerated and might block the way to the EU.[105] In the last week of March, several delegations from the EU visited Turkey, among them the Socialist Group leader in the European Parliament, Enrique Baron Crespo. He hosted a dinner in honor of Turan Demir, the HADEP leader, and Deputy Mahmut Sakar, and discussed with Prime Minister Ecevit the question of releasing former deputy Zana from prison. Crespo also discussed the question of minority rights and the reforms in the Turkish Penal Code and constitution, especially concerning capital punishment. Crespo was followed by the reporters on Turkey from the Council of Europe Parliamentarians Assembly (COEPA), Andras Barsony and Benno Zierrer. They visited the southeast and were impressed by the positive atmosphere, the fact that daily life was back to normal and that positive developments were taking place in the security and resettlement of local people. They also met Leyla Zana and discussed her imprisonment with the minister of the interior.[106]

The EU continued to track the Turkish government attempts to deal with the Kurds' use of their mother tongue in their media, education and cultural life. Various Turkish commentators advised Foreign Minister Cem to ask the EU to be patient and not to delay negotiations on full membership, despite the obstacles and delays in implementing the right of the Kurds to use their own language.[107]

Two key documents had been prepared by the European Council regarding minorities in European law: (1) the Framework Agreement for the Protection of National Minorities, and (2) the European Charter for Regional or Minority Languages. Turkey claimed that although other EU candidates, namely Poland, Lithuania and Latvia, had not signed these, accession talks with them had begun. Further, neither Belgium nor France had signed the agreement. The French stated that the agreement was contrary to their constitution. The Turkish government said this demonstrated that the minority criteria were problematic even for France, a self-styled champion of freedom worldwide.[108] But the EU did not let up its pressure for the introduction of education and television broadcasts in Kurdish, and every mention of it caused much irritation in Turkey.[109]

ESDI and NATO

Another source of tension between the EU and Turkey was the decision of the EU to establish a 60,000-strong Rapid Reaction Force, in accordance with the European Security and Defense Identity (ESDI) concept and in coordination with NATO, but as a separate entity. Turkey, a NATO member and candidate for the EU, insisted on sending a Turkish unit to the Rapid Reaction Force and on participating in its decision-making command.[110]

In May, Foreign Minister Cem expressed Turkish dissatisfaction with the draft text of the document on the ESDI to be submitted to NATO in June, and was supported by non-EU NATO allies such as Iceland, Canada, and Norway.[111] When the document was submitted, Turkey noted that it could not accept offering the use of NATO facilities and capabilities to the EU automatically. It also stressed that it would be appropriate to provide for the active participation of non-EU NATO allies, including Turkey.[112] The main problem was the EU decision to exclude Turkey from the ESDI decision-making group. The Turkish chief of General Staff, Hüseyin Kivrikoğlu, demanded that measures be taken against this ruling,[113] and the government fully endorsed the military.[114]

In fact, the NATO Council decision of 17 July supported the Turkish position, and confirmed that the EU would not use NATO facilities automatically or in an unlimited way. Every demand from the EU would be evaluated by NATO member countries, including Turkey, with due regard to the veto power of each member state.[115] On the other hand, Turkey wanted to be included in the defense initiative mechanism to be formed within the framework of the ESDI, considering this to be an important step toward full membership of the EU — although this reason was categorically denied by Foreign Minister Cem. The EU suggested that the topic be discussed in the meeting between the fifteen EU countries and the six non-EU European NATO allies in November.[116]

However, no progress was made. Deputy Prime Minister Bahçeli accused the ESDI of trying to establish a European army outside NATO, in which a Turkish contribution of army units was included but Turkey's participation in decision-making was denied. This was not acceptable, Bahçeli said.[117] The efforts to reach a compromise over the ESDI at the NATO ministerial meeting in Brussels failed, as Turkey refused to back down from its request to participate in the ESDI's decision-making and planning.[118] Finally, because of Turkish objections, the agreement between NATO and the EU (ESDI) on this issue was postponed to the following year.[119]

FOREIGN AFFAIRS

Besides matters related to the EU, Turkish foreign policy was geared toward a number of other important areas.

RELATIONS WITH RUSSIA, CENTRAL ASIA, AND THE CAUCASUS

Turkish-Russian relations centered on several issues: the Caucasus and Central Asia, usage of the Bosphorous Straits, and the struggle against terrorism and insurgency being waged by both parties.

Russia expressed concern for calls by some quarters in Turkey for the formation of a "Community of Central Asia and Azerbaijan,"[120] as its apparent ethnic basis could pose a threat to Russian interests in the region. When President Süleyman Demirel proposed the idea of a "Caucasus Pact"[121] Russia responded by convening a summit of the CIS (Commonwealth of Independent States), comprised of the eleven heads of state of the countries of the former USSR and Russian president Vladimir Putin. The intent was clearly to make a show of strength and unity in the face of what was deemed Turkish and Western interference in the Russian sphere of influence. Putin, in his first such meeting as Boris Yeltsin's successor, endeavored to bolster the support of Georgia, Armenia, and Azerbaijan for Russia, and to deter Turkish efforts, by having a mini-summit with these countries during the larger CIS summit.[122] These summits made little impact, however, as apparently several of the CIS countries preferred to opt out of the organization altogether due to a fear of re-Sovietization.[123]

As a result Russia quickly appeared to have come to terms with increasing Turkish influence in the Caucasus and Central Asia, and pursued a policy of engagement rather than obstructionism. During a visit to Ankara in late February, Russian deputy prime minister Ilya Klebanov, met with Prime Minister Bülent Ecevit, National Defense Minister

Sabahattin Çakmakoğlu, and President Süleyman Demirel. The subsequent joint statements reflected a more conciliatory tone than in the past.

A parallel between the Kurdish problem in Turkey and that of Russia in Chechnya was drawn, and the two sides resolved to work together to fight terrorism, and to preserve their respective territorial integrities.[124] Putin assented to Demirel's proposal for a "Caucasus Stability Package." Also on the agenda was the Turkish tender for the license to produce 145 assault helicopters, worth an estimated $4bn. to $4.5bn.[125] The Russians offered to sell Turkey the Ka-52 assault chopper designed by a Russian-Israeli consortium, along with the Vikhr high-precision guided weapons system,[126] and to aid Turkey in developing its own industry so as to produce them itself.

Concerned about the Russian war in Chechnya, Turkey strongly endorsed the US-EU diplomatic efforts aimed at impressing upon the newly elected Putin, to employ a policy of restraint.[127]

Turkey continued to pursue its policy of ever-greater engagement in Central Asia. Foreign Minister Ismail Cem expressed the feelings of affinity between Turkey and Central Asia derived from "the same history, belief, culture, and language."[128] Russia in the meantime, adopted the position that Russian-Turkish cooperation in the region would be a "determining factor in Caucasia, Central Asia, and in international relations," owing to their leading positions and shared interests.[129]

The Turkish role as a major conveyor of energy resources from the East to the West put the issue of the Bosphorous straits on the political agenda. Foreign Minister Ismail Cem stated that Turkey would "not permit the straits to be converted into an oil pipeline" thereby endangering its environment and the city on its banks, simply because oil producing states desired a cheap and easy way to move their product to market.[130] This sensitivity over the Bosphorous did not, however, dampen overall efforts on the part of Turkey to pursue other energy transfer plans. In May 1999 Turkey signed a $2bn.-$3bn. deal with Turkmenistan to build a Trans-Caspian gas pipeline, to carry natural gas from Turkmenistan, across the Caspian Sea, Azerbaijan, and Georgia to Turkey and Europe.[131] In October 2000, President Sezer traveled to Turkmenistan to meet with President Saparmurad Niyazov to discuss the progress of the project.[132]

There were some concerns that beyond Putin's actions in Chechnya, he might also be acting with a heavy hand regarding some of the other republics as well. The Russian war against terrorism was something that Turkey could well understand on one level, having been engaged for many years in a similar fight against Kurdish separatists. However, Turkey insisted that Russia and the West needed to distinguish between legitimate democratic movements of Eastern Turkmenistan, Uzbekistan, and Chechnya, and more problematic "terrorist" movements such as the Taliban in Afghanistan.[133]

RELATIONS WITH THE US

While actively pursuing a policy of closer ties with the US, there were some minor bumps in the road. In March, it was reported by Vice-Admiral Tanır Uzunay, a representative of the Turkish General Staff, that the US was "eavesdropping" on the Turkish military, and other critical institutions, and had become aware of sensitive information.[134] The ensuing debate quickly turned to Turkish lapses in security, the need for a better system, and how best to implement one. The fact that it was the US who was the accused party was quickly sidelined, and Ziya Aktaş of the DSP made a more general statement that "not just America, everyone is eavesdropping on us."[135]

The US continued to press Turkey for greater democratization, individual freedoms, and sensitivity to human rights for its citizens. The issue had a continuing impact on Turkish relations not just with the US, but with the West as a whole. Specifically, the US encouraged Turkey to amend Article 312 of the Turkish Penal Code, which forbade inciting malice and hatred among the people, and which the US viewed as providing unduly broad powers to repress human rights.[136] The Turkish chief public prosecutor, Vural Savaş, stated that Article 312 was an essential instrument in the safeguarding of the "secular Republic."[137] The article was employed to effect the banning from political participation of the leader of the Islamic leaning FP.[138] The US embassy denied that it was attempting to interfere in the internal political and legal affairs of Turkey.[139]

Turkey expressed concern over the convening of a conference on the "Search for a Kurdish Identity" in the US, but the Americans attempted to allay their fears by indication that the conference was organized by a university and did not reflect any change in US policy with respect to Northern Iraq or the Kurds.[140] Foreign Minister Cem also made it known to US secretary of state Madeleine Albright, that the "Armenian massacre" bill that was pending in the US Congress was distressing to Turkey. They were disturbed that efforts to defame Turkey in this way were not only being made by members of the Armenian diaspora in the US but also by the government of Armenia itself.[141] In September, Albright assured Cem during their meeting that President Bill Clinton would do what he could to prevent such "pro-Armenian initiatives" from passing.[142]

The Turkish tender for the production/sale of 145 combat helicopters was still being debated in July. The two companies that remained in the running were the US Bell-Textron Company, and the Russian-Israeli Kamov consortium. Although President Clinton was supportive of the sale there were doubts as to whether the US Congress would permit the deal to be carried out, in light of Armenian and Greek lobbying efforts against it.[143] Such worries were apparently well founded, as the US Senate suspended an authorization to export eight heavy transport helicopters to Turkey, in mid-November. The Turkish government was convinced that this was a result of relentless Greek and Armenian lobbying.[144]

In the wake of the October attack on the USS Cole in Yemen, which killed seventeen American sailors (see chapter on Yemen), the Turkish government announced that it would not permit the US to launch any attacks against the Taliban regime of Afghanistan from the İncirlik airbase in Turkey. Ramız Şen, the chargé d'affaires of the Turkish embassy in Kabul, stated that İncirlik was a NATO airbase and could not be used without Turkish permission. He also expressed Turkey's friendship with Afghanistan, and said "Usama [Bin Ladin] is a problem of the United States, not of Turkey."[145]

The Turkish government adopted a policy of reengagement with Saddam Hussein, and upgraded its representation in Baghdad to the level of ambassador, much to the dismay of the US. Turkey contended that the policy of isolation had been a failure, and thought it better to improve relations with Iraq.[146] Turkey had been damaged economically by the embargo on Iraq and had seen no real benefit in pursuing the policy of the past ten years, claiming to have lost $30bn. in trade since the Gulf War.[147] In addition, the power vacuum created in Northern Iraq enabled the PKK to establish a foothold there, and launch incursions into Turkey, which was answered with a large-scale Turkish counter offensive.[148] The US was sympathetic to Turkish economic difficulties that were in part a result of the embargo, but were in no way inclined to follow a similar course, nor encourage Turkey in its attempted rapprochement with Iraq.

The unusual circumstances surrounding vote-counting in the US presidential election in November of 2000 caused grave doubts in the Turkish government. The Clinton era, by all accounts, had been one of steadily improving relations between Turkey and the US. The worry was that the next president, whoever he would turn out to be, would be plagued by serious legitimacy problems for not having won decisively.[149] The Turkish fear was that such a president would be unable to effectively govern a divided country and an equally divided Congress, rendering the American political scene ripe for the picking of the special interest groups, such as the Greek, and Armenian lobbies.[150] Furthermore, Turkey feared the potential for America to become so bogged down in its own internal problems that its previous support for Turkey in areas such as Cyprus and the Aegean could evaporate, leaving Turkey very vulnerable to European pressure.[151]

With the ultimate, albeit delayed, resolution of the American presidential election in late December, Turkey began to look positively on the outcome. They were satisfied that George W. Bush would continue the process of bettering relations begun under his father, and continued under Clinton. "This expectation stemmed from the fact that Bush's core team knows Turkey very well," wrote one Turkish analyst, "and would likely conduct their foreign policy along sound strategic lines," beneficial to Turkish interests,[152] and typical of a Republican administration.[153] Despite the restored Turkish confidence, questions remained as to how the new Bush administration would handle the sensitive issues such as the ever-present Armenian question, when the Republican speaker of the House, Dennis Hastert pledged to put it on the Congressional agenda.[154]

RELATIONS WITH ISRAEL

Turkish-Israeli relations were marked by ever-greater military cooperation. In March, Israel was awarded a contract worth some $7bn. to produce a thousand Main Battle Tanks (MBT) for the Turkish military, and another contract worth $250m. to upgrade three hundred existing tanks was also in the offing.[155] As mentioned above, the proposed contract for 145 attack helicopters to be produced by a Russian-Israeli consortium grew more likely to be realized, as doubts increased to the viability of the helicopters being purchased from the US.[156] The major obstacle facing even greater defense cooperation between Turkey and Israel was that every time a prospective deal was discussed, Turkey's NATO allies exerted enormous pressure on her to pursue an alternate arrangement with one of them instead.[157] This is what ultimately occurred with respect to the Russian-Israeli KA-52 attack helicopter, which was turned down in favor of the cheaper American AH-1W Twin Cobra.[158] Similarly, under mainly European pressure, several projects already agreed upon were scrapped, such as the MBT upgrade, and a spy satellite deal.[159]

Turkey continued to pursue a policy of relative non-engagement regarding the Arab-Israeli conflict.[160] Its strong strategic relationship with Israel, juxtaposed with its status as a Muslim country, placed Turkey in a difficult position at times. For example, the Palestinian Authority (PA) announced in mid-year that it intended to declare the establishment of an independent Palestinian state on 13 September 2000. If this had occurred (which it ultimately did not), Turkey would have had "to decide whether or not to recognize the new state,"[161] risking the opprobrium of either Israel or the Arab and Muslim world.

In August, when Ankara hosted Israeli, Palestinian, and American diplomatic delegations in an effort to continue the Camp David process, Turkish officials took great pains to make it clear that they were in no way functioning as a mediator. One official described the Turkish role as "a facilitator" and nothing more, emphasizing that it was the US which was conducting the mediation effort.[162] Particularly on the issue of Jerusalem, Turkey was very hesitant to make any comment whatsoever for fear of angering, or alienating Muslim, Christian or Jewish sensibilities.[163]

Throughout the Israeli-Palestinian negotiations, Turkey urged moderation, and discouraged PA President Yasir 'Arafat from making any unilateral moves, as they would obstruct the momentum of the peace process, while refraining from offering any new initiatives of its own, in keeping with its traditional stance.[164] Even with the failure of the Camp David, and subsequent talks between Israel and the Palestinians, and the outbreak of the Intifada in late September (see chapters on Israel, and the PA), Turkey maintained its position as a concerned onlooker, urging the parties to work out their differences, yet refusing at all costs the role of mediator.

There were calls inside Turkey to adopt a more active role in the conflict yet the government continued to maintain its more passive approach.[165] Though Ankara did send financial assistance to the PA,[166] this was not enough to satisfy some quarters in Turkey, many of whom harbored Islamic sympathies.[167] Some expressed the opinion that Turkey had become far too friendly with Israel in the mistaken belief that in doing so Turkey would benefit from the influence of the pro-Israel lobby in the US and so be better shielded from pro-Armenian resolutions.[168] Due to both pressure from the Turkish public, and the rapidly worsening situation, Turkish diplomatic efforts did increase in November and December, with many visits and calls made by Turkish officials to Israel and to the PA, attempting to get the parties back to the negotiating table.

RELATIONS WITH GREECE AND CYPRUS

In the wake of the destruction wrought by the earthquakes of 1999 (see *MECS* 1999, pp. 616–19), Greece and Turkey found common ground upon which to build a new, more friendly dialogue.[169] Despite this "honeymoon atmosphere" the hard issues, and positions of the two sides remained unchanging. Greece and Turkey seemed throughout the year to be more concerned about preserving the new sense of goodwill than actually tackling the disputes that had divided them for so many years.

For Greece, the primary concern, which they often declared to be the only concern, was that of the Aegean Continental Shelf dispute. This multifaceted issue was the product of the very complicated geography of the Aegean. The extremely close proximity to Turkey of so many Greek islands resulted in conflicting claims over territorial waters, airspace, and the right to militarize those islands. These matters were effectively "shelved" since late 1999 due to the "friendly atmosphere" that had developed between the two countries, but during 2000, they began to rear their heads once again.[170]

Greece agreed to permit the Turkish military aircraft to fly in the Aegean's FIR (flight Information Region) provided they identified themselves as "friendly."[171] Greek authorities later decided, however, that Turkey would have to disclose their flight plans in advance, and any failure to do so would give the Greek air force cause to engage the Turkish planes in mock dogfights. This had already occurred on no less than ten occasions in late January and early February.[172] In addition, restrictions on permissible flight paths would be put in place, thereby restricting Turkish aircraft to using flight routes in the southern part of Crete.[173] Turkey was upset with the Greek demands, and stated that it refused to provide such information about flights that would be carried out in international airspace.[174]

Turkey was of the opinion that all the Greek owned Aegean islands must remain "demilitarized in accordance with the (1923) Lausanne Agreement," but Greece held that Limnos was an exception and should open to Greek military use.[175] This disagreement was the direct cause for the Greek withdrawal from joint NATO maneuvers code-named "Destined Glory" held in October.[176] Greece withdrew in the midst of the operation, which cast a shadow over Greek-Turkish relations.

Greece was also of the opinion that its territorial waters extended to twelve miles in accordance with the international agreement it signed in 1982.[177] The bone of contention was that it claimed this applied to all of its islands in the Aegean as well, and that Turkish territorial waters only extended to three miles.[178] Turkey, for its part, claimed a six-mile territorial water limit, and that the Greek islands possessed no claim to territorial waters of their own.[179] A similar situation existed with regard to the claims over airspace: Turkey claimed six miles and Greece claimed ten.

The two countries were unable even to agree on the proper forum for resolving these issues. Turkey asserted that a settlement could only be reached within the confines of bilateral talks based on friendly relations.[180] Greece indicated that it wished the dispute to be adjudicated in the International Court of Justice at The Hague,[181] which Turkey rejected.

There was some mild anxiety in Turkey about what the immediate future of relations with Greece would be prior to the Greek elections that took place on 9 April.[182] When Costas Simitis' PASOK party (Panhellenic Socialist Movement) won reelection, fears of a sudden shift in Greek policy were allayed, and Turkish president Demirel, and the Foreign Ministry, expressed their hopes that relations between the two countries would continue to improve.[183] Prime Minister Simitis had supported Turkish candidacy to the EU at the Helsinki EU summit, and had also helped the cause of the future membership of Cyprus in the organization.[184] Several EU countries, namely Germany, France, The Netherlands, and Italy, were opposed to full Greek Cypriot membership in the EU before the Cyprus issue was solved, hence Simitis' decision not to oppose Turkish candidacy.[185]

As stated above, Greece preferred to confine discussions with Turkey to the issue of the Aegean Continental Shelf issue. This was cause for much consternation to Turkey as it favored direct talks on all outstanding disputes.[186] The Turkish position was that no progress could be made if fundamental issues were never discussed or even recognized as problems.[187]

This standstill amidst the unprecedented period of goodwill and hope became frustrating to both sides. In essence, neither country had taken any new position or, seized upon any new initiative, and certainly was not prepared to make any concession that deviated from long established policies. Officials of the two countries simply continued to applaud the period of good relations, meet with each other periodically, and even signed nine agreements in a span of four months.[188] These agreements were intended to set in motion a meaningful process of problem resolution but failed to do so. They did, however, cause an increase in economic activity, and tourism between the two states.[189]

The issue of Cyprus was the central element in the dispute between Greece and Turkey.[190] None of the concerned parties was happy with the status quo and yet it remained because none of them dared make a concession of any kind. President Rauf Denktaş of the Turkish Republic of Northern Cyprus won reelection in April, shortly after the Greek elections.[191] His position and that of the Turkish government, which backed him, was that there were two separate nations on the island of Cyprus and they should be recognized as such.[192] Denktaş would not even engage in any talks until this was done.[193] The governments of Greece and Greek Cyprus wanted the two parts of Cyprus to be either reunified or confederated. Otherwise, it was possible that only the Greek part of the island would become a member of the EU. The Turkish part of the island could benefit from this status only if it agreed to confederation, or reunification.[194]

Despite the clear importance of the issue it was much easier to avoid it and instead continue basking in the glow of "good neighborly" relations. In September, Turkish foreign minister Ismail Cem, and Greek foreign minister Yeoriyos Papandreou, who met while they were in New York for the 55th session meeting of the UN General Assembly, went so far as to say that "Cyprus was not a Turkish-Greek problem."[195] Turkey had further cause to separate the Cyprus issue from its bilateral relations with Greece. As no solution was likely in the short term, Turkey risked being viewed as the intransigent party, and in so doing might facilitate the admission of Greek Cyprus to the EU, while potentially shutting the door on its own chances of the same.[196]

NOTES

For the place and frequency of publications cited here, and for the full name of the publication, news agency, radio station, or monitoring service where an abbreviation is used, please see "List of Sources." Only in the case of more than one publication bearing the same name is the place of publication noted here.

1. *Hürriyet*, 26 January 2000 (DR).
2. *Hürriyet*, 28 March 2000 (DR).
3. *Milliyet*, 28 December 1999.
4. *Hürriyet*, 19 June 2000 (DR).
5. AA, 11 February 2000 (DR).
6. *Hürriyet* 18 February 2000 (DR).
7. AA, 17 June 2000 (DR).
8. AA, 25 January 2000 (DR).
9. *Hürriyet*, 25 January (DR); AA, 16 February (DR); *Milliyet*, 8 April, 16 May 2000.
10. *Milliyet*, 22 January 2000.
11. *Hürriyet*, 25 February (DR); *Milliyet*, 19 February 2000.
12. *Hürriyet*, 3, 4 March 2000 (DR).
13. Ibid.
14. *Hürriyet*, 4 March 2000 (DR).
15. *Hürriyet*, 2 June 2000 (DR).
16. *Hürriyet*, 5 February 2000 (DR).
17. *Al-Sharq al-Awsat*, 6 February 2000 (DR).
18. AA, 13 February 2000 (DR).
19. *Milliyet*, 3 October 2000.
20. AA, 17 October 2000 (DR).
21. *Milliyet*, 20 January 2000.
22. *Milliyet*, 25 January 2000.
23. *Hürriyet*, 11 February 2000 (DR).
24. AA, 23, 25 February 2000 (DR).
25. AA, 24 May, 11 July, 27 October 2000 (DR).
26. *Hürriyet*, 28 January 2000 (DR).
27. AA, 16 January (DR); *Hürriyet*, 28 January 2000 (DR).
28. AA, 30 January, 7, 18, 21 February 2000 (DR).

29. AA, 26 January 2000 (DR).
30. *Milliyet*, 26 February 2000.
31. *Milliyet*, 20 January 2000.
32. *Milliyet*, 26 January 2000.
33. AA, 21 June 2000 (DR).
34. *Milliyet*, 26 January; AA, 10 February 2000 (DR).
35. AA, 14 February 2000 (DR).
36. *Hürriyet*, 22 February 2000 (DR).
37. AA, 13 March 2000 (DR).
38. AA, 6 March 2000 (DR).
39. AA, 14 March 2000 (DR).
40. AA, 10 April, 15 August 2000 (DR).
41. CTK, 19 January 2000 (DR).
42. AA, 10 March 2000 (DR).
43. AA, 11, 12 December 2000 (DR).
44. AA, 4 January 2000 (DR).
45. AA, 23 May 2000 (DR).
46. AA, 10 December 2000 (DR).
47. AA, 18 January 2000 (DR).
48. *Milliyet*, 8, 13 January; *Hürriyet*, 13 January 2000 (DR).
49. *Hürriyet*, 13 January 2000 (DR).
50. *Milliyet*, 14 January 2000.
51. AA, 16–19 January 2000 (DR).
52. AA, 18 January 2000 (DR).
53. *Milliyet*, 15 January 2000.
54. AA, 15 November 2000 (DR).
55. AA, 20 November 2000 (DR).
56. *Sabah*, 22 November 2000 (DR).
57. AA, 14 December 2000 (DR).
58. AA, 16 August 2000 (DR).
59. *Hürriyet*, 10 February 2000 (DR).
60. AA, 8, 10 February 2000 (DR).
61. AA, 15 February 2000 (DR).
62. AA, 10 May 2000 (DR).
63. AA, 2 March, 29 June, 18 December 2000 (DR).
64. AA, 30 May, 8 December 2000.
65. AA, 5, 25 January 2000 (DR).
66. AA, 23 Feburary 2000 (DR).
67. AA, 23 February (DR); *Hürriyet*, 1, 7 March 2000 (DR).
68. *Milliyet*, 12 October 2000.
69. *Milliyet*, 9 December 2000.
70. *Hürriyet*, 28 November (DR); *Milliyet*, 9 December 2000.
71. AA, 14, 15 November (DR); *Hürriyet*, 15 November 2000 (DR).
72. *Hürriyet*, 17 November 2000 (DR).
73. *Hürriyet*, 15 November 2000 (DR).
74. AA, 15 November 2000 (DR).
75. AA, 28 November 2000 (DR).
76. *Hürriyet*, 14 December 2000 (DR).
77. AA, 21–25, 28 February, 17, 24 September, 6–7 December (DR); *Milliyet*, 20 January, 22, 25 February; *Hürriyet*, 22, 25 February 2000 (DR).
78. AA, 9 April 2000 (DR).
79. *Milliyet*, 21 September 2000.
80. *Sabah*, 11 October 2000 (DR).
81. AA, 28 January 2000 (DR).

82. AA, 10 March 2000 (DR).
83. AA, 11 April 2000 (DR).
84. AA, 9 October, 18 November, 4 December (DR); *Milliyet*, 10 November; *Sabah*, 5 December 2000 (DR).
85. AA, 19 November 2000 (DR).
86. AA, 20 April 2000 (DR).
87. *Milliyet*, 20 November 2000. See also above the chapter on the Kurds.
88. AA, 28 November 2000 (DR).
89. AA, 9 December 2000 (DR).
90. *Milliyet*, 10 December 2000.
91. AA, 18 December (DR); *Hurriyet*, 18 December 2000 (DR).
92. *Sabah*, 19 July 2000 (DR).
93. AA, 17 January 2000 (DR).
94. *Milliyet*, 4 March 2000.
95. *Hürriyet*, 23 March 2000 (DR).
96. *Hürriyet*, 8 April 2000 (DR).
97. AA, 23 February 2000 (DR).
98. AA, 23 March 2000 (DR).
99. *Hürriyet*, 11 May 2000 (DR).
100. AA, 21 June 2000 (DR).
101. AA, 29 June 2000 (DR).
102. *Milliyet*, 15 September, 14 October; AA, 9, 14, 27 October 2000 (DR).
103. *Milliyet*, 12 February 2000.
104. *Milliyet*, 11, 17 February 2000.
105. *Milliyet*, 23 February 2000.
106. AA, 27, 29, 30 March 2000 (DR).
107. *Milliyet*, 4 March 2000.
108. *Milliyet*, 14 March 2000.
109. *Hürriyet*, 21 July 2000 (DR).
110. *Milliyet*, 18, 19 February 2000.
111. AA, 24 May 2000 (DR).
112. AA, 20 June 2000 (DR).
113. *Milliyet*, 22 June 2000.
114. *Milliyet*, 23 June 2000.
115. AA, 10 July 2000 (DR).
116. AA, 27 July, 15 December 2000 (DR).
117. AA, 28 November 2000 (DR).
118. AA, 20 December 2000 (DR).
119. *Milliyet*, 21 December 2000
120. Interfax, 28 January 2000 (DR).
121. *Milliyet*, 26 January 2000 (DR).
122. Ibid.
123. Ibid.
124. AA, 29 Feb 2000 (DR).
125. ITAR-TASS, 29 Feb 2000 (DR).
126. ITAR-TASS, 15 March 2000 (DR).
127. *Hürriyet*, 13 April 2000 (DR).
128. AA, 18 April 2000 (DR).
129. AA, 23 May 2000 (DR).
130. AA, 22 June 2000 (DR).
131. Interfax, 17 October 2000 (DR).
132. Ibid.
133. AA, 22 July 2000 (DR).
134. *Hürriyet*, 10 March 2000 (DR).

135. *Hürriyet*, 7 March 2000 (DR).
136. *Hürriyet*, 23 March 2000 (DR).
137. *Milliyet*, 22 March 2000 (DR).
138. Ibid.
139. Ibid.
140. AA, 19 April 2000 (DR).
141. AA, 13 September 2000 (DR).
142. Ibid.
143. *Hürriyet*, 22 July 2000 (DR).
144. *Milliyet*, 21 November 2000 (DR).
145. *Milliyet*, 16 November 2000 (DR).
146. *Milliyet*, 19 December 2000 (DR).
147. *Sabah*, 7 August 2000 (DR).
148. Ibid.
149. *Milliyet*, 21 November 2000 (DR).
150. Ibid.
151. *Milliyet*, 21 November 2000 (DR).
152. *Milliyet*, 19 December 2000 (DR).
153. Ibid.
154. Ibid.
155. *Hürriyet*, 30 March 2000 (DR).
156. *Rossiyskaya Gazeta*, 29 March 2000 (DR).
157. *Hatzofeh*, 30 August 2000 (DR).
158. Ibid.
159. Ibid.
160. *Milliyet*, 12 July; *Sabah* 7 August 2000 (DR).
161. *Milliyet*, 12 July 2000 (DR).
162. *Milliyet*, 10 August 2000 (DR).
163. Ibid.
164. *Milliyet*, 25 August 2000 (DR).
165. AA, 13 October 2000 (DR).
166. Ibid.
167. Ibid.
168. *Sabah*, 10 October 2000 (DR).
169. AA, 9 October 2000 (DR).
170. *Sabah*, 25 October 2000 (DR).
171. Ibid.
172. *Sabah*, 25 October; *Hürriyet*, 9 February 2000 (DR).
173. *Sabah*, 25 October 2000 (DR).
174. AA, 17 May 2000 (DR).
175. *Sabah*, 25 October 2000 (DR).
176. *Sabah*, 25 October; *Milliyet*, 24 October 2000 (DR).
177. *Sabah*, 25 October; AA, 23 May; *Milliyet*, 24 May 2000 (DR).
178. *Sabah*, 25 October 2000 (DR).
179. Ibid.
180. *Milliyet*, 24 January; AA, 8 October 2000 (DR).
181. AA, 2 March, 11 September, 25 October 2000 (DR).
182. AA, 28 March 2000 (DR).
183. AA, 11, 14 April 2000 (DR).
184. *Hürriyet*, 11 April 2000 (DR).
185. *Milliyet*, 24 Jan 2000 (DR).
186. AA, 24 April, 25 October 2000 (DR).
187. AA, 24 April 2000 (DR).
188. AA, 11 September 2000 (DR).

189. Ibid.
190. Ibid.
191. AA, 20 April 2000 (DR).
192. AA, 8 October 2000 (DR).
193. AA, 11 September; Athens to Vima 9 December 2000 (DR).
194. AA, 11 September 2000 (DR).
195. *Sabah*, 19 September 2000 (DR).
196. *Hürriyet*, 26 December 2000 (DR).

The United Arab Emirates
(Al-Imarat al-'Arabiyya al-Muttahida)

JOSHUA TEITELBAUM

The continued illness of the octogenarian president of the United Arab Emirates (UAE), Shaykh Zayid bin Sultan Al Nuhayyan continued to occupy Emiratis during the year. After spending much of the year overseas for medical treatment, he returned in November, but his activity was still limited by his medical condition. Dubai continued to lead the UAE in technological innovation, announcing that it would soon open "e-government." In foreign and defense affairs, the UAE finally signed a deal worth $6.4bn. to purchase eighty F-16 military aircraft from the US. The dispute between the UAE and Iran over control of three Persian Gulf islands showed no sign of amelioration during the year; the ever friendlier relationship between Saudi Arabia and Iran only increased Emirati concern. All the same, economic relations between the Emirates (particularly Dubai) and Tehran continued apace. Tension with Tehran continued to push the UAE toward advocating the regional rehabilitation of Iraq; it reopened its embassy in Baghdad in April. The Palestinian-Israeli violence which broke out in late September led to a venting of popular sentiment on behalf of the Palestinians; several demonstrations were permitted by the government, an unusual occurrence. In economic issues, increased oil revenues led to a rise in GDP, and some progress was made in economic liberalization.

INTERNAL AFFAIRS

UAE president Shaykh Zayid remained ill during the year. As a result, the crown prince, Shaykh Khalifa bin Zayid Al Nuhayyan, took an ever more active and public role. He represented the UAE at an April summit meeting of the Gulf Cooperation Council (GCC) in Muscat. Although it had appeared in 1999 that the armed forces chief of staff, Lt. Gen. Muhammad bin Zayid Al Nuhayyan, was next in line to become crown prince, observers said during the year that the spotlight had shifted to Shaykh Zayid's second son, Sultan.[1]

The eighty-five-year-old monarch's maladies led to a stream of concerned visitors. President Husni Mubarak of Egypt visited Zayid in Geneva in June, as did King 'Abdallah II of Jordan in July. That same month, Zayid, it was announced, left Geneva for tests in the US. The "tests," however, turned out to be a kidney transplant, which he underwent in Cleveland.[2] Zayid was expected to return to Abu Dhabi after a short while, but in late September he fell in the Cleveland hospital and broke his hip. He finally flew home in late November, but planned festivities were postponed, probably due to his frail condition. The leaders of Egypt and Bahrain flew to Abu Dhabi to greet the president, and Zayid moved to remove concerns for his health by publicizing these meetings and others with concerned citizens. However, the televised coverage of these meetings showed Zayid seated, never standing.[3]

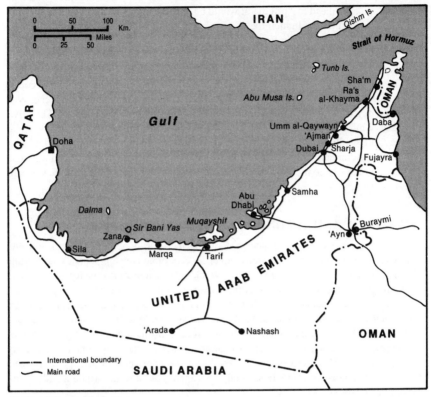

United Arab Emirates

Eager to exploit the possibilities of the Internet, Dubai, which prided itself on innovation, announced in April that it would be introducing "e-government" in order to reduce expenditure and lighten the administrative burden. The initiator of the project was Shaykh Muhammad bin Rashid Al Maktum, crown prince of Dubai and the UAE minister of defense, who warned all government officials who would stand in the way of progress: "If any top officials resist this revolution... we will say: 'Thank you very much,' and show them the door."[4] Public prosecutors in Dubai reported that they had begun to interrogate suspects over the Internet. But an attempt by a couple to get divorced by e-mail was rejected after the intervention of the Dubai personal status court.[5] The UAE minister of information, Shaykh 'Abdallah bin Zayid, stated in April that press censorship in the Gulf would end in about five years, because of increased Internet usage. In a further development, Internet service in Dubai was interrupted in June when a British expatriate hacked into the state-run Etisalat system. By the end of the year, he was still awaiting trial.[6]

ECONOMIC AND ADMINISTRATIVE DEVELOPMENTS

Real GDP growth was an estimated 5% during the year, double the growth of 1999, thanks to increased oil revenue (see chapter on economic developments in the Middle East).[7] Dubai announced in February that it would set up a free trade zone for e-commerce, technology, and the media. Ra's al-Khayma announced that it sought to set up a similar zone. In March, Dubai launched a high-tech financial market, and that same month Abu Dhabi announced that it would have a World Trade Center by 2003. In a move to increase efficiency, Shaykh Muhammad of Dubai turned up unannounced at a number of government departments in February. Muhammad said he found many officials neglecting their public duty. There were empty offices, absent managers, and too many police officers at the Dubai courts, reported the official news agency. As a result, Muhammad sacked several officials.[8]

The pace of economic liberalization gained some momentum during the year. In April, a company began to offer commercial leases on land to all nationals. Dubai removed a ban on foreign majority ownership of companies, but only for GCC nationals.[9]

FOREIGN AFFAIRS

Following seven years of negotiations, the UAE finally signed a deal on 5 March worth $6.4bn. to purchase eighty F-16 Desert Falcon Block 60 multi-role military aircraft from the American firm, Lockheed Martin. The UAE was scheduled to take delivery between 2004 and 2007. General Electric Aircraft Engines was granted the contract to supply the engines for the aircraft, and Northrop Grumman the radar and targeting systems. Negotiations had been lengthy because the US was hesitant to give the UAE access to source codes and other technology, and because the two sides had difficulty agreeing on the finance package. But it became clear to both sides that the deal was necessary. The UAE realized that it could depend only on the US to come to its defense in the event of an attack (Iran being the most likely candidate), and it was able to extract concessions from the US, which agreed to supply AMRAAM missiles and advanced electronic warfare systems. For its part, the US was anxious to conclude the deal because Congress had not been prepared to appropriate funds for the development of the Block

60 aircraft, and the agreement with the UAE provided the necessary cash. As the US Air Force wrote in a memorandum to Congress defending the sale, "it would 'keep a vital defense industrial base asset alive and protect skilled aerospace workers for seven years at no cost to the US taxpayer.'"[10]

The deal cemented the security relationship between the two countries, putting it on a footing similar to the security relationship between Riyadh and Washington. The purchase of the US aircraft would require US training and maintenance, a development which would facilitate a US deployment to the UAE if that should ever be necessary. Secretary of Defense William Cohen said as much during an April visit to Abu Dhabi. The aircraft, he declared, "will further link our two nations in a strategic relationship that will enhance the stability throughout the Gulf." During the visit, Cohen also noted that the UAE had agreed to let the port of Jabal 'Ali serve as a liberty port for American sailors and marines.[11]

The conflict between the UAE and Iran over control of the three Persian Gulf islands of Abu Musa, Greater Tunb and Lesser Tunb continued unabated throughout the year. In a statement read out in late January to the consultative council of the federation by his son, Deputy Prime Minister Sultan, Shaykh Zayid stated that the UAE sought to solve the conflict by peaceful means, and expressed his support for the tripartite committee formed by the GCC in July 1999 to mediate between the two countries (see *MECS* 1999, p. 631). Iran responded that it sought a resolution of the conflict via direct negotiations. In late February, the UAE information minister, 'Abdallah bin Zayid, expressed the Emirates' impatience with the work of the committee, which was comprised of the foreign ministers of Saudi Arabia, Oman, and Qatar. He expressed his hope that the committee would "activate its work" following the victory of reformers in the Iranian elections and "reach a settlement to the problem." He also expressed his disappointment that Iran "always makes excuses not to receive the tripartite committee."[12] Iran had also rejected international adjudication by the International Court of Justice (ICJ) in The Hague, preferring only bilateral negotiations. While Iranian foreign minister Kamal Kharrazi had said in July that Iran would receive the committee, *al-Sharq al-Awsat* reported in December that Tehran had told Gulf officials that it would not in fact receive the committee.[13] Since it had possession of the islands, Iran was in no hurry to resolve the dispute, and Saudi Arabia, the only military threat to Iran in the region, was not about to go to war on behalf of the UAE claim to the disputed islands.

In March, *Jane's Defence Weekly* published satellite images of Abu Musa and analyzed them. Its conclusion: the Iranian presence on the island was not a major security threat to the UAE. According to the magazine, there was "no evidence of a control tower, hardened aircraft shelters, helicopter facilities, or any sign of sustained fighter and attack aircraft capability." It further stated that the single port facility on the island was "rudimentary." All the same, the magazine qualified its assessment, noting that the images did show a series of ten escarpments which could hide large articulated vehicles, and might be capable of housing anti-ship missile launchers and associated radar. It concluded: "As it stands, if Abu Musa is a dagger pointed at the heart of the Emirates (and the West's oil supply), it has yet to be sharpened."[14]

The April visit of Iranian minister of defense Ali Shamkhani to Saudi Arabia, where he was to discuss a security pact (see chapter on Saudi Arabia), moved Shaykh Khalifa to lash out at the idea. "As for security agreements with Iran, we think that the question of our islands is an obstacle to any security agreement in the region."[15]

In May, the Emirati press accused Iran of "stealing" Emirati oil by drilling in the

Dorra offshore oil field, which was subject to rival claims by Tehran, Riyadh, and Kuwait. "GCC countries should review their relationship with Iran...before this country attacks (and occupies) another region in the Arab Gulf," wrote *al-Khalij*.[16] Iran, in turn, announced in July and September that UAE ships had been seized for smuggling oil out of Iraq. *Iran News* accused the UAE of having failed to respond to the Gulf détente policies of President Mohammad Khatami, and instead trying to close ranks with Iraq. (Iran itself, however, was also engaged in the smuggling of Iraqi oil, according to senior British sources).[17]

In December, on the occasion of the UAE National Day, Zayid expressed his disappointment that Tehran refused to accept the jurisdiction of the tripartite committee. He stated that Iran's "occupation" of the islands was hobbling Iranian relations with the GCC countries, and demanded that it either join serious negotiations or agree that the dispute be referred to the ICJ.[18]

Despite the acrimony, business was business, and economic relations between the two countries continued apace. More than fifty Iranian companies participated in an April international expo in Sharja. A report issued in May by the Abu Dhabi customs office noted that the value of UAE re-exports to Iran in the first quarter of 2000 placed Iran third - after Saudi Arabia and Qatar — in Abu Dhabi re-exports. Re-exports from Dubai were also significant. In October, Ahmad Bati, deputy director general of the Dubai Ports Organization, stated that 2001 would see the UAE set up its first trade fair in Iran.[19]

Zayid's concern over the problems with Iran, Iraq, and the Palestinian issue led him to issue several calls during the year for an Arab summit, which had not been held since June 1996 (see *MECS* 1996, pp. 69–79). "History will never forgive leaders of a nation whose destiny lies in unity but who deliberately prefer to disperse and are scared to turn their attention to the situation at hand," the president declared. Like other Arab leaders, Zayid called for summits to be held at regularly scheduled intervals (see chapter on inter-Arab relations).[20]

The UAE reopened its embassy in Baghdad in April. While officials denied that the move signaled a new policy,[21] the timing was of interest: it coincided with the visit of Shamkhani to Riyadh, and may have been a protest at the growing security cooperation between Saudi Arabia and Iran. In June, Iraq announced that it would reopen its embassy in Abu Dhabi.[22]

The UAE continued to take the lead amongst Gulf countries in calling for the lifting of sanctions on Iraq. The aim was to empower Iraq to counterbalance the perceived threat from Iran. In February Shaykh Zayid lamented: "Where are the famous human rights that the West is so fond of preaching, when the Iraqi people have been suffering from the embargo and the continuing sanctions for years?"[23] All the same, a speech by an Emirati representative at the UN millennium summit in September urging Iraq to free Kuwaiti prisoners of war irritated the Iraqis: "We have never heard such words from an Emirati official," wrote the official *al-Thawra*.[24] The UAE also urged Iraq to cooperate with GCC efforts to achieve a lifting of the embargo.[25]

Where business was concerned, though, the UAE had much less sympathy for Iraq. Ironically, while UAE-flagged ships continued to smuggle Iraqi oil,[26] the Emirates continued during the year to profit from the auctioning off of other tankers caught in violation of the sanctions. Once intercepted by the US-led Multinational Interception Force, the ships were towed to Abu Dhabi. The oil was auctioned off first, with the proceeds going to the UN, but the tankers themselves went to the highest bidder and the profits to the Emirati government.[27]

The UAE continued to undertake high-profile humanitarian missions to Baghdad. On 11 October an Emirates airliner arrived with 30 tons of medicines and medical equipment. The plane also carried a 30-member delegation of Emiratis, headed by the federal health minister, Hamad 'Abd al-Rahman Madfa'a. During the October Arab summit in Cairo (see chapter on inter-Arab relations), the two sides held their highest level meeting since before the 1990–91 Gulf crisis, when Dubai's ruler and UAE vice president Shaykh Maktum bin Rashid al-Maktum sat down briefly with the vice chairman of the Iraqi Revolutionary Command Council, 'Izzat Ibrahim.[28]

The Palestinian disturbances, which began in late September, focused the attention of the Emirates leadership, as they did throughout the Arab world (see chapter on inter-Arab relations). The government issued permits for demonstrations and marches, which were peaceful in nature. Hundreds of students rallied inside the grounds of the American University of Dubai, Sharja University City, and the state university in al-'Ayn. Students at Sharja University tried to take their demonstration into town, but were halted by police. Public demonstrations were also held in cordoned-off parts of Ras al-Khayma and Abu Dhabi.[29]

Moved by the Palestinian children confronting Israeli forces with stones, in October UAE newspapers published an advertisement by a lawyer seeking fifty truckloads of one-cubic-inch size stones and half a million home-made slingshots to be transported to Jordan for delivery to Palestinian youth. "We want the rocks from our mountains to be thrown at the Israeli aggressors by the brave Palestinian youths in the West Bank and Gaza, said Siddiq Fath 'Ali al-Khaja.[30] The government also lent its support, sending medical aid and pledging $150m. at the Cairo summit to support the uprising.[31]

Disappointment with what he saw as the one-sided policy of the US, Shaykh Zayid called for international involvement alongside the US in the peace process. "It is inconceivable that one single state can take on the role of arbiter and decide by itself the outcome of the Palestinian issue," Zayid stated during an early December meeting with Palestinian Authority (PA) President Yasir 'Arafat in Abu Dhabi. On another occasion, he accused the US of bias toward Israel.[32] According to al-Ittihad, Emiratis were boycotting US goods, leading by mid-December to a drop in demand of 50% for items made in America. The boycott had also affected US fast-food chains, said the paper.[33]

NOTES

For the place and frequency of publications cited here, and for the full name of the publication, news agency, radio station, or monitoring service where an abbreviation is used, please see "List of Sources." Only in the case of more than one publication bearing the same name is the place of publication noted here. However, all references to al-Ittihad are to the Abu Dhabi daily; all references to al-Bayan are to the Dubai daily.

The author thanks Itamar Inbari for his excellent work in assembling source material for this chapter.

1. CR, United Arab Emirates, June 2000, p. 12.
2. MENA, 8 June (DR); AFP, 9, 13 July, 28, 30 August 2000.
3. AFP, 20, 27 September; 26, 27, 29 November 2000; CR, United Arab Emirates, February 2001, p. 11.

4. AFP, 4 April, 23 May 2000.
5. AFP, 2, 14 May 2000.
6. AFP, 22, 25, 26 June, 25 December 2000.
7. *CR*, United Arab Emirates, February 2001, p. 5.
8. AFP, 6, 21 February, 6, 26 March, 10 May 2000.
9. *CR*, United Arab Emirates, June 2000, p. 16.
10. AFP, 5, 6 March; AP, 6 March; UPI, Reuters, 14 March; *CR*, United Arab Emirates, June 2000, pp. 13–14.
11. *WF*, 11 April 2000.
12. AFP, 31 January, 27 February 2000.
13. AFP, 19 March; 16 July; 30 December 2000.
14. AFP, 7 March; IRNA, 7 March 2000.
15. AFP, 22, 23 April 2000.
16. AFP, 12 May 2000.
17. IRNA, 25 July (DR); AFP, 13 September; *The Times*, 5 July 2000.
18. *CR*, United Arab Emirates, February 2001, p. 12.
19. IRNA, 22 April, 11 May, 10 October 2000 (DR).
20. AFP, 22 January, 30 April 2000.
21. AFP, 20, 22 April 2000.
22. AFP, 24 June 2000.
23. AFP, 15 February 2000.
24. AFP, 11 September 2000.
25. AFP, 18 September 2000.
26. *The Times*, 5 July 2000.
27. AFP, 20, 21 February, 3 May 2000.
28. *CR*, United Arab Emirates, November 2000, p. 16.
29. US Department of State, "UAE: Country Report on Human Rights Practices for 2000," February 2001.
30. Reuters, 5 October 2000; *CR*, United Arab Emirates, November 2000, p. 14.
31. AFP, 13 November; MENA, 23 November 2000 (DR).
32. AFP, 2, 12 December 2000.
33. AFP, 14 December 2000.

Yemen
(al-Jumhuriyya al-Yamaniyya)

JOSEPH KOSTINER

The year 2000 yielded neither changes nor new social and political initiatives in Yemen, but was rather one of ongoing efforts to stabilize existing conditions. During the year, the country's leaders, notably President 'Ali 'Abdallah Salih, sought to consolidate their grip on power and to implement key foreign policies.

In the meantime, Yemeni society was plagued by continual unrest. Political leaders took a hands-off attitude, regarding the riots, tribal fighting and internecine skirmishes as traditional and deep-seated practices which could not be curbed. The depressed economic conditions, tribal opposition to the government, tense relations between northern and southern population groups and a resurgence of militant Islamism contributed to the endemic violence. Kidnappings — mostly of foreign tourists and diplomats — and acts of sabotage and anti-government riots, especially in South Yemen, continued unabated throughout the year.

Salih paid relatively little attention to stopping the violence. He focused instead on strengthening his own presidential position and that of the leading General People's Congress (GPC; al-Mu'tamar al-Sha'bi al-'Amm) party. This was achieved by postponing parliamentary and presidential elections for two years, reinforcing the authority of his appointed consultative council and further eroding the power of the rival Yemeni Socialist Party (YSP; al-Hizb al-Yamani al-Ishtiraki), once the leading party in South Yemen. These measures allowed Salih and his loyal supporters to maintain unchallenged control. The effect was to cause Yemen to retreat from its earlier steps toward democratization, which had been evident in the establishment of a multiparty system and a plan for regular elections (see *MECS* 1990, pp. 712–15). Under such conditions it was hardly surprising that high rates of unemployment and poverty failed to decline, making it impossible to implement much-needed budget cuts and privatization measures.

The one major achievement of Yemen during 2000 was to sign a border demarcation agreement with Saudi Arabia in June. It was supposed to end a long period of border skirmishes and tension with the Saudi kingdom. Yemeni leaders also regarded the agreement as a key to improved relations with other Gulf and Arab states. The agreement was, however, tentative and left a solitary patch of border without clear demarcation. Nor did it bring an end to border clashes, and its actual value remained to be seen.

In the course of the year Yemen did manage to improve its relations with the US. There were promises of aid and of increased commercial and military contacts with Washington. However, the deadly attack in October on the US navy warship USS Cole, which was refuelling in Aden, revived the image of Yemen as a state harboring branches of Islamic terrorist organizations, and therefore unstable and risky for Western interests.

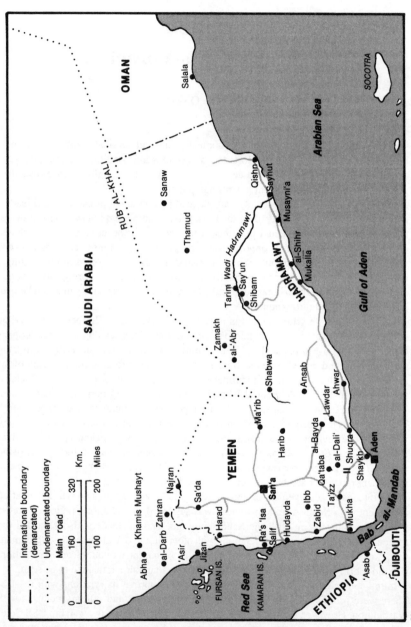

INTERNAL AFFAIRS

SOCIAL UNREST

As in previous years, social unrest of various kinds dominated public life, for several reasons. President Salih believed in the continuing importance of tribal groups in Yemeni society, both as hubs of social and economic activity and as political and administrative units. The regime was relatively weak in rural areas, allowing unrestricted autonomy to the nomadic tribal groups that roamed there. Consequently, tribal chieftains often remained lords of certain provinces, retaining only loose ties with the central government. This made it possible for them to impose their own rules, including levying protection money and kidnapping tourists (see below).

Another cause of unrest was the ongoing tension between North and South Yemen. Six years after the civil war of 1994, which resulted in the defeat of the breakaway of southern regions and their reinclusion in the Yemeni state (see *MECS* 1994, pp. 713–18), feelings of mutual distrust and even hatred festered. Northern political parties and Salih's partisans sought to penetrate and weaken South Yemeni political groupings. The southerners, in their turn, felt economically discriminated against and politically disempowered by the northern-dominated government, and expressed resistance to this hegemony. The situation was thus fraught with potential for conflict.[1]

In recent years Yemen had also become fertile ground for militant Islamism. A number of activists were arrested and put on trial for sabotage. Nevertheless, the Islamist groups retained their followers in Yemen, some of whom were sympathetic to Usama bin Ladin (see *MECS* 1999, p. 642), and they often engaged in acts of terrorism and sabotage. The dire economic conditions and low standard of living for the majority of the populace were an added stimulus to using force to obtain economic benefits.

According to a British journalist, Brian Whitaker, between 1996 and 2000 Yemen witnessed 118 kidnappings involving 147 foreigners. Despite increased security measures, the number of incidents remained constant, averaging ten or eleven a year. They were accompanied by demands for better local facilities for the tribal groups of the kidnappers, such as schools or roads, in return for release of hostages, who were mostly foreign diplomats, aid workers or tourists. Sometimes the kidnapping was intended to force the government to improve its policies toward the tribe of the kidnappers.[2] Thus, in January 2000, a French tourist couple were kidnapped by a tribal group near the town of 'Amran, north of San'a. In early March, the Polish ambassador to San'a was kidnapped in the capital by the local Qiyari tribal group. He was released several days later, but only after the release of the shaykh of that group, Khalid al-Qiyari, who had been detained earlier by the government.[3] In June, northern tribe members abducted a Norwegian diplomat and his son, who were on holiday. The diplomat was killed in a shoot-out between the kidnappers and Yemeni troops trying to rescue the hostages. These events led the government to arrest and try in August and September several dozen people allegedly involved in kidnappings. In spite of this crackdown, Western observers were convinced that abductions motivated by ransom money or local benefits would continue.[4]

Social unrest also took the form of riots and sabotage by different political groups. In February, riots erupted in Dali'i, 45 km. north of Aden. These were provoked by the arrest of about one hundred local people, probably activists of the YSP. The local population rioted in protest against this attempt to weaken the party. In the same month, clashes were reported between an Islamic Jihad group and government forces in the south of the Shabwa province, east of Aden. In July and August, the deputy assistant governor of San'a province was assassinated by a group of armed men. There were also clashes between government forces and villagers in Marib, northeast of Aden.[5] Nevertheless, the Islamist groups that had been most active in 1999 and had dominated the public sphere were relatively weakened by arrests and suppression that year (see *MECS* 1999, pp. 640–42), and their activities decreased for most of 2000.

This situation changed in the last quarter of the year. On 12 October, the USS Cole was the target of sabotage in Aden harbor. Seventeen sailors were killed and the ship was badly damaged. Three Islamist organizations claimed responsibility for the attack: two of them, Muhammad's army (Jaysh Muhammad) and The Islamic Deterrence Force (Quwat al-Dar' al-Islami) were previously unknown. The third, the Aden-Abyan Islamic army (al-Jaysh al-Islami fi 'Adan-Abyan), had already committed various acts of terrorism in Yemen (see *MECS* 1999, pp. 640–42, 643). This group's former leader, Zayn al-'Abidin al-Mihdar, had been executed in October 1999 and its new self-appointed leader, Hatim Muhsin bin Farid, had been put on trial in July for conspiracy.[6] While the actual perpetrators remained unknown, observers noted that they were probably among the "Afghan Arab" followers of Usama bin Ladin. These were the Arab volunteers who had fought the USSR in Afghanistan during the 1980s and had since become intent on attacking US facilities and interests.[7] Yemen subsequently proved to be a base for various militant Arab groups actively hostile to the US.

EROSION OF DEMOCRATIC INSTITUTIONS

In the first weeks of 2000, President Salih announced a campaign against corruption and incompetence in government departments. It was aimed at reducing bribery, eliminating unnecessary jobs and improving the efficiency of public administration. The International Monetary Fund (IMF) had also demanded such improvements. However, other amendments were announced that revealed more old-fashioned political ambitions behind the facade of administrative reform — the consolidation of power in the hands of Salih, his close associates and senior aides. In January, the minister of legal affairs, 'Abdallah Ahmad Ghanim, announced that the size of the Consultative Council would be extended from 59 to 101 members. This council served as a personal advisory body to Salih and was not linked to the Yemeni parliament, the Council of Representatives (CR). The enlargement of the Consultative Council was not at that stage related to new authorities or responsibilities.[8] Instead, it was aimed at providing jobs for some of Salih's supporters, whom he would personally appoint.

The CR did not raise any protests, because a new plan to extend its term of office by two years was then considered and subsequently approved. As a result, parliamentary elections, scheduled for April 2001, were delayed until 2003. This allowed Salih's political party, the GPC, to increase its hold on power as it had an overwhelming majority in the CR. The delayed election was also intended to deal a major blow to the YSP, which was already in decline since the defeat of the south in the 1994 war. The YSP had boycotted the last parliamentary elections in 1997, and its hopes of gaining a parliamentary base were now further frustrated.[9]

In late August, the CR gave its initial approval to the new amendments. It then became evident that matters of treaties and defence would be voted on jointly by the CR and the Consultative Council, whereas the CR alone had hitherto held this responsibility. Likewise, the two bodies would jointly approve new candidates for the CR, another right which had been exclusively that of the CR. Moreover, the new provisions suggested that the CR would become responsible only for "monitoring" the government rather than, as previously formulated, "directing and monitoring" it. The parliamentary body — the elected CR — would therefore lose significant authority. Its members, however, notably the GPC party, owed their parliamentary positions (now confirmed till 2003) to Salih and endorsed the changes. At the same time, presumably to express their loyalty to Salih, 144 out of 301 CR members submitted a proposal to extend the presidential term from five years to seven, a measure that was also endorsed in August. Salih thus derived immediate and direct benefits from the new constitutional amendments.

The Yemeni regime subsequently retreated from its professed democratic process adopted after the unification of the two Yemeni states in 1990 (see *MECS* 1990, pp. 708–12). The extended terms of both the CR and the president, and the strengthening of the Consultative Council at the expense of the CR, attested to the change. The US-based National Democracy Institute, which monitored Yemeni democratization, concluded that: "It appears that Yemen's democratic process has stalled, that the momentum for reform that commenced several years ago has unfortunately diminished."[10]

ECONOMIC CONDITIONS

As in preceding years, the Yemeni government, encouraged by the IMF, announced various measures aimed at reforming its macroeconomic structure. In early 2000, the government approved a bill, ratified by the CR in May, to reform the Central Bank of Yemen. The government also drew up the next five-year plan, scheduled to run from 2001 to 2005. Privatization and private sector expansion were major goals, intended to stimulate real growth by at least 5% per year. President Salih formed a special committee, headed by Prime Minister 'Abd al-Karim al-Iryani, to "devise a privatization program of state-owned companies."[11] The policy to curb corruption (see above) was also part of the government plans.

However, observers stressed the difficulties affecting Yemeni society that could impede, or at least limit, the plans for reform. In particular, most of the Yemeni public was dependent on the government. With a poorly developed private sector and unemployment reaching 20%-40%, the majority of the labor force worked for the government, forming a bloated public sector whose wages took up 60% of the national budget. EU consultants estimated that there were 18,000 "ghost workers" in the civil service. Constrained by the IMF, the government committed itself to cutting 20% of public sector jobs. But in order to curb bribery, in mid-July the government approved a pay rise of 40% for military personnel and 10% for civil servants, since neither group could survive on basic salaries alone and both were prone to engaging in corruption.[12] In addition, in many parts of Yemen the deeply rooted poverty, up to 50% illiteracy and lack of running water were considerable obstructions to large-scale privatization and economic growth.

The decades-old plan to develop the port of Aden and subsequently create a free-trade zone in south Yemen were slowly materializing, but had not yet brought significant changes to the local economy. Meanwhile, the population in Aden kept complaining that it was mostly officials from north Yemen who gained from the jobs and benefits offered by the new project.[13]

FOREIGN AFFAIRS

RELATIONS WITH SAUDI ARABIA

Yemen's relations with Saudi Arabia were a priority in Yemeni foreign and security affairs. Improving border relations with Saudi Arabia would help ameliorate longstanding problems, such as smuggling into Yemen and the intensity and frequency of tribal skirmishes along the border. Moreover, Yemeni leaders were interested in improving economic and strategic relations with the Saudi kingdom. They wanted the Saudis to renew the economic aid that had been cut off because of Yemeni support of Saddam Husayn's invasion of Kuwait in 1990 (see *MECS* 1990, pp. 719–22), and they wished to allay Riyadh's fears about Yemeni policies being opposed to Saudi interests. These concerns had emerged in the 1994 war, when Salih defeated the South Yemeni breakaway entity which was backed by Saudi Arabia. Improved relations with the Saudis were also a key to rapprochement with other Gulf states.

Yemeni and Saudi teams were engaged in negotiations of several years standing over the delineation of the long (over 1,500 km.) and disputed common border. The negotiations did not prevent skirmishes: in December 1999 and mid-January 2000, there were clashes between Saudi and Yemeni border guards, with several Yemeni casualties. The Yemeni foreign minister, 'Abd al-Qadir Ba-Jammal, flew to Jidda for discussions with the Saudi authorities[14] and the border situation subsequently calmed down. However, the actual negotiations did not produce any progress for most of 2000, and unexpected difficulties arose. Yemen was interested in third-party mediation to overcome major hurdles in the discussions. During Salih's visit to Washington in March (see below) senior US officials expressed a readiness to undertake this. The Saudis, however, strongly rejected "outside interference" (see chapter on Saudi Arabia).[15]

To bypass the immediate obstacles, the two parties decided to sign a border agreement based on coordinates, while leaving a long stretch undemarcated. Eventually a border line was to be decided through negotiations, leading to the drawing up of a mutually agreed map. On 26 June, the two sides announced this agreement based on coordinates for both continental and maritime borders. Yemeni leaders hoped that the agreement would not only produce a final delineation, but would lead to improved relations between the two countries in all spheres. Meetings of officials from both sides continued to advance the subject at ministerial and technical levels.[16] However, a renewed border clash in August indicated that pacification on the ground was more problematic.

RELATIONS WITH THE US

President Salih stepped up his efforts to widen and consolidate Yemeni international and commercial ties. In late March, he visited Canada and the US. In Canada, he focused on increasing Canadian foreign aid to Yemen and on the operations of the Canadian Occidental Petroleum Company, which runs the largest oil-producing field in Yemen. In Washington, Salih held talks with President Clinton and senior US officials. Following earlier initiatives, Salih was interested in strengthening military ties with the US (see *MECS* 1999, pp. 645–47) in order to develop a direct security link between Yemen and Washington that would be independent of the traditional US-Saudi Arabian axis and would enhance the Yemeni position. Gen. Henry Shelton (then head of the joint chiefs of staff) participated in the talks, which reportedly focused on aid and regional issues and probably increased military cooperation as well. Despite the improved ties, several issues remained unresolved. Yemen apparently refused to lift travel restrictions on the emigration of members of the region's small Jewish community, although several thousand had already left in recent years. In addition, the US Department of State continued to list Yemen as a state harboring terrorism, as it allowed militant groups like the Palestinian Hamas, the Egyptian Islamic Jihad and the Algerian Armed Islamic Group to maintain branches in the country.[17]

The attack on the USS Cole brought this issue to a head. In the days immediately after the bombing, Yemeni authorities detained about a hundred people in connection with the episode. The US government sent in its own comprehensive team of several hundred persons to investigate the case. Yemen was eager to prove its goodwill and hinted at various Islamist figures who had been detained by the authorities. But no charges were laid. The US expressed dissatisfaction with the Yemeni investigation and unofficially blamed Yemen for its lenience to Islamic terrorist organizations.[18] This impasse continued into 2001.

NOTES

For the place and frequency of publications cited here, and for the full name of the publication, news agency, radio station or monitoring service where an abbreviation is used, please see "List of Sources." Only in the case of more than one publication bearing the same name is the place of publication noted here.

1. *Al-Majalla*, 18 May 2000.
2. *MEI*, 10 March; *al-Quds al-'Arabi*, 7 June 2000.
3. *Ibid.*; Warsaw PAP, 3 March 2000.
4. *CR*, Yemen, 3rd quarter, p. 13; 4th quarter, p. 15; *al-Hayat*, 17 November 2000.
5. *Al-Sharq al-Awsat*, 4 April; *CR*, Yemen, 2nd quarter, pp. 12–13; 3rd quarter, 2000, pp. 12–13.
6. *Al-Sharq al-Awsat*, 29 June 2000.
7. *Al-Hayat*, 16 November 2000.
8. *Al-Sharq al-Awsat*, 31 January 2000.
9. *CR*, Yemen, 1st quarter, 2000, pp. 14–16.
10. *MEI*, 1 September; *CR*, Yemen, 3rd quarter, 2000, pp. 12–14.
11. *Al-Hayat*, 26 January 2000.
12. *FT*, 7 January; *CR*, Yemen, 3rd quarter, 2000, p. 17.
13. *GSNL*, 10 January 2000.
14. *Al-Quds al-'Arabi*, 25 January — BBC Monitoring, 27 January 2000.
15. *CR*, Yemen, 3rd quarter, 2000, pp. 13–14.
16. Interview with Yemen's chief negotiator, Husayn 'Ali al-Jayshi, *al-Sharq al-Awsat*, 27 June, 7 July; Salih on the treaty, *al-Majalla*, 23 July 2000.
17. *CR*, Yemen, 2nd quarter, 2000, pp. 14–15.
18. *FT*, 20 October; *MEI*, 22 December 2000.

INDEX

635